THE WORLD OF BUSINESS

Lawrence J. Gitman
San Diego State University

Carl McDaniel
University of Texas, Arlington

SOUTH-WESTERN College Publishing

An International Thomson Publishing Company

Acquisitions Editor: Rob Jared
Developmental Editor: Ann Torbert
Sponsoring Editor: Alice Denny
Production Editor: Eric Carlson
Designer: Joseph M. Devine
Production House: GTS Graphics
Video Production: Paradigm Communications Group
Video Writer/Producer: Mark Di Stasi
Video Writer: Becky Jones
Media and Technology Editor: Sheri Lajti
Photo Researcher: Kathryn A Russell, Pix, Inc.
Photographer Chapter and Part Openers: Joyce Photography
Photo Editor: Jennifer Mayhall

GB60BA
Copyright © 1995
By South-Western College Publishing
Cinncinnati, Ohio

Library of Congress Cataloging-in-Publication Data

Gitman, Lawrence J.
    The world of business / Lawrence J. Gitman, Carl McDaniel.—2nd
ed.,
        p. cm.
    Includes bibliographical references and index.
    ISBN 0-538-83625-3
    1. Management—United States. 2. Marketing—United States.
3. Business enterprises—United States—Finance. 4. Accounting—
United States. 5. Business—Data processing. 6. International business.
I. McDaniel, Carl D.
HD70.U5G53 1995
650—dc20   94-17198
                                      CIP

I(T)P   1 2 3 4 5 6 7 8 VH 1 0 9 8 7 6 5 4
Printed in the United States of America

International Thomson Publishing

South-Western College Publishing is an ITP Company. The ITP
trademark is used under license.

This book is dedicated to
Introduction to Business instructors,
those men and women whose important work
is shaping the real world of business.

BRIEF CONTENTS

CONTENTS

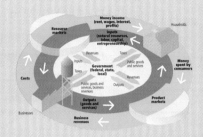

**PART 2
THE BUSINESS ENVIRONMENT   74**

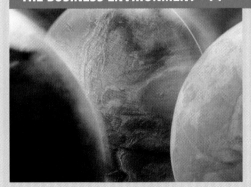

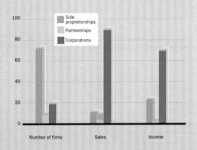
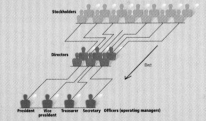

PART 3
BUSINESS STRUCTURES   170

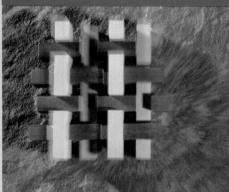

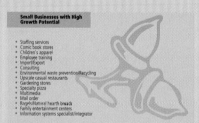

PART 4
MANAGEMENT 240

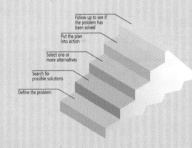

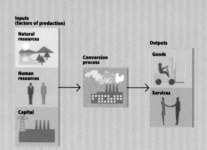

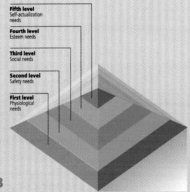

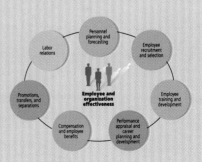

PART 6
MARKETING MANAGEMENT 438

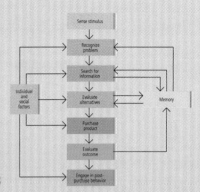

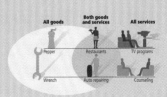

PART 7
MANAGEMENT INFORMATION TOOLS 564

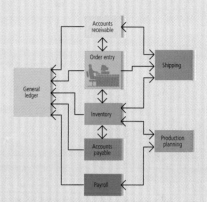

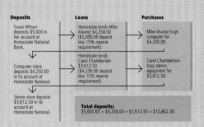

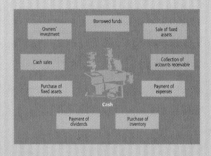

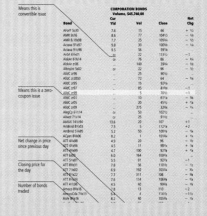

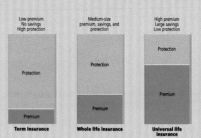

PREFACE

TO THE INSTRUCTOR

Quality, value, ethics, global business, and *entrepreneurship* are but a few of the many important terms and concepts in today's business vocabulary. This second edition of *The World of Business* offers value for students and instructors by carefully weaving the threads of ethical, global, and entrepreneurial behavior into the fabric of business. Like any product sold in a competitive market, this book has been carefully researched, developed, designed, and produced.

A CAREFULLY DEVELOPED TEXT

The World of Business has been developed and revised to provide students with one of the most lively, interesting, stimulating, and up-to-date textbooks they will use during their college careers. To meet the market need, we've created an intellectually sound textbook at the highest standard of quality. The book has been written with both the student and the instructor in mind.

Our market research shows that, above all, instructors design their courses to explain the functions of business. They are also interested in exploring current trends in business and exposing their students to career opportunities. With those points in mind, we have stressed core ideas, currency, and careers.

We have taken special care to achieve a fine balance between breadth and depth of coverage. Because this is the only course in which students are exposed to *all areas* of business, subjects must receive more than a quick once-over. We have done extensive research to ensure that the right material is covered in sufficient depth to provide a solid foundation for future study. Before each chapter was written, current literature on the subject was thoroughly reviewed. Traditional concepts were updated with the latest findings and contemporary business practices.

Breadth is also important, because students need to appreciate the interplay among the functional areas of business. They also need to understand how business interacts with government and how international activities affect firms. Students need to appreciate how the various components of, say, the banking system fit together and interact. They must also come to appreciate how the key functional areas of business affect society.

A DELIGHTFUL AND ENJOYABLE BOOK TO READ

As a busy instructor, perhaps teaching over a hundred students and several different subjects, you recognize the importance of choosing the right textbook. The first criterion for success is that the book hold the reader's interest. There's probably no greater hindrance to learning (and teaching) than a dull textbook. Thus we've invested extensive effort in making *The World of Business* a truly pleasurable and captivating reading experience. We've tried to accomplish this in a variety of ways:

- *A lively, informal writing style developed over the years by two highly experienced and successful authors:* Careful attention to language and the use of hundreds of real-world examples make *The World of Business* readable and engaging.
- *A prologue that sets the tone:* Students must learn from the start that business operates in an ever-changing environment. Successful organizations plan for the future and understand how emerging trends will affect them. To help students understand the ever-changing world of business, we feature examples through the text in eight critically important areas that will impact tomorrow's organizations. These trend areas are explained in detail in the Prologue.
- *Fascinating examples of major trends:* Two carefully researched examples of business trends are featured in each chapter. These boxes were unanimously well-received and praised in the first edition, and we have included the feature again in this edition.

    Most of the stories in the trends boxes are new in the second edition. They were chosen for their importance to business,

their timeliness, and their interest to students. These trends complement the multitude of real-world examples woven into the text. Examples of **social and demographic trends** are engaging and relevant to everyone; for business, these trends will determine who will buy what, how much, and where. **Trends in technology** have radically affected how we live and how we do business. Indeed, technology itself has become a giant business. **Trends in global competition** are changing the status of the United States as the premier economic power. To compete in the global marketplace, the way we do business will change. New to this second edition, **trends in quality management** relate both to productivity and profitability and apply to all aspects of a firm's operations. **Trends in service businesses** involve the unique challenges of providing services, rather than goods, in developed economies. **Small business trends** preview new opportunities and challenges that are on the horizon for entrepreneurs in a global economy. **Trends in business ethics and social responsibility** are critically important because firms operate within communities, not in a vacuum. Managers can make socially conscious decisions that are good for both businesses and society. Finally, **trends in business today** are interesting stories about business and helpful hints for students. The specific trends boxes and topics are set in bold italic type in the detailed table of contents.

- *Videos that bring the text to life:* The videos that accompany the text focus on real people in real jobs. Each part opens with two videos: one that describes the general topics to be covered in that part of the book and a second that profiles a company in a related business. Videos at the beginnings of chapters look at the educational and business experience of a recent college graduate working in the area of business about to be discussed. The young employees featured in the videos come from a variety of backgrounds—mostly business majors. They discuss how they found their jobs and how they put to use on the job what they learned in their college coursework. *These videos clearly illustrate to your students how the material they are about to read has everyday relevance to a recent former student.* The videos serve as a springboard to help enliven the classroom experience. Brief sections at the beginnings of parts and chapters in the textbook provide text background for these videos.

- *Special emphasis on career opportunities:* A **Career Appendix** at the end of each part of *The World of Business* begins with a general discussion of careers relevant to the material just completed (such as management, marketing, or finance). We then feature a Dream Career. The dream career is one that offers excitement, advancement, high earnings, and self-fulfillment. The reviews of specific jobs that follow include information on the skills and education required, where the best opportunities can be found, the employment outlook through 2000, and the salary range. At the end of the text, the Epilogue provides tips on how to find one's first career position. We then follow with suggestions for holding that first position and advancing from it.

- *An outstanding design:* A book's design is important. When accompanied by relevant content and sound writing, the design can attract students to read and learn. A great deal of thought went into the design of *The World of Business.* This beautiful book reflects the work of artists and editors whose shared vision was a stimulating but uncluttered appearance. We are proud of the subtleties of the clean and cohesive look and believe that it will be a pleasure for students to read.

- *A creative, customized art program:* We incorporate 240 illustrations and nearly 170 full-color photographs throughout *The World of Business* to illustrate concepts and drive home key points.

A PROFESSIONAL LEARNING TOOL

Creating a book that's a pleasure to read is an important step in developing an effective learning tool. Still, pedagogical devices are necessary to complete the task. Every chapter in *The World of Business* offers:

- *An Integrated Learning System:* Each chapter contains learning goals that challenge the student to explain, discuss, understand, and clarify the concepts presented. Each objective is identified by a numbered icon: ▼, which is repeated in the chapter next to relevant text discussions. The numbered objectives are also identified in the *Instructor's Resource Manual, Test Bank,* and *Study Guide.* The integrated learning system enables you and your students to find and focus on mastery of stated objectives.

- *Numerous full-color photos and illustrations:* An integral part of the book's design, the illustrations present critical data and ideas in a clear, engaging manner. The photos are unusually interesting and are linked to the text by thought-provoking and informative captions.

- *Concept checks:* These questions, at the end of each major section in each chapter, prompt students to review key concepts in the material just covered.

- *Key terms:* Students' business vocabularies will be built on critical terms that are set off in boldface type. The key terms are also defined in the margin for quick review and are listed for quick reference at the end of each chapter. The terms can also be found in a glossary at the end of the book.

- *A comprehensive summary:* A summary—tied to the learning goals—appears at the end of every chapter. Each learning goal is listed and followed by relevant summary information.

- *Discussion questions:* At the end of every chapter, we present a series of thought-provoking questions designed to stimulate class discussion.

- *Case studies:* Brief, lively, and timely cases are written in a style that will enhance student learning. Case topics were carefully selected to be up-to-the-minute and challenging. They include such topics as K-mart's expansion into Central Europe, the ethics of a company's move out of an inner-city neighborhood, reviving Los Alamos as an industrial research and development center, management techniques in the development of Microsoft's Windows NT, and the ethics of advertising malt liquor.

A TEXTBOOK MODEL OF FLEXIBILITY

The structure of *The World of Business*, including chapter sequence and topical coverage, reflects the issues relevant to today's—and tomorrow's—business environment. The structure also gives instructors tremendous support and freedom. The Prologue introduces the eight trends that are featured throughout the book. Part One explores the economics of business in chapters on business systems and the business economy. Part Two provides a solid overview of the business environment in a brand-new chapter on our multicultural society and its implications for business, along with chapters on global business and the important topics of social responsibility and business ethics. Part Three looks at business structures: the forms of business organization and an exploration of entrepreneurship, small businesses, and franchises. At the end of these three parts, the stage is set for the entrance of the functional business disciplines.

The remainder of *The World of Business* covers the major content areas, in this sequence:

Part Four   Management
Part Five   Human Resources
Part Six   Marketing Management
Part Seven   Management Information Tools
Part Eight   Finance

Part Nine covers further dimensions of business in two chapters, one on the legal and tax environment of business and the second on risk and insurance. The text concludes with the Epilogue, which discusses how to find and hold that first job after graduation.

Each of these nine parts has been designed to stand alone as a logical, highly teachable unit. Although the chapters have been sequenced in the most popular order, many other sequences are possible. For example, the Legal and Tax Environment (Chapter 23) could easily be covered before Money and Financial Institutions (Chapter 20). Our flexible chapter design allows instructors to conveniently and effectively create other course structures.

CHANGES IN THE SECOND EDITION

Throughout the text we have carefully updated in-text examples with recent happenings from the business world. We have also replaced most of the trends boxes and end-of-chapter cases in the book; those that remain we feel are classic teaching and learning vehicles. In addition, we have made the following specific changes within individual chapters:

- *Chapter 1:* Updated material on communism and the political situation in Eastern Europe. Updated discussion of automation and computerization in the section entitled "The Technology Revolution." Added a section on the importance of *knowledge workers* in the modern economy. Introduced the concept of *reengineering* in the section on the changing corporate scene.
- *Chapter 2:* Changed the discussion of GNP to follow the new government usage of *GDP*. Revised the material on the service sector, to consider the issues of *service sector productivity* and the *export of services*. Added a new section on the dislocation of the work force, including *downsizing* and the resulting *white-collar unemployment*.
- *Chapter 3:* This *new chapter* titled "Our Multicultural Society and Its Implications for Business" discusses the important demographic and cultural changes taking place in the United States, and it considers their implications for regions, the business community, and society at large. The chapter then looks, in turn, at the demographic and marketplace patterns associated with

significant groups in our diverse society: African-Americans, Hispanic-Americans, Asian-Americans, and Native Americans. Finally, the chapter explores some of the key effects of cultural diversity in the American workplace.

- *Chapter 4:* Updated material to reflect changing trade developments and laws, specifically *GATT,* the *G7 countries,* leveling the playing field with Japan, the *Maastricht Treaty, NAFTA,* and *international franchising.*
- *Chapter 5:* Added the concept of a *glass ceiling* in the gender discussion and expanded the discussion of what the *Americans with Disabilities Act* means for U.S. business.
- *Chapter 6:* Updated material on trends in mergers and acquisitions, including LBOs. Added brief coverage of *S corporations* and *limited liability companies.*
- *Chapter 7:* Revised small business material to include technology as an important factor. Expanded and updated franchising material, to include new information on types of franchising, franchising opportunities for women and minorities, and pitfalls to be aware of in franchising.
- *Chapter 8:* Revised and strengthened the material on leadership styles.
- *Chapter 9:* Added discussions of *reengineering* the corporation and *"partnering"* (virtual corporations).
- *Chapter 10:* Added coverage of *environmental issues* in manufacturing, *continuous improvement, concurrent engineering,* and *flexible plants.* Expanded material on quality management, which now includes *benchmarking* and quality measurement, including *ISO 9000.*
- *Chapter 11:* Added section on *equity theory.*
- *Chapter 12:* Added information on the new *Family and Medical Leave Act of 1993,* the affirmative action record of the 1980s, benefits of employee training, and a partial sample performance appraisal form.
- *Chapter 13:* Added coverage on *labor problems in small firms* and the effects of

reengineering/downsizing on the work force.
- *Chapter 14:* Added material on *middle-aged, "older,"* and *single consumers.*
- *Chapter 15:* Expanded material on *importance of new products* to a firm's profitability and added section on value marketing.
- *Chapter 16:* Reorganized material on vertical marketing systems and market coverage. Added new section, "What's 'In Store' for Retailing's Future?" including discussion of *advanced store technology* and *global retailing.*
- *Chapter 17:* Added section on *advertising regulation,* including *industry self-regulation* and federal regulation, and material on *combining push and pull strategies.*
- *Chapter 18:* Added material on *CD-ROMs.* Expanded coverage of both *local* and *wide area networks,* including the *Internet.* Expanded and revised material on *telecommuting.*
- *Chapter 19:* Added discussion of *international accounting standards, government regulatory organizations,* and *common-size financial statements.* Now includes exhibits of *sample statement of cash flows* and *sample common-size income statement.*
- *Chapter 20:* Added discussion of *M1, M2, M3* and of pressure on banks to make *minority loans.* Updated material on the S&L crisis, problems in banking, international banking, and the future of banking, including *expansion of banking services, mergers and interstate banking,* and *regulatory reforms.*
- *Chapter 21:* The order of the chapters on financial management and the securities markets was switched, so that in this edition financial management comes first. Expanded capital budgeting coverage to include *qualitative factors* involved in the capital budgeting decision. Added new section on *cost of capital,* following the material on leverage which has been condensed. Revised and updated coverage of *venture capital.*
- *Chapter 22:* Added new material on *mu-*

nicipal bonds, underwriting, laws that regulate the securities markets, and securities order types (*market order, limit order, stop-loss order*). Revised discussions of *market averages* and *market indexes,* and ethical issues, including up-to-date examples of some well-known ethical lapses in finance.

- *Chapter 23:* Added new sections on *arbitration* and *mediation* and on *deregulation of the telecommunications industry.* Updated tax material for *new tax law.*
- *Chapter 24:* Added material on *Superfund* and on *title insurance.* Updated *issues in health insurance.*

INSTRUCTOR'S RESOURCES SECOND TO NONE

The World of Business reflects an awareness of the tremendous importance of the first course in business. We've created teaching materials to minimize classroom preparation time and to maximize the student's understanding and appreciation of the world of business and *The World of Business.* The particular emphasis on vocabulary building and integrated learning goals throughout the package ensures that students will succeed in meeting learning objectives and mastering key terms. The package is thorough:

- *Instructor's Resource Manual:* This volume is a comprehensive guide to building a system of customized instruction. The manual begins with sample course outlines and a discussion of learning and teaching strategies for the course. Following this overall introduction to the textbook are detailed lecture outlines for each chapter. Each outline suggests a way to organize lectures, bring in outside examples, and encourage class discussion. Special emphasis is placed on how major chapter points can be reinforced through transparencies, discussion questions, trend areas, and so on. Also included are suggested homework assignments for students and classroom exercises. Answers to discussion questions are included for each chapter, as

well as answers to end-of-chapter cases. Teaching tips and creative ideas for classroom activities are included as well. The goal in designing this manual was to integrate the pieces of the package to support the instructor's classroom lectures and discussions while creating a high level of interest for students. The *Instructor's Resource Manual* is also available on computer disk so that you can customize it to fit your own teaching style and needs.

- *Videodisc Technology:* Videodisc is the ultimate multimedia approach to classroom presentations. Its flexibility and ease of use make it a dynamic tool for instructors. *The World of Business* videodisc contains text-integrated video, definitions, transparencies, and animated illustrations for classroom projection. The videos and other segments can be viewed in any order, and with an optional computer and South-Western software, a complete video "script" of a classroom presentation may be prepared ahead of time. An accompanying *Videodisc Instructor's Guide* describes how to integrate this technology in the classroom. A compatible "CAV-type" videodisc player is required to use this ancillary.
- *Videos tied to the textbook:* As noted earlier, Part Overview, Business Profile, and Career Profile videos have been produced to support and be integrated in the textbook. The video segments are 3 to 5 minutes in length and include all sizes and types of businesses.
- *Test Bank:* Containing over 3,600 test items, the test bank was carefully reviewed by instructors who teach the Introduction to Business course to ensure that questions are well-written, varied, and valid. A grid at the beginning of each chapter of the printed test bank shows which test items relate to which learning objectives in the chapter. The test bank is available in both IBM-compatible and Macintosh disk formats.
- *Color transparencies:* A wealth of colorful acetate transparencies—200 in this edition—are available to enhance lectures

and discussions. About one quarter of them reproduce key illustrations from the textbook. The remaining three-quarters are customized teaching transparencies developed to add interest to classroom lectures.

- *Student Study Guide:* Each part opens with a list of the chapters in that part and a discussion of the purpose of the part. For each chapter, the *Study Guide* includes a chapter outline and learning objectives. This opening material is followed by self-tests tied to the learning objectives, including true/false, multiple-choice, and matching-definitions tests, and a short-answer essay section that reviews the chapter's highlights. Each chapter ends with two experiential exercises. The answer key to all of the self-tests is included at the end of each chapter of the *Study Guide*.
- *Business Simulation Software:* South-Western College Publishing offers software simulations that can be used with *The World of Business*. User's guides are available to reinforce concepts as they are learned.

ACKNOWLEDGMENTS

Preparing a major textbook and its supplements requires the help, advice, and support of many individuals. Special thanks goes to subject matter experts Tom Lumkin, University of Texas at Arlington, for his advice on the management sections of the text, and to Richard A. Hatch, San Diego State University, for his help with the chapter on computers and information systems. Marlene G. Bellamy, aided by Amy Balser Bloomenthal, provided research and writing assistance on many aspects of the text, including many of the Trends boxes. Carl McDaniel also owes a debt of gratitude to Roseann Reddick for keyboarding his portion of the manuscript.

Sincere appreciation is also extended to those who prepared supplementary items in *The World of Business* package. The *Study Guide* was written by Jerome Kinskey and Scott King of Sinclair Community College. Gene Hastings of Portland Community College prepared the *Test Bank*. Elizabeth Elam

of CUNY-Baruch College revised the *Instructor's Resource Manual* for the new edition. Mark Di Stasi, Suzanne Warden, and Becky Jones of Paradigm Communication Group oversaw the research, writing, and production of the video part and chapter openers integrated throughout the textbook. They worked with various business professors to select appropriate companies and recent graduates for the videos.

Special recognition goes to the professionals at South-Western College Publishing who assisted in making the second edition of *The World of Business* a reality. The skills of developmental editor Ann Torbert contributed significantly to this textbook. Sponsoring editors Alice Denny and Dennis Hanseman provided excellent editorial support and coordination. Production editor Eric Carlson took a complicated project and skillfully navigated it through the production process. Development and production of the videos and videodisc were ably handled by media and technology editor Sherie Lajti. Finally, we are indebted to our acquisitions editors Randy Haubner and Rob Jared, who put both time and money on the line in support of this project.

We do not want to overlook the many instructors who contributed their expertise to development of *The World of Business*. Without the cooperation and assistance of this group of highly motivated instructors of the Introduction to Business course, our job would have been more difficult. Our sincere thanks go to the more than five hundred instructors who took the time to share their expertise with us in a very detailed research questionnaire preceding the first edition of the book. Thanks, too, to the reviewers of the previous edition:

Abraham Axelrod, Queensborough Community College
Alec Beaudoin, Triton College
Marcel Berard, Community College of Rhode Island
Harvey Bronstein, Oakland Community College
Pete Ciolfi, Brevard Community College

Steve Floyd, Manatee Community College
Martin Lecker, Rockland Community College
Robert Litro, Mattatuck Community College
Roger Luft, Eastern Illinois University
Jim E. Moore, Front Range Community College
Robert Redick, Lincoln Land Community College
Bill Searle, Asnuntuck Community College
Jonnie Williams, Grand Rapids Junior College

We also wish to acknowledge and thank the following instructors whose enthusiasm for teaching impelled them to submit their great ideas for teaching introduction to business, for inclusion in the second edition *Instructor's Manual*:

James S. Cleveland, The Sage Colleges
Jim Codling, Mary Holmes Jr. College
Bruce L. Conners, Kaskaskia College
Brian P. Cooke, Santa Fe Community College
Sarah S. Dickson, South Puget Sound Community College
Joseph Fox, Spartanburg Technical College
Marlin Gerber, Kalamazoo Valley Community College
Joyce Goetz, Austin Community College
Kathleen C. Jacobs, Wesley College
Janice M. Karlen, Fiorello H. LaGuardia Community College
William P. McClary, Empire State College
Dorothy Minkus-McKenna, Long Island University
Frankie Lee Schesser, Chaffey College
Thomas L. Severance, MiraCosta College
Timothy G. Wiedman, Thomas Nelson Community College
Sandra Young, Shenango Valley School of Business
Nancy Zeliff, Northwest Missouri State University.

We are also most grateful to the following reviewers who suggested ways to make this edition of the book an even better teaching and learning vehicle:

Xenia Balabkins, Middlesex Community College
John C. Bowdidge, Southwest Missouri State College
Tommie Gillespie, Central State University
Robert Grau, Cuyahoga Community College
Kurt A. Heppard, U.S. Air Force Academy
James V. Isherwood, Community College of Rhode Island
Gene Johnson, Clark College
Jerry Kinskey, Sinclair Community College
Joyce Stockinger, Portland Community College
Robert Ulbrich, Parkland College
Rod Wise, Central State University

Finally, we thank our families for their continuing encouragement and support.

Lawrence J. Gitman
Carl McDaniel

ABOUT THE AUTHORS

Lawrence J. Gitman, Professor of Finance at San Diego State University, is the author of a number of best-selling textbooks, including *Principles of Managerial Finance, Personal Financial Planning,* and *Fundamentals of Investing.* His *Investment Fundamentals: A Guide to Becoming a Knowledgeable Investor* was selected as one of 1988's best personal finance books by *Money* magazine. Professor Gitman, who received his Ph.D. from the University of Cincinnati, has served on the faculties of The University of Tulsa and Wright State University. In addition, he has earned the professional credentials of Certified Financial Planner (CFP) and Certified Cash Manager (CCM). His research has appeared in *Financial Management,* the *Financial Review,* the *Journal of Risk and Insurance,* and many other publications. He is past president of the Academy of Financial Services, the Midwest Finance Association, and the FMA National Honor Society. An avid bicyclist, he lives with his wife and two children in La Jolla, California.

Carl McDaniel, Professor of Marketing at the University of Texas, Arlington, has been a classroom teacher for over twenty years and is the winner of two outstanding teaching awards, the most recent of which was given by the Academy of Business Administration. His research has appeared in the *Journal of Marketing Research,* the *Journal of Marketing,* and the *California Management Review,* among many others. In addition to *The World of Business,* he has co-authored *Principles of Marketing* and *Contemporary Marketing Research.* Before receiving his Ph.D. from Arizona State University, Professor McDaniel worked as a district sales manager for Southwestern Bell. He has also been co-owner of a marketing research firm, and his business experience is reflected in this book. In his spare time, Professor McDaniel enjoys skiing and fishing.

TO THE STUDENT

We wrote *The World of Business* with you in mind. Your study of the many exciting aspects of business described in this book will open the door to the wide, wide world of business. We hope it will motivate you to pursue further business studies and choose a career in business, small or large.

Whatever your career path, we urge you to open your mind, relax, and enjoy this textbook. Its exciting format, lively writing style, interesting illustrations, and many learning tools should make your first exposure to the study of business pleasant as well as highly informative.

To help you understand the career opportunities that await you in the business world, we've included two items that relate specifically to careers: The first is videos that tell the stories of recent college graduates and their experiences so far in the business world. Profiles of these young men and women are included in the textbook at the start of each chapter. These videos clearly show you how the material you are about to read has everyday relevance in the job world. The second item related to careers is the career sections at the end of each part. These sections preview specific jobs and describe where opportunities can be found, what skills are required, the employment outlook through the year 2000, and salary ranges. Also, the book's Epilogue will help you prepare for finding the right job.

The glossary at the end of the book and the marginal definitions throughout the chapters will help you define and understand key business terms. For your convenience, at the end of each chapter, key terms are listed along with the page number on which they are first discussed.

At the end of each major section of the text, we have included Checkpoints. These review questions are there to encourage you to stop and think about the material you have just read. We urge you to take the time as you do your assigned reading to stop and try to answer the checkpoint questions. Be honest with yourself in assessing what you have truly mastered and what you need to reread or review before you go on to the next section.

For extra help, the *Student Study Guide* for *The World of Business* is an option available to further enrich your first exposure to business. For each chapter, the guide includes chapter outlines and highlights, self-tests with answers, and a set of experiential exercises. This guide should ease and augment your learning experience.

Now a bit of advice: You will see that most of the young graduates profiled in the videos chose to major in business disciplines in college, and they discuss how the learning that took place in their college courses has helped them in their careers. Those graduates who were liberal arts majors have had to learn some things on the job that their business-major classmates learned in school. Nevertheless, many of the non-business majors mentioned in their interviews that what they found especially useful in business were two skills developed in their college courses: the ability to clearly think through a problem and the ability to communicate well with others, both in writing and orally. Of course, we hope you choose a business discipline as a major, but wherever your talents take you, please be sure to take seriously the need to develop your thinking and communicating skills along the way. They'll be of great use to you in your eventual career—and in life generally.

We applaud you for choosing to learn about the business world. We're confident that this textbook and the study guide will greatly enhance your learning experience. Perhaps they will even help inspire you to pursue further studies in business. We hope you'll enjoy the world of business!

Lawrence J. Gitman
Carl McDaniel

PROLOGUE
Trends in Business

As we rush toward the twenty-first century, the pace of change seems faster and faster. The businesses that will be still competing in the next century are the ones that best adapt to the ever-changing business environment. The one thing we know is that tomorrow's businesses will be quite different from today's.

To understand how fast our lives can change, consider the world of 1975. The Volkswagen beetle was the hot imported car. Japanese imports were just starting to be sold in the United States. The personal computer was an idea yet to be born. Business communication was primarily by telephone or mail—Federal Express and "faxing" were unknown. There were no videocassette recorders or video cameras for personal use, and cellular phone technology was not widely used.

These and other changes in the way we live and work affect business organizations. To survive in tomorrow's business world, businesspeople must do their best to continually answer the question "What will tomorrow hold?" Managers, workers, and tomorrow's graduates must have visions, goals, and ideas based on their best guess of what the future will be. How can they even guess? The smart ones look at today's trends and the issues that seem to be changing fastest, and try to imagine where they'll lead.

To help you look ahead, this prologue examines seven areas where change will affect tomorrow's business: trends in the social and demographic profile of our country, technology, global competition, service businesses, small business, business ethics and social responsibility, and quality management. Throughout the text special theme boxes will give you specific examples of these trends, and an eighth category will focus on interesting stories from other areas of business.

To be successful in the 1990s, business organizations must understand how the trends discussed on the following pages will affect their organizations. In turn, managers and small-business owners must create plans to take advantage of opportunities arising from these and other trends. Businesspeople must also be aware of pitfalls and challenges created by the ever-changing business environment and react accordingly. As the late Washington Redskins coach George Allen once said, "The future is now." Businesses must be nimble enough to change with today's trends. Those that do not will not survive.

SOCIAL AND DEMOGRAPHIC TRENDS

T R E N D S

Social and Demographic

During America's first 150 years, four basic values strongly influenced attitudes and lifestyles. The first was self-sufficiency: Every person stood on his or her own two feet. The second was upward mobility: People could—and did—move up the social and economic ladder, largely through success in business. Next came the Protestant work ethic: hard work, dedication to family, and thrift. The fourth value was conformity: No one wanted to be too different from his or her neighbors.

Today some of these values simply don't hold. Our government has turned self-reliance into a "psychology of entitlement," the notion that the government owes each person a good standard of living. Also, many Americans have lost the habit of saving for their future needs.

Until recently the dream of upward mobility was widespread. Most Americans believed they had a good chance for advancement and felt they were more likely to succeed than their parents. This was especially true for the "baby boomers," the generation born between 1945 and 1960. With the coming of age of the "baby bust" generation—those born between 1961 and 1981—this belief is changing. Unlike the preceding generations, the "busters" are afraid that they may not experience the American Dream. The slower growth of the economy has resulted in fewer jobs and lower wages. The median income of Americans under 25 declined 10.8 percent from 1980 to 1990, while that of other age groups increased 6.5 percent. Many worry that they may not, in fact, match their parents' economic success.[1]

Value differences between the "boomers" and the "busters" can create workplace conflicts. Where the older generation tended to focus primarily on their careers, the "busters" are typically less workaholic. They seek balance in their lives; personal satisfaction comes first for many. "Boomer" managers may perceive "busters" as less dedicated and loyal workers; they must find new ways to motivate their younger employees.

These changes are just a few examples of the trends that may provide rich opportunities and potential pitfalls for American businesses. *Social and demographic trends* affect how and why people live and behave as they do, which in turn affects buying decisions.

THE CHANGING ROLE OF FAMILIES AND WORKING WOMEN

The social trend that perhaps has had the greatest effect on business has been the growing number of women getting jobs outside the home. Today about 60 percent of all women of working age are in the work force, compared to about 45 percent in 1970.[2] The size of the paychecks they earn is growing as well. More women are choosing to delay marriage and to return to work after they have children, thereby increasing their

■ With more women in the workforce than ever before, the traditional dynamic of the family is changing. Many companies are offering new benefits, such as on-site day care centers, to meet the needs of their employees.

earning potential. As a result, the number of affluent households is expected to increase sharply through the year 2000.[3]

With two incomes, families have more purchasing power than ever before. Many of today's families can buy luxury items that were unthinkable a generation ago. Manufacturers can build more quality into products because families now have the money to pay extra for it. Shopping patterns have changed as well. Today, for example, men shop for groceries and women buy their own cars. Studies show that men and women tend to buy different brands. No longer can companies like Sara Lee, Procter & Gamble, and Honda appeal just to the sex that has traditionally bought their products.

Dual careers have also created a *poverty of time*. The hours spent working and commuting to work, taking care of family, doing housework, shopping, sleeping, and eating leave few hours for anything else. Many workers today feel that they do not have time for themselves after meeting work and family responsibilities. As a result, many timesaving strategies have become popular with consumers. For example, videocassette

■ **Exhibit 1**
U.S. Population Growth Rates by Age Group, 1980–1990

Source: U. S. Department of Commerce, Bureau of the Census, *Statistical Abstract of the United States: 1992,* 112th ed. (Washington, D.C.: Government Printing Office, 1992), p. 14.

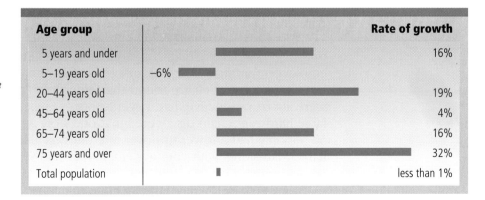

Age group	Rate of growth
5 years and under	16%
5–19 years old	–6%
20–44 years old	19%
45–64 years old	4%
65–74 years old	16%
75 years and over	32%
Total population	less than 1%

recorders (VCRs) let us manage our own television program schedules. Automatic teller machines free us from the limits of bankers' hours. Mail-order, cable TV, and computer shopping services let us shop from home for just about anything, at any time of day.

With more women in the workforce, many companies find they need new types of family benefits to attract and keep employees. Flex-time, job sharing, telecommuting, and child care and elder care are among the benefits offered by an increasing number of corporations. Such policies are good business. The Conference Board, a business research group, found that companies that implement these benefits have lower turnover and absenteeism and increased productivity. They also attract a higher-quality workforce.[4]

A SNAPSHOT OF THE UNITED STATES IN THE 1990s

Social trends like these are extremely important, but they are no more significant than demographic trends. *Demography* is the study of vital statistics such as ages, births, deaths, and locations of people. So how are demographic trends affecting the U.S. population?

For one thing, the population of the United States is growing at a slower rate than in the past. The 1990 census revealed that the U.S. population grew to 250 million in 1990, from 227 million in 1980. This change represented an annual growth rate of less than 1 percent. Population growth estimates expect a continuation of this pattern. But the slow growth rate masks an array of differences.

The "baby boomlet" of the 1980s—when many baby boomers themselves started families—resulted in a modest increase in the number of children under age 10. The number of 20- to 44-year-olds grew by 19 percent between 1980 and 1990, while the number of 10- to 19-year-olds fell by 11 percent (see Exhibit 1). The biggest spurt has come among those over 75. This number has grown by 32 percent since 1980.[5]

In general the U.S. population is becoming older overall. Population forecasters estimate that by 2020 over one-third of the population will be 50 years old or older. And about 5 percent of that group will be 85 or older. Smart businesses are already focusing on an aging marketplace. For example, a higher number of retirees means expanded markets for leisure activities, from hobbies to travel. Companies are changing their advertising campaigns to feature older models. They are taking the needs of older consumers into account when designing products.

The number of workers over 50 is increasing, and companies are discovering that they are a valuable resource. Studies show that older employees perform equal to or better than their younger counterparts. Days Inn, a motel chain, found that older telephone reservations clerks were just as productive, had lower turnover rates, and cost less to train. A large hardware chain discovered that one store staffed with workers over 50 not only had a lower turnover rate but was also 18 percent more profitable than stores with younger employees and 9 percent above the company average. As a result, it plans to recruit more older workers.[6]

Along with a slow growth rate in population, the United States has had a rate of new household formation under 2 percent, the lowest since the

Great Depression. This rate measures the number of new households set up—as, for example, when a young adult moves out of the family home and into his or her own apartment, or when a couple gets a divorce. Growth in household formation is likely to slow even more as we move through the decade.

This change will profoundly affect businesses. They will no longer be able to count on growing markets to fuel sales increases. Thus the 1990s are shaping up as a struggle for market share and profits. Companies will be able to do well in the United States only by taking competitors' customers or by tapping into specialized niches, such as the growing elderly market. Or they can gain new customers by buying them. For example, in 1993 toy maker Mattel, whose products appeal to older children, acquired Fisher-Price, the leader in educational toys for infants and toddlers.[7] If a business cannot count on many new customers coming into the marketplace, it may make sense to buy customers in either existing or new markets.

AMERICANS ON THE MOVE

Just as changing age patterns in a population open new markets, population shifts can do the same. The average American moves every six years. All types of businesses do well in areas that are experiencing a large influx of new residents. On the other hand, in areas where more people are moving out than moving in, many businesses must either move or close down.

Over time different regions of the country gain or lose in popularity. Areas that attracted large numbers of new residents five years ago may today be experiencing low or negative growth. This is true in some areas of California, for example, in response to the state's slow recovery from the 1990-1991 economic downturn. Thousands of jobs have been lost, due in large part to cutbacks in defense and aerospace spending. Many businesses are moving out of state, looking for a more favorable business climate. They are relocating to regions that offer such features as fewer governmental regulations and better and more affordable living conditions for employees.

GROWING MINORITY POPULATIONS

Another demographic trend of note is the rapid growth of minority populations. Minorities now account for about 25 percent of the population in the United States. The three largest minority groups are African-Americans (12 percent), Hispanic-Americans (9 percent), and Asian-Americans (4 percent). By 2023, the Bureau of Census Projections estimates, this number will grow to about 35 percent.

Perhaps the richest gift that business can give to American society is to show, by example, that racial and ethnic harmony in the workplace can translate into a highly productive and creative force. Business can help create a work environment that is open, diverse, and free—an environment that is nonracist and nonsexist and believes in equal opportunity for all.

From a different perspective, growing minority markets represent opportunities for business. The diverse cultural backgrounds of minorities create demands for products customized for their needs. Not only will new goods and services be created to satisfy minority consumers, but unique promotional campaigns and special retail stores will as well. Our multicultural society is discussed in greater detail in Chapter 3.

A CHANGING AGRICULTURAL ENVIRONMENT

Perhaps no other American institution seems so wholesome and tranquil as the family farm. The U.S. government has supported farming since the passage of the Homestead Act in 1862. Except during the Great Depression of the late 1920s and 1930s, family farming prospered. Then, at the end of World War II, the number of family farms began to decline quite rapidly. Small farmers simply couldn't make a living. In 1920 approximately 30 percent of the workers in the United States worked on farms. Today the number is slightly less than 3 percent. The family farm is rapidly becoming a thing of the past.

Big has become better in farming. The use of machines in farming has drastically reduced the number of workers needed to plant and harvest America's crops. New machines and technology have also made American farming the most efficient and productive on earth. Although farms with annual sales of more than $500,000 account for only 1 percent of the number of farms, they contribute 30 percent of total agricultural production and 45 percent of the farm income.[8]

TRENDS IN TECHNOLOGY

TRENDS

Technology

Just as technology has changed farming, so it has changed daily life for all of us. New types of packaging allow us to keep juices, milk, and even whole dinners on the shelf without refrigeration. New types of ice cream and other products are made without harmful cholesterol and fat. We have VCRs and portable radios and TVs to provide us with entertainment. Factories use robots to increase the efficiency of production and reduce the monotony of some assembly line work. Technology has also changed the way we bank (automated teller machines), the way we communicate (cellular phones, video conferencing, fax machines), and the way we play (video games, simulated golf courses, fantasy football games). New diagnostic medical techniques and laser surgery have enabled people to live happier, healthier, and longer lives.

Two types of technology that continue to have an enormous impact on business are computers and communication. In recent years the amount of information we can put on an electronic chip has increased significantly, driving down the cost of personal computers and making them very fast. Computers are also becoming more powerful, more portable, and easier to use. Some can even recognize voice commands and read handwriting. Computers are also an integral part of numerous products, including medical instruments, household appliances, automobiles, and airplanes.

■ The information super-highway will change the way we live and do business by linking computer, phone, and cable television technologies.

New types of technology are changing the way businesspeople communicate. Instead of face-to-face meetings, people can meet electronically. Video-conferencing systems allow managers at different sites worldwide to see and talk with each other using computers and video cameras. This not only saves on travel costs, but also improves employee productivity. Similarly, teleconferencing provides the same advantage, but without the ability to see the participants. The computer screen transmits documents such as diagrams, memos, and financial statements that participants can discuss as if they were in a conventional meeting. Eliminating the time constraints of meetings is possible with electronic conferencing and groupware. This technology creates electronic databases, forums, and conferences that are available 24 hours a day. For example, a company can set up an electronic suggestion box or have ongoing, multisite electronic brainstorming sessions.[9]

The next major technological revolution will be in wireless communications. Cellular technology is already well established. A similar new wireless phone technology, personal communications services (PCS), will lower the cost of mobile phones and pagers to further expand the market for wireless communication. These technologies, together with fiber optics, will expand the "electronic information superhighway," a network linking computer, phone, and cable television technologies. The ability to transmit documents and audio and video data will open up a new world of communication and information services for businesses and individuals. Forward-looking companies are already jockeying for position.

During the rest of the decade many opportunities will exist for businesses creating new technology, for those using it, and for those helping other people learn to use it. Technology will continue to raise our standard of living and provide us with a wealth of new products.

TRENDS IN GLOBAL COMPETITION

The world economy is no longer a series of separate national economies, but one global economy. Advances in technology and communications have allowed more companies than ever before to participate in the world arena. Large U.S.-based multinational corporations have operations in many countries. For example, Gillette manufactures in 57 locations in 28 countries and markets in over 200 countries. Likewise, foreign companies—Honda and Toyota, for example—build factories in the United States. Partnerships between multinational companies are on the rise as companies look for new ways to compete in the global marketplace.

■ New trading blocs throughout the world are lowering tariff boundaries and opening new markets. The North American Free Trade Agreement (NAFTA) will encourage more cross-border trade among Canada, Mexico, and the United States and strengthen economic ties among the three countries.

For example, Hitachi, Ltd., and Texas Instruments have several joint ventures for research and development. Financial markets, small businesses, and service companies are also moving into international markets at an increasing rate.

Around the world, nations are working to remove barriers to growth. We have seen the emergence of important new trading blocs in North America and Western Europe. Latin American countries have adopted economic policies that encourage cross-border trade and foster closer ties with the United States. Canada, Mexico, and the United States have created a free trade zone and are formalizing the economic reality through the North American Free Trade Agreement (NAFTA). The twelve Western European countries that form the European Union opened a new era of free trade and open markets when tariff barriers among them fell at the end of 1992. And in Eastern Europe, countries are testing economic as well as political freedom.

The United States remains the world's premier economic power. But the rest of the world is gaining on us. To overcome world competitors, U.S. managers must rethink time-honored ways of doing things. Workers must become better educated and trained. Business must learn to convert its technology into new products and services. And government must help rather than hinder U.S. companies' attempts to compete in the global marketplace. If Americans don't embrace the global marketplace and become better and bigger participants in it, U.S. stature will only erode further.

TRENDS IN SERVICE BUSINESSES

TRENDS

Service Economy

Roughly eight of every ten U.S. workers are employed in providing services, and 90 percent of the 36 million new jobs created in the United States in the past 20 years have been in the service sector. Service businesses include automobile repair shops, hair salons, stock brokerages, lawyers, physicians, restaurants, hotels, airlines, movie theaters, and many other types of businesses you're familiar with. The service sector accounts for about 75 percent of the value of everything produced in the United States during the year.[10]

The main difference between services and goods is that services are intangible. They cannot be touched, seen, tasted, heard, or felt in the same manner as goods can be. Thus it's harder to judge the quality of services than to judge the quality of goods. For example, if you had your appendix removed, stayed in the hospital for two days, and paid a fee of $1,500, how would you know if you got service worth the price you paid?

More than ever before service organizations are attempting to deliver consistent, quality service. Quality in services cannot be engineered at a manufacturing plant and then delivered intact to the customer. But this is a challenge to even the best-managed firms. Some service firms—the Disney organization, American Express, Federal Express, McDonald's, Fidelity Investments, SAS Airlines, Marriott Hotels—have succeeded in earning reputations for good service.

The future of service organizations is bright. More and more people will work in service businesses as compared with manufacturers and sellers of goods. Professional services, such as health care, law, accounting, engineering, and architecture, will try to improve quality and customer satisfaction.

SMALL BUSINESS TRENDS

Small-business ownership is part of the American Dream. Each year about 250,000 new businesses are launched. Their owners start with high hopes and ambitions. Being in business for themselves gives them a feeling of independence and freedom of choice. Small businesses have played an important role in our economy, and they will continue to do so. Because small businesses thrive in areas of the economy where large businesses could not afford to operate, they give consumers wider choices in the marketplace. For example, a mom-and-pop general store might do quite well in McDaniel, Maryland (pop. 150), but a Safeway supermarket would not have enough business to justify keeping its doors open. Small businesses fill voids all over the United States.

Small-business owners find that they go through two managerial stages. In the first stage, when the firm is small, the owner maintains control over all aspects of its operation. As the company grows, the role of the owner must change. In the second stage, one person can't do it all. Many of the decisions and day-to-day operations must be turned over to others, freeing the owner to plan and direct the overall operation of the company, which are the most important management tasks.

In times past, small-company owners could focus almost exclusively on the business of manufacturing a product or servicing customers. Customers were acquaintances; competitors were often just down the block. But no more. Today's global economy forces the owner/manager to expand far beyond the four walls of a factory or office. Small-business owners must now play some new roles, including public relations expert and international trade specialist. They must also be aware of the legal ramifications of their actions, from hiring to entering into contracts and advertising.

Today opportunities abound for people willing to take risks and put long, hard hours into their own business. As you can see, the small business owner of today must wear many hats in order to succeed.

TRENDS IN BUSINESS ETHICS AND SOCIAL RESPONSIBILITY

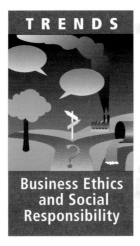

Business Ethics and Social Responsibility

Ethics refers to the moral rules or values generally governing the conduct of a person or a group. A businessperson must consider the ethical aspects of any decision. Today's business ethics are actually a subset of the values held by society as a whole. Like everybody else, businesspeople have social responsibilities. They develop their values through family and educational and religious institutions, as well as social movements. A businessperson with a mature set of ethical values accepts personal responsibility for decisions that affect the full community.

The players in the world of business—including you and me—are the ones who make the decisions and determine the rules. How do we do this in an ethical manner? There is no cut-and-dried answer. But one way to examine the ethics of a business decision is to ask yourself several key questions:

1. Have I defined the problem accurately?
2. Can I discuss the problem with the affected parties before I make my decision?
3. Am I confident that my position will be as valid over a long period of time as it seems now?
4. Could I disclose, without qualm, my decision or action to my boss, my company president, my family, and society as a whole?

A "yes" answer to these four questions is a good indication that the decision is ethical.

Ethics and social responsibility go hand-in-hand. Social responsibility is the concern of businesses for the welfare of society as a whole. Socially responsible companies are managed by people with good ethical values. Today more organizations than ever before are socially conscious. They engage in a variety of activities to benefit society: They hire and train the disadvantaged, donate funds to charities and schools, sponsor community projects, refrain from polluting the environment, use recyclable packaging, and fight illiteracy and school dropout rates, among many other activities.

In summary, business is very much a human institution. It is carried on by, and for, people, and is affected by the traditions and standards of

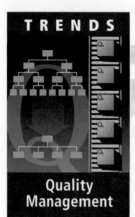

■ Local business and community leaders refurbished this West Baltimore mural depicting African-American heroes to signal their commitment to improving the neighborhood.

those who came before. We can't avoid making decisions about what is right or wrong, whether in our personal lives or in our business lives. What we must do is try our best to do what is right for ourselves and others.

TRENDS IN QUALITY MANAGEMENT

Quality control was once considered primarily a production responsibility. Today, managing for quality is a company-wide goal affecting all departments. *Total quality management (TQM)* refers to the application of quality principles to all aspects of a company's operations. It focuses on improving operations to achieve greater efficiency. A commitment to TQM relates directly to profitability. It results in lower costs, fewer errors, better manufacturing processes, and more efficient administrative systems. As quality increases, so does productivity.

A notable example of TQM in action is Ford Motor Company. Ford, whose motto is "Quality is Job 1," achieved significant cost reductions in the labor, overhead, and materials required to produce its cars. It redesigned its cars so that they need fewer parts. The company also encouraged employees to find ways to improve efficiency and reduce costs. As a result, it needs one-third fewer worker-hours to build its cars than rival General Motors, a savings of about \$800 per car.[11]

TRENDS IN BUSINESS TODAY

In addition to the seven major trends described above, there are many interesting concepts and exciting developments in other areas of the business world. For example, companies are developing new ways to finance their businesses, adopting new management practices, and looking for different ways to train workers. The *Business Today* boxes feature interesting anecdotes or company stories about business in general.

A LOOK AHEAD

This Prologue has quickly sketched the key trends affecting business now and in the future. Two of these areas are so important that we have devoted entire chapters to the topics—international business, Chapter 4, and social responsibilities and business ethics, Chapter 5. All of the trends will be highlighted in boxes throughout the book. For example, one might show how technology is changing business operations; another might describe the effect of demographics on human-resource management or labor relations.

Your journey through **The World of Business** will be both challenging and exciting. A career in business offers great opportunities. At the end of each major section, a special "career appendix" offers a glimpse of specific opportunities available in that area of business. The information in these sections can help you match your aptitudes and interests with the right kind of job for you. Most career sections also describe a "dream job"—a job considered one of the most interesting and challenging in that area. Finally, the epilogue at the end of the book tells you how to get and hold that first job once you have graduated.

Even if you plan to be a social worker, artist, government employee, or schoolteacher, you need to understand basic business principles. An artist, for instance, must manage finances and have some human-relations skills to achieve success. Mental health clinics, branches of government, and schools require sound financial management, quality personnel administration, and marketing skills. As you can see, everyone needs a basic understanding of business.

Part 1

The Economics of Business

Overview

Business in the United States combines human ingenuity, physical resources, and environmental assets within a framework of governmental restraints. The main goal of this system is to produce goods or provide services as efficiently and cost-effectively as possible in order to maximize profits. This can be quite a challenge in our rapidly changing world. Companies must understand and adapt to new technologies, new classes of consumers, and the expanding global marketplace.

One hallmark of our capitalist system is competition. In the early days of mass production, automaker Henry Ford was able to compete effectively simply by turning out cars faster and cheaper than other factories. Now, though, it is more difficult to maintain a competitive edge. A new program to increase employee motivation may be just as important to a company's success as mastering the intricacies of doing business in developing countries.

There is no formula for success in business, but a thorough study of the subject will certainly be beneficial. Are you an independent, entrepreneurial type, or would you prefer to be part of an efficient, well-trained team? Would you be happier owning your own business or working for a large firm? Knowing the many forms business can take—from the locksmith down the street to multinational conglomerates like Procter & Gamble— you will be better prepared to choose your career path. A basis in economics is also important. It would be impossible to run a successful business of any size without understanding such economic concepts as inflation, unemployment, and the principles of supply and demand.

Another lesson to be learned from studying business is the necessity of planning. Your great idea for a product will remain just that—an idea— unless you formulate a solid plan for development, production, and marketing. At the same time, a company's business strategy must be flexible enough to allow for unexpected changes. Contingency plans should be included that will allow the company to weather a period of slow sales or a downturn in the economy and the resultant higher costs and tighter credit.

Ready-made solutions are as rare in business as they are in your personal life. This is as it should be, because business is grounded in the real world. It does not exist above it or outside it. Recognizing this, more and more corporations are showing increased concern for the environment, the consumers who buy their products, and their workers. They realize that business has a social responsibility, and that they must consider all of their actions in terms of society as a whole.

The constantly changing economic environment makes business an arena for creativity and inventiveness. New problems arise every day, demanding new solutions. The first part of this book gives you an overview of the history of American business, describes the various economic systems, and introduces you to the basic theories of economics. These are the foundations of a solid business education.

Company Profile

KMPG Peat Marwick has every right to refer to itself as "The Global Leader" in the accounting profession. With 800 offices in 125 countries, it is the largest public accounting firm in the world and the first ever to reach $6 billion in annual revenues. Among top-ranked accounting firms, it represents the largest share of audited companies in sales and assets worldwide.

The company reached this level of accomplishment by positioning itself as a market-driven firm. It is committed to being responsive to its clients' needs and understanding their businesses from the inside out. Ultimately, that meant structuring the corporation in a way that would provide client services that go far beyond traditional accounting functions.

KMPG Peat Marwick has reorganized its international network to reflect its status as a global business advisory firm. The new structure concentrates on six lines of business in ten worldwide geographic areas. The lines of business are: financial services, health care and life sciences, information and communications, manufacturing, retailing and distribution, and special markets and designated services. The new structure is supported by the Center for Professional Excellence, an internal education department designed to enhance the company's teamwork approach to servicing clients.

KPMG Peat Marwick believes its market-focused strategy will allow it to deliver unmatched value to its clients and lead to growth and greater profit for the firm. This "Global Leader" is committed to setting new standards for the accounting profession.

Business Systems

chapter 1

Learning Goals

After studying this chapter, you should be able to:

1. Gain an appreciation for the study of business.
2. Understand the term *business*.
3. Recognize how the four basic inputs and the two basic outputs of the business system are related.
4. Discuss the differences among basic economic systems.
5. Understand how gross domestic product, productivity, and standard of living measure the performance of economic systems.
6. Trace the historical development of U.S. business.

Career Profile

As a busy college student, Chad Mattix used his computer for everything from composing term papers to balancing his budget. When minor equipment or software problems arose, he was frustrated by the scarcity of companies offering advice and technical aid geared to student computing needs. Recognizing an unfilled niche, he and three others joined forces to develop a small business that provides a wide range of support to other computer users on campus. The partners' complementary backgrounds contributed to the company's success. Some members provided business savvy, others technical expertise.

Pinnacle Computer Corporation is still going strong. Two years out of college, Chad is now president of the company, which recently began offering its services to small and medium-size businesses. Pinnacle designs work-group applications for internal communications through e-mail (electronic mail) and project management programs. The goal is to use computer technology to better manage small companies' work loads and streamline their communications. Pinnacle works closely with clients, identifying their processes and then determining the best means of automating them.

Chad's role as president requires that he focus on several aspects of the business, including sales, accounting, operations, and legal issues. His degree in finance has been a big help, but he feels that a broader background in other areas of business studies, such as sales and marketing, would have better prepared him for the challenges he now faces.

Chad believes entrepreneurs will find more opportunities as major corporations reduce the size of their workforces and turn to outside companies to perform jobs once done in-house. Pinnacle Computer Corporation plans to continue expanding its customer base—and profits—by keeping abreast of new technology and the changing needs of their clients. Judging by their success thus far, it is a potent recipe for success.

This chapter is the beginning of our journey; it will introduce you to the world of business. It has two goals: to help you appreciate the study of business and to give you some background that will be useful as you read the rest of the book. After a brief discussion of why and how to study business, the chapter describes the basic inputs and outputs of the business system and their circular flow through the economy. It then discusses the differences among basic economic systems: capitalism, socialism, and communism. It next looks at how the performance of economic systems can be measured and, finally, at the development of the U.S. business system.

THE STUDY OF BUSINESS

 Businesses are dynamic organizations. They grow and contract as they move through different life cycle stages. Changes in the economy and the marketplace require businesses to rethink existing strategies and apply new methods and tools. Successful companies continually seek new markets and better ways to do things. Take, for example, Blockbuster Entertainment Corporation, the country's largest video rental chain. Recognizing that new forms of technology could make video rentals obsolete, company Chairman Wayne Huizenga is transforming Blockbuster into a global entertainment company. Since 1992, Blockbuster has added three retail music chains, two movie studios, and children's indoor play centers. It has plans for a large entertainment and sports complex in Florida.[1]

It's wise to look for better ways to do business when you're at the top of your game. Many companies don't do so, however, until things start to sour. Chrysler Corporation was one such company. On the verge of bankruptcy in the 1970s, Chrysler has since made a spectacular comeback. Once viewed as stodgy and unresponsive to customer preferences, the revitalized carmaker has had a recent string of successful new car introductions. The company revamped its operations, adopting "lean management" techniques pioneered by the Japanese. Chrysler now brings together engineering and manufacturing employees on product-development teams. Relying on suppliers for design and preassembled units, rather than doing everything in-house, reduces costs and time. As a result, the new Neon subcompact cost about $1.3 billion to develop, compared to $3.5 billion for GM's Saturn.[2]

WHY STUDY BUSINESS?

Studying business is important for people just starting their careers. Whether you want to be a social worker, engineer, government employee, or manager, you need to understand basic business principles. This is also true whether you plan to work for a profit-oriented company like Chrysler or a not-for-profit organization like the United Way or Girl Scouts of America. A *not-for-profit organization* exists to provide a social service rather than to earn a profit. But to be efficient, it too must operate as a business, competing for people's scarce volunteer time and donations.

■ Different careers require different skills. A manager must be able to communicate effectively with people and motivate them to perform, while a computer specialist will need a solid technical background.

Selecting a Career

A primary reason to study business is to learn about career opportunities. Most jobs are found in private business, but many government bodies and not-for-profit organizations also offer challenging positions.

Some careers focus on people skills and some on technical skills. By studying business, you will learn which career paths focus on which skills. An accountant, for example, must have an eye for detail and enjoy working with numbers. A salesperson must enjoy meeting and interacting with people. Often a production manager must have training in engineering as well as business.

Understanding the Role of the Worker

Another reason to study business is to understand the role of the worker. Most students choose to work for a company or organization instead of running their own business. If you understand the nature of business, you will have a clearer picture of where you fit into the overall operation. You will know what rewards are available and the training required to advance in your chosen career path.

Becoming an Independent Businessperson

The pride of owning a business is often available to those willing to make some sacrifices. One of the first tasks in opening a new business is to get financing. Banks and other financial institutions want to see a sound business plan before they loan funds. A person who knows about business can create a better plan.

A small-business owner usually can't afford to hire specialists like full-time accountants, human-resource managers, or market researchers. The owner must perform these functions instead. Business training helps the owner perform these tasks well. Also, a person with sound business skills is more likely to succeed as an owner.

Appreciating the Relationship between Business and Society

Citizens need to know what responsibility business has to society. As Chapter 5 explains, business does not cause all of society's ills, nor is it able to cure them. But by understanding the impact of business on society, we can think intelligently about the proper role of business in dealing with society's problems.

Becoming a More Informed Consumer

It has been said that people can increase their standard of living by a third by making wise consumer decisions. For example, buying a car with a history of few breakdowns costs less in the long run than buying a car with a poor service record. Consumers who know how products are manufactured and moved to the marketplace and how prices are determined understand better how to purchase the right products. In turn, they motivate businesses to produce the goods and services they want and need.

HOW TO STUDY BUSINESS

You can study business both formally and informally. An informal study would include working in an industry; reading books, magazines, and newspapers; and talking about business with other people. All of these activities build your knowledge of business.

The formal study of business can take many forms. The most common is a degree program offered by a college or university, from an associate degree at a two-year college to a bachelor's degree at a four-year school and the advanced master's degree (MBA) and doctorate (DBA or Ph.D.). Many business schools combine formal study with work experience in the form of cooperative programs and internships to bridge the gap between classroom theory and the realities of the business world.

Concept Check
- What are some important reasons to study business?
- Why is it important to be an informed consumer?

People who know how products are produced can make better purchases

---

THE NATURE OF BUSINESS

2   What does the term *business* mean to you? To some people it means large companies and their activities; to others it means small enterprises owned by families; to yet others it means jobs. In its most far-reaching sense, **business** is the economic process in which productive resources (basic inputs) are assembled and used to create goods and services (basic outputs) that can satisfy society's needs and wants.

business Economic process that involves assembling and using productive resources to create goods and services that can satisfy society's needs and wants.

In this sense business is as much a part of the Cuban and Chinese systems as it is of the U.S. system. Regardless of a nation's political structure, goods and services must be produced and distributed. What distinguishes U.S. firms from Cuban or Chinese firms is our use of individual decision making, based on the profit motive, to determine the output of goods and services. In some societies central planning determines a good deal of the output. But more and more nations, including Eastern European countries and the Commonwealth of Independent States (formerly the Soviet Union), are moving to free-market economies that allow individual decision making.

■ A piano converts inputs—pressure on its keys—into outputs—musical notes. Business can be viewed as the economic equivalent of this process, with production resources being used to create needed goods and services.

Producing goods and services that consumers want, at fair prices and with a no-nonsense approach, is a major strength of the United States. The spirit that enables U.S. businesses to do these things is found at both small firms and our largest companies. Ford Motor Company, for example, is committed to producing high-quality automobiles and trucks. McDonald's insists on cleanliness and consistent service at its thousands of fast-food outlets throughout the world.

BASIC INPUTS

3

factors of production
Four basic inputs used by business: natural resources, labor, capital, and entrepreneurship.

natural resources
Commodities that are useful inputs in their natural state.

Businesses make use of four basic inputs: natural resources, labor, capital, and entrepreneurship. These inputs, known as **factors of production**, are common to all productive activity in all economic systems.

Natural Resources
Commodities that are useful inputs in their natural state are known as **natural resources**. They include farmland, forests, mineral and oil deposits, and water. Sometimes natural resources are simply called *land*, although, as you can see, the term means more than just land. Today, urban sprawl, pollution, and limited resources have raised questions about resource use. Conservationists, ecologists, and government bodies are proposing laws to control land planning and resource conservation.

Labor

labor Economic contributions of people working with their minds and muscles.

capital Tools, machinery, equipment, and buildings used to produce goods and services and get them to the consumer.

The economic contributions of people working with their minds and muscles are called **labor**. This input includes the talents of everyone—from restaurant cooks to nuclear physicists—who performs the many tasks of manufacturing and selling goods and services.

Capital
The tools, machinery, equipment, and buildings used to produce goods and services and get them to the consumer are known as **capital**. Some-

times the term *capital* is also used to mean the money that buys machinery, factories, and other production and distribution facilities. However, because money itself produces nothing, it is *not* one of the basic inputs. Instead, it is a means of acquiring the inputs. Therefore, in this context, capital does not include money.

Entrepreneurship

entrepreneurs Risk takers who seek profit by combining natural resources, labor, and capital to produce goods or services.

Entrepreneurs are people who combine the inputs of natural resources, labor, and capital to produce goods or services for intended profit. These people must make all the decisions that set the course for their firms; they must create products and production processes. Because they are not guaranteed a profit in return for their time and effort, they must be risk takers. Of course, if their firms succeed, the rewards may be great.

One very successful entrepreneur is Bill Gates, founder of Microsoft Corporation. Gates, now in his late thirties, dropped out of Harvard in 1975 to establish his computer software company. When he started Microsoft, he recognized that a computer chip called the microprocessor would make it possible to produce computers small and cheap enough for people to use in their homes and offices. Six years later he convinced IBM to let him sell DOS (disk operating system), which is the internal software that makes an IBM personal computer work. With DOS, other manufacturers could make IBM-compatible computers. Today, DOS is used in over 120,000 personal computers.

Gates transformed Microsoft into a major power in the computer industry. It had 1993 sales of over $4.1 billion, about 15,000 employees, and a market value (based on the price of its common stock) of $23 billion. It offers the broadest array of products in the personal computer software business, with a market share of about 30 percent. Along the way, Bill Gates has amassed a personal fortune of over $7 billion, most of it in Microsoft stock.[3] Such are the rewards for the successful entrepreneur. On the other hand, as Chapter 7 will show, entrepreneurs work hard and take many risks.

BASIC OUTPUTS: GOODS AND SERVICES

goods Tangible items manufactured by businesses.

Firms use the basic inputs to produce the basic outputs desired by customers: goods and services. **Goods** are the tangible items made by businesses, including the packaging, the brand name, and the item itself. General Motors goods are more than just the Chevrolets and Buicks made by the firm. GM is in the business of providing personal transportation. Hence the cars, trucks, and buses it makes are only the tangible, or outer, form of what the company provides. It also provides maintenance, through dealers, to help keep the vehicles on the road.

services Intangible items provided by organizations for their customers.

Services are intangible items, things that can't be held, touched, or seen before they are acquired. Examples of services are hairstylists cutting hair, dry cleaners cleaning clothes, attorneys drawing up wills, and accountants filling out tax forms. Many service firms are small enterprises, but a number are large. Examples of large service firms are Price Waterhouse and Company (certified public accountants), Prudential Insurance, and Hyatt Hotels.

REWARDS

profit Reward to businesses for providing what consumers are willing to buy.

What motivates entrepreneurs and other business owners? Why are they willing to take the financial risks involved in business? There is no single answer to this question, but one motivator is well known: profit. **Profit** is the reward to businesses for providing what consumers are willing to buy. It is the return that business owners receive for assembling the basic inputs and taking the risks of business ownership. Technically, profit is the amount of money remaining from a firm's sales revenues after deducting production costs, interest costs, and taxes.

Profit is one measure of a firm's success. It tells potential investors which firms and industries are good investments. People with money to invest move their money into firms with high profits and out of those with low profits.

Profit also benefits society. Firms that meet customer demands and desires are able to grow. Growth provides more jobs, which means more consumer spending, which in turn creates even more jobs.

Besides entrepreneurs, other suppliers of inputs must also receive rewards. If they did not, the stream of inputs available for production would soon dry up. Labor, for example, must be compensated, because people generally will not work without pay. Payment for labor services is called *wages*, payment for the use of natural resources is called *rent*, and payment for capital is called *interest*.

THE CIRCULAR FLOW OF INPUTS, OUTPUTS, AND MONEY

People in households provide the basic inputs (natural resources, labor, capital, and entrepreneurship) to businesses. That is, businesses and all the inputs they use are owned by households—by individuals. Thus profits end up in the hands of the people who own the businesses.

circular flow Flow of inputs from households to businesses in return for money in the form of rent, wages, interest, and profits and flow of outputs from businesses to households in return for money in the form of spending.

We can view the business system in terms of the **circular flow** of inputs, outputs, and money (see Exhibit 1-1). The upper half of the exhibit shows a two-way flow between households and businesses through the *resource markets*—the markets for natural resources, labor, capital, and entrepreneurship. Households directly or indirectly (through their ownership of businesses) own all these inputs and supply them to businesses. The businesses pay for the inputs in the form of rent, wages, interest, and profits. These four types of payment represent income to the households supplying the inputs. As the lower half of the exhibit shows, the households use the money they receive from the businesses to buy outputs in the product markets—the markets for goods and services, or products. The circular flow of inputs, outputs, and money makes up the lifeblood of the business system.

Concept Check

- What are the basic inputs and outputs of an economic system?
- Explain the concept of circular flow.

Natural resources, Labor & Capital

▓ Exhibit 1-1
The Circular Flow of
Inputs, Outputs, and
Money

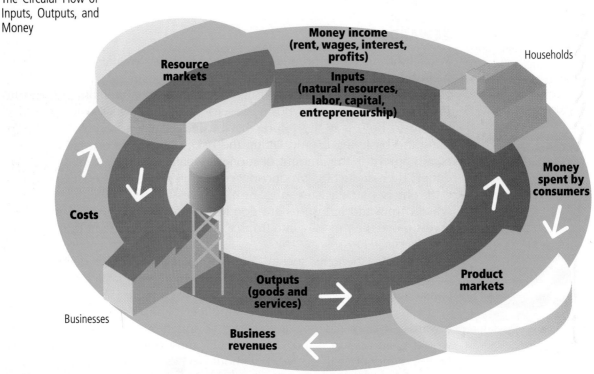

ECONOMIC SYSTEMS

4 During this century, the world has seen intense competition among three
very different economic systems: capitalism, socialism, and communism.
Most of the world's people have lived and worked under one of these
three. Yet, remarkably, within the past few years communism has stum-
bled. By understanding the nature of each system, you can see why communism is losing its appeal.

CAPITALISM

capitalism Economic system based on competition in
the marketplace and private
ownership of the factors of
production.

Capitalism, also known as the *private enterprise system,* is based on competition in the marketplace and private ownership of the factors of production (resources). In a competitive economic system a large number of
people and businesses freely buy and sell products in the marketplace. In
pure capitalism all the factors of production are owned privately, and the
government does not try to set prices or coordinate economic activity.

The first advocate of this system was the Scottish economist Adam
Smith. In 1776 he wrote *The Wealth of Nations,* in which he explained
why a capitalist system has little need for government planning, intervention, or control. Smith believed that economic freedom is essential for
growth. He believed that people will work hard if they receive enough

■ Capitalism in the United States is characterized by private ownership of businesses and competition in the marketplace. This competition helps keep prices low and encourages the development of new and more diverse products.

financial reward. A worker who isn't satisfied with the money earned will produce something else. For example, a cobbler would quit making leather shoes and start making leather jackets if he could make twice as much money per year.

As if guided by an invisible hand, the economy grows and prospers as people try to improve their economic well-being. When products are scarce, prices tend to be high. Producers will make and sell high-priced merchandise because they earn more money doing so. As more such items are produced, the scarcity disappears. The invisible hand then guides the production of other needed goods and services for the society.

A capitalist system offers certain economic rights: the right to own property, the right to make a profit, the right to make free choices, the right to compete. The right to own property is central to capitalism. Profit is the main incentive in this system, and it encourages entrepreneurship. Profit is also necessary for producing goods and services, building plants, paying dividends and taxes, and creating jobs. The freedom to choose whether to become an entrepreneur or to work for someone else means that people have the right to decide what they want to do on the basis of their own drive, interests, and training. The government does not create job quotas for each industry or give people tests to determine what they must do.

In a capitalist system competition is good for both businesses and consumers. It leads to better and more diverse products, keeps prices stable, and increases the efficiency of producers. Producers try to produce their goods and services at the lowest possible cost and sell them at the highest possible price. But when profits are high, more firms enter the market to seek those profits. The resulting competition among firms tends to lower prices. Producers must then find new ways of operating more efficiently if they are to keep making a profit—and stay in business.

Economists see four types of competition within capitalism. They are perfect (pure) competition, monopoly, monopolistic competition, and oligopoly. We'll look at each of these in turn.

Perfect Competition

Four things define **perfect (pure) competition**:

- A large number of small firms are in the market.
- The firms sell similar products; that is, each firm's product is very much like the products sold by other firms in the market.
- Buyers and sellers in the market have good information about prices, sources of supply, and so on.
- It is easy to open a new business or close an existing one.

In a perfectly competitive market firms sell their products at prices determined solely by forces beyond their control. Since the products are very similar and since each firm contributes only a small amount to the total quantity supplied by the industry, price is determined by supply and demand. A firm that raised its price even a little above the going rate would lose customers. In the wheat market, for example, the product is essentially the same from one wheat producer to the next. Thus none of the producers has control over the price of wheat.

Perfect competition is an ideal. No industry shows all its characteristics. But the stock market and some agricultural markets, such as wheat and corn, come closest to perfect competition. A farmer, for example, can sell all of his crop through national commodity exchanges at the current market price.

Pure Monopoly

At the other end of the spectrum is **pure monopoly**, the market structure in which a single firm accounts for all industry sales. This structure is characterized by **barriers to entry**—factors that prevent new firms from competing equally with the existing firm. Often the barriers are technical or legal conditions. Polaroid, for example, has held major patents on instant photography for years. When Kodak tried to market its own instant camera, Polaroid sued, claiming patent violations. Polaroid collected millions of dollars from Kodak. Another barrier may be one firm's control of a natural resource. DeBeers Consolidated Mines Ltd., for example, controls most of the world's supply of uncut diamonds.

Public utilities like gas, water, and electricity are pure monopolies. Some monopolies are created by a government fiat that outlaws competition. The U.S. Postal Service is currently one such monopoly.

Monopolistic Competition

Three characteristics define the market structure known as **monopolistic competition**:

- Many firms are in the market.
- The firms offer products that are close substitutes but still different from one another.
- It is relatively easy to enter the market.

perfect (pure) competition Form of capitalism in which a large number of small firms sell similar products, buyers and sellers have good information about the market, and entry or exit is easy.

pure monopoly Form of capitalism in which a single firm accounts for all of an industry's sales.

barriers to entry Factors that prevent new firms from competing equally with the existing firm in a monopoly.

monopolistic competition Form of capitalism in which a large number of firms offer products that are close but not identical substitutes and entry is relatively easy.

Under monopolistic competition, firms take advantage of product differentiation. Industries where monopolistic competition occurs include clothing, food, and similar consumer products. Companies use advertising to distinguish their products from others. Such distinctions may be significant or superficial. For example, Burger King claims that its broiled burgers are better than McDonald's grilled ones, and Tylenol is advertised as being easier on the stomach than aspirin.

Firms under monopolistic competition have more control over pricing than do firms under perfect competition, because the products are not viewed by consumers as exactly the same. However, firms must demonstrate those product differences to justify their prices to customers.

Oligopoly

oligopoly Form of capitalism in which a few firms produce most of the output and large capital requirements limit the number of firms.

An **oligopoly** has two characteristics:

- A few firms produce most or all of the output.
- Large capital requirements or other factors limit the number of firms.

Boeing and McDonnell Douglas (aircraft manufacturers) and USX (formerly U.S. Steel) are major firms in different oligopolistic industries.

With so few firms in oligopolies, what one firm does has an impact on the other firms. Thus the firms in an oligopoly watch one another closely for new technologies, product changes and innovations, promotional campaigns, pricing, production, and so on. Sometimes they go so far as to coordinate their pricing and output decisions, which is illegal. Many antitrust cases—legal challenges arising out of laws designed to control anticompetitive behavior—occur in oligopolies.

SOCIALISM

socialism Economic system in which the basic industries are owned by the government or by the private sector under strong government control.

Socialism is the economic system in which the basic industries are owned by the government or owned by the private sector under strong government control. A socialist state controls such critical, large-scale industries as transportation, communication, and utilities. Smaller businesses may be privately owned. To varying degrees the state also determines the goals of businesses, the prices and selection of goods, and the rights of workers. Socialist countries typically provide for their citizens a higher level of services, such as health care and generous unemployment benefits, than do capitalist countries. As a result, however, taxes and unemployment can be quite high in these countries.

Socialism is the economic system of many countries, including Great Britain, Denmark, Israel, and Sweden. However, socialism operates differently from country to country. In Denmark, for example, most businesses are privately owned and operated, but two-thirds of the population is sustained by the state through government welfare programs.

COMMUNISM

communism Economic system in which the factors of production are owned collectively and the people receive economic benefits according to their needs and contribute according to their abilities.

Developed in the late nineteenth century by Karl Marx and others, **communism** is the economic system in which the factors of production are owned collectively rather than individually. The people receive economic benefits according to their needs and contribute to society according to their abilities. Marx, a German economist, expected a social revolution that would result eventually in a classless society. Government would wither away, and the people would then run the society for the good of everyone. The true test for communism began in 1917, when Russia was knocked out of World War I by the Germans. Vladimir Lenin, a follower of Marx, rose to power and established a communist regime. Communism later spread from Russia to other countries in Eastern Europe, as well as to China, North Korea, and Cuba.

The late 1980s and early 1990s was a period of great change in all communist countries. Their failure to maintain healthy economic growth finally produced tremendous change. In 1991 the former Soviet Union became a confederation of independent states, of which Russia is the largest. Today communism is being replaced by some aspects of a free market system throughout Eastern Europe and some of the former Soviet states.

Economic reform is not easy. In fact, changing from communism to a freer market is a gut-wrenching and uncertain process. In Russia, political turmoil and economic chaos followed the fall of communism. The people were unprepared for competition and capitalism. Factory managers who were used to being told how much to produce and where to ship the goods were forced to find customers for their wares. Workers used to loafing on the job suddenly had to produce or lose their jobs. During this transition period, continuing political unrest and fighting between regional factions contributed to the weakening of the Russian economy. Unemployment rose. Personal income fell sharply, while problems with supply and demand for goods pushed prices higher.

Only time will tell what kinds of economic reforms take place in the former communist nations. As of late 1993 the Russian government was preparing a new round of free market reforms designed to force companies to become more competitive in the world market. Additionally, farmers on some collective farms were offered the opportunity to buy for themselves the land they had farmed with others. However, there were signs that some countries were beginning to undo the moves toward a market economy. Poland, for example, once again elected a communist government.

Yet the newly established private sector is already showing signs of becoming more firmly entrenched. With no central economy to control the flow of goods and services throughout the former Soviet Union and Eastern Europe, many entrepreneurs are finding ways to bridge the gap. Many Russians seek the chance to earn more than the average factory salary of $30 per month or to supplement it with income from other businesses. For example, large numbers of traders travel to Poland regularly with goods bought at state stores that they resell at higher prices. Perhaps the next step for some will be setting up their own stores or factories.[4] American entrepreneurs, too, are discovering new market opportunities in Russia, as the nearby Small Business Trends box shows.

TRENDS

Small Business

American Entrepreneurship Is Alive in Russia

Large multinationals like Coca Cola and RJR Nabisco, as well as smaller companies, are opening offices in Russia in record numbers. But when managers from these firms arrive in Russia, they find that the fledgling free enterprise system does not offer all—or even many—of the comforts of home. Even when services like dry cleaning and video rentals exist, the quality is inferior. To the rescue of these frustrated foreigners comes a group of American entrepreneurs whose businesses provide the desired goods and services.

Often the ideas for their businesses come from their own experiences while living in Russia. Alexander Malchik discovered during business trips to Russia that good coffee was hard to find. In partnership with Montana Coffee Traders, based in his hometown of Whitefish, Montana, he opened a gourmet coffee business in Moscow in March 1992. The business was profitable within two months. By fall 1993 it supplied coffee beans to foreign businesses, luxury hotels, and supermarkets. Likewise, Lisa Dobbs recognized that Westerners had difficulty finding good, healthy, and affordable food. The result was Moscow Catering Co./Kalitnikovsky Produkti. Her firm was an instant success and, in addition to catering services, now sells prepared foods.

The influx of foreign companies also created a need for employee housing. While looking for his own lodgings, management consultant Michael Oster found most available apartments were overpriced and did not have the features desired by Westerners. His real estate and development company, with offices in Moscow and St. Petersburg, rents apartments from Russians, remodels them for the Western market, and sublets them.

Starting a business in Russia isn't easy. It can take six months to register a company with the government. Most small companies can't afford the high cost of renovated commercial facilities and must rent older, less attractive space. After overcoming these stumbling blocks, however, these entrepreneurs are on their way to success as they meet the growing demand from both Westerners and Russians for previously unavailable, high-quality goods and services.[5]

MIXED ECONOMIES

mixed economies
Economies that use more than one economic system, typically capitalism and socialism.

Canada, Great Britain, and Sweden, among others, are **mixed economies**. That is, they use more than one economic system. Typically, the government is basically socialist and owns basic industries. In Canada, for example, the government owns the communications, transportation, and utilities industries, as well as some of the natural-resource industries. It also supplies health care to its citizens. But most other activity is carried on by private enterprises, as in a capitalist system.

The United States, surprisingly, is also considered a mixed economy. The few factors of production owned by government include some public lands, the Postal Service, and some water resources. But the government is extensively involved in the economic system through taxing, spending, and welfare activities. The economy is also mixed in the sense that the country tries to achieve many social goals—income redistribution and social security, for example—that may not be attempted in purely capitalist systems.

Some people believe that the U.S. government is too involved in the economy. They note that the average worker now must work over five months just to pay one year's federal, state, and local taxes. Although the public seems to favor reducing the role of government, it is a difficult goal to achieve and not likely to happen soon.

THE PERFORMANCE OF ECONOMIC SYSTEMS

5 Various measures show how well an economic system is performing, whether it is capitalist, socialist, communist, or mixed. These measures include gross domestic product, productivity, and the standard of living.

Gross Domestic Product

gross domestic product (GDP) Monetary value of all final goods and services produced within a nation annually.

Gross domestic product (GDP) is the monetary value of all final goods and services produced within a country each year. This measure is considered the best guide to a country's economic health because it shows how fast output is growing (or not growing). Prior to December 1991 the United States measured its total output in terms of gross national product (GNP). GNP includes both domestic and overseas operations in the value of all final goods and services produced by a nation's economy. GDP measures only domestic production, and most economists consider it a better measure than GNP of a country's economy. Because GDP is used by most other countries, this change makes it easier to compare U.S. economic growth to that of other countries. Recently the GDP of the United States has been growing at a slow but steady rate. In 1993, for example, GDP was almost 5 percent higher than GDP in 1992, after adjustment for inflation. (Inflation, a general increase in prices, is covered in more detail in Chapter 2.)

Productivity

productivity Output of goods and services per unit of labor.

Another measure of economic well-being is **productivity**, the output of goods and services per unit of labor. Productivity increases when we get more output from the same or less input. For example, if a single worker produces 50 tables one month and 75 tables the next month, productivity has increased.

Productivity can be increased by giving workers more and better equipment. A worker can move more dirt per hour with a bulldozer than with a shovel. Education and training can also enhance productivity. During the 1980s U.S. productivity lagged behind that of other countries. In the 1990s it has has been steadily increasing as investments in new technologies are paying off. As we will see in Chapter 2, improved service sector productivity is a major reason for these gains.

Standard of Living

How well do people live in the United States? We can tell by examining the **standard of living**, the level of material affluence of a country, as measured by its output of goods and services divided by its total population. The United States, France, Canada, West Germany, Japan, and Britain have the highest standard of living in the world, along with Saudi Arabia and a few tiny oil-based kingdoms. In contrast, the standard of living in Eastern European countries, including the countries of the former Soviet Union, is less than half that of the United States.

Our standard of living changes over time. In the 1950s and 1960s, most families managed very well on one paycheck. Now more families need a second paycheck to maintain their standard of living. America's standard of living is not shared equally. About one in four households have incomes under $15,000, half are in the $15,000 to $50,000 range, and another quarter have incomes over $50,000.[6]

Concept Check

- Explain the four types of competitive environments.
- Compare and contrast capitalism, socialism, and communism.
- What is a mixed economy? Give some examples.
- Describe several measures of economic well-being.

[handwritten notes: pure perfect Competition, Monopolistic, Oligopoly, Monopoly]

[handwritten notes: GDP prod. S.O.L.]

DEVELOPMENT OF THE U.S. BUSINESS SYSTEM

6 From the beginning, anyone in our country who had the ability could take part in business activities. In fact, some of the most famous Americans were businesspeople first: Benjamin Franklin was a printer only a short

■ The colonial economy revolved around home-based industry. Families were large, and the members worked together to produce most of the goods they required, from cloth to butter to hand-forged tools. When the family had satisfied its needs, any surplus was sold or traded.

time after running away from home at age seventeen; Abraham Lincoln was a storekeeper before studying law and entering politics. Business activities range from starting a company to buying part ownership in it or lending it money. This book provides many examples of the variety and creativity of U.S. business activity.

THE COLONIAL ERA

In colonial times (before 1800) most businesses were family enterprises. And most colonial families were self-sufficient. Family members made cloth, grew crops, and hunted wild game. They built and furnished their houses. Large families were useful, and children were expected to help with the work. Once the family had all it needed, any surplus it produced could be sold or traded. This was the beginning of the market system. As production processes grew more efficient, more surplus goods came to the marketplace.

THE INDUSTRIAL REVOLUTION

Industrial Revolution
Massive shift from home-based industries to the factory system, which began in England in the mid-1700s and in the United States in the mid-1800s.

The **Industrial Revolution** was a massive shift from home-based industry. Begun in England in the mid-1700s, it ushered in the factory system, which brought all the materials, machinery, and labor together in one place.

English law prohibited the export of machinery and technology at this time. But Samuel Slater, a young Englishman, memorized the details for constructing textile machines and built the first U.S. cotton mill in Pawtucket, Rhode Island. He is credited with starting the factory system in the United States. The system developed rapidly in the late 1800s, at the same time that businesses were becoming more organized and jobs were becoming more specialized. Interchangeable parts, the telegraph, and agricultural machines also changed the scope of American business.

During the 1800s railroads and public transportation, new markets on the frontier, and new industries such as textiles and agricultural implements began to emerge. Large urban areas became centers of business activity. Large financial institutions developed to finance the new business activities.

The Industrial Revolution gave us several business concepts still in use today. One was, of course, *mass production*, the production of large quantities of standardized products at a relatively low price. Another was *mass marketing*, which helped distribute, throughout a large trade area, the quantities of goods created by mass production. Merchandise was carried by rail cars to distant markets, and new institutions, like the department store, were created. A third business concept that came out of the Industrial Revolution was *concentrated financial resources*, the money amassed by banks, insurance companies, and other financial institutions for use in large-scale investments.

CAPTAINS OF INDUSTRY

In the second half of the nineteenth century, certain key people had a profound effect on U.S. businesses. These *captains of industry*, as they were called, developed the largest and most powerful companies in the United States. John D. Rockefeller founded Standard Oil; Andrew Carnegie founded U.S. Steel. Others with great influence were Cornelius Vanderbilt (shipping and railroads), Jay Gould (railroads), J. P. Morgan (banking and finance), and Andrew Mellon (banking, mining, and aluminum manufacturing). Using new technologies to build their firms, these people were entrepreneurs—risk takers—in the truest sense of the word.

The role of these entrepreneurs in shaping industry cannot be overemphasized. Their adventurousness accelerated the growth of the U.S. economy in the late 1800s. By creating new companies, they added thousands of jobs to the marketplace. Spending by new workers created even more jobs. The new goods and services produced by the captains of industry—such as steel, clothing, and transportation—enhanced the quality of life.

MASS PRODUCTION AND SPECIALIZATION

The Industrial Revolution brought the concept of mass production, but the industrialists of the first few decades of the 1900s perfected the system. In 1913 Henry Ford introduced the assembly line in his automobile factory. This innovation was a major breakthrough in production technology. By using fixed work stations, giving workers specialized tasks, and bringing work to the worker, Ford was able to greatly improve productivity. Because of the assembly-line technique, the cost of Ford automobiles fell to under $200 at a time when most other automobiles cost well over $1,000. Thus the automobile age started in the United States.

Ford recognized that gains could be achieved by allowing workers to focus all their efforts on one specific task rather than on several tasks. The concept of *labor specialization* became the hallmark of the mass-production era.

MATURITY AND CHANGE

In the past six decades, business has undergone many changes. Consumers' buying habits and expectations have changed. Government regulations have been enacted in response to the problems of the Great Depression and later economic events. Labor unions have become more and then less powerful. New technology and major production changes have become common in all industries. A new type of employee, the knowledge worker, has become a major force in the workplace. Mergers became a major trend in the 1980s, subsided, and are again gaining momentum. Entrepreneurship is growing. The workplace is experiencing dramatic changes as today's corporations adopt new strategies for success that present exciting opportunities for the future.

Consumer Spending Patterns

Consumers now spend more on such services as doctors, restaurants, hair salons, and air travel than on physical goods, such as dresses or books. They now hire others to perform tasks that they used to handle themselves. Car washes, lawn-care and housecleaning services, delicatessens in grocery stores, and even day care for children and senior citizens are common businesses used by Americans these days. Indeed, service industries are now the fastest-growing segment of the economy.

Government Regulation

The collapse of the U.S. economy in 1929 and its ongoing weakness during the Great Depression led President Franklin D. Roosevelt to press for new government regulation of business. Laws enacted in the 1930s aimed to control some of the risky investing that led to the stock market crash and the pricing practices that restricted competition. Many additional laws affecting business were enacted through the early 1970s. Consumer protection, worker protection, environmental protection, taxation, and energy administration were the major focuses of these laws. During the 1980s and early 1990s there was less additional regulation of business than in prior decades. (Regulation of business is discussed in more detail in Chapters 5 and 23.)

Labor Unions

In the 1930s labor unions began to play a major role in U.S. business. The Congress of Industrial Organizations (CIO) had split from the American Federation of Labor (AFL) in 1935. The AFL and CIO competed nationally for members by seeking to win bigger concessions from business owners. This competition continued until the AFL and CIO merged in 1955. (The labor-union movement is discussed in more detail in Chapter 13.)

The Technology Revolution

During the 1980s alone, U.S. companies spent $1 trillion on new manufacturing and communication technologies.[7]

automation Replacement of workers with machines.

The resulting increase in **automation** (the replacement of workers with machines) has created a technology revolution. Computers are central to this technology revolution. Today they are involved in almost every aspect of business. Some guide machines used in manufacturing processes. For example, Nucor, a steel manufacturer, uses computer-controlled mini-mills to produce steel with one-twelfth of the labor required ten years ago in traditional mills.[8]

At other companies computers move vast amounts of information both inside and outside the organization. Departments such as purchasing, inventory, and production that used to function separately are now linked electronically. And more businesses are establishing electronic links to suppliers and customers, creating a chain of interrelated organizations. Technological advances will continue to change the way we work, allowing more jobs to include decision-making and innovation. Chapter 10 provides further insights into the U.S. drive to automate production and computerize firms of all kinds.

■ Knowledge workers, such as this petroleum technician, are valuable assets for many companies. Their understanding of new technologies allows them to discover innovative solutions to age-old problems.

Knowledge Workers

New technology, by itself, does not change how we work. It provides the *tools* that allow companies to find better ways to reduce costs, shorten production time, and provide better customer service. The technology revolution has made *knowledge*—how to apply technologies—a critical resource. Some business consultants consider it as important as the traditional factors of production (land, labor, and capital).

In the future the ability to use knowledge will determine a company's success. This requires a new breed of employee—**knowledge workers**, who manage, use, or operate the new technology. Highly educated and technologically savvy, these workers add value by bringing innovative solutions to problems.

Knowledge workers are a diverse group. Some are involved mostly in "brainwork," while others work with their hands. Examples of knowledge workers include computer engineers and programmers, medical technicians, paralegals, research scientists, accountants, and equipment-repair technicians. Regions with large numbers of knowledge workers are rapidly emerging as the country's new growth regions, as the following Social Demographics Trends box shows.

knowledge workers
Highly trained employees who manage, use, or operate new technologies.

Where the Jobs Are

All around America new clusters of high-technology companies are stealing the spotlight from traditional technology centers like California's Silicon Valley and Massachusetts' Route 128. Two burgeoning technology capitals, Raleigh–Durham, North Carolina, and Austin, Texas, ranked first and fifth in *Fortune* magazine's 1993 survey of the best cities for business. Minneapolis–St. Paul has a large concentration of health care and medical instrumentation companies. Salt Lake City and Philadelphia have also attracted many biomedical enterprises. The Orlando and Tucson regions are home to many companies in the laser and electro-optics industries.

Why do these and other new growth areas attract businesses? All have strong university systems that generate a high level of intellectual energy. They offer highly regarded programs related to the needs of the region's high-technology employers. The University of Texas at Austin, for example, is known for its computer, physics, engineering, health sciences, and business administration departments. This has been a drawing card for many companies in the computer and electronics industries, including IBM, Apple, Motorola, Hewlett-Packard, and Dell Computer, Austin's premier start-up company. Raleigh–Durham has three major universities: Duke, the University of North Carolina–Chapel Hill, and North Carolina State. Together they manage a central research institute where university scientists and corporate researchers work on research and development projects. Business and government organizations in such industries as chemicals, biotechnology, and pharmaceuticals—DuPont, Ciba–Geigy, Sumitomo, and the National Institutes of Health, to name a few—have facilities in the area's Research Triangle Park, one of the country's premier high-tech campuses.

The university contribution is three-fold. First, the opportunity for collaboration between academic and industry researchers fosters the transfer of ideas from the campus to commercial application. New trends surface sooner. Second, the university provides employers with a pool of well-trained knowledge workers. Third, strong university systems offer the continuing education knowledge workers need to understand increasingly complex and frequently changing technological developments.

Both leading technology companies and start-up ventures gravitate to these new regions. They find that the dynamic business atmosphere fosters creativity, speeding up the product development process.[9]

The Merger Era

In a merger, one firm takes over another (usually a smaller one), causing it to lose its identity. The acquiring firm takes over the other's property and assumes its debts. A significant period of merger activity occurred in the United States during the 1980s, when the dollar value of the mergers completed during the decade was $1.3 trillion, an amount equal to the annual economic output of Germany. Many of the mergers of the 1980s were motivated solely by financial objectives. These mergers were often unfriendly, with "corporate raiders" pursuing firms they believed were badly managed. They financed these deals using very high levels of debt, later selling off parts of the acquired company to repay the debt.

Merger activity dropped in the late 1980s but is now increasing again. This new wave of mergers looks quite different from that of the prior decade. The transactions are generally friendly and driven by strategic objectives, such as entrance into new markets or increased market share. Merger activity is especially high in industries that are in transition, such as telecommunications, media, and health care.[10] Many mergers also involve overseas companies, continuing a trend that started in the 1980s; they aim to create effective global competitors. Ford, for example, bought Jaguar to compete more effectively in Europe and to add an upscale sports car to its product line. Of course foreign companies are also buying American companies. Sony's acquisition of Columbia Pictures made it a major player in the entertainment business.

A merger can saddle the new firm with great financial complexity and wrenching change. Some mergers have succeeded, others have not. Companies with a well-defined strategic goal tend to do best. For example, Quaker Oats bought Stokely-Van Camp in 1984 for its food products, especially Gatorade. Gatorade has become Quaker's largest brand and is currently the world's best-selling sports drink.[11] (The topic of mergers is explored further in Chapter 6.)

Entrepreneurship in the 1990s

The greatest surge in entrepreneurship since the days of Carnegie and Rockefeller is happening today. Many people, including college students, have begun their own businesses. They believe that, compared with corporate managers, entrepreneurs have more fun, get more satisfaction from their work, and make a lot more money. Another reason for the increased number of entrepreneurial ventures is the large number of corporate restructurings and downsizings. Many corporate managers who lose their jobs prefer to start their own companies rather than work for someone else.

Yet starting a new company can be a daunting, lonely task. Entrepreneurs sometimes work harder than seems humanly possible. For example, Rachelle Nacht put her personal life on hold for three years when she started Mortgage Match, Inc., a mortgage brokerage firm, in 1990. Like many successful entrepreneurs, she was a compulsive worker who put in 20-hour days trying to do everything herself.[12] And workaholics Guy Robinson and LaVerne Parker, partners in a software firm, kept postponing their wedding because something always came up at work. Friends finally arranged to have the ceremony during lunch at their office![13] (The rewards and risks of entrepreneurship are examined further in Chapter 7.)

The Changing Corporate Scene

The 1990s are evolving into a decade of tremendous change for business. More and more companies are discovering that they must be adaptable and flexible to survive. All over the country and the world companies are "reinventing" themselves to meet the pressures of global competition. They are learning to use technology more effectively, shedding business units that no longer fit with corporate strategy, downsizing existing operations, and even completely changing their organizational structure and business operations.

Reengineering involves a total rethinking and redesigning of business processes to achieve dramatic improvements in cost, service, or time. Companies look at themselves as if they were a brand-new entity and decide how the business should ideally be run. They then get rid of old methods and implement new ways to accomplish their goals. Reengineering is especially popular in industries undergoing major market changes, such as financial services and telecommunications. (We'll look at reengineering in more detail in Chapter 9.)

Companies also are streamlining operations. By the year 2000 the average company will employ fewer people. The traditional large organization with many layers of managers and covering a complete range of business operations is giving way to networks of specialists. Also called *modular corporations,* these companies focus on what they do best—designing and marketing products, for example. They contract with outside specialists for other needed services, such as manufacturing, distribution, and accounting.[14] As you can see, tomorrow's businesses will probably look quite different from those we know today.

Concept Check
- Describe the Industrial Revolution in the United States.
- Explain the differences between mergers of the 1980s and 1990s.
- Describe some of the important emerging trends for businesses.

OVERVIEW OF THIS BOOK

This book offers a picture of the business world. It emphasizes not only the business system as a whole, but also each of the key functional areas of business: management, marketing, finance, accounting, and information systems. The duties and interrelationships of the managers in these areas help explain the principles and practices of business operations. The book shows these principles and practices at work in businesses that are large and small, for-profit and not-for-profit, domestic and international. The book also offers glimpses of many real-world business situations and decisions.

This chapter has sketched the development of the business world. Later chapters cover the subject in more depth. Chapter 2 explains the economic aspects of business. Part Two discusses the business environment: our multicultural society, the global nature of business today, and the social responsibility of business and ethics among businesspeople. Part Three examines how businesses are structured. Parts Four and Five explain how businesses are managed. Part Six shows how companies market their products. Part Seven introduces you to the tools of the information age, accounting and computers. Part Eight explains how companies finance their operations. The book ends, in Part Nine, with a look at the legal and tax environments of business, and at risk and insurance.

■ SUMMARY

1. Gain an appreciation for the study of business.

Economic strength results when firms produce goods and services that consumers want at reasonable prices and with a no-nonsense approach. How U.S. firms do this is the subject of the book. The study of business can help students select a career, understand the roles of workers in organizations, become more informed consumers, and appreciate the relationship between business and society. Students can also learn the advantages and pitfalls of establishing an independent company.

2. Understand the term *business.*

Business has many meanings. Essentially, though, it is the process of assembling and using productive resources to create the goods and services that satisfy society's needs and wants. Business is as much a part of the Soviet Union and the People's Republic of China as it is of the United States.

Business is studied informally and formally. Informally, people learn through their work and through reading and talking with other people. Formally, they study the subject in colleges and universities.

3. Recognize how the four basic inputs and the two basic outputs of the business system are related.

Businesses make use of four productive resources, also known as basic inputs or factors of production: natural resources, labor, capital, and entrepreneurship. They produce two basic outputs: goods and services (often called products).

The rewards for business owners are profits. The rewards for labor are wages, those for natural resources are rent, and those for capital are interest.

Households provide the basic inputs to businesses and are the consumers of its basic outputs. The flow of goods and services between households and businesses is known as the circular flow.

4. Discuss the differences among basic economic systems.

The major economic systems are capitalism, socialism, and communism. Economies that rely on more than one system are mixed economies.

Under capitalism individuals have the right to own property, to make a profit, to compete, and to make free choices. Within capitalism are four types of competitive environments: perfect (pure) competition, monopoly, monopolistic competition, and oligopoly.

In socialist economies basic industries are owned and operated or strongly controlled by government. Under communism, the factors of production are owned collectively rather than individually, and the people receive economic benefits according to their needs and contribute to society according to their abilities.

5. Understand how gross domestic product, productivity, and standard of living measure the performance of economic systems.

Gross domestic product (GDP) is the monetary value of all final goods and services produced within a country each year. It is a comprehensive measure of a country's economic health. Productivity is the output of goods and services per unit of labor. If we get more output with the same or less labor, then productivity has increased. New and better equipment and well-trained and motivated workers often improve productivity. A country's standard of living is measured by its per-person output of goods and services.

6. Trace the historical development of U.S. business.

In colonial times businesses were mainly family enterprises. Families began to sell or trade their surpluses, creating a market system. Eventually, the Industrial Revolution introduced factories. Railroads and public transportation, new markets, and new industries began to emerge. The Industrial Revolution created the concepts of mass production, mass marketing, and concentrated financial resources.

The captains of industry emerged in the second half of the nineteenth century. They developed the largest and most powerful companies in the United States. They also perfected the system of mass production. Labor specialization became the hallmark of the mass-production era.

From 1930 to the present business has undergone many changes. Consumers' buying habits have changed, government regulation of business has increased, and labor unions have grown and then declined. The technology revolution has brought increased automation and computerization. A new class of employee, the knowledge worker who manages and operates the new technologies, is emerging. Mergers became an important part of the business world in the 1980s. The 1990s promise the return of entrepreneurship, as well as major changes in how corporations are organized and operated.

■ DISCUSSION QUESTIONS

1. Do you think a hospital, museum, or orchestra is really a business? Explain.

2. What would happen in the U.S. economic system if the entrepreneurs vanished?

3. Discuss how a product that you recently bought moved through the circular flow.

4. Why is the U.S. system called a mixed economy? Isn't it really capitalistic?

5. What is the importance of the factory system in the business history of the United States?

6. Do you think the merger era was good for our economic system? Why or why not?

■ CASE

The New "Private" Schools

More and more, private sector companies are taking over services formerly provided mostly by government or nonprofit organizations. For

example, many cities and towns now hire private firms to provide trash collection services. The newest area to be privatized is the public school system. In November 1993 Minneapolis hired Public Strategies Group to manage its 98 schools. Former state finance commissioner Peter Hutchinson heads the consulting firm and will, in effect, be the superintendent of schools. The city will pay Public Strategies a flat fee, using money targeted for school administrative jobs.

Minneapolis is the largest school district thus far—6,800 employees and 44,000 students—to turn to a private firm to run its schools. Baltimore gave Education Alternatives Inc. (EAI), another Minneapolis-based consultant, control over nine of its 177 schools in 1992. EAI has improved academic performance at these schools, considered among the city's toughest. In late 1993 San Diego was considering hiring EAI to manage some of its underperforming schools.

Private firms avoid the massive bureaucracy and union problems that plague many large urban school systems. They operate schools more like businesses, setting goals and holding teachers accountable for student performance. They, in turn, are accountable to the school districts, which can terminate the management contract by giving the agreed-upon notice.[15]

Questions

1. Do you think it is appropriate for private firms to manage public schools? Why? What are some of the advantages and disadvantages of this approach?
2. Are there other fields where private companies are or could be taking over government or nonprofit organizations? Has the government assumed responsibility for jobs once done by private companies?

Chapter 2

The Business Economy

Learning Goals

After studying this chapter, you should be able to:

1 Understand the importance of economics and circular flow.

2 Discuss how economic growth, gross domestic product, and business cycles are related.

3 Explain the economic goals of full employment and price stability.

4 Describe inflation, the two indexes used to measure it, and its two main causes.

5 Discuss how and why the government uses monetary and fiscal policy to achieve its macroeconomic goals.

6 Understand the basic microeconomic concepts of demand and supply and how they establish prices.

7 Describe the four key economic issues of the 1990s.

 ## Career Profile

Recruiters for KPMG Peat Marwick, the largest public accounting firm in the world, visited Tricia Huff's campus during her senior year in college. She met with them and, as a result, was offered a position as an assistant staff accountant after graduating with a bachelor's degree in business. Her primary responsibility at KPMG Peat Marwick is to test clients' financial statements. In the four months since she started with the company, she has already dealt with a national life insurance corporation, a local leasing corporation, and a nonprofit organization.

Tricia emphasizes that it is the basic technical accounting skills she developed during her college classes that have helped her most at KPMG Peat Marwick. She plans to build on that foundation by continuing to update and expand her audit skills in order to reach her career goal of becoming an accounting professional.

Overview

We now turn to the economy, which is the framework in which businesses operate. This chapter begins by looking at basic economic principles. It discusses three major macroeconomic goals—economic growth, full employment, and price stability— and how government uses policy to achieve them. It next looks at microeconomics to show how demand and supply determine prices. Finally, it explores four economic issues facing the U.S. economy in the 1990s: the national debt, the global economy, improving service sector productivity, and the dislocation of the work force.

THE STUDY OF ECONOMICS

economics Study of how people use scarce or limited resources to produce and distribute goods and services.

Economics is the study of how people use scarce resources to produce and distribute goods and services. The resources of a person, a firm, or a nation are limited. Hence, economics is the study of choices—what people, firms, or nations choose from among the available resources. Every economy is concerned with what types and amounts of goods and services should be produced, how these should be produced, and for whom. These decisions are made by the marketplace, the government, or both. In the United States the government and the free-market system together guide the economy.

WHY STUDY ECONOMICS?

You probably know more about economics than you realize. Every day the news has many stories related to the economy: A union wins wage increases at General Motors; the Federal Reserve Board lowers interest rates; Wall Street has a record day; the President proposes higher income taxes; consumer spending rises as the economy recovers from a recession; retail prices rise.

■ Economics is the study of choices. The personal economic decisions you make—what you spend your money on—are factors in determining what types of goods and services are produced and distributed.

The state of the economy affects both people and businesses. How you spend your money (or save it) is a personal economic decision. Whether you continue in school and whether you work part-time are also economic decisions. Every business also operates within the economy. Based on their economic expectations, businesses decide what products to produce, how to price them, how many people to employ, how much to pay these employees, how much to expand the business, and the like.

macroeconomics Study of the economy as a whole.

Economics has two main subareas. **Macroeconomics** is the study of the economy as a whole. It looks at *aggregate* data, data for large groups of people, companies, and products considered as a whole. In contrast, **microeconomics** focuses on individual parts of the economy, such as households or firms.

microeconomics Study of particular markets.

Both *macro* and *micro*, as they're called, offer a valuable outlook on the economy. For example, a domestic carmaker might use both to decide whether to introduce a new line of cars. It would consider such macro-economic factors as the national level of personal income, the unemployment rate, interest rates, fuel costs, and the sales level and types of imported cars. From a microeconomic viewpoint, the manufacturer would judge consumer demand for new cars versus the existing supply, competing models, labor and material costs and availability, and current prices and sales incentives.

ECONOMICS AS A CIRCULAR FLOW

Another way to see how sectors of the economy interact is to view business as a circular flow of inputs and outputs between households and businesses. We saw this model in Chapter 1. Exhibit 2-1 adds a third entity, government, to the flow.

Let's review the exchange by following the purple circle around the inside of the diagram. Households provide inputs (natural resources, labor, capital, entrepreneurship) to businesses, which convert these inputs into outputs (goods and services) for consumers. In return, consumers receive income from rent, wages, interest, and ownership profits (green circle). Businesses receive income from consumer purchases of goods and services.

The other important exchange in Exhibit 2-1 takes place between governments (federal, state, and local) and both individuals and businesses. Governments provide many types of public goods and services (highways, schools, police, courts, health services, unemployment insurance, Social Security) which benefit individuals and businesses. Government purchases from businesses also contribute to business profits. The contractor who repairs the local stretch of state highway, for example, is paid by government for the work. As the diagram shows, government receives taxes from individuals and businesses to complete the flow.

Changes in one flow affect the others. If government raises taxes, households have less to spend on goods and services. Lower spending causes businesses to reduce production, and economic activity declines; unemployment may rise. But cutting taxes can stimulate economic activity. Keep the circular flow in mind as we continue our study of econom-

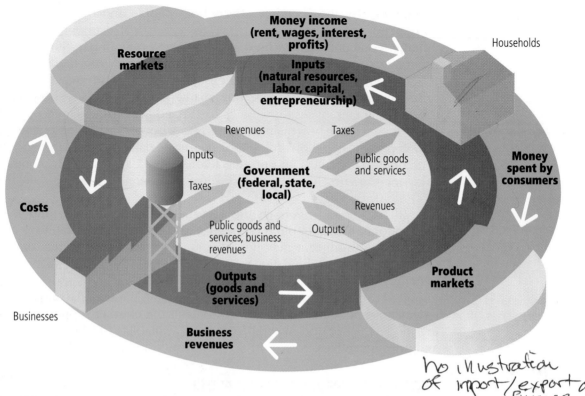

Exhibit 2-1
Economics as a Circular Flow

ics. The way economic sectors interact will become more evident as we explore macroeconomics and microeconomics.

handwritten: no illustration of import/export or finance

Concept Check

- What is economics?
- What is the difference between macroeconomics and microeconomics?
- How do resources flow among the household, business, and government sectors?

MACROECONOMICS: THE BIG PICTURE

Have you ever turned on the radio or television and heard something like, "Today the Labor Department reported that for the second straight month unemployment decreased"? Statements like this are macroeconomic news. Understanding the national economy and how changes in government policies affect households and businesses is a good place to begin the study of economics. Let's look first at macroeconomic goals and how they can be met.

MACROECONOMIC GOALS

The United States and most other countries have three main macroeconomic goals: economic growth, full employment, and price stability. A nation's economic well-being depends on carefully defining these goals and choosing the best economic policies to reach them.

Economic Growth

Perhaps the most important way to judge a nation's economic health is to look at its production of goods and services. The more that are produced, the higher the nation's standard of living. An increase in a nation's output of goods and services is **economic growth**.

Economic growth is usually a good thing, but it also has a bad side. Increased production yields more pollution. Growth may strain public facilities, such as roads, electricity, schools, and hospitals. Thus the government tries to apply economic policies that will keep growth to a level that does not reduce the quality of life.

As we saw in Chapter 1, the most basic measure of economic growth is the *gross domestic product (GDP)*. GDP is the total monetary value of all goods and services produced within a nation each year. It is reported quarterly and is used to compare trends in national output. When GDP rises, the economy is growing.

There are two ways of expressing GDP. **Nominal GDP** uses current market prices—today's posted prices for goods and services. **Real GDP** adjusts the nominal GDP for price changes (for inflation) as measured from a specified year. Real GDP is considered the more meaningful measure of economic growth.

The *rate* of growth in real GDP is also important. As Exhibit 2-2 shows, while real GDP in the United States has steadily increased, the annual percentage *rate* of growth—the amount of the increase—has varied widely. When the rate of growth was close to or below zero, the U.S. economy was stagnant or declining.

economic growth Increase in a nation's output of goods and services.

nominal GDP Measure of GDP that uses current market prices.

real GDP Measure of GDP that adjusts for price changes.

■ **Exhibit 2-2**

U.S. Gross Domestic Real Product versus Rate of GDP Growth

Source: U.S. Department of Commerce.

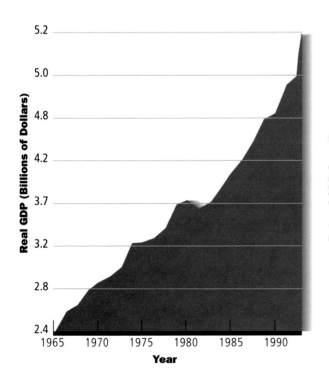

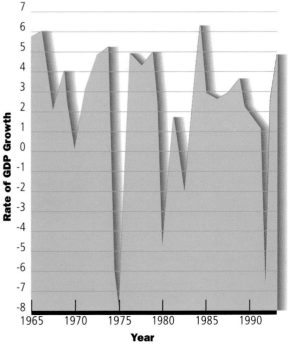

■ **Exhibit 2-3**
Per Capita GNP in Various Countries

Source: World Bank, *The World Bank Atlas, 1994* (Washington, D.C.: World Bank, 1994).

Country	Per-capita GNP	Country	Per-capita GNP
Austria	$22,110	India	310
Brazil	2,770	Israel	13,230
Bulgaria	1,350	Italy	20,510
Cameroon	860	Japan	28,220
Canada	20,320	Mexico	3,740
Chile	2,730	Netherlands	20,590
China (mainland)	380	Philippines	770
Czech Republic	2,440	Poland	1,960
Egypt	630	Russian Federation	2,680
Ethiopia	110	Singapore	15,750
France	22,300	Switzerland	36,230
Germany	23,030	United Kingdom	17,760
Gabon	4,450	United States	23,120

GDP can be used to compare the economies of different countries. Because countries vary in size, this comparison is based on *per capita* (per person) rather than total GDP. Exhibit 2-3 lists per capita GDP figures for various countries (all expressed in U.S. dollars). GDP should be evaluated in context with other aspects of a nation's economy. Taken by itself, rapid GDP growth might seem good. But if prices are also rising rapidly and purchasing power is shrinking, the standard of living may not be improving.

The level of economic activity is constantly changing. These changes upward and downward are called **business cycles**. Business cycles vary in length, in how high or low the economy moves, and in how much the economy is affected. GDP traces the patterns as economic activity expands and contracts. An increase in business activity results in rising output, income, employment, and prices. Eventually these all peak, and output, income, and employment decline. A decline in real GDP that lasts for two consecutive quarters (each a three-month period) is called a **recession**. It is followed by a recovery period when economic activity once again increases.

The most recent recession began in 1990 and ended in March 1991. Although it was relatively short, it has taken the economy much longer to recover than after prior recessions. The pace of economic expansion differed considerably among the regions. Most states in the Southeast were enjoying economic growth, but larger states, including California and many Middle Atlantic and Northeastern states, were still struggling to recover in late 1993.[1]

Businesses must monitor and react to changing business cycles. During the 1980s the economy was growing rapidly. Companies expanded in these boom years, investing in new factories to keep up with customer demand. However, when the economy went into recession in 1990–91, many companies found themselves with more capacity than the demand

business cycles Changes upward and downward in business activity.

recession Period of decline in GDP that lasts six months or longer.

for their products or services required. By fall 1993 U.S. businesses were, on average, using only about 82 percent of production capacity.[2]

Full Employment

full employment Having jobs for all who are willing and able to work.

Another macroeconomic goal is **full employment**, or having jobs for all who want to and can work. Full employment doesn't actually mean 100 percent employment. Some people choose not to work for personal reasons (attending school, raising children) or are temporarily unemployed while they wait to start a new job. Thus the government defines full employment as a situation where about 94 to 96 percent of those available to work actually have jobs.

unemployment rate Percentage of the total labor force that is not working but actively looking for work.

Measuring Unemployment. To determine how close we are to full employment, the government measures the **unemployment rate**. This rate measures the percentage of the total labor force that is not working but is *actively looking for work.* It excludes "discouraged workers," those not seeking jobs because they don't think they can find them.

Each month the Department of Labor releases statistics on employment. These figures help us understand how well the economy is doing. Exhibit 2-4 shows that the U.S. labor force now totals about 129 million workers. To really understand the state of the economy, we have to look at the unemployment rate shown in Exhibit 2-5. From 1955 to 1970, unemployment stayed between 4.5 and 5.5 percent. It climbed as high as 9.2 percent in 1973 and 9.7 percent in 1982, both recession years, and then declined steadily through the 1980s. Although twice as many people were out of work as in the 1950s and 1960s, the unemployment rate was not much worse because so many more people were in the labor force.

Exhibit 2-4
Labor and Unemployment Trends

Source: U.S. Department of Labor.

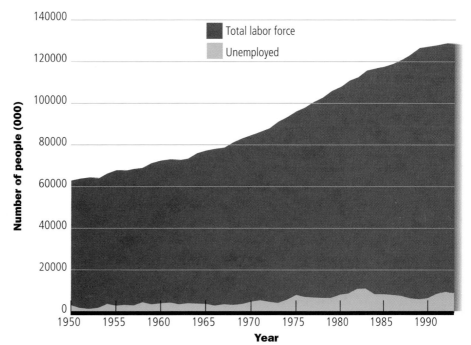

■ **Exhibit 2-5**
U.S. Unemployment Rate
Source: U.S. Department of Labor.

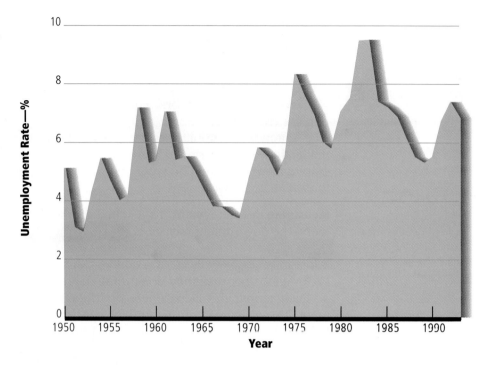

By the winter of 1991, however, the U.S. economy was in a recession. After rising in 1992, the unemployment rate fell in 1993; at year-end the rate was 6.7 percent.

Types of Unemployment. Economists classify unemployment into four types: frictional, structural, cyclical, and seasonal. The categories are of small consolation to someone who is unemployed, but they help economists think about and understand the problem of unemployment in our economy.

frictional unemployment Short-term, voluntary unemployment, unrelated to the business cycle.

Frictional unemployment is freely chosen, short-term, and unrelated to the business cycle. It includes people who are unemployed while waiting to start a better job, as well as those entering or reentering the job market. This type is always present and has little impact on the economy.

structural unemployment Involuntary unemployment caused by the mismatch between available jobs and the skills of available workers.

Structural unemployment is also unrelated to the business cycle but is involuntary. It is caused by a mismatch between available jobs and the skills of available workers in an industry or a region. For example, if the birth rate declines, fewer teachers will be needed. Or the available workers in an area may lack the skills that employers want. Retraining and skill-building programs are often required to reduce structural unemployment.

cyclical unemployment Unemployment caused by a downturn in the business cycle.

Cyclical unemployment, as the name implies, occurs when a downturn in the business cycle reduces the demand for labor throughout the economy. In a long recession cyclical unemployment is widespread. The government can partly counteract cyclical unemployment with programs that boost the economy.

In the past, cyclical unemployment affected mainly lower-skilled workers and those in heavy manufacturing. Typically, they would be rehired when economic growth increased. Beginning with the 1990-1991 recession, however, companies eliminated positions at all levels. For the

■ Department store Santas are subject to seasonal unemployment. They are hired on a temporary basis only during the Christmas season.

first time large numbers of white-collar workers are also unemployed. This issue is discussed further later in the chapter.

The last type is **seasonal unemployment**, which occurs during specific seasons in certain industries. Employees subject to seasonal unemployment include retail workers hired for the Christmas buying season, lettuce pickers in California, and restaurant employees in Orlando during the summer.

seasonal unemployment Periodic unemployment caused by seasonal variations in certain industries.

Price Stability

4

The third macroeconomic goal is to keep overall prices for goods and services fairly steady. The general upward movement of prices is called **inflation**. Inflation's higher prices reduce **purchasing power**, the value of what money can buy. If prices go up but income doesn't rise or rises at a slower rate, a given amount of income buys less. For example, if the price of a basket of groceries rises from $30 to $40 but your salary remains the same, you can buy only 75 percent as many groceries ($30 ÷ $40). Your purchasing power declines by 25 percent ($10 ÷ $40).

inflation General upward movement of prices.

purchasing power Value of what money can buy.

Inflation affects both personal and business decisions. When prices are rising, people tend to spend more, before their purchasing power declines further. Businesses that expect inflation often increase their supplies, and people often speed up planned purchases of cars and major appliances.

demand-pull inflation Increase in prices that occurs when the demand for goods and services is greater than the supply.

Types of Inflation. There are two types of inflation. **Demand-pull inflation** occurs when the demand for goods and services is greater than the supply. Would-be buyers have more money to spend than the amount needed to buy available goods and services. Their demand, which exceeds the supply, tends to pull prices up. The higher prices will stimulate supply, eventually creating a balance between demand and supply.

cost-push inflation Increase in prices caused by increases in production costs.

Cost-push inflation is triggered by increases in production costs, such as materials and wages. These increases push up the prices of final goods and services. Wage increases are a major cause of cost-push inflation, creating a "wage-price spiral." For example, assume the United Auto Workers union negotiates a three-year labor agreement that raises wages 3 percent per year and increases overtime pay. Car makers would then raise the car prices to cover their higher labor costs. Also, higher wages will give auto workers more money to buy goods and services, and this increased demand may pull up other prices. Workers in other industries will demand higher wages to keep up with increased prices, and the cycle will push prices even higher.

How Inflation Is Measured. The rate of inflation is most commonly measured by looking at changes in the **consumer price index (CPI)**. The CPI is an index of the prices of a "market basket" of goods and services purchased by typical urban consumers. It is published monthly by the Department of Labor. Major components of the CPI, which are weighted by importance, are food, clothing, transportation, housing, health, and recreation.

consumer price index (CPI) Index of the prices of a "market basket" of goods and services bought by typical urban consumers.

The CPI sets prices in a base period at 100. The base period, which now is 1982-1984, is chosen for its price stability. Current prices are then expressed as a percentage of prices in the base period. A rise in the CPI means prices are increasing. For example, the CPI was 146.7 in February 1994, meaning that prices had increased 46.7 percent from the 1982-1984 base period. The CPI had risen 2.5 percentage points above the February 1993 CPI of 144.2.

Like GDP, the CPI has fluctuated considerably. The rate of inflation from 1960 to 1993, as measured by the CPI, is shown in Exhibit 2-6. It was stable in the early 1960s, with average yearly increases of 1.3 percent. But inflation started to climb steadily after 1965. Fuel price increases were the main contributor to double-digit inflation in 1974 and from 1979 to 1981.

▓ Exhibit 2-6

Change in Consumer Price Index, 1960–1993

Source: Bureau of Labor Statistics.

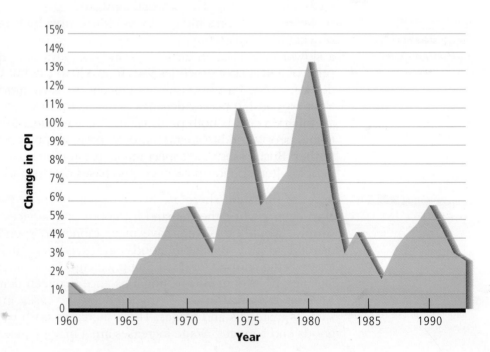

The inflation rate decreased throughout the 1980s to a low of 1.9 percent in 1986. Then wage increases, especially in the service sector, pushed inflation upward again. Increases in food prices, labor costs, and energy costs kept inflation rising to about 6 percent in 1990. It tapered off during the 1990-1991 recession, dropping to about 3 percent for 1992 and 2.7% for 1993.

producer price index (PPI) Index that measures the prices paid by producers and wholesalers for commodities.

Changes in wholesale prices are another important indicator of inflation. The **producer price index (PPI)** measures the prices paid by producers and wholesalers for such commodities as raw materials, partially finished goods, and finished products. From January through October 1993, wholesale prices rose only 0.4 percent, compared to 1.2 percent for 1992. This, together with the CPI's modest increase, was viewed by economists as a positive sign that inflation was under control, despite the increase in economic growth that typically pushes up prices.[3]

Actions in one part of the economy have a ripple effect on the others. Usually economic events act as economists would expect. Sometimes they do not. Clearly, the interaction of factors makes it hard enough to describe the economy's condition, let alone to make accurate forecasts. This difficulty is what causes many to view economics as an art as much as a science.

Concept Check

- How is economic growth measured? Which statistic is more meaningful—nominal GDP or real GDP?
- What is a business cycle? How do businesses adapt to periods of contraction and expansion?
- Why is full employment usually defined as a target percentage below 100 percent? How is unemployment measured?
- What is the difference between demand-pull and cost-push inflation?

ACHIEVING MACROECONOMIC GOALS

5 To reach our macroeconomic goals, we must often choose among conflicting alternatives. Sometimes political needs override economic ones. For example, bringing inflation under control may call for a politically difficult time of high unemployment and low growth. Or, in an election year, politicians may resist raising taxes to curb inflation.

Still, the government must try to guide the economy to a sound balance of growth, employment, and price stability. The two main tools it uses are monetary policy and fiscal policy.

MONETARY POLICY

monetary policy Government programs for controlling the amount of money in circulation in a nation's economy.

Federal Reserve System (the Fed) Central banking system in the United States which prints money and controls the amount in circulation.

Monetary policy refers to a government's programs for controlling the amount of money circulating in the economy. Changes in the money supply affect both the level of economic activity and the rate of inflation. The **Federal Reserve System** (the Fed), the central banking system, prints money and controls how much of it will be in circulation. The money supply is also controlled by the Fed's regulation of certain bank activities.

■ The housing industry is sensitive to changes in interest rates. When rates are up, construction slows down. This can have a ripple effect throughout the economy.

(Chapter 20 discusses in detail the structure of the Federal Reserve System and how it controls the money supply.)

When the Fed increases or decreases the amount of money in circulation, it affects interest rates (the cost of borrowing money and the reward for lending it). Interest rates, in turn, affect consumer and business decisions to spend or invest. The housing industry, business, and investments react most to changes in interest rates.

The Fed can use monetary policy to contract or expand the economy. With **contractionary policy**, the Fed restricts, or tightens, the money supply. The result is higher interest rates, slower economic growth, and higher unemployment. Thus contractionary policy reduces spending and, ultimately, lowers inflation. For example, the Fed used a restrictive monetary policy to bring inflation from 13.5 percent in 1980 to a low of 1.9 percent in 1986.

With **expansionary policy**, the Fed increases, or loosens, growth in the money supply. An expansionary policy stimulates the economy. Interest rates decline, so business and consumer spending go up. Unemployment rates drop as businesses expand. But increasing the money supply also has a negative side: Higher spending pushes prices up, increasing the inflation rate.

contractionary policy Monetary policy used to restrict the money supply and slow economic growth.

expansionary policy Monetary policy used to increase the money supply and stimulate economic growth.

FISCAL POLICY

fiscal policy Government program of taxation and spending, which can be used to stimulate the economy.

The other economic tool used by the government is **fiscal policy**, its program of taxation and spending. By increasing its spending or by cutting taxes, the government can stimulate the economy. Look again at Exhibit 2-1. The more government buys from business, the greater business revenues and output are. Likewise, if consumers or businesses have to pay less in taxes, they will have more income to spend for goods and services.

Exhibit 2-7
The Federal Budget

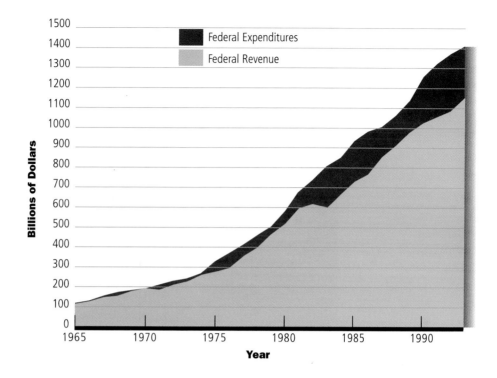

Tax policies in the United States therefore affect business decisions. High corporate taxes can make it harder for U.S. firms to compete with companies in countries with lower taxes. As a result, companies may choose to locate facilities overseas to reduce their tax burden.

If the government spends more for programs (social services, education, defense) than it collects in taxes, the result is a **federal budget deficit**. To balance the budget, the government can cut its spending, increase taxes, or do some combination of the two. When it cannot balance the budget, it must make up any shortfalls by borrowing (just like any business or household).

Exhibit 2-7 shows the gap between federal spending and tax revenues in recent years. The result is a rapidly rising burden of national debt. The **national debt** is the cumulative total of past deficits, minus any surpluses. By mid-1993 it totalled $4.35 trillion. People have widely differing opinions about controlling the federal deficit. Some believe that deficits allow economic growth, high employment, and price stability. Others believe that unlimited deficits and high levels of national debt have a bad impact on the U.S. economy. Businesses must compete with the government for the funds necessary for growth. This complex topic is the subject of a later section devoted to economic issues of the 1990s.

federal budget deficit Shortfall when total expenditures for government programs exceed the revenues received from taxes.

national debt Cumulative total of past budget deficits, minus any surpluses.

Concept Check
- What are the two kinds of monetary policy? How does the government use monetary policy to achieve its macroeconomic goals?
- What is fiscal policy? What fiscal policy tools can the government use to achieve its macroeconomic goals?

■ The price of any product, and how much of it is manufactured, depends upon supply and demand in the marketplace.

MICROECONOMICS: A NARROWER VIEW

6 Now let's shift our focus from the whole economy to *microeconomics,* the study of particular markets. This field of economics is concerned with how prices and quantities of goods and services behave in a free market. It stands to reason that people, firms, and governments try to get the most from use of their limited resources. Consumers want to buy the best quality at the lowest price. Businesses want to keep costs down and revenues high to earn larger profits. Governments also want to use their revenues to provide the most effective public goods and services possible. These groups choose among alternatives by focusing on the prices of goods and services.

THE BASICS OF DEMAND AND SUPPLY

As consumers in a free market, we influence what is produced. If a product is popular, high demand attracts other producers. They want to compete for our dollars by supplying a similar item at a lower price, of better quality, or with different features.

The Nature of Demand

demand Quantity of a good or service that people are willing to buy at various prices.

demand curve Graph of the relationship between quantity demanded and price.

Demand is the quantity of a good or service that people are willing to buy at various prices. The higher the price, the lower the quantity demanded, and vice versa. A graph of this relationship is called a **demand curve**.

Let's assume you own a store that sells sweatshirts. From past experience you know how many sweatshirts you can sell at different prices. You have shown this information on the demand curve in Exhibit 2-8. The *x-axis* (horizontal axis) shows the quantity of sweatshirts, and the *y-axis* (vertical axis) shows the related price of those sweatshirts. For example, if the price of the sweatshirt is $20, customers will buy (demand) 500 sweatshirts.

In the graph the demand curve slopes downward and to the right. This means that, as the price of a sweatshirt falls, people will want to buy more of them. The graph also shows that, if you put a large number of sweatshirts on the market, you will have to reduce the price to sell all of them.

The Nature of Supply

supply Quantity of a good or service that businesses will make available at various prices.

supply curve Graph of the relationship between quantity supplied and price.

Demand alone is not enough to explain how the market sets prices. We must also look at **supply**, the quantity of a good or service that businesses will make available at various prices. The higher the price, the greater the amount a producer is willing to supply, and vice versa. A graph of the relationship between various prices and the quantities a producer will supply is a **supply curve**.

We can again plot the quantity of sweatshirts on the x-axis and the price on the y-axis. Exhibit 2-9 shows that 900 sweatshirts will be available

■ **Exhibit 2-8**
Demand Curve for
Sweatshirts

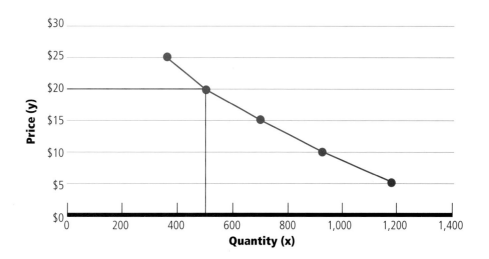

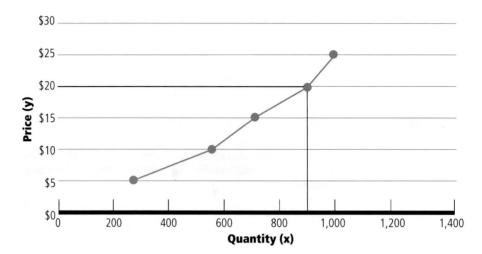

at a price of $20. Note that the supply curve slopes upward and to the right, the opposite of the demand curve. If consumers are willing to pay higher prices, manufacturers of sweatshirts will buy more inputs (yarn, dye, machinery, labor) and produce more sweatshirts. The quantity supplied will be higher at higher prices, because producers can earn higher profits.

How Demand and Supply Interact to Determine Prices

In a stable economy, the number of sweatshirts that consumers demand depends on their price. Likewise, the number of sweatshirts that suppliers provide depends on price. But what is the price that matches consumer demand for sweatshirts with the quantity suppliers will produce?

To answer this question we need to look at what happens when demand and supply interact. By plotting both the demand curve and the supply curve on the same graph (Exhibit 2-10), we see that they cross at a certain quantity and price. At that point, labeled E, the quantity demanded equals the quantity supplied. This is the point of **equilibrium**. The equilibrium price is $15; the equilibrium quantity is 700 sweat-

equilibrium Point at which quantity demanded equals quantity supplied.

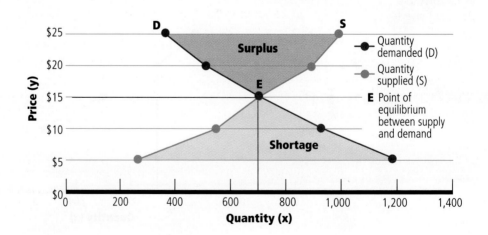

shirts. At that point there is a balance between the amount consumers will buy and the amount the manufacturers will supply.

Market equilibrium is achieved through a series of quantity and price adjustments that occur automatically. The gold area in Exhibit 2-10 is the surplus that results when the price is above equilibrium. At prices above $15, suppliers produce more sweatshirts than consumers are willing to buy. To sell more sweatshirts, prices will have to fall. Thus a surplus pushes prices downward until equilibrium is reached. When the price falls below equilibrium, the quantity of sweatshirts demanded rises above the available supply. The resulting shortage (beige area in Exhibit 2-10) forces prices upward until equilibrium is reached at $15.

Companies must continually monitor supply and demand characteristics of their markets. Changes often mean rethinking marketing and production strategies, as the Global Competition Trends box shows.

T R E N D S

Global Competition

An Abundance of Aluminum

As Russia and other former Soviet republics began exporting aluminum to the West, U.S. aluminum producers were faced with serious competition in the global marketplace. Prior to 1991 the Soviet republics exported 250,000 metric tons or less; in 1992, they shipped almost 1.25 million metric tons.

The output from these lower-cost entrants to the global market swelled aluminum inventories to about double the desired level. But continuing recessions in the major industrialized nations, such as Japan and Europe, greatly reduced demand. The per-pound price of aluminum fell from $1.10 in early 1989 to a record low of about $0.47 in November 1993. Even though demand in the United States increased 9 percent in 1993, U.S. aluminum companies were not free to raise their prices because of the intense competition. As a result, profits at Aluminum Company of America (Alcoa), the largest aluminum producer in the world, dropped sharply, and third-largest Reynolds Metals Co. had losses for four consecutive quarters. About 15 percent of total U.S. production capacity was shut down.

In response to this changing market, U.S. aluminum companies began looking for expanded uses for the metal, new customers, and more ways to cut production costs. They worked with U.S., Japanese, and European car manufacturers to develop more aluminum auto parts. Because aluminum is lighter than steel, increasing the aluminum content can help car companies meet U.S. fuel-efficiency requirements. They stepped up marketing programs to packaging companies in Asia and Latin America. In addition, Western producers—who voluntarily cut production by 1.8 million tons—met with the Russians to discuss how to restore an equilibrium of supply and demand. They offered to help modernize factories if Russia would also curtail production.

Some industry analysts believe that the companies that survive this current crisis will be better positioned for the future. They predict that high inflation in Russia will eliminate its cost advantage. Growth in Japanese and European economies, when they begin to recover from recession, will boost demand. And no one is adding production capacity. The industry hopes that by 1998 there might be a shortage in aluminum that would again boost prices.[4]

- Define demand and supply and draw them on a quantity (x)–price (y) graph.
- How can a firm use the principles of demand and supply to make decisions about the quantity to produce?

ECONOMIC ISSUES OF THE 1990S

You can see that firms and individuals are affected by both macroeconomic and microeconomic decisions. The U.S. economy is always changing in response to such decisions and to the actions of individuals, businesses, and governments.

Steady growth in its economy during the 1980s kept the U.S. a world leader. But as we move through the 1990s, the gap between our economy and those of other industrialized countries is shrinking. The United States is the acknowledged world leader in some industries; pharmaceuticals and aerospace are two. In many others—electronics, computers, motor vehicles, heavy equipment—U.S. companies do not dominate as they did ten years ago. They share the world marketplace with major foreign corporations, many of whom have captured significant market shares.

The United States remains the world's largest exporter of goods and services and still ranks first in manufacturing productivity. But during the 1980s the United States fell behind Germany and Japan in the rate of productivity growth. Fortunately, U.S. productivity has been improving steadily since 1991. Non-farm business productivity rose 2.8 percent in 1992, the largest annual gain since 1972, and 1.9 percent in 1993.[5] The United States also lags in capital investment. From 1988 to 1992 the average annual investment in business facilities of U.S. firms was about 15 percent of GDP. Comparable investment figures for other countries were 33 percent in Japan, about 25 percent in Asia's newly industrializing economies (South Korea, Hong Kong, Taiwan, Singapore), and about 21 percent for the European Economic Community. Capital investment helps businesses prepare for new technologies and sets the stage for future growth.[6]

In today's fast-paced global economy U.S. firms must work harder than ever to stay ahead of foreign competitors. They must sell more goods and services abroad. In addition, they must develop, manufacture, and sell products that compete more effectively with imports. Our standing in the future will be affected by how we handle four big economic issues: the federal budget deficit and national debt, the global economy, improving productivity in the service sector, and retraining the workforce. Success in dealing with these issues will keep us in the forefront of the business world in the next century.

THE FEDERAL BUDGET AND THE NATIONAL DEBT

Over the past decade reducing the federal budget deficit has become a national priority. This is not a new problem; we have had deficits almost every year since the 1930s. But before 1975 the yearly budget deficit was rather small, equal to no more than 3.5 percent of GDP. It began to climb in the 1980s and reached $290.2 billion in 1992 (4.9 percent of GDP) before declining slightly to $255 billion in 1993.[7] Because each year's budget deficit was added to those that went before, the national debt tripled between 1980 and 1990.

Causes of the Budget Crisis

Who's to blame for the budget crisis? Deficit spending has long been an accepted form of fiscal policy. The government traditionally spends more to stimulate a weak economy and spends less when the economy is expanding. But after the 1982 recession the government spent more while the economy prospered. Congress and President Ronald Reagan both said they wanted to decrease the deficit, but their actions did not match their words. Taxes were cut while spending increased greatly for defense. The biggest increase came in entitlement programs like Social Security and Medicare for the elderly; welfare and Medicaid for the poor; unemployment; pensions for federal, military, and civilian workers; and price supports for farmers. Since 1964 these programs have grown about 12 percent per year because of formulas that automatically raise the benefit payments. Today they account for half of all federal spending.[8] Interest payments on the national debt also added to annual deficits.

There have been many legislative attempts to reduce the deficit. The 1985 Gramm–Rudman–Hollings Balanced Budget and Emergency Deficit Control Act was supposed to reduce the deficit to zero by 1993 by decreasing the deficit limits each year. When the targets were not achieved, Congress changed the limits. A $500 billion budget deficit package was signed by Congress and President Bush in 1990. However, as mentioned earlier, the deficit continued to rise, in large part due to entitlements and to the economic effects of recession. Reducing the deficit was also a priority for President Clinton, who signed another deficit-reduction bill in August 1993. Its goal was to reduce the deficit to about $180 billion (2.2 percent of GDP) by 1998.[9]

Many economists and politicians believe the key to deficit reduction is reducing entitlement program spending. But this strategy is very controversial. Obviously, recipients such as the elderly, the poor, farmers, and veterans are opposed to any benefit cuts. The politicians that represent them do not want to alienate these voter groups by curtailing entitlements.[10] At this point it is too early to tell if the federal government has made any real progress in curbing the deficit.

THE UNITED STATES AND THE GLOBAL ECONOMY

After World War II the United States was the world's biggest economic power. It did not have to give much thought to what was happening in other nations' economies. But during the past twenty-five years, a number of other countries—mainly Japan and Germany—have also become major economic powers. Strong economic growth in Asian and Latin American countries such as Brazil, Mexico, China, Korea, and Taiwan further increases competition in world markets.

As these and other developing nations are integrated into the global economy, their residents want a higher standard of living. This creates

■ Pepsi Cola has had great success in selling their soft drinks around the world. Many other American corporations are also looking to foreign countries to find new markets for their products.

new markets for all types of U.S. goods and services. Total U.S. exports jumped 81 percent from 1985 to 1992.[11] We are exporting more to emerging economies. China now accounts for 15 percent of the total U.S. consumer goods exports, up from 5 percent in 1987. Over time the rising demand for sophisticated goods and services should create more jobs in the United States.[12] However, imports of foreign goods now account for 25 percent of U.S. purchases. U.S. corporations are facing increased competition, especially in consumer goods, from Asian and Latin American low-cost producers.[13]

Global competition is good for American business. It leads to improved productivity by forcing corporations to change faster and to be more innovative and efficient. In industries that compete internationally— for example, steel, consumer electronics, and car manufacturing—U.S. companies are moving quickly to develop better, lower-cost ways to design and produce goods that are priced competitively.

The United States has grown to depend more on other nations. Every year more companies, both large and small, expand their international sales and operations. Many receive large portions of their revenues from international sales; Coca Cola (80 percent), Gillette (70 percent), and Microsoft (50 percent) are some well-known examples. However, the fortunes of U.S. corporations are now linked closely to economic health in other countries. In 1992 and 1993 slow growth and high unemployment in the European Union (EU) sharply reduced the demand for U.S. goods and services.

IMPROVING SERVICE SECTOR PRODUCTIVITY

About eight out of ten American workers today provide services rather than produce goods. They work in industries like financial services, communications, transportation, education, wholesale and retail trade, health care, entertainment, food service, law, consulting, and government agencies. Truck drivers who deliver goods to stores are service employees, as are university professors, FBI agents, advertising copywriters, accountants, and airline reservation agents.

The Shift to Services

The shift from a manufacturing economy to a service-based economy is not new. If we define a service-based economy as one with more than half of all jobs in the service sector, the United States has been a service economy since 1950. What *is* new is the fast growth in service jobs. The service sector is responsible for almost all new job creation since 1980.

Why have service jobs increased? First, U.S. manufacturing output has gone up steadily (although at a slower rate than in many foreign countries). Today we have about the same number of production workers—12 million—as in 1946. But with the help of automation they now produce five times more goods.[14] Because manufacturing firms require service firms to buy, market, distribute, and sell most goods, service companies must hire more employees to handle the increased volume.

A second reason for the growth in service jobs is the trend toward using outside providers to replace such service employees as engineers and cafeteria workers. Firms also are using temporary employees to cover seasonal increases in demand. And service firms themselves need to buy services, which has a snowball effect. For example, a manufacturing firm may hire a software developer to design an inventory control program. The software firm in turn requires accounting and legal services.

Technological innovation and development of new services have also expanded the service sector. Service firms now offer complex computer and communication systems unknown ten years ago. And rapid change in the business world has spawned a booming consulting industry, which gives advice on everything from using new technology to setting up employee benefits.

Closing the Productivity Gap

For many years U.S. service sector productivity gains were extremely low, less than 1 percent annually. From 1987 until mid-1991, service productivity actually decreased. Since then it has surged, reaching 3.2 percent in late 1992—about the same as manufacturing productivity growth.[15] For overall productivity in the U.S. to continue to improve, the service sector must continue to become more productive.

The productivity gap between services and manufacturing has several causes. For one thing, service firm productivity is harder to measure. Increased value from improved customer convenience and service may not result in improved profitability. In addition, though service firms invested heavily in technology, the benefits were slow to appear. At first automation often increased the bureaucracy and the paperflow, actually decreasing productivity. Now that companies have learned how to manage the new technologies efficiently, productivity is improving steadily.

Exporting Services

An important result of high U.S. service sector productivity is the increase in service exports. Service exports now account for 28 percent of total exports and are one of the fastest growing segments of the economy. From 1990 to 1993 they grew an average of 12.6 percent per year, double the growth in goods, and reached about $190 billion in 1993. In 1992 the service industries had a trade surplus of $59 billion (compared to a $96 billion trade deficit in goods). Service exports also created about 1.7 million new jobs from 1986 to 1992.[16]

Tourism—spending by foreign tourists in the U.S.—represents about one-third of all service exports. Among the other leading service exports are entertainment; information technology; and business, technical, and financial services (legal, accounting, insurance, architecture, construction, and engineering services).

Like productivity, service exports are hard to measure. In many cases American firms export ideas, such as product designs, to their own foreign manufacturing facilities. And services such as bank fees for making foreign loans and fees charged by securities firms to manage stock and bond portfolios for overseas investors are not currently included. Recognizing the significance of service exports to the overall foreign trade picture, in March 1994 the Commerce Department added service trade to its monthly foreign trade report.[17]

DISLOCATION OF THE WORK FORCE

Unfortunately our improved productivity has come at a great cost in human terms. In just the first nine months of 1993, almost 450,000 people lost their jobs. This staggering number far exceeds layoffs during 1991, a recession year. What is more troubling is the permanent nature of most of these job cuts. In the 1980s layoffs were a way to reduce costs until demand increased and companies would hire again. Today, in addition to reductions in demand, job cutbacks are the result of cost reduction strategies to help firms remain competitive.

Downsizing is affecting most industries, including computer manufacturers and pharmaceutical companies, former leaders in job creation. IBM, once considered one of the most secure places to work, has reduced its work force by over 25 percent since 1986. Defense contractors have been especially hard hit due to reductions in military spending since the end of the Cold War. The Bureau of Labor Statistics estimates that by 1997 this "peace dividend" will result in cuts by military contractors of over 300,000 jobs. Another million jobs could be lost at their suppliers.[18] Adapting defense-related technological expertise to peacetime uses is one response to this situation as the nearby Business Today Trends box shows.

Another key difference in the current round of layoffs is the type of worker who is unemployed. Highly skilled workers, middle managers, executives, and other professionals who were once considered immune have lost their jobs. White-collar unemployment reached an all-time high—an estimated 3.1 million in mid-1993. Fewer of these workers will be rehired because their jobs no longer exist. Job security, particularly at large corporations, is a thing of the past.

The causes of this new unemployment are similar to reasons for our improved productivity. Global competition has forced change upon U.S.

Missiles to Modems

In 1986 about half of Rockwell International's revenue came from military contracts. The company was best known for building the B-1 bomber, missiles, and space shuttles. But defense spending fell after the end of the Cold War, and Rockwell lost 40,000 jobs from 1986 to 1993.

Rockwell's management, led by Chief Executive Officer Donald Beall, saw the writing on the wall ten years ago. Accurately predicting the decline in military spending, he began to revamp the company. He focused on four key business units: electronics, automotive products, graphics equipment, and aerospace. He sold any businesses that did not fit and bought companies with significant market share in these areas.

Beall decided that the corporate organization was too cumbersome to remain competitive. Rockwell reduced management from seven to three levels and slashed headquarters staff by over 50 percent. Executives were required to study new techniques to manage knowledge workers. By investing in new manufacturing technology, research and development, and employee training, the firm improved efficiency and productivity.

Its Laurinburg, North Carolina, automotive plant is an example of the company's success. The plant features a program of worker-directed manufacturing. It formed a partnership with a local community college to train new, unskilled workers in the latest production techniques. Employees are encouraged to continually upgrade their skills. They earn pay increases as they master new jobs. Only five years after adding truck transmissions to its product line, the plant achieved a 16 percent market share against long-established competitors.

Rockwell's strategic shift has paid off handsomely. Today it derives less than a quarter of its sales from government contracts. This figure should drop further as its non-defense products continue to grow at a rapid pace. It is a leader in telecommunications equipment, producing 80 percent of all computer modems and fax machines sold worldwide. It manufactures about two-thirds of the high-speed newspaper presses in the U.S. The company's profitability increased about 20 percent in 1993, no small accomplishment in a weak economy.[19]

corporations so they can compete more effectively in international markets. In addition to restructuring operations in the U.S., many have also transferred jobs overseas to take advantage of lower-cost labor in other countries. Advances in communications technology allow companies to locate facilities in countries with a surplus of well-educated, highly motivated workers. For example, California software company Quarterdeck Office systems hires Irish programmers and staffs a technical support operation in Dublin. Texas Instruments, Motorola, and IBM have sizable programming operations in India. AT&T Bell Laboratories manufactures telephones in Singapore and Indonesia.[20] The increased use of outside firms for functions previously handled in-house and the emergence of a contingent workforce also contribute to unemployment. Companies are using part-time and temporary workers on a contract basis to cut labor costs and save on fringe benefits.

Training for the Future

Finding new jobs is becoming increasingly difficult for unemployed workers. Their skills may no longer be in demand, perhaps replaced by technology, or may be too specialized for another employer. Many older, experienced workers lose jobs to younger applicants who can be hired for lower salaries.

Companies need better-trained, more adaptable workers who can handle more than one type of job. In addition to technological skills employees also need good communication and decision-making skills. As companies reduce the number of management layers, more responsibilities are shifting downward. Because technology changes rapidly, continuing education will be more important than ever.

Yet most companies have made little or no investment in workplace education. The skills taught in training programs, many of which are government sponsored, often do not meet the needs of local employers. Dislocated workers need to be retrained to fill available jobs. This calls for cooperation among business, academia, and the government. The United States needs more successful training programs like that at Cincinnati Technical College (CTC). Working with about 600 local companies that provide cooperative positions for its students, CTC offers two-year technical training programs geared to employer requirements in fields ranging from civil engineering to accounting to aviation maintenance. About 98 percent of its graduates find skilled jobs, and many are hired by the companies where they do their co-op work.[21]

Increasingly, the ability of the United States to stay competitive will depend on how well we use our human capital. Preparing today's work

■ Students at Cincinnati Technical College benefit from training programs especially geared to employer requirements in various fields. About 600 local companies worked with the school to develop the program and often hire its graduates.

force for tomorrow's challenges will lead to job growth in the United States. Domestic companies will keep operations here, and a highly skilled labor pool will attract foreign business investment.

Concept Check

- What are some of the reasons for the federal budget crisis? How does this crisis affect interest rates?
- What does a service-based economy mean for U.S. business?
- Discuss the major reasons for the recent high level of unemployment. How do today's unemployed workers differ from those in the past?

■ SUMMARY

continued

1. Understand the importance of economics and the circular flow.

Economics is the study of how individuals, businesses, and governments use scarce resources to produce and distribute goods and services. The two major areas in economics are macroeconomics, the study of the economy as a whole, and microeconomics, the study of particular markets. The individual, business, and government sectors of the economy are linked by a series of two-way flows. The government provides public goods and services for the other two sectors and receives income in the form of taxes. Changes in one flow affect the other sectors.

2. Discuss how economic growth, GDP, and business cycles are related.

A nation's economy is growing when the level of business activity, as measured by gross national product, is rising. GDP is the total value of all goods and services produced in a year. Changing levels of GDP create business cycles. An increase in GDP usually indicates a strong economy. A recession occurs when real GDP declines for at least two consecutive quarters.

3. Explain the economic goals of full employment and price stability.

The goal of full employment is to have a job for all who can and want to work. How well a nation is meeting its employment goals is measured by the unemployment rate. There are four types of unemployment: frictional, structural, cyclical, and seasonal. Price stability is the ability to keep the overall prices of goods and services from moving much either up or down.

4. Describe inflation, the two indexes used to measure it, and its two main causes.

Inflation is the general upward movement of prices. When prices rise, purchasing power falls. The rate of inflation is measured by changes in the consumer price index (CPI) and the producer price index (PPI). There are two main causes of inflation. If the demand for goods and services exceeds the supply, prices will rise. This is called demand-pull inflation. Higher production costs, such as materials and wages, can also increase the final price of goods and services, which is cost-push inflation.

5. Discuss how and why the government uses monetary policy and fiscal policy to achieve its macroeconomic goals.

Monetary policy refers to actions by the Federal Reserve System to control the money supply. When the Fed restricts the money supply, interest rates rise, the inflation rate drops, and economic growth slows. By expanding the money supply, the Fed stimulates economic growth.

The government also uses fiscal policy—changes in levels of taxation and spending—to control the economy. Reducing taxes or increasing spending stimulates the economy; raising taxes or decreasing spending does the opposite. When the government spends more than it receives in tax revenues, it must borrow to finance the deficit. Some economists favor deficit spending as a way to stimulate the economy; others worry about our high level of national debt.

6. Understand the basic microeconomic concepts of demand and supply and how they establish prices.

Demand is the quantity of a good or service that people will buy at a given price. Supply is the quantity of a good or service that firms will make available at a given price. When the price increases, the quantity demanded falls but the quantity supplied rises. A price decrease yields increased demand but a lower supply. At the point where the quantity demanded equals the quantity supplied, demand and supply are in balance. This equilibrium point is achieved by market adjustments of quantity and price.

7. Describe the four key economic issues of the 1990s: national debt, globalization, service sector productivity, and dislocation of the work force.

The national debt rose to new heights during the 1990s as the gap between federal spending and tax revenues widened. Concern over rising national debt produced laws to control and reduce the deficit, although these laws have not yet had much effect.

The United States now competes in a global economy. Economic conditions in other countries affect demand for U.S. exports. Newly industrialized nations in Latin America and Asia create new markets for U.S. goods but also produce low-cost goods that compete with American products.

The service economy now accounts for eight out of ten jobs in the United States. Productivity in this sector was slow to improve until recently. But the increase in U.S. service exports is balancing the loss of manufacturing exports.

To stay competitive the United States will need a highly skilled work force. This will require retraining the many workers who have lost their jobs due to global competition, technology, and corporate restructuring.

■ DISCUSSION QUESTIONS

1. Assume that the U.S. economy is sluggish and the government wants to stimulate it just before a national election. Which type of policy—monetary or fiscal—is it more likely to use? Why?

2. What are the current trends in the economy with regard to GDP growth, unemployment, and inflation? What do they tell you about the level of business activity and the business cycle? If you owned a personnel agency, how would this information affect your decision making?

3. In 1993 the federal government passed a budget package with tax increases and spending reductions designed to reduce the federal deficit. Has this program been successful?

4. As a manufacturer of in-line roller skates, you are questioning your pricing policies. You note that, over the past five years, the CPI has increased an average of 3 percent per year, and the price of a pair of skates increased an average of 5 percent per year for the first three years and 2 percent for the next two years. What does this information tell you about demand, supply, and other factors influencing the market for these skates?

5. IBM, once America's premier computer manufacturer, laid off 60,000 employees in 1993. Based on what you have learned about economics and what was happening in the economy at the time, how would you classify the unemployment resulting from this program? Why? What are some of the other economic issues that influenced IBM's management? How might their decision affect other aspects of the economy?

Gatortronics

While still in college, you create a computer game, "Gatortronics." You and your friends spend a lot of time playing it. The object of the game is for your alligator to eat as many pizzas as possible. Your economics professor hears about the game, plays it, and encourages you to sell the program commercially. But she tells you that you should first calculate the equilibrium point to see if you can charge enough to make a profit on the game.

You make copies of the game and place them in different computer stores all over town at different prices. At the end of the month, you collect the following data on sales of your game:

Price	$100	$80	$60	$40	$20
Number sold	2	5	11	20	32

You also find out how other software companies price similar games. Your study of costs yields the following data:

Price	$100	$80	$60	$40	$20
Number available	32	20	11	5	2

Questions
1. Graph the supply and demand curves. What is the equilibrium point for your software?
2. If you price your game at $80, what will happen? At $20?
3. What additional factors should you consider when you set the price for the game? What are some situations that would cause you to change the price?

Your Career in Business

There are more types of jobs in business than in any other field. Unlike engineering, social work, or most other fields, business can satisfy many interests, personality types, challenges, and compensation levels. The needed education ranges from a two-year degree to a Ph.D.

All business careers require a few skills. For instance, communication skills are important for almost any business position. No matter what you know, if it can't be communicated to others, you may not advance very far. Moreover, good communication skills help you sell your ideas to others. Public speaking and the ability to make presentations are also useful skills.

Usually, a businessperson must be able to pay attention to details when examining records and preparing reports. Some basic math and accounting skills will help with budgets and statistics.

Many business positions require managing the work of others. Successful supervisors have good human-relations skills. They understand the interactions of work groups, motivation techniques, and morale building. Good managers can communicate well, develop plans, organize human and material resources, and create systems to make certain that work matches plans.

Today's workplace is very dependent on information technology. Companies therefore require computer-literate employees. Those with advanced computer skills will be in great demand.

The business environment is changing rapidly, and today's college graduates will change jobs—and careers—many times. You should continually increase your portfolio of transferrable skills—those that apply to many types of companies and positions—so that you can move into new areas as opportunities arise. Take advantage of on-the-job training and continuing education courses. The more skills you have, the more valuable you are to an employer.

If you are thinking of a career in business, you should consider the following questions:

- Are you willing to let people working for you make decisions?
- Can you make yourself understood in group discussions?
- Do you work calmly and efficiently under pressure?
- Will you work more than eight hours a day and sometimes take work home?
- Can you identify key points in masses of information?
- Are you patient with other people?
- Are you self-disciplined and self-controlled?
- When you are planning, can you generally take a broad view?
- Do you have good analytical skills?

- Have you considered how a professional business position might change your lifestyle?

This list is not comprehensive. Its goal is just to get you thinking about whether a business career is really for you. Positive answers to all the questions are a step in the right direction. Negative answers to all of them probably mean you should look elsewhere for a career.

Testing the Waters: Part-Time Work while Attending School

One good way to see how you feel about a business career is to work part-time for a company while in school. You will be viewing the organization from the bottom up, but you can still see how the firm operates. Talk to workers and managers and get their ideas about the company and their careers. Part-time work can provide you with some great insights, enhance your resume, and put some money in your pocket.

Consider the case of Joe Alfrey. When he was an undergraduate finance major at the University of San Diego, he worked part-time as a waiter. Although waiting tables would not seem to be related to a finance career, Joe found his work experience valuable. He learned how to deal with many types of people, set priorities, and solve problems—skills that are important in business. While getting his Masters in Business Administration in finance at San Diego State University, he worked part-time as a financial analyst for a biotechnology company and joined it full-time after graduation. However, after several years he discovered that an entrepreneurial career, perhaps in the food business, was more to his liking. His earlier work experiences helped him to reach this decision.[1]

You can also work as a consultant or take free-lance assignments in some fields. If you have computer skills, you might moonlight at "computer camps," where kids learn how to operate computers. You can also sell your services to people who need help with their computer, such as writers who are trying to set up new word-processing programs. If you are a whiz at programming, you might make a customer's data base "user friendly." One young consultant did a thriving business translating computer symbols to plain English. Desktop publishing and computer graphics are other areas with good potential for part-time work. You can find opportunities like these by checking the yellow pages and contacting computer consultants. They often need part-time help.

Lawn or house painting services are surprisingly profitable and good businesses for students because demand is highest in the summer. To start these businesses, you need basic equipment (lawn mower and other gardening tools or ladders, brushes, rollers, and tarps) and fliers to advertise your services. The secret to success is to know what *not* to do. For example, don't try to compete with the twelve-year-old down the street who does quick-and-dirty mowing, and don't do battle with the high-priced, professional lawn services. Instead, do the work neither one wants to do: trimming, weeding, occasional seeding and fertilizing, and even sweeping the driveway.

Jobs like these might not make you a fortune or pave your career path, but there's something to be gained from almost any business experience. Operating a lawn service, for example, will sharpen your understanding of how to find customers, position yourself within a market, and build a client base.

You can gain real-world experience in many ways. The part-time catering business Constance Collins ran while she was in college turned into a full-time business after graduation.[2] Students at many colleges have used their talents to start profitable part-time home- or dorm-based ventures. Don't be surprised if your idea becomes the basis for a full-time business. After all, two college kids named Jobs and Wozniak started their company part-time, working out of a garage, and Apple Computer was born.

Working for the Government

If you decide that a business-oriented career is for you, don't rule out working for the government. Many business specialties, such as management or accounting, have a counterpart in government. The federal government is the largest single employer, but more people work for the fifty state governments. Local governments employ almost three times as many people as state governments do.

Altogether, government provides about 17 million jobs.

Among the occupations in government agencies are accountant, computer programmer and computer systems analyst, office manager, purchasing agent, and urban and regional planner. These jobs usually require at least a four-year college degree in a field related to the occupation. Purchasing agents are concentrated in the federal government. Urban and regional planners are much more

likely to work for local governments. The other positions are found at all levels of government.

Government employees enjoy a number of fringe benefits. The most common are paid vacation and sick leave, paid holidays, medical insurance, retirement plans, and tuition aid. Others are job security and advancement opportunities. A government is less likely to be affected by temporary economic setbacks than a private company, and government positions often have clearly defined career ladders. But the major benefits of government employment may be intangible: the opportunity to serve the public good and have a direct impact on other people.

Government service has some disadvantages too. One is the inability to measure achievement in terms of profit and loss. The final goal of most private companies is to make money by offering some good or service. The marketplace provides constant feedback about their success. But government programs can rarely show a clear-cut success, and even the most successful programs have critics. Politics also has a major effect on government workers. Politicians control the budget and make the final decisions. And the same controls that provide job security can protect the job of someone you think you should replace. Promotion is often sure but slow. Government also doesn't offer the extremely high salaries and bonuses that go to a few very successful private workers.

The federal government, every state, most cities, and many counties have agencies that provide information about how jobs are filled. Counseling to help you determine which occupations you are best prepared for may also be available. The names of the agencies differ a good deal. You can learn the ones you need to know from gov-

ernment directories in the library. The government section of a telephone book may also indicate whom to contact for job information.

Two other government agencies also try to help job seekers. One is the Job Service, which provides employment information and counseling for government and nongovernment jobs. The other is the library: Besides directories and job announcements, it has many other books and some magazines that give advice on finding work.

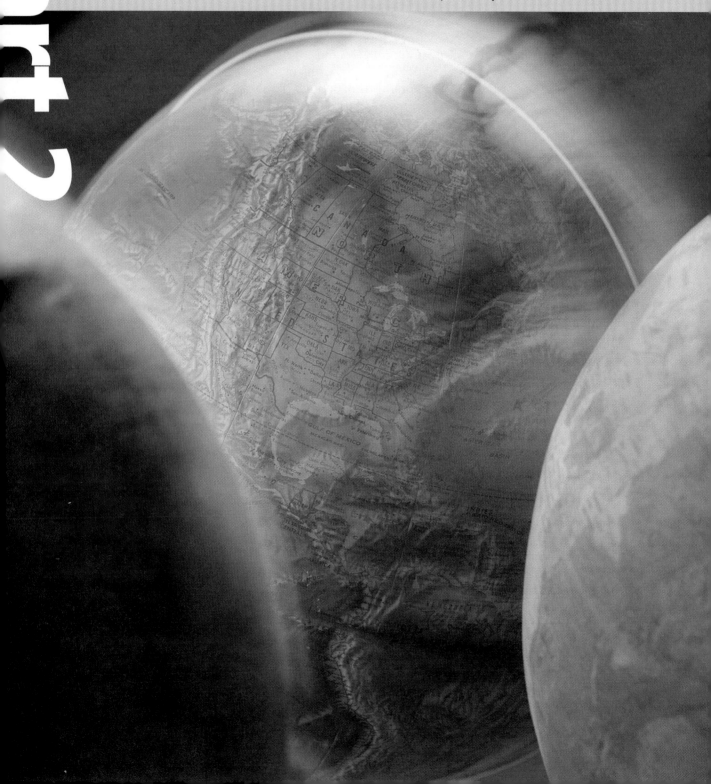

The Business Environment

Part 2

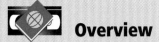

Overview

Scientists believe that the chlorofluorocarbons used in our refrigerators and air conditioners have caused depletion of the atmosphere's ozone layer. This could lead to such problems as an increase in cases of skin cancer worldwide. That is one example of how our actions can have a serious impact on people and places far from where we live. Corporate executives must be sensitive to this fact, especially in today's global economy. They should consider the economic, social, and environmental repercussions their decisions may have.

The obligations of business begin here at home. The United States is becoming more culturally and ethnically diverse by the day. This presents a challenge to business on two fronts. First, corporations will have to learn how to target their goods and services to new markets. Second, as the workforce begins to reflect the changing makeup of the population, it will be important to understand how to motivate and communicate with employees of differing values and cultures. This is known as "managing diversity." The overall aim is to enhance performance and satisfaction by increasing the respect employees have for each other, both as individuals and members of groups.

These lessons take on even greater importance when doing business internationally. In order to take advantage of new foreign markets in developed and developing nations, corporations will have to be sensitive to the cultures of the countries they do business in. Depending on the country, companies may have to tailor their products to appeal to consumers and businesses from different backgrounds.

Another concept that is transforming the way business is done is social responsibility. There is a growing feeling that businesses should act in a socially and ethically correct manner. This can range from showing more concern for the environment to setting up new programs to hire disabled workers. Conducting business in a socially responsible manner can improve a company's public image at the same time that it encourages a more favorable climate for business by helping to prevent further government regulations.

The following chapters examine the ways business is responding to the new demands of our multicultural society, the expanding global market, and the popular notion that companies have an obligation to do the right thing. You will see that it all boils down to a simple truth: We are all citizens of the same planet. Business is not excused from the laws and ethical values that control the behavior of individuals. Whether at home or abroad, businesspeople should ask themselves how the decisions they make will affect society as a whole. Both society and business will benefit from such concern.

The Business Environment

The health industry has come under fire recently. People both inside and outside the industry are calling for change. Critics cite high costs, poor service, and unequal access to treatment as proof that an overhaul is necessary. In the midst of this debate, United Medical Resources continues to go quietly about the business of providing quality service to its customers.

United Medical Resources is an employee benefits administrator. The company processes claims for corporations with self-funded or flexible-benefit health plans. It services over 120 corporations and their 120,000 employees located throughout the United States. Chief executive officer Vickie Buyniski established the privately held company in 1983. Under her leadership, United Medical Resources' revenues have grown from a first-year total of $380,000 to over $6 million today.

The success of UMR is built upon each employee's commitment to the company's key principles: customer satisfaction, quality performance, and service. Ms. Buyniski says that these three components make up the yardstick that United Medical Resources uses to evaluate its performance.

UMR strives to find the health care program that best matches the needs of each of its clients. It is this kind of service that has made United Medical Resources a success in a turbulent industry.

Our Multicultural Society
and Its Implications for Business

Chapter 3

Learning Goals

After studying this chapter, you should be able to:

1 Appreciate and understand the increasing cultural diversity of the United States.

2 Identify key characteristics and trends among African-Americans and opportunities to serve this market.

3 Identify key characteristics and trends among Hispanic-Americans and opportunities to serve this market.

4 Identify key characteristics and trends among Asian-Americans and opportunities to serve this market.

5 Understand how companies are managing cultural diversity in the workplace.

Career Profile

Kristin Knapp is Vice President of Public Relations of AIESEC, the largest student organization in the world. She rose to this leadership position while serving as a volunteer with AIESEC during college. Though Kristin majored in public relations, it was her classes in international business that prepared her for the environment in which she operates every day. Kristin works with five other people from different AIESEC chapters throughout the United States, helping undergraduates become more aware of foreign cultures through business opportunities. She also interfaces with AIESEC's corporate sponsors— such as AT&T, Arthur Andersen, IBM, and GE— to develop outside ties that will benefit AIESEC.

AIESEC has over 820 chapters in 78 countries. The organization seeks to promote cultural understanding while developing tomorrow's global leadership. This objective is met through two programs. The core program involves an international exchange of members for practical work internships in foreign markets. The other program is the global theme project, in which all of AIESEC's chapters host projects relating to a common theme. These projects are designed to give the students a better perspective on global business and the different cultures of the world. In fact, one recent theme of the project was education toward international and cultural understanding.

Kristin feels that it is vital that companies be aware of differences among cultures, given the global nature of business today. U.S. firms must be open to new ideas from other cultures if they are to target effective marketing and promotional campaigns at people of different backgrounds. Businesses can no longer hope to reach everyone with a single promotional strategy. Many potential customers would be unreceptive to such a unicultural approach. The more specific advertisers are in addressing their customers' needs and wants, the more successful they will be. Kristin believes that an understanding of cultural differences can help businesses achieve the goal of satisfying their customers.

Diversity is a term we see and hear all around us these days. This chapter looks at what diversity is and how it affects U.S. business. First, the chapter considers the expected changes in the racial and ethnic makeup of the United States in the next decade, including the implications for regions, business, and society at large. Next, the chapter examines three significant groups—African-Americans, Hispanic-Americans, and Asian-Americans. Finally, the chapter explores how companies are managing cultural diversity in the workplace.

OUR MULTICULTURAL SOCIETY

 The United States is undergoing a major transition as it becomes ethnically diverse. During the 1990s it will change from a society dominated by whites and rooted in Western ways to a society that includes three large racial and ethnic minorities: African-Americans, Hispanic-Americans, and Asian-Americans. All three minorities will grow both in size and share of population; the white majority will decline as a percentage of the total population. Society's beliefs, values, and social norms—its *culture*—will change to reflect the changing makeup of the population. The United States is quickly moving from a largely Western culture to **multiculturalism,** the recognition and acceptance of a variety of cultural expressions. Multiculturalism occurs when the ethnic groups in an area, whether a city, county, or country, are roughly equally represented.

multiculturalism The recognition and acceptance of a variety of cultures that are roughly equally represented in a particular region.

The U.S. population grew from 226 million in 1980 to over 253 million in 1994. Much of that growth took place in minority groups. The 1990 census found that whites represented eight in ten Americans, down from nine in ten in 1960. By 1994 about a quarter of the population were members of minority groups.[1]

■ The changing ethnic makeup of the United States is reflected in the wide assortment of cultural celebrations that take place around the country.

■ Exhibit 3-1

Multicultural Makeup of the United States

Source: U.S. Department of Labor—Bureau of the Census Projections.

1994

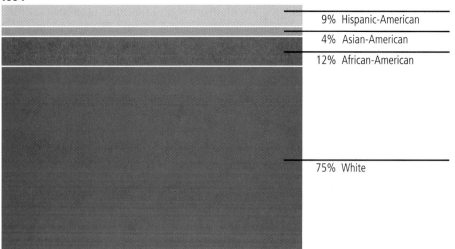

9% Hispanic-American

4% Asian-American

12% African-American

75% White

2023

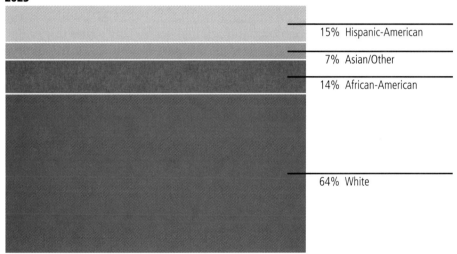

15% Hispanic-American

7% Asian/Other

14% African-American

64% White

Demographic shifts will be even more pronounced in the future. Exhibit 3-1 shows the 1994 population mix and the forecasted population mix for 2023. Note that of the three major ethnic groups, Hispanics will be the fastest-growing segment of the population. The diversity of the American population is projected to stabilize around the year 2023, as the birthrate among minorities levels off.

THE IMPACT OF IMMIGRATION

During the last decade 8.7 million people immigrated to the United States. Many who were already here resented these immigrants, because unemployment was high and social services strained. A 1992 survey found that 68 percent believed that immigration was bad for the country.[2]

Unlike past waves of immigration, the new immigrants have been mainly from Asia and Latin America. Like the existing workforce, these immigrants have been split between the highly skilled and well educated and those with minimal skills and little education. On balance, the economic benefits of being an open-door society far outweigh the costs. For example, the United States is reaping a bonanza of highly educated foreigners. In the late 1980s, 1.5 million college-educated immigrants joined the U.S. workforce. High-tech industries are depending on immigrant scientists, engineers, and entrepreneurs to remain competitive. Also, the immigrants' links to their old countries are boosting U.S. exports to such fast-growing regions as Asia and Latin America.

Even immigrants with less education are contributing to the economy as workers, consumers, business owners, and taxpayers. Some 11 million immigrants are employed, and they earn at least $240 billion a year. They're paying more than $90 billion in taxes—a lot more than the estimated $5 billion that immigrants receive in welfare.[3] Immigrant entrepreneurs, from the corner grocer to the local builder, create jobs for other immigrants and those born here. Vibrant immigrant communities are revitalizing cities and older suburbs that would otherwise be suffering from a shrinking tax base.

The Immigration Act of 1990 (IMMACT 1990) has increased the diversity among immigrants—especially at the upper end of the socioeconomic scale. The law allows people who have no family in the United States to immigrate if they have highly prized work skills or are ready to make a significant business investment. The law nearly tripled the number of visas (to 140,000 a year) for engineers and scientists, executives and managers, and other people with skills in demand. Investor immigrants, who will each put at least $1 million into the economy, account for 10,000 of those visas.

The results are noticeable: About 40 percent of the 200 researchers in the Communications Sciences Research wing at AT&T Bell Laboratories were born outside the United States. In Silicon Valley, California, much of the technical workforce is foreign-born. At Du Pont Merck Pharmaceutical, a joint venture based in Delaware, a new drug for treating hypertension was invented by a team that included two immigrants from Hong Kong and a scientist whose parents migrated from Lithuania.

The next generation of scientists and engineers at high-tech companies in the United States will be dominated by immigrants. The number of native-born citizens getting science Ph.D.s has remained about the same, but the number of foreign-born students receiving science doctorates more than doubled between 1981 and 1991, to 37 percent of the total.[4]

ETHNIC/CULTURAL DIVERSITY BY REGION

Regardless of their educational level, immigrants tend to join their peers, and their peers tend to live in large coastal cities. California, New York, Texas, Florida, Illinois, and New Jersey are expected to be home to three of every four new immigrants, who will be joining already-large minority populations in those states. In California, non-Hispanic whites will become a minority within the next two decades.[5]

Ethnic groups are not equally dispersed across the United States. Four of New York City's five boroughs are among the ten most ethnically diverse counties in the country.[6] San Francisco County is the most diverse in the nation. The proportions of major ethnic groups are closer to being equal there than anywhere else.

The least multicultural region is a broad swath stretching from northern New England through the Midwest and into Montana. These counties have few people other than whites. The counties with the very lowest level of diversity are found in America's agricultural heartland—Nebraska and Iowa.

BUSINESS OPPORTUNITIES AND ETHNIC GROUPS

The ethnic diversity of a region depends on its employment and business opportunities. Today minorities own about a tenth of the nation's 14 million firms.[7] During the past decade every large minority group increased the number of businesses owned and rates of business ownership. This change occurred despite the obstacles many would-be minority entrepreneurs have faced in attempting to borrow money to start and operate small businesses.

Some minority groups have much higher rates of business ownership than others. The number of firms owned by Asians grew by 89 percent during the past decade, not far behind the rate of Asian population growth. The number of firms owned by Hispanics grew by 81 percent. Business growth was only 38 percent among businesses owned by African-Americans. But that growth was still faster than the 13 percent rate of this group's population growth between 1980 and 1990.[8] We'll take a closer look at minority-owned businesses in Chapter 7.

The high rate of business ownership among Asians is due to several factors. First is their high level of educational attainment. In 1992 about 40 percent of adult Asian-Americans had completed college, compared with only 23 percent of white Americans.[9] Asian-Americans also have rather high incomes, so they have more capital with which to launch small businesses. Finally, a large share of Asian-Americans are recent immigrants, many of whom came to the United States specifically to go into business.

Examples of successful immigrant minorities abound. Paul Yuan, for example, left Taiwan with his wife in 1975, seven days after they were married. They settled in Seattle with several thousand dollars in life savings and no work visas. Yuan was a college graduate but for two years worked in Chinese restaurants. In 1978 he became a legal resident and opened his own travel agency while working nights as a hotel dishwasher. In 1994, at 45 years of age, Yuan owns a thriving Seattle travel business.

Similarly, in 1965 Humberto Galvez, 21, left Mexico City for Los Angeles. He started pumping gas and busing tables, working his way up the ladder with a lot of bumps along the way. After starting and selling a chain of nineteen El Pollo Loco charbroiled chicken restaurants in the Los Angeles area, he now owns six Pescado Mojado seafood diners, employing 100 workers.

Taken together, minority groups are rapidly becoming a larger portion of America's business owners. They generate more income and employment in the U.S. economy as money earned in their businesses is spent and re-spent.

SOCIAL IMPLICATIONS OF MULTICULTURALISM

Multiculturalism will have a profound impact on society as a whole. If we count men and women as separate groups, all of us are now members of at least one minority group.[10] Without fully realizing it, we have left the time when the nonwhite, non-Western part of our population could be expected to assimilate to the dominant majority. In the future everyone will have to do some assimilation.

As minority groups grow, no single group will have the political power to dictate solutions. Agreement on how to resolve almost any public issue is likely to be hard to obtain. Reaching a consensus will require more cooperation than it has in the past.

The U.S. economy continues to move away from manufacturing and jobs requiring physical skills toward services and jobs requiring mental skills. More than ever, a college education will be the way for minorities to gain broader opportunities in U.S. society. As educational attainment becomes more important for individual success, differences in educational attainment will produce sharply different socioeconomic profiles for different racial and ethnic groups. This trend could create a population polarized by both race and economic opportunity. Unless the current pattern changes, whites and Asian-Americans could increasingly dominate high-income, high-status occupations, leaving African-Americans and Hispanics with low-income, low-status occupations. Even if job discrimination suddenly disappeared, lower educational attainment would keep many minorities from entering newly opened doors.

- Explain what is meant by the United States becoming a multicultural society.
- What has been the impact of immigration on the United States?
- Describe the social implications of multiculturalism.

AFRICAN-AMERICANS

African-Americans, numbering 31 million in 1994, are the largest minority group in the United States. The proportion of the population that is African-American will continue to grow well into the next century because of differences in birthrates (22.1 births per 1,000 persons among African-Americans, versus 14.8 for whites). Also, the death rate among African-Americans is lower than among the general population because their average age is younger. The median age of this group was 28.2 years in 1994, nearly five years younger than the median for all citizens.

■ People Colors Crayons is an example of a product in tune with the multicultural changes in society. They offer a wider selection of skin tones than standard crayon sets.

Courtesy of Lakeshore Learning Materials, P.O. Box 6261, Carson, CA 90749.

The immigration of African-Americans from abroad is minimal compared with the large numbers of immigrants from Latin America and Asia. Immigration accounted for only about 30 percent of the increase in the African-American population.

GEOGRAPHIC CONCENTRATION

At the beginning of the twentieth century over 90 percent of all African-Americans lived in the South. The growing industrial base in the North, combined with the lack of economic opportunity and racial oppression and violence in the rural South, started a massive movement of African-Americans. Most moved to the Northeast and the Midwest. In the 1970s African-Americans began to migrate back to the South and West from declining northern industrial cities. Today 53 percent of all African-Americans live in the South, 19 percent each in the Midwest and Northeast, and 9 percent in the West.[11]

The largest concentration of African-Americans in a metropolitan area is in New York City (see Exhibit 3-2). The areas of greatest population growth among African-Americans are outer suburbs surrounding central metropolitan areas. For example, the African-American population of

		1990 African-American population (in thousands)	Percentage of population that is African-American
1	New York, NY	2,250	12.53
2	Chicago, IL	1,332	16.53
3	Washington, D.C. –MD–VA	1,041	26.56
4	Los Angeles–Long Beach, CA	992	6.83
5	Detroit, MI	943	20.22
6	Philadelphia, PA	929	15.76
7	Atlanta, GA	736	25.98
8	Baltimore, MD	616	25.86
9	Houston, TX	611	16.47
10	New Orleans, LA	430	34.75
11	St. Louis, MO–IL	433	17.31
12	Newark, NJ	422	58.46
13	Dallas, TX	410	10.57
14	Memphis, TN–AR–MS	399	40.64
15	Norfolk–Virginia Beach–Newport News, VA	398	28.51

Exhibit 3-2
African-American
Population Centers
Source: 1990 U.S. Census.

Gwinnett County, Georgia, north of Atlanta, increased 344 percent during the 1980s. In contrast, Gwinnett County's total population only doubled. Although the majority of both African-Americans and whites live in metropolitan areas, they tend to live in different communities. Half of whites, compared with just over a quarter of African-Americans, lived in suburban areas in the early 1990s.

Suburban African-Americans are an important consumer market because they tend to have greater educational attainment and more disposable income than African-Americans who live in cities. Black families who live in the suburbs of large metropolitan areas have an average income of more than $32,000.[12] That is 55 percent higher than the average income of African-Americans living in the central cities of those same metropolitan areas.

INCOME PATTERNS OF AFRICAN-AMERICANS

A substantial and growing African-American middle class has been overshadowed by the image of the low-income African-American. The concentration of poor African-Americans in densely populated urban areas makes them highly visible. They represent less than 30 percent of the U.S. poor, but they make up more than 40 percent of the poor in central cities.[13]

It is a myth that African-Americans have little discretionary income. Total expenditures by this group currently top $270 billion a year. Increasingly, marketers are finding this market segment very rewarding. The median income of dual-income African-American families is over $35,000, and about 13 percent of African-American families have incomes over $50,000.[14] Who are these affluent consumers? Like affluent whites, they tend to be well-educated (32 percent are college graduates), home owners (77 percent), in the prime earning ages (66 percent between 35 and 55), married (79 percent), and suburbanites.[15]

THE AFRICAN-AMERICAN MARKETPLACE

The three biggest minority groups—African-Americans, Hispanic-Americans, and Asian-Americans—now have total buying power of $445 billion, making them an important focal point for American businesses.[16] Selling to minority markets is quite challenging because of ethnic and cultural differences and preferences. First, managers must realize that ethnic markets are not homogeneous. There is not an African-American market or a Hispanic-American market any more than there is a white-American market. Yet there are many niches within ethnic markets that require well-defined strategies.

For example, African Eye, which offers designer women's fashions from Africa, recently attracted a thousand women to a fashion show near Washington, D.C. The show featured the latest creations by Nigerian designer Alfadi. African Eye's dresses and outfits blend African and Western influences and, priced at $50 to $600, are aimed at a small portion of the market. Says Mozella Perry Ademiluyi, the president and cofounder of African Eye: "Our customer is professional, 30 to 65, has an income level of $30,000-plus, and often is well-traveled. They don't just want to wear something that is African. They want something that is well-tailored, unique, and creative as well."[17]

An alternative to the niche strategy is to maintain a brand's core identity while straddling different languages, cultures, ages, and incomes with different promotional campaigns. Levi Strauss, for example, publishes *501 Button-Fly Report* for 14- to 24-year-olds. It has Spike Lee interviewing spelunkers (cave explorers), roadies, cemetery tour guides, and others on what they do in their jeans. For men ages 25 and up, Levi's runs separate ads on sports programs and in magazines, showing adults in pursuits like touch football and outings with the kids. A Hispanic campaign, in TV and outdoor advertising, follows two men through their day, from working to teaching a boy to play softball. *"Levi's siempre quedan bien"*—"Levi's always fit well"—is the theme.

AFRICAN-AMERICANS AS CONSUMERS

African-American spending patterns are somewhat different from those of other groups. The average African-American family spends about $20,000 per year on consumer goods. This is about 35 percent less than the average non-African-American household. But African-American consumers spend more than other consumers on certain products, such as rental appliances, boys' shoes and clothing, home repair and maintenance supplies and services, and taxi fares.[18]

Consumption differences are not limited to just product categories, but to specific brands as well. For example, Procter and Gamble's Crest toothpaste is the best seller in the United States. Yet African-Americans buy more of Colgate Palmolive's Colgate brand. Chrysler's research showed that white consumers were typically sold on performance and quality when shopping for a car, but African-American buyers were more committed to style and American-made models.

PRODUCTS FOR THE AFRICAN-AMERICAN MARKET

Progressive firms are creating new and different products for the African-American market. Many times African-Americans are the first to realize unique product opportunities. For example, Olmec Corp. is a New York-based toy manufacturer that was created by Yla Eason when she couldn't find an African-American superhero doll to buy her son. Her $2 million company markets more than sixty kinds of African-American and Hispanic dolls. Eason now has a distribution partnership with Hasbro. Today, both Mattel and Tyco Industries market dolls that are more than Barbies in darker plastic. Tyco just introduced Kenya, who wears beads to adorn her cornrows. Like a Mattel doll called Chani, Kenya comes in a choice of three complexions: light, medium, and dark. A new boy doll in the product line is named Jamal.

In health and beauty aids, manufacturers owned by African-Americans—such as Soft Sheen, M&M, Johnson, and ProLine—target black consumers. Huge corporations like Revlon, Gillette, and Alberto-Culver also have either divisions or major product lines for the African-American market. Alberto-Culver, for example, has a hair-care line with seventy-five products for this segment. In fact, hair-care items are the largest single category within the African-American health and beauty aid category.

Recently Dallas-based JC Penney added two clothing sections to more than 100 stores, one called the African Collection (authentic African clothing), and the other called Africa Today (U.S.-styled clothing made of African fabrics). It also issued a specialty catalog that offers many of the same clothes by mail. Macy's flagship store in Manhattan is selling Cross Colours, a line of brightly colored clothing that its tags describe as ethnically inspired. Nike and Converse began selling jogging suits and other exercise wear that feature African prints.

Not all products created for the African-American market have been viewed in a positive manner. In fact, some products have drawn such a negative reaction that they were withdrawn from the market immediately, as the Ethics Trends box on the next page indicates.

REACHING AFRICAN-AMERICAN CONSUMERS

Many of the nation's largest retailers target African-Americans as customers. To better reach African-American consumers, Kmart appointed

Stop Hurting African-American Consumers

Uptown cigarettes were developed by R.J. Reynolds to appeal to African-American smokers. The impetus was research that showed a significant percentage of African-American smokers switching from RJR's Salem to brands like Lorillard's Newport, with lighter menthol flavoring. So Uptown was developed for the "taste preferences of black smokers." But two weeks before its planned introduction, the cigarette was attacked by the African-American community and health officials, including then-Secretary of Health and Human Services Louis Sullivan, an African-American. R.J. Reynolds dropped the product.

Another controversial product category aimed mainly at African-Americans is malt liquor. It is a product much like beer, but with up to 6 percent alcohol, versus 3.5 percent for most beer. "The growth in the industry has been fastest in ethnic markets in major cities," says John Derolito, president of United Beers of Brooklyn. "We're going where the market is."

The mom-and-pop stores that dot inner cities have become the main sellers of the malt liquors, which seldom appear in well-to-do areas. The corner groceries in these areas are more accessible than liquor stores to underage drinkers. The owner of a small supermarket in Harlem estimates that he sells up to twenty cases of malt each week, compared with just three cases of beer. "It's status," says a youth counselor with the Manhattan Valley Youth Program. "The attitude is, 'You're a man if you've got a 40 in your hand.'" Forty-ounce cans of malt liquor sell for about $1.50. Most liquor makers preach moderation, but some malt marketers imply that their products are a cheap drunk.

The most aggressive malt liquor marketer is the small brewer McKenzie River, with its St. Ides brand. The St. Ides message has been quantity, with ads routinely presenting a 40-ounce bottle as a single serving. McKenzie River has also pitched the beer as enhancing sexual performance. The company's other promotional tactics were even more controversial among regulators and inner-city community activists. The company's sales representatives routinely put stickers on containers of St. Ides warning consumers "Caution: Most powerful malt" or touted it as "No. 1 strongest malt"—a violation of federal rules. They stopped doing so in 1991.[19]

the minority-owned advertising agency Burrell Inc. to develop special advertising. Their "Looking Good" advertising campaign was designed to reach African-American women between 18 and 49. The ads appear in such national ethnic magazines as *Ebony, Essence,* and *Class;* in African-American local newspapers; and on radio stations in ten markets.

Spiegel, the large catalog retailer, joined with the publisher of *Ebony* to develop a fashion line and catalog aimed at African-American women. Spiegel found that this group spends 6.5 percent of family income on apparel, compared with an average of 5 percent for all women. This catalog, to be called *E Style,* features clothes designed especially for African-

American women. Pizza Hut, a PepsiCo subsidiary, is making minority-owned franchises a priority. Pizza Hut is estimated to have about 300 minority-owned stores. It now includes the nation's largest African-American-owned fast-food franchise company: Larry Lundy, until recently the chain's vice president of restaurant development, bought thirty-one stores in the New Orleans area for a price estimated at $15.5 million.[20]

Shopping malls are also being developed for the African-American market. Researchers have found that African-Americans in an average trip to a mall spend $51.21, or 5.1 percent more than whites.[21] On the eastern edge of Atlanta, the South DeKalb Mall restyled itself as an "Afrocentric retail center." It boosted both the share of African-American-owned stores—to over a third in 1994—and the number of African-American store managers—to 85 percent from 65 percent. It increased the number of vendor carts run by minorities and doubled the number of cultural shows. Almost all the mall's advertising is now aimed at African-Americans. Several mall retailers tailor their goods to blacks. Camelot Music more than doubled its selection of gospel, jazz, and rhythm-and-blues music. The Foot Locker store stocks styles that sell well in African-American markets, such as suede and black athletic shoes and baseball shirts from the "Negro League" of the 1930s. For many local residents the mall has become a focal point for racial pride. People shop there out of loyalty to the neighborhood, and they delight in seeing signs of African-American culture.

Although many African-Americans would like to start their own businesses, they have found many obstacles in their paths. However, some have proved that it is possible to start a successful business and to help the community as well, as the following Small Business Trends box shows.

TRENDS
Small Business

A Medical Maverick

Back in the late 1980s, a pair of tickets to the annual dinner dances of Syracuse's big hospitals cost $400—a royal sum for a young physician like Jennifer Daniels. But Dr. Daniels, just back from running medical clinics on Indian reservations in the West, scraped together the money to attend several of the events. "I let them know I was spending my last 10 cents for the tickets," recalls Dr. Daniels, "and I wanted to meet all the VIPs."

That she did. Often the only African-American in attendance, she was escorted from table to table saying, "Hi, I'm Dr. Daniels. I want to open a family practice on the South side." The connections ("That's how I met the mayor," she says) paid off. She believes they helped her cut through the red tape when applying for building permits. Also, the mayor's links to the banking community may have opened some financial doors.

The result is that Dr. Daniels is living her dream. She runs her own family-health practice in a poor, inner-city neighborhood in Syracuse, on a piece of land that was once a vacant lot where police met their informants. It's part of the neighborhood where she grew up—mostly black, heavily populated, and without any other doctor for miles around.

Like most successful small-business owners, Dr. Daniels called on a powerful combination of drive, ingenuity, and old-fashioned emphasis on spending money wisely. She says she has several formulas for usually getting what she goes after: When first deciding to pursue something, she says, "I think of three or four outcomes I can be happy with. And if I can only find one outcome I will find satisfactory, I pass it up." Another personal rule is to "do only things that I feel are very important and in areas where no one else has any desire to do the same thing." Citing her medical practice, she notes: "The land was inexpensive because nobody else wanted it. I don't spend money advertising because I'm in a physician-shortage area. And I don't waste time or money commuting because I live three blocks away, in an area where no other doctor wants to live."

Now nearly two years old, the practice has been making money since its sixth week. It has enabled Dr. Daniels recently to pay back more than half of the $190,000 loan used for construction of her medical building. And it has made the young doctor a role model in the city's black community.[22]

Concept Check

- Describe the socio-demographic characteristics of African-Americans.
- Discuss the African-American marketplace.
- How do firms reach and serve the African-American consumers?

HISPANIC-AMERICANS

3 Those people whose families come from the area of the Western Hemisphere south of the United States—Mexico, Central America, the West Indies, and South America—have traditionally been called Hispanic-Americans. The umbrella term for this area of the Western Hemisphere is Latin America. Therefore, some people suggest that the term *Latino* is more appropriate for this quite diverse group of people. Although most ancestors of Hispanic-Americans spoke Spanish, some spoke Portuguese, French, or other native languages. We'll use the term Hispanic in this book, because at this point it is the term that is more generally accepted in U.S. culture.

Currently the Hispanic-American population is around 24 million. Within the next twenty years Hispanics should become the nation's largest minority group. By 2010 the United States is projected to be home to 39 million Hispanics. That is 12.9 percent of the U.S. population, compared with a projected 12.5 percent share for African-Americans.[23]

HISPANIC SUBGROUPS

The concept of multiculturalism is nowhere more evident than in the Hispanic culture. Mexican-Americans are 60 percent of Hispanic-Americans and are highly concentrated in the Southwest. Puerto Rican-Americans are the second-largest Hispanic subgroup, at just 12 percent, and they dominate the Hispanic population of New York City. Cuban-Americans are the majority of Hispanics in south Florida, although they are just 5 percent of

■ Hispanic-Americans are expected to become the nation's biggest minority group within the next 20 years. Restaurant owner Roberto Reyes hopes to draw customers from south Florida's large and affluent Cuban-American community.

all Hispanic-Americans. The remaining 23 percent of Hispanics trace their lineage to South America, Central America, or Spain.[24]

Mexican-Americans are the youngest Hispanic subgroup, with a median age of just 24. Cuban-Americans are the oldest, with a median age of 39. Cuban-Americans are also the best educated: 20 percent of them who are 25 or older have attended at least four years of college. This college-educated share slips to 15 percent for "other" Hispanics, 10 percent for Puerto Rican-Americans, and 5 percent for Mexican-Americans.[25]

GEOGRAPHIC CONCENTRATION

Four states now have more than a million Hispanic residents: California, Texas, New York, and Florida. By the year 2000 two more states will join this club: Illinois and New Jersey (see Exhibit 3-3). Twenty states had at least 100,000 Hispanic-Americans in 1990.[26]

The greatest metropolitan concentration of Hispanic-Americans is in Los Angeles County, where over 3 million Hispanics live. Dade County (Miami) is a distant second, with more than 950,000 Hispanics. Cook County (Chicago) ranks third, with almost 700,000. About two-thirds of all Hispanics live in just twenty-five metropolitan areas. Today the number of Hispanics in California, Texas, New York, and Florida is greater than the entire U.S. Hispanic population of 1980. The 1990 census showed that 70 percent of the Hispanic population is still concentrated in those four states. However, future censuses will show a greater dispersion of the Hispanic population.

INCOME PATTERNS OF HISPANIC-AMERICANS

The total purchasing power of the Hispanic market in the United States is over $170 billion annually. Median family income for Hispanic-Americans

Exhibit 3-3
States with the Greatest Hispanic Population, in Thousands
Source: Woods & Poole Economics, Inc.

		1990	2000
1	California	7,737	10,144
2	Texas	4,358	5,979
3	New York	2,216	2,681
4	Florida	1,585	2,412
5	Illinois	905	1,193
6	New Jersey	740	952
7	Arizona	691	1,073
8	New Mexico	581	825
9	Colorado	425	594
10	Michigan	288	378
	Total U.S.	22,449	31,066

in 1994 was about $30,000, compared with $40,000 for the general population. Twenty-one percent of all Hispanic households have incomes of over $35,000, and 8 percent have incomes over $50,000. Some Hispanic communities are quite affluent. In Miami over 33 percent of the Hispanic households have incomes greater than $35,000, which is higher than the national average.[27]

However, incomes are not equally distributed among Hispanic subcultures. According to the 1990 census, the median income of Cuban-Americans was $31,300, the highest of any Hispanic group. The comparable figures for Mexican-Americans and Puerto Rican-Americans, according to the U.S. Census Bureau, were $22,200 and $19,900.[28] Puerto Rican-Americans living in New York City unfortunately have a poverty rate of 41 percent, compared with the national average of 14 percent.[29]

Miami has the second-highest total of Hispanic-owned businesses—trailing only Los Angeles. But Miami's Hispanic businesses reported $500 million more in revenues than those in Los Angeles. Analysts attribute the higher per-business ratio to Miami's established Cuban-American community.[30]

THE HISPANIC MARKETPLACE

The diversity of the Hispanic population and the language differences create many challenges for those trying to serve this market. Hispanic-Americans, especially recent immigrants, often prefer products from their native country. Therefore, many retailers along the southern U.S. border import goods from Mexico. In New York City more than 6,000 *bodegas* (grocery stores) sell such items such as plantains, chorizo sausage, and religious candles to Puerto Rican-Americans. They also serve as neighborhood social centers. Fresh produce is usually very important to Hispanic groups because of the tradition of shopping every day at open-air produce markets in their native country. Many Hispanic-Americans are loyal to brands found in their homeland. If these are not available, Hispanic consumers will choose brands that reflect their native values and cultures. Research shows that Hispanic shoppers are often not aware of many mainstream American brands.[31] For instance, Procter & Gamble noted that many retailers in Southern California were importing its Ariel detergent from Mexico. Ariel is offered in more than fifty countries and is one of the world's leading detergents. P&G has been trying to get Hispanics to switch to a new, U.S.-made version of Ariel called Ariel Ultra. Although the product has several key benefits over the imported Ariel, sales are slow. Ariel Ultra is selling well to white consumers, but Mexican-Americans prefer the original version. Tradition seems to be the primary motivation.

REACHING HISPANIC-AMERICAN CONSUMERS

Advertising to Hispanic-Americans often means choosing between English and Spanish languages. It's a difficult decision: Researchers disagree on which language is appropriate for different kinds of advertising. One study of language use found that most Hispanic-Americans think and speak in Spanish in common situations. But 80 percent of Mexican-born permanent residents speak at least some English, and 90 percent of first-generation, U.S.-born Mexican-Americans speak English well. A growing number of upwardly mobile, assimilated Hispanic-Americans use English in their business and professional lives.[32] So choice of language probably depends on the group one wishes to sell to.

Nor can companies assume that they can simply use Spanish instead of English to promote their products to Hispanic-Americans. They must take other steps to make sure their message will be understood and be relevant. First, the translation must be correct. Coors beer blundered in converting the slogan "Get loose with Coors" into Spanish; it translated as "Get the runs with Coors."[33] Advertisers who are ignorant of subtle dialect differences among Hispanic groups frequently run into trouble. In its early marketing efforts, Tang, the instant breakfast drink, billed itself as *jugo de china*, which is a Puerto Rican term for orange juice. But to all other Hispanics the phrase is meaningless; *jugo de naranja*—juice of oranges—would be a better choice. Another Hispanic subsegment was puzzled by a phrase that translated as "low asphalt" and wondered why it would be an attractive feature for a cigarette.[34]

Today marketers are carefully targeting major segments of the Hispanic market. A series of Campbell Soup ads, for instance, features a woman cooking, but the ads differ in such details as the woman's age, the setting, and the music: In the version for Cuban-Americans, a grandmother cooks in a plant-filled kitchen to the sounds of salsa and merengue music. In contrast, the Mexican-American ad shows a young wife preparing food in a brightly colored, "Southwestern-style" kitchen, with pop music playing in the background.

Most promotional dollars targeting the Hispanic market are spent to encourage Hispanics to buy mainstream goods and services. For example,

Hispanics are 27 percent more likely than non-Hispanics to buy contact lenses (probably because of the relative youth of the Hispanic market). There is no such thing as a Hispanic contact lens. But Pearle Vision Centers advertises in Spanish in selected markets.

Radio, television, and other media preferences vary from market to market. A survey of 5,000 households in ten markets in the continental United States, conducted by San Antonio-based Hispanic Marketing Research & Communications, found that 60 percent of the Hispanic market listens to Spanish-language radio—at least once in a while, 40 percent of the nation's Hispanics watch Spanish-language television, and Spanish-language newspapers are read by 20 percent of the nation's Hispanics. In Miami, which has two daily Spanish-language newspapers and dozens of weeklies, 35 percent of the Hispanic market reads them exclusively.[35]

Coca Cola is one of the largest promoters to Hispanic-Americans in the United States. Its *El Super Concurso de el Magnate* sweepstakes for Coca-Cola Classic was one of the largest media merchandising promotions ever directed at Hispanic consumers. It generated more than half a million viewer responses. Commercials for Coke's promotion were aired exclusively on the Spanish-language Telemundo television network. They featured Andres Garcia, the popular star of Telemundo's *El Magnate novela* (a Spanish soap opera). Coca-Cola also recently sponsored other national promotions for Hispanic-Americans, including a tie-in with "*MTV Internacional.*"[36]

Perhaps the most visible types of retailers serving the Hispanic market are grocery stores. The first step is to offer more full-service meat counters, better produce, and bilingual signage. But developing a retail store for Hispanic-Americans is becoming increasingly more difficult. One reason is that immigration from Latin American countries is increasing. As a result, supermarkets must cater to more people with different product preferences. In the Los Angeles area, for example, although 80 percent of the Hispanics are from Mexico, many other countries are now represented. A second complicating factor for retailers is **acculturation**—the process of adapting to the local culture. Customers may be immigrants, but they may also be second- and third-generation Hispanic-Americans whose buying habits have moved closer to those of whites.

An example of success in finding the right mix for Hispanic grocery stores is Vons, a California supermarket chain. The company formed a separate eight-person management team to develop a format for Hispanic-American customers. The team decided on a target customer it would plan its Tianguis stores for: an unacculturated Hispanic who has been in the United States for less than two years and does not speak English. When the first Tianguis store opened, it had a fiesta-like atmosphere. Stands served Mexican foods, walls were splashed with bright colors, shoppers were serenaded with live mariachi bands, and shelves were stocked with *empanadas*, handmade tortillas, and other items usually found only in specialty shops. Making the extra effort to cater to its prospective customers' needs has paid off. In less than three years Tianguis became one of the most profitable chains in the crowded and competitive Los Angeles grocery retail market.[37]

acculturation The process of adapting to the local culture.

Concept Check

- Describe the socio-demographic characteristics of Hispanic-Americans.
- Discuss the Hispanic marketplace.
- How do firms reach and serve the Hispanic consumers?

ASIAN-AMERICANS

4   In 1994 the Asian-American population will reach 8 million. During the past decade the Asian-American population growth rate was 108 percent. This growth rate was twice that of Hispanic-Americans, six times that of African-Americans, and twenty times that of white Americans.[38] Like Hispanic-Americans, Asian-Americans are not a monolithic group; there are thirteen submarkets within the Asian-American community. The five largest are: Chinese (1.6 million), Filipino (1.4 million), Japanese (848,000), Asian Indians (815,000), and Koreans (799,000).

Immigration accounted for nearly three-fourths of the Asian-American population increase during the 1980s and early 1990s.[39] Of the two major streams of immigrants, one consists of people originally from Asian coun-

■ Asian-American households are the most affluent in the country. One reason for this is the high rate of business ownership among this ethnic group.

tries that already had large numbers of people in the United States (for example, China, Korea, and the Philippines). This group tends to be educated and ready to move quickly into the mainstream of U.S. society. The other stream is immigrants and refugees from some of the war-torn countries of Southeast Asia: Vietnam, Laos, and Cambodia. Many in this group begin their American lives on welfare and lack the education and skills to move out of poverty.

GEOGRAPHIC CONCENTRATION

Fully 56 percent of Asian-Americans live in the West, compared with 21 percent of all Americans. Nearly four out of ten Asian-Americans live in California, and about one out of ten lives in Hawaii. Another 18 percent live in the Northeast, 14 percent in the South, and 12 percent in the Midwest. Twelve states—California, Hawaii, New York, Illinois, New Jersey, Texas, Massachusetts, Pennsylvania, Virginia, Florida, Michigan, and Washington—have over 100,000 Asian-Americans.[40]

Asian-Americans are highly urbanized: 93 percent live in a metropolitan area. Among those living in "metros," about half live in central cities and half in suburbs. That figure contrasts with the one for whites, who are twice as likely to live in suburbs as in central cities.

The high level of Asian immigration to the United States has created a youthful population. The average age of Asian-Americans is just 30, compared with 36 for whites. As Asian-Americans age into their peak earning years, businesses can expect their already high incomes to increase further.

INCOME PATTERNS OF ASIAN-AMERICANS

Asian-American households are more affluent than any other racial or ethnic group, including whites. The median household income of Asians was about $33,000 in 1994. Fully 32 percent of Asian-American households have incomes of $50,000 or more, compared with only 29 percent of white households.[41] The high household incomes of Asians may be due in part to their concentration in Los Angeles, San Francisco, and Honolulu, where salaries are high to compensate for the high cost of living. A second reason is that 78 percent of all Asian-Americans live in families (households of two or more related persons), compared to only 70 percent for whites.[42] More married couples means more two-income families.

A third reason for the high household incomes of Asian-Americans is their high level of education. Among adults aged 25 or older, 14 percent of Asians have been to college for five or more years, compared with only 9 percent of all Americans. An additional 21 percent of Asians have completed four years of college, versus only 13 percent of all Americans.

A final reason for higher incomes is the high rate of business ownership among Asian-Americans. During the past decade they have created new businesses faster than any other U.S. population group.[43] Different groups tend to gravitate toward different specialties. The Chinese, for instance, are often found in retail, wholesale, and financial enterprises, but rarely in construction or transportation. The Japanese prefer construction and transportation to retail and service establishments. Retail-oriented Korean-Americans have become a major force in food marketing.

Why does the Asian-American community start so many new businesses? A key factor is the Asian immigrants' tradition of self-employment. They turn to their fellow immigrants for help in raising money to start businesses. Asian-Americans pool their money in a *keh*, or cooperative, typically made up of about twenty members. Members contribute a fixed sum (which could range from $100 to $1,000) every month, and the total is awarded in full to a different member each month. Once the monthly payout cycle has been completed for the *keh*, it disbands. *Kehs* are a source of interest-free venture capital as well as a forum for exchanging business tips. There is little chance that a member would dare to stop contributing to the pot after getting his or her share. Reneging on a financial pledge to others violates Asian concepts of personal and family honor.

Asian businesses are typically family owned and operated. During start-up, when money is scarce, they often draw on unpaid workers from the extended family. Extended kinship networks also enable immigrant households to share rents or mortgages, provide free child care, and ensure economic security against loss of employment by other household members.

Many of the businesses serve internal markets in the Asian-American community. Business owners tend to employ people from their own subgroup. In San Francisco's Chinese community, a dollar turns over five or six times before it leaves the community.[44]

THE ASIAN-AMERICAN MARKETPLACE

Asian-Americans are more comfortable with technology than the general population. They are far more likely to use automated teller machines, and many more of them own VCRs, compact disc players, microwave ovens, home computers, and telephone answering machines.[45] Asian-American consumers show no reluctance to buy American products, even when Asian or other foreign alternatives are available. Indeed, a recent study found that Ford was the auto of choice for nearly a third of Asian-American respondents. The second choice was Toyota, at 21.9 percent. Only 9.1 percent owned Hondas.[46]

Asian-American subgroups often differ dramatically in their product preferences. For example, most Asian-Americans drink lots of soda, but Koreans do not. Only half of the Koreans surveyed reported drinking soda in the previous three months. When they do drink soda, Koreans drink more 7-Up than any other. In this they differ from Asian-Americans in general, whose top soda preferences are Coke (55 percent) and Pepsi (18 percent). Another example of differing preferences among subgroups is perfume usage. Asian Indians were the biggest perfume users; nearly seven out of ten had used some kind of fragrance in the previous three months. Japanese used perfume the least (about 36 percent). Overall, Chanel was the preferred perfume brand among all Asian-Americans.[47]

A number of products have been developed specifically for the Asian-American market. For example, Kayla Beverly Hills salon draws Asian-American consumers because the firm offers cosmetics formulated for them. Anheuser-Busch's agricultural-products division markets rice to Asian-Americans, who are rice connoisseurs. The company developed eight varieties of California-grown rice, each with a different label, to cover a range of nationalities and tastes. Its "Taste the Tradition" ads, devised by multiethnic Los Angeles agency Muse Cordero Chen, played up the brands' similarities to Asian-grown rice, which is stickier than the kind most Westerners eat. The ads captured such nuances as the differences in Chinese, Japanese, and Korean rice bowls. Sales of Anheuser-Busch's Asian rice brands are now growing more than 10 percent a year.[48]

REACHING ASIAN-AMERICAN CONSUMERS

Cultural diversity within the Asian-American market complicates efforts of businesses to promote their products. Although Asian-Americans embrace the values of the larger U.S. population, they also hold on to the cultural values of their particular subgroup. Consider expensive consumer goods such as automobiles or televisions. In Japanese-American homes, the husband alone makes the decision on such purchases nearly half the time; only about 5 percent of the time does the wife make the decision. In Filipino families, however, by far the most decisions are made by husbands and wives jointly or with the input of other family members.[49] The company wishing to sell consumer goods to Asian-Americans must decide whether to focus promotional efforts primarily at men or at the family.

Misunderstanding the cultural differences among Asian-Americans can lead to some embarrassing gaffes. Metropolitan Life Insurance angered potential customers when it ran an ad in a Korean magazine showing a family in traditional dress—Chinese dress, that is. During Chinese New Year Coors got complaints for reinforcing sexual stereotypes in an ad showing an exotic-looking woman wrapped in the folds of a silk dragon. A spokesperson says the brewer's advertising has since gotten away from "women and dragons."[50] In another case a company placed a Chinese-language ad to wish the community a happy new year—but ran the Chinese characters upside down. Such problems create business opportunities for advertising agencies like Lee Liu and Tong Inc. of New York City, which specializes in the Asian-American market. The agency attracts mainstream advertisers who want to avoid embarrassing gaffes.[51]

The main promotion medium for reaching Asian-Americans is ethnic newspapers. In contrast, Hispanic-Americans prefer radio.[52] Several Asian-language national newspapers are published in cities with large Asian populations.

Asian-Americans spend over $38 billion a year on retail purchases.[53] Many of these dollars flow to other Asian-Americans who operate flower shops, grocery stores, appliance stores, and other small businesses.[54] For instance, at first glance the Ha Nam supermarket in Los Angeles' Koreatown might be any other grocery store. But next to the Kraft American singles and the State Fair corn dogs are jars of whole cabbage kimchi. A snack bar in another part of the store cooks up aromatic mung cakes, and an entire aisle is devoted to dried seafood. In most U.S. supermarkets, bags near the checkout counter are filled with charcoal for barbeques; at Ha Nam they are filled with rice.

Because Asian-Americans have a tendency to live in neighborhoods of people with the same ethnic background, specialized retail centers have naturally evolved. In suburban Orange County, California, Vietnamese immigrants have improved a once-barren area: An indoor mall, called Asia Garden, is packed on Sunday mornings. About 50,000 weekend shoppers patronize the 800 shops and restaurants, buying herbal medicine and dining on snail-tomato-rice-noodle soup. In the mornings people may attend Buddhist ceremonies in makeshift temples. In the evenings they can applaud Elvis Phuong, a popular entertainer who, like his namesake, wears skintight pants and a sneer.

- Describe the socio-demographic characteristics of Asian-Americans.
- Discuss the Asian-American marketplace.
- How do firms reach and serve Asian-American consumers?

NATIVE AMERICANS

We have discussed African-, Hispanic-, and Asian-Americans in some detail because they are the largest ethnic minority groups in the United States. Another group that must be singled out, largely because of its role in U.S. history, is Native Americans. The strong bonds that these people still feel to their native culture are renewing their communities. They have not yet erased the poverty and other ills that affect many Native Americans, but many now living on and off the reservations have made educational and economic progress. A college-educated middle class has emerged, Native American business ownership has increased, and some tribes are creating good jobs for their members.

The 1990 census counted nearly 1.9 million Native Americans, up from fewer than 1.4 million in 1980. This 38 percent leap exceeds the growth rate for most other minority groups.

Native Americans have some important competitive advantages because of the "sovereignty" granted to reservations. Many local, state, and federal laws do not apply on the reservations. They have no sales or property taxes, so cigarettes, gasoline, and other items can be sold for low prices. Reservations can also offer lucrative activities not permitted off the reservations, such as gambling.[55]

In addition to the groups discussed above—African-Americans, Hispanic-Americans, Asian-Americans, and Native Americans—our society is enriched by people from other parts of the world, such as Eastern and Western Europe, the former Soviet Union, and Australia. All of these groups, as citizens, as workers, and as consumers, help create the rich interwoven fabric of the United States.

■ Native Americans living on and off the reservations are making educational and economic progress. These Navajo businesspeople have opened their own restaurant.

CULTURAL DIVERSITY IN THE WORKPLACE

5 Cultural misunderstandings happen every day in the workplace. Consider these examples:

A Hispanic manager starts a budget-planning meeting by chatting casually and checking with his new staff on whether everyone can get together after work. His boss frets over the delay and wonders why he doesn't get straight to the numbers. Hispanic culture teaches that building relationships is often critical to working together, while the dominant American culture encourages "getting down to business."

A second-generation Asian woman appears for an employment interview. Deferring to authority, she keeps her eyes down, rarely meeting the interviewer's. The interviewer, a white American male, thinks, "She's not assertive, not strong enough. Maybe she's hiding something or is insecure." Meanwhile, the Asian woman views the persistent eye contact of the interviewer as domineering, invasive, and controlling. Neither person trusts the other.[56]

■ The diversity of the American workforce presents a challenge to some companies. They must learn to motivate and communicate with employees of varied cultural backgrounds.

To avoid misunderstandings such as these, businesspeople need to understand multiculturalism and appreciate what it contributes to the business environment. Multiculturalism affects the world of business in two important ways: As we saw earlier in the chapter, various ethnic groups offer businesses an opportunity to generate revenue by selling goods and services tailored to their needs. Also, multiculturalism creates diversity in the workplace. One recent study of 645 firms found that three-quarters of the respondents were concerned about increased diversity; of these, about one-third felt that diversity affected their corporate strategy. Why are companies so concerned? The two primary reasons cited relate to company personnel. First, they worry that supervisors do not know how to motivate their diverse work groups. Second, they are uncertain about how to handle the challenge of communicating with employees whose cultural backgrounds result in differing assumptions, values, and even language.[57]

In almost every business today, managers must improve their company's productivity. They cannot hope to meet this goal until they learn how to manage an ethnically diverse workforce. This task is so important that about half of all Fortune 500 firms already have diversity managers. Most others are considering adding such a position.[58]

Developing an efficient multicultural workforce requires companies to make positive efforts, such as the following:

1. *Develop programs that promote awareness of cultural differences:* Education and training budgets should include programs, seminars, and workshops that will help make supervisors and employees aware of cultural differences. Such training can help avoid some misunderstandings, like those cited at the beginning of this section.

2. *Promote positive attitudes toward differences among ethnic groups:* Company newsletters, publications, and bulletin boards are ideal promotion tools to inform all employees of various special ethnic observances and events. These can feature cultural events observed each year, such as Black History Month (February), Asian Pacific Heritage Week (first or second week in May), and National Hispanic Heritage Week (second week in September).

3. Foster flexible communications: Use different channels of communications to establish maximum understanding of messages. Sending a memo, conducting a one-on-one consultation, and holding a group discussion are examples of different approaches. Studies have shown that certain modes of communication are more effective than others with various ethnic groups and with various individuals.

4. *Involve representatives of all minority groups in the decision-making process:* Free-flowing communication networks throughout an organization allow minority concerns to reach the levels where decisions are approved. Encourage feedback from minority employees to obtain different perspectives regarding decisions that affect their performance at work.

5. *Recognize that there are no "one size fits all" solutions:* Some solutions may involve introducing policies for more flexible dress codes or allowing minorities to celebrate holidays, such as Martin Luther King, Jr.'s birthday.

6. *Challenge stereotypes and assumptions about minority groups:* Allowing overgeneralizations and stereotypes to linger in the workplace will only generate misunderstandings. Personnel development courses or workshop discussions on cultural differences are the best tools to eliminate conflicts.

7. *Include minority groups in all after-work engagements and company-sponsored events:* Encourage minority group members to become involved in social organizations and activities that will enhance career development, as well as in the planning of such events. These efforts will be seen as favorable to all employees and can help to build positive intergroup relations.[59]

Successful diversity programs are good for businesses. Levi Strauss, for example, is recognized as one of the most ethnically diverse companies in the world. About 60 percent of its employees belong to minority groups. Levi Strauss spends $5 million a year on its "Valuing Diversity" educational programs. The programs are designed to get employees thinking about how to become more tolerant of personal differences, and, ultimately, to see the importance of them.

Levi Strauss promotes diversity in every corridor. Ads for job openings "strongly encourage" minorities to apply. When job seekers interview at Levi Strauss, they often find a person across the desk who looks like them. "You get a feeling there's opportunity here because of the diversity at senior levels," says internal audits manager Loraine Binion, an African-

American. The company also supports in-house networking groups of blacks, Hispanics, and other minorities. A diversity council, made up of two members of every group, regularly meets with Levi's executive committee on raising awareness of diversity issues. Managers' bonuses are even tied to meeting the corporate goal that employees aspire to appreciate diversity.[60]

Promoting diversity in the workforce makes good marketing sense for Levi's too. "It's tough to design and develop merchandise for markets you don't understand," says Dan Chew, manager of corporate marketing. Then there's the flip side: "When you make a point of valuing other people's contributions, some good ideas for products make their way back to headquarters." For instance, Levi's credits an Argentine employee for thinking up its Dockers line of casual pants, now worth more than $1 billion a year.[61]

Later, in Chapter 12, we will discuss other issues associated with managing diversity in the workplace.

Concept Check

- Why has cultural diversity affected the workplace?
- What is meant by "managing diversity"?

■ SUMMARY

Key Terms

acculturation 93

multiculturalism 78

1. Appreciate and understand the increasing cultural diversity in the United States.

Much of the growth in the U.S. population from 1980 through 1994 occurred in minority markets, and this will continue into the next century. Immigration has served as a major source of growth in minority markets. On balance, immigrants are a boon to the U.S. economy. The Immigration Act of 1990 will further encourage the immigration of wealthy and highly educated persons to the United States.

Regional differences in multiculturalism can be observed. San Francisco County is the most ethnically diverse in the nation. Four of New York City's five boroughs are among the ten most ethnically diverse areas. The areas with the least multiculturalism run from northern New England through the Midwest into Montana.

The multicultural nature of the United States means that no longer can various ethnic groups be expected to assimilate into white, Western culture. In the future no single ethnic group will be large enough to dictate political policy. As the United States continues to become a service-dominated economy, education will be the means for minorities to participate fully.

2. Identify key characteristics and trends among African-Americans and opportunities to serve this market.

In 1994 the 31 million African-Americans were the largest minority group. The proportion of the population that is African-American will continue to grow into the next century. Today more than half of all African-Americans live in the South, although significant African-American populations also

live in the industrial Midwest and Northeast. The African-American population, with a median age of 27.9, is younger than the U.S. population as a whole. Although poor African-Americans in urban areas are highly visible, there is a substantial and growing black middle class. The median income of dual-income black families is over $35,000. Expenditures by African-Americans now top $270 billion annually.

New products have been created to reflect African-Americans' unique desires, hopes, customs, and preferences. Health and beauty aids constitute one product category that has developed special lines for African-Americans. In addition, "Afrocentric products" stress the special heritage and culture of African-Americans. National magazines and local newspapers aimed at the African-American market are important media for advertising these products. Numerous special stores and shopping areas cater to this market.

3. Identify key characteristics and trends among Hispanic-Americans and opportunities to serve this market.

The Hispanic-American population is about 24 million, and it is growing much faster than the general population. Four states now have over a million Hispanic citizens; over 3 million Hispanic-Americans currently live in Los Angeles County alone. The Hispanic market consists of three diverse subgroups: Mexican-American, Puerto Rican-American, and Cuban-American. Cuban-Americans are concentrated in Florida, Puerto Rican-Americans in New York City, and Mexican-Americans in the Southwest. Mexican-Americans are the youngest, with a median age of 24; Cuban-Americans are the oldest at 39. Cuban-Americans are the most highly educated subgroup. The total purchasing power of the Hispanic market is over $170 billion per year. Median family income for Hispanic-Americans is about $30,000, compared with $40,000 for the general population.

Companies have found that Hispanic-Americans, especially recent immigrants, often prefer products from their native countries. Subtle differences in culture and language often make it necessary for companies to design different promotional programs for the main Hispanic submarkets. Spanish-language broadcasting outlets and publications are the most effective means of reaching them. Special retail chains and stores have developed for Hispanic-American consumers.

4. Identify key characteristics and trends among Asian-Americans and opportunities to serve this market.

By the end of 1994 there were almost 8 million Asian-Americans. During the past decade the Asian-American population growth rate was 108 percent, higher than that of any other ethnic group. There are thirteen submarkets within the Asian-American community. Fifty-six percent of all Asian-Americans live in the West, and most Asian-Americans live in a metropolitan area. The average age of Asian-Americans is 30. They are the most affluent of any racial or ethnic group, including whites. The main reason for their affluence is their high education level. Asian-Americans also have the biggest rate of business ownership among minority groups.

Asian-Americans tend to be good customers for technologically advanced products. As with the Hispanic-American market, the Asian-

American market is divided into subgroups based on country of origin, with definite product preferences among these subgroups. Cultural differences also complicate promotion, although Asian-Americans as a whole embrace traditional U.S. values. Various ethnic newspapers help marketers reach the shopping areas serving their own ethnic group.

5. Understand how companies are managing cultural diversity in the workplace.

Many companies are actively managing cultural diversity in the workplace to increase efficiency and employee satisfaction with their work environment. Special programs created by firms promote awareness of cultural differences and a positive attitude toward differences among ethnic groups. These programs also teach supervisors how to motivate diverse work groups and how to effectively communicate with persons of differing values and cultures. Managing diversity requires challenging stereotypes and assumptions about ethnic groups. The overall aim is to increase knowledge and respect of others, both as members of groups and as unique individuals, which in turn is expected to enhance employee satisfaction and performance.

■ DISCUSSION QUESTIONS

1. What does it mean to say that America is becoming a multicultural society?

2. What has been the economic impact of immigrants in the past fifteen years?

3. Because Asian-Americans can get interest-free loans from a *keh*, do you believe they have an unfair advantage over other ethnic groups in creating new businesses? Why or why not?

4. Suppose you have seen the following statement in the newspaper: "People are basically the same everywhere, and we all want the same things. There is no need to create special products and promotions for ethnic groups. Everyone, for example, likes Coca-Cola." Write a letter to the editor replying to the assumptions made here.

5. Describe the ethnic mix of the U.S. population in 1994 and the projected mix for 2023. What are the implications of the changes?

6. Why do you think "managing diversity" in the workplace has become such an important issue for businesses?

■ CASE

Valuing Differences at Digital Equipment

Digital Equipment sells computers and computer networks worldwide. It has 120,000 employees in sixty-four countries. Over 50,000 of these employees are outside the United States, and over 50 percent of the company's revenue is generated outside the United States. The company has multiple manufacturing sites in Europe and the Pacific Rim, as well as plants in Mexico, Canada, and the United States. Digital Equipment calls its management approach to dealing with employees and all of their differences "Valuing Differences." Digital's Valuing Differences philosophy encourages employees to pay attention to their differences as unique individuals and as members of groups. It seeks to raise employees' level of comfort with differences and to capitalize on differences as a major asset to the company's productivity.

Digital's Valuing Differences work is done in a variety of ways. The company sponsors and supports a wide range of activities, such as awareness and skills training, "Celebrating Differences" events, and the leadership groups and support groups. But the most innovative aspect of the Valuing Differences approach is the emphasis placed on personal development through small-group dialogue in ongoing groups called core groups. Each of these programs works as follows:

Awareness and Skills Training: External consultants and in-house trainers conduct sessions that help employees raise their levels of awareness about the issues of diversity in their workplace. Some of the sessions are specifically focused on learning about the cultural norms of different cultural groups. Digital's most popular in-house training course is "Understanding the Dynamics of Difference," a two-day course designed to introduce employees to basic Valuing Differences concepts.

Celebrating Differences Events: Each year, various organizations within the company plan and sponsor a calendar of cultural and educational events. Employees celebrate Black History Month, Hispanic Heritage Month, Gay and Lesbian Pride Week, International Women's Month, and so forth. These events give employees an opportunity to learn about different groups at regularly scheduled times throughout the year.

Leadership Groups and Support Groups: Members of "same—differences" interest groups come together regularly to provide one another with needed emotional and career support. Some of these groups are referred to as "efficacy" groups because their members participated in efficacy training—a program designed to help minority employees learn how to deal effectively in the dominant culture. In addition, Digital supports task-oriented leadership groups. Sometimes these are also "same—differences" interest groups. For example, white women or black men may form a task force that meets on a regular basis to recommend and monitor changes in company practices that affect Digital's work climate and culture.

Core Groups: Digital also supports an informal network of small, ongoing discussion groups. These core groups consist of seven to nine employees who agree to meet monthly to examine their stereotypes, test the differences in their assumptions, and build significant relationships with people they regard as different.[62]

Questions

1. What do you think was the motivation for Digital's "Valuing Differences" program?
2. What other actions could Digital take to manage diversity?
3. Do you think that the "same—differences" groups could backfire and result in the emergence of old prejudices and stereotypes?

Global Business

Chapter 4

Learning Goals

After studying this chapter, you should be able to:

1 Understand the importance of international trade and discuss the position of the United States in the world economy.

2 Understand some of the measures of international trade.

3 Explain why nations trade.

4 Understand the barriers to international trade, and list the major arguments for and against tariffs.

5 Explain economic integration and trade pacts.

6 Specify ways for businesses to enter into foreign trade.

7 Describe the impact of culture and political climate on international trade.

8 Explain the trade role of multinational corporations.

 Career Profile

Kirk Perry has had a clear vision of his career since his sophomore year in college, when he told his counselor that he wanted to work for Procter & Gamble. He and the counselor developed a plan to help Kirk achieve his goal. They mapped out the courses Kirk would enroll in, the extracurricular activities he would pursue, and the work load he would be expected to shoulder for the next two years as a double major in marketing and finance. Kirk's commitment paid off: He was hired by P&G following his graduation from college and is now a brand manager in the company's health-care advertising division, a position with a tremendous amount of responsibility.

Procter & Gamble is an international company. Most of their products are for the consumer market, and at least one of these products—such as Crest, Scope, Cover Girl, Tide, and Bounty—can be found in approximately 98 percent of the homes in the U.S. and more than 50 percent of households worldwide. Kirk works closely with P&G's advertising agency to develop advertising strategies and principles for the health-care product line.

Companies take their business global in hopes of greater sales and profits. By entering new territories, they increase their market potential. Kirk is well aware that the future of Procter & Gamble lies in countries with developing economies and consumer bases, such as China. While there is certainly some risk involved in investing in these countries, they are home to billions of potential customers. Kirk believes that P&G products will be as popular there as they are in the rest of the world.

Overview

Doing business abroad promises great rewards for firms that can do it well. This chapter opens our view of business from the U.S. economy to the world. It first looks at the importance of international trade and the advantages it offers. Then it looks at barriers to trade and at efforts to undo those barriers. Next it shows how businesses can enter the global market and what political and cultural factors they must take into account. Finally, it inspects the role of multinational companies.

THE IMPORTANCE OF INTERNATIONAL TRADE

For trade to occur, people must communicate. Communication aids understanding and cooperation, which may someday lead to world peace. In the meantime, as this chapter shows, international trade improves relationships with friends and allies, helps ease tensions among nations, and—economically speaking—bolsters economies, raises people's standard of living, and improves the quality of life. The value of international trade is over $4 trillion a year and growing. This section takes a look at some key aspects of international trade: exports and imports, the balance of trade, the balance of payments, and exchange rates.

EXPORTS AND IMPORTS

exports Goods and services sold to other countries

imports Goods and services bought from other countries.

The developed nations (those with mature communication, financial, educational, and distribution systems) are the major players in international trade. They account for about 70 percent of the world's exports and imports. **Exports** are goods and services made in one country and sold to others. **Imports** are goods and services that are bought from other countries. The United States is both the largest importer and the largest exporter in the world. Today, one of every six manufacturing jobs in the United States depends directly on foreign trade. And for every billion dollars' worth of products we sell abroad, we create about 25,000 new jobs at home.[1]

Each year, the United States exports more food, animal feed, and beverages than the year before. A third of U.S. farm acreage is devoted to crops for export. The United States is also a major exporter of engineering products and other high-tech goods, such as computers and telecommunications equipment. For more than 40,000 U.S. companies (the majority of them small), international trade offers exciting and profitable opportunities. Among the largest U.S. exporters are Boeing Company, General Motors Corporation, General Electric Company, Ford Motor Company, and IBM.[2]

Despite our own impressive list of resources and great variety of products, imports to the United States are also growing. Some of these imports are raw materials that we don't have, such as the manganese, cobalt, and bauxite used to make airplane parts, exotic metals, and military hardware. More modern factories and lower labor costs in other countries make it cheaper to import industrial supplies (like steel) and production equipment than to produce them at home. Most of the favorite hot beverages of Americans—coffee, tea, and cocoa—are imported. We also import Scotch

■ One factor contributing to the U.S.'s unfavorable balance of trade is American consumers' preference for Japanese brands of automobiles, cameras, and electronic equipment.

whiskey, English bicycles, German and Japanese automobiles, Italian and Spanish shoes, Central American bananas, Philippine plywood, Hong Kong textiles, and French wines.

BALANCE OF TRADE

balance of trade
Difference between the value of a country's exports and the value of its imports over some period.

trade surplus An excess of exports over imports.

trade deficit An excess of imports over exports.

The difference between the value of a country's exports and the value of its imports during a certain time is the country's **balance of trade.** A country that exports more goods than it imports is said to have a *favorable* balance of trade, called a **trade surplus.** A country that imports more than it exports is said to have an *unfavorable* balance of trade, or a **trade deficit.** When imports exceed exports, more money flows out of the country than into it. Thus, countries strive to have more exports than imports.

Although U.S. exports have been booming, we still import more than we export. We have had an unfavorable balance of trade throughout the past decade. In 1993 the United States had a trade deficit of approximately $110 billion.[3] About half of the deficit is accounted for by Japan. That means that Americans purchased about $50 billion more from Japanese companies than Japanese consumers bought from U.S. firms. Part of the problem is that most U.S. companies still avoid the export market. Many medium-size and small producers think "going global" is more trouble than it's worth. And as we've seen, Americans are buying more foreign goods than ever before. As long as we continue to import more than we export, the United States will continue to have a trade deficit.

BALANCE OF PAYMENTS

balance of payments
Difference between a country's total payments to other countries and its total receipts from other countries.

The difference between a country's total payments to other countries and its total receipts from other countries is its **balance of payments.** This figure includes the balance of trade and then some. The balance of payments is the summary of a country's financial transactions with other countries. It includes imports and exports (balance of trade), long-term investments in overseas plants and equipment, government loans to and from other countries, gifts and foreign aid, military expenditures made in other countries, and money transfers in and out of foreign banks.

From the beginning of this century until 1970, the United States had a trade surplus. But in the other areas that make up the balance of payments, U.S. payments exceeded receipts. Much of this was due to the large U.S. military presence abroad. Hence, almost every year since 1950, the United States has had an unfavorable balance of payments. And since 1970, both the balance of payments *and* the balance of trade have been unfavorable. What can a nation do to reduce an unfavorable balance of payments? It can foster exports, reduce its dependence on imports, decrease its military presence abroad, or reduce foreign investment.

EXCHANGE RATES

exchange rate Value of one currency in terms of another.

The **exchange rate** is the value of one currency in terms of another. For example, the U.S. dollar was worth 113 Japanese yen and 5.34 French francs on April 13, 1993. Government actions and supply and demand can influence the exchange rate between any two currencies. The value of a currency depends on how strong international banks and investors think the country's economy is. They consider the leaders' attitudes toward business, the country's inflation rate, the balance of payments, the balance of trade, wage rates, and productivity.

Exhibit 4-1
Cost of a Big Mac in Foreign Countries

Source: "Big Mac Currencies," *The Economist,* 17 April 1993, p. 79.

	Prices in local currency*	Actual exchange rate 4/13/93	Price of Big Mac in dollars
United States	$2.30	—	$2.30
Argentina	Peso3.60	1.00	3.60
Belgium	BFr109	35.2	3.10
Britain	£1.81	1.46	2.65
Canada	C$2.86	1.39	2.06
Denmark	DKr25.75	6.69	3.85
France	FFr18.5	5.83	3.17
Germany	DM4.60	1.71	2.69
Holland	Fl5.45	1.91	2.85
Japan	¥391	104	3.77
Mexico	Peso8.10	3.36	2.41
Russia	Ruble2,900	1,775	1.66
Sweden	SKr25.5	7.97	3.20
Switzerland	SwFr5.70	1.44	3.96
*Average U.S. price			

devaluation Reduction of a currency's value relative to another.

Devaluation is the reduction of a currency's value relative to another currency. During the past decade, the U.S. dollar has been devalued relative to most of the currencies of the industrialized world. Devaluation of the dollar makes U.S. goods sell for less abroad and reduces costs for visiting foreigners. On the other hand, devaluation increases the price U.S. consumers pay for imported goods and makes foreign vacations more expensive. Exhibit 4-1 shows what you would have paid for a McDonald's Big Mac in April 1993 in a number of different countries. As you can see, devaluation has made the Big Mac an expensive item for the American tourist with a hamburger craving! Devaluation also makes it more expensive for U.S. firms to purchase assets abroad and less expensive for foreign firms to buy U.S. assets.

Concept Check

- Explain the difference between balance of trade and balance of payments.
- Describe the position of the United States in world trade.
- Explain the impact of currency devaluation.

WHY NATIONS TRADE

3 One might argue that the best way to protect workers and the domestic economy is to stop trade with other nations. Then the whole circular flow of inputs and outputs could stay within our own borders. But if we decided to do that, where would we get resources like cobalt or coffee beans? Some things we just can't produce. And some things, like steel, we can't produce at the low costs we're used to. The fact is that nations are good at producing different things. It's the same with people: You might be better at balancing a ledger than repairing a car. You benefit by

■ In terms of trading, Kenya has an absolute advantage in coffee. Because of its soil and climate, it can produce and sell coffee beans at a lower cost than almost any other country.

"exporting" your bookkeeping services and "importing" the car repairs you need from someone who can do that well. The term that economists use to explain specialization like this is *advantage*.

ABSOLUTE ADVANTAGE

absolute advantage Ability to produce and sell a product that no other country can produce or that no other country can produce at such a low cost.

A country has an **absolute advantage** when it can produce and sell a product at a lower cost than any other country or when it is the only country that can provide it. The United States, for example, has an absolute advantage in reusable spacecraft and other high-tech items.

Say that the United States has an absolute advantage in air traffic control systems for busy airports and that Brazil has an absolute advantage in coffee. The United States does not have the proper climate for growing coffee, and Brazil lacks the technology to develop air traffic control systems. Both countries would gain by exchanging air traffic control systems for coffee.

COMPARATIVE ADVANTAGE

principle of comparative advantage Idea that all countries will benefit from producing and trading what each can produce best.

Even if the United States had an absolute advantage in both coffee and air traffic control systems, it should still specialize and engage in trade. Why? Because of the **principle of comparative advantage,** which says that each country should specialize in the products that it can produce most readily and cheaply and trade those products for the products that foreign countries can produce most readily and cheaply. The result will be more products available and lower prices for those products than if each country produced everything it needed by itself.

To illustrate, say that the United States has an absolute advantage over Outer Mongolia in producing two items: golf carts and bicycles. It can produce golf carts three times as efficiently as Outer Mongolia and can produce bicycles twice as efficiently. In this case, although the United States has a comparative advantage in the production of golf carts, Outer Mongolia has a comparative advantage in bicycles. Any time the United States spends making bicycles is time it cannot spend producing golf carts. For efficiency, each country should specialize in the production of only one good. By specializing in what it is really good at (golf carts) and letting Outer Mongolia make the bicycles, the United States assures that the total production of both goods is as great as it can possibly be.

Thus comparative advantage acts as a stimulus to trade. If your country and my country allow us to trade whatever goods and services we choose, without government regulation, we have free trade. **Free trade** is the policy of permitting the people of a country to buy and sell where they please, without restrictions. That doesn't mean we get things "for free"—you'll still charge me for your shirt buttons carved from old Coke bottles and I'll charge you for copper-roofed birdhouses. But our governments won't restrict our trade by limiting the numbers of buttons and birdhouses we trade or by regulating the prices in our exchanges.

free trade The policy of permitting people of a country to buy and sell where they please, without government restriction.

protectionism The policy of protecting home industries from outside competition through the setting of trade barriers.

The notion of free trade is based on the principle of comparative advantage. The opposite trade policy is **protectionism,** protecting home industries from outside competition through the setting of artificial barriers such as tariffs and quotas. In the next section, we'll look at the various barriers, some natural and some created by governments, that restrict free trade.

Concept Check

- Describe the concept of comparative advantage.
- Explain the difference between absolute advantage and comparative advantage.
- Describe the policy of free trade and its relationship to comparative advantage.

BARRIERS TO INTERNATIONAL TRADE

4 International trade is carried out by both businesses and governments—as long as no one puts up trade barriers. In general, trade barriers keep firms from selling to one another in foreign markets. The major obstacles to international trade are natural barriers, tariff barriers, and nontariff barriers.

NATURAL BARRIERS

Natural barriers to trade are physical or cultural. For instance, even though raising beef in the relative warmth of Argentina may cost less than raising beef in the bitter cold of Siberia, the cost of shipping the beef from South America to Siberia might raise the price too much. *Distance* is thus one of the natural barriers to international trade. Jet airplanes cut the time needed to ship goods long distances, but weight is a factor. Thus air cargo is limited to products with a high value per pound. For example, it would not make sense to ship coal or gravel by air. However, orchids, seafood, computers, and replacement parts for machinery are often moved this way. With advances in technology, liquified natural gas, asphalt, and other hard-to-transport products can now be moved by ship or barge—something not feasible fifteen or twenty years ago. Further improvements in technology should help lower other distance barriers as well.

Language is another natural trade barrier. People who can't communicate can't reach the understandings needed for trade. And once trade begins, language problems may result in the wrong goods being shipped.

TARIFF BARRIERS

tariff Tax levied by a nation on imported goods.

A **tariff** is a tax imposed by a nation on imported goods. It may be a charge per unit, such as per gallon of oil or per new car; it may be a percentage of the value of the goods, such as 5 percent of a $500,000 shipment of shoes; or it may be a combination. No matter how it is assessed, any tariff makes imported goods more costly, so they are less able to compete with domestic products.

protective tariff Tax levied on imports to make them less attractive to buyers than domestic goods.

Protective tariffs make imports less attractive to buyers than domestic products are. The United States, for instance, has protective tariffs on imported poultry, textiles, sugar, and some types of steel. U.S. carmakers want a 25 percent protective tariff placed on imported minivans. On the other side of the world, Japan has a tariff on U.S. cigarettes that makes them cost 60 percent more than Japanese brands. U.S. tobacco firms believe they could get as much as a third of the Japanese market if there were no tariffs on cigarettes. With tariffs, they have under 2 percent of the market.

Arguments For and Against Tariffs

Congress has debated the issue of tariffs since 1789. The main argument against tariffs is that they discourage free trade, and free trade lets the principle of comparative advantage work most efficiently. The main argument for tariffs is that they protect domestic businesses and workers.

One of the oldest arguments in favor of protectionism is the infant-industry argument. It says that tariffs protect new domestic industries from established foreign competitors. A tariff gives the struggling industry time to become an effective competitor. A tariff protected the infant U.S. motorcycle industry against British firms. But then the Japanese drove most European and American producers from the market. Harley-Davidson is the only remaining U.S. motorcycle maker.

A second argument for tariffs is the *job-protection argument.* Supporters—especially unions—say we should use tariffs to keep foreign labor from taking away U.S. jobs. U.S. jobs are lost, they say, when low-wage countries sell products in the United States at prices lower than those U.S. manufacturers can afford to charge. The higher prices charged by the U.S. firms help pay the higher wages of U.S. workers. Those who take this view tend to be more vocal during times of high unemployment.

Defense suppliers and the military often use the *preparedness argument* for tariffs. They say that industries and technology that are vital to maintaining our military might should be protected. In the event of war, these industries will be needed; thus they must be protected during peacetime. U.S. shipbuilders, gunpowder manufacturers, and uniform manufacturers are helped by this sort of tariff.

An argument against tariffs is that they raise prices, which decreases consumers' purchasing power. Over the long run tariffs may also be too protective, if they cause domestic companies to stop innovating and fall behind technologically. An example is the Italian car builder, Fiat. Protective tariffs helped keep Fiat's Italian market share very high as recently as 1989. As Europe's trade barriers fell, foreign competitors moved in with cars that Italian drivers prefer. Fiat is now desperately trying to catch up. It is spending $29 billion to revamp factories and design new models.[4]

NONTARIFF BARRIERS

Besides tariffs, governments use other tools to restrict trade. Among them are import quotas, embargoes, and buy-national regulations.

Import Quotas

import quota Limit on the quantity of certain goods that can be imported.

Limits on the quantity of certain goods that can be imported are **import quotas**. The goal of setting quotas is to limit imports to the optimum amount of a given product. The United States, for instance, restricts total steel imports from twenty-nine countries to a bit less than 20 percent of the U.S. market. The Federal Trade Commission estimates that consumers pay an extra $20 billion a year for steel, cars, and textiles whose prices are kept artifically high by quotas.[5]

Import quotas can cut two ways, of course. Japan, France, and Brazil have import quotas against many U.S. goods. The Japanese dropped import quotas on U.S. beef and oranges in early 1993.

Embargoes

embargo Complete ban on importing a product into a country or exporting it to a foreign country.

The complete ban against importing or exporting a product is an **embargo**. Often embargoes are set up for defense purposes. For instance, the United States does not allow twenty-seven high-tech products, such as supercomputers and lasers, to be exported to countries that are not allies. Although this embargo costs U.S. firms billions each year in lost sales, it keeps enemies from using the latest technology in their military hardware.

Buy-National Regulations

Government rules that give special privileges to domestic manufacturers are called buy-national regulations. One such regulation in the United States bans the use of foreign steel in building U.S. highways.

■ The U.S. recently lifted its long-standing trade embargo against Vietnam. Many companies have already positioned themselves to take advantage of the new market.

Other buy-national regulations use national standards that are different from international standards, such as requiring bottles to be quart size rather than liter size. The most subtle buy-national regulations simply make it hard for foreign products to enter the market. The French seem most adept at using this tactic. For example, to reduce imports of foreign video recorders, at one time France ruled that all of them had to be sent through the customs station at Poitiers. This customs house is located in the middle of the country, was woefully understaffed, and was open only

a few days each week. What's more, the few customs agents at Poitiers opened each package separately to inspect the merchandise. Within a few weeks, imports of video recorders in France came to a halt.

Concept Check

- Discuss the concept of natural trade barriers.
- Describe several tariff and nontariff barriers to trade.

PREVENTING UNFAIR TRADE

U.S. firms don't always get to compete on an equal basis in international trade. To make things even—"to level the playing field"—Congress has passed antidumping laws.

ANTIDUMPING LAWS

dumping Charging a lower price for a product (perhaps below cost) in foreign markets than at home.

Dumping is charging a lower price for a product (perhaps below cost) in foreign markets than in the firm's home market. The company might be trying to win foreign customers, or it might be seeking to get rid of surplus goods. Or, to help create an export market, some governments subsidize certain industries so they can sell their goods for less. For example, Japanese steel is sold below cost in world markets and losses are covered by government subsidy.

When the variation in price can't be explained by differences in the cost of serving the two markets, dumping is suspected. Most industrialized countries have antidumping regulations. They are especially concerned about *predatory dumping*, the attempt to gain control of a foreign market by destroying competitors with impossibly low prices. Many businesspeople feel that Japan has engaged in predatory dumping of semiconductors in the U.S. market.

If a government decides that imports are being sold for less than fair value and that domestic industry is being hurt, it can impose extra duties, or fines. These are calculated as the difference between the U.S. price and the price in the country of origin. In the steel industry import quotas alone were not sufficient to stifle foreign competitors. In 1993, the U.S. Commerce Department imposed dumping duties of up to 109 percent on steel imports from nineteen nations. Experts estimate that a foreign company's steel is effectively barred from the U.S. market once dumping duties greater than 15 percent are imposed.[6] Similarly, dumping duties of 87 percent have recently been applied to all South Korean dynamic random access memory (DRAM) semiconductors.[7] These chips are a basic component of most computer equipment.

Consumers tend to benefit from low prices. So, a low price is not in itself enough reason to impose an antidumping duty. A domestic industry must be injured as well. Unless a domestic industry is suffering, the price is allowed to stand. Developing nations, which generally lack mature industries, tend not to have antidumping regulations.

INCREASING GLOBAL TRADE

It might almost seem that governments act only to restrain global trade. On the contrary, governments and international financial organizations work hard to increase it.

GATT

General Agreement on Tariffs and Trade (GATT) Multinational agreement passed in 1947 to reduce tariffs and other barriers to international trade.

After World War II, many nations wanted to make international trade easier. In 1947 they adopted the **General Agreement on Tariffs and Trade (GATT)** to reduce tariffs and other barriers. GATT offers a basic set of rules for trade negotiations. It also created an agency that oversees and carries out the rules. The 105 member countries of GATT meet periodically to review recommendations, settle disputes, and study new ways to reduce tariffs and end nontariff barriers. Each periodic meeting opens a new *round* of trade talks. The Uruguay Round of trade talks, which began in 1990, has been stalled largely because Europeans balked at removing protection for their agricultural goods. However, a new GATT agreement was reached on December 15, 1993, to reduce tariffs on 8,000 manufactured goods. The agreeement is expected to boost world output by $270 billion a year by 2005 and create millions of new jobs in America.[8] The guiding principle of GATT negotiations is fairness to all member countries. Any trade advantage a GATT member gives to one country must be given to all GATT members. GATT has been successful in reducing tariff barriers on manufactured goods, which have fallen from an average of 40 percent in pre-GATT days to 5 percent today. However, as tariffs fell, other nontariff barriers have emerged to take their place.

THE GROUP OF SEVEN

Group of Seven (G7) The seven economic superpowers, who meet regularly to set broad economic policies.

The seven economic superpowers—the United States, Germany, Japan, Britain, France, Italy, and Canada—comprise the **Group of Seven (G7)**. Their foreign ministers and central bankers meet at least four times each year to set broad policies on interest rates, exchange rates, economic policy, and trade. Each year the heads of government of the G7 countries, along with their finance ministers, hold an *economic summit.* The summit meetings put the power of world political leaders behind global economic initiatives ranging from trade talks to operations designed to combat the illegal drug trade. For example, the July 1993 Economic Summit, held in Tokyo, produced an accord to eliminate tariffs on a wide range of manufactured goods. Also, in March 1994 G7 met in the United States to discuss ways to boost employment throughout the world.

Boosting exports is critically important for the United States. Exports have accounted for more than one-third of America's economic growth and two-thirds of all new domestic jobs since 1987.[9] Also, jobs created by exports pay, on average, 13 percent more than jobs rooted solely in the domestic economy. Foreign trade creates good jobs.

LEVELING THE PLAYING FIELD WITH JAPAN

Tariff and nontariff barriers imposed by Japan have long been a major source of frustration for U.S. business. Recall that about half of the U.S. trade deficit is accounted for by Japan. Trade barriers there cost the United States as much as $18 billion in annual exports.[10] At the Tokyo economic summit, President Clinton told Japanese officials that the U.S. wants Japan to slash its trade surplus by half and raise its imports of U.S. manufactured goods by one-third by 1996. Previous administrations believed that if Japan would open its markets to competition, U.S. businesses would get their fair share. The Clinton administration believes that the Japanese market must be pried open by government action or threats of retaliation. The new policy is called *managed trade*. It requires the Japanese government to reach target market shares for U.S. imports in five major product categories. For example, managed trade in the semiconductor industry has resulted in an increase in the U.S. share of the Japanese chip market from 7 percent in 1986 to 20 percent today.[11]

FINANCIAL INSTITUTIONS THAT FOSTER WORLD TRADE

World Bank International bank that offers developing nations low-interest-rate loans to help build infrastructure and relieve debt.

Two international financial organizations are instrumental in fostering global trade. The **World Bank** (formally the International Bank for Reconstruction and Development) has offered low-interest loans to developing nations. The purpose of the loans was to help build the infrastructure of developing countries—roads, power plants, schools, drainage projects, hospitals, and the like. Now the World Bank offers loans to help developing nations relieve their debt burdens. To receive these debt-relief loans, the countries must pledge to lower trade barriers and aid private enterprise.

International Monetary Fund (IMF) International bank that gives short-term financing to countries with balance-of-trade problems.

The **International Monetary Fund (IMF)** is also an international bank. It gives short-term loans to countries with a bad balance of trade. The IMF was founded in 1944 by forty-four countries and later became affiliated with the United Nations. The main goals of the IMF are to help steady exchange rates and oversee money exchanges by countries. Now the IMF is also making long-term loans to very poor nations to help them strengthen their economies.

Concept Check

- Describe the purpose and role of GATT.
- Explain the purpose of G7 and the economic summits.
- What are the roles of the World Bank and the IMF in world trade?

ECONOMIC INTEGRATION AND TRADE PACTS

5 Nations that frequently trade together may decide to formalize their relationship. The governments meet and work out agreements for a common economic policy. The result is economic integration.

preferential tariff Tariff that offers advantages to one nation (or several) over other nations.

free-trade zones Areas formed by trade associations in which there are few, if any, duties or rules to restrict trade among the partners.

customs unions Associations with reduced tariff and nontariff barriers for member nations and with common policies for trade outside the union.

One thing the nations may agree on is a **preferential tariff**, which gives advantages to one nation (or several nations) over others. For instance, members of the British Commonwealth pay a lower tariff when they trade with Great Britain than do others. In other cases, nations may form free-trade associations. In the **free-trade zones** they set up, there are few, if any, duties or rules to restrict trade among partners. But outsiders would have to pay the tariffs set by individual members.

Nations may also integrate through **customs unions**. Tariff and nontariff barriers are reduced among the members, and common policies are established for trade outside the union. The European Union, also called the European Community (EC) and the European Common Market, is the best-known customs union. Its first members in 1958 were Belgium, France, Italy, Luxembourg, the Netherlands, and West Germany. Since then, six other European nations have become full or partial members: Denmark, Great Britain, Ireland, Greece, Portugal, and Spain. New members will continue to join. Other large customs unions include the Latin American Integration Association, the Council of Mutual Economic Cooperation, made up of Eastern European countries, and the League of Arab States. All of these customs unions foster trade among members and deal as a unit with nonmembers.

UNITED EUROPE

United Europe Trade agreement of the European Community that standardizes trade rules and taxes.

The EC removed many internal trade barriers on its way to **United Europe**. Members standardized trade rules and taxes and got better access to government contracts. Health and safety standards were coordinated through 300 regulatory changes. The goal was to end the need for a special product made for each country. Goods marked "GEC" ("goods for EC") can be traded freely, without being retested at each border. Duties, customs procedures, and taxes are also standardized. A driver hauling cargo from Amsterdam to Lisbon now can clear four border crossings by showing a single piece of paper. Prior to 1992 the same driver would have carried two pounds of papers to cross the same borders.

Some economists have called the European single market concept the "United States of Europe." It is an attractive market, with 320 million consumers and purchasing power almost equal to that of the United States.[12] But the EC will probably never be a "United States of Europe." The *Maastricht treaty* which proposed binding the EC countries together in finance, defense, economics, and foreign policy by 1999 has been ratified by all twelve member nations. Yet nations continue to worry about local identities being submerged in a united Europe. With nine different languages and their own national customs, Europeans will always be more diverse than Americans. Thus product differences will continue. It will be a long time, for instance, before the French begin drinking the instant coffee that Britons enjoy. Or consider washing machines: British homemakers want front-loaders, and the French want top-loaders; Germans like lots of settings and high spin speeds; Italians like slower speeds.

Although a united Europe creates vast opportunities, American business faces the possibility of a protectionist movement by United Europe

■ Some U.S. firms are well prepared to compete in the united European market. Because of its early and aggressive international expansion, Coca-Cola is already considered a classic European brand.

against outsiders. American companies realize that they have to be perceived as European or risk tough trade barriers. For example, European automakers have proposed holding Japanese imports at roughly their current 10 percent market share. The Irish, Danes, and Dutch, who don't make cars and whose home markets are wide open, would be unhappy about a restricted supply of Toyotas and Datsuns. But Renault and Peugeot, now protected by a 3 percent French quota on Japanese cars, will face tougher competition if the quota is raised at all.

Indeed, a number of big American companies are already more "European" than the Europeans. Coca-Cola and Kellogg are considered classic European brand names. Ford and GM compete for the largest market share in auto sales on the continent, and IBM and Digital Equipment dominate their markets. General Electric, AT&T, and Westinghouse, already strong in Europe, have invested heavily in new manufacturing facilities throughout Europe.

Although many U.S. firms are well prepared to contend with united European competition, the rivalry is perhaps more intense there than anywhere else in the world. In the long run, it is questionable whether Europe has room for eight mass-market automakers, including Ford and GM, when the United States sustains just three. Similarly, an integrated Europe probably doesn't need twelve national airlines.

THE NORTH AMERICAN FREE TRADE AGREEMENT

North American Free Trade Agreement (NAFTA) Treaty that eliminates trade barriers among the United States, Canada, and Mexico.

The **North American Free Trade Agreement (NAFTA)** is a treaty among the governments of the United States, Canada, and Mexico that will phase out barriers to trade in goods and services in North America and eliminate barriers to investment. As tariffs and other trade barriers are eliminated, the treaty will create an open market of more than 360 million consumers with a combined gross domestic product of more than $6 trillion in annual output.[13] Despite opposition in the United States that focused on potential job losses, reduced American wages, and environmental hazards, the treaty was ratified by Congress and signed into law by President Bill Clinton in late 1993. Canada, the largest U.S. trading partner, entered a free-trade agreement with the United States in 1988. Thus, most of the new opportunities for U.S. business under NAFTA are in Mexico, America's third largest trading partner. Mexican consumer demand is such that U.S. exports to Mexico tripled from 1989 to 1993.[14] When the treaty went into effect in 1994, tariffs on about half the items traded across the Rio Grande River immediately disappeared. The pact also removed a web of Mexican licensing requirements, quotas, and tariffs that used to limit transactions in U.S. goods and services. For instance, the pact allows U.S. and Canadian financial-services companies to own subsidiaries in Mexico for the first time in fifty years.

The first industries to benefit from the treaty are likely to be autos, textiles, capital goods, financial services, construction equipment, electronics, telecommunications, and petrochemicals. Sales of companies in such industries have been rising for some time as a result of Mexico's growing economy: In 1983 Caterpillar sold only 12 pieces of heavy construction equipment to Mexico; in 1993 it shipped over 1,200. NAFTA removes tariffs on Caterpillar equipment sold in Mexico while maintaining duties against Japanese rival Komatsu. As protections are lifted from the Mexican car industry, Rockwell International will sell more door latches, sunroofs, and window mechanisms. It already plans to build a new plant in Mexico.

NAFTA could boost U.S. exports to Mexico by $10 billion a year, expand Canada-Mexico trade by 30 percent, and create 600,000 new jobs in Mexico.[15] Yet the NAFTA agreement may not benefit everyone equally, as the following Ethics and Social Responsibility Trends box shows.

TRENDS

Business Ethics and Social Responsibility

Is NAFTA Good for U.S. Workers?

Most economists agree that lowering trade barriers is good. As foreign countries sell more to the United States, they will use the revenue to buy U.S. exports. Often they will also set up shop and create jobs in the United States, as the Japanese and Germans are doing. A recent example is a BMW plant that will bring 2,000 jobs to South Carolina. Other benefits of free trade include a freer exchange of technology and managerial ideas. Although the net benefit is hard to quantify, economists project that free trade between the United States and Mexico will lift output in both countries and create tens of thousands of new U.S. jobs.

If goods trade freely, prices and production costs will tend to equalize. To compete, countries must specialize where they have a relative edge. Low-wage countries, like Mexico, will make labor-intensive goods. Those with capital will do better with technology-intensive products. Thus, low-skilled work should

flow from the United States to Mexico—or the wages of low-skilled U.S. workers must fall.

In the 1980s, factory workers whose companies competed with foreign rivals often were laid off or were forced to take wage cuts. The glut of job candidates helped hold down pay among the 64 million workers who never went beyond high school. Wages of the college-educated held up better to foreign competitors.

The increase in global trade bears much of the blame for unprecedented income inequality between the most- and least-educated parts of the U.S. work force. Declining pay for those at the bottom may not slow U.S. growth, since average incomes should rise as those at the top do better. But widening inequality poses other problems. The poverty rate could stay up. The tab for welfare and unemployment could mount, inflating taxes. Ultimately, resentment of the wealthy could reach a boiling point. "One possibility is for us to become a class society like those in Latin America," which have unequal distributions of wealth and chronically unstable governments, says Richard B. Freeman, an economist at Harvard University. "That's the direction we're headed."[16]

Concept Check

- Explain the concept of United Europe.
- Describe the pros and cons of NAFTA.

ENTERING THE INTERNATIONAL MARKET

6 The North American Free Trade Agreement will stimulate many big American and Canadian companies to enter international trade. But many small firms are still afraid to enter the international market. Why? They don't know how, they fear not getting paid, or they just feel that it is more trouble than it's worth. Most small firms lack information about tariffs, quotas, and demand for their product in international markets. Thus they have a hard time making the right marketing decisions. Also, many small firms don't want to deal in foreign currencies because of the complexities. Small firms *can* succeed in foreign markets, however. And they have many ways to enter international trade: exporting, licensing, contract manufacturing, joint ventures, direct foreign investment, and counter-trade.

EXPORTING

A firm that decides to take the international plunge will probably begin with exporting. The one difference between export sales and domestic sales is the need to deal in a foreign currency.

Exporters who need help can call on the U.S. Department of Commerce's Foreign Commercial Service Division. It has offices in sixty-seven foreign countries and sixty-eight locations in the United States. It offers

■ Most companies entering the international market begin by exporting their products to other countries. With trade barriers falling, this can be a very profitable move, even for smaller firms.

export counseling, market research assistance, sales leads, and conferences.

A company that doesn't want to get involved in the details of exporting can use an *export-management company (EMC)*. EMCs are U.S.-based firms that specialize in exporting a certain type of product or exporting to a certain country. Some 2,000 such companies exist in the United States. They act as marketing agents for domestic companies in international markets. Usually EMCs charge a 15 percent commission for their services. A would-be exporter could also sell its goods to an *export-trading company (ETC)*. The ETC would then resell the goods overseas, adding a markup for itself. Whether a company uses an EMC or an ETC, or begins without outside help, exporting can be very profitable. For example, Vita-Mix Corporation, an Ohio-based manufacturer of blenders, faced stagnating sales in the early 1990s. It turned to exporting, with immediate success. Two years after going global, exports accounted for 20 percent of Vita-Mix's $15 million in sales.[17] The firm now ships blenders to 20 countries, from Norway to Venezuela.

LICENSING

licensing Agreement in which a firm (licensee) buys or rents the right to use the patent, trademark, production process, brand name, product, or company name of another firm (licensor).

Another effective way for a firm to move into the global arena with relatively little risk is to sell a license to manufacture its product to someone in a foreign country. **Licensing** is the legal process whereby a firm (the *licensor*) agrees to let another firm (*the licensee*) use its manufacturing process, trademarks, patents, trade secrets, or other proprietary knowledge. The licensee, in turn, agrees to pay the licensor a royalty or fee agreed on by both parties.

U.S. companies have eagerly embraced the licensing concept. For instance, Philip Morris licensed Labatt Brewing Company to produce Miller High Life in Canada. The Spalding Company receives more than $2 million annually from license agreements on its sporting goods. Fruit-of-the-Loom lends its name through licensing to forty-five consumer items in Japan alone, for at least 1 percent of the licensee's gross sales.

The licensor must make sure it can exercise the control over the licensee's activities needed to ensure proper quality, pricing, distribution, and so on. Licensing may also create a new competitor in the long run, if the licensee decides to void the license agreement. International law is often ineffective in stopping such actions. Two common ways of maintaining effective control over licensees are shipping one or more critical components from the United States or locally registering patents and trademarks by the U.S. firm, not by the licensee.

Franchising is one form of licensing that has grown rapidly in recent years. Over 350 U.S. franchisors operate more than 32,000 outlets in foreign countries, bringing in sales of $6 billion. Over half the international franchises are for fast-food restaurants and business services. As with other forms of licensing, maintaining control over franchisees is important. For instance, McDonald's was forced to take legal action to buy back its Paris outlets, since the restaurants were dirty and provided poor service and food. Because of the damage to McDonald's reputation, the chain had only 67 outlets in all of France, compared to 270 in Great Britain and 270 in Germany. To reestablish itself, McDonald's decided to project French style and class. The first outlet to appear after McDonald's repurchased its franchise was in a handsome, turn-of-the-century building on one of Paris' grand boulevards.

CONTRACT MANUFACTURING

contract manufacturing Private-label manufacturing in which a foreign company produces goods to which the domestic firm attaches its brand name.

Firms that want to pursue the international market more directly may decide to contract for the production of their goods by foreign manufacturers. Such private-label manufacturing by a foreign company is called **contract manufacturing**. The foreign company produces the goods, and the domestic firm's brand name is put on them. Marketing may be handled by either the domestic company or the foreign manufacturer. Levi Strauss, for instance, entered into an agreement with the French fashion house of Cacharel to produce a new Levi's line called "Something New," for distribution in Germany.

Contract manufacturing lets a company "test the water" in foreign markets. It can develop brand loyalty without a large investment in equipment. After establishing a solid base, the company can become more directly involved.

JOINT VENTURES

joint venture Business owned by two or more firms or investors (or governments)

In world trade, a **joint venture** lets two or more firms or investors (including governments) share ownership of a business. The owners may share patents, trademarks, or control over manufacturing and marketing. Many joint ventures come about when no single firm will assume the financial risk for an enterprise. Large, long-term investments are natural candidates for joint ventures. Examples are factories built abroad and mining operations for natural resources like bauxite, iron ore, and petroleum. With natural resources, one firm may do the mining, another supply the transportation, and yet another do the refining. Developing countries often insist on joint ventures to gain access to technology or to put their own people into managerial positions.

Joint ventures also can be very risky. Many fail. Others fall victim to a takeover, in which one partner buys out the other. In a survey of 150 companies involved in joint ventures that ended, three-quarters were found to have been taken over by Japanese partners. Joint ventures can be seen as "a race to learn": The partner that learns fastest comes to dominate the relationship and can then rewrite its terms. Thus, a joint venture becomes a new form of competition. The Japanese excel at learning from others; U.S. and European companies are not as good at it.[18]

In a successful joint venture, both parties gain valuable skills from the alliance. In the General Motors-Suzuki joint venture in Canada, for example, both parties have contributed and gained. The alliance, CAMI Automotive, was formed to manufacture low-end cars for the U.S. market. The plant, run by Suzuki management, produces the Geo Metro/Suzuki Swift as well as the Geo Tracker/Suzuki Sidekick sport utility vehicle. Through CAMI, Suzuki has gained access to GM's dealer network and an expanded market for parts and components. GM avoided the cost of developing low-end cars and obtained models it needed to revitalize the lower end of its product line and to lower its average fuel economy rating. GM also has learned how Japanese carmakers use work teams, run flexible assembly lines, and manage quality control.[19]

DIRECT INVESTMENT

direct foreign investment Active ownership of a foreign company or foreign manufacturing or marketing facilities.

Active ownership of a foreign company or of overseas manufacturing or marketing facilities is **direct foreign investment**. Direct investors have either a controlling interest or a large minority interest in the firm. Thus they have the greatest potential reward but also the greatest potential risk. Federal Express, for example, lost $1.2 billion on its attempt to build a hub in Europe. It created a huge infrastructure but could not generate the package volume to support it.[20]

A firm may make a direct foreign investment by acquiring an interest in an existing company or by building new facilities. It might do so because it has trouble transferring some resource to a foreign operation or getting that resource locally. One important resource is personnel, especially managers. If the local labor market is tight, the firm may buy an entire foreign firm and retain all its employees instead of paying higher salaries than competitors. Sometimes firms make direct investments because then can find no suitable local partners. Also, direct investments avoid the communication problems and conflicts of interest that can arise with joint ventures. IBM, for instance, requires total ownership of foreign investments because it does not want to share control with local partners.

The United States is a popular place for direct investment by foreign companies. In 1993 the value of foreign-owned business in the United States was over $425 billion. Britain is the biggest foreign investor in the U.S. economy, followed, in order, by Japan, the Netherlands, Canada, and Germany.

COUNTERTRADE

countertrade Trading arrangement in which part or all of the payment for goods or services is in the form of other goods or services.

International trade does not always involve cash. Today countertrade is a fast-growing way to conduct international business. In **countertrade**, part or all of the payment for goods or services is in the form of other goods or services. Countertrade is a form of barter (swapping goods for goods), an age-old practice whose origins have been traced back to cave dwellers. The U.S. Commerce Department says that roughly 30 percent of all international trade involves countertrade. In fact, both India and China have made billion-dollar government purchasing lists, with most of the goods to be paid for by countertrade.

A common type of countertrade is straight barter. For example, PepsiCo sends Pepsi syrup to Russian bottling plants and in payment gets Stolichnaya vodka, which is then marketed in the West. Another form of countertrade involves compensation agreements. Typically, a company will provide technology and equipment for a plant in a developing nation and agree to take full or partial payment in goods produced by that plant. For example, General Tire Company supplied equipment and know-how for a Rumanian truck tire plant. In turn, the company received tires from the plant, which it sold in the United States under the Victoria brand name. Pierre Cardin gives technical advice to China in exchange for silks and cashmeres. In these cases, both sides benefit even though they don't use cash.

Concept Check
- Discuss several ways that a company can enter international trade.
- Explain the concept of countertrade.

POLITICS AND CULTURE IN INTERNATIONAL TRADE

7 Whether a domestic firm is thinking of simple export, direct foreign investment, or countertrade, it should understand the politics and culture of the country in which it plans to do business. Often political and cultural factors are more important in completing a sale than the price or even the product. If two companies are selling the same basic product, the company with more insight into the foreign culture is likely to make the sale.

POLITICAL CONSIDERATIONS

Government policies range from prohibiting private ownership and suppressing individual freedom to maintaining little central government and granting great personal freedom. But as private-property rights increase, government-owned industry and centralized planning tend to decrease.

In addition to the basic political structure of a country, nationalism is also a concern. **Nationalism** is the sense of national consciousness that boosts the culture and interests of one country over those of all other countries. Strongly nationalistic countries, such as Iran or New Guinea, often discourage investment by foreign companies.

Political risk is another danger for companies thinking about exporting to or investing in foreign countries. Rapid political changes sometimes disrupt a country's economic system. The new government may attack for-

nationalism Sense of national consciousness that puts the interests of one's country ahead of international considerations.

■ By the year 2000 Campbell Soup would like half of their revenues to come from foreign sales. To accomplish this, they have tailored their products for different cultures from around the world.

eign corporations as remnants of the Western-dominated colonial past, as happened in Cuba, Nicaragua, and Iran. Even if such changes do not directly hurt firms and their employees, they can have drastic effects. In the past few decades, coups in Ghana, Ethiopia, and Iraq, to name a few, have seriously hampered foreign companies.

In a hostile climate, a government may *expropriate* a foreign company's assets, taking ownership and compensating the former owners. Even worse is *confiscation*, which does not involve payments to the owner. Iran confiscated a number of assets of U.S. firms when the Shah was deposed in 1979.

CULTURAL CONSIDERATIONS

If a firm doesn't understand a country's culture, it has little chance of successfully doing business there. *Culture* is the set of shared beliefs, values, and social norms that determines what is acceptable in a society. Culture includes family organization, the language, the educational system, and the social class system.

An example of how culture can influence one's view of the world is shown in Exhibit 4-2, taken from a Japanese airline route map. Note that the United States is upside down and backward, which reflects the view of the world as seen from the island of Japan. On their map of their world, Japan is in the center and "right side up."

History offers many examples of mismatches between product and culture. For instance, a U.S. company sent cake mixes for fluffy, frosted cakes to Great Britain. But in England cakes are eaten at teatime—using fingers, not forks—and they need to be dense and not too messy or crumbly. Often, American companies must alter products for local tastes. For example, Domino's most popular pizza in Japan is topped with grilled chicken, spinach, onion and corn. It also offers pizza with curry flavoring

■ **Exhibit 4-2**
The Japanese View of North America

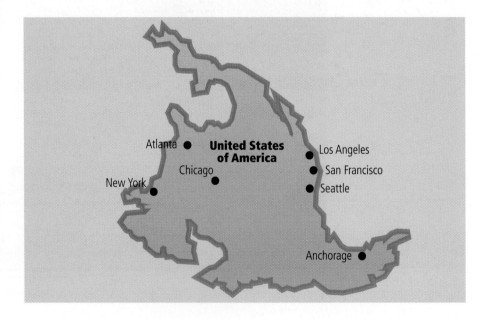

and one topped with squid or seaweed.[21] One of Campbell's most popular canned soups in Hong Kong is watercress and duck gizzard.[22]

At first, Procter & Gamble's launch of Ace detergent in Mexico was a failure. Developed for U.S. washing machines, the product had a low-suds formula. But many Mexicans wash their clothes in a basin of water or in rivers, and they judge a detergent by its suds. Procter & Gamble researched the problem and changed the formula to be more sudsy. The company also switched from cardboard boxes to plastic bags, which keep the detergent drier and are cheaper. Besides, many Mexicans shop every day and can afford only small amounts of detergent each time. Now the 100-gram bag of Ace, enough to wash just one basket of clothes, is a top seller throughout Latin America.

Color is another cultural factor. Colors have different meanings in different countries, and firms doing business in the international market need to be aware of these. When PepsiCo changed the color of its vending equipment from deep royal blue to light ice blue, sales in Southeast Asia plunged. In that part of the world, light blue is associated with death and mourning. Pepsi lost its lead to Coke because of the color change.

Changing the color, taste, size, shape, or functions of products is often necessary to meet the demands of consumers and businesses with different cultural backgrounds. One common factor, however, across all business cultures in developed nations is the relentless pursuit of quality improvement in both products and services, as the following Trends in Quality Management box shows.

TRENDS

Quality Management

A Yen for Creativity

New and better products call for creativity and imagination. Yet the Japanese business culture of rigid management systems and consensus decision making often stifles, rather than encourages, creativity. Yoshiharu Fukuhara, President of Shiseido, Japan's largest cosmetics manufacturer with sales of about $5 billion annually, believes that creativity is the key to long-run survival. "Until now," he notes, "Japan has relied on its technological advances and high quality to sell products. But in the next era, that alone will not be enough. We must begin to make products that also have spirit."

Fukuhara asked his managers just how much they were willing to break out of their velvet cocoons to evolve into visionary risk takers. The replies were simply hushed respect for their leader. Fukuhara decided that radical steps were needed to improve creativity and individual expression.

At a Shiseido management retreat, the doors swung open to reveal a darkened conference room. As Argentine tango music throbbed, twenty division heads of Shiseido filed in, to find goldfish in beakers on tables. A leader dressed in black announced: "This goldfish is Shiseido." He instructed the managers to analyze the creature and its role in the world, and to draw parallels with their company. Some asked for magnifying glasses. All jotted down notes.

In another session, the executives watched Ushio Amagatsu, leader of a

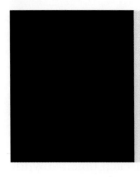

renowned dance troupe called Sankaijuku that performs an avant-garde Japanese dance known as Butoh. Clad in a white loincloth, his skin painted an eerie white, Amagatsu held participants spellbound as he slowly and excruciatingly contorted his body. To drive home the importance of equilibrium and patience, he instructed everyone to balance an egg on end. About half succeeded.

Will these techniques overcome Japanese cultural barriers to creativity? Only time will tell.[23]

Concept Check
- Explain how political factors can affect international trade.
- Describe several cultural factors that a company involved in international trade should consider.

THE IMPACT OF MULTINATIONAL CORPORATIONS

8

multinational corporations Corporations that move resources, goods, services, and skills across national boundaries without regard to the country in which they are headquartered.

Corporations that move resources, goods, services, and skills across national boundaries without regard to the country in which their headquarters are located are **multinational corporations**. Some are so rich and have so many employees that they resemble small countries. For example, the sales of both Exxon and General Motors are larger than the gross domestic product of all but twenty-two nations in the world. Multinational companies are heavily engaged in international trade. The successful ones take political and cultural differences into account.

Today, dozens of America's top names—including General Electric, Gillette, Xerox, Dow Chemical, and Hewlett-Packard—sell more of their products outside the United States than they do at home. U.S. service companies—such as McDonald's, Service Master (cleaning services), and Federal Express—are close behind.

A multinational company may have several worldwide headquarters, depending on where certain markets or technologies are. Britain's APV, a maker of food-processing equipment, has a different headquarters for each of its worldwide businesses. Hewlett-Packard recently moved the headquarters of its personal computer business to Grenoble, France. Siemens A.G., Germany's electronics giant, is relocating its medical electronics division headquarters from Germany to Chicago. Honda is planning to move the worldwide headquarters for its power-products division to Atlanta, Georgia. The largest multinational corporations in the world, by industry, are shown in Exhibit 4-3.

Large multinationals have advantages over other companies. For instance, multinationals can often overcome trade problems. Taiwan and South Korea have long had an embargo against Japanese cars for political reasons and to help domestic carmakers. Also, Japan observes the Arab embargo of Israel. Yet Honda USA, a Japanese-owned company based in the United States, sends Accords to Taiwan and Korea and Civic sedans to Israel. Another example is Germany's BASF, a major chemical and drug manufacturer. Its biotechnology research at home is challenged by the environmentally conscious Green movement. So BASF moved its cancer and immune-system research to Cambridge, Massachusetts.

Another advantage for multinationals is their ability to sidestep regulatory problems. U.S. drugmaker Smith Kline and Britain's Beecham decided to merge, in part so they could avoid licensing and regulatory hassles in their largest markets. The merged company can say it's an insider in both Europe and the United States. "When we go to Brussels, we're a member state [of the European Union]," one executive explains. "And when we go to Washington, we're an American company, too." [24]

Multinationals can often save a lot in labor costs, even in highly unionized countries. For example, Xerox started moving copier rebuilding work to Mexico, where wages are much lower. Its union in Rochester, New

Exhibit 4-3
The World's Largest Multinational Corporations by Industry

Source: "The World's Largest Industrial Corporations," *Fortune,* 26 July 1993, p. 190.

Industry	Company	Country	Company Sales ($ millions)
Aerospace	Boeing	U.S.	$30,414
Apparel	Levi Strauss Associates	U.S.	5,570
Beverages	PepsiCo.	U.S.	22,084
Building materials, glass	Saint-Gobain	France	14,297
Chemicals	E. I. DuPont de Nemours	U.S.	37,386
Computers, office equipment	IBM	U.S.	65,096
Electronics, electrical equipment	General Electric	U.S.	62,202
Food	Philip Morris	U.S.	50,157
Forest and paper products	International Paper	U.S.	13,600
Industrial and farm equipment	Mitsubishi Heavy Industries	Japan	23,011
Jewelry, watches	Citizen Watch	Japan	3,328
Metal products	Pechiney	France	12,344
Metals	IRI	Italy	67,547
Mining, crude-oil production	Ruhrkohle	Germany	15,712
Motor vehicles and parts	General Motors	U.S.	132,775
Petroleum refining	Exxon	U.S.	103,547
Pharmaceuticals	Johnson & Johnson	U.S.	13,846
Publishing, printing	Matra-Hachette	France	10,416
Rubber and plastic products	Bridgestone	Japan	13,860
Scientific, photo, control equipment	Eastman Kodak	U.S.	20,577
Soaps, cosmetics	Procter & Gamble	U.S.	29,890
Textiles	Toray Industries	Japan	7,862
Tobacco	RJR Nabisco Holdings	U.S.	15,734
Toys, sporting goods	Nintendo	Japan	5,213
Transportation equipment	Hyundai Heavy Industries	S. Korea	6,518

York, objected because it saw that members' jobs were at risk. But it agreed to change work styles and improve productivity to keep the jobs at home.

Multinationals can also shift costs from one plant to another. When European demand for a certain solvent declined, Dow Chemical shifted production in its German plant to another chemical that had been imported from Louisiana and Texas. Computer models help Dow make decisions like these so it can run its plants more efficiently.

Finally, multinationals can tap new technology from around the world. Xerox has introduced some eighty different office copiers in the United States that were designed and built by Fuji Xerox, its joint venture with a Japanese company. Versions of the superconcentrated detergent that Procter & Gamble first formulated in Japan in response to a rival's product are now being sold under the Ariel brand name in Europe and tested under the Cheer and Tide labels in the United States. Also consider Otis Elevator's development of the Elevonic 411, an elevator that is programmed to send more cars to floors where demand is high: It was developed by six research centers in five countries. Otis's group in Farmington, Connecticut, handled the systems integration; a Japanese group designed the special motor drives that made the elevators ride smoothly; a French group perfected the door systems; a German group handled the electronics; and a Spanish group took care of the small-geared components. Otis says the international effort saved more than $10 million in design costs and cut the design process from four years to two.

Concept Check

- Define the term multinational corporation.
- Discuss the role of multinational corporations in international trade.

■ SUMMARY

1. Understand the importance of international trade and discuss the position of the United States in the world market.
International trade improves relations with friends and allies, helps ease tensions among nations, and helps bolster economies, raise people's standard of living, and improve the quality of life.

The United States is still the largest importer and exporter in the world. One of every six manufacturing jobs in the United States depends on foreign trade. A third of our farm acreage is devoted to crops for export.

2. Understand some of the measures of international trade.
Two concepts important to international trade are the balance of trade (the differences in value of a country's exports and imports over some period) and the balance of payments (the difference between a country's total payments to other countries and its total receipts from other countries). The United States now has both a negative balance of trade and a negative balance of payments.

Key Terms

absolute advantage 112

balance of payments 109

balance of trade 109

contract manufacturing 124

countertrade 126

customs unions 119

devaluation 111

direct foreign investment 125

dumping 116

embargo 115

exchange rate 110

continued

3. Explain why nations trade.

Nations trade because they gain by doing so. The principle of comparative advantage states that each country should specialize in the goods it can produce most readily and cheaply and trade them for those that other countries can produce most readily and cheaply. The result is more goods at lower prices than if each country produced by itself everything it needed. Free trade allows trade among nations without government restrictions.

4. Understand the barriers to international trade, and list the major arguments for and against tariffs.

There are a number of barriers to international trade. The three major types are natural barriers, such as distance and language; tariff barriers, or taxes on imported goods; and nontariff barriers. The nontariff barriers to trade include import quotas, embargoes, and buy-national regulations. The main argument against tariffs is that they discourage free trade and keep the principle of comparative advantage from working efficiently. The main argument for using tariffs is that they help protect domestic companies, industries, and workers.

5. Explain economic integration and trade pacts.

Some major efforts to build international trade are the General Agreement on Tariffs and Trade (GATT), the World Bank, and the International Monetary Fund (IMF). Economic-integration plans, which include preferential tariffs, free-trade zones, and customs unions, are intergovernment agreements on common economic policy. The best-known customs union is the European Union, which removed most internal trade barriers at the end of 1992. It is now sometimes called United Europe. The United States, Canada, and Mexico have signed a similar free-trade agreement entitled the North American Free Trade Agreement (NAFTA).

6. Specify ways for businesses to enter into foreign trade.

There are a number of ways to enter the global market. The major ones are exporting, licensing, contract manufacturing, joint ventures, direct investment, and countertrade.

7. Describe the impact of culture and political climate on international trade.

Domestic firms entering the international arena need to consider the politics and culture of the countries they plan to do business with. For example, government trade policies can be loose or restrictive, countries can be nationalistic, and governments can change. In the area of culture, many products fail because companies don't understand the culture of the country in which they are trying to sell their products.

8. Explain the trade role of multinational corporations.

Multinational corporations engage heavily in international trade. These firms are often so wealthy and populous that they resemble small countries. Many countries encourage multinationals to invest there.

■ DISCUSSION QUESTIONS

1. What do you think the U.S. government should do to correct our balance of trade problem? What should it do to correct our balance of payments problem?

2. Should the United States protect its businesses from foreign businesses that produce useful goods at a cost lower than domestic producers?

3. Recent rounds of the GATT have taken many years to conclude. Why do you think this is so? What can world leaders do to speed up the process?

4. Do you think that the United States is "leveling the playing field" with Japan? If not, what should be the next step?

5. Describe the current status of United Europe.

6. What do you think is the best way for a small company to enter international trade? Why?

7. Do you think that countertrade will grow? Why or why not?

8. Explain how political and cultural factors can increase or decrease a company's international sales.

9. What sort of impact has the presence of foreign multinationals had on the U.S. economy? Give some examples.

10. Name some U.S. multinational companies that have been successful in world markets. How do you think they have achieved their success?

■ CASE

A Red Letter Day in Prague

For Don MacNeill, K mart Corp.'s top manager in Central Europe, it will be a moment good enough to make up for months of toil and trouble. "Can you imagine?" he asks as he stands outside K mart's partially refurbished store in central Prague, capital of the new Czech Republic. "Can you imagine a big red 'K' right up there? I'm looking forward to that. I really am."

It won't happen right away. K mart bought the huge Maj department store as part of a thirteen-store chain that sprawls across much of the former Czechoslovakia. But the going has been "very slow," says MacNeill, who is managing director and chief operating officer for K mart's activities in the Czech Republic, Slovakia, and Eastern Europe.

In 1991, the Czech government offered K mart an opportunity to select the best stores in the biggest cities from the huge state-owned Prior chain. Moreover, K mart would be plunging into a pool essentially free of fellow American cut-rate retailing competitors: no Wal-Marts, no Targets, not a single super-warehouse store in all the land. And the Czech and Slovak market sits at the center of Central Europe, within a day's drive of tens of millions of other shoppers.

So K mart put down nearly $120 million to buy and renovate thirteen stores. That is a small sum compared with the $3 billion facelift K mart is carrying out in North America, but it marks a significant step nonetheless—and one fraught with problems.

For one thing, what K mart bought was a chain of stores only in theory. The Czechoslovak retailing sector, once a monstrosity of central planning, broke apart soon after the Communist collapse in 1989. By the time K mart came along, most of the stores were either winging it alone or limping along as clusters of three or four.

What passed for inventory made the Americans cringe. Warehouses by the dozen bulged with sweaters, dresses, and underwear from the mid-1980s. "When an item didn't sell," Mr. MacNeill explains, "it was simply sent back to the warehouse and then returned to the shelves a few years later for another try." This was terrifying stuff for a company that unloads slow-selling items at giveaway prices by announcing "blue-light" specials that last 30 minutes or less.

Turning the old Prior stores into real K marts involves dozens of details, some of which mean changing old habits. Sales clerks in one store were sent to the floor wearing tags announcing: "I'm here for you." The problem was, many of them weren't. "It didn't take us long to realize the clerks were finding places to hide," Mr. MacNeill recalls. "They felt a little shy about getting out among the customers. Their hiding spots are gone now."

That's why K mart isn't yet ready to put its name on any of the stores it bought.[25]

Questions

1. Do you think that K mart underestimated the importance of culture when it purchased the old Prior stores?
2. Should K mart have simply stayed in Western Europe where customers, clerks, and managers are more like those in the United States? Why or why not?
3. What are some of the tasks facing management before the stores are ready for the K mart sign?

Chapter 5

Social Responsibility
and Business Ethics

Learning Goals

After studying this chapter, you should be able to:

1 Explain the concept of social responsibility.

2 Present arguments for social responsibility.

3 Describe the aspects of social responsibility.

4 Discuss the effects that environmental, consumer, employee relations, and financial responsibility issues have had on business.

5 Understand the relationship between ethics and social responsibility.

6 Explain the role of ethics in business decision making.

Career Profile

Katie Cook began her career at United Medical Resources facing the challenge—and opportunity—of helping the company define exactly what its corporate communications department would be. She obtained her position as Corporate Communications Coordinator after being recommended to the president of UMR by another organization where she'd served as an intern. Katie describes it as being in the right place at the right time.

United Medical Resources is a managed care, third-party health benefits administrator. It aids companies in designing employee benefit plans and acts as a consultant by advising them on what types of health care packages will best meet their needs.

Katie's college background in liberal arts and economics prepared her for the variety of work she performs at United Medical Resources. She uses her technical skills in writing, editing, and page layout to prepare company newsletters, press releases, and speeches. In addition, her experience in analyzing and interpreting complicated information will be an asset to her throughout her career.

Overview

More and more people are asking what responsibility business has to society. This chapter addresses that issue. It defines social responsibility and explains why business should want more than just to make a profit. It looks at four broad issues affecting business: the environment, consumerism, employee relations, and financial responsibility. Finally it discusses how companies merge the issues of ethics and social responsibility.

THE IMPORTANCE OF SOCIAL RESPONSIBILITY

 Social responsibility is the concern of businesses for the welfare of society as a whole. It consists of obligations beyond those required by law or union contract. This definition makes two important points. First, social responsibility is voluntary. Beneficial action required by law, such as cleaning up factories that are polluting air and water, is not voluntary. Second, the obligations of social responsibility are broad. They extend beyond stockholders to workers, suppliers, consumers, and communities.

social responsibility
Concern of businesses for the welfare of society as a whole.

Social responsibility is the obligation of every employee in a company. A manager who leads a model personal life may still allow the company to pollute a river. This manager might think pollution is a public problem, one to be solved by society. However, the concept of social responsibility says the manager—and every other employee—must consider all of the firm's acts in terms of society as a whole.

THE RIGHT-TO-EXIST ARGUMENT

It seems logical to us today that businesses should be socially responsible. Many argue that society, through laws granting the right to own private property, gives businesses the right to exist. A firm is like a citizen of a country and thus has rights and duties.

Yet society can change its view of business rights and duties. In fact, today a new "social contract" seems to be giving businesses a broader social role. And businesses seem to be accepting this role. For instance, the chairman of Wisconsin Energy said that business executives should be making the world better, that they should do more than the average citizen.[1] Herman Miller, the large office furniture manufacturer, no longer uses tropical woods, such as rosewood, from endangered rain forests in its office desks and tables.[2]

MAKING A PROFIT—AND MORE

Some argue that business accomplishes its social responsibility by producing efficiently. The most notable proponent of this traditional view is economist Milton Friedman. In the mid-1990s, though, many businesses are taking a larger view of their impact on our communities and the environment. The old notion was often "If we can do it and make a profit and it isn't illegal, then go for it." Today, many executives are saying, "Yes, we can do it and make a profit and it's not illegal—but is it right?" For example, Lever Brothers has switched from plastic bottles that clogged landfills

■ Herman Miller, a large manufacturer of office furniture, recognizes its social responsibilities. The company no longer uses tropical woods from endangered rain forests to make its desks and tables.

to new "bag-in-a-box" containers for Wisk laundry detergent and Snuggle fabric softener. Gallo has stopped selling low-priced wine in skid-row areas. Conoco plans to buy only double-hull tankers in the future to cut down on oil spills.

Concept Check
- Explain the concept of social responsibility.
- Is making a profit the only responsibility of a business?

THE CASE FOR SOCIAL RESPONSIBILITY

2 Firms become socially responsible for several important reasons. These include creating a better environment for business, avoiding further government regulation, using available resources, and improving the firm's public image.

A BETTER ENVIRONMENT FOR BUSINESS

A good argument for social responsibility is that it creates a better environment for business. Workers who are satisfied with job conditions, for instance, are more efficient. If they are being paid enough, their purchasing power increases. Growing incomes mean more demand for additional goods and services. What's more, labor strife decreases, and turnover and absenteeism decline.

AVOIDANCE OF FURTHER GOVERNMENT REGULATION

A related argument for social responsibility is that such self-policing helps prevent further government regulation. Today, businesses must cope with a huge number of regulations. Many come from agencies trying to protect consumers and workers: the Consumer Product Safety Commission, the Environmental Protection Agency, the Equal Employment Opportunity Commission, the Federal Trade Commission, the Food and Drug Administration, and the Occupational Safety and Health Administration. Businesses that abuse their power can expect more regulation by these agencies and others—and all of society pays for that regulation.

BETTER USE OF BUSINESS RESOURCES

Businesses also have resources—plants and equipment, capital, and human resources—that can be applied to social problems. The argument is that businesses should use these resources, as good corporate citizens, for socially responsible projects. For instance, they can pay some of their best people to work on important community projects. Some firms, such as General Motors, Dow Chemical, and Tenneco, do this now. For years, Bell System companies have "loaned" executives to such projects as the United Way and Junior Achievement. Companies can also hire people with few skills and little education and help them improve. Firms that do these things do them not just because they have the resources but also because they believe it is the "right" thing to do.

Some companies donate money and equipment to worthy causes. G. D. Searle, for example, offers free heart disease drugs to poor patients. Honeywell spent $142,000 to fund a prenatal and early childhood project in a poor Minneapolis neighborhood with high rates of infant death and child abuse. Campbell Soup Company donated an expensive piece of equipment to Reed College, which specializes in training teachers, for its chemistry program. As social responsibility continues to become a part of doing business, such corporate programs will grow.

AN IMPROVED PUBLIC IMAGE

Businesses that become socially responsible improve their public image. Companies like Coca-Cola, Phillips Petroleum, and McDonald's advertise their efforts in the area of social responsibility. The payoff from a good reputation is large. It puts the company first in the minds of consumers and helps keep it there. Often a good image means that customers are willing to pay a little more for the company's products. A solid reputation also helps attract and retain good employees.

The flip side of the coin is that consumer groups sometimes boycott the products and stocks of companies that, in their view, act irresponsibly. Jesse Jackson's Operation PUSH urged a boycott of Nike products because it felt Nike unfairly used black athletes to attract inner-city kids. The ads influenced the children to buy shoes they could not afford. PUSH wanted Nike to deposit funds in black-owned banks, hire a black advertising agency, and put an African American on its board of directors. But Nike spends millions each year to help inner-city neighborhoods, so it did not give in to PUSH.

- How can socially responsible actions help business avoid more regulation?
- Just because business has the resources, should it use them on socially responsible acts?

ASPECTS OF SOCIAL RESPONSIBILITY

3 Peter Drucker, a management expert, said that we should look first at what an organization does to society and second at what it can do for society. This idea suggests that social responsibility has two basic dimensions: legality and responsibility.

ILLEGAL AND IRRESPONSIBLE BEHAVIOR

The idea of social responsibility is widespread today. Thus it is hard to imagine a company that would continually act in illegal and irresponsible ways. But such actions do occur sometimes. For example, Abbott Laboratories, manufacturers of Similac baby formula, raised the price of Similac eighteen times from 1980 through 1993. The total price increase for the formula was 207 percent during this period—six times the increase in the consumer price of milk, its basic ingredient. In 1993, Abbott was selling over $1.1 billion worth of Similac each year. But Abbott's huge Similac sales came from price agreements with competitors and cash grants to the American Academy of Pediatrics. Abbott recently settled a $140 million Florida antitrust suit. Abbott still faces antitrust actions by the Federal Trade Commission and nine state court lawsuits related to baby formula pricing.[3]

Businesses are often tempted to take illegal and irresponsible actions when the punishment is light and the risk is low. Assume a company knows that it is required to install pollution-control equipment at a cost of $750,000. The highest fine for not installing the equipment is only $10,000.

It would cost less—in financial terms—to be fined than to install the equipment. The Occupational Safety and Health Administration sets up and enforces safety and health standards. It has few inspectors and about five million businesses to watch. A company stands a chance of being inspected about once every seventy-seven years. Thus the temptation to ignore the law can be very strong.

IRRESPONSIBLE BUT LEGAL BEHAVIOR

Sometimes companies act irresponsibly, yet their actions are legal. For example, RJR Nabisco spends over $35 million each year promoting Camel cigarettes. Most ads show the slick cartoon character, Joe Camel, shooting pool, riding a motorcycle, or engaged in some activity that appeals to America's youths. A report in the *Journal of the American Medical Association* notes that Joe Camel is a recognized cartoon character among persons under 18 years old.[4] Despite appeals by the U.S. Surgeon General, RJR Nabisco has refused to drop the Joe Camel character. Do the ads work? Evidently so—Camel is one of the top three most preferred brands (along with Marlboro and Newport) of smokers under 18 years old.[5] Though Nabisco's behavior is legal, many consider it extremely irresponsible.

LEGAL AND RESPONSIBLE BEHAVIOR

The last category is the one in which most business activities fall. Most firms act legally, and most try to be socially responsible. Yet competition at home and abroad places real pressure on firms to balance social responsibility, commitment, and profitability. Firms that find it necessary to downsize, for example, can ill afford to do more for society.

▓ **Exhibit 5-1**
America's Most Admired Corporations

Source: Jennifer Reese, "America's Most Admired Corporations," *Fortune*, 8 February 1993, p. 45. ©1991 The Time Inc. Magazine Company. All rights reserved.

Rank	Last Year	Company
1	1	**Merck** Pharmaceuticals
2	2	**Rubbermaid** Rubber & plastic products
3	3	**Wal-Mart Stores** Retailing
4	8	**3M** Scientific, photo & control equipment
5	7	**Coca-Cola** Beverages
6	9	**Procter & Gamble** Soaps, cosmetics
7	5	**Levi Strauss Associates** Apparel
8	4	**Liz Claiborne** Apparel
9	15	**J. P. Morgan** Commercial banking
10	12	**Boeing** Aerospace

Many business leaders feel they should do even more to help society. A survey of executives from the 1,000 largest American corporations asked, "Should corporations become more directly involved in solving such social problems as substance abuse, homelessness, health care, and education?" Sixty-nine percent of the executives said yes.[6]

Many companies are trying to do more. For example, Bristol-Myers, Coca-Cola, General Motors, Exxon, Ford Motor, Citicorp, J. P. Morgan, and many others have agreed to help the National Black MBA Association persuade young African-Americans to look for executive jobs. The group, which has about 2,000 members, hopes to build a scholarship fund handing out $450,000 a year by the end of the decade.

Each year *Fortune* magazine publishes a list of the most admired U.S. corporations (see Exhibit 5-1). Although being admired and being socially responsible are not the same, they are related. At the least, one would not expect a socially irresponsible firm to make the top ten. As the exhibit shows, the most admired firms come from many industries.

What are the issues that firms must consider in their efforts to be socially responsible? Social issues do change over time. But among the most important issues facing business today are environmental problems, consumerism, employee relations, and financial responsibility—which are discussed in the following sections.

Concept Check
- What are the three aspects of social responsibility?
- Give an example of legal but irresponsible behavior.

ENVIRONMENTAL ISSUES AFFECTING BUSINESS

4 The world's forests are being destroyed fast. Every second, an area the size of a football field is laid bare. Plant and animal species are becoming extinct at the rate of seventeen per hour. A continent-size hole is opening up in the earth's protective ozone shield. Each year we throw out 80 percent more refuse than we did in 1960, causing over half of the nation's landfills to reach their capacity.[7] The United States and the world face some very big environmental problems. A recent study found that 80 percent of American consumers consider protecting the environment more important than keeping prices down.[8] In other words, we are willing to pay for a clean environment. On the other hand, Americans are also willing to pay to be able to throw things away. For example, consumers don't seem to mind that Bic Corporation's annual output of four million pens, three million razors, and 800,000 plastic lighters ends up in landfills.[9] Ray Winter, president of Bic, notes, "We really haven't seen any demand for increased recyclability for our products. We can't get our distributors to carry the pen refills that we already make. If Wal-Mart won't carry [the refills] what's the point?"[10] The point is simply that disposable packages and products harm our ecosystem.

■ The depletion of the ozone layer is one environmental issue affecting business. A survey showed that environmental concerns have a bearing on the purchase decisions of 96 percent of consumers.

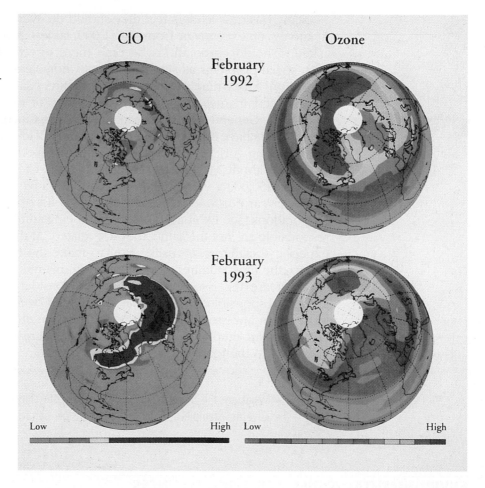

ECOLOGY

Ecology is the study of living things and their environment. The *ecosystem* is the ecological community and the environment taken together. Because we are part of the ecosystem, each human act is closely linked with other acts in the chain of life.

Sometimes even the best things have bad consequences. For instance, motor vehicles let us quickly transport people and materials across great distances. But their widespread use also gives us air pollution, gasoline shortages, and depletion of the raw materials needed to produce the vehicles. Likewise, the irrigation of desert land in the high plains of Texas and in areas of Arizona and California has increased agricultural production. But the amount of water underlying these areas has fallen drastically in the past twenty years, raising the prospect of too little water for all the homes, businesses, and farms. Some people have found business opportunities in looking for ways to deal with the environmental problems facing the world today, as the following Global Business Trends box shows.

Using the Marketplace to Save Nature

To help protect delicate ecosystems in other parts of the world, one unique organization is using the free market system and the profit motive. A pioneer in environmental protection is Cultural Survival Enterprises (CSE), a human rights organization in Cambridge, Massachusetts. It aims to defend people whose traditional cultures are threatened by modern economic life—like the Indians of the Amazon Basin, where every day 1,400 acres of rain forest are cleared for timber, cattle raising, or mining. Charles M. Peters of the New York Botanical Garden has shown that a Peruvian rain forest is worth more alive than dead: The fruit and rubber it produces are fourteen times as valuable as its timber. Cultural Survival Enterprises, headed by anthropologist Jason Clay, helps natives form cooperatives to harvest and sell rain forest products.

CSE's biggest product is Rainforest Crunch, a peanut-brittle-like confection studded with cashews and Brazil nuts. It's sold as candy and is also used in Ben & Jerry's Rainforest Crunch Ice Cream. In addition, Clay has imported samples of 350 resins, oils, and pigments of proven usefulness in products from soap to furniture polish. Seventy-five corporations, including Body Shop, Mars, Safeway, and Canada's Loblaw supermarkets, have been working with the samples; seventeen are now steady customers.

More than nine million pounds of shelled Brazil nuts come to the U.S. annually. What sets CSE apart from competitors is its effort to put the profit into the hands of forest residents, giving them less reason to sell out to miners and loggers. Says Clay: "Poverty is as much a destroyer of the rain forest as greed. These people don't want to live in Stone Age zoos."

CSE takes the same approach in Africa and Asia—selling killer-bee wax and honey from Zambia, for example. Clay is eyeing the mushrooms, berries, tars, and resins found in North America's old-growth forests; some Native Americans have claims to a big share of revenue from products grown on their old lands. In this new environmentalism, entrepreneur and activist become one and the same.[11]

POLLUTION

When the environment is contaminated with the by-products of human activity, the result is *pollution*. Among the many pollutants are liquid and solid waste, discharges of gas and particles into the air, noise, heat, poison, and radiation. Some pollutants last a long time; some decompose rather quickly. Many pollutants (iron, for example) don't harm humans but kill plants and fish. Some pollutants, like DDT and mercury, become concentrated in the food chain. One animal eats several plants or animals that contain the pollutant, and thus the pollutant builds up in the larger animal. Years after the pollutant was released, the larger animal shows the effects. Humans, of course, may suffer a great deal, because they are at the top of the food chain.

Acid Rain

Acid rain, which falls mostly in the East and in Canada, contains a high level of acidity. Sulfur oxides released into the atmosphere, largely by coal-burning utilities in the Midwest, have been blamed for acid rain. Scientists are still debating how much damage acid rain does to trees and lake and river life.

If any industry should be concerned about acid rain, it is the paper industry. It uses wood pulp to make paper. Yet Champion International and International Paper, two large paper producers, report no damage to forests they own in areas where acid rain falls.

The U.S. Clean Air Act of 1990 is the first major triumph for those who believe the marketplace can play a big role in cleaning up the environment. To attack acid rain, the law requires huge reductions in emissions of sulfur dioxide by U.S. power plants. A utility may use any means it likes to cut emissions. Those that do more than their share can sell their "surplus" to companies not meeting the standards. This system gives companies an incentive to exceed what the law requires: They can create a valuable asset in tradable pollution permits, which inefficient companies can buy. That rewards innovation and frees the government from being a constant watchdog. Amendments to the Clean Air Act require that sulfur oxide "scrubbers" be installed in new power plants. Sulfur oxides in the air have dropped 32 percent since 1977, although the use of coal to produce power is up over 50 percent. Even with no new laws, sulfur oxide levels will fall as new plants are built and old ones are shut down.

Ozone

Ozone is a form of oxygen that shields life on earth from the ultraviolet rays of the sun. Scientists believe that the ozone is disappearing from a large section of the atmosphere, leaving a continent-size hole. They think chlorofluorocarbons (CFCs) released into the atmosphere are to blame. CFCs are used in refrigerators, air conditioners, and foam containers. Already new laws restrict the availability of freon (which contains CFCs) to individual consumers.

Although scientists disagree about how fast the hole is growing, they agree that something needs to be done about ozone depletion. The U.S. Senate has approved an international treaty that says industrial countries must cut their use of CFCs in half by 1998. The Environmental Protection Agency (EPA) recommended a total phaseout of CFCs. Substitutes are now being tested for cost and effectiveness.

Ozone in the atmosphere is good; ozone at ground level is bad. Sunlight and heat react with gasoline fumes and other compounds to form ozone. If the air is still, as it often is during summer heat waves, smog hangs close to the ground and ozone readings increase. Ozone can make even healthy people cough and feel chest pains. Long-term exposure to ozone may cause permanent damage to the lungs. Sadly, most big U.S. cities don't meet the EPA's clean-air standards. Tired of waiting for the federal government to enforce its rules, California is considering state laws that would help clean up the air.

Global Warming

A recent EPA study reports that the earth's average temperature is likely to rise between 1.8 and 3.6 degrees Fahrenheit in the next century. As the global economy expands, the world burns more coal, oil, and natural gas. The by-product, carbon dioxide, is the chief culprit in global warming (also called the greenhouse effect). Global warming will probably upset the balance of forces that makes the earth a good place for living things. Although a few degrees seems like a small increase, it could have drastic effects on ocean levels, rainfall, vegetation, agriculture, and our way of life on earth.

U.S. businesses and government are making progress in cutting back on use of the fossil fuels that contribute to global warming. During the past twenty years, our economy has grown about 45 percent. But our energy use has barely increased. In the long run, alternative fuel sources, such as wind and solar power, will have to be used more.

BUSINESS RESPONSE TO ENVIRONMENTAL PROBLEMS

■ Esprit clothing company's Ecollection was created with the idea that the best fashion statement is one that positively affects the world around us— aesthetically, culturally, and environmentally. The clothing is made of organically grown cotton and flax (linen) that is colored using natural dyes.

A recent survey found that 59 percent of those polled believe their health has been affected by the environment. Environmental concerns have a bearing on the purchase decisions of 96 percent of consumers.[12] The business community knows that society wants and expects its help with pollution and other environmental problems. Which companies are most friendly to our environment and which are the worst? *Fortune* magazine did an extensive study of American manufacturers with sales of over $400 million annually.[13] The authors scored companies from zero (worst) to ten (best) in twenty different performance categories. These included things like a company's emissions of toxic chemicals, as well as its written environmental policies, goals, and employee incentives. The scores were sup-

plemented with interviews with government officials, company executives, environmental groups, and other experts. The results are shown in Exhibit 5-2.

Dow Chemical, a company whose name was once synonymous with war chemicals napalm and Agent Orange, is now among America's top ten environmental champions. Four times a year, eight environmental advocates from around the world gather at the company's Midland, Michigan, headquarters to consult with senior managers and board members. Dow is the only major U.S. corporation that regularly lends its ear to such a high-level group.

At the plant level, Dow managers carry on this same kind of consultation with local environmental groups. They have an incentive to do so: Their salaries and bonuses are pegged to, among other things, how well environmental goals are met.

During the past twenty years, furniture maker Herman Miller has found a way to recycle or reuse nearly all the waste left over from the manufacturing process. Fabric scraps are sold to the auto industry to reuse as lining for cars; luggage makers buy Miller's leather trim for attache cases; stereo and auto manufacturers use vinyl for sound-deadening material. Headquarters is powered by a facility that turns wood scraps into energy and shaves $450,000 off the gas bill. Miller even has a thriving secondhand furniture business, which buys back its old furniture and refurbishes and resells it. That's how the company has reduced solid waste 80 percent since 1982.[14]

American Telephone & Telegraph is also steering an impressive environmental course. In 1990 the telecommunications company established goals for reducing air emissions, CFCs, solid waste, and hazardous waste. AT&T managed to eliminate virtually all its ozone-depleting substances by May 15, 1993, a year and a half before the company's goal, and two and a half years ahead of the worldwide ban.[15]

Many small companies are also environmentally active. The Seventh Generation catalog, published in South Burlington, Vermont, lists many

■ **Exhibit 5-2**
Who Scores Best on the Environment?

Source: Fay Rice, "Who Scores Best on the Environment?" *Fortune,* 26 July 1993, pp. 114–116.

The 10 leaders	The 10 most improved	The 10 laggards
AT&T	Ciba-Geigy	American Cyanamid
Apple Computer	Hewlett-Packard	Boeing
Church & Dwight	Johnson & Johnson	BP America
Clorox	S. C. Johnson & Son	E. I. DuPont de Nemours
Digital Equipment	Minn. Mining & Mfg. (3M)	General Electric
Dow Chemical	Nalco Chemical	International Paper
H. B. Fuller	Polaroid	Louisiana-Pacific
IBM	Shell Oil	Maxxam
Herman Miller	Sun	Monsanto
Xerox	Union Camp	USX

environmentally sensitive products. The list includes recycled paper products, organic baby foods, energy-saving fluorescent lights, and drain-cleaning enzymes safe for waterways. Ringer Inc. of Minneapolis markets nontoxic lawn and garden care products. Baubiologie of Pacific Grove, California, sells safe building materials, such as natural paints and stains.

design for disassembly (DFD) Making products with simple parts and materials so they are easy and cheap to take apart and recycle.

The latest in recycling technology is called **design for disassembly (DFD)**. It means that manufacturers simplify parts and materials so they can easily snap them apart and sort and recycle them. Glue and screws are enemies of DFD. "Pop-in, pop-out" two-way fasteners are used instead. Whirlpool, Digital Equipment, Electrolux, 3M, and General Electric are starting to build DFD into their products. BMW, for instance, now uses only five types of plastics in its cars instead of twenty, to reduce the cost of sorting disassembled cars.

responsible consumption Efficient use of resources by consumers and businesses with a view to the future.

The scarcity of environmental resources seems to be one of the facts of life. Scientists estimate that by the year 2010 the world's population will be so huge that nature and technology will have trouble meeting its needs. That means that we need to change our ways: to be prepared for energy crises and water shortages, to use less of scarce resources, to use more responsible products in place of those that are ecologically damaging. The goal is **responsible consumption**, the efficient use of resources by consumers and businesses with a view to the future.

Concept Check

- Explain the concept of ecology, and give an example.
- What is responsible consumption?

CONSUMER ISSUES AFFECTING BUSINESS

consumerism Organized effort by citizens, businesses, and government to protect consumers.

Another aspect of social responsibility is protection of consumers, or **consumerism**. This is another area in which society wants business to assume social responsibility. There are three sources of consumer protection. The first is consumer-oriented groups. They provide information that helps consumers make decisions about purchases. They also take a stand for consumers on public issues. The second source is government, through laws and regulations relating to consumers. The third source is business, when it tries to meet its social responsibilities.

THE GROWTH OF CONSUMERISM

The first U.S. consumer protection law, passed in 1872, made it a crime to cheat consumers through the mail. Another law, passed in 1883, banned the sale of unwholesome tea and the import of spoiled food and drink.

In 1962 President John F. Kennedy, in a special message to Congress, outlined what he saw as the four rights of consumers:

- The right to safety: protection against goods that may harm health or life

- The right to be informed: protection against fraudulent, deceitful, or grossly misleading information, advertising, labeling, and other practices, and access to the facts needed to make informed choices
- The right to choose: access to a variety of products at competitive prices
- The right to be heard: assurance that consumer interests will get full, sympathetic consideration in the creation of government policy

Consumerism peaked from the late 1960s through the mid-1970s, led by Ralph Nader and others. The consumer movement was based in large part on Kennedy's outline of consumer rights. The consumer movement has been less active in the 1980s and 1990s, for two reasons. First, consumers seem more satisfied with the goods and services they can buy. Second, American business is now exercising greater concern with and involvement in social responsibility issues. This awareness has helped managers foresee and prevent problems that anger consumers.

BUSINESS RESPONSE TO CONSUMERISM

Only a small portion of firms have been guilty of consumer abuse. Billions of honest exchanges occur every day. Indeed, many companies are trying new ways to respond to consumers' needs. General Motors, Ford, and Chrysler, for example, now have panels made up of volunteers to settle consumer disputes that are not resolved locally. GM interviews more than 2.5 million people annually to determine its customers' needs and problems, including the sales and service experience at GM dealerships. Also, GM has a new program to help physically-challenged individuals purchase vehicles that meet their special needs. The program even provides a $1,000 reimbursement to cover the cost of special driving equipment.[16]

Companies are also trying to improve product quality. Reynolds Metals, for instance, has hired a vice president whose only task is to ensure high product quality. At General Motors, quality audits have shown a 56 percent improvement for cars and a 37 percent improvement for trucks

■ In response to the special needs of some of its busy customers, the Hertz rental car company started the #1 Club Gold program. Members arriving at the airport are transported directly to their rental vehicle—avoiding long lines in the terminal—and the return procedure is also streamlined.

between 1988 and 1993.[17] Today, on average, there is less than one-half of one defect-per-vehicle difference between GM vehicles and those produced by Japanese manufacturers. Service businesses try to keep up quality through careful hiring and training and a strong commitment to excellence. Marriott states that every action it takes should be aimed at better customer service. Hertz #1 Club Gold program allows members to skip endless lines at rental counters. The customer goes directly to the courtesy bus at the airport and tells the driver his or her last name. The customer is dropped off at the reserved car which is already running—with the heater or air conditioner on, depending on the temperature. As they exit, customers show their driver's license and are on their way.[18]

The push for quality in both services and products is found throughout the world. In fact, meeting rigid quality standards may determine if a company can compete in world markets, as is shown in the following Quality Management Trends box.

T R E N D S

Quality Management

The Passport to Quality

A set of quality standards is rapidly becoming the passport required for success in the international marketplace. The standards were created in the late 1980s by the International Organization for Standardization. The set of five technical standards, known collectively as ISO 9000, was designed to offer a uniform way of determining whether manufacturing plants and service organizations implement and document sound quality procedures.

To register, a company must undergo an audit of its manufacturing and customer service processes, covering everything from how it designs, produces, and installs its goods to how it inspects, packages, and markets them. More than fifty countries, including the United States and those in the European Community (EC), have endorsed the standards.

There is no legal requirement that companies adopt the standards, but some experts say the guidelines eventually will largely determine what may be sold to and within the EC. Several EC industries—toys, construction products, gas appliances, machinery, some medical devices—have already announced timetables for adopting ISO standards. The regulations would apply to EC companies making those goods as well as to the manufacturers that supply parts or materials to those companies.

Companies should not view ISO registration as some trade barrier thrown up by the Europeans, however. The standards also are being integrated into the requirements for manufacturers that make products under contract for several U.S. government agencies including NASA, the Department of Defense, the Federal Aviation Administration, and the Food and Drug Administration.[19]

One excellent way to improve quality is for companies to communicate better with their customers. Whirlpool Corporation now has a twenty-four-hour "cool line." Customers can call toll-free from anywhere in the country to ask about company products or to complain. John Smale, Procter & Gamble's recently retired chairman, listened to tapes of P&G's hot line as he drove to and from work. Burger King's hot line handles up to 4,000 calls a day. Of those calls, 60 to 70 percent are complaints, 20 to 30 percent are compliments, and about 10 percent are questions or requests. A warning goes out to franchises if the number of similar complaints goes over preset guidelines.

Perhaps the business world's attitude toward consumerism is best expressed by business leaders themselves:

Every decision involves giving up something to get something. . . . The real intelligent course involves being sure that you deliver the quality the customer expects, not sacrificing quality to increase earnings. And if you make that call correctly, you may make a little less today but you're likely to make more in the future. So I think when an individual's goals or a corporation's goals are very much out of line with society's goals, they're in trouble. . . . The fact is you can't be a large, successful corporation and be working against the public will; not for long.
—*Richard Hecker, Chairman and CEO, DuPont*

The only way for a corporation to exist . . . is to be part of the whole society. We depend upon a healthy environment to sell our products, to hire people, to have customers to sell to. . . . I really do think, particularly the large corporations, if they are going to survive as entities, the only way to do that is feel a responsibility to the communities that [they] operate in . . . whether that's the country [they] operate in or a local community.
—*David T. Kearns, Chairman and CEO, Xerox*

Corporations can be short-sighted and worry only about our mission, products, and competitive standing. But we do it at our peril. The day will come when corporations will discover the price we pay for our indifference. We must realize that by ignoring the needs of others, we are actually ignoring our own needs in the long run. We may need the goodwill of a neighborhood to enlarge a corner store. We may need well-funded institutions of higher learning to turn out the skilled technical employees we require. We may need adequate community health care to curb absenteeism in our plants. Or we may need fair tax treatment for an industry to be able to compete in the world economy. However small or large our enterprise, we cannot isolate our business from the society around us. Nor can we function without its goodwill.
—*Robert D. Haas, President and CEO, Levi Strauss*[20]

If companies across the country adopt the philosophy of these three executives, then consumerism might die for lack of issues. Such philosophies, universally adopted, would go a long way toward making U.S. firms more competitive in world markets.

Concept Check

- Define consumerism, and discuss its current state.
- List the four basic rights of consumers.

EMPLOYEE RELATIONS ISSUES AFFECTING BUSINESS

discrimination Unfair and unequal treatment of certain classes of people.

A third major area in which businesses can show social responsibility is employee relations. Abuses in this area are various sorts of **discrimination**—the unfair and unequal treatment of certain classes of people.

DISCRIMINATION BY RACE, NATIONAL ORIGIN, AND RELIGION

The unfair treatment of people because of their race is *racism*. In recent years much effort has been made to overcome discrimination against racial minorities. Today it is illegal for organizations to discriminate on the basis of race. But the degree to which the American people have overcome racial discrimination in the workplace and in society at large is a matter of debate.

Another form of discrimination occurs when a group is treated unfairly because of its national origin or religion. An example is the exclusion of Jews from membership in many country clubs.

The group most likely to be discriminated against varies widely from place to place or from industry to industry. In New York City, for instance, Puerto Ricans are often discriminated against; in many Texas cities, Mexican-Americans are the ones discriminated against.

The landmark law banning discrimination is the Civil Rights Act of 1964. When the act was amended in 1972, the Equal Employment Opportunity Commission (EEOC) was created to help enforce the original law. The Civil Rights Act bans employment discrimination on the basis of race, sex, age, religion, color, or national origin. These requirements for nondiscriminatory treatment are called equal employment opportunity requirements. They apply to all private and public organizations.

A 1977 amendment to the Civil Rights Act required that firms doing business with the federal government make special efforts to recruit, hire, and promote women and members of minority groups. These require-

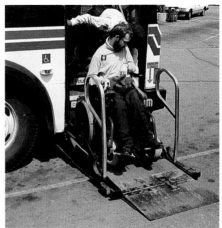

■ The Civil Rights Act of 1964 makes it illegal to discriminate against a person because of his or her race, sex, age, religion, color, or national origin. The Americans with Disabilities Act of 1970 seeks to make it easier for disabled people to get around independently and to do their jobs.

affirmative action Laws
that require firms to make
special efforts to recruit, hire,
and promote women and
members of minority groups.

ments are called **affirmative action**. Equal employment opportunity and
affirmative action have given hope and opportunity to many minorities in
the United States. Today, about two-thirds of the world's industrialized
nations have started or are setting up affirmative action programs.

DISCRIMINATION ON THE BASIS OF GENDER

The unfair treatment of people because of their gender is *sexism*. Discrimination of this type has generally been directed against women. In
employment, it occurs when men and women perform the same or very
similar jobs for different levels of pay or when they are segregated by type
of activity. In 1993, women still earned only 70 cents for every dollar
earned by men. This is up a dime since 1963—which means that women's
earnings have gained on men's by a ratio of one-third of one percent a
year over the past three decades.[21]

About three-fourths of the employed women in the United States have
typically female jobs. These jobs include secretary, household worker,
bookkeeper, elementary school teacher, and waitress. Only 11 percent of
employed women hold managerial or administrative jobs. Many women

glass ceiling A barrier of
subtle discrimination that impedes upward movement.

perceive a **glass ceiling**, or barrier of subtle discrimination, barring them
from moving up into the highest ranks. One recent study of 439 top-rank-
ing women at America's largest companies found that 90 percent still feel
that the glass ceiling is intact.[22] The survey respondents claimed that
"being a woman" more than any other issue was the greatest single career
obstacle they had to overcome.

Men can also be victims of sexism. For example, airlines have traditionally preferred female to male flight attendants. Women have also been
preferred as librarians, receptionists, and nurses.

Sexual Harassment

Sexual harassment is also a violation of the Civil Rights Act. The law bans
unwelcomed sexual advances and requests for sexual favors that hurt a
person's ability to do his or her job. It is also illegal for a supervisor to
promise a promotion in return for sexual favors and then not promote the
employee because he or she refused the sexual offer. Recently the courts
ruled that people also have the right to work in a place free of sexually
offensive pictures.

A survey of America's 1,000 largest corporations found that sexual
harassment complaints had been filed in 90 percent of these companies
during one year. The average amount each firm spent because of sexual
harassment was $6.7 million.[23] This figure includes the costs of employ-
ees quitting their jobs because of harassment, staying at their jobs but not
working as well, taking a leave of absence, or seeking help within or outside the company. The figure does not include legal costs or costs resulting from destructive behavior or sabotage. The vast majority of sexual
harassment complaints are filed by women, but not always. Recently in
Los Angeles a jury awarded a man $1 million because he was sexually
harassed by his female boss.[24]

AGE DISCRIMINATION

As Americans live longer, *ageism*—the unfair treatment of people because of their age—will probably increase. The elderly have been especially hurt by discrimination. Although federal laws ban age discrimination before age seventy, workers older than seventy still suffer from it. Often they are forced to leave their jobs even when they are healthy and doing well at their work.

Ageism is not limited to the elderly. Many large companies won't hire anyone over thirty-five for management jobs. They claim that a person thirty-five or older would be out of step in their promotion sequence.

Age discrimination cases are now often tried by juries. These juries are made up of people who have parents, relatives, and friends who fear losing their jobs just because they are getting older. Thus juries rarely come down on the side of large, faceless corporations. Age discrimination cases are the fastest-growing part of discrimination law.

Early retirement programs have also come under fire as a form of age discrimination. Du Pont, USX (formerly U.S. Steel), Gardner-Denver Corporation, Dresser Industries, and the National Geographic Society have faced legal challenges to their early retirement programs. The only successful company defense to the lawsuits has been that the programs are completely voluntary.

DISCRIMINATION AGAINST THE DISABLED

People with mental and physical disabilities are often denied job opportunities that they can handle just as well as the nondisabled. But the physical barriers to employing disabled people are starting to come down. For example, many companies are making their buildings accessible by wheelchair. Employers' attitudes seem to be improving as well.

In 1990 Congress passed the *Americans with Disabilities Act (ADA)* which took effect in 1992. This law requires public transportation systems, such as city buses, to accommodate people with disabilities, including those in wheelchairs. Now disabled persons have a means to get to and from work and can move toward independence. The law also requires any employer of twenty-five or more persons to make reasonable accommodations for the disabled. Today we are seeing more wheelchair ramps and automatic doors in buildings. Affected workers and job applicants are taking action. The Equal Employment Opportunity Commission (EEOC) received over 12,000 complaints during the law's first year. About 20 percent of the cases were resolved during the year, with disabled workers collecting over $11 million from employers.[25]

The ADA does have several important flaws. It does not require employers to hire qualified disabled employees. Nor does it set a deadline for installing accommodation facilities for the disabled. Remedy must be sought in court or at the EEOC, both often lengthy processes. Of the estimated 22.4 million people with a work disability, only 61 percent have found jobs.[26]

HELPING THE DISADVANTAGED

People who do not normally qualify for even the lowest-level jobs are termed disadvantaged, unemployable, or hard-core unemployed. They may not really be unemployable or even unemployed, although they typically spend a great deal of time without work. Besides the disabled, the disadvantaged and unemployable include high-school dropouts, people under twenty-two years of age, people over fifty-five years of age, the poor, minorities, ex-convicts, and people with alcohol or drug problems.

The disadvantaged have some unique problems. Many haven't applied for jobs for years because they consider their chances of getting a decent job very slim. They also may not know how to fill out job applications and other forms. And they may live a long way from the employment offices of major firms and have no means of transportation. Companies like General Motors, Honeywell, and AT&T now have successful programs for hiring and training the disadvantaged.

Concept Check
- Describe and discuss several forms of discrimination.
- Who are the disadvantaged, and how can business help them?

FINANCIAL RESPONSIBILITY ISSUES AFFECTING BUSINESS

A fourth area of social responsibility for business is financial activities. Abuses in this area have been much in the news. Companies and individual employees have been challenged on the issues of excessive executive compensation and insider trading.

EXCESSIVE EXECUTIVE COMPENSATION

Today it is common for top executives of big companies to receive $1 million or more in annual income. In 1992, seven executives received over $30 million.[27] In addition to salaries, these people get year-end bonuses, options to buy company stock at below-market prices, gifts of stock, and bonuses for good performance. The total of these payments plus salary is called *compensation.*

One study of the seventy top executives found that only 10 percent of their salaries related to changes in corporate profits, sales, or assets.[28] That is, whether the company performed well or not, 90 percent of the salary would be paid. And executive salaries, on average, continue to rise regardless of the state of the economy. Today the average CEO's salary is thirty-five times that of the average worker. Executive recruiters claim the reason is a shortage of good top managers and the resulting competition to acquire and hold top executives.

Of course, not all executives are overpaid. Many have done an excellent job in guiding their firm's long-run success. Without their talents, thousands of workers would not have jobs. And some companies, such as

Eastman Kodak, Itel, Wells Fargo, and Anheuser-Busch, tie executive compensation very closely to company performance. The better the company does, the better the CEO does.

INSIDER TRADING

Wall Street stock traders usually make decisions based on information and rumors. Generally, if an investor wants to work hard enough, he or she can uncover the same data. As long as the investor has equal access to the information available to stock traders, there is no ethical problem. However, some high-powered financial traders, such as Ivan Boesky, Dennis Levine, and Michael Milken, made money by using information not available to others. Usually such "inside" information concerns one company taking over another, which often leads to a big jump in the stock price. A Wall Street trader who learns of the takeover before the general public can earn a huge profit by buying stock in the target company. Such *insider trading* is illegal.

Concept Check
- What is "excessive" executive compensation?
- Explain the concept of insider trading.

BUSINESS ETHICS

There is no doubt that certain behaviors, such as insider trading, are both illegal and unethical. Yet, ethical conduct in many other areas of business is often difficult to define in concrete terms.

ETHICS

business ethics
Standards for judging the rightness or wrongness of conduct in business practices, institutions, and actions.

Ethics is a set of standards for judging whether something is right or wrong. **Business ethics** involves such standards in business practices, institutions, and actions. When a corporation is criticized for discharging too many pollutants, it is being judged on ethical grounds. When a company is praised for hiring the disadvantaged, its ethics are judged positively. It is seen as contributing to human good.

Society expects businesspeople to act ethically. Their actions should not have unjust or harmful consequences, and they should not lead to social condemnation, loss of customer goodwill, disapproval by peers, or court action.

GUIDES TO ETHICAL CONDUCT

A businessperson must consider the ethical implications of any decision. Yet ethics aren't always clear-cut. At times, ethics depend on the situation and the time. Nevertheless, all of us must have an ethical base for both business and our personal lives.

■ This ad from the Phillips Petroleum Company focuses on its concern for the environment. More and more companies are realizing that ethical behavior and social responsibility can be a selling point.

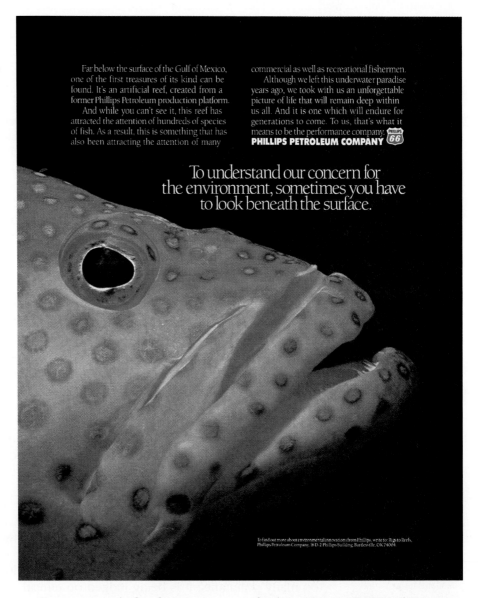

Far below the surface of the Gulf of Mexico, one of the first treasures of its kind can be found. It's an artificial reef, created from a former Phillips Petroleum production platform.

And while you can't see it, this reef has attracted the attention of hundreds of species of fish. As a result, this is something that has also been attracting the attention of many commercial as well as recreational fishermen.

Although we left this underwater paradise years ago, we took with us an unforgettable picture of life that will remain deep within us all. And it is one which will endure for generations to come. To us, that's what it means to be the performance company.

PHILLIPS PETROLEUM COMPANY 66

To understand our concern for the environment, sometimes you have to look beneath the surface.

To find out more about environmental innovations from Phillips, write to: Rigs to Reefs, Phillips Petroleum Company, 16-D-2 Phillips Building, Bartlesville, OK 74004.

One approach for forming a set of ethics is to examine the consequences of an act. Who is helped or hurt? How long-lasting are the consequences? What actions produce the greatest good for the most people? An example will show how complex the answers can be. Since 1939, the Maxwell House Coffee Company operated the world's largest coffee-processing plant in Hoboken, New Jersey.[29] For over a decade, rumors of a plant shutdown circulated. With health-conscious consumers cutting out caffeine, U.S. coffee drinking has been dropping steadily. Maxwell House's four U.S. plants were running at only 55 percent of capacity.

Thus it was no surprise when the company decided to combine all East Coast manufacturing—either at the Hoboken plant or at its Jacksonville, Florida, plant. The city of Hoboken wanted the plant to stay open. Maxwell House brought the area $520 million in direct sales and 600 manufacturing jobs. The plant was indirectly responsible for another

3,000 jobs in the area, plus $75 million in personal income and $90 million in regional business each year.

To keep the plant, Hoboken offered Maxwell House $7.1 million in tax breaks and another $2.5 million in reduced operating costs. Two days later, word leaked out that the firm's management had gone back to Jacksonville to get some breaks on labor costs. It wasn't long before the president of Maxwell House told the 600 workers in Hoboken that the world's largest coffee-processing plant would close in eighteen months. Hoboken had made a good offer. But the operating costs in Jacksonville were lower and would stay lower.

A day after the announcement, a local store started selling T-shirts with the legend "Maxwell House. The Last Drop Was Bitter." The first five dozen sold out overnight. Of course, the Hoboken employees were upset about the decision. Yet the company chose to do the greatest good for the greatest number of people. Its stockholders' earnings would improve because of the savings in operating costs. And the Jacksonville workers and their community would benefit.

A second approach to ethical behavior stresses rules. Do any rules, such as "Always treat others as you would like to be treated," apply in the situation? For example, ServiceMaster offers care and maintenance services for hospitals, schools, and factories. Top management always stresses empathy for the worker. It promises dignity to its janitors, groundskeepers, and launderers. Former chairman and CEO William Pollard expressed the company policy as follows: "Most people want to do a good job. If they're helped in determining what the job is, given the right tools, recognized for and praised for performance, they're going to respond."[30]

The last approach is to develop moral character. Morality is a relative concept; that is, moral standards may not agree from person to person. A person who is considered moral meets the standards of good behavior set by his or her peer group or by the larger society. In business, the standards and values of society as a whole are those that usually apply.

MAKING ETHICAL DECISIONS

Fortunately, most businesspeople have moved beyond a self-centered, childlike morality that is based on what will be immediately punished or rewarded. Businesspeople use the values they've acquired from family, educational, and religious institutions, as well as ideas from social movements like women's rights or environmental safety.

A businessperson with a mature set of ethical values accepts personal responsibility for decisions that affect the full community, including:

- Employees and the organization
- People directly affected by company activities, such as customers, suppliers, and stockholders
- Society at large

Many companies are writing down their codes of ethics. They also are beginning to help employees develop ethical values through training programs, counseling, and reporting systems. In the late 1980s, few companies had ethics officers. Today about 20 percent of America's large corporations have them.[31] Typically, ethics officers are at the vice presidential level.

Companies are using innovative techniques to teach employees about ethical behavior. Citicorp has developed an ethics board game, which teams of employees use to solve hypothetical problems. General Electric employees can tap into specially designed interactive software on their personal computers to get answers to ethical questions. At Texas Instruments, employees are treated to a weekly column on ethics over an international electronic news service. One popular feature is a kind of Dear Abby mailbag. With answers provided by the company's ethics officer, it deals with the troublesome issues employees face most often. Managers at Northrop are rated on their ethical behavior by peers and subordinates through anonymous questionnaires.[32]

One of the most effective tools ethics officers employ is a hot line through which workers on all levels can register complaints or ask about questionable behavior. Raytheon Corporation's hot line receives some 100 calls a month. Around 80 percent involve minor issues that can be resolved on the spot or referred to the human resources department. Another 10 percent of callers are simply looking for advice. But about ten times a month callers report some serious ethical lapse that must be brought to the attention of senior management.[33]

An important key to ethical behavior in organizations is top management. Younger executives and other employees tend to follow the lead of top management. If everyone knows unethical actions will not be accepted or excused, the company has taken a giant step in the right direction.

MERGING ETHICS AND SOCIAL RESPONSIBILITY

Can a firm be ethical yet not act responsibly? This question is still being debated, but the answer seems to be no. Today, most business leaders believe that ethics and social responsibility are intertwined. For instance, hiring the disadvantaged would be socially responsible. But hiring the disadvantaged for jobs that will soon be abolished would be unethical. Ethics concerns the rules by which social responsibility is carried out. Thus, it is hard to separate the rules of the game from the game itself.

ORGANIZING FOR SOCIAL RESPONSIBILITY

6

social audit Systematic assessment of company activities that have social impact.

To get a clear picture of their social responsibility and ethics, many companies undertake a **social audit**. This audit is a step-by-step assessment of and report on company activities that have social impact.

There is no best way to conduct a social audit. In one company, the CEO asked his public affairs group to figure out how to do one. Naturally, the public affairs group wanted to increase the company's role in community affairs. Thus it wanted to evaluate the link between social programs and long-range profits. In another company, the president wanted to satisfy his own conscience. Thus the issues chosen for the social audit were personally important to him.

To offset these problems, many large corporations use outside social auditors. These are experts who can impartially judge company policies and actions from a social viewpoint. A list of topics often examined in social audits appears in Exhibit 5-3.

Many companies also have a committee within the board of directors to decide which social programs they should work on. General Motors, for instance, has a public-policy committee composed of five members of the GM board. The committee meets once a month to make recommendations to GM's top management. A few other companies that use board members to guide their social responsibility policies are Ford, IBM, Kimberly-Clark (maker of Kleenex), and Philip Morris.

The result is that companies are having a good effect on society. For instance, Quaker Oats was thinking of building a major food plant in Danville, Illinois. It told the city's leaders that passing an open-housing ordinance would show that the city wanted to work for social progress. The ordinance passed. Two days later Quaker Oats approved the plan to

Exhibit 5-3
Topics Included in a
Social Audit

Education
- Gives direct financial aid to schools, including scholarships, grants, and tuition refunds
- Donates equipment and skilled employees to schools
- Aids in counseling and remedial education

Employment and training
- Actively recruits the disadvantaged
- Offers special training, remedial education, and counseling
- Provides day-care centers for children of working mothers
- Supports government accident, unemployment, health, and retirement systems, where needed

Civil rights and equal opportunity
- Ensures employment and advancement opportunities for minorities
- Facilitates equality of results by continued training and other special programs
- Encourages adoption of open-housing ordinances
- Provides financing and managerial assistance to minority enterprises and participates with minorities in joint ventures

Ecology and the environment
- Engineers new facilities for minimum environmental effects
- Cooperates with local, state, regional, and federal agencies to develop better systems of environmental management
- Develops more effective programs for recycling and reusing disposable materials

Conservation and recreation
- Augments the supply of renewable resources, like trees, with more productive species
- Preserves animal life and the ecology of forests and similar areas
- Provides recreational and aesthetic facilities for public use
- Improves the yield of scarce materials and recycles to conserve the supply

Culture and the arts
- Gives direct financial support to art institutions and the performing arts
- Participates on boards to give advice on legal, labor, and financial management problems

build the new plant in Danville. As more businesses put extra time, money, and effort into socially responsible projects, both society and the world of business will benefit.

- Define business ethics, and give examples of ethical and unethical behavior.
- Discuss several guidelines for ethical decision making.
- Explain the relationship between ethics and social responsibility.

■ SUMMARY

1. Explain the concept of social responsibility.
Social responsibility is the concern of business for the welfare of society as a whole. It is a voluntary obligation to society that extends to every employee in a company.

2. Present arguments for social responsibility.
Businesses accept social responsibility because (1) society has given them the right to exist and can change its rules for business whenever it wishes; (2) businesses must do more than just produce goods and services; (3) social responsibility can create a better environment for business; (4) when businesses assume social responsibility, the need for government regulation decreases; (5) businesses have the resources to deal with social problems; and (6) socially responsible businesses have a better public image.

3. Describe the aspects of social responsibility.
Social responsibility has two basic dimensions: legality and responsibility. The combinations considered here are actions that are illegal and irresponsible, irresponsible but legal, and legal and responsible.

4. Discuss the effects that environmental, consumer, employee relations, and financial responsibility issues have had on business.
Among the environmental issues that affect business are technological advances that have led to problems of scarcity and overuse. Pollution is another major concern. Business and government action has reduced many forms of pollution, but more must be done. The concept of responsible consumption is to use resources with a view to the future.

Consumer protection comes from consumer-oriented groups, government, and business. In the United States, consumer-protection laws have a long history, beginning in 1872. Since the mid-1980s, consumerism has returned to the grass-roots level. Many businesses support consumerism.

Employee relations are concerned mainly with the problem of discrimination because of race, national origin, gender, age, or physical or mental disability. The disadvantaged—those who cannot meet normal standards for getting even the lowest-level jobs—are a special problem. Business and government have both tried to reduce discrimination and help the disadvantaged.

Financial responsibility questions involve excessive executive compensation and insider trading. One way to solve the problem of excessive executive compensation is to tie payment to company performance. The federal government has cut down insider trading by punishing some of the biggest names in finance.

5. Understand the relationship between ethics and social responsibility. Today, most executives believe that social responsibility is an ethical issue. Managers often feel they must put aside their personal ethics to achieve corporate goals. This problem can be solved if top management supports ethical codes.

6. Explain the role of ethics in business decision making. A number of companies now use social audits to assess and report on company activities that have social impact. Some companies have even set up committees to decide which social programs to undertake. Others have enacted innovative programs to teach employees about mature ethical behavior.

■ DISCUSSION QUESTIONS

1. Do you think business ethics can be taught? Explain.

2. How might stockholders react to the use of corporate resources for socially responsible causes?

3. What are the limits to the social responsibilities of a business?

4. It has been said that businesses will solve pollution problems without government interference. Do you agree or disagree with this statement? Explain.

5. It has been said that it is difficult to make a profit and be ethical at the same time. Do you agree or disagree with this statement? Explain.

6. Do you think consumerism is dead? Why or why not?

include 4 rights of consumer
3 main sources of consumer

■ CASE

Stride Rite on the Move

Between 1990 and 1994, Stride Rite received fourteen public-service awards, praising the firm for "improving the quality of life" in its community and the nation. While doing good, Stride Rite also has done well. It posted a profit, usually a record one, for thirty-two consecutive quarters.

Stride Rite, manufacturer of Keds sneakers and Sperry Top-Sider shoes, has been socially active on many fronts. It has contributed 5 percent of its pretax profit to a charitable foundation, sent 100,000 pairs of sneakers to strife-torn Mozambique, paid Harvard graduate students to work in a Cambodian refugee camp, given scholarships to inner-city youths, permitted employees to tutor disadvantaged children on company time, and been a pioneer in setting up on-site day-care and elder-care facilities. Executives are proud of the many plaques for good deeds hanging in Stride Rite's gleaming Cambridge, Massachusetts, headquarters.

But just a few miles away, in Boston's rough, inner-city Roxbury neighborhood, stands another Stride Rite building: a weather-beaten, red-brick structure surrounded by empty lots, crumbling roads, and chain-link fences. It once housed corporate headquarters and employed 2,500 people making the company's shoes. Today, the building is just a distribution center employing only 175 workers. In late 1994, even they will be gone. Stride Rite plans to close the warehouse—and another one in nearby New Bedford—and move the operations to Kentucky.

In the past decade, Stride Rite has prospered partly by closing fifteen factories, mostly in the Northeast and several in depressed areas, and moving most of its production to various low-cost Asian countries. The company still employs 2,500 workers in the United States, but that number is down from a peak of about 6,000.

The labor cost savings of producing shoes in Asian countries is huge. Andy Li, a Taiwan contractor who has found subcontractors to work for Stride Rite, says skilled workers in China earn $100 to $150 a month, working 50 to 65 hours a week. Unskilled workers—packers and sorters—get $50 to $70 a month. By comparison, Stride Rite's U.S. workers average $1,200 to $1,400 per month in wages alone, plus modest fringe benefits.

Donald Gillis, executive director of Boston's Economic Development and Industrial Corporation, tried to persuade Stride Rite to stay in Roxbury. He says, "The most socially responsible thing a company can do is to give someone a job." Stride Rite contends it has little choice but to pull its distribution centers out of Roxbury and New Bedford. "It was a difficult decision," says Ervin Shames, Chairman of Stride Rite. "Our hearts said, 'Stay,' but our heads said, 'Move.'" Stride Rite will save millions of dollars, he adds, by going to the Midwest. When the company profiled its retailers, he says, "the average customer tended to be in the Midwestern or Southern part of the nation."

The new central location will make shipping generally more efficient. Now, most Stride Rite shoes are shipped from the Far East to Los Angeles and Seattle and then trucked to Boston and New Bedford, where they are sorted and labeled and then dispatched to retailers nationwide. The new distribution center in Louisville will eliminate up to 1,200 miles on some truck routes and will speed deliveries.

Stride Rite contends that it has been socially responsible but also has to balance the demands of two masters—shareholders and society. If a company doesn't stay competitive, its executives contend, it can't grow, it would provide fewer jobs, it would earn too little to afford its community programs, and, at worst, it might jeopardize its survival. "Putting jobs into places where it doesn't make economic sense," Chairman Shames says, "is a dilution of corporate and community wealth."[34]

Questions

1. Do you agree with Ervin Shames? Why or why not?
2. Do you agree with Don Gillis? Why or why not?
3. Do you think that Stride Rite is being socially responsible, or do you think the firm's reasons are just "window dressing" to cover the massive layoffs?
4. Some argue that companies like Stride Rite are "cutting their own throats" because if people don't have jobs they can't purchase the company's products. Comment.

Your Career in the International Business Environment

If you dream of faraway places, if you thrive on challenges and new experiences, if you cherish the differences that make each culture special—an international career may be for you.[1] But beware. A career in international business is not all glamour and excitement and may not always mean a foreign assignment. Not all international jobs are in Paris.

It takes a certain kind of person to adapt to the changes, stresses, and risks that are part of an international career. If you have trouble understanding why someone from another part of the United States acts a certain way, you can expect even more trouble when trying to negotiate with a Japanese or European client. On the other hand, if words like *adventuresome, self-confident, independent, quick-thinking, adaptable, curious, and open-minded* apply to you, the chances are good that you would make a good internationalist.

Working in a foreign country is a wonderful opportunity for learning and growth. Besides the adventure of exploring a new culture and making new friends, living and working abroad offers endless chances for personal and professional growth. You can learn to communicate in a foreign language, acquire new patterns of social interaction, and develop new skills in management and decision making.

Speak the Language

Learning a foreign language is a must. Learning a language is for direct communication and, more importantly, for understanding how the people of that culture think. A knowledge of the language is also the surest way to become accepted in a foreign country. Even if the people speak English as a second language, the fact that you can speak their language, even though with a limited vocabulary and an American accent, says a great deal about your sincere interest in doing business.

Beware of Culture Shock

Living and working abroad can be hard. Language, food, customs, and living conditions are not what you're used to. Subtle differences in thought, behavior, and emotions also put you at a disadvantage. Culture shock is inevitable. It affects everyone living in a foreign culture to some degree, especially those who work in a local firm.

Culture shock gradually decreases with time. Most people adapt to their new living and working environment within six months.

Consider a Short-Term International Job

One easy way to test the international waters is to take a short-term job in Europe. Getting a permit to work in the United Kingdom (England, Scotland, Wales, Northern Ireland) is very simple. In 1993, more than 5,000 students and recent graduates got permits to work there for up to six months. Most worked as waiters, hotel staff, bartenders, secretaries, or retail clerks. Then they returned to earn a graduate degree or start a career in the United States, with an international flavor to their resume.

Applicants must be full-time students or recent graduates. There is a $96 application fee, and a professor has to complete a multiple-choice reference form. Students graduating in the spring must enter the United Kingdom by December 31.

The program is operated by the nonprofit Council on International Educational Exchange (CIEE) in New York, which sponsors the exchange with the British Universities North America Club (BUNAC). Each summer, BUNAC sends thousands of British students to work in America. But this is no travel plan. All CIEE provides is a work permit. Getting airline tickets, housing, and a job is up to you.

CIEE also sponsors work exchanges with France, Germany, Ireland, Australia, New Zealand, Costa Rica, Jamaica, and Canada. The organization is hoping to begin exchange programs in Spain, Latin America, and central and eastern Europe as well. Still, most students choose the United Kingdom because it requires no foreign language skills, it's relatively close to home, and the wages generally are higher.[2]

Another opportunity for a short-term job is an international internship. International internships are much more abundant than you might think. There are opportunities for almost every specialty, including business, medicine, education, and law. Some are paid, some unpaid, and some you pay for. Most are abroad, although many are in the U.S. with private and government organizations. Some are tied to college programs that last a full semester, while others are designed to last a summer. A few can last up to two years.

One program offered by the Peace Corps allows participants to combine a year of on-campus work with a standard two-year assignment as a Peace Corps volunteer. The objective is to earn a master's degree upon completion. Most "official" international organizations, such as the World Bank and United Nations, also offer internships. At the U.N., internships are volunteer but offer perhaps the best experience among all government and volunteer agency jobs.

Many nonprofits working in international development sponsor internships as well. These programs tend to be volunteer and less structured than larger government efforts. Indeed, a big advantage to nonprofit programs is that interns often can arrange their own work schedules and choose which offices to work in.

Once you have an internship under your belt, finding a full-time international job

after graduation becomes much easier. For instance, the U.N.'s Food and Agriculture Organization (FAO) actively seeks recent graduates "who have had a relevant, industry-specific internship or volunteer experience with an international organization."[3] The corporate world values internships as well. Strong language and communication skills, plus some knowledge of the host country, are among the qualifications for employees being considered for overseas assignments.[4]

The best way to prospect for international internships and volunteer spots is to send a letter of inquiry, along with your resume, to organizations you've targeted through your research. They'll usually respond with detailed information about their programs, including eligibility requirements and application deadlines.

Know Where to Look for an International Job

International careers generally fall into one of two categories: business or government. Students with good preparation in international business often do well in government positions or in the not-for-profit sector. On the other hand, students geared toward a career in government may not have the skills in finance and marketing to go into the business world.

U.S. government positions include the Foreign Service, for which you must qualify by taking an examination. Positions are also available in the armed services and in such government organizations as the U.S. Agency for International Development, the International Trade Administration, and the Peace Corps, as noted above.

Some U.S.-based international organizations in the not-for-profit sector include CARE, Save the Children, Catholic Relief, Voice of America, and the United Nations. All like to have internationalists on their payroll.

In the business world, banking is at the core of most international transactions. Worldwide banks like Citibank, Chase Manhattan, BankAmerica, and Manufacturers Hanover all need people trained in international business. Other financial institutions, like American Express and Merrill Lynch, also have big international divisions. Many of these firms hire foreign nationals for their overseas positions. The Americans in their international offices often work as liaisons, handling overseas accounts, seeking international markets, or working with international portfolios.

Export/import positions are opening up around the world as companies expand their markets and seek new sources of parts and materials for manufacturing. Even small and medium-size U.S. firms are finding that their products are in demand outside the United States. Companies like Procter & Gamble, Carnation,

Johnson & Johnson, R. J. Reynolds, Firestone, Sears, Ford, Goodyear, Monsanto, and Kodak all do plenty of business outside the United States. Their products have become household words as far away as Japan, Brazil, and Australia.

Taking Advantage of NAFTA

Job opportunities for U.S. graduates will be found both north and south of the border because of NAFTA. The top five states currently exporting to Mexico are Texas, California, Michigan, Illinois, and Arizona. The six corresponding Mexican border states where trade activity is greatest are Tamaulipas, Nuevo Leon, Coahuila, Chihuahua, Sonora and Baja California.[5]

Although most Americans won't see hiring opportunities created in these Mexican states (NAFTA won't allow free access to jobs in other countries), company-sponsored new hires who have skills not found in the host country are welcome. That means engineers and computer specialists likely will get first priority, say recruiters. And while Spanish language skills are critical in many positions, they aren't always essential.

Projected boom areas in the U.S. include El Paso and south Texas, Las Cruces, N.M., Tucson, Arizona, and San Diego, says Briane Carter, career services director at the University of Texas-El Paso (UTEP). These areas have

been heavily developed in recent years through *maquiladora* (twin-plant) operations. Maquiladora plants were created to develop a manufacturing relationship between Mexico and the U.S. in which tax incentives are given to factories that partially assemble products in Mexico and complete the assembly process in the U.S.

Canadians are very aware that many jobs and industries will leave their country for Mexico after tariffs and trade barriers are cut, says John Jenkins, an international marketing professor at Wilfred Laurier University in Waterloo, Ontario.[6] Nevertheless, Canadian NAFTA negotiators say that in the long run, their economy will gain from the agreement. They'll lose out in labor-intensive industries, says Jenkins, but they expect to secure a competitive advantage in such "cultural industries" as telecommunications and publishing. For recent U.S. graduates, potential jobs in those industries may be available "up north," as will positions with American companies actively selling goods to Canadian customers.

When asked which industries will benefit most from NAFTA, trade experts seem to agree on six: telecommunications, environmental protection/cleanup, health care, transportation/logistics, financial services, and consulting. The Mexican telephone and information transfer system must be updated quickly, for example, and St. Louis-based

■ Working with the Peace Corps is good preparation for an international career.

Southwestern Bell Telephone Company is already under contract to help. In transportation, truckers now can make deliveries directly into border states. In future years, they'll be allowed to traverse Mexico and Canada to make in-country pickups and deliveries.

In financial services, Mexican companies hoping to do business in the U.S. likely will bow to the accounting and financial practices of their U.S. partners. As a result, demand for well-trained finance and accounting graduates will be excellent. If you become familiar with Mexican financial procedures and know Spanish, you'll rise to the top of the list.

And in consulting, NAFTA regulations will be constantly changing as new provisions are phased in and out. So companies and individuals who are well versed on the shifting landscape will be in demand as consultants. In

fact, they'll be worth their weight in gold to businesses trying to cross the NAFTA "financial mine field," say current consultants.

To advance your NAFTA-related hirability, start preparing now, career counselors advise. Extensively research the initialed NAFTA agreement, and seek opportunities to write papers on the subject for classes, regardless of your major. You might review the economic, social, linguistic, historic, or political aspects of the agreement, allowing you to become proficient in one or more of these areas.

Get involved in professional trade associations as a student member and join related clubs. Look for any available opportunity to use your campus setting as a NAFTA information generator. And be on the lookout for internships and summer jobs in regions expected to boom as the agreement takes effect. This will require lots of re-

search and cold calling to chambers of commerce and small businesses.

If becoming part of one of the largest trading alliances is your career goal, then don't wait for others to get the same idea. Establish a foothold now, and you'll leave the competition in the dust.

Business Structures

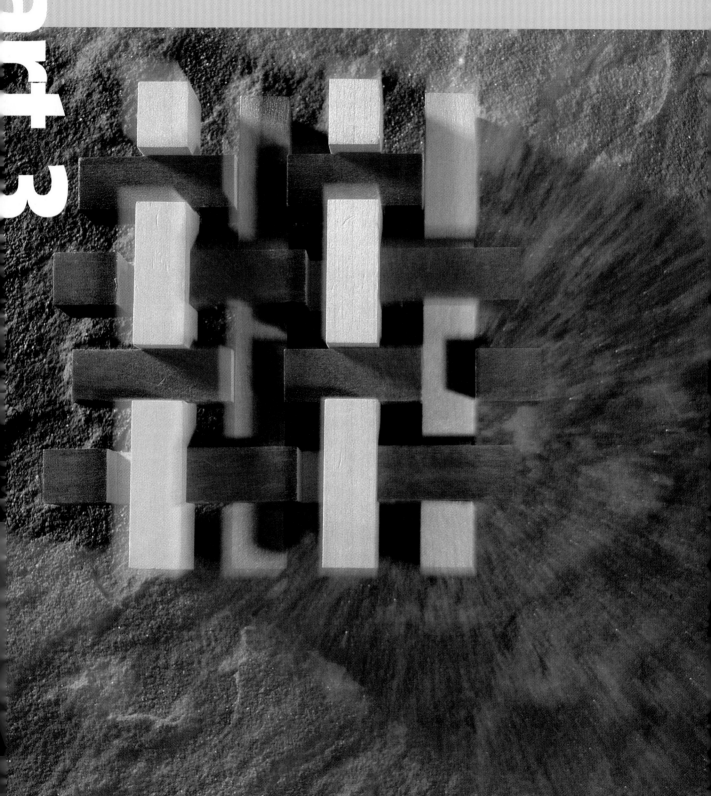

Overview

The 1980s has been called "the decade of financial engineering" because of the many mergers, acquisitions and leveraged buyouts it saw. Some corporations restructured in order to save money or reduce competition; others wanted to grow more quickly or acquire new technology. Deals were made at a furious pace, and purchase prices reached new highs. Americans were fascinated by the details of high-profile takeovers like Kohlberg Kravis Roberts' $25 billion acquisition of RJR Nabisco.

But while battles between corporate giants may grab headlines, the fact is that small businesses are the backbone of our country's economy. Businesses with less than 100 employees account for 98 percent of U.S. companies and employ one-third of all workers. These firms may be owned and managed by a single person, by a group of partners, or by many individuals who buy stock and provide capital for a corporation. One alternative to starting a business from scratch is to buy into a franchise operation. Franchising is one of the fastest growing segments of the economy and offers tremendous opportunities.

The structure of a business reflects its goals. Whichever organizational approach is chosen, however, small business owners usually work long hours and assume considerable obligations in order to make their dreams of success a reality. The following chapters will examine the many forms a business can take, from sole proprietorship to international corporation. They also cover entrepreneurship, franchising, and the basics of small business ownership. Such knowledge will certainly be valuable to anyone contemplating a business career, but any business owner will tell you that there's no better teacher than experience.

Subway is also the fastest growing franchise. Most of the company's seven thousand stores are located in the United States, but Subway is also expanding into the international market. Shops can be found in Canada, Australia, Japan, Israel, Ireland, Mexico, Portugal, and South Korea.

Subway founder Fred DeLuca credits his company's success to the commitment of the individual franchise owners, saying that they are the people "who make it happen." Even in a thriving franchise operation like Subway, the people who buy and run the local stores have to be willing to work long and hard to make their stores successful. One thing that should encourage them is the fact that franchise businesses, in general, tend to do better than independent businesses. According to the U.S. Department of Commerce, the success rate for franchise businesses is 92 percent, compared to only 23 percent for independent businesses. And after ten years, franchise businesses have a 90 percent success rate, compared to 18 percent for independent businesses.

Subway has big plans for the future. The company has set out to equal or exceed the number of outlets operated by the largest fast-food company in every market that it enters. With its long history of success and its current momentum, it is likely to reach that goal.

Subway

In 1965, Subway was a one-store operation in Bridgeport, Connecticut. Today, it is a major contender in the fast-food industry. The company's specialties are sub sandwiches served on fresh-baked bread and made-to-order salads. It's a healthy alternative to traditional fast food and has helped make Subway the number one franchise of any kind, according to *Entrepreneur* magazine.

Forms of Business Organization

Chapter 6

1. Define the three main forms of business organization.

2. Understand the factors to consider in choosing a form of business organization.

3. Discuss the advantages and disadvantages of sole proprietorships.

4. Define the different types of partnerships, and discuss the advantages and disadvantages of partnerships.

5. Describe the organizational structure, advantages, and disadvantages of corporations.

6. Discuss cooperatives, joint ventures, quasi-public corporations, and limited liability companies.

7. Understand the basics of mergers and acquisitions and recent merger trends.

Career Profile

Matt Yorke started Adept Entertainment, a disc jockey/music service, while still in college. His part-time pursuit has since blossomed into a full-blown career. Matt decided early on to focus on the college market and continues to do so. The business strategy he has developed allows him to provide an excellent program of entertainment for his clients at a reasonable and competitive rate while also clearing a good profit.

Matt started college as an economics major, later switching his course of study to management. The broad-based curriculum provided him with knowledge of many different aspects of business. This knowledge helps Matt deal with the various challenges he faces as the owner of a small company. Matt feels that the best preparation he had for his current situation was a course in entrepreneurship that blended what he had learned in his previous economics and management classes. The course inspired Matt to start Adept and gave him the tools to turn it into a prosperous business.

Adept Entertainment is a sole proprietorship. As the owner, Matt has assumed personal liability for any losses the business might experience in exchange for greater control and freedom than he would have working for a larger company. Now, though, Matt is considering franchising his successful formula. If he does, he will likely change Adept's organization to a partnership, or perhaps even a corporation, in order to generate funding for the expansion.

Overview

The first five chapters set forth the broad framework for our study of business: U.S. and world business systems, the economic environment in which businesses operate, our multicultural society and its implications for business, the global marketplace, and social responsibility and ethical issues. Now we will consider a more specific topic: the different ways a business can be organized. Anyone who decides to start a business must choose the form of business organization that will fulfill the goals of the firm and its owners. The three main forms of business organization—sole proprietorships, partnerships, and corporations—all have advantages and disadvantages. Some other forms of business organization—cooperatives, joint ventures, quasi-public corporations, and limited liability companies—have arisen for special situations. Finally, the chapter explores the impact of corporate restructuring and the merger and acquisition boom of the 1980s and 1990s.

TYPES OF BUSINESS ORGANIZATION

   When you start a business, you have many decisions to make. The first is the form of organization best suited to the needs of your business. To choose wisely, you must ask some important questions: Who will be responsible for the firm's debts and taxes? How will the business be taxed? How easily will it find financing? How much operating control do the owners want? Can the firm attract employees? What are the costs of the chosen form? The answers determine which type of organization you will choose.

Most businesses start as sole proprietorships. Many of them become partnerships or corporations as they expand. As shown in Exhibit 6-1, the sole proprietorship is by far the most popular form of private business ownership. It accounts for about 72 percent of all businesses. Corpora-

▦ Exhibit 6-1

Comparison of Forms of Business Organization

Source: U.S. Bureau of the Census, *Statistical Abstract of the United States, 1992,* 112th edition (Washington, D.C.: Government Printing Office, 1992), p. 520.

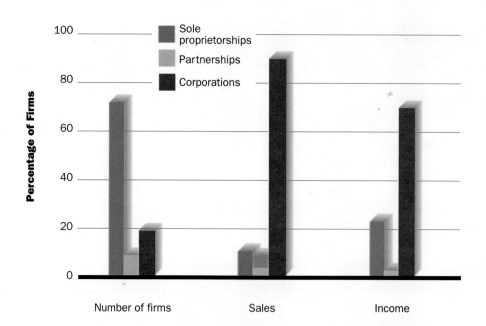

◼ In a sole proprietorship, the owner assumes personal financial liability in exchange for direct control of his or her business.

tions rank second, accounting for about 19 percent of all businesses. They are followed by partnerships, which represent about 9 percent of all businesses. However, as Exhibit 6-1 illustrates, corporations do much better than both sole proprietorships and partnerships in terms of sales and profits. They account for 90 percent of total sales and 74 percent of total profits.

Concept Check
- What are the major forms of business organization?
- How do they compare in terms of number of businesses, sales, and profits?

SOLE PROPRIETORSHIPS

3

sole proprietorships
Businesses established, owned, operated, and often financed by a single individual.

You are probably familiar with **sole proprietorships**, businesses that are established, owned, operated, and often financed by one person. The neighborhood florist, drugstore, hardware store, shoe repair shop, dry cleaner, and ice cream store are usually sole proprietorships. Small service businesses—such as lawyers, consultants, real estate agents, and accountants—often operate as sole proprietorships. Most sole proprietorships operate in five broad areas, as shown in Exhibit 6-2.

 The sole proprietor has complete responsibility for all business decisions. In most cases, he or she also works in the firm.

ADVANTAGES OF SOLE PROPRIETORSHIPS

Sole proprietorships have several advantages that make them popular:

✗ • *Ease and low cost of setting up:* The sole proprietorship is the easiest business form to set up. When the owner has the start-up funds,

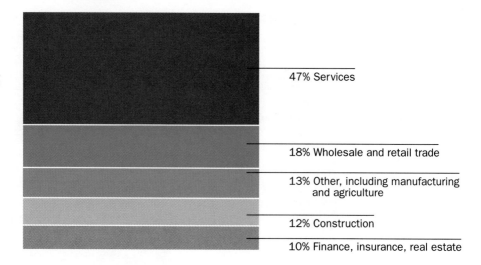

■ **Exhibit 6-2**
Most Popular Types of
Sole Proprietorships

Source: U.S. Bureau of the Census,
*Statistical Abstract of the United States,
1992,* 112th edition (Washington, D.C.:
Government Printing Office, 1992), p.
519.

47% Services

18% Wholesale and retail trade

13% Other, including manufacturing
and agriculture

12% Construction

10% Finance, insurance, real estate

he or she gets the required local licenses and permits (if any) and just starts business. This form of business can usually be set up without the help of an attorney. Thus sole proprietorships are the least expensive type of firm to start.

- *Profits that all go to the owner:* The owner of a sole proprietorship gets all the profits of the business. The owner tries to operate the business as efficiently as possible to increase its profits.

- *Direct control of the business:* The sole proprietor is his or her own boss, with responsibility for all business decisions. Direct control lets the owner keep the details secret, if desired (within the limits of the law, of course). A single owner can quickly adjust to changing business conditions. Independence is another big advantage of the sole proprietorship. As Chapter 7 explains, many people form sole proprietorships for lifestyle reasons.

- *Freedom from government regulation:* All businesses are subject to some government control, but sole proprietorships generally have more freedom than other business forms. Their formation is not controlled by law. But they still must obey the rules of government agencies, such as the Occupational Safety and Health Administration, the Environmental Protection Agency, the Internal Revenue Service, and local licensing agencies. For instance, no business may dump toxic waste, regardless of the organizational form.

- *No special taxation:* Proprietorships do not have to pay special franchise or corporate taxes. Their profits are taxed as personal income of the owner. (Taxation of sole proprietorships is discussed in more detail below.)

- *Ease of dissolution:* With no co-owners or partners involved, the proprietor can close or sell the business at any time. Thus owners often use sole proprietorships to test new business ideas before setting up a corporation, which is less flexible and more expensive to form.

DISADVANTAGES OF SOLE PROPRIETORSHIPS

Of course, sole proprietorships also have several disadvantages:

- *Unlimited liability:* In the eyes of the law, the sole proprietor and the firm are identical. Thus the owner is responsible for all business debts of the sole proprietorship—even when they are more than the value of the business. In the event of a lawsuit or failure of the business, the owner can be held personally liable and may be legally required to sell personal property—house, car, investments—to satisfy the claims against the business.

- *Difficulty in raising capital:* With unlimited liability, sole proprietors may have a hard time raising funds for their business. That's because business assets are not protected from the claims of personal creditors. For instance, a sole proprietor who doesn't pay a contractor for work done on her home could have some business assets seized or sold to satisfy the contractor's claims. This type of exposure increases the risk to any business lender. To finance their business, owners must often use personal funds—borrowing on life insurance, taking a second mortgage on their home, withdrawing money from savings and investments. Many make personal sacrifices that lower their standard of living. Even the successful sole proprietor must often take in partners or merge with another company to get the funds needed to expand.

- *Limited management expertise:* The success of a sole proprietorship is tied directly to the owner's talents. The owner of a sole proprietorship is fully responsible for all business decisions and must be a "jack-of-all-trades." But not all owners are equally skilled in all the areas required to run a business. For instance, an inventor who creates a new product may not be a good production manager or salesperson or accountant.

- *Personal time commitment:* A sole proprietor must be willing to make sacrifices to run a successful business. If an employee gets sick, the owner is usually the one who takes over. It is not unusual for the business to dominate the owner's life. Many sole proprietors work twelve or more hours a day, six or seven days a week.

- *Trouble in hiring qualified employees:* The sole proprietor may have trouble finding and keeping good employees. The small size of the business often limits the incentives it can offer. Chances for employee development and promotion may be limited. Sole proprietorships rarely provide fringe benefits because of their high cost. And job security is low because of the uncertainty of the business.

- *Unstable business life:* The life span of a sole proprietorship is uncertain and depends on the owner's continuing ability to keep operating the business. Sole proprietors sometimes lose interest in their business, run into financial trouble, or want to move on to something new. When a proprietor dies or is disabled, the business may cease to exist. This potential lack of continuity often makes it hard for a proprietor to obtain funds and hire staff.

- *Losses that all go to the owner:* The sole proprietor receives all profits but is also responsible for all losses. However, tax law allows these business losses to be deducted from other types of personal income, which somewhat reduces the pain.

TAXATION OF SOLE PROPRIETORSHIPS

As noted earlier, the sole proprietorship is neither a legal entity nor a taxable one. The profits of the business are reported on the owner's individual tax return. Business income is combined with all other personal income and taxed at personal income tax rates. The tax rates on personal income range up to 39.6 percent. The ability to combine business and personal income may provide a tax break. At some levels of taxable income, the personal rate is lower than the corporate rate, and vice versa.

Concept Check

- What is a sole proprietorship?
- Why do so many businesspeople choose this form of organization?
- What are the drawbacks to being a sole proprietor?

PARTNERSHIPS

4

partnership Association of two or more persons as co-owners of a business.

Another major form of business organization is the partnership. The Uniform Partnership Act, the law that governs partnerships in most states, defines a **partnership** as "an association of two or more persons to carry on as co-owners of a business for profit."

■ One must choose one's partners carefully when entering into a partnership agreement. An ideal partnership brings together people with complementary backgrounds rather than similar experience.

Some advantages of partnerships come quickly to mind. When you have a partner, you are not tied to the business as you would be in a sole proprietorship. Someone else helps manage and operate the firm and brings extra skills. Setting up a partnership takes a more formal agreement than starting a sole proprietorship, but partnerships are still quite easy to form. The co-owners agree to do business as partners and to get the required permits and licenses before starting operations.

Partnerships aren't as popular in the United States as the other forms of business, as we saw in Exhibit 6-1. Still, some types of professional service organizations have traditionally been partnerships. Many accounting firms, investment banks, stock brokerages, real estate companies, and law firms are set up as partnerships. Corporations and other businesses can also form partnerships, usually for a special project. These "joint ventures" are discussed later in this chapter.

PARTNERSHIP AGREEMENTS

partnership agreement Written statement of the terms and conditions of a partnership.

Although it is easy to start a partnership, serious conflicts sometimes arise between the partners. Such problems can hurt the business and personal relationships of the partners. Thus it is a good idea to write out the rules of the partnership, usually with the help of a lawyer. This **partnership agreement** puts in writing the terms and conditions of the partnership: what each partner contributes in money, talent, or equipment; the management duties of each; how the partners will be compensated (salary, share of profits); how partnership interests can be sold; and procedures for resolving conflicts, dissolving the business, and distributing its assets.

As in a marriage, choosing the right partner is critical. Ideally, partners should complement each other's skills: a technical and manufacturing expert with a financial and marketing specialist, for instance. Those who advise partnerships find that problems typically arise not for legal reasons but because partners don't pay enough attention to factors like goals, personalities, business values, and work habits. Even married couples who are business partners benefit from written rules.

TYPES OF PARTNERSHIPS

There are three basic types of partnerships: general, limited, and master limited. Each is structured to meet a different set of business goals.

General Partnerships

general partnership Partnership in which all partners share in the management and profits.

In a **general partnership,** all partners share in the management and profits. They co-own assets, and each can act on behalf of the firm. Each general partner has unlimited liability for all the business debts and contracts of the firm. Professional firms—architects, attorneys, accountants, and investment bankers—often organize as general partnerships. Recently, however, many of these partnerships are reevaluating this business form because of liability issues, as is shown in the following Service Economy Trends box.

The Perils of Partnerships

In March of 1992 the prestigious New York law firm of Kaye, Scholer, Fierman, Hays & Handler, accused by federal regulators of withholding damaging information during an investigation of its client Lincoln Savings & Loan, settled out of court for $41 million. The firm's insurance covered only $25 million of the total, so its 109 partners had to pay the remaining $16 million out of their own pockets. Why? Because in a professional partnership arrangement, partners share the power and the profits garnered by a firm but are also personally liable for the firm's misdeeds.

The penalty paid by Kaye Scholer is part of a wave of large court damage awards against U.S. accountants and attorneys. The total of such awards in 1992 alone was close to $1 billion. As a result of this phenomenon, many professional partnerships are looking for ways to limit their shared liability. Many have decided to abandon their partnership structure in favor of incorporation. That way, payments resulting from court judgments against the corporation would be made with corporate funds and only by executives responsible for the offense.

But as these professionals move to protect themselves, many of their clients feel threatened. If lawyers and accountants are no longer held personally responsible for their work, clients have less assurance that they will receive quality service and may have more problems settling malpractice suits. On the other hand, if professionals cannot limit their personal liability, clients with high-risk cases may find no lawyer or accountant willing to help them.

This flight from partnerships is partly due to the fact that they are not well suited to large firms. Partners in small firms can feel secure sharing liability collectively because they work together closely and know each other well. In recent years, however, many accounting, law, and architectural firms have expanded into huge enterprises with hundreds of partners and branches throughout the nation and the world. If these firms retain a partnership structure, a partner in Dallas can be held liable for the mistakes of a partner in New York whom he has never met. Many observers predict that ever-increasing liability risks may make the partnership a thing of the past.[1]

limited partnership Partnership that has two types of partners—general and limited.

general partners Those partners in a limited partnership who have unlimited liability.

limited partners Those partners in a limited partnership whose liability is limited to the amount of their investment and who do not participate in day-to-day management of the firm.

Limited Partnerships

A **limited partnership** has two types of partners: one or more **general partners,** who have unlimited liability, and one or more **limited partners,** whose liability is limited to the amount of their investment. In return for limited liability, limited partners agree not to take part in the day-to-day management of the firm. The limited partners thus help finance the business, but the general partners keep control of it.

This form of business organization was popular for tax reasons until the tax laws changed in 1986. Limited partnerships were formed to finance investment in specific ventures, such as oil and gas drilling, real estate, sports teams, and Broadway plays. However, they are not used much today.

Master Limited Partnerships

A newer form of business organization is the **master limited partnership (MLP)**. It is a hybrid: taxed like a partnership, operated like a corporation, and traded on a stock exchange. Master limited partnerships can be created by combining several limited partnerships. In some cases, corporations or divisions of corporations have formed master limited partnerships to take advantage of the tax benefits. Master limited partnerships are permitted by the Tax Reform Act of 1986 and receive some tax benefits through 1997. With the exception of energy and real estate MLPS, most are required to convert to corporations by the end of 1997. Master limited partnerships first formed in the real estate and oil industries but now are used in a variety of industries. The Boston Celtics basketball team is owned by a master limited partnership that trades on the New York Stock Exchange. Other examples include Mauna Loa Macadamia, Sahara Casino, Perkins Family Restaurants, and Cedar Fair (amusement parks).[2]

ADVANTAGES OF PARTNERSHIPS

All types of partnerships have some advantages in common:

- *Ease of formation:* Partnerships rank between sole proprietorships and corporations on this score. The partners have to agree to do business together and write a partnership agreement. But no complex state laws govern how most partnerships are set up.
- *Availability of capital:* Because the financial resources of more than one person are available to partnerships, they can get capital more easily than sole proprietorships. The financial strength of the partners also increases the firm's ability to find more funds.
- *Diversity of skills and expertise:* Ideal partnerships bring together people with backgrounds that complement one another, rather than people with similar experience. Combining partner skills to set goals, manage the overall direction of the firm, and solve business problems helps the firm succeed.
- *Flexibility:* Like sole proprietors, general partners are active in managing their firm. Thus partnerships can quickly respond to changes in the business environment.
- *Relative freedom from government control:* Partnerships have to obey state rules for licensing and permits. Otherwise, the government has little control over partnership activities.

DISADVANTAGES OF PARTNERSHIPS

Despite these advantages, there are reasons to avoid setting up a partnership:

- *Unlimited liability:* All general partners have unlimited liability for the debts of the business. In fact, any one partner can be held personally liable for all partnership debts and legal judgments (like malpractice), regardless of who caused them. As with a sole proprietorship, business failure can lead to a loss of the general partners' personal assets. Unlimited liability is considered the main disadvantage of partnerships.

- *Potential for conflicts between partners:* Each partner is an agent for the partnership. Thus one partner can take an action, such as signing a contract, that binds all the other partners. This joint responsibility can strain the relationships between partners and, if unresolved, can end the partnership.
- *Limited life:* Partnerships must be ended or reorganized when someone who owns more than 50 percent of the partnership dies, becomes incapacitated, or withdraws. A partnership may keep operating for a limited time so the remaining partners can form a new partnership. To avoid this problem, most partnerships have a *buy-sell agreement* that allows surviving partners to buy a deceased partner's interest. Often such a purchase is funded with the proceeds of a special life insurance policy (discussed in Chapter 24).
- *Sharing of profits:* The partners must share the profits of the business, although they don't have to share equally. Deciding on a fair division of profits can be a problem. If each partner contributes about the same amount in time, expertise, and capital, the profit-sharing formula may be simple. But if the partners contribute different sorts of things, the process is more difficult. For instance, in a real estate development partnership, one partner may provide the money and the other the "sweat equity" (hard work and management). In such a case, it is hard to place a value on the contribution of each partner.
- *Difficulty in leaving a partnership:* Partnerships are easier to form than to leave. It may be hard to sell a partnership interest if one partner wants to leave. If the remaining partners can't afford to buy the interest, they must find an acceptable purchaser. Specific guidelines for transfer of partnership interests are often included in partnership agreements. Selling limited partnership units can be even more difficult.

TAXATION OF PARTNERSHIPS

Partnerships must file partnership returns with the Internal Revenue Service, reporting the amount of profit and how it was divided among the partners, but they pay no income taxes. Each partner's profit is reported on the partner's personal income tax return and is taxed at personal tax rates. In the event of a partnership loss, each partner's share of the loss can sometimes be used to offset personal income.

The partnership form of organization, particularly the master limited partnership, can provide big tax savings. As with sole proprietorships, the tax advantage depends on the level of taxable income. Some MLP income is tax-deferred. When the MLP shares are sold, they are treated as a capital gain (the difference between the sale price and the original purchase price). The maximum tax on capital gains is currently (1993) 28 percent, versus the top rate of 39.6 percent for ordinary income.

- What is a partnership? Describe briefly the three types of partnerships, and explain the difference between a general partner and a limited partner.
- What are the main advantages and disadvantages of partnerships, and how do they compare to sole proprietorships?
- Compare and contrast the taxation of sole proprietorships and partnerships.

CORPORATIONS

5 When people think of business, most think of major, well-known corporations like Boeing, Apple Computer, and Procter & Gamble. Corporations are not the most popular form of business organization in terms of number of firms. But they account for the largest share of both sales and income.

corporation Legal business entity with a life separate from its owners, which limits the owners' liability.

The term **corporation** was first defined by Chief Justice John Marshall in 1819 as "an artificial being, invisible, intangible, and existing only in contemplation of the law." In other words, the corporation is a legal entity with an existence and life separate from its owners. Thus the owners' liability is limited. A corporation is subject to the laws of the state in which it is formed. The state issues a charter that gives the corporation the right to operate as a business and specifies its business goals. A corporation can own property, enter into contracts, sue and be sued, and engage in business operations under the terms of its charter. Unlike sole proprietorships and partnerships, corporations are taxable entities.

■ Large corporations are the most important non-governmental force in our economy. With their extensive resources and access to capital, they provide many of the goods and services we rely upon.

Corporations range in size from large multinational corporations with thousands of employees and sales in the billions to small firms with a few employees and revenues under $25,000. Many individuals and small businesses incorporate to benefit from the advantages of this form of business organization.

THE INCORPORATION PROCESS

Setting up a corporation is more complex than starting a sole proprietorship or partnership. Most states base their laws for chartering corporations on the Model Business Corporation Act of the American Bar Association. But states do have different registration procedures, fees, taxes, and laws regulating corporations.

A firm doesn't have to incorporate in the state where it is based. It may benefit by comparing the rules in several states before choosing a state of incorporation. Although it is a small state with few corporations actually based there, Delaware's pro-corporate policies have made it the state of incorporation for about 187,000 companies, including half of the Fortune 500.

Five main steps are involved in incorporating a business:

1. Selecting a name for the firm
2. Writing the articles of incorporation and filing them with the state, usually with the secretary of state
3. Paying the fees and taxes
4. Holding an organizational meeting
5. Adopting bylaws, electing directors, and passing the first operating resolutions

ARTICLES OF INCORPORATION

articles of incorporation Legal description of a corporation filed with the state in which it is incorporated.

The **articles of incorporation** are written on a form authorized or supplied by the state. Although they vary from state to state, the articles of incorporation must cover the name and address of the corporation; its goals; types of stock and number of shares of each type; life of the corporation (usually "perpetual," meaning with no time limit); minimum investment by the owners; methods for transferring shares; and names and addresses of the first board of directors and the incorporators.

bylaws Legal and managerial guidelines of a corporation.

The corporate charter is issued on the basis of the information in the articles of incorporation. Once the charter is issued, an organizational meeting is held to adopt bylaws, elect directors, and pass initial operating resolutions. **Bylaws** provide the legal and managerial guidelines for operating the firm.

THE CORPORATE STRUCTURE

As Exhibit 6-3 shows, corporations have their own organizational structure with three important components: stockholders, directors, and officers.

▓ Exhibit 6-3
Organizational Structure
of Corporations

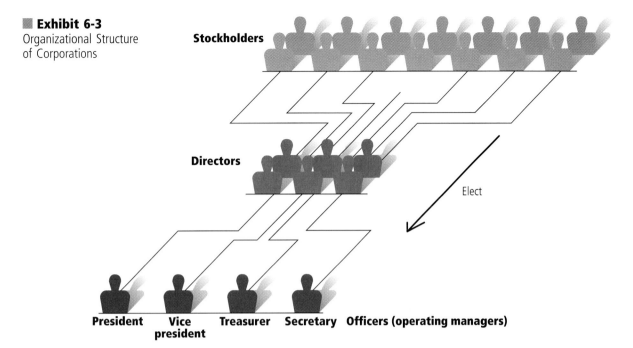

Stockholders

Directors

Elect

President Vice president Treasurer Secretary Officers (operating managers)

▓ Exhibit 6-4
Sample Stock Certificate

Source: Reprinted courtesy of Chevron
Corporation; © Chevron Corporation,
1984.

Stockholders

stockholders Owners of a
corporation, who hold shares
of stock that provide certain
rights; sometimes called
shareholders.

The owners of a corporation are its **stockholders,** sometimes called *shareholders,* who hold shares of stock that provide certain rights. They get some of the corporation's profits, in the form of dividends, and they can sell or transfer their ownership in the corporation (the shares of stock) at any time. A sample stock certificate is shown in Exhibit 6-4. Stockholders attend annual meetings, elect the board of directors, and vote on matters that affect the corporation, as the charter and bylaws specify. They generally have one vote for each share of stock owned.

Board of Directors

Those who govern a corporation are its **board of directors.** The directors, who are elected by the stockholders, handle overall management of the corporation. They set major corporate goals and policies, elect corporate officers, and oversee the corporation's operations and finances. The number of directors varies: Small firms may have as few as three; large corporations generally have fifteen to twenty-five.

In large corporations, the board of directors usually includes corporate executives and *outside directors* (not employed by the organization) who are chosen for their professional and personal expertise. Because they are independent of the firm and have varied experience, outside directors can bring a fresh view to the corporation's activities. Outside directors for major corporations are paid an annual fee of $10,000 to $20,000 or more for their work on the board.

Officers

The **officers** of the corporation are high-level employees responsible for achieving corporate goals and policies. Also called top management, the officers are elected by the board. They include the president and chief executive officer (CEO), vice president, treasurer, and secretary. Sometimes officers are also board members and stockholders. A company's top management hires and directs other employees, who are responsible for the firm's day-to-day operations.

CORPORATE OWNERSHIP

There are four types of corporate ownership. The common stock of a **privately owned firm** is not available to the general public. A **closely owned firm** belongs to a small group of investors (such as a family). The common stock of a **publicly owned firm** belongs to a broad group of unrelated individual and institutional investors or even another corporation. When most or all of a corporation's stock is controlled by another firm (the **parent company**), the corporation is called a **subsidiary.** Unlike a division or operating unit, a subsidiary is a chartered corporation in its own right. Some well-known closely owned corporations include Levi Strauss, United Parcel Service, Hallmark Cards, and Estée Lauder. Clothing retailer The Gap, a publicly owned corporation, is the parent of subsidiaries Banana Republic, Inc., and The Pottery Barn.

Most small corporations are privately or closely owned. Most large corporations are publicly owned, and their shares are actively traded. But in the late 1980s, many large corporations "went private," which means that management or a group of major stockholders bought back the stock. If the corporation has fewer than 500 stockholders and no longer trades shares on the public stock exchanges, it doesn't have to publish financial information. This confidentiality allows management to closely control the corporation's activities. Examples of companies that went private since 1988 are Budget Rent a Car, Montgomery Ward, and Del Monte Foods.

The amount of influence that stockholders have depends on the size of the corporation and the number of stockholders. In a large corporation like AT&T, with 1.35 billion shares and about 2.5 million stockholders, most stockholders have very little influence. In small firms, the stockholder usually has greater influence over management.

ADVANTAGES OF CORPORATIONS

Certain features let corporations merge financial and human resources into enterprises with great potential for growth and profits. Among these advantages are:

- *Limited liability:* This is one of the main advantages of incorporation. Because the corporation is a legal entity that exists apart from its owners, a stockholder's liability for the debts of the firm is limited to the amount of stock owned. If the corporation goes bankrupt, creditors can look only to the assets of the corporation for payment.

- *Ease of transferring ownership:* Stockholders of public companies can sell their shares to someone else at any time. The transfer of ownership does not affect the status of the corporation, as it would in a sole proprietorship or a partnership.

- *Unlimited life:* The life of a corporation is unlimited. Corporate charters specify a number of years of life, but they also include rules for renewing the charter. The corporation is separate from its owners, so the death or withdrawal of a stockholder does not affect its existence.

- *Ability to attract additional financing:* Corporations can raise money by selling new shares of stock. Dividing ownership into smaller units makes it more affordable to a larger group of investors—from those who want a small amount to others who invest much larger amounts. Provided there are buyers (and there usually are), investors' funds are not tied up indefinitely. The larger size and the stability of corporations also helps them get bank loans. The availability of financing lets corporations grow much larger than sole proprietorships and partnerships.

DISADVANTAGES OF CORPORATIONS

The corporation might seem to have more advantages than the other two forms of business organization, but it does have some disadvantages as well:

- *Double taxation of profits:* Corporations must pay federal and state income taxes on their profits. Any profits paid to stockholders in the form of dividends are also taxed as personal income to them. Therefore, the same income is taxed twice.

- *Cost and complexity of formation:* Setting up a corporation takes many steps. Writing and filing the articles of incorporation usually require the services of a lawyer. Each state has filing fees and may also have license and registration fees. The filing requirements and costs vary from state to state.
- *More government restrictions:* Corporations are regulated more than sole proprietorships and partnerships. For instance, corporations must register in each state where they want to do business. Before selling stock to the public, they must register with the Securities and Exchange Commission (SEC). Unless it is closely held, the firm must publish financial reports on a regular basis. It must also file other special reports with the SEC and with state and federal agencies. These reporting requirements impose substantial costs. Publishing information on corporate operations may also give an advantage to competitors or takeover firms.

TAXATION OF CORPORATIONS

As noted earlier, corporations must pay income taxes on their profits. Under the current (1993) tax code, corporate tax rates range from 15 to 35 percent, compared to 15 to 39.6 percent on personal income. However, corporations receive certain tax deductions (such as for operating expenses) that reduce their taxable income. We will learn more about taxation in Chapter 23.

fiscal year The 12-month period used by a firm for accounting purposes.

Corporations must file their tax returns and pay income taxes within 2-1/2 months after the close of their **fiscal year,** the 12-month period used for accounting purposes. Businesses may choose a fiscal year other than the calendar year. They usually base their fiscal year on the pattern of seasonal operations, choosing a year-end date when inventories are low and easy to count. For example, retail operations usually have a fiscal year ending January 31, when inventories should be low due to the holiday selling season.

S Corporations

S corporation Business entity that provides limited liability to its stockholders but whose profits and losses are taxed as the personal income of the stockholders.

For some small corporations, double taxation of corporate profits is a major disadvantage. To avoid this problem, firms that meet certain size and ownership constraints can set up an **S corporation**. S corporations are organized like corporations, with stockholders, directors, and officers. But, like partnerships, their income and losses flow through to the stockholders and are taxed as the personal income of the stockholders, who retain the important corporate advantage of limited liability.

THE ROLE OF CORPORATIONS IN THE U.S. ECONOMY

Corporations play an important role in the U.S. economy. As we saw in Exhibit 6-1, corporations account for only 19 percent of all businesses but generate about 90 percent of the revenues and 74 percent of the income.

Rank 1993	Company	Sales ($ millions)	Profits* ($ millions)
1	GENERAL MOTORS Detroit	133,621.9	2,465.8
2	FORD MOTOR Dearborn, Mich.	108,521.0	2,529.0
3	EXXON Irving, Texas	97,825.0	5,280.0
4	INTL. BUSINESS MACHINES (IBM) Armonk, N.Y.	62,716.0	(8,101.0)
5	GENERAL ELECTRIC Fairfield, Conn.	60,823.0	4,315.0
6	MOBIL Fairfax, Va.	56,576.0	2,084.0
7	PHILIP MORRIS New York	50,621.0	3,091.0
8	CHRYSLER Highland Park, Mich.	43,600.0	(2,551.0)
9	TEXACO White Plains, N.Y.	34,359.0	1,068.0
10	E.I. DU PONT DE NEMOURS Wilmington, Del.	32,621.0	555.0
11	CHEVRON San Francisco	32,123.0	1,265.0
12	PROCTER & GAMBLE Cincinnati	30,433.0	(656.0)
13	AMOCO Chicago	25,336.0	1,820.0
14	BOEING Seattle	25,285.0	1,244.0
15	PEPSICO Purchase, N.Y.	25,020.7	1,587.9
16	CONAGRA Omaha	21,519.1	270.3
17	SHELL OIL Houston	20,853.0	781.0
18	UNITED TECHNOLOGIES Hartford	20,736.0	487.0
19	HEWLETT-PACKARD Palo Alto	20,317.0	1,177.0
20	EASTMAN KODAK Rochester, N.Y.	20,059.0	(1,515.0)
21	DOW CHEMICAL Midland, Mich.	18,060.0	644.0
22	ATLANTIC RICHFIELD Los Angeles	17,189.0	269.0
23	MOTOROLA Schaumburg, Ill.	16,963.0	1,022.0
24	USX Pittsburgh	16,844.0	(259.0)
25	RJR NABISCO HOLDINGS New York	15,140.0	(145.0)

* A number in parentheses indicates a loss rather than a profit.

Exhibit 6-5

The 25 Largest U.S. Industrial Corporations, Ranked by 1992 Sales

Source: "The Fortune 500," *Fortune*, 19 April 1993, p. 184.

Thus they are the most important nongovernmental force in our economy. Just scan Exhibit 6-5, which lists the largest industrial companies in the United States, and you will see many familiar names that affect daily life.

We tend to think of corporations as the large firms that make the headlines in *The Wall Street Journal*. However, over 80 percent of all U.S. corporations take in less than $500,000 a year. Small businesses incorporate to take advantage of such features as limited liability, unlimited life, and the ability to attract capital for growth. But size is indeed a benefit for many corporations, which have the resources to provide many of the goods and services we need. Could you imagine trying to make automobiles or jet engines as a sole proprietorship or partnership? In 1993, the top 1,000 industrial and service corporations, as listed by *Business Week,* accounted for $4 trillion in sales—an average sales level of $420 million each. Clearly, it would be impossible to grow and operate such a company as a sole proprietorship or partnership.

Concept Check

- What is a corporation?
- What are the three key groups in the corporate structure, and what are the responsibilities of each?
- Summarize the advantages and disadvantages of corporations. Which features have enabled corporations to dominate the business scene?

SPECIALIZED FORMS OF BUSINESS ORGANIZATION

6 In addition to the three main forms of business organization, several specialized types of business organization play a role in our economy. These are cooperatives, joint ventures, quasi-public corporations, and limited liability companies.

COOPERATIVES

cooperative Organization formed by individuals or businesses with similar interests to reduce costs and gain economic power through collective ownership.

Cooperatives are formed by people with similar interests in order to reduce costs and gain economic power. The member-owners pay annual fees and get a share of any profits.

A cooperative is a legal entity with several corporate features, such as limited liability, an unlimited life span, an elected board of directors, and

■ Citrus fruit growers who are members of Sunkist's agricultural cooperative pay dues to support market development and national advertising. By joining forces, smaller growers are able to compete effectively with large producers.

an administrative staff. Unlike a corporation, a cooperative does not keep profits. Instead, it distributes all profits to its members in proportion to their contribution. Since the coop keeps no profits, it pays no taxes.

There are two types of cooperatives. *Seller cooperatives* are popular in agriculture. Individual producers join to compete more effectively with large producers. Member dues support market development, national advertising, and other activities. Some familiar agricultural cooperatives are Sunkist (citrus fruit), Calavo (avocados), Blue Diamond (almonds), and Ocean Spray (cranberries).

Another form is the *buyer cooperative*, which buys in volume for the best possible prices. Food cooperatives are one example. College bookstores are also often operated as buyer cooperatives. At the end of the year, members get shares of the profits based on how much they bought.

Recently, small businesses have turned to cooperatives as a way to lower costs. By joining together for discounts, small companies are able to increase their efficiency and compete with larger domestic and foreign corporations. The National Cooperative Bank, which specializes in loans to co-ops, estimates that there about 20,000 cooperatives with two million members. Cooperatives are especially popular with fast-food franchises, and most have now followed the lead of Kentucky Fried Chicken, which formed its Food Service Purchasing Co-op in 1980. By reducing purchasing costs, these and similar cooperatives help the chains operate more profitably. Employers' Health Purchasing Co-op Inc., is a Seattle co-op formed to combine small companies into a larger group with more clout to negotiate with health insurers. High-tech companies are trying co-ops as well. Aldus Corp., the Seattle software company that developed a desktop-publishing program called PageMaker, has asked over 140 independent software firms to become part of a co-op that customizes PageMaker for specific professions. The co-op will market and distribute the software. Aldus benefits from increased sales of the basic program and the applications in new markets, while the co-op members get the profits from customizing the program.[3]

JOINT VENTURES

joint venture Entity formed by two or more companies to undertake a specific project.

In a **joint venture,** two or more companies form an alliance to pursue a specific project, usually for a specific time. There are many reasons for joint ventures. The project may be too large for one party to handle on its own. That was the case in the Trans-Alaska Pipeline, which cost over $20 billion. Another reason for joint ventures is that a company can gain access to new markets, products, or technology by working with a firm whose expertise complements its own. For example, Singapore Telecommunications International (STI) and Comcast, a U.S. cable television company, formed Cambridge Cable Ltd. to provide cable television and phone services in England. Many U.S. and foreign car manufacturers—Chrysler and Mitsubishi, Nissan and Mercury, and Ford and Mazda, for example—have formed joint ventures to expand their product lines. Mazda recently

From Rivalries to Alliances

In just three years, Toshiba Corporation has become the world's second-largest maker of color flat-panel displays for portable computers. But they didn't do it alone. Five years ago the company teamed up with IBM to form Display Technologies Inc. (DTI), which developed the technology for the displays and also manufactures them. This strategic alliance combined the strengths of these two major corporations. Toshiba was well-known for its manufacturing ability but wanted help to design the complex chips that make the colors on the screens vivid and the images clear. IBM was a proven chip designer but lacked the manufacturing ability to make the screens. So, each invested more than $250 million in DTI. The new company has been so successful that Toshiba and IBM hope to see their investment paid back in five years rather than the eight or ten they had anticipated.

Toshiba is currently involved in more than two dozen partnerships and joint ventures. These have allowed the firm to weather a severe economic slowdown in Japan. Such partnerships are becoming increasingly common in the 1990s, as rapid advances in technology have blurred the boundaries between the computer, telecommunications, and electronics industries. Developing the key components of this new technology involves astronomical costs. For instance, Toshiba estimates that its new random-access memory chip will require more than $1 billion to develop. Such costs, as well as the broad research capabilities necessary for high-tech R & D, are more than most companies can handle alone.

According to Toshiba president Fumio Sato, "The technology has become so advanced, and the markets so complex, that you simply can't expect to be the best at the whole process any longer." So, American companies such as Apple, AT&T, and Motorola are following Toshiba's lead and teaming up with former competitors, in order to gain a dominant position in the international high-tech market.[4]

began using a New Jersey Ford plant to manufacture trucks, rather than import them. Today, many joint ventures are technology-oriented and involve alliances between multinational companies, as the above Technology Trends box shows.

QUASI-PUBLIC CORPORATIONS

quasi-public corporation Business operated and often subsidized by a unit of local, state, or federal government.

Another type of corporation is the **quasi-public corporation.** A business that is too risky or lacks the profit potential to attract private investors can be operated by local, state, or federal government. Government financial support may also be required. The Tennessee Valley Authority, a rural electrification program started in the 1930s by the federal government, was one of the first quasi-public corporations. The Massachusetts and Pennsylvania turnpike authorities are state-owned quasi-public companies. Public ownership at the local government level is used to provide services when profit is not a consideration. Examples include water and

■ This water-treatment plant in Oakland, California, is a quasi-public corporation. The government built and operates the facility in order to provide a needed service to the citizens of the community.

sewer systems, parking garages, and civic and cultural facilities. The Museum of the State of New York in Albany and the Los Angeles County Museum of Art are examples of government-owned cultural organizations.

LIMITED LIABILITY COMPANIES

limited liability company (LLC) Business entity that provides liability protection to its owners but is taxed like a partnership.

A new type of business entity is the **limited liability company (LLC).** Like the S corporation, it provides liability protection but is taxed like a partnership. First authorized by Wyoming in 1977, LLCs gained popularity after a 1988 tax ruling that treats them like partnerships for tax purposes. The combination of limited liability and favorable tax treatment makes them attractive for many types of small businesses. Thirty-five states allow formation of LLCs, and thousands are now in existence.

The LLC permits flexibility in allocating both management control and income. Unlike the S corporation, it does not limit the number or type of owners. To qualify for LLC status, the organization must have fewer corporate characteristics—for example, centralized management, limited owners' liability, unlimited life—than noncorporate ones. Businesses that may wish to use or convert to LLC status include many start-up situations, existing general and limited partnerships, professional firms, and international ventures.[5]

Concept Check

- How do cooperatives differ from other forms of business organization?
- What are some of the reasons that businesses form joint ventures?
- Explain why quasi-public corporations are set up.
- Describe the advantages of the limited liability corporation.

CORPORATE GROWTH THROUGH MERGERS AND ACQUISITIONS

7 As noted in Chapter 1, many large merger and acquisition transactions took place in the 1980s, and they are again popular in the 1990s. Although mergers have been a part of American business since the 1880s, the recent boom of "merger mania" was different. Many companies were bought by corporate raiders for financial reasons rather than for an interest in the business itself. The frantic pace of merger activity slowed after 1989 but began to increase again in 1992. Today's mergers focus on strategic rather than financial objectives. Companies are acquiring other firms for their specialized knowledge of markets or technology, for example.

corporate restructuring Expanding or contracting a firm's operations or changing its ownership structure.

merger Combination of two or more firms to form one new company, which often has a new corporate identity.

acquisition Purchase of a firm by a corporation or investor group.

MERGER AND ACQUISITION BASICS

With all the merger and acquisition activity during the 1980s, many new terms were coined. They describe various forms of **corporate restructuring**—expanding or contracting a firm's operations or changing its ownership structure. A **merger** occurs when two or more firms combine to form one new company, which often takes on a new corporate identity. In an **acquisition,** a corporation or an investor group buys a corporation, and the identity of the acquired company may be lost. In Sprint's 1992 $3 billion acquisition of Centel Corp., Sprint was the *acquirer* and

■ Today's mergers and acquisitions often focus on strategic rather than financial objectives. Merck, the world's largest drug manufacturer, paid $6 billion to buy Medco Containment Services, a fast-growing mail-order company that shipped more than $2 billion of drugs in 1992. This acquisition gives Merck access to Medco's extensive distribution network and will make the company more competitive in the changing health-care industry.

Centel the *target*. Normally, the acquiring company finds a target company and, after analyzing the target carefully, negotiates with the management or stockholders of the target company.

If the top managers of the target company like the deal, they will recommend that stockholders approve it. This is called a **friendly merger.** Mergers can also be unfriendly. A **hostile takeover** occurs when the target's management or directors don't like the acquiring company's offer and try to block the transaction. PSI Resources, an Indiana public utility, fought off a hostile takeover by Ipalco Enterprises, another Indiana utility. It instead entered into a friendly merger with Cincinnati Gas and Electric.[6] Hostile takeovers and management defenses are discussed in more detail later in this chapter.

Types of Mergers

The three main types of mergers are horizontal, vertical, and conglomerate. A **horizontal merger** results when companies in the same industry merge to reduce costs, expand product offerings, or reduce competition. For example, in 1993 Primerica (now called Travelers Inc.) expanded its financial services empire by acquiring the Shearson brokerage unit from American Express as well as Travelers Insurance. The New York Times Co. purchased Affiliated Publications, Inc., publisher of the Boston Globe, to increase its market share in New England. The banking industry also experienced many horizontal mergers as banks looked for ways to expand into new regions and take advantage of economies of scale (cost savings as a result of running larger operations).

In a **vertical merger,** a company buys a firm in its same industry that is involved in an earlier or later stage of the production or sales process. Buying a supplier of raw materials, a distribution company, or a customer gives the acquiring firm more control. Merck & Co., the world's largest drug manufacturer, acquired Medco Containment Services, a high growth mail-order drug distributor, for $6 billion in 1993. This transaction made Merck the largest integrated pharmaceutical producer and distributor. It put Merck in an excellent competitive position to benefit from proposed changes in the health care industry.[7]

A **conglomerate merger** combines companies in unrelated businesses to reduce risk. Combining with a company whose products have a different seasonal pattern or that respond differently to the business cycle can result in a more stable pattern of sales. General Electric Co., for example, manufactures aircraft engines, appliances, power systems, and other industrial products; owns National Broadcasting Company (NBC); and offers insurance, financing, securities brokerage, and other financial services through GE Capital Services' subsidiaries.

Conglomerates are often formed as a **holding company.** The stock of the operating companies is owned by a parent corporation that may provide financial and administrative support but is not involved in operations. For instance, Dart Group is a holding company that owns Crown Books, Trak Auto, Shoppers Food Warehouse, Dart Group Financial, and Cabot-Morgan Real Estate.

friendly merger Combining of firms in which the target company supports the proposal of the acquiring company.

hostile takeover Combining of firms in which the target company does not welcome the proposal of the acquiring company and tries to block the transaction.

horizontal merger Combining of firms in which companies in the same industry merge to improve operations.

vertical merger Combining of firms in which a company acquires a firm in the same industry that is involved in an earlier or later stage of the production or sales process.

conglomerate merger Combining of firms in unrelated industries to reduce risk by diversifying operations.

holding company Firm that holds the stock of various operating companies and may provide financial and administrative support but not be involved with day-to-day operations.

Conglomerate mergers were popular in the 1970s and 1980s, a time when bigger meant better. Many corporations grew by acquiring companies in unrelated businesses. The trend today is to take a more focused approach. Many companies are selling off units that don't fit with their redefined corporate strategy. For example, in 1992 Sears decided to sell its financial services unit, Dean Witter Discover. Sears found that the idea of one-stop shopping for consumer goods and financial services did not work; it now has refocused its attention on its original retail business.

Motives for Corporate Restructuring

Companies undertake mergers and acquisitions for various reasons. Often mergers are used to improve the overall performance of the merged firms. Improvement can result from cost savings, elimination of overlapping operations, increased market share, or reduced competition. Growth, widening of product lines, and the ability to quickly acquire technology or management skill are other motives. Acquiring a company is often a faster, less risky, and less costly way to grow than developing products internally or expanding geographically. For instance, in 1993 AT&T entered the wireless communications field and also gained the possibility of providing local phone service by acquiring McCaw Cellular, the largest U.S. cellular operator, for $12.6 billion.[8] Dean Foods, the largest private label frozen vegetable processor in the U.S., agreed to acquire Birds Eye from the Kraft General Foods unit of Philip Morris in late 1993. The purchase not only doubled its frozen vegetable sales but gave Dean a new and growing product line, prepared frozen vegetables with sauces.[9]

The 1980s has been called the decade of "financial engineering." Most big transactions of that time were done for financial rather than strategic motives. A new form of acquisition called **leveraged buyouts (LBOs)** became popular then. LBOs are corporate takeovers financed by large amounts of borrowed money—as much as 90 percent of the purchase price. LBOs can be started by outside investors or by the corporation's management. Believing that the company is worth more than the value of all the stock, they buy the stock and take the company private. The purchasers expect to generate cash flow by improving operating efficiency or by selling off some units for cash that can be used to pay the debt. LBOs are rare today. Many of these transactions did not live up to investor expectations. Nor did operations generate enough cash to repay the debt. Take, for example, the 1988 RJR Nabisco deal, the largest LBO. Investment firm Kohlberg Kravis Roberts (KKR) paid nearly $25 billion to acquire RJR Nabisco because of its major consumer brands. But today the investors face losses due to intense competition and weakened demand in the food and tobacco industries.[10]

A form of corporate restructuring related to LBOs is **divestiture.** Parts of a company are sold for either strategic or financial reasons: getting rid of poorly performing units, getting cash for expansion, streamlining operations, or selling off units that no longer fit the company's goals. Today, many companies divest for strategic reasons. In 1992 Bristol-Myers Squibb decided to focus on its health care products and sold its Drackett unit

leveraged buyouts (LBOs) Mergers financed by large amounts of borrowed money.

divestiture Selling selected operating units for either strategic or financial reasons.

(maker of Windex and other well-known cleaning products) to S.C. Johnson & Son Inc., who wanted to increase its market share in cleaning products.[11]

Strategies for Fighting Hostile Takeovers

As noted earlier, merger proposals are not always supported by the target company's management. In such a case, the acquiring company or investor group can make a **tender offer,** a direct offer to buy some or all of the target company's shares at a price above the market price. To stop this sort of hostile takeover, the management of the target firm can use certain defensive strategies. Informing stockholders of management's reasons for opposing the takeover may discourage them from "tendering" their shares. Going deeply into debt to buy another company or divesting certain operating units may make the target less attractive to the acquirer.

Many new takeover defenses, some with colorful names, developed in the 1980s. The **white knight strategy** is to find an acquirer (the "white knight") friendlier to management than the acquiring firm. The target firm tries to merge with a firm that will let existing management keep operating the company. In the PSI Resources and Cincinnati Gas and Electric merger, Cincinnati Gas was the white knight.

A **poison pill strategy** is used to make a firm less attractive as a takeover candidate. A company could go further into debt to make the company financially riskier. It could give existing stockholders special voting rights or rights to buy more shares at a below-market price in the event of a takeover attempt. Kroger Co., a large supermarket chain, used a poison pill strategy in 1988 to prevent takeover attempts by KKR and the Dart Group. It borrowed $4 billion and paid it out as a dividend to its shareholders. This made Kroger a very highly leveraged company and served as a successful defense against the raiders.[12]

A **golden parachute strategy** promises expensive compensation packages to certain managers if they lose their jobs in a takeover. A golden parachute is another way to put a large financial burden on a company if it is acquired.

NEW TRENDS IN MERGERS AND ACQUISITIONS

Unlike the "financial engineering" and hostile takeover era of the 1980s, the merger and acquisition wave of the 1990s is driven by strategic motives. Now we are seeing a return to friendly mergers based on sound economics. Most are financed with stock (equity) and cash, rather than high levels of debt that can lead to financial ruin. More mergers will involve cross-border transactions with companies in different countries. For example, in 1994 Swiss drug firm Sandoz AG announced it would acquire Gerber Products Co., the baby-food maker, for $3.7 billion.

Many of today's transactions are driven by regulatory and technological changes. A 1992 law allows utility companies to sell power across state lines. Utilites are merging to gain economies of scale. In 1992, Entergy expanded its customer base in the Southeast by acquiring Gulf States Util-

tender offer Direct offer to buy some or all of a target company's stock at a price above the market price.

white knight strategy Defense against hostile takeover in which the target firm finds a more suitable acquirer.

poison pill strategy Defense against hostile takeover in which the target firm acts to make itself less desirable for acquisition.

golden parachute strategy Promise of expensive compensation packages to managers if they lose their jobs in a takeover, intended to make a firm less attractive as a takeover target.

ities for $2.3 billion.[13] In health care, the insurance reform movement provides incentives for companies to combine forces to become more competitive. Columbia Healthcare Corp. increased its revenues from $1 billion to $10 billion by purchasing two much larger companies, Galen Health Care and Hospital Corporation of America.[14]

The telecommunications industry is responsible for much of the increased merger activity. There has been a convergence of communication technologies—phone, cable, wireless, and computer—leading to mergers between companies with complementary technologies. These alliances allow the new firm to offer a wider range of information and communication services. In October 1993, Bell Atlantic, the third largest regional phone company, announced its intent to acquire Tele-Communications Inc. (TCI), the world's biggest cable television company, for about $26 billion. This merger would have created one company with the capability to develop and transmit interactive video services. Previously, phone and cable companies were seen as competitors in the information technology marketplace. The deal eventually fell apart, but there are certain to be other, similar combinations of firms in the personal communication services industry. Some may take place as mergers or acquisitions, others as joint ventures, as firms look to expand in this fast-moving field.[15]

Acquiring a minority interest in a company is another trend that is gaining popularity. Especially in the computer, communications, consumer electronics, entertainment, and publishing industries, companies use this technique to form alliances. They may establish links with customers, competitors, and suppliers, often on a global basis. For example, in June 1993 British Telecommunications (BT) purchased a 20 percent equity interest in MCI Communications, creating a joint venture to build a worldwide phone and computer network for multinational firms. BT benefits from MCI's marketing expertise and U.S. market share; MCI gets BT's international network and cash to fund future acquisitions of other telecommunication and multimedia companies. As a result, each improves its competitive position against rival AT&T.[16]

Concept Check

- What are the three types of corporate mergers?
- How can a firm defend itself against a hostile takeover?
- Discuss and compare corporate restructuring during the 1980s and 1990s.

■ SUMMARY

1. Define the three main forms of business organization.
A sole proprietorship is a business owned and operated by an individual. A partnership is an association of two or more people who operate a business as co-owners. A corporation is a legal entity with an existence separate from its owners.

2. Understand the factors to consider in choosing a form of business organization.

Key Terms

acquisition 194

articles of incorporation 184

board of directors 186

bylaws 184

closely owned firm 186

continued

When choosing a form of organization for a business, evaluate the owner's liability for the firm's debts, the ease and cost of forming the business, the ability to raise funds, the taxes, the degree of operating control the owner can retain, and the ability to attract employees.

3. Discuss the advantages and disadvantages of sole proprietorships.
The advantages of sole proprietorships include ease and low cost of formation, the owner's rights to all profits, the owner's direct control of the business, relative freedom from government regulation, the absence of special taxes, and ease of dissolution. Disadvantages include unlimited liability of the owner for debts, difficulty in raising capital, limited managerial expertise, large personal time commitment, unstable business life, difficulty in attracting qualified employees, and the owner's personal absorption of all losses.

4. Define the different types of partnerships, and discuss the advantages and disadvantages of partnerships.
The three types of partnership are the general partnership, limited partnership, and master limited partnership. In a general partnership, the partners co-own assets and share in the profits. Each partner is individually liable for all debts and contracts of the partnership. The operations of a limited partnership are managed by one or more general partners, who have unlimited liability. Limited partners are financial partners whose liability is limited to the amount of their investment; they do not participate in the firm's operations. The master limited partnership is operated like a corporation and has units that are traded on a stock exchange, but it is taxed like a partnership.

The advantages of partnerships include ease of formation, availability of capital, diversity of managerial expertise, flexibility to respond to changing business conditions, and relative freedom from government control. Disadvantages include unlimited liability for general partners, potential for conflict between partners, limited life, sharing of profits, and difficulty in leaving a partnership.

5. Describe the organizational structure, advantages, and disadvantages of corporations.
A corporation is a legal entity chartered by a state. Its organizational structure includes stockholders, the board of directors, and officers. Stockholders are the corporation's owners. They can sell or transfer their shares at any time and are entitled to receive profits in the form of dividends. The stockholders elect the board of directors, who govern the firm; the officers are top-level employees who carry out the goals and policies set by the board.

Advantages of corporations are limited liability, ease of transferring ownership, stable business life, and ability to attract financing. The main disadvantages are double taxation of profits, the cost and complexity of formation, and government restrictions.

6. Discuss cooperatives, joint ventures, quasi-public corporations, and limited liability companies.
Cooperatives are collectively owned by individuals or businesses with similar interests to achieve more economic power. All profits are distrib-

uted to members in proportion to the volume of business they do through the cooperative. Two types of cooperatives are seller and buyer cooperatives.

Joint ventures are formed by two or more companies to undertake a special project. They can be set up in various ways, such as partnerships or special-purpose corporations. By sharing managerial expertise, technology, products, and financial and operational resources, companies can reduce the risk of new enterprises.

Quasi-public corporations are businesses run by a government unit for the benefit of the public. They require government support because they may be too risky or lack the profit potential to attract private investors.

Limited liability companies provide limited liability for their owners but are taxed like a partnership. For many small businesses, the limited liability company is a good form of organization.

7. Understand the basics of mergers and acquisitions and mergers trends in the 1980s and 1990s.

Mergers occur when two companies combine to form one company; in an acquisition, one company or investor group buys another. There are three types of mergers. A horizontal merger involves companies in the same industry that merge to have more economic power, to diversify, or to win more market share. A vertical merger involves the acquisition of a firm that serves an earlier or later stage of the production or sales cycle, such as a supplier or distribution outlet. In a conglomerate merger, unrelated businesses come together to reduce risk through diversification.

Companies merge for strategic reasons, such as growth, diversification of product lines, increased market share, or greater buying power. The other main motive for merging is financial restructuring—cutting costs, selling off units, laying off employees, refinancing the company—to increase the value of the company to its stockholders. Leveraged buyouts, which are financed mostly by borrowed money, are a form of financial merger.

Mergers can be friendly or hostile. Management faced with a hostile takeover can defend itself by using strategies that make it unattractive to the acquiring company: increasing its debt burden, selling off operating units, finding a white knight, or using poison pills or golden parachutes.

Mergers and acquisitions of the 1980s tended to be large deals, and many were done for financial rather than strategic reasons. Although many corporate restructurings did improve efficiency, others—particularly financially motivated transactions—were not successful. The current trend is toward friendly, strategic mergers financed with equity and cash. Merger activity is especially high in industries undergoing regulatory and technological change, such as utilities, health care, and telecommunications.

■ DISCUSSION QUESTIONS

1. Choose a business you would like to start. What form of business organization do you think is best suited to your company? Why? What factors influenced your decision?

2. Say that you are the sole proprietor of a paper recycling company. You are offered the chance to buy a hazardous-waste disposal business. Would buying the new company cause you to rethink the form of business organization? Why?

3. Assume that you have been a salesperson in a bicycle shop for the last few years, that you have $7,500 in savings, and that you want to go into business for yourself. You also know you'll need a partner. What are the characteristics of the person you would seek?

4. You own 3 percent of the stock of a medium-size high-tech corporation. Recent performance has been disappointing, and from the annual report you learn that profits are again flat. The company has been losing market share because it has cut spending on research and development. Yet top management salaries have increased 15 to 20 percent in each of the last three years. You are angered by this information. What are some actions you could take to influence management?

5. Based on your understanding of the merger and acquisition activity of the 1980s, do you think corporate takeovers benefit society more than they harm it? Why or why not? Do you think mergers enhance U.S. productivity, or are they destructive?

■ CASE

Recipe for Success

Two sisters from Cleveland are finding out that there's more to business success than just having a great product. Heather and Hope Wilson discovered early on that choosing the right form of business organization is very important to a young company.

Two years ago, the Wilson sisters decided to start their own business when their homemade candy sold out at a charity bake sale. A local candy store owner offered to buy as much Frosted Swirl as they could make. The sisters formed a partnership and began manufacturing the candy in their own kitchen. The product sold quickly, and soon other stores were placing orders.

When a regional grocery store chain said it wanted to buy Frosted Swirl, the Wilson sisters knew they'd have to buy more equipment. But they didn't have enough money. To raise funds, they formed a corporation, Frosted Swirl Enterprises, and sold stock to friends and family. With the proceeds, they bought ovens and other equipment to mass-produce the candy. Today they have four ovens and five employees, and they produce Frosted Swirl and four other candies for regional distribution. Now a wholesaler wants to distribute Frosted Swirl throughout the United States. The sisters are considering further expansion of their company.

Questions
1. What were the advantages to the Wilsons of beginning as a partnership? What were the disadvantages?
2. For what reason did they decide to form a corporation? What are the advantages and disadvantages to the Wilsons of this form of ownership?

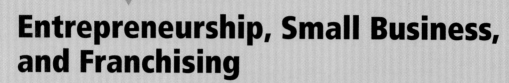

Entrepreneurship, Small Business, and Franchising

Learning Goals

After studying this chapter, you should be able to:

1 Define entrepreneurship, discuss why people become entrepreneurs, and describe the characteristics of successful entrepreneurs.

2 Understand what a small business is, and explain the economic importance of small businesses.

3 Describe the advantages and disadvantages of small business ownership.

4 Discuss the growing importance of women and minority business owners.

5 Describe the role of the Small Business Administration.

6 Discuss start-up and management considerations.

7 Define franchising, understand its importance, and recognize its advantages and disadvantages.

 Career Profile

Subway is one of the fastest-growing franchise businesses in the world, and managing one of the sandwich stores is a fast-paced, demanding job. Just ask Dean Dameron. In the five years he's been with the Subway organization, he's worked as a sandwich/salad prep person, an assistant manager, and a night manager. This "through the ranks" experience has given Dean a thorough knowledge of scheduling, product ordering, customer and employee relations, and the evaluation of food and labor costs. It is knowledge he now puts to good use in his current position, store manager.

Subway prides itself on promoting from within, and Dean Dameron is proof of the wisdom of this policy. This means of advancement gives employees confidence in themselves and trains them in all aspects of running a store. When other employees see people like Dean advance to higher positions, it encourages them to continue to do a good job.

An electronic media and communications major in college, Dean also took a variety of introductory level business courses. He utilizes the skills he learned at school to help him interact with customers, employees, and suppliers. His business background and communications skills have made him a better manager. This, combined with his on-the-job training and determination, will allow him to continue his rise in this fast-growing company. His aspiration is to own his own Subway franchise one day.

The 1990s has been called the decade of the entrepreneur. Small business in the United States has grown recently, helped by population and economic trends. Advances in technology make it possible for small companies to compete successfully with large corporations. As a result, small, flexible companies are prospering. This chapter begins with a discussion of entrepreneurship. Then it looks at the importance of small businesses in the economy, their advantages and disadvantages, and the role of the Small Business Administration. Next, it gives guidelines for starting and managing a small business. Finally, it explores franchising as a route to small business ownership.

ENTREPRENEURSHIP

entrepreneur A person who takes the risk of starting and managing a business in order to make a profit.

The entrepreneurial spirit plays an important role in the U.S. economy. People with the drive and creativity to start their own businesses are the foundation of the U.S. business system. The person who takes the risk of starting and managing a business to make a profit is an **entrepreneur**. As the examples in this chapter show, entrepreneurs are found in all industries. They come from all backgrounds and age groups and have different motives for starting companies.

Many of today's large companies were founded by entrepreneurs with vision and the drive to implement their ideas: Henry Ford started Ford Motor Company to mass-produce an affordable automobile. George Eastman developed the first Kodak camera while he was a bank clerk. King C. Gillette's safety razor launched the Gillette Company, a leader in personal care products. More recently, Steven Jobs and Steve Wozniak founded Apple Computer in a garage. Frederick Smith's idea for a new type of air freight service led to the development of Federal Express. And Ted Turner has made Turner Broadcasting System a major broadcast and cable television and publishing empire.

■ Ted Turner is a very successful entrepreneur. Through his vision and drive, Turner Broadcasting System has become a broadcast, cable television, and publishing empire.

Not all entrepreneurs want to own large firms. In every community, entrepreneurs have started small businesses just for personal satisfaction and the lifestyle. Virginia Lewey is a *lifestyle entrepreneur.* Formerly a partner in a Chicago law firm, she gave up a six-figure income to start Logan Beach, a café. She wanted a freer lifestyle, where she could wear jeans to work and have control over her business.[1]

On the other hand, the goal of *growth-oriented entrepreneurs* is to start a business that will grow into a major corporation. Most high-tech companies are formed by growth-oriented entrepreneurs. Larry Ellison cofounded Oracle Systems Corp in 1977 after reading an article on relational databases in an IBM publication. Oracle developed its database program three years ahead of IBM. By 1993 the company was a leader in software for corporate database programs. Ellison is now moving Oracle into multimedia communications products and is at the forefront of new technology for the information superhighway.[2]

Of course, many entrepreneurs start firms on a small scale and then expand beyond their first expectations. Howard Schultz's fast-growing Starbucks coffee bar and mail order business started with one store in Seattle. When visiting Italy in 1983, he realized there was a market in the U.S. for attractive coffee bars selling premium coffee drinks and beans. By 1993, his company had about 250 retail outlets on the West and East Coasts and was adding 70 to 90 new stores a year in other geographical areas.[3]

As you can see, the term *entrepreneur* covers a lot. It is often used in a broad sense to include most small-business owners. But there is a difference between entrepreneurship and small-business management. Entrepreneurship involves taking a risk, either to create a new business or to greatly change the scope and direction of an existing firm. The entrepreneur is typically an innovator with an idea for a new product who starts a company to pursue it. Thus some small-business owners are entrepreneurs. Others are managers who bought an existing business and made a conscious decision to stay small. The two groups share some of the same characteristics, and the reasons for becoming an entrepreneur or a small-business owner are very similar. Entrepreneurs generally take a longer-term view than the small-business owner. But otherwise the differences are not always clear.

WHY BECOME AN ENTREPRENEUR?

According to a recent survey, one out of every eight people has a secret desire to start a company. When those with a positive interest were contacted a year later, 25 percent had actually formed their own business. What prompted them to follow their instincts? Exhibit 7-1 shows how entrepreneurs in another survey ranked some important goals in starting a business: doing work they like, being their own boss, making more money (profits and personal income), and building a successful organization. Two other important basic motives are feeling personal satisfaction with your work and building the lifestyle that you prefer.

■ **Exhibit 7-1**
Entrepreneurs' Goals

Source: *New Business in America: The
Firms and Their Owners* (Washington,
D.C.: The NFIB Foundation, 1990), p. 18.

Goal	Percentage choosing goals as most important
The kind of work I want to do	26%
Avoid working for others	18
Make more money	18
Build a successful organization	29

■ **Exhibit 7-2**
Entrepreneurs' Personal
Objectives

Source: *New Business in America: The
Firms and Their Owners* (Washington,
D.C.: The NFIB Foundation, 1990), pp.
31–32, 61–62.

Goal	Percentage of entrepreneurs who	
	Rate goal important when starting business	Indicate business fulfills goal after 3 years
Have a challenge	73%	78%
Gain respect/recognition	41	63
Build something for family	74	58
Earn lots of money	46	20
Have greater control over my life	78	61
Fulfill others' expectations	21	41
Use my skills and abilities	81	83
Take best alternative available/have steady employment	81	52
Live where and how I like	52	58

Do entrepreneurs feel that going into business for themselves is worth it? The answer is a resounding yes. In one survey of people who had been in business three to four and a half years, 82 percent said they would do it over again. However, the way they ranked personal goals changed over time. Exhibit 7-2 compares their reasons for going into business with how well they felt the business fulfilled these goals after three years. It seems that the financial aspects were less fulfilling and the personal challenges slightly more fulfilling than expected.

CHARACTERISTICS OF THE SUCCESSFUL ENTREPRENEUR

Not everyone who wants to start a business is cut out for the entrepreneurial life. Being an entrepreneur requires special drive, perseverance, and a spirit of adventure. Having a great concept is not enough. An entrepreneur must also be able to develop and manage the company that implements the idea. Some entrepreneurs thrive on the early stages of the company's development and would rather move on to something new than manage the firm once it is established.

The Entrepreneurial Personality

Many of the studies on the entrepreneurial personality have found similar traits. But note that having many of the common traits does not guarantee success.

Entrepreneurs like to be independent, and they have a high need for achievement. They are self-starters who prefer to lead rather than follow. They have great self-confidence and persevere in the face of opposition. Entrepreneurs are aware of the challenges of starting a business, but they have faith in their ability to resolve problems and are good decision makers. Entrepreneurs must be risk takers. However, most successful entrepreneurs prefer a moderate degree of risk, in which they have a chance to control the outcome, over highly risky ventures that depend on luck.

Creativity is another entrepreneurial trait. To compete with larger firms, entrepreneurs need to have creative product designs, marketing strategies, and solutions to managerial problems. Good interpersonal and communication skills are also essential. These skills help entrepreneurs deal with employees, customers, and other businesspeople, such as bankers, accountants, and attorneys.

Entrepreneurs *are* the company; they cannot leave problems at the office at the end of the day. Studies have found that most entrepreneurs tend to work longer hours and take fewer vacations once they have their own company. Of course, entrepreneurs often work longer hours than corporate employees, especially at the beginning. Nancy Olson opened her first Imposters Copy Jewelry store in San Francisco. For several years she worked 80 hours a week. But her efforts paid off as her business grew from one store in 1985 to 105 stores throughout the United States.[4]

Entrepreneurs must also have a strong sense of commitment, a high energy level, and the willingness to make personal sacrifices to achieve their goals. For example, Scott Cook and Tom Proulx started Intuit Inc. in 1983. Convinced that available financial planning programs were too complex for the average person, they developed Quicken, an easy-to-use personal finance program. Cook and Proulx firmly believed that there was a large market for their program but couldn't get financing because lenders thought the program was too simple compared to its competitors. Rather than give up, they worked without salaries; found two small investors; used savings, credit card cash advances, and loans from family to keep the company alive. Intuit almost went bankrupt in 1985, but Cook was able to convince several banks to buy Quicken and resell it to customers. Mail order and then retail distribution followed. By 1993, Intuit was a $100 million public company, and Quicken is one of the most popular personal financial planning programs.[5]

Managerial Ability and Technical Knowledge

A person with all the characteristics of an entrepreneur might still be unable to run a successful business. Entrepreneurs need managerial ability to organize a company, develop operating strategies, get financing, and manage day-to-day activities. They also need technical knowledge to carry out their ideas. For instance, an entrepreneur may have a great idea for a new computer game and be a self-confident, hard-working, motivated person with good interpersonal skills. But without a detailed knowledge of computers, it would be nearly impossible for him or her to produce a computer game that would sell.

Managerial skills and technical knowledge can be learned. Working for a company in your field of interest is one way to develop skills, understanding, and experience before going out on your own.

- What is an entrepreneur? What are some major factors that motivate entrepreneurs to start businesses?
- Describe the personality traits and other skills characteristic of successful entrepreneurs.

SMALL BUSINESS

2   Small businesses are important to the U.S. economy. About 98 percent of the businesses in the United States have fewer than 100 employees. In fact, entrepreneurs have been forming small businesses since the founding of this country. The Industrial Revolution resulted in the creation of large businesses operating on a regional or national scale. Small businesses became unable to compete with the more cost-efficient larger firms. But recently there has been a renewed interest in entrepreneurship and small business.

Let's look at some of the main reasons behind the increase in small business formation. First, many employees have been forced to look for

■ There has lately been an increase in the formation of small businesses. One reason for this is that new technology, such as low-cost computers, makes it possible for small businesses to compete in industries that were formerly closed to them.

other jobs or careers due to recent major corporate restructurings and downsizings. Others are leaving the corporate world in mid-career in search of independence and a better lifestyle. Large corporations no longer represent job security or offer as many fast-track career opportunities. This has encouraged many new college and business school graduates to start their own companies or look for work in small firms. Thomas Madonia, a 1990 graduate of Emory University, had trouble finding a job in a weak economy. So using computer skills he developed as a hobby, he and a partner formed Atlanta Multigraphics. The firm provides computer graphics and animation services—for example, recreating accident scenes or architectural walk-throughs—for businesses.[6]

Other reasons for starting small businesses include the desire to gain personal satisfaction from work and the potential for profit. Also, as we discuss later in this chapter, more women and minorities are turning to business ownership as the best route to success.

Another major factor is rapidly changing technology—computers and automation especially—that gives individuals and small companies the power to provide services and make goods. This technology costs less today, making it easier for small companies to compete in industries that were formerly closed to them. The availability of overnight shipping services reduces the need for warehouses.[7] As mentioned in earlier chapters, the trend today is away from vertically integrated firms to specialized companies that contract with other firms for services. This "outsourcing" creates opportunities for smaller companies, many of whom provide major corporations with products and services.

WHAT IS A SMALL BUSINESS?

How many small businesses are there in the United States? Estimates range from about 4 million to almost 20 million, depending on how government agencies and other groups define a business and the size limits they use. The database of the federal Small Business Administration, which uses the number of business enterprises, lists about 5.1 million firms with fewer than 500 employees as of 1990.

So what makes a business "small"? As we've seen, there are different interpretations, and the range is extremely broad. But a **small business** generally is

small business Business that is owned by an individual or small group of investors, independently managed, locally based, and of little influence in its industry; its size may vary, from fewer than 500 to fewer than 100 employees.

- Independently managed
- Owned by an individual or a small group of investors
- Based locally (although the market it serves may be widespread)
- Not a dominant company (thus it has little influence in its industry)

Small businesses in the United States can be found in almost every industry group, as shown in Exhibit 7-3. Small businesses include the following:

- *Wholesale and retail trade: Retailers* are firms that sell goods or services directly to the end user. *Wholesalers* link manufacturers and retailers or industrial buyers; they assemble, store, and distribute products ranging from heavy machinery to produce. Small businesses

■ **Exhibit 7-3**
Types of Small Business,
by Industry

Source: U.S. Small Business Administration, *Small Business Data Base* (Washington, D.C.: Government Printing Office, 1992).

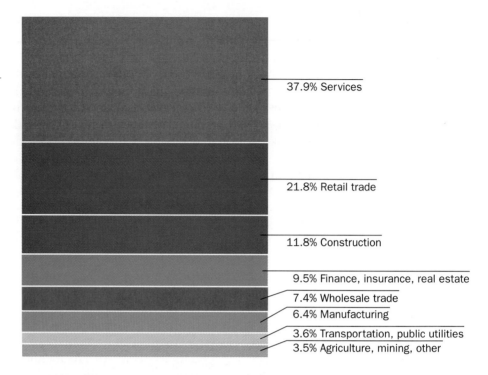

37.9% Services

21.8% Retail trade

11.8% Construction

9.5% Finance, insurance, real estate

7.4% Wholesale trade

6.4% Manufacturing

3.6% Transportation, public utilities

3.5% Agriculture, mining, other

such as Hydro-Scape, a San Diego-based wholesale distributor of irrigation equipment, dominate this broad category. About 85 percent of all wholesale firms have fewer than twenty employees. Most retailers also qualify as small businesses, whether they operate one store or a small chain. They typically sell to special markets not well served by large department store and discount chains. For example, Wolfman-Gold & Good, a twelve-year-old specialty tableware store in New York City, emphasizes value, wide selection, and custom and personalized orders.

- *Services:* Service firms also include a wide range of businesses. They are often small; very few service-oriented companies are considered national in scope. They include repair services, restaurants, specialized software companies, accountants, travel agencies, and management consultants. One type of service business that has become popular in recent years is the temporary help agency. With so many corporations cutting back staffing, "temp" agencies have moved beyond their traditional clerical and health-care markets into specialized areas, including attorneys, executives, and high-technology personnel. For example, On Assignment Inc. provides chemists, biologists, and other scientists on an as-needed basis. This concept has worked so well that the company now has twenty-seven offices around the United States.[8]

- *Manufacturing:* This category is dominated by large companies, but many small businesses produce goods. Machine shops, printing firms, clothing manufacturers, beverage bottlers, electronic equipment manufacturers, and furniture makers are often small manufacturers. In some industries, small manufacturing businesses have an advantage, since they can focus on customized products that would not be profitable for larger manufacturers.

- *Construction:* A large percentage of the nation's construction firms are small businesses. Firms employing under twenty people account for about 90 percent of all these companies. They include independent builders of industrial and residential properties and thousands of contractors in such trades as plumbing, electrical, roofing, and painting.

- *Agriculture:* Agriculture-related industry, including forestry and fisheries, is another category dominated by small businesses. The SBA estimates that 99 percent of all agricultural firms have fewer than 100 employees. Because it is hard for small farms to compete with large ones, many grow unusual products for specialty markets, such as certain plants for florists and fruits that were previously imported. For example, Ecke Poinsettia Growers in Encinitas, California, supplies most of the country's poinsettia plants. And The Green House, another Encinitas company, provides packaged fresh herbs for supermarkets.

THE ECONOMIC IMPORTANCE OF SMALL BUSINESSES

Small businesses play a big role in the U.S. economy. They account for about 40 percent of the gross domestic product and retail sales. Small businesses are also an important source of jobs. Firms with fewer than 500 employees provide jobs for over half of the labor force, with almost 40 percent in companies with under 100 employees. Within certain industries, the percentage is even higher. Data from the Small Business Administration shows that about 99 percent of all employees in construction, wholesale trade, and retail trade work in firms with under 500 employees. Even more important, businesses with fewer than 500 employees created almost all of the 5.8 million new jobs from 1987 to 1992. During that same period, 2.3 million jobs were lost in companies with over 500 employees.[9]

Small businesses also create more new goods and services than large firms. According to a recent study, small businesses produce about 2.4 times as many innovative products as large firms. During this century, small businesses have introduced synthetic insulin, the photocopier, the Polaroid camera, the helicopter, the personal computer, the zipper, and soft contact lenses. These firms stay close to their customers and can respond quickly to changes in their markets.

In addition to their direct contributions, small businesses have influenced the business world in other ways. Many large companies have been upstaged by small, innovative newcomers who are not hampered by bureaucracy. In the computer industry, start-ups like Microsoft, Dell, Oracle, and Compaq have pushed IBM from its leadership role. Biotechnology is another area where small companies, not large pharmaceutical firms, lead in new product development. Size is no longer necessary for success.

■ Biotechnology is one field in which small firms, unhampered by bureaucracy, lead large companies in new-product development. Synthetic insulin, for example, was introduced by a small corporation.

3   ADVANTAGES OF SMALL BUSINESS

Small businesses have advantages directly related to their size:

- *Greater flexibility:* Because most small businesses are owner-operated, they can react more quickly to changing market forces. They can develop product ideas and market opportunities without going through a lengthy approval process. An example is Zoom Telephonics. Founded in Boston as a telephone products firm, it got off to a successful start. But demand for its original product, a telephone speed dialer, disappeared when lengthy access codes were no longer needed to use long-distance carriers like Sprint and MCI. The company almost went bankrupt but quickly geared up to make different products. It turned to high-speed, low-priced fax modems that send text and graphics quickly to facsimile machines. These products are especially attractive to home-based and small businesses. Zoom is now one of the leading companies in a growing market.[10]

- *More efficient operation:* Small businesses are less complex than large organizations. They have fewer employees doing things that are not directly related to producing or selling the company's product (such as personnel management, accounting, and legal work). Thus they can keep their total costs down. If they need such help, small businesses can use outside specialists. This approach lets many small businesses make profits with lower prices than large firms can charge. Again, Zoom Telephonics is a good example. It keeps cost low by designing the products in-house and using contract firms for partial assembly.[11]

- *Greater ability to serve specialized markets:* Small businesses excel in serving specialized markets. Large firms tend to focus on goods and services with an established demand and the potential for high sales. Many products would not exist were it not for the small firm's ability to provide them cost-effectively. In-Land Technologies Services (ITS), a custom metal fabrication company, makes products too specialized for the customers to build themselves and too small for other firms to produce economically.[12] Another small company that serves its customers well is Singular Publishing Group, Inc., a San Diego-based medical publisher. Started in 1990 by Sadanand Singh, it focuses on highly technical, cutting-edge medical books. These books are too specialized for a larger publisher; their audience is limited. Singular maintains a database of potential customers throughout the world. When it publishes a new book, it directs its marketing efforts to those who have a particular interest in a book's topic.[13]

- *More personal service:* Another advantage of small businesses is their ability to give the personal touch. In businesses like gourmet restaurants, health clubs, fashion boutiques, and travel agencies, customers place a high value on personal attention. The owner-manager, through this direct relationship with customers, also gets feedback on how well the firm is meeting the needs of its market. Saloom Furniture in Gardner and Winchendon, Massachusetts, builds only custom orders of dining room furniture. And the company regularly seeks customer input. This personalized approach has allowed the company to grow rapidly; it was on *Inc.* magazine's list of the 500 fastest-growing private companies in 1991, 1992, and 1993.[14]

DISADVANTAGES OF SMALL BUSINESS

Small businesses also face several disadvantages:

- *Limited managerial skill:* Small business owners may not have the wide variety of skills they need to respond quickly to change. Many people start businesses without much business background. Some may have experience in one area of business but not in the specific type of business they choose to start. Others have the technical skills but not the management ability. For example, Beth Tondreau had the artistic and creative ability required to start her own book design firm in 1985. What she lacked was business knowledge; she did not have a sense of what she needed to charge for her services. She eventually hired a consultant to help her determine an appropriate pricing structure.[15] Later, this chapter discusses how these problems can be overcome when starting and managing a small business.

- *Fund-raising difficulty:* Another big problem for small businesses is getting adequate financing. Small firms must compete with larger, more established firms for the same pool of investment funds. Getting loans can be difficult, because new businesses are obviously more risky than established ones. And the interest rates charged by banks and private investors are usually higher for small firms than for large ones. During an economic downturn, lenders apply tougher credit standards to small firms, which makes it harder for them to stay afloat. The owner's personal resources are generally the main form of financing. Sources of financing are examined in greater detail later in the chapter.

- *Burdensome government regulation:* Because they have limited staff and financial resources, small firms can be greatly affected by government rules. Many are forced to hire outside consultants to help prepare the required reports. New federal, state, and local regulations have added to this burden. Environmental restrictions are especially burdensome. In 1990 Congress expanded the federal rules for clean water and toxic wastes, generating many new laws. In 1994 new laws restricting use of freon in refrigeration units will take effect. The number of local laws has increased as well, particularly with regard to noise pollution and traffic related to home-based businesses. Employment regulations are another area of concern. And firms that have more than 50 employees are subject to the federal family-leave act.[16]

- *Extreme personal commitment of the owner:* Starting and managing a small business require a major commitment by the owner. More than half of the first-year entrepreneurs in one survey devoted more than sixty hours per week to their company. Many worked more than seventy hours. Long hours, the need for owners to do much of the work themselves, and the stress of being personally responsible for the success of the business are big disadvantages. Virginia Lewey's café was open twelve to fifteen hours a day, and that didn't include setup and cleanup time. Until she found a reliable assistant, she had to take full responsibility for the entire operation and could not take time to market the restaurant.[17]

4   TRENDS IN SMALL BUSINESS OWNERSHIP

Social and demographic trends, combined with the challenges of operating in the fast-paced business climate of the 1990s, have given rise to a new type of entrepreneur. Today more of those starting businesses have corporate backgrounds, management experience, and a college education. A shift toward older entrepreneurs, starting second or third careers, is expected to continue. Another important trend is the growth in firms owned by women and by minorities.

■ More women and minorities are starting small businesses. By paying attention to the needs of her customers and working hard, Patsy Brown has made a success of Papa's Grocery, a store she opened in Los Angeles in 1984.

Women-Owned Businesses

Today, more women than ever before are part of the work force. As they gain experience, more are starting businesses. A recent survey of executive and professional women found that about 40 percent plan to go into business for themselves or are seriously considering self-employment, as the following Social and Demographic Trends box demonstrates.

TRENDS

Social and Demographic

If You Can't Join 'Em, Beat 'Em

Many women working for big corporations feel they are being held back from promotions to top management positions because of their gender. Up against this "glass ceiling," some women are choosing to quit their corporate jobs and start their own businesses.

However, they often find that the discrimination they had hoped to escape still plagues them. Many face exclusion from government contracts and unequal access to credit. When Roxanne Givens, the president of Legacy Management and Development Corporation in Edina, Minnesota, tried to obtain financing for her company, the bank refused to use her financial statement but agreed to use that of her brother. Adele Cepeda, an investment manager who left a Wall Street firm to start a company with two female colleagues, was told by a bank to look to her family for start-up funds. Cepeda, undaunted, went on to run a successful business which in 1992 had $40 million in assets. Women find it especially challenging to get a foot in the door in traditionally male-dominated industries. Enita Nordeck, the founder of Unity Lumber Products in Yuba, California, has not been permitted to join an all-male forest products association, where she might make important connections or do business informally over a game of golf.

Women entrepreneurs are also venturing into the international arena, where they frequently have difficulty gaining acceptance as professionals. In Saudi Arabia in 1992, religious police asked two American businesswomen to leave a trade show, citing a law that forbids women from mixing with unrelated men. M.J. Witt, the owner of a Chicago television programming concern, was asked to dinner in Tokyo by an important Japanese executive with whom she hoped to do business. But he took her to a romantic restaurant and refused to talk about business, instead asking about her personal life and grabbing for her hand across the table. Many businesswomen abroad are learning to combat such discrimination. Mary Ann Carlile wears her wedding ring, even though she's divorced, in order to "keep discussion on business." Others use their initials, rather than a first name, in early correspondence with foreign contacts, in order to make gender a non-issue. At best, say international experts, women who want to do business abroad must simply work harder than their male counterparts.[18]

As of 1992, approximately 7 million women in the United States ran their own businesses, accounting for a third of the businesses in the country. And the National Association of Women Business Owners (NAWBO) estimated that by the end of 1992, women-owned businesses employed more people than all the Fortune 500 companies combined. More women are moving into nontraditional fields (like manufacturing, transportation, and communications) as well.

Still, women-owned businesses accounted for only 14 percent of gross receipts for 1992 and were granted only 1 percent of federal government contracts. One reason is the high concentration of women in service and retail trades, which generally earn lower profits. In addition, women often run very small businesses, as reflected by the fact that nine out of ten women-owned companies are sole proprietorships. Women-owned businesses also tend to be newer than those owned by men, so they have not had as much time to achieve their sales and earnings potential or to form essential support networks.

Several government agencies have stepped in to help women entrepreneurs by offering incentives to banks that agree to finance women's start-ups. Under the Illinois Women's Finance Initiative, the state pays $1 to a bank for every dollar the bank lends to a woman entrepreneur. The city of Chicago has gone even further, paying $4 for every dollar lent. The Small Business Administration has a program that teaches businesswomen how to win federal government contracts.

Minority-Owned Businesses

Firms owned by minorities—nonwhite people—are another area of small business growth. They increased 63 percent from 1982 to 1987. One reason for this growth has been the increase of minorities in the population as a whole. The three groups that most often own businesses are those discussed in Chapter 3—African-Americans, Hispanic-Americans, and Asian-Americans. Nearly all minority-owned firms are small businesses, and about 95 percent are sole proprietorships. Women are well represented among minority entrepreneurs. For instance, about a third of all African-American entrepreneurs are women.

Minorities, especially African-Americans and Hispanics, have faced barriers to entrepreneurship, such as low family income, lack of education, and racial discrimination. Trade associations such as the National Alliance of Black Entrepreneurs and the U.S. Hispanic Chamber of Commerce provide training, networking, educational seminars, and similar services to help minority entrepreneurs.

Many minority business owners in the United States are finding that hard work and business skills are bringing them success. Yet, despite the success of many, minority-owned businesses tend to fail more often in their early years than other small businesses do. Problems include a lack of management skills and trouble getting financing. The federal government's Small Business Administration provides loan guarantees and also has programs just for minority-owned businesses. Many states offer financing programs for these firms. For instance, the Pennsylvania Minority Enterprise Corp. offers financial assistance to the state's minority-owned small businesses and has recently formed the Keystone Minority Capital Fund for businesses in the western part of the state. The Massachusetts Minority Enterprise Investment Corporation is an association that makes loans to minority-owned businesses. For example, Skyline Communications Corp., a minority-owned mail and package delivery company, was unable to get bank loans so was financed for its first five years by loans from the owner's family and friends. It then received expansion funding from the association.[19]

- What is a small business? Why are small businesses becoming so popular?
- What are the major economic contributions of small businesses? In which industries are most small companies found?
- Discuss the major advantages and disadvantages of small business ownership.
- Why are women- and minority-owned businesses important? What special problems do they face?

THE SMALL BUSINESS ADMINISTRATION

5

Small Business Administration (SBA) Main government agency that helps small businesses through a broad range of activities.

The **Small Business Administration (SBA)** is the main government agency that helps small businesses. The agency's mission is to help people start and manage small businesses, to help them win federal contracts, and to speak on behalf of small business. Through its 110 local offices, the SBA advises and helps small businesses in the areas of finance and management.

FINANCIAL ASSISTANCE PROGRAMS

The SBA offers two main types of financial assistance to small businesses who meet the agency's qualifications: loan guarantees and direct loans. It provides guarantees of up to $750,000 for loans made by private lenders, usually banks. Direct loans are made directly to small businesses using funds set aside each year by Congress. These loans cannot exceed $150,000 and are used mostly for special purposes, such as aid to firms in high-unemployment areas. A new program designed for very small businesses was introduced in 1992. The Microloan Program provides funding to local nonprofit agencies like the Coalition for Women's Economic Development in Los Angeles and the Arkansas Enterprise Group. The agencies then make loans ranging from several hundred dollars to a maximum of $25,000.[20]

There are also SBA guarantee programs for specific purposes. The SBA offers guaranteed loans to small businesses that export goods or that have been hurt by foreign competition. It also guarantees private loans for small businesses that are installing pollution control equipment.

SBA financing has increased quite a bit recently. For fiscal year 1993, the SBA made about 28,000 direct and guaranteed loans totaling almost $6.1 billion. This amount is about 33 percent higher than in 1991. Of these loans, about 15 percent were awarded to minority-owned businesses. The Microloan Program, though local intermediary agencies, loaned $6.7 million to more than 600 borrowers in 1993.

The SBA also works with small firms to help them win a share of government business. The set-aside program reserves certain government contracts for small businesses. The 8(a) program directs about $4 billion a year in federal contracts to minority-owned firms. The SBA also coordinates the Small Business Innovation Research program. Under this program, large government agencies must reserve a certain percentage of their research contracts for technology-related small businesses.

MANAGEMENT ASSISTANCE PROGRAMS

The SBA also provides a wide variety of management advice. It has a toll-free number to provide general information. Its Office of Business Development and local Small Business Development Centers offer advice, training, and educational programs. Business development officers counsel small-business owners.

The SBA's Business Development Library provides publications on most business topics. Its "Starting Out" series has more than thirty brochures on how to start a business in different fields (from ice cream stores to fish farms). The SBA also offers free management consulting through two volunteer groups, the Service Corps of Retired Executives (SCORE) and the Active Corps of Executives (ACE). Executives in these programs use their business background to help small-business owners.

The SBA is committed to helping minority-owned businesses. Its Office of Minority Small Business and Capital Ownership Development coordinates all minority activities. The SBA also makes a special effort to help veterans go into business for themselves. Veterans who served in Vietnam between 1964 and 1975 qualify for direct loans.

Concept Check

- What is the Small Business Administration?
- Describe the financial and management assistance programs offered by the SBA.

STARTING AND MANAGING A SMALL BUSINESS

6 You may have decided that you'd like to go into business for yourself. If so, what's the best way to go about it? You can (1) start from scratch, (2) buy an existing business, or (3) buy a franchise. The first two options are covered in this section. Franchising is covered in the following section.

Starting a business is only the first step—you must also be able to keep it going. Many businesses fail each year. The SBA estimates that about a quarter of all new businesses fail after two years, half after three years, and two out of every three by the end of the sixth year.

Businesses close down for many reasons. Economic factors—business downturns and high interest rates—are the most common. Financial causes—inadequate capital, low cash balances, and high expenses—are second. Lack of experience—inadequate business knowledge, manage-

■ Dating services are businesses with high growth potential. They are popular with singles, who now make up about 40 percent of the adult population in the United States.

ment experience, and technical expertise—ranks third. Many of the causes of business failure are interrelated. For example, low sales and high expenses are often directly related to poor management.

FINDING THE IDEA

Finding the right business idea means deciding whether you have the personal traits you need to succeed and then choosing the type of business that is best for you. The career section that follows this chapter includes a self-assessment questionnaire and other information to help you make these decisions.

Entrepreneurs get ideas for the businesses they form from many sources, as shown in Exhibit 7-4. It is not surprising that prior jobs provide the most ideas. Starting a firm in a field where you have experience improves the chance for success. W. L. Gore, a chemist at DuPont, saw new uses for Teflon, DuPont's nonstick coating product. He left the company to develop Gore-Tex, a Teflon-based waterproof fabric. Today W. L. Gore & Associates is a $1 billion per year business.[21]

Choosing a business from among those with high growth potential can also increase the success rate. Growth potential changes from year to year, depending on market trends. For example, the growing senior, single, and preteen populations are demographic trends that create business opportunities. Services appealing to seniors include financial and investment services, travel, and health care. Dating and travel services are popular with singles, who now account for about 40 percent of the adult population. Preteen children are themselves a $14.4 billion market, not including the purchases made by their families.[22] Each December, *Entrepreneur* magazine lists its "hottest businesses" for the coming year. Services are among the top choices now, as shown in Exhibit 7-5.

■ Exhibit 7-4
Sources of New Business Ideas

Source: *New Business in America: The Firms and Their Owners* (Washington, D.C., The NFIB Foundation, 1990), p. 19.

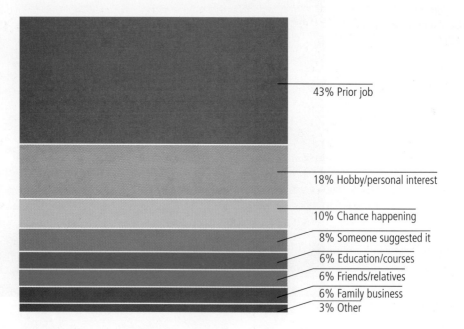

43% Prior job

18% Hobby/personal interest

10% Chance happening

8% Someone suggested it

6% Education/courses

6% Friends/relatives

6% Family business

3% Other

■ **Exhibit 7-5**
Small Businesses with
High Growth Potential

Source: Guen Sublette, "15 Hottest
Businesses for 1994," *Entrepreneur,*
December 1993, pp. 71–88.

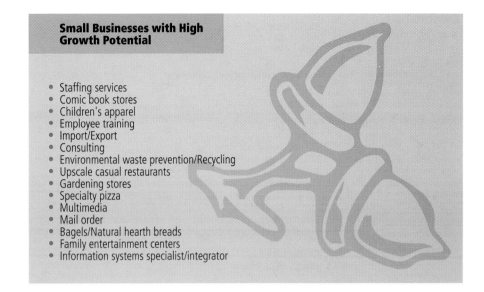

Small Businesses with High Growth Potential

- Staffing services
- Comic book stores
- Children's apparel
- Employee training
- Import/Export
- Consulting
- Environmental waste prevention/Recycling
- Upscale casual restaurants
- Gardening stores
- Specialty pizza
- Multimedia
- Mail order
- Bagels/Natural hearth breads
- Family entertainment centers
- Information systems specialist/integrator

CHOOSING A FORM OF ORGANIZATION

A person starting a new business must decide whether it will be a sole proprietorship, a partnership, a corporation, or a limited liability company. (The advantages of each type of business organization were discussed in Chapter 6.) The choice depends on the type of business, number of employees, capital requirements, tax considerations, and level of risk.

DEVELOPING THE BUSINESS PLAN

Once you have the basic concept for a product, you must judge its chances for success and set goals for the business. The planning process is one of the most important steps in starting a business. It should result in a formal, written business plan that describes in detail the idea for the new business and how it will be carried out.

Key features of a business plan are a general description of the company, the qualifications of the owner(s), a description of the product, an analysis of the market (demand, customers, competition), and a financial plan. It should focus on the uniqueness of the business and explain why customers will be attracted to it. Exhibit 7-6 is a brief outline of what should be included in a business plan.

Writing a good business plan may take many months. Many business-people, in their eagerness to begin doing business, neglect planning. They immediately get caught up in day-to-day operations and have little time for planning. But taking the time to develop a good business plan pays off. Writing the plan forces you to carefully analyze your concept and make decisions about marketing, production, staffing, and financing. A venture that sounds good at the idea stage may not look so good after closer analysis. The business plan also serves as the first operating plan for the business.

■ **Exhibit 7-6**
Outline for a Business
Plan

Source: Adapted from Justin G. Longe-
necker and Carlos W. Moore, *Small
Business Management* (Cincinnati: South-
Western, 1991), p. 158.

Executive summary One- to three-page overview of the total business plan. Written after the other sections are completed. Highlights their significant points and, ideally, creates enough excitement to motivate the reader to read on.

General company description Explains the type of company and gives its history if it already exists. Tells whether it is a manufacturing, retail, service, or other type of business.

Products and services plan Describes the good and/or service and points out any unique features. Explains why people will buy the good or service.

Marketing plan Shows who will be your customers and what type of competition you will face. Outlines your marketing strategy and specifies what will give you a competitive edge.

Management plan Identifies the "key players"—the active investors, management team, and directors. Cites their experience and competence.

Operating plan Explains the type of manufacturing or operating system you will use. Describes the facilities, labor, raw materials, and processing requirements.

Financial plan Specifies financial needs and contemplated sources of financing. Presents projections of revenues, costs, and profits.

Legal plan Shows the proposed type of legal organization—proprietorship, partnership, or corporation. Points out special, relevant legal considerations.

The most popular use of business plans is to persuade lenders and investors to finance the venture. The detailed information in the business plan helps them decide whether to invest. Even though the business plan may have taken months to write, it must capture the potential investor's interest in only a few minutes. The basic business plan should be adapted with a particular reader in mind, tailored to that type of investor and his or her investment goals.

FINANCING THE BUSINESS

Once the business plan is complete, the next step is to get the financing needed to set up the business. The amount depends on the type of business and the entrepreneur's planned investment. Businesses started by lifestyle entrepreneurs require less financing than growth-oriented businesses. Many of these businesses were started with an investment of less than $50,000. Of course, manufacturing or high technology companies generally require a larger initial investment.

debt Borrowed funds that must be repaid with interest over a stated period.

equity Funds raised through the sale of owner-ship interests in a business.

The two forms of business financing are **debt**, borrowed funds that must be repaid with interest over a stated time period, and **equity**, funds raised through the sale of stock in the business. Those who provide equity funds get a share of the profits. Lenders usually limit debt financing to no more than a quarter to a third of the firm's total needs. Thus equity financing usually amounts to about 65 to 75 percent of total start-up financing.

Once the business is running, it is likely to have an ongoing need for both short- and long-term financing. Short-term financing sources include trade credit, bank lines of credit, and SBA loans. These sources are used to meet operating expenses, inventory costs, and payroll. Long-term financing is used to buy fixed assets like plant, machinery, and computers. The main sources of long-term financing are banks, supplier and customer credit, the SBA, private investors, venture capital, and sales of stock. Chapter 21 will provide additional information on financing a business.

BUYING A SMALL BUSINESS

Another route to small business ownership is buying an existing business. Although this approach is less risky, it still requires careful and thorough analysis. Several important questions must be answered: Why is the owner selling? Does he or she want to retire or move on to another challenge, or are there some problems with the business? Is the business operating at a profit? If not, can the problems be corrected? What are the owner's plans after selling the company? Depending on the type of business, customers may be more loyal to the owner than to the product. They could leave the firm if the current owner decides to open a similar business. To protect against this situation, a "noncompete clause" can be included in the contract of sale.

Many of the same steps for starting a business from scratch apply to buying an existing company. A business plan that thoroughly analyzes all aspects of the business should be prepared. Get answers to all your questions, and determine, via the business plan, that the business is a good one. Then you must negotiate the purchase price and other terms and get financing. This can be a difficult process, and it may require the use of a consultant.

MANAGING AND STAFFING THE BUSINESS

Whether you start a business from scratch or buy an existing one, managing a small business is nearly always a challenge. Often the owner must be a jack-of-all-trades, getting involved in all areas of the business–from personnel to production and maintenance.

One way to ease the burden is to hire outside consultants. Nearly all small businesses need a good certified public accountant (CPA), who can help with financial record keeping, tax planning, and decision making. An accountant who works closely with the owner to help the business grow is a valuable asset. An attorney who knows about small business law can provide legal advice and draw up essential documents. Consultants in other areas, such as marketing, employee benefits, and insurance, can be hired as needed. Outside directors with business experience are another way for small companies to get advice. Resources like these free the small-business owner to concentrate on planning and day-to-day operations.

The main job of the small-business owner is to carry out the business plan. This may not be as easy as it sounds. The small-business owner must be ready to solve problems as they arise and move quickly when market conditions change. Hiring, training, and managing employees is another crucial responsibility.

Attracting good employees can be hard for the small firm, which may not be able to match the salaries, benefits, and advancement potential offered by larger firms. To overcome these disadvantages, small-business owners must promote employee satisfaction. Comfortable working conditions, flexible hours, opportunities to help make decisions, and a share in profits and ownership are some of the ways to do this. For example, Starbucks, the coffee company, promotes employee loyalty by offering full benefits to its part-time workers.[23]

Over time, the owner's role changes. As the company grows, others make many of the day-to-day decisions. Then the owner can focus on managing employees and making plans for the firm's long-term success. The owner must always watch performance, evaluate company policies in light of changing conditions, and start new policies as required. The type of employees needed may also change as the firm grows. A larger firm may need more managerial talent and technical expertise.

Later chapters of the book present detailed discussions of management, production, human resources, marketing, accounting, computers, and finance, all of which are useful to small-business owners.

OPERATING INTERNATIONALLY

More and more small businesses are discovering the benefits of looking beyond the United States for markets. Currently only about 10 percent of small businesses export their products, but the number is increasing each year. Small businesses decide to export because of foreign competition in the United States, new markets in growing economies, economic conditions (such as recession) in the United States, and the need for increased sales and higher profits.

Expanding into overseas markets can be hard. It requires learning about exporting, developing distribution resources, understanding the methods of doing business in other countries, and financing the venture. A good place to start is the nearest U.S. and Foreign Commercial Services office of the Department of Commerce. Trade specialists in these offices provide export counseling. They help with market research and refer small-business owners to local organizations that can help. Its National Trade Data Bank is a database with information on foreign demand for specific goods. Each year the Department of Commerce sponsors trade shows and conferences that are a good place to meet potential buyers. Banks with export services and international divisions can also provide leads. Trade associations are another good source of export information and advice. Even some states have agencies to encourage exporting. Going overseas to visit trading partners and customers personally is also recommended.

Many small businesses hire international trade specialists to get started selling overseas. They have the time, knowledge, and resources that most small businesses lack. *Export trading companies* buy goods at a discount from small businesses and resell them abroad. *Export management companies (EMCs)* act on a company's behalf. For fees of 5 to 15 percent of gross sales and multi-year contracts, they handle all aspects of exporting, including finding customers, billing, shipping, and helping the company comply with foreign regulations. When Gemini Manufacturing, an Arkansas company, decided to sell its golf bags in Europe it turned to Marco International, an EMC, to speed the process. European sales now account for about 10 percent of Gemini's revenues.[24]

Concept Check

- What personal qualifications are important for someone who is considering small business ownership?
- Why is it important to develop a business plan? What should be included in such a plan?
- How should the purchase of an existing business be analyzed?
- Why should a small business consider exporting?

FRANCHISING

7

franchising Business arrangement between a company that supplies a good or service and the individual or company that sells the good or service in a specified area.

franchisor Company that supplies the franchised product.

franchisee Individual or company that sells the franchised good or service in a certain area.

You probably deal with many franchised businesses, among them food companies like McDonald's, Taco Bell, Burger King, Little Caesar's Pizza, and Dunkin' Donuts. Many other types of businesses are also franchises, including Goodyear Tire Centers, Pearle Vision, Decorating Den, Mail Boxes Etc., Jazzercise, Jiffy Lube, Midas Muffler, Kwik-Kopy, Hertz, and your local GM and Ford dealers.

Franchising, one of the fastest-growing segments of the economy, is the third route to small business ownership. It is a way to become self-employed without starting the business from scratch. **Franchising** is a business arrangement between a **franchisor**, the company that supplies the product, and the **franchisee**, the individual or company that sells the

■ McDonald's began franchising in the 1950s, at the start of the franchise boom. Now, approximately 560 million franchises of every stripe employ 8 million workers and provide more new jobs than the Fortune 500 companies.

product in a certain geographic area. With a franchise, the entrepreneur buys a package: a proven product, proven operating methods, and training in managing the business.

franchise agreement
Contract authorizing the franchisee to use the franchisor's business name and its trademark and logo in exchange for specified payments.

The **franchise agreement** is a contract allowing the franchisee to use the franchisor's business name and its trademark and logo. It outlines the rules for running the franchise, the services provided by the franchisor, and the financial terms. The franchisee agrees to keep inventory at certain levels, buy a standard equipment package, keep up sales and service levels, follow the franchisor's operating rules, take part in the franchisor's promotions, and maintain a business relationship with the franchisor. In return, the franchisor generally provides use of a proven company name and symbols, building plans and help in finding a site, guidance and training, management assistance, managerial and accounting procedures, employee training, wholesale prices on supplies, and financial assistance. Financial terms require a minimum cash investment, which can sometimes be paid in installments; payment of an initial fee; and monthly payments, usually a percentage of sales.

Franchises can be grouped into two major categories: *Product and trade name franchises* give the franchisee the right to manufacture or sell well-known products under the franchisor's trademark. Examples include automobile dealers, gasoline service stations, and soft-drink bottling plants. These franchises account for about 70 percent of all franchise sales revenues but only 23 percent of business units (and the number is declining). In a *business-format franchise,* which includes restaurants, business services, lodging, and retail outlets, the franchisee buys the right to the name, trademark and logo, and a complete system for doing business. As more types of companies use franchising to expand, the number of business-format franchise units rose 13 percent from 1989 to 1992, and sales grew 29 percent.

Most franchises offer an established business concept and the support of a large corporation. Thus they tend to reduce the risk of business ownership. Less than 4 percent of all franchise outlets close each year. About 85 percent of franchise units are operated by the same franchisee after five years. A 1991 Gallup survey found that 94 percent of franchise owners considered their franchise operation successful, and about 75 percent were satisfied with their overall franchising experience.

GROWTH OF FRANCHISING IN THE UNITED STATES

Many of today's major names in franchising, such as McDonald's and Kentucky Fried Chicken, started in the 1950s. Franchising grew rapidly in the 1960s and 1970s as more types of businesses—clothing, business services, convenience stores, and many others—used franchising to distribute their goods and services. Growth continued in the 1980s, with sales revenue for the decade increasing 155 percent and the number of franchise units growing by 56 percent. According to the International Franchise Association (IFA), about 560 million franchise outlets employ 8 million workers and account for 35 percent of all retail sales in the United States. Fran-

Exhibit 7-7
Franchise Sales by Type
of Business

Source: International Franchise Association, "Franchise Fact Sheet," 9 November 1993.

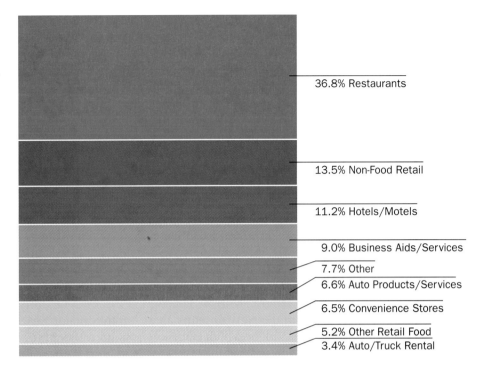

36.8% Restaurants

13.5% Non-Food Retail

11.2% Hotels/Motels

9.0% Business Aids/Services

7.7% Other

6.6% Auto Products/Services

6.5% Convenience Stores

5.2% Other Retail Food

3.4% Auto/Truck Rental

chises are a major source of U.S. job growth, providing more new jobs than the Fortune 500 companies.

As Exhibit 7-7 shows, restaurants account for the largest share of business format franchise sales, followed by other retailers and hotels. But service-oriented businesses, led by business services, are the fastest-growing sector of franchising. The number of franchised service outlets increased 21 percent in just the two years from 1988 to 1990. The increase in the number of working women and two-income households has translated to more demand for convenience services (like fast-food restaurants and car repair), child care, and home repair and cleaning services. Consumers have also had more disposable income to spend on recreation through travel, lodging, car rental, and retail video and music franchises.

OPPORTUNITIES FOR WOMEN AND MINORITIES

According to the IFA, women and minorities have become the fastest-growing group of franchise owners. This trend is expected to continue through the 1990s. Because more women and minorities now have business education and experience, high-growth franchisors have begun to recruit them. Minority and women franchisees account for 25 percent of McDonald's U.S. franchisees.[25] About 15 percent of Burger King franchisees are minorities, and General Nutrition Centers has almost 40 percent.

Many franchisors also have special programs to provide financial aid for these franchisees. For example, Kentucky Fried Chicken (KFC), a unit of PepsiCo, has a guaranteed loan program for minority franchisees that finances up to 95 percent of total cost. This program has helped KFC increase the number of minority franchisees to 10 percent of its total. Burger King's smaller Expressway restaurants are attractive to minority franchisees because they require less capital to start: $150,000 to $300,000, compared to $500,00 or more for a standard outlet.

Many trade associations assist women and minority franchisees. Chicago-based Women in Franchising promotes opportunities for women and minorities and sponsors seminars to teach them how to enter the field. The International Franchise Association sponsors the Women's Franchise Network and the Alliance for Minority Opportunities in Franchising. One satisfied woman franchisee is Sherry Cohen. She owned a travel agency and decided in 1990 to become a Uni-Globe Travel (International) Inc. franchisee. As part of a national chain, she receives help training employees and has access to lower prices on travel packages than she did as an individual agency. Since joining Uni-Globe, her business has doubled.[26]

The largest African-American franchise start-up was accomplished by Larry Lundy, who in February 1992 bought thirty-one Pizza Hut restaurants in the New Orleans area. Another major African-American franchisee is NDI Video, which owns twenty-three Blockbuster Entertainment outlets in Baltimore and upstate New York and plans to build about twenty more stores by 1995.[27] Hispanic franchisees include José Canchola, who owns four McDonald's restaurants, and Vivian Dominguez, with ten KFC outlets in New Mexico.

INTERNATIONAL FRANCHISING

Franchising, like other areas of business, is part of the global marketplace. The IFA estimates that almost half of its members now franchise internationally, and many more plan to do so within five years. The most popular types of international franchises are restaurants, hotels, business services, educational products, car rentals, and nonfood retail stores.

International franchising has grown rapidly. In 1971, 156 companies had a total of 3,365 foreign units. Today over 400 companies have more

■ With trade barriers crashing down and new markets opening every day, an increasing number of businesses are franchising internationally. KFC, for example, has outlets across the globe, including this one in Saudi Arabia.

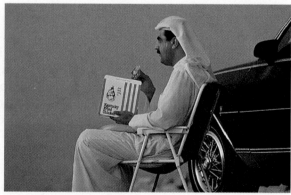

than 35,000 international franchise outlets. Six geographic areas account for about 90 percent of all foreign franchises: Canada, Japan, continental Europe, Australia, the United Kingdom, and other Asian countries. Mexico and other Latin American nations and Eastern Europe are becoming popular as well. Burger King has plans for at least thirteen outlets in Poland, and Domino's Pizza also expects to open outlets there.[28]

Franchisors in foreign countries face many of the same problems as other firms doing business abroad. In addition to tracking the market and currency changes, they must be aware of the local culture, language differences, and political risks, as the Global Competition Trends box shows.

T R E N D S

Global Competition

Un Big Mac, Por Favor

The Indian government in 1993 granted the McDonald's Corporation permission to open twenty restaurants throughout the country. There is, however, one hitch: four out of five Indians are Hindu and do not eat beef. McDonald's claims that this is not a problem; they will simply substitute another meat in their famous burgers. It is likely to be lamb, which is very popular in India.

McDonald's is no stranger to the international marketplace: as of 1992, 4,400 of its 13,400 restaurants were located outside the United States (including 1,000 in Japan) and accounted for 40 percent of its profits. The chain is one of many that are expanding their foreign operations as the domestic fast-food market nears saturation. And common to all their international marketing strategies are efforts to adapt their menus to local tastes. Kentucky Fried Chicken in Australia is testing the "Smorgasbar," a deli case filled with side dishes such as peas and gravy, a national favorite. The store also offers home delivery in two of its restaurants and plans to expand that service to an additional twenty stores. Pizza Hut, which operates 440 outlets in Australia, offers barbecue and Asian sauces as well as an all-you-can-eat dessert bar, all of which are unavailable in the United States. It's no wonder these chains are trying so hard to please: the typical Australian spends approximately U.S. $15.50 per week on fast food, or about 20% more than the average American.

Since 1989, when President Carlos Salinas de Gortari authorized American franchises to operate in Mexico, more than 150 American companies have opened branches there. Now anyone living in one of the country's major cities can lunch at Burger King, have a new muffler installed at Midas, treat themselves to a cone at Baskin Robbins, and watch a video from Blockbuster while enjoying a Domino's Pizza for dinner. Some critics have warned that this franchise boom is eroding the national culture and the sense of a Mexican identity. The historian Lorenzo Meyer rejects this notion, pointing to the fact that several franchisers were initially unsuccessful in the country because they failed to include offerings typical to Mexican menus. One chain, however, met with criticism for the opposite reason: Taco Bell. Declared the social commentator Carlos Monsivais, "For us to import tacos is like the people of Alaska to start importing ice."[29]

ADVANTAGES AND DISADVANTAGES OF FRANCHISING

As we have seen, franchising has grown a lot in the past twenty years. It offers advantages and disadvantages to both the franchisor and the franchisee.

The franchisor benefits from being able to expand without making a major investment, since franchisees finance their own units. The franchisor gives up a share of profits to the franchisee, but it gets ongoing revenues in the form of royalty payments. On the other hand, although many franchisees are highly motivated managers who know the local market, the franchisor has less control over them than over company employees.

Advantages to the Franchisee

How can someone decide between buying a franchise or starting a similar nonfranchise business? The advantages and disadvantages of the franchise must be compared to the risk of starting a new business. There are three main advantages of franchising:

- *Management training and assistance:* The franchisee with little personal experience gets a crash course from the franchisor. The structured training program quickly trains the owner how to start and operate the business. Ongoing training programs for managers and employees are another plus. For example, Dairy Queen's district managers are an important resource for new store owners. They provide training and advice on how other franchisees solved similar problems.

- *Recognized name, product, and operating concept:* A franchise gives the owner a widely known and accepted business. Consumers know they can depend on the product offered by such franchises as Pizza Hut, Hertz, and Holiday Inn. The franchisee doesn't have to break new ground. He or she gets a business with a proven track record, set operating procedures, standard goods and services, and national advertising. As a result, the franchisee's risk is reduced, and the opportunity for rapid increases in income can be high.

- *Financial assistance:* Starting a business can be costly, and entrepreneurs often have limited resources. Franchise companies provide financial assistance in several ways. First, by being linked with a nationally known company, the franchisee generally has a better chance of getting funds from a lender. Also, the franchisor typically gives the franchisee advice on financial management, referrals to lenders, and help in preparing loan applications. Many franchisors also offer payment plans, short-term credit for buying supplies from the franchise company, and loans to buy real estate and equipment. For example, Sir Speedy, a printing franchise, helps its franchisees with long-term loans for equipment. Franchisees also save on purchases because the franchisor can pass along volume discounts.

Disadvantages for the Franchisee

Although franchising has many advantages, prospective franchisees should consider these disadvantages:

- *Costs of franchising:* The costs of starting a franchise v[...]
  ing on the type of business. They may include a non[...]
  application fee; a one-time franchise fee; purchases of land[...]
  ing, and equipment; and funds for supplies and operating exp[...]
  Franchise fees are higher for better-known franchises, but e[...]
  newer companies charge $10,000 to $25,000 or more. Total start-up
  costs for *Money* magazine's top franchising prospects range from
  $2,000 for Jazzercise to $610,000 for an average McDonald's. The
  franchisee must also pay ongoing fees or royalties, which are usually a percentage of sales. These fees can range from 2 percent to
  20 percent. Fees for local and national advertising are also charged
  as a percentage of sales. Other fees for management advice may also
  be charged.
- *Restricted operating freedom:* A franchisee gives up some freedom
  by agreeing to conform to the franchisor's operating rules and facilities design. Inventory and supplies must also conform to franchisor
  standards. In many cases, purchases must be made from either
  approved suppliers or the franchisor. In addition, the franchisee is
  restricted to a specific territory or site, which may limit growth. Many
  franchisees find this lack of control bothersome. But failure to conform to franchisor policies can mean loss of the franchise. Also, most
  franchise contracts run at least ten years. A product or concept that
  is popular today may lose its appeal in five years, leaving the franchisee with an obsolete business. Or increased competition, as
  occurred with frozen yogurt and quick-lube franchises, may reduce
  profitability.

SUCCESSFUL FRANCHISES

If you decide that franchising is for you, the next step is to choose the
right one from among the 2,500 U.S. franchisors. It's important to pick an
industry that you enjoy and where you perhaps have some experience.
The financial commitment may be significant, and it may take some time
until the business makes a profit. Franchise companies that sell products
with high consumer demand and that provide a lot of support for their
franchisees offer the best prospects for success. Stay away from franchise
sectors—such as car rentals, hotels, and some types of fast-food restaurants—that can't absorb more outlets.

The fastest-growing areas of franchising include the following: educational products and services; cleaning services; business services such as
copying centers, personnel and temporary help agencies, and business
training; health-related services; and personal and home services. Other
markets with good potential are automotive services such as detailing,
parts, and repair; ethnic and specialty restaurants; and entertainment-
related franchises such as video rentals. Franchises that emphasize convenience and leisure activities are also very popular. Would-be franchisees
would do well to check recent issues of *Entrepreneur* and other small
business magazines for their ideas on promising franchise opportunities.

When buying a franchise, as with any business, you should thoroughly ...vestigate the franchise company. The Federal Trade Commission (FTC) ...quires the franchisor to provide a *Uniform Franchise Offering Circular* *(FOC)* to any prospective franchisee. This disclosure document includes ...e number of units, names of franchisees, and any past litigation against ...e franchisor. The FTC and franchise trade groups are trying to improve ... amount of information franchisors provide, including financial data ...h as sales and earnings and better start-up and operating cost data. ...eting with current and past franchisees is an excellent way to find out ...ow well the franchisor helped franchisees and if it provided the expected services.

Purchasing a franchise does not guarantee success. Many franchisees have been disappointed in the results of their franchise outlets, which have not lived up to the promises of the franchisor. The franchisor may run into financial difficulties, as did Nutri/System Inc., a weight-loss franchise company, which could not keep up with payments on its bank loans. The franchisees could no longer count on the franchisor for diet foods, a major source of income, and for other services.[30] In some cases, franchisees have sued franchisors. For example, the lawsuit filed by Postal Instant Press (PIP) franchisees says that the company misled them; breached contracts by reducing technical support, advertising, and other services; and misrepresented or omitted facts to get franchisees to buy or renew their franchises.[31]

Concept Check
- Describe franchising and the main parties to the transaction.
- Discuss the role of franchising in the U.S. economy.
- What are the major advantages and disadvantages of franchising?

■ SUMMARY

Key Terms

debt 222

entrepreneur 204

equity 222

franchise agreement 226

franchisee 225

franchising 225

franchisor 225

small business 209

Small Business
  Administration (SBA)
  217

1. Define entrepreneurship, discuss why people become entrepreneurs, and describe the characteristics of successful entrepreneurs.
Entrepreneurship involves taking the risk of starting and managing a business to make a profit. Entrepreneurs are innovators who start firms either to have a certain lifestyle or to develop a company that will grow into a major corporation. People become entrepreneurs for four main reasons: the opportunity for profit, independence, personal satisfaction, and lifestyle. Successful entrepreneurs are hardworking, independent, self-motivated, creative, and self-confident, with a high need for achievement and a willingness to take moderate risks. They have good interpersonal and communication skills. Managerial skills and technical knowledge are also important for entrepreneurial success.

2. Understand what a small business is and explain the economic importance of small businesses.
A small business is independently owned and operated, has a local base

of operations, and is not dominant in its field. The Small Business Administration further defines small business by size, according to the industry. Small businesses play an important role in the economy. About 98 percent of U.S. businesses have fewer than 100 employees. Small businesses are found in every field, but they dominate the construction, wholesale, and retail categories. Most new private-sector jobs created in the United States over the past decade were in small firms. Small businesses also create about twice as many new goods and services as larger firms.

3. Describe the advantages and disadvantages of small business ownership.

Small businesses have flexibility to respond to changing market conditions. Because of their streamlined staffing and structure, they can be efficiently operated. Small firms can serve specialized markets more profitably than large firms and provide a higher level of personal service. Disadvantages include limited managerial skill, difficulty in raising the capital needed for start-up and expansion, the burden of complying with increasing levels of government regulation, and the major personal commitment required on the part of the owner.

4. Discuss the growing importance of women and minority business owners.

Women are starting businesses at a faster rate than any other group. Currently they own about 30 percent of all businesses. Women often choose self-employment for lifestyle reasons and to overcome limited opportunities in large firms. Minority-owned businesses are another high-growth category. Minorities view business ownership as a way to overcome racial discrimination and economic hardship. Both women and minorities have faced barriers to entrepreneurship, such as discrimination, lack of formal business education, and limited business experience. Special training programs and financial assistance have helped increase business ownership among women and minorities.

5. Describe the role of the Small Business Administration.

The Small Business Administration is the main federal agency serving small businesses. It has several types of loan programs for small businesses: private lender loan guarantees, direct loans, and guarantees for export loans. Through its set-aside programs, it helps small businesses get government contracts and research and development grants. The SBA offers a wide range of management assistance services, including courses, publications, and consulting. It has special programs for veterans, minorities, and women.

6. Discuss start-up and management considerations.

One of the most important steps for small-business owners is to develop a formal business plan. This written plan describes in detail the idea for the business and how it will be implemented. The plan is also of use in getting both debt and equity financing for the new business.

At first, small-business owners are involved in all aspects of the firm's operations. Wise use of outside consultants can free up the owner's time to focus on planning and strategy in addition to day-to-day operations.

Other key management responsibilities are finding and retaining good employees and monitoring market conditions.

7. Define franchising, understand its importance, and recognize its advantages and disadvantages.

Franchising involves a franchisor, the supplier of goods or services, and a franchisee, the individual or company that buys the right to sell the franchisor's products in a specific area. Franchising is one of the fastest-growing segments of the economy. With a franchise, the entrepreneur buys a package business with a proven product and operating methods. Advantages include management training and assistance; use of a recognized name, product, and operating concept; and financial assistance from the franchisor. Disadvantages are the costs of franchising and reduced operating freedom due to the need to conform to the franchisor's standard procedures.

■ DISCUSSION QUESTIONS

1. Would you make a good entrepreneur? Evaluate your strengths and shortcomings, taking into account your personal situation (stage of life, family situation, experience, objectives, and so on). Would you prefer a life-style or a growth-oriented opportunity? Name several types of businesses you would consider starting, and explain why you chose them.

2. After working in marketing with a major food company for twelve years, you are becoming impatient with corporate "red tape" (regulations and routines). You have an idea for a new snack product for nutrition-conscious consumers and are thinking of starting your own company. What are the entrepreneurial characteristics you will need? What other factors should you consider before quitting your job?

3. Suzanne Chen is a software developer for a medium-size company that develops educational and personal finance software. She has an idea for a new computer game based on the stock market. Describe how she should prepare a business plan that would convince investors to back her. What other alternatives to starting her own company should she consider?

4. Your uncle, Joe Chambers, has just been laid off from his job as senior vice president of a local bank that was acquired by a larger bank. His seventeen years' experience entitles him to severance pay of $200,000. He has a chance to buy a small printing company for $400,000. What are the important factors he should consider in deciding whether this is a good business to buy?

5. You are a personnel manager for a hospital and have decided you want to own a personnel agency for nurses and other health-care workers. You can either start your own company or buy a franchise. What are the advantages and disadvantages of each option? Given your personal situation, which would you choose? Why?

■ CASE

Child's Play

Anna and Don Bell are tired of the rat race and have decided to open their own business. Anna, vice president of information systems at a Fortune 500 company, knows that parents are concerned about preparing their children to cope in an increasingly computer-oriented world. Don, an elementary school teacher, wants to stay in the education field.

Anna's research shows that there are several ways to market computer education. They can offer after-school computer classes for school-age children. They can also reach younger children by contracting with day-care centers and preschools to provide on-site classes. In either case, they can operate the business from their home at first to save costs, taking the computers to the class sites and arranging for part-time space if they offer an after-school program.

The Bells have two options to get started: open their own children's computer school or buy a franchise from Computertots, a high-growth company with about 125 franchisees nationwide. The franchise would require start-up costs of about $40,000. Royalties are 6 percent of annual revenues, plus 1 percent for advertising. The level of annual revenues will depend on the marketing strategy they choose. Computertots provides curriculum packages and ongoing training and support. Each month franchisees receive the "Share Fair Packet," with marketing ideas that worked for other franchisees, and *Tot Times*, a franchisor newsletter with articles on current educational issues and trends. The franchisor does not help with financing.

The Bells' other choice is to open their own children's computer center. Anna and Don spend their evenings debating the pros and cons of each choice.[32]

Questions

1. What are the advantages to the Bells of franchising? What are the disadvantages?
2. What are the advantages to starting an independently owned business? What are the disadvantages?
3. How should the Bells investigate and evaluate these options? Which choice would you recommend to the Bells? Why?

Your Career as an Entrepreneur

Do you have what it takes to own your own company? Or would you be better suited to work for a corporation? To find out, you need to determine whether you have the personal traits for entrepreneurial success. If the answer is yes, you need to identify the type of business that is best for you.

Know Yourself

Owning a business is challenging and requires a great deal of personal sacrifice. You must take a hard and honest look at yourself before you decide to strike out on your own. The quiz on pages 237–239 can help you evaluate your entrepreneurial strengths and weaknesses and determine what type of career—corporate employee, franchisee, or independent business owner—is right for you. Choose the answer that best matches your feelings now.

Which Business Is for You?

If you are well suited to owning your own company, the next question is what type of business to start. You need to consider your expertise, interests, and financial resources. Start with a broad field, then choose a specific good or service. The business can involve a new idea or a refinement of an existing idea. It may bring an existing idea to a new area.

To narrow the field, ask yourself the following questions:

- What do I like to do?
- What am I good at?
- How much can I personally invest in my business?
- Do I have access to other financial resources?
- What is my past business experience?
- What are my personal interests and hobbies?
- How can I use my experience and interests in my own business?:
- Do I want or need partners?

Spending time on these and similar questions will help you identify some possible business opportunities and the resources you will need to develop them.

Prior job experience is the number-one source of new business ideas. Starting a firm in a field where you have specialized product or service experience improves your chance for success. For example, their work at Aldus, a leader in desktop publishing software, gave Jeremy Jaech and a colleague the technical knowledge and marketing savvy to start Shapeware, a Seattle company that makes computer-assisted drawing software. At Aldus, Jaech was part of a successful software company, learning how the software marketplace works and what types of products customers wanted. Within three years Shapeware had revenues of $12 million and raised $4.3 million in venture capital for future expansion.[1]

Personal interests and hobbies are another major source of ideas. Gourmet food enthusiasts have started many restaurants and mail-order food businesses. His passion for fine wines led Marvin Shanken into publishing. He bought *Wine Spectator* magazine for $40,000 in 1979 and built it into the most popular magazine in its field. Today M. Shanken Communications, Inc., publishes six specialty publications.[2] Likewise, Jean Leinhausen turned an interest in specialty crafts into an $8 million business by forming ASN Publishing, a Southern California company that publishes and distributes needlework instruction and pattern books.[3] In all these three cases, the basis for the new business was the entrepreneur's existing skills and interests.

What's Your Career Niche?

1. The most important reward for me for a job well done is:
   a. Praise from the boss.
   b. A feeling of satisfaction.
   c. Compliments from my co-workers.
   d. A cash bonus.
2. When I've moved in the past, my friendships have tended to:
   a. Remain firmly rooted with friends back home.
   b. Slowly change as I make new friends and lose touch with old ones.
   c. Break off cleanly when I leave and start anew as I settle in.
3. When something goes wrong, my tendency is to:
   a. Step in and personally make sure the problem is corrected
   b. Find out what went wrong and set up a system to avoid a repeat in the future.
   c. Work harder so the problem is soon forgotten.
4. I tend to give my best work effort when:
   a. I'm an equal member of a team.
   b. I'm in charge of things.
   c. I work closely with a supervisor who is my mentor.
   d. I'm assigned a task to do by myself.
5. My idea of relaxing is:
   a. Trying out a new recipe for dinner.
   b. Staying home and watching TV.
   c. Working on a project I brought home from work.
6. Whether I'm at work or play, my approach is to:
   a. Immerse myself in a specific activity as much as possible.
   b. Spread my interest equally over as wide an area as I can.
   c. Focus in on several areas that draw my interest.
7. If I won $50,000 in a lottery, I'd seriously consider:
   a. Buying a luxury sports car with a cellular phone.
   b. Taking a well-deserved vacation.
   c. Investing in something my accountant would appreciate as much as I would.
   d. Paying off all my debts.
8. My definition of disposable income is:
   a. The amount of money I have left over after paying my bills.
   b. What's left after setting aside enough money to cover my expenses, plus 10 percent for a "rainy day."
   c. It depends. I save up until I have enough for a major purchase, then start saving again.
9. Flying on a business trip is a good opportunity for:
   a. Catching up on sleep.
   b. Doing work I brought from the office.
   c. Reading something that is both entertaining and informative.
10. If I were setting up a trust fund for my grandchild, I would invest the major portion of my funds in:
    a. A venture capital fund that offers a high return at moderate risk.
    b. Blue chip stocks offering steady growth and low risk.
    c. Certificates of deposit with a guaranteed rate of return.
11. My own personal business plan extends through:
    a. The current pay period.
    b. The next quarter.
    c. The end of the year.
    d. The next five years.
    e. The day I can retire.

Entrepreneurial comedians Jerry Saslow and Mollie Allen entertain movie extras for a living.

12. If I vacation in a foreign country, I prefer to:
   a. Sign up for a package tour in advance.
   b. Use a guidebook and make my own arrangements beforehand.
   c. Wait until I arrive to decide where to stay and what to see.
   d. Stay in the same places and revisit the sites I've enjoyed before.

13. When I get a phone message from someone I don't know, I usually:
   a. Call them back myself.
   b. Have my secretary return the call to find out the purpose.
   c. Disregard the message and see if they call back.

14. When I go to a social gathering, I like to:
   a. Gravitate toward people I know.
   b. Strike up a conversation with someone I haven't met before.
   c. Seek out a quiet spot and hope no one takes offense.

15. If I suddenly found out I owed $15,000 to the IRS, I would:
   a. Fire my accountant.
   b. Get a second job.
   c. Take out a loan.
   d. Discuss the situation with the IRS and try to work something out.

16. When someone asks my advice on a sticky problem, my response is often:
   a. Offer sympathy and secretly rejoice that it's not my problem.
   b. Tell them how I would handle it if I were in their shoes.
   c. Refer them to someone who has more experience in the area.

17. If I find myself torn between staying late at work and leaving on time, the determining factor is:
   a. Realizing that the work will keep until tomorrow and that I've done enough for today.
   b. Noticing that the boss is still there and feeling I should stay at least as late as he or she does.
   c. Deciding whether I'm making any progress on the task and staying with it if I am.

d. Whether I have any-
   thing planned for the
   evening.
18. When I see a piece of
    trash in front of my home,
    my inclination is to:
    a. Pick it up and put it in
       the trash barrel.
    b. Leave it for the street
       cleaner scheduled to
       come by the next day.
19. When it comes to buying
    a new car, I like to:
    a. Buy a new model as
       soon as it hits the
       showroom.
    b. Wait until the year-end
       clearance sale and then
       shop for a good deal
       on one of several
       models.
    c. Give the company a
       year or two to work the
       bugs out before I spend
       my money.
20. If it's up to me to choose
    a restaurant, I like to:
    a. Go to an old favorite.
    b. Ask friends for their
       suggestions.
    c. Follow the recommen-
       dation of a newspaper
       or magazine critic.
    d. Stop at an interesting
       looking place I've seen
       on the way home.

Scoring

1. a=2, b=4, c=1, d=3
2. a=1, b=4, c=7
3. a=5, b=3, c=1
4. a=2, b=8, c=4, d=6
5. a=4, b=2, c=6
6. a=2, b=6, c=4
7. a=8, b=2, c=6, d=4
8. a=2, b=4, c=6
9. a=1, b=5, c=3
10. a=7, b=3, c=1, d=5
11. a=8, b=7, c=5, d=3, e=1
12. a=1, b=5, c=7, d=2
13. a=8, b=4, c=1
14. a=3, b=7, c=1
15. a=8, b=1, c=2, d=5
16. a=3, b=5, c=1
17. a=1, b=2, c=7, d=3
18. a=6, b=2
19. a=8, b=4, c=1
20. a=1, b=3, c=5, d=8

Your Score

Category Range
Corporate Player 26–60
You like to share responsibilities with others. You'd probably be happiest working in an
established company.

Franchise Candidate 61–100
You enjoy working on your
own, but you also like having
the support of others. You
should consider franchising as
a career option.

Entrepreneur 101–133
Your independent spirit
makes you a good candidate
for starting your own business. Good luck!

Source: Quiz developed by Adia Personnel Services and
published in "What's Your Career Niche," *Franchising
Opportunities,* February 1990, pp. 24-25.

239

Part 4

Management

Overview

One key to the success of any size company is a well-defined and easily understandable mission statement. In order for all of a firm's employees to work toward a common goal, they must first know what that goal is. Henry Ford realized this over 70 years ago. The original mission statement of his Ford Motor Company was simply "to produce and market passenger cars at low cost, so nearly every family can buy one."

Another visionary, Walt Disney, dreamed of a "magic kingdom" where families could enjoy themselves in a wholesome and exciting setting. Again, a simple mission statement, but as with the Ford automobile, Disneyland and Disney World might never have become a reality without the hard work of a dedicated team of employees. Both Disney and Ford understood this. They made sure to hire the most competent people they could find at all levels of their organizations. In this way, both men were able to ensure that their products would be top-notch.

In the past, major corporations structured their internal organization in a fashion similar to a high-rise building. Every "floor," or level, represented another layer of management. If a company has too many floors, though, the decision-making process is slowed, and processing information "up the chain" takes a great deal of time. Corporate downsizing, or "right" sizing, as it is sometimes called, is a response to this problem. In downsizing, the structure of a company is reorganized, and many of the middle layers of management are eliminated. This tends to strengthen the company and make it more competitive. The responsibilities of individual employees increase, and the "team" concept takes on even more importance for the organization.

A lean, effective structure will mean nothing, however, unless the company's production process functions efficiently. This is true whether a firm produces goods or provides a service. It is for this reason that operations management is such a crucial element of today's corporations. Operations managers work closely with marketing, finance, accounting, and other areas of the company to decide upon the best way to convert the firm's inputs into outputs. They are often responsible for managing as much as three-fourths of a company's revenue-producing assets.

The following chapters will explore the role of the manager within a company, the different organizational structures used in business, and manufacturing and the production process. These topics are important fundamentals for any business education.

Andrew Jergens Company

When a company makes the decision to expand its operations into the global marketplace, how well the company manages its growth often determines its success. New challenges arise along with the new opportunities offered by globalization. Consider the evolution of the Andrew Jergens Company. More than a century ago, Mr. Jergens began producing soap at his company in Cincinnati, Ohio. Today, the company's products can be found the world over, and its product line has expanded to include bar and liquid soaps, hand and body lotions, and bath additives.

Perhaps the most important factor in Jergens' growth from a small, regional company into a multinational concern was a change in corporate ownership. In 1988 the Kao Corporation of America purchased the Andrew Jergens Company. KCOA also owns a chemical company, an information systems company, and cosmetic companies. KCOA's parent is the Kao Corporation, headquartered in Tokyo, Japan. The union of Jergens and Kao was successful because both companies share the goal expressed in the Jergens mission statement: "Serve consumers with unique personal care products that enrich the quality of their everyday lives."

Jergens is constantly looking toward the future, anticipating how it can better serve its loyal customers and expand its presence in the marketplace. The company recently established a new, state-of-the-art research and development center. This facility represents the company's commitment to developing new and better products. KCOA is helping out in this respect, by linking Kao's advanced technology with the trusted name and tradition of Jergens.

Effective management, constant innovation, and a strong parent company have made Jergens' transition into the global marketplace a smooth one, allowing the company to fulfill its mission statement in ways Andrew Jergens could never have imagined.

The Managerial Process

chapter 8

1. Briefly explain the nature of management and the roles of managers.
2. Identify the four managerial skills, and describe their usefulness at various levels of the organization.
3. List the steps in the problem-solving process.
4. Explain the four managerial functions: planning, organizing, directing, and controlling.
5. Describe three management leadership styles.
6. Discuss management by objectives.

Career Profile

Upon graduating from college, Brad Hoeweler worked as a staff accountant for a public accounting firm, putting to use his double major of accounting and finance. After gaining valuable experience there, he signed on as an assistant to the president of Gidding-Jenny, a retail clothing store owned by his family. Then, when the president departed, Brad assumed that position.

Gidding-Jenny is a clothing retailer. Its product line begins where department stores' end and ranges up to designer fashions. As president, Brad is responsible for store operation and the purchasing of merchandise, as well as personnel, marketing, forecasts, and budgets. He is involved in every aspect of the business, from customer relations to the planning of the company's short- and long-term goals.

Brad changed the firm's management style by introducing a team sales strategy. The buying and operations managers now meet weekly to discuss issues that need to be resolved. The buyers inform the operations managers when shipments will be arriving and what they will include. This allows the operations managers to make room for the new merchandise and to pull together the elements needed to display it. Using the team sales strategy, the buyers and operations managers work together to anticipate and avoid problems. Most decisions are made collectively at these meetings. If a consensus cannot be reached, Brad makes the final decision.

Gidding-Jenny generates approximately $6.5 million in annual sales. Brad's goal is to make it an even bigger success. He envisions expanding the store and perhaps opening others. He understands that his success, and that of Gidding-Jenny, depends upon how well the buying and sales personnel meet customers' needs and do their parts to make the store run smoothly. Through effective management, he will continue to provide his staff with the tools and guidance they need to perform their jobs to the best of their abilities.

Overview Chapter 8 begins by describing the roles of managers and the levels of management. Next it looks at the skills required to be a good manager, including problem solving. It then explains the key activities of a manager: planning, organizing, directing, and controlling. Next it looks in detail at three leadership styles. Finally it considers the technique of management by objectives.

THE NATURE OF MANAGEMENT AND THE WORK OF MANAGERS

 A manager's job typically involves a number of planned and unplanned activities. Many of them take little time to accomplish, but most require communication. A manager interacts most often with in-house people—but also with people outside the organization. Many of these activities involve solving problems by making decisions. Some of these decisions are made after a quick analysis of a situation; others involve more study.

KEY FUNCTIONS OF MANAGEMENT

management Process of coordinating a firm's human and other resources to accomplish its goals.

managers Employees of a firm who are responsible for coordinating resources.

Management is the process of coordinating a firm's human and other resources to achieve an organization's objectives. **Managers** are the employees who are responsible for coordinating resources. Management activities are focused in four key areas: planning, organizing, directing, and controlling. Although these activities are discussed separately later in the chapter, in practice they form a tightly integrated cycle of thoughts and actions. As we'll see, the managerial process is (1) thinking about a problem and designing a plan to deal with it, (2) implementing the plan, (3) leading by personal example, and (4) reviewing the results and making any needed changes.

MANAGERIAL ROLES

In performing their duties, managers play different roles. (A *role* is a set of activities or a pattern of behavior that a person is expected to perform.) Managers have three basic roles: informational, interpersonal, and decisional. In practice, these roles often overlap. Managers must be adept at stepping into and out of various roles as situations or conditions change.

Informational Roles

A manager's contacts with other managers and with subordinates are the basis for the informational roles. The manager may be both an information seeker and an information distributor. As an information seeker, a manager looks for information that will help the firm achieve its goals. An article in *Chain Store News,* for example, might tell a district manager for Shop Rite how and where to place mirrors and electronic equipment to reduce shoplifting and robberies. As an information distributor, a manager transmits important information to others (such as managers and subordinates). The Shop Rite district manager might pass along the magazine's suggestions to store layout and design specialists.

A third part of the informational role is being a spokesperson. A spokesperson releases information to people outside the department, and possibly outside the firm, who can help accomplish its goals. The Shop Rite district manager, for example, might tell the local police and newspapers of the chain's new robbery-prevention steps.

Interpersonal Roles

The manager's interpersonal roles consist of relationships with other people. In these roles, the manager may serve as a figurehead, leader, or liaison.

The role of figurehead is mostly ceremonial. An example would be Dave Thomas, the founder of Wendy's Hamburgers, who appears in television commercials for the company. James Near, Chief Executive Officer and Chairman of Wendy's, actually runs the company.

In the leader role, the manager takes charge of the goals of a department or other group. For example, in the mid-1980s Wendy's store managers weren't getting the respect they needed and were passing their frustrations along to their crews. The crews, feeling unappreciated, made the customer feel the same. Customers left Wendy's in droves. As sales fell, store labor was cut and sales fell even further. Morale took a nose dive, quality became spotty, and consistency in operations was nonexistent. James Near was hired by Dave Thomas to turn the company around. Mr. Near began by raising employee training to uniformly high standards, seeing that everyone, from the newest kid on fries all the way up to the manager, received the same basic training. Next, Mr. Near worked to make "store manager" truly a status position, giving managers more control and freedom in making day-to-day decisions. Compensation and benefits were also improved. Managers and crews were refocused to look at their restaurants from the customer's point of view. Today, Wendy's sales, profits, and employee retention are higher than ever.[1]

In the liaison role, a manager makes contacts with other people inside and outside the organization to accomplish the group's tasks. For example, John Wright, manager of a local restaurant, may telephone a wholesale paper supplier to inquire about buying larger and thicker dinner napkins.

Decisional Roles   ~~sets goals~~

The manager's decisional role is a big part of his or her job. Managers must make decisions to improve operations, handle disagreements among workers, and allocate resources efficiently. For example, Compaq Computer was founded on the premise of offering highly engineered personal computers (PCs) for which customers would willingly pay a premium price. By the end of the 1980s, however, the technology had become more standardized, making it easy for almost anyone to enter the PC business. In addition, PC prices had plummeted. Purchasing a PC had become a matter of going to the local superstore, and people were no longer interested in spending for a premium product. In order for Compaq to catch up with the market and stop losing money, it would need a new strategy, practically overnight.

■ This plant manager combines all three of the traditional management skills in order to be effective. He functions at various times as an information distributor, a leader and liaison, and a decision maker.

In response, the Compaq board of directors fired co-founder and chief executive Rod Canion and hired Eckhard Pfeiffer. Mr. Pfeiffer notes:

I spent endless hours with the Compaq management team, and together we came to the conclusion that to remain one of the top three PC suppliers in the world, we must stop being only a high-end player and bring our costs and prices down 35 to 50 percent. So we needed to develop new low-priced products and at the same time lower the cost and prices of our traditional high-end products in order to satisfy our existing customer base. Most important, we had to go from being a business-centered company to being a customer-centered company.[2]

The ability and willingness to take decisive action is a key aspect of the manager's job.

LEVELS OF MANAGEMENT

Do the managers of small companies and of large companies like Compaq Computers perform similar roles and functions? Yes, all managers must plan, organize, direct, and control their operations. But the frequency and type of role vary, depending on the size of the organization and the level at which a manager works. A top executive acts as a figurehead or a spokesperson more often than the manager of a small produc-

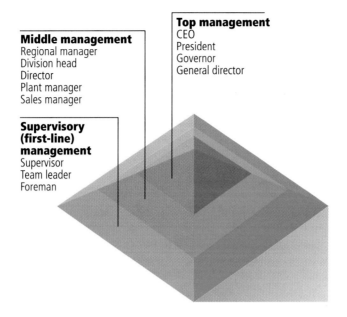

Exhibit 8-1
Three Basic Levels of
Management

Top management
CEO
President
Governor
General director

Middle management
Regional manager
Division head
Director
Plant manager
Sales manager

**Supervisory
(first-line)
management**
Supervisor
Team leader
Foreman

tion unit does. The production supervisor is more often involved in handling worker disputes or resolving conflicts between employees.

Most firms have three levels of managers: top (or executive), middle, and supervisory (see Exhibit 8-1). The diagram is shaped like a pyramid because there are fewer managers at each higher level. **Top managers** are the small group at the head of the organization. Top managers design and approve the firm's basic policies and represent the firm to other organizations. They set overall strategy and long-range goals. Deciding on strategy and goals includes deciding which industries to compete in, how much of the market to seek, and what to do with profits. It also includes defining company values and ethics. **Middle managers** are the ones who carry out the plans and policies of top managers. In doing so, they oversee lower-level managers. **Supervisors** are the lowest level of management but the most numerous. They manage the operating employees, or the rank-and-file workers. Although supervisors have some responsibility for the firm's resources, most of their time is spent leading, motivating, and controlling workers.

top managers Relatively small group of managers at the head of an organization.

middle managers Managers who are concerned with implementing the plans and policies of top managers and who oversee lower-level managers.

supervisors Lowest level of managers, responsible for managing operating employees.

Concept Check
• What are the three basic managerial roles?
• Discuss the three levels of management and how they differ.

MANAGERIAL SKILLS

2   Just as roles vary by management level, so too do the needed managerial skills. (A *skill* is the ability to do something competently.) A manager needs four types of skills: technical, human relations, conceptual, and political.

TECHNICAL SKILLS

technical skills Specialized knowledge and ability that a person brings to a job.

The specialized knowledge and ability that a person brings to a job are **technical skills.** Operating a filtration system in a brewery, preparing a financial statement, programming a computer, and designing an office building are examples of technical skills.

Managers need both supervisory skills and the technical skills of a nonsupervisory position. For example, a vice president of information systems is very likely to be a competent computer programmer or systems analyst as well as to be able to perform informational, interpersonal, and decision roles.

HUMAN-RELATIONS SKILLS

human-relations skills Skills used in working with people to accomplish the organization's goals.

Human-relations skills are those used in working with people to accomplish the organization's goals. A manager with good human-relations skills is typically a leader who can communicate well and motivate others. The ability to work with people, a sensitivity to their needs, and a

■ Tommy Lasorda, manager of the Los Angeles Dodgers baseball team, has developed excellent human-relations skills. He responds to the individual needs of his players in order to draw out their best performances. His ability to motivate and inspire veterans as well as rookies has led to a very successful management career.

willingness to let subordinates make some decisions on their own are prime examples of good human-relations skills.

Tommy Lasorda, manager of the Los Angeles Dodgers baseball team, is known for his human-relations skills. He can manage veteran players as well as develop rookies. With some players he must push, encourage, and provide firm direction and leadership. Other players may need very little attention. The point is that Lasorda must be able to treat each player differently.

CONCEPTUAL SKILLS

conceptual skills Ability to view an organization as a whole, to understand how its parts fit together, and to see how it relates to other organizations.

Viewing an organization as a whole, understanding how its parts fit together, and seeing how it relates to other organizations are **conceptual skills**. Being able to diagnose situations and create solutions to problems are important examples. Using sound judgment to solve problems and make decisions is another.

Steven Jobs foresaw the personal computer revolution when he cofounded Apple Computer Corporation. He led and inspired the team that created the widely acclaimed personal computer Apple's Macintosh. Yet Jobs' technical and conceptual skills weren't enough. He lacked human relations and political skills to remain at the helm of Apple Computer. The company's board ousted him in 1985. His new venture, Next Incorporated, suffers from a lack of a conceptual vision. The company has not yet earned a profit and has nearly exhausted $125 million in cash from backers such as Ross Perot and Canon Incorporated of Japan. In 1993, Next quit producing personal computers because they weren't competitive with others on the market.[3]

POLITICAL SKILLS

political skills Ability of a manager to get enough power to reach his or her goals.

Political skills are the ability of a manager to get enough power to reach his or her goals. A person with good political skills has the right connections, impresses the right people, and maintains good relations with others. A manager with political skills can also negotiate to his or her advantage.

Political skills can be used for the good of the organization or for self-interest. Say that Sammy Kane, a production supervisor, believes worker morale will improve if vending machines are installed in the lounge. Then workers won't have to go across the street to get drinks and snacks. Sammy decides that the best way to get the vending machines is to have a good relationship with the plant manager. In casual conversations, he compliments her about the high productivity of the workers. He says they work hard because she tries to keep their morale high. Sammy is "playing politics" to get the vending machines installed. After he has a good relationship with the plant manager, he mentions how nice it would be to have vending machines in the lounge. The plant manager decides to install the machines. Sammy's political skills have helped to bring this change about.

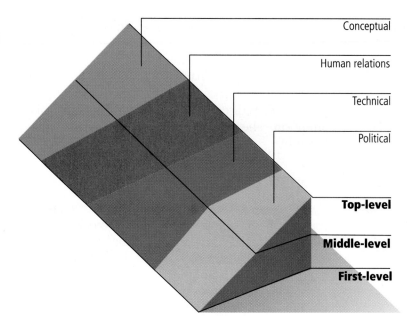

■ **Exhibit 8-2**
Managerial Skills Needed
at Each Level of Man-
agement

Conceptual

Human relations

Technical

Political

Top-level

Middle-level

First-level

SKILLS BY MANAGERIAL LEVEL

All four managerial skills are important. But their usefulness may vary by managerial level. Technical skills tend to be used most at lower levels of the organization. Conceptual skills are called into play more by managers with greater authority and responsibility, because they must see "the big picture." Human-relations skills are needed throughout the organization, at every managerial level. First-level managers may need them most, because of the heavy leadership demands of supervisory positions. Middle managers, on the other hand, often need the most political skill, because they often want to rise to top-level management. At the supervisory level, political skill is aimed mostly at steering the organization toward its goals. At the top, political tactics are focused on getting and holding power. Middle managers use political skills for both reasons—to win favor and to acquire and retain power. Exhibit 8-2 shows the degree of each skill used at the three main managerial levels.

All four management skills can be learned. Formal classes and exercises help managers at all levels hone their skills. Experience on the job plus formal management training helps create effective managers.

3   ## PROBLEM SOLVING AND DECISION MAKING

Of the four essential managerial skills, the conceptual skills of problem solving and decision making are hardest to develop through training. (*Decision making* is choosing among alternatives.) A manager's normal workday involves solving problems, making decisions, and communicating those decisions to others.

Of course, many problems are routine and can be solved by following set procedure. For example, suppose a personnel manager from American

Exhibit 8-3
Problem-Solving Process

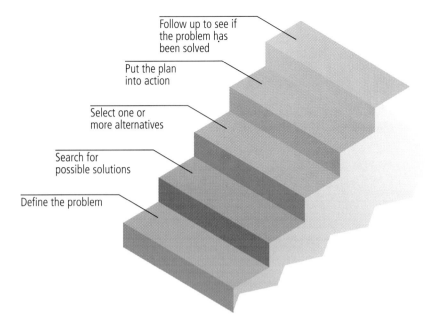

Follow up to see if
the problem has
been solved

Put the plan
into action

Select one or
more alternatives

Search for
possible solutions

Define the problem

Express gets a request for a new accounting supervisor in the Phoenix office. The manager will put into motion a standard recruiting plan.

Sometimes problems are unique or unforeseen and thus cannot be planned for. For example, a strike by employees concerned about hazardous working conditions would be an unexpected problem. To try to follow a routine procedure would be impractical and inappropriate.

Faced with a unique or unexpected problem, the manager must search for a solution. The first step is to clarify and define the problem. Once the problem is understood, the manager searches for alternatives; he or she outlines possible solutions and then evaluates them. Next, the manager makes a decision, choosing one or more alternatives. The manager then puts the plan into action. Finally, the manager follows through to see whether the plan has indeed solved the problem. Exhibit 8-3 summarizes these steps in the problem-solving process.

Concept Check

- Describe the four managerial skills and how they are used at each level of management.
- What are the steps in the problem-solving process?

PLANNING

4 Managerial work can be divided into four functions: planning, organizing, directing, and controlling. We will study them individually, but managers often perform more than one of these functions at a time. All of them require good decision-making and communication skills.

planning Managerial activity of deciding what needs to be done, how, when, and by whom.

Planning begins by setting goals and then designing strategies, policies, and methods for achieving the goals. Specifically, planning is decid-

■ Planning is one of the most important managerial functions. In planning meetings, work is divided and delegated, and timetables are set. Such meetings are the foundation of a successful project.

ing what needs to be done and how, when it will be done, and by whom it will be done. It helps an organization improve its competitive position. The planning process is the foundation for other managerial activities.

PURPOSES OF PLANNING

Many successful managers change their plans as they go along. Yet few would want—or dare—to proceed without planning. Plans and goals provide a framework for activities and a "measuring stick" which can be used to measure progress and success.

Planning provides several advantages to managers. First, it greatly increases their chances of success. Having a course of action helps them reach a specific goal. Second, it helps them coordinate their decisions and programs with those of other managers. Third, planning encourages the development of capable, forward-looking employees and managers.

proactive managers
Managers who anticipate problems, threats, and opportunities and take advance action.

Such managers are called **proactive managers**. They can anticipate problems, threats, and opportunities and take action in advance, rather than waiting for problems to develop. Norman Augustine, chairman of defense contractor Martin Marietta Corporation, has been riding a defense-spending roller coaster for the past decade. At a time when many contractors are leaving the defense market, Norman Augustine is moving his company deeper into the troubled industry. As a proactive manager, he recently bought General Electric's Aerospace Division for $3.05 billion. The purchase makes Martin Marietta the world's biggest defense electronics company. Mr. Augustine believes that he needs a huge corporation to survive the defense industry shake-out. He feels that changing world politics will one day again create heavy demand for his company's products.[4]

reactive managers
Managers who do not re-
spond to problems until the
damage has been done.

In contrast, **reactive managers** do not respond to problems until the damage has been done. Of course, managerial skill is needed in reactive situations, too—if only to remedy problems in the most efficient way. (Needless to say, even the most proactive managers are sometimes surprised by totally unexpected problems.) However, a proactive style is clearly better than a reactive one. A proactive style can often prevent problems before they occur. The best that a reactive manager can hope for is to minimize the damage from each crisis that arises.

PLANNING THROUGH OBJECTIVES

mission General purpose
or reason for an organization's existence.

An organization's **mission** is its general purpose or reason for existence. The mission of a hospital, for example, is to provide high-quality medical care for the surrounding community. The U.S. armed services exist to protect our country from foreign invasion and to protect our interests abroad. In the 1920s, Henry Ford established the following mission for the Ford Motor Company: to produce and market passenger cars at low cost so nearly every family could buy one.

objectives Measurable
targets to be achieved within
a certain time frame.

Objectives, which are based on an organization's mission statement, are measurable targets to be achieved within a certain time frame. For instance, Fuddrucker's Restaurants has an objective of attaining a high rate of repeat business. One method it uses to get repeat business is to sell specially marked plastic cups that, throughout the year, can be brought in and refilled with free soft drinks with a meal purchase.

TYPES OF PLANNING

You probably have done some personal planning of one sort or another. For example, you may have planned to get a college degree and then start working in the career of your choice. You may have marriage and a family somewhere in your plans as well. You do short-term planning too: You have a paper due in two weeks, you're scheduled to work at your job forty hours in that time, and you have a date this Friday night. Your short-term plans support your long-term ones. You need a passing grade on the paper to get through the course and eventually get your degree; your job helps pay tuition; the date might lead to fulfillment of the marriage and family goal. Without realizing it, you've been doing strategic and tactical planning. All businesses do the same.

Strategic Planning

strategic planning Creation of long-range, comprehensive objectives and
development of long-term
courses of action and allocation of resources to achieve
those objectives.

Strategic planning is creating long-range (one to five years), comprehensive objectives and figuring out what will need to be done and what resources will be needed to achieve those objectives. Strategic planning takes into account the organization's environment as well as the organization itself. Smart managers stay alert for new trends, such as those discussed in the Prologue, and ask themselves how such trends might affect the firm's strategic plan.

Strategies are formulated by top managers and put into action by lower-level managers. They help answer questions about what products, services, and locations a firm should offer its customers; what market opportunities exist; and what resources are needed to offer the right goods and services to customers. A strategic plan for Panasonic, for example, might focus on extensive research to provide leading edge electronic products for the consumer entertainment market.

Tactical Planning

tactical planning Short-range, detailed planning based on strategic planning decisions.

usually form of budget.

Tactical planning is short-range (often less than one year), detailed planning based on strategic decisions. It focuses on current operations. One of Panasonic's tactical plans might be to reduce production costs by lowering the number of individual parts needed to manufacture its big screen television sets.

Some tactical plans take the form of policies, procedures, and rules. *Policies* are guidelines for making decisions in particular situations. *Procedures* are steps to be followed in accomplishing a task. *Rules* are specific plans that prescribe how to carry out policies.

Consider the Panasonic *policy* of offering high-quality goods. To implement this policy, managers might follow the *procedure* of getting the quality of a new product approved by corporate headquarters before offering it to the public. The *rule* might be that every compact disk player has to pass four quality inspections.

Contingency Planning and Crisis Management

All organizations must have strategic and tactical plans, which usually need to be changed as the environment changes. One way of preparing

■ **Exhibit 8-4**
Characteristics of Strategic, Tactical, and Contingency Planning

Characteristic	Type of planning		
	Strategic planning (long-range)	Tactical planning (short-range)	Contingency planning (when certain conditions arise)
Time frame	One to five years or longer	One week to one year	When event occurs
Level of management	Top management (CEO, vice presidents, directors, division heads)	Lower or supervisory management (unit supervisors, first-line supervisors, assistant foremen, and middle management)	Top management and middle management
Coverage	External environment and entire organization	Smaller structural units and offices	External environment and entire organization
Purpose and goal	Establish mission and long-term goals	Implement and activate plans	Meet unforeseen challenges and opportunities
Content	Broad and general (objectives and policy statements)	Detailed (timetables, procedures, rules)	Both broad and detailed
Accuracy and predictability	Uncertain	Reasonably certain	Reasonably certain once event occurs

contingency plans Plans that identify courses of action to be taken if events disrupt the completion of a strategic or tactical plan.

for unforeseen circumstances is to develop a contingency plan. **Contingency plans** identify alternative courses of action to be taken if events undercut a strategic or tactical plan (see Exhibit 8-4). *USA Today*, for instance, is one of the nation's leading national newspapers. It must have contingency plans to meet unforeseen problems and take advantage of opportunities. What if the cost of newsprint suddenly triples? What if the people in Europe suddenly become very interested in a paper like *USA Today* in their own languages? Management needs to be prepared to deal with problems and seize opportunities as they arise.

crisis management Scramble for answers to business problems within a short time frame.

Sound contingency planning reduces the need for **crisis management**, which is the scramble for answers to business problems within a very short time frame. Explosions, product failures, tainted products, unethical employee actions, hurricanes, floods, and fires require quick and decisive actions. In many instances, crisis management produces bad decisions. When bad publicity hits, the company should begin a campaign to minimize it right away. The company should also seek to resume normal operations as quickly as possible.

INVOLVEMENT IN PLANNING

All levels of management are involved in the planning process (see Exhibit 8-4). But top-level managers spend more time planning than middle- and lower-level managers do. For the most part, lower-level managers and technical employees carry out the strategies and policies issued by top managers. For example, local sales managers at Southwestern Bell submit sales forecasts. The data are then compiled and modified by the regional managers and, finally, by the vice president of marketing. Top-level managers then set tactical goals based on the sales forecasts. The tactical plans are formulated in light of Southwestern Bell's strategic plan.

Concept Check

- Why is it important to plan?
- How do proactive and reactive managers differ?
- Compare and contrast strategic, tactical, and contingency planning.

ORGANIZING

4

organizing Managerial activity of arranging a firm's human and material resources to carry out its plans.

A second activity of management is **organizing**, or arranging a firm's human and material resources to carry out its plans. The purpose of organizing is to coordinate the efforts of all parts of the company. Organizing provides the structure of people, positions, departments, and activities.

Sometimes companies over-organize; the result is bureaucracy. For example, there are 332 regional Girl Scout councils scattered around the United States, each one with an office and a paid staff overseen by a volunteer board. This structure is then overseen by the national office, Girl Scouts USA. The sprawling bureaucracy of Girl Scouts of America eats up most of the profits of Girl Scout cookie sales. For example, Troop 265 of Wallingford, Connecticut, sold $498 worth of Girl Scout cookies (166

■ General Electric boosted efficiency and productivity in many of its divisions by modernizing their organization. Quality control is emphasized, and teams of seven to eight workers rotate jobs and make decisions about how their work should be done. This organic structure will allow the company to adapt rapidly to changes in the industry.

boxes). But only $67 of the troop's sales remained in its bank account. The small amount of earnings wasn't even enough to buy all of the badges the girls earned during the year. Annually, the sale of Girl Scout cookies generates over $400 million in revenue. Yet the bureaucracy consumes over $357 million of the profit.[5]

STRUCTURE AND DESIGN

The formal structure of an organization is the arrangement of positions, departments, and major work units and the relationships that exist among these elements. Managers can arrange these elements for the most efficient flow of work and information. They do so by

- Dividing up the tasks (*division of labor*)
- Grouping jobs and employees (*departmentalization*)
- Shifting and redefining authority and responsibility (*delegation*)

These and other key features of organizational structure are discussed in Chapter 9.

CHANGE AND REORGANIZATION

Hospitals, government agencies, businesses, and other organizations are always changing. Many changes are the result of carefully laid plans. Other changes come in response to financial distress. The ability to make organizational changes effectively and efficiently is often a key to organizational survival and success.

Some industries experience little technological, customer, or competitive change. Examples are the industries that produce cement, railroad box cars, and small electric motors. Companies operating in an environment of little change tend to have more formal and rigid organizational structures. For the most part, their procedures are standardized, and jobs are specialized.

Other industries are more likely to face rapid change. These firms benefit from a more *organic* form of organization, with little standardization and lots of adaptability. John Welch, CEO of General Electric, has transformed GE from a rigid, stodgy company to a highly organic one. Welch says, "We no longer have the time to climb over barriers between functions like engineering and marketing, or between people—hourly, salaried, management, and the like. Geographic barriers must evaporate. Our people must be as comfortable in Delhi and Seoul as they are in Louisville or Schenectady. The lines between the company and its vendors and customers must be blurred into a smooth, fluid process with no other objective than satisfying the customer and winning in the marketplace."[6]

Regardless of how slowly or rapidly the environment changes, organizations do reorganize over time. An example is some of the large public accounting firms. Recently they have changed from a structure based on the type of accounting service (such as audit, tax, general accounting, management consulting) to one based on type of client (not-for-profit, health care, banking). Each customer group has its own auditors, tax specialists, and consultants. The top partners in some firms have even delegated additional authority and responsibility to client-group managers, so they can more quickly react to the environment. Each client group becomes a separate center accountable for its own profits and expenses.

Concept Check

- Define organization and its purpose.
- Describe an organic form of organization.

DIRECTING

4

directing Managerial activity of guiding others to achieve specific objectives.

After an organization's structure has been created and plans have been developed, employees must work to carry out those plans. Managers must set in motion these activities. The third management activity, **directing,** is guiding others in order to achieve specific goals. From the employee's point of view, the directing activity is often what makes a manager seem effective or not.

The skills of directing are essential for getting employees to do their jobs properly. The key elements are *leadership, communication,* and *motivation.* The manager has to understand what motivates workers to complete their tasks. Incentives, such as recognition or a pay boost, encourage people to perform at their best. A high level of performance is more likely when the manager's leadership is encouraging and when communication is nonthreatening and supportive. The managerial activities of planning and organizing are performed most often by managers at higher levels of the organization. Lower-level managers and supervisors spend most of their time directing and controlling.

5 LEADERSHIP

leadership Ability to influence and direct others to attain specific organizational goals.

The ability to influence and direct others in order to attain specific organizational goals is **leadership**. Successful leadership depends on the leader's ability to communicate and influence behavior, the followers' responsiveness to the leader's directives, and the nature of the task.

Leadership Style

leadership style Relatively consistent behavior pattern that characterizes a leader.

autocratic leadership style Decision style in which managers make all the decisions and order employees to implement the solutions.

Effective leaders are relatively consistent in the way they attempt to influence the behavior of others. The manager who makes all the major decisions in one situation is not likely to share decision making in another. Likewise, a manager who is considerate in one situation is not likely to be insensitive in another. **Leadership style** is the relatively consistent pattern of behavior that characterizes a leader. Much of the consistency occurs because a leadership style is based somewhat on an individual's personality. Despite this consistency, some managers can modify their style as the situation requires.

Three common decision styles are autocratic, participative, and free-rein (see Exhibit 8-5). Each has its own blend of employee involvement. Managers who try to solve all the problems themselves and order employees to implement the solutions use the **autocratic leadership style**.

Exhibit 8-5
Management Leadership Styles

Amount of authority held by the leader

Autocratic style
- Manager makes most decisions.
- Manager acts in authoritative manner.
- Manager is usually concerned about subordinates' attitudes toward decisions.
- Emphasis is on gettting task accomplished.
- Manager tells people what to do and is assertive.
- Approach is used mostly by military officers and some production line supervisors.

Participative style (democratic, consensual, consultative)
- Manager shares decision making with group members.
- Manager encourages discussion of issues and alternatives.
- Approach encourages teamwork.
- Manager is concerned about subordinates' ideas and attitudes.
- Manager coaches subordinates and helps coordinate efforts.
- Approach is found in many successful organizations.

Free-rein style (laissez-faire)
- Manager turns over virtually all authority and control to group.
- Manager leads group by providing ideas and information.
- Members of group are presented with task and given freedom to accomplish it.
- Members can do anything they want as long as their actions don't violate company policy.
- Approach works well with highly motivated, experienced, educated personnel.
- Approach is found mostly in high-tech firms, laboratories, and colleges.

Amount of authority held by group members

■ Certain management styles are better suited to certain business environments than others. The participative style is common among research scientists, such as those on this semiconductor research team. In a more dynamic environment, such as Bill Gates' Microsoft software company, a free-rein style might work better. Microsoft's many technically skilled employees are allowed to find their own methods of accomplishing the tasks they are assigned.

participative leadership style Decision style in which managers share decision making with group members through a democratic process, consensus, or consultation.

Information flows in one direction only, from manager to employee. An autocratic style may help a company that hasn't been performing up to its potential. An unusual, yet successful, autocratic leadership style is Robert Levine, chief executive officer of Cabletron Corporation. He feels so strongly about keeping meetings short that Cabletron's conference rooms have no chairs—only waist-high tables. A woman who worked in Cabletron's telephone-sales operation recalls the firm as "an extreme pressure-cooker situation."[7] A young salesman who earned more than $100,000 a year says he was fired two years ago for arriving 30 minutes late to a daylong training session.[8] Mr. Levine's aggressive attitude also applies to decision making. Steps that might require months at other companies are often taken in days. David Kirkpatrick, chief financial officer, recalls that Mr. Levine approved the construction of a factory in Scotland "in two short meetings over three days, in which he didn't ask for the details."[9]

When autocratic leaders are liked and respected, they are considered knowledgeable and decisive. Many successful managers are autocrats. But when autocrats are disliked, they are perceived as being heavy-handed. Perhaps that is why the autocratic style is losing ground in most organizations. Most of the new breed of managers are willing to share authority with the group.

Leaders who share decision making with group members are using a **participative leadership style**. There are three types of participative leadership. *Democratic leaders* let the group make the final decision. The manager collects information and then the group votes on what action to take. Sometimes physicians or scientific teams at places like Bell Labs use this approach. *Consensual leaders* encourage group discussion about an issue and then make a decision that reflects the general agreement (consensus) of group members. All workers who will be affected by a decision have a chance to provide input. A decision is not considered final until all parties involved agree with the decision. *Consultative leaders* confer with subordinates before making a decision, but they retain the final authority to make decisions.

A participative style does have some problems. It often results in time-consuming committee work. And sometimes participative management is carried to extremes. Subordinates are consulted about trivial things the manager could easily handle. Yet, when kept in bounds, the participative style is well suited to managing competent people who are eager to assume responsibility.

Historically, managers in Western Europe have been easy-going, collegial, participative-style managers. Yet the new United Europe and stiff global competition have resulted in a tougher new management style as the Global Competition Trends box shows.

TRENDS

Global Competition

Europe's Tough New Managers

Marco Tronchetti Provera got his job the old-fashioned way: He married into the Pirelli family, one of Italy's richest. A decade later he joined the family business, which is Europe's second-largest tiremaker. Tronchetti rose quickly, leaping over several more experienced managers to become managing director in February 1992. When he took over, Pirelli was on the brink of bankruptcy.

Tronchetti began a series of moves that would have been unthinkable in Europe a few years ago. He closed 12 plants, sold a huge division, fired 170 senior managers, moved the company's headquarters from Milan's plush Piazzale Cadorna to a modest building on the corner of a 74,000-acre factory site outside town, and hired actress Sharon Stone to lead a European image campaign. Almost as an encore, he and the chairman's daughter separated. Pirelli is still losing money, but a lot less than before.

The changing of the guard cuts all across European industry. Says Michel de Rosen, an ambitious executive at Rhone-Poulenc, the soon-to-be-privatized chemicals giant: "In the past, an advanced degree from the right school was enough to get you the top job. Now performance counts for much more."

Global competition lies behind all of this change. Between 1983 and 1993, Europe's share of world markets dropped 14.4 percent, to 13.9 percent, while Asia's fast-growing nations—not even counting Japan—have seen their share rise from 4.6 percent to 8.1 percent, according to the International Monetary Fund. Even worse, Europe has failed at creating strong companies in the high-tech industries that will dominate the next century.

Europe still has a long way to go in overcoming the competitive drag of its too-generous social welfare system and its laid-back approach to management. But if the trend toward a new management style continues, and even picks up, Europe could become a model of how to manage in the new global economy.[10]

free-rein (laissez-faire) leadership style Decision style in which managers turn over all authority and control to employees.

Managers who use a **free-rein** or **laissez-faire** (translated as "leave it alone") **leadership style** turn over all authority and control to the group. Group members are given a task and free rein to figure out how best to perform it. The manager doesn't get involved unless asked. Subordinates are allowed all the freedom they want as long as they do not violate company policy.

A problem with the free-rein style is that it often frustrates subordinates. They perceive the free-rein manager as being uninvolved and indifferent to what is happening. Free-rein managers run the risk of being replaced, because they appear to contribute so little to running the department.

Each of these three leadership styles—autocratic, participative, free-rein—has good and bad points. The one that seems most popular today is the participative style, perhaps partially because it is the typical style of the Japanese companies that have become so successful in the global marketplace.

Also, different management styles often work better in different business environments. In stable environments, such as concrete manufacturing which changes very little and employs a large number of low-skilled workers, an autocratic management style may work best. On the other hand, in a dynamic environment such as computer software development, which changes rapidly and employs primarily technically skilled employees, a free-rein style of management may provide the most productive work environment.

The effectiveness of a leader also depends on whether he or she is job-centered or employee-centered. **Job-centered managers** focus on what is needed to complete a task. They plan and organize the workplace, assign work duties, inspect worker output, and closely follow work rules and procedures. **Employee-centered** managers tend to be more concerned about their subordinates than about the details of the tasks. They assume that if people are happy in their work, the work will be done well. These managers understand and appreciate the personal needs of their employees. They develop meaningful work-related relationships with them and try to expand their capabilities as individuals and as a group.

Job-centered managers tend to be autocratic in their dealings with employees. Employee-centered managers tend to be democratic. That is, job-centered managers tend to make decisions and issue orders, with little or no input from subordinates. Employee-centered managers permit subordinates to take part in work decisions. Each approach may be good for certain kinds of work. For example, production line managers tend to be job-centered; managers of chemistry research labs tend to be employee-centered. But usually, effective managers combine the two approaches.

job-centered managers Managers who direct their efforts toward what is necessary for completing a task.

employee-centered managers Managers who are more concerned about their subordinates than about the details of their group's tasks.

COMMUNICATION

Managers must communicate with their subordinates and with others to transmit their ideas and directives. They are also communicating when they receive information they need to make decisions. In fact, the effectiveness of a supervisor rests heavily on his or her communication skills. Most daily activities of a supervisor are dominated by contacts with subordinates, superiors, and other supervisors.

Communication can be formal or informal. Formal communication includes messages transmitted through meetings, memos, posters, reports, closed-circuit television, and electronic mail (on computers). In *horizontal* channels of communication, messages are passed to people at the same organizational level. In *vertical* channels, messages are passed up and down the management structure. For instance, when Lou Gerstner was brought in from RJR Nabisco to head IBM, he held numerous meetings with top managers at the company. Soon after taking the reins, he also began vertical communications by having meetings at IBM plants and sales offices.

In addition to formal communication, considerable informal interaction takes place at work. Informal communication systems, also called grapevines or rumor mills, often parallel formal systems. But they usually involve face-to-face communication. Casual conversations during lunch breaks are a type of informal communication. (Chapter 9 looks at the informal organization in more detail.)

Keys to Effective Communication

Here are several rules of good communication:

- Know what you want to say before you say it. Have a clear idea about what you hope to accomplish by communicating.
- Remember that communication is more than just words. A person's tone of voice, a smile or frown, and gestures can say more than words.
- Be mindful of your audience. Consider the other person's needs and interests.
- Always follow up. Make sure your message was understood. Get a reaction to what you said.
- Be a good listener as well as a good speaker. When people start talking, they often stop listening. Listening helps avoid such costly mistakes as half-filled orders, rescheduled meetings, and needlessly repeated work.

MOTIVATION

motivation Stimulation and direction of behavior through encouragement, incentives, and reinforcement.

Effective managers must be able to motivate their subordinates to perform well. **Motivation** is the stimulation and direction of behavior. Through encouragement, incentives, and reinforcement, managers can motivate people to work harder and better. One major incentive is money. Salespeople who work on commission are likely to work harder and better than those who work for fixed salaries, for example. Another incentive is clear, supportive feedback about performance. Employees who are not told about their mistakes are unlikely to correct them. Those who are told in a supportive way usually try to improve their job performance. Recognizing workers for a "job well done" encourages other workers to do well and shows that "management cares."

■ By reengineering their work processes, Kodak improved the morale and productivity of the employees in its black-and-white film department. The employees, known as "zebras," now work in self-directed teams that are part of "the flow." This increased freedom stimulated the workers' motivation, and profits rose accordingly.

Managers can increase worker motivation in various ways. One is to give rewards: promotions, wage increases, praise, recognition. Another is to design challenge and variety into jobs—for instance, by giving workers more interesting and more difficult (but achievable) tasks. A third way to increase worker motivation is to change certain aspects of the work environment. For example, Chrysler gave skilled workers new and better tools for building its New Yorker model. As a result, model defects decreased greatly. These motivational techniques can make the work and the work environment more pleasant. If employees have a chance to satisfy personal needs, they will work harder. (Motivation is discussed more in Chapter 11.)

Concept Check

- Explain directing.
- Explain the three management leadership styles.
- Describe the differences between formal and informal communication systems.
- Define motivation, and explain its importance.

CONTROLLING

DIRECTING
(steering toward a goal)

4

controlling Managerial activity of ensuring that the organization's goals are being met, by monitoring progress toward them and correcting deviations from the plan if necessary.

The manager's **controlling** activity is the process of ensuring that the organization's goals are being met. It includes monitoring progress toward those goals and correcting deviations from the plan if necessary. The three basic steps of control are establishing performance standards, measuring performance (of employees and of the organization), and taking corrective action if needed (see Exhibit 8-6).

Performance standards are the levels of performance the company wishes to attain. They are based on established objectives. To be useful, they should be expressed in very specific terms. Liz Claiborne, the clothing manufacturer, might establish a goal of making 1,000 pairs of twill pants per month as one of its performance standards. Also, the company might hold supervisors to the performance standard of responding to all seamstresses' grievances within two working days. Actual performance is then measured against the standards to see if corrective action needs to be taken.

Feedback is essential to controlling. Most companies have a reporting system that points up performance standards that are not being met. A feedback system helps managers see problems before they get out of

■ **Exhibit 8-6**
Elements of Managerial Control

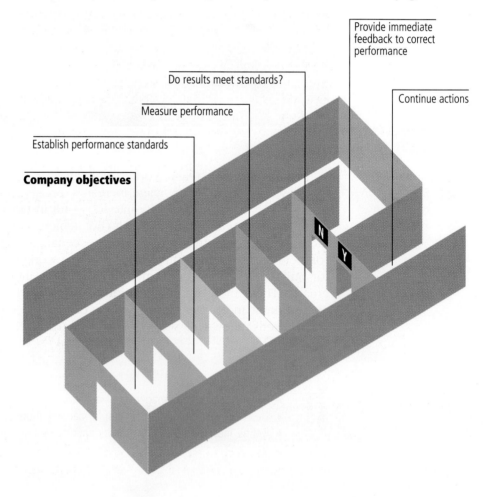

Provide immediate feedback to correct performance

Continue actions

Do results meet standards?

Measure performance

Establish performance standards

Company objectives

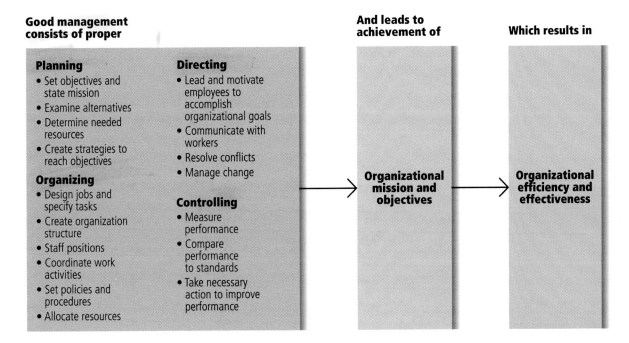

Good management consists of proper		And leads to achievement of	Which results in

Planning
- Set objectives and state mission
- Examine alternatives
- Determine needed resources
- Create strategies to reach objectives

Organizing
- Design jobs and specify tasks
- Create organization structure
- Staff positions
- Coordinate work activities
- Set policies and procedures
- Allocate resources

Directing
- Lead and motivate employees to accomplish organizational goals
- Communicate with workers
- Resolve conflicts
- Manage change

Controlling
- Measure performance
- Compare performance to standards
- Take necessary action to improve performance

Organizational mission and objectives

Organizational efficiency and effectiveness

Exhibit 8-7
What Managers Do and Why

hand. If a problem exists, they can take corrective action. Toyota uses a simple but effective control system on its automobile assembly lines. Each worker serves as the customer for the process just before his or hers. The worker becomes a quality-control inspector. If a piece isn't installed properly, it won't be accepted by the next worker. Any worker can alert the supervisor to a problem by tugging a rope that turns on a warning light (feedback). If the problem isn't corrected by the time the next piece comes down the line, the worker can stop the line by pulling the rope a second time.

Why is controlling important? First, it lets managers determine the success of their planning, organizing, and leading activities. Second, control systems direct everyone's behavior toward important goals. Third, control systems coordinate the activities of all members of the organization. They provide methods to integrate resources and measure activities. In a sense, control is the mechanism for making sure the other three managerial functions—planning, organizing, and directing—are operating smoothly. Exhibit 8-7 summarizes these functions of management.

Concept Check
- Describe the control process.
- Why is control important?

CONTROLLING YOUR LIFE IN THE WORKPLACE

In many offices today, people never seem to have enough time to complete the day's work. Every manager knows how it is: The data for the annual report are due by 5 p.m. The fax is spitting out word of a pending corporate reorganization. Jim in accounting drops by to report a "little problem" with some of the first-quarter numbers. The secretary is at home sick, and the temporary secretary has put the chairman on hold by mistake.

Time pressure and stress—the two go hand in hand. Stress is a physical and emotional condition that comes from trying to adapt to the environment. A study found that the average manager is interrupted every eight minutes by co-workers. Interruptions, once one of life's minor problems, are the leading cause of on-the-job stress. A certain amount of stress will increase motivation and performance. But beyond a point, stress impairs performance. The negative effects of stress are physical and mental. Physical stress can result in loss of weight or excessive weight gain, fatigue, ulcers, and heart problems. Mentally one can become depressed, anxious, and unable to sleep. It's important, therefore, to learn to deal with both time pressures and stress.

TRENDS

Business Today

Work Smart

Here are some tips for managing your time:

- *Plan ahead:* This is first and most obvious. Write out your goals for the day, the week, the month, the quarter.
- *Establish priorities:* Keep in mind the 80-20 rule: 20 percent of one's effort delivers 80 percent of the results. Find and focus on that 20 percent.
- *Learn to say no:* Managers waste a lot of time by taking on too much.
- *Delegate wherever possible:* Never do something yourself that can be done by somebody else.
- *Batch:* That is, do similar things together. For example, set aside an hour for returning phone calls instead of allowing yourself to be interrupted every few minutes.
- *Finish up:* Many projects drag on and on because there is no force toward closure.

If stress builds up despite your efforts to manage time better, try these:

- *Get plenty of exercise:* Exercise helps reduce some of the tension created by job stress. It also helps the body ward off future stress-related disorders. A physically fit, well-rested person usually can tolerate more frustration than can a tired, physically run-down person.
- *Eat properly:* The body's nutritional needs increase a great deal during periods of stress. The body is depleted of vitamins and minerals, and its ability to resist further stress decreases. Caffeine, sugar, and salt can compound the problem by increasing the production of stress chemicals.
- *Learn to relax:* Relaxation is the opposite of stress. Learning to relax is a good way to counter the effects of stress on the body. People who practice relaxation skills regularly are likely to be more psychologically and physiologically stable, less anxious, and in greater control of their lives than people who do not. A relaxed state can be achieved through

progressive muscle relaxation, use of pleasant mental pictures, and deep breathing.

- *Get support from friends, family, and co-workers:* Few people can function alone when experiencing prolonged stress. Social support from other people—encouragement, understanding, and friendship—is an important strategy for coping successfully with job stress.[11]

MANAGEMENT BY OBJECTIVES

6

management by objectives (MBO) Program in which employees help set goals for their own performance and at specified intervals check their performance against the goals.

Over the past forty years, thousands of organizations have tried to improve managerial performance through the use of **management by objectives (MBO)**. Introduced by Peter Drucker, a well-known management consultant, MBO is a program in which employees help set their own goals. Then, at specified times, they check their performance against the goals.

The MBO approach is based on the idea that every person and every job in an organization exists for a reason. That reason can be expressed as an objective for the person and the job. (Some examples of MBO objectives are shown in Exhibit 8-8.) The employee and the supervisor discuss the job and its objectives so they both clearly understand what is expected of the employee. MBO is versatile: Among the organizations using it are Texas Instruments, the Salvation Army, Walt Disney Company, and the U.S. Department of Health and Human Services.

MBO programs vary greatly from organization to organization. They tend, though, to have a few common characteristics:

- The employee and the supervisor work out a mutual understanding of the employee's job and responsibilities. They devote special attention to areas that can be improved.

▨ Exhibit 8-8
Examples of Objectives for an MBO Program

Position	Objective
Collections manager	To reduce the number of outstanding past-due accounts by 8 percent in nine months
Marketing manager	To introduce new Model XK in the $200-$300 price range by November 1 and to reach 10,000 units in annual sales volume by June 15
Production manager	To reduce product defects from 8 percent to 2 percent by December 15
Sales manager	To reduce salespersons' costs by 5 pecent by consolidating sales districts (and thereby reducing travel expenses) by April 1
Personnel manager	To computerize all remaining personnel files by March 1

- The employee and the supervisor devise, agree on, and record the specific objectives to be attained. They set time limits and target dates for attaining each objective.
- They devise action plans for accomplishing the objectives.
- At periodic performance reviews, they decide whether the objectives have been met. They may set new objectives or modify the unmet ones.
- The supervisor offers rewards (raises, promotions, bonuses) for successfully attaining the objectives.

At first glance, MBO seems rather simple. But it is not as easy as it looks. The objectives must be realistic and measurable. Supervisors must also realize that objectives are often reached by group effort, not just by individuals.

If MBO is handled well, it can bring several benefits beyond the accomplishment of specific objectives. Among these benefits are better relationships, planning and control systems, interpersonal communication, and employee motivation. MBO, however, is not without some problems. Sometimes it is very difficult to align goals within and across departments in complex organizations. Sometimes there may also be mismatch between organizational and individual objectives. MBO can require a lot of meetings and huge amounts of documentation, especially when starting a new MBO program. Finally, the increased paperwork often causes managers to resist the MBO concept.

Concept Check
- Explain the management by objectives process.
- What are some possible benefits and drawbacks of MBO?

■ SUMMARY

Key Terms

autocratic leadership
   style 258

conceptual skills 249

contingency plans 255

controlling 264

crisis management 255

directing 257

employee-centered
   managers 261

free-rein (laissez-faire)
   leadership style 260

human-relations skills
   248

continued

1. Briefly explain the nature of management and the roles of managers.
Management is the process of coordinating a firm's human and other resources to accomplish organizational goals. Managerial roles are informational, interpersonal, and decisional. Most firms have three levels of management: top, middle, and supervisory. Top managers establish overall strategy and long-range goals. Middle managers implement the plans and policies of top managers. Supervisors manage operating employees.

2. Identify the four managerial skills, and describe their usefulness at various levels of organization.
A successful manager effectively uses four basic skills: Technical skills consist of the specialized knowledge and abilities that a person brings to a job. Human-relations skills are those required to work with people to accomplish organizational goals. Conceptual skills are those used to view

the organization as a whole and see how the parts fit together. Political skills are those used by a manager to reach his or her objectives, such as having the right connections and impressing the right people. Technical skills tend to play a larger role at the lower organizational levels. Conceptual skills are needed more as the manager advances in the organization. Human-relations skills are important at every level. Political skills are most often used by middle managers.

3. List the steps in the problem-solving process.

A manager's typical workday involves solving problems, making decisions, and communicating those decisions to others. Some problems are routine and can be dealt with according to established procedures. Unforeseen problems require that the manager become aware that an unusual problem exists, clarify and define the problem, outline possible solutions, weigh and evaluate the solutions, choose the best one, implement it, and follow through to see if it succeeds.

4. Explain the four managerial functions: planning, organizing, directing, and controlling.

The four managerial functions form a tightly integrated cycle consisting of thinking about a problem and making a decision, taking action, reviewing the decision and employee performance, and making needed adjustments.

Planning is future oriented. It requires setting objectives and designing the strategies, policies, and methods for achieving them. It is handled by managers who are either proactive (looking forward) or reactive (responding to existing problems). Strategic planning is long-range and comprehensive. Strategic plans are designed by top managers and carried out by lower-level ones. Tactical planning is short-range and detailed. It is based on strategic planning decisions and focuses on current operations. Tactical plans can take the form of policies, procedures, or rules. Contingency plans are courses of action to be taken if events disrupt the completion or accomplishment of a plan.

Organizing is the process of arranging the firm's human and material resources to carry out its plans. Organizations are constantly changing. Rapid change calls for flexible organization structures.

Directing is guiding others to achieve certain goals. Its key elements are leadership, communication, and motivation. Leadership effectiveness depends on leadership style and whether a manager is job-centered or employee-centered. Communication systems may be formal or informal. Formal systems may be either vertical or horizontal. Informal systems are commonly referred to as grapevines. Motivation can be increased through rewards, job challenges and variety, and changes in the work environment.

Controlling ensures that the organization's objectives are being attained. Its basic steps are setting performance standards, measuring performance, and taking corrective action. An essential element of control is feedback.

5. Describe the three management leadership styles.

A manager's decision style is how he or she interacts with employees and involves them in solving problems. An autocratic manager tries to solve problems without consulting employees. He or she issues orders to implement actions to solve the problem. A participative manager shares decision making with group members. There are three participative decision styles: democratic, consensual, and consultative. A free-rein manager turns over almost all authority and control to the group.

6. Discuss management by objectives.

Many firms have tried to improve employee performance through the use of management by objectives (MBO). The objectives are set by employees and their managers working together. Performance is evaluated on the basis of how well the employee meets the objectives.

■ DISCUSSION QUESTIONS

1. Why do organizations need managers?

2. Choose a job you've had. List the top-, middle-, and lower-level managers, indicate their job titles, and briefly describe their duties.

3. Being a middle manager may be more stressful than being a first-level or top-level manager. Why might this be true?

4. From your own job experience, provide examples of problem-solving and leadership styles.

5. Assume you are a supervisor of twenty to twenty-five assembly-line workers. Which decision style would be best for choosing three workers to schedule for overtime work? Which would be best for identifying ways of reducing waste? Which would be best for setting the department's summer vacation schedule? Explain your answers.

6. Use the activities of the president of your college or university to illustrate the three managerial roles presented in the chapter. Provide examples of each type of role (list people, places, events, and so on).

7. Using a McDonald's restaurant manager as an example, give a sample decision for each of the managerial functions: planning, organizing, directing, and controlling.

8. Is your most recent work supervisor employee-centered or job-centered? Briefly explain the differences in these two leadership approaches in terms of motivating employees and communicating job requirements to them.

9. Identify at least ten ways that your college controls your campus life.

10. How do students use the four major management functions to accomplish their goal of graduating?

■ CASE

Managing in Tough Times

In a world of unceasing change, the new manager must balance the tremendous demands of work with demands from the rest of his or her life—and help others do the same. It isn't easy. No one knows that better than Rick Hess, 40, of M/A-Com, a Lowell, Massachusetts, defense company that makes microwave communications equipment and is trying to build business in the private sector. M/A-Com's chief operating officer said to the staff in April, "I went home last night and told my wife the next year will be hell. I suggest you go home and tell yours. It's tough times."

A typical day for Hess starts at 7 a.m. and ends at 7 p.m. He goes home, tucks his four young kids in, and then does paperwork until bed, typically about 11. He tries to leave weekends for his family. It helps, he found, to keep his work in perspective. "I'm a fairly patient person," he ways. "I get angry but don't display it. I try to look at the long term. I always have a goal, and I focus on that and don't get upset with the day to day."

Hess knows his people are under a lot of stress, too, and that part of the manager's job is to make sure they avoid burnout. He stays close to them, takes them to lunch, tries to find out what's going on in their lives. He plays softball or basketball with them one night a week. "I want to know if someone's wife is having a baby so I don't give him a job that requires him to work an 80-hour week. The worst thing I can do is give someone an assignment he's bound to fail."

To motivate his people Hess constantly tries to get them to challenge themselves, another important skill of the new manager. "Don't rule people out because they don't have experience," he says. "Don't trap people in cubbies. Give people a reach if they have potential. Let a technical guy go and talk with customers and grow." Hess likes ambitious people because he understands that he won't be able to go to his next job until someone is ready to take his.[12]

Questions

1. How would you describe the leadership style of Rick Hess?
2. Would you say that Rick Hess is a job-centered or employee-centered manager? Why?
3. Do you think that MBO would be effective at M/A-Com? Why or why not?

Internal Organization of the Firm

1 Describe the factors to consider in building a formal organization.

2 Explain the bases for organizing departments within an organization.

3 Explain the difference between the formal and informal organization, and describe the informal organization's functions.

4 Describe organizational authority and the sources of authority.

5 Understand line and staff and other organizational design choices.

6 Understand how the environment affects organizational development.

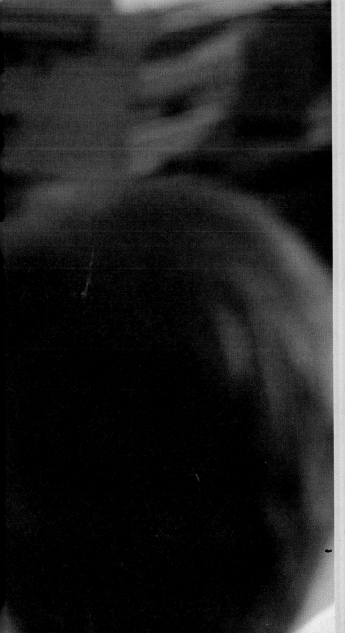

Career Profile

Richard Zinnecker's first job out of college was a challenging one for a recent graduate: He took a position in the accounting department of a company that had filed for reorganization under Chapter 11 bankruptcy laws. The firm had worked out a plan in bankruptcy court to pay off part of its debts, and Richard's department was responsible for implementing it. He and his team successfully turned the company around, and eventually it was making a profit again.

Richard then moved into the position of comptroller for Advanced Office Systems, an office automation company. The firm sells products that help make offices more efficient—fax machines, copiers, and computer peripherals like modems. Richard was once again immediately faced with the challenge of assisting in the reorganization of a company. Utilizing his previous experience, he helped Advanced Office Systems grow by 30 percent in the first year of its reorganization.

Richard's main task as comptroller is to monitor the money coming into and going out of the company. He is in charge of order entry, accounts receivable, accounts payable, check approval, collection calls, and establishing and building relationships with banks and vendors. Another important aspect of his job is evaluating the operations of the different departments, and then, in conjunction with the department managers, determining ways to make them more efficient. Efficiency is important to Richard, because he recognizes that a well-organized company is usually a successful company.

Richard's double major in finance and accounting prepared him for his career, with all its responsibility. He learned to analyze data and derive the proper conclusions from it, a skill he draws upon every day. Richard was also president of his college's Business Tribunal. He reported to the dean and the assistant dean to discuss issues like funding and accreditation. This taught him more about finance and also gave him valuable experience in interacting with people in authority.

Chapter 9 begins by exploring the basics of the formal and informal organizational structure. The focus then turns to how delegating authority and assigning responsibility bring an organization to life. Next the chapter explores the ways organizations are built. The chapter concludes with a look at how factors outside the firm affect organizational design.

THE NATURE OF THE FORMAL ORGANIZATION

 A formal organization consists of two or more people working together with a common objective and a clarity of purpose. Formal organizations also have lines of authority, channels for information flows, and some means of control.

ORGANIZATION STRUCTURE

Structure implies order and design. *Organization structure,* then, is the order and design of relationships within the firm. Human, material, financial, and information resources are deliberately connected to form the business organization. Some connections are long lasting, such as the links among people in the finance or marketing department. Others can be changed at almost any time, as when a committee is formed to study a problem.

organization chart
Depiction of the relationships among tasks and those given authority to do those tasks in a formal organization.

An **organization chart** is a picture of the structured relationships among tasks and those given authority to do those tasks. In the organization chart in Exhibit 9-1, each figure represents a job, which includes several tasks. The sales manager, for instance, must hire salespeople, set sales territories, motivate and train salespeople, and control sales operations. The chart also shows the general type of work done. The vice president of operations, for instance, is in charge of manufacturing (through over-

Exhibit 9-1
Organization Chart for a Typical Appliance Manufacturer

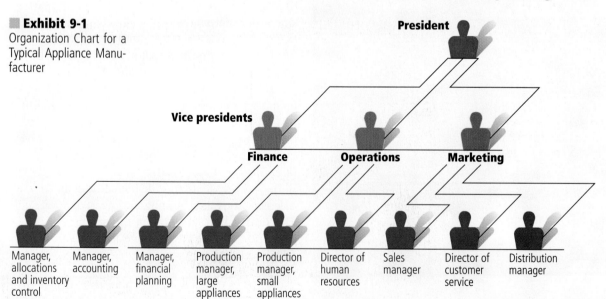

President

Vice presidents

Finance   Operations   Marketing

Manager, allocations and inventory control | Manager, accounting | Manager, financial planning | Production manager, large appliances | Production manager, small appliances | Director of human resources | Sales manager | Director of customer service | Distribution manager

sight of production managers) and staffing (through oversight of the director of human resources).

Organization charts show the *formal* relationships among people, jobs, and departments. The *informal* relationships can be quite different. At times they can be even more effective than the formal ones. At a large H. J. Heinz tomato-processing plant, the supervisor of the kitchens and the personnel specialist were friends. They attended sporting events and hunted and fished together. During the canning season, in the summer, the plant hired hundreds of temporary workers. Many of them were migrant laborers. A few college students would also be hired for the summer. The kitchen supervisor preferred using the college students in his department, because they quickly learned what to do. Because of his friendship with the personnel specialist, he almost always had a chance to interview the college students before the other supervisors did. An organization chart does not specify these day-to-day relationships, which are discussed in more detail later in the chapter.

STRUCTURAL BUILDING BLOCKS

The design of an organization structure depends on the firm's core competency or capability. The *core competency* is the activity or set of activities that forms the basis for an organization's existence. For example, Southwest Airlines' core competency is short-haul passenger airline flights. Core competencies form the basis for organizing work activities. Four major building blocks help firms design an organization structure to accomplish their work activities. The building blocks are division of labor and specialization, departmentalization, span of control, and the managerial hierarchy.

■ The main basis for the existence of Southwest Airlines is to provide short-haul passenger airline flights. This, then, is Southwest's core competency. A company's core competency will determine the structure of the firm and the organization of work activities.

Division of Labor and Specialization

After the core competency has been identified, it is broken down into smaller work activities. Workers are then assigned to perform each of the subtasks. The process of dividing the work and assigning tasks to workers is the **division of labor**. In a fast-food restaurant, for instance, some employees take and fill orders, others prepare food, a few clean and maintain equipment, and at least one supervises the rest. In an auto assembly plant, some workers may install rearview mirrors, and others may mount bumpers on bumper brackets. These are very specific subtasks.

division of labor Process of dividing work and assigning tasks to workers.

Dividing the core competency into smaller work activity units that can be repeated is **specialization of labor**. Workers who become specialists in one task, or a small number of tasks, develop greater skill in doing that job. This leads to greater efficiency and consistency in production and other work activities.

specialization of labor Dividing the firm's primary task into subunits that can be repeated easily and efficiently.

2 DEPARTMENTALIZATION

Over the years, organizations often expand from one product and a few employees to many products and hundreds or thousands of employees. As the firm grows, it organizes people, products, and resources into groups to better achieve its goals. **Departmentalization** is grouping jobs under the authority of one manager for the purposes of planning, coordination, and control. Organization charts like that in Exhibit 9-1 show departmentalization.

departmentalization Grouping jobs under the authority of one manager for the purposes of planning, coordination, and control.

There are five basic ways for a firm to organize:

- *Functional organization:* based on function (marketing, finance, production, sales, and so on)
- *Product organization:* based on goods or services produced or sold (such as outpatient/emergency services, pediatrics, cardiology, orthopedics, obstetrics/gynecology)
- *Process organization:* based on the production process used (such as lumber cutting and treatment, furniture assembly, furniture finishing, shipping)
- *Customer organization:* based on customer type (such as railroad, aircraft, automotive, military customer groups)
- *Geographic organization:* based on sales territories or regions (such as U.S. and Canadian marketing, European marketing, South American marketing)

Each of these forms is shown in Exhibit 9-2.

Once the organization has been departmentalized, people may be assigned to a department either because they all do the same type of work or because they are jointly responsible for some product, client, or market. Decisions about how to departmentalize affect the way management assigns authority, distributes resources, rewards performance, and sets up communication. The method of departmentalization that is chosen also affects the quality of the organization's goods and services.

Exhibit 9-2
Five Ways to Organize

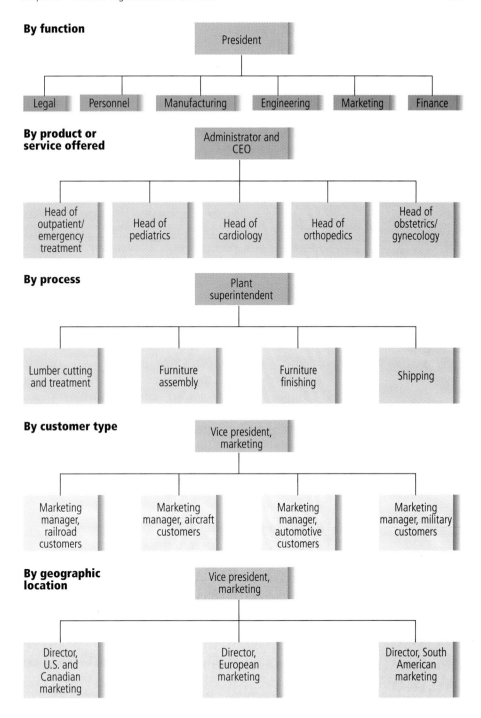

By function

President

Legal | Personnel | Manufacturing | Engineering | Marketing | Finance

By product or service offered

Administrator and CEO

Head of outpatient/ emergency treatment | Head of pediatrics | Head of cardiology | Head of orthopedics | Head of obstetrics/ gynecology

By process

Plant superintendent

Lumber cutting and treatment | Furniture assembly | Furniture finishing | Shipping

By customer type

Vice president, marketing

Marketing manager, railroad customers | Marketing manager, aircraft customers | Marketing manager, automotive customers | Marketing manager, military customers

By geographic location

Vice president, marketing

Director, U.S. and Canadian marketing | Director, European marketing | Director, South American marketing

Span of Control

Once a firm has established its departmental organization, it must decide how many managers are needed to supervise the work. The answer depends on how many employees each manager can supervise. The number of employees reporting directly to a manager is the manager's **span of control** (sometimes called *span of management*). It can be as narrow as two or three employees or as wide as fifty or more. No one span of control applies to all jobs, but a good rule of thumb is five to nine people.

span of control The number of employees reporting directly to a manager.

If hundreds of employees perform the same job, one supervisor may be able to manage as many as eighty. Such might be the case at a clothing plant, where hundreds of sewing machine operators work from identical patterns. But if employees perform complex and different tasks, a manager can probably supervise only a small number (eight or fewer). A supervisor at a pharmaceutical company, for instance, might oversee just a few research chemists. Span of control is affected by various factors:

- *Nature of the task:* The more complex the task, the narrower the span of control.
- *Location of the workers:* The more locations, the narrower the span of control.
- *Ability of the manager to delegate responsibility:* The greater the ability to delegate, the wider the span of control.
- *Amount of interaction and feedback between the workers and the manager:* The more feedback and interaction required, the narrower the span of control.
- *Level of skill and motivation of the workers:* The higher the skill level and motivation, the greater the span of control.

The Managerial Hierarchy

Two aspects of the organization that are closely related to span of control are the managerial hierarchy and the chain of command. **Managerial hierarchy** refers to the levels of management within the organization. Generally the management structure is in the shape of a pyramid, with the three basic levels described in Chapter 8: top, middle, and supervisory.

managerial hierarchy Levels of management within the organization: top, middle, supervisory.

The main feature of the managerial hierarchy is that each unit is controlled and supervised by a manager in a higher unit. The person with the most formal authority is at the top of the hierarchy. Managers at the top have most of the power. The amount of power decreases as you move down the pyramid. At the same time, the number of employees increases as you move down from level to level.

chain of command Series of superior-subordinate relationships within a hierarchy.

An organization with a well-defined hierarchy has a clear **chain of command**. The chain of command defines the relationships of authority from one level of organization to the next, from top to bottom. It is shown in the organization chart. When someone skips his or her boss to speak to a higher-ranking official, that person is said to be violating the chain of command.

unity of command Principle that everyone in an organization reports to and gets instructions from only one boss.

flat organization structure Organization structure with a wide span of control, few managerial levels, and a short chain of command.

tall organization structure Organization structure with a narrow span of control, many managerial levels, and a long chain of command.

A related principle is **unity of command**, in which everyone reports to and gets instructions from only one boss. Unity of command guarantees that everyone will have a direct supervisor and also will not be taking orders from a number of different supervisors. Unity of command and chain of command give everyone in the organization clear directions and help coordinate people doing very different jobs.

Managerial hierarchy and the chain of command determine the shape of a firm's organization. A wide span of control results in a **flat organization structure**, with few managerial levels and a short chain of command. Colleges and universities tend to have flat structures. Only two or three levels of administration stand between the faculty and the president. A narrow span of control results in a **tall organization structure**, with many managerial levels and a long chain of command. Military organizations usually have many levels (or ranks) of managers (officers) and thus are tall structures. Exhibit 9-3 shows typical flat and tall structures.

REENGINEERING THE ORGANIZATION

The tall organization structure lets managers carefully sift information before making decisions. The result, though, is slow decision making. In today's global marketplace, what counts is speed. Companies must be

■ Exhibit 9-3
Wide versus Narrow
Span of Control

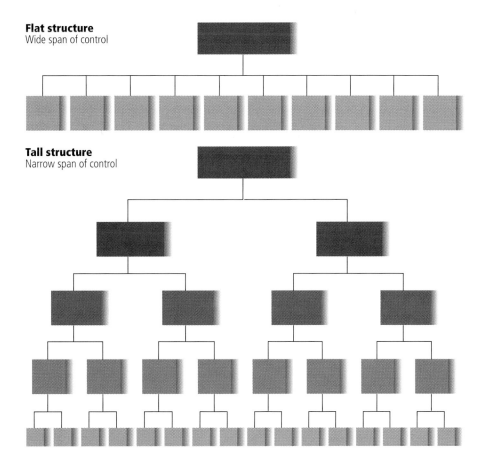

Flat structure
Wide span of control

Tall structure
Narrow span of control

able to launch new products quickly and change existing ones for big customers. A good solution is flatter companies in which information flows quickly, decisions come fast, and teamwork is the rule. Also, most organization structures today are based upon specialization of labor and fragmented work tasks. The larger the organization, the more specialized the work may be and the more it may be broken into separate steps. This rule applies not only to manufacturing jobs but to some clerical jobs as well. Insurance companies, for instance, typically assign a separate clerk to process one line of a standardized form. Each clerk then passes the form to another clerk, who processes the next line. These workers never complete a job; they just perform piecemeal tasks.

reengineering The re-design of business processes to improve operations.

Some of the old ways of doing business simply don't work anymore. To meet the challenges of the future, companies are increasingly turning to **reengineering**—the redesign of business processes to improve operations. An even simpler definition of reengineering is "starting over." In effect, top management asks, "If we were a new company, how would we run this place?" The purpose of reengineering is to identify and abandon the outdated rules and fundamental assumptions that guide current business operations. Every company has many formal and informal rules based on assumptions about technology, people, and organizational goals that no longer hold. Thus, the goal of reengineering is to redesign business processes to achieve improvements in cost control, product quality, customer service, and speed. The process of reengineering almost always results in a flatter organization structure.

GTE undertook reengineering of its telephone operations which account for about 80 percent of its $20 billion annual revenue. Facing new competitive threats, GTE figured it had to offer dramatically better customer service. The company examined its operations from the outside in. It concluded that customers want one-stop shopping—one number to fix an erratic dial tone, question a bill, sign up for call waiting, or all three, at any time of day.

GTE set up its first pilot "customer care center" in Garland, Texas, in late 1992. The company started with repair clerks, whose job had been to take down information from a customer, fill out a trouble ticket, and send it on to others who tested lines and switches until they found and fixed the problem. GTE wanted that done while the customer was still on the phone—something that previously had happened in just one of every 200 calls. The first step was to move testing and switching equipment to the desks of the repair clerks. GTE stopped measuring how fast they handled calls and instead tracked how often they cleared up a problem without passing it on.

The next step was to link sales and billing with repair, which GTE is doing with a push-button phone menu that allows callers to connect directly to any service. Operators have new software that lets them handle virtually any customer request. So far in the pilot program, says GTE vice president Mark Feighner, the company has seen a 20 to 30 percent increase in productivity.[1]

Concept Check

- Explain the importance of division of labor and specialization to an organization.
- What are five different ways to organize?
- Explain the difference between span of control and the chain of command.
- Describe the differences between a tall and a flat organization structure.
- What is reengineering the organization, and why is it so important in today's business environment?

THE INFORMAL ORGANIZATION

3

informal organization
Relationships within an organization that are based on friendship or circumstances, that result in informal channels of communication, and that do not show up on an organization chart.

We've considered the features of formal organization. Yet many relationships within an organization do not show up on an organization chart. These unrecorded relationships are based on friendship or circumstance. They result in informal channels of communication known as the **informal organization**. The relationships may be between people at the same level or between people at different levels and in different departments. Some are work-related, such as those among people who carpool or ride the same train to work. Others are not, such as those among people who belong to the same church or health club. Informal channels of communication sometimes are called *grapevines, rumor mills,* or *intelligence networks.*

FUNCTIONS OF THE INFORMAL ORGANIZATION

The informal organization has several functions: First, it offers friendship and social contact. Second, through interpersonal relationships and informal groups, it gives employees more control over their work environment

■ The company softball team is an example of an informal organization that exists within the formal organization of a firm. Informal organizations provide the status and recognition that the formal organization cannot. Informal organizations also create informal leaders, whose abilities can often be used by managers for the good of the formal organization.

and thus improves their job performance. Third, the informal organization provides status and recognition that the formal organization cannot offer. Fourth, it can help orient new employees by informally passing along rules, responsibilities, basic objectives, and job expectations. Finally, the grapevine often transmits information quickly and takes it places where the formal system does not reach. At British Airways, when the company announced that it was firing 22,000 workers, many employees knew before their supervisor whether or not they still had a job. This information came through the grapevine. Sometimes managers even use the grapevine to transmit information prior to formal announcements and get feedback ahead of time.

PROBLEMS OF THE INFORMAL ORGANIZATION

Although the informal organization can help the organization achieve its goals, it can also create problems. *Group norms* (goals or standards) may conflict with company standards, for instance. Informal groups often resist change, especially technological change. Also, the grapevine can spread incorrect information. Consider the student intelligence network on a college campus. Its information about instructors and their course requirements, especially in regard to term papers and exams, is often inaccurate. You might not like to have your grades depend on it.

USING THE INFORMAL ORGANIZATION

The informal organization is important for both individuals and firms, so managers need to recognize it and learn to use it well. One of the best ways of capturing its good points is to bring informal leaders into the decision-making process. For instance, Digital Equipment Corporation, the computer manufacturer, asked employees to suggest simpler ways to move materials through the factories. The ideas they generated saved millions of dollars. Managers can also put informal leaders on committees concerned with safety and health, productivity, and technological change. Through this participation, the abilities of informal leaders are shared with the formal organization.

Concept Check

- What is the informal organization?
- How can the informal organization affect the formal organization?

BRINGING AN ORGANIZATION TO LIFE: AUTHORITY AND RESPONSIBILITY

4   The organization structure that looks good on paper is put to the test when it comes to life through the actions of employees. Managers exercise their authority and discharge their responsibilities to help achieve the organization's goals. The distribution of authority makes the joint effort of managers and workers possible.

MANAGERS' AUTHORITY AND INFLUENCE

authority The right, granted by the organization to a manager and acknowledged by the employees, to request action.

In most organizations, some employees have to account for work done by others. If the workers don't complete their tasks properly or on time, those who are responsible for the work must take the blame. By exercising **authority**, a person who is responsible for the work of others gets them to do their jobs. Authority is power granted by the organization and acknowledged by the employees. Authority can also be considered the right to act. Managers give subordinates some authority to do their jobs. For instance, certain hospital employees have the right to enter an operating room; others have the right to dispense medicine; still others have the right to bill the patient. Certain employees of a college have a right to determine students' grades.

Authority is the *right* to influence others and request action. Employees' positions affect their formal authority. The higher a person advances within an organization, the greater his or her formal authority. One of the clearest examples is the military. A general has more formal authority than a colonel, who in turn has more than a captain.

power The ability to influence others to take action.

Power, on the other hand, is the *ability* to influence others to carry out orders or to do something they would not have done otherwise. Authority and power are not the same. The source of authority is a position in the formal organization. Power does not come strictly from a person's formal position. It is the ability to influence others regardless of one's position in the organization. The members of a group may grant someone power because they feel that person can lead them. And sometimes managers may lack the power to influence behavior except by "pulling rank"—reminding employees of the formal authority prescribed by their position.

People with informal authority tend to get things done by persuasion rather than command. This form of power is called *influence*. In business, influence involves guiding employees in a suitable, agreed-on direction. Today it is an important element of supervisory leadership. The visible use of authority is less acceptable than it was in the past.

SOURCES OF POWER

Formal authority may give a manager the right to ask an employee to analyze a report and make a recommendation. Informal authority may give a person the right to tell someone else the best way to do something. But neither formal nor informal authority guarantees that others will comply. Only power ensures that a person's requests will be acted on.

There are five key types of power:

- *Legitimate power:* the authority to influence others because of one's position in the organization. A worker who states "I ought to do as my boss says" is reflecting legitimate power. Most employees accept the manager's authority to conduct a performance review, for instance.

■ As President, Bill Clinton utilizes all five of the key types of power in order to govern the country and represent the United States in international politics. Depending upon the situation, he may call upon the power that comes with his office or his personal power.

- *Reward power:* the ability to control rewards given to others. Someone with this power can give salary increases or recommend someone for promotion.
- *Coercive power:* the ability to punish others. It might include giving someone the worst working hours, demoting someone, making verbal threats, humiliating someone, or firing the person.
- *Expert power:* the ability to influence others because of special skills or knowledge. Doctors, lawyers, engineers, scientists, and computer specialists often have expert power.
- *Referent power:* power ascribed to a person because their personal qualities and success have made them an influential figure. Ross Perot has had this type of power.

The first three types of power result from a person's position within the organization (position power). The latter two are based on an individual's personal skills (personal power).

Power is based on people's perceptions. A worker who believes the boss can reward or punish, has expertise, controls information, or has personal appeal will give the boss power. Even if the boss has power based on position, informal leaders with personal power may still have more influence. The wise manager will identify group members with informal authority (power) and work with them to achieve the organization's goals.

DELEGATION AND ACCOUNTABILITY

delegation Distribution of job duties and authority to subordinates.

responsibility Obligation to perform delegated duties and to handle one's assigned authority.

accountability Obligation to report back to one's supervisor the results of responsibilities undertaken.

In any large organization, top managers cannot keep all the authority and make all the decisions. They must delegate some of their duties and their authority to lower-level managers. **Delegation** is the sharing of job duties and authority with subordinates.

Accepting delegated duties and authority gives lower-level managers **responsibility**. Responsibility obliges them to take on the duties and the authority they're given. It also makes them accountable for their actions. **Accountability** is the obligation to report back, or "account for," the results of one's responsibilities. For instance, when a store manager tells a salesclerk to change prices, the clerk assumes the responsibility of using the new prices in the future. The clerk is also held accountable for doing so. If he or she uses an old price, the difference between it and the higher new price might be taken from the clerk's paycheck. However, the manager still has overall responsibility for performing the task—using the new prices.

Concept Check
- What is the difference between authority and influence?
- Explain the concept of power and its sources.

CHOICES IN DESIGNING ORGANIZATIONS

5

The amount of authority that is delegated within a firm is closely related to the way the organization is structured. There is no single best way to design an organization. A number of issues have to be decided, as discussed below.

LINE AND STAFF ARRANGEMENTS

line organization Organizational design with direct, clear lines of authority and communication flowing from the top managers downward.

staff personnel People in an organization who provide advice and specialized support services to line personnel.

line-and-staff organization Organizational design that combines the direct flow of authority of a line organization with staff groups who support the line departments.

Line organization is a design with direct, clear lines of authority and communication flowing from the top managers downward. If the line managers at a store like Radio Shack have the technical skills and knowledge needed to solve merchandising problems, the line organization may be fine. But in larger stores, like Bloomingdale's or JC Penney, the line managers need technical help. For instance, they may need a specialist in store design or fashion shows. These helpers, called **staff personnel**, provide advice and specialized support services to line managers.

Most firms use a **line-and-staff organization**. This arrangement combines the direct flow of authority of a line organization with staff groups who provide advice and services to the line departments. In day-to-day affairs, the line managers pursue the firm's primary task. The staff special-

Line functions

Staff functions

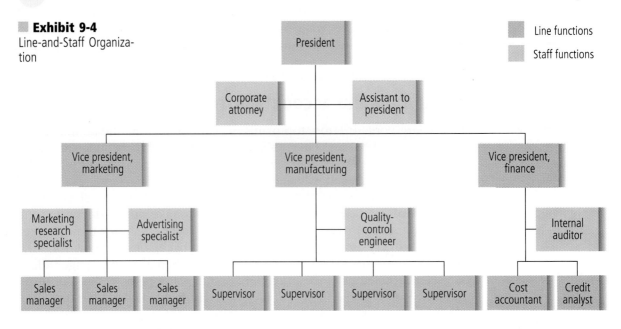

Exhibit 9-4
Line-and-Staff Organization

Line functions

Staff functions

ists help line employees achieve the firm's goals. The chief elements of *line* organization are the production, marketing, and financial functions. *Staff* personnel include legal, consulting, public relations, personnel, and other specialists. Exhibit 9-4 is an organization chart showing line-and-staff relationships. Your local telephone company, for instance, may have the following line departments: plant and installation, business office, and traffic (long distance and local operators). Its staff departments could be engineering, personnel, and legal.

Position and Authority

Line and staff managers may not always be easy to tell apart. The main differences are their authority and specialized knowledge.

line authority Right to make decisions and issue orders about line functions.

staff authority Right to advise and assist line managers and staff people.

   Line authority is the right to make decisions and issue orders about line functions like production, marketing, and finance. It flows from the top downward through each position. **Staff authority** is the right to advise and assist line managers and other staff people. It is based mostly on specialized knowledge. For instance, the lawyer for labor relations at General Dynamics attends executive meetings on labor and collective-bargaining problems. During the negotiating process, he often advises the executive in charge of negotiating labor agreements.

   People in the line organization need managerial skills and the ability to make full use of staff members' expertise. But sometimes line managers may not want help from staff specialists. American Can Company once sent staff scientists to do research on plastic products for the Dixie Cup division. But Dixie's line managers were experts on wood-fiber products, and they refused to heed the results of the research done by staff plastics experts. In the end, some disgruntled plastics scientists were transferred or left the company.

This story is an example of *line-staff conflict*. With no direct authority, staff specialists may push line managers to accept new ideas. The line managers may strongly resist the new ideas or may fail to tell the specialists about line problems. To forestall conflicts, line managers and staff specialists need to admit that both can help the organization succeed.

Functional Authority

functional authority
Combination of line and staff authority in which specialists are given the authority to supervise some specialized area of activity.

One way to make the line-staff relationship work better is to develop **functional authority**. This combination of line and staff authority gives staff members the direct authority to supervise some specialized area of activity. Functional authority combines similar activities into one organization structure that exercises authority using both line and staff considerations.

Functional authority is common in labor and industrial relations departments. In a unionized company, one or more specialists may be given the job of dealing with the union on a continuing basis. The manager of Whirlpool's plant in Evansville, Indiana, lets the director of labor relations negotiate, administer, and interpret labor agreements. During contract negotiations, the company's labor relations specialists may ask for information from line managers and other staff specialists. If the contract has to be changed (for instance, to add a second shift), the plant manager lets the labor relations specialists work out any problems with the union.

CENTRALIZATION AND DECENTRALIZATION

centralization Practice of assigning only a limited amount of authority to lower-level managers.

Delegation rarely means giving total authority to lower-level managers. **Centralization** occurs when most of the decision-making authority is located (centralized) at the top of the organizational pyramid (see Chap-

■ The decentralized organization of Federal Express gives lower-level managers greater freedom to make decisions. Problems are solved quickly this way, and managers are more motivated. This system works for Federal Express because its employees are willing and able to assume greater responsibility.

decentralization Practice of assigning considerable authority and decision-making freedom to lower-level managers.

ter 8). As a result, only limited authority is given to lower-level managers. **Decentralization** is the process of pushing decision-making authority down the organizational pyramid, giving lower-level managers more authority and decision-making freedom.

Firms like CBS and Polaroid are fairly centralized. Centralization lets top managers develop a broad view of things and exercise tight financial controls. Centralization may also mean that lower-level managers don't get a chance to develop their skills and that problems may take a while to solve.

Several factors must be considered in deciding how much authority to delegate. Five important ones are the size of the organization, the speed of change in its environment, managers' willingness to give up authority, employees' willingness to accept more authority, and the organization's geographic dispersion. Decentralization is usually desirable when:

- The organization is very large, like Exxon, Ford, and General Electric.
- The firm is in a dynamic environment where quick, local decisions must be made, as in many high-tech industries.
- Employees are willing and able to take more responsibility. Some companies, such as Federal Express and Pitney Bowes, are known for young management teams that are eager to try new things.
- The company is spread out geographically, such as JC Penney, Mobil Oil, and Procter & Gamble.

A company that decentralizes can expect some benefits, including quicker decisions, because problems are solved at lower levels; faster development of lower-level managers; less need for top managers to be involved in the minor details; and motivated lower-level managers, who like their greater freedom to make decisions. But decentralization can be risky. If lower-level managers don't have needed skills, they may make costly mistakes. For this reason, some companies, such as Kraft-General Foods, Penn Central, and Clark Equipment, have begun to recentralize.[2]

In practice, the amount of authority delegated to lower-level managers varies from organization to organization—and from function to function within an organization. Manufacturers often decentralize production and centralize their financial decision making. For many years, this has been the strategy of General Electric, General Motors, and Motorola. Firms also have found that technology affects structure, as the Trends in Technology box describes.

COMMITTEE ORGANIZATIONS

committee organization Organization structure in which authority and responsibility are held by a group of workers rather than a single manager.

A **committee organization** is a structure in which authority and responsibility are held by a group of workers rather than a single manager. Committees are normally part of a regular line-and-staff organization. A group can broaden the view of a problem and expand the range of possible solutions. Also, with more people working on a task, more information can be gathered and analyzed. Committees are given varying degrees

TRENDS

Technology

High-Tech Structure

Technology can really change a company's structure. A traditional span of control is ten or fewer, but technology can create spans of hundreds. Spans that large require decentralized organization.

Aetna Life & Casualty Company recently overhauled its process of issuing an insurance policy. In 1992, Aetna had twenty-two business centers, with a staff of 3,000. It took about fifteen days to get a basic policy out of the office, in part because sixty different employees had to handle the application. Now, the operation has been pared down to 700 employees in four centers—and customers get their policies within five days. How? Because a single rep sitting at a personal computer tied to a network can perform all the steps necessary to process an application immediately. When all the relevant information is gathered, the policy is passed along the network to headquarters in Hartford, where it's printed and mailed within a day.

The technology has also given Aetna's sales force more autonomy. The old hierarchy of supervisors and agents has been replaced by work teams of about seventeen people. At Aetna's Tampa office, the new system for issuing policies saved $40 million and improved productivity by 25 percent.

Arthur Andersen and Company is a leader in applying technology to professional services. The accounting and consulting firm links its 40,000 professionals with thousands of clients around the United States and in up to 200 other countries. According to executives, "Even those in the know may not have the best answer to a complex question." So the firm is developing an electronic bulletin board to let any professional send a query to the entire Arthur Andersen system. Solutions or information that anyone in the company may have for special problems will be instantly available. The firm, as you might guess, is highly decentralized. Each local office is as independent as possible. Partners say that Arthur Andersen's edge is "empowering people to deliver better quality technology-based solutions to clients in a shorter time."[3]

of authority and responsibility. Sometimes the committee's role is only advisory; at other times the committee has full responsibility for making and implementing a decision.

Committees can make coordination of tasks much easier. At Toyota, product and manufacturing engineers work together in a committee. Thus factory machinery is developed in tandem with new car prototypes. Testing a new design often leads to changes in the car, which trigger changes in the assembly line. But since Toyota completes the two processes at the same time, the production plan stays on schedule.

Committee organizations have some drawbacks. Groups normally take longer to reach decisions than individuals. Groups may also reach decisions that committee members can agree on but that are not the best solutions. Committees are sometimes dominated by people with a strong personality or higher formal authority. Finally, it's impossible to hold a single person accountable for a decision; in a sense, everyone—but no one—is responsible.

■ In a matrix organization, members of different departments are assigned permanently to cross-functional teams. Hallmark, for example, brought together artists, designers, printers, and financial personnel to create new lines of greeting cards. The company expects to cut its new-product development time in half by using this system.

PROJECT MANAGEMENT AND MATRIX ORGANIZATION

project management
Temporary organization structure that brings together people from various parts of a company to work on a special project.

Firms in high-tech industries, such as aerospace, electronics, and electrical equipment, developed a couple of new organization structures. **Project management** brings together people from various parts of a company to work on a special project. When Bell Helicopter decides to bid on a government helicopter project, for instance, it pulls together people from several departments to estimate costs, develop technology, establish schedules, and write the bid. A senior engineer may direct the project at this stage. If Bell wins the contract, the project team will grow. People in the company who can help design and build the helicopter will join the team. When the contract is finished, the managers and workers will return to their regular departments, and the project director may receive another special project to direct. As this example shows, project management is temporary. Project teams may be located at sites away from company headquarters for the duration of the project.

matrix organization
Permanent organization structure that brings people from different departments to work on special projects.

When project management is used for several projects over some time, the company may decide to formalize the arrangement. **Matrix organization** is the permanent organization structure that collects people from different departments to work on special projects. This type of structure has both vertical and horizontal authority relationships, as shown in Exhibit 9-5. Indeed, the word *matrix* comes from the cross-hatching of horizontal lines (the project team) with vertical lines (the line-and-staff organization). The firm illustrated in Exhibit 9-5 has four special project

Exhibit 9-5
Matrix Organization

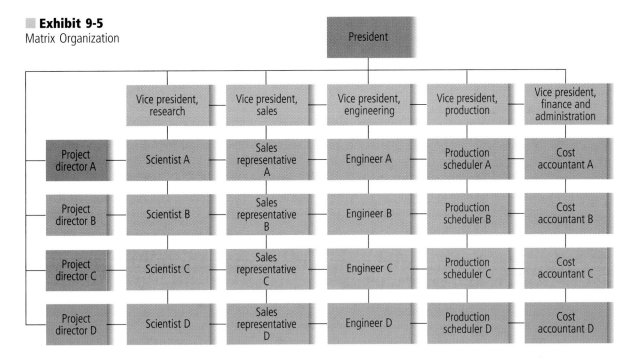

groups (A, B, C, D). Even if it had only one, authority and responsibility would still flow both vertically and horizontally.

Horizontal authority in this kind of structure is represented by the director of a single project. The director is in charge of all aspects of that project, from research and design through sales and accounting. Vertical authority might be represented by the vice president for production, who would oversee production schedules for a number of projects. This arrangement is an exception to the principle of unity of command. Instead, it features overlapping, or dual, authority. A production scheduler, for instance, might report directly to the project director and indirectly to the vice president for production.

Advantages of Project Management and Matrix Organizations

A big advantage of these structures is teamwork. By pooling the skills of various specialists, the company can tackle more complex tasks. Here are some other advantages:

- *Efficient use of resources:* Project managers use only the specialized staff they need to get the job done, instead of building large groups of underused specialists.
- *Flexibility in conditions of change and uncertainty:* The project structure is flexible, and the group can be disbanded quickly when it is no longer needed.
- *Ability to balance conflicting objectives:* The customer needs a finished product and predictable costs. The organization needs high profits and the development of technical capability for the future. These twin goals serve as a focal point for directing activities and overcoming conflicts.

- *Improved motivation and commitment:* Most employees like the excitement of working on a special project. Thus they are more productive than they would be in a stable department.
- *Opportunities for personal development:* The project structure gives people the freedom they need to develop as managers.[4]

Disadvantages of Project Management and Matrix Organization

Project and matrix arrangements pose two major problems. First, they may cause conflicts between the horizontal and vertical authority figures and confusion among team members over lines of authority. The second problem is that if people are assigned to several different projects over a short time, they may never develop the expertise, loyalty, or teamwork needed to do their best. Despite these potential drawbacks, matrix organizations work very well in high-tech industries.

INTRAPRENEURING

intrapreneurs Creative, risk-taking individuals allowed to work as entrepreneurs within an organization.

As we saw in Chapter 7, entrepreneurs tend to be risk takers. Many large corporations are trying to encourage this sort of behavior for entrepreneurial types within the organization, who are called **intrapreneurs**. They tend to be creative, inventive risk takers who focus on creating new products or devising new uses for old ones. The corporation provides resources and freedom to succeed or fail; failure is viewed as a learning experience. This strategy keeps the entrepreneurial spirit alive in a large company. It also helps the company keep creative employees who might become restless in the usual corporate structure. Many major technology-oriented corporations have intrapreneurial units, such as the one that created IBM's personal computer. Some intrapreneurial units grow into separate companies, as was the case with Apple Computer's software development group.

The 3M Company had the most notable success with intrapreneuring. Spencer Silver, a scientist in 3M's research labs, made an adhesive that stuck only a bit. Since 3M was looking for a better adhesive, not a worse one, many wrote off the discovery. But Silver believed his adhesive must have some use. For five years, he kept looking for that use. Finally, a 3M chemical engineer and church choir member named Arthur Fry found a problem to fit Silver's solution. Fry used little slips of paper to mark his place in the hymnal. But these would fall out or slip down into the book. Fry thought, "If only I had a little adhesive on these bookmarks . . ." He suddenly realized that Silver's adhesive was perfect for temporarily sticking paper to paper. Fry worked out a way to apply the adhesive to paper, and the Post-it note was on its way.[5]

THE VIRTUAL CORPORATION

Intrapreneuring is a way to foster, within a large organization, the entrepreneurial spirit that often thrives in smaller organizations. Some small businesses are finding a way to avoid the problems of large organization structure by forming complementary partnerships with others. Many

■ The 3M company has long encouraged intrapreneurs within its organization. It provides resources and the freedom to experiment for creative employees who might become restless in the usual corporate environment. This philosophy led to the invention of the Post-it note, which was the creation of a 3M research scientist and a 3M chemical engineer.

virtual corporation
Network of independent companies linked to share skills, costs, and market access.

entrepreneurs, with limited capital, are turning to a new form of organization called the virtual corporation. The **virtual corporation** is a network of independent companies linked by information technology to share skills, costs, and access to one another's markets, as the Small Business Trends box on the next page demonstrates.

The virtual corporation is not limited to smaller entrepreneurial firms. Companies like AT&T, Corning, Apple Computer and Intel are utilizing the virtual corporation concept. Partnering—the key attribute of the virtual corporation—will assume even greater importance, says James R. Houghton, chairman of Corning Inc.[6] Corning may be the most successful U.S. company at putting together alliances. Its nineteen partnerships, accounting for nearly 13 percent of earnings in 1993, have let the company develop and sell new products faster, providing size and power without the growth in organization structure.

Embracing the Virtual Corporation

The virtual corporation has neither central office nor organization chart. It has no hierarchy, and no vertical integration.

In the concept's purest form, each company that links up with others to create a virtual corporation will be stripped to its essence. It will contribute only what it regards as its "core competencies," the key capabilities of a company. It will mix and match what it does best with the best of other companies and entrepreneurs. A manufacturer will manufacture, while relying on a product design firm to decide what to make and on a marketing company to sell it.

An example of a virtual corporation is Kingston Technology of Fountain Valley, in southern California, one of the world's leading upgraders of personal computers. Instead of growing as its business grew, adding new capacity or branching into new businesses, Kingston stayed small. It created a solid network of partners and farmed work out to them. This isn't merely subcontracting. Kingston and its partners lead complementary corporate lives, sharing capital, know-how, and markets. Because each specializes in what it does, Kingston has been able to concentrate on its core competency.

For example: One recent Tuesday, a Los Angeles branch of ComputerLand received a call from Bank of America. It wanted 100 IBM PCs pronto. The problem: They needed lots of extra memory and other upgrades, the better to run Windows, Microsoft's operating system, and link into the bank's computer network. ComputerLand called Kingston, which moved into action. Within hours it had designed an upgrade system—its specialty—and relayed the "specs" to a key partner, Express Manufacturing. Express, which specializes in assembling electronic parts, cleared its manufacturing lines, filled Kingston's order, and sent the finished systems back that very afternoon. By evening, Kingston had tested all the components and sent them, via Federal Express, to ComputerLand. By the weekend, Bank of America's computers were up and running.

Normally that turnaround might have taken ten days. But Express could accommodate its partner because the two are virtual extensions of each other.[7]

- Explain the concepts of line-and-staff authority and functional authority.
- What is the difference between centralized and decentralized organizations?
- Distinguish among committee, project management, and matrix forms of organization.
- Why is intrapreneuring important to some companies?
- Explain the concept of the virtual corporation.

ENVIRONMENTAL EFFECTS ON ORGANIZATIONAL DESIGN

6 As we've seen, businesses are created to offer some product needed in the marketplace. They are structured in the best way to meet that need. But internal organization isn't everything. At some point, the firm has to interact with other companies and people in the external environment. As noted in the Prologue, the external environment consists of social, political, economic, and technological factors that affect company operations. The "others" in a firm's environment include competitors, government agencies, suppliers, consumers, labor unions, and financial institutions.

Other organizations have a big influence on the firm's structure. For instance, the requirements of the federal government's Equal Employment Opportunity Commission have caused many firms to create an affirmative action office within the personnel department.

The environment of some firms is fairly stable; changes take place very slowly. The environment of other firms changes rapidly and creates great uncertainty. The clothing industry, for instance, often faces sudden change. In fact, fashion designers must constantly anticipate changes in trends and consumer tastes. Once the cloth has been cut, the designer and the clothing maker have committed many resources to one clothing style.

To minimize threats to growth and survival, firms may have to become more flexible. Procter & Gamble found itself facing some strong competitors, such as Colgate-Palmolive and Campbell Soup. The company's 4,000-member sales force was not as efficient as the competition's. P&G had eleven national sales forces, each selling a product line like detergents or foods. Numerous P&G salespeople visited each retailer. Today, one sales team sells all P&G products to a single retail account. For its largest customers, P&G sends a team with people from finance, distribution, and manufacturing to create a coordinated effort. For example, a team of a dozen attends solely to the needs of Wal-Mart. Some environmental changes require such major adjustments; others don't.

Concept Check

- What factors comprise the external environment?
- How does environmental change affect an organization?

■ SUMMARY

1. Describe the factors to consider in building a formal organization.
An organization is a group of people brought together to achieve certain goals. Organization structure is the order and design of relationships among employees, jobs, and departments. Several major building blocks of any organization structure are division of labor and specialization, departmentalization, span of control, and the managerial hierarchy.

The process of dividing the work and assigning tasks to workers is the division of labor. Specialization of labor means that work is divided into smaller and smaller subunits until it can be repeated easily and efficiently. The span of control is the number of employees reporting directly to a supervisor.

The managerial hierarchy refers to the number of levels of management within the organization. The chain of command is the clear, unbroken line of authority from the highest to the lowest level of the organization. Unity of command means that no person has more than one supervisor.

Today, many companies are reengineering their organizations. Reengineering asks the question, "If we were beginning this company today, how would we design it?" The goal is to redesign business processes to achieve cost savings, improvement in response time, and better product quality, customer service, and profits.

2. Explain the bases for organizing departments within an organization.

Departmentalization is the grouping of jobs under the authority of one manager for the purposes of planning, coordination, and control. There are five forms of departmentalization: functional, product, process, customer, and geographic. Functional designs are based on such functions as marketing, finance, and production. A product organization is based on goods or services sold. A process organization is based on processes used within the firm. Customer-based structures consider the types of customers served. Geographic departmentalization is based on sales territories.

3. Explain the difference between the formal and informal organization, and describe the informal organization's functions.

Many relationships within an organization do not show up on the organization chart. These informal channels of communication are known as the informal organization. Informal channels of communication sometimes are referred to as grapevines. The informal organization offers social contact, helps improve job performance, provides personal recognition, passes along information about "how things are done," and transmits information quickly.

4. Describe organizational authority and the sources of authority.

An organization's structure comes to life through the authority exercised by managers and the responsibilities discharged by both managers and subordinates. Authority is the right to influence others and request action. Authority is often delegated to subordinates, who then become responsible for handling the authority and accountable for carrying out the actions associated with the authority. Power is the ability to influence others. The five types of power—legitimate, reward, coercive, expert, and referent—have different sources. Delegation is the distribution of job duties and authority to subordinates. Responsibilities are the obligations to perform duties.

5. Understand line and staff and other organizational design choices.

A line organization contains direct, clearly understood lines of authority and communication that flow from the top managers downward. A staff organization consists of the people who provide specialized support services to line managers. The main differences between line and staff managers are their authority and specialized knowledge. The possibility of line-staff conflict is sometimes avoided by developing functional authority, a combination of line and staff authority that gives a specialist the direct authority to supervise some specialized area of activity.

The amount of authority and responsibility delegated to lower-level managers depends in part on the degree of centralization in the organization. Whether the organization should be centralized or decentralized depends on its size, how rapidly its external environment is changing, the willingness of managers to give up authority, the willingness of subordinates to accept greater responsibility, and its geographic dispersion. Often the degree of centralization varies from function to function within an organization.

Project management and matrix organization are relatively new arrangements developed by high-tech firms. They bring together people from different functional areas of the firm to work on a project team. Intrapreneuring offers entrepreneurial opportunities to creative employees within the corporate structure. The virtual corporation is a network of independent companies linked by information technologies to share skills, costs, and one another's technologies. Partnering is the key attribute of the virtual corporation.

6. Understand how the environment affects organizational development.

Organizations must interact with other organizations and with individuals in the external environment. This interaction influences the structure of the firm. Some firms operate in a fairly stable environment; others operate in a rapidly changing environment. Organizations may have to adopt flexible structures to cope with change.

■ DISCUSSION QUESTIONS

1. Why is organizing an important process? Give an example of how being disorganized can cause severe performance problems.

2. After you graduate and get your first job, which type of organization structure do you believe would be best for you? Would you prefer to work within the same structure throughout your career, or do you think another design would be better later on?

3. Draw an organization chart of the firm you work for, your college, or a campus student organization. Show the lines of authority and formal communication. Describe the informal relationships that you think are important for the success of the organization.

4. Is there such a thing as too much specialization? Give an example. What are the results?

5. Assume that you're responsible for your school's homecoming activities. How might you departmentalize your workers by function? By process? How might you use the matrix concept?

6. As the person in charge of homecoming, would you centralize or decentralize your operation? Explain why.

7. Why do you think that reengineering has become popular? Give an example of a company that has gone through reengineering.

8. What is meant by the virtual corporation? Why might this concept appeal to entrepreneurs?

9. Assume that you manage a department in which a line employee responsible for producing television sets refuses to take advice from a staff employee. How would you approach the problem and resolve the conflict?

10. Why is there no ideal span of control?

11. How can the informal organization help or possibly hinder a firm in achieving its main goals?

■ CASE

Reviving Los Alamos

It is a tense time for the Los Alamos faithful, once considered the elite of the defense-research establishment. Home to J. Robert Oppenheimer and the Manhattan Project, Los Alamos was the birthplace of nuclear weapons. For fifty years the lab, overseen by the federal government and the University of California, has been a major contractor to the military. From its beginning as a secret post office box in 1943, Los Alamos has grown into a 43-square-mile, high-tech megalopolis of 11,000 workers, a $1 billion-a-year budget, and about 2,000 buildings in the New Mexico mountains housing everything from plutonium to lasers.

Yet Los Alamos—the height of U.S. technological prowess—is suddenly in the same boat as many of America's major, old-line corporations. Fat, slow, and riddled with operational and administrative excess, the lab has found itself in bureaucratic meltdown at a time when the military's nuclear-weapons complex is shrinking and the nation has lost its appetite for huge research projects at taxpayer expense.

The lab hopes to recast itself as a research and development partner for U.S. industry. And it must do so at competitive prices. But problems loom ahead.

Los Alamos, for example, builds into its projects costs for the lab's massive ongoing environmental cleanup, costs so high that "no one in the world could afford to do business with them," says one executive working with the lab. And Los Alamos knows only one way to operate: the bureaucratic way. The executive recalls negotiating a research agreement between a consortium of companies and the lab. The consortium had one lawyer; Los Alamos had a dozen government attorneys who kept arguing among themselves and almost killed the deal.

Motorola University, a consulting group, was brought in to help reengineer Los Alamos. The consultants produced a blistering 25-page critique: Cynicism and skepticism prevailed among the staff, the lab was too hierarchical, bad news never traveled upward, and pay wasn't tied to performance. Simple decisions, Motorola found, required seven signatures at Los Alamos. A senior manager must approve buying a dozen doughnuts for a meeting. An organization chart of the lab is so confusing it amazes even those who maneuver through the system daily. Hiring a new employee can take as long as a year. And oversight by the Energy Department gets ludicrous, lab managers complain. "We have checkers checking the checkers," says one.

At its heart the lab's operational problems revolve around deep divisions between the lab's vaunted scientific and technical workers and the support and service personnel. Both sides say the other is paid too much for too little work. Scientists complain they spend too much time fretting over everything from plumbing to personnel. Nonscientists gripe that the scientists constantly change the requirements for a job and don't trust them to do the job right. To compete successfully in the business marketplace, Los Alamos has many problems to solve.[8]

Questions

1. Do you think that the concept of reengineering can be successfully applied to nonprofit organizations such as Los Alamos?
2. Could the concept of the virtual corporation be applied at Los Alamos? If so, how?
3. What kind of leadership style would probably be most successful with the lab's scientists? With its support personnel?

Production and Operations Management

Learning Goals

After studying this chapter, you should be able to:

1 Understand why production and operations management is so important in both manufacturing and service firms.

2 Describe the role of technology in mass production, and discuss the changing face of operations management.

3 Discuss the various production processes.

4 Explain how automation affects manufacturing and service industries.

5 List the factors to consider in production planning.

6 Discuss the major methods of inventory management.

7 Identify two key aspects of production control.

8 Explain how quality control affects production and operations.

 # Career Profile

Time and hard work are what it takes to become a member of a corporate management team. Bill Kammer is pursuing this goal within the engineering department at the Andrew Jergens Company. Currently Bill is a manufacturing systems electrical engineer. He works on the manufacture, development, and implementation of control systems at various Jergens facilities. These control systems are the electrical and mechanical components that help navigate a product through an assembly line. Once the systems are in place, Bill and his team constantly evaluate them to see how they can improve them. They also provide technical support by monitoring the systems, making sure they do what they were designed to do.

Bill's job brings him into contact with many different departments at Jergens, from marketing to maintenance to manufacturing. This gives him an excellent opportunity to learn the structure of the company and hone his communication skills, which are vital to any good manager. In addition, he evaluates new computer software that could benefit the engineering department and the company. He then passes on this information to the members of his work team. This, too, is a way to develop management skills.

Every day Bill relies upon the knowledge he acquired as an electrical engineering major in college, and in the statistics and business management courses he took outside his major. His first position after graduation was as an electrical engineer for a heavy industrial corporation, and the experience he gained on that job also helps him now. Bill's education combined with his work experience prepared him well for the day-to-day tasks of operations management. He plans to continue working hard and gaining knowledge, keeping his sights set on a management position with Jergens.

Overview

Every organization creates some type of goods or services and thus has a production function. Every firm must consider how its products will be made or its services will be delivered. Thus every firm needs operations management. This functional area must work closely with marketing, finance, accounting, and other areas. This chapter begins with an overview of manufacturing and today's manufacturing and operations environment. Next it considers basic production processes and the role of automation. Then it examines key aspects of the production process. Finally it considers inventory and production control and quality control. Throughout the chapter, examples show how American manufacturers and service companies are changing their operations to improve productivity and regain a competitive edge.

THE PRODUCTION PROCESS

In a manufacturing company, the production process and its outputs are usually obvious. General Electric's appliance division, for instance, converts steel, rubber, copper, and other inputs into dishwashers, washing machines, and dryers. In a service company, the production process involves a less obvious conversion. For example, Columbia Health Care converts medical personnel, equipment, and supplies into health care for patients. Exhibit 10-1 shows the inputs and outputs for some other types of businesses.

Production, the creation of goods and services, is an essential function in every firm. Through the production process, the firm converts inputs (natural resources, human resources, and capital) into outputs (goods and services) by changing the inputs in some way, as depicted in Exhibit 10-2. Managing the conversion process is the role of **operations management**.

production Creation of goods and services by converting inputs to outputs.

operations management Managing the conversion process that turns inputs into goods and services.

■ Goods and services are created through the production process. In this process, inputs are converted into outputs. ALCOA, for example, converts natural resources, human resources, and capital into aluminum.

Type of Organization	Input	Output
Airline	Pilots, crew, flight attendants, reservations system, ticketing agents, customers, airplanes, fuel, maintenance crews, ground facilities	Movement of customers and freight
Grocery store	Merchandise, building, clerks, supervisors, store fixtures, shopping carts, customers	Groceries for customer sales
High school	Faculty, buildings, classrooms, library, auditorium, gymnasium, students, staff, supplies	Graduates, public service
Manufacturer	Machinery, raw materials, plant, workers, managers	Finished products for consumers and other firms
Restaurant	Food, cooking equipment, serving personnel, chefs, dishwashers, host, patrons, furniture, fixtures	Meals for customers

■ **Exhibit 10-1**
Production Inputs and Outputs

All students of business, regardless of their career goals, should understand operations management. Today operations management personnel work closely with other major functions of the firm, such as marketing, finance, accounting, and human resources. The trend is also toward improved cooperation among design, production, and quality control within the operations management area.

Operations managers face the challenge of combining people and other resources to produce high-quality goods and services, on time and at a low cost. They must decide what products to make (with input from marketing), how these products should be designed, and what production processes should be used. The job of the operations manager in the short term is to make the best use of facilities. In the longer term, it is to look for ways to improve production.

▮ MANUFACTURING IN THE UNITED STATES

The United States is one of the most productive countries in the world. We produce about one-fourth of the world's goods with only 5 percent of its people. During the 1980s our productivity growth fell behind that of other nations, particularly Germany and Japan. But it has improved in recent years as companies recognized the need to focus on operations management. For 1993, business production rose 3.1 percent, the best since 1972.

A Historic View

mass production
Ability to produce many goods at once.

Mass production, the ability to manufacture many goods at once, was a product of the Industrial Revolution. It relied on five advances:

■ **Exhibit 10-2**
Production Process for
Goods and Services

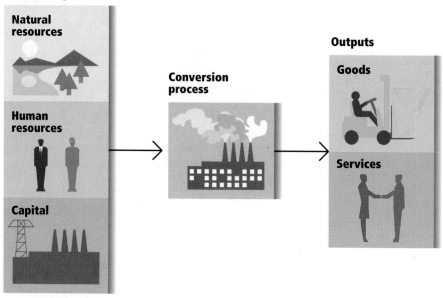

Inputs
(factors of production)

Natural resources

Human resources

Capital

Conversion process

Outputs

Goods

Services

mechanization Use of
machines for work previously
done by people.

standardization Use of
interchangeable parts.

specialization Division of
the production process into
the smallest possible activities so that each worker performs only one task.

assembly lines Conveyor
systems that move products
to each work station in the
production process.

automation Use of ma-
chines to do work with minimum human intervention.

- **Mechanization:** The use of machines for work that had been done by people. Replacing human effort with machines increases productivity. For instance, one bulldozer can move as much dirt as hundreds of workers with shovels.

- **Standardization:** The use of interchangeable parts. One benefit of standardization is ease of repair. A part can be replaced with another standardized part.

- **Specialization:** Dividing the production process into the smallest possible activities so each worker performs only one task. The concept was promoted in the early 1900s by Frederick W. Taylor, the founder of scientific management. (Chapter 11 discusses Taylor's work in more detail.)

- **Assembly lines:** A conveyor system that moves products to each work station in the production process. In 1913, Henry Ford and Charles Sorenson created the assembly line. A conveyor belt moved Model T cars past the workers, each of whom had a specialized task, such as attaching parts, welding, or painting. Assembly time dropped from 12.5 to 1.5 hours, and car prices fell as well.

- **Automation:** The use of machines to do work with minimum human intervention. In many of today's highly automated factories, workers operate machines that do the actual work.

Manufacturing's Changing Role

Today, American companies are rethinking old ways of producing goods to compete with foreign goods. The Japanese, especially, have focused on improving *production*. They pioneered a flexible, or lean, system of manufacturing, in which response time is quick and customer demand drives the process.

Another Japanese concept is *kaizen*, or **continuous improvement.** The idea is that teams of workers from various departments (not just manufacturing) look for small, inexpensive changes that improve production processes. Over time, many small changes can add up to considerable savings. Freudenberg-NOK put *kaizen* to work at an Indiana auto parts plant. The recommended solutions—for example, eliminating a production line bottleneck, changing a work area layout, adding a fan to cool engine mounts so they can be painted more quickly—improved productivity. The company estimates that its $2 million investment in these changes will have a direct payback of $12 to $20 million.[1]

Businesses also are shifting away from large, inflexible plants with high fixed costs to smaller, more efficient facilities. These plants are better equipped to meet the demand for a variety of high quality products and to provide better customer service. Ultra Pac Inc., a small company with 300 employees, competes with Mobil and Tenneco in the recyclable food container market. Within three days of receiving an order, the firm can make and ship up to 500 different containers, including specialized models. This quick turnaround time, about one third less than its larger rivals, has increased Ultra Pac's market share.[2] Some large companies, among them Intel, Eaton Corp., and Carrier, are opening small plants with 125 to 250 highly-skilled employees who are given more responsibility and "cross-trained" to do various jobs.[3]

Smaller, flexible plants are part of the movement toward "agile manufacturing systems." **Concurrent engineering**—the use of cross-functional teams that design both the product and its manufacturing process at the same time—is a step in this process. Benefits include reduced product costs and development time, simplified product designs, and fewer component parts. At Boeing Co., teams are simultaneously designing the 777 airplane and the machinery to produce it. This will reduce costly rework later.[4]

The role of operations management within the firm is one more area of change. For many years, it was viewed as less important than areas like marketing and finance. Careers in operations management were considered less glamorous. Yet operations managers control about three-fourths of a firm's assets (including supplies, wages, and benefits). Now that top management realizes what a big role they play, operations managers are getting higher salaries and status.

ENVIRONMENTAL ISSUES

Industrial and service firms today must review all their operations to ensure compliance with an increasing number of federal, state, and local pollution control regulations. For example, the 1990 Clean Air Act bans ozone-damaging chlorofluorocarbons (CFCs) by 1996. Because it is less costly to prevent pollution than to clean it up, manufacturers are designing products and production processes that prevent or reduce pollution.

continuous improvement (kaizen) Idea, originated in Japan, that teams of workers look for small, inexpensive changes to improve production processes.

concurrent engineering Using cross-functional teams to design both the product and its manufacturing process at the same time.

Ford and other car manufacturers have replaced CFCs in vehicle air conditioning systems with hydrofluorocarbons, which don't deplete ozone. Refrigerator manufacturers are also phasing out CFCs.[5]

Service companies, too, are looking for ways to make their operations more environmentally-friendly. Restaurant chains such as Domino's Pizza, McDonald's, and Burger King have performed environmental audits and instituted procedures to reduce the amount of garbage they generate. Hallmark Cards' focus on the "3 R's"—reduce, reuse, and recycle, with the emphasis on reduce—could save the company an estimated $5 to $7 million annually.[6]

3   BASIC PRODUCTION PROCESSES

Operations managers classify production processes in two ways. The first way describes how inputs are converted into outputs. The second tells about the timing of the process.

Converting Inputs to Outputs

There are two basic processes for converting inputs into outputs. In the first, the basic input (raw material) is *broken down* into one or more outputs (products). For instance, bauxite (the input) is processed to extract aluminum (the output). Other examples are petroleum refining (where crude oil is converted into gasoline, kerosene, and petrochemicals) and meat packing (where an animal is divided into different cuts of meat, hide, and by-products).

The other type of process is just the opposite: The basic inputs (parts or raw materials) are either *combined* to create the output (a new product) or *transformed* into the output (a different product). An airplane, for instance, is made up of thousands of parts. Iron and other minerals are combined and transformed by heat into steel.

Continuous, Repetitive, and Intermittent Production

Timing of the production is another method of classification. A **continuous process** uses long production runs that may last days, weeks, or months without equipment shutdowns. It is best for high-volume, low-variety products with standardized parts, such as nails, glass, and paper. Petroleum products, chemicals, and steel are also made this way. Per-unit costs are low, and production is easy to schedule.

The **repetitive** process is similar. It uses *modules*, premade parts or units, in the assembly process. For instance, the repetitive process is used to make washing machines. First the motor is assembled as a separate module, and then it is installed into the machine.

In an **intermittent process,** short production runs are used to make batches of different products. Machines are shut down to change them to make different products at different times. This process is best for low-volume, high-variety production. A firm that produces goods in response to customer orders, called a *job shop*, uses an intermittent process. For instance, a print shop handles a variety of projects, including newsletters,

continuous process
Production process that uses long production runs without shutting down equipment.

repetitive process Production process that uses preassembled modules.

intermittent process
Production process that uses short production runs for batches of different products.

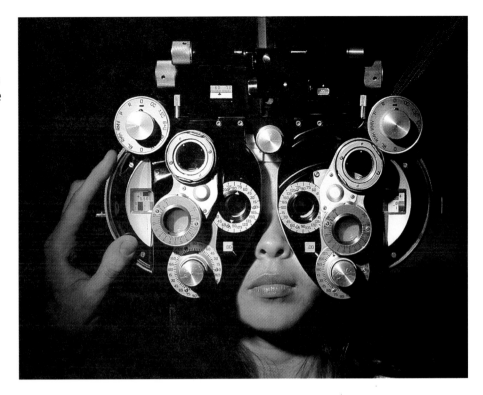

 Service companies, such as optometrists, generally use the intermittent process of production. This is necessary because their services are customized to suit each customer.

brochures, stationery, and reports. Each print job varies in quantity, type of printing process, binding, color of ink, and type of paper.

Service companies generally use repetitive or intermittent rather than continuous processes. For instance, meals prepared at a gourmet restaurant, physical examinations or surgical operations performed by a physician, and consultations with a tax accountant are customized to suit each customer. They use the intermittent process. Note that their "production runs" may be very short—one order of grilled salmon or one eye exam at a time.

Concept Check

- What is operations management, and why should U.S. manufacturers improve production methods?
- What are the five major technological advances that contributed to the development of mass production?
- What are the two ways to convert inputs to outputs? How are continuous, repetitive, and intermittent production processes different?

AUTOMATION IN TODAY'S WORKPLACE

4 Automation is one way firms can improve their efficiency and ability to compete. The advantages of automation include more flexibility, reduced costs, and an ability to combine production steps. Recently, automation has grown out of advances in computer technology.

■ ANDI is an automated airplane inspector that is currently in development at Carnegie Mellon Research Institute. The robot will perform the tedious chore of checking airplanes for tiny flaws in their aluminum skin. It is more accurate than human inspectors but is not intended to replace them. "It's a tool for their tool kits," says one of the scientists who developed ANDI.

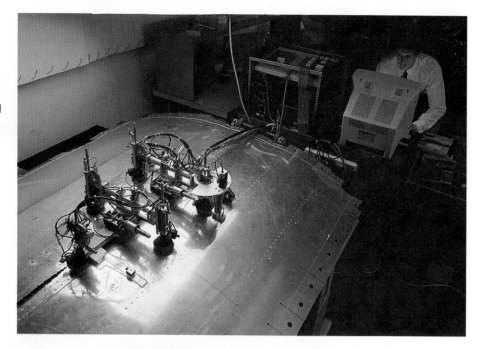

MANUFACTURING AUTOMATION

Although automation has displaced some workers, it has also created new jobs and even new industries that need workers. It has greatly improved productivity and greatly reduced costs. Automation is taking place in all areas, from product manufacturing to computerized inventory control to shipping. Russell Athletic Co., a major manufacturer of athletic apparel, spent $500 million to automate its factories. Computerized lasers cut fabrics, robots sew clothes together, and computers sort the finished items by color. As a result, product costs fell and profits tripled from 1983 to 1993.[7]

However, although automation may solve some problems, it may, in fact, create new ones. For example, in 1987 automotive parts manufacturer Federal-Mogul installed automated equipment to reduce climbing labor costs. Although the plant could make the parts faster, the new equipment was geared to large production runs. This put Federal-Mogul, which assembles 1,800 different parts, at a disadvantage in responding to changing customer needs. The firm reverted to its old, lower-tech system, which was better suited to its small-batch production requirements. Also, technological resources must be integrated with human resources to be successful. For example, when Corning automated a ceramics plant, it found that employee motivation declined. When the firm found ways to give workers more responsibility and involve them in decisions, productivity improved 25 percent in one year.[8]

computer-aided design (CAD) Use of computers to design and test new products and modify existing ones.

CAD/CAM Systems

Advances in computer technology have transformed design and manufacturing. In **computer-aided design (CAD)**, computers are used to design and test new products and modify existing ones. Engineers use computers to draw products and look at them from different angles. They can analyze the products, make changes, and test prototypes before making even one item. Likewise, **computer-aided manufacturing (CAM)** uses computers to develop and control the production process. Computers analyze the steps required to make the product. They then send instructions to machines that produce it.

computer-aided manufacturing (CAM) Use of computers to develop and control production processes.

CAD/CAM systems integrate design, testing, and manufacturing. Their scope ranges from designing the product to instructing machines to make it and controlling the flow of materials. For instance, a linked CAD/CAM system connects Ford Motor Company and AlliedSignal, one of its parts subcontractors. Computers at Ford send the design for connecting rods to computers at an AlliedSignal plant in Kansas City, Missouri. Based on the design specifications, AlliedSignal's computers then transmit instructions to make the part to the appropriate machine tool in the factory.[9]

CAD/CAM systems Computer systems that integrate the entire design, testing, and manufacturing process.

Using CAD/CAM, a manufacturer can easily explore different designs through computer simulation and resolve problems early in the process. The results are shorter design time, reduced costs, and improved quality. Although the design process itself may account for only 5 to 8 percent of a product's cost, the design decision can lock in 70 percent or more of the total cost.

Robotics

Robots are computer-controlled machines that can perform tasks independently. *Robotics* is the technology involved in designing, constructing, and operating robots. The first robot, or "steel-collar worker," was used by General Motors in 1961.

robots Computer-controlled machines programmed to perform tasks independent of human control.

Robots can be mobile or fixed in one place. Fixed robots have an arm that moves and does what the computer instructs. Robots may be quite simple, with limited movement for a few tasks such as cutting sheet metal and spot welding. Or they may be complex, with hands or grippers that can be programmed to perform a series of movements. Some robots even have sensing devices for sight and touch.

Robots often operate with little or no human intervention. Replacing human effort with robots is most effective for tasks requiring consistency, accuracy, speed, or strength. General Motors uses robots to spray paint its cars, a job that presents a health hazard to humans. A self-propelled robot inspector developed by Carnegie Mellon University for the Federal Aviation Administration moves over jet aircraft looking for loose rivets and tiny cracks in the aluminum shell. The robot detects defects difficult for humans to spot.[10]

Flexible Manufacturing Systems

flexible manufacturing system (FMS) Manufacturing system that integrates computers, robots, machine tools, and materials- and parts-handling machinery.

A new way to automate a factory is to blend computers, robots, machine tools, and materials- and parts-handling machinery into a **flexible manufacturing system (FMS)**. Such systems combine automated work stations with computer-controlled transportation devices. Automatic guided vehicles (AGVs) move materials between work stations and into and out of the system.

A flexible manufacturing system is expensive. But once the machines are in place, they take little labor to operate and provide consistent product quality. And the system can be changed easily and inexpensively. FMS equipment can be programmed to perform one job and then quickly be reprogrammed to perform another. These systems work well when small batches of a variety of products are required or when each product is made to customer specifications. For instance, Solectron, a California electronics manufacturer, makes specialty circuit boards for 75 customers. By reprogramming robots and other machinery, it can make different types of circuit boards on each of its production lines.[11]

Computer-Integrated Manufacturing

computer-integrated manufacturing (CIM) Manufacturing system that uses computer systems to automate the entire manufacturing process.

Combining the new automation techniques results in **computer-integrated manufacturing (CIM)**. CIM includes computerized manufacturing processes (like robots and FMS) with other computerized systems used before manufacture (CAD/CAM, inventory control, parts ordering). With CIM, when a part is redesigned in the CAD system, the changes are quickly transmitted to the machines producing the part, as well as to all other departments that need to know.

A good example of CIM in action is the joint manufacturing plant opened by John Deere & Co. and Hitachi Construction Machinery in North Carolina. At the plant, which makes hydraulic excavating equipment, sophisticated computer systems integrate the entire manufacturing process, from order entry and purchasing to shop-floor control, scheduling, and accounting.[12]

AUTOMATION IN SERVICE BUSINESSES

Service businesses also use automation to improve customer service and productivity. Measuring productivity and quality is harder, however, because services are less standardized than goods and may require more workers relative to equipment.

Retail stores of all kinds use *point-of-sale terminals* that track inventories, identify items that need to be reordered, and tell which products are selling well. *Optical scanners*, both hand-held and at cashier stations in grocery stores and at retailers, read bar codes, automatically record the price and the item, and update inventory records. Libraries, music stores, and video rental stores also use optical scanners. The benefits of point-of-sale terminals and optical scanners are quicker checkout and more efficient and accurate inventory management. Wal-Mart, the leader in retailing automation, has its own satellite system connecting point-of-sale terminals to distribution centers and headquarters. Frank's Nursery and Crafts, a Detroit-based chain of stores, uses a satellite system to speed up credit authorization, cutting long checkout lines.[13]

Automation is being applied in the health care industry as well. At the University of Wisconsin Hospital and Clinics in Madison, robot-dispensed medicines are delivered to patients by automatic carts.[14] Robots have also moved into the operating room and perform hip replacement surgery.

They can make more precise adjustments than human surgeons.[15] Physicians and hospitals in rural areas can use computer links to regional medical centers to get advice on diagnosis and treatment. These and similar applications have improved many service operations in the past decade.

Concept Check

- What are these major types of manufacturing automation: CAD/CAM systems, robots, flexible manufacturing systems, computer-integrated manufacturing?
- What are the benefits of automation in the service sector?

PRODUCTION PLANNING

5 An important part of operations management is *production planning.* It means deciding what types and amounts of resources are needed to make the product. Good production planning balances goals that may conflict: providing good customer service while keeping costs down, keeping profits up while maintaining adequate inventories. Sometimes accomplishing these goals is quite difficult, as the following Business Today Trends box shows.

TRENDS

Business Today

Devilish Problems

Production planning can be difficult when a company markets a new product. A common worry is that no one will buy the new item, leaving the company with a surplus of useless merchandise. But what happens when a product is successful beyond a company's wildest dreams?

That's exactly what happened to the Nabisco Biscuit Co. when it introduced SnackWell's Devil's Food Cookie Cakes. The fat-free chocolate and marshmallow cookies were an instant success with health-conscious consumers who craved sweets. A year after the cookies first appeared, Nabisco was still unable to meet consumer demand. The shortage of SnackWells led supermarkets to ration their supplies and even resulted in a television commercial, in which three angry women corner a Nabisco baker and demand to know why he can't make more SnackWells. All joking aside, the shortage has cost Nabisco a significant amount of money in lost sales.

An obvious solution to the problem would be for Nabisco to make more of the cookies. But it can't. The marshmallow, chocolate icing, and glaze used to coat SnackWells would stick to a conveyor belt, so the company must use custom-made machinery available at only one bakery. In addition, it takes four hours to make each devil's food cookie, compared to 30 minutes for Nabisco's popular Chips Ahoy! brand.

Dealing with surplus demand problems teaches a company how to improve its future production planning. Nabisco, for example, will sell its newest SnackWell, the Double Fudge Cookie Cake, only in northeastern states until it can accurately gauge the public's demand for the product. According to one company spokesman, "We've learned our lesson."[16]

There are three phases of production planning. *Long-term* planning has a time frame of three to five years. It focuses on what products to produce, how many, and where. *Medium-term* planning decisions cover about two years. They concern the layout of production facilities, the source of parts (whether to make or buy), and human resources (the number of workers needed and the number of shifts to be worked). *Short-term* planning, with a one-year time frame, converts these broader goals into specific production plans and materials management strategies.

Four important factors in production planning are site selection, facilities layout, make-or-buy decisions, and purchasing decisions.

SITE SELECTION

One big decision that must be made early in production planning is where to put the facility. Site selection affects operating costs, the price of the product, and the company's ability to compete. For instance, the costs of shipping raw materials and finished goods can be as much as 25 percent of a product's total cost. Putting facilities where these and other costs are as low as possible is part of a firm's success. Mistakes made at this stage can be expensive. It's hard to move a plant or service facility once production begins.

Quantitative Factors

The costs of locating in various sites are different. Thus an analysis of the numbers is a good place to start the site selection process.

■ Site selection is an important decision for any business. This lumber mill is located close to the source of all of the raw materials it needs to operate, which allows it to keep shipping costs down. These savings can then be passed on to its customers.

Labor costs are very important to both manufacturing and service businesses. Matters to be weighed include the size of the regional labor pool, workers' skill levels, training needs, local wage rates, worker productivity, and unionization. For example, Utah is now home to many high-tech companies, especially in the software and biotechnology fields. Companies are attracted by the state's well-educated and motivated work force and its pro-business attitude.[17] Other high-technology firms have moved to Texas and North Carolina.

Being close to customers and raw materials is also important. Shipping costs are less, so a firm can give customers better service at a lower cost. Companies that use heavy or bulky raw materials are especially concerned about being near suppliers. Mining companies want to be near ore deposits, oil refiners near oil fields, paper mills near forests, and food processors near farms. Castle and Cooke processes and packages Dole pineapple products near pineapple fields in Hawaii, for example.

A related issue is access to highways, railroads, airlines, and waterways. These are routes for raw materials, finished products, and commuting workers. General Motors built its Saturn plant in Spring Hill, Tennessee, in part because of good rail and highway access to parts suppliers and customers. Firms that provide on-site service—retail stores, gasoline stations, movie theaters, dry cleaners—need convenient, visible locations with adequate parking or public transportation.

Another factor is the cost and availability of energy. In many industries, especially heavy manufacturing, energy costs are a large part of the total product cost. In the Northeast, where most electricity is generated by oil, electricity is more expensive than in the Northwest, which has many low-cost hydroelectric plants.

Taxes can also play a role in site selection. State corporate income taxes, property taxes, and sales and payroll taxes are a cost of doing business that varies quite a bit. Also, many states and localities use tax exemptions, reductions, and the like to attract new businesses. Utah, for instance, offers attractive tax rates and a Centers of Excellence program that funds technology start-ups.

Qualitative Factors

Some site selection matters are not easily measured. The quality of life in a community—education, recreation, cultural activities, climate, public services—matters more to some companies than to others. High-tech companies place quality of life high on their list of priorities. A good quality of life helps them attract and keep well-educated and highly skilled workers.

The Site Selection Decision

Once the firm chooses a region of the country and evaluates all the quantitative and qualitative factors, it selects a specific community and a site. As with most other production-related decisions, the main goal is to keep costs down. The final choice is usually the one with the lowest costs that meets the firm's qualitative standards and production goals.

Most states and many communities actively recruit new businesses. They form development agencies that try to convince companies of the merits of their locale, find potential sites, and work out tax and other financial incentives. For example, many states actively campaigned for Mercedes-Benz's $300 million, 1,500-worker U.S. assembly plant. Mercedes management looked at transportation costs, access to export facilities, and the availability of skilled and semiskilled workers. It chose Alabama over 34 other states. In addition to meeting Mercedes' general criteria, it offered the best incentive package, including job training programs and tax breaks.[18]

FACILITIES LAYOUT

A second important factor in production planning is facilities layout. Ideally, processes, equipment, and work areas are arranged in the most efficient pattern. Some firms, for instance, use U-shaped production lines, rather than long, straight ones, to allow workers to move more quickly from one area to another.

Service organizations must also consider layout, but they are more concerned with how it affects customer behavior. In a department store, for instance, should the freight elevator be placed in the center or at the edge of the store? In the center, it would be more convenient for moving merchandise into the departments. But it would also block customer views of merchandise.

There are three main types of facility layouts: process, product, and fixed position layouts. Product and fixed position layouts are illustrated in Exhibit 10-3.

Process Layout

process layout Facility layout that groups together all workers who perform similar tasks and moves products from one work station to another.

The **process layout** arranges work flow around the process, grouping together all workers who perform similar tasks. Products pass from one work station to another (but not necessarily to every work station). For instance, all grinding would be done in one area, all assembling in another, and all inspecting in yet another. The process layout is best for firms that produce small numbers of a wide variety of products.

Product Layout

product (assembly-line) layout Facility layout in which work stations or departments are arranged in a line, through which products pass in sequence.

For a continuous or repetitive production process, the **product (assembly-line) layout** is used. When large quantities of a product need to be processed on an ongoing basis, the work stations or departments are arranged in a line. Automobile and appliance manufacturers and food-processing plants usually use a product layout. Service companies may also use a product layout for routine processing operations. For example, overnight film processors use assembly-line techniques.

Fixed-Position Layout

fixed-position layout Facility layout in which the product stays in one place and workers and machinery move to it as needed.

Some products cannot be put on an assembly line or moved about in a plant. A **fixed-position layout** lets the product stay in one place and the workers and machinery move to it as needed. Products that are difficult or impossible to move—ships, airplanes, and construction projects (houses, roads, bridges)—are typically produced using a fixed-position layout. Lim-

■ Exhibit 10-3
Facility Layouts

**Product layout
Assembly of television sets**

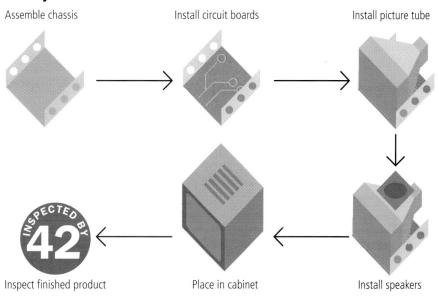

Assemble chassis → Install circuit boards → Install picture tube

Inspect finished product ← Place in cabinet ← Install speakers

**Fixed position layout
Construction of a stadium**

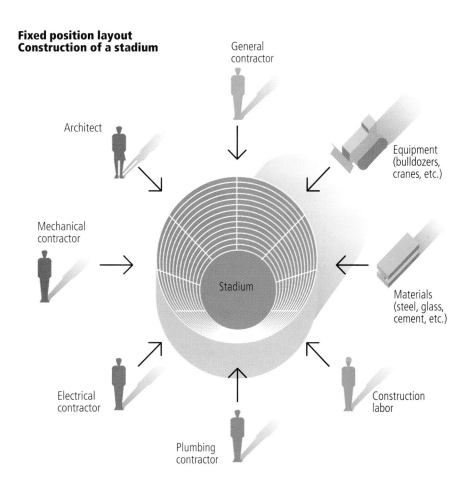

General contractor

Architect

Equipment (bulldozers, cranes, etc.)

Mechanical contractor

Stadium

Materials (steel, glass, cement, etc.)

Electrical contractor

Plumbing contractor

Construction labor

ited space at the project site often means that parts of the product must be assembled at other sites. The fixed-position layout is also common for on-site services, such as landscaping, pest control, and house painting.

MAKE-OR-BUY DECISIONS

make-or-buy decision
Question of whether a firm should make the parts needed in manufacturing its products or buy them from outside sources.

Another decision the firm must make is whether it should make its own parts or buy them from an outside source. This is the **make-or-buy decision**. Standard items, such as screws, bolts, rivets, and nails, are usually cheaper to buy. Other important factors in the make-or-buy decision are whether outside sources can provide high-quality supplies and whether the firm needs to hide special design features from competitors. The quantity of items needed is another consideration. It may be more cost-effective to buy a part that is used in only one of many products than to make it.

MINIMIZING COSTS THROUGH PURCHASING DECISIONS

The purchasing function (called *procurement* in some companies) is a big part of any firm's production strategy. The cost of materials and supplies for manufacturers is over half of sales revenues.

Four main types of costs should be considered when production decisions are made: raw materials and parts, labor, equipment, and energy. All are related. A firm could reduce its equipment costs by buying low-efficiency electrical equipment but might get higher electric bills. The key is to consider all costs together. Exhibit 10-4 compares the cost components for three different production methods that produce the same quality and quantity. All things considered, the least costly method is B. As you can see, choosing a method on the basis of only one or two types of cost could result in a bad decision.

Various departments send requests for supplies, raw materials, and parts to the purchasing department. The purchasing department selects suppliers, negotiates contracts, and develops purchasing strategies, such as when to buy and in what quantity.

VENDOR RELATIONSHIPS

The purchasing agent finds the supplier (vendor) that can fill the order at the best price and meet other criteria, such as quality and delivery time. A vendor located near the purchaser can usually deliver goods quickly. Thus the purchaser can keep fewer goods on hand (inventories) and reduce costs. Tight scheduling usually requires close cooperation between purchaser and supplier.

In the past, the relationship between purchasers and vendors was frequently competitive and antagonistic. During contract negotiations, each side would try to get better terms at the expense of the other. Purchasers used many suppliers and switched among them. Today the trend is toward using fewer suppliers and making longer-term commitments to

■ **Exhibit 10-4**
Costs of Alternate Production Methods

Cost component	Production method		
	A	**B**	**C**
Raw materials and parts	$ 50,000	$ 45,000	$ 35,000
Labor	150,000	100,000	80,000
Equipment	40,000	75,000	150,000
Energy	10,000	20,000	30,000
Total	$250,000	$240,000	$295,000

them. Thus purchasers now evaluate things like the vendor's financial strength, technical ability, and management and sales force.

Vendors and purchasers become partners working toward mutually beneficial goals. With high-volume, long-term contracts, vendors can invest in better equipment and more capacity. Purchasers make sure that vendors understand their requirements. Purchasers sometimes help vendors with training, engineering, and production. With this kind of relationship, vendors tend to become highly involved with the purchaser and often appear to be part of the purchaser's business.

One company who uses these strategies is Xerox, whose purchased materials account for 70 percent of product cost. Because it competes on quality, Xerox must have suppliers who meet its high standards. It spends $500,000 annually on supplier training and enters into two- to five-year contracts rather than change vendors frequently. Over the past 10 years, Xerox's investment in its suppliers has paid off. It has reduced defective parts from 10,000 to 225 per million, cut lead time from 39 to eight weeks, and cut costs 45 percent.[19]

Concept Check

- List the quantitative factors that affect selection of a site for a facility. List the qualitative factors that affect the decision.
- Describe the three types of facilities layout. What type of firm would use each of these layouts?
- What factors should be considered when deciding whether to make or buy parts or components?
- What are some important considerations in selecting vendors? What are the benefits of cooperative relationships with vendors?

INVENTORY MANAGEMENT

6 A firm's *inventory* is the supply of goods it holds for use in production or for sale to customers. **Inventory management** is deciding how much inventory to keep on hand and ordering, receiving, storing, and keeping track of it. The goal of inventory management is to keep down the costs of ordering and holding inventories while maintaining enough supply for

inventory management
Process of determining the right amount of inventory and of ordering, receiving, storing, and keeping track of it.

production and sales. Inventory is a big investment for many companies, as much as 40 percent of the total. Inventory management is thus a major responsibility of the operations manager.

Good inventory management enhances product quality, makes operations more efficient, and increases profits. Poor inventory management can result in dissatisfied customers, financial difficulty, and even bankruptcy. Campbell Soup implemented a new computerized inventory system called continuous product replenishment, CPR. Grocery stores now send daily reports on what products were purchased by consumers the prior day and what is left in stock. Campbell compares that information to historic patterns and tells its factories how much to deliver and when. Sales at outlets using CPR increased 30 to 40 percent more than at stores not connected to the system. Store buyers also like CPR because they can reduce the amount of inventory they keep, in some cases by as much as 55 percent.[20]

TYPES OF INVENTORY

As part of its product planning, a company lists the physical *specifications,* the characteristics, of the products it will make. The specifications take different forms, depending on the product. In a machine shop, they might be engineering drawings that show what the product looks like, what it's made of, and what variations are acceptable. At a restaurant, the specifi-

■ Effective inventory management lowers the costs of ordering and storing inventory while maintaining enough supply for production and sales. This shoe manufacturer must plan carefully to ensure that it has enough raw materials on hand to provide for a smooth flow of finished product.

cations would be the recipes and requirements about food appearance and quality. Raw material specifications describe the raw materials to be used and their quality. For instance, they might state whether one style of Levi jeans is made of ten-ounce or twelve-ounce denim. Specifications should also tell whether substitutions are permitted. In a construction project, aluminum nails could be a substitute for galvanized nails.

bill of material List of components required to make a product.

A **bill of material** then lists the components and the number of each required to make the product. The bill of material is used to decide how much inventory is needed to produce the desired quantity.

There are three basic types of inventory, each with a place in the production process. *Raw material inventory* is items bought by the firm for use in making a finished product (including manufactured items bought from another company). *Work-in-process inventory* is all items in production, partly finished goods at some stage of completion. *Finished goods inventory* consists of items that have been completed but not yet sold.

LEVELS OF INVENTORY

Deciding how much inventory to keep on hand is one of the biggest challenges facing operations managers. With large inventories, the firm can meet most production and customer demand. The purchasing agent may also buy in large quantities to take advantage of quantity discounts. But large inventories tie up the firm's money, are expensive to store, and can become obsolete. One way to determine inventory levels is to look at three costs: the cost of holding inventory, the cost of reordering frequently, and the cost of not keeping enough inventory on hand. Managers must measure all three costs and try to minimize them.

perpetual inventory Continuously updated list of inventory levels, orders, sales, and receipts for all major items of a firm's inventory.

To control inventory levels, managers often track the use of certain inventory items. Most companies keep a **perpetual inventory**—a continuously updated list of inventory levels, orders, sales, and receipts—for all major items. Campbell Soup's CPR system is based on a perpetual inventory. Today companies often use computers to track inventory levels, calculate order quantities, and print purchase orders at the right times.

MATERIALS REQUIREMENT PLANNING

materials requirement planning (MRP) Computerized information system for controlling inventory by comparing forecasts of production needs to inventory on hand.

A popular computerized system for controlling inventory, as well as production, is **materials requirement planning (MRP)**. MRP uses a master schedule to ensure that the materials, labor, and equipment needed for production are at the right places in the right amounts and at the right times. The schedule is based on forecasts of demand for the company's products. It says exactly what will be manufactured during the next few weeks or months and when the work will take place. Sophisticated computer programs coordinate all the elements of MRP. The computer comes up with materials requirements by comparing production needs to inventory on hand. Orders are placed so items will be there when they are needed for production. The goal of MRP is to assure a smooth flow of finished products.

MRP is especially valuable for firms that make complex products. Car makers, for instance, use MRP to coordinate the arrival of nuts, bolts, windshields, hubcaps, and other parts. They also need to coordinate the arrival of subassemblies—transmissions, brakes, engines—and to schedule the assembly of everything into the finished product, the automobile.

JUST-IN-TIME SYSTEMS

just-in-time (JIT) system Inventory system that schedules materials to arrive just as they are needed.

Many U.S. manufacturers have recently adopted the **just-in-time (JIT) system**, a Japanese concept. This system is used to minimize inventories. It is based on the belief that materials should arrive exactly when they are needed for production, rather than being stored on site. Thus a JIT system greatly reduces or ends inventory holding costs. Manufacturers use MRP schedules to determine what parts will be needed and when, and then order them so they arrive "just in time." The goal is to keep the production process running smoothly. Under the JIT system, inventory is "pulled" through the production process in response to customer demand.

The JIT system is part of an overall manufacturing strategy and not simply a goal in itself. It requires teamwork between vendors and production and purchasing personnel. Any delay in deliveries of supplies could bring production to a halt. Modular or virtual corporations, who turn to outside companies for parts and services critical to their operations, depend on just-in-time concepts for their success.

JIT works best where production schedules are relatively stable. Companies with repetitive manufacturing processes—IBM, Hewlett-Packard, Westinghouse, Corning, and John Deere, to name a few—have applied JIT techniques with good results. In a recent survey of 1,035 manufacturers using JIT, 86 percent said that it provided definite benefits.[21] At one Corning auto parts plant, implementation of JIT resulted in reduction of storage areas by two-thirds.

MANUFACTURING RESOURCE PLANNING

manufacturing resource planning (MRPII) Computerized system that integrates data from many departments and generates management reports.

Manufacturing resource planning (MRPII) expands MRP. It uses a complex computer system to integrate data from many departments, including finance, marketing, accounting, engineering, and manufacturing. MRPII can generate a business plan for the firm, as well as management reports, forecasts, and financial statements. Using MRPII, a company can translate its resource needs—facilities, equipment, materials, personnel—into financial needs. The system lets managers assess the impact of production plans on profitability and make more accurate forecasts. If plans in one department change, the effects of these changes on other departments are transmitted throughout the company.

Concept Check

- Why is inventory management important? What are the goals of inventory management?
- Describe materials requirement planning (MRP) and just-in-time (JIT) systems. What are the advantages of using JIT?
- Discuss manufacturing resource planning (MRPII) and its uses.

PRODUCTION CONTROL

Every company needs to have systems in place to see that production is carried out as planned and to know when it is not. The coordination of materials, equipment, and human resources to achieve production efficiency is called **production control.** Two of its key aspects are routing and scheduling.

production control
Coordination of materials, equipment, and human resources to achieve production efficiency.

ROUTING PRODUCTION

Routing is the first step in production control. It sets out a work flow, the sequence of machines and operations, as a product progresses from start to finish. Routing depends on the type of goods and the facility layout.

Once the work flow is set, *route sheets* are written that guide jobs through the production facility. These sheets contain information about the specific steps and their order. Route sheets may also include information about the operation, such as the time needed to prepare the machine to produce the given items.

Routing and layout patterns affect schedules and costs. Caterpillar once kept bins of parts in several locations, waiting to be moved between buildings. By developing a logical flow for parts and relocating all processes for a group of parts to one location, the company saved time and reduced the possibility of damage.[22]

SCHEDULING PRODUCTION

Closely related to routing is scheduling, or specifying and controlling the time allowed for each step in the production process. The production manager prepares timetables showing the most efficient sequence of pro-

■ The production of "Our Welcoming Web," the Cincinnati Museum of Natural History's first traveling exhibit, required careful scheduling. It was necessary to coordinate the creation of the exhibit, its shipping and advertising, and the special educational programs and tours each site offered in conjunction with the show.

duction and then tries to ensure that materials are in the right place at the right time.

Scheduling is important to both manufacturing and service firms. The production manager in a factory schedules materials deliveries, work shifts, and production processes. A trucking company schedules drivers, clerks, and truck maintenance and repair. Scheduling at a college means deciding when to offer courses in which classrooms with which instructors. A museum must schedule its special exhibits, ship the works to be displayed, advertise, and conduct educational programs and tours.

Scheduling techniques range from simple to complex. Giving line numbers at the post office or making appointments with job applicants are simple ones. Two more complex scheduling tools, frequently used by production and operations managers, are Gantt charts and the critical path method.

Gantt Charts

Gantt charts Scheduling technique that uses bar graphs plotted on a time line to show the relationship between scheduled and actual production.

Named after their originator, Henry Gantt, **Gantt charts** are bar graphs plotted on a time line that show the relationship between scheduled and actual production. Exhibit 10-5 is an example. The left-hand side of the chart lists the activities required to complete a job. Both the scheduled time and the actual time for each activity are shown, so the manager can easily judge progress. In this chart, scheduling, designing, ordering, and delivering materials have been completed. Scheduling and delivering materials both began late but were completed early. Designing began ahead of schedule, but was completed after its scheduled end date. Ordering began and ended late. At the October 8 review date, machining components had not yet begun. Thus it was already behind schedule.

Exhibit 10-5
A Typical Gantt Chart

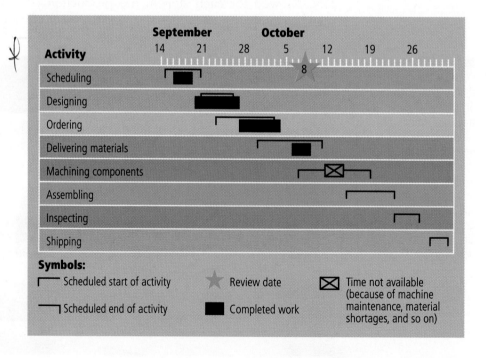

Symbols:
- ⌐ Scheduled start of activity
- ¬ Scheduled end of activity
- ★ Review date
- ■ Completed work
- ⊠ Time not available (because of machine maintenance, material shortages, and so on)

Gantt charts are most helpful when there aren't many tasks, when task times are relatively long (days or weeks rather than hours), and when the job routes are short and simple. One of the biggest shortcomings of Gantt charts is that, like other graph-based models, they are static. They also fail to show how tasks are related. These problems can be solved by using the critical path method.

The Critical Path Method

To schedule big projects, production and operations managers need to break complex operations into smaller tasks. The smaller tasks are easier to analyze and control. An important scheduling tool is the **critical path method (CPM)**, which breaks projects into a sequence of events.

To determine a critical path, the manager identifies all the activities required to complete the project, the relationships among the activities, and their order. Arrows connect the activities, and time and cost estimates are assigned to each. Then the manager determines the **critical path**, the longest path through the activities. All noncritical activities can be completed at the same time as the critical path activities. Delays in these other activities don't necessarily delay the project, because the critical path activities take more time. The sum of the activity times on the critical path gives the total amount of time needed to complete the project.

To better understand how CPM works, look at Exhibit 10-6, a CPM diagram for constructing a house. Each activity is represented by an arrow. The numbers next to each arrow represent the days needed to complete the activity. Thus the first activity is building the foundation, which takes five days. The arrows also show the sequence of activities. In the example, the foundation and frame must be finished before the electrical wiring and the siding can begin. The red arrows represent the critical path, the fastest possible time to build the house (thirty-eight days total). Noncriti-

critical path method (CPM) Scheduling technique that breaks a project into a sequence of activities and estimates the total time needed to complete the project.

critical path Longest path through the activities identified in the production process.

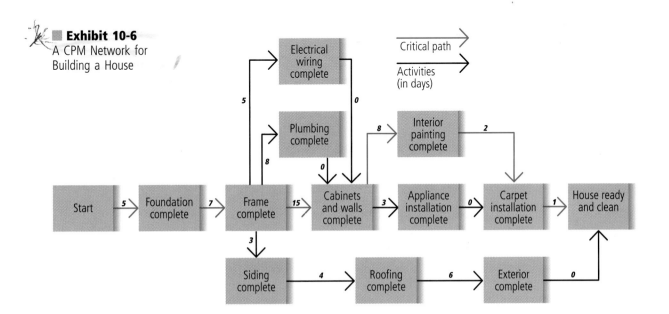

Exhibit 10-6
A CPM Network for Building a House

cal activities (represented by black arrows) can be delayed a bit or done early. Short delays in installing appliances or roofing won't delay completion of the house, because these activities do not lie on the critical path.

CPM diagrams help managers assess how delays in certain activities will affect completion of the project. Scheduling construction of sophisticated factories or equipment can be quite complex, with thousands of activities and events. Thus managers often use computers to develop and use CPM diagrams.

Concept Check

- What is routing?
- Describe the scheduling process and the tools—Gantt charts and the critical path method—used by operations managers.

MANAGING FOR QUALITY

8 The ability to produce high-quality goods and services is more important today than ever. Many U.S. industries—such as automobiles, steel, and home electronics—lost customers to foreign companies. The cause was largely a lack of attention to quality. As a result, today many American companies, both large and small, have joined the crusade for quality.

To a consumer, quality is how well a product serves its purpose. From the company's viewpoint, quality is the degree to which the product conforms to a set of standards. **Quality control** is creating quality standards and measuring finished goods or services against those standards. Once quality control was simply a matter of inspecting products before they went out the door. Today it's a company-wide commitment that supports other business goals.

quality control Creating quality standards and measuring finished goods or services against those standards.

total quality management (TQM) The application of quality principles to all aspects of a company's operations to achieve greater efficiency and profitability.

Total quality management (TQM) refers to the use of quality principles in all aspects of a company's operations. It emphasizes that *all* employees involved with the product or service—marketing, purchasing, accounting, shipping, everyone—can contribute to its quality. It focuses on improving operations to achieve greater efficiency. And it puts customer satisfaction first.

One of the first to say that quality control should be a company-wide goal was an American, Dr. W. Edwards Deming. His ideas were adopted by the Japanese in the 1950s but largely ignored in the United States until the 1970s. Deming helped Japanese firms set up the quality-control programs that made them so successful. He believed that quality control must start with top management, who must foster a culture of quality. Teamwork between managers and workers helps to identify ways to improve production processes. This leads to better quality than simply inspecting the final product for defects. Deming played a key role in making Ford a leader in quality improvements.

■ The Ritz Carlton Hotel Company has been a recipient of the Malcolm Baldrige National Quality Award. Companies apply for the award, created by Congress in 1987, to publicly confirm their commitment to total quality management.

QUALITY, PRODUCTIVITY, AND COSTS

Quality was once the responsibility of a quality-control department. Management believed that quality and productivity were two different things.

Today management believes that quality and productivity are linked. Defective products are a waste of time and materials. With a high rate of rejects, more production is needed to fill orders, which costs more. Defective parts increase the rate of equipment failure and the amount of useless downtime (time when machines are not running). Customer dissatisfaction with poor quality and missed delivery schedules results in lost sales. Warranty costs and the potential for product-liability lawsuits are also higher when quality is poor. Clearly, investing in quality helps a business stay competitive and profitable over the long run. The links among quality, costs, and productivity are summarized in Deming's quality chain reaction, depicted in Exhibit 10-7.

To improve quality, it must be an issue throughout the production process. It should be a feature of product planning and design and all stages that follow. Finding and correcting problems early in the process saves money. Designing products for better quality, simpler operation, and easier repair also reduces the need for customer service after the sale.

In the manufacturing sector, quality is fairly easy to define and mea-

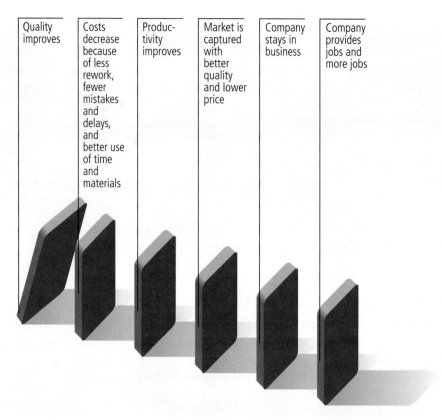

Quality improves

Costs decrease because of less rework, fewer mistakes and delays, and better use of time and materials

Produc-tivity improves

Market is captured with better quality and lower price

Company stays in business

Company provides jobs and more jobs

sure, because tangible products have characteristics that can be defined and measured. But in the service sector, quality is much harder to define, let alone measure. The Service Economy Trend box on the next page describes some efforts at using TQM in the health care field.

Recently, many in the business community have complained that TQM has not produced the anticipated gains. Perhaps expectations have been too high. TQM does not work well at companies who see it as a "quick fix." In fact, though, TQM remains a desirable management strategy. It is most successful when companies view TQM as a sound way to operate a business.[23] It should be part of an overall program that includes evaluation of administrative and manufacturing procedures, employee involvement, and benchmarking.

benchmarking Measuring the products, services, and procedures of one's own company against the best companies to identify areas for improvement.

Benchmarking involves measuring your company's products, services, and procedures against the best of its competitors to identify areas for improvement. For example, Engelhard, a New Jersey manufacturer of specialty chemicals, wanted to cut its cycle time. It arranged to study the continuous production processes of IBM and DuPont. Dow Chemical benchmarks internally so that departments can learn from each other. Service companies also use benchmarking. Prudential Insurance based its employee evaluation and incentive system on what it learned at MCI and Motorola.[24] Exhibit 10-8 summarizes the key steps in a TQM program.

Surgery for Hospital Costs

The Henry Ford Hospital in Detroit used to admit its chemotherapy patients a day early to prepare for their treatment. Now, the hospital simply instructs the patients to drink the necessary liquids at home and to come in on the day their treatment begins. Changing this procedure cuts one day off a patient's hospital stay and about $250 off the cost of treatment. These changes at Henry Ford are part of a national trend: the health care industry is following in the footsteps of other businesses and exploring total quality management techniques. Doctors, nurses, and administrators are working together, examining all the steps involved in the treatment of conditions ranging from basic infections to open-heart surgery. Their goal is to eliminate unnecessary steps that drive up costs yet do not improve the quality of care. At Henry Ford, for example, a team followed textbook quality management techniques, drawing flow charts of the entire chemotherapy treatment process. This overview allowed them to identify possible areas for change.

Some experts predict that total quality management can potentially lead to significant reductions in the cost of health care. The accounting and consulting firm Ernst & Young reports that when hospitals examine complex procedures such as hip replacement and open-heart surgery, they usually find that 15 to 25 percent of their costs are used for steps that do not improve patient care.

Such reform efforts are spurred by a basic change in consumer attitudes towards health care. Instead of seeking the most advanced technology without considering the price, consumers are now demanding both lower prices and higher quality care. As a result, doctors must compete to win patients. This competition will surely increase with the move to reform America's health care system.

Yet total quality management in the health care field is a relatively new idea and faces many obstacles. Examining medical procedures is a lengthy process that involves extensive testing, data analysis, and cooperation between many departments of a hospital. Changes in established procedure cannot be made lightly, as the health of patients must never be endangered.[25]

MEASURING QUALITY

Companies can take one of two routes to publicly confirm their commitment to total quality management: apply for a state or national award program or for ISO 9000 certification. The prestigious Malcolm Baldrige National Quality Award, created by Congress in 1987, has been a major force in encouraging companies to implement TQM concepts. Past recipients include some well-known names—Xerox, IBM, the Cadillac division of General Motors, Federal Express, The Ritz-Carlton Hotel Company, and two units of AT&T—as well as other firms such as Granite Rock Co., a recent winner in the small business category.

▨ Exhibit 10-8
Five Keys to Making
Total Quality Work

Source: Adapted from Rahul Jacob, "TQM:
More than a Dying Fad?" *Fortune*, 18
October 1993, pp. 66–68, 72.

Five Keys to Making Total Quality Work

1. Chief Executive Officer must be involved.

2. Avoid tunnel vision; focus on what the customer wants.

3. Link TQM to a few clear strategic goals.

4. Demand a financial payback—and don't wait forever.

5. Don't adopt someone else's quality program off-the-shelf without adapting it to fit your company.

Many states now have award programs based on the Baldrige criteria. Especially helpful for small businesses, these local programs are often a stepping-stone to the Baldrige. In 1992, almost half the Baldrige applicants were small businesses, up from 18 percent in 1988.

ISO 9000, described in Chapter 5, is another quality program gaining in popularity. Receiving this certification for a company's business unit indicates that it meets the quality requirements of the International Organization for Standardization. The number of U.S. companies with ISO 9000 certification jumped from about 200 in 1992 to almost 14,000 by mid-1993. Because ISO 9000 is an international program, many major corporations such as DuPont, General Electric, Eastman Kodak, and British Telecommunications now require their suppliers to get certification so that their products are accepted worldwide.[26]

Many companies have discovered that merely preparing to enter the Baldrige competition or apply for ISO 9000 speeds up quality improvements and helps a firm define its quality procedures. All Baldrige applicants, for example, get feedback on their quality programs, and award winners share their experiences with other companies.

QUALITY-CONTROL TECHNIQUES

Companies can overcome and avoid quality problems in many ways. One of the best is to get departments to cooperate. Breaking down the barriers between departments leads to broader solutions to quality problems. Also, linking product design with process design has improved quality at many companies.

Automated machinery for production and inspection, such as robots with optical scanners, is another method of quality control. But the defects that are found must then be tracked back to their source, not just corrected after the fact.

statistical quality control (SQC) System that uses statistical techniques to test for quality.

Statistical Quality Control

One popular method is **statistical quality control (SQC)**, a system that uses statistical techniques to test for quality. First used by Bell Telephone Laboratories in the 1920s, statistical quality control was then developed by Deming in Japan. It is based on the assumption that most quality problems result from problems with the manufacturing process, not with the workers.

Because inspecting or testing 100 percent of the output is not cost-effective, SQC checks a sample of the output for defects. It uses statistics to assess overall quality. Quality problems can then be corrected.

Quality Circles

Improving quality is much easier when all members of the organization are involved. **Quality circles**, a technique used by almost all Japanese companies, brings together small groups of employees to discuss, analyze, and recommend solutions to quality problems in their area. Each circle, or group, usually has five to fifteen members and meets regularly. Members are trained in group communication, problem solving, and statistical quality control. Lockheed was the first American company to use quality circles.

Management and workers must both understand what quality circles can and cannot do. For instance, quality circles do tend to improve productivity, increase savings by solving problems, and improve worker morale. But they cannot solve problems associated with poor product decisions. And quality circles will not work where managers fear loss of control or can't accept suggestions from workers. Quality circles haven't done as well here as in Japan, partly because of differing labor, management, and work cultures. Whirlpool and General Electric have replaced quality circles with other types of incentive programs that promote the exchange of ideas leading to quality improvements.

quality circles Technique that brings together small groups of employees to discuss, analyze, and recommend solutions to quality problems in their area.

Concept Check

- Define quality control. Why is improving quality a priority for most American companies today?
- What are the relationships among quality, productivity, and costs?
- What are some popular quality-control techniques?

▦ SUMMARY

1. Understand why production and operations management is so important in both manufacturing and service firms.

Production and operations management is managing the conversion of inputs—natural resources, human resources, and capital—into outputs—goods and services. Finding out how to produce high-quality goods or services on time and at a low cost is an important part of a firm's overall strategy.

2. Describe the role of technology in mass production, and discuss the changing face of operations management.

Key Terms

assembly lines 304

automation 304

benchmarking 326

bill of material 319

CAD/CAM systems 309

computer-aided design (CAD) 308

continued

continued

Five technological advances contributed to the development of mass production: mechanization, standardization, specialization, assembly lines, and automation.

Lower productivity growth and more competition from foreign manufacturers led American manufacturers to reevaluate their production methods. More are adopting flexible production systems that permit quick response to customer needs. Product design is being coordinated with process design. Information systems permit the linking of production with a firm's other departments, for better coordination and control. Operations management is no longer considered an isolated activity but is now integrated with other functions.

Today manufacturers must comply with many laws covering air, water, and solid-waste pollution. Since manufacturing processes are a major cause of pollution, companies are developing environmentally safe production methods that prevent or reduce pollution.

3. Discuss the two main production processes.

Two basic production processes transform inputs into outputs. One breaks down raw material into one or more outputs, and the other combines or transforms inputs to create the final product. Production processes can be continuous, repetitive, or intermittent.

4. Explain how automation affects manufacturing and service industries.

Automation in the production process is advancing with computer technology. Three major types of automation in manufacturing are CAD/CAM systems, robotics, and flexible manufacturing systems. Computer-integrated manufacturing combines these systems to automate the whole manufacturing process. The benefits of automation are greater flexibility, better productivity and quality, lower costs, and the ability to integrate production systems with other areas of the company.

Service businesses also use automation in many ways. Computer systems for accounting, record keeping, scheduling, and many other activities are part of almost every business today.

5. List the factors to consider in production planning.

The goal of production planning is to satisfy customers while minimizing costs. Choosing the site for a manufacturing or service facility is one element. Important cost-based factors are nearness to customers and materials sources, labor availability, availability and cost of transportation, energy costs, and taxes. Qualitative factors include quality of life and environmental regulations.

Other factors in production planning are facilities layout (whether to use process, product, or fixed-position layout), make-or-buy decisions, and control of costs through purchasing decisions.

6. Discuss the major methods of inventory management.

The goal of inventory management is to keep the costs of ordering and holding inventory down while keeping enough stock on hand to meet production and sales demands. Materials requirement planning uses a master schedule to determine when parts are needed. With just-in-time systems, companies schedule parts to arrive just before they are needed. Manufacturing resource planning integrates data from production and other departments to generate management reports.

7. Identify two key aspects of production control.

Key aspects of production control are routing and scheduling. Routing determines the sequence of operations throughout the production process. Facility layout is a factor in routing. Techniques for scheduling production include Gantt charts and the critical path method.

8. Explain how quality control affects production and operations.

Quality control is measuring finished goods against clients' needs or against the firm's own standards. Today both manufacturing and service companies consider quality important. When all personnel are concerned with quality, the concept is called total quality management (TQM). Companies can affirm their commitment to TQM by applying for the Baldrige award or similar state awards and by seeking ISO 9000 certification. Two popular techniques are statistical quality control and quality circles.

■ DISCUSSION QUESTIONS

1. Classify each of the following production processes as continuous, repetitive, or intermittent: printing designs on white T-shirts ordered in minimum quantities of 144, manufacturing motorcycles, brewing beer. Explain your classifications.

2. Computers, robots, and other forms of automation are being used to produce goods and services more and more often. What are some of the advantages of automation? Why would some workers be opposed to automation? On the whole, do you think automation has helped or hindered U.S. businesses? Explain.

3. Would your community be attractive to new companies? Using the criteria presented in the chapter, evaluate your community and discuss its advantages and disadvantages. What types of firms might want to locate there?

4. What key trade-offs would you consider when trying to decide whether to make or buy a key input, one used to make nearly all your firm's products?

5. If you were in charge of purchasing for your company, what general strategy would you use to buy the best-quality items at the lowest cost with the best delivery schedule? How would you evaluate each potential vendor?

6. Is it better to place infrequent large orders or to place frequent small orders? Explain your answer.

7. Design a CPM diagram for promoting and staging a rock concert.

8. You own a small company that designs specialized computer software. How would you measure quality from both the company's and the client's viewpoint? Describe your quality-control program, including your quality standards.

■ CASE

If the Shoe Fits

Allen-Edmonds Shoe Corp., a Wisconsin manufacturer of expensive men's and women's shoes, was losing business because some retailers could not wait up to eight weeks for shoe orders. President John Stollenwerk wanted to institute procedures that would reduce production time, cut costs, and thereby increase customer satisfaction.

The first step was to automate the firm's main plant. Carts of unfinished shoes had been pushed by workers between work stations. Replacing these with a conveyor system to move the shoes reduced work-in-process inventory from 5,000 to 1,200 pairs of shoes. Workers liked the system, which brought the work to them. It also lowered the investment in inventory by $400,000 and shortened the time to make a pair of shoes at that plant from three and a half days to eight hours.

Encouraged by that successful change, Stollenwerk turned to just-in-time production techniques to further improve the company's overall operating efficiency. These practices, he hoped, would cut investment in inventory and speed up the manufacturing process. However, what works at large companies does not always succeed at smaller ones, especially companies with many products produced in small lots. For example, Allen-Edmonds makes 41,000 different styles, colors, and sizes of shoes and frequently changes product lines.

To make the just-in-time system work, Allen-Edmonds needed the cooperation of its suppliers, the leather tanners. Although the leather sole manufacturers agreed to deliver weekly rather than monthly, the European tanneries providing hides for shoe uppers were unwilling to process hides in small batches to suit Allen-Edmonds, one small customer.

Just-in-time theory emphasizes quality and teamwork. Stollenwerk therefore changed the compensation system at one plant from piecework, which stresses doing individual jobs quickly, to hourly pay. But employees did not adapt well to the new plan; productivity fell as some workers took more breaks and slacked off. Morale dropped as well. After the company lost $1 million in 1990, it went back to piecework because the workers needed the discipline of that system. Both productivity and profits increased.

The just-in-time program did bring some benefits to Allen-Edmonds. It reduced inventory costs by $3.5 million and average order time to about three weeks, which pleased customers. However, Stollenwerk maintains that there is still no good just-in-time system for small manufacturers with shorter production runs.[27]

Questions

1. Why did automation succeed but just-in-time fail at Allen-Edmonds? What should management consider before implementing new management strategies?

2. Does Allen-Edmonds practice total quality management? Give specific examples to support your answer.

3. What are some other techniques that Allen-Edmonds could use to shorten production time?

Your Career in Management

Many students in business schools choose management as their major. Management principles and practices apply in any kind of organization, regardless of the product or process. A person who wants to become a manager needs a strong background in psychology, sociology, group dynamics, social psychology, and human relations.

Managers must respect the individuality, dignity, and needs of the people who report to them. They must also be able to motivate others to perform needed tasks. In turn, good managers are always motivated to do the best possible job. They also are confident—and their confidence is based on continual self-evaluation of their abilities and past successes.

The late 1990s and beyond will be a good time for college graduates to seek careers in management. But they need to realize that college graduation does not lead immediately to a management position. A path often followed is to become a management trainee. Trainees learn about company policy, the nature of the industry, operating procedures, and organization structures. They may also spend some time on the production line, work in a warehouse, or fill some other blue-collar job. The training program may last from several weeks to several years. After completing the program, new managers may specialize in such fields as sales, production, accounting, personnel, industrial relations, credit, finance, and research and development. Middle-level and upper-level managers are chosen from the ranks of sales managers, production managers, controllers, human-resource managers, and so on.

Dream Career: Hotel and Motel Management

Hotel and motel management is a sophisticated field. Managers must understand computers, finance, and labor relations. They also need to know the seven other areas that make up the backbone of the operation: rooms, food and beverage, personnel, sales and marketing, hotel accounting, conventions, and catering. The emphasis in hotel and motel management has evolved from technical skills to management skills. Recently, the industry has become much more competitive because more companies are now going after the same number of travelers.

The preferred way to advance is through the management training program of a major hotel chain. Prospective managers have six to fifteen months of intensive training, rotating through all the major departments. The fastest way to become a general manager is to specialize in room sales or food and beverage, which are the most operations-oriented areas.

- *Places of employment*: Throughout the country and abroad, with most jobs in medium-size to large cities.

- *Skills required*: A two-year degree for some jobs, but the quickest route into management is a four-year degree. A second language is mandatory for employment overseas, and it helps in some U.S. metropolitan areas.
- *Employment outlook through 2005*: Good.
- *Salaries*: $17,000–$25,000 for trainees; $33,000–$40,000 for assistant managers; $53,000–$80,000+ for general managers in major cities.

Where the Opportunities Are

City Manager

With the increase in urban problems—decay of the inner city, for example—cities have a great need for people with managerial skills. City managers are usually appointed by a governing body, such as a city council, and they are responsible to that body. The major duties of city managers are managing tax collection and disbursement, law enforcement, and public-works projects; hiring department heads and supporting staffs; and preparing annual budgets (to be approved by city officials). Other duties may include collecting rents, designing traffic controls, and planning for expansion.

- *Places of employment*: Generally, cities with populations over 50,000,

although some smaller communities now hire city managers.

- *Skills required*: Master's degree in public administration, although some cities accept people with a four-year degree and several years' experience as an assistant city manager.
- *Employment outlook through 2005*: Very good. More and more cities are seeking professional managers rather than politicians to handle complex city affairs.
- *Salaries*: $20,000–$40,000 for assistant city managers; $40,000–$100,000+ for city managers, with the higher figure for medium-size to large cities.

Quality-Control Manager

If significant numbers of a product break down during the warranty period, the cost of repairs eats into corporate profits. Thus many firms hire quality-control people for all phases of the design and manufacturing process. Others spend their money on inspection procedures. A quality-control manager supervises quality-control inspectors. The inspectors decide whether products and materials meet quality standards. To do so, they either examine every item produced or check a sample of the items.

- *Places of employment*: Everywhere, but the best opportunities are where

high-tech industries are concentrated, as in Austin, Boston, and Marin County, California.

- *Skills required*: Two-year degree for inspectors; two-year or four-year degree plus experience for managers; four-year degree or master's degree for quality-control engineers.
- *Employment outlook through 2005*: Above average in high-tech industries.
- *Salaries*: $20,000–$40,000 for inspectors; $30,000–$50,000 for managers; $60,000+ for managers with an engineering degree and an MBA.

Retail Food-Store Manager

In all types of food stores—supermarkets, small grocery stores, convenience stores, specialty food stores—managers coordinate operations. Their duties often include planning work schedules and controlling advertising, ordering, pricing, hiring, and especially customer relations. Managers may assist clerks and stockers in their daily tasks or may supervise and assist in such departments as the delicatessen, film processing, check cashing, and catering. Other responsibilities may include store security, personnel matters, expense control, and competitive strategies.

- *Places of employment*: Throughout the country.
- *Skills required*: Two-year

or four-year degree. In small or family-owned stores, managers may learn the business through experience. But for the most part, formal education is essential.

- *Employment outlook through 2005:* Average.
- *Salaries:* $19,000–$23,000 for trainees; $60,000–$80,000 for general managers of very large food stores.

Purchasing Manager

If materials, supplies, and equipment are not on hand when they're needed, the entire work flow of an organization could stop. Keeping a big enough supply on hand is the purchasing manager's responsibility. It includes more than just buying goods and services, however. Market forecasting, production planning, and inventory control are all part of the job. Purchasing managers supervise purchasing agents or industrial buyers, who do the actual buying. Over half of all purchasing managers work for moderate-size to large manufacturers. The rest work in government agencies, construction companies, hospitals, and schools.

- *Places of employment:* Throughout the country, especially in large industrial and government centers, such as Washington, D.C., Atlanta, Chicago, Pittsburgh, and Los Angeles.
- *Skills required:* Generally,

a two-year or four-year degree, but many employers now require an MBA.

- *Employment outlook through 2005:* Good in general; very good with MBA.
- *Salaries:* $26,000–$30,000 for junior purchasing agents (but less for entry-level purchasing agents in the federal government); $45,000–$80,000 for purchasing managers.

Radio or TV Station Manager

The manager of a small radio or TV station may also be the owner and may play an active role in the four major departments: programming, engineering, sales, and general administration. At large stations in metropolitan areas, station managers may be called director of directors, since they oversee the directors of programming, continuity, radio and television, public service, and so on. In either case, station directors control all aspects of production, from budgeting to programming, and they inform, educate, and entertain audiences.

- *Places of employment:* New York, Chicago, and Los Angeles for the most opportunities, but throughout the country in medium-size to large cities.
- *Skills required:* Four-year, specialized degree in broadcasting, mass com-

munication, telecommunications, speech, or journalism; an emphasis in programming, management, and marketing may also be acceptable.

- *Employment outlook through 2005:* Good, especially in cable television. The competition at higher levels is vigorous.
- *Salaries:* $22,000–$35,000 for managers in small communities; $35,000–$75,000+ for managers in large cities.

Facility Manager

Before the term facility management was developed, it was thought that these were the people you called when light bulbs needed replacing or the windows were dirty. Nothing could be further from the truth. When you look at a firm's balance sheet, the first large expense you usually see is salaries. The second is facilities. Well-managed work sites not only save the organization money but also contribute to productivity. With stricter environmental rules—and heightened public sensitivity—companies are more interested in providing attractive, healthy, safe buildings. Facility managers play a big role in the operation, maintenance, and in some cases planning of everything from office complexes to factories.

- *Places of employment:* Throughout the country and especially in large cities.
- *Skills required:* Two-year

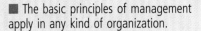 The basic principles of management apply in any kind of organization.

or four-year degree. Several universities now offer a four-year program in facilities management.

- *Employment outlook through 2005:* Very good, especially with larger companies.
- *Salaries:* $20,000–$30,000 to start; $55,000+ for senior facilities managers.

Industrial Production Manager

Production managers are usually responsible for all production in a factory. In large plants with several operations—aircraft assembly, for instance—a manager is in charge of each operation, such as machining, assembly, or finishing. Production managers are typically responsible for production scheduling, staffing, equipment, quality control, inventory control, and coordination with other departments. Production managers, in essence, plan the production schedule. They

determine which machines will be used, whether overtime or extra shifts are necessary, the sequence of production, and related matters.

- *Places of employment:* Throughout the United States.
- *Skills required:* Two-year or four-year degree, depending on employer. More are requiring a four-year degree, and some are requiring an MBA.
- *Employment outlook through 2005:* Very good with undergraduate engineering degree and MBA.
- *Salaries:* $23,000–$30,000 for assistant production managers; for production managers, $35,000–$55,000. Some employers give performance bonuses.

Management Careers: A Final Note

This career appendix doesn't exhaust the list of managerial positions. There are managers for every possible business function: traffic managers, public-relations managers, office managers, department managers, and administrators at all levels.

The opportunities for advancement from line operations, sales positions, or general administrative work are many for those who wish to move up and take more responsibility. Higher-level managers need many more administrative skills than lower-level managers do, but most companies train people for those positions. Many companies also encourage potential managers to continue their education. Some even pay tuition. The future looks promising for those willing to make the effort to move into management.

Human Resources

Part 5

Overview

Motivating employees to achieve the company's goals can be one of the most difficult tasks a firm faces. Different workers are driven to perform by different needs. Some are motivated by money, others by a desire for recognition, and still others by a sense of responsibility and duty. Human relations are the dynamics of how people interact with one another and how managers interact with employees to inspire effectiveness. Managers who are most successful at motivating workers understand human relations and have good communication skills.

Even so, corporate culture in America has traditionally inhibited give-and-take between managers and employees. This is changing, though, as American companies expand into the global marketplace and are exposed to foreign management styles. The Japanese style, in particular, has been very influential. American companies are realizing the need for more compassionate human-resource management. Developing and keeping satisfied, productive workers has become another weapon in the arsenal of the successful corporation.

Human-resource managers generally have three goals. The first is to provide competent, well-trained employees for the company; the second is to make employees as effective as possible; and the third is to satisfy employees' personal needs by helping them achieve successful careers. Ultimately, reaching all three goals is good for both the employees and the company.

Workers in certain trades are represented by collective bargaining units called unions. These organizations negotiate agreements with company management on behalf of their members working within the company. Labor-management relations can be critical to the success of a company and a worker's career. Today, corporations and unions are working more closely together than in the past. The declining workforce and the increase in health-care costs are two trends that led to this new cooperation.

The following chapters will explore different ways of motivating employees, group behavior, current trends in the field of human resources, and the history and future of the labor movement in America. Human-resource management is an invaluable area of business operations that can be exciting and rewarding to the individual who chooses it as a career.

Company Profile

Good Samaritan Hospital began as Saint John's Hotel for the Invalids. In 1866, two Cincinnati-area bankers offered to donate a larger facility to the Sisters of Charity, the order of Catholic nuns that established the facility. This gift gave the Sisters a new, 95-bed hospital where patients were guaranteed treatment regardless of their ability to pay.

The name "Good Samaritan" truly reflected the intentions of the Sisters and their benefactors. That spirit of inclusiveness still permeates the hospital today, not only in patient care but also in employee relations. A member of the national Sisters of Charity Health Care System, Good Samaritan is acutely aware of the important role its employees play in delivering the highest quality care possible to the hospital's patients.

Good Samaritan's commitment to both patients and staff has created an outstanding facility. What started as a small private general hospital over 140 years ago is now the largest private, teaching, and research health-care facility in Cincinnati. Good Samaritan also has one of only two Level One Trauma Centers in the Cincinnati tri-state area. It is capable of handling every type of emergency situation.

At Good Samaritan, the entire staff, from administrators to health-care providers, shares equally in the original mission established for the hospital.

Motivation, Leadership, and Group Behavior

Learning Goals

After studying this chapter, you should be able to:

1 Understand Taylor's concept of scientific management.

2 Describe what Mayo's Hawthorne studies revealed about worker motivation.

3 Discuss Maslow's hierarchy of needs.

4 Describe Theory X, Theory Y, and Theory Z.

5 Explain job motivators, job-maintenance factors, worker expectations, and equity theory.

6 Distinguish between job enlargement and job enrichment, and explain their effects on workers.

7 Explain the nature of work groups, group socialization, and group cohesiveness.

8 Discuss the importance of group leadership.

Career Profile

People sometimes find jobs in unusual ways. Just ask Edwin Bowman, who was hired after meeting someone from AT&T while waiting to board a plane. Edwin's inquisitiveness at the airport, coupled with his college education in finance and management, eventually led to a position as an account manager with AT&T Global Information Solutions.

Edwin works with various financial institutions through the data services division of Global Information Solution's Financial Business Unit. His primary responsibility is to sell AT&T products that will help banks address problems such as improving the efficiency of their mortgage loan application process. After the products are installed and the client is completely informed about how the equipment operates, Edwin follows up to make sure that the customer is completely satisfied with the purchase.

AT&T G.I.S. takes a team approach to servicing clients. Team members work together to determine and meet the needs of their customers in a productive and timely manner. Each person on the team is a potential leader. The specific project and the skills and talents of the employees assigned to it dictate who will assume the role.

Customer and employee satisfaction are linked at AT&T G.I.S. If the clients are happy, the employees will also be happy, because AT&T G.I.S. bases its employees' levels of compensation and recognition on their success in pleasing customers. This gives Edwin and his associates extra incentive to make every effort to meet clients' needs.

This chapter begins by exploring the nature of worker motivation and organizational culture. It then studies leadership. Next it discusses interpersonal relationships among workers. It ends with a study of group behavior.

UNDERSTANDING WORKER MOTIVATION

People are a firm's most important resources. Managers and workers can be put to good use or wasted. The firm suffers when good employees become bored or unhappy, lose interest, and leave the organization. But they'll stay if they have interesting tasks, feel like part of an effective team, and are recognized for their contributions.[1]

Good managers have many skills for dealing with employees. They understand people's work habits and attitudes. They can motivate people to achieve the organization's goals and can provide direction through leadership. To succeed, managers must understand **human relations**, how people interact with one another and how managers interact with employees to improve effectiveness. Human-relations skills include the ability to motivate, lead, communicate, build morale, and teach others. Good managers are also students of **organizational behavior**, human behavior in an organized setting.

How can managers and the organization promote enthusiastic job performance, high productivity, and job satisfaction? Many studies of human behavior in organizations have aimed to find out. Among the first of such studies were those by Frederick Taylor.

human relations How people interact with one another and how managers interact with employees to make the organization and the employees more effective.

organizational behavior Human behavior in an organized setting.

▼ TAYLOR'S SCIENTIFIC MANAGEMENT

In the factories and machine shops of the 1880s, management and labor usually did not see eye to eye. Wages were relatively high, because of a labor shortage in America. But ethnic differences between factory workers, mostly immigrants, and the Anglo-Saxon managers fostered hostility. Another problem was the piecework system: workers were paid according to how many pieces of work they produced. Management reduced the rate of pay per piece if production increased. Workers responded by doing less work in a ten-hour day than they were able to.

Frederick Taylor was a low-level manager at Midvale Steel Company in Philadelphia. He wanted to resolve the conflict between management and labor. To management, a day's work was the most one could force a person to do in a day; to labor, it was the least the person could get away with. Taylor reasoned that there must be a true technical measure of a day's work. It occurred to him that worker productivity depended not just on how hard a person worked but on how the work was done. If a person could be taught a better way to work and be paid for increased productivity, everybody would profit—labor, management, even consumers.

One by one Taylor studied the jobs in the plant and redesigned the

■ A good manager understands human relations and is a student of organizational behavior. He or she is always seeking new methods of motivating employees to achieve the company's goals.

equipment and the methods. For instance, he realized that a special crew could sharpen all the cutting tools. Then individual machinists wouldn't have to sharpen their own. They could keep working. Taylor studied each job with a stopwatch, breaking down every task into separate movements. An instruction sheet was then prepared that said exactly how each job should be done, how much time it should take, and what motions and tools should be used.

Taylor's ideas led to dramatic increases in productivity at Midvale. He told his story to a wider audience in a book, *The Principles of Scientific Management.* His pioneering work of breaking jobs down into their component parts contributed to specialization and the assembly-line method of production. Yet "scientific management" didn't increase workers' job satisfaction. Taylor had a great knack for machinery, but he failed to realize that people are motivated by more than money and that repetition in a job is boring.

MAYO'S HAWTHORNE STUDIES

Elton Mayo, who has been called America's first industrial psychologist, was interested in Taylor's notion of "scientific management." Mayo was studying fatigue among workers at a Western Electric plant in Hawthorne, Illinois. He observed two groups making the same telephone part. For one group, the shop lighting was improved; for the other it was left alone. In both groups, to Mayo's surprise, production increased a little. Mayo couldn't understand why the group with better lighting wasn't much more productive than the other group.

Mayo extended his research to a group making telephone relays. He explained the purpose of his study to the workers, gave them veto power over changes in their routine, and encouraged them to work in their own way. He discovered that performance improved, not because of changes in lighting, but because management was paying attention to their efforts and interested in their well-being. The employees worked better because their employer was listening to their opinions. The phenomenon of an improved attitude leading to improved work performance became known as the **Hawthorne effect**.[2]

Hawthorne effect Improved work performance resulting from an improved attitude.

Concept Check

- What were Frederick Taylor's contributions to the study of management?
- What was unusual about Elton Mayo's Hawthorne research findings? What were the implications?

HOW NEEDS MOTIVATE: MASLOW'S HIERARCHY

3 Mayo's studies proved that workers are not motivated by money alone. In fact, pay is often a weak motivator. Many researchers have explored what motivates people. Among them was psychologist Abraham Maslow, who proposed a theory of motivation based on universal human needs.

■ Praise and recognition are important to an employee's feeling of self worth. To satisfy this need, Bell Labs has created a program that rewards its scientists for their contributions to the company.

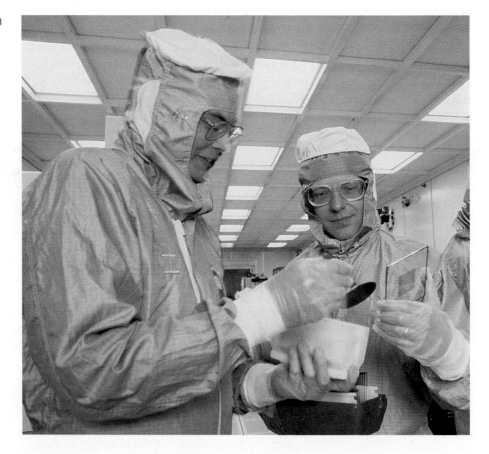

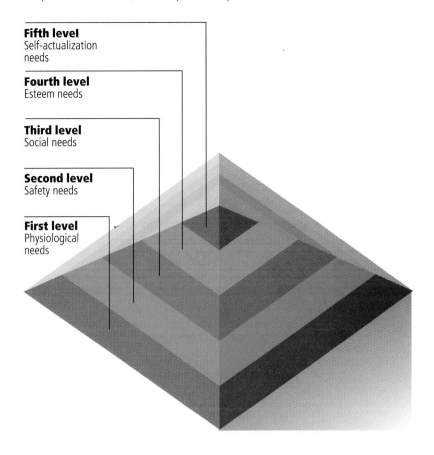

■ **Exhibit 11-1**
Maslow's Hierarchy of
Human Needs

Fifth level
Self-actualization
needs

Fourth level
Esteem needs

Third level
Social needs

Second level
Safety needs

First level
Physiological
needs

UNIVERSAL NEEDS

needs theory of motivation Theory that people act to satisfy their unmet needs.

hierarchy of needs Sequence of five human needs, as proposed by Maslow—physiological, safety, social, esteem, and self-actualization needs.

The **needs theory of motivation** states that people act to satisfy their unmet needs. When you're hungry, for instance, you look for and eat food. Maslow proposed a **hierarchy of needs**, a sequence consisting of physiological, safety, social, esteem, and self-actualization needs, as shown in Exhibit 11-1. According to his theory, a person's behavior is motivated by unsatisfied needs. Once a need is satisfied, its importance to the individual diminishes. A higher-level need then is more likely to motivate the person. Research studies have shown that this is true sometimes, but not always.

Physiological Needs

physiological needs Most basic human needs for food, shelter, and clothing; first level of needs in Maslow's hierarchy.

The most basic human needs are **physiological needs**, the needs for food, shelter, and clothing. In large part it is the physiological needs that motivate a person to find a job. People need to earn money to provide food, shelter, and clothing for themselves and their families.

Safety Needs

safety needs Needs for security, protection from physical harm, and avoidance of the unexpected; second level in Maslow's hierarchy.

Once people have met their most basic needs for physiological well-being, they reach the second level in Maslow's hierarchy, which is **safety**

needs. People need to feel secure, to be protected from physical harm, and to avoid the unexpected. In work terms, these needs are for job security and protection from work hazards.

After Citibank in New York said it had to eliminate 2,000 jobs in its home office, two employees killed themselves. The bank's medical director claimed that higher stress was also contributing to more employee car accidents. Hypertension among workers was so high that Citibank installed blood pressure monitors at seven of its U.S. bank sites.[3] These actions will help Citibank's workers meet their safety needs.

Social Needs

social needs Needs for belonging (acceptance by others) and for giving and receiving friendship and love; third level in Maslow's hierarchy.

Physiological and safety are physical needs. Once these are satisfied, people turn to needs involving other people. Maslow's third level is **social needs**, needs for belonging (acceptance by others) and for giving and receiving friendship and love. Informal social groups on and off the job help people satisfy these needs. So do school friends and family members.

Even formal work groups can help meet workers' social needs. For instance, Aetna Life organized self-managed teams—combining clerks, technical writers, underwriters, and financial analysts—to handle customer requests and complaints. New "team" furniture, designed by Steelcase, establishes small areas that Steelcase calls neighborhoods, where workers who perform the same tasks, such as handling telephone inquiries, are grouped together.

Esteem Needs

esteem needs Needs for the respect of others and for a sense of accomplishment and achievement; fourth level in Maslow's hierarchy.

The fourth level of needs in Maslow's hierarchy is **esteem needs**—needs for the respect of others and for a sense of accomplishment and achievement. Satisfaction of these needs is reflected in feelings of self-worth. Having a job is often very important in satisfying esteem needs. People who have been unemployed for a long time often lack self-respect and feel that they lack the respect of others.

When a person's reputation and sense of self-worth are equally strong, the person's need for esteem is satisfied. Praise and recognition from managers and others in the firm contribute to the sense of self-worth. For instance, TRW Inc.'s space and defense business recently chose its first nineteen "technical fellows." Each fellow got a cash bonus, a plaque, and a big research budget to pursue projects of personal interest. IBM, Bell Labs, and 3M have similar reward programs for their scientists.[4]

Self-Actualization Needs

self-actualization needs Needs for fulfillment, for living up to one's potential, and for using one's capabilities to the highest degree; fifth and highest level in Maslow's hierarchy.

The highest level of needs in Maslow's hierarchy is **self-actualization needs**—needs for fulfillment, for living up to one's potential, and for using one's abilities to the utmost. The Army recruiting slogan "Be all that you can be" is aimed at the human need for self-actualization. For a carpenter, self-actualization could mean designing and building a beautiful set of cabinets. A manager who develops and maintains an effective department might also feel self-actualized.

MASLOW'S CONTRIBUTIONS

If nothing else, Maslow's needs hierarchy has prompted managers to carefully consider human needs. It has dramatized how satisfying needs can motivate employees. The needs hierarchy has also helped managers realize that it is hard to motivate people by appealing to satisfied needs. For instance, overtime pay would probaly not motivate an employee who already earns plenty.

Maslow's needs hierarchy has helped, but it should not be taken too literally. Not everybody satisfies needs step by step. For instance, some people will try to gain esteem before satisfying their social needs. Another problem with the hierarchy is that it oversimplifies motivation. It implies that people strive to satisfy their needs one at a time. In reality, people usually try to satisfy more than one group of needs at a time.

Concept Check
- List and discuss the needs found in Maslow's hierarchy.
- Why did Maslow refer to his theory as a hierarchy?

MANAGEMENT STYLES FOR MOTIVATING EMPLOYEES

4 THEORIES X AND Y

Douglas McGregor, one of Maslow's students, started his study of motivation with two somewhat contradictory assumptions: that in general people do not like to work, and that work is a natural activity. From these assumptions, he devised two theories of what motivates workers and what management styles are appropriate. These two approaches, known as Theory X and Theory Y, reflect his two very different assumptions.

Theory X assumes the following:

Theory X Management theory that assumes people do not like to work and that managers must closely control workers' behavior.

- The average person dislikes work and will avoid it if possible.
- Because people don't like to work, they must be controlled, directed, or threatened with punishment to get them to make an effort.
- The average person prefers to be directed, avoids responsibility, is relatively unambitious, and wants security above all.

This view of people suggests that managers must constantly prod workers to perform and must closely control their on-the-job behavior. Carrying Theory X to an extreme, some managers have even spied on employees, as the Business Ethics and Social Responsibility Trends box on the next page shows.

McGregor believed that a management style based on Theory X is inappropriate. He recognized that most of today's workers have moved beyond physiological and safety needs to higher levels of needs. Theory X managers tell people what to do, are very directive, like to be in control, and show little confidence in employees. They foster dependent, passive, resentful subordinates. McGregor's warning is to "watch out for self-fulfilling prophecies": Management creates the conditions that cause

Putting Theory X to Work

True or false:
___ I am very strongly attracted to members of my own sex.
___ I believe in the second coming of Christ.
___ I have no difficulty starting or holding my urine.

Most people would not volunteer such information. But people who want to be a security guard at Target Stores must answer those and 701 other questions. Sibi Soroka passed the test and landed a job. Afterward, though, he felt "humiliated" and "embarrassed" at having to reveal "my innermost beliefs and feelings." So in a class-action suit, he has accused Target of illegal prying. That dispute over workplace privacy highlights a hot employment issue of the mid-1990s.

New snooping technology is leading to more frequent and foolproof spying. Some organizations are bugging and tapping workers, monitoring them at their computer, even using special chairs to measure wiggling (wigglers aren't working). General Electric says it uses tiny fish-eye lenses installed behind pinholes in walls and ceilings to watch employees suspected of crimes. Du Pont says it uses hidden long-distance cameras to monitor its loading docks around the clock. At airlines like Delta, computers track who writes the most reservations. Safeway Stores in Oakland, California, has dashboard computers on its 782 trucks. The computers record driving speed, oil pressure, engine RPMs, idling time, and when and how long a truck is stopped. If anything is abnormal, the driver is questioned.

Procter and Gamble's security department's activities have included watching employees with video cameras, monitoring their telephone calls from P&G offices and their homes, and following them on business trips. One former executive describes "bosses seizing and scrutinizing personal medical records to pry into an employee's personal life." One brand manager reported that while lunching at a local restaurant, he and colleagues discussed an ad already on the air. Later that day, the manager's boss, who wasn't present at lunch, scolded him for talking about the ad in public.

Employers have lots of good reasons for checking up on workers. Court cases have led to the so-called negligent hiring theory, which holds a boss liable for a worker's crimes or negligence on the job if the employer fails to screen for personality quirks or past misdeeds. Another goal is preventing theft.[5] These measures are based on the assumptions of Theory X.

employees to fit Theory X descriptions. By assuming that employees are lazy, unmotivated, and in need of strict control, managers reinforce the conditions that made employees act that way in the first place. And managers who think workers are lazy and irresponsible may lose or frustrate the best ones.

In contrast, **Theory Y** is based on the following assumptions:

- Work is as natural as play or rest.
- The threat of punishment isn't the only way to get people to work. People will be self-directed and self-controlled and will try to achieve organizational goals if they believe in them.

Theory Y Management theory that assumes people like to work and that they will do so when managers encourage learning and self-development.

- Workers can be positively motivated. They will try to accomplish organizational goals if they believe they'll be rewarded for doing so.
- Under proper conditions, the average person not only accepts responsibility but also seeks it.
- Most workers have a relatively high degree of imagination and creativity and are willing to help solve problems.

Managers who follow Theory Y recognize individual differences and encourage workers to learn and develop their skills. A secretary might be given the responsibility for generating a monthly report. The reward for doing so might be recognition at a meeting, a special training class to enhance computer skills, or a pay increase. In short, the Theory Y approach builds on the idea that worker and organizational interests are the same. For instance, Mark Athon, a sales representative for a chemical company, surpassed his monthly sales quota with a big order of janitorial cleaner. Athon got his regular sales commission plus a bonus. He benefited from the reward, and the firm gained from the increase in sales.

COMPARING THEORIES X AND Y

At first, you might conclude that Theory Y is always better than Theory X. It is better in some cases, especially with well-educated workers. Many firms in high-tech industries—such as Dresser Industries, Texas Instruments, and TRW Systems—use Theory Y in both day-to-day management and management-training programs.

The more controlled and authoritarian approach of Theory X can be just as effective in some conditions. Army basic training, for instance, would never work under Theory Y. Some assembly-line workers may be more productive under a Theory X manager, at least in the short run. But their attitude toward the work and fellow workers will usually suffer in the long run.

In reality, most companies operate somewhere between the extremes suggested by Theory X and Theory Y. The Theory Y approach is not always best because some employees need more structure and supervision oversight. Even firms that support self-direction sometimes mistrust the extent of employees' willingness to work. Theory Y represents an ideal that may not always reflect the practical reality of the workplace.

JAPANESE MANAGEMENT STYLE

The assumptions of Theories X and Y have helped managers in U.S. firms motivate and lead employees. Japanese managers, however, have a different approach. Of course, not every Japanese manager leads in the same way. But researchers have uncovered a general style used by many of them. It includes:

- *Making decisions by consensus:* This is more than the participative decision style discussed in Chapter 8. When faced with an important decision, such as changing a production process, the Japanese involve all who would likely be affected. Sixty to eighty people could

■ A key component of the Japanese management style is an emphasis on consensus decision making. Employees are likely to be more committed to carrying out a decision they have had a hand in, but this approach can also lead to a lack of creativity and original thinking.

be involved. Consensus decision making is cumbersome and time-consuming. But employees are more likely to support the decision, understand it better, and be more committed to carrying it out.

- *Maximizing worker development:* Japanese leadership practices stem from an interest in developing people. Employees can have long-term, and sometimes lifetime, employment. Managers offer each employee ample coaching and training. Employees are rewarded for focusing on long-term results and being cooperative and loyal. Companies sponsor many cultural, athletic, and recreational facilities. In short, Japanese managers use a people-oriented style of leadership to achieve long-term results.

- *Recognizing employees as experts:* Japanese managers assume that employees are intelligent enough to work without a lot of supervision and rules. The first step in improving productivity is getting workers' opinions on how to do it.

- *Focusing on long-term results:* The Japanese leadership style emphasizes patience. Japanese managers are willing to listen to ideas that are likely to pay off in the long run. Short-term results are less important. Also, because Japanese workers know their jobs are secure, they're less likely to resist new technology.[6]

Does Japanese-style management work? Yes and no. The Japanese have proved to be very successful in their business ventures. They are strong competitors for Americans, Europeans, and virtually all other businesspeople in the world. In electronics (Sony, Pioneer, Sharp), automobiles (Toyota, Nissan, Honda), and cameras (Nikon, Canon, Minolta), the Japanese dominate.

On the other hand, the Japanese management style rewards conformity in thinking and behavior. Creativity suffers because of the emphasis on

Factor	Traditional U.S. management	Japanese management	Theory Z (combination of U.S. and Japanese management)
Length of employment	Relatively short-term; worker subject to layoffs if business is bad	Lifetime; layoffs rarely used to reduce costs	Long-term but not necessarily lifetime; layoffs "inappropriate"; stable, loyal work force; improved business conditions don't require new hiring and training
Rate of evaluation and promotion	Relatively rapid	Relatively slow	Slow by design; manager thoroughly trained and evaluated
Specialization in a functional area	Considerable; worker acquires expertise in single functional area	Minimal; worker acquires expertise in organization instead of functional area	Moderate; all experience various functions of the organization and have a sense of what's good for the firm rather than for a single area
Decision making	On individual basis	Input from all concerned parties	Group decision making for better decisions and easier implementation
Responsibility for success or failure	Assigned to individual	Shared by group	Assigned to individual
Control by manager	Very explicit and formal	More implicit and informal	Relatively informal but with explicit performance measures
Concern for workers	Focuses on work-related aspects of worker's life	Extends to whole life of worker	Is relatively concerned with worker's whole life, including the family

■ **Exhibit 11-2**
Differences in Management Approaches

work-group harmony, obedience, and consensus decision making. Japan still imports more foreign technology than it exports. Japanese industry often copies, and further develops, the ideas and technology of others.

Also, Japanese young people are less likely to want lifetime employment at one company than their parents and grandparents did. They are more concerned with their own careers and less interested in being part of a group. Just as we have learned from the Japanese, they have learned from Western business practices and lifestyles (such as being so preoccupied with your job that no time is left for family). The Japanese management style will have to adapt to these young professionals and their attitudes toward work and career.

THEORY Z

Theory Z Management theory that combines U.S. and Japanese management styles.

For these same reasons, U.S. firms could not simply import Japanese management techniques. Instead, William Ouchi (pronounced O-chee), a management scholar at the University of California, Los Angeles, has developed a management theory that combines U.S. and Japanese business practices. He calls it **Theory Z**. Exhibit 11-2 compares the traditional

U.S. and Japanese management styles with the Theory Z approach. Theory Z emphasizes long-term employment, slow career development, moderate specialization, group decision making, individual responsibility, relatively informal control over employees, and concern for workers. Theory Z has many Japanese elements, but it reflects U.S. cultural values.

Theory Z has been well received, but there is not yet much evidence to support its success. However, many U.S. firms—among them Union Carbide, Delta Airlines, IBM, and Procter & Gamble—do use elements of Theory Z. They expect that Theory Z will help improve organizational performance, worker motivation, and relationships between workers and managers.

MANAGEMENT OF CORPORATE CULTURE

corporate culture Set of attitudes, values, and standards of accepted behavior that distinguishes one organization from another.

Corporate culture is the set of attitudes, values, and standards of accepted behavior that distinguishes one organization from another. Corporate culture is the accumulated history of an organization, including the visions of its founders.

Corporate culture is greatly influenced by top management and can change when a new CEO takes command. In effect, the culture is the boat and the CEO steers it. But corporate cultures are enmeshed in history and usually change slowly. Redefining a corporate culture is a difficult, time-consuming task. For example, Tenneco hired an outside CEO, Michael Walsh, to redefine its corporate culture. He came with experience: He had been successful in reformulating the culture of Union Pacific railroad.

When Walsh arrived at Tenneco he discovered, among other things, that Tenneco's profitable auto-parts and chemicals divisions didn't strive as hard as they might for higher earnings because their profits were routinely combined with the company's money-losing farm-equipment operation. He found that inventories were bloated because some plant managers kept production lines rolling with little regard to what dealers actually sold. Shipping labels on some wares were so uninformative that customers had trouble figuring out what was inside. Quality control was a joke. At that point, Walsh understood what he had to do: Rip out layers of stifling protocol, wipe away acceptance of the status quo, and undo years of built-up cynicism about efforts to improve. Says Walsh: "I arrived to find a big behemoth of the sort that tries two things on anyone who wants change: It waits you out or wears you out."[7]

But Walsh made progress against the monster. He decided on a simple strategy: Set higher targets on every measure of performance and make missing them unacceptable. The new culture is called "no-excuses management." It requires that executives meet targets despite outside economic forces. Progress is reviewed weekly and monthly.[8]

Jeffrey Sonnenfeld of Emory University has identified and labeled four types of corporate culture: academies, clubs, fortresses, and baseball teams.[9] An *academy* is a company that provides excellent management and skills training. It expects its employees to use this training to move steadily through the ranks of management. The culture stresses long-term career advancement. New employees are typically young college gradu-

■ In terms of corporate culture, United Parcel Service (UPS) is a "club." Managers train in all parts of the operation, rather than specializing, and commitment to the good of the company is more important than personal achievement.

ates who are shaped to the company mold. A classic academy is Xerox. Every manager spends at least sixty hours each year in management training school, with twenty hours devoted to people management.

In *clubs,* everyone strives to fit into the group. Commitment to the company, doing things for the good of the group, is emphasized over personal achievement. Clubs groom managers as generalists instead of narrow specialists. A typical club is United Parcel Service. Chief executive John W. Rogers and his management committee began as clerks, drivers, and management trainees. Instead of learning more and more about these specialties, they learned a little of everything. Rogers, after thirty-two years with UPS, still does his own photocopying, eats lunch in the cafeteria alongside packagers and junior managers, and shares a secretary. "When decisions have to be made, we get everyone's opinion, and the company feels like a family to a lot of us," says John Tranfo, a staff vice president who will soon be celebrating his fortieth year at UPS. "In management, we have hardly any turnover," he adds.

Baseball teams seek out talent of all ages and experience. They reward people on the basis of what they produce. The emphasis is on short-term results rather than long-term commitment. Baseball teams don't spend resources on training. Either you come in with skills, or you learn them quickly on the job. Many accounting and law firms and consulting, advertising, and software development companies could be classified as baseball-team companies. The managers think of themselves as free agents, much like professional athletes. If one company doesn't give them the freedom or rewards they think they deserve, they leave for another one— or form their own.

Fortresses are companies that are struggling to keep afloat. Many are academies, clubs, or baseball teams that have failed and are trying to come back. Others, including retailing and natural-resource companies,

IMP ✗

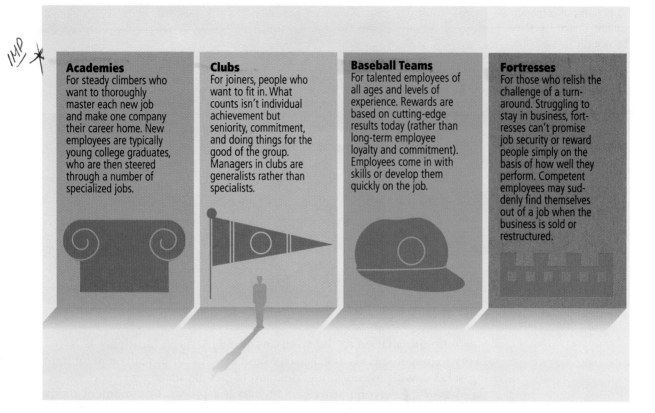

Academies
For steady climbers who want to thoroughly master each new job and make one company their career home. New employees are typically young college graduates, who are then steered through a number of specialized jobs.

Clubs
For joiners, people who want to fit in. What counts isn't individual achievement but seniority, commitment, and doing things for the good of the group. Managers in clubs are generalists rather than specialists.

Baseball Teams
For talented employees of all ages and levels of experience. Rewards are based on cutting-edge results today (rather than long-term employee loyalty and commitment). Employees come in with skills or develop them quickly on the job.

Fortresses
For those who relish the challenge of a turn-around. Struggling to stay in business, fortresses can't promise job security or reward people simply on the basis of how well they perform. Competent employees may suddenly find themselves out of a job when the business is sold or restructured.

■ **Exhibit 11-3**
Which Organizational Culture Is for You?
Source: Jeffrey Sonnenfeld, Emory University.

are always in a boom-or-bust cycle. Fortresses cannot promise job security or reward employees on the basis of how well they perform. Good employees may lose their jobs when the company is sold or restructured. As bad as this sounds, Bruce McKinnon, senior vice president of Microband Wireless Cable of New York, enjoys working for fortresses. In the past six years he's worked at three other cable television companies. He was hired each time as "a portable warlord to help them back on track. . . . I like the fact that there's adrenaline flowing, because you're doing an overhaul, not just a refining, and you have the chance to really create something."

Of course, many companies can't be neatly classified in any one way. Many have a blend of corporate cultures. Within General Electric, the Kidder Peabody unit and the NBC unit both have baseball-team qualities. GE's aerospace division operates more like a club; the electronics division is an academy; the home-appliance unit is a fortress. Still other companies are in transition. Apple Computer started out as a baseball team but is becoming an academy as it matures. And with deregulation, banks—once the clubbiest of firms—are fast evolving into baseball teams.

Before you take your first job after graduation, carefully consider the culture of potential employers. (Exhibit 11-3 summarizes the employee view of each culture.) If you are a risk taker, you will probably thrive at a baseball-team company but not perform as well at an academy. On the other hand, if you are a team player who craves security, you won't be happy at a baseball-team company. Think about your personality and the type of environment that makes you happy. Compare this information to what you see of the employer's corporate culture. This will get your career off to a good start.

- Explain Theory X and its applications.
- Discuss Theory Y and why it is applied more than Theory X.
- Describe Theory Z.
- Explain the Japanese style of management.
- Define corporate culture, and give several examples.

MOTIVATION FOR EFFECTIVE PERFORMANCE

5 Arnie Davis, an engine assembler, hasn't missed a day of work in ten years. Brenda Shelton, an attorney, takes legal documents home each night for further study. Why do these people work so hard? Most adults want to be productive. Many also believe that work is good in itself and essential for physical, social, and economic well-being. Placing a high value on work is known as the *work ethic*. People who share this value get to work on time, try to do a good job, suggest work improvements, and respond well to supervision.

Hard-working, eager employees with high morale are an ideal. They do exist some of the time, in some companies more than others and under the leadership of some managers more than others. To some extent, peo-

■ Jim Henson Productions has created a series of Muppet Meeting Films that are designed to motivate salespeople and energize business meetings. The films use humor to inspire employees to perform at their best. Many companies find such motivational materials to be quite effective.

Muppet, Muppet Meeting Films, video titles, and character names and likenesses are trademarks of Jim Henson Productions. ©1994 Jim Henson Productions.

ple's attitudes toward work depend on individual characteristics, such as personality and upbringing. But they also are influenced by factors that relate specifically to the job.

MOTIVATION AND MAINTENANCE FACTORS

job satisfiers According to Herzberg, job factors, such as recognition and responsibility, that motivate workers to work harder.

According to management scholar Frederick Herzberg, **job satisfiers**— the factors that satisfy and motivate workers—are achievement, recognition, the work itself, responsibility, advancement, and growth (see the left side of Exhibit 11-4). All these factors should be part of the actual job. They correspond more or less to Maslow's esteem and self-actualization needs.

A job with many satisfiers will usually motivate workers, provide job satisfaction, and prompt effective performance. But a lack of job satisfiers doesn't always lead to dissatisfaction and poor performance. A lack of job satisfiers may only discourage workers from doing their best.

job-maintenance factors According to Herzberg, aspects of the work environment, such as working conditions and salary, that are required to keep workers in a job.

In contrast to job satisfiers are **job-maintenance factors**, aspects of the work environment that lie outside the job itself but that are required to keep workers at the job. These factors include company policy, supervision, working conditions, interpersonal relationships at work, salary and benefits, and job security (see the right side of Exhibit 11-4).

Disappointment with any of the job-maintenance factors will turn them into job *dissatisfiers*. Job-maintenance factors rarely motivate workers. Good working conditions, for instance, will keep employees at a job but won't make them work harder. But poor working conditions, which are job dissatisfiers, may make employees quit.

Job-maintenance factors can help satisfy workers' physiological, safety, and social needs. Salary and benefits, for instance, enable workers to eat, live in a safe place, and get health care if needed. Protective clothing (working conditions) can help reduce safety hazards. Rest breaks can provide time for chatting with co-workers (interpersonal relationships), a social need.

Although Herzberg's ideas have been widely supported, some of them are disputed. Salary is a case in point. Other researchers have found that many employees view salary as a motivator, not just a potential job dissatisfier. Chaparral Steel Company, for instance, has a profit-sharing plan that gives employees big bonuses over their annual income. Though base

■ **Exhibit 11-4**
Factors That Affect
Worker Motivation

Job satisfiers (motivators)	Job-maintenance factors (potential job dissatisfiers)
Achievement	Company policy
Recognition	Supervision
Work itself	Working conditions
Responsibility	Interpersonal relationships at work
Advancement	Salary and benefits
Growth	Job security

pay has not increased for several years, the profit-sharing plan has been a very strong motivating force. It has encouraged employees to think in terms of the whole company rather than just their own job and department.

Of all the possible job rewards—pay increases, promotions, job security, recognition, and others—pay increases are the most clear-cut, well understood, and highly valued. Most people agree that businesses should pay for good performance. It follows that the best-performing workers should be given the largest pay increases. A pay increase tied to performance, rather than to seniority, is a *merit increase.* Suppose that you work for a company that gives raises to employees who reach certain levels of production within the budget and with no accidents. The expectation of such an increase will encourage you to work hard. In that case, a merit increase is a motivator because it is a reward that reinforces a high level of performance.

EXPECTATIONS AND JOB OUTCOMES

Good attitudes toward work and good job performance usually bring about *job satisfaction.* Workers at all levels can experience the pleasure of doing a good job. Job satisfaction is experienced by carpenters' helpers, supermarket clerks, operators of amusement-park rides, and presidents of major corporations. It goes along with high morale (the mental attitude toward work and people). High **morale** is expressed in confidence, cheerfulness, and so on. Much of this positive feeling flows from the work itself.

morale Mental attitude toward work and people.

Employees come to expect certain things about the organization—namely, that it will provide financial and other rewards in exchange for their work toward organizational goals. Management expects employees to put forth enough effort to yield a certain amount of production in return for a given amount of reward (money and other benefits). Usually the firm tries to let employees know what it expects through training, job descriptions, and production standards. Employees develop expectations about rewards through information about wage rates, job transfer opportunities, and the job promotions of others.

psychological contract Unwritten expectations of an employee or an employer.

Workers and managers also have many unwritten expectations. These unwritten expectations form an agreement known as the **psychological contract**. When the employee and the firm meet each other's unwritten expectations over and over, this psychological contract strengthens the employee's attachment to the firm. On the other hand, if the worker and the company fail to meet each other's expectations, their breaking of the psychological contract may bring about lower morale and productivity.

expectancy theory Management theory that motivation and job performance depend on how employers view their workers.

Victor Vroom, a management scholar, has studied the relationship between expectations and worker motivation. His work, called **expectancy theory,** explains that employees are motivated by their expectations, or their estimates of the chances, of receiving a reward for achieving some goal (outcome). An employee who believes that hard work is likely to produce a bonus or a promotion will work hard. An employee who believes that hard work is unlikely to lead anywhere is

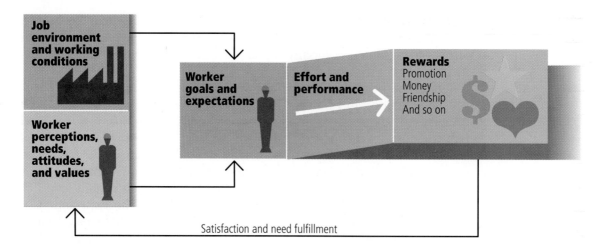

Satisfaction and need fulfillment

■ **Exhibit 11-5**
Cycle of Worker Motiva-
tion and Behavior

equity theory Manage-
ment theory that explains
motivation as related to
workers' perceptions of how
fairly they are treated compared with coworkers.

likely to make only a small effort (see Exhibit 11-5). According to Vroom's expectancy theory, then, motivation and job performance depend on how employees view their chances of success.

EQUITY THEORY

A different explanation of a worker's motivation to perform is called equity theory. **Equity theory** is concerned with individuals' perceptions about how fairly they are treated compared with their coworkers. Equity means fairness; motivationally, it means employees' perceived fairness of rewards or treatment at work. When individuals compare their rewards to those given to others doing similar jobs and feel inequities exist, they will react in one of the following ways to achieve satisfaction:

- *Increase their performance, to justify higher rewards.* This occurs when they perceive a positive inequity—for instance, when they are aware that they are being treated more favorably by their boss.
- *Decrease their performance, to compensate for lower rewards.* This occurs when they perceive a negative inequity—when their pay, for instance, seems too low by comparison with others.
- *Change the compensation* they receive, through legal or other action or by inappropriate behavior such as theft.
- *Modify their comparisons.* For example, workers might persuade low performers who are receiving equal pay to increase their efforts, or they might discourage high performers from working so hard.
- *Distort reality.* Workers might psychologically rationalize that the perceived inequities are justified.
- *Leave the inequitable situation*—by quitting the organization or by changing jobs or careers.[10]

Inequities arise out of many different situations, and they occur in promotions, benefits, work assignments, job ratings, employee recognition, and transfers. Many of them are emotionally charged, ranging from racial problems to sex discrimination. On a daily basis, even minor managerial decisions can lead to perceived inequities.

6 JOB ENRICHMENT

Herzberg has extended motivation theories by proposing a job enrichment theory. The basic notion of job enrichment is that making jobs more pleasant will motivate workers to perform better.

The concepts of job enlargement and job enrichment are closely related. **Job enlargement** is the expansion of the number of tasks involved in a job. When variety increases, job satisfaction usually does too. A General Mills cereal plant in Lodi, California, has successfully tried job enlargement for line workers. They now get to schedule production and operate and maintain their machinery. During the night shift, the factory runs smoothly with no managers.

Job enrichment is the redesign of jobs to provide workers with more authority, responsibility, and challenge and with the opportunity for more personal achievement. Job responsibilities are often expanded so workers plan and evaluate their own performance. At AT&T, this concept has been used with great success. Installers of telephone switching systems have participated with AT&T management in defining the nature of the job. They have also helped decide what is acceptable and unacceptable performance. Of course, not all workers want more responsibility or greater challenges, so job enrichment cannot be used for everyone.

Job rotation is the assignment of workers to several jobs over time. When one job is mastered, the worker moves to a new one. New challenges prevent boredom. Job rotation can lead to job enlargement. It is also a good way to train lower-level managers. AT&T, General Mills, and MCI routinely rotate lower-level managers. Schlumberger, the giant oil-well servicing company, expects middle- and lower-level managers to change jobs at least every two years.

A more general approach to making jobs pleasant is captured in the term **quality-of-work-life programs**. These programs are designed to enhance job performance and worker commitment to the organization. Job enlargement, job enrichment, and job rotation are part of many quality-of-work-life programs. So are many other types of "perks." At Apple Computer, for instance, managers in stressful jobs can get a massage in the office, take part in a horseback-riding club, or take aikido (karate) lessons.

job enlargement Expansion of the number of tasks involved in a job so workers have more job satisfaction.

job enrichment Redesign of jobs to provide workers with greater authority, responsibility, and challenge and a chance for more personal achievement.

job rotation Reassignment of workers to several different jobs over time.

quality-of-work-life programs Processes and techniques designed to enhance job performance and commitment to the organization.

Concept Check

- Discuss Herzberg's job satisfiers and job-maintenance factors.
- Describe Vroom's theory of the relationship between worker expectations and motivation.
- Discuss equity theory and give an example.
- Explain the concept of job enrichment.

INTERPERSONAL RELATIONSHIPS AND GROUP BEHAVIOR

7

Organizations want to motivate groups as well as individuals. Every organization contains *groups,* social units of two or more people who share the same goal and cooperate to achieve it. Some groups are informal,

work groups Groups created to accomplish a specific task.

formed by people who associate with one another by choice. **Work groups** are those created to accomplish various tasks. Work groups can be organized in just about any way: They can be committees, task forces, teams, crews, or work gangs.

For example, the General Electric plant in Bayamon, Puerto Rico, has organized its employees in teams. The plant manufactures arrestors—surge protectors that guard power stations and transmission lines against lightning strikes. The facility employs 172 hourly workers, just 15 salaried "advisers," and one manager. That's it: three layers, no supervisors, no staff. A conventional plant would have about twice as many salaried people. Every hourly worker is on a team with ten or so others; they meet weekly. Each team "owns" part of the work—assembly, shipping and receiving, etc. But team members come from all areas of the plant, so that each group has representatives from both upstream and downstream operations. An adviser sits in the back of the room and speaks up only if the team needs help.

Hourly workers change jobs every six months, rotating through the factory's four main work areas. In six months they'll begin their second circuit of the plant, and everyone on the floor will know his or her job and how it affects the next person in line. The reward for learning is a compensation plan that pays for skill, knowledge, and business performance. In just a year the work force became 20 percent more productive than its nearest company equivalent on the mainland.[11]

The standards used to determine whether a group member's actions are acceptable are **norms**. Norms are derived from an organization's culture and tend to be established by the people in the work group. In their

norms Standards of behavior or performance.

■ Socialization is the process by which the norms of the workplace are communicated to a new employee. By watching and talking with others, the employee learns what behaviors are expected of him or her, such as working late or on weekends.

research at the Hawthorne plant, Mayo and his associates watched four-teen workers in one of the production rooms for several months. They found that the workers had set their own norm about what a fair day's work was. Employees who performed at or near the norm were highly regarded by most of the group. Those who performed much above or below it were called rate busters or chiselers and were avoided. The amount of work considered acceptable by the group was less than the amount considered acceptable by the company, however. The group's norm was what determined the amount of work done.

GROUP SOCIALIZATION

socialization Process by which a new group member learns the basic goals of the group and the preferred means of achieving these goals.

Work norms are conveyed through the process of **socialization**, which means "learning the ropes" of a new position. It is the process by which organization members become aware of their organization's culture. Specifically, socialization is the process by which a new group member learns some important things:

- The basic goals of the group.
- The preferred means for reaching these goals.
- The person's responsibilities within the group.
- The behavior patterns expected for effective performance within the group. For instance, the group may expect its members to work nine to ten hours a day and, when necessary, on Saturdays.
- The basic rules and attitudes that help maintain the group's identity and integrity. For instance, the group may have an informal dress code, want its reports prepared in a certain style, or expect its members to complain about the food in the company cafeteria.

Work socialization occurs both formally in training programs and infor-mally by watching and talking with other group members. Group perfor-mance is related to how rapidly new members are socialized. The sooner new members learn their jobs and perform them correctly, the better the group's overall performance will be.

GROUP COHESIVENESS

group cohesiveness De-gree to which the members of a group want to remain in it and the tendency of group members to resist outside in-fluences.

Group cohesiveness refers to the degree to which group members want to stay in the group and the tendency of group members to resist outside influences (such as a change in company policies). A cohesive group may perform better than one that lacks cohesiveness. But cohesiveness can also result in reduced productivity. In the Hawthorne studies, Mayo found that one very cohesive group had norms leading it to produce less than the company wanted. But at Saab, a Swedish auto manufacturer, group cohesiveness has the opposite effect. Cohesive engine-assembly teams are more productive.

Several factors make work groups more cohesive:

- Similarity of members' interests
- Degree to which members depend on one another in the perfor-mance of group tasks

- Goals of the work group
- Existence of a common threat to the group
- Leadership within the group
- Degree of member participation in making decisions that affect the group *As Long As Has Good Effect*

Social interaction promotes cohesiveness.

The manager of a work group can influence several of these factors. He or she can strongly influence group performance by developing a highly cohesive group. But building cohesiveness tends to be much easier in a small group of fifteen or fewer employees. Group cohesiveness may take several weeks or months to develop.

Work group cohesiveness can benefit the organization in several ways: more output, enhanced worker self-image because of group success, more company loyalty, less employee turnover, and reduced absenteeism. On the other hand, cohesiveness can also lead to restricted output, resistance to change, and conflict with other work groups in the organization. At the extreme, employees can become united as a group against management. The pilots, mechanics, and flight attendants at Eastern Airlines were strongly united against the company's chairman, Frank Lorenzo, who finally stepped down as chairman when the airline was bankrupt.

8   EFFECTIVE LEADERSHIP FOR GROUP PERFORMANCE

Pierre du Pont was twenty years old when he first reported for duty at his family's powder works. The year was 1890. In a dingy shed that passed for a laboratory, du Pont could find little modern equipment—and even less managerial responsibility. After eight frustrating years, he teamed up with two cousins to buy the family business for $12 million. Over the next seventeen years—first as treasurer, then as president—he turned the company into a vast, modern corporation. He was aided in this task by a troop of inspired lieutenants, whom he brilliantly led.

Recall from Chapter 8 that *leadership* is the ability to influence and direct others for the purpose of attaining specific goals. Effective leadership means setting objectives and defining the activities that will achieve them, strengthening the ties among group members to keep the group together, and setting an example with positive behavior and attitudes. Leaders must guard against doing anything that could destroy the group, such as showing favoritism. To keep the group together, they must encourage workers, be friendly and responsive, and try to reduce tensions when disagreements arise. In these ways, they build and preserve group cohesiveness—a sense of solidarity, a desire to remain in the group, and a tendency to resist outside influences.

informal leaders Leaders who emerge from a group because they understand member concerns and can communicate these concerns to others.

In many situations, the manager, as formal leader, keeps the group together. But often **informal leaders** emerge from the group. They become leaders because they understand member concerns and can communicate these to others. Informal leaders can be very influential in getting the group to meet its goals and in building group cohesiveness.

A striking example of both formal and informal leadership is provided by Mary Kay Cosmetics Company, as is shown in the Business Today Trends box.

T R E N D S

Business Today

Lessons In Leadership

Each summer, more than 36,000 Mary Kay beauty consultants (saleswomen) converge on Dallas. They arrive, driving pink Cadillacs, from towns and cities all over the United States. Their destination is a three-day sales rally called Seminar—part convention, part glitzy show.

In 1963, Mary Kay Ash (now chairman emeritus) and son Richard Rogers (now chairman) started the company. Its growth has been remarkable, from first-year sales of $198,000 to over $613 million in 1993. The company has built a sales force of 300,000. More than 6,500 of them drive Cadillacs and other cars worth over $90 million, compliments of the company as a reward for meeting sales goals. Seventy-four saleswomen have earned commissions of $1 million or more over the course of their careers.

How does Mary Kay do it? By giving people recognition, not just cash. The most successful, such as Anne Newbury, are featured in film clips of the kind political parties use to introduce nominees. Over her twenty-four-year career, Newbury has earned $2 million. "I don't know about you," she tells the audience, "but I had always dreamed of driving Cadillacs ever since I was young. My first Cadillac came easily. . . ."

Special treatment of its sales staff is the key to the company's success. Emotional compensation matters almost as much as cash. To women who've made their pile, it probably matters more. At Seminar, their efforts are recognized. Color-coded suits, sashes, badges, crowns, bees, and other emblems show how far each woman has come. (Bumblebees are favorites, since they denote success against tough odds: according to the laws of aerodynamics, bees shouldn't be able to fly.) Sales director Deborah Robina wears a bracelet reading "$1,000,000." Its band is gold, the numerals written in 32 diamonds. The amount is how much she and the group of saleswomen she leads sold last year, and she's proud of it. Women with lower sales wear metal lapel bars giving the amount: "$25,000." Like generals inspecting ribbons, they immediately see who's done what.

The consultants find Mary Kay Ash uniquely approachable. One consultant noted, "Mary Kay calls you her daughter and looks you dead in the eye. She makes you feel you can do anything. She's sincerely concerned about your welfare." Amazingly, she is. When Shirley Hutton's daughter was ill with a kidney stone, Ash phoned twice to visit with the girl. By such touches, every "daughter" in the company learns a lesson: When somebody takes an interest in you, it feels good.

Recognition from Ash is what her salespeople crave most. She personally crowns four Queens of Seminar—women who have excelled at sales or recruiting. She kisses them and puts roses in their laps. She pats hands, looks deeply into teary eyes. Everything about Mrs. Ash is straight and stripped of false emotion. She is the giver and receiver of true love, on a massive scale.[12]

FITTING INTO THE GROUP

Sometimes a new supervisor has trouble developing effective relationships with peers, subordinates, and his or her boss. These new relationships can perhaps be developed more easily through mentoring and networking.

mentoring Teaching a newer, younger employee about the firm.

When older, more experienced people in the firm take new, younger people "under their wing," a **mentoring** relationship exists. The younger person learns about the firm from the older colleague. The senior person can explain many of the unwritten do's and don'ts of the job, as well as the corporate culture. The younger person who has a mentor may be able to learn about the organization more quickly and with fewer mistakes. Mentoring, then, can aid employee motivation and job performance.[13]

networking Using informal contacts inside and outside an organization.

Informal contacts inside and outside the organization make up a network of friends and professional colleagues. In part, **networking** means setting up the informal links inside the firm discussed in Chapter 8. Outside the firm, networking means building relationships by joining trade or professional associations, attending university-sponsored conferences or management development programs, or even just eating lunch at a place that attracts other businesspeople. Through networking, people often become aware of job opportunities (many times, before the formal announcement), major organizational problems, and competitors' plans. Networking doesn't always produce grand results, but it is worth doing.

Concept Check
- What is a work group, and what are several key characteristics of groups?
- Discuss mentoring and networking and their importance to workers and to the firm.

■ SUMMARY

1. Understand Taylor's concept of scientific management.
Frederick Taylor wanted to find an objective way to measure a day's work. He conducted time-and-motion studies and broke down every operation into separate movements. Taylor's ideas led to dramatic increases in productivity. But his concept of scientific management meant designing jobs that involved repetition, which lowered worker morale.

2. Describe what Mayo's Hawthorne studies revealed about worker motivation.
Elton Mayo discovered that employees' attitudes improved when they were taken into the employer's confidence. The result was better work performance. This phenomenon became known as the Hawthorne effect.

3. Discuss Maslow's hierarchy of needs.
Abraham Maslow drew on the views of Taylor and Mayo when he devel-

oped his needs theory of motivation. He believed that people act in order to satisfy their needs. He classified human needs in a hierarchy: physiological needs, safety needs, social needs, esteem needs, and self-actualization needs. Once a lower-level need is satisfied, a higher-level need becomes more important.

4. Describe Theory X, Theory Y, and Theory Z.

The authoritarian Theory X approach assumes that people dislike work and must be prodded to do it. Theory Y assumes that work is a natural activity and that workers are positively motivated. Although Theory Y may be more appealing, Theory X does sometimes work. So does a combination of the two.

Theory Z is an attempt to combine U.S. and Japanese management styles. In general, Japanese firms offer lifetime employment opportunities and rely on group decision making. U.S. companies tend to employ people for a shorter time and to rely more on individual decision making.

5. Explain job motivators, job-maintenance factors, worker expectations, and equity theory.

Several factors affect worker motivation and job satisfaction. Job satisfiers are the factors that motivate workers to do more. They relate to the job itself and correspond to esteem and self-actualization needs. Job-maintenance factors tend to lie outside the job but are necessary to keep workers at it. They generally relate to physiological, safety, and social needs. Workers may also be motivated by their expectations about job rewards and outcomes. Money can be an important motivator. Equity theory relates workers' motivation to perceptions of whether they are treated fairly compared to co-workers.

6. Distinguish between job enlargement and job enrichment, and explain their effects on workers.

Job enlargement means expanding the number and variety of tasks to make the jobs more interesting and satisfying. Job enrichment means redesigning jobs to provide workers with more authority and responsibility. It gives workers a chance for more personal achievement and recognition.

7. Explain the nature of work groups, group socialization, and group cohesiveness.

Every organization has groups. Some are set up on purpose. Others develop informally. Workers in groups set norms and value group members who conform to them.

Group socialization is how a new member learns about group goals, his or her responsibilities, and the group's general rules and attitudes. Socialization occurs through formal training, talking with group members, and observing their actions.

Group cohesiveness is the degree to which group members want to stay in the group and the group's ability to resist outside influences. A cohesive group usually produces more, fosters better worker self-image, and is more loyal to the company.

8. Discuss the importance of group leadership.

Effective leadership means setting goals and defining the activities that will achieve them, strengthening the ties among group members to keep the group together, and setting an example with positive behavior and attitudes.

■ DISCUSSION QUESTIONS

1. Do you think the concept of "scientific management" is applicable today? Why or why not?

2. How are job satisfaction and employee morale linked to job performance? Do you work harder when you are satisfied with your job? Explain your answer.

3. Review the assumptions of Theories X and Y. Under which set of assumptions would you prefer to work? Is your current or former supervisor a Theory X manager or a Theory Y manager? Explain by describing the person's behavior.

4. Theory Z is built in part on characteristics of Japanese management. How appropriate are Japanese managerial practices for the management of U.S. firms?

5. Is money a job satisfier or a job-maintenance factor for you? Explain.

6. Both individual motivation and group participation are needed to accomplish certain goals. Describe a situation you're familiar with in which cooperation achieved a goal that individual action could not. Describe one in which group action slowed progress and individual action would have been better.

7. Explain the differences between equity theory and expectancy theory.

8. Have you ever used networking to reach a personal goal? If so, explain how you did it.

9. Have you ever been an informal leader? If so, were you effective? Describe the situation.

■ CASE

Tension in the Build Lab

David Cutler, wearing white Reeboks, white trousers, and a T-shirt with the legend "Over the Line," blasts through the door leading to Microsoft Corp.'s Build Lab. He is checking on the progress of the biggest, most complex, and possibly most important program ever designed for a desktop computer. He is not happy.

It is 10:20 Monday morning, and the daily "build" of the program, called Windows NT, isn't finished yet. As leader of the NT team, Cutler insists that a new build, or test version, of NT be stitched together electronically each morning. Today he is angry about the delay and still angry about a botched test the day before. After glaring at a computer screen he storms out of the lab, leaving a distinct chill. Two builders dip into a king-size jar of antacid tablets.

Cutler is a leader who doesn't believe in bottling up emotion. "The way you let off stress is to let it out," he says. Yet he is also the sort of leader who slogs through the mud with his troops. "You really don't take [Cutler's outbursts] personally," said Mitchell Duncan, his chief builder. "He's not attacking your character. Dave gets in at 6 a.m. He's there every weekend. He's there in the trenches."

Consisting of a staggering 4.3 million lines of code and costing more than $150 million to develop, NT is considered by many to be the most ambitious computer program ever tried. NT's supporters hope they can use the program to empower not just speedier personal computers but also new kinds of PC networks that can displace far more expensive mainframes and minicomputers.

The first version of NT was so complex it had thousands of defects ("bugs"), raising fears that the kit would be a disgrace. And Microsoft had announced its plans to ship hundreds of thousands of copies by a certain date. In an all-out effort to clean up NT, the NT team went on a "death march." The workload increased, the briefings and builds were extended to Saturdays and Sundays, dinners were brought in, and a fair number began sleeping at work—under desks, in lounges, and on the floor.

Many on the NT team had never faced such a deadline in their lives. For 18 percent of the staff, this was the first job out of college. Johanne Caron, a 28-year-old who was writing part of the "DOS shell" (the layer of instructions that allowed existing DOS programs to run on NT), found herself on the edge. Her basic code affected a crucial part of NT. If anyone criticized her work, she said, "I'd jump down their throat." Meanwhile, her marriage was falling apart. "I put all my energy in my job," she says. "I didn't even try to save the marriage."

As for Cutler's troops, they are divided in their feelings about the future. Many eagerly anticipate working on the next version of NT, while others sense that a chapter of their lives has ended. Some are tired, almost to the breaking point. After nearly two years in "ship mode," with one deadline after another looming, says Charles Whitmer, a graphics programmer, "A lot of people are angry, tired, and burned out."[14]

Questions
1. Describe Cutler's management style. Might a different style have been more effective?
2. How would you describe the corporate culture of Microsoft? Would a different culture work better?
3. What do you think was motivating Johanne Caron? Why? What about her priorities?

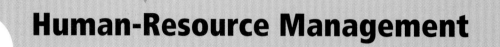

Human-Resource Management

chapter 12

Learning Goals

After studying this chapter, you should be able to:

1 Describe the human-resource function.

2 Describe the federal laws and agencies that affect human-resource management.

3 Discuss human-resource planning.

4 Explain how employees are recruited and selected.

5 Describe how employees are trained and developed.

6 Explain how performance appraisals and career development are used in human-resource management.

7 Explain the forms of compensation and fringe benefits available to employees.

8 Discuss promotions, transfers, and separations.

9 Describe key human-resource issues of the 1990s.

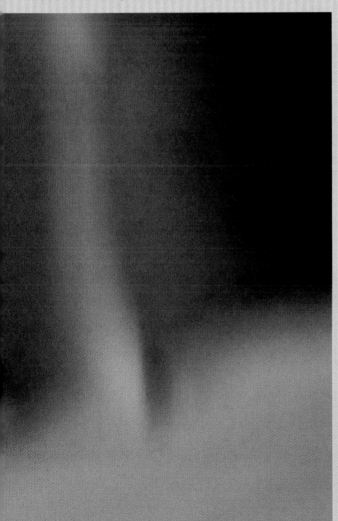

 # Career Profile

While attending college, Sharon Evans worked as a part-time clerk/typist in the human-resources department at Good Samaritan Hospital. Shortly after she graduated, the hospital needed to fill the position of Employee Relations Representative and Employment Recruiter. Sharon was offered the job because of her previous work experience and because she had received her bachelor's degree in personnel industrial relations.

Sharon is responsible for recruiting and evaluating potential employees for several areas of the hospital. The business office and the nursing, physical therapy, and X-ray departments all rely on her for qualified staff members. This has given her a good understanding of the multitude of positions available in the hospital and the types of people required to fill them. Her biggest challenge so far has been learning to work with such a wide variety of personalities.

Sharon is truly committed to the field of human relations. The classes she had in college that have come in most handy have been those that dealt with human-resource management and recruiting. But Sharon realizes that in order to continue to be effective in her position, she must continue to learn. By keeping up with the latest developments in her field, she constantly improves her professional skills. Her knowledge and enthusiasm are assets to Good Samaritan Hospital, and will serve her well throughout her career.

Overview

Chapter 12 starts by exploring some recent trends in managing a firm's most important resources—its employees. It then looks at the relationship between personnel specialists and other managers. The chapter then discusses laws affecting human-resource management. The focus turns next to human-resource planning, followed by employee recruitment and selection, training and development, performance evaluation, career development, compensation and benefits, and promotions, transfers, and separations. The chapter ends with a look at human-resource issues for the 1990s.

THE CHANGING WORKPLACE

The American workplace has changed a lot in the past decade. Perhaps the most important cause of change has been the federal government. It has reached into firms' management of employees through congressional legislation, agency guidelines, and decisions of the Supreme Court. Three areas of government regulation have demanded the attention of human-resource managers recently: equal employment opportunity, especially for people with disabilities; pensions and retirement issues associated with the aging work force; and job safety and health care.

A second factor behind changes in the workplace is the changing labor force. The biggest change has been an increase in the number of working women. About 61 percent of all women between sixteen and sixty-five years of age are now working outside the home. By the year 2000, white men will make up only 39 percent of the labor force—down from 50 percent in the late 1970s. As you learned in Chapter 3, the workforce is becoming more culturally diverse. As a result, many traditional aspects of organizational culture are giving way.

■ New government regulations, the changing makeup of the labor force, and the growth of mechanization and computerization have altered the way firms manage their employees. As many aspects of traditional organizational culture disappear, human-resource matters take on new importance for companies hoping to stay competitive in world markets.

A third factor in the changing workplace is the emphasis on improving efficiency in order to stay competitive in world markets. Computerized manufacturing systems and robots have greatly reduced the need for production workers in the steel, auto, farm equipment, and tire industries. Sophisticated computer and office communication systems have also reduced the need for file clerks, bookkeepers, and even typists. The trade-off is that new high-tech equipment and systems call for more highly trained workers.

Concept Check

- What is the role of the federal government in human-resource matters?
- How has America's labor force changed?

THE HUMAN-RESOURCE FUNCTION

Raw materials, capital, employees, and information are the resources of an effective organization. Those who manage human resources work in the personnel area. In the past, the personnel department has helped recruit, test, hire, train, and evaluate people. Personnel managers have developed policies on paying, promoting, and firing employees. They have also been concerned with employee benefit programs, union-management relations, and compliance with laws regarding employees.

human-resource management Process of hiring, developing, motivating, and evaluating people to achieve organizational goals.

Today employees are thought of as an important asset rather than just a cost of doing business. Hence, the personnel function has been replaced by the concept of human-resource management. **Human-resource management** is the process of hiring, developing, motivating, and evaluating people in order to achieve organizational goals. Various policies, procedures, and programs are designed to bring about a proper match between jobs and individuals. In this new approach, the goal is to satisfy employee needs and develop their skills as much as possible, to improve their efficiency, and to find and keep quality employees who can meet organizational goals. The human-resource approach often takes the form of programs for developing employee interests and talents.

HUMAN-RESOURCE GOALS AND ACTIVITIES

The human-resource function has several goals. The first is to provide competent, well-trained employees for the company. A second is to make employees as effective as possible. A third is to satisfy employees' needs by helping them achieve successful careers. A human-resource department can achieve these goals only if its managers clearly understand the objectives and strategies of the whole organization.

Exhibit 12-1 illustrates the main activities in human-resource management: planning and forecasting the need for people; recruiting and selecting employees; training and developing them; appraising their performance; helping develop their careers; compensating them; providing

■ Exhibit 12-1
Human-Resource Management Function

fringe benefits; processing promotions, transfers, and separations; and dealing with labor unions. (The labor-relations function is discussed in detail in Chapter 13.)

HUMAN-RESOURCE SPECIALISTS AND OTHER MANAGERS

The human-resource department typically plays a staff role, supporting the line organization. Human-resource specialists perform many tasks that help managers make decisions about employees. Basic human-resource policies (like whether to promote primarily from within the organization) and overall human-resource objectives (like hiring goals) are decided by top managers. Given this overall direction, human-resource specialists can design specific personnel programs and procedures. Middle- and supervisory-level managers in manufacturing, marketing, and other areas then carry out these programs and use the specific procedures to deal with problems like tardiness. The human-resource responsibilities of the three levels of managers are summarized in Exhibit 12-2.

Let's look at an example of how human-resource specialists support other managers. Barry Corbet is a manager in the public relations department at H. J. Heinz, the international food company. He needed another data-entry clerk. First he sent an employee requisition form to the human-resources department. Judy Wagner, a specialist in the employment office, placed an ad in the help-wanted section of the local newspaper. The job was also posted in-house. Judy interviewed and tested people who applied for the job. The three applicants who met the minimum hiring requirements were taken to Barry for in-depth interviews. He decided to hire Fran Kriter. Fran was then referred back to the human-resource department to get her payroll and personnel records set up. Throughout

▓ Exhibit 12-2
How Three Levels of
Management Are
Involved in the Human-
Resource Function

**Top
managers**

Approve
human-resource policy

**Human-resource
specialist**

Designs
human-resource
program

**Middle- &
supervisory-level
managers**

Implement
human-resource
practices

these events, Barry and Judy were mindful of two very important human-resource policies issued by Anthony O'Reilly, the Heinz CEO. One policy says Heinz is an "equal opportunity employer," which means it does not unfairly discriminate in employment decisions. The other directs that the company "attempt to hire the most qualified individuals available for every vacant and new position."

Concept Check

- What are the goals of the human-resource function?
- Discuss the activities of human-resource management.
- Explain the relationship between human-resource specialists and other managers.

LAWS AFFECTING HUMAN-RESOURCE MANAGEMENT

 Federal laws help ensure that job applicants and employees are treated fairly and not discriminated against. Hiring, training, and job placement must be unbiased. Promotion and compensation decisions must be based on performance. These laws help all Americans who have talent, training, and the desire to get ahead.

FEDERAL LAWS

Exhibit 12-3 summarizes the main federal laws affecting the employment relationship. Several are concerned with giving equal employment opportunity to all workers. *In general, federal law prohibits discrimination based on age, race, gender, color, national origin, religion, or disability.*

Fair Labor Standards Act Federal law that sets the minimum wage.

Several laws govern wages, pensions, and unemployment compensation. For instance, the **Fair Labor Standards Act** sets the minimum wage, which increased to $4.25 per hour in 1991. Many minimum-wage jobs are found in service businesses, such as restaurants and car washes. The **Pension Reform Act** protects the retirement income of employees and retirees. Federal tax laws also affect compensation, including employee profit-sharing and stock-purchase plans.

Pension Reform Act Federal law that protects the retirement income of employees and retirees.

Occupational Safety and Health Act Federal law that requires employers to provide a workplace free of health and safety hazards.

Employers must also be sensitive to laws concerning employee safety, health, and privacy. The **Occupational Safety and Health Act** requires employers to provide a workplace free of health and safety hazards. For

■ The Family and Medical Leave Act went into effect in 1993. Under this act, firms must provide twelve weeks of unpaid leave a year to employees to allow them to deal with such personal matters as the birth or adoption of a child or the serious illness of a family member.

Americans with Disabilities Act Federal law that prohibits discrimination against disabled persons.

instance, manufacturers must require employees working on loading docks to wear steel-toed shoes so their feet won't be injured if materials are dropped. Drug and AIDS testing and the use of lie detectors are also governed by federal laws. (These topics are discussed later in the chapter.)

One of the most recent employment laws is the **Americans with Disabilities Act,** which came into full force on July 26, 1994. To be considered disabled, a person must have a physical or mental impairment that greatly limits one or more major life activities. More than 33 million Americans fall into this category. Employers may not discriminate against disabled persons. They must make "reasonable accommodations" so qualified disabled employees can perform the job, unless doing so would cause "undue hardship" for the business. Altering work schedules, modifying equipment so a wheelchair-bound person can use it, and making buildings accessible by ramps and elevators are considered reasonable. Two companies often praised for efforts to hire the disabled are McDonald's and DuPont. During the first year the Disabilities Act was in force, the Equal Employment Opportunity Commission (the federal agency that enforces the act) received nearly 12,000 disability discrimination complaints. The aggrieved persons collected over $11 million.[1]

Family and Medical Leave Act Federal law that requires employers to grant unpaid leave to certain employees for family and medical reasons.

Another new law affecting employers and employees is the **Family and Medical Leave Act** which was passed and went into effect in 1993.[2]

Law	Purpose	Agency of enforcement
Social Security Act (1935)	Provides for retirement income and old-age health care	Social Security Administration
Fair Labor Standards Act (1938)	Sets minimum wage, restricts child labor, sets overtime pay	Wage and Hour Act Division, Department of Labor
Equal Pay Act (1963)	Eliminates pay differentials based on gender	Equal Employment Opportunity Commission
Civil Rights Act (1964), Title VII	Prohibits employment discrimination based on race, color, religion, gender, or national origin	Equal Employment Opportunity Commission
Age Discrimination Act (1967)	Prohibits age discrimination against those over 40 years of age	Equal Employment Opportunity Commission
Occupational Safety and Health Act (1970)	Protects worker health and safety, provides for hazard-free workplace	Occupational Safety and Health Administration
Vietnam Veterans Readjustment Act (1974)	Requires affirmative employment of Vietnam War veterans	Veterans Employment Service, Department of Labor
Employee Retirement Income Security Act (1974) — also called Pension Reform Act	Establishes minimum requirements for private pension plans	Internal Revenue Service, Department of Labor, and Pension Benefit Guaranty Corporation
Pregnancy Discrimination Act (1978)	Treats pregnancy as a disability, prevents employment discrimination based on pregnancy	Equal Employment Opportunity Commission
Immigration Reform and Control Act (1986)	Verifies employment eligibility, prevents employment of illegal aliens	Employment Verification Systems, Immigration and Naturalization Service
Americans with Disabilities Act (1990)	Prohibits employment discrimination based on mental or physical disabilities	Department of Labor
Family and Medical Leave Act (1993)	Requires employers to provide unpaid leave for childbirth, adoption, or illness	Equal Employment Opportunity Commission

▓ Exhibit 12-3
Federal Employment Laws

The law applies to employers with 50 or more employees. It requires these employers to provide unpaid leave of up to twelve weeks during any twelve-month period to workers who have been employed for at least a year and work a minimum of 25 hours a week. The reasons for the leave include the birth or adoption of a child; the serious illness of a child, spouse, or parent; or a serious illness that prevents the worker from doing the job. Upon return, the employee must be given his or her old job back. The worker cannot collect unemployment while on leave. Companies can deny leave to a salaried employee in the highest-paid 10 percent of its workforce, if letting the worker take leave would create a "serious injury" for the firm.[3]

THE ROLE OF GOVERNMENT AGENCIES

Several federal agencies oversee employment, compensation, and related laws. These agencies include the Equal Employment Opportunity Commission (EEOC), the Occupational Safety and Health Administration (OSHA), the Office of Federal Contract Compliance Programs (OFCCP), and the Wage and Hour Division of the Department of Labor. The two agencies that enforce employment discrimination laws are the EEOC and the OFCCP.

Equal Employment Opportunity Commission Federal agency that investigates and resolves charges of employment discrimination.

The **Equal Employment Opportunity Commission**, created by the 1964 Civil Rights Act, investigates and resolves charges of discrimination. It also files lawsuits on its own against employers. Violators can be forced to promote, pay back wages to, or provide additional training for employees against whom they discriminated. Sears, Motorola, and AT&T have had to make large back-pay awards and to offer special training to minority employees who the courts ruled had been discriminated against.

Office of Federal Contract Compliance Programs Federal agency that polices firms with U.S. government contracts to make sure job applicants and employees get fair treatment.

affirmative action programs Programs set up by employers to expand job opportunities for women and minorities.

The **Office of Federal Contract Compliance Programs** oversees firms with U.S. government contracts to make sure that applicants and employees get fair treatment. One big part of its job is to review federal contractors' affirmative action programs. Employers set up **affirmative action programs** to expand job opportunities for women and minorities. In the case of a major violation, the OFCCP can recommend cancellation of the firm's government contract.

CORPORATE AFFIRMATIVE ACTION OFFICERS

Many firms have appointed an affirmative action officer to help see that they comply with antidiscrimination laws. At firms like Coca-Cola, Snap-on Tools, Hilton Hotels, and Santa Fe Southern Pacific Railroads, the affirmative action officer makes sure that job applicants and employees get fair treatment. He or she often reports directly to the company president rather than to the vice president of human resources.

protected classes Specific groups of people with legal protection against employment discrimination under various federal laws.

Affirmative action officers watch for signs of *adverse impact*, or unfair treatment of certain classes of employees. **Protected classes** are the specific groups (women, African-Americans, Native Americans, and others) who have legal protection against employment discrimination.

One example of adverse impact is a job qualification that tends to weed out more female applicants than male applicants. Say that an airline automatically rules out anyone under five feet seven inches who wants to be a pilot. Many more female applicants than male applicants would be rejected, because women tend to be shorter than men. But height has nothing to do with a pilot's ability, so this height requirement would be discriminatory.

The overall affirmative action record of the past decade was mixed. The employment of women in professional occupations continues to grow. But minority representation among professionals did not increase, even though professional jobs were among the fastest-growing of the decade. Technical jobs have the most equitable utilization rates of minorities, but they grew slowly during the past ten years.[4]

Concept Check

- What are the key federal laws affecting employment?
- List and describe the functions of the two federal agencies that enforce employment discrimination laws.
- What is affirmative action?

HUMAN-RESOURCE PLANNING

3

human-resource planning Creating a strategy for meeting a firm's future human-resource needs.

Firms need to have the right number of people, with the right training, to do the organization's work when it needs to be done. Human-resource managers are the ones who must determine future human-resource needs. Then they assess the skills of the firm's existing employees to see if new people must be hired or existing ones must be retrained. Creating a strategy for meeting future human-resource needs is called **human-resource planning**.

The human-resource planning process (pictured in Exhibit 12-4) begins with a review of corporate strategy and policy. By understanding the mission of the organization, planners can forecast its human-resource needs. When JC Penney moved its headquarters from New York City to Dallas, for instance, much human-resource planning was necessary. Planners had to decide which employees to transfer, when to do so, and how to orient them to their new environment.

JOB ANALYSIS AND DESIGN

job analysis Study of the tasks required to do a job well.

Human-resource planners must know what skills different jobs require. Information about a specific job is typically assembled through a **job analysis**, a study of the tasks required to do a job well. This information is used to specify the essential skills, knowledge, and abilities. For instance, when General Dynamics was awarded the contract for the F-16 fighter plane, several new jobs were created for industrial engineers. Job analysts from the company's human-resource department gathered information from other department heads and supervisors to help recruiters hire the right people for the new jobs.

job description List of the tasks and responsibilities of a job.

job specification List of the qualifications a person must have to fill a job.

The tasks and responsibilities of a job are listed in a **job description**. The skills, knowledge, and abilities a person must have to fill a job are spelled out in a **job specification**. These two documents help human-resource planners find the right people for specific jobs.

WORK SCHEDULES AND THE ALTERED WORKWEEK

Scheduling work is an important part of human-resource planning. Most people work an eight-hour shift. The standard eight-hour workday is often 8 a.m. to 5 p.m. with a one-hour lunch period. In some parts of the

■ Exhibit 12-4
Human-Resource Plan-
ning Process

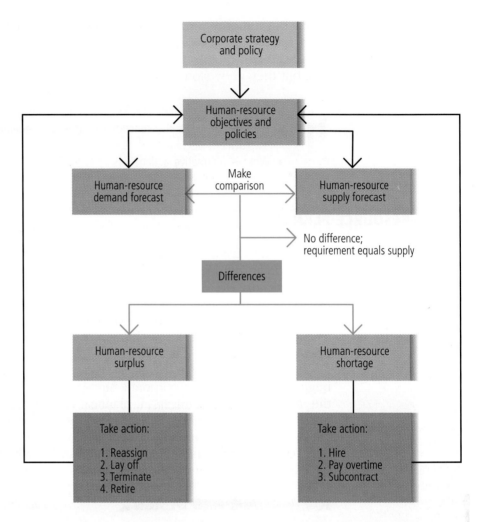

country and in some industries, the standard workday is 9 to 5. And many
companies have the need for two or three different shifts per day.

Organizing one shift a day is easier than organizing more than one. But
even the standard eight-hour workday can create scheduling problems.
Consider the Yellow Freight Line terminal in Orlando, Florida. Freight
tends to arrive early in the morning and late in the afternoon. So dock-
workers were very busy early and late but tended to be idle in the middle
of the day. Yellow Freight put some workers on a split shift, which gives
them time off during the middle of the day. The changing seasons can
also create planning problems. H. J. Heinz, for instance, has to have three
or four times as many factory workers during the harvest and canning season to get all the vegetables processed.

Recently many firms have experimented with **altered workweeks** to
get away from the standard eight-hour day, five-day week work schedule.
One variation is the **compressed workweek**. Either the normal number
of hours is squeezed into fewer than five days or employees work fewer
hours and fewer days. Kraftco's Sealtest Foods has a four-day week with
ten-hour days, Lipton Tea has a three-day week with twelve-hour days,

altered workweeks Ma-
jor departures from the standard eight-hour-a-day,
five-days-a week work
schedule.

compressed workweek
Workweek of either the normal number of hours
squeezed into fewer than
five days or fewer hours and
fewer days per week.

and Scoville Manufacturing (producer of housewares and automotive products) has a four-day week with nine-hour days. A workweek with three twelve-hour days has not been very popular except in hospitals.

flextime Work schedule in which employees work during a core period of the day and schedule the rest of their work hours as they please.

Flextime is another type of work scheduling system. All employees work during a core period of the day (say from 9:30 a.m. to 2:00 p.m.), when the load is greatest. But they can schedule the rest of their work time as they please. This type of arrangement has been used successfully at the Social Security Administration offices in Baltimore and at the Hewlett-Packard Company. Aetna Life and Casualty Company offers both a compressed workweek and flextime without a specific core time. Gerri Tyler, a systems software manager for US West, Incorporated, found that flextime raised morale, productivity, and client satisfaction in her department. Other companies also have found a link between becoming more customer-oriented and being more employee-oriented, as the Quality Management Trends box shows.

TRENDS

Quality Management

Employees Have Lives Too

Duke Power Company in Charlotte, North Carolina, gave Sharon Allred Decker a challenging assignment: consolidate the customer-service functions of its ninety-eight offices and make the company more responsive to customers. Decker launched a service center that operates around the clock, seven days a week. But she did more than that: She reasoned that Duke Power's employees would be more responsive to customers if they felt they were treated well by the company—and she acted on that belief.

To improve the quality of life at work, Decker convinced Duke Power to open a fitness center and to join a partnership to build a daycare center. Early on, Decker listened to employees who hated working swing shifts: days one week, evenings the next, and then nights. She came up with twenty-two separate schedules and let workers bid on them yearly, based on seniority. The changes make it easier for employees to arrange care for children and aging parents. The employee turnover rate is now quite low; most who leave transfer to other jobs in the company.

These days it is rare to find a midsize or large company that does not offer some form of child-care assistance or flexible scheduling. A survey of over a thousand U.S. businesses found that 78 percent offer child-care support; 60 percent, some form of flexible scheduling; 20 percent, elder-care programs; and 9 percent, on-site child-care. Flextime is the most popular option, chosen by about 25 percent of all eligible employees.

Improving the quality of workers' lives reaps benefits for companies as well. WMX Technologies in Oak Brook, Illinois, sponsors parent support groups that address topics from discipline to schoolwork. The company estimates such counseling saves it $1,600 a year per participant by lowering absentee and turnover rates and use of medical benefits. Corning Glass says its family-friendly programs have cut turnover in half since 1986. Having an employee-friendly reputation also helps with recruiting. Surveys show that people will even trade higher pay for more flexibility in their lives.[6]

- Explain job analysis, description, and design.
- What is meant by an altered workweek? Give some examples.

EMPLOYEE RECRUITMENT AND SELECTION

4   When a firm creates a new position or an existing one becomes vacant, the firm starts looking for people with the needed qualifications. The two sources of job applicants are the internal and external labor markets. The *internal labor market* is made up of current employees; the *external labor market* is the pool of potential applicants outside the firm.

Most companies try to fill positions beyond entry level from within the company. The internal search for job applicants usually results in some kind of reassignment. People can be promoted (upward mobility), transferred (movement at the same level), or demoted (downward movement).

If qualified candidates cannot be found inside the company, the external labor market must be tapped. The external search process involves finding potential applicants, providing information about job openings, and trying to attract qualified prospects to the firm.

RECRUITING METHODS AND JOB INFORMATION

recruitment Attempt to find and attract qualified applicants in the external labor market.

Recruitment is the attempt to find and attract qualified applicants in the external labor market. A company may advertise, prospect on college campuses, or use employment agencies or executive search firms. The type of position that's open determines which recruitment method will be used and which segment of the labor market will be searched. A company would not recruit an experienced engineer the same way it would recruit an entry-level janitor.

Unskilled workers do such jobs as warehouse stocking and loading and unloading large shipments of goods. They are usually recruited through newspaper advertising, employee referrals, employment agencies, and the job-placement services of the U.S. Training and Employment Service (USTES). The Texas Employment Commission and the Iowa State Employment Service are examples of state agencies that are members of USTES. Radio ads for jobs have also been used successfully by Mercy Hospital in San Francisco, Apple Computer, and many other companies.

With the information they get from USTES or from help-wanted ads, prospective employees usually apply directly to the employer at the job site. There they get more specific information about the time and place of work, the wage rate, the times of rest breaks, and the types of equipment they will use. The labor market for nonmanagement workers is usually the area within thirty miles of the job site.

Positions that require specialized skills and knowledge—such as chemist, engineer, or systems analyst—call for a different recruitment strategy. For entry-level managerial and professional positions, many firms—such as Ford, Procter & Gamble, and General Electric—send

■ College job fairs are one way companies recruit employees for entry-level managerial and professional positions. It is here that students commonly make the contacts that lead to a job after graduation.

recruiters to college campuses. The recruiters conduct preliminary interviews with thousands of students who are nearing graduation. They give students annual reports, specially prepared company brochures, and descriptions of available jobs. They ask students about their interests and goals and the type of company in which they would like to begin their career. If a student's interests and the firm's interests seem to match, the student is invited to company headquarters for a more in-depth interview.

Many firms rely on private employment agencies for positions above the entry level. **Employment agencies** help job applicants and employers by coming up with acceptable matches. Employers list openings with agencies, and applicants seek jobs through them. When an applicant is hired through an agency, either the applicant or the employer pays a fee to the agency. Often the fee is one month's salary, but sometimes it's more.

Exhibit 12-5 shows what contacts managers use to get their jobs. Want ads and friends and relatives are good sources. So are employment agencies and **executive search firms**, which operate much like employment agencies. But executive search firms differ in that they work mainly with employers to recruit people for middle-management or top-management positions. Often the person a search firm finds is already employed and not seeking a new job. Through the search firm, the potential employer tries to lure the person away from the other company. This technique is sometimes called "pirating employees," and search firms are often dubbed "headhunters."

employment agencies
Private firms that help match job applicants with job openings.

executive search firms
Private firms that work mainly with employers to recruit people for middle- and top-management jobs.

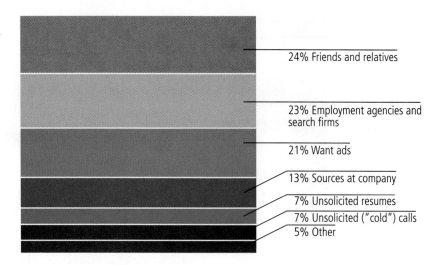

24% Friends and relatives

23% Employment agencies and
search firms

21% Want ads

13% Sources at company

7% Unsolicited resumes

7% Unsolicited ("cold") calls

5% Other

THE EMPLOYEE SELECTION PROCESS

After people have been attracted to the firm and applied for a job, employment specialists begin the selection process. Each stage of the process is harder for the applicant than the one before. The applicant can be rejected at any stage. Also, employers must make difficult choices among the many applicants that may be suited for the position. Exhibit 12-6 shows the stages in the employee selection process.

Initial Screening

The first two stages in the selection process—the preliminary interview and the employment application form—make up the initial screening. The preliminary interview tends to be rather short, often less than fifteen minutes. It is designed to weed out obviously unqualified candidates, and it usually follows a set list of questions. Employment application forms also tend to be short and only capture a limited amount of information. Persons are often selected for a preliminary interview based upon their resume. The *resume* provides the employer an overview of an applicant's personal and work history.

Employment Tests

After the initial screening, an applicant may be asked to take one or more employment tests. These tests may measure general intelligence and knowledge, aptitude for the work, skill levels, work interests, attitudes, and personality. For example, some tests measure attitudes toward authority, attitudes toward subordinates, and willingness to be a team player. Some tests show how well the person can perform job tasks. A typing test, for instance, measures an applicant's ability to type quickly and accurately. In addition, two types of employment tests are often used these days: drug and AIDS tests.

Many employers use drug tests to weed out people who have a problem with substance abuse. In 1993, a study found that 85 percent of all medium and large companies conduct drug tests on at least some employ-

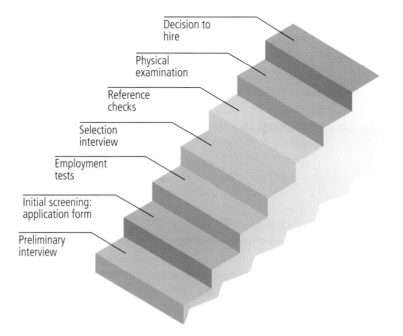

Decision to hire

Physical examination

Reference checks

Selection interview

Employment tests

Initial screening: application form

Preliminary interview

ees and job applicants. About 2.5 percent of those tested showed signs of drug use.[7] Some firms test employees, too. Anyone who is found to be an abuser may be placed in a rehabilitation program. Employers take these steps because they are concerned about safety, productivity, and worker health.

Drug testing is controversial. First, there is the issue of privacy. Many say that requiring employees to provide a urine sample for testing violates a person's right to privacy. Also, some say what people do off the job is no one else's business. Employers counter that a person on drugs does less work and is absent more often. A drugged worker on a production line may also be a safety hazard to himself or herself and to others. A second issue concerning drug testing is the accuracy of testing and laboratory analysis. Careless or inadequate procedures may indicate drug use when, in fact, the person has not used drugs.

Testing for AIDS is also controversial. Those who test positive are considered by law to be handicapped and therefore to be in a protected class. AIDS testing is also a privacy issue. Why should employers know whether a person has AIDS, especially if it doesn't affect the ability to do a specific job? Employers answer that the health-care costs for a single AIDS patient (which the employer may end up paying) can be huge.

For many years lie detector, or polygraph, tests were used by many employers to check applicants' honesty. But in 1988 Congress passed the Polygraph Protection Act, which bans lie detector tests by private employers. Instead, some employers now check credit histories to gauge applicants' character. For instance, Nordstrom (a department store chain), TRW, and Abbott Laboratories routinely check credit records. Barry's Jewelers, a California-based jewelry store chain, recently screened sixty-two job candidates. It rejected sixteen, including three for problems arising from credit reports.[8]

Selection Interview

The most widely used tool in hiring decisions is the selection interview, an in-depth discussion of the applicant's work experience, skills and abilities, education, and personal interests. For a managerial or professional position, the applicant might be interviewed for more than an hour by several people. A traditional sort of question asked in a selection interview might be "Why would you enjoy working for our company?" Today many companies stress "behavioral questions," which require detailed accounts of actual situations. S.C. Johnson, maker of Johnson's Wax, is an example. Instead of asking "How would you reprimand an employee?" a Johnson's interviewer might now say, "Give me a specific example of a time you had to reprimand an employee. Tell me what action you took. And what was the result?" Interviewers are trained to ask follow-up questions and to record not only what a candidate says but whether he or she squirms—or lights up with enthusiasm.

Recruiters look for dozens of characteristics among the students they interview. You might be surprised at the things that *don't* matter. Foreign language skills, physical fitness, and a willingness to travel aren't highly regarded by most recruiters. Even a good sense of humor isn't that important. "A sense of humor is weighed low by us during interviews because students are nervous and can't easily throw out a quick witticism or comeback," says M. Alana Demers, employment manager for Public Service of New Hampshire. "Students who try to exhibit humor in an interview usually defeat themselves."[9]

The book's epilogue presents a number of other tips on beginning your business career.

TRENDS
Business Today

Eight Key Skills that Recruiters Seek

When interviewing new college graduates, corporate recruiters look for the following skills. The list is based on a study of corporate recruiters from 739 companies. The skills are listed in order, from most to least important.

1. *Written communication skills:* Writing skills are carefully assessed by recruiters, for good reason. "There seems to be a marked decline in written communication skills among managers, and many companies are hoping to stop that descent by hiring students who can write," says Wayne Davis, corporate staffing representative at Baxter Healthcare in Deerfield, Illinois. "We ask for writing samples and give writing tests" when students are invited for on-site meetings, says Robert Conner of Transamerica in Los Angeles. Even English majors should be prepared to polish their grammar, vocabulary, and penmanship, he says. "Few students realize that writing in a business format is much different from writing to a friend or writing an essay for class."

2. *Decision-making skills:* Students who can discuss important decisions they've made in their lives and explain how those decisions relate to achieving their goals will impress recruiters. "Knowing why a student decided on a certain major, college, or coursework can communicate a

sophisticated pattern of life planning," says Irv C. Pfeiffer, IBM's Chicago-based college relations manager for the West and Midwest. Some recruiters look for evidence that students can make good choices. "I say to students, 'Describe the last critical decision you made; what was your thought process and the outcome?'" says Tami Simmons, assistant employment manager at Campbell Soup in Camden, New Jersey. "Their answers are revealing."

3. *Attitude toward work:* This category is assessed differently at every company. Yet there are some common characteristics of people with a good work ethic: They are self-starters, they strive for perfection, they do more than what's required. To judge work ethic, JC Penney runs many students through its eleven-week summer internship program. Erle Johnson at Westinghouse says he looks for signs in interviews that students "are willing to go all out," a trait also mentioned by other recruiters.

4. *Oral communication skills:* Mumblers who don't speak up and ramblers who don't know when to shut up will have a tough time landing job offers. Finding a balance between the two extremes is crucial. So is an ability to think on your feet, organize your thoughts, and then present a logical argument that's easily understood. At Hallmark Cards, communication skills are more highly valued for potential marketers than for prospective accountants. "But if a student hopes to move into management eventually, she must demonstrate a broad base of technical and communications skills," says Cindy Aitken, a placement manager for Hallmark.

5. *Good judgment:* Judgment is assessed in many ways. Students often are asked to describe times when they've spotted a potential problem and then sought help from others to reach a solution. Simmons at Campbell Soup says she waits for students to reveal their judgment themselves. "Anyone who asks about starting salaries early on or who downgrades past jobs" shows a clear lack of judgment, she says.

6. *Maturity:* Another trait that's often tough to identify in a thirty-minute meeting is maturity. It shows up most often in a student's style. "I see it in the depth of student answers when asked about career goals," says Davis at Baxter Healthcare. He adds, "Are their responses thoughtfully considered before spoken?" Maturity also shows up in how students see themselves. "There's a fine line between confidence and arrogance," says M. Alana Demers at New Hampshire Public Service. "Maturity isn't something you can fake."

7. *Well-developed work habits:* Work habits are the specific techniques students have developed in past jobs. "Are they well organized? Do they use a daily to-do list? Do they have impact on others through their presence? We look at how these characteristics would fare in a realistic work setting," says Davis of Baxter Healthcare. Kathy Brumitt at Anheuser-Busch seeks graduates who can plan ahead, motivate others, start projects, and work well as part of a team. "Have they accomplished past work objectives, and how much did they have to stretch themselves?"

8. *Interpersonal skills:* Being able to relate well to others in the business world pays off in promotions and bigger paychecks. "Our surveys show that executives who have advanced the fastest here have strong interpersonal skills," says Davis at Baxter Healthcare.[10]

Reference Checks

Most employers try to check applicants' background and references. They at least try to check applicants' current employment and salary. Many request transcripts to check courses taken and grade-point average. Some employers get background reports from credit rating companies, which can provide information on indebtedness, reputation, character, and lifestyle.

Reference checks have become controversial in recent years. Many former employers don't feel good about hurting someone's chances for a job by saying something critical. Others give even bad employees good reviews just to get rid of them. When checking references, a recruiter must try to judge whether the former employer is avoiding straight answers—and if so, why. Federal laws allow some rejected applicants to demand access to the background information that a recruiter compiled and then sue both the source of that information and the recruiting employer.

Physical Examination

Generally justified.
— Baseline for insurance.
need for WORKERS COMP.

The physical exam is the final step in the employee selection process. Although not all companies require it, those that do cite several reasons. For one thing, the exam can tell whether an applicant has the physical requirements for a position. It may uncover medical problems that would limit the applicant's ability to do a specific job. The exam can also set a baseline of the applicant's health for future insurance or compensation claims. By identifying health problems, an exam can pinpoint people who might be absent often and detect diseases that could be transmitted to other workers. In the largest organizations, the exam is usually performed by their own medical department. Smaller companies retain an outside doctor to perform the exam, which is almost always paid for by the employer.

Concept Check
- List several sources of potential employees.
- Describe the employee selection process.

EMPLOYEE TRAINING AND DEVELOPMENT

5 The human-resource department tries to match an employee with a job, but rarely is the match perfect. Thus the firm must train employees to perform their jobs well.

EMPLOYEE ORIENTATION

employee orientation program Training program designed to acquaint new employees with the company.

Once a person is hired, he or she can go through orientation. An **employee orientation program** is designed to acquaint new employees with the company. It deals with small but important matters, such as how to get a parking sticker, what the lunch hours are, policies on personal telephone calls and mail, paydays, and holidays. Orientation programs at large firms are often conducted by human-resource specialists. They may include tours of the buildings, talks by department heads, videotape presentations, and lots of printed information. But the supervisor of the "new hire" still has a big responsibility for orientation. The supervisor introduces the person to his or her new colleagues and helps familiarize the person with the workplace.

TRAINING AND DEVELOPMENT PROGRAMS

After orientation, the worker's formal training program usually begins. The purpose of training is to enhance a person's ability to do the job. Training programs are developed very carefully to meet a company's needs. Those needs determine the training goals, which are often stated in terms of what the trainee will be expected to do on the job. In a construction firm, for instance, one goal may be to teach trainees how to read blueprints and order needed materials.

Once the training goals have been set, a training program is designed. Someone decides what information needs to be given to the trainees, what materials will be used, and how the information will be delivered. Very often, the best way to train people is to give them a chance to practice the skills they'll need or to let them experience a situation similar to the one they'll face on the job. JC Penney has found that newly hired clerks do better when they are given time to practice using checkout terminals before being put on the sales floor.

At the end of the training program, it is assessed in terms of how well the company's needs were met. A typical question at this point would relate directly to the stated goals: Have the construction workers learned to read blueprints and order needed materials? Have the clerks learned to operate a checkout terminal without making mistakes?

A vast majority of companies have found that employee training produces big dividends. Workers feel better about themselves and their jobs, productivity increases, costs decline, and customers receive better service. Yet most companies offer no employee training. Just 15,000 employers—a mere 0.5 percent of the total—account for 90 percent of the $30 billion spent on training annually.[11] Labor Secretary Robert Reich says, "American companies have got to be urged to treat their workers as assets to be developed, rather than as costs to be cut."[12] Some companies do an excellent job of training workers. Large firms that offer the best employee training are Motorola, Target, Federal Express, General Electric, Corning, and Solectron.[13]

ON-THE-JOB TRAINING

on-the-job training Employment training that takes place at the job site and tends to be directly related to the job.

Training can be classified broadly as either on-the-job or off-the-job training. Supervisors and co-workers usually handle **on-the-job training**. It takes place at the job site and tends to be directly related to the job. Some of the methods used are specific job instructions, coaching (guidance given to new employees by experienced ones), special project assignments, and job rotation (work at several different jobs over some period).

■ One popular form of off-the-job training is programmed instruction. In this method, which is often computerized, the subject or process to be learned is broken down into manageable sequences. When a trainee gives the correct response to a question about the material, he or she is allowed to move on to the next segment of the program. A trainee who answers incorrectly is given an explanation of the material and asked to try again.

The employee who receives on-the-job training gets quick feedback. The employee can take corrective action shortly after a mistake is pointed out. Also, on-the-job training is inexpensive. Trainees produce while learning, and no expensive classrooms or learning tools are needed.

OFF-THE-JOB-TRAINING

off-the-job training Employment training that takes place away from the job site.

Some companies recognize that it is often necessary to train employees away from the workplace. This is **off-the-job-training**. Several popular methods are classroom and vestibule training and programmed instruction.

Classroom Training

Classroom training allows many trainees to be taught by just a few teachers. It may use lectures, films, videotapes, and other audiovisual media.

For managers, classroom training might also include case studies. Trainees analyze a lot of information about a business problem, like how to market a new product, and then present a course of action.

Vestibule Training

vestibule training Off-the-job training in which trainees learn on the actual equipment they will use or on models of it.

Vestibule training teaches trainees how to operate the actual equipment (or a model) that they will use on the job, but they are actually trained off the job. Vestibule training thus combines the advantages of on-the-job training and off-the-job training. It is necessary when on-the-job training is too costly or dangerous. For instance, putting new assembly-line workers right to work could slow production. Vestibule training brings them up to speed. Training pilots—where safety is a concern—is another good use of vestibule training.

Vestibule training may involve just setting up a separate room with the equipment the trainees will be using on the job. Or it may involve using equipment simulators. In pilot training, for instance, the airplane simulator enables the crew to learn how to fly without the distraction of air traffic control chatter. Also, the crew can practice hazardous flight maneuvers in a safe, controlled environment.

Programmed Instruction

With programmed instruction, subject matter is broken down into organized, logical sequences. The trainees are given a segment of the information and then respond by writing an answer or pushing a button on a machine. When they give a correct response, they can move on to the next segment of material. When they give an incorrect response, they get an explanation and are asked to try again. Computer-assisted instruction is a version of programmed instruction often used to teach more complex topics. An advantage of programmed instruction is that employees can work at their own pace. Also, they can skip over what they already know and concentrate on new and unfamiliar material. Programmed instruction is often used by salespeople to build their product knowledge and by repair people to learn how to maintain equipment.

Concept Check

- Discuss human-resource training and development.
- What are several forms of off-the-job training?

PERFORMANCE EVALUATION AND CAREER DEVELOPMENT

6

performance appraisals Comparisons of actual and expected performance.

Giving employees feedback on their work is one good way to improve their performance. In many organizations, feedback is given through the performance evaluation (or appraisal) process. **Performance appraisals** are comparisons of actual performance with expected performance. Appraisals often also measure effort, attitudes, dedication to the job, and team playing. Companies use them to make decisions about training,

■ **Exhibit 12-7**
An Employee Perfor-
mance Appraisal Form

Employee's Name		Date Employed
Last	First	
Position Title		Date Assigned Present Position
Department		Period of Review
		From To

PERFORMANCE FACTORS	Rating Key 1. Consistently Below Expectations 2. Below Expectations 3. Meets Expectations 4. Exceeds Expectations 5. Consistently Exceeds Expectations 6. Unobservable or Not Applicable

1. **QUALITY OF WORK:** How accurate, neat and complete is the individual's work?   1 2 3 4 5 6
    Consider the degree work meets acceptable standards.
    Examples or reasons for giving this rating are:

2. **PRODUCTIVITY:** Does individual produce an acceptable amount of work? Consider   1 2 3 4 5 6
    how person effectively uses available working time, plans and prioritizes work,
    sets and accomplishes goals, and completes assignments on schedule.
    Examples or reasons for giving this rating are:

3. **KNOWLEDGE OF JOB:** Is individual familiar with duties and requirements of   1 2 3 4 5 6
    position as well as methods, practices, and equipment to do the job? Consider
    knowledge gained through experience, education and specialized training. Con-
    sider if person maintains current knowledge about changes in policy and pro-
    cedure; keeps abreast of new developments and major issues in field.
    Examples or reasons for giving this rating are:

compensation, promotion, and other job changes. Performance appraisals also help employees judge the progress they are making toward their goals. An employee whose progress is disappointing may seek adjustments in his or her job or even seek a position with another company. A portion of a sample performance appraisal form is shown in Exhibit 12-7. Performance factors included on the form are: quality of work, productivity, knowledge of job, adaptability, dependability, inititative and resourcefulness, judgment, relationships with people, and attendance and punctuality. Managers are further evaluated on leadership ability, appraisal and development of people, planning and organization, and communication skills.

PERFORMANCE PLANNING

To do a performance appraisal, the employee and the manager need to agree on common goals. They do so by *performance planning,* which involves setting goals for the job, figuring out how to tell whether the goals have been met, determining how the employee will achieve the goals, and setting a time limit for them to be met. For instance, Sam Collins, a sales representative for Caterpillar, has these goals: a 20 percent increase in total sales and a 10 percent increase in the number of customers. He has six months to raise total sales and a year to get more customers. To reach the first goal, Sam plans to contact existing customers twice as often (one sales call will be made by telephone). He plans to call on at least five potential customers each week to pursue his second goal.

Several methods could be used to assess Sam Collins's sales performance. One would be to judge whether his sales goals were met. This approach focuses on results. A second method would be to place each of his job behaviors on a scale ranging from excellent performance to unacceptable performance, as shown in Exhibit 12-7.

CAREER PLANNING AND DEVELOPMENT

Career planning and development has recently become an important part of human-resource management, especially for managerial and professional employees. A *career* is the sequence of jobs that someone has until retirement. A career may focus on an occupation, like accounting, or it may consist of a series of diverse jobs (such as plant manager, sales manager, global planner) within a business, an industry, or a government agency. A career typically has four stages: (1) *entry,* (2) several years of *skill* and *technical development,* leading to (3) the *midcareer years* of success and improving performance, and ending in (4) *late career* with stable performance.

Career planning is a lifelong process. From time to time, a person needs to assess his or her strengths and weaknesses, gather information about occupations and companies, and plan job goals and longer-range career objectives. Sometimes career changes are forced on employees when they are fired or passed over for promotion. Although career planning is up to the individual, many firms now provide career counseling services.

ASSESSMENT CENTERS

assessment center Evaluation of managerial talent through an intensive period of exercises and tests.

One way to identify employees with managerial potential is to send them through an **assessment center**. An assessment center is not a location but a series of tasks, such as interviews, case-problem discussions, job simulations, and decision exercises. They tend to last from one day to one week. Trained observers assess the managerial candidates and then recommend promotion or more training. Assessment centers were pioneered by AT&T. They have been used successfully by American Airlines, Boise Cascade, and Federal Express, among many other firms.

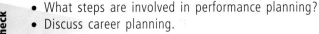

- What steps are involved in performance planning?
- Discuss career planning.
- Describe an assessment center.

EMPLOYEE COMPENSATION

 Compensation, which includes both pay and benefits, is closely linked to performance appraisals. Employees who perform better tend to get bigger pay increases. Several internal and external factors affect a person's pay.

INTERNAL INFLUENCES: JOB EVALUATION

Wages, salaries, and benefits usually reflect the importance of the job. The jobs that management considers more important are compensated at a higher rate. Likewise, different jobs of equal importance to the firm are compensated at the same rate. For instance, if a drill-press operator and a lathe operator are considered of equal importance, they may both be paid $18 per hour.

job evaluation Systematic comparison of jobs to determine reasonable pay rates.

To set wages and salaries, firms can use **job evaluation**, a systematic comparison of jobs on the basis of their required skills, responsibility, and experience. Each evaluation has three steps:

1. A thorough job analysis
2. An identification of *compensable factors*—aspects of the job that the organization values—including knowledge, specialized training, work complexity, problem-solving ability, and equipment use
3. Selection of a method for evaluating jobs according to the compensable factor

One commonly used evaluation method ranks sets of jobs by overall value and difficulty. Another assigns points to each compensable factor and adds the points to arrive at a total that's used to determine what that job is worth.

EXTERNAL INFLUENCES: COMPETITIVE COMPENSATION

In deciding how much to pay workers, the firm must also be concerned with the salaries paid by competitors. If competitors are paying much higher wages, a firm may lose its best employees. Larger firms conduct salary surveys to see what other firms are paying. Wage and salary surveys conducted by employer associations or the U.S. Department of Labor can also be useful.

An employer can decide to pay at, above, or below the going rate. Most firms try to offer competitive wages and salaries within a geographic area or an industry. If a company pays below-market wages, it may not be able to hire skilled people.

PAY SATISFACTION AND COMPARABLE WORTH

Pay is an important motivator for workers, as Chapter 10 explains. Satisfaction with pay helps keep performance levels high and absenteeism and turnover low. Employees who are satisfied with their pay also tend to be satisfied with their job and their employer.

comparable worth Concept that employees should be paid the same for jobs that are similar in worth to the employer.

An important compensation issue is **comparable worth**. Many people think employees should be paid the same for jobs that are similar in worth to the employer, even if the jobs are different in terms of knowledge required, equipment used, working conditions, and other factors. Say that a senior secretary for a brewery gets $22,000 a year and a forklift operator gets $31,000. What if the company's job evaluation produces the same point totals for the two jobs? The jobs would be of comparable worth, but the two salaries are quite different. Traditionally, lower-paying jobs have been occupied mostly by women and higher-paying jobs mostly by men. To solve this problem, the courts have forced some state and local governments to pay women the same as men for jobs of comparable worth.

METHODS OF PAYMENT

wages Payments to lower-level employees based on the number of hours worked.

salary Payment to managerial and professional employees, set through job evaluation and not tied to any specific number of work hours.

piecework payment Method of payment in which employees are paid by the amount they produce.

Employees are usually paid on the basis of the amount of time they work, the amount they produce, or some combination of time and output. Lower-level workers, such as machinists and assembly-line employees, are usually paid hourly **wages**. Managerial and professional employees are usually paid biweekly or monthly **salaries**. Rates for specific jobs are set through a job evaluation, using the company's pay ranges and making adjustments for such external factors as general economic conditions and rates paid by competitors. Salaries and wages are also determined by merit and performance appraisals.

In some firms, employees are paid by the amount they produce. These **piecework payment** plans usually increase pay as performance increases. For instance, a tire maker at Goodyear might be paid $7.00 for each tire up to twenty tires a day and $8.50 per tire over that. A worker who made twenty-five tires in a work shift would thus earn $182.50.

Firms use other types of incentive systems as well. The *commissions* paid to salespeople are a percentage of each item's selling price. A salesperson who sold a drilling machine for $6,000 and received a 5 percent commission would get $300. A *bonus* is a payment for reaching a specific goal. Typically, bonuses are paid once a year. For instance, a factory manager may offer all workers a $100 year-end bonus if there are no serious on-the-job accidents during the year.

Another form of incentive pay is a *sharing of costs-savings* plan. Employees get a share of any extra profits resulting from their cost-cutting suggestions. Say that employee suggestions result in savings of $200,000. Typically, the workers get 75 percent of the savings, and the rest goes to the firm. In this example, workers would share $150,000 ($200,000 × 75%).

A firm that offers *profit sharing* pays employees a portion of the profits over some preset level. Many firms have adopted this type of incentive plan. Union Carbide, for instance, shares profits that reflect an 8 percent or better return on capital. Employees who have profit-sharing plans are thought to identify more closely with the company and its profit goal. Thus they are more likely to reduce waste and increase productivity.

- What is meant by job evaluation?
- Discuss pay satisfaction and comparable worth.
- Describe the various ways to compensate employees.

FRINGE BENEFITS AND EMPLOYEE SERVICES

fringe benefits Employee benefits beyond wages or salaries, including insurance, pensions, and paid sick leave.

As noted above, compensation is more than just wages and salaries. It also includes fringe benefits and employee services.

Fringe benefits include insurance, pension plans, and paid sick leave. Some other fringe benefits are required by law: unemployment compensation, worker's compensation, and Social Security, which are all paid for in part by employers. *Unemployment compensation* provides former employees with money for a certain period while they are unemployed. To be eligible, the employee must have worked a minimum number of weeks, be without a job, and be willing to accept a suitable position offered by the state Unemployment Compensation Commission. Some state laws permit payments to strikers. *Worker's compensation* pays employees for lost work time caused by work-related injuries and may also cover rehabilitation after a serious injury. *Social Security* is mainly a government pension plan, but it also provides disability and survivor benefits and benefits for people undergoing kidney dialysis and transplants. Medicare (health care for the elderly) and Medicaid (health care for the poor) are also part of Social Security.

Many employers also offer fringe benefits not required by law. Among these benefits are paid time off (holidays, sick days, and vacations), insurance (life, health and hospitalization, and disability), profit-sharing plans, pensions, stock-purchase options, and bonuses.

PENSIONS

pensions Retirement income paid to former workers.

One of the most expensive fringe benefits is **pensions**—retirement income paid to former workers. For most people, the two sources of retirement income are Social Security and pensions.

Most employees participate in Social Security through a payroll tax. A percentage of the employee's pay is deducted from each paycheck. The employer pays an equal amount. The amount deducted and the maximum tax per year have increased over the past few years. They have increased because more Americans are becoming eligible for benefits, people are living longer, and the amount paid to retirees is increasing.

Many employers provide private pension plans to supplement Social Security. These plans are governed by the Employee Retirement Income Security Act (ERISA) of 1974. The act specifies that employers who offer a pension plan must set aside money now for the payment of pension benefits in the future. The act also talks about *vesting,* or guaranteeing employees some pension benefit if they leave the job before the usual retirement age. All employees must be fully vested in any pension plan (must be eligible to get 100 percent of what has been put into their

■ One of the most expensive fringe benefits a company can offer is a pension. This is compensation that is paid to employees after they retire from the firm. The Employee Retirement Income Security Act of 1974 sets the rules for employers who offer such private pension plans, assuring that the workers' contributions to the fund will be available to them when they retire.

account) by the time they have fifteen years of service with the firm. Also, employers must give employees certain retirement and pension information at least once a year.

Funding and vesting are required by law because of past abuses. Unethical firms would take money from employee paychecks for future pension benefits but would not put the money into a pension fund. When the employees retired, there would be no fund. The company itself would be unable to pay benefits. Before the law requiring funding and vesting, employees could do little about this kind of abuse.

STOCK-PURCHASE OPTIONS

stock-purchase options Employee rights to buy a set number of shares of the firm's stock at a fixed price by a certain time.

Stock-purchase options give employees (usually executives) the right to buy a set number of shares of the company's stock at a fixed price by a certain time. The employees gain as long as the stock price goes up. Companies like Avis, Dell Computer, and Lincoln Electric offer stock-purchase options to all employees. Stock ownership by employees can strengthen team spirit and incentive to work hard. Employees understand that they will benefit from company profitability. Thus, they are as anxious as the company owners and managers to see the company succeed.

Options are attractive to both employees and stockholders for the following reasons:

- Executives must put up some of their own money, as do the stockholders.
- The value of the option is the same as that of the stockholders' stock. Thus executives and stockholders are equally at risk.
- Options are a form of profit sharing, which links executives' financial success to that of the stockholders.

EMPLOYEE SERVICES

employee services
"Extra" services offered by companies to improve employee morale and working conditions.

Employee services are the extras that companies offer in order to improve employee morale and working conditions. Among them are social and recreational programs, free parking, merchandise discounts, tuition reimburment for college courses, company newsletters, and day-care centers. The benefits and services offered by some of America's largest companies are shown in Exhibit 12-8.

Concept Check
- List and describe several forms of fringe benefits.
- What is the difference between fringe benefits and employee services?

PROMOTIONS, TRANSFERS, AND SEPARATIONS

 It is part of the human-resource function to deal with employees' job moves—both within and out of the company. Employees move three different ways: promotions, transfers, and separations.

PROMOTIONS

promotion Upward move in an organization to a position with more authority, responsibility, and pay.

A **promotion** is an upward move in an organization to a position with more authority, responsibility, and pay. Promotion decisions are usually based on seniority (length of service) and merit. Union employees usually prefer a strict seniority system to preserve union strength. Nonunion employees, especially managers, think promotions should be based mostly on merit. But both seniority and merit are used to justify promotions.

The American military may have the most thorough, formal program for making promotion decisions. The performance evaluations and personnel files of potential officers are sent to a special decision-making committee called the Promotion Board. This board consists of high-ranking officers who have been selected and trained to make promotion decisions. They review thousands of evaluations and make their decisions according to clearly drawn criteria from the Pentagon. A typical officer being reviewed is evaluated at least nine times by various board members and may be evaluated as many as fifteen times. Promotion decisions are based entirely on the information included in the formal evaluation and the personnel file.

Exhibit 12-8
Benefits and Services Offered by Some of America's Largest Companies

Source: Adapted with permission from "Happy Campers," *Advertising Age*, 28 January 1991, p. 28, copyright © Crain Communications, Inc., 1991; and "The Company Cure," *Fortune*, 6 September 1993, p. 14.

Company	Maternity leave	Paternity leave	Vacation days after 1 year	Overtime pay	Christmas bonus	Child-care assistance	Elder-care assistance	Telecommuting	Dress codes	Flexible hours	Summer hours	Minorities on board	Women on board
Time Warner	✓	✓*	20**	✓**		✓	✓	✓		✓	✓**	0 of 24	0 of 24
Ralston Purina	✓		10							✓	✓	0	0
Sears, Roebuck	✓		10						✓§	✓		1 of 16	3 of 16
General Motors	✓	✓*	10	✓	✓	✓				✓**		1 of 18	2 of 18
Warner-Lambert	✓	✓*	10	✓		✓	✓	✓		✓	✓	1 of 16	1 of 16
Eastman Kodak	✓	✓*	10	✓		✓	✓	✓		✓	✓	2 of 15	2 of 15
Ford Motor Co.	✓	✓*	10	✓		✓	✓	✓§		✓**		2 of 17	1 of 17
K mart	✓	✓*	10	✓	✓				✓	✓		2 of 11	2 of 11
AT&T	✓	✓	10			✓	✓	✓		✓		0 of 18	2 of 18
Kellogg	✓	✓	10	✓		✓	✓	✓	✓	✓		2 of 13	2 of 13
R. J. Reynolds Tobacco	✓		10	✓		✓	✓	✓				NA	NA
Procter & Gamble	✓	✓*	10			✓				✓		1 of 17	1 of 17
Pepsi-Cola USA**	✓		10	✓†			✓				✓	1 of 14	1 of 14
Oscar Mayer Foods	✓	✓*	10	✓				✓	✓§	✓		2 of 22	4 of 22
Johnson & Johnson	✓	✓*	10	✓	✓	✓	✓	✓		✓		1 of 18	2 of 18

* Unpaid leave
** Does not apply to all employees
† Various restrictions apply
§ Informal policy

TRANSFERS

transfer Sideways move in an organization to a position with about the same salary and at about the same level.

A **transfer** is a sideways move in an organization to a position with about the same salary and at about the same level. Employees may seek a transfer for personal enrichment, for a more interesting job, for more convenience (better hours, location of work, and so on), or for a job that offers more chances for advancement. Employers may transfer workers from a position where they are no longer needed to one where they are needed. Or the goal may be to find a better fit for the employee within the firm.

SEPARATIONS

separation Employee's leave-taking, due to resignation, layoff, termination, or retirement.

A **separation** occurs when an employee leaves the company. The cause may be resignation, layoff, termination, or retirement.

Resignation

resignation Voluntary departure of an employer from a job.

A **resignation** occurs when an employee decides to leave the firm. The employee may want a job with better pay, working conditions, promotion opportunities, geographic location—or may have some other reason.

Layoff

layoff Temporary separation of an employee from a job, arranged by the employer.

A **layoff** is a temporary separation arranged by the employer, usually because business is slow. Layoffs can either be planned, such as seasonal reductions of employees, or unplanned, as when sales decrease. Generally, employees with the least seniority are laid off first.

There are several alternatives to a layoff. With a *voluntary reduction in pay,* all employees agree to take less pay so that everyone can keep working. Other firms arrange to have all or most of their employees take vacation time during slow periods. Other employees agree to take *voluntary time off,* which again has the effect of reducing the employer's payroll and avoiding the need for a layoff. Control Data Corporation avoids layoffs with what it calls a *rings of defense* approach. Temporary employees are hired with the specific understanding that they may be laid off at any time. When layoffs are needed, the first "ring of defense" is the temporary workers. Permanent Control Data employees know they probably will never be laid off.

Termination

termination Permanent separation of an employee from a job, arranged by the employer.

A **termination** is a permanent separation arranged by the employer. Reasons for terminations include failure to meet performance expectations, violation of the rules, dishonesty, sexual harassment, absenteeism, laziness, or insubordination (disobedience).

Most companies follow a series of steps before terminating an employee. First, the employee is given an oral warning. The second step is a written statement that the employee's actions are not acceptable. If the employee fails to improve, he or she is suspended from work for a time. If the employee persists in wrongdoing after suspension, his or her employment is terminated.

Companies must make certain that they have their facts straight when terminating an employee. Various lawsuits underscore that point. For example, Don Hagler, a 41-year veteran of Procter & Gamble, sued P&G when the company fired him after publicly accusing him of stealing a $35 company telephone. Hagler said that the phone was his property and that P&G libeled him by posting notices on company bulletin boards accusing him of theft. A Texas jury awarded Hagler $15.6 million.[14]

Another method of terminating an employee is **dehiring**, or getting the employee to quit. A supervisor who wants to get rid of an unwanted employee may try to make the employee's work environment so uncomfortable that he or she chooses to leave. Then the supervisor is spared the unpleasant chore of discharging the employee.

dehiring Method of termination in which the employer makes the job so unpleasant that the employee quits.

Retirement

retirement Permanent separation of an employee from the company, usually at the end of his or her career.

Retirement is a permanent separation from the company, usually arranged by the employee at the end of his or her career. Mandatory retirement ages of sixty-five or seventy used to be common. Retirement was often like a dismissal. But in 1987 the Age Discrimination in Employment Act was amended to ban discrimination on the basis of age for anyone over forty, to remove the upper age limit, and to make retirement an option for employees who are still able to work. There are a few specific exceptions, in such occupations as fire fighter and police officer.

Workers in companies with too many employees may be offered early-retirement incentives. This option offers retirement benefits to younger employees or adds extra retirement benefits or both. Employees can thus retire more comfortably without working longer. Companies like Xerox, IBM, ITT, Hewlett-Packard, and Phillips Petroleum have used early-retirement plans to reduce their work forces.

Retirement can be an emotional period for an employee. Some look forward to having time to relax and enjoy the fruits of their labor without worrying about work problems. But for others, retirement is very hard. Once-busy employees have to cope with being "nonproductive" and having nothing to do. More companies are offering preretirement counseling to help employees cope with this change.

Concept Check
- Distinguish between a promotion and a transfer.
- Discuss the types of employee separations.

HUMAN-RESOURCE ISSUES OF THE 1990S

9 Several issues and trends will confront human-resource managers for the rest of the decade. They include the changing nature of the work force and of work, employee stress and health, and climbing human-resource costs.

Three changes in the nature of the workforce present problems: growing worker illiteracy, the aging of the workforce, and its changing makeup, as discussed in Chapter 3. Human-resource managers have

■ As part of its wellness program, Johnson & Johnson built a fitness center for its employees. The company also offers seminars on such subjects as losing weight, quitting smoking, and stress management. A study by the company showed that employees who participated in the program were absent from work less and had lower medical costs than nonparticipants.

responded by emphasizing more basic education and training, more retirement planning, and more opportunities for members of protected classes to be promoted.

As discussed in Chapter 6, corporations themselves have been changing because of mergers and acquisitions. Firms that restructure must decide where to put workers in the new organization or whether to terminate their employment. Corporate restructurings have made it harder for workers to switch jobs. They have also resulted in huge layoffs in some industries, such as banking and steel. The pace of mergers and acquisitions has now slowed some. But many companies restructured in the 1980s are fighting for economic survival, putting jobs at risk.

Changes in the workplace have also caused higher levels of employee stress. Some workplace stress stimulates better performance. Many workers find that they get more work done with some time pressure. On the other hand, too much stress can lead to reduced productivity, drug and alcohol abuse, and more absenteeism and turnover.

wellness programs
Company-sponsored programs that help employees in personal areas of their lives.

Employee assistance programs are ways to fight these problems. Many companies are offering **wellness programs**, which offer help in such areas as losing weight, quitting smoking, and managing stress. Some firms have built expensive fitness centers and hired staff to oversee a wellness program. Coors Brewing Company found that health insurance costs were 13 percent lower for employees in its wellness program. In a five-year study, Johnson & Johnson found that people in its wellness program were absent from work less and had lower hospital costs than nonparticipants.[15] Even if they can't show that the programs cut costs, companies report that wellness programs are popular with employees. In fact, com-

panies with a new wellness program generally have fewer union grievances than they did before.

Wages and benefits tend to increase and rarely, if ever, decrease. This
has also been the case for things like health insurance, pensions, and
Social Security. Of these, the cost of health care has gone up most in
recent years. Many employers have tried to contain health care costs without limiting the quality and availability of services.

One approach to controlling costs is called a **cafeteria benefits plan**.
Employees are allowed to choose their own benefits—with two conditions. First, the company sets the cost limits per employee. Second, each
benefit plan must include certain items, such as Social Security, worker's
compensation, and unemployment insurance. Otherwise, employees can
pick and choose from the options. A young married employee might
choose life insurance and help with college tuition. An older employee
might choose a better pension plan.

Human-resource management has become very complex. As a result,
top management has become more involved and supportive. Carefully
designed human-resource practices can greatly reduce an organization's
exposure to lawsuits. Several firms found guilty of employment discrimination have been forced to make large cash awards to current and former
employees. Top executives have come to realize that the human-resource
function can have a major impact on the firm's profits.

Concept Check
- Discuss the changing nature of the workforce.
- What are wellness programs?
- Describe a cafeteria benefits plan.

cafeteria benefits plan
Benefits plan in which employees choose their own
benefits, up to a certain cost
per employee.

■ SUMMARY

1. Describe the human-resource function.

Human-resource management is the process of hiring, developing, motivating, and evaluating people to achieve organizational goals. The
process begins with a job interview and ends when the employee leaves
the firm. The overall goals of the human-resource function are to provide
competent, well-trained employees to the various departments in the
company; to make human resources more effective; and to satisfy
employees' needs by helping them achieve successful careers. Human-
resource planning involves defining future needs for workers, examining
the number and qualifications of existing employees, and creating a strategy for meeting future human-resource needs.

The human-resource department has a staff role that supports the line
organization. Basic human-resource goals are defined by top management. The human-resource department sets policies and procedures that
are then carried out by operating managers. The human-resource department keeps employee records as a service to operating managers. It also

Key Terms

affirmative action
   programs 376

altered workweeks 378

Americans with
   Disabilities Act 374

assessment center 391

cafeteria benefits plan
   401

comparable worth 393

compressed workweek
   378

dehiring 399

employee orientation
   program 386

employee services 396

continued

helps make sure that employment discrimination doesn't take place and that highly qualified job applicants are available.

2. Describe the federal laws and agencies that affect human-resource management.

A number of federal laws (listed in Exhibit 12-3) affect human-resource management. Federal law prohibits discrimination based on age, race, gender, color, national origin, religion, or disability. One of the newest laws is the Americans with Disabilities Act, which became fully operational in 1994. The law bans discrimination against disabled workers and requires employers to change the work environment to accommodate the disabled. Another new law is the Family and Medical Leave Act. The law requires employers, with certain exceptions, to provide employees up to twelve weeks a year of unpaid leave. The leave can be for birth or adoption of a child or due to serious illness of a family member.

Federal agencies that deal with human-resource administration are the Equal Employment Opportunity Commission (EEOC), the Occupational Safety and Health Administration (OSHA), the Office of Federal Contract Compliance Programs (OFCCP), and the Wage and Hour Division of the Department of Labor. The two agencies that enforce employment discrimination laws are the EEOC and OFCCP. Many companies employ affirmative action officers to ensure compliance with antidiscrimination laws.

3. Discuss human-resource planning.

Job analysis and design are important components of successful human-resource planning. The tasks and responsibilities of a job are usually listed in the job description. The skills, knowledge, and abilities needed for the job are given in the job specification.

Another important consideration in human-resource planning is the scheduling of work. Factors that complicate scheduling include multishift operations, changes in work flow, and workweek plans like compressed schedules and flextime.

4. Explain how employees are recruited and selected.

Employee recruitment and selection take place when a new position is created or an existing one becomes vacant. Qualified applicants can be found in either the internal or the external labor market.

After people have been attracted to the firm and applications have been received, employment specialists begin the selection process. First comes the initial screening, which includes a preliminary interview and completion of an application form. Then the applicant may be asked to take one or more employment tests. At this point, reference checks are also done, and applicants may undergo a physical examination. The selection interview is the most widely used tool for making the hiring decision.

5. Describe how employees are trained and developed.

Training and development programs aim to increase the knowledge and skill of employees. Such programs generally are concerned with orienting new employees to the firm, improving the performance of employees in their current jobs, and preparing employees for more job responsibilities and promotions. Training can be broadly classified as either on-the-job or off-the-job. Off-the-job methods include classroom training, vestibule training, and programmed instruction.

6. Explain how performance appraisals and career development are used in human-resource management.

Performance appraisals begin with performance planning: specifying job goals, identifying the means of telling whether the goals have been met, determining how the employee can achieve the goals, and setting the time frame within which the goals are to be achieved.

Career development includes assessing one's progress from time to time, gathering information about different occupations and companies, and planning immediate job goals and longer-range career objectives. Assessment centers are used to identify employees with managerial potential.

7. Explain the forms of compensation and fringe benefits available to employees.

Employees are usually paid for the amount of time worked, the amount of output produced, or some combination of the two. Workers are usually paid wages, whereas professionals and managers are paid a salary. Compensation incentive systems include piecework, commissions, bonuses, sharing of costs savings, and profit sharing.

Fringe benefits and employee services are forms of nonwage compensation. Some fringe benefits are required by law. Others are voluntarily provided by employers. One of the most important and expensive benefits is the pension. Federal law requires that employees with fifteen years of service be fully vested in (have full access to) their pension plans. Stock options are the right to buy shares in the company at a fixed price by a fixed time in the future.

8. Discuss promotions, transfers, and separations.

Promotions are upward moves in an organization. They include increased authority, responsibility, and salary. Transfers are lateral moves, usually at the same salary and level. Separations may be a resignation, layoff, termination, or retirement. A resignation is a voluntary separation of an employee from a company. A layoff is a temporary separation arranged by the employer. When an employer fires an employee, it is a termination. Retirement is a permanent separation from the company, usually initiated by the employee at the end of his or her career.

9. Describe key human-resource issues of the 1990s.

Work force changes of the 1990s include increasing worker illiteracy, aging of the work force, and women and minorities becoming a majority of the work force. Employee stress has increased in the work environment. To combat stress and absenteeism, companies have developed wellness programs. Climbing benefit costs have prompted many employers to offer a cafeteria benefits plan.

■ DISCUSSION QUESTIONS

1. What are the uses and drawbacks of such selection tools as skill tests, intelligence tests, personality tests, drug tests, AIDS tests, and physical exams?

2. Explain how the employee selection process might differ between hiring a custodial employee and hiring a chemist.

3. What kind of training and development program would be best for assembly-line workers? For first-line supervisors? For industrial sales representatives? For maintenance workers? For computer programmers?

4. How important is training likely to be in the future? What changes that are facing organizations will increase the importance of training?

5. In what circumstances may an employer wish to pay different wages to people doing the same job? In what circumstances may an employer wish to pay the same wages to everyone doing the same job?

6. Why do you think pay secrecy is so common?

7. You are applying for a job as a manager and are at the point of negotiating salary and benefits. What questions would you ask your prospective employer concerning benefits? Describe the benefits package you would try to negotiate for yourself.

8. When does an organization benefit by keeping its older employees? Discuss some strategies for keeping older workers on the job.

9. Would reducing the number of employee resignations always be a good thing? Why or why not?

■ CASE

Creating Stars at Bell Labs

Wanted: Bright, but merely average, workers who can be turned into star performers—not just for an hour, or a day, but for good.

Many management experts maintain that such a transformation is impossible. A company's most productive employees, they say, have high IQs, driving personalities, superior work ethics, and other assets that can't be taught. Accordingly, companies try to hire people with these desired qualities instead of attempting to teach new tricks to those already on staff.

But a few companies are now asserting they can do the impossible after all. As a notable example, Bell Laboratories, the research arm of American Telephone & Telegraph Co., says that it has trained 248 engineers in its switching systems business unit to emulate the work and social habits of the unit's best performers.

Bell Labs called for the engineers to learn—from each other, no less—such mundane things as how to empty their in-baskets efficiently, how to take constructive criticism, and how to ask for help instead of wasting time by insisting on solving problems themselves. The result: Engineers who went through the program boosted their productivity by 10 percent in eight months, saving Bell Labs three times the money spent on the program after one year, and more than six times after two years.

Bell Labs engineers concede that some people simply don't want to learn. But they insist that anyone open to improvement can learn to be a star. "I was a little leery" at first, says engineer Jerry Yingling. But after his first class, he saw that engineers have different ways of solving the same problems—some more efficient than others—and that they can learn new methods from each other.[16]

Questions

1. Do you think that an average employee can be made into a star simply by emulating a star?
2. If so, would the technique work as well for nonprofessional workers? Remember, Bell Labs was training engineers.
3. Comment on the following: "If you look at what really drives people [to succeed], it's amost all attitudes and values," according to Warren Bennis, a business administration professor at the University of Southern California. For a mere middle performer to become a star, "the need, the drive, the ambition has got to be there."

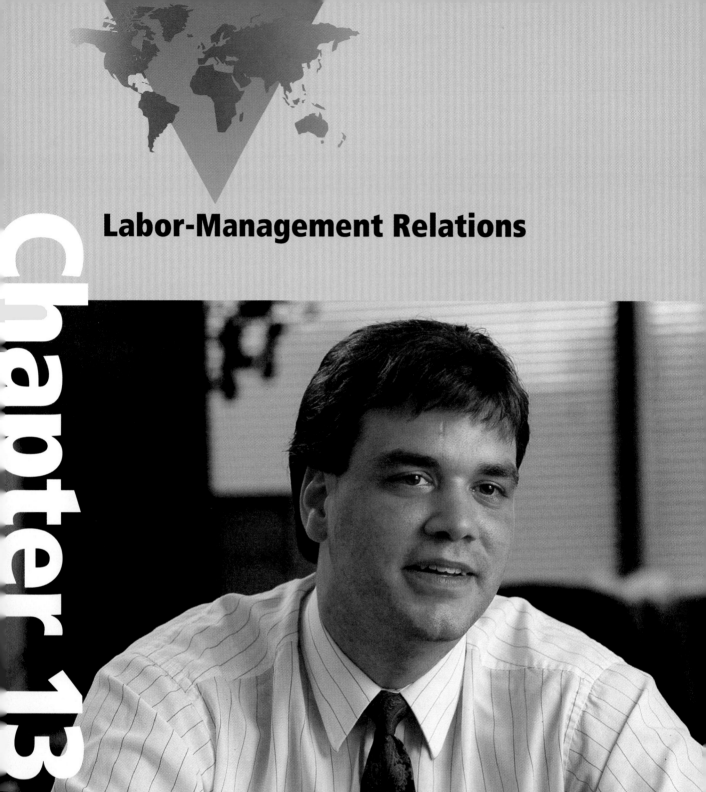

Labor-Management Relations

Learning Goals

After studying this chapter, you should be able to:

1. Understand the history of the U.S. union movement, and describe labor organizations today.
2. Understand the role of federal legislation in the growth of unionism and collective bargaining.
3. Explain the union organizing process.
4. Explain the collective bargaining process.
5. Understand the important issues and items in labor agreements.
6. Discuss the grievance procedure.
7. Identify and describe the economic weapons of unions and management.
8. Discuss trends affecting the American work force and labor-management relations.

 Career Profile

There are very few entry-level positions in the field of labor-management relations. Knowing this, John Owens took advantage of the co-op work-study program at his college. While still in school, he began working for LensCrafters' personnel department in order to gain practical experience. He learned firsthand about benefits and compensation during his internship at the headquarters of this international company. This helped him to get the job he wanted in labor relations shortly after graduation.

John is now senior labor relations specialist at the University of Cincinnati. UC offers both undergraduate and graduate programs to a student body of over 36,000. Some of the school's more noted programs are in law, nursing, music, engineering, and medicine.

The university is also one of the largest employers in the state of Ohio. John is responsible for interpreting labor contracts and managing the negotiations related to them. His work involves five different labor organizations, ranging from a clerical union to the bargaining unit that represents the professors at the university. He conducts policy and procedure reviews and meets with managers and supervisors regarding discipline and grievance procedures. He also works with the various departments within the university to set up training programs designed to foster quality employee relations.

The courses John took to obtain his degree in industrial relations/personnel and his participation in the school's work-study program provided him with a considerable amount of experience in labor-management relations prior to graduation. This combination of theory and practical experience has been a key resource for him. Indeed, he feels that such a background is essential in order to advance quickly in his field.

Overview

Chapter 13 begins with a brief history of the American labor movement. Next it describes the laws that are the framework of labor and management relations in this country. It then describes the current status of unions and their functions. You will next discover why employees join unions and how union contracts are negotiated and administered. The weapons both labor and management use to gain control are discussed. The chapter concludes with a look at trends in the American work force and the future of labor-management relations.

EMERGENCE OF LABOR UNIONS

labor union Organization that represents workers in labor disputes over wages, hours, and working conditions.

employee associations Labor organizations whose members work in federal, state, county, and municipal government agencies.

collective bargaining Process of negotiating labor agreements that provide for compensation and working conditions mutually acceptable to the union and to management.

A **labor union** is an organization that represents workers in their disputes with management over wages, hours, and working conditions. Labor organizations whose members work in government agencies are called **employee associations**. Other labor organizations represent professional employees, such as baseball players, engineers, teachers, news reporters, and pilots.

Whether the labor organization is a union or an association, its hallmark is collective bargaining. **Collective bargaining** is the process of negotiating labor agreements between union members and management.

EARLY AMERICAN UNIONS

The forerunners of unions began to develop toward the end of the 1700s. That was when the United States was changing from an agricultural to an industrial economy. The guilds or societies, as they were called, were made up of skilled craftsmen who pushed for better working conditions. They resisted shop owners who wanted to lower wages. Many of the early guilds threatened to stop working unless business owners paid higher wages, provided some of the tools needed for work, and shortened the workday. Employers opposed these efforts, often successfully.

Knights of Labor First major national labor organization, founded in 1869.

In 1869 a small group of clothing workers secretly founded the Noble Order of the Knights of Labor. The **Knights of Labor** was the first major national labor organization. By about 1880 its local assemblies had more than 500,000 members. But it was never very good at improving the life of the working person. It was more concerned with broad social issues, economic programs, and reforms.

EMERGENCE OF THE AMERICAN FEDERATION OF LABOR

American Federation of Labor (AFL) Labor union, founded in 1881, that organized workers within skilled trades and encouraged unions to function much like businesses.

Many of the craft groups within the Knights of Labor were unhappy with its philosophy and activities. In 1881 they broke away and formed the Federation of Organized Trades and Labor Unions, which five years later was renamed the **American Federation of Labor (AFL)**. Under Samuel Gompers, who was its president for more than thirty-five years, the AFL dropped the philosophy of the Knights of Labor. In its place, the AFL pressed for better recognition and more power for member unions; collective bargaining; and temporary work stoppages (*strikes*) to improve wages, hours, and working conditions.

The AFL consisted of numerous local unions joined together under the banner of one large union. The member unions of the AFL were **craft unions,** representing workers in a single craft or occupation, such as bricklaying or carpentry. Each had *exclusive jurisdiction* over its trade or craft—that is, each had the right to organize all the workers within a skilled trade or craft. Each union could also develop its own constitution and program of collective bargaining.

craft union Union that represents workers in a single craft or occupation.

Gompers emphasized *business unionism,* an approach that encouraged unions to function much like businesses. The union and the company would negotiate and sign a contract, or a written labor agreement, much as two business firms might reach a written sales agreement.

DEVELOPMENT OF THE CONGRESS OF INDUSTRIAL ORGANIZATIONS

The AFL was the major force on the labor scene for nearly fifty years. But with the Great Depression in 1930 came severe unemployment in the building trades and a loss of power for the AFL. Then, just as the economy got stronger and things began to improve for the AFL, a crisis developed. Mass-production workers wanted to set up **industrial unions**, unions that represent workers in a single industry, regardless of their occupation or level of skill. The AFL insisted on craft unions.

industrial union Union that represents workers in a single industry, regardless of their occupation or skill level.

Under the leadership of John L. Lewis, the United Mine Workers of America challenged the AFL's position. For several decades, the UMW had been a member of the AFL. But it had developed as a mining-industry union, containing skilled and unskilled workers. Thus it went against the AFL's doctrine of exclusive jurisdiction. Lewis argued that a union organized along industry lines was better than a craft union for representing workers in large-scale, mass-production industries.

Congress of Industrial Organizations (CIO) Labor union that broke away from the AFL in 1935 and organized workers along industry lines.

In 1935 Lewis took his union and a handful of others and left the AFL. They formed the **Congress of Industrial Organizations (CIO)**. The CIO made a big effort to organize unions in several mass-production industries, including the auto and steel industries. Its membership drives were very successful. After a brief period, the AFL counterattacked and also recruited thousands of industrial workers to its ranks.

THE AFL AND CIO: RIVALRY AND MERGER

Until the early 1950s, the AFL and the CIO competed for new members and tried to steal the other's members. This effort cost a lot of money and produced few gains. Finally the two decided to end their war. On December 5, 1955, the AFL and CIO merged into one. George Meany became its president. The combined AFL-CIO spoke for more than 16 million workers.

THE U.S. LABOR MOVEMENT TODAY

In 1945, the high-water mark for the U.S. labor movement, union members accounted for 35.5 percent of all employed Americans. Today that share stands at 16.2 percent, or 20,741,000 workers (see Exhibit 13-1).[1]

■ On December 5, 1955, the American Federation of Labor merged with the Congress of Industrial Organizations, ending a long-standing feud. AFL president George Meany and CIO president Walter Reuther shook hands and raised a gavel simultaneously, signaling the formation of the largest labor group in the world, with 16,000,000 members.

The decline would have been sharper had unions in service industries and in the public sector not experienced rapid growth in recent years.

Today, labor unions may represent an industry or skilled trade or a geographic area. There are still craft unions (often found in the building trades) and industrial unions (such as the United Auto Workers and the United Steelworkers of America). A more recent type is the **conglomerate union**, which represents a wide variety of workers and industries. For instance, the Teamsters Union represents not only truck drivers but also nurses, teachers, police officers, sanitation engineers, firefighters, and secretaries. A group of many unions organized across the country is a **national union.** And there are **international unions**, which have members outside the United States, usually in Canada. Examples are the International Typographical Union and the International Ladies Garment Workers Union.

conglomerate union Union, such as the Teamsters Union, that represents a wide variety of workers and industries.

national union Group of many unions in a particular industry, skilled trade, or geographic area.

international union Union with membership outside the United States.

local union Branch of a national union, organized in a specific area or plant.

Local Labor Unions

National and international unions are made up of **local unions**—branch unions that represent a specific area or even a specific plant. A local union linked with the United Auto Workers, for instance, would follow the national union's rules. Local unions number more than 60,000 in the United States. The national union usually sets the number of local officers,

■ **Exhibit 13-1**
Membership in National
Union and Employee
Associations

Source: Data for 1930 through 1987 from
Courtney Gifford, *Directory of U.S. Labor
Organizations*, 1988–1989 ed. (Washington, D.C.: Bureau of National Affairs,
1989), p. 2. Current data supplied by
telephone from the Bureau of National
Affairs on November 5, 1993.

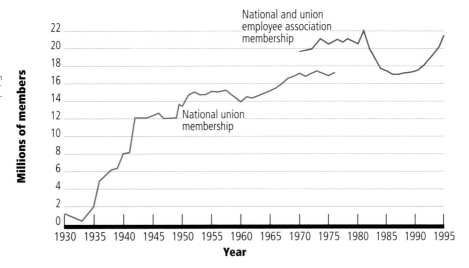

Note: After 1978, the Bureau of Labor Statistics consolidated union and employee association membership data.

election procedures, the schedule of local meetings, financial arrangements with the national organization, and the local's role in negotiating labor agreements.

The three main functions of the local union are collective bargaining, worker relations and membership services, and community and political activities. Collective bargaining takes place every two or three years. On a day-to-day basis, local union officers and **shop stewards** in the plant represent union members to management when workers have complaints. Union issues are discussed at monthly meetings. Financial and other reports are given, officers are elected, committee appointments are announced, and special events are planned. Members may also get a union newsletter and other information from the national union at these meetings.

shop stewards Elected union officials who represent union members to management when workers have complaints.

The AFL-CIO Today

Today the AFL-CIO is an umbrella organization for most U.S. labor unions. It represents nearly a hundred unions and employee associations. The organizations in the AFL-CIO represent nearly 80 percent of all **rank-and-file** union members—those who are not elected officials of the union. (However, one of the largest labor organizations, the National Education Association, does not belong to the AFL-CIO.)

rank-and-file Union members who are not elected officials.

The AFL-CIO federation now represents 11 percent of the U.S. work force, or about 70 percent of all U.S. unions and employee organizations. Membership is down a third from 16.4 percent in 1975, despite absorbing the 1.3 million-member Teamsters union several years ago.[2] In 1993 only 10 of the 86 member unions reported membership gains during the past two years. The organization does not interfere with the affairs of member unions and does not take part in collective bargaining. It does run union organizing drives and such political activities as lobbying.

For already hard-hit unions, the 1980s and the early 1990s were a tough time. Many major employers went off-shore, bankrupt, or out of business, and survivors responded to intensified global competition by increasing efforts to produce more goods using fewer workers. As a result, some of the biggest unions lost almost half their members: The United Steelworkers of America, for example, shrank from one million in 1983 to 555,000 in 1993.[3] In the future, new forms of labor organizations may result, as the following Social and Demographic Trends box describes.

TRENDS

Social and Demographic

Labor Organizations for a Changing World

The decline in union membership is a result of changing social and demographic trends. Today's workers are often turning to a different type of labor organization instead of the traditional labor union.

An example is the Black Caucus at Xerox Corporation. African-American employees—hourly and management workers alike—meet periodically to discuss such issues as salary equity and advancement. They then present their complaints to the company's chairman. Another example is 9 to 5: The Association for Working Women. This group doesn't have much clout in collective bargaining, but it lobbies for women's concerns and runs public-relations campaigns and research to support its causes.

The emergence of such groups reflects a shifting work force. Today's more skilled workers, increasing numbers of them women, are scattered among myriad small firms and are more likely to spend their days in offices, not factories. They may work side by side with management and prefer to see themselves and their careers in individualistic terms. Yet traditional unions, say corporate critics, cling to old ways of protecting their narrow membership: rigid work rules, pattern bargaining across industries (rather than bargaining customized for the particular situation), and general antagonism to management.

"The problem is that unions in America don't match what people want," argues Dan Lacey, editor of a newsletter called *Workplace Trends*. "People want some kind of intermediary in the workplace, but they don't want to pay dues and wear a satin jacket." To his mind, many unions, in failing to adapt to a changing workplace, behave almost like some hidebound companies: "They know there's a demand, but they never come up with the right product."

For many workers, crossing a picket line just doesn't carry the severe stigma it once did. Fewer Americans have family or friends in unions. And, particularly when unemployment is high, an honest day's work—or any work—can have more appeal than solidarity and brotherhood.[4]

Concept Check

- Trace the development of the labor movement in the United States.
- What is the AFL-CIO, and how does it operate?
- What are the functions of a local union?
- What is the trend in union membership?

THE LEGAL ENVIRONMENT OF UNIONS

 Union activities have not always been businesslike. To a great extent, the way unions operate today—and the respectful relationship between unions and employers—is the result of laws passed over the past few decades.

NORRIS-LAGUARDIA ACT (ANTI-INJUNCTION ACT)

injunction Court order banning certain activities.

Before 1932, a company faced with striking or picketing workers could get the courts to order them back to work. It did so by requesting an **injunction**, a court order banning certain activities. Only rarely did a judge deny the employer's request for an injunction. Union members who didn't obey could be fined or sent to prison.

yellow-dog contracts Agreements by employees that, as a condition of being hired, they would not join a labor union; declared unenforceable by the Norris-La-Guardia Act.

Employers also used the courts to enforce **yellow-dog contracts**. In these, as a condition of being hired, employees agreed not to join a labor union. Employees who broke a yellow-dog contract could be fired and blacklisted. **Blacklists** of workers who were involved with unions were passed among employers to keep the workers from being hired.

blacklists Lists of workers involved with unions, circulated among employers to keep those workers from being hired.

The **Norris-LaGuardia Act** of 1932 (also known as the Anti-Injunction Act) largely ended the use of injunctions by employers. It banned their use to prevent strikes, among other things. The act also said yellow-dog contracts could not be enforced.

Norris-LaGuardia Act Federal legislation passed in 1932 that ended the use of injunctions by employers and declared yellow-dog contracts unenforceable.

WAGNER ACT (NATIONAL LABOR RELATIONS ACT)

Wagner Act Federal legislation passed in 1935 that allowed the formation of unions and provided for certification elections.

The Norris-LaGuardia Act opened the door to more union organizing, especially in mass-production industries. But employers were still not required to bargain with unions. Unions urged Congress to pass a law that would require employers to deal with them.

Congress responded with the National Labor Relations Act of 1935, commonly known as the **Wagner Act**. This law encouraged the formation of unions and the use of collective bargaining. It also provided a means for peacefully resolving disputes over union representation. The cornerstone of this important act is in Section 7:

Employees shall have the right to self-organization, to form, join, or assist labor organizations, to bargain collectively through representatives of their own choosing, and to engage in other concerted activities for the purpose of collective bargaining or other mutual aid or protection.

unfair labor practices Measures designed to keep workers from joining a union; banned by the Wagner Act.

The Wagner Act also protected workers from the employer by identifying **unfair labor practices**. For instance, an employer cannot discriminate against an employee who is involved in union activities. Nor can an employer fire an employee for joining a union. The **National Labor Relations Board (NLRB)** enforces the Wagner Act. More than forty offices of the NLRB are scattered throughout the United States. Administrative judges and field examiners investigate charges of employer or union wrongdoing and supervise elections held to decide on union representation.

National Labor Relations Board (NLRB) Federal agency that investigates charges of unfair labor practices and supervises union certification elections.

TAFT-HARTLEY ACT (LABOR-MANAGEMENT RELATIONS ACT)

Taft-Hartley Act Federal legislation passed in 1947 that prohibited unions from engaging in unfair practices.

Employers resisted the Wagner Act, and in some cases disobeyed it, until the Supreme Court upheld the law in 1937. Many employers saw the Wagner Act as too pro-labor. In 1947 Congress amended it with the Labor-Management Relations Act, commonly known as the **Taft-Hartley Act.** This act:

- Defined unfair union practices
- Outlined the rules for dealing with strikes of major economic impact
- Broadened employer options for dealing with unions
- Further defined the rights of employees as individuals

Among the unfair union practices banned by the Taft-Hartley Act were excessive or discriminatory fees and dues. (For example, monthly dues of $200 would be too much for a union member who earns only $2,000 per month.) Also, the act made it unlawful for picketing union members to block nonstriking employees from entering the business to go to work.

Emergency Strike Procedures

Right after World War II, union strike activity grew dramatically. Lengthy strikes disrupted business, and many firms and citizens suffered. In response, Congress put national emergency strike procedures into the Taft-Hartley Act. The President of the United States can thus declare a national emergency if a strike threatens the health and safety of Americans. And the President can temporarily stop the strike by having a federal judge issue an injunction. The injunction forces the strikers back to work for up to eighty days (known as the *cooling-off period*) while the employer and labor negotiators try to resolve their differences. If they don't reach an agreement within eighty days, the strike can resume. The President cannot issue a second injunction.

Federal Mediation and Conciliation Service

conciliation Process in which a specialist helps management and the union focus on the issues in dispute and acts as a go-between.

Congress also created the Federal Mediation and Conciliation Service as part of the Taft-Hartley Act. This service helps unions and employers negotiate. Agency specialists, who serve as impartial third parties between the union and the employer, use two processes: conciliation and mediation. In **conciliation**, the specialist helps management and the union focus on the issues and acts as a go-between.

mediation Process in which a third-party specialist holds talks with union and management negotiators to help bring about concession and compromise.

The specialist takes a stronger role in **mediation**. The mediator (the specialist) holds talks with union and management negotiators at separate meetings and at joint sessions. The mediator also suggests compromises. Mediators cannot issue binding decisions. Their only tools are communication and persuasion. (The process of labor negotiation is discussed in more detail later in the chapter.)

LANDRUM-GRIFFIN ACT (LABOR-MANAGEMENT REPORTING AND DISCLOSURE ACT)

Shortly after the AFL-CIO merger in 1955, some national unions, such as the Teamsters and the Bakery Workers, were accused of poor financial management, rigged elections for officers, and bribery of union officials. After an investigation, Congress passed the Labor-Management Reporting and Disclosure Act of 1959, often called the **Landrum-Griffin Act**. Unlike the Wagner and Taft-Hartley acts, this law deals mostly with the internal affairs of labor unions. It contains a bill of rights for union members, a set of rules for electing union officers, and safeguards to help make unions financially sound. It also requires that unions file detailed annual financial reports with the U.S. Secretary of Labor. The Department of Labor enforces the Landrum-Griffin Act.

During the early 1990s, the Department of Labor and the U.S. Attorney General investigated the Teamsters Union. The union agreed to such reforms as letting all union members elect top officials and submitting to review by a court-appointed board.[5]

Landrum-Griffin Act Federal legislation passed in 1959 that dealt mostly with the internal affairs of labor unions, such as the rights of union members and rules for electing officers.

Concept Check
- Discuss the key points of the Norris-LaGuardia Act and the Wagner Act.
- List the key points of the Taft-Hartley Act.
- Describe the key points of the Landrum-Griffin Act.

UNION ORGANIZING

3 Unions can be formed or gain new members in two ways:

- The unionized employer hires more workers, who choose, or are required, to join the union.
- The employees of a nonunion employer form or join a union.

A nonunion employer becomes unionized through an *organizing campaign*. The campaign is started either from within, by unhappy employees, or from outside, by a union that has picked the employer for an organizing drive. Once workers and the union have made contact, a union organizer tries to convince all the workers to sign *authorization cards*. These cards prove the workers' interest in having the union represent them. In most cases, employers resist this card-signing campaign by speaking out against unions in letters, posters, and employee assemblies. However, it is illegal for employers to interfere directly with the card-signing campaign or to coerce employees into not joining the union.

Once the union gets signed authorization cards from at least 30 percent of the employees, it can ask the National Labor Relations Board for a **union certification** election. This election, by secret ballot, determines whether the workers want to be represented by a union. The NLRB posts an election notice and defines the **bargaining unit**—that is, employees who are eligible to vote and who will be represented by the particular union if certified. Supervisors and managers cannot vote. The union and the employer then engage in a preelection campaign through speeches, memos, and meetings. Both try to convince workers to vote in their favor. (The benefits usually stressed by the unions in an organizing campaign are listed in Exhibit 13-2.) The election is conducted by the NLRB. If a majority vote for the union, the NLRB certifies the union as the exclusive

union certification election Election, by secret ballot, that determines whether workers want to be represented by a union.

bargaining unit Group of employees eligible to vote in a union election and represented by a particular union.

■ **Exhibit 13-2**
Benefits Stressed by
Unions in Organizing
Campaigns

Almost always stressed	Often stressed	Seldom stressed
Grievance procedures	More influence in decision making	Higher-quality products
Job security		Technical training
Improved benefits	Better working conditions	More job satisfaction
Higher pay	Lobbying opportunities	Increased production

decertification election
Election that allows workers
to end their representation by
a union.

bargaining agent. The employer then has to bargain with the union over wages, hours, and other terms of employment. The complete organizing process is summarized in Exhibit 13-3. After one year, if the union and the employer don't reach an agreement, the workers can petition for a **decertification election.** It is similar to the certification election, but it allows workers to vote out the union. Decertification elections are also held when workers become dissatisfied with a union that has represented them for a longer time. Recently the number of decertification elections has increased from fewer than 100 to about 1,000 a year. Still, fewer than 1 percent of union members are affected by this type of election.

Concept Check

• Describe the union organizing process.

■ **Exhibit 13-3**
Union Organizing Process

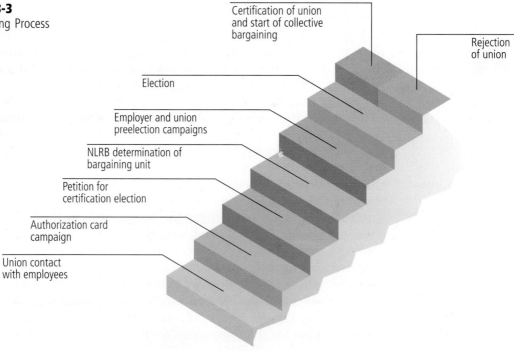

Certification of union and start of collective bargaining

Rejection of union

Election

Employer and union preelection campaigns

NLRB determination of bargaining unit

Petition for certification election

Authorization card campaign

Union contact with employees

NEGOTIATING UNION CONTRACTS

4 As noted earlier, collective bargaining is the process of negotiating, administering, and interpreting labor agreements. Union contracts covering almost 3.1 million workers were negotiated in 1993. Typically, both management and union negotiating parties are made up of only a few people. One person on each team is the chief spokesperson.

Bargaining begins with union and management negotiators setting a *bargaining agenda,* a list of contract issues that will be discussed. Much of the bargaining over the specifics takes place through face-to-face meetings and the exchange of written proposals. Demands, proposals, and counterproposals are exchanged during several rounds of bargaining. The resulting contract must then be approved by top management and by union members (see Exhibit 13-4).

■ **Exhibit 13-4**
Process of Negotiating
Labor Agreements

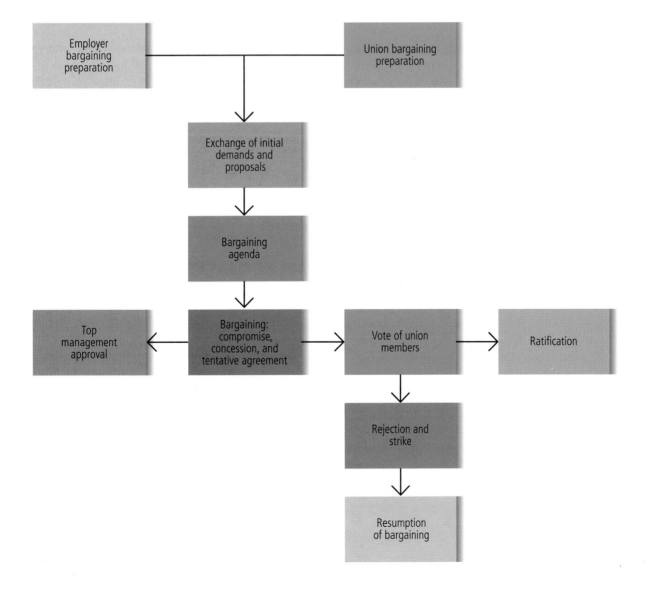

THE SUBSTANCE OF BARGAINING

5 The labor agreement negotiated by the union and the employer may range from a few pages to as many as 500. Some parts of the agreement have to be there, such as wages, hours, and working conditions. Employers must discuss and settle these issues. Other issues are optional. Demanding that the dates and times of union membership meetings be announced over the plant's intercom system is an example of an optional item.

Union Security

One of the key issues in a contract is union security. At one extreme is the **closed shop**, a place where only union members can be hired. The union serves, in effect, as an employment agency for the firm. The Taft-Hartley Act made closed shops illegal.

The most common form of union security today is the **union shop**. Nonunion people can be hired, but then they must join the union, normally within thirty or sixty days.

An **agency shop** does not require employees to join the union. But to keep working there, employees must pay the union a fee to cover its expenses in representing them. Whether or not a worker joins the union, it must fairly represent everyone.

The Taft-Hartley Act permitted the states to pass even stricter laws about union security. Any state can make all forms of union security illegal. Twenty-one states now have **right-to-work laws** (see Exhibit 13-5).

closed shop Place of employment where only union members can be hired; made illegal by the Taft-Hartley Act.

union shop Place of employment where nonunion people can be hired but must join the union within a specified period.

agency shop Place of employment where the employee does not have to join the union but must pay the union a fee.

right-to-work laws State laws that allow employees to work at a unionized company without having to join the union.

■ Exhibit 13-5
States with Right-to-Work Laws

States without right-to-work laws
States with right-to-work laws

In these states, employees can work at a unionized company without having to join the union. This is commonly known as an **open shop** arrangement. Workers don't have to join the union, and they don't pay dues or fees to the union.

Closely related to union security is the *dues checkoff*. When this clause is in the labor contract, the employer deducts union dues from members' paychecks. The funds are sent to the union at the end of each pay period. The automatic checkoff ensures that union dues will be paid on time.

Management Rights

When a company becomes unionized, management loses some of its decision-making rights. But management still has certain rights that can be negotiated in collective bargaining.

One way to resist union meddling in management matters is to put a *management-rights clause* in the labor agreement. Most union contracts have one. A typical clause gives the employer all rights to manage the business except as specified in the contract. For instance, the contract might say that seniority must be considered in deciding who to promote.

Another common management-rights provision is a lengthy list of areas that are not subject to collective bargaining. This list might secure management's right to schedule work hours; hire and fire workers; set production standards; determine the number of supervisors in each department; and promote, demote, and transfer workers. These rights, also known as *management prerogatives,* are not governed by any hard and fast rules. They differ from one contract to another.

Wages

Much bargaining effort goes into wage increases and fringe-benefit improvements. Once agreed to, they remain in effect for the life of the contract.

Some contracts provide for a **cost-of-living adjustment (COLA)**. Wages increase automatically as the cost of living goes up. A typical COLA clause might call for a wage increase of 1¢ per hour for each two-fifths of a point rise in the consumer price index. Often the adjustments are made only after the cost of living rises a certain amount, typically 6 percent in a year.

Other contracts provide for *lump-sum wage adjustments*. The workers' base pay remains unchanged for the contract period (usually two or three years). But they each may receive a bonus (or lump sum) once or twice during the contract. The lump-sum amount depends on the profitability of the firm and might range from $200 to $2,000.

To save money and jobs, the union and management might agree to a *two-tier wage system*. The starting pay of newly hired workers is far below that of workers who have been employed for some time. Both groups of workers may receive wage increases over the years. Ford Motor Company and the United Auto Workers reached an agreement in 1993 that new workers would only receive 75 percent of the standard $18-per-hour base pay for the first three years of employment.[6]

The union and the employer are usually both concerned about the firm's ability to pay higher wages. The ability of a firm to pay depends greatly on its profitability. But even if profits have declined, average to above-average wage increases are still possible if labor productivity increases.

Benefits

Besides asking for wage increases, unions usually want better fringe benefits. In some industries, such as steel and auto manufacturing, fringe benefits are 40 percent of the total cost of compensation. Benefits may include higher wages for overtime work, holiday work, and less desirable shifts; insurance programs (life, health and hospitalization, dental care); payment for certain nonwork time (rest periods, vacations, holidays, sick time); pensions; and income-maintenance plans. A fairly common income-maintenance plan is *supplementary unemployment benefits,* a fund set up by the employer to help laid-off workers.

give-backs
Worker benefits removed from union contracts.

Before the mid-1980s, unions gradually extended the list of benefits. But because of poor economic conditions, major technological changes, government deregulation, and increased competition, many unions have found themselves in a weaker bargaining position. Thus they have lost some of the benefits. These union **give-backs**, also called *concession bargaining,* have taken place in the auto, airline, steel, mining, and construction industries.

Job Security and Seniority

Cost-of-living adjustments, supplementary unemployment benefits, and certain other benefits give employees some financial security. But most financial security is directly related to job security—the assurance, to some degree, that workers will keep their jobs. Of course, job security depends primarily on the continued success and financial well-being of the company.

seniority Length of an employee's continuous service with a firm.

Seniority, the length of an employee's continuous service with a firm, is discussed in about 90 percent of all labor contracts. Seniority is a factor in job security; usually unions want the workers with the most seniority to have the most job security. Seniority also serves other purposes in collective bargaining. One is to determine an employee's eligibility for vacations. It is also important in calculating severance pay (additional pay given to employees who leave the company) and pension benefits. Seniority in these areas is called *benefit rights.* Another purpose is to determine job assignments. People with job rights seniority have first choice of higher-paying jobs, the preferred shift, overtime work, and job transfers.

Concept Check

- Explain the collective bargaining process.
- What do unions want from collective bargaining?
- What are management rights?

GRIEVANCE AND ARBITRATION

6

grievance Formal complaint by an employee or a union that management has violated some part of the labor contract.

The union's main way to police the contract is the grievance procedure. A **grievance** is a formal complaint, by an employee or by the union, that management has violated some part of the contract. Under a typical contract, the employee starts by presenting the grievance to the supervisor, either in person or in writing (see Exhibit 13-6). A shop steward may be at the meeting or may just get a copy of the grievance.

If the problem isn't solved, the grievance is put in writing (if it hasn't already been). The employee, one or more union officials, the supervisor, and perhaps the plant manager then discuss the grievance. If the matter still can't be resolved, another meeting takes place, with higher-level representatives of both parties. If top management and the local union president can't resolve the grievance, it goes to arbitration.

arbitration Settlement of labor-management disputes by having a third party make a binding decision.

Arbitration is the settling of a labor-management dispute by having a third party—a single arbitrator or a panel—make the decision. The deci-

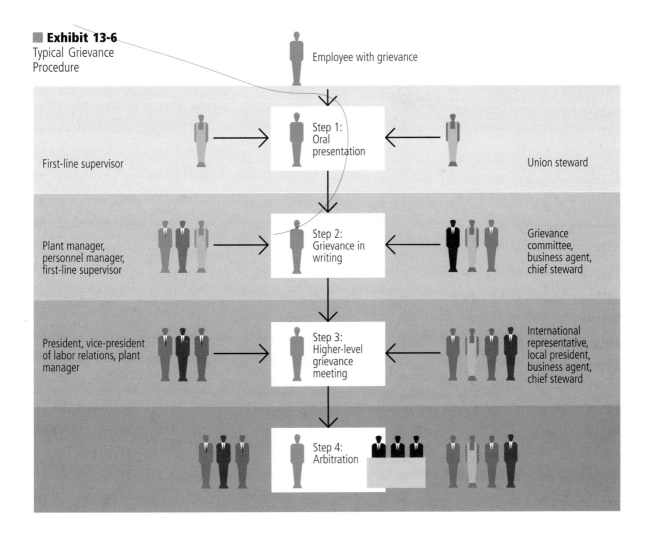

Exhibit 13-6
Typical Grievance Procedure

Employee with grievance

First-line supervisor → **Step 1: Oral presentation** ← Union steward

Plant manager, personnel manager, first-line supervisor → **Step 2: Grievance in writing** ← Grievance committee, business agent, chief steward

President, vice-president of labor relations, plant manager → **Step 3: Higher-level grievance meeting** ← International representative, local president, business agent, chief steward

Step 4: Arbitration

■ A strike is a union's most powerful weapon. It is used to put pressure on an employer to concede to the union's demands for higher wages and better benefits. During a strike, union members often picket in an effort to convince the employer to shut down and to persuade customers and suppliers not to do business with the firm.

sion is binding on the union and the employer. The arbitrator reviews the grievance at a hearing and then makes the decision. Only sometimes can the decision be appealed through the courts.

A much-publicized example of arbitration took place in the sports world. For the past decade, major league baseball owners have been trying to control players' pay. In the mid-1980s, after double-digit pay increases, owners decided simply to stop bidding on free agents. (Free agents are players with six or more years in the majors. They can sell their skills to the club that bids the most.) Players' salaries plunged from more than 38 percent of league revenues to about 31 percent in 1990. The players' union filed a grievance, and arbitrators ruled that team owners had violated the labor contract. They fined the owners $102.5 million.

Concept Check
- Describe the grievance procedure.
- Explain the arbitration process.

WEAPONS OF LABOR-MANAGEMENT CONFLICT

7 Both sides to labor-management conflicts have powerful weapons. Unions can fight with strikes, product boycotts, picketing, and corporate campaigns.

Employers can fight with lockouts, strikebreakers, bankruptcy, and mutual-aid pacts. Exhibit 13-7 lists the weapons of both sides.

UNION WEAPONS

strike Temporary work stoppage.

The **strike** is the most powerful union weapon, but it is usually the action of last resort. Although a strike may hurt the employer, it also means loss of pay to employees. On the average, fewer than 2 percent of U.S. workers are involved in strikes each year. And with few exceptions, strikes tend to last under a month.

Strikes occur most often over such economic issues as wages, pensions, vacation time, and other benefits. They usually result from a strike vote of the union membership. A strike normally starts right after the old union contract has expired, if management and labor can't agree on new contract terms. Sometimes a group of union members or an entire local union will strike without the approval of the national union, while the contract is still in effect. This action, which is often illegal because it violates the contract, is called a **wildcat strike**. A strike by workers not directly involved in a collective bargaining dispute, to support strikers who are, is a **sympathy strike**.

A different form of refusal to work is the **sick-out**. A sick-out occurs when a group of employees claim they are not working because of illness. Employers must pay sick leave to workers during a sick-out, and operations are disrupted. During the busy 1990 Christmas season, after a bitter contract dispute

wildcat strike Strike by local members of a national union while the labor contract is in effect, in violation of the contract.

sympathy strike Strike mounted by workers not directly involved in a collective bargaining dispute to support strikers who are directly involved.

sick-out Union weapon in which members claim they are not working because of illness.

■ **Exhibit 13-7**
Weapons of Unions and Management

Union		Management	
Strike	Employees refuse to work.	**Lockout**	Employer refuses to let employees enter plant to work.
Boycott	Employees try to keep customers and others from doing business with employer.	**Strike-breakers**	Employer uses nonunion employees to do jobs of striking union employees.
Picket	Employees march near entrance of firm to publicize their view of dispute and discourage customers.	**Mutual-aid pact**	Employer receives money from other companies in industry to cover some of income lost because of strikes.
Corporate campaign	Union disrupts stockholder meetings or buys company stock to have more influence over management.	**Bankruptcy**	Employer cancels labor agreement.

that had lasted many months, hundreds of American Airlines pilots called in sick. Thousands of flights had to be canceled. The airline ran full-page advertisements in newspapers around the country apologizing to travelers and blaming the pilots. But a new contract signed in February 1991 gave the pilots a very good salary structure.

The union's most often used weapon is **picketing**. When a union calls a strike, it usually sets up picket lines to advertise the strike and discourage the employer from staying open. Union members line up and parade back and forth in front of the employer's site. Picketers carry signs saying the employer is unfair. They try to persuade nonstriking workers to stop working and other people (customers and suppliers) to stop doing business with the company.

A **primary boycott** is the union's effort to keep people from doing business with a firm involved in a labor dispute. If the Oil, Chemical, and Atomic Workers Union has a contract dispute with Shell Oil Company, the union can tell its members not to buy Shell products. The union may also start a publicity campaign to convince other customers not to buy from Shell. If the boycott hurts sales, it may force the company to give in to union demands.

A 1988 ruling by the Supreme Court gave unions the right to use **secondary boycotts**. A secondary boycott targets companies doing business with a firm that is the subject of a primary boycott. For instance, Cesar Chavez organized a grape boycott to force California growers to accept the United Farm Workers as the bargaining agent for farm laborers. At one time, over 17 million Americans quit buying grapes. In some states, a secondary boycott was organized against Kroger stores, because they still bought grapes from California growers.

The **corporate campaign** is a fairly new union weapon. Often a union tries to disrupt the stockholder meetings of a company it wants to pressure. Sometimes a union buys a great deal of stock in a company with which a dispute is in progress, so it can have more influence. A union may also threaten to withdraw great sums of money from banks that do business with the firm. The goal of a corporate campaign, or any other union weapon, is to make the employer give in to union demands. Recent union corporate campaigns have been conducted against the Diamond Walnut Cooperative, Fisher Scientific, Hood Furniture Company, and the Frontier Hotel (Las Vegas).

MANAGEMENT WEAPONS

Management has its own weapons in labor disputes. One of the most effective is the **lockout**, the refusal to let workers enter a plant or building to work. If the workers can't do their jobs, they don't get paid. Also, management can hire temporary workers during a lockout. But sometimes a lockout can benefit the union. Overhead costs (costs for lease payments and management salaries) continue whether a plant is open or closed, putting pressure on management to end the lockout.

Strikebreakers (or "scabs") are nonunion employees hired to replace striking union workers. If suitable strikebreakers can be found, the company can stay open and keep earning profits. The problem with strikebreaking is finding qualified people. Recently both International Paper Company and Caterpillar Incorporated replaced strikers with permanent replacements. In

picketing Union weapon in which union members form a line in front of an employer's site and try to persuade others to stop doing business with the firm.

primary boycott Effort to keep people from buying the products of a firm with which the union has a dispute.

secondary boycott Boycott of companies doing business with a firm that is the subject of a primary boycott.

corporate campaign Attempt to disrupt the business dealings of a firm with which a labor dispute is in progress.

lockout Refusal by management to let workers enter a plant or building to work.

strikebreakers Nonunion employees hired to replace striking union workers; also called scabs.

■ Eastern Airlines declared bankruptcy when it was struck by the Machinists, Pilots, and Flight Attendants unions in 1989. The company then hired nonunion pilots and other employees as part of its reorganization. This is one weapon management has at its disposal to limit the damage a strike can do to a company.

mutual-aid pact Pooling of resources within an industry to help cover the costs of a member company whose workers go on strike

1993, Kroger hired unemployed members of the United Auto Workers as permanent replacements for strikers in Detroit.

Another weapon used by employers in some industries is the **mutual-aid pact**. Companies in the industry pool their financial resources into a fund that can be used to help cover the costs of any member company whose workers go on strike. These pacts have been used with success in the airline, tire, and newspaper industries.

Finally, under provisions of the Bankruptcy Code of 1978, a company can file for *bankruptcy* in the face of a strike and petition for time to reorganize the business. Eastern Airlines filed for bankruptcy in March 1989, within a week of strikes by the Machinist, Pilots, and Flight Attendants unions. Replacement pilots and other nonunion employees were hired as part of Eastern's reorganization. The company, however, finally went out of business. A company in bankruptcy is controlled by a trustee. When the union tries to improve wages and benefits, those who are still owed money usually urge the trustee to reject the demands.

Small businesses can find it hard to resolve labor-management conflict. Whereas large companies have professionally trained human resource man-

agers to help resolve conflicts, most small firms do not. Owners of small companies often say, "It's my plant; I own it; I created it and no one is going to tell me how to run it," says Melvin Wells, chief administrative law judge at the National Labor Relations Board.[7] "Many small business owners got to where they are because they are good at controlling. It's a little scary to give up that control," says Labor Secretary Robert Reich.[8] In 1993, two-thirds of unfair labor practice complaints filed with the National Labor Relations Board are filed against firms with fewer than one hundred workers.[9] The following Small Business Trends box illustrates the labor troubles of some small firms.

TRENDS

Small Business

No Winners

Nearly four years into his company's labor dispute, a bitter Art Nevill wonders if the business will be able to survive. Sales at the company he runs and half-owns, Refuse Compactor Service Inc., have slipped from nearly $7 million in 1989 to only about $2 million in 1993. And no one can put a price tag on the emotional toll. A deteriorating labor situation at Refuse Compactor culminated in a strike. It left Jesus Vela, a former welder at the company, finding only day-to-day work and separated from his wife. At home, "little problems would become big problems," he laments in Spanish.

The labor conflict at Refuse Compactor shows what can go wrong when a proud, independent owner faces workers making demands on that independence. But Nevill wasn't an easy man to work for. "He used to scream at you every day," says Javier Soriano, who joined Refuse as a welder in 1976. Soriano tells of asking Nevill to give Vela, who spoke no English, a 25-cent raise to $6.50 an hour. "Art said he could do it if he took the money from me," Soriano says.

In the spring of 1989, Tony Abuanza and another employee told plant manager George Miller that the workers wanted more pay, an extra week of vacation, and another holiday. Miller told them to put their request in writing. But workers apparently took that as rejection. A week later, the company received a letter from the UAW, saying that workers had signed cards seeking a vote on representation from the union. Within weeks, the workers, hoping for higher pay and relief from workplace pressure, voted the union in, 29-17.

Relations between Refuse Compactor and its workers deteriorated quickly. Soriano says that in a meeting with about a dozen workers, Nevill told them that "the [expletive] union will never tell me what to do in my shop," adding, "How would you like it if I told you what to do in your house?" Seeing his 20-year-old creation slip into outsiders' hands, Nevill presented a "final" offer, and called workers in to argue that the union was a bad idea.

As Nevill fought back, the union, worried that its support was dwindling, turned its threat into reality: On November 17, 1989, the workers called a strike. Neither side expected more than a two-week impasse. At $100 a week in strike pay from the UAW, it would be tough for the workers to live. At the same time, the UAW felt that it couldn't show weakness lest it demonstrate to other business owners that a hard line would soften union demands.

As the strike dragged on for weeks and then months, morale decayed. Gradually, the number of pickets shrank to 17, with many workers leaving to find other employment or return to Mexico. The business began to suffer, too. Customers coming to the gate had to wait until strikers moved out of the driveway. Eventually they declined to come. Truck drivers were prodded to keep away. Many did.

The company's work force has dropped from more than 60 to about 15. The UAW local has spent far more than it can ever hope to recoup in union dues. NLRB investigators have been poring over company records, trying to determine how much it owes in back pay to the strikers. The union claims that Refuse should pay over $300,000. Nevill is considering filing for bankruptcy if the back pay claim is too high. Both sides remain disillusioned. The striking workers have long since given up hopes of working for Refuse again. Meanwhile, Nevill considers his business to be "back to 1975" in size. Concludes the owner: "I hope I never see another employee or another NLRB person in my life."[10]

Concept Check

- What weapons can the unions use in a labor conflict?
- What weapons does management have?

THE FUTURE OF LABOR-MANAGEMENT RELATIONS

8

Several trends are affecting business and the American labor movement. These are some of the more important ones:

- *Changing mix of ages, sexes, and races in the labor force and therefore in union membership:* The ratio of female to male workers continues to increase in the United States. Women's share of the labor force will grow to 47 percent by the year 2000, up from 45 percent in 1990. During the 1990s, the number of middle-age workers will grow by 9 million. The African-American labor force will grow twice as fast as the white labor force. The number of Hispanics will increase at four times the pace of whites.[11] Women have always been less prone than white men to join unions. Minorities are slightly more likely to join. Thus unions may have to switch targets. Also, older union workers sometimes find their interests at odds with those of younger union members. A changing membership may mean the need to focus on different union issues.

- *Unprecedented power for employees due to new union contracts in some industries:* Contracts at Inland Steel, LTV, Northwest Airlines, and TWA have set up formal mechanisms for worker input. In some cases, employees also stand to exercise significant control over key aspects of corporate decision-making, such as capital investment,

mergers, asset sales, and even hiring senior management. Pacts at
LTV and Inland Steel gave workers or their representatives seats on
the board of directors, profit sharing, and strong job-security guarantees in return for simpler work rules and job reductions through
attrition. As TWA struggles through Chapter 11 bankruptcy, its unions
agreed to $660 million in concessions in exchange for 45 percent of
the company's equity. They got four of the fifteen board seats and
the right to name one of two vice-chairmen.[12] The result is that, with
more power to influence the company, employees may feel less
need for protection through labor unions.

- *Restructuring of corporate America through mergers, acquisitions, down-
  sizing, bankruptcy, and plant closings:* In nearly all these situations, the
  number of workers declines, which translates to a decline in union
  members.
- *Technological change and innovation, especially in manufacturing:*
  Such change means fewer workers are needed on the assembly line.
  Job security, income protection, and retraining of workers have become
  as important as wage increases to labor unions.
- *Foreign competition and plants moving to countries with cheaper labor:*
  This change poses very real threats to union and nonunion companies in
  the United States. Much higher wages make U.S. firms less competitive.
- *Continuing increases in the cost of health care:* Growing numbers of
  people are not covered by health care insurance. In 1991, nearly $700
  of the price of each new car was the cost of health care insurance for
  auto makers.
- *Rapid growth of evening and weekend work for dual-income families:*
  The result is a so-called "split-shift" family. Today, one out of every six
  working mothers with children under fourteen holds a night job or
  works on a rotating shift. The same is true for one out of five working fathers. Thus one out of every six two-income families with children under six has work hours that don't overlap.[13] There is no room
  in a worker's schedule for the unexpected, such as a sick child or a
  school play. The main cause is the growth in service businesses, which
  need the most shift and weekend labor. Union membership has not
  been a top priority among split-shift parents.

These trends suggest that in the mid-1990s unions may need to cooperate
more with employers. They may need to be more willing to link pay and performance. But union-management cooperation will give workers greater control over their jobs and indeed, in running the company. An example of the
gains to be achieved through cooperation is Ford Motor Company. Ford sold
nearly as many vehicles in 1993 as it did in 1983, using half as many production workers. The most important factor in Ford's increased productivity was
increased cooperation of its work force. Over a period of years Ford persuaded its employees to work harder and smarter, and to help management find ways to cut costs. Ford now takes one-third fewer worker-hours to
build cars than General Motors, giving Ford a cost advantage of $795 per
vehicle.[14]

On the other side, management may need to give union leaders a broader role in decision making, as noted above. The National Association of Manufacturers, whose members account for 85 percent of U.S. manufacturing output, has strongly endorsed employee participation in decision making.[15] Wise managers will see the advantages. After all, if a company goes out of business, both management and labor lose.

Concept Check

- Describe changes in the American workforce.
- Why may unions become more cooperative with management during the remainder of the decade?

■ SUMMARY

1. Understand the history of the U.S. union movement, and describe labor organizations today.

The forerunners of U.S. labor unions were guilds formed to further craftsmen's interests. Partly because of the courts, employers often succeeded in opposing these groups. The Knights of Labor was one of the first national labor organizations, but it was not very good at improving the lot of workers.

In 1881, many of the craft groups left the Knights of Labor to form the American Federation of Labor. Under Samuel Gompers, the AFL pursued such practical matters as union rights and better wages, hours, and working conditions for members.

In 1935 John L. Lewis and the United Mine Workers of America left the AFL to form the Congress of Industrial Organizations. Until the early 1950s, AFL and CIO unions competed for membership. The two groups merged as the AFL-CIO in 1955.

Today the U.S. labor movement consists of the AFL-CIO labor federation, national and international unions, and local unions. As an umbrella organization, the AFL-CIO represents about one-tenth of the total U.S. work force. A national union consists of many local unions in a particular industry, skilled trade, or geographic area. The main functions of the local unions are collective bargaining, worker relations and membership services, and community and political activities.

2. Understand the role of federal legislation in the growth of unionism and collective bargaining.

The courts have gradually taken a bigger role in the settlement of labor disputes. The Norris-LaGuardia Act banned employers' use of injunctions and yellow-dog contracts. In 1935 Congress passed the Wagner Act, which encouraged the creation of unions, defined unfair labor practices, and established the National Labor Relations Board. This act was amended in 1947 by the Taft-Hartley Act, which placed some restraints on union activities. In 1959 Congress passed the Landrum-Griffin Act, which dealt mainly with the internal affairs of unions.

continued

3. Explain the union organizing process.

A company is unionized through an organizing campaign. When the union gets signed authorization cards from 30 percent of the firm's employees, the NLRB conducts a union certifying election. A majority vote is needed to certify the union as the exclusive bargaining agent. The union and the employer then begin collective bargaining and have one year in which to reach an agreement.

4. Explain the collective bargaining process.

Collective bargaining is the process of negotiating, administering, and interpreting labor agreements. Both union and management negotiators prepare a bargaining proposal. The two sides meet and exchange demands and ideas. Bargaining consists of compromises and concessions that lead to a tentative agreement. Top management then approves or disapproves the agreement for the management team. Union members vote to either approve or reject the contract.

5. Understand the important issues and items in labor agreements.

One of the most important issues for the union in negotiating an agreement is union security. Closely related is the dues checkoff. To protect its rights, the employer often includes a management-rights clause in the labor agreement. Much of the effort that goes into negotiations is devoted to deciding on wage increases and fringe-benefit improvements. Job security, another union concern, is assured mainly through seniority provisions.

6. Discuss the grievance procedure.

The main way the union polices the labor contract is through the grievance procedure. Typically, in the first step the employee presents the grievance to the supervisor, perhaps in the presence of the shop steward. Later steps involve higher and higher levels of union and company officials. If the issue isn't settled at any of these levels, the grievance may go to arbitration.

7. Identify and describe the economic weapons of unions and management.

The union's main way to pressure the employer is the strike. It also uses boycotts and picketing. Management's main ways to put pressure on labor are the lockout, strikebreaking, mutual-aid pacts, and bankruptcy.

8. Discuss trends affecting the American work force and labor-management relations.

Workers are getting older, the ratio of female to male employees is increasing, and the African-American and Hispanic labor forces are growing much faster than the white labor force. New contracts are giving workers unprecedented decision-making power. Financial restructuring of American business has reduced the number of workers in many organizations. Technology has reduced the demand for assembly-line workers. Foreign competition threatens unions as well as employers. Health care costs are becoming a bigger part of total labor costs. More evening and split-shift work in dual-income families is creating "split-shift" families. As a result of these trends, unions and employers are finding reasons to try to work together.

■ DISCUSSION QUESTIONS

1. Can unions be considered a monopoly? Explain.

2. Would you join a labor union? Why or why not? What would you say to co-workers who disagreed with you and were trying to persuade you to follow them?

3. From 1935 to early 1974, unions won from 55 to 60 percent of the certification elections. Since 1974, unions have been winning slightly less than 50 percent of such elections. Why are unions less successful today? Why have employers been winning more of these elections?

4. The "right-to-work" issue resulting from the Taft-Hartley Act has created an ongoing debate. What are the arguments for and against the "right-to-work" clause? What is your personal position?

5. Do current rules for representation elections favor the employer or the union? What changes, if any, would you recommend in the rules about what is fair or unfair during an organizing campaign? Explain your answer.

6. You are the president of a small firm (thirty employees). You are not unionized, but you would like to have an appeals process that is like a grievance procedure. Discuss what this appeals process might be.

7. Should employees of the federal government be allowed to strike? If not, why? If so, which ones? Why not the remainder? How should labor disputes in the public sector be resolved?

8. Many recent union contracts have included a cost-of-living adjustment. If this adjustment adds to inflation, does it benefit the workers or not? Explain.

9. Have you or a member of your family ever been a union member? If so, name the union and describe it in terms of size, member characteristics, strike history, and bargaining effectiveness.

■ CASE

Skiing into a Grievance

Station KARL, Channel 10 in Denver, requires all on-air personalities to seek written permission before accepting any free-lance work or activities, including charity appearances. The reason is that KARL has an interest in the image of its on-air employees. KARL understands why outsiders seek appearances from on-air personalities: these people are already known to the public. But that public image is the stock in trade, the capital, of KARL's news department. Also, the Federal Communications Act bans broadcasters from soliciting gifts (payola) in exchange for air time, and KARL's policy helps prevent payola.

Don Frankin was KARL's lead newscaster. He was asked to participate in a fund-raising event for the Muscular Dystrophy Association. A number of eligible bachelors were being asked to take part in "The Great Date."

Each bachelor would come up with his own date package, which would be "sold" to the highest bidder. The bachelor would be part of the date package. Among the other bachelors were people employed by other TV and radio stations. Frankin agreed to participate. He planned a date package consisting of two round-trip tickets to Switzerland on Swiss Air, a one-week stay at a Swiss hotel, and the use of ski equipment during the stay.

Larry Walther, vice president of KARL, first learned of Frankin's involvement in the event from a newspaper article. Walther called the article to the attention of the general manager of KARL-TV, Bill Smith. They decided to call in Frankin to find out what was happening. In their own words, it was strictly a "fact-finding mission."

The meeting was attended by Frankin, Walther, and William Choate, shop steward of the American Federation of Television and Radio Artists (AFTRA), of which Frankin was a member. Frankin and Choate repeatedly asked Walther if there was any problem with Frankin's participation in the fund-raising event. Frankin asked if station management had any concerns, because he was there to answer any questions they had. Walther said that he didn't know if there were any concerns, that he was just seeking information.

This conversation concluded with Choate urging Walther to let them know before the event if there was any problem so it could be remedied. Walther responded by saying that he had read the article and had listened to Frankin and Choate and heard their explanation. He was going to think about the situation and decide what action he needed to take. Walther left both Frankin and Choate with the impression that he would get back to them. He never did.

The bachelor auction took place more than two weeks later. Frankin's date package was sold for $2,250 after a bidding war. Frankin and his package were bought by a woman Frankin had been dating. Frankin went on the trip with her. He never made a secret of it. Other people in the newsroom knew about it. Frankin even had to schedule vacation time with Walther to take the trip. Nobody ever told him not to go.

When Frankin returned, he got an official written reprimand from the company, signed by Walther. The gist of the letter was that Frankin was in trouble because he did not bother to seek management opinion or approval for this or other outside events. There had been no message from the company at all before this warning letter.

AFTRA filed a grievance on Frankin's behalf. They sought the immediate removal of the letter from all KARL-TV files, a formal written apology to Don Frankin, a formal statement from the company that it would stop all discriminatory practices, and confirmation that Larry Walther had been formally reprimanded for his actions in this matter.

During the arbitration hearing, general manager Bill Smith conceded that he had never signed permission for an employee to engage in charity activities and that he had made no decision approving or disapproving Frankin's fund-raising activities. According to Smith, KARL disciplined Frankin strictly because he had acted without permission.[16]

Questions

1. Did Don Frankin take proper action in his meeting with Walther? Should he have asked for written permission at that time?

2. You are the arbitrator. What are your conclusions and recommendations?

3. Should white-collar employees join labor unions? Why or why not?

Your Career in Human-Resource Management

If you would like a career in business and enjoy working with people, consider human-resource management. This field requires the ability to get along with different types of people and to communicate effectively. You do not have to be outgoing to have strong interpersonal skills. In fact, a quiet, friendly manner can be an asset. Take speech, writing, and other communication courses in college to strengthen your interpersonal skills.

A career in human-resource management offers many challenges and opportunities. For instance, if you choose this field, you will have a chance to help ensure that all employees are treated fairly. Decisions about who to hire, promote, and train; about how much to pay; and about how to help dissatisfied employees must all be made fairly. When employees sense that the employer is unfair, their work attitudes and behaviors suffer. Absenteeism, low motivation, lack of concern for the quality of products, lack of commitment, and even sabotage may result. These attitudes and behaviors affect costs, productivity, and profits. As a communicator and an advocate, the human-resource professional helps the organization succeed.

Dream Career: Manager of Corporate Training

The training and development of employees is an area of great importance for the 1990s. U.S. companies spend over $215 billion a year on formal and informal training. That's only slightly less than the $240 billion spent nationally each year on elementary, secondary, and higher education. Technical training in robotics and automation and basic education for those who have not finished high school are two areas of growth in the field of training.

A manager of corporate training supervises specialists who design training programs, conduct those programs, and assess them. The training manager may also oversee a reimbursement program for employees who take outside courses, arrange for special noncredit courses for employees on college campuses, and represent the firm in designing apprenticeship programs with labor unions.

- *Places of employment:* Any relatively large firm (1,000 or more employees).
- *Skills required:* Four-year or master's degree with a major in human-resource management, adult education, psychology, or occupational education.
- *Employment outlook through 2005:* Very good.
- *Salaries:* $25,000–$30,000 to start for corporate training specialists; $50,000–$75,000 for managers; higher salaries for those with more experience or an advanced college degree.

Where the Opportunities Are

Job Analyst

A very important part of human-resource management is job analysis. This involves studying an organization's jobs to set pay rates, conducting employee performance appraisals, and designing training programs. A job analyst may also work with industrial engineers to spell out the tasks of new jobs. The end result of an analyst's job is job descriptions, which explain the duties, training, and skills that each job requires.

- *Places of employment:* Mostly in larger cities. Any organization that has a fully staffed human-resource department will likely employ one or more job analysts.
- *Skills required:* Two- or four-year college degree with almost any major. Very good interpersonal (or interviewing) and written communication skills are essential. A job analyst should enjoy detail work. This is usually considered an entry-level job in the human-resource department.
- *Employment outlook through 2005:* Good.
- *Salaries:* $25,000–$45,000.

Director of Labor Relations

Unionized firms with several hundred union employees employ an experienced person as chief spokesperson in dealings with the union. This person negotiates the labor agreement, meets with union officials to resolve grievances, and serves as the firm's main link to the union. At times the director of labor relations will interact with government agencies, such as the National Labor Relations Board, the Federal Mediation and Conciliation Service, and the Department of Labor. In addition to effective communication and negotiation skills, this person needs to know a lot about labor law, wage determination, and report and document preparation.

- *Places of employment:* Unionized firms anywhere in the country, but particularly manufacturing firms in the Northeast and Midwest and on the West Coast.
- *Skills required:* In larger firms a law degree; preferably a master's degree in industrial relations in most medium-size to large companies.
- *Employment outlook through 2005:* Fair.
- *Salaries:* $40,000–$90,000, depending greatly on experience and educational background.

Plant Health and Safety Officer

The Occupational Safety and Health Act of 1970 requires that manufacturing facilities and offices be safe and healthy places to work. Virtually all firms that employ 500 or more workers have a safety officer. This person conducts safety inspections, keeps accident and injury records, provides safety training, and may help design safety features into equipment.

- *Places of employment:* Any business or other type of establishment that employs several hundred or more people. Even large office buildings often have a health and safety officer.
- *Skills required:* Four-year degree with a major in industrial engineering, safety engineering, industrial hygiene, occupational nursing, industrial administration, or some area of business administration.
- *Employment outlook through 2005:* Very good, especially in manufacturing firms and health care organizations.
- *Salaries:* $30,000–$60,000. The higher salaries are associated with positions requiring an engineering background.

Human-Resource Development Specialist

The past decade has seen much corporate restructuring through mergers, acquisitions, and retrenchments. Some firms have created internal consulting jobs for people who can smooth corporate change and development. The duties of a development specialist include counseling employees about their performance, conducting stress-management programs, mediating disputes between departments, helping employees find new jobs, and counseling employees with personal or career problems.

- *Places of employment:* Large organizations, which are most likely to be located in metropolitan areas.
- *Skills required:* Master's (even doctoral) degree in psychology, business administration, human-resource management, industrial or organizational psychology, or related behavioral or social sciences.
- *Employment outlook through 2005:* Good. Only very large firms are likely to hire human-resource development specialists.
- *Salaries:* $35,000–$80,000. The lower salaries are for people with a master's degree; the higher salaries are for those with experience or a doctoral degree.

College Recruiter

Many firms, especially large ones, recruit graduates from colleges and universities. A corporate college recruiter is involved in employment planning and assessing human-resource needs for professional, technical, and managerial employees; selecting colleges to visit; traveling to those colleges to interview graduating students; performing preliminary screening of these appli-

cants; and recommending applicants to line managers for in-depth interviews. The job can involve a lot of travel, especially in the late fall and early spring. The recruiter may also be responsible for developing recruiting brochures for distribution to applicants through college placement offices across the country.

- *Places of employment:* Any firm, government agency, or other type of organization that hires large numbers of college graduates.
- *Skills required:* Four-year college degree with almost any major. Very good oral and written communication skills are essential.
- *Employment outlook through 2005:* Good, although fewer positions are available in manufacturing firms. This job is usually reserved for those who know about the organization.
- *Salaries:* $25,000–$65,000. Larger firms in metropolitan areas pay higher salaries.

Employment Interviewer

Whether looking for a job or trying to fill one, you could find yourself turning to an employment interviewer for help. Working primarily in private personnel-supply firms or in state employment offices, employment interviewers act as brokers, matching applicants' skills with

■ A manager of corporate training oversees the design and implementation of new training programs.

available job openings.

The employer places a "job order" with the personnel agency, describing the job and its requirements, such as education and experience. Employment interviewers search through the records they have of jobseekers, to find the best match of applicant and job. Computers often are used to keep records and match jobs and employees, but they are no substitute for personal contact between interviewer and applicants. Since the personnel-supply firm usually is paid by the employer to recruit workers for specified jobs, the employment interviewer's expertise is judged by the quality of job applicants he or she sends to the company. Therefore, the employment interviewer must maintain a good file of qualified job seekers. Evaluation of employee job skills, checking of background and references, and sometimes testing job skills are important parts of the job.

Employment interviewers must have good people skills: They must be able to maintain good relations with employers, in order to keep a steady flow of job orders coming. Also, they must be able to counsel job applicants. They sometimes offer tips on how to present a positive image and on interviewing techniques, and they sometimes have to offer tactful but persuasive counsel if an applicant's job or salary requests do not match his or her qualifications or are more than the market will bear.

Many personnel-supply firms specialize in placing applicants in particular kinds of jobs, such as secretarial, word processing, and computer programming. Some firms specialize in placing professionals in such fields as engineering, accounting, law, management, and health. Still other firms specialize in supplying office help on a temporary basis. Indeed, temporary agencies have seen a boom as, increasingly, employers are hiring temporary employees, in order to reduce the costs of pay and benefits associated with hiring permanent employees.

Employment interviewers who work in the public sector in state jobs find that some applicants are hindered by problems such as poor language skills, lack of educa-tion, drug or alcohol abuse, or a prison record. In some states, it is the employment interviewer's responsibility to counsel hard-to-place applicants and to refer them to the appropriate resources for literacy or language instruction, vocational training, and other assistance. In other states, specially trained job counselors perform that task.

Desirable characteristics for employment interviewers, whether in the private or the public sector, are good communication skills, sales ability, a desire to help people, and office skills, including a knowledge of computers. A friendly manner is an asset because personal interaction plays a large role in the job.

- *Places of employment:* Across the United States, in medium to large cities.
- *Skills required:* Usually a college degree in both public and private sector jobs. For personnel-supply firms that place professionals, a master's or even a doctoral degree in the profession may be a prerequisite.
- *Employment outlook through 2005:* Will keep pace with general job growth in the economy. More opportunities in private-sector personnel-supply firms, particularly those that supply temporary help, than in the public sector.
- *Salaries:* Average in the private sector, $17,000–$25,000, with those work-ing on commission and those who place professional workers earning considerably more. Average in the public sector, $13,000–$20,000.

Part 6

Marketing Management

Overview

Marketing is much more than advertising an item or a service to the public. It includes everything from consumer research and product development to pricing, packaging, customer service, and distribution strategies. Marketing managers put an incredible amount of time into developing a product before it ever reaches the shelf or display rack.

Essentially, marketing strategy encompasses four areas: product, placement, price, and promotion. Corporations assign people to analyze and develop what they hope will be the perfect marketing plan for each product they sell. Often, this process begins with a basic question: How will this product be accepted in today's—and tomorrow's—social and cultural environment?

Demographics are important when analyzing potential markets for a product or service. A current major demographic trend is the so-called "graying" of America. A fourth of all Americans are over 50 years old. If that doesn't seem significant, consider that these "older" Americans control 80 percent of the nation's wealth! That translates into a lot of purchasing power.

Marketing is used in not-for-profit organizations as well as for-profit businesses. It applies to both consumer and industrial products and services. The following chapters cover all aspects of marketing. You will discover that it is an area of business that makes use of employees' diverse talents and interests, from sociology, to statistics, to accounting. Perhaps the one constant of the marketing environment is that it's always changing.

 ## Seta, Appleman & Showell

Anticipating and adapting to the ever-changing marketing environment has been the key to success for Seta, Appleman & Showell. S.A.S. is one of the Midwest's largest creative and marketing communications firms. Since beginning as an art studio in 1966, S.A.S. has evolved to become a design, sales promotion, and marketing group. Its client list is diverse. The company represents everything from manufacturers of consumer package goods, pharmaceuticals, and automobiles to industrial concerns and business-to-business operations. Many of Seta's clients, in fact, are Fortune 500 companies, which are attracted by Seta's impressive business philosophy: "To gain a thorough understanding of our client's design and marketing needs, to have a clear vision of project objectives, and achieve our target results with optimum effectiveness."

S.A.S. has built this philosophy on a foundation of research, strategy, teamwork, and education. The company feels that an understanding of the company's industry is necessary whether creating a single design element or a complete marketing program. A well-defined marketing strategy helps ensure that the elements being created achieve results for the client. Seta assigns an interdisciplinary team to every job. Clients then have the opportunity to work directly with the writers, artists, marketing managers, and production personnel handling their project. This approach helps eliminate miscommunication between the client and the studio. It also helps both parties achieve their project goals in a more direct manner.

Seta, Appleman & Showell recognizes that in order to stay ahead of the competition, it must emphasize the importance of continuing education for its staff. Technological advancements, such as the computerization of design functions, have profoundly changed the way Seta interacts with its clients and outside vendors. The training and support the company provides for its employees make Seta an even greater asset to its clients.

Seta, Appleman & Showell is a company that has successfully defined its market. With its attitude of anticipating, understanding, and embracing change, S.A.S. has a prosperous future ahead of it.

The Marketing Process and Marketing Research

Chapter 14

Learning Goals

After studying this chapter, you should be able to:

1 Explain the marketing concept.

2 Describe the four elements of the marketing mix.

3 Understand how the marketing environment can affect marketing decisions.

4 Explain how consumers make decisions.

5 Explain how markets can be segmented.

6 Understand how marketing research is used to minimize marketing risk.

 Career Profile

The classified ads were a valuable resource for Jamie Beresh when she started her job search. Upon graduating from college with a degree in graphic design, Jamie looked in the help-wanted section of a local newspaper and read an ad for a job that was ideal for someone with her background and ambitions. She answered the ad and was eventually hired as the art director for the South Dakota Gold Company.

This multimillion-dollar company designs and manufactures authentic Black Hills gold jewelry. It is Jamie's responsibility to design national advertisements that run in trade magazines. She also produces marketing materials such as flyers and catalogs. Her efforts help to promote new product lines the firm develops.

Test marketing plays a vital role in the introduction of new products at the South Dakota Gold Company. The firm first has a small number of distributors sell a new line. If the line does well, the company introduces it to more distributors. If the product fails to take off, a decision is made to either rethink the design and test the revised version or abandon the product completely. South Dakota Gold doesn't introduce a new product line on a large scale until it has proven itself in a test market. This process reduces the company's financial risk.

Marketing research also helps Jamie design her ads. Who is buying the company's product? How old are they? What is their gender? Their income level? The answers to these and several other questions give Jamie a good idea of how to create an ad that will appeal to those who have purchased the product in the test market. Her interpretation of the research material and her understanding of the product are the foundation for the ad's design. Following this, Jamie works with jewelry designers, photographers, printers, and magazine publishers to come up with the final product, a national ad.

Jamie's college courses in graphic design gave her the skills she needs for her job, but it was the classes she took in marketing, advertising, and marketing research that helped her make the most of these skills in the world of business.

Overview Chapter 14 begins by explaining the functions of marketing and the marketing concept. It then discusses target markets and the marketing mix. A discussion of the environmental factors that affect marketing decisions follows. Next, consumer buying behavior is explained. You will then learn how market segmentation helps firms identify their best potential customers. The chapter ends with a description of marketing research and how it improves marketing decisions.

THE "RIGHT" PRINCIPLE AND EXCHANGE

marketing Process of planning and executing the conception, pricing, promotion, and distribution of ideas, goods, and services to create exchanges that satisfy individual and organizational objectives.

exchange Process in which two parties give something of value to each other to satisfy their needs.

Marketing is the process of getting the right goods or services to the right people at the right place, time, and price, using the right promotion techniques. This concept is referred to as the *"right" principle*. This is how the American Marketing Association defines **marketing**: the process of planning and executing the conception, pricing, promotion, and distribution of ideas, goods, and services to create exchanges that satisfy individual and organizational objectives. An **exchange** takes place when two parties give something of value to each other to satisfy their needs. In a typical exchange, a consumer trades money for a good or service.

To encourage exchanges, marketers follow the "right" principle. If your local Chrysler dealer doesn't have the right car for you when you want it, at the right price, you will not exchange money or credit for a new car. Think about the last exchange (purchase) you made: What if the price had been 30 percent higher? What if the store or other source had not been so accessible? Would you have bought anything? The "right" principle tells us that marketers control many factors that determine marketing success.

THE FOUR UTILITIES

utility Ability of a good or service to satisfy consumer desires.

form utility Transforming a good or service into a more desirable or usable form.

place utility Having a good or service where consumers would like to buy or use it.

time utility Having a good or service available when consumers want it.

possession utility Making it possible for consumers to complete a transaction and gain the right to use the product.

Through the process of exchange, marketing creates utility. As defined by economists, **utility** means the ability of a good or service to satisfy consumer desires. There are four types of utility: utility of form, time, place, and possession.

Form utility is the result when a good or service is transformed into something more desirable or usable. Form utility is created mainly through the production process. For instance, smelting bauxite to create aluminum creates form utility; converting the aluminum into soft drink cans results in greater form utility. Marketing is only somewhat involved in developing form utility. To the extent that marketing tells production what consumers want, it aids in producing form utility. Choosing the sizes of a product to offer (for example, gallons, quarts, and pints of milk) is another way marketing can help create form utility.

The other three types of utility are created only through marketing. **Place utility** means having the product where consumers would like to buy it or use it. **Time utility** is having the good or service available when they want it. **Possession utility** means making it possible for the consumer to complete a transaction and gain the right to use the product.

■ Dominos Pizza, from a marketing standpoint, has all four types of utility covered. The company offers a product customers want —pizza—in the sizes they want it (form utility); it opens stores in areas where they will do well (place utility); and the company's famed delivery service ensures that customers have access to the product when and where they want it (time and possession utilities).

Marketing creates place utility through distribution. A set of Revereware cookware would have little value for you if it were sitting in a warehouse in Philadelphia and you wanted to cook dinner in Chicago. Time utility is created by storage. Marshall Field's, a Chicago-based department store chain, buys Revereware sets and stores them in warehouses and on the shelves of their stores until you are ready to buy. By advertising the Revereware, perhaps on sale, and offering credit and other services, Marshall Field's facilitates possession utility.

Through the exchange process, marketing creates utility for consumers and brings revenue to the company. All parties are satisfied and (typically) better off than before the exchange took place. For the profit-oriented company, marketing stimulates sales revenue. For the not-for-profit business, it stimulates client contact and funds. The more efficient a firm's marketing effort, the greater its market share and profits (assuming expenses are kept down). Greater market share and profits give the firm more clout. A highly profitable firm, for instance, can outbid competitors for the best employees. It also has more resources to invest in ventures that can generate future profits. Thus good marketing helps ensure the firm's long-run survival.

Concept Check

- List and explain the four types of utility.
- How do the four types of utility relate to marketing?

THE MARKETING CONCEPT

marketing concept
Idea that a firm first identifies consumer needs and then produces goods or services that satisfy them.

production orientation
Idea that the firm should produce what it does best and then aggressively try to sell the product, based primarily on price.

If you study today's best firms, you'll see that they have adopted the **marketing concept**. This is the idea that a firm first identifies consumer needs and then produces the goods or services that will satisfy them. The marketing concept is oriented toward pleasing consumers by offering value.

In contrast, around the time of the Industrial Revolution, firms focused on raising output (through mass production) and producing goods of uniform quality. The result was lower costs. Most firms then had a **production orientation**, which assumes that people want to buy products at the lowest price possible. It assumes that price is their main concern. Basically the focus of a production orientation is the firm's own capabilities. It does not take into account the desires and needs of consumers. Production-oriented managers assess the firm's resources and ask, What can we do best? What can our engineers design? What is economical and easy to produce given our equipment?

There is nothing wrong with assessing a firm's capabilities. In fact, such assessments are necessary in planning. But the production orientation does not consider whether what the firm produces most efficiently also meets the needs of the marketplace. The firm might produce 100,000 widgets and then find that no one wants to buy them. Hence the need for the marketing concept.

THE FUNCTIONS OF THE MARKETING DEPARTMENT

The marketing concept is applied by the entire organization. But it is the job of the marketing department to assess demand for the firm's products, to generate more demand, and to service the demand. Exhibit 14-1 shows these three functions and their related activities. Demand is *assessed* through marketing research and sales forecasting. It is *generated* through product planning, pricing, advertising, sales promotion, personal selling, and publicity. It is *serviced* through order processing and handling, warehousing, inventory management, and transportation. These functions are discussed in more detail in this chapter and in Chapters 15 through 17.

Marketing department

Functions	Assessing demand	Generating demand	Servicing demand
Activities	Marketing research Sales forecasting	Advertising Sales promotion Pricing Personal selling Product planning Publicity	Inventory management Order processing and handling Warehousing Transportation

Marketing functions • General administration
of other depts. • Financing & Risk Taking

■ **Exhibit 14-1**
Functions and Activities
of the Marketing Depart-
ment

consumer orientation
Idea that planning should
identify a product's likely
consumers and supply goods
or services designed to meet
their needs and wants.

CONSUMER ORIENTATION

It would be foolish to try to sell electric space heaters to people living at the equator. If you wanted to sell space heaters, you would do better in a cooler climate. Firms do better when they identify the group of people (or firms) most likely to buy their product and when they produce something that will meet the needs and wants of those consumers. This kind of planning has a **consumer orientation**. A consumer-oriented firm often does research to explore consumer needs. It wants to better understand the target customer or to get reactions to new product ideas.

Consumer orientation doesn't mean that a company's new-product development team sits idly waiting for market researchers to bring them ideas. Companies with strong basic research skills, such as Du Pont and General Electric, rely on marketing to help refine new ideas to suit consumer needs. One example is 3M's Post-it Notes. After the product was invented, market researchers found plenty of sales potential under certain conditions. First, the color should contrast with white, the color of most documents. Second, at least two sizes should be made—one for long notes and the other for short notes. One year after introduction, the Post-it Note tray was introduced because market researchers found the note pads were getting lost on customers' desks. Now 3M sells over $150 million worth of Post-it Notes a year.

GOAL ORIENTATION

goal orientation
Idea that a firm should be
consumer oriented only to
the extent that being so also
achieves corporate goals.

The second aspect of the marketing concept is **goal orientation**. A firm should be consumer oriented only to the extent that it also achieves organizational goals. In profit-making firms, these goals usually are financial, such as getting a 15 percent return on invested money.

Companies often have service goals as well. Caterpillar Tractor Company tries to provide 24-hour parts delivery anywhere in the world. It usually meets its goal. But that isn't always good enough for Caterpillar equipment owners, who have huge sums of money tied up in their equipment. They lose a lot of income if equipment sits idle waiting for parts. Thus Caterpillar owners would like parts delivery anywhere in the world in six hours or less. However, Caterpillar couldn't meet its financial goals if it had to build new parts warehouses all over the world and stock them all with inventory. Caterpillar is a well-managed, consumer-oriented firm, but it knows its limits. Marketing managers with a goal orientation meet the needs of consumers but not at the expense of profit and overall objectives.

Concept Check

- Discuss the concept of production orientation.
- What is meant by consumer orientation?
- Why is goal orientation an important part of the marketing concept?

CREATING A MARKETING STRATEGY

A company can't succeed unless it has a well-planned marketing strategy. The two main steps in creating a marketing strategy are to define the target market and to develop a marketing mix.

DEFINING A TARGET MARKET

target market Specific group of consumers toward which a firm directs its marketing efforts.

The **target market** is the specific group of consumers toward which a firm directs its marketing efforts. It is selected from the larger overall market. For instance, Carnival Cruise Line says its main target market is "blue-collar entrepreneurs," people with an income of $25,000 to $50,000 a year who own auto supply shops, dry cleaners, and the like. Unlike other cruise lines, it does not seek affluent retirees. Quaker Oats targets its grits to blue-collar consumers in the South. Kodak targets Ektar color print film, designed for use only in rather sophisticated cameras, to advanced amateur photographers. The Limited Inc. has several different types of stores, each for a distinct target market: Express for trendy younger women; Lerner for budget-conscious women; Lane Bryant and Roaman's for full-size women; and Henri Bendel's for upscale, high-fashion women. These target markets are all part of the overall market for women's clothes.

Identifying a target market helps a company focus its marketing efforts on those who are most likely to buy from it. Concentrating on potential customers lets the firm use its resources efficiently.

CONSUMER AND INDUSTRIAL PRODUCTS

consumer products Goods and services purchased and used by the end user.

industrial products Products bought for use in producing other goods and services, for operating a business, or for reselling to other organizations.

Marketing strategies for consumer products and industrial products are usually very different. **Consumer products** are those goods and services bought by the end user. **Industrial products** are those bought for use in producing other products, operating a business, or reselling to other organizations. Consumer products and industrial products are distributed, sold, and purchased quite differently.

Industrial products usually pass directly from the producer to industrial buyers, such as other manufacturers, or to institutions like hospitals and schools. Consumer goods are often sold first to a wholesaler, who then sells them to a retailer. The decision to buy a consumer good is usually made by one or two people. For instance, a husband and wife might jointly choose a new VCR. On the other hand, the decision to build a new factory in a distant city is usually made by a committee of managers.

When the marketing department understands how most of the target audience views a product, its can plan a marketing strategy to fit. A Duncan yo-yo is not marketed like a BMW automobile. A Gardner-Denver air compressor is not marketed in the way economic forecasting is. Also, two different marketing strategies may be needed for a single product. A personal computer is a consumer good when sold to an individual and an industrial good when sold to an accounting firm.

DEVELOPING A MARKETING MIX

Once the target market—whether consumer or industrial—has been selected, marketing efforts turn toward giving those consumers what they want. The blend of product offering, pricing, promotional methods, and distribution system that will reach a specific group of consumers is called the **marketing mix**. Distribution is sometimes referred to as place, thus giving us the **four p's** of the marketing mix: product, price, promotion, and place. Every target market requires a unique marketing mix to satisfy the needs of the target consumers and meet the goals of the firm. A strategy must be constructed for each of the four p's and blended with that of other elements. Thus the marketing mix is only as good as the weakest part. An excellent product with a poor distribution system could be doomed to failure.

A successful marketing mix requires careful tailoring. For instance, at first glance you might think that McDonald's and Wendy's have roughly the same marketing mix. After all, they are both in the fast-food business. But McDonald's targets parents with young children. It has Ronald McDonald, special children's Happy Meals that it promotes heavily, and playgrounds. Wendy's is targeted more to an adult crowd. Wendy's doesn't have playgrounds but does have carpeting (a more adult atmosphere), and it pioneered fast-food salad bars.

Product Strategy

Marketing strategy typically starts with the product. You can't plan a distribution system or set a price if you don't know what you're going to market. Marketers use the term "product" to refer to both *goods*—such as tires, stereos, clothing—and *services*—e.g., hotels, hair salons, restaurants. (In fact, the gross domestic product accounted for by services is much greater than that for products.) Thus the heart of the marketing mix is the good or service. Creating a **product strategy** means choosing a brand name, packaging, colors, a warranty, accessories, and a service program.

Marketers view products in a much larger context than you might imagine. They include not only the item itself but also the brand name and the company image. The names Yves St. Laurent and Gucci, for instance, create extra value for everything from cosmetics to bath towels. That is, prod-

marketing mix Blend of product offering, pricing, promotional methods, and distribution system that will reach a specific group of consumers.

four p's The four elements of the marketing mix: product, price, promotion, and place.

product strategy Decisions about specific elements of a product or service, such as brand names, packaging, warranty, and service.

ucts with those names sell at higher prices than identical products without the names. We buy things not only for what they do, but also for what they mean. (Product strategies are discussed further in Chapter 15.)

Product strategy is equally valid for goods and for services. In fact, service providers are scouting for ways to develop stronger customer orientation, as the Trends in Service Economy box shows.

"Calling Dr. Mickey"

Peter Betts, President of East Jefferson General Hospital in suburban New Orleans, has learned a lot from Disney University in Orlando, Florida. Patients have become "guests" and employees "team members." Of course, no one wants to be in a hospital. But Betts wants people to leave his institution with the same positive feelings as visitors to Disney World. In the process, he also wants to reduce hospital costs and improve employee relations and quality of service.

Every two weeks, East Jefferson holds "guest relations training" for about 20 to 40 new team members—every full-time, part-time, temporary, or contract employee. They are hand-delivered to the room by their immediate supervisors. At the welcoming session, Betts preaches service philosophy. "When Dave [Thomas] goes to Wendy's how do you think they treat him?" he asks. "Remember, the people who come here own the place."

Service is judged by direct contact between the guest and hospital—such as if the food shows up on time and the nurse comes when the button is pushed, he says. "If Mrs. Jones doesn't get her food tray, don't blame food service," he instructs in an upbeat, but pointed manner. "All she wants is her food. Get it for her."

"We have mystery visitors trying to catch people doing something right," he tells the new hires. "When you see someone lost, don't give directions, stop and take them there."

The new intensive care unit has a central non-public corridor where employees move supplies and equipment. Similar to tunnels at the Magic Kingdom, the hall keeps "off-stage" activity hidden. It also allows a lot of the supplies and support machinery to be pulled out of the guests' rooms so the rooms are more open and inviting.

Similar to Disney, East Jefferson employees adhere to a strict dress code that—among other things—mandates the length of skirts, trousers, and fingernails, and dictates what jewelry and makeup is (and mostly isn't) allowed. "Denim, spandex, leather, and sheer or clinging fabrics are not part of the E.J.G.H. look," team members are warned.

East Jefferson has critical care nurses standing in line for jobs, and other hospitals are hiring E.J.G.H.'s services. "Other hospitals in town have turnover rates of 30, 40, to 50 percent. Ours was 10.3 last year, and it's getting smaller," Betts says. It seems the Disney magic can work wonders in many environments.[1]

Pricing Strategy

pricing strategy Decisions about how to price a good or service, determined by demand and by cost.

Pricing strategy is based on demand for the product and the cost of producing it. Some special considerations can also influence the price. Sometimes, for instance, a special introductory price is used to get people to try a new product. Some firms enter the market with low prices and keep them low, such as Carnival Cruise Lines and Suzuki cars. Others enter a market with very high prices and then lower them over time, such as producers of compact disk players and personal computers. (You can learn more about pricing strategies in Chapter 15.)

Distribution Strategy

distribution strategy Decisions about how to deliver a good or service to the consumer or industrial user.

Distribution is the means (the channel) by which a product flows from the producer to the consumer. (It is examined in detail in Chapter 16.) One aspect of **distribution strategy** is deciding how many stores and which specific wholesalers and retailers will handle the product in a geographic area. Cosmetics, for instance, are distributed in many different ways. Avon has a sales force of several hundred thousand who call directly on consumers. Clinique and Estee Lauder are distributed through selected department stores. Cover Girl and Del Laboratories use mostly chain drugstores and other mass merchandisers. Redken sells through beauticians. Revlon uses several of these distribution channels.

Promotion Strategy

promotion strategy Decisions about how to advertise and sell a good or service.

Many people feel that promotion is the most exciting part of the marketing mix. **Promotion strategy** covers personal selling, advertising, public relations, and sales promotion. Each element is coordinated with the others to create a promotional blend. An advertisement, for instance, helps a buyer get to know the company and paves the way for a sales call. A good promotion strategy can dramatically increase a firm's sales. (Promotion is the topic of Chapter 17.)

Public relations plays a special role in promotion. It is used to create a good image of the company and its products. Bad publicity costs nothing to send out, but it can cost a firm a great deal in lost business. Good publicity, such as a story on television or in a magazine about a firm's new product, may be the result of much time, money, and effort spent by a public-relations department.

Sales promotion directly stimulates sales. It includes trade shows, catalogs, contests, games, premiums, coupons, and special offers. McDonald's contests offering money and food prizes are an example. The company also issues discount coupons from time to time.

Concept Check

- What is a target market, and why should a company have one?
- What is the difference between consumer and industrial products?
- What is meant by the marketing mix?

THE MARKETING ENVIRONMENT

3 Over time, the environment in which consumers live, work, and decide what to buy changes. New consumers become part of the target market, and others drop out. Those who remain may have tastes, needs, incomes, lifestyles, and buying habits different from those of the original target consumers.

The business environment changes as well, as discussed in the Prologue. As these environments evolve, the marketing mix must change. Managers can control the marketing mix, although they cannot control elements in the business environment that reshape the target market. The companies that best predict opportunities or threats in environmental change have the best chance of long-run survival.

THE SOCIAL/CULTURAL ENVIRONMENT

The social/cultural environment shapes the values of a society or particular groups within society. Today's consumers are demanding and discriminating. They insist on high-quality goods that save time, energy, and often calories. U.S. consumers rank the characteristics of product quality as (1) reliability, (2) durability, (3) easy maintenance, (4) ease of use, (5) a trusted brand name, and (6) a low price. Shoppers are also concerned about nutrition and want to know what's in their food. In the late 1980s, barely a third of grocery shoppers read labels on the foods they bought; today half of them do.[2]

Today's shoppers also care about the environment. Eight in ten U.S. consumers regard themselves as environmentalists, and half of those say they are strong ones.[3] Four out of five shoppers are willing to pay 5 per-

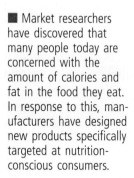

■ Market researchers have discovered that many people today are concerned with the amount of calories and fat in the food they eat. In response to this, manufacturers have designed new products specifically targeted at nutrition-conscious consumers.

cent more for products packaged with recyclable or biodegradable materials. Many marketers predict that by the year 2000 it will be very hard to sell a product that isn't environmentally friendly.

In the 1990s, fewer consumers say expensive cars, designer clothes, pleasure trips, and "gold cards" are necessary components of a happy life. Instead, they put value on nonmaterial accomplishments, such as having control of their lives.[4] Many families often feel a *poverty of time*. They have few hours to do anything but work and commute to work, handle family situations, do housework, shop, sleep, and eat. In a recent study of 1,010 people, half said they would sacrifice a day's pay for an extra day off each week. Of those surveyed, 21 percent said they had "no time for fun anymore," and 33 percent said they don't accomplish what they set out to do each day.[5]

A primary reason that Americans have less time is the growth of dual-income families. Approximately 58 percent of all females between 16 and 65 years old are now in the work force. Female participation in the labor force will grow to 63 percent by 2005.[6] This phenomenon has probably had a greater effect on marketing than any other social change.

Although they have less time for family activities, dual-career families typically have greater household incomes. Their purchase roles (which define what items are traditionally bought by the man or the woman) are changing, as well as their purchase patterns. Consequently, new opportunities are being created. For example, small businesses are opening daily that cater to dual-career households by offering specialized goods and services. For example, San Francisco Grocery Express, a warehouse operation, uses computers to take customers' telephone orders. Customers refer to a catalog listing grocery items and prices. Later, vans deliver the food to the purchasers' front doors. Household cleaning and lawn care services are also becoming popular among time-stressed middle-class families.

THE DEMOGRAPHIC ENVIRONMENT: THE UNITED STATES IN THE MID-1990s

demography Study of vital statistics, such as ages, births, deaths, and locations of people.

Demographic factors—another uncontrollable variable in the external environment—are also extremely important to marketers. **Demography** is the study of people's vital statistics, such as their ages, births, deaths, and locations. Demographics are significant because the basis for any market is people.

The U.S. population is growing at a slower rate—less than 1 percent, with a rate of new household formation under 2 percent—than at any time since the Great Depression. These rates will decline even more as we move through the decade. At least twelve states are expecting no growth at all. This phenomenon will profoundly affect consumer goods marketers, because they can no longer count on expanding overall markets to fuel sales increases. But the slow rate of growth masks an array of differences among various ethnic and age groups. Consumer goods marketers will be able to prosper in the domestic market only by taking competitors' customers or tapping into specialized niches, such as the growing elderly or ethnic markets, before competitors do.

The mid-1990s are being characterized as a struggle for market share and profits. Several of the big consumer goods mergers—for example, R.J. Reynolds with Nabisco and Kraft with General Foods—were partially driven by demographics. In other words, these companies gained new customers by acquiring their competitors. If a marketer can't count on many new customers entering the marketplace, buying existing customers may make sense.

Middle-Aged Consumers

The "Pepsi generation" has matured. As the age of today's average consumer moves toward 40, consumption patterns also change. People in their early 40s tend to focus on their families and finances. As this group grows, its members will buy more furniture, to replace the furniture they bought when just starting their working lives. Sales of financial products, such as mutual funds, should prosper. The demand for family counselors and wellness programs should also increase. Because middle-aged consumers buy more reading materials than any other age group, the market for books and magazines should remain strong. During the remainder of the 1990s, merchants will offer more products and services aimed at middle-aged markets. Styles and retail stores will have a more conservative look, and commercials will feature more middle-aged actors. Health clubs will appeal to aging consumers who want to stay fit.

Older Consumers: Not Just Grandparents

Today's 50-plus consumers are wealthier, healthier, and better educated than those of earlier generations. Although they make up only a quarter of the population, 50-plus consumers buy half of all domestic cars, half of all silverware, and nearly half of all home remodeling.[7] Despite stereotypes to the contrary, a full 85 percent of mature citizens report themselves to be in good or excellent health. And many choose not to just stay at home. Eight out of every ten travel dollars spent in the United States are spent by people over 50 years old.[8]

By early in the next century, over a third of the U.S. population will be part of the 50-plus age group.[9] Smart marketers are already actively pursuing it. Aging consumers create some obvious opportunities. JC Penney's Easy Dressing clothes are a catalog line of Velcro-fastened clothing for women with arthritis or other ailments who may have difficulty with zippers or buttons. Sales from the first catalog, distributed in 1992, were three times higher than expected. Other retailers are adding more rest stops in stores and arranging shelving so customers needn't bend over.

The Growing Singles Market

More of us are living alone than in the past. The 1990 census showed that about 23 million people in the United States live by themselves—since 1970, a 91 percent jump for women and a 156 percent increase for men.[10]

Two trends lie behind this singles surge: Unprecedented numbers of adults never marry, and by some estimates, over half of all couples divorce.

It's an attractive market but a tough one. Studies show singles share such traits as a tendency to spend more than married adults on travel, convenience foods, and restaurants. But this vast, fragmented group includes everyone from carefree 21-year-olds to elderly widows. They are also widely scattered geographically, although the greatest concentration of single households is in the Midwest. There is also the delicate task of getting a message across without offending. Campbell made that mistake with its Soup for One line. "Our consumers told us Soup for One is a lonely name. They are eating alone, and they don't need to be reminded," says Robert Bernstock, a vice president in the soup division.[11] After years of mediocre sales, the Soup for One label was removed, and sales of the single-serving sizes have improved.

Consumers on the Move

The average U.S. citizen moves every six years.[12] Population shifts, as well as changing age patterns, open new markets. Areas experiencing a large influx of people create many new marketing opportunities for all types of businesses in those regions. Conversely, significant out-migration from a city or town may force many of its businesses either to move or to close down. The greatest gains in population during the past decade were in the Far West and in the Mountain states.

THE ECONOMIC ENVIRONMENT

The economic areas of greatest concern to most marketers are the distribution of consumer income and the economic uncertainty of inflation and recession. Over the past decade, disposable (after-tax) incomes have risen. More people can afford the "good life." About two-thirds of all American households earn a "middle-class" income.[13] The U.S. government puts the rough boundaries for a middle-class income at $18,000 (comfortably above poverty level) to about $75,000 (just short of wealth). When incomes are generally rising, marketers promote higher-quality, higher-priced goods and services.

Fortunately, the United States has not had a high rate of inflation for almost a decade. The mid-1990s have been marked by an inflation rate of under 5 percent. But firms have cut jobs and tightened their belts, to become more competitive. The result has been a fair amount of economic uncertainty, even within the middle class. In times of inflation or economic uncertainty, consumers try to make more economical purchases, although most resist an actual decrease in their standard of living. Instead, they reduce their brand loyalty and tend to buy whatever is on sale. Consumers also take advantage of coupons when prices are on the rise. Recessions (periods of reduced economic activity) also cause consumers to seek bargains and stock up. They stock up because recessions often lead to large-scale unemployment.

THE TECHNOLOGICAL ENVIRONMENT

Marketers must stay aware of new technology to avoid being left behind by the competition. For instance, SABRE is a computerized reservations system that American Airlines created from technology developed by another company. It gave American a big advantage over other airlines. The system, used by thousands of travel agents, shows American's flights first on the computer screen.

Managers must understand how to link new technology with opportunities to meet the needs of the target market. Technology is useless if it doesn't provide value to the company or the customer or both.

THE COMPETITIVE ENVIRONMENT

Both large and small firms must work hard to maintain their profits and market share. Competitors' aggressive actions are one reason. Others are slowing population growth, rising costs, and tightening resources.

To prosper, firms must seek a competitive edge. An example is Coca-Cola. The brand name Coca-Cola is the most powerful and best recognized in the world. Coke, itself, sells for a very modest price. It is almost universally liked. The per capita consumption goes up almost every year in virtually every country. In the United States, on average, every man, woman and child in the country drinks 296 eight-ounce servings of Coke products a year.[14] (In American Samoa, average consumption is 500 servings a year!) Also, Coke is sold in almost every country in the world, except Cuba. Yet Coke maintains its huge marketing budget. It knows it must keep looking for new product opportunities and must keep its name and image ever in the public eye.

NOT-FOR-PROFIT MARKETING

Analyzing the marketing environment and creating a marketing mix are activities not restricted to profit-oriented companies. The application of marketing principles and techniques is also vital to not-for-profit organizations. Marketing helps not-for-profit groups identify target markets and develop effective marketing mixes. In some cases, marketing has kept symphonies, museums, and other cultural groups from having to close their doors. In other organizations, such as the American Heart Association and the U.S. Army, marketing ideas and techniques have helped managers do their jobs better. The Army, for instance, has identified the most effective ways to get young men and women between the ages of eighteen and twenty-four to visit a recruiter.

Most managers in not-for-profit organizations have little or no background in marketing or business administration. Yet they are often expected to generate and manage large sums of money. Until recently, the idea of applying marketing to not-for-profit organizations was often viewed as radical. But the use of marketing knowledge creates satisfied customers and clients and enables not-for-profit organizations to reach their goals. Now marketing earns their profound respect.

■ Marketing techniques can be applied to social issues and causes. Effective market research can lead to campaigns such as this one, aimed at discouraging pregnant women from smoking. This helps effect changes in society's behavior.

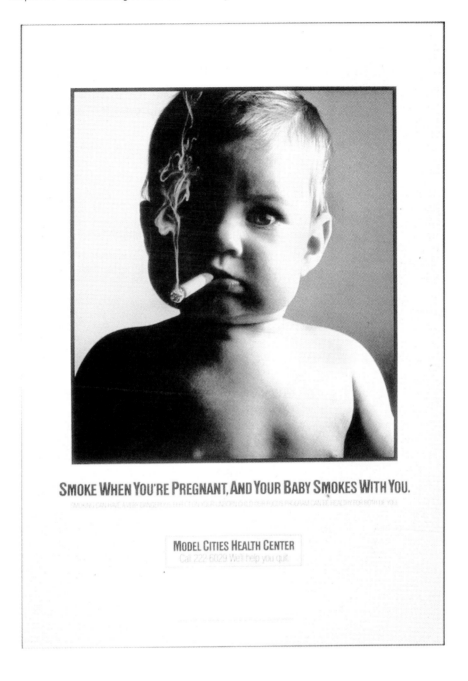

SMOKE WHEN YOU'RE PREGNANT, AND YOUR BABY SMOKES WITH YOU.

MODEL CITIES HEALTH CENTER

What kind of help do not-for-profit organizations need? The chief need is money. Even not-for-profit organizations must meet expenses. Without money, the organization will cease to exist. Fine-arts groups, like Chicago-based The Masters of American Dance, must attract enough donations and sell enough tickets to pay for performers, utilities, set designs, and many other things. Most states and many cities market themselves to increase business development, tourism, and convention business—all to improve the local economy. Another goal for not-for-profit organizations is greater exposure to their target market so they can better serve clients.

social marketing Application of marketing theories and techniques to social issues and causes.

Not-for-profit marketing is also concerned with **social marketing—** that is, the application of marketing to social issues and causes. The goals of social marketing are to effect social change (for instance, by creating racial harmony), further social causes (for instance, by supporting the local police), and evaluate the relationship between marketing and society (for instance, by asking whether society should allow advertising on television shows for young children). Individual organizations also engage in social marketing. The Southern Baptist Radio and Television Convention promotes brotherhood and goodwill by promoting religion and good deeds. Social marketing against drunk driving, the use of drugs, and smoking has also increased in recent years.

Concept Check

- Explain several social/cultural factors that have had an impact on marketing.
- What is meant by demographics? Give some examples of demographic trends.
- What are the most important elements of the economic environment to marketers?

CONSUMER BEHAVIOR

4

consumer behavior Actions people take in buying and using products.

An organization cannot reach its goals without understanding **consumer behavior.** Consumer behavior is the actions people take in buying and using goods and services. Marketers who understand consumer behavior can create a more effective marketing mix. For instance, they can have a better idea of how a price increase will affect a product's sales.

To understand consumer behavior, marketers must understand how consumers make buying decisions. The decision-making process has several steps, which are shown in Exhibit 14-2. The entire process is affected by a number of personal and social factors. A buying decision starts with a stimulus. A *stimulus* is anything that affects one or more of our senses (sight, smell, taste, touch, or hearing). A stimulus might be the feel of a sweater, the sleek shape of a new-model car, the design on a package, or a brand name mentioned by a friend. The stimulus leads to problem recognition: "This sweater feels so soft and looks good on me. . . . Should I buy it?" In other words, the consumer decides at this step that there's a purchase need.

The consumer next gets information about the purchase. What other styles of sweaters are available? At what price? Can this sweater be bought at a lower price elsewhere? Next, the consumer weighs the options and decides whether to make a purchase. If the consumer buys a product, he or she expects certain outcomes. These outcomes may or may not become reality. Maybe the sweater lasts for years and years. Or maybe the shoulder seams pull out the first time it's worn. Finally, the consumer assesses his or her experience with the product and uses this information to update expectations about future purchases.

■ Exhibit 14-2
Consumer Decision-
Making Process

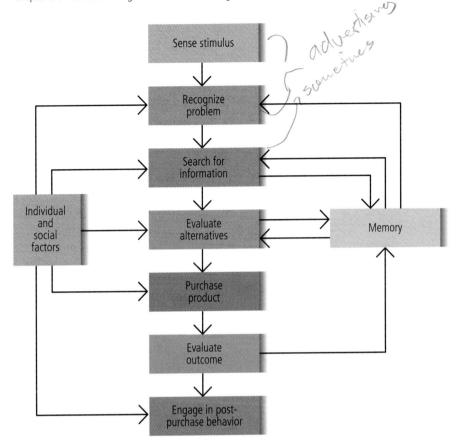

[handwritten margin notes: Social Factors, Culture, Social class, Reference group, Opinion leader, Individual factors, needs, perceptions, motivations, attitudes]

[handwritten notes near top right: advertising, sometimes]

INFLUENCES ON CONSUMER DECISION MAKING

As Exhibit 14-2 shows, individual and social factors can influence the consumer decision-making process. *Individual factors* are within the consumer and are unique to each person. They include perception, beliefs and attitudes, values, learning, self-concept, and personality. Companies often conduct research to better understand individual factors that cause consumers to buy or not to buy. For instance, Hyatt hotels found that people who stayed at Hyatt while on business chose other hotels when they traveled on vacation with their children. Hyatt was perceived as a businessperson's hotel. So Hyatt came up with a program called Camp Hyatt, which caters to children with a year-round program that varies by season. It combines attractive rates that appeal to parents with lots of activities for kids.[15]

Social factors that affect the decision-making process include all interactions between a consumer and the external environment: family, opinion leaders, social class, and culture. Families may be the most important of these social factors. Yet families have limited resources, so many buying decisions are compromises. Since a number of decisions have input from several family members, marketing managers sometimes promote products using a family theme, such as Camp Hyatt.

- Describe the consumer decision-making process.
- Explain how individual and social factors can influence consumer decision making.

MARKET SEGMENTATION

5

market segmentation
Process of separating, identifying, and evaluating the layers of a market in order to design a marketing mix.

The study of consumer behavior helps marketing managers better understand why people buy what they buy. Other techniques are used to identify the target markets that may be most profitable for the firm. One is **market segmentation,** the process of separating, identifying, and evaluating the layers of a market to design a marketing mix. For instance, a market might be broken into two groups: families with children and families without children. Families with young children are likely to buy hot cereals and presweetened cereals. Families with no children are more likely to buy health-oriented cereals. You can be sure that cereal companies plan their marketing mixes with this difference in mind.

■ Age is one of the variables used to separate the population into markets. One important segment is children 4 to 12 years old. Marketers have discovered that they spend or influence the spending of over $130 billion a year.

Form	General characteristics
Demographic segmentation	Age, education, gender, income, race, social class, household size
Geographic segmentation	Regional location (e.g., New England, Mid-Atlantic, Southeast, Great Lakes, Plains States, Northwest, Southwest, Rocky Mountains, Far West); population density (urban, suburban, rural); city or county size; climate
Psychographic segmentation	Lifestyle, personality, interests, values, attitudes
Benefit segmentation	Benefits provided by the good or service
Volume segmentation	Amounts of use (light versus heavy)

■ **Exhibit 14-3**
Forms of Market Seg-
mentation

FORMS OF MARKET SEGMENTATION

The five basic forms of market segmentation are demographic, geographic, psychographic, benefit, and volume. Their characteristics are
summarized in Exhibit 14-3 and discussed in the following sections.

Demographic Segmentation

**demographic segmen-
tation** Division of a market
by such variables as age, education, gender, income, and
household size.

Demographic segmentation uses such variables as age, education, gender, income, and household size to differentiate among markets. This
form of market segmentation is the most common. The U.S. Census
Bureau provides a great deal of demographic data. For example, marketing researchers can use census data to find areas within cities that contain
high-income consumers, the most singles, the highest concentration of
blue-collar workers, and so forth.

You don't have to be an adult to have market clout. Children 4 to 12
years old spend or influence the spending of over $130 billion a year.[16]
Preteens spend over $1 billion annually on such play items as toys, bikes,
and roller blades; $3.2 billion on food and beverages; about $800 million
on movies and spectator sports; over $500 million on consumer electron-
ics; and $620 million at the video arcade.[17] The teen market spends or
influences the spending of nearly $250 billion *per day*.[18]

Other age segments are appealing targets for a wide range of marketers. People between 35 and 44 are likely to have school-aged children
at home and to outspend all other age groups on food at home, housing,
clothing, and alcohol. Those between 45 and 54 spend more than any
other group on food away from home, transportation, entertainment, education, personal insurance, and pensions. People from 55 to 64 spend
more than those 45 to 54 on health care.[19]

Certain markets are segmented by gender. These include: clothing,
cosmetics, personal care items, magazines, jewelry, and footwear. Gillette,
for example, is one of the world's best-known marketers of personal care

products for men. It has been much less successful marketing to women. But other marketers that have traditionally focused on men—such as Smith & Wesson, the gun manufacturer, and Anheuser-Busch, the beer marketer—have had recent success in marketing to women.[20]

Income is another popular way to segment markets. Income level influences consumers' wants and determines their buying power. Many markets are segmented by income, including housing, clothing, automobiles, and alcoholic beverages. Budget Gourmet frozen dinners are targeted to lower-income groups, whereas the Le Menu line is aimed at higher-income consumers.

Geographic Segmentation

geographic segmentation Division of a market based on region of the country, city or county size, market density, or climate.

Geographic segmentation means segmenting markets by region of the country, by city or county size, by market density, or by climate. (*Market density* is the number of people or businesses within a certain area.)

Many companies segment their markets geographically to meet regional preferences and buying habits. Pizza Hut, for instance, gives Easterners extra cheese, Westerners more ingredients, and Midwesterners both. Both Ford and Chevrolet sell more pickup trucks and truck parts in the middle tier of states than on either coast. The well-defined "pickup truck belt" runs from the upper Midwest south through Texas and the Gulf states. Ford "owns" the northern half of this truck belt, and Chevrolet the southern half.

Psychographic Segmentation

psychographic segmentation Division of a market based on personality or lifestyle.

Race, income, occupation, and other demographic variables help in developing strategies but often do not paint the entire picture of consumer needs. Demographics provides the skeleton, but psychographics adds meat to the bones. **Psychographic segmentation** is market segmentation by personality or lifestyle. People with common activities, interests, and opinions are grouped together and given a "lifestyle name." A popular system is Values and Life-Styles (VALS-2), designed by SRI International in Menlo Park, California. VALS identifies lifestyle types in the U.S. population.

Psychographic segmentation helps marketers understand and focus on certain market segments. For instance, a large computer software company found that management information system (MIS) managers were its biggest customers. Wanting to know more about this group, the software company interviewed 200 MIS managers. The firm found that its target customers belong to lifestyle groups that seek motivation and approval from the outside world. These customers look for variety and excitement in life and are in awe of wealth, power, and prestige. The software company used this information to develop a plan for promoting its products to the target market.

Benefit Segmentation

benefit segmentation Division of a market based on what a product will do rather than on consumer characteristics.

Benefit segmentation is based on what a product will do rather than on consumer characteristics. For years Crest toothpaste was targeted toward consumers concerned with preventing cavities. Recently Crest subdivided its market. It now offers regular Crest, Crest Tartar Control for people who want to prevent cavities and tartar buildup, and Crest for kids. Another toothpaste, Topol, targets people who want whiter teeth—teeth without coffee, tea, or tobacco stains. Sensodyne toothpaste is aimed at people with highly sensitive teeth.

Volume Segmentation

volume segmentation
Division of a market based on the amount of product bought.

simplest

The fifth main type of segmentation is **volume segmentation,** which is based on the amount of product purchased. There are heavy, moderate, and light users, as well as nonusers, for just about every product.

Heavy users often account for a very large portion of a product's sales. Thus a firm might want to target its marketing mix to the heavy-user segment. The average heavy user of soup, for instance, is worth about $8.34 of profit to Campbell's. Light users are worth pennies.[21] Frequent-flyer programs are the airlines' way of targeting heavy users of air travel. Through market research, Frito-Lay found that heavy users of Light Doritos, Cheetos, and Ruffles potato chips were thirty-five to fifty-four years old, college educated, white-collar workers with an annual income of more than $35,000. Using demographic segmentation, Frito-Lay then found individual supermarkets across the country whose customers matched this profile. The company heavily stocked its light products in these supermarkets and increased promotional spending in these key neighborhoods.[22]

Concept Check
- Define market segmentation.
- List and discuss the five basic forms of segmentation.

MARKETING RESEARCH

6

marketing research
Collecting, recording, and analyzing data important in marketing goods and services and communicating the resulting information to management.

How do companies get most of their information about customers? By doing **marketing research,** which involves collecting, recording, and analyzing data important in marketing products and communicating the information to management. The information includes the preferences of markets, the perceived benefits of products, and consumer lifestyles. Most of the examples of marketing techniques in this chapter were based on marketing research. Research helps companies make better use of their marketing budgets. Marketing research has a range of uses, from fine-tuning products to discovering whole new marketing concepts.

For example, the Olive Garden restaurant chain is completely based on marketing research, from the decor to the wine list. Every new menu item is put through a series of consumer taste tests before being added to the menu.

Hallmark Cards uses marketing research to test messages, cover designs, and even the size of the cards. Hallmark's experts know which kind of cards will sell best in which places. Engagement cards, for instance, sell best in the Northeast, where people are big on engagement parties. Birthday cards for "Daddy" sell best in the South, because even adult Southerners tend to call their fathers Daddy.

DATA GATHERING

Two types of data are used in marketing research: primary and secondary. **Primary data** are collected directly from the original source to solve a problem. **Secondary data** have already been collected for a project other than the current one. Secondary data can come from a number of sources, among them government agencies, trade associations, research bureaus, universities, commercial publications, and internal company records. Company records include sales invoices, accounting records, data from previous research studies, and historical sales data.

Secondary data can save companies time and money because they don't have to collect new information. But since secondary data were gathered to meet some other need, they may not fully meet the current need. For instance, the maker of Seven Seas salad dressing wanted to know whether consumers would buy a new blend for Caesar salads. It had data on consumer preferences for other flavors and for the Caesar salad dressings then on the market. It didn't have data on the one question that mattered: How would consumers respond to Seven Seas' particular blend? The only way to answer the question was to get primary data. Consumers were asked to taste the new blend and then compare it to others they had tried.

primary data Research data collected directly from the original source for the current project.

secondary data Research data collected for a project other than the current one.

■ **Exhibit 14-4**
Types of Interview Research

Type of Interview	Where/How Conducted	Cost	Drawbacks
Door-to-door	Respondents' homes	High: interviewer time plus transportation costs	Hard to find people with time or willingness to let interviewer into home
Mall-intercept	Shopping malls	Less than door-to-door	People at malls may not be typical
Telephone	By phone	Less than preceding two types	Cannot reach everyone. Respondents can't be shown things or be observed. Easy for people to hang up.
Focus groups	Conference room in research facility, with interviewer	Fairly inexpensive	Some respondents may be swayed by opinions of others
Mail	By mail	Relatively inexpensive	Low response rate (25% considered good) Researchers can't clarify unclear responses

Some form of survey research is usually used to gather primary data. People from various groups are questioned in an effort to determine their attitudes or behaviors. Survey research uses five kinds of interviews: door-to-door, mall-intercept, telephone, focus group, and mail. These are described in Exhibit 14-4.

Of the five, **focus groups** are the most popular of the interview techniques. They bring together people from a target market to discuss specific products and other marketing concepts. The people are recruited at malls or by telephone. Their discussions are held in a conference room and are usually tape-recorded. The room is often equipped with one-way mirrors so marketers can watch the sessions. Focus group members might be asked to describe what they like about their favorite brand of a particular product or to discuss how much of it they consume. In this sort of discussion, researchers have some freedom to explore issues that come up, and group members can interact. Thus focus group research is good for getting new product or advertising ideas and shedding light on reasons for consumer behavior. Focus groups usually have eight to ten participants. Therefore, focus group findings are typically compared with results of other survey research studies that contain many more respondents.

Marketing research is not just an American phenomenon. It is used all over the world, as the Global Competition Trends box shows.

focus groups Groups of people from target markets who are brought together to discuss products and other marketing ideas.

TRENDS
Global Competition

Asking Natasha's Opinion

Opinion research in the former Soviet Union dates back to the 1960s, during a brief thaw in the political and economic climate under Khrushchev. For instance, large-scale youth surveys were conducted under the direction of Dr. Boris Grushin, then head of the Soviet Institute of Public Opinion at the *Komsomolskaya Pravda* newspaper. VNIIKS, All-Union Institute for Market Research, attached to the Ministry of Home Trade, also started doing research on issues of supply and demand around the same time.

With a few exceptions, most of the opinion surveys conducted before 1985 were designed to bolster the Communist Party line. Usually, only positive and favorable findings were published. In addition, little concern was given to proper sampling procedures or interview techniques. Most of this early research was based on questionnaires distributed at respondents' places of work, which provided respondents little faith in the promise of anonymity.

The dissolution of the Soviet Union has brought profound changes in marketing research there. Research organizations, reformed or newly established, sprang to life to take the public pulse, document social change, and serve the needs of a wide variety of clients.

There are basically three types of research organizations in the former Soviet Union today. The first type conducts almost exclusively marketing research projects. It includes groups that at one time or another were affiliated with government industry and trade agencies, as well as new joint ventures with foreign partners. For example, VNIIKS is now affiliated with a Finnish research institute, and INFOMARKET is owned by the Russian Ministry of Metallurgy and a Dutch research company.

The second type has a more scholarly orientation. It concentrates on public opinion research and social trends. Examples are the Institute of Sociology and the Institute of Applied Social Research. Universities such as Moscow State University and the University of Vilnius have also started centers of public opinion research.

The third type of research organization seeks to combine marketing and opinion research. Their clientele is diverse, ranging from various government and legislative branches to Western media, advertising agencies, and corporations. The All Commonwealth Center for Public Opinion and Market Research, and Vox Populi, headed by Boris Grushin, are two of the best known of this kind.

Currently available research services include surveys in Russia and the individual republics; consumer panels; opinion leader panels; and ad hoc studies covering a wide range of social, economic, political, and marketing or business-related topics. Data collection techniques include face-to-face interviewing, surveys by mail, and even telephone interviewing among elites or opinion leaders.[23]

SINGLE-SOURCE RESEARCH

single-source research
Marketing research that monitors the promotion that panel members are exposed to and what they buy.

Managers are always seeking better information in order to make more effective decisions. **Single-source research** monitors virtually all the advertising and promotion that panel members are exposed to and what they buy. Advertising campaigns, coupons, displays, packages, and product prices are all measured.

The single-source system uses two electronic monitoring tools—television meters in homes and laser scanners in stores—in various test cities. Panel members in the test cities hand the checkout clerk a special card. When the clerk waves the card over the scanner, the scanner "reads" the UPC codes (the coded series of bars) on products and identifies everything bought by that panel member. Single-source research can thus test the precise impact on sales of TV commercials, ads in special editions of magazines, coupons with different price discounts, and direct price discounts.

Concept Check

- Describe two types of data gathering.
- Why is single-source research becoming so important to marketers?

■ SUMMARY

Key Terms
benefit segmentation 460

consumer behavior 456

continued

1. Explain the marketing concept.
Marketing includes those business activities that are designed to satisfy consumer needs and wants through the exchange process. Marketing managers use the "right" principle—getting the right goods or services to

the right people at the right place, time, and price, using the right promotional techniques.

Today many firms have adopted the marketing concept. They identify consumer needs and wants and then produce goods or services that satisfy them. The bases of the concept are a consumer orientation and a goal orientation.

2. Describe the four elements of the marketing mix.
To carry out the marketing concept, firms create a marketing mix—a blend of products, distribution systems, prices, and promotion. Marketing managers use this mix to satisfy target consumers. The mix can be applied to nonbusiness as well as business situations.

3. Understand how the marketing environment can affect marketing decisions.
The external environment is always changing and cannot be controlled by marketing managers. But they must understand the environment in order to choose an effective marketing mix. One important aspect of the external environment is social and cultural factors. A second uncontrollable aspect is demographic factors. Many marketers are now developing specific mixes to reach changing target audiences.

A third factor in the environment is economic variables. The three areas of greatest concern to marketers are the distribution of consumer income, inflation and economic uncertainty, and recession. Other environmental concerns for marketing managers are developing technology and global competition.

4. Explain how consumers make decisions.
Consumer behavior is what people do in buying and using goods and services. The consumer decision-making process consists of the following steps: responding to a stimulus, recognizing a problem or opportunity, seeking information, evaluating alternatives, judging the purchase outcome, and engaging in postpurchase behavior. A number of factors influence the process. Individual factors are those within the individual consumer, unique to each person. Social factors include all interactions between a consumer and the external environment, such as family, social classes, and culture.

5. Explain how markets can be segmented.
Success in marketing depends on understanding the target market. One technique used to this end is market segmentation. The five basic forms of segmentation are demographic (population statistics), geographic (location), psychographic (personality or lifestyle), benefit (product features), and volume (amount purchased).

6. Understand how marketing research is used to minimize marketing risk.
Much can be learned about consumers through marketing research, which involves collecting, recording, and analyzing data important in marketing goods and services and communicating the results to management. Mar-

keting researchers may use primary data, which are gathered through door-to-door, mall-intercept, telephone, focus group, and mail interviews. They may also use secondary data, which are obtained from previous projects and a number of sources. Secondary data save time and money, but they may not meet researchers' needs. Both primary and secondary data give researchers a better idea of how the market will respond to the product. Thus they reduce the risk of producing something the market doesn't want.

■ DISCUSSION QUESTIONS

1. Can the marketing concept be applied effectively by a sole proprietorship, or is it better for larger businesses with more managers? Explain.

2. How would the marketing mix differ for each of the following organizations: United Airlines; Henrietta's Hair Styling Salon; Caterpillar Tractor Co.; Revlon (cosmetics); the American Cancer Society chapter in Evanston, Illinois (population 80,000); Burger King; George and Harry's machine-tool rebuilding shop.

3. Give an example of how the changing environment has caused a company to alter its marketing mix. Can some companies survive without worrying about the external environment?

4. Why is it important for organizations to understand consumer behavior? Give some examples.

5. "Market segmentation is the most important concept in marketing." Why do you think some marketing professionals make this statement? Give an example of each form of segmentation.

6. When would a marketer want to consider using primary research? Secondary research?

7. Do you think marketing research is an invasion of privacy? Should it be against the law? Explain.

8. Can marketing research be carried out in the same manner all over the world? Why or why not?

■ CASES

"I Saw That at Spring Break"

The annual rite of spring break has become a paradise for the movie studios. When the students hit town, the studios are out in force with trailers, movie-related stunts, in-your-face contests, autograph-signing actors, and T-shirts and other freebies. And with good reason. Spring break is considered the single largest marketing event in the college market, drawing two million students each year.

These students comprise one of the biggest captive audiences a marketer can find. And unlike concerts, football games, or other events that draw big crowds to one site, when spring break ends, the students disperse across the country, carrying marketers' messages with them.

"Spring break is a great buzz, a 'start-talking' point for movies," said Charlotte Kandel, senior vice president of worldwide publicity and promotion at Warner Bros. Warner promotes summer releases at spring break. "Kids are big talkers," Kandel said. "Once they get home and we start running the trailers and TV spots, they remember, 'Oh yeah, I saw that at spring break'."

"Poster publications"—promotional fliers that open up into posters—are on display in hotel rooms and at poolside. Table tents direct students to watch *Preview Theater,* a 60-minute special running on local channels in hotel rooms and on video screens at nightclubs. Movie posters are up in hotel lobbies, nightclubs, and comedy clubs. And banners stretch across palm trees and pool decks.

College students comprise a disproportionate percentage (24%) of movie audiences, so they are a particularly important market for the studios. Moviegoing is a major form of entertainment for college students. The average college student sees 1.8 movies at theaters each month, plus more titles on videos.

Yet the value of spring break promotions is difficult to measure. Industry executives generally agree spring break is not as important to marketing plans as, say, promotional screenings sponsored by radio stations and newspapers, because screenings run closer to a movie's release. Still, executives who commit to spring break marketing year after year swear by it.

Executives at 20th Century Fox said they put their time into creating take-home items, tied to movies, that students will keep, use, and remember them by. "We look for the newest cutting-edge items that kids are wearing and using," said Alan Amman, vice president of field operations and promotions for the company.

"What we're doing is participating in their fun times," said Michael Hogan, president of Hogan Communications, which has been organizing spring break promotions for studios for the past decade. "Students love the free T-shirts," he says. "And later, when the movie comes out, they remember the name from spring break and start wearing the shirts because nobody else has one."[24]

Questions

1. Do you think movie studios follow the marketing concept? Why or why not?
2. What type of promotion are the studios using at spring break? Give some examples.
3. What other types of goods and services would be a "natural" to promote at spring break locations?

Product and Price Strategies

Learning Goals

After studying this chapter, you should be able to:

1. Explain the product concept.
2. Describe a product classification system for consumer and industrial goods.
3. Explain the roles of branding, packaging, and labeling in creating a product.
4. Explain the process of new-product development.
5. List the stages of the product life cycle.
6. Describe the role of pricing in marketing.
7. Explain how prices can be set.
8. Explain price skimming and penetration pricing.
9. Understand the pricing tactics used by marketers to maintain a competitive position.

Career Profile

A position with a toy manufacturer during a work-study program in college gave Matthew Fenton a thorough understanding of how to market products to children. This experience, along with his double major in marketing and management, helped him land a job as an associate brand manager at Van Melle U.S.A.

Van Melle is an international company based in Breda, Holland. The century-old family business manufactures and markets candy. Van Melle U.S.A. is the U.S. branch of the operation. It oversees the marketing of two products: Mentos, the best-selling mint candy in the world, and AirHeads, the number-one fifteen cent, non-chocolate children's candy in the United States.

Brand recognition is important when selling candy to children. It is essential to stand out from the competition and catch kids' eyes. Packaging is a big part of Van Melle's sales strategy. The company recognizes that children are attracted to products that look outrageous. An interesting package design may convince a child to pick your product out of a display containing over a hundred other items.

Matthew's current tasks include package design, display design, coordinating research tests, analyzing promotional programs, and analyzing competitors. The continuing profitability of Mentos and AirHeads is one of the key measures of his job performance. Gradually, he will become more involved in long-term strategic planning for the company.

Matthew finds children's marketing very exciting. He enjoys the challenge of coming up with new ways to promote Van Melle's products to kids. He had to spend an additional year in college in order to participate in the work-study program that gave him his first real-world experience in business, but in the long run that investment has paid high dividends for his career.

Overview

Chapter 15 begins by exploring the nature of products and ways to classify them. It then explains the key roles of branding, packaging, and labeling in creating a product. Next it explains the steps involved in new-product development. Once a product is placed on the market, it enters the product life cycle, which is also discussed. We then turn our attention to the role of pricing in the marketing mix. The chapter explains how prices are set and presents two key strategies for pricing new products. Chapter 15 ends with a discussion of the tactics used to fine-tune pricing strategies.

WHAT IS A PRODUCT?

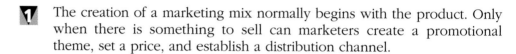

The creation of a marketing mix normally begins with the product. Only when there is something to sell can marketers create a promotional theme, set a price, and establish a distribution channel.

■ In marketing terms, a product is any good or service that satisfies wants. Many products are a melding of goods and services. If you want to enjoy a day of skiing, you need the proper equipment (products as goods) and a ski lift to get you to the top of the mountain (product as service).

■ **Exhibit 15-1**
Product Concept: Tangible and Intangible Attributes

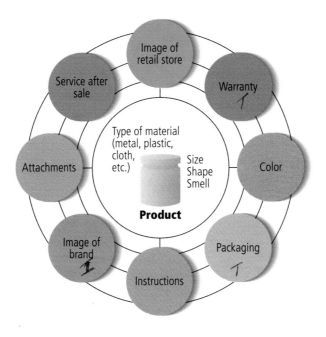

■ **Exhibit 15-1**
Product Concept: Tangible and Intangible Attributes

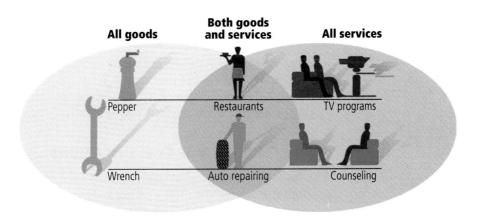

■ **Exhibit 15-2**
Blends of Goods and Services

product Any want-satisfying good or service, along with its perceived tangible and intangible attributes and benefits.

In marketing, a **product** is any good or service, along with its perceived attributes and benefits, that satisfies wants. Attributes can be tangible or intangible. Among the tangible attributes are packaging and warranties (see Exhibit 15-1). Intangible attributes are symbolic, such as brand image. People often buy things for what they mean, not for what they are. Why else would a man on the hottest day of the summer wrap a tie around his neck? The benefits of that tie are symbolic (a badge of taste or rank), not tangible.

THE BLEND OF GOODS AND SERVICES

Products are often a blend of goods and services (see Exhibit 15-2). A Honda Accord (a good) would have less value without maintenance (a service). Burger King sells such goods as sandwiches and french fries. It also offers a service by preparing the food and keeping the dining area clean.

The more tangible something is, the more likely we are to call it a good. For instance, a Coke, a Corvette, Morton salt, and *Rolling Stone* magazine are easy to classify as goods. The more intangible something is, the more likely we are to call it a service. Haircuts, TV programs, and marriage counseling are usually thought of as services. Services generally cannot be physically held; they can only be experienced.

WHAT MAKES SERVICES DIFFERENT?

A good image is important in selling a service because there are few objective standards for measuring service quality. Goods can be judged by their weight, size, color, and so on. But services must often be judged subjectively. Also, services are usually completed before their quality can be judged. Defective services cannot be returned. Furthermore, some services, such as plumbing and TV repair, are not used very often. Thus people often choose a service company on the basis of its reputation rather than personal experience.

Service output is also hard to standardize. You may like your haircut one time and not the next, even though the same stylist cut it both times. A lawyer may win a case for you, but using the same lawyer in the future will not guarantee success.

Finally, services cannot be saved or stored. Once Flight 97 takes off for New York, the service is used up. Empty seats bring in no revenue. This aspect of services is especially important to airlines, hotels, and amusement promoters, who may cut prices to attract buyers at slow times.

2 CONSUMER PRODUCT CLASSIFICATIONS

Because most things sold are a blend of goods and services, the term *product* can be used to refer to both. After all, consumers are really buying packages of benefits. The person who buys a plane ride is looking for a quick way to get from one city to another (the benefit). Providing this benefit requires goods (a plane, food) and services (ticketing, maintenance, piloting).

Marketers must know how consumers view the types of products their companies sell. They can then design the marketing mix to appeal to the selected target market. Marketers have devised product categories to help define target markets. The first level distinguishes between individual consumers and business buyers. Subgroups exist within those two classifications.

As you learned in Chapter 14, products that are bought by the end user are called *consumer products*. They include electric razors, sandwiches, cars, stereos, magazines, and houses. Consumer products that get used up, such as hair mousse and potato chips, are called *consumer nondurables*. Those that last for a long time, such as washing machines and shoes, are *consumer durables*.

▓ Exhibit 15-3
Classifying Consumer Products by the Effort Expended to Buy Them

Another way to classify consumer products is by the amount of effort consumers are willing to make to acquire them. The three major groupings in this scheme are convenience products, shopping products, and specialty products (see Exhibit 15-3).

Convenience Products

convenience products Relatively inexpensive products that require little shopping effort.

Relatively inexpensive items that require little shopping effort are **convenience products**. Soft drinks, candy bars, milk, bread, and small hardware items are examples. We buy them routinely without much planning. This does not mean that such products are unimportant or obscure. Many, in fact, are well known by their brand names—such as Pepsi-Cola, Pepperidge Farm breads, Domino's pizza, Sure deodorant, and UPS shipping.

Shopping Products

shopping products Products that are bought after a brand-to-brand and store-to-store comparison.

Products that are bought after a brand-to-brand and store-to-store comparison of price, suitability, and style are **shopping products**. Examples are furniture, automobiles, a vacation in Europe, and some items of clothing. Convenience products are bought with little planning, but shopping products may be chosen months or even years before their actual purchase.

Specialty Products

specialty products Products for which consumers search long and hard and for which they refuse to accept substitutes.

Products for which consumers search long and hard and for which they refuse to accept substitutes are **specialty products**. Expensive jewelry, designer clothing, state-of-the-art stereo equipment, limited-production automobiles, and gourmet dinners fall into this category. Since consumers are willing to spend much time and effort to find specialty products, distribution is often limited to one or two sellers in a given region, perhaps Neiman-Marcus, Gucci, or the Porsche dealer.

TYPES OF INDUSTRIAL PRODUCTS

capital products Industrial products that are usually large and expensive and have a long life span.

expense items Industrial products that are smaller and less expensive than capital products and typically have a life span of less than a year.

Products bought by businesses or institutions for use in making other products or in providing services are called *industrial products*. They are classified as either capital products or expense items. **Capital products** are usually large, expensive items with a long life span. Examples are buildings, large machines, and airplanes. **Expense items** are typically smaller, less expensive items that usually have a life span of less than a year. Examples are printer ribbons and paper. Industrial products are sometimes further classified in the following categories.

Installations

Installations are large, expensive capital items that determine the nature, scope, and efficiency of a company. Capital products like General Motors' Saturn assembly plant in Tennessee represent a big commitment against future earnings and profitability. Buying an installation requires longer negotiations, more planning, and the judgments of more people than buying any other type of product.

Accessories

Accessories do not have the same long-run impact on the firm as installations, and they are less expensive and more highly standardized. But they are still capital products. Minolta copy machines, IBM personal computers, and smaller machines such as Black and Decker table drills and saws are typical accessories. Marketers of accessories often rely on well-known brand names and extensive advertising as well as personal selling.

Component Parts and Materials

Component parts and materials are expense items built into the end product. They may be custom-made items, such as a drive shaft for an automobile, a case for a computer, or a special pigment for painting U.S. Navy harbor buoys. Other component parts may be standardized for sale to many industrial users. Integrated circuits for personal computers and cement for the construction trade are examples of standardized component parts and materials.

Raw Materials

Raw materials are inputs to the final product that have undergone little or no processing. They, too, are expense items. Examples include lumber, copper, and zinc. Most buyers of raw materials have specific uses in mind. Generally they want ample supplies in the right grade. For instance, International Paper requires a certain type of log in specified lengths to make paper.

Supplies

Supplies are expense items that do not become part of the final product. They are bought routinely and in fairly large quantities. Supply items run the gamut from pencils and paper to paint and machine oil. They have little impact on the firm's long-run profits.

Services

Services are expense items used to plan or support company operations, such as janitorial cleaning and management consulting. Industrial services are usually sold on a personal basis. Buyers must be convinced of their need for the special skills of an outside firm or the cost-effectiveness of hiring a certain one.

3 BRANDING

Most industrial and consumer products have a brand name. If everything came in a plain brown wrapper, life would be less colorful and competition would decrease. Companies would have less incentive to put out better products because consumers would be unable to tell one company's products from those of another.

brand Product identifier in the form of words, names, symbols, or designs.

The product identifier for a company is its **brand**. Brands appear in the form of words, names, symbols, or designs. They are used to distinguish a company's products from those of its competitors. Examples of well-known brands are Kleenex tissues, Jeep automobiles, and IBM computers.

trademark Legally exclusive design, name, or other identifying mark associated with a company's brand.

A **trademark** is the legally exclusive design, name, or other identifying mark associated with a company's brand. No other company can use the same trademark. Coming up with a new trademark or brand name is not an easy task. Marketers are always on the lookout for new names or even for certain letters of the alphabet that can "push consumers' hot buttons," as the following Trends in Business Today box shows.

T R E N D S

Business Today

The ABCs of Brand Names

Suppose that you are given the task of naming a new Polaroid camera. What names might you suggest? New York consulting firm Delano, Goldman & Young, given that task, came up with the brand name Captiva for Polaroid's new instant camera. The name is meant to suggest the ideas "captivating" and the "capture" of an image on film. Besides that, says Frank Delano, chairman of the firm, Captiva fits the trend in choosing product names that are international sounding, often ending in vowels.

If one vowel is good, two are even better. Thus Oldsmobile's Aurora and Achieva and Nissan's Altima, beginning and ending in vowels, have names that naming consultants feel sure will be noticed. But what of foreign-sounding names that do not end in vowels? Dr. Delano claims that General Motors dropped its Calais line of cars in part because of the name. He says the name "meant nothing. It may sound French, but it's not a person, it's not a place, it's not even a French word. It was just a word that didn't say anything about the product." Calais is, in fact, the name of a French port, but the brand name clearly didn't pique Mr. Delano's interest.

As is true with colors, names and even letters go in and out of fashion. For example, says Delano, the letter X saw its heyday in earlier decades with Exxon and Xerox but has now been overused. What is an exciting sound right now, says Delano, is the letter Z, as used in Prozac and Zoloft, rival antidepressant prescription drugs.

But what letters should companies be thinking about, in order to stay ahead of the curve? According to Delano, they would do well to concentrate on Q and J, which he says are up-and-coming letters because they are untapped areas. As anyone who has played the game of Scrabble® knows, successful use of those letters, as with the letters X and Z, is more difficult than using other letters but can bring great reward.[1]

The two major types of brands are manufacturer (national) brands and dealer (private) brands.

Manufacturer (National) Brands

manufacturer brands Brands owned by national or regional manufacturers and widely distributed; also called national brands.

Brands owned by national or regional manufacturers and widely distributed are **manufacturer brands**. (These brands are sometimes called national brands, but since some of the brands are not owned by nationwide or international manufacturers, *manufacturer brands* is a more accurate term.) A few well-known manufacturer brands are Polaroid, Liz Claiborne, Nike, and Sony.

Manufacturer brands can bring new customers and new prestige to small retailers. For instance, a small bicycle repair shop in a midwestern college town got the franchise to sell and repair Schwinn bicycles. The shop's profits grew quickly, and it became one of the most successful retail business in the university area. Because manufacturer brands are widely promoted, sales are often high. Also, most manufacturers of these brands offer frequent deliveries to their retailers. Thus retailers can carry less stock and have less money tied up in inventory.

Dealer (Private) Brands

dealer brands Brands that carry the wholesaler's or retailer's name; private brands.

Brands that carry the wholesaler's or retailer's name rather than that of the manufacturer are **dealer brands**. Sears has several well-known dealer (or private) brands, including Craftsman, Diehard, and Kenmore. The Independent Grocers Association (IGA), a large wholesale grocery organization, uses the brand name Shurfine on its goods. Dealer brands tie consumers to particular wholesalers or retailers. If you want a Kenmore washing machine, you must go to Sears.

Although profit margins are usually higher on dealer brands than on manufacturer brands, dealers must still stimulate demand for their products. Sears' promotion of its products has made the company one of the largest advertisers in the United States. But promotion costs can cut heavily into profit margins. And if a dealer-brand item is of poor quality, the dealer must assume responsibility for it. Sellers of manufacturer brands can refer a disgruntled customer to the manufacturer.

Generic Products

generic products Products that carry no brand name, come in plain containers, and sell for much less than brand-name products.

Many consumers don't want to pay the costs of manufacturer or dealer brands. One popular way to save money is to buy **generic products**. These products carry no brand name, come in plain containers, and sell for much less than brand-name products. They are typically sold in black and white packages with such simple labels as "liquid bleach" or "spaghetti." Generic products are sold by 85 percent of U.S. supermarkets. Sometimes manufacturers simply stop the production line and substitute a generic package for a brand package, though the product is exactly the same. The most popular generics are garbage bags, jelly, paper towels, coffee cream substitutes, cigarettes, and paper napkins.

Brand Loyalty

brand loyalty Preference
for a particular brand.

A consumer who tries one or more brands may decide to buy a certain brand regularly. The preference for a particular brand is **brand loyalty**. It lets consumers buy with less time, thought, and risk. Brand loyalty ensures future sales for the firm. It can also help protect a firm's share of the market, discourage new competitors, and thus prolong the brand's life. Brand loyalty to most or all of a company's products is a marketer's dream come true.

Why do people continue buying the same brands? A recent study found the following motivations (in rank order of importance): good past experience with the brand, good price for value, high quality, and based upon a personal recommendation.[2] If consumers perceive a product to be of high quality, they may be willing to pay more for it. The brands Americans view as having the highest quality are shown in Exhibit 15-4.

■ **Exhibit 15-4**
America's 25 Highest Quality Brands in Rank Order

Source: Terry Lefton, "How the Big Brands Rank," *Brandweek,* 29 March 1993, p. 28.

Brand name

1. Disney World/Disneyland
2. Kodak Photographic Film
3. UPS
4. Hallmark Greeting Cards
5. Fisher-Price Toys
6. AT&T Long Distance Telephone
7. Mercedes Automobiles
8. Arm & Hammer Baking Soda
9. Chiquita Bananas
10. Levi's Jeans
11. Lego Toys
12. Hershey's Milk Chocolate Bar
13. Federal Express
14. Tylenol Pain Reliever
15. Rubbermaid Kitchen Products
16. Harley Davidson Motorcycles
17. Playskool Toys
18. Michelin Automobile Tires
19. Tupperware Kitchen Products
20. IBM Personal Computers
21. Campbell's Soup
22. Dole Bananas
23. Universal Studios Florida
24. Sony Television
25. Wal-Mart

PACKAGING

Packaging can be quite important in marketing a product. One basic function of packaging is to protect the product from breaking or spoiling and thus extend its life. A package should be easy to ship, store, and stack on a shelf and be convenient for the consumer to use. Wholesalers and retailers prefer packages that help cut shipping costs and reduce shoplifting. The package should also be easily disposable. Increasingly, consumers and environmental groups are concerned about the impact of packaging on the environment.

Many new packaging methods have been developed recently. Aseptic packages keep foods fresh for months without refrigeration. Examples are Borden's "sippin' packs" for juices, the Brik Pak for milk, and Hunt's/Del Monte's aseptic boxes for tomato sauce. Some package developers are creating "micro-atmospheres" that allow meat to stay fresh in the refrigerator for weeks. A patch on the lid of Armour's Dinner Classics changes from blue and white to all blue when the food is properly cooked in a microwave oven. And Oscar Mayer now uses Zip-Pak resealable packaging on its lunch meats.

A second basic function of packaging is to help promote the product by providing clear brand identification and information about the product's features. For example, Ralston Purina Company's Dog Chow brand, the leading dog food, was losing market share. The company decided that the pictures of dog breeds on the package were too old-fashioned and rural. With a new package, featuring a photo of a dog and a child, sales have increased.

Packaging can help link a firm's products to one another. Planters Nuts and Weight Watchers, for instance, have both made packaging changes to better sell several related products under a single brand name. Standardizing the labels and colors of the packages visually reinforces the *family brand concept*—using the same brand name on a variety of products. Ralston Purina uses its "checkerboard squares" on everything from chicken feed to cereal.

Packaging also can be used to convey product messages. When the price of fancy seafood rose rapidly, consumers of Wakefield frozen seafood noticed. In response, the company developed a new, more elegant box featuring a photo of seafood in a silver serving dish. This change helped position the product as a high-quality one worth the higher price.

A major part of any package is the label. Congress has been concerned with labeling since it passed the Food and Drug Act of 1906. This act banned false labeling of foods and drugs. Eventually, Congress realized that the legislation was too vague. In 1967 it passed the Fair Packaging and Labeling Act. This act requires labels and packages to give enough information about product ingredients and composition to help the consumer make an informed decision. The law helps consumers make rational comparisons of prices and other factors and makes it illegal to deceive consumers. A new labeling law was passed in 1991 to improve and clarify food labeling. The law controls the health claims on labels and now requires nutritional labeling. It also requires standard definitions for such terms as *light, low fat,* and *low salt.*

CUSTOMER SERVICE

A product strategy is not complete without attention to customer service. A product that doesn't work properly is useless. A VCR, for instance, that refuses to play back a recorded tape is of no value.

The two basic components of customer service are the warranty and the repair service. If products need repair, we expect them to be fixed quickly. Companies that offer poor repair service rarely get repeat sales. A **warranty** guarantees the quality of a good or service. An **implied warranty** is an unwritten guarantee that the product is fit for the purpose for which it was sold. All sales have an implied warranty under the Uniform Commercial Code (a law that applies to commercial dealings in most states). An **express warranty** is made in writing. Express warranties range from simple statements, such as "100 percent cotton" (a guarantee of raw materials) and "complete satisfaction guaranteed" (a statement of performance), to extensive documents written in obscure language.

Congress passed the Magnuson-Moss Warranty–Federal Trade Commission Improvement Act (1975) to help consumers understand warranties and to help them get action from manufacturers and dealers. A **full warranty** means the manufacturer must meet certain minimum standards, including repair "within a reasonable time and without charge" of any defects and replacement of the merchandise or a full refund if the product does not work "after a reasonable number of attempts" at repair. Under the law, any warranty that does not live up to this tough standard must be "conspicuously" promoted as a limited warranty.

Service businesses have also tried to ensure customer satisfaction. American Airlines, for instance, gives customers vouchers for free travel when they are bumped from a flight or if their luggage gets misplaced. American Express spends hundreds of millions of dollars on the latest technology to maintain its service quality. It also has over a hundred programs to recognize and reward employees who take good care of customers. The U.S. Postal Service guarantees delivery of its Express Mail by 3 p.m. the next day. Service companies that foster good service generally find that it pays off in more customer loyalty and sales.

warranty Guarantee of the quality of a good or service.

implied warranty Unwritten guarantee that a good or service is fit for the purpose for which it was sold.

express warranty Written guarantee of the quality of a good or service.

full warranty Warranty that meets certain minimum federal standards, including repair or replacement of defective products.

Concept Check

- Explain the difference between goods and services.
- Describe the three categories of consumer products and five types of industrial products.
- Distinguish between manufacturer brands and dealer brands.
- What is a warranty?

NEW-PRODUCT DEVELOPMENT

[4]

new product Product that has a new brand name but is introduced into a product category new to the organization.

flanker brand Product that uses a new brand name but is introduced into a product category in which the organization already has products.

line extension Product using an existing brand name in an existing category but produced in a new flavor, size, or model.

franchise extension Product introduced in a new category using an existing brand name.

Marketers have several different terms for new products, depending on how the product fits into a company's existing product line. When a firm introduces a product that has a new brand name and is in a product category new to the organization, it is classified as a **new product**. For example, disposing of the hot oil used to cook tempura was a problem for Japanese households. Pouring it down the drain clogged plumbing lines and polluted Japan's waterways. So S.C. Johnson developed Tempura Oil Solidifier, which enables the oil to be disposed of as a solid waste.

If the product that is developed uses a new brand name but is introduced into a category in which the organization already has products, the new item is called a **flanker brand**. Procter & Gamble introduced Luv diapers after experiencing great success with Pampers. Hampton Inns and Embassy Suites are flanker brands for Holiday Inns.

A new flavor, size, or model using an existing brand name in an existing category is called a **line extension**. Diet Cherry Coke and caffeine-free Coke are line extensions. Johnson & Johnson line extensions for Tylenol include Tylenol Extra-Strength caplets, Tylenol Extra-Strength liquid, Tylenol Sinus caplets, Tylenol Allergy and Sinus caplets, Tylenol Cold Formula caplets, Tylenol Cold Formula liquid, and Tylenol "No Drowsiness" Cold Formula caplets. The strategy of expanding the line by adding new models has enabled companies like Seiko (watches), Kraft (cheeses), Oscar Mayer (lunch meats), and Sony (consumer electronics) to tie up a large amount of shelf space and "share of mind" in a product category.

A product in a new category using an existing brand name is a **franchise extension**. Examples of franchise extensions are Reynolds plastic wrap (an extension from Reynolds aluminum), Fisher-Price shampoo and baby bath (extension from toys), IBM copiers (extension from computers), and Liz Claiborne cosmetics (extension from clothing). Franchise extension allows the organization to build on the consumer awareness, goodwill, and image of its established brand name. It also reduces the amount of money the firm needs to invest in advertising the new product. It quickly conveys to the consumer many of the attributes of the old product, allowing the company to enter the new category from a position of strength. But consumers' perceptions of the new item must be consistent with their perception of the brand name. Consumers view Arm & Hammer's laundry detergent as a logical franchise extension of the company's baking soda. Yet Arm & Hammer underarm deodorant was a flop.

IMPORTANCE OF NEW PRODUCTS TO MANAGEMENT

New products pump life into corporate sales, letting the firm not only survive but also grow. Companies like Allegheny Ludlum (steel), Corning (fiber optics), Dow (chemicals), Hewlett-Packard (computers), and Stryker (medical products) get most of their profits from new products. Companies that lead their industries in profitability and sales growth get 49 percent of their revenues from products developed within the last five

■ Ford Motor Company's CAD design system is lowering the automaker's new-product development costs. Using a powerful computer, designers can test many elements of new models without building expensive mockups. Changes can be made at the touch of an electronic pen.

years. Merck, for example, introduced Mevacor, a cholesterol-lowering drug, in 1988. By the mid-1990s Mevacor was producing sales of about $600 million annually. The least successful firms get only 11 percent of their sales from new products.[3]

Creating successful new products is not easy. For instance, Johnson & Johnson introduced more than 200 new products in the past five years. But only two of them were "home runs" with sales of over $100 million.

THE PRODUCT DEVELOPMENT PROCESS

Developing new products is both costly and risky. To increase their chances for success, most firms use the product development process shown in Exhibit 15-5 and summarized here:

1. *Set new-product goals:* Usually the goals are financial. A company may want to recover its investment in three years or less. Or it may want to earn at least a 15 percent return on the investment. Nonfinancial goals may include using existing equipment or facilities.

2. *Develop new-product ideas:* Smaller firms usually depend on employees, customers, investors, and distributors for new ideas. Larger companies use these sources and more structured marketing research techniques.

    Excellent product ideas are often generated from the comments of focus groups. A few examples are the interior design of the Ford Taurus, Stick-Up room deodorizers, Dustbusters, and Wendy's salad bar. In the industrial market, machine tools, keyboard designs, aircraft interiors, and backhoe accessories evolved from focus groups.

    Brainstorming is also used to generate new-product ideas. The goal of **brainstorming** is to have the group think of as many ways to vary

brainstorming Process for generating new ideas by having a group think of as many ideas as possible, with criticism and evaluation held until later.

a product or solve a problem as possible. Criticism is avoided, no matter how ridiculous an idea seems at the time. The emphasis is on sheer numbers of ideas. Evaluation of those ideas is postponed to later steps of development.

3. *Screen ideas and concepts:* As ideas emerge, they are checked against the firm's new-product goals and its long-range strategies. This procedure is called **screening**. Many product concepts are rejected, for various reasons: they don't fit well with existing products, needed technology is not available, the company doesn't have enough resources, or the sales potential is low. There is great market potential for a safe, fast-acting weight-reducing product, for instance. Much less potential exists for a dog collar with a built-in radio.

4. *Develop a preliminary profit plan:* If a product concept makes it through the screening stage, the firm prepares a preliminary profit plan. A rough financial statement outlines general sales estimates as well as developmental expenses, production costs, and financing charges. From these figures, management can estimate if a new-product concept will meet its financial goals.

5. *Create a marketing mix:* If a concept looks as if it could be profitable, it is ready for the main part of the development process. The product, the marketing strategy, and the communication plan all begin at once. Plans for promotion, for instance, do not wait until the product is fully developed.

The type and amount of product testing varies, depending on how easy it is to make the item and how easy it will be for consumers to use it. If Seven Seas is testing a new salad dressing flavor, it already has a lot of experience. Thus it will go directly into advanced taste tests and perhaps home-use tests. But if Seven Seas

screening Checking new ideas against the firm's new-product goals and long-range strategies.

decided to develop a new line of soft drinks, it would most likely do a great deal of testing. It would study many aspects of the new product before actually making it.

The marketing strategy is refined while testing takes place. Channels of distribution are selected. Pricing policies are developed and tested. The target market is further defined, and demand for the product is estimated. Management also continually updates the profit plan.

As the marketing strategy and product tests mature, a communication strategy develops. Logo and package wording are created. Communication strategy also includes promotion themes and introduction of the product to the sales force. The projected cost of the communication strategy may be revised for the profit plan.

6. *Test market the new product:* Test marketing allows management to evaluate various strategies and to see how well the parts of the marketing mix fit together. Few new-product concepts reach this stage. For those that do, the firm must decide whether to introduce the product on a regional or national basis. Test-market cities all over the country are chosen. No one has yet found a "magic city" in which local success guarantees national success.

   Big companies, like McDonald's, have the luxury of testing a product in a limited area without going to much effort. It simply adds the test item to the menu. McDonald's has been testing fried chicken for over six years in various parts of the country. Recently it began testing a variety of new sandwiches.

7. *Introduce the product:* A product that passes test marketing is ready for market introduction, called *national rollout,* which requires a lot of logistical coordination. Various divisions of the company must be encouraged to give the new item the attention it deserves. Packaging and labeling in a different language may be required. Sales training sessions must be scheduled, spare parts inventoried, service personnel trained, advertising and promotion campaigns readied, and wholesalers and retailers informed about the new item. If the new product is to be sold internationally, it may have to be altered to meet the requirements of the target countries. For instance, electrical products may have to run on different electrical currents. As you can see, market introduction is not a simple task.

The total cost of development and initial introduction can be staggering. For example, it cost Gillette over $200 million to develop and start manufacturing the Sensor razor and another $110 million for first-year advertising alone![4] A grocery industry task force concluded that, on average, manufacturers pay $5.1 million to get a new product or line extension on grocery shelves nationally.[5] Forty-six percent of spending is for advertising and promotion to persuade consumers to try the product. Another 16 percent is for promotions directed at wholesalers and retailers. Research and development and market analysis costs consume 18 percent. Making the product is the least expensive step.

- Explain the differences among a franchise extension, line extension, and flanker brand.
- What are the steps in the new-product development process?

THE PRODUCT LIFE CYCLE

5

product life cycle Series of stages in a product's sales and profits over a period of time, consisting of introduction, growth, maturity, and decline (and death).

After a product reaches the marketplace, it enters the **product life cycle**—a pattern of sales and profits over some period. The cycle typically has four stages: introduction, growth, maturity, and decline (and death). These stages are pictured in Exhibit 15-6. As the product moves through these stages, the firm must keep revising the marketing mix to stay competitive and meet the needs of target customers.

STAGES OF THE LIFE CYCLE

Introduction

When a product enters the life cycle, it faces many obstacles. Although competition may be light, the *introductory stage* usually features frequent product modifications, limited distribution, and heavy promotion. The failure rate is high. Production and marketing costs are also high, and sales volume is low. Hence profits are usually small or negative.

An example of a new product is General Mills' China Coast restaurants. Currently, restaurants provide about a third of General Mills' $7.8 billion in annual revenues. General Mills is parent to 587 Red Lobster (seafood) and 365 Olive Garden (Italian) restaurants, each of which grosses more than $2.7 million annually, on average.[6] Company executives believe each China Coast restaurant could do as well. Although the restaurants will all look alike, including a turquoise pagoda roof, the menus will be somewhat customized to local tastes. Before entering a market, a General Mills

■ **Exhibit 15-6**
Stages in the Product
Life Cycle

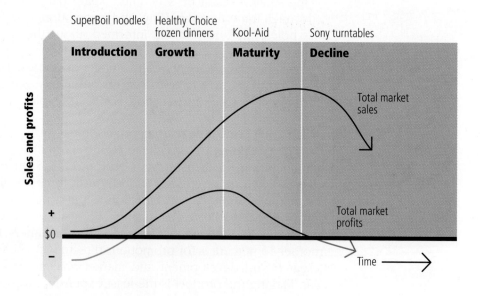

crew will sample food at competing restaurants, to measure the local spice level. Will China Coast be successful? Only time will tell.

Growth Stage

If a product category survives the introductory stage, it advances to the *growth stage* of the life cycle. In this stage, sales grow at an increasing rate, profits are healthy, and many competitors enter the market. Large companies may start to acquire small pioneering firms that have reached this stage. Emphasis switches from primary demand promotion to aggressive brand advertising and communicating the differences between brands. For example, the goal changes from convincing people to buy compact disk players to convincing them to buy Sony versus Panasonic or RCA.

Distribution becomes a major key to success during the growth stage, as well as in later stages. Manufacturers scramble to acquire dealers and distributors and to build long-term relationships. Without adequate distribution, it is impossible to establish a strong market position.

Toward the end of the growth phase, prices normally begin falling and profits peak. Price reductions result from increased competition and from cost reductions from producing larger quantities of items (economies of scale). Also, most firms have recovered their development costs by now, and their priority is in increasing or retaining market share and enhancing profits.

Maturity

After the growth stage, sales continue to mount—but at a decreasing rate. This is the *maturity stage*. Most products that have been on the market for a long time are in this stage. Thus most marketing strategies are designed for mature products. One such strategy is to bring out several variations of a basic product (line extension). Kool-Aid, for instance, was originally offered in three flavors. Today there are over ten, plus sweetened and unsweetened varieties.

Decline (and Death)

When sales and profits fall, the product is in the *decline stage*. The rate of decline is governed by two factors: the rate of change in consumer tastes and the rate at which new products enter the market. Sony turntables are an example of a product in the decline stage. The demand for turntables has now been surpassed by the demand for compact disk players and cassette players.

Death may follow decline, but it is not inevitable. Sometimes modifying a product or its perceived uses lets it enter a new growth phase. The use of creative marketing strategies to prolong the life of a product is called **innovative maturity**. Tactics include:

innovative maturity
Use of creative marketing strategies to prolong the life of a product.

- *Promoting more frequent use of the product by current consumers:* AT&T's "Reach Out and Touch Someone" campaign has stimulated the use of long-distance calling for all types of occasions.
- *Developing more varied use of the product by current consumers:* Jell-O is promoted for use in salads. Arm & Hammer baking soda

is suggested for brushing teeth, deodorizing refrigerators and sinks, and cleaning dentures.

- *Creating new consumers for the product by expanding the market:* General Electric created an artificial intelligence program to pinpoint problems in locomotives. With modifications, the program is now being used by Kidder Peabody and Company, investment bankers, to identify corporate takeover targets.
- *Developing new product features and refinements:* The laundry detergent industry has relied on this strategy to extend the life cycles of brands, adding whiteners, brighteners, bleaches, scents, and various other ingredients and attributes. Unscented Bounce, Charmin-Free, and decaffeinated beverages are products with deleted ingredients.
- *Making a dramatic new guarantee:* Spray 'n Wash shifted from declining sales to rapidly growing sales almost immediately after offering this guarantee: "If Spray 'n Wash doesn't remove a stain from a shirt—any shirt—we'll buy you a new shirt."
- *Developing new distribution channels:* For years Woolite fabric cleaner was sold only in department stores. Then American Home Products introduced the product in supermarkets and grocery stores without changing the product, the price, or the promotional appeal. Sales tripled in the first year.

THE PRODUCT LIFE CYCLE AS A MANAGEMENT TOOL

■ Exhibit 15-7
Strategies for Each Stage of the Product Life Cycle

The product life cycle may be used in planning. Marketers who understand the cycle concept are better able to forecast future sales and plan new marketing strategies. Exhibit 15-7 is a brief summary of strategic needs at various stages of the product life cycle.

Category	Introduction	Growth	Maturity	Decline
Marketing objectives	Encourage trial Establish distribution	Get triers to repurchase Attract new users	Seek new users or uses	Reduce marketing expenses Keep loyal users
Product objectives	Establish competitive advantage	Maintain product quality	Modify product	Maintain product
Distribution objectives	Establish distribution network	Solidify distribution relationships	Provide additional incentives to ensure support	Eliminate trade allowances
Promotional objectives	Build brand awareness	Provide information	Reposition product	Eliminate most advertising and sales promotions
Pricing objectives	Set introduction price (skimming or penetration pricing)	Maintain prices	Reduce prices to meet competition	Maintain prices

Marketers must be sure that a product has moved from one stage to the next before changing its marketing strategy. A temporary sales decline should not be interpreted as a sign that the product is dying. Pulling back marketing support can become a self-fulfilling prophecy that brings about the early death of a healthy product.

Concept Check

- Describe the stages in the product life cycle.
- What is meant by innovative maturity?

PRICE STRATEGY

 Part of the product development process is setting the right price. **Price** is the perceived value that is exchanged for something else. Value in our society is most commonly expressed in dollars and cents. Thus price is typically the amount of money exchanged for a good or service. Note that *perceived value* refers to the time of the transaction. After you've used a product you've bought, you may decide that its actual value was less than its perceived value at the time you bought it. The price you pay for a product is based on the *expected satisfaction* you will receive and not necessarily the *actual satisfaction* you will receive.

price Perceived value that is exchanged for something else.

Although price is usually a dollar amount, it can be anything with perceived value. When goods and services are exchanged for each other, the trade is called *barter.* If you exchange this book for a math book at the end of the term, you have engaged in barter. The price you pay for the math book will be this book.

IMPORTANCE OF PRICE TO MANAGEMENT

Price is important in determining how much a firm earns. The prices charged customers times the number of units sold equals the *gross revenue* for the firm. Revenue is what pays for every activity of the company (production, finance, sales, distribution, and so forth). What's left over (if anything) is profit. Managers strive to charge a price that will allow the firm to earn a fair return on its investment.

A price must be chosen that is not too high or low. And the price must equal the perceived value to target consumers. If consumers think a price is too high, sales opportunities will be lost. Lost sales mean lost revenue. If prices are too low, consumers may view the product as a great value, but the company may not meet its profit goals.

PRICING OBJECTIVES

Firms need to set pricing objectives that are realistic, measurable, and attainable with the resources they have. But pricing goals vary: Firms may try to set a price that will allow them to keep or increase their share of the market. Sometimes the objective is to set a price that will meet the competition. Three other common objectives are maximizing profits, achieving a target return on the investment, and offering good value at a fair price.

Maximizing Profits

profit maximization
Production of units of output for as long as the revenue from selling them is greater than the cost of producing them.

Profit maximization means producing a product as long as the revenue from selling it exceeds the cost of producing it. In other words, the goal is to get the largest possible profit from the product.

Here's an example: Carl Morgan, a builder of houses, sells them for $100,000 each. His revenue and cost projections are shown in Exhibit 15-8. Notice in column 3 that the cost of building each house drops for the second through the fifth house. The lower cost per house results from two things: First, by having several houses under construction at the same time, Morgan can afford to hire a full-time crew. The crew is more economical than the independent contractors to whom he would otherwise subcontract each task. Second, Morgan can order materials in greater quantities than usual and thus get quantity discounts on his orders.

Morgan decides that he could sell fifteen houses a year at the $100,000 price. But he knows he cannot maximize profits at more than seven houses a year. Inefficiencies creep in even at the sixth house. (Notice in column 3 that the cost of building the sixth house is higher than the cost of building any of the first five houses). Morgan can't supervise more than seven construction jobs at once, and his full-time crew can't handle even those seven. Thus Morgan has to subcontract some of the work on the sixth and seventh houses. If he were to produce more than seven houses, he would need a second full-time crew.

The table also shows why Morgan should construct seven houses a year. Even though the profit per house is falling for the sixth and seventh houses (column 4), the total profit is still rising (column 5). But at the eighth house, Morgan would go beyond profit maximization. That is, the cost of the eighth unit would be greater than its selling price. He would lose $15,000 on the house, and total profit would fall to $154,000 from $169,000 after the seventh house.

■ **Exhibit 15-8**
Revenue, Cost, and Profit Projections for Morgan's Houses

(1) Unit of Output (house)	(2) Selling price (revenue)	(3) Cost of building house	(4) Profit on house	(5) Total profit
1st	$100,000	$76,000	$24,000	$24,000
2nd	100,000	75,000	25,000	49,000
3rd	100,000	73,000	27,000	76,000
4th	100,000	70,000	30,000	106,000
5th	100,000	70,000	30,000	136,000
6th	100,000	77,000	23,000	159,000
7th	100,000	90,000	10,000	169,000
8th	100,000	115,000	(15,000)	154,000

Many accounting systems are not sophisticated enough to notify management that the profit-maximizing point has been reached. Thus many companies have turned to pricing goals that are easier to measure.

Achieving a Target Return on Investment

target return on investment Pricing objective in which the price is set to give the company the desired profitability in terms of return on its money.

One pricing objective used by many companies is **target return on investment**. The price is set to give the company the desired profitability in terms of return on its money. Among the companies that use target return on investment as their main pricing objective are 3M, Procter & Gamble, General Electric, and Du Pont.

To get an idea of how target return works, imagine that you are a marketing manager for a cereal company. You estimate that developing, launching, and marketing a new hot cereal will cost $2 million. If the net profit for the first year is $200,000, the return on investment will be $200,000 ÷ $2,000,000, or 10 percent. Let's say that top management sets a 15 percent target return on investment. (The average target return on investment for large corporations is now about 14 percent.) Since a net profit of $200,000 will yield only a 10 percent return, one of two things will happen. Either the cereal won't be produced, or the price and marketing mix will be changed to yield the 15 percent target return.

Value Marketing

value marketing Offering the target market a product or service of high quality at a fair price and with good customer service.

Value marketing has become a popular pricing strategy in the mid-1990s. **Value marketing** means offering the target market a high-quality product at a fair price and with good service. It is the notion of offering the customer a good value. Value marketing doesn't mean high quality if it's available only at high prices. Nor does it mean bare-bones service or low-quality products. Value marketing can be used to sell a variety of products, from a $44,000 Infiniti Q45 from Nissan to $2.99 packages of L'eggs hosiery.

A value marketer does the following:

- *Offers products that perform:* This is the price of entry, because consumers have lost patience with shoddy merchandise.
- *Gives consumers more than they expect:* Soon after Toyota launched Lexus, the company had to order a recall. The weekend before the recall, dealers phoned every Lexus owner in the United States, personally making arrangements to pick up their cars and offering replacement vehicles.
- *Gives meaningful guarantees:* Chrysler offers a 70,000-mile power train warranty. Michelin recently introduced a tire warranted to last 80,000 miles.
- *Avoids unrealistic pricing:* Because consumers couldn't understand why Kellogg's cereals commanded such a premium over other brands, Kellogg's market share fell 5 percent in the late 1980s. Likewise, Compaq maintained a 35 percent price premium over other personal computer brands, even though other similar PCs were steadily decreasing in price. Compaq lost market share and profits, and ultimately the CEO resigned.

- *Gives the buyer facts:* Today's sophisticated consumer wants informative advertising and knowledgeable salespeople.
- *Builds long-term relationships:* American Air Lines' AAdvantage program, Hyatt's Passport Club, and Whirlpool's 800-number hot line all help build good customer relations.[7]

Concept Check

- Explain the concept of price.
- What is meant by target return on investment, and how does it differ from profit maximization?
- What is value marketing?

PRICE DETERMINATION

7 After setting a pricing objective, the company must set a specific price on the product. Two techniques that are often used to set a price are markup pricing and breakeven analysis.

MARKUP PRICING

markup pricing Addition of a certain percentage to a product's cost to arrive at a new price.

One of the most common forms of pricing is **markup pricing**. This method adds a certain percentage to a product's cost to arrive at the new price. (The new price is thus *cost plus markup.*) The cost is the expense of manufacturing the product or acquiring it for resale. The markup is the amount added to the cost to cover expenses and leave a profit. For example, an item that costs $5 and sells for $7 carries a markup of 29 percent:

Cost to retailer	$5
Markup	+2
Retail price	$7

$$\text{Markup percentage} = \frac{\text{Markup}}{\text{Retail price}}$$

$$= \frac{\$2}{\$7}$$

$$= 29\%$$

Several elements influence markups. Among them are tradition, the competition, store image, and stock turnover. Traditionally department stores used a 40 percent markup. But today competition has forced retailers to respond to consumer demand and meet competitors' prices. A department store that tried to sell household appliances at a 40 percent markup would lose customers to such discounters as Wal-Mart and Target. However, a retailer trying to develop a prestige image will use markups that are much higher than those used by a retailer trying to develop an image as a discounter.

THE BREAKEVEN CONCEPT

Manufacturers, wholesalers (companies that buy from manufacturers and sell to retailers and institutions), and retailers (firms that sell to end users) need to know how much of a product must be sold at a certain price to cover all costs. The point at which the costs are covered and additional sales result in profit is the **breakeven point**.

To find the point at which it breaks even, the firm measures the various costs associated with the product:

breakeven point Point at which costs are covered and additional sales result in profit.

- Some costs do not vary with different levels of output. These are called **fixed costs**. The rent on a manufacturing facility is a fixed cost. It must be paid whether production is one unit or a million units.

fixed costs Costs that do not vary with different levels of output.

- **Variable costs** are costs that change with different levels of output. Wages and expenses of raw materials are considered variable costs.

variable costs Costs that change with different levels of output.

- The **fixed-cost contribution** is the selling price per unit (revenue) minus the variable costs per unit.

fixed-cost contribution Selling price per unit (revenue) minus the variable costs per unit.

- **Total revenue** is the selling price per unit times the number of units sold.
- **Total cost** is the total of the fixed costs and the variable costs.
- **Total profit** is total revenue minus total cost.

total revenue Selling price per unit times the number of units sold.

total cost Sum of total variable costs plus total fixed costs.

total profit Total revenue minus total cost.

Knowing these amounts, the firm can figure the breakeven point:

$$\text{Breakeven point in units} \quad = \quad \frac{\text{Total fixed cost}}{\text{Fixed-cost contribution}}$$

Let's see how this works: Grey Corporation, a manufacturer of after-shave lotion, has variable costs of $3 per bottle and fixed costs of $50,000. Grey management believes the company can sell up to 100,000 bottles of after-shave at $5 a bottle without having to lower its price. Grey's fixed-cost contribution is $2 ($5 revenue per bottle minus $3 variable costs per bottle). Therefore, $2 per bottle is the amount that can be used to cover the company's fixed costs of $50,000.

To determine its breakeven point, Grey applies the previous equation:

$$\text{Breakeven point in bottles} \quad = \quad \frac{50{,}000 \text{ fixed cost}}{\$2 \text{ fixed-cost contribution}}$$
$$= \quad 25{,}000 \text{ bottles}$$

Grey Corporation will therefore break even when it sells 25,000 bottles of after-shave lotion. After that point, at which the fixed costs are met, the $2 per bottle becomes profit. If Grey's forecasts are correct and it can sell 100,000 bottles at $5 a bottle, its total profit will be $150,000 ($2 per bottle × 75,000 bottles).

By using the equation, Grey Corporation can quickly find out how much it needs to sell to break even. It can then calculate how much profit it will earn if it sells more units (as pictured in Exhibit 15-9). A firm that is operating close to the breakeven point may change the profit picture in a

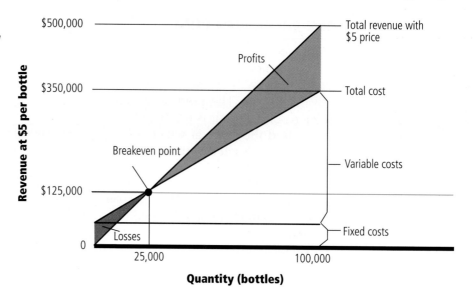

Exhibit 15-9
Breakeven Point for Grey
After-Shave at $5 a
Bottle

couple of ways. Reducing costs would lower the breakeven point and
expand profits. Increasing sales would not change the breakeven point
but would provide more profits.

8   PRICING NEW PRODUCTS

The firm's pricing objectives offer guidelines for new-product pricing
strategies. The two main strategies are price skimming and penetration
pricing. Both let the company develop an appropriate price for a new
product.

Price Skimming

Charging a high introductory price for a new product is the strategy of
price skimming. As the product moves through its life cycle, the price
usually is lowered because competitors are entering the market. As the
price is lowered, more and more consumers can buy the product. Among
the products priced this way are personal computers, cellular mobile telephones, and compact disk players.

Skimming is often used in the following situations:

- *When a product is legally protected by a patent or copyright:* In this
  situation, competitors cannot enter the market and charge lower
  prices for a similar product.
- *When the product is the result of a major technological breakthrough:*
  Competitors cannot quickly duplicate such a product.
- *When production cannot be expanded quickly:* Technological difficulties, raw materials shortages, or limited numbers of skilled workers can all hold down production. Hummel figurines, for instance,
  are sold at skimming prices because only a few people can produce
  them.

price skimming Pricing
strategy of charging a high
introductory price for a new
product.

■ Price skimming is the strategy of charging a high introductory price for a new product. This allows the manufacturer to find out how much consumers are willing to pay and to create an image of quality and prestige. Cellular phones were initially quite expensive, but prices for them have fallen as more and more competitors enter the market.

Price skimming has four important advantages: First, a high initial price can be a way to find out what buyers are willing to pay. Second, if consumers find the introductory price too high, it can be lowered. Third, a high introductory price can create an image of quality and prestige. Fourth, when the price is lowered later on, consumers may think they are getting a bargain.

For most products, skimming is a short-range strategy. To sell to a mass market, a company must eventually reduce new-product prices. When Hewlett-Packard (HP) first introduced its laser printer for personal computers, it set a high price—around $4,000. HP had a good head start on competitors, and no close substitute was available. The high-priced printer was sold mainly to computer professionals and business users with serious needs for desktop publishing. Distribution was through a select group of authorized HP computer dealers whose salespeople could explain the printer. When other firms entered the market with similar printers, HP added features and lowered its price. It also did more advertising and contracted with mail-order firms to reach new target markets. Then, just as competitors were entering the market to go after budget-oriented buyers, HP introduced a smaller model at a lower price. This strategy of changing prices over the course of the product life cycle is very typical of skimming.

Very high prices are also typical of rent-to-own retail stores. In fact, the total retail price is usually higher than a skimming price because of interest fees and other rental charges. Because rent-to-own stores usually serve a low-income market, the people who can least afford it pay the highest prices, as the Business Ethics and Social Responsibility Trends box shows.

TRENDS

Business Ethics and Social Responsibility

Rent to Own—Pay Forever

Rent-A-Center is a chain that rents refrigerators, furniture, diamond pinkie rings, and assorted other merchandise to America's urban and rural poor. Since buying Rent-A-Center in 1987, London-based Thorn has expanded it briskly. Thorn now thoroughly dominates the industry, which is known as *rent-to-own* because renters who make every weekly payment, usually for 78 weeks, become owners. Rent-A-Center USA controls 25 percent of the $2.8 billion U.S. rent-to-own market.

For low-income customers, Rent-A-Center has tremendous appeal. The chain gives them immediate use of brand-name merchandise, and the weekly payments are usually less than $20. But critics charge that Rent-A-Center employees, scrambling to meet ambitious sales targets set by Thorn, routinely encourage unsophisticated customers to rent more goods than they can afford. Although in theory customers can eventually own the goods outright, the company says three out of every four are unable to meet all their payments. When customers fall behind in payments, Rent-a-Center repossesses the goods and re-rents them. Their failure is partially responsible for Thorn's success. The company earns considerably more by renting, repossessing, and then re-renting the same goods than it does if the first customer makes all the payments. An ex-manager of a California Rent-A-Center store recalls one particular Philco VCR, for example, that he says retailed for about $119—but that brought in more than $5,000 in a five-year period.

Customers who do manage to make every installment may end up paying several times the item's retail value—at an effective annual interest rate, if the transaction is viewed as a credit sale, that can top 200 percent. In Utah, for example, Rent-A-Center customers pay a total of $1,003.56 over eighteen months for a new Sanyo VCR with a suggested retail price of $289.98. That amounts to an effective annual interest rate of a breathtaking 231 percent.

Rent-A-Center denies that its transactions are credit sales. Since most customers don't end up buying the product and they can cancel at any time, the firm argues, it doesn't charge interest at all.

Rent-A-Center says its customer base is 25 to 30 percent African-American and 10 to 15 percent Hispanic, and just 15 percent are on welfare or government subsidies. But former store managers consistently maintain that the total on government assistance is more than 25 percent, with some claiming up to 70 percent. Indeed, they unanimously report that sales always spiked on "Mother's Day," as they call the day when welfare mothers get their checks.[8]

Penetration Pricing

penetration pricing Pricing strategy of selling a new product at a low price in the hope of achieving large sales volume.

A company that doesn't use price skimming will probably use **penetration pricing**. This strategy sells new products at low prices in the hope of achieving a large sales volume. Penetration pricing requires better planning than skimming does because of the need to gear up for mass production and marketing. When Texas Instruments entered the digital-watch market, its Lubbock, Texas, facilities could produce 6 million watches a year. This amount met the entire world demand for low-priced watches. If the company had been wrong about demand, its losses would have been huge.

Penetration pricing has two big advantages. First, the low initial price may induce consumers to switch brands or companies. Using penetration pricing on its jug wines, Gallo has lured customers away from Taylor California Cellars and Inglenook. Wal-Mart has consistently taken business from Sears by setting prices lower.

economies of scale Tendency for the cost per unit to decrease when large quantities of the item are produced.

The second advantage of penetration pricing is that it may discourage competitors from entering the market. Their costs would tend to be higher, so they'd need to sell more at the same price to break even. Producing large quantities of a single item tends to give **economies of scale**. The cost per unit decreases when large quantities of the item are produced. A Rolls-Royce costs over $100,000; a Mazda Miata costs about $18,000. The price difference is due in part to the huge difference in production of the two cars. The yearly production of Rolls-Royce is about 1,500 units, which is hardly one day's production of the Miata.

9 SPECIAL PRICING TACTICS

Sometimes management will fine-tune the company's pricing strategy by using special pricing tactics. These include leader pricing, cash rebates, and price bundling.

Leader Pricing

leader pricing Pricing strategy of pricing products below the normal markup or even below cost to attract customers.

loss leader Product priced below cost.

Pricing products below the normal markup or even below cost to attract customers to a store where they wouldn't otherwise shop is **leader pricing**. A product priced below cost is referred to as a **loss leader**. Retailers hope that this type of pricing will increase their overall sales volume and thus their profit.

Items that are leader priced are usually well known and priced low enough to appeal to many customers. They also are items that consumers will buy at a lower price, even if they have to switch brands. Supermarkets often feature coffee and bacon in their leader pricing. Department stores and specialty stores also rely heavily on leader pricing.

Cash Rebates

cash rebates Price reductions made after consumers buy the product.

Price reductions made after products are purchased are **cash rebates**. They are a good way for manufacturers or retailers to lower prices temporarily. The automobile industry is a common user of rebates.

Bundling

bundling Pricing strategy of grouping two or more products together and pricing them as one.

Bundling means grouping two or more related products together and pricing them as a single product. Marriott's special weekend rates often include the room, breakfast, and one night's dinner. Department stores may offer a washer and dryer together for a price lower than if each unit were bought separately.

The idea behind bundling is to reach a segment of the market that is not effectively reached when the products are sold separately. Some buyers are more than willing to buy one product but have much less use for the second. Bundling the second product to the first at a slightly reduced price thus creates some sales that otherwise would not be made. Aussie 3-Minute Miracle Shampoo is typically bundled with its conditioner because many people use shampoo at a more rapid rate than conditioner and then don't need a new bottle of conditioner.

unbundling Pricing strategy of reducing the bundle of services that accompany a basic product.

Another approach is to reduce the bundle of services that accompanies the basic product. This is called **unbundling**. Rather than raise the price of hotel rooms, some hotel chains have started charging registered guests for parking. To help hold the line on costs, some department stores require customers to pay for gift wrapping.

CONSUMER PRICE PERCEPTIONS

Psychology often plays a big role in how consumers view prices. Two strategies used by marketers to influence consumer perceptions are odd-even pricing and prestige pricing.

Odd-Even Pricing

odd-even pricing Setting a price below the next whole number to influence consumers' perceptions of a product.

Setting a price just below the next whole number to influence consumers' perceptions of a product is called **odd-even pricing**. Retailers believe that consumers favor odd prices for most products. Instead of pricing a stereo system at $500, the seller will price it at $499.95 or $495. In theory, customers will view the price as $400-plus rather than $500 and be more attracted to the stereo.

Odd-even pricing may seem to involve trivial amounts of money, but the totals are significant. A retailer who could sell as many units at the even price is not maximizing profits. For a retailer who grosses $30 million a year, odd pricing may reduce profits by $100,000.

Odd prices are used to imply bargains, and even prices denote quality or status. One would not find a hand-tooled leather sofa at $6,999.95. Instead it would be $7,000. Fine jewelry, watches, and clothing are priced at even amounts.

Prestige Pricing

prestige pricing Raising the price of a product so consumers will perceive it as being of higher quality, status, or value.

Raising the price of a product so consumers will perceive it as being of higher quality, status, or value is **prestige pricing**. This type of pricing is common where high prices indicate high status. In the specialty shops on Rodeo Drive in Beverly Hills, which cater to the superrich of Hollywood, shirts that would sell for $15 elsewhere would have to sell for at least $50. Otherwise, customers would perceive them as being of low quality.

Concept Check
- Give an example of markup pricing.
- Explain the concept of breakeven pricing.
- What is the difference between penetration pricing and price skimming?
- List and explain some special pricing tactics.

■ SUMMARY

1. Explain the product concept.

Products are any want-satisfying goods or services, along with their perceived tangible and intangible attributes and benefits. The less tangible something is, the more likely we are to call it a service. Most items are usually a combination of goods and services. Services are often marketed differently from goods.

2. Describe a product classification system for consumer and industrial goods.

The two broad categories of products are consumer products and industrial products. Consumer products are goods and services that are bought and used by the end users. They can be classified as convenience products, shopping products, or specialty products, depending on how much effort consumers are willing to exert to get them.

Industrial products are those bought by organizations for use in making other products or in rendering services. They are classified as capital products or expense items and are subclassified as installations, accessories, component parts and materials, raw materials, industrial supplies, and industrial services.

Key Terms

brainstorming 481

brand 475

brand loyalty 477

breakeven point 491

bundling 496

capital products 473

cash rebates 496

convenience products 473

dealer brands 476

economies of scale 495

expense items 473

express warranty 479

fixed-cost contribution 491

fixed costs 491

flanker brand 480

continued

3. Explain the roles of branding, packaging, and labeling in creating a product.

Products usually have brand names. Brands identify products by words, names, symbols, designs, or a combination of these things. The two major types of brands are manufacturer (national) brands and dealer (private) brands. Generic products carry no brand name. Often the promotional claims of well-known brands are reinforced in the printing on the package. Packaging is an important way to promote sales and protect the product. The labels on packages provide information about product ingredients and composition.

4. Explain the process of new-product development.

To succeed, most firms must continue to put out new products. But new-product development can be risky. Many new products fail. The steps in new-product development are setting goals, exploring ideas, screening ideas, making a preliminary profit plan, creating a marketing mix, test marketing, and introducing the product.

5. List the stages of the product life cycle.

After a product reaches the marketplace, it enters the product life cycle. This cycle typically has four stages: introduction, growth, maturity, and decline (and possibly death). Profits usually are small in the introductory phase, reach a peak at the end of the growth phase, and then decline. Innovative maturity involves prolonging the life of a product through creative marketing.

6. Describe the role of pricing in marketing.

Price indicates value, helps position a product in the marketplace, and is the means for earning a fair return on investment. If a price is too high, the product won't sell well, and the firm will lose money. If the price is too low, the firm may lose money even if the product sells well. Prices are set according to pricing objectives. Among the most common of these objectives are profit maximization, target return on investment, and value pricing.

7. Explain how prices can be set.

A cost-based method for determining price is markup pricing. A certain percentage is added to the product's cost to arrive at a new price. The markup is the amount added to the cost to cover expenses and earn a profit. Breakeven analysis determines the level of sales that must be reached before total cost equals total revenue. Breakeven analysis provides a quick look at how many units the firm must sell before it starts earning a profit. The technique also reveals how much profit can be earned with higher sales volumes.

8. Explain price skimming and penetration pricing.

The two main strategies for pricing a new product are price skimming and penetration pricing. Price skimming involves charging a high introductory price and then, usually, lowering the price as the product moves through its life cycle. Penetration pricing involves selling a new product at a low price in the hope of achieving a large sales volume.

9. Understand the pricing tactics used by marketers to maintain a competitive position.

Pricing tactics are used to fine-tune the base prices of products. Among these tactics are leader pricing, cash rebates, bundling, odd-even pricing, and prestige pricing.

Sellers that use leader pricing set the prices of some of their products below the normal markup or even below cost to attract customers who might otherwise not shop at those stores. Cash rebates are used to lower prices temporarily. Bundling is grouping two or more products together and pricing them as one. The notion is that the seller will sell more items than if each was priced separately.

Setting a price at an odd number tends to create a perception that the item is cheaper than the actual pricing. Prices that are even denote quality or status. Raising the price so an item will be perceived as having high quality and status is called prestige pricing.

▓ DISCUSSION QUESTIONS

1. Describe the product attributes of the following: a McDonald's hamburger, your income tax return prepared by H&R Block, a set of Craftsman screwdrivers from Sears, a box of corn flakes.

2. Name at least one new product in each of the following areas that has become important in the last ten years: automobiles, food, medicine, communications.

3. Name three types of products for which the brand name is very important. Then name three types of products for which you would never consider investing money to develop a brand identity.

4. Which of the following items might have good consumer acceptance as generic products: automobile tires, ice cream, staples, scientific calculators, running shoes, panty hose, gasoline, men's briefs? Explain your answer.

5. Under what circumstances would a jeans maker market the product as a convenience product? A shopping product? A specialty product?

6. Dick Storinger, the owner of Oakton Pharmacy, needed a personal computer to keep track of prescriptions, print labels, and maintain his financial records. At Computercraft, Dick tried out a few models and decided on the small one that his daughter bought for her work in graduate business school. Did Storinger buy a consumer product or an industrial product? Explain.

7. What kind of pricing objectives would be best for a store featuring high-fashion designer clothes? Explain at least two approaches.

8. What pricing strategy would you most likely consider if you were going to market a new product and knew that your competition couldn't start producing a similar product for a year? Explain.

9. How can something as obvious as a retail price have a psychological dimension?

10. "Even though rent-to-own customers pay three to four times retail for a product, it is the only means for many low-income families to acquire TVs, VCRs, and furniture. Therefore, the end justifies the means." Comment.

■ CASE

The Beech Starship

It was a bold concept: a sleek airplane made not from metal but from carbon-plastic, with startling L-shaped wings and twin turboprop engines mounted near the rear of the plane, to push rather than pull it through the air.

Raytheon Co.'s Beech unit invested a decade and a small fortune on the plane, called it Starship, and marketed it as a flashy but fuel-efficient alternative to the corporate jet. But Starship has made a hard landing in the marketplace. In one of the most expensive flops in commercial aviation, Raytheon officials now concede they have quietly written off much of the development cost of the plane, estimated by some analysts to approach $500 million. Only twenty-three Starships have been sold through 1993—fewer than half of the fifty orders claimed by Raytheon before the first sale in 1990. Not one Starship was sold in 1993.

"For the pilot and the passenger, it has really got everything," says Dennis Murphy, sales manager at Elliott Flying Services, in Des Moines, Iowa. But "for the money, the performance isn't there," Mr. Murphy adds. "For $5 million, you can buy a jet. Starship just doesn't fit in today's market."

Raytheon counted on Starship's fuel efficiencies to attract frugal buyers. But as the plane developed, energy prices fell and became less of an issue. Starship's relative slowness as a non-jet became a liability, as speed remained important for business buyers. Starship's space-age design was also expected to be an attraction for corporate chiefs. But it "turns out the older-generation CEO-level manager is very conservative—he doesn't want people pointing at him when he lands," a Raytheon executive says.

Burt Rutan, who designed the first Starship models and helped flight-test the plane, says Beech selected "the most expensive method, hand-laying each layer" of carbon-impregnated fabric for the fuselage. According to Rutan, manufacturing costs were so high "they'll never recover their investment. ...They expected break-even at about 500 units."[9]

Questions

1. What factors led to the Starship's failure? What were the warning signals that management missed? How could this problem be avoided in the future?

2. At what stage of the new product development process should development of the Starship have been stopped?

3. Raytheon is thinking of bringing out a revised version of the Starship with improved stability, handling, avionics, and a roomier interior. It also is cutting the price to $4.3 million. Is developing a new model simply throwing good money after bad? Why or why not?

Distribution Management

Learning Goals

After studying this chapter, you should be able to:

1 Describe the role of distribution channels.

2 Explain why different channels are used for consumer products and industrial products.

3 Decide when a marketer would use exclusive, selective, or intensive distribution.

4 Discuss the functions of wholesalers and their relationships to manufacturers and others in the distribution channels.

5 Distinguish among the types of wholesalers.

6 Contrast the different kinds of retail operations.

7 Explain the goals and functions of physical distribution.

Career Profile

Cummins Engines Company is one of the largest designers and manufacturers of fuel-efficient diesel engines. The company sells and distributes its products in over 130 countries around the world. It is Donna Guyer's job to review customer requirements and match Cummins parts to their needs. She examines the products the company has in inventory and those due from manufacturing and then decides how best to fill the clients' orders.

Because they are industrial goods, Cummins' products have a shorter distribution channel than many retail items. The company supplies parts and service to their own distributors and also to original equipment manufacturers. In this twofold process, engines go directly to the manufacturers, and spare parts go to the "after market," which consists of over 143 distributors in over 500 locations worldwide. These distributors then provide parts and service to end users.

Donna's degree in operations management has helped her immensely in the area of distribution. While in college she learned to analyze and solve problems using both case studies and live business studies. Cummins Engines has provided Donna with additional training, putting her through such courses as Engine Familiarization, in which she learned to take apart a diesel engine and put it back together, and Supplier Ethics, which addressed the subject of dealing responsibly and ethically with suppliers. In addition, Donna is pursuing an MBA to further her career in distribution management.

Chapter 16 explores the means by which goods and services flow from producers to consumers. It begins by explaining what distribution channels are and by describing the most common consumer and industrial channels. Next it describes three types of channel systems. Wholesaling and retailing are then discused. The chapter ends with a look at physical distribution.

DISTRIBUTION CHANNELS

distribution channel
Series of marketing organizations through which goods and services pass on their way from producers to end users.

manufacturers Firms that convert raw materials and component parts to finished products.

agents Sales representatives of manufacturers and wholesalers.

brokers Middlemen who bring together buyers and sellers.

industrial distributors Independent wholesalers that buy related product lines from many manufacturers and sell them to industrial users.

wholesalers Firms that sell finished goods to retailers, manufacturers, and institutions.

retailers Firms that sell goods to consumers and to industrial users for their own consumption.

A **distribution channel** is a series of marketing organizations through which goods and services pass on their way from producers to end users. The firms that most often appear in the channels are:

- **Manufacturers**, firms that convert raw materials to finished products.
- **Agents**, sales representatives of manufacturers and wholesalers, and **brokers,** who bring together buyers and sellers. Both are usually hired on a commission basis by either a buyer or a seller. Agents and brokers are go-betweens whose job it is to make deals. They do not own or take possession of the goods.
- **Industrial distributors**, independent wholesalers that buy related product lines from many manufacturers and sell them to industrial users. They often have a sales force to call on purchasing agents, make deliveries, extend credit, and provide information. Industrial distributors are used in such industries as aircraft manufacturing, mining, and petroleum.
- *Industrial users,* firms that buy products for internal use or for producing other products. They include manufacturers; utilities; airlines; railroads; and service institutions, such as hotels, hospitals, and schools.
- **Wholesalers**, firms that sell finished goods to retailers, manufacturers, and institutions (such as schools and hospitals). Historically, their function has been to buy from manufacturers and sell to retailers.
- **Retailers**, firms that sell goods to consumers and to industrial users for their own consumption.
- *Consumers,* the end users of consumer goods.

Exhibit 16-1 shows eight different ways marketing entities can be linked. For instance, a manufacturer can sell to a wholesaler that can sell to a retailer that in turn can sell to a customer. In any of these distribution systems, goods and services are physically transferred from one organization to the next. As each takes possession of the products, it may take legal ownership of them. As the exhibit indicates, distribution channels can handle either consumer products or industrial products.

CONSUMER PRODUCTS CHANNELS

Consumer products channels tend to be more complex than industrial products channels. The difference occurs because consumer products tend to be less expensive than industrial products. Most of the time, the lower the price of a good, the more steps involved in distributing it.

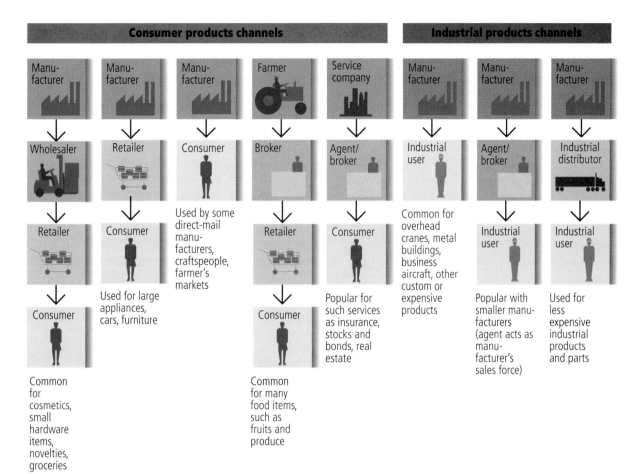

| Consumer products channels | | | | | Industrial products channels | | |

Manu-facturer → Wholesaler → Retailer → Consumer

Common for cosmetics, small hardware items, novelties, groceries

Manu-facturer → Retailer → Consumer

Used for large appliances, cars, furniture

Manu-facturer → Consumer

Used by some direct-mail manu-facturers, craftspeople, farmer's markets

Farmer → Broker → Retailer → Consumer

Common for many food items, such as fruits and produce

Service company → Agent/broker → Consumer

Popular for such services as insurance, stocks and bonds, real estate

Manu-facturer → Industrial user

Common for overhead cranes, metal buildings, business aircraft, other custom or expensive products

Manu-facturer → Agent/broker → Industrial user

Popular with smaller manu-facturers (agent acts as manu-facturer's sales force)

Manu-facturer → Industrial distributor → Industrial user

Used for less expensive industrial products and parts

■ **Exhibit 16-1**
Channels of Distribution for Industrial and Consumer Products

To understand these economics, let's look at an example. Say that the hypothetical Ace Comb Company makes its combs in New York City. The combs sell for 30¢ each to consumers, and convenience stores all over the country sell about 50 combs each per month. If Ace had to ship one box only to each of the 2,000 convenience stores in California, the shipping costs would be more than the manufacturing costs. For Ace and the stores to make a profit, the combs would have to sell for more than 30¢ apiece. Instead, Ace sells 50,000 combs per shipment to a wholesaler in Los Angeles. The wholesaler adds a small profit, then sells the combs along with many other items to the California convenience stores. Even with the wholesaler's costs added in, the retail cost per item is low because several items are shipped together from the wholesaler to the retailers. Also, the combs are shipped in one large lot from New York to California.

INDUSTRIAL PRODUCTS CHANNELS

It is not only the price of an item that determines how complex a distribution channel is. Industrial products channels tend to be more direct than consumer products channels because many industrial products are custom-made for the end user. Thus the manufacturer must have direct

contact with the buyer. For instance, Wichita Clutch Company custom-
makes clutches for Marion Machine Company. The clutches are for huge
shovels used in strip-mining. Wichita Clutch's engineers work with Marion's designers to produce clutches to exact specifications. The two firms
need no go-between to arrange the sale.

DISTRIBUTION FACILITATORS

The members of distribution channels negotiate with each other; they buy
and sell products and transfer titles of ownership. Other organizations
help move merchandise from producers to final users but do not perform
negotiating functions. They are not members of distribution channels.
Instead, they are *distribution facilitators*. For instance, a truck line that
ships goods from one channel member to another is a distribution facili-
tator. Banks facilitate distribution by extending credit to members of distribution channels. Also, market-research firms help determine which
retail stores are likely to sell the most of a product. All three of these facilitators help create a smooth flow of merchandise from producer to end
user, but they are not members of distribution channels.

THE FUNCTIONS OF DISTRIBUTION CHANNELS

Why do distribution channels exist? Why can't every firm sell its products
directly to the end user or consumer? Why are go-betweens needed?
Channels serve a number of functions:

Channels Reduce the Number of Transactions

Channels make distribution simpler by reducing the number of transactions required to get a product from the manufacturer to the consumer.
Assume for the moment that only four students are in your class. Also
assume that your professor requires five textbooks, each from a different
publisher. If there were no bookstore, twenty transactions would be necessary for all students in the class to buy the books (see Exhibit 16-2). If
the bookstore serves as a go-between, the number of transactions is
reduced to nine. Each publisher sells to one bookstore rather than to four
students. Each student buys from one bookstore instead of from five publishers.

Dealing with channel members frees producers from many of the
details of distribution activity. Producers are traditionally not as efficient or
as enthusiastic about selling products directly to end users as channel members are. First, producers may wish to focus on production. They may feel
that they cannot both produce and distribute in a competitive way. Some
firms also may not have the resources to invest in distributing their products.

Channels Ease the Flow of Goods

Channels make distribution easier in several ways. The first is by *sorting,*
which consists of the following:

- *Sorting out.* Breaking many different items into separate stocks that
  are similar. Eggs, for instance, are sorted by grade and size.

■ Exhibit 16-2

How Distribution Chan-
nels Reduce the Number
of Transactions

Without a middleman:
5 publishers × 4 students = 20 transactions

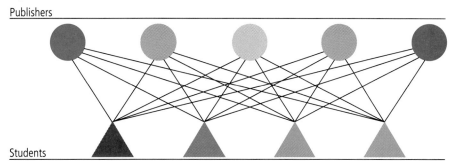

With a middleman:
5 publishers + 4 students = 9 transactions

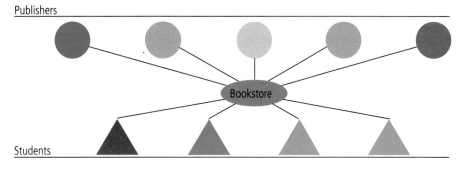

- *Accumulating:* Bringing similar stocks together into a larger quantity. Twelve large grade A eggs could be placed in some cartons and twelve medium grade B eggs in other cartons.
- *Allocating:* Breaking similar products into smaller and smaller lots. (Allocating at the wholesale level is called *breaking bulk*.) For instance, a tank-car load of milk could be broken down into gallon jugs. The process of allocating generally is done when the goods are dispersed by region and as ownership of the goods changes.

Without the sorting, accumulating, and allocating processes, modern society would not exist. We would have home-based industries providing custom or semi-custom products to local markets. In short, we would return to a much lower level of consumption.

A second way channels ease the flow of goods is by locating buyers for merchandise. A wholesaler must find the right retailers to sell a profitable volume of merchandise. A sporting goods wholesaler, for instance, must find the retailers who are most likely to reach sporting goods consumers. Retailers have to understand the buying habits of consumers and put stores where consumers want and expect to find the merchandise. Every member of a distribution channel must locate buyers for the products it is trying to sell.

Channel members also store merchandise so goods are available when consumers want to buy them. The high cost of retail space often means that goods are stored by the wholesaler or the manufacturer.

One way in which channels make distribution easier is by sorting. In this instance, bulk amounts of different types of candy from different manufacturers are brought together by a channel member and recombined into assortment packs. The middleman performs an important function by providing an outlet for the candy manufacturers' products and offering consumers more choices.

Channels Perform Needed Functions

The functions performed by channel members help increase the efficiency of the channel. Yet consumers sometimes feel that the go-betweens create higher prices. They doubt that these intermediaries, or *middlemen,* perform useful functions. Actually, if channel members did not perform important and necessary functions at a reasonable cost, they would cease to exist. If firms could earn a higher profit without using certain channel members, they would not use them.

A useful rule to remember is that, although channel members can be eliminated, their functions cannot. The manufacturer must either perform the functions of the middlemen itself or find new ways of getting them carried out. Publishers can bypass bookstores, for instance, but the function performed by the bookstores then has to be performed by the publishers or by someone else.

Concept Check

- Define the term distribution channel.
- Give examples of three consumer products channels and three industrial products channels.
- Why are channels of distribution necessary?
- Can channel functions be eliminated?

VERTICAL DISTRIBUTION SYSTEMS AND MARKET COVERAGE

Efficient distribution channels are the ones in which all the channel members work smoothly together and do what they're expected to do. A manufacturer expects wholesalers to promote its products to retailers and to perform several other functions as well. Not all channels have a leader or a single firm that sets channel policies. But all channels have members who rely on one another.

VERTICAL MARKETING SYSTEMS

vertical marketing system Planned, organized, formalized distribution channel.

To increase the efficiency of distribution channels, many firms have turned to vertical marketing systems. In a **vertical marketing system**, firms are aligned in a hierarchy (manufacturer to wholesaler to retailer). Such systems are planned, organized, formalized versions of distribution channels. The three basic types of vertical marketing systems are corporate, administrative, and contractual.

Corporate Distribution Systems

corporate distribution system Vertical marketing system in which one firm owns the whole channel of distribution.

In a **corporate distribution system**, one firm owns the entire channel of distribution. Corporate systems are tops in channel control. A single firm that owns the whole channel has no need to worry about channel members. The channel owner will always have supplies of raw materials and long-term contact with customers. It will have good distribution and product exposure in the marketplace.

forward integration Acquisition by a manufacturer of a middleman closer to the target market.

Examples of corporate systems abound. Evans Products Company (a manufacturer of plywood), for instance, bought wholesale lumber distributors to better market its products to retail dealers. This move was an example of forward integration. **Forward integration** occurs when a manufacturer acquires a middleman closer to the target market, such as a wholesaler or retailer. A wholesaler could integrate forward by buying a retailer. Other examples of forward integration include Sherwin-Williams, a paint maker that operates over 2,000 paint stores, and Hart Schaffner and Marx, a long-established menswear manufacturer that owns over a hundred clothing outlets. Or a manufacturer might integrate forward by buying a wholesaler. For decades, Pepsi-Cola focused on supplying syrup and concentrate to independent bottlers. But in the 1980s, it decided it could best satisfy retailers' demands by serving them itself. After spending several billion dollars to buy out independent bottlers, Pepsi-Cola today owns bottling and distributing operations that account for half the soda in its system, compared to just 21 percent a decade ago.[1]

backward integration Acquisition by a wholesaler or retailer of control over production of the products it sells.

Backward integration is just the reverse: It occurs when a wholesaler or retailer gains control over the production process. Many large retail organizations have integrated backward. Sears has part ownership of production facilities that supply over 30 percent of its inventory. Recently, Wal-Mart bought McLane Company, a Texas wholesaler with a reputation as one of the best specialty distributors of cigarettes, candy, and perishables in the United States. With McLane, Wal-Mart can avoid outside distributors and can lower overall costs.[2]

Administrative Distribution Systems

administrative distribution system Vertical marketing system in which a strong organization takes an informal leadership role in setting the policies of the distribution channel.

An **administrative distribution system** is one in which a strong organization takes over as leader and sets channel policies. The leadership role is informal; it is not written into a contract. Companies like Gillette, Hanes,

Campbell's, and Westinghouse are administrative system leaders. They can often influence or control the policies of other channel members without the costs and expertise required in setting up a corporate distribution system. They may be able to dictate how many wholesalers will be in the channel or require that the wholesalers offer sixty-day credit to retail customers, among other things.

Contractual Distribution Systems

contractual distribution system Vertical marketing system consisting of a network of independent firms that coordinate their distribution activities by contractual agreement.

The third form of vertical marketing is a **contractual distribution system**. It is a network of independent firms at different levels (manufacturer, wholesaler, retailer) that coordinate their distribution activities through a written contract. The franchise is a common form of the contractual system. The parent companies of McDonald's and Chemlawn, for instance, control distribution of their products through the franchise agreement each franchisee signs.

3 MARKET COVERAGE

market coverage Number of dealers used to distribute a product in a particular area.

All types of distribution systems must be concerned with **market coverage**. How many dealers will be used to distribute the product in a particular area? The three degrees of coverage, as shown in Exhibit 16-3, are exclusive, selective, and intensive. The type of product determines the intensity of the market coverage.

exclusive distribution Market coverage consisting of one or two dealers per area.

When a manufacturer selects one or two dealers per area to market its products, it is using **exclusive distribution**. Only items that are in strong demand can be distributed exclusively, because consumers must be willing to travel some distance to buy them. If Wrigley's chewing gum were sold in only one drugstore per city, Wrigley's would soon be out of business. However, Bang and Olufsen stereo components, Jaguar automobiles, and Adrienne Vittadini designer clothing are distributed exclusively with great success.

Jaguar markets its automobiles using exclusive distribution. The company allows only one or two dealers per geographical area to sell its cars. This degree of market coverage works for Jaguar, because its cars are in demand. Consumers are willing to travel some distance to purchase them.

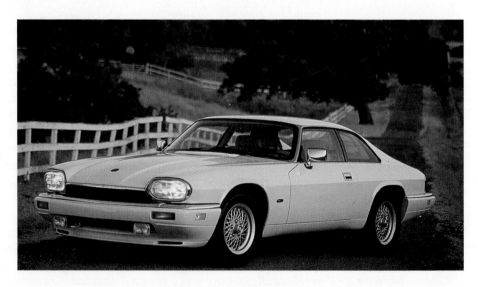

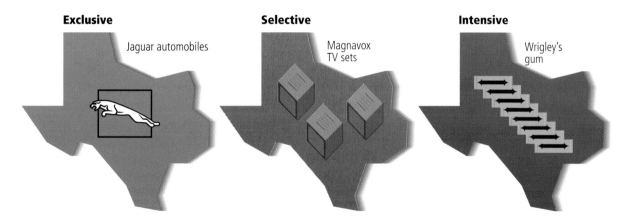

Exclusive — Jaguar automobiles
Selective — Magnavox TV sets
Intensive — Wrigley's gum

■ **Exhibit 16-3**
Degrees of Market Coverage

selective distribution
Market coverage consisting of a limited number of dealers (but more than one or two) per area.

intensive distribution
Market coverage in which a manufacturer's products are sold virtually everywhere.

A manufacturer that chooses a limited number of dealers in an area (but more than one or two) is using **selective distribution**. Since the number of retailers handling the product is limited, consumers must be willing to seek it out. Timberline boots, a high-quality line of footwear, are distributed selectively. So are Magnavox TV sets, Maytag washers, Waterford crystal, and Wrangler clothing. When choosing dealers, manufacturers look for certain qualities. Magnavox may seek retailers that can offer high-quality customer service. Wrangler may look for retailers with high-traffic locations in regional shopping malls. All manufacturers try to exclude retailers that are a poor credit risk or that have a weak or negative image.

A manufacturer that wants to sell its products everywhere there are potential customers is using **intensive distribution**. Such consumer goods as bread, tape, and light bulbs are often distributed intensively. Usually these products cost little and are bought frequently, which means that complex distribution channels are necessary. Coca-Cola is sold in just about every type of retail business, from gas stations to supermarkets.

Concept Check
• What are the three types of vertical marketing systems?
• Name the three degrees of market coverage.

WHOLESALING

4 Wholesalers are channel members that buy finished products from manufacturers and sell them to retailers. Retailers in turn sell the products to consumers. Manufacturers that use selective or exclusive distribution normally sell directly to retailers. Manufacturers that use intensive distribution often rely on wholesalers.

Wholesalers also sell products to institutions that use them in performing their own mission. Among these institutions are manufacturers, schools, and hospitals. A manufacturer, for instance, might buy typing paper from Nationwide Papers, a wholesaler. A hospital might buy its cleaning supplies from Lagasse Brothers, one of the nation's largest wholesalers of janitorial supplies.

Sometimes wholesalers sell products to manufacturers for use in the manufacturing process. A builder of custom boats, for instance, might buy batteries from a battery wholesaler and switches from an electrical wholesaler. Some wholesalers even sell to other wholesalers, creating yet another stage in the distribution channel.

About half of all wholesalers offer financing for their clients. They sell products on credit and expect to be paid within a certain time, usually sixty days. Other wholesalers operate like retail stores. The retailer goes to the wholesaler, selects the merchandise, pays cash for it, and transports it to the retail outlet.

breaking bulk Breaking down large shipments of goods into smaller, more usable quantities.

Many wholesalers store merchandise and provide it to retailers on an as-needed basis. Part of this storage function usually involves **breaking bulk**—breaking down large shipments into smaller, more usable quantities that can be sold to retailers. A boxcar full of Chiquita bananas may be shipped to a produce wholesaler, who breaks the shipment into smaller lots and in turn sells them to supermarkets.

Because wholesalers usually serve limited areas, they are often located closer to retailers than the manufacturers are. Retailers can thus get faster delivery at lower cost from wholesalers. A retailer who knows that a wholesaler can restock store shelves within a day can keep a low level of inventory on hand. More money is then available for other things, since less cash is tied up in items that are sitting on the shelves or in storerooms.

Wholesalers also provide an unofficial information function. They usually know their retail market and can tell manufacturers about market trends. They can also tell retailers about new products.

5 TYPES OF WHOLESALERS

The three main types of wholesalers are merchant wholesalers, manufacturers' sales branches, and agents and brokers (see Exhibit 16-4).

■ **Exhibit 16-4**
Types of Wholesalers

Wholesalers

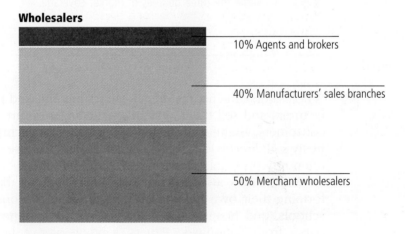

10% Agents and brokers

40% Manufacturers' sales branches

50% Merchant wholesalers

Sam's Club, operated by Wal-Mart, was one of the victors in the fierce competition between warehouse clubs. Warehouse clubs sell merchandise in bulk to members who pay annual membership fees. Because members can be small businesses or individuals, the clubs are classified as both wholesale and retail organizations.

Merchant Wholesalers

Independent wholesalers that buy goods from manufacturers on their own account and then resell them to other businesses are **merchant wholesalers**. These wholesalers operate warehouses where they receive the merchandise, take title to it, store it, and later ship it to buyers. By taking title to the merchandise, they own it. Thus they can set policies for it and dispose of it in any manner they choose. Many merchant wholesalers are full-service wholesalers carrying groceries, hardware, or furniture. They not only carry merchandise but also may have a sales force, offer credit, make deliveries, advise clients, and service the products they sell. Merchant wholesalers account for about half of all wholesale sales.

merchant wholesalers Independent wholesalers that buy products from manufacturers on their own account and then resell them to other businesses.

Manufacturers' Sales Branches

Wholesalers that perform many of the same functions as full-service merchant wholesalers but that are owned and completely controlled by a manufacturer are **manufacturers' sales branches**. They account for about 40 percent of all wholesale sales and are the fastest-growing form of wholesaling. The main reason for their popularity is that they let manufacturers keep close control over inventory. This control has been useful in such industries as clothing, transportation equipment, and forest products.

manufacturers' sales branches Wholesalers owned and completely controlled by a manufacturer.

Some manufacturers set up sales branches because they are dissatisfied with merchant wholesalers. Manufacturers may decide that the merchant wholesalers are not promoting the manufacturer's products as much as they should or that the inventories they carry are too small.

manufacturers' repre-
sentatives (manufac-
turers' agents) People
who represent noncompeting
manufacturers and function
independently rather than as
salaried employees of the
manufacturers.

Agents and Brokers

Agents represent manufacturers and wholesalers. **Manufacturers' repre-**
sentatives (also called **manufacturers' agents**) represent noncompeting
manufacturers. These salespeople function as independent agents rather
than as salaried employees of manufacturers. They do not take title to or
possession of merchandise. They get commissions if they make sales—
and nothing if they don't. They are found in a variety of industries, including electronics, clothing, hardware, furniture, and toys.

Brokers bring together buyers and sellers. Like agents, they do not take
title to merchandise, they receive commissions on sales, and they have little say over company sales policies. They are found in markets where the
information that would join buyers and sellers is scarce. These markets
include real estate, agriculture, insurance, and commodities.

TRENDS

Business Today

Wholesalers or Retailers

By 1993, warehouse clubs sales had soared to over $35 billion annually, from
more than 650 stores. A *warehouse club* sells a limited selection of brand name
appliances, household items, and groceries on a cash-and-carry basis to members, usually small businesses and groups. Members pay an annual membership fee. Merchandise is typically sold in bulk-size cartons or in smaller containers wrapped together. For example, members can buy five-pound boxes of
cheese, cartons of 1,000 ketchup "tear-packs," or shrink-wrapped packages of
a dozen boxes of pencils. Although small-business members can find high-volume office supplies like legal pads and copier paper, they still must shop at the
traditional office supply store for some of their needs.

Because warehouse clubs act as a wholesaler to small businesses and a
retailer to group customers, the question arises: How should a warehouse club
be classified? The answer is that it is both a wholesaling and a retailing organization. According to James Degen, a Santa Barbara, California, wholesale
club consultant, about 70 percent of club members are retail group members
(i.e., federal employees, employees of local businesses, and so forth). From
this perspective a wholesale club is a retail organization. On the other hand,
wholesale members account for over 60 percent of all wholesale club sales.
This might lead to classifying the clubs as wholesalers.

Competition in the warehouse club market has been severe. In a war of
attrition requiring huge amounts of capital and operating on razor-thin profit
margins, the operators of warehouse stores have seen the number of chains
shrink. In late 1993 K mart, worn down by competition and no profits, sold
most of its Pace Club stores to Wal-Mart, operator of Sam's Clubs. Two other
large wholesale club chains, Price and Costco, merged to survive. The only
national chains today are Sam's Clubs and Price-Costco.[3]

Concept
Check

- Describe the functions of a wholesaler.
- Distinguish among merchant wholesalers, manufacturer's sales branches, and
  agents and brokers.

RETAILING

6 Some 30 million Americans are engaged in retailing. Of this number, almost 16 million work in service businesses like barber shops, lawyers' offices, and amusement parks. Most retailers are involved in small businesses like shoe stores, restaurants, and clothing stores. But most sales are made by the giant retail organizations, such as Sears, Wal-Mart, K mart, and JC Penney. Half of all retail sales come from fewer than 10 percent of all retail businesses. This small group employs about 40 percent of all retail workers.

Retailers feel the impact of changes in the economy more than many other types of businesses. Mergers and acquisitions, recession, and high levels of consumer debt have weakened many retailers. Survival depends on keeping up with changing lifestyles and shopping patterns.

TYPES OF RETAIL OPERATIONS

There is a great deal of variety in retail operations. The major types of retailers are described in Exhibit 16-5, which divides them into two main categories: in-store and nonstore.

The first nine types of retailing in Exhibit 16-5 (everything but catalog stores and hypermarts) are traditional *in-store retailing*. Examples include Sears, Wal-Mart, K mart, Saks, Dayton Hudson, and many others. These retailers get most of their revenue from people who come to the store to buy what they want. Many also do some catalog and telephone sales.

Nonstore retailing includes vending, direct selling, and direct response marketing. Vending uses machines to sell food and other items, usually as a convenience in institutions like schools and hospitals.

Direct selling involves face-to-face contact between the buyer and seller, but not in a retail store. Usually the seller goes to the consumer's home. Sometimes contacts are made at the place of work. Mary Kay Cosmetics, Avon, Herbalife, and Amway each employ over 100,000 direct salespeople. Some companies, like Tupperware and Longaberger baskets, specialize in parties in a person's home. Most parties are a combination social affair and sales demonstration. The hostess usually gets a discount and a special gift for rounding up a group of friends. The trend seems to be away from door-to-door canvassing and toward these party plans. But the sales of many direct-sales companies have suffered as women continue to enter the work force on a full-time basis.

Direct-response marketing is conducted through media that encourage a consumer to reply. Popular direct-response media are catalogs, direct mail, television, newspapers, and radio. The ads invite a person to "call the toll-free number now" or to fill out an order blank. Direct-response marketing includes K-Tel selling "golden oldies," Ronco offering its Vega-matic vegetable slicer, and Ed McMahon shouting from an envelope that "you may have just won $10 million." It also includes the catalogs sent out by Lands' End, L. L. Bean, J. Crew, Lillian Vernon, and countless others.

Know (handwritten)

Type of retailer In-store retailing	Description	Examples
Department store	Houses many departments under one roof, each treated as separate buying center to achieve economies of buying, promotion, and control	JC Penney, Saks, May Company, Rich's, Bloomingdale's
Specialty store	Specializes in category of merchandise and carries complete assortment	Toys 'R' Us, Radio Shack, Zales Jewelers
Variety store	Offers variety of inexpensive goods	Ben Franklin, Woolworths
Convenience store	Offers convenience goods with long store hours and quick checkout	7-Eleven, Circle K
Supermarket	Specializes in wide assortment of food, with self-service	Safeway, Kroger, Winn Dixie
Discount store	Competes on the basis of low prices and high turnover; offers few services	Wal-Mart, Target, K mart
Off-price retailer	Sells at prices 25 percent or more below traditional department store prices in spartan environment	Ross, T. J. Maxx, Clothestime
Factory outlet	Owned by manufacturer; sells close-outs, factory seconds, and canceled orders	Levi Strauss, Ship 'n Shore, Dansk
Wholesale club	Warehouse-type operation that sells food and general merchandise to small businesses and individual members at deeply discounted prices for cash	Sam's, Costco
Catalog store	Sends catalogs to customers and displays merchandise in showrooms where customers can order from attached warehouse	Best, Service Merchandise, Lurias
Hypermart	Offers huge selection of food and general merchandise with very low prices; sometimes called "mall without a wall"	Hypermart USA, American Fare
Nonstore retailing		
Vending machine	Sells merchandise by machine	Canteen
Direct selling	Sells face-to-face, usually in person's home	Fuller Brush, Avon, Amway
Direct response marketing	Attempts to get immediate consumer sale through media advertising, catalogs, or direct mail	K-Tel, L. L. Bean, Ronco

(Handwritten notes in margin: "Don't have Set up depts (NOT MGD)" near Variety store; "DEPT STORE + SUPER MKT COME TOGETHER" near Hypermart; "wide range of services." and "New Wal Marts WINN DIXIE" near Hypermart row)

■ **Exhibit 16-5**
Types of Retailers

In-home shopping allows the consumer to consider several options and then buy something without fighting traffic and the crowds in a retail store. Many offer toll-free phone lines, open around the clock.

CREATING A RETAIL STRATEGY

Retailing is a very competitive business. Managers have to develop an effective strategy to survive. The key tasks in building a retail strategy are defining a target market, developing a product offering, creating an image

■ **Exhibit 16-6**
Tasks Involved in Creating a Retail Strategy

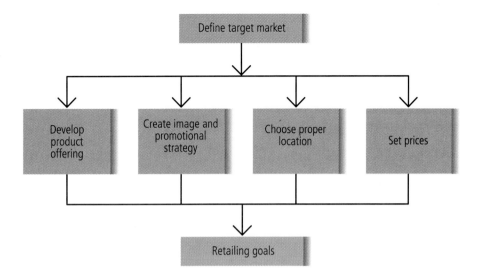

and a promotional strategy, choosing a location, and setting prices (see Exhibit 16-6).

Defining a Target Market

The first task in creating a retail strategy is defining the market to be served. This task is also one of the most important. Successful retailing has always been based on knowing the customers. In some cases, retailing chains have stagnated because management lost sight of whom they should be serving. Sears, for instance, has had trouble determining exactly whom it wants to serve. In other cases, the market that the firm should be serving is different from the one first chosen. Zayre found that its Hit or Miss clothing chain was, at first, a miss. It was meant to appeal to teenagers seeking low-cost clothes. The chain was not profitable until it was repositioned to reach professional women seeking values in clothing.

Developing a Product Offering

A second basic task in creating a retail strategy is to develop a product offering. The product offering is also called the *merchandise mix.*

First, a buying organization must be created to buy the products that will be sold. In large retail firms, a formal buying department has well-defined purchasing authority and responsibility. In smaller firms, the buying entity is more informal. It is not separate from the rest of the firm and does not need extra staff. In very small companies, buying may be done by an outside firm that has excellent sources of supply and knowledge of market trends.

After the buying organization is set up, the retailer must decide what to buy. This decision is based on market research, data on what has sold in the past, customer requests, suppliers' marketing efforts, and other sources.

■ The striking design of Mikasa's New Jersey retail store is intended to set it apart from the housewares manufacturer's factory outlets. The company recognizes the importance of image and atmosphere in developing a retail strategy. Mikasa set out to create a unique showcase for the Lifestyle store's exclusive selection of high-end merchandise.

Finding sources of supply and assessing their wares is the next step in developing a product offering. When the retailer finds desirable products, it negotiates a purchase contract. Sometimes a manufacturer won't sell to a retailer if it feels the retailer's image doesn't fit the product's image. For instance, JC Penney was only recently able to pick up such labels as Oshkosh B'Gosh, Maidenform, Henry Grethel, and Van Heusen. Before, these clothing manufacturers wouldn't sell to Penney's because of its somewhat downscale and dowdy image. JC Penney now tries to portray itself as a fashion-conscious, upscale retailer.

Creating an Image and Promotional Strategy

The third task in developing a retail strategy is to create an image and a promotional strategy. Promotion combines with the store's merchandise mix, service level, and atmosphere to make up a retail image. *Atmosphere* refers to the physical layout and decor of the store. They can create a relaxed or busy feeling, a sense of luxury, a friendly or cold attitude, and a sense of organization or clutter.

Choosing a Location

The next task in creating a retail strategy is figuring out where to put the store. First a community must be chosen. This decision depends on the strength of the local economy, the nature of the competition, the political climate, and so forth.

Then a specific site must be chosen. One important decision is whether or not to locate in a shopping center. A free-standing store can be used by large retailers like K mart and Target and sellers of shopping goods like furniture and cars. Customers will seek out these retailers. Such a location also has the advantages of low-cost land or rent and no direct competitors close by. On the other hand, it may be harder to attract customers to a free-standing location. Another disadvantage is that the retailer can't share costs for promotion, maintenance, and holiday decorating, as do stores within a mall.

Setting Prices

Another strategic task of the retail manager is to set prices. The strategy of pricing was presented in Chapter 15. Retailing's goal is to sell products, and the price is critical in assuring that sales take place.

Price is also one of the three key elements in the store's image and positioning strategy. Higher prices often imply quality and help support the prestige image of such retailers as Lord and Taylor, Saks Fifth Avenue, Gucci, Cartier, and Neiman Marcus. On the other hand, discounters and off-price retailers offer a good value for the money.

WHAT'S "IN STORE" FOR RETAILING'S FUTURE?

Predicting the future is always risky, but technological advancements, a shift in the retailer's role from distribution center to marketer, and global retailing are seen as some of the more important trends for retailing's future.

Advanced Store Technology

Several new technologies are emerging in retailing that will profoundly affect the industry. Some of the following technologies are already in stores and some will be rolled out nationally over the next few years: LED cart handles advertising store specials; coupon-dispensers on shelves; in-store radio stations; *Headline News* and product commercials on monitors at checkouts; machines at checkouts that print coupons for products similar to those you've just bought; debit cards; and cash registers that send information to a store database that keeps track of individual customers' purchases.[4] Marketers and food manufacturers like these advanced technologies because the store is the only place where the product, the advertiser's message, and the consumer all come together in one place.

As the Trend in Technology box on the next page shows, firms are also using technology to track customers' movements inside stores.

From Distribution Centers to Marketers

Supermarket retailing consultant Glen Terbeek predicts that by the year 2000 retailers, especially supermarkets, will become true marketers rather than marketers that act as distribution centers.[5] For instance, branded packaged goods and staples won't be sold in supermarkets. Instead, they will be delivered directly to consumers at home. Consumers would use hand scanners to record products' bar codes and update electronic shop-

Spying for Sales

More retailers are spying on their customers. But this time, instead of trying to spot shoplifters, they're looking for ways to increase sales. No longer content with rudimentary surveys at the checkout, hundreds of retailers nationwide are turning to electronic and infrared surveillance equipment with names like VideOcart, ShopperTrak, and Datatec. The goal is to provide retailers with data about shoppers' traffic patterns that can be used to change buying habits.

Take Bashas' Markets Inc. in Chandler, Ariz. High-tech surveillance showed that only 18 percent of the grocery store's customers went past the greeting cards, which are high-profit items. So George Fiscus, the store-layout manager, moved the section, sandwiching it between the floral department and an aisle with peanut butter, jelly, and health foods, which regularly drew 62 percent of the store's traffic. Nestled in their new home, the greeting cards showed a sales jump of 40 percent.

Sometimes the information does little more than confirm the intuition of the retailer. An astute grocery buyer or merchandiser often knows which sections are most heavily traveled. But the real value comes from being able to measure the effects of altering display space or moving products from aisle to aisle. And the data can also help stores pinpoint "dead spots," or infrequently visited sections, and reveal some merchandising missteps.

K mart Corp., in an effort to improve service and sales at its discount stores, is testing a new radarlike system that tracks customer traffic. The system, developed by the Datatec Industries, uses beams of infrared light to count customers as they pass under sensors mounted over the store entrance and on the ceiling at certain locations inside the store. K mart hopes to use the so-called Shopper-Trak system to improve service by sending salespeople to crowded departments and opening more checkout lanes before long lines form. The retailer also hopes to use the information to convert browsers into buyers. Departments with little traffic, for instance, could be promoted more heavily with advertised specials, in-store events such as its familiar "blue-light specials," and better displays at the ends of aisles. However, the system can merely uncover problems—and store officials will have to solve them. "At that point," says David M. Carlson, senior vice president, "you're up to the question of the skill and talent of the merchant."[6]

ping lists. Magazine ads would also carry bar codes so consumers could scan pages to put new products on their lists.

With the boring parts of grocery shopping taken care of almost automatically, consumers could then visit stores for things they enjoy buying—fresh produce, meats, or the fixings for a dinner party. Supermarkets would sell concepts and solutions rather than just ingredients. For instance, the products for a spaghetti dinner would all be grouped in one part of the store. Other possible categories would be *kids' lunch, diet, bridge club, tight budget,* or *new and exciting.*

But the future growth in convenience retailing will be primarily in home shopping. Already home shopping is a $3 billion a year industry—

and growing at 20 percent a year. The merger of Home Shopping Network and QVC in 1993 created a home shopping mega-network that is already available to 60 million viewers, or two-thirds of all television households. Upscale retailers such as Saks Fifth Avenue, have already found success on QVC. A 500-channel Television Shopping Mall will allow retailers to create the look and feel of their stores on the air. R. H. Macy plans to take one channel and call it "TV Macy's." On a catalog-based channel, called Catalog, Spiegel and Time Warner will sell products from Crate and Barrel, Nature Company, and Eddie Bauer, among others. The ultimate in home shopping—interactive television—should be available by the end of the decade. Nordstrom's, the department store chain, plans to be among the first to use interactive home shopping. Viewers will be able to ask for information as well as place orders from home.[7]

Global Retailing

Retailing is becoming more global. Major retailers are seeing attractive opportunities in Mexico, Japan, a United Europe, and the newly capitalistic societies of Eastern Europe and Russia.

Franchises are also seeking new growth abroad, especially in emerging nations like Mexico, Turkey, and Venezuela.[8] Franchising is popular in Eastern European countries, too. Pizza Hut recently opened its first franchise in Hungary and regularly has as many as 150 customers lined up outside. Fifteen more Pizza Huts will open in Hungary, as well as twenty-two KFC and forty Dunkin' Donuts outlets.[9]

In Asia, China and Japan are also relaxing trade and retailing restrictions, making their countries likely targets for U.S. retailers. The first McDonald's franchise outlet in China was an overnight success, and Domino's Pizza plans to open outlets near Hong Kong. Japan has recently relaxed retail laws, making it easier for large retailers like Toys R Us to locate among the traditional mom-and-pop stores. Retailers in the United Kingdom are so worried about warehouse clubs such as Sam's and Price-Costco, that they have filed a lawsuit to restrict their entry into the market.[10]

Concept Check

- Name five types of retailers, and discuss their operations.
- Describe the key tasks in creating a retailing strategy.
- Discuss the trends that will shape the future of retailing.

PHYSICAL DISTRIBUTION

The success of companies like Sam's Warehouse Club is partly based on having a good physical distribution system. **Physical distribution** consists of all activities concerned with transporting raw materials, component parts, and finished inventory so that they arrive at a designated place when needed and in usable condition.

Physical distribution is part of the marketing mix. Retailers don't sell products they can't deliver, and salespeople don't (or shouldn't) promise

physical distribution
All business activities concerned with transporting raw materials, component parts, and finished inventory so they arrive at a designated place when needed and in usable condition.

deliveries they can't make. Late deliveries and broken promises may mean loss of a customer. Accurate order filling and billing, timely delivery, and arrival in good condition are important to the success of the product.

Physical distribution is also part of the price of the product. Physical distribution has two main goals: good service and minimal costs. But a firm must be careful not to cut costs so much that it cannot deliver good service. One health-care products firm learned this lesson. It cut its distribution costs to 5 percent below the industry average and used wholesalers to distribute its products. At the same time, the firm's main competitor increased its distribution costs but sold directly to major drug chains. The competitor reduced turnaround time on orders and increased inventory for faster delivery. The logical result was that the health care products firm lost market share, despite having lower prices. On the other hand, a household products firm promised delivery in three days. It had to increase inventory 15 percent to meet this goal and to increase prices to cover the costs of inventory and transportation. Later the company found that its customers were happy with a ten-day delivery schedule. As you can see, marketers must weigh the impact of any cost savings against the quality of the distribution system.

ORDER CYCLE TIME

order cycle time Time between placing an order and receiving the order in good condition.

Perhaps the best measure of distribution service is **order cycle time**, or the time between when an order is placed and when it is received in good condition. A long order cycle time can mean lost sales. When Gillette introduced its Sensor shaving system, it was an immediate success. By the end of the first three months, Gillette had shipped eight million Sensors, a level the firm did not plan to hit until the end of the first year. Orders were pouring in, but Gillette couldn't fill them. Some retailers waited up to ninety days for the razors. Smaller retailers couldn't get any. The lengthy order cycle time cost Gillette millions of dollars. To meet demand, Gillette stepped up production in the United States and added production capacity in Europe.

THE FUNCTIONS OF PHYSICAL DISTRIBUTION

Distribution managers are responsible for carrying out several functions. They need to choose a warehouse location and type, set up a materials-handling system, maintain an inventory control system, set up procedures for processing orders, and choose among the available modes of transportation (see Exhibit 16-7).

Choosing Warehouse Location and Type

Deciding where to put a warehouse is mostly a matter of deciding which markets will be served and where production facilities will be located. A *storage warehouse* is used to hold goods for a long time. For instance, Jantzen makes bathing suits at an even rate throughout the year to provide steady employment and hold down costs. It then stores them in a warehouse until the selling season.

■ **Exhibit 16-7**
Functions of Physical
Distribution

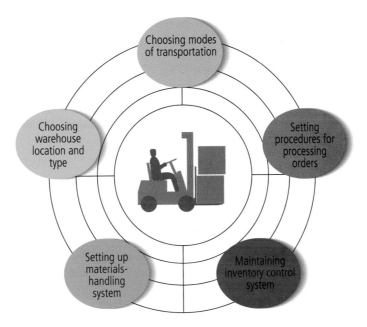

Choosing modes
of transportation

Choosing
warehouse
location and
type

Setting
procedures for
processing
orders

Setting up
materials-
handling
system

Maintaining
inventory control
system

distribution centers
Warehouses that specialize
in changing shipment sizes
but do not store goods.

Distribution centers are a special form of warehouse. They specialize in changing shipment sizes but not in storing goods. Such centers
make bulk (put shipments together) or break bulk. They strive for rapid
inventory turnover. When shipments arrive, the merchandise is quickly
sorted into orders for various retail stores. As soon as the order is complete, it is delivered. Distribution centers are the wave of the future,
replacing traditional warehouses. Companies simply can't afford to have a
lot of money tied up in idle inventory.

Setting Up a Materials-Handling System
A materials-handling system moves and handles inventory. The goal of
such a system is to move items as quickly as possible while handling them
as little as possible. When Kodak built a new plant for making photographic coated paper, for example, it designed a way to minimize materials handling. It built a ten-level concrete rack to hold the one-ton rolls of
raw paper. A computer handles inventory control and commands
machines that can retrieve and carry the rolls without damage and then
load the paper on the assembly line.

Maintaining an Inventory Control System
The third function of physical distribution is inventory control. The goal is
to provide a continuous flow of goods and to match the quantity of goods
kept in inventory as closely as possible with demand. Inventory control is
a critical function. A producer cannot afford to run out of an item that
could stop production. But the inventory on hand should not be too large.
The costs of storing raw materials, parts, and finished products for a year
can be huge. In industries where product models change yearly, as with
cars, large inventories can also depress new-product sales. Dealers have
to offer large discounts to get customers to buy last year's model instead

of the new one. Also, goods may go stale or become obsolete if they are stored too long. Then the firm has to mark down the prices.

To improve inventory management, many firms are turning to a just-in-time (JIT) inventory system, as described in Chapter 10. Such systems are complex. They require better planning and information, closer supplier relations, and better production and distribution facilities. But as computers and fax machines are making JIT systems more workable, more companies are able to use these cost-effective systems.

Setting Procedures for Processing Orders

Another highly important distribution activity is order processing. Slow shipment, incorrect merchandise, and partially filled orders create much dissatisfaction. The flow of goods and information must be monitored so mistakes can be corrected before the merchandise is shipped and the customer billed.

Choosing Modes of Transportation

A final function of physical distribution is to decide how merchandise will be shipped. A transportation manager can choose among several shipping methods: air, highway (truck), rail (train), water (barge or ship), and occasionally pipeline. Each method has advantages and disadvantages (see Exhibit 16-8).

Air. Normally the fastest way to ship merchandise is by air freight, or cargo-carrying airplanes. At first glance, air seems the most expensive method. But when other factors are taken into account—for instance, the ability to eliminate a warehouse because of the speed of air delivery—the total cost of distribution may be less than any other method.

Merchandise shipped by air freight usually is of high value (computers, diagnostic equipment, critical replacement parts) or is perishable (flowers and pineapples from Hawaii, lobsters from Maine).

Highway. Trucks are the most flexible way to haul freight. Many truck lines provide door-to-door service in almost every community of the United States. Trucks may even be faster than airplanes for distances under 250 miles. Goods carried by truck don't have to be transported to and from airports.

Trucks are often used in combination with other modes of transportation. A popular approach is **containerization**, packing and sealing goods in large, standard-size containers. The containers can be loaded on trucks, trains, planes, and ships—whatever it takes to reach the destination—without being unpacked. When containerized goods are transported by truck to railroad terminals and loaded on trains, the service is called *piggyback service*. When the goods are transported by either trucks or trains and then airplanes, it is called *birdyback service*. When the goods are transported by either trucks or trains and then ships, it is called *fishyback service*.

containerization Packing and sealing goods in large, standard-size containers that are transported without being unpacked until they reach their final destination.

■ Exhibit 16-8
Relative Advantages of
the Basic Modes of
Transportation

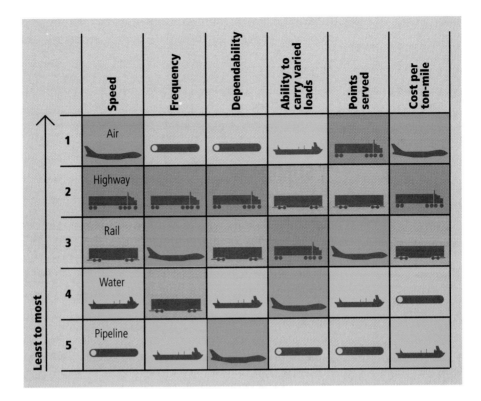

Rail. For almost a century, railroads have been the backbone of the U.S. freight system. But the completion of the interstate highway system and growth of truck lines has almost wiped out rail service to smaller markets, though some service still operates between larger cities.

A unique rail service is the *unit train*. This type of train goes only between two points, carrying a single bulk commodity, such as coal. Every day, for instance, Burlington-Northern runs a coal unit train with almost a hundred cars from the coalfields of Wyoming to an electric power generator for the city of San Antonio, Texas.

Water. Other major carriers of bulk goods are the vessels that travel the waterways. Deep-water ships use the oceans. Barges tend to use the inland waterways (rivers, lakes, and canals). Large tugboats greatly increase the capacity of many barge lines. Also, special barges now handle such items as asphalt, corrosive chemicals, and even refrigerated commodities like some fruits and vegetables.

Pipeline. A continuous flow of products is maintained by pipelines, the slowest mode of transportation. Pipeline routes are inflexible, and capacity is limited by the diameter of the pipe. But weather is almost never a problem. Gases, liquids, and some soluble solids are the main products moved through pipelines. Coal, for instance, is moved in a watery mixture called a slurry. Goods going through pipelines move in one direction to storage terminals at the receiving end.

Concept Check

- Describe the goals of physical distribution.
- Explain the functions of physical distribution.

■ SUMMARY

1. Describe the role of distribution channels.

Distribution deals with how products reach consumers. Distribution channels are series of marketing entities through which goods and services pass on their way from producers to end users. Distribution systems focus on the physical transfer of goods and services and on their legal ownership at each stage of the distribution process.

2. Explain why different channels are used for consumer products and industrial products.

Consumer products channels are usually more complex than industrial products channels. Most industrial products are more expensive than most consumer products. Usually, the higher the price, the simpler the channel needed to distribute the product. Many industrial products are custom-made for end users. Others are sold through industrial distributors.

3. Decide when a marketer would use exclusive, selective, or intensive distribution.

The degree of intensity depends in part on the type of product being distributed. Exclusive distribution (one or two dealers in an area) is used when products are in high demand in the target market. Selective distribution has a limited number of dealers per area, but more than one or two. The channel is used for consumer shopping goods, some specialty goods, and some industrial accessories. Intensive distribution occurs when the manufacturer sells its products in virtually every store willing to carry them. It is mainly for consumer convenience goods.

4. Discuss the functions of wholesalers and their relationships to manufacturers and others in the distribution channels.

Wholesalers typically sell finished products to retailers and to other institutions, such as manufacturers, schools, and hospitals. They also provide a wide variety of services, among them storing merchandise, financing inventory, breaking bulk, providing rapid delivery to retailers, and supplying market information.

5. Distinguish among the types of wholesalers.

The three main types of wholesalers are merchant wholesalers, manufacturers' sales branches, and agents and brokers. Merchant wholesalers buy from manufacturers and sell to other businesses. Full-service merchant wholesalers offer a complete array of services to their customers, who are retailers. Manufacturers' sales branches perform many of the same functions as full-service merchant wholesalers, but they are owned and completely controlled by the manufacturers. Agents and brokers are essentially independents who provide buying and selling services. They receive commissions according to their sales.

6. Contrast the different kinds of retail operations.

Some 30 million Americans are engaged in retailing. Retailing can be either in-store or nonstore. In-store retail operations include department stores, mass-merchandising shopping chains, specialty stores, discount stores, off-price retailers, factory outlets, and catalog showrooms. Nonstore retailing includes vending machines, direct sales, and direct response marketing. Creating a retail strategy is important in all kinds of retailing and involves defining a target market, developing a product offering, creating an image and a promotional strategy, choosing a location, and setting prices. Advanced technology, convenience retailing, and global retailing are trends that will affect the future of retail operations.

7. Explain the goals and functions of physical distribution.

Physical distribution consists of all business activities concerned with transporting raw materials, component parts, or finished inventory so they arrive in a designated place when needed and in usable condition. Its two main goals are good service and minimal costs.

The functions of physical distribution include choosing a warehouse location and type, setting up a materials-handling system, maintaining an inventory control system, setting procedures for processing orders, and choosing modes of transportation (air, highway, rail, water, or pipeline).

▪ DISCUSSION QUESTIONS

1. Consider the following statement and discuss: "The only thing that middlemen really do is increase prices for consumers."

2. Trace the channel for some product you are familiar with. Tell why you think the channel evolved as it did.

3. Explain how you would try to distribute a novelty item you invented that would appeal to college students.

4. If you were going to open a small business, would you rather operate at the retail or wholesale level? Why?

5. Why do you think the same brand and model of some popular stereo equipment can be found in audio equipment (specialty) stores, discount stores, and catalog showrooms?

6. What factors would you consider important in choosing a retail location? How would you go about collecting this information?

7. Chapter 15 categorized consumer products as convenience, shopping, and specialty products. What are the relationships between these categories and the types of retail stores discussed in this chapter?

8. Why is the minimization of costs not always the best goal for physical distribution? What about maximization of service?

9. What do you see as the future of retailing?

■ CASE

Please Don't Squeeze the Small Retailer

Seeking to cut its distribution costs, Procter & Gamble is considering requiring retailers to buy its products, such as Tide laundry detergent, Crest toothpaste, and Charmin toilet tissue, only in large quantities. Those that need smaller amounts would effectively be forced to pay a premium to buy through wholesalers. Retailers say the new rules would represent a big change from the current system. Retailers say they can now choose among a wide range of quantities and volume discounts when buying directly from P&G. But under one P&G proposal, retailers would have to order either 500 cases at a time or full truckloads, which typically contain more than 1,800 cases of most of the company's products.

Retailers say P&G has told them it plans to overhaul its distribution system, largely because of the cost of handling small orders that go directly to individual stores rather than to warehouses. People close to P&G say that although nearly all of its sales volume comes from retailers that buy 500 or more cases of products at a time, these large shipments are impractical to manage and so are broken down into smaller orders. Many such retailers, lacking warehouse space, would be forced to buy those smaller quantities of P&G products from wholesalers—and pay a premium for their services—or obtain warehousing facilities.

The new rules could wind up hurting P&G in some stores if angry retailers retaliate. "For a lot of retailers, it'll be a reason not to favor P&G on how they stock their shelves and on merchandising and promotional programs," said an executive with a drugstore chain.

P&G is making a concession to customers that want some flexibility: The company will allow them to order truckloads containing a mixture of products, retailers say. As a rule, P&G ships truckloads containing only identical or related products—such as Charmin toilet tissue and Bounty paper towels. Customers will, however, have to pay a premium for truckloads containing several kinds of products, such as Tide detergent and Duncan Hines cake mix. P&G has told customers it believes it will be able to provide this service by streamlining the links between its manufacturing plants and regional distribution centers. However, P&G will provide an incentive for customers to order single-product truckloads directly from P&G plants by giving them a special discount.[11]

Some small retailers cannot afford to purchase and warehouse truck-load-sized orders, whether single-product or mixed. Like P&G's Charmin tissues, they may end up feeling squeezed.

Questions
1. Do you think P&G's plan is a good way for the company to cut its distribution costs?
2. What other techniques could P&G use to lower its costs of distribution?
3. Do you see any ethical issues in the case? If so, what are they?

Promotional Strategies

Learning Goals

After studying this chapter, you should be able to:

1 Describe the goals of promotional strategy.

2 Define the promotional mix, and explain its elements.

3 Describe the types of advertising.

4 Evaluate the media that advertisers use.

5 Describe the selling process.

6 Distinguish among the various types of sales promotion.

7 Understand how public relations fits into the promotional mix.

8 Discuss the factors that affect promotional mix.

Career Profile

Jeff Fulwiler is approaching a career in business from a creative perspective. A liberal arts major in college, Jeff augmented his artistic skills with business savvy gained from marketing and advertising courses. He found a job as a graphic designer with Seta, Appleman & Showell, a premier creative and marketing communications firm, immediately after graduation. Recently, he was promoted to senior graphic designer. In this position he heads up several design teams working on a variety of projects.

Most of Jeff's design work is executed on computer. He had some exposure to computers in college, but it wasn't until he started working at S.A.S. that he really began to learn to use them for graphic design. He trained first on computer tutorials, and then under the guidance of one of the company's senior artists.

The team approach to projects at S.A.S. has helped Jeff expand his interpersonal communication skills. This is important, because part of his job is dealing with a diverse group of clients. He must be able to understand what these clients want to say with their designs. He must also be able to pinpoint what specific target audiences feel about a client's product or image. It is the art classes he had in college that gave him the creative discipline required for such a position, but he's also enhanced his artistic skills with business savvy.

Jeff is prepared to continue putting in long hours at the office and on his own time to keep up with the changing technology of his field. He feels this is the best way to reach his goals and prepare himself for the challenges he will encounter along the way.

Overview

Promotion, the topic of this chapter, is the last element of the marketing mix. First the chapter considers the goals of promotion. Next it explains the elements of the promotional mix: advertising, personal selling, sales promotion, and public relations. The chapter ends with a discussion of how marketing managers choose a promotional mix.

PROMOTIONAL STRATEGY

promotion Marketing activity that stimulates demand for a firm's goods or services.

differential advantage Set of unique features of a company and its products that the target market perceives as important and better than the competition.

Very few goods or services can survive in the marketplace without good **promotion**, which builds demand for those products. Marketers promote everything from aircraft to zoos.

Once the product has been created, promotion is often used to convince target customers that it has a **differential advantage** over the competition. A differential advantage is a set of unique features that the target market perceives as important and better than the competition. Such features may be high quality, fast delivery, low price, good service, and the like. Lexus, for example, is seen as having a quality differential advantage over other luxury cars. So, promotion for Lexus stresses the quality of the vehicle. On the other hand, despite massive advertising budgets, brewers did not explain the differential advantage of dry beers such as Bud Dry, Coors Dry, and Michelob Dry. Despite strong initial sales, brewers now consider dry beer an "also ran."[1]

▼ PROMOTIONAL GOALS

promotional strategy Plan for informing, persuading, or reminding the target market about a good or service to stimulate action.

Most firms undertake promotion of some sort. The meaning of the Latin root word is "to move forward." Hence actions that move a company toward its goals are promotional in nature. Because company goals vary widely, so do promotional strategies. In a broad sense, **promotional strategy** is the plan for informing, persuading, or reminding the target market about a product. The goal is to stimulate action. In a profit-oriented firm, the desired action is for the consumer to buy the promoted item. Mrs. Smith's, for instance, wants people to buy more frozen pies. Not-for-profit organizations seek a variety of actions with their promotions. They tell us not to litter, to buckle up, to join the Army, to attend the ballet.

Promotional goals include creating awareness, getting people to try products, providing information, explaining the organization's actions, retaining loyal customers, increasing the use of products, and identifying potential customers. Any promotional campaign may seek to achieve one or more of these goals.

Creating Awareness

All too often, firms go out of business because people don't know they exist or what they do. Small restaurants often have this problem. Simply putting up a sign and opening the door is rarely enough. Promotion through ads on local radio or TV, coupons in local papers, fliers, and so forth can create awareness of a new business or product.

■ A good promotional strategy will create awareness of your product or service and get people to try it. Methods of promoting a product range from buying television ad time to placing coupons in local newspapers. Here, Smartfood Popcorn takes a more direct approach, using a costume and free samples to attract potential customers.

Even companies with large promotion budgets can see their efforts backfire. Recall the pink bunny that keeps on going . . . and going . . . and going? Is it in an ad for Duracell or Eveready Energizer batteries? If you said Duracell, you're wrong but hardly alone. The bunny ad was voted television's most popular ad in an annual survey of 4,700 consumers. But 40 percent claimed it was a Duracell ad.[2] In effect, Energizer is advertising for Duracell. The mix-up is fairly common. When number-two brands challenge bigger rivals by mocking them in ads, consumers often remember the ad, the product—and the number-one brand name rather than the name of the challenger.

Getting Consumers to Try Products

Promotion is almost always used to get people to try a new product or to get nonusers to try an existing product. Sometimes free samples are given away. Lever, for instance, mailed over 2 million free samples of its Lever 2000 soap to target households. Coupons and trial-size containers of products are also common tactics used to tempt people to try a product. But the largest share of the promotional budget for new items typically goes to advertising. Cheseborough-Pond's spent $40 million to promote several new anti-aging Pond's skin care products in 1994. Of that, approximately $23 million was spent on advertising, and the remainder on coupons and other types of sales promotion.[3]

Providing Information

Informative promotion is more common in the early stages of the product life cycle. An informative promotion may explain what ingredients (like fiber) will do for your health, tell you why the product is better (high definition television versus regular television), inform you of a new low price, or explain where the item may be bought.

People typically will not buy a product or support a not-for-profit organization until they know what it will do and how it may benefit them. Thus an informative ad may change a need into a want or stimulate interest in a product. Consumer watchdogs and social critics applaud the informative function of promotion, since it helps consumers make more intelligent purchase decisions. Star-Kist, for instance, lets customers know that its tuna is caught in dolphin-safe nets.

Explaining an Organization's Actions

Companies that are having big public relations problems may turn to promotion to present their side of the issue. For instance, when over 300 people suffered from food poisoning in Idaho, Washington, and Nevada from eating Jack-in-the-Box hamburgers, the company quickly turned to promotion to explain its corrective actions. It ran advertising in Seattle and other major markets apologizing for the problem and explaining new policies to prevent a recurrence. Also, Jack-in-the-Box president Robert Nugent held a news conference to explain the company's position and to answer questions.[4]

Keeping Loyal Customers

Promotion is also used to keep people from switching brands. Ads remind them about the brand, as in Campbell's slogan "Soups are mmmmm good," and American Airlines' "Something special in the air." Marketers also remind users that the brand is better than the competition. Dodge Ram trucks claim that they have superior safety features. For years, Pepsi has claimed it has the taste that consumers prefer. America West Airlines brags of its on-time ratings month after month. Such advertising reminds customers about the quality of the product.

Firms can also help keep customers loyal by telling them when a product or service is improved. Blockbuster Entertainment Corporation has begun promoting the rental of CD-ROM drives at 52 of its stores in northern California. Linking the CD-ROM drive with a personal computer, customers can experience more lifelike video games. The hope is that after renting the equipment and programs, customers will want to buy their own machinery. If they do, Blockbuster will have positioned itself to become a major rental supplier of the 5-inch compact discs that contain the programs. Its stores already carry more than 200 CD-ROM titles.[5]

Increasing the Amount and Frequency of Use

Promotion is often used to get people to use more of a product and to use it more often. When smoking was banned on domestic flights, Wrigley's began promoting its chewing gum as a good alternative to smoking. The most popular promotion to increase the use of a product may be frequent-flyer programs. American Airlines, the pioneer, has enrolled over three million frequent flyers. Hotel chains like Marriott and Hyatt now have frequent-user programs.

Identifying Target Customers

Promotion helps find customers. One method is the direct response coupon. For instance, *The Wall Street Journal* and *Business Week* include direct-response coupons for more information on computer systems, corporate jets, color copiers, and other types of business equipment, to help target those who are truly interested.

Instead of coupons, some firms use toll-free 800 numbers. Sharp Electronics says, "Find out how you can put a serious computer in your briefcase. Without taking everything out of it. Call 1-800-BE-SHARP."

THE PROMOTIONAL MIX

> **promotional mix** Combination of advertising, personal selling, sales promotion, and public relations used to promote a product.

The combination of advertising, personal selling, sales promotion, and public relations used to promote a product is called the **promotional mix**. Each firm creates a unique mix for each product. But the goal is always to efficiently and effectively deliver the firm's message to the target audience. These are the elements of the promotional mix:

- *Advertising:* any paid form of nonpersonal promotion by an identified sponsor
- *Personal selling:* face-to-face presentation to a prospective buyer
- *Sales promotion:* marketing activities (other than personal selling, advertising, and public relations) that stimulate consumer buying, including coupons and samples, displays, shows and exhibitions, demonstrations, and other types of selling efforts
- *Public relations:* linking of organizational goals with key aspects of the public interest and programs designed to earn public understanding and acceptance

In the sections that follow, each of these elements of the promotional mix is explained in more detail.

Concept Check
- List and discuss the goals of promotion.
- What is the promotional mix?

ADVERTISING

> **advertising** Any paid form of nonpersonal presentation by an identified sponsor, which may be transmitted by any of a number of different media.

Most Americans are bombarded daily with advertisements to buy things. **Advertising** is any paid form of nonpersonal presentation by an identified sponsor. It may appear on television or radio, in newspapers, magazines, books, or direct mail, or on billboards or transit cards.

The money that big corporations spend on advertising is mind-boggling. Nearly 10¢ of every dollar spent on perfume and cosmetics goes to advertising. Even the missile and space industry spends nearly 2¢ of every sales dollar on ads. Companies like Procter & Gamble, Kraft-General Foods, Philip Morris, or General Motors spend an average of over $100,000 per hour. Many of the ad dollars are spent in the prime evening hours on network television. Estimated advertising expenses in this country in 1993 were over $150 billion. A Super Bowl 30-second commercial in 1994 cost $900,000.[6]

Advertising has a big place in our society and much power to influence thought and action. But it lacks a direct feedback mechanism. A potential buyer can't ask an ad how something works, for instance. Thus advertising can't adapt as easily to individual consumers as personal selling can. For example, a consumer shopping for a car can respond right away with questions about the sales presentation.

③ TYPES OF ADVERTISING

product advertising
Advertising of a specific good or service.

comparative advertising
Product advertising in which the company's product is compared with competing, named products.

reminder advertising
Advertising used to keep the product name in the public's mind.

institutional advertising Advertising that creates a favorable picture of a company and its ideals, services, and roles in the community.

advocacy advertising
Advertising that takes a stand on certain social or economic issues.

The form of advertising most people know is **product advertising**, which features a specific good or service. It can take many different forms. One special form is **comparative advertising**, in which the company's product is compared with competing, named products. Coca-Cola and Pepsi-Cola often use comparative advertising. MCI claims that the only major difference between it and AT&T is that AT&T is more expensive. Another special form is **reminder advertising**, which is used to keep the product name in the public's mind. It is most often used during the maturity stage of the product life cycle. It assumes that the target market has already been persuaded of the product's merits and just needs a memory boost. Miller beer, V-8 vegetable juice, and the FTD florist association use reminder promotion.

In addition to product advertising, many companies use **institutional advertising**. This type of advertising creates a positive picture of a company and its ideals, services, and roles in the community. Instead of trying to sell specific products, it builds a desired image and goodwill for the company. Some institutional advertising supports product advertising that targets consumers. Other institutional advertising is aimed at stockholders or the public. **Advocacy advertising** takes a stand on a social or economic issue. It is sometimes called *grass-roots lobbying*. Energy companies often use this type of advertising to influence public opinion about regulation of their industry.

In designing any type of advertising, decisions must be made in two main areas: the message and the media. Neither choice is easy.

DESIGNING THE ADVERTISING MESSAGE

The message is a key part of advertising. It's what the firm wants the public to know about the product. Designing an advertising message is not an easy task. For this reason, most firms hire an advertising agency and let its creative people develop a *theme*. Examples include "For all you do, this Bud's for you" and Visa International's " .... but you'll have to bring your Visa card because they don't take American Express." Advertising themes are often quite general, so that the firm can develop a number of sub-themes or minicampaigns. Dodge used "An American revolution" as a

GERMANS CAN SIT THROUGH FIVE-HOUR OPERAS BY WAGNER. THEY OBVIOUSLY KNOW SOMETHING ABOUT ENDURANCE.

The citizens of Germany pursue a curious national passion. Contemplating the thunder of Wagner's epic *Ring* Cycle.

It's monumental stuff. But by the time the fat lady finally tortures her last High C, the audience has endured four long nights, and 15 hours, of music. And if you're not in the mood, it can be some of the most grueling punishment this side of the Kalahari Desert.

But if you're someone who would frankly prefer the Kalahari Desert, we suggest another form of German entertainment: The legendary endurance motorcycles of BMW.

These are the R100GS and PD. Machines that are all guts and glory. That dare to measure themselves against the craggy, eternal truths of the world's most unwelcoming environments.

The engine they share is the famous boxer. A tenacious 980cc fire-breather that puts 60 thundering horses at your command. Fine-tuned to tolerances that would delight a diamond cutter, this powerplant has made history on the road and off. Making the BMW enduros the fastest machines in their class.

If cratered rock and pockmarked deserts are your idea of paradise lost, these are the machines to take you there. They thrive on the roughest terrain ever carved by a glacier or brewed by a volcano. Of course, they also handle interstates with the easy grace you'd expect only of a BMW.

And while you're traveling mile after rugged mile, tucked comfortably into the back of your mind will be the reassurance of BMW's three-year, unlimited-mileage, limited warranty.* A sense of security that's reinforced by your automatic membership in the BMW Motorcycle Roadside Assistance Plan.**

You don't have to track the trackless wastes to find such mean machines. Just call 800-345-4BMW to pinpoint the authorized dealer in your hemisphere. Then take a seat and enjoy the performance. **WORTH THE OBSESSION.**

■ This ad for BMW motorcycles is an example of product advertising that features a specific good or service. It is the most prevalent type of advertising, and it takes many forms.

major campaign theme and then promoted its supercharged Daytona Turbo Z with the subtheme "Pure adrenalin." The themes point up the perceived benefits of a product. Market research is used to find out what those benefits to consumers are.

Advertising messages are developed in three stages: (1) generation, (2) evaluation, and (3) execution. *Message generation* is the creative development of things to say about the product. It draws on the firm's promotional goals, the product's image, and the desired positioning of the product.

Message evaluation normally involves market research to find the best theme among those that have been developed. A good message is one that makes a positive impression on the target market. It must also be unique; consumers must be able to differentiate it from competitors' messages (remember the Energizer bunny). Most important, a good advertising message is believable. A theme that makes wild claims is a waste of money—or worse, if it creates ill will for the advertiser. Volvo lost market share after its "monster-truck crushing" ads were exposed as false.

Message execution means developing copy and illustrations for the campaign. Copy is the written or spoken part. Illustrations (drawings, photographs) are used to support the copy. Finally, the advertising format must be developed for print media and television. Copy and illustrations must be balanced on the page or on the screen. Headline sizes and colors must be chosen. Sometimes message execution can lead to controversy, as the Business Ethics and Social Responsibility Trends box shows.

Can a Camel Be Too Cute?

The staff of the Federal Trade Commission has recommended that the FTC seek an outright ban of R.J. Reynolds's highly effective Joe Camel advertising campaign on the grounds that the six-year-old campaign entices minors to smoke. One study, published in December 1991 in the *Journal of the American Medical Association,* found that more than half the children aged three to six in one survey were able to match the Joe Camel logo with a photo of a cigarette. Six-year-olds were almost as familiar with Joe Camel as they were with a Mickey Mouse logo.

The popularity of the bad-boy cartoon camel has been one of R.J. Reynolds's few marketing successes of late, due largely to the character's appeal to young smokers. Thanks to the labors of Reynolds's beast of burden—the "Smooth Character" appears in hip poses wooing ladies—Camel was one of the few full-priced cigarettes to increase its market share in 1993. In 1993, Camel was one of the most heavily advertised tobacco brands at $23 million, according to Leading National Advertisers. Camel is the number-eight cigarette brand in the country, with 3.7 percent of the market.

The dapper dromedary's youth appeal is broadly accepted. Even RJR openly acknowledges that the campaign was designed to enliven the brand's image and that it appeals to younger smokers—but those of legal age. RJR notes that the percentage of high school students who have tried cigarettes has dropped since the ads first appeared, undercutting the claim that the ads are luring kids to smoke.

While any action against Joe Camel would be a victory for antismoking forces, critics say that the government's delay in taking action highlights a faint-hearted approach to tobacco regulation. Lung cancer and other smoking-related diseases kill 434,000 people a year, according to the Centers for Disease Control and Prevention in Atlanta. Yet critics say the government seems more interested in cracking down on marketers of dietary supplements.

Former FTC officials and lawyers say the FTC may have a tough time proving its case. "They've got a major hurdle to deal with in the First Amendment," says Stuart Friedel, a partner at Davis & Gilbert and a former FTC trial attorney. "To seek to ban a form of advertising because it's unfair is extraordinarily unusual, aggressive and, in my mind, not supportable by the weight of law." The notion of unfairness means that the advertising is unfair to children because it encourages them to smoke. Tobacco industry lawyers say that the FTC's definition of unfairness is so broad that there is virtually no chance it will be able to ban the Camel ads.[7]

---

4   CHOOSING ADVERTISING MEDIA

advertising media
Channels through which advertising is carried to prospective customers; include newspapers, magazines, radio, TV, outdoor advertising, direct mail.

The channels through which advertising is carried to prospective customers are the **advertising media**. Both product and institutional ads appear in all the major advertising media: newspapers, magazines, radio, television, outdoor advertising, and direct mail. Each company must decide which media are best for its products. Two of the main factors in making that choice are the cost of the medium and the audience reached by it.

CPM (cost per thousand) Rate at which advertising costs are quoted, figured per thousand members of an audience.

In advertising, costs are usually given in terms of **CPM (cost per thousand** members of an audience). The cost of a thirty-second ad on the "CBS Evening News" is about $60,000, a CPM of $5.70. The nature of the audience is a second big factor in choosing media. "Monday Night Football," for instance, is a good medium for reaching college-educated men. A heavy-metal radio station might be a good medium for a producer of acne products.

Choosing a medium means weighing the strengths and weaknesses of each. These are summarized in Exhibit 17-1 and discussed on the following pages.

Newspapers

The most popular advertising medium in the United States today is newspapers. They account for about 25 percent of all advertising dollars. Their popularity makes sense, since about half of all American adults read a newspaper every day.

Newspapers are an excellent medium for selling products in local markets. In fact, local advertising makes up the bulk of newspaper promotions. But one problem with this type of advertising is the high "noise level." Newspaper ads compete not only with other ads but also with news and entertainment stories, sports results, and comics that may be on the same page. Newspaper ads also have a short life span, because they are tossed out with yesterday's news.

Magazines

There are magazines for almost every interest group and market segment, from art lovers and astronomers to veterinarians and welders. About 5.5 percent of all advertising revenue is directed to magazines. Magazines have a higher CPM than newspapers. But they often have a lower cost per potential customer, because they appeal to special audiences. Makers of clothing and accessories for teenage girls will find that most newspapers have a lower CPM than the magazine *Sassy* does. Yet almost every reader of *Sassy* has some interest in the latest teen fashions. At most, 10 or 15 out of 100 newspaper readers could be expected to share this interest. Also, the details of a product, especially colors, show up very well in magazine advertising.

Radio

More than 11,000 radio stations share U.S. airwaves. Indeed, every corner of the country can be reached by radio. It accounts for 7 percent of all advertising sales. The major networks—ABC, CBS, Mutual, and NBC—offer both news and entertainment programs. Programming ranges from all news to call-in talk shows, classical music, "oldies," and hard rock.

Every station positions itself in the marketplace, and this positioning helps advertisers reach specific target markets. High-priced automobiles may be promoted on "beautiful music" FM stations, for example. Some stations depend on disk jockeys and other radio personalities to build loyal audiences. These personalities can be effective in selling to local customers.

Medium	Strengths	Weaknesses
Newspapers	Geographic selectivity and flexibility Short-term advertiser commitments News value and immediacy Constant readership High individual market coverage	Little demographic selectivity Limited color facilities Short-lived
Magazines	Good reproduction, especially color Message permanence Demographic selectivity (reaches affluent audience) Regionality Local-market selectivity Special-interest possibilities Relatively long advertising life	Long-term advertiser commitments Slow audience buildup Limited demonstration capacities Lack of urgency Long lead time for ad placement
Radio	Low and negotiable costs High frequency Immediacy of message Relatively little seasonal change in audience Highly portable Short scheduling notice Short-term advertiser commitments Entertainment carryover	No visuals Advertising message short-lived Background sound Commercial clutter (a large number of ads in a short time)

Television	Widely diversified audience
	Creative visual and audio opportunities for
	  demonstration
	Immediacy of message
	Entertainment carryover
		High cost
		Little demographic selectivity
		Advertising message short-lived
		Consumer skepticism about
		  advertising claims

Network	Association with programming prestige	Long-term advertiser commitments

Local	Geographic selectivity
	Associated with programs of local origin
	  and appeal
	Short lead time
		Narrow audience on independent
		  stations
		High cost for broad geographic
		  coverage

Outdoor advertising	Repetition possibilities Moderate cost Flexibility	Short messages Lack of demographic selectivity Many distractions when observing the message

Direct mail	Very efficient with good mailing list
	Can be personalized by computer
	Can reach very specific demographic
	  market
	Lengthy message with photos and
	  testimony
		Very costly with poor mailing list
		May never be opened

■ Exhibit 17-1
Strengths and Weak-
nesses of Major Media

Television

Television is second only to newspapers in the share of advertising dollars (22 percent). But TV is the leader in national advertising. TV advertisers get huge audiences and pay a low CPM. Before remote-control channel changers, very little could draw viewers' attention away from the TV. But remote controls let viewers switch easily to shows on other channels or mute the sound of TV commercials.

Although many TV markets can be segmented by lifestyle, the products advertised on TV must usually have broad appeal. Food, car, and appliance ads usually do well. Television also has many of the advantages of personal selling. For instance, a Maytag dishwasher can be demonstrated on television almost as if it were being shown in each viewer's home.

Outdoor Advertising

Outdoor advertising is an inexpensive medium with great flexibility. But it accounts for only 1 percent of advertising spending. Outdoor advertising includes the transit cards in buses and subways, posters, and billboards, which are the most common form of outdoor advertising. Billboards can pinpoint a fairly specific geographic market. But they allow little or no control otherwise over who sees them. They also are limited to short messages, since they have only a few seconds to grab viewers' attention. Billboards are often a good way to reach ethnic and minority groups that may not read magazines or newspapers as much as other groups do.

Direct Mail

Direct mail is a popular medium, consuming 18 percent of all advertising dollars. Direct mail can be the most efficient medium an advertiser uses or the least efficient, depending on the quality of the mailing list and of the mailing piece. Good mailing lists are available from list brokers for about $75 to $100 per 1,000 names. Prestigious lists or lists of people who have bought merchandise through the mail in the past few months normally cost $200 per 1,000 names.

Direct mail can reach a huge market. For instance, American Express sent out over half a billion pieces of mail in 1993. It is little wonder, then, that many of the Fortune 500 firms have been attracted to this form of selling. General Mills (Talbots), American Can (Fingerhut, Figi's, Michigan Bulb), R.J. Reynolds (Harry and David, Jackson & Perkins), and Quaker Oats (Joseph A. Bank Clothiers, Herrschners, Brookstone) are large companies with direct-mail operations. About 7,000 different catalogs are published each year, and 7 billion copies are mailed out. JC Penney alone puts out twenty-eight catalogs a year, amounting to 200 million pieces that bring in $1.6 billion in sales.

Other Media

Other important media include the yellow pages (7 percent of total ad revenue) and business papers like *The Wall Street Journal* and *Barron's* (2 percent of total advertising dollars). The remaining advertising dollars are devoted to many minor media. These include ads on trucks, in farm publications, and on grocery carts.

Direct marketing (or **direct-response marketing**) is promoting a product directly to a buyer and getting an immediate response. Home Shopping Network is a major direct-response marketer. Direct marketing approaches include telephone sales; direct mail; catalogs; and TV, radio, or newspaper ads that invite the consumer to call a toll-free number or fill out a coupon. About 75 percent of all U.S. households place a direct-response order each year.

Electronic direct marketing involves the use of such technologies as videotext, videodisks, electronic mail, and interactive television. Compucard, for instance, lets consumers order goods directly from manufacturers through their home computers. The firm offers more than 60,000 items at prices as much as 50 percent below manufacturers' suggested retail price. The advantage of electronic direct marketing is that it shortcuts the drawn-out process of mail-order selling.

ADVERTISING AGENCIES

Companies that help create ads and place them in the proper media are **advertising agencies**. Many companies rely on agencies to both create and monitor their ad campaigns.

Full-service advertising agencies offer the five services shown in Exhibit 17-2. The creative department develops promotional themes and messages, writes copy, designs layouts, takes photos, and draws illustrations. The media services group selects the media mix and schedules advertising. The research department may conduct market research studies for clients or help in developing new products or gauging the firm's or product's image. Merchandising advice may include developing contests and brochures for the sales force. Campaign design and planning is often wholly in the hands of the agency. But some firms prefer to do much of the work in-house, relying on the agency only for scheduling media and evaluating the campaign.

ADVERTISING REGULATION

Besides planning advertising campaigns and scheduling media, advertising agencies must also cope with the growing role and scope of advertising regulation.

Self-Regulation in the Advertising Industry

To avoid increasing government regulation, advertising industry leaders in 1971 set up procedures for self-regulation. The **National Advertising Division (NAD)** of the Council of Better Business Bureaus is a complaint bureau for consumers and advertisers. The **National Advertising Review Board (NARB)** is an appeals board that may be used if the issue reaches a deadlock or the losing party wishes to appeal.

direct marketing (direct-response marketing) Variety of approaches, such as catalogs, direct mail, and telephone sales, used to promote a product and get an immediate response from the buyer.

advertising agencies Companies that help create ads and place them in the media.

National Advertising Division (NAD) Division of the Council of Better Business Bureaus that handles advertising complaints from consumers and advertisers.

National Advertising Review Board (NARB) Group to which deadlocked or unsatisfactory cases from the NAD can be appealed.

■ **Exhibit 17-2**
Functions of an Advertis-
ing Agency

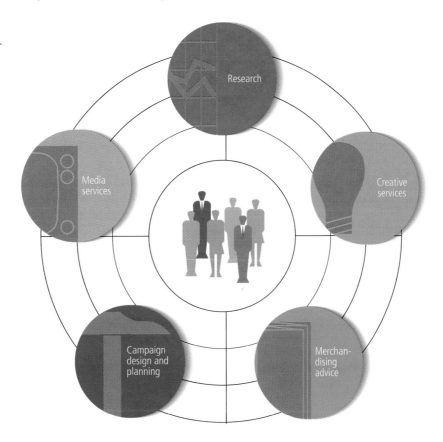

■ **Exhibit 17-2**
Functions of an Advertising Agency

After receiving a complaint about an advertisement, NAD starts investigating. It collects and evaluates information and then decides whether the ad's claims are substantiated. If the ad is deemed unsatisfactory, NAD negotiates a change or discontinuation of the advertisement with the advertiser. For instance, Procter & Gamble recently filed a truth-in-advertising complaint with NAD against the makers of Arm & Hammer baking soda toothpaste for claiming, "Two out of three dentists and hygienists recommend baking soda for healthier teeth and gums." P&G argued that there was no scientific basis for the statement. Arm & Hammer eventually agreed to change the statement to "healthy" rather than "healthier" teeth and gums.[8]

Advertising managers want to avoid having to drop or modify advertisements or commercials. This action is expensive for the following reasons: Controversy can create ill will for the company; the ad must be remade; and if a substitute commercial is unavailable, the timing of the campaign may be destroyed.

Federal Regulation of Advertising

Federal Trade Commission Federal agency that oversees advertising of products sold across state lines.

When self-regulation doesn't work, in the United States the **Federal Trade Commission** (FTC) steps in. The FTC's main concern is with deception and misrepresentation in advertising. The FTC defines deception as "a representation, omission, or practice that is likely to mislead the consumer acting reasonably in the circumstances, to the consumer's detriment." The courts have ruled that deception can also cover what the consumer infers from the advertisement, not only what is literally said.

The FTC's traditional remedy for deceptive advertising is the cease-and-desist order. This order bans use of the advertising claims found to be false or deceptive. In some cases, the FTC requires a corrective message. **Corrective advertising** is an advertisement run to correct the false impressions left by previous advertisements. For example, after investigating several diet-program companies for false and deceptive advertising, the FTC required them to revise their weight-loss claims to reflect accurately the programs' success in helping customers keep off the weight they lose.

corrective advertising
Advertising run to correct false impressions left by previous ads.

Concept Check

- Define five different types of advertising, and give examples.
- Explain some of the strengths and weaknesses of the six main advertising media.
- Describe the services offered by advertising agencies.
- Names the groups that regulate advertising and what remedies they may prescribe.

PERSONAL SELLING

5

personal selling Face-to-face sales presentation to a prospective customer.

Advertising acquaints potential customers with a product and thereby makes personal selling easier. **Personal selling** is a face-to-face sales presentation to a prospective customer. About 6.5 million people are engaged in personal selling in the United States. Slightly over 45 percent of them are women. Sales jobs range from salesclerks at clothing stores to engineers with MBAs who design large, complex systems for manufacturers. The number of people who earn a living from sales is huge compared, for instance, with the half a million workers employed in the advertising industry.

Many college students say they are "turned off" by the thought of a career in sales. Many feel that salespeople are ill trained, aggressive, deceitful, arrogant, and lacking in talent and brains. All of us have run into salespeople at one time or another who have some (or many) of these traits. But these are often salespeople representing fly-by-night companies selling directly to consumers. They are not professional salespeople.

THE PROFESSIONAL SALESPERSON

Companies that recruit college graduates to enter the field of selling want to develop professional salespeople. A professional salesperson has two main qualities: complete product knowledge and creativity. The professional knows the product line from A to Z and understands what each item can and can't do. He or she also understands how to apply the prod-

■ Personal selling involves a face-to-face sales presentation to a prospective customer. A professional salesperson knows every aspect of the product line he or she is selling and is able to devise creative ways to tailor the product to the customer's needs.

uct to meet customers' needs. For instance, a sales rep may find a way to install conveyor equipment that will lower the cost of moving products in the prospective customer's plant.

Professional salespeople develop long-term relationships with their clients. Most salespeople rely on repeat business, which depends, of course, on trust and honesty. Most professional selling is not high-pressured. Instead, the sales process is more a matter of one professional interacting with another, such as a salesperson working with a purchasing agent. Professional salespeople are largely sources of information and creative problem solvers. They cannot bully a professional buyer into making an unwanted purchase.

SALES POSITIONS

College graduates have many opportunities in sales. Among them are the following:

- *Selling to wholesalers and retailers:* When a firm buys products for resale, its main concerns are buying the right product and getting it promptly. Often retailers expect the manufacturer's salesperson to stock the merchandise on the shelves and to set up promotional materials approved by the store. Sometimes these sales jobs are entry-level training positions that can lead to better opportunities.

- *Selling to purchasing agents:* Purchasing agents are found in government agencies, manufacturing firms, and institutions (hospitals and schools). Purchasing agents look for credibility (can the salesperson deliver merchandise of the proper quality when needed?), service after the sale, and a reasonable price. The message the salesperson must get across is one of complete dependability and reliability.
- *Selling to committees:* The form of selling that may demand the most professionalism and creativity is selling to a buying committee. When a purchase decision is so important that it will have a big impact on the buyer's long-run success, it is usually made by a committee. When United Airlines decides to order 100 new airplanes, for instance, a committee decides what type of plane to buy. A committee sales presentation requires careful analysis of the potential buyer's needs. It commonly includes an audiovisual display.

THE SELLING PROCESS

Selling is a process that can be learned. Scholars have spelled out the steps of the selling process, and professional salespeople use these steps all the time. The process consists of prospecting for and qualifying customers, approaching customers, presenting and demonstrating the product, handling objections, closing the sale, and following up on the sale (see Exhibit 17-3).

■ **Exhibit 17-3**
The Selling Process

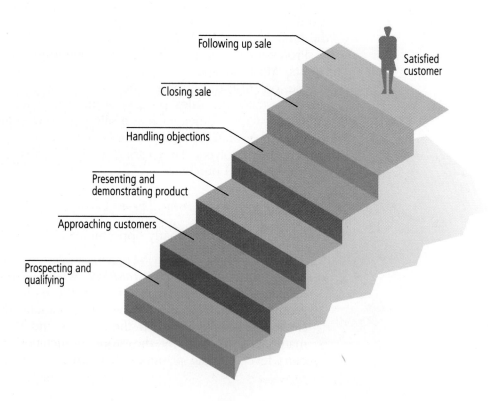

Following up sale

Satisfied customer

Closing sale

Handling objections

Presenting and demonstrating product

Approaching customers

Prospecting and qualifying

Prospecting and Qualifying

To start the process, the salesperson looks for **sales prospects**, those companies and people who are most likely to buy the seller's offerings. This activity is called **prospecting**. Because there are no sure-fire methods for prospecting, most salespeople try many ways to find prospects.

The most likely source of prospects for many companies is the inquiries generated by advertising and promotion. Inquiries are also known as **sales leads**. Leads usually come in the form of letters, cards, or telephone calls. Some companies supply salespeople with prospect lists. These lists are compiled by the company from external sources, such as Chamber of Commerce directories, newspapers, public records, club membership lists, and professional or trade publication subscription lists. Another good source of leads is meetings, such as professional conventions and trade shows. Sales representatives attend such meetings to display and demonstrate their company's products and to answer the questions of those attending. Another source of prospects is the firm's files and records. One source is correspondence with buyers. Another is records in the service department that identify those who might be prospects for new models of equipment they already own. Finally, friends and acquaintances of salespeople can often supply leads.

One rule of thumb about prospects is that not all are "real" prospects. Just because someone has been referred or has made an inquiry does not mean that the person is really a prospect. Salespeople can avoid wasting time and increase their productivity by qualifying all prospects. **Qualifying questions** are used to separate prospects from those who do not have the potential to buy. The following three questions help determine who is a real prospect and who is not: (1) Does the prospect have a need for our product? (2) Can the prospect make the buying decision? (3) Can the prospect afford our product?

Approaching Customers

After identifying a prospect, the salesperson explains the reason for wanting an appointment and sets a specific date and hour for it. At the same time, the salesperson tries to build interest in the coming meeting. One good way is to impart an interesting or important piece of information—for instance, "I think my product can cut your shipping and delivery time by two days."

Presenting and Demonstrating the Product

The presentation and demonstration can be fully automated, completely unstructured, or somewhere in between. In a fully automated presentation, the salesperson would show a movie, slides, or a filmstrip and then answer questions and take any orders. A completely unstructured presentation has no set format. It may be more of a casual conversation, with the salesperson presenting product benefits that might interest the potential buyer.

So-called **canned presentations**—presentations that are memorized—are sometimes used to sell products to end users. Someone selling replacement windows to homeowners might use a canned presentation. They are

sales prospects Companies and people most likely to buy a salesperson's offerings.

prospecting Looking for sales prospects.

sales leads Inquiries about a firm's products generated by the firm's advertising and promotion.

qualifying questions Questions used by salespeople to find genuine sales prospects.

canned presentations Memorized sales presentations.

rarely used in industrial sales, however. Instead, industrial salespeople often use organized presentations, whose major points are outlined ahead of time. Beechcraft salespeople, for instance, use a checklist in their presentations, but they can change the formula as needed. Thus their presentations cover the important points and vary to suit the circumstances.

Handling Objections

Almost every sales presentation, structured or unstructured, meets with some objection. Rarely does a customer say "I'll buy it" without asking questions or voicing concerns. The professional salesperson tries to anticipate objections so they can be countered quickly and with assurance. A Canon salesperson selling a Laser Class FAX-L770 might well run into concern about the price. The response could be "Yes, the L770 is more expensive than some others, but it has expandable memory so more information can be received into memory or stored for transmission as your needs grow. And with Canon's Hyper-Smoothing feature, incoming faxes are clearer. Also, Canon's exclusive cartridge system stores everything that can run out or wear out in one neat, disposable unit." Being able to handle objections shows the salesperson's confidence in the product and assures the customer that the product will meet his or her needs.

Closing the Sale

After all the objections have been dealt with, it's time to close the sale. Even old pros sometimes find this part of the sales process awkward. Perhaps the easiest way to close a sale is to ask for it: "Ms. Jones, may I write up your order?" Another technique is to act as though the deal has been concluded: "Mr. Bateson, we'll have this equipment in and working for you in two weeks." If Mr. Bateson doesn't object, the salesperson can assume that the sale has been made.

Following Up the Sale

The salesperson's job isn't over when the sale is made. In fact, the sale is just the start. The salesperson must write up the order properly and turn it in promptly. Often this part of the job is easy. But an order for a complex piece of industrial equipment may be a hundred pages of detail. Each detail must be carefully checked to ensure that the equipment is exactly what was ordered.

After the product is delivered to the customer, the salesperson must make a routine visit to see that the customer is satisfied. This follow-up call may also be a chance to make another sale. But even if it isn't, it will build goodwill for the salesperson's company and may bring future business. Repeat sales over many years are the goal of professional salespeople.

Concept Check
- Describe the professional salesperson.
- Explain the selling process.

■ Sales promotion takes many forms. LEGO recently promoted its building blocks by setting up the LEGO Imagination Center, a huge display of LEGO structures, in Bloomington, Minnesota's Mall of America.

SALES PROMOTION

6

sales promotions
Marketing events or sales efforts—other than advertising, personal selling, and public relations—that stimulate consumer buying.

Sales promotion helps make personal selling and advertising more effective. **Sales promotions** are marketing events or sales efforts—not including advertising, personal selling, and public relations—that stimulate consumer buying.

COUPONS, SAMPLES, PREMIUMS, CONTESTS, AND SWEEPSTAKES

coupons Price reductions designed to stimulate immediate sales.

Five of the most popular forms of sales promotion are coupons, samples, premiums, contests, and sweepstakes. **Coupons** are price reductions designed to bring in immediate sales. Physically, they are part of an ad or a package. They can be redeemed for goods or cash. Over 90 percent of U.S. households use coupons regularly. About 280 billion coupons were issued in 1993; they saved shoppers a total of $4 billion.[9] On average, American families use about eight coupons per week.

Coupons are best for getting nonusers to try a brand or existing users to buy more often. Despite their popularity, coupons have a few bad points. First, they are costly to the advertiser. A single-page, four-color insert in Sunday newspapers across the country costs well over $500,000. What's more, over 95 percent of the coupons issued are not redeemed. Finally, the market is glutted with coupons, so they are becoming less effective.

■ Sales promotions are special marketing events designed to stimulate consumers to buy certain products. They can take many forms. Manufacturers of automotive products, like Valvoline, often sponsor auto racing teams, which gives them the opportunity to place their logos in highly visible and dynamic locations.

samples Free gifts of a product that are distributed to consumers to gain public acceptance of the product.

premiums Gifts or prizes to consumers who buy a product, which add value to the purchase.

contests Skilled competitions among consumers for various prizes.

sweepstakes Consumer competitions whose winners are picked on the basis of chance.

Samples are free gifts of a product that are distributed to build public acceptance. Samples of food products, for instance, are offered to grocery shoppers on Fridays and Saturdays in many large stores. Samples are usually paired with coupons to encourage an immediate purchase.

Premiums, another form of sales promotion, offer gifts or prizes to people who buy a product, thereby adding value to the purchase. *Sports Illustrated* once offered a sneaker with a built-in telephone to anyone who subscribed to the magazine for thirty months. Membership in the Quality Paperback Book Club begins with an offer of three books for $1 each.

Another way manufacturers generate interest in products is by sponsoring contests or sweepstakes. **Contests** are skilled competitions among consumers for various prizes. Entrants may write a jingle about a product or explain briefly why the product is desirable. Nintendo, for instance, pitted video-game experts against all comers in thirty markets around the country. As many as 700 players per hour went through the video obstacle course. Winners got new and upcoming Nintendo releases.

Sweepstakes are also consumer competitions, but the winners are picked by chance. Miller Genuine Draft sponsored a "Do That Spring Party Thing" sweepstakes that sent forty-eight young-adult winners and their guests on a trip to the Bahamas. Sweepstakes are used mainly for marketing consumer goods, and they often increase product demand. As the following Trends in Global Competition box describes, they occasionally produce trouble.

You—and All Your Neighbors—Could Be a Millionaire

Pepsi's advertisements were splashed for weeks all over Philippine newspapers, radio, and TV: "Today, you could be a millionaire!" From her tin-roofed shack in one of Manila's slums, Victoria Angelo couldn't resist. The unemployed mother of five and her husband, Juanito, who pedals people about in his three-wheeled cab for about $4 a day, began drinking Pepsi with every meal and snack. Each morning, the family prayed for a specially marked bottle cap. And each night, they and their neighbors flocked around a small television to see if their prayers were answered.

And then, a miracle! The nightly news announced that anyone holding a bottle cap marked 349 had won up to one million pesos, about $40,000, tax-free. Spreading her collection of caps on a table, Victoria Angelo screamed, "We are a millionaire!"

But her dream has become a nightmare for New York-based Pepsico Inc. Instead of a single one million-peso winner, up to 800,000 bottle caps marked 349 had been printed. Tens of thousands of Filipinos soon began demanding billions of dollars that Pepsi refuses to pay.

The dispute—on which Pepsi has spent millions of dollars—has sparked a cola war, Philippines-style. Pepsi records show that 32 delivery trucks have been stoned, torched, or overturned. Armed men have thrown bombs at Pepsi plants and offices. In the worst incident, police say, a grenade tossed at a Pepsi truck bounced off and killed a schoolteacher and a five-year-old girl and wounded six other people. Local Pepsi executives use round-the-clock bodyguards and vary office hours and travel. Heavily armed guards ride shotgun on Pepsi trucks.

Suing Pepsi has become the choice of a new generation. At last count, more than 22,000 people had filed 689 civil suits seeking damages from Pepsi, the company says. More than 5,200 criminal complaints of fraud and deception have been filed.

Kenneth Ross, spokesman for Pepsi-Cola International, which owns 19 percent of the local bottling company, said the company's position is clear. "We will not be held hostage to extortion and terrorism," he said in a telephone interview from Purchase, NY. "And that's exactly what we have faced in the Philippines."[10]

TRADE SHOWS AND CONVENTIONS

trade shows Meetings that give manufacturers and wholesalers the chance to display their products to a large audience of potential buyers at a relatively low cost.

An important form of sales promotion is **trade shows** and conventions. These meetings give manufacturers and wholesalers the chance to display their wares to a large audience of potential buyers at relatively low cost. Trade shows and conventions cover almost every type of product sold. About 6,000 of them are held each year in the United States, and they are attended by about 80 million people.[11]

POINT-OF-PURCHASE DISPLAYS

point-of-purchase (POP) displays Promotional devices designed to stimulate immediate sales.

Promotional devices designed to stimulate immediate sales are **point-of-purchase (POP) displays**. They include signs attached to store shelves, ads on grocery bags, in-store announcements, even shipping crates used as a platform for stacks of the product. They sometimes double or triple a company's sales.

The main problem with POP displays is getting retailers to use them. About $50 billion a year is spent on POP displays, and over half that amount is wasted. POP materials are bulky and arrive unassembled. Since retailers have a limited amount of space, they may not be inclined to assemble and use the displays. When POP displays are used, they are about the least costly kind of sales promotion.

Other Forms of Sales Promotion

Sales promotion can take many other forms: corporate logos on hot-air balloons, shopping center carnivals, auto racing sponsorships, products showcased in movies, sponsorships of rides and exhibits at Walt Disney World. A new type of promotion is to pipe scents into stores to put shoppers in a buying mood. (Women tend to prefer floral scents. Men favor the aroma of backyard barbecue.)

Concept Check

- How is sales promotion different from advertising?
- Describe three types of sales promotion.

PUBLIC RELATIONS

7

public relations Any communication or activity intended chiefly to win goodwill or prestige for a company or person.

publicity Information about a company or product that appears in the news media and is not directly paid for by the company.

Like sales promotion, public relations can be a vital part of the promotional mix. **Public relations** is any communication or activity designed to win goodwill or prestige for a company or person. Its main form is **publicity**, information about a company or product that appears in the news media and is not directly paid for by the company. Publicity can be good or bad. Children dying from eating tainted Jack-in-the-Box hamburgers is an example of negative publicity.

Naturally, public relations departments of firms try to create as much good publicity as possible. They furnish company speakers for business and civic clubs, write speeches for corporate officers, and encourage employees to take active roles in such civic groups as the United Way and the Chamber of Commerce. The main tool of the public relations department is the *press release,* a formal announcement of some newsworthy event connected with the company. The event may be the start of a new program, the introduction of a new product, or the opening of a new plant, for example.

Public relations departments are also charged with protecting a company's good name. Sometimes the legal staff joins in. Procter & Gamble has brought several suits against Amway distributors and others for spreading rumors that P&G supports the Church of Satan. Amway sells a number of products in categories dominated by P&G.[12] The Amway distributors involved were fined and required to stop making untrue statements about P&G.

Concept Check

- Explain the difference between public relations and publicity.
- What functions does a public relations department perform?

FACTORS THAT AFFECT THE PROMOTIONAL MIX

8 Promotional mixes vary a great deal from one product and industry to the next. Advertising and personal selling are usually a firm's main promotional tools. They are supported by sales promotion. Public relations helps develop a positive image for the organization and its products. The specific promotional mix depends on the nature of the product, market characteristics, available funds, and push and pull strategies.

THE NATURE OF THE PRODUCT

Selling toothpaste differs greatly from selling overhead industrial cranes. Personal selling is most important in marketing industrial products and least important in marketing consumer nondurables (consumer products that get used up). Broadcast advertising is used heavily in promoting consumer products, especially food and other nondurables. Print media, on the other hand, are used for all types of consumer products. Industrial products may be advertised through special trade magazines. Sales promotion, branding, and packaging are roughly twice as important (in terms of percentage of the promotional budget) for consumer products as for industrial products.

MARKET CHARACTERISTICS

When potential customers are widely scattered, buyers are highly informed, and many of the buyers are brand-loyal, the promotional mix should be a blend of more advertising and sales promotion and less personal selling. But sometimes personal selling is required even when buyers are well informed and geographically dispersed, as is the case with mainframe computers. Industrial installations and component parts may be sold to knowledgeable people with much education and work experience. Yet a salesperson still must explain the product and work out the details of the purchase agreement.

Salespeople are also required when the physical stocking of merchandise—called **detailing**—is the norm. Milk and bread, for instance, are generally stocked by the person who makes the delivery, rather than by store personnel. This practice is becoming more common for convenience products as sellers try to get the best display space for their wares.

detailing Physical stocking of merchandise by delivery personnel rather than store personnel.

AVAILABLE FUNDS

Money, or the lack of it, is one of the biggest influences on the promotional mix. A small manufacturer with a tight budget and a unique product may rely heavily on free publicity. The media often run stories about new products.

If the product warrants a sales force, a firm with little money may turn to manufacturers' agents. They work on commission, with no salary, advances, or expense accounts. The Duncan Company, which makes parking meters, is just one of the many that rely on manufacturers' agents.

PUSH AND PULL STRATEGIES

push strategy Manufacturer's use of aggressive personal selling and advertising to convince a wholesaler or retailer to carry its merchandise.

Manufacturers may use aggressive personal selling and trade advertising to convince a wholesaler or a retailer to carry and sell their merchandise. This approach is known as a **push strategy** (see Exhibit 17-4). The wholesaler, in turn, must often push the merchandise forward by persuading the retailer to handle the goods. This strategy relies on extensive personal selling to channel members, on trade advertising, and on price incentives to wholesalers and retailers. The retailer then uses advertising, displays, and other promotional forms to convince the consumer to buy the "pushed" products. This concept also applies to services. For example, the Jamaican Tourism Board targets promotions to travel agencies, which are members of their distribution channel.

pull strategy Manufacturer's attempt to stimulate consumer demand to get wider distribution of a product.

At the other extreme is a **pull strategy**, which stimulates consumer demand in order to obtain product distribution. Rather than trying to sell to the wholesaler, the manufacturer using a pull strategy focuses its promotional efforts on end consumers. As they begin demanding the product, the retailer orders the merchandise from the wholesaler. The wholesaler, confronted with rising demand, then places an order from the manufacturer. Thus, stimulating consumer demand pulls the product down through the channel of distribution (see Exhibit 17-4). Heavy sampling, introductory consumer advertising, cents-off campaigns, and couponing are part of a pull strategy. For example, using a pull strategy,

■ **Exhibit 17-4**
Push and Pull Advertising Strategies

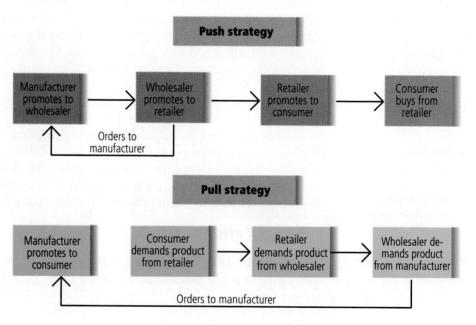

the Jamaican Tourism Board may entice travelers to come to their island by offering discounts on hotels or airfare.

Rarely does a company use a pull or a push strategy exclusively. Instead, the mix will emphasize one of these strategies. For example, pharmaceutical company Marion Merrell Dow uses a push strategy, through personal selling and trade advertising, to promote its Nicoderm patch nicotine withdrawal therapy to physicians. Sales presentations and advertisements in medical journals give physicians the detailed information they need to prescribe the therapy to their patients who want to quit smoking. Marion Merrell Dow supplements its push promotional strategy with a pull strategy targeted directly to potential patients through advertisements in consumer magazines and on television. The advertisements illustrate the pull strategy in action: Marion Merrell Dow directs consumers to ask their doctors about the Nicoderm patch.

Concept Check

- Explain how the nature of the product, market characteristics, and available funds can affect the promotional mix.
- Distinguish between push and pull strategies.

■ SUMMARY

1. Describe the goals of promotional strategy.

Promotion aims to stimulate demand for a company's goods or services. Promotional strategy is designed to inform, persuade, or remind target audiences about those products. The goals of promotion are to create awareness, get people to try products, provide information, explain the organization's actions, keep loyal customers, increase use of a product, and identify potential customers.

2. Define the promotional mix, and explain its elements.

The unique combination of advertising, personal selling, sales promotion, and public relations used to promote a product is the promotional mix. Advertising is any paid form of nonpersonal promotion by an identified sponsor. Personal selling consists of a face-to-face presentation in a conversation with a prospective purchaser. Sales promotion consists of marketing activities—other than personal selling, advertising, and public relations—that stimulate consumers to buy. These activities include coupons and samples, displays, shows and exhibitions, demonstrations, and other selling efforts not in the ordinary routine. Public relations is the marketing function that links the policies of the organization with the public interest and runs a program designed to earn public understanding and acceptance.

3. Describe the types of advertising.

Institutional advertising creates a positive picture of a company. Advocacy advertising takes a stand on controversial social or economic issues. Prod-

Key Terms

advertising 535

advertising agencies 542

advertising media 538

advocacy advertising 536

canned presentations 547

comparative advertising 536

contests 550

corrective advertising 544

coupons 549

CPM (cost per thousand) 539

detailing 553

differential advantage 532

direct marketing (direct-response marketing) 542

Federal Trade Commission 543

continued

uct advertising features a specific good or service. Comparative advertising is product advertising in which the company's product is compared with competing, named products. Reminder advertising is used to keep a brand name in the public's mind.

4. Evaluate the media that advertisers use.

The main types of advertising media are newspapers, magazines, radio, television, outdoor advertising, and direct mail. Newspaper advertising delivers a local audience but has a short life span. Magazines deliver special-interest markets and offer good detail and color. Radio is an inexpensive and highly portable medium but offers no visual appeal. Television reaches huge audiences and has visual and audio opportunities yet can be very expensive. Outdoor advertising requires short messages but is only moderately expensive. Direct mail can reach targeted audiences, but it is only as good as the mailing list.

5. Describe the selling process.

Personal selling is a direct sales presentation to a prospective buyer. It is a big part of the promotional mix for many firms. Professional salespeople are knowledgeable and creative. They also are familiar with the selling process. This process consists of prospecting and qualifying, approaching customers, presenting and demonstrating the product, handling objections, closing the sale, and following up on the sale.

6. Distinguish among the various types of sales promotion.

Sales promotions are one-time marketing events or sales efforts. They do not include advertising and personal selling. The most popular sales promotions are coupons, samples, premiums, contests, and sweepstakes. Trade shows and conventions and point-of-purchase displays are other types.

7. Understand how public relations fits into the promotional mix.

Public relations is concerned mostly with getting good publicity for companies. Publicity is any information about a company or product that appears in the news media and is not directly paid for by the company. Public relations departments furnish company speakers for business and civic clubs, write speeches for corporate officers, and encourage employees to take active roles in civic groups. These activities help build a positive image for an organization, which is a good backdrop for selling its products.

8. Discuss the factors that affect promotional mix.

The factors that affect promotional mix are the nature of the product, market characteristics, available funds, and push versus pull strategies. Personal selling is used more with industrial products, and advertising is used more heavily for consumer products. With widely scattered, well-informed buyers and with brand-loyal customers, a firm will blend more advertising and sales promotion and less personal selling into its promotional mix. A manufacturer with a limited budget may rely heavily on publicity and manufacturers' agents to promote the product.

A pull strategy relies mostly on advertising and sales promotion to the end user; a push strategy requires personal selling to channel members.

■ DISCUSSION QUESTIONS

1. If you were a medium-size manufacturer of specialized machinery, what important issues would you have to consider in designing a promotional strategy? Where would you place the most emphasis?

2. Describe how the promotional mix would change at each stage of the product life cycle for a new consumer product for which you expected wide use.

3. Do you think it's fair for a marketer to run ads naming competitors' products and suggesting that they are inferior? Explain.

4. Choose a current advertising campaign and explain why you think it works or doesn't work. Is it integrated with other forms of promotion?

5. Discuss a recent advocacy ad that you have seen or heard. Do you feel it was effective?

6. How can advertising, sales promotion, and publicity support one another? Give an example.

7. "Public utilities should not be allowed to promote their offerings, because such promotion raises our utility bills." Discuss.

8. In what ways do the functions and responsibilities of a professional salesperson differ from those of a retail clerk?

9. Do small-business owners need to know much about personal selling? Why or why not?

■ CASE
Promoting Colt 45—Cynicism or Inspiration?

The TV commercial begins with a message of hope and reformation, delivered in hip, stream-of-consciousness narration over bleak, grainy shots of an inner-city neighborhood. "I was the first one in my family to go to college," says the earnest young African-American man in shirt and tie. "It was a night-school thing, which is cool, because now I can do some good things. Give back what I earned." He sits on a front porch and beckons to a young friend to join him. "And the brothers, they see me and maybe they'll want to do something better for themselves, y'know," the role model says.

It may look like an ad for Big Brothers or the United Negro College Fund. But the college grad and his front-porch pal sip from bottles of Colt 45 malt liquor in the ad from G. Heileman Brewing Co. It marks a sharp departure from the campaign Colt 45 has used since the mid-1980s, featuring the older-appeal, middle-aged leading man, Billy Dee Williams, beautiful women, and the tag line, "Colt 45. It works every time."

The new ad is part of a controversial effort to hone a hipper image for Colt 45 and appeal more directly to the malt-liquor market's most important customers: young inner-city African-Americans. It is re-opening the debate over the ethics of aiming high-octane malt liquor at young drinkers in the inner city. Deutsch/Dworin, the New York ad agency that created the new Colt 45 commercials, says they are meant to portray the values and concerns of inner-city consumers. But critics call them cynical, just a more subtle version of Mr. Williams's glitzy spots linking the drink with romantic and financial prowess.

"It's too bad, and it's in poor taste," says David Grant, a communications official with the Institute on Black Chemical Abuse, speaking of the new approach. "It's inaccurate to portray someone like the gentleman, with this sense of mission, yet acting as a proponent of malt liquor right there on the street."

Many brewing-industry executives see nothing wrong with such efforts. Targeting low-income African-Americans for malt liquor is no different from selling the Mercedes-Benz line to white, affluent suburbanites, their argument goes. It reeks of paternalism and racism to suggest it is inappropriate, says Donny Deutsch, executive vice president and creative director at Deutsch/Dworin. Why should Colt 45 shy away from portraying its core consumers just because more than 90 percent of them are male and black?

"I don't understand why beer can't be segmented with intelligence, respect, honesty, and relevance" to black consumers, Mr. Deutsch says. "Just like you can target to affluent businessmen, you should be able to target urban downscale white women, or urban black men, or children. That's marketing. Who are these people who are sitting as judge and jury on who should be targeted?"

Makani Themba, a public-policy analyst at the Marin Institute in San Rafael, California, says the spots have been calculated to send two dangerous messages: "That the way to appropriately bond is through malt liquor, and that malt liquor is a better alternative to the other dangerous things that are out there. Various visual cues add up to an appeal to underage drinkers, she maintains. The younger guy in the porch scene looks barely out of his teens, in Ms. Themba's view, especially given the way he treats the other character as a mentor.

The ad also includes a shot of a pair of sneakers dangling over a telephone-pole wire. When gang members badly beat an opponent, they hang up his sneakers for all to see, Ms. Themba says. In the ad, she maintains, this suggests that the younger character is saying no to street dangers by engaging in a safer activity—drinking malt liquor. Mr. Deutsch counters that he has never heard of such a thing. The image of the dangling sneakers, he says, "was literally picked up as they were shooting," in Los Angeles, and any underlying message was unintended. The agency says, moreover, that everyone who appears in the spots is at least 25 years old.[13]

Questions
1. Do you agree with Donny Deutsch? Why or why not?
2. Should Heileman change its target market? Why or why not?
3. If the target market is unchanged, what other means could be used to promote the product? What about an alternative advertising campaign?

Your Career in Marketing

Marketing is critically important to American businesses. Top management realizes that a company must understand the marketplace and consumer needs and wants if it is to grow and compete effectively.

Marketing offers a rich variety of career opportunities, from marketing research to creative advertising. Some positions are desk jobs—for instance, market research analyst and product manager. Others—especially those in sales, public relations, and advertising—require wide contact with the public and with other firms.

For the past few decades, business graduates have been employed mostly in marketing, often in sales. The outlook for careers in marketing will continue to be very bright through the year 2000.

Dream Career: Advertising Account Manager

Advertising account managers make sales to client firms. They are also responsible for keeping clients satisfied so they will stay with the advertising agency. These managers work on a day-to-day basis with clients and serve as the link between clients and the agency's creative, media, and research departments.

Account managers must understand each client's target consumers very well. To be successful, they have to help design the best possible advertising for their clients, advertising that will make their clients' business grow. They also have to be able to identify the strengths and weaknesses of the brands to which they are assigned. Finding brand differences is important too, because these differences are what help set apart the clients' products.

Human nature being what it is, clients can sometimes be difficult. With tact, insight, and a little humor, account managers should always tell clients what the agency believes is right for their business, even if this is not what the clients want to hear.

- *Places of employment:* Mainly New York City and Chicago. Yet there are more than 8,000 moderate-size and smaller agencies, found in every metropolitan area.
- *Skills required:* Four-year degree.
- *Employment outlook through 2005:* Good.
- *Salaries:* $20,000–$25,000 for assistant account executives; $25,000–$55,000 for account executives; $50,000–$100,000 for account supervisors (who manage several account executives).

Where the Opportunities Are

Retail Buyer
All merchandise sold in retail stores, from automobile tires to high-fashion clothing, appears through the decisions of buyers. Buyers for small stores may buy all the mer-

chandise. Buyers for large stores often handle only one or two related lines, such as home furnishings and accessories. Buyers work with a limited budget and thus try to choose merchandise that will sell fast. They must understand customer likes and dislikes and foresee fashion and manufacturing trends.

- *Places of employment:* Throughout the country, with most jobs in major metropolitan areas.
- *Skills required:* Two-year degree for some jobs; four-year degree for most.
- *Employment outlook through 2005:* Good.
- *Salaries:* $20,000–$60,000, plus bonuses for some buyers.

Market Researcher

Market researchers provide information that marketing managers use to make decisions. Statisticians determine sample sizes, decide who is to be interviewed, and analyze data. Account executives in research firms sell research projects to advertising agencies, manufacturers, and retailers. They also act as go-betweens for research firms and clients in planning studies, giving progress reports, and presenting results. Field supervisors hire research field workers to do the interviewing. They are in charge of gathering data quickly, economically, and accurately.

- *Places of employment:* Mostly large research firms in New York City, Chicago, Dallas, and California. Other opportunities are with manufacturers and large retailers throughout the country.
- *Skills required:* For research statisticians, an MBA; for account executives, a four-year degree; for field supervisors, usually a four-year degree but sometimes a two-year degree.
- *Employment outlook through 2005:* Fair to good in the places mentioned here; fair elsewhere.
- *Salaries:* $23,000–$40,000 for research statisticians; $25,000–$50,000+ for account managers; $15,000–$30,000 for field supervisors.

Manufacturers' Representative

Manufacturers' sales reps sell mainly to other businesses: factories, railroads, banks, wholesalers, retailers, hospitals, schools, libraries, and other institutions. Most of these salespeople sell nontechnical products. Those who deal in highly technical goods, such as electronic equipment, are often called sales engineers or industrial sales workers. Some manufacturers' sales positions require much travel.

- *Places of employment:* Throughout the country.
- *Skills required:* For selling nontechnical products, usually a four-year degree; for selling technical products, a technical undergraduate degree and an MBA.
- *Employment outlook through 2005:* Very good.
- *Salaries:* $18,000–$50,000+ for nontechnical sales reps; $26,000–$60,000+ for technical sales reps. Many companies also pay commissions or bonuses to salespeople.

Travel Agent

Many travelers seek help from travel agents, specialists who have the information and ability to make the best possible travel arrangements given the tastes and budget of their customers. Travel agents check fare schedules and ticket prices, often via computer terminals. They also use other guides and fact sheets to get information on hotel accommodations and other tourist needs. A benefit of this career is free or low-cost travel to visit places that want to attract more tourists.

- *Places of employment:* Throughout the country, but concentrated in major population centers. Only 20 percent of all agencies are located in small towns and rural areas.
- *Skills required:* Two-year degree.
- *Employment outlook through 2005:* Good.
- *Salaries:* $18,000–$35,000.

■ A manufacturer's sales rep should have good people skills and be prepared to travel.

Wholesaler Sales Representative

Wholesaler sales reps visit buyers for retail, industrial, and commercial firms and for schools, hospitals, and other institutions. They offer samples, pictures, or catalogs that list the items their company stocks. Some of these salespeople check the retailers' stock to find what should be ordered. Some help retail store personnel improve and update systems for ordering and taking inventory. Sales reps who handle technical equipment, such as air-conditioning equipment, may help with installation and maintenance.

- *Places of employment:* Usually large cities (where the wholesalers are), but sales territories may be almost anywhere.
- *Skills required:* Either a two-year or four-year degree, depending mainly on the product line and market.
- *Employment outlook through 2005:* Good.
- *Salaries:* $22,000–$85,000, with the higher figure for experienced people in growth industries.

Public Relations Agent

Public relations agents help firms, government agencies, universities, and other organizations build and maintain a positive public image. They may handle press, community, or consumer relations; interest-group representation; fund-raising; speech writing; or plant tours. They often represent employers in community projects.

- *Places of employment:* Manufacturing firms, public utilities, transportation companies, insurance companies, trade and professional associations, and government agencies, mainly in large cities.

More than half of the roughly 2,000 public relations firms are in New York City, Chicago, Los Angeles, and Washington, D.C.

- *Skills required:* Four-year degree.
- *Employment outlook through 2005:* Very good.
- *Salaries:* $22,000–$75,000+, with the higher figure for public relations directors.

Product Manager

In large manufacturing firms, one key product may account for millions of dollars in sales. Such a product is too important to leave its success to chance. Product managers oversee its marketing program and are responsible for meeting profit objectives. They must coordinate the activities of the distribution department, market researchers, advertising agencies, and so on to assure that the product has the right marketing mix. Working with many departments without direct authority over any of them requires good human relations and planning skills.

- *Places of employment:* Major population centers and industrial centers.
- *Skills required:* Four-year degree usually, but some employers require an MBA.
- *Employment outlook through 2005:* Good.
- *Salaries:* $28,000–$70,000, with the higher figure for group product managers.

Advertising Media Planner

Advertising media planners supervise all media purchases and determine when commercials will be shown and which media will be used. They also select, recommend, and evaluate the publications and programs that expose the advertising to best advantage. Media planners are responsible for achieving the right exposure in a campaign. They must be good negotiators, because media rates can be flexible. Skilled planners can stretch their clients' media budgets.

- *Places of employment:* Mainly New York City and Chicago for large advertising agencies, but every metropolitan area for moderate-size and smaller agencies.
- *Skills required:* Four-year degree or MBA.
- *Employment outlook through 2005:* Fair.
- *Salaries:* $25,000–$50,000, with the higher amounts at major New York agencies.

Distribution Traffic Manager

Distribution traffic managers are responsible for in-bound raw materials and products and out-bound finished goods. They deal with methods of handling time in transit, packaging costs, warehouse costs, costs of intraplant movement, and avoidance of waste and damage. Most importantly, perhaps, traffic managers must understand the costs and services of the carriers to reduce expense and increase service.

- *Places of employment:* Throughout the country, especially big industrial centers.
- *Skills required:* MBA.
- *Employment outlook through 2005:* Very good.
- *Salaries:* $30,000–$60,000, with the higher figure for senior traffic managers.

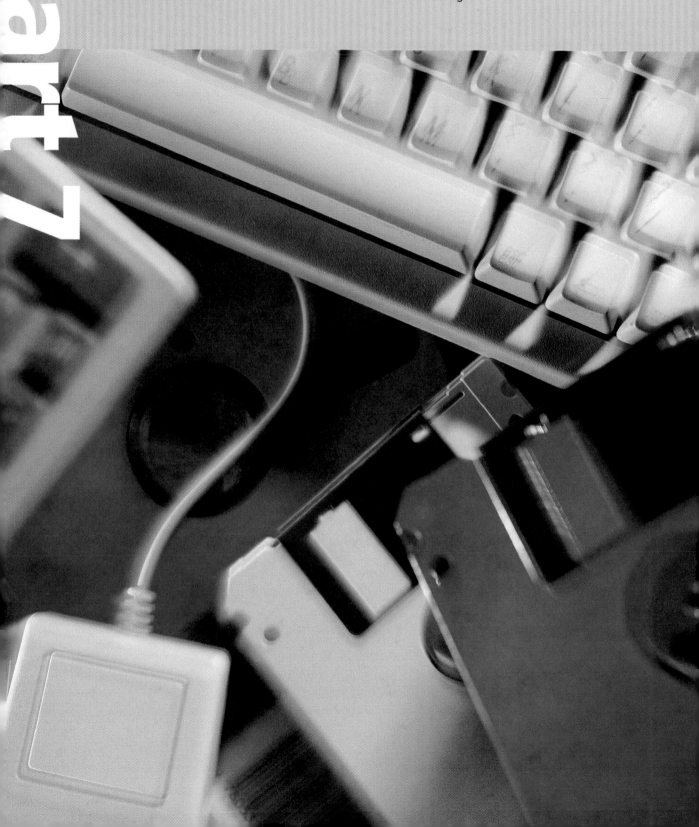

Management Information Tools

Part 7

Overview

Computers have become the tool of the trade in business today. They are used to perform extremely complex operations as well as everyday jobs like word processing and creating spreadsheets. Through a network of linked computers, one manager can transmit important news to literally hundreds of thousands of people, from office to office and city to city. In fact, information can be shared around the world almost as easily as from one floor of an office building to another!

With our growing dependence on computers and electronic information, the quality and confidentiality of data has become a great concern. Employees should be sensitive to how certain data are saved—personnel files and financial or marketing documents, for instance. This kind of information typically isn't intended for general consumption. The accessibility of computer records must be protected as carefully as if they were paper copies in a locked file cabinet. Many new security systems have been designed to address this problem.

Financial and managerial accounting are two areas of business that rely heavily on computers and management information systems. Accounting is the gathering, classifying, and summarizing of data. This information is then presented in a form that is useful to managers, creditors, investors, and government agencies, who use it to analyze a company's performance. Because computers can quickly and accurately process huge amounts of data, they are very useful to accountants of all types. They streamline the routine aspects of the job, allowing accountants to spend more time interpreting information.

Successful tradespeople make full use of their tools. Businesspeople, likewise, must understand and employ the tools available to them. The next section of this book will examine the many uses of computers in business. It will also look at accounting, the standard financial language for businesses.

International Business Machines

The world of management information systems is a rapidly changing one. No company knows that better than International Business Machines. IBM (nicknamed Big Blue) was a top Wall Street performer for years, until 1991. That was the year IBM posted its first-ever annual loss, due to the expense of restructuring its business divisions.

Critics claimed that IBM had committed the greatest of all corporate sins: It had not responded to its customers' needs. The company had long been known for its large mainframe computer systems, but smaller computers were gaining in popularity. In addition, customers were placing more and more value on software, services, and integration skills.

IBM is now responding to those needs. The firm has reallocated resources to growth businesses, reduced costs, and dedicated additional resources to consulting, systems integration, and related services. Under the leadership of Lou Gerstner, who took over as IBM's chairman and CEO in April 1993, the company is focusing on customer service like never before.

In Gerstner's words, IBM's strengths are technology, people, and customers. He believes that if the company is to succeed, its personnel at every level must remember that "everything starts with the customer." IBM is working hard to make sure all of its customers, whether individual business owners or major corporations, wherever they are in the world, know they can depend on the company. IBM is committed to working with customers to solve their computer and information technology problems, no matter how small or large they may be.

This dedication to its customers marks the beginning of a new era for IBM. IBM's customers and employees, and the company's stockholders, for whom "Big Blue" was such a good investment in the years prior to 1991, all hope they are entering a profitable era for everyone involved.

Computers and Information Systems

Learning Goals

After studying this chapter, you should be able to:

1 Describe the role of information in decision making.

2 Explain the four size categories of computers.

3 Name the parts of a computerized information system.

4 Describe what commonly used microcomputer software does.

5 Discuss the role of computer networks in business information systems.

6 Describe the structure of a typical management information system.

7 Discuss how companies should address the issues of computer security, computer crime, and privacy.

 Career Profile

When Joe Berninger graduated from college, he went to work for IBM as a marketing representative trainee. He spent his first nine months at the company attending classes and seminars that gave him a thorough understanding of the development, manufacture, delivery, and implementation of computer and information technology.

This initial training helps Joe immensely when he meets with clients. His knowledge of IBM's products and services, both from marketing and technical standpoints, is so extensive that he is able to address his clients' concerns with several solutions. He is currently employed as a marketing specialist for the multi-billion-dollar corporation, and his customer relations range from one-on-one meetings to conducting seminars that promote new technologies.

Joe majored in European history in college and minored in business. This broad background in liberal arts and business has proven to be quite beneficial to him. Perhaps the most important skill Joe gained from his major was the ability to write effectively. Writing is something he does often at IBM—mostly in proposals and internal communications.

IBM will be well served by employees like Joe. His commitment to continuous improvement and customer service, his knowledge of the company's products, and his communication skills will help bolster the company's image as a "total solution provider" in the booming and competitive computer industry.

Overview This chapter first discusses the role of information in decision making and the relationship between computers and information systems. Next the components—computer hardware and software—are described. Then commonly used microcomputer software and computer networks are discussed, and centralized management information systems are explained. Finally, we look at responsible use of computers in business. Throughout the chapter, examples show how managers and their companies are using computers to make better decisions in a highly competitive world.

INFORMATION AND DECISION MAKING

The way people make business decisions today has changed a great deal in recent years, largely because of computers. Only twenty-five years ago, well within the careers of many of today's top executives, few companies used computers. Today, nearly every company uses them.

Information has been, and always will be, the basis for good decisions. Every day, managers get information from many sources. Some of it is useful and some is not. To be useful, information must be

- *Relevant:* Some kinds of information are more useful than others in making a certain decision. For instance, when deciding whether to order raw materials, a manager is more likely to need information about inventories and future production plans than about overtime pay.
- *Accurate:* Obviously, inaccurate information can reduce a manager's ability to make good decisions.
- *Complete:* Partial information may cause a manager to focus only on one aspect of a decision. Other important aspects may be overlooked.
- *Timely:* Information that arrives too late is rarely more helpful than no information at all.

information systems Methods and equipment that provide information about all aspects of a firm's operations.

data Numerous facts that are part of an information system.

information Data that have been processed into a meaningful and useful form.

Managers use **information systems**, methods and equipment that provide information about all aspects of a firm's operations, to get the information they need to make decisions.

One function of an information system is to gather **data**, the many facts that describe the company's status. For instance, the fact that a worker finished a unit of production on job 23-M-8735 at 2:17 p.m. on March 7 is a data item. When a manager must make a decision, a long list of data is generally not useful. For the production supervisor, a list of the times during the past hour when each unit was completed is far too detailed. Data must be turned into **information**, a meaningful and useful summary of data. The total number of units produced in the hour would be useful information.

Businesses collect a great deal of data. Only through well-designed information technology systems and the power of computers can managers use such data to make better decisions. Companies are discovering that they can't operate well with a series of separate information systems used to solve specific departmental problems. They need to integrate information systems throughout the firm. Company-wide systems that bring together human resources, operations, and technology are becoming an integral part of business strategy. Technology experts are learning more about the way the business operates, and business managers are learning how using technology effectively can open up new opportunities. Once companies know where they want to go, information systems can help them reach those goals.

Concept Check
- What are information systems? Why are they important?
- What makes information useful?
- Distinguish between data and information. How are they related?

COMPUTERS

computers Machines that accurately process data at very high speeds without direct human intervention.

Information systems existed before computers. But computers greatly improved the quality, quantity, and accessibility of management information. Just as a lathe or a steam shovel helps people do physical work, so a computer helps people do mental work. **Computers** can quickly and accurately do repetitive, often boring tasks.

However, a computer is just a machine. It can't decide what information is needed to make a decision. Nor can it make the kinds of judgments that managers are expected to make. But it can process data millions of times faster than the human brain. Thus computers are used to process data and organize information. Then managers assess the information and make decisions.

programs Instructions, prepared in advance, that allow computers to work continuously.

Computers are very accurate, assuming they have been given correct instructions. They can also follow instructions prepared in advance, called **programs**. Thus they can work continuously without having to stop at every step for more instructions.

The first experimental electronic computers were developed in the 1940s. By the early 1950s, very primitive business computers were on the market. They were expensive and had low reliability and computing power compared with today's computers. By the mid-1960s, reliable computers allowed the first serious business applications. Since then, the cost of computers has fallen dramatically, and their computing power has improved.

TYPES OF COMPUTERS

microcomputers
Computers small enough to fit on an office desk; also called personal computers (PCs) and desktop computers.

laptop (notebook) computers Portable computers smaller than desktop computers.

Most experts divide today's computers into four categories by size. The first type is **microcomputers**, often called *personal computers (PCs)* or *desktop computers*. Microcomputers are now the most widely used type of computer. As their name suggests, they are small enough to fit on an office desk. The most powerful microcomputers are called *workstations*. Smaller, portable microcomputers are called **laptop (notebook) computers**. They work almost exactly like full-size microcomputers. Smaller

■ Thanks to new technology, computers are getting smaller and more powerful. PI Systems Corp. has created the Infolio pen computer, which is portable and smaller than a PC. This allows for mobile data collection, information management, and database applications.

notepad computers
The smallest, handheld computers.

minicomputers Computers about the size of a file cabinet, too large to fit on a desktop but small enough to fit in a typical office.

mainframe computers
Computers typically housed in several large cabinets, which usually require specially built rooms.

yet are **notepad computers,** some of which can read handwritten characters. The basic cost of a microcomputer ranges from under $1,000 to about $10,000, depending on its features.

The second group of computers is **minicomputers**. They are too large to fit on a desktop but small enough to fit in an office. They are often housed in one or two cabinets about the size of a file cabinet. Unlike microcomputers, they can perform different tasks for several users at the same time. The cost of a minicomputer system ranges between $15,000 and $1 million.

The third group of computers is **mainframe computers**. They are typically housed in several large cabinets, each bigger than a file cabinet. Mainframe computers nearly always need a room with special power and cooling systems, raised flooring to cover the maze of cables, and security safeguards to reduce the fire hazard and keep out intruders. A mainframe computer can serve many users at the same time. The cost of a mainframe computer runs between $2 million and $5 million.

supercomputers
Specialized computers, of varying size, that very quickly compute complex scientific problems.

The final group is **supercomputers**, which are used to do complex scientific computations. They can perform many interrelated calculations quickly. Their size has ranged between minicomputers and mainframe computers, but the most recent models are only slightly larger than the typical microcomputer. The cost of a supercomputer now ranges between $10 million and $20 million.

USING COMPUTERS FOR BUSINESS APPLICATIONS

Many people are surprised to find that the size of a computer and its power are not directly related. New microprocessor chips can process 300 million instructions per second, making today's most powerful microcomputers about as powerful as small mainframe computers.

Why, then, would a company spend $2 million for a mainframe computer when it could buy a microcomputer with about the same computing power for $10,000? There is much more to a mainframe computer than its raw computing power. A mainframe computer is specially designed to manage vast amounts of stored information and efficiently handle very high volumes of data. Many users can access data on mainframe computers simultaneously. Still, for certain applications microcomputers are replacing minicomputers and mainframe computers at many companies.

Firms typically use mainframes to store and retrieve data that is directly used by employees in many parts of the company. In a large manufacturing company, for instance, people need to share information about inventories, customers, accounts, and production schedules. All that information can be stored in a central mainframe computer, which can run many large programs at once, handle heavy transaction volumes, and provide very rapid responses to requests. This makes them ideal for use in a company's *computer network*, which links together computers and related equipment such as printers so that employees can share data. (Networks are discussed in greater detail later in the chapter.)

Within the same company, each department may have its own mini- or microcomputer for plans, budgets, and other data. For instance, the marketing department may store and process data from a nationwide consumer survey. The production department may store lists of the parts and materials required to build each of its products.

In many firms, managers keep their own personal programs, files, and documents on microcomputers. A department manager may use a microcomputer to develop a budget for the coming year. A designer may use a microcomputer to create drawings, an advertising copywriter to design ads, a financial analyst to track the firm's financial performance. Most managers use microcomputers to write routine memos and reports and to retrieve data stored in the company's mainframe computer.

Computers have indeed revolutionized the workplace. Among other things, they have greatly increased worker productivity and efficiency. For example, consolidating regional dispatch centers and overall control at a $50 million computer center in Omaha, Nebraska, has paid off for the Union Pacific Railroad. Computerization enabled the railroad to cut total employees by 38 percent while increasing tons hauled by 43 percent. The railroad also saved $40 million a year by reducing idle time for its locomotives.[1]

- What is a computer? What are the four size categories of computers?
- Why might a company purchase a mainframe computer when a less expensive microcomputer may have almost the same computing power?
- Describe the typical tasks of a central mainframe computer, a department's minicomputer, and a manager's microcomputer.

COMPONENTS OF COMPUTERIZED SYSTEMS

3 A computerized information system has two main components: the machines themselves, called **hardware**, and their instructions, called **software**.

hardware Machine component of a computerized information system.

software Program of instructions that make computers perform.

HARDWARE

Modern information systems combine computers, printers, terminals and displays, and many other hardware parts. The list of hardware components can seem endless, but as shown in Exhibit 18-1, there are really only a few main categories: the central processing unit, the auxiliary storage system, the input system, and the output system.

Central Processing Unit

central processing unit (CPU) Part of a computer system that computes.

The **central processing unit (CPU)**, the heart of a computer system, has three parts. The *arithmetic-logic unit (ALU)* does both simple arithmetic (addition, subtraction, multiplication, division) and logical operations (comparisons). The second component of the CPU is the *control unit*. It

■ **Exhibit 18-1**
Computer Hardware Components

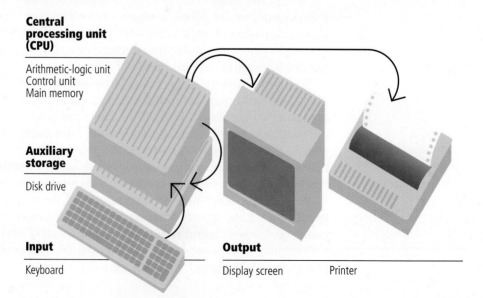

Central processing unit (CPU)

Arithmetic-logic unit
Control unit
Main memory

Auxiliary storage

Disk drive

Input

Keyboard

Output

Display screen   Printer

interprets program instructions and tells other parts of the computer what to do. Third, the *main memory* provides temporary storage for the instructions and data that the computer is processing.

binary numbers Numbers (0 and 1) used to represent all data in a computer's central processing unit.

Instructions and data are stored in the form of **binary numbers**. The binary system allows all data to be represented using only the symbols 0 and 1. Information is stored as bits or bytes. A **bit** (or binary digit) is the amount of memory required to store 0 or 1. A **byte**, eight bits, is the amount of memory required to store the code for one character (the letter *z*, for instance). Amounts of main memory are specified in *kilobytes*, or about a thousand bytes, and *megabytes*, about a million bytes. Most of today's computers contain from four to several hundred megabytes of main memory.

bit Binary digit; amount of memory required to store a single binary 0 or 1.

byte Eight bits; amount of memory required to store the code representing one alphabetic character.

Auxiliary Storage System

auxiliary storage system Hardware that provides long-term storage for programs and data; usually consists of some combination of floppy disk drives and hard disk drives.

The **auxiliary storage system** provides long-term storage for programs and data, usually on a combination of floppy disk drives and hard disk drives. A *floppy disk drive* stores data on a removable, flexible disk with a magnetic coating and a protective covering. Most computer systems today also have one or more *hard disk drives*, which are nonremovable metal disks coated with magnetic material that store much more data than floppy disks. A floppy disk can store from about a third of a megabyte to two megabytes. Hard disks can store from twenty to several thousand megabytes. A new form of storage, the **CD-ROM (compact disk, read-only memory)**, can hold about 680 megabytes. An 18,000-page catalog or an entire encyclopedia fits onto one disk. It uses a laser beam to read data, which can be easily accessed.

CD-ROM (compact disk, read-only memory) Data storage device holding up to 680 megabytes on a single 4 3/4" plastic disk which is read with a laser beam.

Mainframe computer systems sometimes use *magnetic tape drives* for auxiliary storage. Tape storage is much less costly than disk storage. But a tape can be read only from beginning to end. In contrast, any section of a disk or CD can be accessed directly. Tape storage is therefore used mostly for long-term record keeping and other special purposes.

Input and Output Systems

The *input system* enters data and programs into the computer for processing. Most data are entered into the computer through the *keyboard*. Some computer systems also have a *mouse* to ease the task of moving from one place to another on the display during data entry. When the mouse is moved across the desktop, a pointer moves in sync across the display screen.

In computerized business systems, data entry is typically the most expensive process. It also offers the greatest risk of introducing errors. Devices designed to enter data automatically cut input errors and, over time, save costs. These include optical scanners that read bar codes on packages, magnetic scanners that read routing and account codes on bank checks, touch-screen display systems used in fast-food restaurants, and point-of-sale terminals used in department stores.

The *output system* provides the results of processing. The main devices are the display screen and the printer. The *display screen* shows both text and graphics on a TV-like screen. The *printer* creates hard copy, a permanent copy of the output, usually on paper. Printers vary in cost, speed, and quality of output. Today's *laser printers* provide high-speed output with quality like typesetting. The display screen and the printer each have advantages. The display screen is good for quick, temporary access to a small amount of information. The printer is better when a manager needs access to more information or when a permanent record is needed.

COMPUTER SOFTWARE

machine language
Binary codes (0 and 1) used to store data in a computer's main memory.

Computer software, also called a *program*, is the set of instructions that makes a computer operate at one moment as an accounting machine, at another moment as a drawing board, and at another as a text editing tool. Programs can be created in many different programming languages. **Machine language** is the binary (0 and 1) code used to store data in the computer's main memory. But this language is so awkward and error-prone that most programs are written in more English-like, "higher-level" languages and then translated into machine language.

About a thousand higher-level languages are used today. Several are important to business managers. FORTRAN is used to help engineers and scientists solve math problems. BASIC, developed to help beginners learn how to program computers, is part of the operating system on most microcomputers. COBOL, the language used for computerized business information systems in most large companies, was created for accounting and financial data processing. Finally, C is the language of most microcomputer software, such as spreadsheet and word processing packages.

application software
Program that makes a computer do the work that computer users require.

The programs that make the computer do the work that its users require are called **application software**. If clerks need to record customer orders, they use an order-entry application program. If service representatives need to type letters in response to customer inquiries, they use a word processing application program. (Specific types of application software are discussed in the next section.)

system software Program that supports application software with instructions needed by all applications.

operating system
Collection of system software instructions.

System software provides certain complicated program routines that are needed by all applications. With system software, each programmer who writes an application program can use an existing routine to get data from storage or add a word to a screen display. These program routines are part of a collection of programs called an **operating system**, which is often marketed by the computer's maker. Commonly used operating systems include MS-DOS (Microsoft Disk Operating System), Microsoft Windows, IBM's OS/2, Apple's Macintosh system, and Unix.

Concept Check

- Define the two main categories of the components of a computerized information system
- Describe each of the main hardware components of a computer system and the main task of each.
- How is information stored in a computer? Cite four terms used to describe the amount of computer memory storage, and indicate the amount of memory each represents
- What is the difference between application software and system software?

■ The most common types of computer software used in business are word processing, spreadsheet, graphics, database, desktop publishing, and communications. With these, a single employee can perform many different functions in a short amount of time.

MICROCOMPUTER APPLICATION SOFTWARE

4 Companies now use computers for thousands of tasks. Some of the software is so highly specialized that it can be used by only a single company. But several types of software are used in nearly all companies.

Sabrina Tam, a sales representative for a large furniture maker, provides a good example of how the different software can be used. Sabrina gives information about product features to the retail furniture stores in her territory. She earns a commission on sales. Sabrina is considered successful when sales meet the predicted demand for her company's furniture in her territory.

To help her better serve her customers, the company has given Sabrina a computer and some software. The computer is a powerful laptop unit with color display screen and hard disk drive that she can carry into a store owner's office and use during her presentations. She has been trained to use its word processing, spreadsheet, database, graphics, and communications software. Specialized software lets her find product prices, check availability, and enter customers' orders while in their offices.

WORD PROCESSING

word processing Using microcomputers to write, edit, and format documents.

Sabrina uses **word processing** software to write, edit, and format letters to customers and reports to her manager. Before she had the word processor, changes in a document meant completely retyping it. Now she can make changes by typing only the new or altered text. Thus the word processing system saves a great deal of time. The ease of editing also encourages Sabrina to improve documents. Special checkers verify both the spelling and grammar in her documents.

Widely used word processing programs are WordPerfect, Microsoft Word and Word for Windows, and Lotus AmiPro.

SPREADSHEETS

spreadsheet software
Software that automatically calculates rows and columns of numbers.

Sabrina uses spreadsheet software to prepare sales and expense reports for her manager, price estimates and bids for customers, and other materials involving rows and columns of numbers. **Spreadsheet software** automatically calculates the rows and columns. It has many uses, including preparation and analysis of financial statements, sales forecasting, and budgeting. Sabrina's manager asked her to survey major customers and create a spreadsheet that could be used to estimate next year's sales. Sabrina entered the current year's sales into column B of her spreadsheet (see Exhibit 18-2). Her projections went into column C. At the bottom of each column, in the "total" row, she entered a formula that would automatically compute the column total. For instance, the formula entered into cell B12 is "=SUM(B5:B11)," which tells the computer to enter into cell B12 the sum of the values in cells B5 through B11. Sabrina used another formula to get the numbers in column D. Cell D5 is equal to "(C5 − B5)/B5," or the value of cell C5 minus the value of cell B5, divided by the value in cell B5. The answer is a percentage. The minus sign shows that Sabrina expects a negative change, or decrease, in sales of the Honey Wood line. The formulas let Sabrina change any of the numbers in the cells and automatically get new percentages and totals. This feature allows Sabrina to ask "what if" questions. For instance, she could do a second sales forecast that is 10 percent higher than the first.

■ Exhibit 18-2
Sample Spreadsheet

		A	B	C	D
1		Projected Sales by Product Line - District 19			
2					
3			Volume		
4		Product Line	Current	Projected	Increase
5		Honey Wood	43,441	35,000	-19.4%
6		Baroque	5,224,361	6,200,000	18.7%
7		Classic Oak	8,983,004	9,400,000	4.6%
8		Broadloom	92,495	240,000	159.5%
9		Modern	334,923	290,000	-13.4%
10		Provincial	4,903,027	5,500,000	12.2%
11		Broadway	284,043	410,000	44.3%
12		TOTAL	19,865,294	22,075,000	11.1%

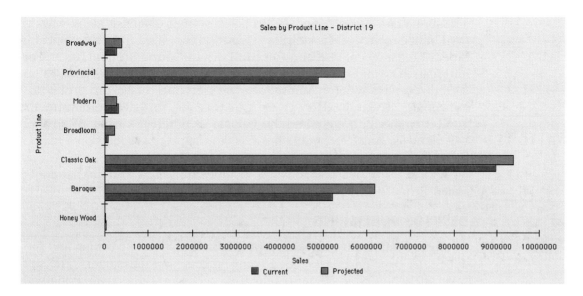

■ **Exhibit 18-3**
Graph Prepared with
Spreadsheet Program

Spreadsheets are very useful business tools. They are widely used to check the effects of different assumptions. Popular spreadsheet programs include Lotus 1-2-3, QuattroPro, and Excel.

GRAPHICS

Sabrina uses *graphics software* to create tables and graphs for customer presentations. For instance, she can depict a customer's profits from sales of her line of furniture. She can show profits for last year and then use similar graphs to show the potential profits from orders this year. Her graphics package, called *presentation graphics software,* is the simplest type. Yet the graphs it produces are more detailed than those produced by other types of programs. Sabrina can also use the graphics feature of the spreadsheet program to illustrate her projections. Exhibit 18-3 is a bar graph of current versus projected sales for each product line.

Widely used graphics systems include Harvard Presentation Graphics, Lotus Freelance Graphics, and Microsoft PowerPoint.

DATABASES

database software
Software that organizes information so it can easily be sorted.

Sabrina uses **database software** to keep records on the 473 customers in her territory. Basic information on each customer includes store name, address, name of owner or manager, telephone number, fax number, date of most recent call, furniture lines carried, and yearly volume of purchases. The records also include notes from previous sales calls, information on each customer's special needs, and a list of the products purchased before. All these data are stored in the customer file. Within the file, the entry for each customer forms a record. Within each record are several columns, or *fields,* each for a single piece of information about that customer—the store name, street address, city, and so on.

Sabrina can organize records in her customer database many ways to more efficiently cover her territory. For instance, she can list customers in order of most recent visit and value of last year's furniture purchases. This information would help her focus on high-volume customers she has not visited recently. When new products are introduced, she can group customers by ZIP code. Each group can then be sorted according to the goods commonly bought and the volume of purchases. This information will allow Sabrina to schedule her visits to the best prospects on a region-by-region basis.

Widely used database software includes dBase IV, Paradox, and File-Maker Pro.

DESKTOP PUBLISHING

desktop publishing
Using microcomputers to design and produce published materials, including both text and graphics.

Sabrina's company uses **desktop publishing** software to design and produce sales brochures, catalogs, advertisements, and newsletters. The software allows multiple columns of text to be set up on a page, along with titles, pictures, and graphs. For mailings to her customers, Sabrina sometimes uses her word processor to prepare text and a graphics program to prepare illustrations. Then she gives a floppy disk containing her text and graphs to a company designer, who uses a desktop publishing program to make a very handsome mailing piece. The company saves both time and money by not sending materials out to typesetters and other specialists.

Widely used desktop publishing programs include PageMaker, Ventura Publisher, QuarkXPress, FrameMaker, and Microsoft Publisher.

COMMUNICATIONS

modem Hardware that connects a computer to a phone line so users in different locations can transfer data.

Sabrina uses her computer's communications software and a telephone link to transfer customer orders, sales reports, expense reports, and other information to and from the home office. Her computer communicates through a **modem**, hardware that connects a computer or a terminal to the telephone line. With a modem and communications software, Sabrina can call up her company's central computer system (which also has a modem and communications software) and transfer data. Systems like this are often used to connect microcomputers to larger company computers.

Concept Check

- Discuss the main use of the five most common types of microcomputer application software.
- How do word processing software, desktop publishing software, and spreadsheet software differ? If you had to produce a full-page table of numbers, which of these three software packages would you choose?

COMPUTER NETWORKS

5 One big trend in business computing is the use of networks to deliver information to managers. Computer **networks** are widespread collections of terminals, computers, and other equipment that use communications channels to share data. Networks have been widely used for about twenty years, but microcomputers have made networking much more affordable and popular.

Networks have created new forms of working. For example, employees at different sites can "screen share," working on data as if they were in the same room. Their computers are connected by phone lines, they all see the same thing on their display, and anyone can make changes that are seen by the other participants.[2]

LOCAL AREA NETWORKS

A **local area network (LAN)** lets people at one site exchange data and share the use of hardware and software from a variety of computer manufacturers. Exhibit 18-4 shows a local area network. A recent study by Andersen Consulting estimates that over 85 percent of all businesses use or are planning to install LANs.[3] A key reason for their growth is that they are a more cost-effective way to link computers than terminals linked to a mainframe computer. At Motorola, the shift to networks has saved the company's computer group about $20,000 per month.[4]

There are two types of LANs. *Client/server systems* have a specialized computer, called the *file server*, that handles only network communications and holds its programs and databases. The individual users who swap data are called *clients* and have PCs with special software that allow them to communicate with the server. A server might be used, for instance, to manage access to a hard disk system that holds the central database for 50 users. In a *peer-to-peer system*, users can access other user's data and resources without going through a central server. These networks are becoming more powerful and sophisticated. They are popular with small businesses because they are easy to set up, less expensive than client/servers, and do not require a computer dedicated just to the network. However, they are slower than server-based systems and depend on the availability of each user's equipment. If someone with a key database goes on vacation, that information may not be accessible to other users. Client/server LANs can handle more tasks and users and offer better data security, making them better for large groups.[5]

LANs can help companies reduce staff, streamline operations, and cut processing costs. At Talking Rain Beverage Company, a Preston, Wash-

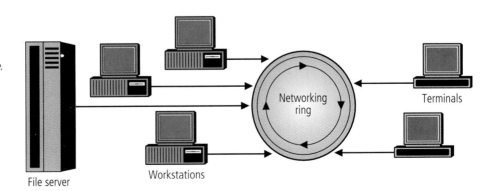

File server   Workstations   Terminals

ington, bottled water business, a LAN links 11 PCs. Its sales manager can access information from the sales reps and prepare regional reports. These are shared with the reps and help generate new customer leads. Because all financial and payroll data is on the LAN, the company no longer needs to hire an outside payroll manager.[6]

An important new application of network technology is *workflow automation.* This is both a way to analyze the flow of information through an organization and a type of software that automatically moves information to the right place. Using this software improves productivity because it gives employees accurate information when they need it, moving documents from person to person automatically. For example, with a workflow automation system, an employee would fill out an expense report form that would automatically proceed to the necessary managers for approval, "notify" the computer to process the check, confirm to the employee that payment is on its way, and file the report.[7]

WIDE AREA NETWORKS

wide area network (WAN) Computer network connecting computers at different work sites, allowing them to exchange data and share hardware and software.

A network that connects computers at different sites is called a **wide area network (WAN)**. It uses phone lines, satellites, and microwaves to connect the computers. Transmissions take place almost instantly, in less than a second. Long-distance telephone companies, such as AT&T, MCI, and US Sprint, operate very large WANs. Companies also connect LANs at various locations into WANs.

■ Each store in the Frank's Nursery and Craft chain is linked to the company's headquarters by satellite. This is an example of a wide area network. Through the network, orders are transmitted automatically to the head office by handheld scanners, credit card transactions are approved in just a few seconds, and headquarters can even control the volume of the background music in each store.

Like LANs, WANs can reduce costs and improve efficiency. At American Healthcare Management, a chain of for-profit hospitals, setting up a WAN linking all the hospitals allowed management to get current financial and operating information. Corporate managers could quickly access daily and monthly reports of patient and financial statistics, focus on problem areas, and take corrective action immediately. With better financial controls, the company was able to reduce costs and speed up collections from insurance companies and patients.[8]

An especially useful application of WANs is for inventory and sales systems. For example, the route salespeople at PepsiCo's Frito-Lay division use hand-held order-entry computers to immediately send data about the store's current supply and inventory by satellite to a mainframe computer at headquarters. Salespeople now have the authority to adjust prices as market situations change. The system, which cost $40 million for the hand-held computers, has increased Frito-Lay's market share and reduced waste, in terms of products going stale, by $40 million per year.[9]

One of the largest WANs is the Internet, a network of private, university, and government computers with thousands of databases and libraries. As of fall 1993, it had over 17 million users worldwide and was growing at about 15 percent a month. Originally established as a Defense Department network so researchers at widespread universities and laboratories could share information, universities and high-technology firms are still major users. The network is not well organized for business uses, but this is changing as more commercial users join.[10]

ELECTRONIC MAIL

electronic mail (E-mail)
Computer networks through which written messages are recorded and transmitted.

One service provided on most computer networks is **electronic mail (E-mail)**. It is similar to postal mail or interoffice mail, except that messages are recorded and transmitted electronically. They are delivered immediately anywhere within the network. E-mail replaces standard mail as well as many phone conversations aimed at getting information or an answer to a simple question. (The Internet is essentially a global E-mail service.) E-mail can also be used to transfer computer files and place orders. It gives large and small businesses an affordable, convenient option to telephone or mail service.

At VeriFone, which manufactures terminals and manages networks used to approve credit card purchases, "P-mail," or paper mail, is not used at all inside the company. All employees are reachable via the Internet. Salespeople in the midst of difficult negotiations can query other managers and receive advice a short time later. Because it has offices worldwide, a group working against a deadline can send a project to another group in an earlier time zone, keeping work going around the clock.[11]

The arrival of the information superhighway will increase the number of people using E-mail and other types of information links, raising new ethical issues about using information technology, as the Business Ethics and Social Responsibility Trends box on the next page shows.

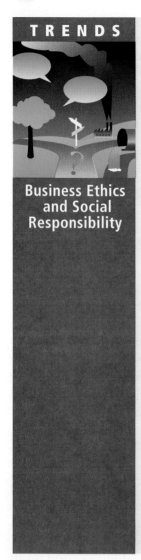

TRENDS

Business Ethics and Social Responsibility

Virtual Reality Check

When the telegraph machine was invented in the late nineteenth century, author Mark Twain quipped, "Now that Maine and Texas can talk to each other, what are they going to say?" Perhaps a similar question could be posed about the information superhighway: Now that we have this new technology, how will we use it? Indeed, politicians, legal experts, and philosophers have suggested that we are making great advances in the communications field without thinking about the legal and ethical issues that are involved.

The most basic concern is how to govern *cyberspace,* the sphere in which people interact by way of computer networks. The House Telecommunications Subcommittee will play a central role in drafting the laws that determine the rights and responsibilities of network users. Regulating how well people obey these laws will be difficult. There is no personal contact in cyberspace, and users only have to identify themselves with a log-on. Unfortunately, some users have already abused the system by violating the trust of others. The *Los Angeles Times,* for example, had to recall one of its Moscow bureau reporters after he was caught reading co-workers' E-mail. One way to prevent such snooping is "public key" cryptography that encodes computer messages and data so that only the designated recipient can access them. Law enforcement agencies advocate a federally mandated system of encoding, with a "trapdoor" that would allow agents to decode suspected criminal communications. Opponents of such a system argue that it would give the government too much power and also be a fundamental threat to our personal privacy.

But personal privacy is already being threatened by the expanding electronic superhighway. Until recently, our financial, medical, and tax records were stored in separate computers. Now, however, computer networking can pool this data, thereby creating detailed portraits of individuals that could be used in loan and job applications as well as criminal investigations.

It is perhaps ironic that these advances in communications technology, made to facilitate the dissemination of information, result in efforts to regulate its flow.[12]

Concept Check

- What is a computer network? How do a LAN and a WAN differ?
- What are some benefits companies gain by using networks? Give specific examples. Discuss briefly the problems that companies must consider when using networks.
- What is E-mail, and how is it used?

MANAGEMENT INFORMATION SYSTEMS

6 In large companies, a **management information system (MIS)** collects and stores the company's key data and produces the information needed by managers for analysis, control, and decision making. A large company's MIS might have five components: a data processing system, a man-

**management informa-
tion system (MIS)**
Computer system that col-
lects and stores key data and
produces information needed
by managers for analysis,
control, and decision
making.

**data processing
system** Part of an MIS system that updates the records
in a database and processes
large amounts of data into
the information required by
managers.

batch processing Updating a database by collecting
the data over some period
and then processing them all
at the same time.

on-line processing
Updating a database by processing each transaction
when the data about it become available.

agement reporting system, decision support systems, office automation systems, and expert systems.

DATA PROCESSING SYSTEMS

In an MIS, permanent records are normally stored in a database. It is similar in many ways to a microcomputer database, but it is vastly larger. In fact, all the company's key data are stored in a single huge file, so access to all of them is very efficient.

The data in an MIS change from time to time. A **data processing system** converts large amounts of data into the desired information required by managers. It collects data and updates the records in the database.

The database can be updated in two ways. In **batch processing**, data are collected over some time and then all processed together. Firms with hourly-wage payrolls often use batch processing to process timecards once a week. In the early days of business computing, nearly all systems used batch processing. Batch processing uses computer resources very efficiently. It needs relatively little computing power, and it can use inexpensive magnetic tape, rather than disks, for auxiliary storage. It is well suited to applications such as payroll that require periodic rather than continuous processing.

In **on-line processing**, data are processed whenever they become available. If you call a travel agent to make an airline reservation, the agent enters your reservation directly into the airline's computer and quickly receives confirmation of it. On-line processing has always been more costly than batch processing. But today the difference may be small. On-line processing also has a big advantage: It can keep the company's data absolutely current. (With batch processing, the data are only as current as the most recent batch run.) Because absolutely current data are needed for management decision making, many large companies use on-line processing systems. The data processing systems of large companies are custom designed to keep the records they need. But some applications in the areas of accounting and finance, human-resource management, sales and marketing, and manufacturing are nearly universal.

Accounting and Finance Applications

Most accounting information systems have subsystems for order entry, accounts receivable (for billing customers), accounts payable (for paying bills), payroll, inventory, and general ledger (for determining the financial status and profitability of the business). The relationships among these subsystems are diagrammed in Exhibit 18-5. These subsystems are sometimes treated as separate, but they are really parts of a single large system used to keep track of a company's activities.

As you can see in Exhibit 18-5, the entire accounting system grows out of the order entry system. When taking an order from a customer, a clerk checks the accounts receivable system to see whether the customer still owes money on an earlier purchase. If the customer's account is okay, the clerk checks the inventory system to see whether the ordered goods are

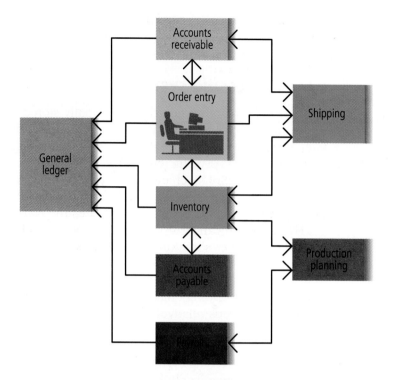

available for shipment. If the goods are available, they are shipped. The accounts receivable system is thus triggered to bill the customer. If the goods are not available for shipment, some must be made. Then raw materials and labor will be required. Inventory must be checked and perhaps ordered. If more inventory is ordered, the accounts payable system will be notified to pay for the materials when they are received and billed. When labor is scheduled, the payroll system is notified to pay the workers. All of these systems transmit data to the general ledger, which is used to keep track of profits from operations.

Financial planning systems project revenues and expenses over some period of time. Cash planning systems are the ones that project a company's cash surpluses and shortages. Even in a very profitable company, cash may not always come in when it's needed. Cash planning systems predict the timing and amounts of cash shortages (and surpluses) so managers can arrange financing (or investments). Computerized systems are also widely used to analyze the financial outcome of various courses of action and to provide information to other decision makers.

Human-Resource Management Applications
The key application for human-resource management is the payroll system. This system produces paychecks and keeps payroll records. It also provides information needed to plan future hiring needs. Computer information systems may keep records of employee skills and abilities. Job performance evaluations kept in computer memory may be used to decide on raises and promotions.

Sales and Marketing Applications

The most common applications in sales are order entry and processing systems. Entering an order starts a complex process using a wide variety of data. The output of a sales information system includes reports on the performance of salespeople. Marketing applications include forecasting sales and generating reports and analyses of sales.

Manufacturing Applications

As shown in Chapter 10, computers are widely used in manufacturing. The key applications are inventory and production scheduling. Workers, machines, and raw materials are limited and expensive resources. Scheduling systems help make sure that the right amounts of each are there when required. Material requirements planning (MRP) systems are often used to schedule not just raw materials, but all aspects of production. Computer-integrated manufacturing (CIM) systems use many of the same data to control the delivery of raw materials to work stations and other aspects of the manufacturing process. In fact, some CIM systems use computer-controlled robots throughout the assembly process.

MANAGEMENT REPORTING SYSTEMS

management reporting system System that uses collected data to produce decision-making information in the form of reports.

The **management reporting system** uses data collected by the data processing system to produce reports that managers can use to make decisions. The most common types of reports are:

- *Detail reports:* These have one entry for each transaction in the data processing system. For instance, a payroll detail report would have one line for each employee showing exactly how his or her paycheck was determined. Payroll office personnel would use this report to answer employee questions about their paychecks.
- *Summary reports:* These contain only summary information. A payroll summary report might include things like total labor cost by department, overtime as a percentage of total payroll cost by department, and a comparison of current labor costs with those in the prior year. Higher-level managers usually need only summary reports.
- *Exception reports:* These tell about cases that fail to meet some standard. An accounts receivable exception report might list all customers whose accounts are overdue. Collection personnel would use the report to focus their work.
- *Demand reports:* These are more often screen displays produced only when a manager requests them. (Detail reports, summary reports, and exception reports are typically printed and sent out on some schedule.) For instance, a production supervisor may use a microcomputer to call up a report on the day's hourly production. A travel agent might use a terminal to get information on flights from Cleveland to Atlanta.

DECISION SUPPORT SYSTEMS

decision support system System that provides several kinds of decision-making information and allows its users to ask "what if" questions.

A **decision support system** is a tool for answering "what if" questions, questions about what would happen if the manager made certain changes. In simple cases, a manager can create a spreadsheet and try changing some of the numbers. For instance, a manager could create a spreadsheet to show the amount of overtime required if the number of workers increases or decreases. *Simulation*, a more complex "what if" tool, uses equations to represent a real-world process. The manager enters into the computer the values that describe a particular situation, and the program computes the results.

OFFICE AUTOMATION SYSTEMS

office automation system Tools—such as word processing, E-mail, or fax—used by a company for better communication.

An **office automation system** is a communication tool. Today's office automation systems make good use of the microcomputer networks in many companies. The key elements include:

- *Word processing systems* for producing written messages
- *E-mail systems* for communicating directly with other employees
- *Departmental scheduling systems* for planning meetings and other activities
- *Cellular phones* for providing telephone service away from the office, as in cars

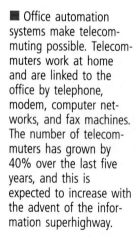

■ Office automation systems make telecommuting possible. Telecommuters work at home and are linked to the office by telephone, modem, computer networks, and fax machines. The number of telecommuters has grown by 40% over the last five years, and this is expected to increase with the advent of the information superhighway.

- *Pagers* that notify employees of phone calls; some pagers have the ability to display more extensive written messages sent from a computer network
- *Voice mail systems* (the oral version of E-mail) for recording, storing, and forwarding phone messages
- *Facsimile (fax) systems* for delivering messages on paper within minutes
- *Electronic bulletin boards* and *computer conferencing systems* for discussing issues with others who are not present.

Office automation systems enable managers to handle most of their own communication. At one time each manager may have had a secretary to take dictation, type, answer the phone, and help with other clerical and administrative tasks. Many managers now write their own routine memos and letters instead of relying on a secretary. Several managers may share a pool of word processing specialists, who prepare long or complex documents, and administrative assistants, who help with other kinds of work.

Businesses and managers use office automation systems in many ways. For instance, the Hats Off restaurant in Hudson, Massachusetts, was having problems handling its many phone calls about the restaurant's specials. It now faxes daily menus to customers. Not only did sales increase, but with fewer phone calls it was able to manage with one less hostess.[13] Office automation systems have proved their worth to business travelers as well. As managing director of consumer products for AT&T, Harriet Donnelly travels frequently. She stays in touch with her office and clients using a notebook computer with a built-in fax modem and E-mail software, a pager that can store short messages, and a cellular phone. Several times a day she checks her voice mail for messages, returning many of the calls in the evening. Then she responds to E-mail messages and pager messages from people who don't have E-mail. With fax and modem capabilities, she can easily transmit written documents directly from her computer. Having all the right equipment at hand makes it easier for her to be productive in any country she visits.[14]

Office automation systems also make telecommuting possible. An estimated 7.6 million people work at home, using microcomputers and other high-tech equipment to keep in touch with the office. Instead of spending time on the road twice a day, telecommuters work at home two or more days a week. The Trends in Business Today box on the next page discusses telecommuting in more detail.

EXPERT SYSTEMS

expert system Computer system that gives managers advice like that they would get from a human consultant.

An **expert system** gives managers advice like that they would get from a human consultant. *Artificial intelligence* is what lets a computer system solve problems more or less as humans do. The use of expert systems is growing as more applications are found. To date, expert systems have

TRENDS

Business Today

Home Sweet Office

Lee Taylor works for PDR Information Services in Santa Clara, California. Yet he lives in an isolated cabin near Telluride, Colorado. Taylor is one of a growing number of "telecommuters," people who are employed by companies but work at home, thanks to recent advances in communications technology. They keep in touch with their offices with the aid of telephones, modems, computer networks, and fax machines. For some, the possibility of working at home means they can avoid a slow commute to work in heavily populated cities. For others, it means the chance to live in a beautiful resort area or a small town. According to the research firm Link Resources, the number of telecommuters has grown by 40 percent in the last five years. These numbers are expected to increase further in the next decade with the development of the information superhighway.

Telecommuting benefits not only workers but also the places where they choose to live. Small towns like Steamboat Springs, Colorado, and Buffalo, Wyoming, are gaining affluent, professional residents without having to provide them with jobs. In addition, these towns often enjoy the luxury of serving as testing grounds for new communications technology. A few years ago, Telluride had relatively limited phone service. Now InfoZone, a program sponsored largely by telecommunications companies, allows Telluride's residents access to the Internet and will soon provide them with a communitywide information system.

Telecommuting is one answer to employee demands for more flexible hours and work schedules. And, despite the doubts of some skeptics, studies have shown that most people working at home have increased their productivity (and many are also working longer hours). Still, not all jobs are suited to telecommuters, particularly those that require extensive interaction with coworkers. Also, some who try telecommuting give it up because they find it too isolating.

As more and more people choose to work at home, American businesses will need to rethink their operating and management strategies. The effects of telecommuting on the economy and on the quality of our lives must be studied thoroughly.[15]

been used to help explore for oil, schedule employee work shifts, and diagnose illnesses. Soon they may even make snow. SKI Ltd.'s Killington Resort in Vermont uses sophisticated information systems in most of its operations, from marketing to snowmaking. The company may add artificial intelligence to its computer-controlled snowmaking system, which involves monitoring weather data and regulating the equipment. Another potential use is in staffing decisions. Converting the existing information system to an expert system would shift some of the decision making to the computer, which would reassign employees to various areas at the resort as peak staffing needs change during the day.[16]

- What are the main components of a management information system? What does each one do?
- Describe the four applications of data processing systems found in most large American companies.
- Describe some of the key elements of office automation systems. How can this equipment help employees work more efficiently?

USING COMPUTERS RESPONSIBLY

Many inventions have changed the way we live. Think what life would be like without cars, phones, planes, and TV. Computers have also become a common feature of our lives today. It's rare to buy something or to transact business without using computers in some way: scanning prices at a checkout, checking a credit card through a network, getting cash from an automatic teller machine, using a spreadsheet to determine how much bank financing a company needs, using a word processor to prepare a contract. The widespread use of computers has raised questions about how computers should be used. Of special concern are the issues of computer security, computer crime, and privacy.

Protecting the information stored in computers is no easy task. With the ever-increasing dependence on computers, companies must develop both emergency disaster-recovery plans and plans covering extended periods of time in the event of a major fire, earthquake, or flood. For example, in April 1992 the collapse of tunnels under the Chicago River flooded the basement of the Chicago Board of Trade's (CBOT) building. Because the building lost all power, the CBOT, a specialized securities exchange, could not get price quotes or make securities transactions. Fortunately, the CBOT had a disaster plan. It had backup tapes of its data, which it sent to another location with similar equipment that could handle its data processing. Because of its contingency plan, the CBOT was able to resume operations in just a few hours.[17]

Disasters are not the only threat to data. A great deal of information, much of it confidential, can easily be tapped or destroyed by anyone who knows about computers. Firms are taking steps to prevent computer crimes, which cost large companies as much as $600,000 per year. The most common computer crimes are software piracy, unauthorized access and use, and malicious damage. *Software piracy* is the copying of copyrighted software programs by people who haven't paid for them. Some say there is one illegal copy for every legal copy of a commercial program. But piracy deprives of revenue the company that developed the program—usually at great cost. Thus software firms take piracy seriously and go after the offenders. Many also make special arrangements with large companies that need the same program for many employees. Firms can get multiple copies of programs at a lower cost rather than use illegal copies.

Another type of computer crime is unauthorized access and use. Using the company's computer to type a term paper for a class or prepare a resume is not doing much harm. But gaining access to a bank's computer system and transferring funds into one's personal account is a very serious crime. Copying confidential information about a new product and providing it to a competitor is equally serious. Links between computers, using modems and networks, also make it easier for someone outside the organization to gain access to a company's computers. Once information goes over a network to suppliers, customers, or bankers, the potential exists for unauthorized access. To protect data, companies can encode confidential information so only the recipient can decipher it. Special authorization systems can help stop unwanted access from inside or outside. These can be as simple as a password or as sophisticated as fingerprint or voice identification.

A third type of computer crime is deliberate damage to the information in a computer system. For example, an unhappy employee in the purchasing department could get into the computer system and delete information on past orders and future inventory needs. The sabotage could severely disrupt production and the accounts payable system. Willful acts to destroy or change the data in computers are hard to prevent. To lessen the damage, companies often keep a backup copy of critical information.

computer virus Computer program that copies itself into other software and thereby spreads to other computer systems, corrupting them.

A **computer virus**, a computer program that copies itself into other software and can spread to other computer systems, is another form of damage. For example, a "worm" virus was introduced into the Internet in November 1988. The "worm" destroyed the memories of 6,000 computers before it was disabled.[18] Viruses can hide for weeks or months before starting to damage information. Usually they attack at times determined by the person who wrote them. Some viruses announce their presence. Others just produce error messages that could result from nonvirus reasons as well. A virus that "infects" one computer or network can be spread to another computer by sharing disks. To protect data from virus damage, software developers have created "vaccination" programs that detect and remove viruses.

Concept Check

- What are some common types of computer crimes?
- What steps can firms take to protect information from destruction and from unauthorized use?
- What is a computer virus?

■ SUMMARY

1. Describe the role of information in decision making.

When making decisions, managers compare information about the company's current status to its goals and standards. Some of the information is provided by information systems, which collect data and process it.

continued

2. Explain the four size categories of computers.

Microcomputers are small enough to fit on a desktop. Minicomputers are too large for a desktop but small enough to fit into a normal office. Mainframe computers are large enough to require a specially outfitted room of their own. Supercomputers are specialized for scientific computations, and in size they range between microcomputers and minicomputers.

3. Name the parts of a computerized information system.

A computerized information system includes hardware and software. Hardware components include the central processing unit, the auxiliary storage system, the input system, and the output system. The central processing unit (CPU) consists of an arithmetic-logic unit, main memory, and a control unit. Software falls into two main categories: application software and system software.

4. Describe what commonly used microcomputer software does.

The most commonly used microcomputer application software does word processing, spreadsheets, graphics, databases, desktop publishing, and communications. Word processing systems aid in composing, editing, and formatting documents. Spreadsheets automatically manipulate rows and columns of numbers, making analysis easier. Graphics systems create graphs and drawings. Database systems store and retrieve records and create data presentations. Desktop publishing programs help create professional-looking documents with text and graphics. Communications systems can be used to share data among computer systems.

5. Discuss the role of computer networks in business information systems.

Local area networks (LANs) and wide area networks (WANs) are used to tie together computers so they can share data and expensive hardware. Today companies use networks extensively to improve operating efficiency. Networking techniques, like electronic mail, allow employees to communicate with each other quickly, regardless of their location.

6. Describe the structure of a typical management information system.

A management information system (MIS) consists of the following: a data processing system for collecting and organizing data; a management reporting system that provides information based on the data to the managers who need it; decision support systems to provide special information to managers who request it; office automation systems to aid in communication; and expert systems to provide advice in certain areas.

7. Discuss how companies should address the issues of computer security, computer crime, and privacy.

Companies are more dependent on computers than ever before. They need to protect data and equipment from natural disasters and computer crime such as software piracy, unauthorized access and use, and malicious damage.

■ DISCUSSION QUESTIONS

1. Some people view the spread of computers as a threat to the job security of secretaries. Others note that many secretarial jobs have been changed to higher-status administrative assistant jobs. Explain why you find one view more persuasive than the other.

2. Which application software systems would most help a full-time business student? What tasks would those software systems support?

3. Discuss the move toward using smaller computers but putting them on more people's desks. What are the advantages? The disadvantages? Be specific.

4. Describe an information system that would help a student choose and register for courses. What information does a student need to choose courses? What are the sources of that information?

5. You have just bought a new computer system and need to get some software, but you have a tight budget. A friend has offered to copy some programs for you, including some that don't allow copying. Discuss the ethical issues involved in accepting your friend's offer. What would you decide to do, and why?

■ CASE

Traci's Boutique

With a retailing degree and three years' experience in the highly competitive boutique business, Traci Steffinski decided to open her own small store in a city with a large university. The boutique sells an international collection of handcrafted jewelry, scarves, belts, and clothing. Because her merchandise is reasonably priced, the boutique has been very successful, attracting a variety of customers, including students. After two profitable years, she is ready to open a second, larger boutique closer to campus.

Until now, Traci has managed the business without a computer. She realizes that with two stores she should computerize her operations. Traci has listed the activities that are involved in running her business: writing to potential suppliers for catalogs, ordering merchandise, approving credit card purchases, letting customers know about special sales and the new store, developing accounting and inventory systems, and hiring an artist to design an announcement and newspaper ads. Before opening the second store, Traci will need to hire additional staff and set up systems for paying them and tracking sales. She will also be traveling to more trade shows to find new items to sell.

Questions
1. List the types of hardware and software that Traci will need. Be specific. Explain why each item will be needed and how will it be used.
2. Outline the steps Traci should take to develop her computer systems for inventory, financial information, and customer information.

3. How could Traci use spreadsheet software to run her business? Can you identify enough uses to justify an expense of, say, $300 for the software? Explain.

4. Should Traci also invest in office automation equipment, and why? If so, what types of systems would you recommend?

Accounting

Chapter 19

Learning Goals

After studying this chapter, you should be able to:

1 Understand the role and uses of accounting information.

2 Distinguish between financial and managerial accounting and public and private accountants.

3 Discuss the accounting equation, double-entry bookkeeping, and the accounting cycle.

4 Describe the balance sheet and its key parts.

5 Describe the income statement and its key parts.

6 Understand the role of the statement of cash flows.

7 Explain how common-size financial statements and ratio analysis can be used to spot a firm's financial strengths and weaknesses.

 Career Profile

Diane Weidner began her relationship with American Financial Corporation as a student in a co-op work-study program. Upon graduation she accepted a full-time position with the company and is now an accountant in its finance and corporate reporting department. American Financial Corporation is a diversified holding company with investments in property and casualty insurance, tax-sheltered annuity programs, fresh and prepared food products, and the entertainment industry. The company operates in all fifty states and many foreign countries.

Diane gathers accounting data from subsidiaries and affiliates and uses this information to prepare financial statements for the Securities and Exchange Commission. The same information is also used in preparing AFC's annual shareholder report. Diane's task is to take very complicated material and put it into a readable format. She condenses and consolidates raw accounting data into financial statements and accompanying explanatory footnotes.

After Diane's co-op experience sparked her interest in accounting, she took courses such as nonprofit accounting and taxation to broaden her knowledge base. She feels that one course in particular, accounting theory, best prepared her for her present position by teaching her how to use critical thinking skills to analyze accounting problems. This same course, she believes, also helped her prepare for and pass the CPA exam.

Overview

Accounting is the standard financial language for businesses. It is a set of procedures and guidelines for companies to follow when preparing financial reports. This chapter starts by discussing why accounting is important for businesses and for users of financial information and presenting an overview of the accounting field. Basic accounting procedures are explained next. Then the two main financial statements—the balance sheet and the income statement—and their key parts are described, followed by a brief discussion of the statement of cash flows. Finally, several ways to analyze financial statements are presented.

THE ROLE OF ACCOUNTING

Your Great-Aunt Helen wants to buy you a few shares of stock, to encourage your interest in business. Her stockbroker suggests two computer companies, and you are to choose one of them. The product lines of the

■ Accounting is the standard financial language of business, and accountants perform a wide range of important functions. They classify and summarize financial information, prepare and analyze financial reports, design and manage financial systems, and help plan the firm's financial strategy.

companies are nearly identical. Where can you get more information to help you make your choice? Someone suggests that one way to learn more about them is to study their financial statements. The companies send you their financial statements upon request, but now you're even more mystified. What do all those numbers mean, and how can you use them to make your decision? You can find the answers by studying accounting.

accounting Process of collecting, recording, classifying, summarizing, reporting, and analyzing financial activities.

Accounting is the process of collecting, recording, classifying, summarizing, reporting, and analyzing financial activities. It results in reports that describe the financial condition of an organization. All types of organizations—businesses, hospitals, schools, government agencies, civic groups—use accounting procedures. Accounting provides a framework for looking at past performance, current financial health, and possible future performance. It also provides a framework for comparing the financial performances of different firms. Understanding how to prepare and interpret financial reports will let you evaluate the two computer companies and choose the one that is more likely to be a good investment.

As Exhibit 19-1 shows, the accounting system converts the details of financial transactions (sales, payments, and so on) into a form that people can use to make decisions. Data becomes information, which in turn becomes reports. These reports describe a firm's financial position at one point in time and its financial performance during a certain period. Financial reports include *financial statements,* such as balance sheets and

■ Exhibit 19-1
The Accounting System

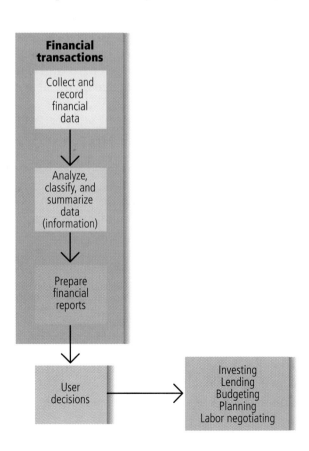

income statements, and special reports, such as sales and expense breakdowns by product line.

Financial statements are the chief element of the **annual report**, a yearly document that describes a firm's financial status. Annual reports usually discuss the firm's activities during the past year and its prospects for the future. Some large firms show revenues and profits by division to give a more detailed picture. Annual reports and quarterly updates are the basic source of information for stockholders, analysts, and investors.

THE USERS OF FINANCIAL REPORTS

Financial reports are used by many different people inside and outside the organization. Managers need financial information to track the firm's progress and to make day-to-day and long-term plans. Unions use financial data as a basis for contract negotiations. Investors need financial information to judge potential profits. Creditors, such as bankers or suppliers, review a firm's financial statements before deciding whether to lend it money or extend credit for purchases. Government agencies, such as the Internal Revenue Service and the Securities and Exchange Commission, require financial reports derived from accounting information.

ACCOUNTING VERSUS BOOKKEEPING

People sometimes confuse accounting with bookkeeping. **Bookkeeping** is the system used to record a firm's financial transactions. It is a routine, clerical process. Accounting is a much broader concept. The transactions recorded by bookkeepers are used by accountants, who classify and summarize financial information and prepare and analyze financial reports. Accountants also develop and manage financial systems and help plan the firm's financial strategy.

2 AREAS OF ACCOUNTING

The field of accounting is divided into four main areas: financial accounting, auditing, managerial accounting, and tax accounting. **Financial accounting** focuses on preparing the financial reports used by managers and outsiders to track the firm's performance and compare it with that of other firms.

The process of reviewing the records used to prepare financial statements is called **auditing**. Internal audits are performed by the firm's accountants. They make sure that everyone is following accounting policies and procedures. Independent audits are performed by outside accountants. They provide a formal *auditor's opinion* saying whether the report has been prepared in accordance with general accounting rules. This written opinion is an important part of the annual report.

As the term implies, **managerial accounting** provides financial information that can be used to evaluate and make decisions about current and future operations. For instance, the sales reports prepared by managerial accountants show how well marketing strategies are working. Production cost reports help departments track and control costs. Managers may prepare very detailed financial reports for their own use and provide summary reports for top management.

The fourth branch of accounting is **tax accounting**. Tax accountants develop tax strategies and prepare tax returns. They also assess the tax consequences of business deals. Tax specialists must be up-to-date on tax laws and other rulings that affect tax strategies and payment.

tax accounting Branch of accounting that develops tax strategies, prepares tax returns, and assesses the tax consequences of business deals.

2 THE ACCOUNTING PROFESSION

The accounting profession has grown rapidly since 1960. This growth is due to the increased complexity, size, and number of businesses and to frequent changes in the tax laws. The nearly 1.4 million accountants in the United States are classified as either public accountants or private (corporate) accountants.

Public Accountants

public accountants Independent accountants who provide accounting services to organizations and individuals for a fee.

Independent accountants who serve organizations and individuals on a fee basis are called **public accountants**. Public accountants offer a wide range of services, including preparation of financial statements and tax returns, independent auditing of financial records and accounting methods, and management consulting. There are over 40,000 public accounting firms in the United States, ranging from sole practitioners to firms with thousands of partners and offices throughout the world. The largest public accounting firms, called the *Big Six*, are Arthur Andersen, Coopers & Lybrand, Deloitte and Touche, Ernst & Young, KPMG Peat Marwick, and Price Waterhouse. Almost all the Fortune 500 industrial companies employ Big Six accounting firms. Many large accounting firms have groups that focus on the special needs of clients in one industry, such as financial services, electronics, health care, or entertainment.

Management consulting has become an important source of revenue for public accountants. Many large public accounting firms have separate management services groups that advise clients on mergers and acquisitions, international trade, information technology, loan applications, employee benefits and compensation, and government contracts. International accounting is another growth area for public accounting firms. Most Big Six firms have offices in a hundred countries. Accounting for multinational corporations is quite challenging, because of different currencies and economic environments.

Private Accountants

private accountants Accountants employed within business organizations.

Accountants employed within organizations are **private accountants**. They may do financial accounting, auditing, managerial accounting, or tax accounting. Their activities include preparing financial statements, auditing company records, developing accounting systems, preparing tax returns, and providing financial information for management decision making.

Certification Programs: CPAs and CMAs

certified public accountant (CPA) Professional accountant certified by the American Institute of Certified Public Accountants.

Professional accountants have earned a certificate as either a public accountant or a management accountant. To become a **certified public accountant (CPA)**, an accountant must have a bachelor's degree and pass a test prepared by the American Institute of Certified Public Accountants. The test is given twice a year. It takes two and a half days and covers accounting theory and practice, auditing, and business law. Each state also has requirements for CPAs. Most require one to three years of hands-on experience in a public accounting firm. Almost all states require CPAs to keep studying for continuing certification. Only CPAs can provide the auditor's opinion on a firm's financial statements. Most CPAs first work for public accounting firms. Many later become private accountants or financial managers.

certified management accountant (CMA) Professional accountant certified by the National Association of Accountants.

The second type of professional accountant is the **certified management accountant (CMA)**. The CMA certificate was developed for private accountants by the National Association of Accountants. Requirements for the CMA are similar to those for the CPA. They include having a bachelor's degree, passing a test that takes two and a half days, and having two years' management accounting experience. Continuing education is also required to keep CMA status.

Financial Accounting Standards Board (FASB)

Comparing the financial reports of an organization to its past reports and to the reports of other organizations is an important way to analyze its health. To make comparisons easier, accountants follow rules known as **generally accepted accounting principles (GAAP)**. When a financial report is prepared "in accordance with GAAP," users know that it conforms to standards agreed on by accountants.

generally accepted accounting principles (GAAP) Standardized rules of accounting for preparation of financial statements, established by the Financial Accounting Standards Board.

The independent **Financial Accounting Standards Board (FASB)** defines the GAAP used in the United States. The seven-member board was created in 1972 to establish standards for accounting procedures. It has representatives from the accounting profession, business, universities, and government. It publishes its accounting principles, called *accounting standards*, as issues arise and in response to changes in the financial environment. It also issues interpretations that explain or clarify existing standards. A similar group, the *Governmental Accounting Standards Board*, sets accounting standards for state and municipal governments.

Financial Accounting Standards Board (FASB) Seven-member board that establishes standards for accounting procedures.

At the present time, there are no international standards, although the International Accounting Standards Committee is trying to develop them. Because accounting practices vary from country to country, multinational companies must make sure that the company's financial statements conform to their own country's accounting standards and to those of the parent company's country. Also, many countries have special accounting requirements that must be met before the company can be listed on local stock exchanges. Of course, the same holds true for companies that wish to be listed on stock exchanges in the United States, as the Trends in Global Competition box shows.

Daimler Bends to the Rules

Until recently, no German companies had listed stock on a U.S. stock exchange. They were unwilling to conform to American accounting standards, which are much more stringent than their own. The Securities and Exchange Commission (SEC), which regulates all American securities markets, requires companies to give potential investors a clear picture of their financial workings and performance so they can compare different investment opportunities. Germany has no agency equivalent to the SEC, and German companies do not have to disclose as much to their shareholders. In the past, these lax rules allowed many German firms to hide profits to reduce their tax liability and to accumulate hidden reserves of money inside their subsidiaries.

Finally, in March 1993, Daimler-Benz, one of the world's largest industrial companies and maker of Mercedes' automobiles, announced that it would list its shares on the New York Stock Exchange (NYSE). For the first time, the secret world of German accounting practices was opened to the scrutiny of American financial analysts.

Daimler-Benz must now translate its financial reports into American accounting language and must follow SEC regulations for financial disclosure. It must issue financial results quarterly by division and must apply uniform accounting standards to all subsidiaries. Because of these new guidelines, financial analysts predicted that Daimler-Benz's reported annual earnings would increase substantially. Indeed, one of the company's first actions was to reveal hidden reserves of $2.5 billion (in German currency, 4 billion deutsche marks), which it recorded as a one-time extraordinary profit for 1992.

Why did Daimler-Benz finally decide to conform to the rules of the SEC? Doing so gives the company direct access to American investors, an important source of capital. Some industry observers feel the weak European economy prompted the move. But according to the company's Chief Financial Officer, Gerhard Liener, "Anglo-Saxon [accounting] principles are…getting nearer to becoming the world's accounting standard. We have to adapt or risk becoming provincial." In any case, it is expected that other German companies will follow Daimler-Benz's lead.[1]

Government Regulatory Organizations

Two government agencies that are involved in the development of accounting principles are the *Securities and Exchange Commission (SEC)* and the *Internal Revenue Service (IRS)*. The SEC regulates the disclosure of financial information by companies with publicly-owned securities. The IRS publishes regulations covering the definition of income for federal income tax purposes. Because these rulings may differ from financial accounting principles, many businesses keep separate financial and tax accounting systems.

- Explain why accounting is important to the main users of financial information.
- What are the four major areas of accounting?
- What is the difference between public and private accountants? How are they certified?

BASIC ACCOUNTING PROCEDURES

3   Using generally accepted accounting principles, accountants record and report financial data in similar ways for all firms.

THE ACCOUNTING EQUATION

assets Things of value owned by a firm.

liabilities Debts; what a firm owes to its creditors.

owners' equity Total amount of the owners' investment in the firm, less any liabilities; net worth.

accounting equation Mathematical statement of the relationship among the three main accounting elements: Assets = Liabilities + Owners' equity.

The accounting procedures used today are based on those developed in the late fifteenth century by an Italian monk, Brother Luca Pacioli. He defined the three main accounting elements as assets, liabilities, and owners' equity. **Assets** are things of value owned by a firm. They may be *tangible*, such as cash, equipment, and buildings, or *intangible*, such as a patent or trademarked name. **Liabilities**—also called debts—are what a firm owes to its creditors. **Owners' equity** is the total amount of the owners' investment in the firm, minus any liabilities. Another term for owners' equity is *net worth*.

The relationship among these three elements is expressed in the **accounting equation**:

$$Assets \ = \ Liabilities \ + \ Owners' \ equity$$

The accounting equation must always be in balance (that is, the total of the elements on either side of the equal sign must be equal).

Suppose you start a bookstore and put $10,000 in cash into the business. At that point, the business has assets of $10,000 and no liabilities. This would be the accounting equation:

$$Assets \ = \ Liabilities \ + \ Owners' \ equity$$
$$\$10,000 \ = \ \$0 \ + \ \$10,000$$

The liabilities are zero and owner's equity (the amount of your investment in the business) is $10,000. The equation balances.

DOUBLE-ENTRY BOOKKEEPING

double-entry book-keeping System of bookkeeping in which every transaction changes two accounts or records.

To keep the accounting equation in balance, every transaction must be recorded as two entries. As each transaction is recorded, two accounts or records are changed. This method is called **double-entry bookkeeping**.

Suppose, after starting your bookstore with $10,000 cash, you borrow another $10,000 from the bank. The accounting equation will change as follows:

Assets   = Liabilities + Owner's equity
$10,000 = $0   + $10,000   Initial equation
$10,000 = $10,000   + $0   Borrowing transaction
$20,000 = $10,000   + $10,000   Equation after loan

Now you have $20,000 in assets—your $10,000 in cash and the $10,000 loan from the bank. The bank loan is also recorded as a liability of $10,000, because it's a debt you must repay. Making two entries keeps the equation in balance.

Next you spend $10,000 on books to sell. These form your inventory, which is an asset. When this transaction is recorded, the accounting equation stays the same. You have simply exchanged one asset (cash) for another (inventory).

In your first month of business you sell all of the books for $15,000. (You don't sell your inventory at cost, of course, or you would soon go out of business.) Now a major change takes place in the accounting equation:

Assets   = Liabilities + Owner's equity
$20,000 = $10,000   + $10,000   Equation after loan
$ 5,000 = $0   + $ 5,000   Profit on sale of books
$25,000 = $10,000   + $15,000   Equation after loan and
                                           sale of books

Assets increase by $5,000, the difference between the amount you got from selling the books and the amount you paid for them. Because the bank loan remains unchanged, the profit from the sale increases owner's equity. The accounting equation and double-entry bookkeeping are a logical way to record your company's transactions.

THE ACCOUNTING CYCLE

Exhibit 19-2 shows the five steps in the accounting cycle: analyzing documents, recording transactions, posting them to the proper accounts, preparing a trial balance, and preparing the financial statements. These steps can be performed by hand or by computer.

The first step in the accounting cycle is to analyze the data collected from many sources. All transactions with a financial impact on the firm— sales, payments to employees and suppliers, interest and tax payments, purchases of inventory, and the like—must be documented. The accountant must review the documents to make sure they're normal and complete. Next each transaction is recorded in a **journal,** a listing of financial transactions in chronological order (see Exhibit 19-3). Then the journal entries are classified into **accounts**, which are records of increases and decreases in specific asset, liability, and owners' equity items. The accounts are next posted to the **ledger**, which contains all of a company's accounts. For instance, each transaction that increases or decreases cash would be posted in the cash account section of the ledger, as shown in

journal Listing of financial transactions in chronological order.

accounts Categories of items that appear in the financial statements.

ledger Accounting record that contains all of a company's separate accounts.

trial balance Summary of ledger totals for each account, used to confirm the accuracy of the accounting figures.

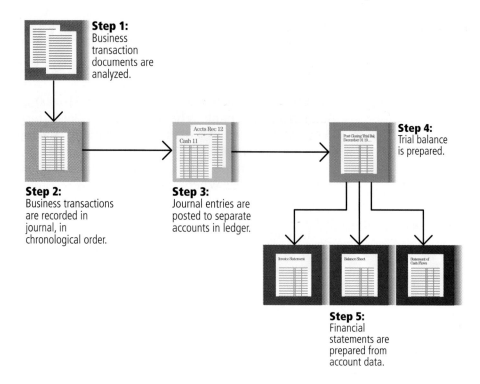

■ **Exhibit 19-2**
The Accounting Cycle

Step 1: Business transaction documents are analyzed.

Step 2: Business transactions are recorded in journal, in chronological order.

Step 3: Journal entries are posted to separate accounts in ledger.

Step 4: Trial balance is prepared.

Step 5: Financial statements are prepared from account data.

Exhibit 19-3. The ledger totals for each account are summarized in a **trial balance**, which is used to confirm the accuracy of the figures. Finally, these values are used to prepare financial statements.

COMPUTERS IN ACCOUNTING

Because they can quickly and accurately handle large amounts of data, computers have become part of the accounting activity in almost all firms. They streamline the routine aspects of accounting so the accountant can focus on interpreting financial information. With computerized accounting systems, an entry generates the appropriate changes to other related parts.

Computerized accounting programs do many different things. Tax programs use accounting data to prepare tax returns and tax plans. Microcomputer software packages help even very small firms automate their accounting systems. Computerized point-of-sale terminals used by many retail firms automatically record sales and do some of the bookkeeping. The Big Six and many other large public accounting firms develop accounting software for themselves and for clients.

Concept Check

- Explain the accounting equation and its relationship to double-entry bookkeeping.
- Describe the five-step accounting cycle.
- What role do computers play in accounting?

Journal page

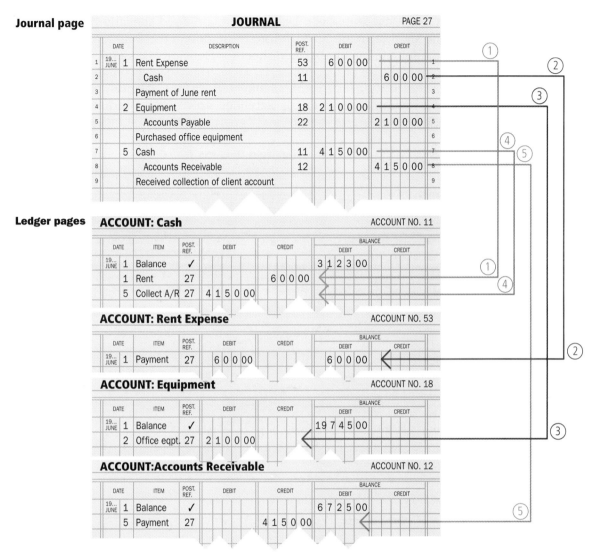

Ledger pages

■ **Exhibit 19-3**
Sample Journal and
General Ledger Pages

THE BALANCE SHEET

4

balance sheet Financial
statement that summarizes a
firm's financial position at a
specific point in time, providing detail on the items that
make up the accounting
equation.

The **balance sheet** summarizes a firm's financial position at a specific
point in time. It presents details of the accounting equation—assets, liabilities, and owners' equity—in that order. Total assets are equal to total
liabilities plus owners' equity. Balance sheets are generally prepared quarterly (every three months) but may be prepared only at year-end.

The assets are listed in order of their **liquidity**, the speed with which
they can be converted to cash. The most liquid assets come first, and the
least liquid are last. Because cash is the most liquid asset, it is listed first.
Buildings, on the other hand, have to be sold to be converted to cash, so

liquidity Speed with which
an asset can be converted to
cash.

they are listed after cash. Liabilities are arranged similarly: Liabilities due
in the short term are listed before those due in the long term.

Exhibit 19-4 is the balance sheet for Delicious Desserts, Inc., an imag-
inary bakery, as of December 31, 1995. The basic accounting equation is
reflected in the three totals highlighted on the balance sheet: Assets of
$155,650 equal the sum of liabilities and owners' equity ($70,150 +
$85,550).

▪ **Exhibit 19-4**
Sample Balance Sheet

Delicious Desserts, Inc. Balance Sheet as of December 31, 1995			
Assets			
Current assets:			
Cash		$15,000	
Marketable securities		4,500	
Accounts receivable	$45,000		
Less: Allowance for doubtful accounts	1,300	43,700	
Notes receivable		5,000	
Inventory		15,000	
Prepaid expenses		6,750	
Total current assets			$89,950
Fixed assets:			
Bakery equipment	$56,000		
Less: Accumulated depreciation	16,000	$40,000	
Furniture and fixtures	$18,450		
Less: Accumulated depreciation	4,250	14,200	
Total fixed assets			54,200
Intangible assets:			
Goodwill		$7,000	
Trademark		4,500	
Total intangible assets			11,500
Total assets			**$155,650**
Liabilities and Owners' Equity			
Current liabilities:			
Accounts payable	$30,650		
Notes payable	15,000		
Accrued expenses	4,500		
Income taxes payable	5,000		
Current portion of long-term debt	5,000		
Total current liabilities		$60,150	
Long-term liabilities:			
Bank loan for bakery equipment			
Total long-term liabilities		10,000	
Total liabilities			$70,150
Owners' equity			
Common stock (10,000 shares)		$30,000	
Retained earnings		55,500	
Total owners' equity			85,500
Total liabilities and owners' equity			**$155,650**

ASSETS

Assets can be divided into three broad categories: current assets, fixed assets, and intangible assets. They are listed on the balance sheet from most to least liquid.

current assets Assets that can or will be converted to cash within the next twelve months.

Current assets are those that can or will be converted into cash within the next twelve months. They are important because they provide the funds used to pay the firm's current bills. They also represent the amount of money the firm can quickly raise. Current assets include the following, listed in this order:

1. *Cash:* Funds on hand or in a bank that are immediately available for use. Cash is the most liquid asset.

2. *Marketable securities:* Temporary investments of excess cash in bonds and stocks that can readily be converted into cash if needed.

3. *Accounts receivable:* Amounts owed to the firm by customers who bought goods or services on credit.

4. *Notes receivable:* Written promises of a customer or employee to pay the company a certain amount on or before a certain date. Typically they arise from credit sales or loans.

5. *Inventory:* Stock of goods being held for production or for sale to customers. In a manufacturing company, inventory consists of raw materials, work-in-process, and finished goods awaiting sale. In wholesale and retail businesses, most inventory is merchandise for sale to customers. Delicious Desserts would have raw materials (flour, eggs, sugar, spices) on hand but very little work-in-process or finished goods, because of its short production process and perishable products.

■ Any buildings a company owns are considered fixed assets. Fixed assets decrease in value because they tend to wear out and become outdated over time. Depreciation charges spread the original cost of a fixed asset over the number of years it is expected to produce revenues for the firm.

fixed assets Assets used by a firm for longer than a year.

depreciation Process that allocates the original cost of a fixed asset to the years in which it is expected to generate revenues.

intangible assets Long-term assets, such as trademarks and patents, that have no physical existence.

Fixed assets are long-term assets used by the firm for more than a year. They tend to be used in production and include land, buildings, machinery, equipment, furniture, and fixtures. Except for land, fixed assets wear out and become outdated over time. Thus they decrease in value every year. This declining value is accounted for through depreciation. **Depreciation** assigns the original cost of a fixed asset to the years in which it is expected to produce revenues. A portion of the cost of a depreciable asset—a building or piece of equipment, for instance—is charged to each of the years it is expected to provide benefits. This practice helps match the asset's cost against the revenues it provides. Since it is impossible to know exactly how long an asset will last, estimates are used. They are based on past experience with similar items or IRS guidelines for assets of that type. Notice that, through 1995, Delicious Desserts has taken a total of $16,000 in depreciation on its bakery equipment.

Intangible assets are long-term assets with no physical existence. Common examples are patents, copyrights, trademarks, and goodwill. *Patents* and *copyrights* shield the firm from direct competition, so their benefits are more protective than productive. For instance, no one can use more than a small amount of copyrighted material without permission from the copyright holder. *Trademarks* are registered names that can be sold or licensed to others. Delicious Desserts' intangible asset is a trademark valued at $4,500. *Goodwill* occurs when a company pays more for an acquired firm than the value of its tangible assets, as shown in the Trends in Business Today box.

TRENDS
Business Today

What's in a Name?

In this era of multi-billion dollar acquisitions, goodwill can become a major consideration for companies. The price difference between purchase price and the value of tangible assets arises from such factors as the company's reputation, its ownership of a marketable brand name, and managerial skill. Under generally accepted accounting principles in the United State, companies must *amortize*, or write off, goodwill against future earnings each year for up to 40 years. This reduces reported earnings. (Amortizing an intangible asset is similar to the process of depreciating a tangible asset.)

Measurement of goodwill is very subjective. For instance, how do you put a dollar value on a particular brand name such as Reebok? And there is no guarantee that a popular brand will stay that way. Yet companies are willing to pay significant premiums to acquire desirable brands or companies with excellent reputations. The 1993-1994 bidding war between QVC Network Inc. and Viacom Inc. for control of Paramount Communications Inc. demonstrates the considerable impact goodwill has on future earnings. As of late 1993, the book value of Paramount's assets was just over $4 billion. The two rivals had pushed the price for the company to $9.8 billion. Depending on the value assigned to movie star contracts and movies and book rights, goodwill could reach almost $5.8 billion! If Viacom, the winner, writes off this goodwill over 20 years, its

profits will be $290 million lower *each year,* or $145 million if over the maximum 40-year period.

In either case, the amortization of goodwill would place an enormous handicap on the acquiring firm. RJR Nabisco Inc., which in the 1980s went through a leveraged buyout at a price that included a sizable premium for its brand names, has had a difficult time generating earnings at expected levels. Reduced reported earnings also make it harder for a company to raise funds from investors. As a result, some financial analysts are now focusing more on a company's cash flow than just on profits.[2]

LIABILITIES

As noted earlier, liabilities are the amounts a firm owes to its creditors (lenders). They are listed on the balance sheet according to time. Those liabilities coming due sooner—current liabilities—are presented first, followed by long-term liabilities.

current liabilities Debts due within one year of the date of the balance sheet on which they're listed.

Current liabilities are those due within a year of the date of the balance sheet. These short-term claims may strain the firm's current assets, because they must be paid in the near future. The main current liabilities are listed in this order:

1. *Accounts payable:* Amounts owed for inventories, supplies, services, or other things bought on credit and due within a year. This account is the liability counterpart of accounts receivable. (*Receivables* are amounts due from customers who bought goods on credit. *Payables* are amounts the firm owes for credit purchases.) If Delicious Desserts buys $2,000 worth of flour and sugar on credit terms that require full payment by the end of the following month, that amount would be shown as an account payable until the company pays it.

2. *Notes payable:* Short-term loans from banks, suppliers, or others that must be repaid within a year. As with notes receivable, notes payable are backed up by written promises to pay certain amounts, plus interest, on certain dates. In the case of notes payable, the company owes the money to a creditor. For example, Delicious Desserts has a six-month, $15,000 loan from its bank that is a note payable.

3. *Income taxes payable:* Taxes owed for the current operating period but not yet paid. Taxes are often shown separately because they are a large amount.

4. *Current portion of long-term debt:* Any repayment on long-term debt due within the year. Delicious Desserts is scheduled to repay $5,000 on its equipment loan in the coming year.

long-term liabilities Debts that come due more than one year after the date of the balance sheet on which they're listed.

Long-term liabilities come due more than one year after the date of the balance sheet. They include bank loans (such as Delicious Desserts' $10,000 loan for bakery equipment), mortgages on buildings, and the company's bonds sold to others.

OWNERS' EQUITY

Owners' equity is the owners' total investment in the business, including both amounts put in by the owners and amounts left over from profitable operations. For sole proprietorships and partnerships, amounts put in by the owners are recorded as capital. In a corporation, the owners provide capital by buying the firm's common stock. For Delicious Desserts, the total common stock investment is $30,000. **Retained earnings** are the amounts left over from profitable operations since the firm's beginning. They are total profits minus all dividends (distributions of profits) paid to stockholders. Delicious Desserts has $55,550 in retained earnings.

retained earnings Total profits of a firm since its beginning minus all dividends paid to stockholders.

Concept Check

- What is a balance sheet? What are the three main categories of accounts on the balance sheet? How do they relate to the accounting equation?
- Define the three broad categories of assets and the main accounts included within each of them. How are assets arranged on the balance sheet?
- Distinguish between current and long-term liabilities. What are the main types of current liabilities?
- What is owners' equity? What are retained earnings, and how do they relate to owners' equity?

THE INCOME STATEMENT

5 The balance sheet shows the firm's financial position at a certain point in time. The **income statement** summarizes the firm's revenues and expenses and shows its total profit or loss over a period of time. It is sometimes called an *operating statement*, because it summarizes the results of the firm's operations. Most companies prepare monthly income statements for management and quarterly and annual statements for use by investors, creditors, and other outsiders. The three key parts of the income statement are revenues, expenses, and net profits or losses. The income statement for Delicious Desserts for the year ended December 31, 1995, is shown in Exhibit 19-5.

income statement Summary of revenues and expenses, showing profit or loss.

REVENUES

Revenues are the dollar amount of sales plus any other income received from sources like interest, dividends, and rents. The revenues of Delicious Desserts arise from sales of its bakery products.

Revenues are determined starting with **gross sales**, the total dollar amount of a company's sales. Delicious Desserts had two deductions from gross sales. *Sales discounts* are price reductions given to customers that pay their bills early. For example, Delicious Desserts gives sales discounts to restaurants that buy in bulk and pay at delivery. *Returns and allowances* is the dollar amount of merchandise returned by customers because they didn't like a product or because it was damaged or defective. **Net sales** is the amount left after deducting sales discounts and

revenues Dollar amount of sales plus any other income received from other sources.

gross sales Total dollar amount of a company's sales.

net sales Dollar amount left after deducting sales discounts and returns and allowances from gross sales.

■ Exhibit 19-5
Sample Income
Statement

Delicious Desserts, Inc.
Income Statement
for the Year Ended December 31, 1995

Revenues

Gross sales	$275,000	
Less: Sales discounts	2,500	
Less: Returns and allowances	2,000	
Net sales		$270,500

Cost of Goods Sold

Beginning inventory, January 1	$ 18,000	
Cost of goods manufactured	109,500	
Total cost of goods available for sale	$127,500	
Less: Ending inventory December 31	15,000	
Cost of goods sold		112,500

Gross profit   **$158,000**

Operating Expenses

Selling expenses

Sales salaries	$31,000	
Advertising	16,000	
Other selling expense	18,000	
Total selling expenses		$ 65,000

General and administrative expenses

Professional and office salaries	$20,500	
Utilities	5,000	
Office supplies	1,500	
Interest	3,600	
Insurance	2,500	
Rent	17,000	
Total general and administrative expenses		50,100

Total operating expenses	115,100

Net profit before taxes   **$42,900**

Less: Income taxes   10,725

Net profit   **$32,175**

returns and allowances from gross sales. Delicious Desserts' gross sales were reduced by $4,500, leaving net sales of $270,500.

EXPENSES

expenses Costs incurred by a business in the course of generating revenues.

cost of goods sold Total expense incurred in purchasing or producing a firm's goods or services.

Expenses are the costs of generating revenues. Two types are recorded on the income statement: cost of goods sold and operating expenses.

The **cost of goods sold** is the total expense of buying or producing the firm's goods or services. For manufacturers, cost of goods sold includes all costs directly related to production: purchases of raw materials and parts, labor, and factory overhead (utilities, factory maintenance, machinery repair). For wholesalers and retailers, it is the cost of goods bought for resale. For all sellers, cost of goods sold includes all the expenses of preparing the goods for sale, such as shipping and packaging.

Delicious Desserts' cost of goods sold is based on the value of inventory on hand at the beginning of the accounting period, $18,000. During the year, the company spent $109,500 to produce its baked goods. This figure includes the cost of raw materials, labor costs for bakery workers, and the cost of operating the bakery area. Adding the cost of goods manufactured to the value of beginning inventory, we get the total cost of goods available for sale, $127,500. To determine the cost of goods sold for the year, we subtract the cost of inventory at the end of the period:

$$\$127,500 - \$15,000 = \$112,500$$

The amount a company earns after paying to produce or buy its products but before deducting operating expenses is the **gross profit (gross margin).** It is the difference between net sales and cost of goods. Since service firms do not produce goods, their gross profits equal net sales.

The other major expense category is **operating expenses**. These are the expenses of running the business that are not related directly to producing or buying its products. The two main types of operating expenses are selling expenses and general and administrative expenses. **Selling expenses** are those related to marketing and distributing the company's products. They include salaries and commissions paid to salespeople and the costs of advertising, sales supplies, delivery, and other items that can be linked to sales activity, such as insurance, telephone and other utilities, and postage. **General and administrative expenses** are the business expenses that cannot be linked to either cost of goods sold or sales. Examples of general and administrative expenses are salaries of top managers and office support staff; office supplies; fees for accounting, consulting, and legal services; insurance; rent; and utilities. Delicious Desserts' operating expenses totaled $115,100.

NET PROFIT OR LOSS

The final figure—or *bottom line*—on an income statement is the **net profit** (also called net income) or **net loss**. It is calculated by subtracting all expenses from revenues. If revenues are more than expenses, the result is a net profit. If expenses exceed revenues, a net loss results.

Several steps are involved in finding net profit or loss. (These are shown in the right-most column of Exhibit 19-5.) First, cost of goods sold is deducted from net sales to get the gross profit. Then total operating expenses are subtracted from gross profit to get the net profit before taxes. Finally, income taxes are deducted to get the net profit. As shown in Exhibit 19-5, Delicious Desserts earned a net profit of $32,175 in 1995.

Net profits can be paid out as dividends to stockholders or they can be kept by the firm. The portion that is kept is added to the retained earnings account on the balance sheet, where it increases owners' equity. The retained earnings account is thus the main link between the income statement and the balance sheet.

gross profit (gross margin) Amount a firm earns after paying to produce or buy goods but before deducting operating expenses; the difference between net sales and the cost of goods.

operating expenses Expenses of operating a business that are not directly related to the production or purchase of its products.

selling expenses Expenses directly related to marketing and distributing the company's products.

general and administrative expenses Business expenses that are neither cost of goods sold nor selling expenses.

net profit Amount by which revenues exceed expenses; net income.

net loss Amount by which expenses exceed revenues.

Net profit is often used as a basis for financial decisions, but it is important to understand what is behind the financial statements. For example, if you look at financial statements of major league baseball teams, you might think they are in dismal financial health. Closer investigation reveals that the statements of these privately-held entities, although they follow GAAP, don't tell the whole story. The owners want to show losses, which provide them with tax write-offs and help in negotiating player salaries and stadium fees. One way to achieve this is to find ways to keep revenues low and increase expenses. For example, Anheuser-Busch, owner of the St. Louis Cardinals, uses a separate corporation for its stadium concession revenues.[3]

ANALYZING PROFITS

Studying a firm's net profit (or loss) is one way to assess its financial success. But accounting techniques can produce differing amounts on the bottom line. When analyzing a firm's profits, you must be aware of the accounting methods used. You must also understand that profit is not cash.

Calculating Depreciation

Businesses can charge part of the cost of a fixed asset against the annual revenues it generates. Such *depreciation* is an accepted expense. But accountants differ in their estimates of the useful life of an asset. They also use different methods to calculate the amount to be treated as an expense each year. These decisions clearly affect the firm's net profit. The shorter the estimated life of an asset, the higher the amount of depreciation expense deducted each year. That means lower profit—something companies may not wish to show in a financial report. But there's a tempting trade-off: lower profit also means lower taxes.

Valuing Inventory

Putting a value on inventory is another area of accounting choice. On a balance sheet, the greater the value of inventory, the greater the value of current assets and hence owners' equity. On an income statement, high inventory value increases cost of goods sold and decreases profit.

The two most widely used methods for setting the value of inventory are LIFO and FIFO. The **last-in, first-out (LIFO)** method uses the cost of the most recently bought or produced goods to calculate cost of goods sold. For accounting purposes, the cost of the most recent goods would be deducted first, working backward from there as needed. It doesn't matter which products are actually sold. The **first-in, first-out (FIFO)** method uses the cost of the earliest bought or produced goods to calculate cost of goods sold.

The choice of LIFO or FIFO can affect the value of inventory on the firm's balance sheet. To see how, suppose that prices rise during a certain period. If the firm is using LIFO, the oldest inventory, which has a lower value, remains at the end of the period. With FIFO, the remaining inventory would be the newest, and most expensive, items. The use of FIFO results in higher profits, because the cost of goods sold is lower. Thus total

last-in, first-out (LIFO) Inventory valuation method that assigns the cost of the most recently bought or produced goods to the items sold.

first-in, first-out (FIFO) Inventory valuation method that assigns the cost of the earliest bought or produced goods to the items sold.

■ From an inventory standpoint, a grain silo works on a FIFO (first in, first out) basis, but there is no requirement that the cost flow method match the actual movement of goods. An accountant may use FIFO to show higher profits on the balance sheet, or LIFO to keep profits down and thus lower the firm's tax bill, depending on the firm's needs.

profits are higher. Many companies use LIFO to keep down their profits and thus their taxes.

The footnotes to a firm's financial statements explain whether it has used LIFO or FIFO. Companies may choose either method, but they cannot switch from one to another without good reason. If they could switch at will, firms could mislead investors, creditors, and tax agencies by raising or lowering profits.

As discussed earlier in the chapter, there are different national accounting standards in other countries. Inventory valuation is one area of difference. The United States is one of only a few industrialized countries that allows the use of LIFO in valuing inventory. Our tax laws generally favor the use of LIFO rather than FIFO. Many U.S. companies are not willing to give up LIFO to conform to international accounting standards.

Profit Is Not Cash

It is very important to recognize that *profit does not represent cash.* The income statement is a summary of the firm's operating results during some time period. It does not present the firm's actual cash flows during the period. Those are summarized in the *statement of cash flows,* which is discussed briefly in the next section.

Profit and cash are different for two main reasons. First, most firms recognize revenues at the point of sale, not when they get paid. They may be paid days or months later. Similarly, most firms record expenses when they contract to buy something, not when they actually pay for it. Depreciation is the second cause of differences between profit and cash. Depreciation is treated as an expense, but it reduces profits and taxes without any loss of cash.

- What is an income statement? How does it differ from the balance sheet?
- Describe the key parts of the income statement. Distinguish between gross sales and net sales.
- Define the two types of expenses. How is cost of goods sold calculated? How is net profit or loss calculated?
- Why is it important to be aware of how depreciation and inventory were handled when analyzing a firm's profits? Explain why profit is not the same as cash.

STATEMENT OF CASH FLOWS

6

statement of cash flows Financial statement that summarizes the amounts of money flowing into and out of a firm.

Because profit is not the same as cash, an analysis of the firm's profits cannot show whether it has enough cash to pay its obligations. The **statement of cash flows**, a summary of the money flowing into and out of a firm, is the financial statement used to assess the sources and uses of cash flow during a certain period, typically one year. All publicly traded firms must include a statement of cash flows in their financial reports to stockholders. The statement of cash flows tracks the firm's cash receipts and cash payments. Thus it gives financial managers and analysts a way to spot and respond to cash flow problems.

Using income statement and balance sheet data, the statement of cash flows divides the firm's cash flows into three groups. *Operating flows* are

■ In a small business, a simple ledger such as this may be used to keep track of cash flow—the money flowing into and out of the firm. It records the company's cash receipts and cash payments, the essential data needed to determine a firm's financial well-being.

◼ **Exhibit 19-6**
Statement of Cash Flows

Delicious Desserts, Inc.
Statement of Cash Flows
for 1995

Cash Flow from Operating Activities
Net Profit after tax	$27,175	
Depreciation	1,500	
Decrease in accounts receivable	3,140	
Increase in inventory	(4,500)	
Decrease in accounts payable	(2,065)	
Decrease in accruals	(1,035)	
Cash provided by operating activities		$24,215

Cash Flow from Investment Activities
Increase in gross fixed assets	($5,000)	
Cash used in investment activities		($5,000)

Cash Flow from Financing Activities
Decrease in notes payable	($3,000)	
Decrease in long-term debt	(1,000)	
Cash used by financing activities		($4,000)

Net increase in cash	**$15,215**

those directly related to the production of the firm's goods or services. *Investment flows* are related to the purchase and sale of fixed assets. *Financing flows* result from debt and equity financing.

The 1995 Delicious Desserts' statement of cash flows is presented in Exhibit 19-6. It shows that the company's cash has increased over the last year. And the company had enough cash from operations to purchase inventory and fixed assets and to reduce accounts payable, notes payable, and long-term debt.

Concept Check

• What is the purpose of the statement of cash flows?

ANALYZING FINANCIAL STATEMENTS

7 Users of financial statements can get a lot of information from them. The balance sheet, income statement, and statement of cash flows provide insight into the firm's operations, profitability, and overall financial condition. Two important tools to interpret the numbers in the financial statements are common-size financial statements and ratio analysis.

COMMON-SIZE STATEMENTS

common-size income statement Income statement that expresses each item as a percentage of some given base, such as sales.

The **common-size income statement** is a popular technique for evaluating a firm's profitability. It expresses each item as a percentage of some given base, such as sales. Common-size income statements are particularly useful in evaluating a firm's performance over time. Looking at the

Exhibit 19-7
Common-Size Income
Statement

Delicious Desserts, Inc.
Normal and Common-Size Income Statements
for the Years Ended December 31, 1994 and 1995

	1994		1995	
	Dollar	**Percent**	**Dollar**	**Percent**
Net sales	$235,000	100.0%	$270,500	100.0%
Cost of goods sold	98,500	41.9	112,500	41.6
Gross profit	$136,500	58.1	$158,000	58.4%
Operating expenses				
Selling expenses	$60,000	25.5	$65,000	24.0
General and Administrative Expenses	50,000	21.3	50,100	18.5
Total operating expenses	$110,000	46.8%	$115,100	42.5%
Net profit before taxes	$26,500	11.3%	$42,900	15.8%
Less: Income taxes (at 25%)	6,625	2.8	10,725	4.0
Net profit after taxes	$19,875	8.5%	$32,175	11.9%

relationship of each item to, say, sales provides a clear basis for comparing the firm's profits and expenses to prior years. *Common-size balance sheets* are also sometimes prepared. The base for comparison would be an item that appears on the balance sheet, such as total assets. Besides being useful in evalutating a firm's performance over time, common-size financial statements also allow comparisons between companies, even those of quite different sizes.

Exhibit 19-7 shows Delicious Desserts' normal and common-size income statements for 1994 and 1995. Most profit and expense items represented about the same percentage of sales in both years. However, the 4.3 percent drop in operating expenses, primarily due to the firm's ability to maintain general and administrative expenses at about $50,000, was the primary reason for the 3.4 percent increase in net profit.

TYPES OF RATIO ANALYSIS

ratio analysis Calculation and interpretation of financial ratios to assess a firm's financial performance and condition.

A financial ratio states the relationship between accounts as a percentage. For instance, current assets might be viewed relative to current liabilities or sales relative to assets. **Ratio analysis** means calculating and interpreting financial ratios to assess the firm's performance and condition. The ratios can then be compared through trend analysis or cross-sectional analysis.

In *trend analysis*, ratios are compared over time, typically years. Year-to-year comparisons can highlight trends and point up the need for action. Trend analysis works best with three to five years of ratios.

The second type of ratio analysis, *cross-sectional analysis,* compares the ratios of two or more firms in similar lines of business. One of the most popular forms of cross-sectional analysis compares a firm's ratios to industry averages. These averages are developed by statistical services and trade associations and are updated annually. Some sources of industry averages are the *Almanac of Business and Financial Ratios, Dun & Bradstreet's Key Business Ratios,* and *Robert Morris Associates Statement Studies.* If a firm finds that its ratios are far above or below the industry average, it can seek the causes. Both types of ratio analysis merely highlight potential problems. They do not prove that problems exist.

Ratios can be classified by what they measure: liquidity, activity, debt, and profitability. Delicious Desserts' 1995 balance sheet and income statement (Exhibits 19-4 and 19-5) can be used to illustrate the key ratios in each group.

Liquidity Ratios

liquidity ratios Ratios that measure the firm's ability to pay its short-term debts as they come due.

Liquidity ratios measure the firm's ability to pay its short-term debts as they come due. These ratios are of special interest to the firm's creditors. The three main measures of liquidity are the current ratio, the acid-test (quick) ratio, and net working capital.

current ratio Ratio of total current assets to total current liabilities; measures the firm's ability to pay current debts.

The **current ratio** is the ratio of total current assets to total current liabilities. It measures the firm's ability to pay its current debts as they come due. Traditionally, a current ratio of 2 ($2 of current assets for every $1 of current liabilities) has been considered good enough. Whether it is sufficient depends on the industry in which a firm operates. Public utilities, which have a very steady cash flow, operate quite well with a current ratio below 2. Manufacturers and merchandisers that carry high inventories and have lots of receivables might not find a current ratio of 2 adequate. The current ratio for Delicious Desserts for 1995 is:

$$\text{Current ratio} = \frac{\text{Total current assets}}{\text{Total current liabilities}} = \frac{\$89,950}{\$60,150} = 1.5$$

The ratio of 1.5 means little without a basis for comparison. If the analyst found that the industry average for small bakeries was 2.4, Delicious Desserts would appear to have low liquidity.

acid-test (quick) ratio Ratio of current assets less inventory to total current liabilities; measures the firm's ability to pay current debts without selling inventory.

The **acid-test (quick) ratio** is like the current ratio except that it excludes inventory, which is the least liquid current asset. The acid-test ratio is used to measure the firm's ability to pay its current liabilities without selling inventory. The name *acid-test* implies that this ratio is a crucial test of the firm's liquidity. An acid-test ratio of at least 1.0 is preferred. But again, what is an acceptable value varies by industry. The acid-test ratio is a good measure of liquidity when inventory cannot easily be converted into cash (for instance, if it consists of very specialized goods with a limited market). If inventory is liquid, the current ratio is better. Delicious Desserts' acid-test ratio for 1995 is:

$$\begin{array}{c}\text{Acid-test}\\ \text{ratio}\end{array} = \frac{\text{Total current assets} - \text{Inventory}}{\text{Total current liabilities}} = \frac{\$89,950 - \$15,000}{\$60,150} = 1.2$$

net working capital Difference between total current assets and total current liabilities; measures the firm's overall liquidity.

Because the bakery's products are perishable, it does not carry large inventories. Thus the values of its acid-test and current ratios are fairly close. At a manufacturing company, however, inventory typically makes up a large portion of current assets, so the acid test will be lower than the current ratio.

Net working capital, though not really a ratio, is often used to measure a firm's overall liquidity. It is calculated by subtracting total current liabilities from total current assets. Delicious Desserts' net working capital for 1995 is:

$$\text{Net working capital} = \text{Total current assets} - \text{Total current liabilities}$$
$$= \$89,950 \qquad\quad - \$60,150$$
$$= \$29,800$$

Comparisons of net working capital over time often help in assessing a firm's liquidity.

Profitability Ratios

profitability ratios
Ratios that measure the profitability of the firm.

To measure profitability, a firm's profits can be related to its sales, equity, or stock value. **Profitability ratios** measure how well the firm is using its resources to generate profit and how efficiently it is being managed. The main profitability ratios are net profit margin, return on equity, and earnings per share.

net profit margin Ratio of net profit to net sales; measures the percentage of each sales dollar remaining after all expenses have been deducted.

The ratio of net profit to net sales is the **net profit margin**, also called *return on sales*. It measures the percentage of each sales dollar remaining after all expenses, including taxes, have been deducted. Higher net profit margins are better than lower ones. The net profit margin is often used to measure the firm's earning power. "Good" net profit margins differ quite a bit from industry to industry. A grocery store usually has a very low net profit margin, perhaps below 1 percent, while a jewelry store's net profit margin would probably exceed 10 percent. Delicious Desserts' net profit margin for 1995 is:

$$\text{Net profit margin} = \frac{\text{Net profit}}{\text{Net sales}} = \frac{\$32,175}{\$270,500} = 11.9\%$$

In other words, Delicious Desserts is earning 11.9 cents on each dollar of sales.

return on equity (ROE)
Ratio of net profit to total owners' equity; measures the rate of return that owners receive on their investment.

The ratio of net profit to total owners' equity is called **return on equity (ROE)**. It measures the return that owners receive on their investment in the firm, a major reason for investing in a company's stock. For Delicious Desserts, the return on equity for 1995 is:

$$\text{Return on equity} = \frac{\text{Net profit}}{\text{Total owners' equity}} = \frac{\$32,175}{\$85,500} = 37.6\%$$

On the surface, a 37.6 percent ROE seems quite good. But the level of risk in the business and the ROE of other firms in the same industry must also be considered. The higher the risk, the greater the ROE investors look for. A firm's ROE can also be compared to past values to see how the company is performing over time.

earnings per share (EPS)
Ratio of net profit to the number of shares of common stock outstanding; measures the number of dollars earned per outstanding share of common stock.

Earnings per share (EPS) is the ratio of net profit to the number of shares of common stock outstanding. It measures the number of dollars earned by each share of stock. EPS values are closely watched by investors and are considered an important sign of success. EPS also indicates a firm's ability to pay dividends. Note that EPS is the dollar amount *earned* by each share, not the actual amount given to stockholders in the form of dividends. Some earnings may be put back into the firm. Delicious Desserts' EPS for 1995 is:

$$\text{Earnings per share} = \frac{\text{Net profit}}{\substack{\text{Number of shares} \\ \text{common stock outstanding}}} = \frac{\$32,175}{10,000} = \$3.22$$

Activity Ratios

activity ratios Ratios that measure how quickly a firm's resources are converted into cash or sales.

inventory turnover ratio Ratio of cost of goods sold to average inventory; measures the speed with which inventory is turned into sales.

Activity ratios measure how well a firm uses its assets. They reflect the speed with which resources are converted to cash or sales. A frequently used activity ratio is inventory turnover.

The **inventory turnover ratio** measures the speed with which inventory moves through the firm and is turned into sales. It is calculated by dividing cost of goods sold by the average inventory. (Average inventory is estimated by adding the beginning and ending inventories for the year and dividing by 2.) Delicious Desserts' inventory turnover for 1995 is:

$$\text{Inventory turnover} = \frac{\text{Cost of goods sold}}{\text{Average inventory}} = \frac{\text{Cost of goods}}{(\text{Beg. inventory} + \text{End.})}$$

$$= \frac{\$112,500}{(18,000 + \$15,000)/2} = \frac{\$112,500}{\$16,500} = 6.8 \text{ times}$$

On average, Delicious Desserts' inventory is turned into sales 6.8 times each year, or about once every 54 days (365 days ÷ 6.8). The acceptable turnover ratio depends on the line of business. A grocery store would have a high turnover ratio, maybe twenty times a year, compared to a heavy equipment manufacturer, whose turnover might be only three times per year.

Debt Ratios

debt ratios Ratios that measure the degree and effect of the firm's use of debt to finance its operations.

debt-to-equity ratio Ratio of total liabilities to owners' equity; measures the relationship between the amount of debt financing and the amount of equity financing.

Debt ratios measure the degree and effect of the firm's use of borrowed funds (debt) to finance its operations. These ratios are especially important to lenders and investors. They want to make sure the firm has a healthy mix of debt and equity. If the firm relies too much on debt, it may have trouble meeting interest payments and repaying the loan. The most important debt ratio is the debt-to-equity ratio.

The **debt-to-equity ratio** measures the relationship between the amount of debt financing (borrowing) and the amount of equity financing (owners' funds). It is calculated by dividing total liabilities by owners' equity. In general, the lower the ratio, the better. But it is important to assess the debt-to-equity ratio against both past values and industry averages. Delicious Desserts' ratio for 1995 is:

$$\text{Debt-to-equity ratio} = \frac{\text{Total liabilities}}{\text{Owners' equity}} = \frac{\$70,150}{\$85,500} = 82.0\%$$

The ratio indicates that the company has 82 cents of debt for every dollar the owners have provided. A ratio above 100 percent means the firm has more debt than equity. In such a case, the lenders are providing more financing than the owners.

Concept Check

- How can ratio analysis be used to interpret financial statements?
- Name the two main liquidity ratios and what they indicate.
- Describe the main profitability ratios and the aspect of profitability measured by each. What kinds of information do activity ratios give?
- Why are debt ratios of concern to lenders and investors?

continued

■ SUMMARY

1. Understand the role and uses of accounting information.
Accounting involves collecting, recording, classifying, summarizing, and reporting a firm's financial activities according to a standard set of procedures. The financial reports resulting from the accounting process give managers, investors, creditors, and government agencies a way to analyze a company's past, current, and future performance.

2. Distinguish between financial and managerial accounting and public and private accountants.
Financial accounting is concerned with the preparation of financial reports using generally accepted accounting principles. Managerial accounting provides financial information that management can use to make decisions about the firm's operations. Public accountants work for independent firms that provide accounting services—such as financial report preparation and auditing, tax return preparation, and management consulting—to other organizations on a fee basis. Private accountants are employed to serve one particular organization and may prepare financial statements, tax returns, and management reports.

3. Discuss the accounting equation, double-entry bookkeeping, and the accounting cycle.
The accounting equation states that assets equal liabilities plus owners' equity. Both sides of the equation must be in balance. Thus each transaction is recorded with two entries, one on either side. The process is called double-entry bookkeeping. The accounting cycle has five steps: analyzing documents, recording transactions in journals, posting them to the ledgers, preparing a trial balance, and preparing financial statements.

4. Describe the balance sheet and its key parts.
The balance sheet represents the financial condition of a firm at one moment in time. The key categories of assets are current assets, fixed assets, and intangible assets. Liabilities are divided into current and long-term liabilities. Owners' equity, the amount of the owners' investment in the firm after all liabilities have been paid, is the third major category.

5. Describe the income statement and its key parts.
The income statement is a summary of the firm's operations over some period. The main parts are revenues (gross and net sales), cost of goods sold, operating expenses (selling and general and administrative expenses), taxes, and net profit or loss.

6. Understand the role of the statement of cash flows.
The statement of cash flows summarizes the firm's sources and uses of cash during a financial reporting period. It shows whether the firm had enough cash to pay its obligations.

7. Explain how common-size financial statements and ratio analysis can be used to spot a firm's financial strengths and weaknesses.
Common-size financial statements express each item as a percentage of a given base. They are useful in highlighting changes in performance over time and between companies. Ratio analysis is a way to use financial statements to gain insight into a firm's operations, profitability, and overall financial condition. The four main types of ratios are liquidity ratios, profitability ratios, activity ratios, and debt ratios. Comparing a firm's ratios over several years and comparing them to ratios of other firms in the same industry or to industry averages show trends and highlight financial strengths and weaknesses.

■ DISCUSSION QUESTIONS

1. Rebecca Mardon started a computer consulting business, Mardon Consulting Associates, in January 1995. During the first month, she completed the following transactions:

- Invested $15,000 cash in the business
- Bought $7,000 worth of computer equipment on credit terms that gave her 120 days to pay for it
- Borrowed $5,000 from the bank, to be repaid in two years
- Bought $2,300 worth of office equipment for cash
- Bought $1,250 worth of office supplies on credit terms

Demonstrate the effect of each transaction on the basic elements of the accounting equation: Assets = Liabilities + Owners' equity.

2. You have been hired to help Marbella Enterprises with its year-end financial statements. Based on the following account balances, prepare the company's balance sheet as of December 31, 1995:

Cash	$ 30,250
Accounts payable	28,500
Fixtures and furnishings	85,000
Notes payable	15,000
Retained earnings	64,450
Accounts receivable	24,050
Inventory	15,600
Equipment	42,750
Accumulated depreciation on fixtures and furnishings	12,500
Common shares (50,000 shares at $1)	50,000

Long-term debt	25,000
Accumulated depreciation on equipment	7,800
Marketable securities	13,000
Income taxes payable	7,500

3. The following are the account balances for the revenues and expenses of the Windsor Gift Shop for the year ending December 31, 1995:

Rent	$ 15,000
Salaries	23,500
Cost of goods sold	98,000
Utilities	8,000
Supplies	3,500
Sales	195,000
Advertising	3,600
Interest	3,000
Taxes	12,120

Prepare the income statement for the shop.

4. You own a sporting goods store and are trying to put a value on your inventory and cost of goods sold for the past year so you can prepare financial statements. Beginning inventory and purchases of tennis rackets during the year were as follows:

Date	Transaction	Units	Price per unit
January 1	Inventory	20	$78
March 12	Purchase	15	$80
July 18	Purchase	25	$85
September 24	Purchase	20	$82

On December 31, you have 25 tennis rackets left in stock. Calculate the inventory cost and the cost of merchandise sold and complete this table:

Inventory method	Total cost of merchandise inventory	Total cost of merchandise sold
First-in, first-out (FIFO)	$___	$___
Last-in, first-out (LIFO)	___	___

5. During the year ended December 31, 1995, Lawrence Industries sold $2 million worth of merchandise on credit. A total of $1.4 million was collected during the year. The cost of this merchandise was $1.3 million. Of this amount, $1 million has been paid, and $300,000 is not yet due. Operating expenses and income taxes totaling $500,000 were paid in cash during the year. Assuming that all accounts had a zero balance at the beginning of the year (January 1, 1995), calculate the firm's (1) net profit and (2) cash flow during the year. Explain why there is a difference between net profit and cash flow.

6. Haubner Publications, Inc., has provided the following selected financial information:

Account balances on December 31, 1995

Inventory	$ 72,000
Net sales	450,000
Current assets	150,000
Cost of goods sold	290,000
Total liabilities	180,000
Net profit	35,400
Total assets	385,000
Current liabilities	75,000

Other information

Number of common shares outstanding	25,000
Inventory at January 1, 1995	$ 48,000

Calculate the following ratios for 1995: acid-test (quick) ratio, inventory turnover ratio, net profit margin, return on equity (ROE), debt-to-equity ratio, earnings per share (EPS). What can you tell about the financial performance of the company from these ratios? What other information would you like to have to complete your evaluation?

■ CASE

Wrong Numbers Mean Wrong Decisions

R. S. Bacon Veneer Company was selling $4 million in wood veneer products annually. Its accounting firm, one of the Big Six, produced reports that Bacon's president, Jim McCracken, couldn't make sense of: "We'd get this set of financial documents each month that would have made better sense for General Motors. We wanted to know if we were making money or losing money. But instead, we got all these numbers that were impossible for us to use." When McCracken forwarded these monthly reports to Bacon's bankers, he would include a letter explaining what he thought had really happened during the month.

Using these financial reports, the accounting firm decided that Bacon was on the verge of financial disaster. It advised the company to sell everything and close up shop. McCracken shakes his head: "I'm still amazed that we had the courage to throw them and their reports out the door." Bacon switched to another, smaller accounting firm on the advice of its bankers. The new firm found Bacon basically sound. One of the partners quizzed McCracken about the types of information he needed for management decisions. The result was a report of no more than ten pages. McCracken could now see what each product cost. He used this information to plan ways to diversify. The clear, concise, informative new reports convinced Bacon's bankers to increase the company's credit lines so it could expand. In the next five years, sales went up 300 percent. Profit margins remained more than adequate.[4]

Questions

1. If you were the president of Bacon Veneer, what financial data would you want from the new accounting system?

2. Why might the two accounting firms have come up with such different conclusions about Bacon's health? Why might a Big Six firm not be a good choice for a small business?

3. What role should a small company's banker play in choosing the right accounting firm?

Your Career in the Information Age

The fields of computers/information systems and accounting are among those growing fastest in the United States. Each offers many career opportunities at all levels.

With the increasing reliance on information technology, the number of traditional information-processing jobs—programmers, systems analysts, and computer operators, for instance—has increased. Many new jobs have opened up in areas like computer training and consulting, network administrators, microcomputer sales, service and repair, and telecommunications specialists. Many other opportunities have been created by applying computer technology to existing jobs. Now every industry has computer jobs. Computers have also changed the way managers get data, make decisions, and do their work.

Some degree of computer knowledge is essential no matter what career you choose. If you enjoy working with computers, you may wish to try a career providing the computer-related services that senior managers need, especially development of information systems and decision support systems. A person who chooses a computer-oriented career needs more than just computer and math skills. People skills, organizational skills, analytical skills, and communication skills are all needed to enter one of today's hottest career paths.

New government regulations and the increased demand for good financial information have fueled the need for able accountants and auditors. The Department of Labor projects fast growth in the accounting field. To succeed in this field, you need good math skills and an ability to analyze and interpret facts and figures. Good communication skills—both written and spoken—and computer skills are also important.

Dream Career: Systems Analyst

The people who diagnose computer-related business problems and offer solutions for them are called systems analysts. These experts create information systems for a firm. They view it as a whole, understanding that any single problem and its solution can affect the entire company.

Systems analysts start an assignment by discussing the problem with managers and specialists. They try to define its exact nature and break it down into parts. For instance, if a firm needs a new inventory system, systems analysts will meet with purchasing and manufacturing managers to figure out what data to collect, what computer equipment will be required, and what steps to take to process the information.

Analysts use such techniques as accounting, sampling, and mathematical models to analyze a problem and design a new system. Once a system has been designed, they present it to managers. If a new system is approved by management, systems analysts translate it into hardware needs and instructions for computer programmers. They work with the programmers to set up the system.

Systems analysts need prior work experience. Nearly half of all systems analysts transfer from other careers, especially programming. In many industries, systems analysts begin as programmers and are promoted to systems analyst positions after gaining experience.

- *Places of employment:* Systems analysts work in all types of organizations —manufacturing, consulting, and service firms; the government; and the military. Positions are available in most large urban areas throughout the country.
- *Skills required:* Four-year degree in computer science or a related field like business or engineering. Many positions require an MBA or an advanced degree in computer science.
- *Employment outlook through 2005:* Excellent.
- *Salaries.* $26,000–$34,000 for beginning systems analysts; $35,000–$60,000+ for experienced analysts; $50,000–$80,000+ for managers.

Where the Opportunities Are

Computer Programmer

Computer programmers work in a variety of companies. Software companies use programmers to develop packaged applications programs for both companies and individuals. Hardware manufacturers may use programmers to write systems software for their equipment. Many companies hire programmers to develop customized computer applications. For example, a life insurance company programmer may write software to calculate policy premiums based on life expectancy tables, and a programmer at an educational software firm may develop math and reading games for elementary-school children.

Computer programmers write programs based on design specifications from systems analysts. Then they determine the steps the program must take to accomplish the desired tasks and write the program in a series of coded instructions, using one of the languages developed especially for computers. Next, programmers test the program to be sure the instructions are correct and produce the desired information. They correct any errors and retest the program until it produces the correct results— a process called "debugging." Finally, the programmer prepares instructions for those who will run the program.

- *Places of employment:* Throughout the United States. Areas with many high-tech companies— including the San Francisco and Boston metropolitan areas, North Carolina, Texas, and Southern California—have many opportunities for programmers.
- *Skills required:* Two-year degree. Some employers require a four-year degree.
- *Employment outlook through 2005:* Excellent.
- *Salaries:* $20,000 for beginning programmers; $25,000–$50,000+ for experienced programmers.

Database Manager

The huge growth of governmental and private databases has resulted in a high demand for people who can operate and monitor databases. The database manager (or administrator) normally is not involved in the design or development of the database software. Instead, these managers typically take over once the system has been installed at the organization.

A database manager is responsible for scheduling and coordinating user access as well as overall security. The manager arranges for the preparation of backup files and emergency recovery plans. He or she advises management as to which data should be included in the database, how it should be organized, and how long it

should remain. Many database managers also compile and analyze statistics on use and efficiency of the database and report these findings to management.

- *Places of employment:* Throughout the country, with most opportunities in large urban areas.
- *Skills required:* Four-year program; many organizations also require an MBA.
- *Employment outlook through 2005:* Excellent.
- *Salaries:* $30,000–$45,000 for assistant administrators; $50,000–$62,000 for administrators; $60,000–$75,000 for managers.

Network Administrators

As more companies turn to decentralized computer systems linked into networks, the demand is growing for network administrators to facilitate communications between computers. These specialists help managers define their computing needs and integrate their department's computer systems into the larger system. They purchase the network's equipment (PCs, workstations, printers, scanners, and databases) and maintain the network.

- *Places of employment:* Throughout the country, with most opportunities in large urban areas.
- *Skills required:* BS degree in computer science and computer experience; certification from manufacturers of network systems hardware is desirable.
- *Employment outlook through 2005:* Excellent.
- *Salaries:* $20,000 for entry level; $40,000–$57,000 for midlevel specialists; $71,000+ for managers.

Accountant

About 1.5 million accountants work in the United States today, and the field is still growing. Most accountants (about 60 percent) are involved in managerial accounting for businesses. Another 25 percent work in public accounting firms. The government and educational institutions also employ many accountants.

Managerial accountants work in all types of businesses, from small firms to large multinational corporations. Many are either certified management accountants (CMAs) or certified public accountants (CPAs). They prepare financial statements and other reports for management. They may also specialize in such areas as international, tax, or cost accounting, budgeting, or internal auditing. The top positions for managerial accountants are corporate controller and treasurer. The controller manages the accounting, audit, and budget departments. The treasurer is responsible for cash management, financial planning, and other financial activities.

Public accountants generally earn more than managerial accountants. More than 300,000 public accountants work in accounting firms throughout the United States and abroad. All levels of government have accounting positions as well. Most of these positions carry civil-service rank, and advancement depends on education and experience.

Accountants also establish businesses of their own, hanging out their shingles as CPAs, tax accountants, and accounting consultants.

Opportunities for minorities and women are excellent in the accounting field.

- *Places of employment:* Throughout the country, primarily in large urban areas.
- *Skills required:* Four-year degree in accounting or related field. Many large firms prefer an MA in accounting or an MBA. Computer skills are also important.
- *Employment outlook through 2005:* Excellent.
- *Salaries:* $23,000–$31,000 for beginning accountants and auditors with bachelor's degree; $25,000–$34,000 with master's degree; $33,000–$80,000+ for experienced accountants; $100,000–$300,000 for partners in CPA firms.

Part 8

Finance

Overview

Finance is not just crunching numbers. A good financial manager must be able to evaluate financial data and interpret it in such a way as to maximize its benefit to the company. Numbers alone don't tell the story; it's what they represent that's important, and sound financial management is critical to the success of any business.

For instance, a financial manager, after a thorough study of the matter, will recommend whether and when a company should consider expanding. The manager will also suggest how best to finance the expansion process. New factories and office towers are expensive to build, and companies generally don't have enough savings to completely fund such a major financial commitment on their own.

They will usually go one of two routes to obtain financing: issue additional stock (called equity financing) or borrow the money (called debt financing). Business makes the largest demand on funds in the financial exchange process. This may seem surprising, because we tend to think of business as supporting the economic activity of the country. However, when it comes to financial transactions, households typically supply the funds (through savings accounts and investments), and businesses and governments typically use them.

Commercial banks are one type of financial institution that supplies loans to businesses and consumers, and the way they do business is changing rapidly. "Bankers' hours" are a thing of the past. Drive-up windows are now open early and late for the convenience of customers before and after work, Saturday hours are commonplace, and automated teller machines give customers access to their accounts literally 24 hours a day. These changes are due in part to the deregulation of the banking industry, which increased competition among financial institutions. This, in turn, has led to a new focus on customer service.

The following chapters delve into financial institutions, financial management, and the complexities of the securities market. Each of these areas of business is being transformed by advances in technology and new government regulations. It is an exciting time for those who appreciate the science and art of finance.

PNC Bank Corporation

Pittsburgh-based PNC Bank Corporation is a company that seems to defy conventional labels. On one hand, it is a regional bank that likes to stay close to its customers. PNC serves 70,000 small, middle, and larger-size companies, and two-and-a-half million households consider PNC to be their primary bank. On the other hand, PNC's assets rank it as one of the better-performing big banks in the country. The company's recent acquisition of Sears Mortgage, a $9 billion addition, reinforces its financial strength and depth. For these reasons, PNC has been referred to as a supra-regional bank. It has a solid regional base but also conducts business nationally and internationally.

The chairman and CEO of PNC, Thomas O'Brien, is credited with shaping this new type of banking structure. He is quick to point out, though, that his company does not view itself as a global international bank, nor does it want to become one. PNC has identified its strengths and is aggressively pursuing its growth strategy along those lines. It serves its customers through four core businesses: Corporate Banking, Retail Banking, Investment Management and Trust, and Investment Banking.

Financial organizations, like retail businesses, have realized the need to offer a full range of products and services. PNC Bank Corporation is succeeding in the increasingly competitive financial arena because of its commitment and willingness to meet the needs of every one of its customers, regardless of the size of their accounts.

Financial Institutions

Learning Goals

After studying this chapter, you should be able to:

1. Define money and understand its three main functions.
2. Describe the makeup of the money supply and define M1, M2, and M3.
3. Identify the key members of the U.S. financial system, and explain financial intermediation.
4. Distinguish between depository and nondepository financial institutions, and list the key types of each.
5. Discuss the services offered by commercial banks.
6. List the main functions of the Federal Reserve and the tools it uses to manage the money supply.
7. Describe the role of the FDIC.
8. Understand the reasons for recent banking crises, and discuss the future of banking.

 Career Profile

Dave Melin is a commercial bank officer in PNC Bank Corporation's National Corporate Banking Division. He began his career with PNC Bank directly out of college, starting in the credit and product training program. He is now responsible for managing a large portfolio for approximately fifteen customers. He is aided in this task by his district manager and credit support staff. Dave's function is known as relations management because it is crucial that he build trusting relationships with his clients and other members of PNC's staff.

Dave's major in college was finance, and he feels that the finance and economics courses he took were vital to his success in his current position. He believes that serving as treasurer for his college fraternity was also good training. It gave him a feel for the demands that would be placed upon him in the field of finance.

Dave appreciates and looks forward to the continuing education in regulations, software applications, and management provided by PNC Bank Corporation. He sees it as an opportunity to help refine his analytical talent and further develop his interpersonal skills. This is important to Dave, because these are resources he will rely upon to advance his career.

Overview

This chapter introduces the U.S. monetary system and its financial institutions. First it discusses money, its characteristics and functions, and the components of the U.S. money supply. Next it looks at the U.S. financial system and banking system—especially the development, structure, functions, and services of commercial banks. Then it explains the role of the Federal Reserve System in managing the money supply and clearing checks and the role of the Federal Deposit Insurance Corporation and similar agencies that insure bank deposits. Finally, the chapter discusses changes in the banking industry, the rise of the global bank, and banking in the 1990s.

MONEY

Money is used by people, businesses, and governments to make transactions and measure value. It affects our lives in many ways. We earn it, spend it, save it—and often wish we had more of it. Businesses and governments use money in similar ways. Both require money to finance their operations. By controlling the amount of money in circulation, the federal government can promote economic growth and stability. For this reason, money has been called the lubricant for the machinery of our economic system. Our banking system was developed to ease the handling of money.

■ Money is anything that is accepted as payment for goods and services. Shells, beads, animals, and tobacco have all served as money in different cultures. At one time these huge, circular stones were used as money by the people of Yap Island, in Micronesia.

▼ WHAT IS MONEY?

Without money, goods and services would have to be exchanged directly, a custom called *barter*. Barter can be very inconvenient. Someone who had fish and wanted bread would have to find someone who had bread and wanted fish. Their needs would have to match, and they would have to agree on the quantities to be exchanged. The timing would also have to be right.

These inconveniences led even very primitive societies to develop a money system. Usually something that had value in its own right was used as the basis for exchange. Shells, beads, tobacco, silk, animals, gold, and silver have all served as money. Usually only one item was accepted as the unit in which the value of other goods was stated. The American Plains Indians, for instance, used horses as a basis for exchanging goods. One horse might have been worth 3 steers or 500 arrows or 7 buffalo robes.

Basically, then, **money** is anything—regardless of form—that is acceptable as payment for goods and services. In specific economic terms, money must be generally acceptable in payment for transactions.

money Anything, regardless of form, that is acceptable as payment for goods and services.

WHAT WORKS AS MONEY?

Many early forms of money would not work well today. For instance, a horse can't be divided into smaller units of exchange. Thus it would be hard to buy only two buffalo robes with a horse worth seven buffalo robes. It is also hard to transport a horse over very long distances. And there is the risk that the horse might die. For money to be a suitable means of exchange, it should have four key characteristics: scarcity, durability, portability, and divisibility.

Scarcity is a very important characteristic. Money should be scarce enough to have some value but not so scarce as to be unavailable. Pebbles, which meet some of the other criteria, would not work well as money because they are widely available. Too much money in circulation increases prices (inflation, as discussed in Chapter 2). Governments today control the scarcity of money by limiting the quantity of money produced.

Any item used as money must also have *durability*. A perishable item—milk, for instance—becomes useless as money when it spoils. Even early societies developed forms of money, such as metal coins and paper money, that lasted for a long time.

Large or bulky items, such as boulders or heavy gold bars, cannot easily be transported from place to place. Thus they do not have portability. Again, coins and paper money meet the requirements. Such forms of money help in making transactions, whether they are local or distant.

Finally, how could you purchase a package of gum if the unit of exchange were horses? You'd probably have to trade your horse for a lifetime supply of gum! *Divisibility* is the ability to be divided into smaller parts. All forms of money today are very divisible. A dollar can be split into 100 cents, a Japanese yen into 100 sen, a French franc into 100 centimes. Divisible forms of money help make possible transactions of all sizes and amounts.

▼ THE MAIN FUNCTIONS OF MONEY

Using several types of goods as money would be confusing. Thus societies develop a uniform money system to measure the value of goods and services. For money to be generally acceptable, it must function as a medium of exchange, as a standard of value, and as a store of value.

As a *medium of exchange*, money makes transactions easier. Having one common form of payment in each country is much less complicated than a barter system. Money allows the exchange of goods and services to be a simple process.

Money also serves as a *standard of value*. With a form of money whose value is accepted by all, goods and services can be priced in standard units. Say that glass beads are the basis for a monetary system. A loaf of bread might cost 10 beads, a pound of steak 50 beads, and a shirt 160 beads. Using dollars, these items might cost $1.25, $6.25, and $20.00. Money also allows transactions to be recorded in consistent terms.

As a *store of value*, money is used to hold wealth. It retains its value over time. Someone who owns money can hold on to it for future use rather than exchange it today for other types of assets.

② THE U.S. MONEY SUPPLY

The money supply in the United States has three parts: currency, demand deposits, and time deposits.

currency Cash held in the form of coins and paper money.

- **Currency:** Cash held in the form of coins and paper money. Currency is what usually comes to mind when we think of money. Other forms of currency include traveler's checks, cashier's checks, and money orders. As of October 1993, the U.S. had $326 billion currency in circulation.

demand deposits Money kept in bank checking accounts that can be withdrawn by depositors on demand.

- **Demand deposits:** Money kept in bank checking accounts that can be withdrawn by depositors on demand. As of October 1993, U.S. commercial bank demand deposits totaled about $380 billion, with other checkable deposits (interest-bearing and other special types of checking accounts) totalling $410 billion. Demand deposits represent a promise by the bank to pay, on demand, any amount up to the amount of funds in each depositor's account. Checking accounts provide a convenient way to pay for goods and services. They eliminate the need to carry large amounts of currency. With checks, payments can easily and safely be sent by mail. Checks are the most popular form of payment in the United States.

time deposits Money kept on deposit at banks that earns interest but cannot be withdrawn on demand.

- **Time deposits:** Deposits at a bank or other financial institution that pay interest but cannot be withdrawn on demand. They can take several forms, including savings accounts, money market deposit accounts, and certificates of deposit. Time deposits are the single largest component of the money supply. They totaled about $2.34 trillion as of October 1993.

Because there is a direct link between the size of the money supply and economic growth, the U.S. government monitors and controls the amount of money in circulation. There are three measures of money supply. The basic money supply—currency held by the public, demand deposits, and traveler's checks—is called **M1**. (Currency held by banks is not part of M1.) A broader definition of the money supply is **M2**, which consists of M1 plus most time deposits (those smaller than $100,000). The broadest measure is **M3**, which consists of M2 plus large time deposits (certificates of deposit over $100,000). As Exhibit 20-1 shows, M1 represents about one quarter of the total money supply.

Recently there has been a large outflow of money from banks to other financial service companies such as mutual funds. As a result, defining money supply based only on bank deposits does not provide as good a measure as in the past. The Federal Reserve is considering changing or adding to government measures of money supply.[1]

WHY CREDIT CARDS ARE NOT MONEY

Credit cards are a popular form of payment for goods and services. They are used as a substitute for cash and checks. But credit cards are not money; they are a form of borrowing. The issuer of the credit card gives a short-term loan to the cardholder by directly paying the seller for the cardholder's purchases. The cardholder pays the credit card issuer when billed. The credit card does not replace money; it simply defers payment. Many credit cards allow cardholders to pay only a minimum amount each month and carry forward the unpaid balance, on which interest is charged.

M1 The basic money supply: currency held by the public, demand deposits, and traveler's checks.

M2 An expanded measure of money supply, including M1 plus most time deposits (those smaller than $100,000).

M3 The broadest measure of money supply, consisting of M2 plus large time deposits (certificates of deposit over $100,000).

■ **Exhibit 20-1**
Measures of the Money Supply, October 1993

Source: *Federal Reserve Bulletin*, January 1994, p. A14.

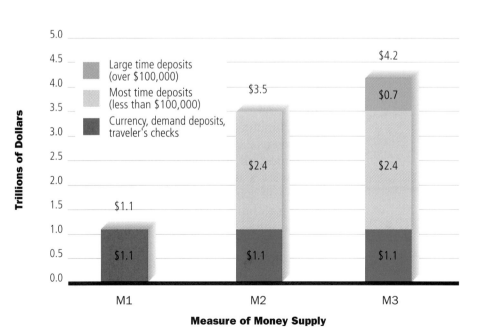

Credit card use has increased a great deal recently. Today about 111 million people carry over 1 billion credit cards, using them to buy almost $500 billion in goods and services each year. Their popularity is due to the convenience of getting one bill for several purchases and the ability to extend the repayment period.

The largest credit card issuers are banks (MasterCard and Visa). Other major issuers include large retail chains (Sears and JC Penney), telephone companies (AT&T and MCI), gasoline companies (Arco and Mobil), and specialized credit card companies (Discover, American Express, and Diners Club). Credit cards are an extremely profitable product. Most cards issued by banks and specialized card companies carry annual fees ranging from $25 to $75 or more. The interest charged on cardholders' unpaid balances averages 18 percent per year (much higher than the rates charged by banks on business loans). Finally, merchants who accept the cards pay to card issuers fees of 1 to 5 percent of the amount of customer credit card purchases.

- What is money? What are its desirable characteristics? Explain its three essential functions.
- Why does the government want to control the money supply? Differentiate between M1, M2, and M3.
- Why are credit cards, which are accepted as a form of payment, not considered money?

THE U.S. FINANCIAL SYSTEM

3 4   The well-developed financial system in the United States supports our high standard of living. The system allows those who wish to borrow money to do so with relative ease. It also gives savers a variety of ways to earn interest on their savings. For instance, a computer company that wants to build a new headquarters in Atlanta might be financed partly with the savings of families in California. The Californians deposit their money in a local financial institution. That institution looks for a profitable and safe way to use the money and decides to make a real estate loan to the computer company. The transfer of funds from savers to investors lets businesses expand and the economy grow.

Almost all Americans take part in the U.S. financial system. Families saving for a house or their children's college education, businesses borrowing to expand their facilities, and state and local governments borrowing to build new schools are all part of the system. The fact that the system serves the needs of 250 million people, millions of businesses, and thousands of government organizations is indeed amazing.

Households are important participants in the U.S. financial system. Statistics show that, overall, households save more than they borrow. Many households do borrow to finance purchases. But on balance, households supply funds to the financial system. Likewise, businesses and governments are overall users of funds. They borrow more money than they save.

FINANCIAL INTERMEDIATION

Sometimes those who have funds deal directly with those who want them. A wealthy realtor may lend money to a client to buy a house, for example. But more often, financial institutions act as intermediaries ("go-betweens") between the suppliers and demanders of funds. They accept savers' deposits and invest them in financial products (such as loans) that are expected to produce a return. This process, called **financial intermediation**, is shown in Exhibit 20-2. Households are shown as suppliers of funds, and businesses and governments are shown as demanders. But a single household, business, or government can be either a supplier or demander, depending on the circumstances.

Financial institutions are the heart of the financial system. They are a convenient vehicle for financial intermediation. They can be divided into two broad groups: *depository financial institutions* (those that accept deposits) and *nondepository financial institutions* (those that do not).

DEPOSITORY FINANCIAL INSTITUTIONS

■ **Exhibit 20-2**
The Financial Intermediation Process

Depository financial institutions include commercial banks, thrift institutions, and credit unions. Commercial banks are the largest group in terms of number, dollars of assets, and deposits.

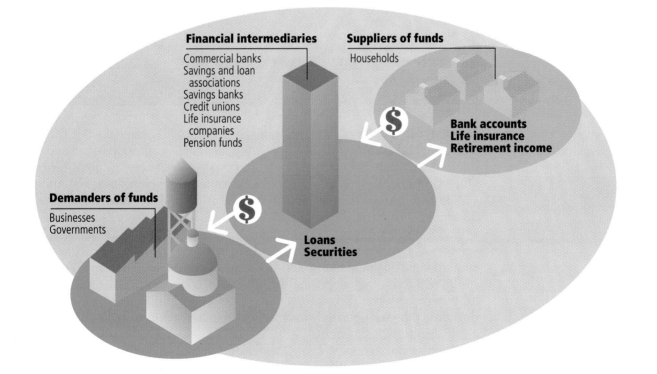

Financial intermediaries
Commercial banks
Savings and loan
  associations
Savings banks
Credit unions
Life insurance
  companies
Pension funds

Suppliers of funds
Households

**Bank accounts
Life insurance
Retirement income**

Demanders of funds
Businesses
Governments

**Loans
Securities**

■ Commercial banks are profit-oriented financial institutions that act as intermediaries between the suppliers and demanders of funds. They accept savings deposits and invest them in financial products (such as loans). The difference between the interest earned on the loans the bank makes and the interest it pays its depositors is the basis of the profit the bank earns.

commercial banks

Profit-oriented financial institutions that accept customer deposits, make loans to consumers and businesses, invest in securities, and provide other financial services.

Commercial Banks

Commercial banks are profit-oriented financial institutions that accept deposits, make loans to consumers and businesses, invest in government and corporate securities, and provide other financial services. About 11,700 U.S. commercial banks accounted for $2.84 trillion in loans and investments (a bank's assets) and $2.35 trillion in deposits as of October 1993. Exhibit 20-3 lists the top fifteen U.S. commercial banks. Among the services they offer are checking and savings accounts, credit cards, consumer loans, business loans, and home mortgage loans. Their main source of funds is customer deposits; the main use of those funds is loans. The difference between the interest earned on loans and the interest paid on deposits, plus fees earned from other financial services, pays the banks' costs and provides a profit.

Commercial banks are no longer the stodgy institutions they once were. Changes in banking laws now let banks provide a wide array of

Rank by Assets, 1993	Bank	Assets, $ millions
1	Citicorp New York	$216,574
2	BankAmerica San Francisco	186,933
3	Nationsbank Charlotte, NC	157,686
4	Chemical Bank New York	149,888
5	J.P. Morgan & Co. New York	133,888
6	Chase Manhattan Corp. New York	102,103
7	Bankers Trust New York Corp. New York	92,082
8	Banc One Corp. Columbus, Ohio	79,919
9	First Union Corp. Charlotte, NC	70,787
10	Key Corp. Cleveland, Ohio	59,655
11	First Chicago Corp.	52,560
12	Wells Fargo & Co. San Francisco	52,513
13	PNC Bank Pittsburgh	52,280
14	First Interstate Bancorp. Los Angeles	51,461
15	Norwest Corp. Minneapolis	50,782

■ **Exhibit 20-3**
Top 15 U.S. Banks, Based on Assets, (as of December 31, 1993)

Source: "The Business Week 1000," *Business Week*, 28 March 1994, pp. 80–90.

financial services, including sales of mutual funds and other securities. Thus the lines between banks and other financial institutions have been erased, increasing the competition for customers. Today's banking system is in a state of flux, facing many challenges. As the Quality Management Trends box indicates, some large banks are finding that total quality management techniques can help improve customer service and increase profitability.

T R E N D S

Quality Management

Banking on Success

In order to stay afloat in the competitive service industry of the 1990s, companies must try to maximize their productivity. Many have streamlined their operations, cutting out largely managerial and bureaucratic positions. But cutting down on the number of employees does not necessarily increase a company's productivity. The key to success, as many have found, is learning to organize and manage workers as effectively as possible. With that goal in mind, companies throughout the nation have launched total quality management programs.

First Chicago Bank's cash management business, which collects receivables for corporate treasuries, launched a TQM program to improve the accuracy and speed of its services. Several times daily, employees empty the locked post office boxes (lockboxes) where the checks arrive. As a result, the checks are processed faster and customers gain an extra day's interest on their deposits.

In addition, the bank teaches its employees about the workings of the entire business, so that they can see beyond the confines of their jobs and make more informed decisions about how to improve their work. The bank even crosses company boundaries to participate in quality improvement campaigns of some of its customers, redesigning forms and redividing work to minimize redundant steps and the margin of error. Aside from raising First Chicago's productivity, these efforts have allowed it to expand its cash management business twice as fast as its competitors.

Another way to improve quality is to boost employee productivity with better technology. For example, Cleveland's Society National Bank, a subsidiary of Key Corp., has installed a voice-mail system for routine customer service work. The system handles about 70 percent of customer phone calls, so that customer service representatives have more time to spend with people who really need human assistance. In addition, laptop computers allow the bank's loan officers the freedom to travel to their customers. According to Executive Vice President Allen Gula Jr., "If you call us and say you want to refinance, we'll meet you in your parking lot at lunch."[2]

Thrift Institutions

thrift institutions Financial institutions (savings banks and savings and loan associations) that offer savings accounts and interest-bearing checking accounts.

Thrift institutions are financial institutions that offer savings accounts and interest-bearing checking accounts. They were formed specifically to encourage household saving and to make home mortgage loans. As of September 1993, the 1,950 thrift institutions in the United States had a total of about $1.13 trillion in loans and investments and $818 billion in deposits.

savings and loan associations (S&Ls) Type of thrift institution chartered by either the federal government or a state government.

Thrifts may be either a savings and loan association or a savings bank. Most (about 1,525) are **savings and loan associations (S&Ls)**. S&Ls can be chartered by either the federal government or a state government. About 30 percent are federally chartered. S&Ls were a major source of home mortgage loans in the United States until recently. Unfortunately, many are now in financial trouble, and their share of the home mortgage market has dropped from 30 to 15 percent.

savings banks State-chartered thrift institutions that tend to make fewer residential real estate loans and more stock and bond investments than S&Ls do.

Savings banks are state-chartered banks that operate much like savings and loan associations. There are about 425 savings banks. Most are located in the Northeast, where this form of bank originated in the 1880s. Compared with S&Ls, savings banks are less active in making residential real estate loans to individuals and more involved in investing in stocks and bonds. Nevertheless, savings banks and S&Ls face many of the same problems.

Credit Unions

credit unions Not-for-profit, member-owned financial cooperatives.

Credit unions are not-for-profit, member-owned financial cooperatives. Members usually have something in common—perhaps their employer, union, professional group, or church. Credit unions offer limited banking services, including loans and interest-bearing checking accounts. Their not-for-profit status makes them tax-exempt. Thus they can pay good interest rates on deposits and offer loans at favorable interest rates. There are about 13,380 credit unions in the United States with over 64 million members.

Before 1978, credit unions were not allowed to make loans with repayment periods of more than twelve years. But then Congress let them make thirty-year real estate loans and issue credit cards. Beginning in 1979, credit unions were permitted to pay interest on checking account balances. These new services have increased their membership and their assets. Credit union assets have been growing much faster than those of commercial banks. In 1992 alone, credit union assets rose 10 percent, compared to 1.9 percent for commercial banks and −9.7 percent for S&Ls. As of December 1992, total credit union assets were $250 billion. Many bankers strongly argue that credit unions now have an unfair advantage. The credit unions respond that they serve people whom banks and thrifts don't want to serve—the small customers who keep several hundred dollars in an account or request a small loan.

NONDEPOSITORY FINANCIAL INSTITUTIONS

Some financial institutions provide a few banking services but do not accept deposits. These nondepository financial institutions include insurance companies, pension funds, brokerage firms, and finance companies. They serve both individuals and businesses.

Insurance Companies

The nation's insurance companies are major funds suppliers. Policyholders make payments (called *premium*s) to buy financial protection from the insurance company. Insurance companies invest the premiums in stocks, bonds, real estate, business loans, and real estate loans for large projects. (The insurance industry is discussed in detail in Chapter 24.)

Pension Funds

Corporations, unions, and governments set aside large pools of money for later use in paying retirement benefits to their employees or members. These **pension funds** are managed by the employers or unions themselves or by outside managers, such as life insurance companies, commercial banks, and private investment advisers. Pension plan members receive a specified monthly payment when they reach a given age. After setting aside enough money to pay near-term benefits, pension funds invest the rest in stocks, bonds, or real estate. They often invest large sums in the stock of the employer. As of mid-1993, pension fund assets exceeded $4 trillion.

pension funds Pools of money set aside to pay retirement benefits to corporate or government employees or to union members.

Brokerage Firms

Brokerage firms are financial organizations that buy and sell securities (stocks and bonds) and provide related advice to clients. During the past ten years, many brokerage firms have also added some banking services. They may offer clients a combined checking and savings account with a high interest rate and also make loans, backed by securities, to clients. (Chapter 21 explains the activities of brokerage firms in more detail.)

brokerage firms Financial organizations that buy and sell securities and provide related advice.

Finance Companies

finance companies
Financial institutions that make short-term loans for which the borrower puts up tangible assets as security.

Finance companies make short-term loans for which the borrower puts up tangible assets (such as an automobile, inventory, machinery, or property) as security. They often make loans to people or businesses that can not get credit elsewhere. To compensate for the extra risk, finance companies usually charge higher interest rates than banks do. *Consumer finance companies* make loans to individuals. Beneficial Corp. and Household International are two of the largest consumer finance companies. *Commercial finance companies*, such as Commercial Investors Trust and General Electric Credit Corp., make loans to promising new businesses with no track record and to firms that are unable to get more bank credit.

Concept Check

- Describe the three main participants in the U.S. financial system. How does financial intermediation work?
- Distinguish among the three types of depository financial institutions.
- List the four main types of nondepository financial institutions.

DEVELOPMENT OF THE U.S. BANKING SYSTEM

During the nineteenth century, banking was regulated very little. Banks' business practices were unsound, and many failed. In 1907, bank failures caused a run on the banks by depositors who wanted to withdraw their money. These runs created cash shortages and caused many other banks to fail. The Panic of 1907 was so severe that Congress had to act. In 1913 it created the Federal Reserve System (the Fed) to correct some of the industry's weaknesses. For most of its history, the country's banking system had been decentralized. The public was afraid of having one large central bank. So the Federal Reserve System was set up as a network of twelve regional banks supervised by the Federal Reserve Board. All banks with national charters had to become members of the system. Membership was optional for state-chartered banks. The Federal Reserve System was granted sole power to issue money.

THE GREAT DEPRESSION AND BANKING REFORM

The banking system worked fairly well from the establishment of the Fed in 1913 until the 1929 stock market crash and the Great Depression that followed. The business failures caused by these events resulted in major cash shortages as people rushed to withdraw their money from the banks. Many cash-starved banks failed because the Fed did not, as expected, lend money to them. The government's actions to prevent bank failures were ineffective. In the next two years 5,000 banks, about 20 percent of the total, failed.

President Franklin D. Roosevelt made strengthening the banking system his first priority. As soon as he took office in 1933, he declared a bank holiday. All the banks were closed for a week so corrective action could be taken.

The Banking Act of 1933 gave the Fed power to regulate banks and reform the banking system. Its most important provision was creation of the Federal Deposit Insurance Corporation (FDIC) to insure deposits in commercial banks. The Federal Savings and Loan Insurance Corporation (FSLIC) was established in 1934 to insure customer deposits at savings and loan associations. The 1933 act also gave the Fed authority to tell banks how much money to keep in reserve, to ban interest on demand deposits, to regulate the interest rates on time deposits, and to keep banks from investing in specified types of securities.

Banking remained a highly controlled industry until the 1980s. Commercial banks, which got most of their funds from demand deposits, focused on short-term lending. Thrift institutions, which had more stable savings account deposits, made mostly long-term real estate loans.

DEREGULATION

During the 1950s and 1960s, inflation was low and interest rates were fairly stable. The Fed limited the interest rates that commercial banks and thrift institutions could pay to savers, so there was no real competition among depository institutions. When inflation and interest rates climbed during the 1970s, however, banks and thrifts could not raise interest rates enough to attract savings. People turned to money market accounts, created by stock brokerage firms like Merrill Lynch. The interest rates on these accounts were not restricted. People withdrew their savings from banks and put them into these new accounts. To meet their needs, many banks had to replace these funds by borrowing at rates higher than those they were earning on their loans. The rules were even more troublesome for thrifts, whose long-term loans were at fixed rates well below the current interest rates.

Major legislation was passed in 1980 and 1982 in response to this crisis. The Depository Institutions Deregulation and Monetary Control Act (DIDMCA) of 1980 was the most significant banking legislation since the 1930s. It wiped out interest rate ceilings. It allowed all depository institutions to pay interest on checking accounts and gave thrifts more freedom to make consumer and commercial loans. Legislation passed in 1982 allowed thrifts to do even more and permitted all depository institutions to offer money market accounts. As a result, most of the distinctions among commercial banks, S&Ls, and other financial institutions were eliminated. Competition intensified. The effect of such deregulation on the banking industry is discussed later in the chapter.

- Describe the major banking reforms of the 1930s.
- Why was banking deregulated in the early 1980s? How did major legislation deregulate the industry?

■ Competition among banks, savings and loans, and other financial institutions increased after the deregulation legislation of the 1980s. All forms of financial institutions began offering a wide array of new services in order to attract more customers.

THE U.S. COMMERCIAL BANKING SYSTEM

5

bank charter License from either the federal government or a state government that lets a bank do business.

national bank Bank chartered by the U.S. Treasury Department.

Commercial banks are an important part of our financial system. In the United States, as in other private enterprise systems, commercial banks are corporations owned and operated by individuals or other corporations. To do business, they must get a **bank charter**, an operating license, from either the federal government or a state government. Thus commercial banks in the United States can be either national or state banks.

National banks are chartered by the Comptroller of the Currency, who is part of the U.S. Treasury Department. These banks must belong to the Federal Reserve System and must carry FDIC insurance on their deposits. About a third of all commercial banks are national banks. They account for about 60 percent of all banking deposits.

state bank Bank chartered by the state in which it is based.

About two-thirds of all U.S. commercial banks are chartered by the state in which they are based. From the customer's viewpoint, **state banks** differ little from national banks. Most are smaller than national banks. Together, state banks account for about 40 percent of total bank deposits. State banks are not required to belong to the Federal Reserve System and are generally less closely regulated than national banks.

The dual banking system of federal and state charters is different from the systems found in other countries. In most, banks are chartered only by the national government. These countries have only a few large banks. For instance, Canada has six nationwide banks and Great Britain five, each with many offices throughout the country. The United States, in contrast, has more than 11,700 commercial banks. The ten largest U.S. commercial banks account for only 25 percent of banking industry deposits.[3]

One reason for the large number of U.S. banks is the restrictions on bank *branches*. The states control the number and type of branches allowed. Interstate branching is banned by federal law. The **bank holding company**, a corporation that owns two or more different banks, was developed to get around this restriction. Today all states except Hawaii allow holding companies to own banks across state lines. In addition, holding companies can provide such services as credit cards, leasing, and financial advice, which banks cannot offer. All major banks are now owned by holding companies. Congress is currently considering proposals to end the prohibition on interstate banking.

bank holding company Corporation that owns two or more different banks, usually allowed to cross state lines to do business.

DEPOSITS

Most banks get a large part of their funds from customer deposits. Customers can withdraw their deposits according to the terms of the specific account in which they are held. The two broad types of deposits are checking accounts and time deposit accounts.

Checking Accounts

Checking accounts are familiar to most people. At any time, depositors can withdraw any amount of funds up to the amount on deposit. Money kept in a checking account is called a *demand deposit*. A special type of checking account, the **negotiated order of withdrawal (NOW) account**, pays interest. These popular accounts can be held by individuals but not by businesses.

negotiated order of withdrawal (NOW) account Interest-bearing checking account that can be held by individuals, but not businesses, and that is subject to service fees and minimum balance requirements.

Most banks charge service fees, such as monthly fees and per-check charges, on checking accounts and NOW accounts. They may also require a minimum balance.

Time Deposits

Time deposits are savings accounts that pay interest. Savings accounts, also called passbook accounts, do not have check-writing privileges. Before 1986, the maximum legal interest rate on savings accounts was 5.5 percent per year. Since then, each financial institution has been allowed to pay whatever rate it chooses. Technically, money cannot be withdrawn on demand from time deposits, but banks usually allow periodic withdrawals from passbook accounts.

money market deposit accounts Savings accounts that allow limited check writing, earn interest at market rates, and are subject to minimum balance requirements.

certificates of deposit (CDs) Time deposits that pay a specified interest rate in exchange for leaving a given amount on deposit for a specified period.

Money market deposit accounts were created in 1982 as part of the government deregulation of financial institutions. They are savings accounts on which the interest rate is set at market rates. They allow limited check-writing privileges (three checks per month). Often they require a minimum starting deposit of about $2,500.

Certificates of deposit (CDs) promise to pay a specified interest rate in exchange for a given amount left on deposit for a specified period. CDs are popular with people who are willing to trade access to their money for a certain time in exchange for an interest rate as much as 2 percent higher than that paid on regular savings accounts.

LOANS AND INVESTMENTS

Banks use their customers' deposits to make loans and investments. The income from them is then used to pay interest to depositors, operating expenses, and taxes. The income left after expenses and taxes is the bank's profit, which may be distributed to stockholders as dividends or reinvested in the bank.

The two categories of loans made by commercial banks are consumer and business loans. *Consumer loans* are loans to individuals. They may be short-term (for under a year) or long-term (for over a year). Consumer loans are made to finance the purchase of a home, car, or other expensive item or to pay for home improvements. *Business loans* give firms both short- and long-term financing to support operations and buy assets. Business loans are discussed further in Chapter 22.

Recently federal regulators have put pressure on banks to increase community development loans to minority and low-income customers. In late 1993 the Clinton Administration proposed regulations that encourage banks to provide more banking services, make more loans, and invest funds in low-income rural and urban communities.[4] The number of investigations of possible discriminatory bank lending practices has also increased. Regulators are using their power to approve regulations to force banks to expand their loans to these groups. For example, in November 1993 the Federal Reserve Board blocked Shawmut National Corp.'s acquisition of a small New Hampshire bank. The Justice Department charged that Shawmut had discriminated against minorities in its mortgage lending. Shawmut settled the case by setting up a $960,000 special fund to compensate those denied mortgages.[5]

MONEY CREATION BY BANKS

When banks make loans, they actually create new money. An example can show how this process works. Say that Susan Wilson deposits $5,000 in a checking account at Homestate National Bank. The bank is allowed to lend this money to someone else, less the portion it must keep on reserve. Assuming the bank must reserve 15 percent of its deposits,

Exhibit 20-4
Example of the Money
Creation Process

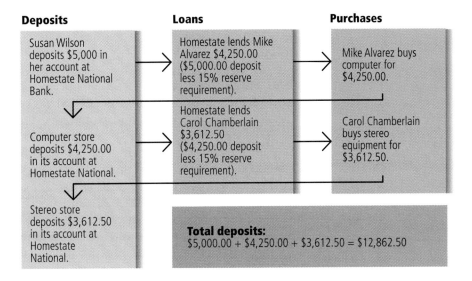

Deposits	Loans	Purchases
Susan Wilson deposits $5,000 in her account at Homestate National Bank.	Homestate lends Mike Alvarez $4,250.00 ($5,000.00 deposit less 15% reserve requirement).	Mike Alvarez buys computer for $4,250.00.
Computer store deposits $4,250.00 in its account at Homestate National.	Homestate lends Carol Chamberlain $3,612.50 ($4,250.00 deposit less 15% reserve requirement).	Carol Chamberlain buys stereo equipment for $3,612.50.
Stereo store deposits $3,612.50 in its account at Homestate National.	**Total deposits:** $5,000.00 + $4,250.00 + $3,612.50 = $12,862.50	

$750 would be held in reserve ($5,000 × 15%). The remaining $4,250 ($5,000 − $750) could be lent to borrowers.

At about the same time, Mike Alvarez applies to the bank for a $4,250 loan to buy a computer for his accounting firm. The bank approves his loan and sets up an account from which he can withdraw the loan proceeds, even though he hasn't deposited any money into the account. In effect, the bank has created a $4,250 demand deposit. Remember that demand deposits are considered part of the money supply.

The store where Mike buys the computer deposits the $4,250 it gets from Mike in its account at Homestate National (or some other bank). The bank can lend 85 percent (and keep 15 percent in reserve), or $3,612.50 ($4,250 × 85%). The whole process could continue. But let's stop at this point. Already Susan Wilson's $5,000 deposit has more than doubled the total value of demand deposits ($5,000.00 + $4,250.00 + $3,612.50 = $12,862.50). This example of money creation is summarized in Exhibit 20-4.

OTHER FINANCIAL SERVICES

Commercial banks offer many other financial services, including money transfer, electronic funds transfer, safety deposit boxes, insurance, investment brokerage, and trust services. Many of these services are also offered by other financial institutions.

Money Transfer

Banks routinely wire funds to other banks throughout the United States and the world. Say that Sara D'Angelo owns a bicycle shop in Omaha, Nebraska. A bicycle wholesaler in New York just informed her that some new French bikes are available at a 30 percent discount from the wholesale price. To get this price, Sara must have the cash in New York by tomorrow. All she has to do is tell her bank to wire the funds from her account to her supplier's account in a New York bank. Such a transfer of funds takes only minutes and usually costs less than $20. Wire transfers are used often by businesses. They are a safe, quick, efficient way to transfer funds.

Electronic Funds Transfer

electronic funds transfer systems (EFTS) Networks of telephone lines and computers that help make financial transactions.

Electronic funds transfer systems (EFTS) make financial transactions with the aid of telephone lines and computers. For instance, a company can use EFTS to deposit its employees' pay directly into their personal bank accounts. Then the company doesn't need to prepare and process checks, and the employees don't need to deposit them. Another form of EFTS uses specially coded plastic cards to transfer cash. Many people now find them more convenient than cash and checks. EFTS cards include credit cards, automated teller machine cards, and debit cards.

automated teller machine (ATM) Electronic banking machine that allows customers to make deposits, withdrawals, and other transactions around the clock, seven days a week.

Suppose you're studying late and you need cash at 11 p.m. for a pizza. Although no bank is open, you can get money you need without borrowing it from friends. You can use an **automated teller machine (ATM)** to withdraw funds from your account. ATMs let customers make deposits, withdrawals, and transactions like loan payments twenty-four hours a day, seven days a week. Most banks have ATMs outside their offices. Some banks put freestanding ATMs in shopping malls, airports, grocery stores, and other high-traffic areas. Because ATMs can perform many of the tasks of human tellers at a much lower cost, some banks are replacing branches with ATMs.

debit cards Plastic cards used to transfer funds from a customer's bank account directly to a merchant's account in payment for goods and services.

Debit cards are another type of EFTS service. They involve the use of *point-of-sale (POS) machines,* electronic machines located at sales outlets that let customers use debit cards to pay for their purchases. With a debit card, funds are transferred from a customer's bank account directly to the merchant's account. The cards used in POS terminals are called debit cards because they cause the money to be removed—or debited—from the customer's account.

Two services that are gaining in popularity are banking at home via telephone and computer. Many routine transactions, such as funds transfer and balance inquiries, can be handled by phone. Any microcomputer can be linked to the bank's computer or an on-line service such as Prodigy, Compu-Serve, or America On-Line using a modem, a device that connects a computer to a telephone. The customer can then pay bills or transfer funds from one account to another.

Other Services

Many banks offer other services to their customers. For instance, all banks have safety deposit boxes that customers can rent for storing valuables they do not wish to keep at home. Through loan officers, banks can also be a source of financial advice. Many banks offer insurance policies that repay loans if the borrower dies or is disabled. Travel, accident, life, and health insurance is often offered through bank cards and other types of credit cards. Some large banks also offer investment brokerage services. Finally, bank *trust departments* manage personal investments or corporate pension funds for a fee. Trust officers also offer estate- and tax-planning services.

Concept Check

- How do national and state banks differ? Discuss why bank holding companies are formed.
- Differentiate among the various types of bank deposits.
- What role do loans and investments play in commercial banks? Describe the money creation process.
- What nondeposit financial services are offered by commercial banks?

THE FEDERAL RESERVE SYSTEM

6 When it was created in 1913, the Federal Reserve System's mission was to control the money supply, to act as a borrowing source for banks, to hold the deposits of member banks, and to supervise banking practices. The Fed's activities have since been broadened. Today the Fed is the most powerful financial institution in the United States.

STRUCTURE OF THE FED

The Federal Reserve System consists of twelve district banks, each located in a major U.S. city. Each has its own president and board of directors, and most have one or two branches. Exhibit 20-5 shows the Federal Reserve

■ Exhibit 20-5
Federal Reserve Districts

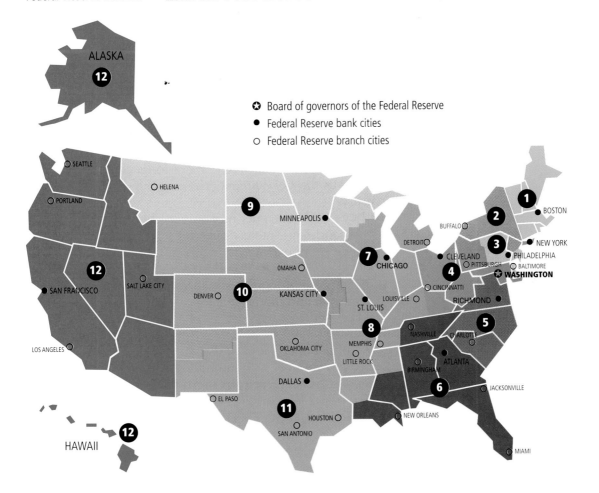

Board of governors of the Federal Reserve
Federal Reserve bank cities
Federal Reserve branch cities

districts and the locations of their branches. All national banks must be members of the Fed. State banks can belong to the Fed if they choose. There are about 6,000 member banks in the Fed system.

The overall operations of the Fed are coordinated by its seven-member Board of Governors, headquartered in Washington, D.C. Each member is appointed to a fourteen-year term by the President of the United States and confirmed by the Senate. Yet the Fed is an independent agency, controlled neither by the President nor by Congress. Instead, they tend to work with the Fed's Board of Governors to set monetary policy—that is, to make decisions about controlling the money supply in order to promote economic growth and stability. The district bank boards focus on regional policy issues.

Among the Fed's activities are these four key functions: carrying out monetary policy, setting rules on credit, distributing currency, and making check clearing easier.

CARRYING OUT MONETARY POLICY

The most important function of the Fed is carrying out monetary policy. The Fed uses its power to change the money supply to control inflation and interest rates, increase employment, and prompt economic activity. To manage the money supply, the Fed has three tools: open market operations, reserve requirements, and the discount rate. Exhibit 20-6 summarizes the short-run effects of these tools on the economy.

Open Market Operations

open market operations Purchase and sale of U.S. government bonds by the Federal Reserve.

Open market operations refers to the purchase and sale of U.S. government bonds by the Fed. It is the most frequently used of the Fed's tools. The U.S. Treasury issues bonds to get the extra money needed to run the government (if taxes and other revenues aren't enough). In effect, Treasury bonds are long-term loans (five years or longer) made by businesses and individuals to the government. The Fed buys and sells these bonds for the Treasury.

When the Fed buys bonds, it puts money into the economy. Banks have more money to lend, and interest rates fall. The declining interest rates generally stimulate economic activity. The opposite occurs when the Fed sells government bonds on behalf of the Treasury. It takes money out of the economy. The Treasury competes with other borrowers, such as consumers and businesses, and therefore interest rates go up.

Reserve Requirements

reserve requirement Percentage of deposits that member banks of the Federal Reserve must hold in reserve.

Fed member banks (all national banks and some state banks) must hold some of their deposits in reserve, without putting them to work in loans or other investments. This **reserve requirement** now ranges from 3 to 10 percent on different types of deposits. Reserves can be held either in cash at the bank or in an account at the Federal Reserve bank in the member bank's district.

When the Fed raises the reserve requirement, banks must hold larger reserves. Then they have less money to lend. Interest rates rise, and eco-

Tool	Action	Effect on money supply	Effect on interest rates	Effect on economic activity
Open market operations	Buy government bonds	Increases	Lowers	Increases
	Sell government bonds	Decreases	Raises	Slows
Reserve requirements	Raise reserve requirements	Decreases	Raises	Slows
	Lower reserve requirements	Increases	Lowers	Increases
Discount rate	Raise discount rate	Decreases	Raises	Slows
	Lower discount rate	Increases	Lowers	Increases

■ **Exhibit 20-6**
The Fed's Monetary Policy Tools and Their Effects

nomic activity slows down. Lowering the reserve requirement makes more money available for loans. As a result, interest rates generally fall, stimulating economic activity.

The Fed seldom changes reserve requirements. In April 1992 it lowered the reserve requirement from 12 to 10 percent for deposits over $46.8 million. By doing so, it signaled its concern that the pace of economic recovery was too slow. By freeing up reserves, it hoped to stimulate the economy by increasing lending and lowering interest rates.

Discount Rate

discount rate Interest rate the Federal Reserve charges member banks to borrow from it.

The Fed is called the "banker's bank" because it lends money to banks that need it. The **discount rate** is the interest rate that the Fed charges member banks. When the discount rate is less than the cost of other sources of funds (such as certificates of deposit), commercial banks borrow from the Fed and then lend the funds at a higher rate to customers. The banks profit from the *spread,* or difference, between the rate charged their customers and the rate paid the Fed.

Changes in the discount rate usually produce changes in the interest rate that banks charge their customers. When the Fed raises the discount rate, interest rates on bank loans rise. Economic growth slows. Lowering the discount rate reduces interest rates on bank loans and encourages economic growth. For example, trying to stimulate a weak economy, the Fed began reducing the discount rate in December 1990, when it lowered the rate from 7 percent to 6.5 percent. This was the first cut in the discount rate since August 1986. It continued reducing the rate to 3 percent in July 1992 but raised it to 3.5 percent in May 1994.

federal funds Excess funds in a bank's Federal Reserve account that may be loaned for a short term to other banks.

federal funds rate Interest rate charged on the loan of federal funds.

Banks often have excess funds in their reserve account at the Fed. Through the Fed, they can loan these funds for a short term—typically overnight—to other banks. These interbank loans are called **federal funds**. The rate charged on them is the **federal funds rate**. It varies with supply and demand, which are directly affected by the Fed's actions. The federal funds rate increases when the demand for funds is greater than the supply of them. It falls when the supply of funds is greater than demand for them. In February and March 1994, the Fed raised the federal funds rate in two steps from 3 to 3.50 percent, ending five years of falling short-term interest rates. As a result, other short-term rates moved upward. The Fed's move to tighten monetary policy was designed to curb inflation.

SETTING RULES ON CREDIT

selective credit controls Power of the Federal Reserve to regulate credit terms on certain types of loans made by banks and other institutions.

The Fed also controls credit terms on some loans made by banks and other lending institutions. This power, called **selective credit controls**, includes consumer credit rules and margin requirements.

Consumer credit rules say what the minimum down payments and maximum repayment periods have to be on consumer loans. Although the Fed hasn't used these rules recently, it has the power to use them to restrict or stimulate consumer credit purchases.

margin requirements Minimum percentage of the value of securities that must be paid in cash by an investor, as determined by the Federal Reserve.

Margin requirements specify the minimum amount of cash an investor must put up to buy securities. The rest of the purchase can be financed through borrowing from a bank or brokerage firm. Say the margin requirement is 50 percent and an investor buys $10,000 worth of stock. The person must put up $5,000 ($10,000 × 50%) in cash. He or she can borrow the balance of $5,000 ($10,000 − $5,000). When the Fed wants to stimulate the securities markets, it lowers the margin requirement. A lower margin requirement lets an investor buy more securities on margin with a given amount of money. When the Fed wants to slow securities trading, it raises the margin requirement. A higher margin requirement means the investor can buy fewer securities on margin with a given amount of money. The Fed does not change this rate often. It has remained at its current level of 50 percent since the late 1960s.

DISTRIBUTING CURRENCY

The Fed distributes to banks the coins minted and the paper money printed by the U.S. Treasury. Almost all paper money is in the form of Federal Reserve notes, which are basically IOUs of the Fed. If you look at a dollar bill, you'll see the words "Federal Reserve Note." The large letter seal on the left indicates which Federal Reserve Bank issued it. Bills bearing a D seal are issued by the Federal Reserve Bank of Cleveland. Those with an L seal are issued by the San Francisco Fed.

MAKING CHECK CLEARING EASIER

Another important task of the Fed is helping banks clear checks. The Fed's check-clearing system lets banks quickly convert checks drawn on other banks—even distant ones—into cash. Checks drawn on banks within the same Fed district are handled locally and reported to the Fed, which transfers funds between the banks on paper. The process is a little more complex for checks drawn on banks outside a bank's Fed district.

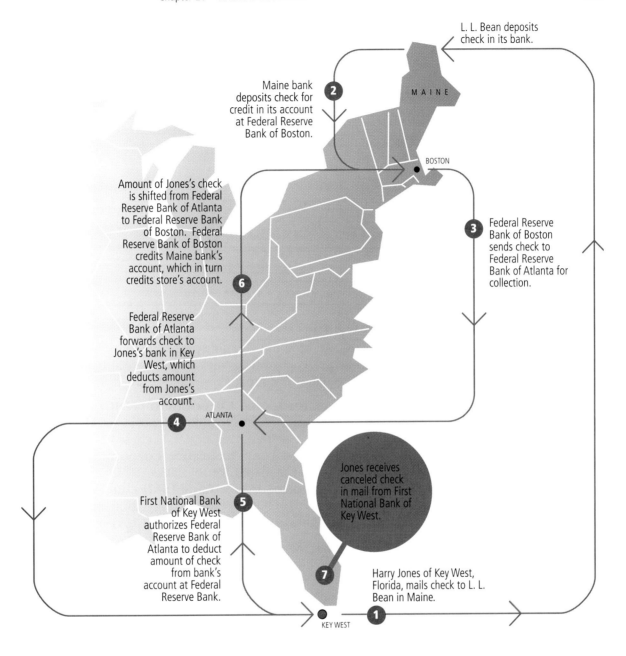

L. L. Bean deposits check in its bank.

2 Maine bank deposits check for credit in its account at Federal Reserve Bank of Boston.

MAINE

BOSTON

3 Federal Reserve Bank of Boston sends check to Federal Reserve Bank of Atlanta for collection.

6 Amount of Jones's check is shifted from Federal Reserve Bank of Atlanta to Federal Reserve Bank of Boston. Federal Reserve Bank of Boston credits Maine bank's account, which in turn credits store's account.

Federal Reserve Bank of Atlanta forwards check to Jones's bank in Key West, which deducts amount from Jones's account.

ATLANTA

4

5 First National Bank of Key West authorizes Federal Reserve Bank of Atlanta to deduct amount of check from bank's account at Federal Reserve Bank.

7 Jones receives canceled check in mail from First National Bank of Key West.

Harry Jones of Key West, Florida, mails check to L. L. Bean in Maine.

1

KEY WEST

■ **Exhibit 20-7**
The Check-Clearing Process

float Advantage gained from the time it takes a check to clear and the amount be withdrawn from the check writer's account.

To illustrate, imagine that Harry Jones of Key West, Florida, has ordered cold-weather gear from L. L. Bean in Maine. Harry encloses a check drawn on his account at the First National Bank of Key West. Exhibit 20-7 shows how the check is cleared.

The time between when the check is written and when the funds are actually deducted from the check writer's account provides float. **Float** is the advantage gained from the time it takes a check to clear and the amount be withdrawn from the check writer's account. Many firms purposely open accounts at banks around the country that are known to have long check-clearing times. By "playing the float," they can keep their funds invested for several extra days. To reduce float, in 1988 the Fed established maximum check-clearing times. Cashier's checks, certified checks, government checks, and checks written on accounts at institutions in the same city in which they are deposited must clear on the next business day. Checks within the same Federal Reserve check-processing region must clear within three business days. Checks drawn on banks in other Fed districts must clear within five or seven business days, depending on the distance between the districts.

Concept Check

- Describe the structure and key duties of the Federal Reserve System.
- Describe the tools used by the Fed to manage the money supply.
- What are the Fed's selective credit controls?
- How are checks cleared through the Fed?

INSURING BANK DEPOSITS

 The many bank failures during the Great Depression led to the formation of insurance corporations to cover deposits in commercial banks, thrifts, and credit unions. The major insurance corporations are:

- The **Federal Deposit Insurance Corporation (FDIC)**, the largest of the insurance corporations, insures the deposits of commercial banks.
- The **Federal Savings and Loan Insurance Corporation (FSLIC)** protected S&Ls until it went bankrupt in 1988.
- The **Savings Association Insurance Fund (SAIF)**, under control of the FDIC, took over the FSLIC's role of insuring thrift institutions.
- The **National Credit Union Administration (NCUA)** insures credit union deposits.

Federal Deposit Insurance Corporation (FDIC) Corporation established in 1933 to insure the deposits of commercial banks.

Federal Savings and Loan Insurance Corporation (FSLIC) Corporation that insured the deposits of savings and loan associations from 1934 to 1988, when it went bankrupt.

Savings Association Insurance Fund (SAIF) Corporation established after the demise of the FSLIC to insure thrift institutions.

National Credit Union Administration (NCUA) Corporation established in 1934 to insure credit union deposits.

ROLE OF THE FDIC

The FDIC is an independent, quasi-public corporation. It is backed by the full faith and credit of the United States government. It insures bank deposits against loss if a bank fails and also regulates certain banking practices. All member banks in the Federal Reserve System must be insured by the FDIC. In fact, about 98 percent of all commercial banks, accounting for 99.5 percent of all commercial bank deposits, belong to the FDIC.

The ceiling on insured deposits is currently $100,000 per account. The insurance premiums, which are a fixed percentage of the bank's domestic deposits, are paid by each insured bank. Until mid-1992, all banks paid the same premium rate, regardless of their risk of failure. At that time, as a result of the large number of bank failures, the FDIC raised its premiums. It also decided to charge weaker banks higher premiums. Some

■ In the classic movie *It's a Wonderful Life,* the bank owned by Jimmy Stewart misplaces some of its clients' funds. Today, such losses would be covered by the Federal Deposit Insurance Corporation, which protects depositors' accounts and regulates certain bank practices.

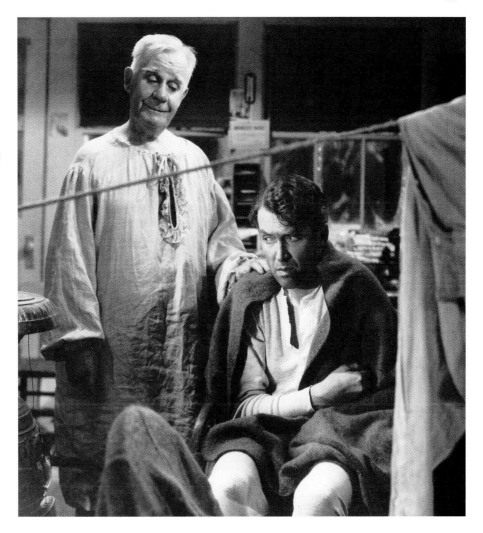

experts argue that some banks take too much risk because they view deposit insurance as a safety net for their depositors. This view is thought to have contributed to the increase in bank and thrift failures.

ENFORCEMENT BY THE FDIC

The FDIC sets guidelines for banks and then reviews the financial records and management practices of member banks at least once a year. These reviews are performed by **bank examiners**, whose visits are unannounced. Bank examiners rate banks on their compliance with banking regulations and their overall financial condition. They focus on loan quality, management practices, earnings, liquidity, and whether the bank has enough capital (equity) to safely support its activities.

When bank examiners conclude that a bank has serious financial problems, the FDIC can take one or more possible courses of action. It can

bank examiners Employees of the FDIC who review the financial records and management practices of member banks at least once a year to assure compliance with FDIC rules.

lend money to the bank, recommend that the bank merge with a stronger bank, require the bank to use new management practices or replace management, buy loans from the bank, or provide extra equity capital to the bank. The FDIC may even cover all deposits at a troubled bank, including those over $100,000, to restore the public's confidence in the financial system.

When a bank fails, the FDIC usually tries to find a stronger bank to acquire it. Typically the FDIC sets up a "bridge bank" to operate the failed bank until the acquirer takes over. If the FDIC can't find a buyer for the failed bank, it sells its assets and returns deposits to their owners, up to the amount of insurance.

For example, when the Bank of New England failed in 1991, the FDIC moved quickly to take control, set up bridge banks for each of its subsidiaries, and take bids for the bank's assets from interested banks throughout the United States. It covered depositors' funds in full, going above the $100,000 insurance limit. The FDIC continued to oversee operations until Fleet Financial acquired Bank of New England in 1992.

Concept Check
- What is the FDIC, and what are its responsibilities?
- What actions can the FDIC take to help financially troubled banks?

CHANGES IN THE BANKING INDUSTRY

8 The banking industry was once a highly protected, conservative industry offering limited services. Now deregulation allows thrift institutions and commercial banks to offer many new products and services. But it also puts them in direct competition with other financial institutions. This change has brought both opportunities and problems.

THE S&L CRISIS

The first crisis in the banking industry hit the S&Ls. It was caused primarily by high interest rates, deregulation, and poor economic conditions. Prior to 1980, S&Ls focused on long-term, fixed-rate home mortgage loans. As interest rates climbed during the 1970s and early 1980s, to attract deposits the S&Ls had to offer higher interest rates on accounts than they earned on existing loans. Congress then deregulated the thrifts, allowing them to make other types of loans to improve profitability. Many already-troubled banks made risky real estate loans and invested in high-yield, high-risk "junk bonds," many of which couldn't be repaid. As a result of high interest rates, poor management, erosion of real estate values by the recession, inadequate regulation, and fraudulent and unethical acts of officers of some major S&Ls, about 2,300 thrifts—50 percent of the total—failed. The agency that insured S&L deposits, the Federal Savings and Loan Insurance Corporation (FSLIC), ran out of funds in 1988 and was replaced by the Savings Association Insurance Fund (SAIF) under control of the FDIC.

To bail out the S&L industry, Congress created two new agencies. One, the Office of Thrift Supervision (OTS), is responsible for regulating the industry. The other, the Resolution Trust Company (RTC), took over more than 700 insolvent thrifts, protected their deposits, and sold the real estate and other assets of these failed institutions. From 1989 to 1993, the RTC sold $350 billion in assets of insolvent thrifts. It has until 1996 to sell the remaining assets under its control. The cost to taxpayers of the massive S&L bailout was estimated at about $200 billion through 1993. Many experts have argued that swift action in the mid-1980s to close insolvent thrifts could have reduced the cost of the bailout to as little as $15 billion.[6]

PROBLEMS IN COMMERCIAL BANKING

In the early 1990s, the commercial banking industry was suffering from many of the same problems that had plagued the thrift industry during the 1980s. The number of bank failures climbed steadily from 1981 through 1990. Profits were squeezed as banks, like S&Ls, had to offer money market accounts at rates that were not much lower than the rates charged on loans. In addition, demand for business loans—a major source of income—dropped as corporations used other, lower-cost sources of funding.

To make up for the decline in business loans, banks began lending to riskier customers, such as developing nations, to managers and companies involved in buying big corporations, and to owners of commercial real estate. The recession in the early 1990s severely depressed property values, leaving many of the nation's largest banks with problem real estate loans. Between 1980 and 1992, about 1,460 commercial banks—about 10 percent of the total—failed. The FDIC stepped in to either arrange for an acquisition by a stronger bank or liquidate the bank and pay depositors directly.

Both large and small banks were affected by the problems in the banking industry. Large banks had too many poor real estate, corporate, and foreign loans. Small banks felt the pinch as many of their depositors transferred funds to larger financial institutions, which they considered too large to fail. Many could not survive the competition and were bought by healthy larger banks that wanted to build market share.

In 1992, the commercial banking industry began to recover. Bank profits rose to record levels. This was due primarily to the large difference between the short-term interest rates banks paid for borrowed funds and to depositors and the higher rates they earned on loans and investments. Other factors contributing to increased profitability were cost-cutting programs, including employee layoffs, and fewer bad loans.[7] Exhibit 20-8 shows that bank failures in 1993 reached a twelve-year low.

Despite these improvements, banks will have to change to stay profitable in the increasingly competitive financial services marketplace. A later section of the chapter discusses some strategies for the future.

■ **Exhibit 20-8**
Number of bank failures,
1984–1993
Source: Federal Deposit Insurance Corp.

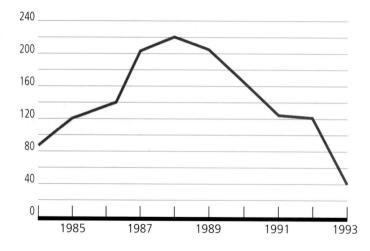

INTERNATIONAL BANKING

As noted in Chapters 2 and 4, the financial marketplace has become international in scope. Money routinely flows across international borders. Multinational corporations need many special banking services, including foreign currency exchange. Starting in the mid-1960s, American banks expanded into overseas markets by opening offices in Europe, Latin America, and the Far East. These banks could provide better customer service, and they had access to more sources of funding.

However, competing against foreign banks was hard. Foreign banks have fewer regulations, making it easier for them to undercut U.S. banks on pricing of loans and services to multinational corporations and governments. From 1983 to 1988, Japanese banks increased their share of international loans from 20 percent to 40 percent, while U.S. banks' market share dropped from 27 percent to 15 percent.

By mid-1993, however, non-U.S. banks were cutting back on their international loans. The Japanese banks' share of the world's business loans dropped to 27 percent.[8] Although Japanese banks are the world's largest, they were among the weakest and least profitable of the world's major banks. This demonstrates the danger of using size as a measure of a bank's quality and safety. Better indicators of bank strength are profitability and a bank's capital ratio (the proportion of a bank's capital, or equity, to its assets). Capital provides a cash cushion to cover losses. A capital ratio over 5 percent is considered adequate. No Japanese bank ranked among the top in either of these categories. The worldwide recession hit both Japanese and European banks very hard. Many reported rising losses from corporate and real estate loans due to the extended economic slowdown. At the same time, U.S. banks were coming out of their crisis, helped by reductions in short-term interest rates. Although Citibank (#22) and BankAmerica (#30) are the only U.S. banks ranked among the top 30 international banks based on size, U.S. banks fared well on the more important capital and profitability ratios.[9]

U.S. banks are expanding their role internationally beyond loans and trade-related services (such as helping international businesses buy materials and borrow and invest money). For example, Citibank has built a 303-branch network in Germany that serves 2.3 million customers. It has established itself as a major force in the retail market, providing better customer service and convenience than the German banks. It introduced telephone banking in 1989, installed many ATMs, and expanded its credit card customer base.[10] Other U.S. banks are hoping to take advantage of their better technological knowledge and information systems to sell more financial services around the world.

THE FUTURE OF BANKING

Although banking has recovered from the crises of the late 1980s and early 1990s, it faces long-term challenges during the 1990s. The profits of 1992 and 1993 resulted mainly from low interest rates. Many fundamental problems still plague the industry. And banks will find that it is not as easy to earn profits if interest rates rise.

A major problem is the declining demand for bank products and services. Banks have lost consumer deposits to mutual funds and business loans to nondepository financial institutions. For example, Merrill Lynch has a business financial services unit with over 3,000 customers and $800 million in loans. And, overall loan demand dropped during the recession, when companies tried to avoid borrowing. However, banks were also more cautious and turned down many loan requests, especially from small businesses. These borrowers, traditionally a good source of bank profits, found other sources eager to make loans. To combat this situation, banks are offering a wider range of services and are pursuing mergers and interstate banking. Regulatory reform is another way to strengthen the industry.[11]

Expansion of Banking Services

One way many banks hope to increase profits is to provide a broader range of services to their customers. A lending relationship can open the door to the sale of other, more lucrative products such as cash management and international trade services. This was the strategic objective behind Bank of America's acquisition of Chicago-based Continental Bank. Bank of America gained access to Continental's many midwestern corporate customers, to whom it can sell a variety of financial products and services, in addition to lending and deposit services. It also plans to use technological advances to help its customers operate more efficiently.[12]

Some banks are looking for niche markets and tailoring their services to serve those customers better. Bankers Trust, a large New York bank, is concentrating on corporate rather than retail customers. Other banks are actively courting small business customers again, as the Small Business Trends box shows.

From Little Acorns Grow . . . Big Loans

Denise Rhone and Carrie Jones, the owners of Sparkle Cleaning Associates in Natick, Massachusetts, decided in 1992 that they wanted to expand their business. They applied for a $50,000 loan at five banks, all of which turned them down. Explained Ms. Rhone, "We had no collateral that banks were interested in." Despite this obstacle, the sixth bank the pair approached, Bank of Boston, gave them their loan. The company was then able to buy carpet-shampoo machines, trucks, and a computer. As a result, Sparkle Cleaning won larger corporate contracts, increased its staff from 25 to 65 employees, and saw its revenues rise to $1 million in 1993.

Unlike some banks, which are concentrating on increasing their consumer loans, Bank of Boston is making an aggressive push into small business lending by offering attractive interest rates and flexible lending terms that competitors aren't matching. The bank is basing this unorthodox strategy on the theory that the economy will improve in the mid-1990s, creating an environment in which small businesses can thrive. It is counting on these small-business customers to generate income from other services such as checking and savings accounts, and it believes that most will remain loyal to the bank as they expand their companies.

This strategy is a major change for Bank of Boston, which like many New England banks was devastated by bad real-estate loans in the late 1980s. These bad loan decisions resulted in regulatory constraints and a reluctance to lend money. But lately bank regulators have begun to encourage other lenders to follow in Bank of Boston's footsteps. In March 1993, banking agencies agreed to allow some large, healthy banks to make loans to small businesses based on their proven records of debt repayment. This "character loan" program was expanded to smaller banks by the comptroller of the currency, which regulates about 3,600 financial institutions throughout the country. With this relaxation of bank rules, perhaps small business will receive a much-needed financial jump-start.[13]

Banks are also moving into new business areas, especially those that provide fee-based, income, rather than earnings from loans. Transaction processing, such as money transfers, is a popular low-risk, fee-based service. Securities sales by banks are growing as banks look for ways to earn fees from depositors looking for higher returns. For example, Mellon Bank acquired Dreyfus, a large mutual fund company, and NationsBank and Dean Witter Discover have a joint venture to sell mutual funds in bank branches. In 1993, Chemical Bank received permission to sell and underwrite corporate bonds. Several major banks, including Bankers Trust, are selling sophisticated financial products formerly available only from Wall Street securities firms.

Mergers and Interstate Banking

Merger activity among banks increased substantially during the early 1990s. Many banks acquired local competitors to increase market share within a region, while others bought out-of-state banks to move into new geographical areas.

As a result of a 1985 Supreme Court decision granting the states the right to form regional banking zones, a new category of bank—the *super-regional bank*—has evolved. Banks like Ohio's Banc One, California's First Interstate Bank, and North Carolina's Wachovia Corp. have created multistate bank networks by rapidly acquiring smaller banks.[14]

More banks are merging because the long-standing state restrictions on interstate banking have been lifted. Although federal law still keeps banks from accepting deposits or setting up branches across state lines, all states except Hawaii can approve interstate holding company mergers. More states are expected to remove interstate banking restrictions in the future.[15] As of March 1994, Congress was considering proposals to remove federal restrictions on nationwide branching. Approval is expected during 1994.

Many people feel that consolidation and interstate banking will strengthen the U.S. banking system. Proponents believe that a national banking system would reduce costs, improve operating efficiency, and increase customer convenience. It is less expensive to operate many branches of one bank than separate subsidiary banks in each state. Industry experts estimates that national branching could cut costs $10 billion per year. Interstate banking also reduces dependence on one region's economy. Texas and New England banks had grave problems when their regional real estate markets collapsed.

Those who oppose interstate banking fear that mergers will concentrate power in large financial institutions. They worry that small banks' personal service and knowledge of the local economy will disappear. Yet smaller banks appear to be surviving. The widespread use of ATM networks allows them to offer their customers the convenience of access to cash outside the bank's service area. Despite bank mergers, industry observers expect that the U.S. will continue to have a large number of financial institutions for the foreseeable future.

Regulatory Reforms

The crises facing thrifts and commercial banks have raised questions about current banking laws and the deposit insurance system. Some regulators favor allowing banks to offer a wide range of financial services because this will strengthen banks and allow them to better compete in the financial arena. A number of proposals were under consideration in early 1994. Reductions in paperwork and reporting requirements would lower bank costs, which are now passed on to consumers. Extending non-discriminatory lending policies to non-bank lenders would level the playing field and make it easier for banks to compete. Allowing banks to sell insurance and other low-risk products would provide a balance to higher-risk lending operations. More liberal interstate banking regulations and nationwide branching are important reforms being debated by Congress.[16]

Concept Check

- What were the main causes of the S&L crisis?
- Describe the problems facing commercial banks in the late 1980s, both here and abroad.
- Discuss some of the ways banks are adapting to the changing financial services marketplace

▓ SUMMARY

1. Define money and understand its three main functions.
Money is anything accepted as payment for goods and services. Its three main functions are as a medium of exchange to make transactions easier, as a unit of account to measure the value of goods and services, and as a store of value to hold wealth.

2. Describe the makeup of the money supply and define M1, M2, and M3.
The three components of the money supply are currency (coins and paper money), demand deposits (checking accounts), and time deposits (interest-earning deposits that can't be withdrawn on demand). M1 is the basic measure of money supply and refers to currency, demand deposits, and travelers checks. M2 includes M1 plus time deposits under $100,000. M3 equals M2 plus large time deposits over $100,000.

3. Identify the key members of the U.S. financial system, and explain financial intermediation.
Households, businesses, and governments are the key members of the U.S. financial system. Financial intermediation is the process by which financial institutions ease the transfer of funds from suppliers to demanders. They accept deposits from savers and invest them in loans or securities to provide funds to demanders.

4. Distinguish between depository and nondepository financial institutions, and list the key types of each.
Depository financial institutions are those that accept deposits; nondepository financial institutions don't accept deposits. Both types provide a wide range of financial services. The main depository institutions are commercial banks, thrift institutions (savings and loan associations and savings banks), and credit unions. Major nondepository financial institutions

Questions
1. How did you apply the Fed's three tools of monetary policy to end the recession?
2. What can you suggest about applying the Fed's monetary tools to relieve the overheated economy?
3. What is the current state of the U.S. economy? What is the Fed doing about it?

Financial Management

Learning Goals

After studying this chapter, you should be able to:

1 Understand the role of finance and the financial manager.

2 Discuss the need for financial planning and the difference between forecasts and budgets.

3 Explain how a firm invests its money, and compare short-term and long-term expenses.

4 Describe the main sources of unsecured and secured short-term financing, and discuss their costs.

5 Distinguish between debt and equity as sources of long-term financing, and describe their relationship to leverage and the cost of capital.

6 Describe the main sources of long-term debt and equity financing, their key features, and their costs.

 Career Profile

Rajive Mohan obtained his first job in a financial institution through a co-op work-study program offered by the two-year college he was attending. He then worked for the United States government, reviewing financial institutions and their compliance with government regulations. He later completed a four-year college program, using his associate degree in business management as a foundation.

Rajive is now on the other side of the table, serving as a Vice President, Compliance Officer, and Internal Auditor with Brentwood Savings Association. In this position, he applies, on a daily basis, the knowledge he gathered from his government job. Because of his previous experience, Rajive saves Brentwood Savings time and money and helps make the government's reviews more efficient.

Rajive certifies that the bank is complying with all federal and state laws and regulations. He also monitors Brentwood's savings, investment, accounting, and loan departments, keeping track of what the bank is spending and what it is getting in return. He works closely with the different departments when they collectively forecast the bank's performance based on certain market trends. Upon reviewing their forecasts, Rajive and other executives determine the budget for the bank during the forecast period in order to assure that it reaches its financial goals.

Rajive's courses in finance and accounting gave him a thorough understanding of the financial side of the world of business. They also prepared him for the responsibilities and daily challenges he faces in managing the future of Brentwood Savings.

Overview

Financial management—raising and spending a firm's money—is both a science and an art. The science part is analyzing numbers and flows of money through the firm. The art is answering questions like these: Is the firm using its financial resources in the best way? Aside from costs, why choose a particular form of financing? How risky is each option? This chapter focuses on financial management of the firm. It starts with an overview of the role of finance and of the financial manager. Next it looks at the basics of financial planning, forecasts, and budgets. A discussion of investment decisions—short-term and long-term expenditures—follows. Finally it considers the firm's sources of short- and long-term financing.

THE ROLE OF FINANCE

All companies, large and small, need money to operate. To make money, they must first spend money. Inventory and supplies must be bought, equipment and facilities acquired, employees paid.

Revenues from sales of the firm's products should be the chief source of funding. But money from sales doesn't always come in when it's needed to pay the bills. Financial managers are the ones who keep track of how money is flowing into and out of the firm (see Exhibit 21-1). They are the ones who decide how the available funds will be used, how much money is needed, and where to get it. **Financial management** is the art and science of managing a firm's money so it can meet its goals.

Financial management is closely related to accounting. In most firms both areas are the responsibility of the vice president of finance or the chief financial officer (CFO). But accountants' main function is to collect and present financial data. Financial managers use financial statements and other information prepared by accountants to make financial deci-

financial management
Determining the most effective ways to acquire and use funds to achieve the firm's goals.

■ **Exhibit 21-1**
Flow of Cash through a Business

Source: Justin G. Longenecker and Cárlos Moore, *Small Business Management*, 8th ed. (Cincinnati: South-Western, 1991), p. 603.

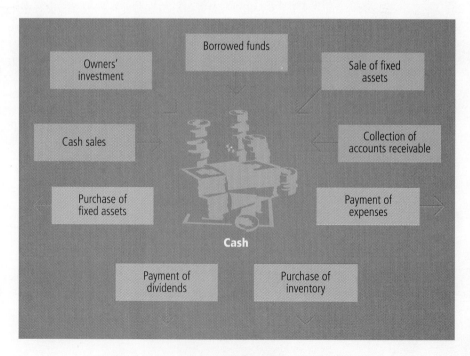

■ A company's financial managers prepare the firm's financial plan. This plan is a synthesis of forecasts for future developments in the firm and budgets that set spending limits based on these forecasts. It is intended to guide the firm toward its goals while maximizing its value.

cash flows Flows of cash into and out of a firm.

sions. Financial managers focus on **cash flows,** the inflow and outflow of cash. They plan and monitor the firm's cash flows to ensure that cash is available when needed.

THE FINANCIAL MANAGER'S RESPONSIBILITIES AND ACTIVITIES

Finance is a central activity in every firm. It may not be as visible as marketing or production, but good management of a firm's finances is just as much a key to its success. All business decisions have financial consequences.

Financial managers have a complex and challenging job. They analyze financial data prepared by accountants, monitor the firm's financial status, and prepare and implement financial plans. CFOs and their staffs coordinate information from such areas as marketing and production to develop and carry out financial strategies. In a small firm, the finance function may be handled by either the accounting department or one or two people. As the firm grows, the finance function grows into a separate department. The finance department oversees day-to-day financial operations (such as financial planning, cash management, credit and collections) and long-term financial activities (such as making investments, fund-raising, and managing the company's pension plan).

The key activities of the financial manager are:

- *Financial planning:* The financial manager prepares the financial plan, which serves as the firm's overall "game plan" for maximizing its value. The financial plan projects revenues, expenditures, and financing needs over a given period. This important document results from the financial planning process, which is discussed in more detail later in the chapter.

- *Investment (spending money):* The financial manager invests the firm's funds in projects and securities that provide high returns in relation to the risks. The goal is to find the combination of current and fixed assets that best uses the firm's precious—and sometimes scarce—financial resources. The firm's future profits and growth may depend on the investments made by the financial manager.

- *Financing (raising money):* The financial manager raises money to pay for the firm's operations and investments. **Internal financing** consists of profits reinvested in the business, which are called *retained earnings* (discussed in Chapter 19). **External financing** is money raised from outside sources, in the form of debt (borrowed funds) and equity (funds raised through the sale of ownership shares in the business). The financial manager also seeks the best balance between debt and equity and between short- and long-term debt.

internal financing Profits reinvested in a business; retained earnings.

external financing Money raised from sources outside the firm.

THE GOAL OF THE FINANCIAL MANAGER

The main goal of the financial manager is *to maximize the value of the firm* to its owners. The value of a publicly owned corporation is measured by the share price of its stock. A private company's value is the price at which it could be sold.

How does the financial manager maximize value? Maximizing profits is one approach, but it should not be the only one. Such an approach favors making short-term gains over achieving long-term goals. What if a firm in a highly technical and competitive industry did no research and development? In the short run, profits would be high, because research and development is very expensive. But in the long run, the firm might lose its ability to compete because of its lack of new products. To maximize the firm's value, the financial manager has to consider both long-term and short-term consequences of the firm's actions.

In seeking to maximize the firm's value, financial managers constantly seek a balance between the opportunity for profit and the potential for loss. In finance, the opportunity for profit is termed **return**; the potential for loss, or the chance that an investment will not achieve the expected level of return, is **risk**. A basic principle in finance is that *the higher the risk, the greater the return that is required*. This widely accepted concept is called the **risk-return trade-off**. Financial managers consider many risk and return factors when making investment and financing decisions. Among them are changing patterns of market demand, interest rates, general economic conditions, market conditions, and social issues (such as environmental effects and equal opportunity employment policies).

return The opportunity for profit.

risk The potential for loss, or the chance that an investment will not achieve the expected level of return.

risk-return trade-off Idea that the higher the risk of an investment is, the greater the return that is required.

Concept Check

- What is the role of financial management in the firm?
- What is the main goal of the financial manager? How does the risk-return trade-off relate to the financial manager's main goal?

FINANCIAL PLANNING

 A *financial plan* is what guides the firm toward its business goals and helps it maximize its value. The financial plan lets the firm estimate the amount and timing of its investment and financing needs.

To prepare a financial plan, the financial manager must first consider existing and proposed products, the resources available to produce them, and the financing needed to support production and sales. Essential to the firm's financial planning are forecasts and budgets.

FORECASTS

The financial planning process starts with financial forecasts, or projections of future developments within the firm. The estimated demand for the firm's products (the sales forecast) and other financial and operating data are key inputs. At Ford Motor Company, economic analysts estimate expected production and sales for each line of cars and trucks. Then financial analysts prepare detailed short- and long-term financial forecasts based on these assumptions.

short-term forecasts
Projections of revenues, costs of goods, and operating expenses over a one-year period; operating plans.

Short-term forecasts, or *operating plans*, project revenues, costs of goods, and operating expenses over a one-year period. Using short-term forecasts, Ford's financial managers would estimate the next year's expenses for inventory, labor, advertising, and other operating activities. These estimates form the basis for *cash budgets*, described below, which predict cash inflows and outflows over the same period.

long-term forecasts
Projections of the firm's financial activities over two to ten years; strategic plans.

Long-term forecasts, or *strategic plans*, typically cover two to ten years and take a broader view of the firm's financial activities. With them, management can assess the financial effects of various business strategies: What would be the financial results of investing in new facilities and equipment? Of developing new products? Of cutting out a line of business? Of acquiring other firms? Long-term forecasts also show where the funding for these activities is expected to come from. Many firms develop five-year strategic plans that are revised from time to time as new information becomes available. Long-term forecasts are supported by short-term forecasts and annual budgets. *Capital budgets*, described below, are based on the long-term forecast. They spell out planned purchases of fixed assets (plant and equipment) for the next few years.

BUDGETS

budgets Formal written forecasts of revenues and expenses.

To plan and control their future financial activities, firms prepare **budgets**. These are formal written forecasts of revenues and expenses. They set spending limits based on forecasts of operations. Budgets are a way to control expenses and compare the actual performance to the forecast.

The budgeting process involves many employees. Each department participates. The complexity of the process depends on the firm's line of business. It would be very different for a small business than for Ford Motor Company. Budgeting at a service company would differ from budgeting at a manufacturing company.

cash budgets Forecasts of a firm's cash receipts and cash expenses.

capital budgets Forecasts for planned fixed-asset outlays over several years.

operating budgets Forecasts of profits, which combine sales forecasts with estimates of production costs and operating expenses.

Firms use several types of budgets. Most cover a one-year period. **Cash budgets** forecast the firm's cash inflows and outflows. Because having enough cash is so critical to their financial health, many firms prepare annual cash budgets subdivided into months or weeks. Then they project the amount of cash needed in each shorter time period. Cash budgets help the firm plan for cash surpluses and shortages. **Capital budgets** forecast outlays for fixed assets (plant and equipment). They usually cover a period of several years. They ensure that the firm will have enough funds to buy the equipment and buildings it needs. **Operating budgets** combine sales forecasts with estimates of production costs and operating expenses to forecast profits. They are based on individual budgets for sales, production, purchases of materials, factory overhead, and operating expenses. Operating budgets then are used to plan operations: dollars of sales, units of production, amounts of raw materials, dollars of wages, and so forth.

As you can see, all budgets begin with forecasts. When actual outcomes differ from budget expectations, management must take action. Budgets are routinely used to monitor and control the performance of a department, a division, or an individual manager. Budgets may need to be revised when performance doesn't match expectations or when the assumptions on which the budget was based no longer hold true. Possible variations can be built into the budgeting process by using different levels of sales or production to prepare several budgets. The financial manager who has a range of possible outcomes and financial consequences to consider can develop a better plan.

Concept Check

- What is a financial plan? What are two types of financial planning documents?
- Distinguish between short-term and long-term forecasts. How are they used by financial managers?
- What are three types of budgets?

HOW ORGANIZATIONS USE FUNDS

3 To grow and prosper, a firm must keep investing money in its operations. The financial manager chooses how best to use the firm's money. Short-term expenses support the firm's day-to-day activities. For instance, athletic apparel maker Nike regularly spends money to buy such raw materials as leather and fabric and to pay employee salaries. Long-term expenses are typically for fixed assets. For Nike, these would include outlays to build a new factory, to buy automated manufacturing equipment, or to acquire a small manufacturer of sports apparel.

SHORT-TERM EXPENSES

Short-term expenses, often called *operating expenses*, are outlays used to support current production and selling activities. They typically result in current assets, which include cash and any other assets (accounts receivable and inventory) that can be converted to cash within a year. The financial manager's goal is to manage current assets so the firm has enough cash to pay its bills and to support its accounts receivable and inventory.

Cash Management: Assuring Liquidity

cash management Making sure that enough cash is available to pay bills as they come due.

Cash is the lifeblood of business. Without it, a firm could not operate. An important duty of the financial manager is **cash management**, or making sure that enough cash is on hand to pay bills as they come due and to meet unexpected expenses.

The cash requirements for a specific period can be estimated from the firm's budget. Many companies keep a minimum cash balance to cover unexpected expenses or changes in projected cash flows. The financial manager arranges loans to cover any shortfalls. If the size and timing of cash inflows closely match the size and timing of cash outflows, the company needs to keep only a little cash on hand. A company whose sales and receipts are fairly predictable and regular throughout the year needs less cash than a company with a seasonal pattern of sales and receipts. A toy company, for instance, whose sales are concentrated in the fall, spends a great deal of cash during the spring and summer to build inventory. It has excess cash during the winter and early spring, when it collects on sales from its peak selling season.

marketable securities Short-term investments that can easily be converted into cash, such as Treasury bills, certificates of deposit, and commercial paper.

Because cash held in checking accounts earns little, if any, interest, the financial manager tries to keep cash balances low and to invest the surplus cash. Surpluses are invested temporarily in **marketable securities**. These short-term investments can easily be converted into cash. The financial manager looks for low-risk investments that offer high returns. Three of the most popular marketable securities are Treasury bills, certificates of deposit, and commercial paper. (*Commercial paper* is short-term debt issued by a financially strong corporation.) Suppose the financial manager of a firm with $7 million in its checking account estimates that $6 million of those funds will not be needed during the next thirty days. The firm could invest this surplus in a marketable security at, say, 3 1/2 percent interest and get back $6 million plus interest of $17,500 at the end of thirty days.

In addition to seeking the right balance between cash and marketable securities, the financial manager tries to shorten the time between the purchase of inventory or services (cash outflows) and the collection of cash from sales (cash inflows). The three key strategies are to collect money owed to the firm as quickly as possible, to pay money owed to others as late as possible without damaging the firm's credit, and to minimize the funds tied up in inventory.

Accounts Receivable

accounts receivable Sales made by the firm for which payment has not yet been received.

Accounts receivable represent sales for which the firm has not been paid. Because the product has been sold but cash has not yet been received, an account receivable represents a use of funds. For the average manufacturing firm, accounts receivable represent about 15 to 20 percent of total assets.

The financial manager uses the firm's credit and collection policies to control accounts receivable. The goal is to collect money owed to the firm as quickly as possible while offering customers credit terms attractive enough to increase sales. *Credit policies* are guidelines for deciding whether to offer credit and, if so, how much and on what terms. *Credit terms* are the specific repayment conditions. They say how long customers have to pay their bills and whether a cash discount is given for quicker payment. For instance, the credit terms *2/10 net 30* mean that full payment is due within thirty days of the invoice date and that a 2 percent discount from the amount due will be given to customers who pay within ten days of the invoice date. A customer buying $1,000 of merchandise under these terms would have to pay $1,000 by day 30 but could pay only $980 if payment were made within ten days of the invoice date.

Another aspect of accounts receivable management is the firm's *collection policies*, the procedures for collecting money that's due the firm. Some firms are more aggressive than others when payments are overdue. The expense of using letters, phone calls, personal visits, collection agencies, or legal action must be weighed against the potential gain. Overly aggressive pursuit of overdue accounts could offend slow-paying customers and result in lost sales.

When setting up credit and collection policies, the financial manager must perform a balancing trick. On one hand are the benefits of increased sales resulting from easier credit policies and more generous credit terms (a longer repayment period or larger cash discount). On the other hand are the problems of financing more accounts receivable or perhaps having more uncollectible accounts receivable. Each firm develops its own credit and collection policies based on such factors as impact on sales, timing of cash flow, experience with bad debt, customer profiles, and industry standards.

Companies that want to speed up collections can use several strategies. They actively manage their accounts receivable, rather than passively letting customers pay when they want to. For example, Hunter Industries, a California manufacturer of irrigation products, encourages customers to pay early by offering higher discounts than its competitors. It also involves its district sales managers, who know customers personally, in the credit approval and collection process.[1]

Companies who sell to international customers need to pay special attention to accounts receivable collection. Sometimes it's easier to sell than to get paid, as the nearby Small Business Trends box explains.

Inventory

Another use of funds is to buy the firm's inventory. In a typical manufacturing firm, inventory is nearly 20 percent of total assets. The cost of inventory includes not only its purchase price, but also ordering, handling, storage, interest, and insurance costs.

Production, marketing, and finance managers usually have differing views about inventory. Production managers want lots of raw materials on hand to avoid production delays. And they don't mind if inventories of finished goods are high, because longer production runs help lower aver-

---

TRENDS

Small Business

Crucial Collections

Small companies are especially eager to increase sales revenue by exporting. Once a firm begins selling its products overseas, however, it typically discovers that collection and cash management strategies for domestic sales are no longer effective. Business practices may differ, and collection time can be very long—90 to 150 days or more, compared to 45 days on average for U.S. customers.

Getting credit information on foreign companies can be difficult. Business owners may have to call credit references themselves and request financial statements, which may be hard to understand. As a result, small exporters may not check international accounts carefully before shipping goods on credit. For example, a small U.S. manufacturer did not verify an African customer's credit references. When it tried to collect its $127,000 bill, it found that the company didn't exist. Gravity Graphics, a New York custom T-shirt company, requires payment before shipping to avoid collection hassles. Customers still pay slowly; some orders are four months old.

One company with a successful international cash management system is Allen Systems, which makes software for mainframe computers. Owner Art Allen, who started the $12.5 million company with $2,000, looks carefully at daily cash management. "As a growing company, we're very vulnerable to cash-flow crises," he says. About half of the firm's $3 million in accounts receivable is from international customers, who used to mail payments to the Naples, Florida, headquarters. Checks took many weeks longer than necessary, and some got lost in the mail. Allen then set up bank accounts in countries where the company operates. Each day he gets status reports on those bank balances. After comparing each location's bank accounts to its projected monthly expenses, he transfers excess funds back to the company's U.S. account and invests them in marketable securities. Such attention to detail is important, because it can take two weeks or more to transfer funds back to the U.S. Although the cost of Allen's system is low, it has helped the company grow and increase profit margins.[2]

---

age costs. Marketing managers typically want lots of finished goods on hand so customer orders can be filled quickly. But financial managers want the least inventory possible without harming production efficiency or sales. Financial managers must work closely with production and marketing to balance these conflicting goals. Techniques for reducing the investment in inventory—efficient order quantities, the just-in-time system, and materials requirement planning—were described in Chapter 10.

LONG-TERM EXPENDITURES

capital expenditures
Investments in long-lived assets, such as land, buildings, and equipment.

A firm also uses funds for its investments in long-lived assets, such items as land, buildings, machinery, and equipment. These are called **capital expenditures**. Unlike operating expenses, which produce benefits within a year, the benefits from capital expenditures extend beyond a

■ One reason firms make long-term capital expenditures is to develop new products. Intel invested millions of dollars over a period of years to finance the creation of its Pentium Chip. During this time the company saw little return on this money. When the chip was completed, however, it was a great success, creating much revenue for the firm.

year. For instance, a printer's purchase of a new printing press with a usable life of seven years is a capital expenditure. It would appear as a fixed asset on the firm's balance sheet. Mergers and acquisitions, discussed in Chapter 6, are also considered capital expenditures.

Firms make capital expenditures for many reasons. The most common are to expand and to replace or renew fixed assets. Another reason is to develop new products. Most manufacturing firms have a big investment in long-term assets. Boeing Company, for instance, puts millions of dollars a year into airplane manufacturing facilities.

Because capital expenditures tend to be costly and have a major effect on the firm's future, they must be carefully assessed. The financial manager selects those long-term expenses that offer the best returns while maximizing the firm's value. This process is called **capital budgeting**.

capital budgeting
Process of evaluating and choosing the long-term expenditures that offer the best returns and meet the goal of maximizing the firm's value.

The Capital Budgeting Process

Capital budgeting is a cooperative effort involving both operating and financial managers. It takes five complex steps. First, managers in various departments develop proposals for projects. Second, the finance staff, with input from line managers, studies each proposal to make sure it's feasible and consistent with the firm's goals and plans. To measure financial feasibility, analysts compare a project's total costs (cash outflows) to the benefits (cash inflows) it is expected to provide over its life. They assess the impact of the proposed investment on the firm's value and the amount of risk it involves. A written report is then sent to the person or committee that makes capital budgeting decisions.

Deciding whether to accept or reject a proposed capital expenditure is the third step. Most firms have a limited capital budget, so they must compare proposals. Often they have a set of standards for judging the proposals. The key factor is usually how much the proposed capital expenditure is expected to add to the firm's value. Projects that are not expected to add to the firm's value are rejected. Those that are expected to add to the firm's value are deemed acceptable. When more projects are acceptable than the budget can fund, the capital budgeting person or group puts together the combination of projects that adds most to the firm's value.

In addition to this quantitative analysis, qualitative factors must also be examined. The project should fit in with the company's overall strategic plan. Some projects, such as pollution control equipment required by government regulations, do not add to a firm's value. In such cases, the firm would look for the least costly alternative. There may be compelling reasons to approve a project even though its return may be below what is usually required. A company may need to do a project to maintain its market share or to accomplish a strategic goal. For example, The Gillette Company's first project in China had a return lower than what it would normally accept. Management decided to proceed because China presented a major market opportunity for Gillette's products, and establishing a strong presence there fit with the company's mission of being a worldwide blade and razor company.[3]

Once a project has been approved and funded, the fourth step takes place: carrying out the project. The final step is follow-up, which involves comparing the project's actual costs and benefits to those that were estimated.

The capital budgeting process keeps many financial managers awake long into the night. If they choose the right projects, their firms prosper. Investment decisions involving new products or the acquisition of another business are especially important. The future of the company may depend on management's ability to correctly estimate how a project will work out.

Concept Check

- Distinguish between short-term and long-term expenses.
- What is the financial manager's goal in cash management? List the three key cash-management strategies.
- What are the goal and role of the financial manager in managing accounts receivable and inventory? Discuss the trade-offs involved when making decisions about accounts receivable and credit and collection policies.
- Describe the firm's main motives in making capital expenditures.

GETTING SHORT-TERM FINANCING

4 How do firms raise the funding they need? They borrow money (debt), sell ownership shares (equity), and retain earnings (profits). The financial manager must assess all these sources and choose the one most likely to help maximize the firm's value.

■ When a company needs to raise money for short-term expenses, the financial manager decides upon the best way to obtain it. Short-term bank loans are one popular method of financing, especially for smaller businesses.

Like expenses, borrowed funds can be divided into short-term and long-term loans. A short-term loan comes due within a year; a long-term loan has a maturity greater than a year. Short-term financing is shown as a current liability on the balance sheet. It is used to finance current assets and support operations. Short-term loans can be unsecured or secured.

UNSECURED SHORT-TERM LOANS

unsecured loans Loans obtained without the borrower's pledge of specific assets as security.

Unsecured loans are given on the basis of the firm's credit and the lender's previous experience with the firm. The borrower does not have to pledge specific assets as security. The three main types of unsecured short-term loans are trade credit, bank loans, and commercial paper.

Trade Credit: Accounts Payable

trade credit Credit extended to the buyer by the seller of products; a form of short-term financing entered as an account payable.

accounts payable Short-term trade credit extended to the buyer by the seller of products.

Trade credit is credit extended to the buyer by the seller. It is a big source of short-term business financing. The credit is entered in the buyer's books as an **account payable**. In effect, it is a short-term loan from the seller to the buyer of goods and services. When Goodyear sells tires to General Motors, GM does not have to pay cash on delivery. Instead, Goodyear regularly bills GM for its tire purchases. Goodyear is extending credit to GM between the time when it receives the tires and when it pays for them. Until GM pays Goodyear, Goodyear has an account receivable from GM—and GM has an account payable to Goodyear.

Bank Loans

Unsecured bank loans are another source of short-term business financing. These loans are often used to finance seasonal (cyclical) businesses. They need bank loans to finance increased inventories just before their strongest sales period and to finance accounts receivable just afterward. For instance, a swimwear maker has strong sales in the spring and sum-

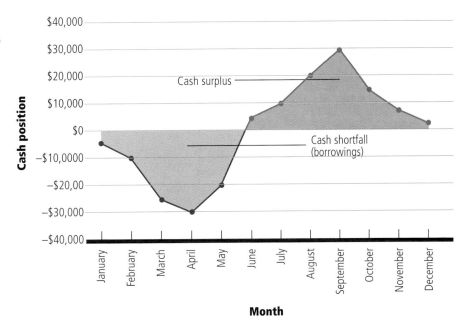

Exhibit 21-2
Swimwear Manufacturer's
Seasonal Cash Flows

mer and lower sales during the fall and winter. It needs short-term bank financing to support the buildup of inventories and receivables during late winter and early spring, as shown in Exhibit 21-2. These bank loans are repaid when the inventory is sold and the receivables are collected.

Unsecured bank loans include single-payment notes, lines of credit, and revolving credit agreements. A **single-payment note** is a one-time loan that is repaid in a lump sum at the loan's maturity date, which is typically 30 to 270 days after the loan is made. The borrower signs a *promissory note*, an agreement to repay the loan amount plus interest at a specified rate on or before maturity. Interest is sometimes payable monthly rather than at maturity.

A **line of credit** is an agreement between a bank and a business. It states the maximum amount of unsecured short-term borrowing the bank will allow over a given period, typically one year. A line of credit is not a guaranteed loan; the bank agrees to lend funds only if it has money available. Usually the firm must repay any borrowing within a year. It must also either pay a fee or keep a certain percentage of the loan amount (10 to 20 percent) in a checking account at the bank.

The third type of bank loan, the **revolving credit agreement**, is basically a guaranteed line of credit. Because the bank guarantees that funds will be available, it charges an extra fee in addition to interest. Revolving credit loans are often arranged for a three- to five-year period.

Firms often obtain annual lines of credit based on their expected seasonal needs. Then they can quickly borrow without having to reapply to the bank each time funds are needed. Suppose the swimwear maker projected a cash shortfall of $80,000 for the period from February to June. The financial manager might get a $100,000 line of credit from the bank. (The extra $20,000 would be there to cover any unexpected expenses.) The

single-payment note
One-time loan repaid in a lump sum at the loan's maturity date; a form of short-term financing.

line of credit Agreement stating the maximum amount of unsecured short-term borrowing a firm may do during a given period if the bank has money to lend when the firm wants it.

revolving credit agreement Guaranteed line of credit.

firm could borrow funds as needed—$10,000 in February, $25,000 in March, $30,000 in April. Then it could gradually repay the loan as cash is collected during the summer months.

Commercial Paper

As noted earlier, **commercial paper** is unsecured short-term debt (an IOU) offered by large, financially strong corporations. Thus it is a short-term investment for firms with temporary cash surpluses, and it is a financing option for major corporations. Commercial paper is issued by these corporations in multiples of $100,000 for periods ranging from 30 to 270 days. It is sold at a discount from its face value, and the interest paid to the buyer is the difference between the price paid and the face value. Say that Ford Motor Credit issues $1 million worth of commercial paper with a ninety-day maturity and sells it for $980,000. At the end of ninety days, the buyer gets $1 million for its $980,000 investment. The interest paid by Ford Motor Credit is $20,000 on $980,000 principal for ninety days, which equals an annual interest rate of 8.2 percent.

Commercial paper is a popular form of financing for big corporations. Many of them use it instead of short-term bank loans. The interest rate on commercial paper is usually 1 to 2 percent below the rate charged by banks to the best business borrowers. Many issuers of commercial paper repay by selling new issues. This process is called "rolling over" commercial paper.

SECURED SHORT-TERM LOANS

The second category of short-term financing is **secured loans**—loans that require the borrower to pledge specific assets as *collateral*, or security. The secured lender can legally take the collateral if the borrower doesn't repay the loan. Commercial banks and commercial finance companies are the main sources of secured short-term loans to business. These loans are used by borrowers who cannot get an unsecured loan.

Secured short-term loans are usually secured by accounts receivable or inventory. Because accounts receivable are normally quite liquid (can easily be converted to cash), they are an attractive form of collateral. The appeal of inventory—raw materials or finished goods—as collateral depends on how easily it can be sold at a fair price.

The amount of a secured short-term loan is a percentage of the value of the collateral, ranging between 30 and 100 percent. The percentage varies with the type and liquidity of the assets being pledged. Say that Homestate National Bank agrees to lend Torrey Pines Publishing an amount equal to 70 percent of the value of its book inventory, which would serve as collateral for the loan.

If a pledge of accounts receivable is used to secure a short-term bank loan, the bank selects the accounts of the borrower that it will accept as collateral. When the borrower collects the receivables that it has pledged, it is trusted to pay those funds to the bank. For instance, Torrey Pines Publishing has total accounts receivable of $450,000. After assessing each customer's payment history, Homestate National Bank concludes that Torrey

Bank borrowing		Factoring	
Monthly receivables	$20,000	Monthly receivables	$20,000
Bank line of credit	$20,000	Amount received (5% discount)	$19,000
Interest cost per 1 month at 12% per year [(12% × $20,000) ÷ 12 months]	$200	Cost of factoring for one month	$1,000
Actual interest cost [($200 ÷ $20,000) × 12 months]	12%	Actual cost of factoring [($1,000 ÷ $19,000) × 12 months]	63.2%

■ **Exhibit 21-3**
Costs of Bank Borrowing versus Factoring

Pines Publishing has $375,000 of acceptable accounts. If Homestate will advance 80 percent of the acceptable collateral, Torrey Pines Publishing can borrow up to $300,000.

Factoring

factoring Outright sale of a firm's accounts receivable to a financial institution that will assume the risks and expenses of collecting the money owed.

Another form of short-term financing using accounts receivable is **factoring**. A firm's accounts receivable are sold outright to a *factor*, a financial institution (usually a commercial bank or commercial finance company) that is in the business of buying accounts receivable at a discount. Factoring is widely used in the clothing, furniture, and appliance industries. For Blue Fish, a small New Jersey apparel company, factoring provided the financing it needed to grow. Although sales were increasing, customers were paying slowly and Blue Fish had couldn't pay suppliers promptly. Rather than give up equity ownership by selling shares of stock to raise the cash, Blue Fish sold its receivables to a factor.[4]

Factoring allows a firm to turn its accounts receivable into cash without worrying about collections. The factor assumes all the risks and expenses of collecting the accounts. Customers of the firm whose accounts have been sold are told to send their payments directly to the factor. Firms that factor all of their accounts can cut out most of their credit and collection operations and thus reduce costs.

Factoring is a costly form of financing, however, because the factor buys the receivables at an often large discount from their actual value. For instance, assume that a factor charges a fee of 5 percent (the discount). If the company sells $20,000 worth of receivables to the factor, it gets only $19,000 (95% × $20,000). The factor keeps all $20,000 it collects. But if customers don't pay on time, the factor—not the company—has the problem. As shown in Exhibit 21-3, factoring costs much more than a bank loan. But often a company has no choice because it has neither the track record to get unsecured financing nor other collateral to pledge as security for a loan.

COSTS OF SHORT-TERM LOANS

prime rate of interest Base rate charged by banks for short-term commercial loans to their most creditworthy business borrowers.

The interest rates on short-term loans are usually tied to the **prime rate of interest**, the base rate banks use in pricing short-term commercial loans to their best—most creditworthy—business borrowers. The prime rate changes with the supply of and demand for short-term funds.

Banks set the interest rates for short-term loans by adding a premium, such as 2 percent, to the prime rate. The result would be referred to as "prime plus 2" or "2 over prime." The interest rate on a *fixed-rate loan* remains the same over the life of the loan. On a *floating-rate loan*, the premium above the prime rate is set when the loan is made, but the interest rate is allowed to change each time the prime rate changes. Say that the prime rate is 7 percent. A firm charged a rate of prime plus 2 percent on a floating-rate loan would pay 9 percent at first. If the prime rate rose to 9 percent, the interest rate on the loan would increase to 11 percent; if it dropped to 6 1/2 percent, the new interest rate would be 8 1/2 percent.

As odd as it may seem, lenders usually charge higher interest rates on secured loans than on unsecured loans. The reason is that secured loans tend to be made to higher-risk borrowers—less creditworthy firms that may be unable to repay the loan or firms that have used up their unsecured borrowing power. To a lender, collateral just reduces losses if the borrower defaults. The collateral in no way reduces the risk that the borrower will default. Another factor raising the cost of secured loans is the potential for increased administrative costs (for keeping detailed records of the collateral, for instance).

Concept Check

- Distinguish between unsecured and secured short-term loans. Briefly describe the three main types of unsecured short-term loans.
- Discuss the two ways that accounts receivable can be used to get short-term financing.
- Define the prime rate of interest. What is the difference between fixed-rate and floating-rate loans? Why are interest rates higher on secured loans than on unsecured loans?

GETTING LONG-TERM FINANCING

5 A basic rule of finance is to match the length of the financing to the period over which benefits are expected to be received from the expenses. Short-term expenses should be financed with short-term financing, and long-term expenses should be financed with long-term financing. Long-term financing sources include both debt (borrowing) and equity (ownership). Equity financing comes either from selling new ownership interests or from retaining earnings.

DEBT VERSUS EQUITY FINANCING

Say that the Boeing Corporation plans to spend $2 billion over the next four years to build and equip new factories to make jet aircraft. Boeing's top management must decide how to raise the money needed to pay for these big projects. It will probably consider several possible sources of long-term financing. Management will assess the pros and cons of both debt and equity.

■ Long-term financing is often a mix of debt and equity. To obtain equity financing, a corporation will sell new issues of common stock, which represent an ownership interest in the company. The company will then use the money raised from the sale of stock to finance its operation. The stockholders will receive a part of the company's profits in the form of dividend payments.

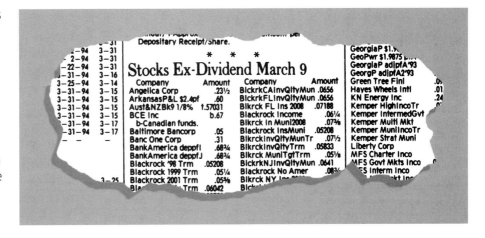

financial risk Chance that the firm will be unable to make scheduled interest and principal payments on its debt.

The main advantage of long-term debt is that the interest on it is a tax-deductible expense. The company's income taxes would thus be lower with debt financing than with equity financing. Also, with debt financing there is no loss of ownership. Creditors do not normally get voting rights. Debt has some disadvantages, however. The big one is **financial risk**— the chance that the firm will be unable to make scheduled interest and principal payments. The lender can force into bankruptcy a borrower that fails to make scheduled debt payments. To protect the lender, most long-term loan agreements have restrictions designed to force the borrower to operate efficiently.

Equity, on the other hand, does not obligate the firm to make dividend payments or repay the investment. From the issuer's viewpoint, stock is a form of permanent financing. It places few restrictions on the firm. Equity financing also increases the total owners' equity, so the firm may be able to borrow more easily and at a lower cost in the future. However, equity financing is costly. Unlike the interest on bonds, dividends to owners are not tax-deductible expenses. Also, the sale of equity increases the number of stockholders and could shift voting control of the company out of management's hands. The chief differences between debt and equity as financing methods are summarized in Exhibit 21-4. When making its long-term financing decision, Boeing's management will weigh these pros and cons—and will also take into account leverage and cost of capital.

leverage Use of debt to finance an investment and increase the company's rate of return.

Leverage

Why would a company increase its financial risk by choosing debt over equity? The answer is **leverage**, the use of debt financing to magnify the firm's rate of return. The use of debt increases risk, but it also increases potential profits. If the firm's earnings are greater than its interest payments on the debt, stockholders will earn a higher rate of return than they would have if equity financing had been used. But leverage works both ways. It magnifies losses as well as gains.

Exhibit 21-5 shows the effect of leverage on stockholders' return. East Company and West Company each need $200,000 to pay for a capital

Tool	Type of financing	
	Debt	**Equity**
Voice in management	Creditors typically have none, unless borrower defaults on payments. Creditors may be able to place restraints on management in event of default.	Common stockholders have voting rights.
Claim on income and assets	Debtholders rank ahead of equity holders. Payment of interest and principal is contractual obligation of firm.	Equity owners have residual claim on income (dividends are paid only after interest and any scheduled principal payments are paid). Firm has no obligation to pay dividends.
Maturity	Debt has stated maturity and requires repayment of principal by specified maturity date.	Company is not required to repay equity, which has no maturity date.
Tax treatment	Interest is tax-deductible expense.	Dividends are not tax-deductible and are paid from after-tax income.

■ **Exhibit 21-4**
Key Differences between
Debt and Equity Financing

East Company		West Company	
Common stock	$ 20,000	Common stock	$ 20,000
Bonds (at 10% interest)	180,000	Bonds	0
Total funds needed	$200,000	Total funds raised	$200,000
Earnings	$50,000	Earnings	$50,000
Less bond interest (10% × $180,000)	−18,000	Less bond interest	−0
Total Earnings	$32,000	Total Earnings	$50,000

East Company: Return to stockholders $= \dfrac{\$32,000}{\$20,000} = 160\%$

West Company: Return to stockholders $= \dfrac{\$50,000}{\$200,000} = 25\%$

■ **Exhibit 21-5**
Effect of Leverage on
Stockholders' Return

expenditure. East Company borrows 90 percent of the money ($180,000) by issuing bonds and raises the other 10 percent ($20,000) by issuing common stock. West Company raises all of the money ($200,000) by issuing new common stock. Each firm earns $50,000 the first year. The outcomes are best compared using the return to stockholders, which is found by dividing the total earnings on the investment by the amount financed with common stock. East Company's greater leverage (debt) earns its stockholders a 160 percent return on their investment. The return on investment earned by West Company's stockholders is only 25 percent. The use of leverage has magnified East Company's return far beyond that of West Company.

Company policies about the mix of debt and equity vary. Some companies are highly leveraged: They have high debt compared to equity. Others have low leverage: They keep debt to a minimum. During the late

1980s the average percentage of debt at U.S. corporations grew steadily. For some companies like Gillette and Coca-Cola, profits grew because of the leverage resulting from higher debt levels. But others weren't so lucky. Many firms that became too highly leveraged in the 1980s couldn't meet scheduled debt payments. Today the trend is to reduce leverage. Over half the 150 large corporations surveyed by the investment firm of Goldman, Sachs & Co. in 1993 said they planned to reduce debt. Many are repaying bank loans with cash flow or equity issues.[5]

Some companies use very little debt, keeping their leverage low. For example, Hormel Foods has only 1.2 percent of its long-term financing provided by debt; Bristol Meyers-Squibb has about 3 percent; Exxon, 15 percent; Hewlett-Packard, 5 percent; and Rubbermaid, 2 percent.

Cost of Capital

capital structure Mix of long-term debt and equity.

The financial manager's long-term financing objective is to select the **capital structure,** or mix of long-term debt and equity, that results in the best balance between risk and cost. The costs of each type of financing differ. In general, the cost of debt financing is the least expensive, and the cost of common equity (common stock) is the most expensive. The cost of preferred stock (which we'll discuss later in this chapter and in the next) falls between the other two.

cost of capital The minimum rate of return the firm must earn on its investments to maintain its market value and attract investors.

A firm's overall **cost of capital** is the minimum rate of return the firm must earn on its investments to maintain its market value and attract investors. It is calculated by multiplying the cost of debt, preferred stock, and equity by the percentage of each in the firm's capital structure. Exhibit 21-6 illustrates this calculation for the hypothetical Carlin Corporation.

The cost of capital is an important financial concept. As a measure of the firm's cost of financing over the long run, it is the minimum rate of return the firm must earn on its investments. An investment that earns a return above the cost of capital will increase the value of the firm, and vice versa.

6 DEBT CAPITAL

■ **Exhibit 21-6**
Calculating the Cost of Capital

Long-term debt is used to finance long-term (capital) expenditures. The maturities of long-term debt typically range between five and twenty years. Three important forms of long-term debt are term loans, bonds, and mortgage loans.

Source of Captial	Proportion (1)	Cost (2)	Weighted Cost [(1) × (2)]
Long-term debt	40%	6%	2.4%
Preferred stock	10	9	0.9
Common stock	50	12	6.0
Totals	100%		9.3%
Weighted cost of capital = 9.3%			

term loan Business loan with a maturity of more than one year.

A **term loan** is a business loan with a maturity of more than a year. Term loans generally have five- to twelve-year maturities and can be unsecured or secured. They are available from commercial banks, insurance companies, pension funds, commercial finance companies, and manufacturer's financing subsidiaries. A contract between borrower and lender spells out the amount and maturity of the loan, the interest rate, payment dates, the purpose of the loan, and other provisions. Term loans may be repaid on a quarterly, semiannual, or annual schedule. The payments include both interest and principal, so the loan balance declines over time. Borrowers try to arrange a repayment schedule that matches the cash flow from the project being financed. Because of the long period involved in term loans, lenders place operating and financial restrictions on the borrower to control the risk that the borrower will default. The borrower might have to keep a minimum level of working capital on hand, might be restricted from selling fixed assets, or might have to limit the total amount of long-term debt.

bonds Long-term debt obligations for corporations and governments.

Bonds are long-term debt obligations (liabilities) for corporations and governments. Like term loans, corporate bonds are issued with formal contracts that set forth the obligations of the issuing corporation and the rights of the bondholders. Most bonds are issued in multiples of $1,000 (par value) for maturities of ten to thirty years. The stated interest rate, or coupon rate, is the percentage of the bond's par value that the issuer will pay each year as interest. Interest is usually paid in two equal payments per year. A $1,000 par value bond with a 10 percent coupon would pay $50 in interest every six months (10% × $1,000 × 1/2 year).

mortgage loan Long-term loan secured by real estate as collateral.

A **mortgage loan** is a long-term loan using real estate as collateral. The lender takes a mortgage on the property, which lets the lender seize the property, sell it, and use the proceeds to pay off the loan if the borrower fails to make the scheduled payments. Long-term mortgage loans are often used to finance office buildings, factories, and warehouses. Life insurance companies are an important source of these loans. They make billions of dollars' worth of mortgage loans to businesses each year.

Costs of Long-Term Loans

The cost of long-term debt financing is generally higher than the cost of short-term financing. That's because the lender is less certain that the long-term borrower will be able to repay the debt. For the higher level of risk, long-term lenders charge higher interest rates. Many long-term loans also have extra fees. For instance, firms issuing bonds through investment bankers must pay the costs of finding investors. Mortgage lenders often charge borrowers a fee equal to about 2 percent of the amount borrowed.

6 EQUITY CAPITAL

Equity is the owners' investment in the business. In corporations, the preferred and common stockholders are the owners. A firm can get equity financing by selling new ownership shares (external financing) or by retaining earnings (internal financing). An advantage of equity financing is its lack of financial risk. The issuer doesn't have to pay out any earnings to the owners or repay their investment.

Selling New Issues of Common Stock

common stock A security that represents an ownership interest in a corporation.

Common stock is a security that represents an ownership interest in a corporation. Corporations sell new issues of common stock through *underwriting* or *rights offerings. Underwriting* means selling a new issue of stock to an investment banking firm for a specified price. (See Chapter 22.) The prospectus for a new issue of common stock is shown in

■ **Exhibit 21-7**
Common Stock
Prospectus

Source: Reprinted by permission of
Chrysler Corporation; Chrysler Corporation
1994.

PROSPECTUS

46,000,000 Shares

Common Stock
($1.00 par value)

Of the 46,000,000 shares of Common Stock being offered hereby, 37,000,000 shares are being offered in the United States and Canada by the U.S. Underwriters (the "U.S. Offering") and 9,000,000 shares are being concurrently offered outside the United States and Canada by the Managers (the "International Offering" and, together with the U.S. Offering, the "Offerings"). The price to the public and the underwriting discount per share are identical for the Offerings. See "Underwriting."

The Common Stock of Chrysler is listed on the New York Stock Exchange under the symbol "C." On February 2, 1993, the last reported sale price of the Common Stock on the New York Stock Exchange Composite Transactions Tape was $38¾ per share.

See "Special Investment Considerations" for a discussion of certain special investment considerations that should be carefully considered by potential investors in the shares of Common Stock.

THESE SECURITIES HAVE NOT BEEN APPROVED OR DISAPPROVED BY THE SECURITIES AND EXCHANGE COMMISSION OR ANY STATE SECURITIES COMMISSION NOR HAS THE SECURITIES AND EXCHANGE COMMISSION OR ANY STATE SECURITIES COMMISSION PASSED UPON THE ACCURACY OR ADEQUACY OF THIS PROSPECTUS. ANY REPRESENTATION TO THE CONTRARY IS A CRIMINAL OFFENSE.

	Price to Public	*Underwriting Discount*	*Proceeds to Chrysler(1)*
Per Share	*$38.75*	*$1.1625*	*$37.5875*
Total(2)	*$1,782,500,000*	*$53,475,000*	*$1,729,025,000*

(1) Before deduction of expenses payable by Chrysler, estimated at $3,000,000.

(2) Chrysler has granted the U.S. Underwriters and the Managers an option, exercisable by the representatives of the U.S. Underwriters for 30 days from the date of the public offering of the shares of Common Stock offered hereby, to purchase a maximum of 6,000,000 additional shares of Common Stock, in the aggregate, solely to cover over-allotments, if any. If the option is exercised in full, the total Price to Public will be $2,015,000,000, Underwriting Discount will be $60,450,000 and Proceeds to Chrysler will be $1,954,550,000. See "Underwriting."

The shares of Common Stock are offered by the several U.S. Underwriters when, as and if issued by Chrysler, delivered to and accepted by the U.S. Underwriters and subject to their right to reject orders in whole or in part. It is expected that the shares of Common Stock will be ready for delivery on or about February 10, 1993.

The First Boston Corporation   Merrill Lynch & Co.

Morgan Stanley & Co.   Salomon Brothers Inc
Incorporated

Lehman Brothers   J.P. Morgan Securities Inc.

PaineWebber Incorporated   Smith Barney, Harris Upham & Co.
               Incorporated

The date of this Prospectus is February 3, 1993.

Exhibit 21-7. It shows that in February 1993, Chrysler Corporation made a public offering of 46 million shares priced at $38.75 each. Underwriters' fees totaled $1.1625 per share, leaving $37.5875 per share for the company (a total of $1.73 billion). The company also incurred several million dollars in issuance costs for printing, legal help, and accounting.

Rights offerings are direct sales of new issues of common stock to the firm's existing common stockholders. They have the right to buy the new stock in proportion to their existing percentage of ownership in the firm. Thus they can maintain their percentage of ownership. If they do not exercise their rights, their percentage of ownership will decrease as new shares are issued. The company is not charged any underwriting fees with a rights issue. Rights offerings are becoming popular with young firms as well as more established ones. Small public companies such as high-tech firms Vitronics Corp., Quadrax Corp., and Artel Corp. used rights offerings to raise equity capital. They found this option attractive because the regulatory approval process is faster than for a common stock issue, and the absence of underwriting fees can mean significant cost savings. A public underwriting could cost $1 million in fees and commissions, compared to less than $500,000 for a rights offering.[6]

Several types of costs may arise when issuing common stock. If the new shares are sold to the public, underwriting costs are a factor. The second cost (discussed below) is dividends paid to stockholders. A third type of cost is *dilution*, which is very hard to measure. It is not an out-of-pocket cost. Instead, dilution refers to the fact that new shares dilute the percentage claim of each existing share on earnings and assets.

Going Public

A firm *goes public* when it first sells its stock to the public. Usually a high-growth company goes public because it needs to raise more funds to finance continuing growth. Going public often lets existing stockholders, usually family and friends who bought the stock privately, earn big profits on their investment. But going public has some drawbacks. For one thing, there is no guarantee an initial offering will sell. An initial public stock offering (IPO) is also expensive. Big fees must be paid to investment bankers, brokers, attorneys, accountants, and printers. Once the company is public, it is closely watched by regulators, stockholders, and securities analysts. The firm must reveal such information as operating and financial data, product details, financing plans, and operating strategies. Providing this information is often costly.

Going public can be successful when a company is well established and market conditions are right. Strong equity markets in 1993 prompted many companies to go public. Among 1993's largest IPOs were spin-offs of two Sears, Roebuck financial subsidiaries: Allstate Insurance ($2.12 billion) and Dean Witter Discover ($796.5 million). Small companies also tapped the equity markets in record numbers. Boston Chicken, a fast-food chain, priced its shares at $20 and saw them jump to $48.50 on the first day before settling down to about $40.[7]

Dividends

Dividends are payments to stockholders of a part of a corporation's profits. A company does not have to pay dividends to stockholders. But if investors buy the stock expecting to get dividends and the firm does not pay them, the investors may sell their stock. If too many sell, the value of the stock decreases. Dividends can be paid in cash or in stock. **Stock dividends** are payments in the form of more stock. Stock dividends may replace or supplement cash dividends. More shares have a claim on the same company after a stock dividend has been paid, so the value of each share often declines.

At their quarterly meetings, the company's board of directors (with the advice of its financial managers) decides how much of the profits to distribute as dividends and how much to reinvest. The firm's basic approach to paying dividends is an important part of its financing strategy and can greatly affect its share price. Dividends give information about the firm's current and future performance. A stable history of dividend payments indicates good financial health. If a firm that has been making regular dividend payments cuts or skips a dividend, investors start thinking it has serious financial problems. The uncertainty often results in lower stock prices. Thus most firms set dividends at a level they can keep paying.

Retained Earnings

Retained earnings, profits that have been reinvested in the firm, have two big advantages over other sources of equity capital: They do not incur underwriting costs, and they do not cause dilution.

Financial managers strive to balance dividends and retained earnings in order to maximize the value of the firm. Often the balance reflects the nature of the firm and its industry. Well-established firms and those that expect only modest growth, like public utilities, typically pay out much of their earnings in dividends. For example, in the year ending February 23, 1994, Boston Edison paid per-share dividends of $1.76, Philip Morris paid $2.60, and Atlantic Richfield paid $5.50. High-growth companies, like those in the computer and biotechnology fields, finance most of their growth through retained earnings and pay low or no dividends to stockholders. For the same period, Apple Computer paid $0.48 per share, while Compaq, another computer manufacturer, and Idec, a biotechnology firm, paid no dividends.

Preferred Stock

Another form of equity is **preferred stock**. Unlike common stock, preferred stock usually has a dividend amount that is set at the time the stock is issued. These dividends must be paid before the company can pay any dividends to common stockholders. Also, if the firm goes bankrupt and sells its assets, preferred stockholders get their money back before common stockholders do. Preferred stock is described in greater detail in Chapter 22.

Like debt, preferred stock increases the firm's leverage because it obligates the firm to make a fixed payment. But preferred stock is more flexible. The firm can miss a dividend payment without suffering the serious results of failing to pay back a debt.

The cost of preferred stock is higher than the cost of debt financing. The reason is that, unlike interest, preferred dividends are not tax-deductible. They must be paid out of after-tax earnings. Also, because the claims of preferred stockholders on dividends and assets are second to those of debtholders, preferred stockholders require higher returns to compensate for the greater risk.

Venture Capital

venture capital Financing obtained, typically by a small, growing firm, from investors that provide money in exchange for stock and a voice in management of the company.

Venture capital is another source of equity capital. It is most often used by small and growing firms that aren't big enough to sell securities to the public. This type of financing is especially popular among high-tech companies that need large sums of money.

Venture capitalists invest in new businesses in return for part of the ownership, sometimes as much as 60 percent. They look for new businesses with high growth potential, and they expect a high investment return within five to ten years. By getting in on the ground floor, venture capitalists buy stock at a very low price. They earn profits by selling the stock at a much higher price when the company goes public. Venture capitalists generally get a voice in management through a seat on the board of directors.

Getting venture capital is tough, even though there are about 300 private venture capital firms in this country. Most venture capitalists finance only about 1 to 5 percent of the companies that apply. In 1992, venture capital firms invested $2.63 billion, double their 1991 investments. Some venture capitalists are moving away from financing brand-new firms. As a result, other sources of venture capital, including private foundations, states, and wealthy individuals, are emerging to help start-up firms find equity capital, as the Service Economy Trends box shows.

TRENDS

Service Economy

Financial Foundations

Stanley Walker, owner of Spencer's Unique Fashion and Spencer's Auto Customizing, used to operate his two businesses out of the back of his truck. He wanted to open up a shop, but the $5,000 he had saved was not nearly enough to pay for a retail location's deposit, rent, and advertising. Then he heard about the Good Faith Fund, a Pine Bluff, Arkansas, organization that grants small, short-term loans to entrepreneurs, with the goal of improving the earnings and business skills of low-income businesspeople.

The Good Faith Fund, in turn, receives the bulk of its funding from an unlikely source: private foundations. Such arrangements are becoming increasingly common, as many foundations now believe that creating jobs in struggling communities is a key to addressing social and economic problems. Foundation awards, called "Program-Related Investments," are generally given to businesses that a traditional lender might dismiss as too risky. They take the form of grants, low-interest loans, equity investments, or donated services.

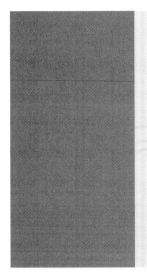

More often, however, foundations do not distribute their monies directly, preferring to go through an intermediary nonprofit organization. That way, they avoid administrative hassles and can award funding more objectively. Many foundations invest in one of the country's two hundred "microenterprise" programs, nonprofit groups like the Good Faith Fund that work to fight poverty, create jobs, teach job skills, and stabilize families and communities. Beverly Smith, the executive director of the Association for Enterprise Opportunity, estimates that such programs have provided over $10 million to entrepreneurs in the past seven years.

Often foundations provide entrepreneurial training and education. According to John Anderson of the Edward Lowe Foundation, "We don't provide money [to entrepreneurs], but we may offer advice on how to get it." One piece of advice they frequently offer is to seek funding locally, and not to overlook possibilities such as church and school groups, arts councils, self-help groups, and other community organizations.[8]

Many states now have publicly funded venture-capital agencies, some of which specialize in funding minority-owned businesses. These organizations can often mean the difference between success and failure for young firms. In 1982, Powersoft Inc., a Boston-area software company, couldn't get funds to expand from either banks or venture capitalists. Owner Mitchell Kertzman turned to the Massachusetts Technology Development Corp., which provided $150,000. With this initial commitment, Powersoft was able to attract another $750,000 in private venture funds. Since then the company has grown from 1 to 170 employees and has sales of $21 million.[9]

Wealthy people may also provide venture capital to small firms. Often called "angels," these investors are motivated by the potential to earn a high return on their investment. Accountants, attorneys, business associates, financial consultants, bankers, and others may help the small firm find an angel. Regional computer database services, such as the Venture Capital Network in New Hampshire and the Venture Capital Connection in Northern California, can be used to match small businesses that need equity with potential investors. Seed Capital Network is a national service that facilitates introductions between investors and business owners. An on-line computer network, American Venture Capital Exchange, allows potential investors with modems to access business plan summaries of companies seeking financing.[10]

Concept Check

- Compare the advantages and disadvantages of debt and equity to the issuer. What roles do leverage and the cost of capital play in determining the mix of debt and equity?
- Discuss the costs involved in issuing common stock. What is the importance of the firm's policy on dividend payments?
- Briefly describe these sources of equity: retained earnings, preferred stock, venture capital.

■ SUMMARY

1. Understand the role of finance and the financial manager.

Finance involves managing the firm's money. The financial manager must decide how much money is needed and when, how best to use the available funds, and how to get the required financing. The financial manager's responsibilities include financial planning, investing (spending money), and financing (raising money). Maximizing the value of the firm is the main goal of the financial manager, whose decisions often have long-term effects.

2. Discuss the need for financial planning and the difference between forecasts and budgets.

Financial planning lets the firm estimate the amount and timing of the financial resources it needs to meet its business goals. The planning process begins with the preparation of forecasts based on the demand for the firm's products. Short-term forecasts are operating plans that project expected revenues and expenses for a year. They are the basis for cash budgets, which show the flow of cash into and out of the firm and are used to plan day-to-day operations. Long-term forecasts project revenues and expenses for two to ten years. These strategic plans allow top management to analyze the impact of different options on the firm's profits. The capital budget is based on the long-term forecast. Operating budgets forecast profits.

3. Explain how a firm invests its money, and compare short-term and long-term expenses.

A firm invests money to support its operations. It invests in short-term expenses—supplies, inventory, and wages—to support current production, marketing, and sales activities. A major focus of the financial manager is managing the firm's investment in these current assets so the company has enough cash to pay its bills and support accounts receivable and inventory. The financial manager tries to collect accounts receivable as quickly as possible, stretch accounts payable, and minimize the investment in inventory. Long-term expenses (capital expenditures) are fixed assets such as land, buildings, and equipment. Because of the large outlay required for capital expenditures, financial managers carefully analyze proposed projects to determine which offer the best returns.

4. Describe the main sources of unsecured and secured short-term financing, and discuss their costs.

Short-term financing comes due within one year. The main sources of unsecured short-term financing (no collateral) are trade credit, bank loans, and commercial paper. Bank loans can be either single-payment notes, lines of credit, or revolving credit agreements. Secured loans require a pledge of certain assets as security for the loan. Pledging accounts receivable or inventory and factoring accounts receivable are forms of secured short-term financing.

The cost of short-term loans is generally interest tied to the prime rate of interest, and for most borrowers it includes a premium above prime. Interest on a fixed-rate loan remains the same over the life of the loan. Interest on a floating-rate loan changes each time the prime rate changes. The cost of unsecured loans is lower than the cost of secured loans.

5. Distinguish between debt and equity as sources of long-term financing, and describe their relationship to leverage and the cost of capital.

Financial managers must choose the best mix of debt and equity for their firm. The main advantage of debt financing is the tax-deductibility of interest. Debtholders also rank ahead of equity owners in their claim on income and assets. But debt involves financial risk because it requires the payment of interest and principal on specified dates. Equity—common and preferred stock—may or may not pay dividends and is considered a permanent form of financing, with no maturity date. Dividends are not tax-deductible. A firm that uses debt benefits from the effect of leverage, which magnifies the company's rate of return. Financial managers also seek the lowest cost of capital, which reflects the firm's financing costs over the long term. The cost of capital represents the minimum rate of return the firm must earn on an investment to maintain the firm's value.

6. Describe the main sources of long-term debt and equity financing, their key features, and their costs.

The main types of long-term debt are term loans, bonds, and mortgage loans. Term loans can be secured or unsecured and generally have five- to twelve-year maturities. Bonds usually have maturities of ten to twenty years. Mortgage loans are secured by real estate. Long-term debt usually costs more than short-term financing because of the greater uncertainty that the borrower will be able to repay the loan.

The chief sources of equity financing are common stock, retained earnings, and preferred stock. New issues of common stock can be sold by an underwriter, or the company can offer existing stockholders the right to buy new shares in proportion to their existing ownership. Selling stock involves three costs: issuing costs (such as underwriters' fees and administrative expenses), dividends, and dilution. Retained earnings are profits reinvested in the firm. Preferred stockholders are also equity owners. Preferred stock increases the firm's leverage. For the issuing firm, preferred stock is more expensive than debt but less expensive than common stock. Venture capital is often a source of equity financing for young companies.

■ DISCUSSION QUESTIONS

1. It has been said that the financial manager's job is to spend money and raise money. Relate these two responsibilities to the balance sheet.

2. You are a financial planner at General Foods Company and have been asked to prepare forecasts and budgets for a new line of high-nutrition desserts. Why is it important for the finance department to prepare these plans for the product-development group? What factors would you consider in developing your projections? How would you assess their impact on the firm's profits?

3. Why is it important for a firm to maintain liquidity? Discuss the pros and cons of meeting all liquidity needs by holding cash.

4. Amy Blumenthal, the cash manager for a chain of sporting goods stores, is studying ways to increase cash. To date, the chain has always paid accounts payable within the credit period. She is now considering extending payments beyond the due date. Discuss the pros, cons, and ethics of stretching accounts payable. What are some other options she should investigate?

5. MGB Designs, Inc., a computer graphics firm, moved into new offices. It had the following expenses. Classify each as either an operating expense or a capital expenditure, and then explain your classifications.

    a. Interior designer's fees
    b. Computer system
    c. Copy machine
    d. Moving costs
    e. The building
    f. Office supplies
    g. Office furniture
    h. Property insurance

6. Which of the following types of companies would be likely to have seasonal borrowing requirements?

    a. National airline
    b. Chain of discount drugstores
    c. Motel in Cape Cod, Massachusetts
    d. Surfboard manufacturer
    e. Video rental store
    f. Garden store in Michigan

7. In February 1994, Duracell raised its quarterly dividend 37.5 percent, from 16¢ to 22¢, and Varian Associates announced that it would start paying quarterly dividends of 6¢ per share. Figgie International, on the other hand, eliminated its quarterly dividend entirely. What signals do these actions send about the financial condition of these firms?

8. You are the chief financial officer of Discovery Labs, a privately held, five-year-old biotechnology company. Discovery has an idea for a new drug that could be a big medical breakthrough. But the firm needs to raise $3 million to fund its development. Discuss the types of long-term financing available to the firm and their pros and cons. What are the key factors you must consider in choosing a financing strategy?

■ CASE

Going It Alone

Manu Gambhir had been writing software programs—and getting paid for his work—since he was in high school. With degrees in computer science and management from the University of Pennsylvania, he was in a good position to land a job with a computer software company. However, Gambhir turned down an offer from Microsoft, where he had worked as a summer intern, to start his own software firm. Deciding that multimedia was a growth area with low barriers to entry, he began to raise money for his own company, InterMedia Interactive Software, Inc. Because Gambhir did not want to bring in outside investors and give up equity in the new company, he worked for nearly two years as a computer consultant until he earned and saved $100,000 of start-up capital.

InterMedia's first two projects were contracts from software publishers for a multimedia game called *Family Circus* and a CD-ROM index for *USA Today* covering two-and-a-half years. The CD-ROM format allowed the index user to access photographs and listen to important speeches.

Recognizing that InterMedia's success depended on developing its own projects, Gambhir approached Simon & Schuster about producing a CD-ROM version of *Lovejoy's College Guide*. With internally generated cash from his earlier contracts, he licensed the Lovejoy name and the right to use the information in electronic form. The result was *Lovejoy's College Counselor,* an interactive college guide that includes videos of college campuses and allows students to quickly identify colleges that meet chosen criteria.

The future for InterMedia looks bright. Revenues were about $500,000 in 1993, and Gambhir expects to reach $2 million in 1994 as the company introduces new products and the popularity of CD-ROM players increases. Through careful budgeting, he has kept project costs low. However, Gambhir's plans include CD-ROMs of popular children's science books that need illustrators, writers, and actors. He estimates that InterMedia needs another $1 million to fund new projects.[11]

Questions

1. Evaluate Gambhir's original financing strategy. What other options could he have used to finance InterMedia's start-up? Discuss the advantages and disadvantages of each alternative.
2. Describe the alternatives now available to InterMedia to raise the $1 million it needs to expand its operations. Which do you recommend, and why? How does the company's current situation change its financing strategy?
3. Suggest some good financial management techniques that Gambhir should use at InterMedia. What should Gambhir's major financial goal be? Does it appear that he is operating the company to meet his goal?

Securities and Securities Markets

Learning Goals

After studying this chapter, you should be able to:

1 Compare common stocks, preferred stocks, bonds, mutual funds, futures contracts, and options.

2 Describe the U.S. securities markets.

3 Explain the key securities market laws and regulatory agencies.

4 Understand investors and their goals.

5 Outline the steps involved in opening a brokerage account and making securities transactions.

6 Identify the main sources of investment information.

7 Understand how to interpret stock, bond, and mutual fund quotations.

8 Discuss current issues facing the securities markets.

 Career Profile

While a finance major in college, Bryan Albach joined an extracurricular organization called the College Finance Association, which proved to be a great resource for launching his career. The CFA sponsers programs that present its members with challenges similar to those they will encounter when they enter the workforce. In The Investment Challenge, for example, Bryan and the other members created and managed investment portfolios. The portfolios were later judged on various criteria, with the best receiving awards. The CFA also introduces its members to speakers in the various areas of finance.

It was while attending one of the association's meetings that Bryan was introduced to a financial consultant from Merrill Lynch who was making a presentation. Through this contact Bryan was able to arrange for an interview with the firm, and he's now employed there as a financial consultant.

As an investment firm, Merrill Lynch raises money for businesses and governments. This funding is created by offering new issues of securities, stocks, and bonds to investors. Merrill Lynch is also one of the world's largest brokerage firms and is committed to helping investors reach their financial goals. Bryan works in the brokerage part of the business, managing money for individuals and companies. After assessing his clients' needs through extensive profiling, he determines where they are presently with their finances and where they would like to be. He then researches the securities market to find the areas most suited to his clients—stocks, bonds, or cash equivalents such as Treasury bills—and creates a financial strategy for them.

Bryan's finance education did not stop when he graduated from college. Before allowing him to trade securities and manage money and investments for clients, Merrill Lynch put him through a two-year training program that prepared him to become a registered investment advisor. Bryan was then teamed with a mentor, one of the firm's senior financial consultants, with whom he worked on a variety of real-life situations while learning from his mentor's experience. This reduces the risk of a new broker making mistakes and also assures the company that their junior trading consultants are learning the successful ways of Merrill Lynch.

Overview

This chapter introduces securities and securities markets. First the different types of securities—common and preferred stocks, bonds, mutual funds, futures contracts, and options—are described. Next the types, operation, and regulation of securities markets are explained. Then the process of buying and selling securities and the popular sources of investment information are discussed. The chapter ends with a brief review of the issues facing the securities markets today.

STOCK: EQUITY FINANCING

securities Certificates issued by corporations or governments that represent either equity or debt investments.

Securities are investment certificates issued by corporations or governments. They represent either equity (ownership in the issuer) or debt (a loan to the issuer). The two types of equity securities are common stock and preferred stock.

COMMON STOCK

As discussed in Chapter 21, *common stock* is a security that represents an ownership interest in a corporation. A share of stock is issued for each unit of ownership. The stockholder (owner) gets a stock certificate to

■ These stock certificates prove that the bearer has an ownership interest in a company. They are issued by a company when an individual purchases a share of the company's stock. A stockholder is entitled to a portion of the company's profits and has voting rights in company matters.

prove ownership. If you own a share of the common stock of General Electric Corporation, you are a partial owner of GE. Your ownership interest isn't very big, because GE has about 927 million shares of stock outstanding. But you are an owner just the same, and your ownership gives you certain rights.

As a stockholder, you have a right to the profits of the corporation. You would get them as dividends on your common stock. *Dividends* are the part of the profits of a corporation that are distributed to stockholders. Dividends can be paid only after all the other obligations of the firm—payments to suppliers, employees, bondholders, and other creditors, plus taxes and preferred stock dividends (discussed later)—have been met. Dividends can be paid in cash or in the form of more shares of stock (called *stock dividends*). Some firms, especially rapidly growing companies and those in high technology industries, pay no dividends. Instead, they reinvest their profits in more buildings, equipment, and new products in order to earn more future profits. As noted in Chapter 19, these reinvested profits are called *retained earnings*.

voting rights Right of common stockholders to cast one vote for each share of stock owned.

Common stockholders also have **voting rights**. They get one vote for each share of stock they own. They can vote on such issues as election of the board of directors, mergers, and selection of an independent auditor.

Potential Returns to Investors

Common stock offers two types of potential returns: dividends and stock-price increases. Dividends are declared annually or quarterly (four times a year) by the board of directors and are typically paid quarterly. For instance, in February 1994 Philip Morris' directors declared a $2.76 annual dividend paid in quarterly installments of 69¢. An investor who owned 100 shares of Philip Morris common stock would be mailed a check for $69 (69¢ × 100) in January, April, July, and October.

An investor can also benefit by selling a stock when its price increases, or *appreciates*, above the original purchase price. Suppose you bought shares of Blockbuster Entertainment Corporation for $10 in July 1992 and sold them for $26 a share in March 1994. The per-share profit of $16 ($26 sales price − $10 original price) represents a 160 percent *rate of return* ($16 profit ÷ $10 original price). Stocks rarely provide such exciting results, however. And common stockholders have no guarantee that they will get any return on their investment.

Advantages and Disadvantages of Common Stock

The returns from common-stock dividends and price appreciation can be quite attractive. Over the long term, common-stock investments have been better than most other types of investments. Another advantage is liquidity: Many stocks are actively traded in securities markets and can be quickly bought and sold.

The disadvantages include the risky nature of common-stock investments. Stockholders may not get any return at all. Stocks are subject to many risks related to the economy, the industry, and the company. These risks can hold down a stock's dividends and its price, making it hard to predict the stock's return.

PREFERRED STOCK

Preferred stock is the second form of equity financing. As described in Chapter 21, preferred stock has advantages over common stock, specifically in the payment of dividends and the distribution of assets if the firm is liquidated. Preferred stockholders get their dividends before common stockholders do. Unlike common stock, preferred stock usually has a dividend amount that is set at the time the stock is issued. This dividend can be expressed in either dollar terms or as a percentage of the stock's par (stated) value. Investors buy preferred stock mainly for these dividend payments rather than for price appreciation. Because the dividends are fixed, the price of preferred stock generally does not change as much as the price of common stock.

Features of Preferred Stock

Preferred stock has features of both common stocks and bonds. Like common stock, it is a form of ownership. Dividends may not be paid on either type of stock if the company has financial hardships. But most preferred stock is *cumulative preferred stock*. Its owners must receive all unpaid dividends before any dividends can be paid to the holders of common stock. Say that a company with a $5 per year preferred dividend missed its annual dividend payment in 1992. It must pay the preferred stockholders $10 ($5 in unpaid preferred dividends from 1992 plus the $5 preferred dividend for 1993) before it can pay any dividends to common stockholders. Preferred stock is like bonds because it provides fixed income to investors, and their claim on income and assets comes before common stockholders (but after bondholders).

Advantages and Disadvantages of Preferred Stock

Investors like preferred stock because of the steady dividend income. Although companies are not legally obligated to pay preferred dividends, most have an excellent record of doing so. But the fixed dividend is also a disadvantage to investors. It limits the cash paid to them. Thus preferred stock has less potential for price appreciation than common stock.

Concept Check

- Define common stock, and describe its features.
- What are the advantages and disadvantages of common stock for investors and corporations?
- What is preferred stock, and how is it different from common stock?

BONDS: DEBT FINANCING

Bonds are long-term debt obligations (liabilities) of corporations and governments. A bond certificate is issued as proof of the obligation. The issuer of a bond must pay the buyer a fixed amount of money—called **interest**, or the *coupon rate*—on a regular schedule, typically every six months. The issuer must also pay the bondholder the amount borrowed—

interest Fixed amount of money that the issuer of a bond must pay bondholders; coupon rate.

principal Borrowed amount of money, on which the issuer of a bond pays interest; par value.

called the **principal**, or *par value*—at the bond's maturity date (due date). Bonds are usually issued in units of $1,000—for instance, $1,000, $5,000, or $10,000.

Say that you buy a Shell Oil bond with a $1,000 par value and a coupon rate of 7 1/4 percent, due in 2002. You will get interest of $72.50 per year (7 1/4% × $1,000), paid as $36.25 ($72.50 ÷ 2) every six months, through 2002. You will also get the $1,000 par value of the bond in 2002.

Bonds do not have to be held to maturity. They can be bought and sold in the securities markets. Unlike common and preferred stockholders, who are owners, bondholders are creditors (lenders) of the issuer. In the event of liquidation, the bondholders' claim on the assets of the issuer comes before that of any stockholders.

The two main types of bonds are grouped by issuer: corporations or the U.S. government.

CORPORATE BONDS

Corporate bonds are issued by corporations. They usually have a par value of $1,000. They may be secured or unsecured, include special provisions for early retirement, and be convertible to common stock. Exhibit 22-1 summarizes the features of some popular types of corporate bonds.

high-yield, or junk, bonds High-risk, high-return bonds.

High-yield, or junk, bonds are high-risk, high-return bonds that became popular during the 1980s, when they were widely used to finance mergers and takeovers. Today, they are used by companies whose credit characteristics would not otherwise allow them access to the debt markets. Because of their high risk, these bonds generally earn 3 percent or more above the returns on high-quality corporate bonds.

■ **Exhibit 22-1**
Popular Types of Corporate Bonds

Bond Type	Characteristics
Mortgage bonds	Secured by property, such as real estate or buildings.
Collateral trust bonds	Secured by securities (stocks and bonds) owned by the issuer. Value of collateral is generally 25 to 35 percent higher than the bond value.
Equipment trust certificates	Used to finance "rolling stock"—airplanes, ships, trucks, railroad cars. Secured by the assets financed.
Debenture	Unsecured bonds typically issued by creditworthy firms.
Convertible bonds	Unsecured bonds that can be exchanged for a specified number of shares of common stock.
Zero-coupon bonds	Issued with no coupon rate and sold at a large discount from par value. "Zeros" pay no interest prior to maturity. Investor's return comes from the gain in value (par value minus purchase price).
High-yield (junk) bonds	Bonds rated Ba or lower by Moody's or BB or lower by Standard & Poor's. High-risk bonds with high returns to investors. Frequently used to finance mergers and takeovers.
Floating-rate bonds	Bonds whose interest rate is adjusted periodically in response to changes in specified market interest rates. Popular when future inflation and interest rates are uncertain.

Secured versus Unsecured Bonds

secured bonds Corporate bonds that pledge specific assets as collateral.

mortgage bonds Bonds secured by a specific property of the issuing corporation.

debentures Unsecured bonds.

Corporate bonds can be either secured or unsecured. **Secured bonds** have specific assets pledged as *collateral,* which the bondholder has a right to take if the bond issuer defaults. **Mortgage bonds** are secured by property, such as real estate, equipment, or buildings. **Debentures** are unsecured bonds. They are backed only by the reputation of the issuer and its promise to pay principal and interest when due. In general, secured bonds are less risky than debentures and therefore have lower interest rates. Of course, a mortgage bond issued by a financially shaky firm is probably less secure than a debenture issued by a sound one.

Convertible Bonds

convertible bonds Bonds that may be exchanged for a specified number of shares of common stock.

Corporate bonds may be issued with an option for the bondholder to convert them into common stock. **Convertible bonds** generally allow the bondholder to exchange each bond for a specified number of shares of common stock. For instance, a $1,000 par value convertible bond may be convertible into forty shares of common stock—no matter what happens to the market price of the common stock. Because convertible bonds could be converted to stock when the price is very good, these bonds usually have a lower interest rate than nonconvertible bonds.

U.S. GOVERNMENT SECURITIES

The U.S. Treasury sells three major types of debt securities, commonly called "governments": Treasury bills, Treasury notes, and Treasury bonds. All three are viewed as risk-free because they are backed by the U.S. government. *Treasury bills* mature in less than a year and are issued with a minimum par value of $10,000. *Treasury notes* have maturities of ten years or less, and *Treasury bonds* have maturities as long as twenty-five years or more. Both notes and bonds are sold in denominations of $1,000 and $5,000. The interest earned on government securities is subject to federal income tax but is free from state and local taxes.

MUNICIPAL BONDS

municipal bonds Bonds are issued by states, cities, counties, and other state and local government agencies.

Municipal bonds are issued by states, cities, counties, and other state and local government agencies. These bonds typically have a par value of $5,000 and are either general obligation or revenue bonds. *General obligation bonds* are backed by the full faith and credit (and taxing power) of the issuing government. *Revenue bonds,* on the other hand, are repaid only from income generated by the specific project being financed. Examples of revenue bond projects include toll highways and bridges, power plants, and parking structures. These usually generate enough revenues to pay the principal and interest on the bonds. Because the issuer of revenue bonds has no legal obligation to back the bonds if the project's revenues are inadequate, they are considered more risky and so have higher interest rates than general obligation bonds.

Municipal bonds are attractive to investors because interest earned on them is exempt from federal income tax. For the same reason, the coupon interest rate for a municipal bond is lower than for a similar-quality corporate bond. In addition, interest earned on municipal bonds issued by governments within the taxpayer's home state is exempt from state income tax as well. In contrast, all interest earned on corporate bonds is fully taxable.

BOND RATINGS

Bonds vary in quality, depending on the financial strength of the issuer. Because the claims of bondholders come before those of stockholders, bonds are generally considered less risky than stocks. But some bonds are in fact quite risky. Companies can *default*—fail to make scheduled principal or interest payments—on their bonds. For instance, in 1992 Olympia and York Developments Ltd., a Canadian real estate firm, could not make interest payments on the bonds it issued to finance its worldwide real estate investments.

bond ratings Letter grades assigned to bond issues to rate their investment quality.

Investors can use **bond ratings**, letter grades assigned to bond issues, to evaluate bond risk. Ratings for corporate bonds are easy to find. The two largest and best-known rating agencies are Moody's and Standard & Poor's (S&P), whose publications are in most libraries and in stock brokerages. Exhibit 22-2 lists the letter grades assigned by Moody's and S&P. A bond's rating may change with events.

POTENTIAL RETURNS TO INVESTORS

Exhibit 22-2
Moody's and Standard & Poor's Bond Ratings

Source: Table from *Fundamentals of Investing*, 5th ed., by Lawrence J. Gitman and Michael D. Joehnk. Copyright © 1993 by Lawrence J. Gitman and Michael D. Joehnk. Reprinted by permission of HarperCollins Publishers.

The two sources of return on bond investments are interest income and gains from sale of the bonds. The price of a bond depends on the current interest rates. If interest rates have fallen since the bond was bought, it will trade at a higher price—at a *premium* over par value—because its interest rate will be more attractive. An investor would realize a gain by

Bond ratings		
Moody's	*S&P*	**Description**
Aaa	AAA	Prime-quality investment bonds: Highest rating assigned; indicates extremely strong capacity to pay.
Aa A	AA A	High-grade investment bonds: Also considered very safe bonds, although not quite as safe as Aaa/AAA issues; Aa/AA bonds are safer (have less risk of default) than single A issues.
Baa	BBB	Medium-grade investment bonds: Lowest of investment-grade issues; seen as lacking protection against adverse economic conditions.
Ba B	BB B	Junk bonds: Provide little protection against default; viewed as highly speculative.
Caa Ca C	CCC CC C D	Poor-quality bonds: Either in default or very close to it.

selling the bond at this time. On the other hand, an investor would real- ize a loss if interest rates rise and thereby lower the bond's price. Such a bond sells at a *discount* from par value. Together, interest income and potential price appreciation provide good returns to bond investors.

ADVANTAGES AND DISADVANTAGES OF BONDS

For investors, bonds can be very appealing. The claims of bondholders rank ahead of the claims of preferred and common stockholders. High- quality bonds can give conservative investors a steady stream of interest income. In recent years, the frequent changes in interest rates have also allowed investors to actively trade bonds to earn returns from price changes. Of course, this type of trading increases the potential for loss.

Concept Check

- What is a bond? Describe the common features of all bonds.
- What are corporate bonds? Discuss secured and unsecured types.
- What are bond ratings? Why are they important to both investors and issuers?
- Discuss the advantages and disadvantages of bonds for investors.

OTHER POPULAR SECURITIES

 Several other types of securities are available to investors. The most pop- ular are mutual funds, futures contracts, and options. Mutual funds have broad appeal. Futures contracts and options are used more by experi- enced investors.

MUTUAL FUNDS

Suppose that you have $1,000 to invest but don't know which stocks or bonds to buy, when to buy them, or when to sell them. By investing in a mutual fund, you can buy shares in a large, professionally managed *port- folio*, or group, of stocks and bonds. A **mutual fund** is a financial service that pools its investors' funds to buy a selection of securities that meet its stated investment goals.

mutual fund Financial service organization that pools the proceeds from sell- ing its shares and invests them in a varied collection of securities.

Mutual funds are the fastest-growing sector of the U.S. financial ser- vices industry. Mutual fund investments grew from $100 billion in 1980 to over $1.4 trillion in 1993, increasing 10 percent from 1992 to 1993 alone. Today about 4,500 publicly traded funds account for about 45 million investors. Some funds invest only in common stocks. Others invest in one or more types of bonds. Balanced funds hold a mix of stocks and bonds. Money market mutual funds invest only in short-term securities, such as certificates of deposit, Treasury bills, and commercial paper.

Each mutual fund focuses on one of a wide variety of possible invest- ment goals. As Exhibit 22-3 indicates, funds exist to meet the needs of nearly all investors. Many large investment companies, like Fidelity Invest- ments, sell a wide variety of mutual funds, each with a different invest-

Fund	Area of Specialization
Dean Witter Developing Group	Small company
Dreyfus Tax-Exempt Bond	Tax-exempt income
Europacific Growth	International
Fidelity Growth & Income	Growth/income
Franklin Global Utilities	Utilities
G.T. Global Health Care	Health care
Invesco Pacific Basin	International-Pacific
Janus Venture	Small companies
Kemper US Government Securities	Government bond
Keystone Precious Metals	Precious metals
Phoenix Balanced	Balanced
T. Rowe Price New Era	Natural resources
Templeton Real Estate Securities	Specialty
United Science and Technology	Technology

■ **Exhibit 22-3**
Investment Objectives of
Selected Mutual Funds

ment goal. Investors can pick and choose funds that match their particular interests. There are even funds that invest with social responsibility in mind, avoiding investments in firms that have an adverse affect on society (the definition of social responsibility may differ among funds). For example, the Parnassus Fund does not invest in the alcohol, tobacco, gambling, nuclear power, or weapons industries. Other funds also avoid companies that fall short on environmental issues.[1]

Mutual funds appeal to investors for three main reasons. First, they are a good way to hold a diversified, and thus less risky, portfolio. Investors with only $500 or $1,000 to invest cannot diversify much on their own. Buying shares in a mutual fund lets them own part of a portfolio that may contain a hundred or more securities. Second, funds are professionally managed. And third, mutual funds may offer higher returns than individual investors could achieve on their own.

FUTURES CONTRACTS

futures contracts Agreements to buy or sell and deliver specific quantities of commodities or financial futures at an agreed price at a future date.

Futures contracts are agreements to buy or sell specified quantities of *commodities* (agricultural or mining products) or *financial futures* (financial instruments) at an agreed-on price at a future date. An investor can buy commodity futures contracts in cattle, pork bellies (large slabs of bacon), eggs, frozen orange juice concentrate, gasoline, heating oil, lumber, wheat, gold, and silver. Financial futures include Treasury securities and foreign currencies, such as the British pound or Japanese yen.

Futures contracts do not pay interest or dividends. The return depends solely on favorable price changes. These are very risky investments, because the prices can vary a great deal.

OPTIONS

options Contracts that entitle their holders to buy or sell specified quantities of financial instruments at a set price during a specified time.

Options are contracts that entitle holders to buy or sell specified quantities of common stocks or other financial instruments at a set price during a specified time. As with futures contracts, investors must correctly guess future price movements in the underlying financial instrument to earn a positive return. Unlike futures contracts, the price paid for an option is the maximum amount that can be lost. But because options have very short maturities, it is easy to quickly lose a lot of money with them.

Concept Check

- What are mutual funds? Why do they appeal to investors?
- Discuss some of the investment goals pursued by mutual funds.
- What are futures contracts? Why are they risky investments?
- What are options? How do they differ from futures contracts?

SECURITIES MARKETS

2 Stocks, bonds, and other securities are traded in the securities markets. These markets streamline the purchase and sales activities of investors by allowing transactions to be made quickly and at a fair price. They make the transfer of funds from lenders to borrowers much easier.

Securities markets are busy places. On an average day, more than 600 million shares of stock in over 8,500 companies change hands. Both individuals and businesses participate in the securities markets. Individuals have many different motives for investing in securities. Many people are motivated by the lure of making a lot of money—and quickly. They hear success stories similar to that of Callaway Golf, a golf club manufacturer whose stock jumped from $23 to $74 per share between March 1993 and 1994. But most investors do not have the same luck. Those who bought American International Petroleum during the same period saw their investment drop from $20 to $1.25 per share. Other investors are more conservative. They choose securities that are expected to provide income or stable long-term growth in value.

Businesses and governments also take part in the securities markets. Corporations issue bonds and stocks to raise funds to finance their operations. They also invest in corporate and government securities. Federal, state, and local governments sell securities to finance specific projects and cover budget deficits.

TYPES OF MARKETS

primary market Market in which new securities are sold to the public.

Securities markets can be divided into primary and secondary markets. The **primary market** is where new securities are sold to the public, usually with the help of investment bankers. In the primary market, the issuer of the security gets the proceeds from the transaction. A security is sold in the primary market just once—when it is first issued by the corporation or government.

secondary market Market in which already-issued securities are bought and sold.

Later transactions take place in the **secondary market**, where "old" (already issued) securities are bought and sold, or *traded*, between investors. The issuers generally are not involved in these transactions. The vast majority of securities transactions take place in secondary markets, which include the organized stock exchanges, the over-the-counter securities market, and the commodities exchanges.

THE ROLE OF THE INVESTMENT BANKER

investment banker Organization that specializes in selling new security issues.

underwriting The process, undertaken by investment bankers, of buying securities from corporations and reselling them to the public.

Investment banking plays a key role in helping firms raise long-term financing. An **investment banker** is a firm that specializes in selling new security issues. These firms act as intermediaries, buying securities from corporations and governments and reselling them to the public. This process, called **underwriting**, is the main activity of the investment banker, which acquires the security for an agreed-upon price and hopes to be able to resell it at a higher price to make a profit. Investment bankers advise clients on pricing and structure of new securities offerings, as well as on mergers, acquisitions, and other types of financing. Well-known investment banking firms include Goldman, Sachs & Co., Merrill Lynch & Co., Morgan Stanley, First Boston, PaineWebber, and Salomon Brothers. Many investment bankers also offer other financial services. For instance, Merrill Lynch is one of the nation's leading securities brokerage firms. Prudential is a major insurance and stock brokerage firm.

ORGANIZED STOCK EXCHANGES

organized stock exchanges Places where securities are bought and sold.

The two key types of securities exchanges are organized stock exchanges and the over-the-counter market. **Organized stock exchanges**, organizations on whose premises securities are resold, account for about 65 percent of the total dollar value of shares traded. The rest is traded in the over-the-counter market.

To make transactions in an organized stock exchange, an individual or firm must be a member and own a "seat" on that exchange. Owners of the limited number of seats must meet certain financial requirements and agree to observe a broad set of rules when trading securities.

The oldest and most prestigious U.S. stock exchange is the *New York Stock Exchange (NYSE)*, which has existed since 1792. Often called the Big Board, it is located on Wall Street in downtown New York City. The NYSE handles over 82 percent of the shares traded on organized stock exchanges. It lists the securities of about 2,360 corporations. In 1993, 66.9 billion shares were traded on the NYSE, with a total dollar value of over $2.3 trillion.[2]

The second largest organized stock exchange, in terms of the number of companies listed, is the *American Stock Exchange (AMEX)*. Like the NYSE, it is a national exchange. The AMEX lists the securities of about 1,000 corporations. But in terms of shares traded, the AMEX is now smaller than some regional exchanges. In 1993, 4.6 billion shares (4 percent of the U.S. total) were traded on the AMEX; they were worth $56.7 billion (about 1.4 percent of the U.S. total). The AMEX's rules are less strict

■ The New York Stock Exchange is the oldest and most prestigious stock exchange in the United States. The trading floor is a frenzied place, as the NYSE handles over 82 percent of shares traded on organized stock exchanges. This added up to 66.9 billion shares in 1993, with a dollar value of over $2.3 trillion.

than those of the NYSE. Thus firms traded on the AMEX tend to be smaller and less well known than NYSE-listed corporations. Some firms move up to the NYSE once they qualify for listing there. Other companies choose to remain on the AMEX. Well-known companies listed on the AMEX include Atari, Amdahl, and The New York Times Co. Companies cannot be listed on both exchanges at the same time.

In addition to the NYSE and AMEX, there are thirteen regional exchanges. They list mostly the securities of firms located in their area. Together, the regional exchanges account for about 7 percent of the total shares traded in the U.S. securities markets. Each regional exchange lists from 100 to 500 companies, and some NYSE companies also list on a regional exchange. Regional exchange membership rules are much less strict than for the NYSE and AMEX. The top five regional exchanges are the Boston, Cincinnati, Chicago, Pacific (in San Francisco), and Philadelphia exchanges. The Chicago and Pacific exchanges rank ahead of the AMEX in number and dollar value of shares traded. An electronic network linking the NYSE, the AMEX, and many of the regional exchanges allows brokers to make securities transactions at the best prices.

Stock exchanges also exist in foreign countries. The Tokyo Stock Exchange is the world's second largest stock exchange, behind the NYSE. The London Stock Exchange ranks third among organized exchanges but fourth in terms of overall worldwide volume behind Nasdaq (described below). Other important foreign stock exchanges include those in Toronto, Montreal, Buenos Aires, Zurich, Sydney, Paris, Frankfurt, Hong Kong, and South Africa. The number of big U.S. corporations with listings on foreign exchanges is growing steadily. For example, about 10 percent of the daily activity in NYSE-listed stocks is due to trades on the London Stock Exchange. Stock exchanges are also developing in emerging capitalist countries such as Russia. But as the Global Competition Trends box explains, making securities transactions there is no simple matter.

TRENDS

Global Competition

Capitalist Comrades

Yulia Kazantseva stands in line for hours, vouchers clutched in hand, waiting to buy shares in Transnational Co. Germes Soyuz, the Russian oil and gas conglomerate. But the shares sell out in two hours, so she returns the next day, only to leave again without shares. Finally, on the third day there are shares, but none of the proper forms needed for the transaction. The salesman sells her the shares anyway.

Welcome to the Russian stock market. The first stocks were traded in post-Communist Russia in 1991, beginning with shares of commercial banks and investment firms. A huge number of companies were privatized in 1992, but the fledgling stock market was not ready to handle the volume of trading that resulted. The problem was compounded when the Russian government awarded a voucher to every Russian citizen, to be exchanged for shares in privatizing enterprises. Yet the large stock exchanges, like the rival Moscow Commodities Exchange and the Russian Commodities and Raw Materials Exchange, do not accept vouchers, nor will they handle small transactions for ordinary citizens.

Into the breach leaped a slew of brokerage firms that provide advice and sell securities to individual investors. However, would-be investors often find that choosing a stock is the least of their worries. Few rules govern the stock market in Russia, so each brokerage firm or exchange establishes its own system. Share prices vary among the different exchanges and brokers. Companies that privatize are required only to publish general descriptions of themselves along with basic statistics, which are often inaccurate. Indeed, the State Privatization Committee warns investors that they buy shares at their own risk.

Despite these problems, interest in investing continues to grow. The major exchanges are now expanding and specializing. However, off-exchange trading continues, and many brokerage firms have enjoyed a great deal of success: The Olma Investment Company, which contracted to sell shares of stock in Germes Soyuz, for example, opened in July of 1992 with a staff of three, and now has eighty employees in eight branches that serve up to 2,000 clients daily.[3]

OVER-THE-COUNTER MARKET

over-the-counter (OTC) market Telecommunications network that links securities dealers throughout the United States for the purpose of buying and selling securities.

Unlike the organized stock exchanges, the **over-the-counter (OTC) market** is not a specific institution with a trading floor. It is a telecommunications network that links dealers throughout the United States. The OTC market is the fastest-growing part of the stock market. The number of shares trading on it doubled between 1990 and 1993, and the dollar value almost tripled. In 1993, 66.5 billion shares were traded, with a total dollar value of $1.35 trillion.

The securities of many well-known companies, some of which could be listed on the organized exchanges, trade on the OTC market. Examples are Apple Computer, Ben & Jerry's, Coors, Lotus Development, MCI, Nordstrom Department Stores, and Starbucks. The stocks of most commercial banks and insurance companies also trade in this market, as do most government and corporate bonds.

National Association of Securities Dealers Automated Quotation (Nasdaq) system Telecommunications system that links OTC dealers with one another and with securities brokers.

The **National Association of Securities Dealers Automated Quotation (Nasdaq) system** is the sophisticated system that links OTC dealers and brokers. Nasdaq provides up-to-date bid and ask prices on about 4,600 of the most active OTC securities. It is the main reason for the popularity and growth of the OTC market. On the NYSE, one specialist handles all transactions in a particular stock. But on the Nasdaq system a number of dealers handle ("make market in") a security. For instance, about forty dealers make a market in Apple Computer stock. Thus dealers compete, improving investors' ability to get a good price. Nasdaq now ranks second in share and dollar volume in the United States (see Exhibit 22-4) and third worldwide.

COMMODITIES EXCHANGES

commodities exchanges Places where futures contracts are traded.

Commodities exchanges provide a place for trading futures contracts. Suppliers of commodities are concerned that the prices will fall before they get their products to market. They want to sell contracts to deliver at some future date some quantity of the product at today's prices. The buyers of these contracts get protection against price increases and assurance that the commodities they need will be available. The parties to a futures contract are obligated to buy or sell the commodity as specified in the contract. Futures contracts can then be actively traded.

Investing in futures contracts is very risky and not recommended for beginners. These contracts offer potentially high returns because the investor may have to put up only 5 to 10 percent of the contract price. Of course, the potential for loss is also great. Over the long run, the average returns to commodities investors have been negative.

MARKET CONDITIONS: BULL MARKET OR BEAR MARKET?

Two terms that often appear in the financial press are "bull market" and "bear market." They refer to the general condition of the market—whether securities prices are rising or falling over time. Market conditions change because of changing investor attitudes, changes in economic activity, and government efforts to stimulate or slow down economic activity.

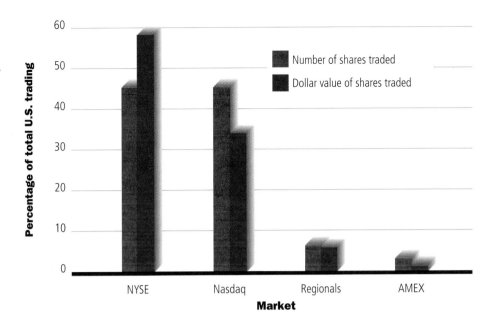

Exhibit 22-4
Where Securities Are
Traded

Source: Data for 1993 provided by New
York Stock Exchange, American Stock
Exchange, and Nasdaq.

bull markets Securities
markets characterized by rising prices.

bear markets Securities
markets characterized by
falling prices.

Securities prices rise in **bull markets**. These markets are normally associated with investor optimism, economic recovery, and government action to encourage economic growth. In contrast, prices go down in **bear markets**. Investor pessimism, economic slowdown, and government restraint are all possible causes. As a rule, investors earn better returns in bull markets. On the other hand, they earn low, and sometimes negative, returns in bear markets.

Bull and bear market conditions are hard to predict. Usually they can't be identified until after they begin. Over the past fifty years, the stock market has generally been bullish, reflecting general economic growth and prosperity. Bull markets tend to last longer than bear markets. The bull market that started in 1982 lasted a full five years, and the bear market that preceded it lasted just over a year and a half.

3 REGULATION OF SECURITIES MARKETS

The securities markets are regulated by both state and federal governments. The states were the first to pass laws aimed at preventing securities fraud. But most securities transactions occur across state lines. Thus federal securities laws are more effective.

The *Securities Act of 1933* was passed by Congress in response to the 1929 stock market crash and subsequent problems during the Great Depression. It protects investors by requiring full disclosure of information about new securities issues. The issuer must file a *registration statement* with the Securities and Exchange Commission (SEC), which must be approved by the SEC before the security can be sold. One portion of the registration statement, the *prospectus*, is a summary that must be given to potential investors.

The *Securities Exchange Act of 1934* expanded the scope of federal regulation. It formally gave the SEC power to control the organized securities exchanges. The act was amended in 1964 to give the SEC authority over the OTC market as well. The amendment included rules for operating the stock exchanges and granted the SEC control over all participants (exchange members, brokers, dealers) and the securities traded in these markets. Each participant must file a registration statement. Corporations with publicly traded stock must file periodic financial reports with the SEC.

Other important legislation regulates investment companies (such as mutual funds) and investment advisers. The *Investment Company Act of 1940* establishes rules and regulations for investment companies and gives the SEC the right to regulate their practices. The *Investment Advisers Act of 1940* requires disclosure about the background of those who provide investment advisory services.

In 1970 the *Securities Investor Protection Corporation (SIPC)* was established to protect customers in the event of financial failure of a brokerage firm. Although monitored by the SEC and Congress, the SIPC is not an agency of the U.S. government. It insures each customer's account for up to $500,000. SIPC insurance does not guarantee that the customer will recover the full dollar value of securities but only that the securities themselves will be returned. Note that the SIPC protects investors only if the brokerage firm fails. It *does not* insure against bad investment advice.

Concept Check

- Distinguish between primary and secondary securities markets. What role does the investment banker play in issuing new securities?
- Describe organized stock exchanges. How does the over-the-counter (OTC) market differ? What role does Nasdaq play?
- Describe futures contracts and the motives for trading them.
- Briefly describe the key provisions of the main federal laws designed to protect securities investors.

INVESTORS AND THEIR GOALS

4 People invest their money for all sorts of reasons. Some want to save for a new home or their children's education. Others want to supplement their income. Still others invest to build up a nest egg for retirement. Businesses also invest, generally to earn income on excess cash. And some companies, such as mutual funds, are in the business of investing.

The two main motives for securities trading are investment and speculation. **Investment** is a long-term strategy. It prefers securities with somewhat predictable levels of return and market values. On the other hand, **speculation** is a short-term strategy that involves the purchase and sale of high-risk securities. Speculators seek high returns within a short time. They invest in the securities of companies with no record of operating success, uncertain earnings patterns, or widely fluctuating share prices.

investment Securities bought for their predictable levels of return and market values over the long term.

speculation Securities bought for high returns within a short time.

Speculative investments include the junk bonds used to finance mergers, futures contracts on silver or other commodities, and options. The stocks of new high-tech companies also provide opportunities for speculation.

TYPES OF INVESTORS

The two types of investors are individual investors and institutional investors. Their characteristics and goals differ, but both groups follow similar basic investment principles.

Individual investors invest their own money in order to achieve their personal financial goals. Over 51 million individuals (about 21 percent of the population) hold about 64 percent of the more than $5 trillion total U.S. equities outstanding, either directly (54 percent) or through mutual funds (10 percent).[4]

institutional investors
Investment professionals who are paid to manage other people's money.

Institutional investors are investment professionals who are paid to manage other people's money. Most of these professional money managers work for financial institutions, such as banks, mutual funds, insurance companies, and pension funds. Others invest the funds of foundations and universities. Institutional investors control very large sums of money. They aim to meet the investment goals of their clients. Institutional investors are a major force in the securities markets. They account for about 65 percent of all trading. More than 10,000 U.S. institutions currently control about $5 trillion in financial assets, which include stocks, bonds, mutual funds, real estate, and foreign securities.[5]

INVESTMENT GOALS

Whether an individual or an institution, every investor should start with this question: "What do I want to achieve with my investment program?" Realistic investment goals are based on the investor's investment motives, financial resources, age, and family situation. Once set, the goals can be used to develop an investment strategy.

risk Chance that an investment will not achieve the expected level of return.

Any investment has **risk,** which in the investment sense is the chance that the investment will not reach the expected level of return. The amount of risk is directly related to the expected return. In other words, investors who want a higher return from their investments must be prepared to accept greater risk. Because most investors dislike risk, they expect higher returns to justify taking more risk. Investors must find their own "comfort level" with regard to risk.

There are many investment goals. The most common of them are income, growth, and safety.

Income

Investors wishing to supplement their income will choose securities that provide a steady, reliable source of income from stock dividends, bond interest, or both. Good choices include low-risk securities such as U.S. Treasury issues, high-quality corporate bonds, preferred stock, and common stock of large, financially sound corporations that regularly pay div-

■ Some investors prefer low-risk securities like high-quality corporate bonds or preferred stock. They hope such securities will provide a steady source of income through interest and dividends. Other investors are interested in growth stocks, whose prices are expected to increase over time. One example of a company whose stock is on the rise is Home Depot. The company is growing fast and provides a high return on investors' money.

dividend yield Measure used to assess the dividends paid on common stock; calculated by dividing the current annual dividend by the market price of the stock.

idends (called *income stocks*). About 80 percent of the NYSE-listed companies pay dividends, and many of them have not missed a dividend payment for decades. Exxon has been paying quarterly dividends since 1882, General Electric since 1899. An advantage of income stocks over bonds and preferred stocks is their potential for growing—rather than fixed—dividends. For instance, companies with high growth in recent per-share dividends include Fluor, Hewlett-Packard, PepsiCola, Bankers Trust, and Bristol Meyers-Squibb.[6]

Dividend yield is a popular way to assess the dividends paid on common stock. It is calculated by dividing the current annual dividend by the market price. For instance, the dividend yield for Mobil on March 3, 1994, was 4.2 percent ($3.40 annual dividend ÷ $80.25 market price). The dividend yield is a good way to compare the returns from different stocks. Say that on March 1, 1994, Jessica Robbins wishes to invest in income stock and is considering the following companies:

Company	Annual dividend	Market price	Dividend yield
Chemical Bank	$1.52	$36.00	4.2%
Commonwealth Edison	1.60	27.125	5.9
Du Pont	1.76	51.75	3.4

Looking only at the dollar amount of the annual dividends, Jessica might choose Du Pont. But by comparing dividend yields, Jessica finds that both

Commonwealth Edison and Chemical Bank provide higher returns on her investment.

Growth

Another important investment goal is growth, or increasing the value of the investment. Many investors try to find securities that are expected to increase in price over time. Generally they choose stocks with above-average rates of growth in earnings and price that are expected to continue. For instance, the earnings of so-called *growth stocks* might increase 15 to 20 percent or more at a time when the earnings of most common stocks are increasing only 5 to 6 percent. Companies with strong records of earnings growth include Gillette, Johnson & Johnson, Microsoft, Nike, and Wal-Mart.[7] Firms that keep and reinvest their earnings to finance growth tend to pay low or no dividends to investors. But they are the ones whose stock price tends to increase the most over time.

Safety

Safety is yet another investment goal. Investors who opt for safety do not want to risk the funds they've invested. They generally choose government and high-quality corporate bonds, preferred stocks, and mutual funds. They avoid common stock because of its frequent price fluctuations. An investor can earn big profits by buying stock when the price is low and selling it when the price is high. But there is no assurance that a stock's price will do what you want or expect it to do. Thus investors who want safety will invest for the long term, choosing the securities of strong companies and waiting patiently for prices to rise.

Developing an Investment Strategy

An investor's strategy may combine several of the above goals. Some securities can fulfill more than one goal. Although a certain stock may be chosen for its regular dividends or bonds for their interest income, they may also provide the benefit of growth through increases in market value.

diversification Combining securities that have different patterns and amounts of return.

Another important part of an investment strategy is **diversification**. It involves combining securities with different patterns and amounts of return. The resulting portfolio is more likely to meet investment goals than any one security is. A portfolio that includes preferred stocks paying high dividends and growth stocks paying modest dividends increases the potential of achieving both income and growth. Investing in a portfolio of securities also greatly reduces risk. Another way to diversify is to invest in companies in different industries.

HOW TO BUY AND SELL SECURITIES

5

stockbroker Person licensed to buy and sell securities on behalf of clients.

Before investing in securities, investors must choose a stock brokerage firm, choose a stockbroker at that firm, and open an account. A **stockbroker** is a person who is licensed to buy and sell securities on behalf of his or her clients. Investors should seek a broker who understands their investment goals and can help in pursuing them.

The two basic types of accounts an investor may open at a brokerage firm are cash accounts and margin accounts. With a *cash account*, security purchases are paid for in full (cost of the securities plus commissions). In a *margin account*, the investor puts up only 50 percent of the cost of the securities. He or she borrows the balance from the broker and pays interest on the loan. The broker holds the securities as collateral for the loan.

When the investor decides to buy or sell a security, the broker makes the transaction. Exhibit 22-5 depicts this process for a stock listed on an organized exchange. To make transactions in the Nasdaq/OTC market,

Exhibit 22-5
How Stockbrokers Execute Trades

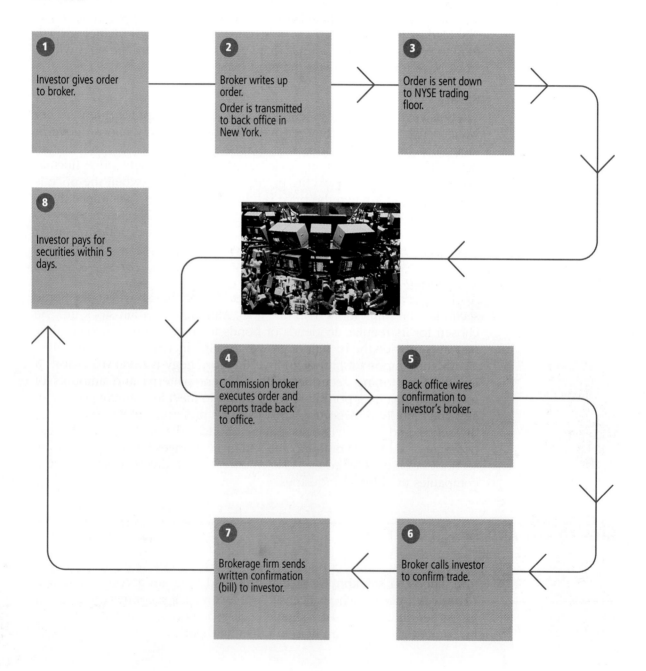

1 Investor gives order to broker.

2 Broker writes up order. Order is transmitted to back office in New York.

3 Order is sent down to NYSE trading floor.

8 Investor pays for securities within 5 days.

4 Commission broker executes order and reports trade back to office.

5 Back office wires confirmation to investor's broker.

7 Brokerage firm sends written confirmation (bill) to investor.

6 Broker calls investor to confirm trade.

the broker uses a computer to find out who deals in the security. He or she then contacts the dealer offering the best price and makes the transaction.

Stocks usually are bought and sold in blocks of 100 shares, called **round lots**. But sometimes an investor can't afford 100 shares of a stock. A purchase of less than 100 shares is called an **odd lot**. Because only round lots are traded on the exchanges, odd lots are grouped together to make up a round lot. An extra fee is charged for odd-lot transactions.

Investors can place three basic types of orders when buying or selling securities. A *market order* is an order to buy or sell a security at the best price available when it is placed. A *limit order* is an order to buy a security at a specified price (or lower) or to sell at a specified price (or higher). If the limit requested by the investor is not reached, the trade is not executed. With a *stop-loss order*, the stock is sold if the market price reaches or drops below a specified level. The stop-loss order is used to limit an investor's loss in the event of rapid declines in stock prices.

Brokerage firms are paid commissions for executing clients' transactions. Although brokers can charge whatever they want, most firms have fixed commission schedules for small transactions. These commissions usually depend on the value of the transaction and the number of shares involved. They typically amount to about 2 percent of the total price of a stock transaction and 1 percent or less on bond transactions. Brokerage firms generally charge a minimum fee of $25 to $30 on bond transactions, regardless of how many bonds are traded. Because their large volume of transactions makes them desirable clients, institutional investors can often negotiate lower commissions on stock and bond trades.

U.S. securities firms are increasing their use of the latest technology to improve the accuracy and speed with which they make securities transactions, as the Technology Trends box explains.

round lots Blocks of 100 shares of stock.

odd lots Blocks of fewer than 100 shares of stock.

TRENDS

Technology

Tools of the Trade

In March 1991 the brokerage firm Salomon Brothers made a huge error: they sold 11 million *shares* of stock instead of the $11 million *worth* of stock they intended to sell. The error cost them around $500,000. How was such a mistake made? It turns out that the vast majority of the 423 billion securities traded in the United States that year were placed with notes scribbled on a scrap of paper. These scribblings were then deciphered by keypunch operators, who entered the data into computers at the end of each day.

To reduce this enormous potential for error, Merrill Lynch, in partnership with Automatic Data Processing, created a professional information system, called Prism. The system allows the firm's brokers to handle questions and transactions while they are on the phone with clients. In fact, they can enter and validate an order, transmit it to the necessary exchange, and have it executed and confirmed on their terminals in less than a minute. Another advantage of Prism is that it's tied into Merrill Lynch's inventory control system, so

that client purchases and sales are instantaneously posted in the firm's inventory of securities.

Such an improvement in technology is invaluable to Wall Street brokerage firms, whose profit depends on the accuracy of information and how fast it is transmitted. Today firms must choose between many high-tech options offered by computer vendors and data processing service companies. Instead of farming out work to service firms that boasted the latest hardware, Bear Stearns chose to bring its information processing in-house and consolidate the existing computer system onto a few hardware platforms. This shift saves the firm from $8 million to $10 million each year. The new system was so successful that Bear Stearns now handles securities clearing for 1,425 outside firms, creating a new source of revenue. Explains Ben Kuenemann of Bear Stearns, "People think computers are different from paper and pencils and adding machines. But they're all just tools. We look at technology as you should any business decision: risk, reward, cost benefit."[8]

Concept Check

- What is the difference between investment and speculation?
- Describe the characteristics of individual and institutional investors.
- Discuss the three main investment goals and the types of securities that would be used to achieve them.

POPULAR SOURCES OF INVESTMENT INFORMATION

6 Good information is a key to successful investing. Studying information about market conditions and investment options should increase returns.

ECONOMIC AND FINANCIAL PUBLICATIONS

Two of the best known publications for economic and financial information are *The Wall Street Journal*, the weekday newspaper providing the most complete and up-to-date coverage of business and financial news, and *Barron's*, a weekly newspaper that carries detailed company analyses. Other excellent sources are such magazines as *Business Week, Financial World, Forbes, Fortune*, and *Money*. Investment professionals use *Financial Analysts Journal* and *Institutional Investor* as well. Newspapers in most cities have sections with business news.

Subscription advisory services also offer investment information and recommendations. Moody's, Standard & Poor's, and Value Line Investment Survey are among the best known. Each offers a wide range of services. Moody's and Standard & Poor's also publish manuals with historical data on most publicly traded companies and monthly stock and bond guides that summarize several thousand issues. Many investment newsletters also give subscribers market analyses and specific buy and sell recommendations.

STOCKHOLDERS' REPORTS

Stockholders' reports are an excellent source of information about a corporation. They include annual reports issued about two months after the end of the company's accounting year, quarterly updates, and other reports filed with the Securities and Exchange Commission.

BROKERAGE FIRM RESEARCH REPORTS

Many stock brokerage firms have big research departments. Their reports range from economic and market forecasts to industry and company analyses. Some research reports focus on a certain industry and recommend securities in that industry to buy, sell, or hold. These reports often forecast prices and potential returns for selected securities.

⑦ SECURITY-PRICE QUOTATIONS

The security-price quotations in *The Wall Street Journal* and other financial media can be hard to understand at first. The quotations typically report the results of the previous day's trading activity. Stock brokerage firms have electronic quotation systems that give up-to-the-minute prices. Investors with personal computers can subscribe to special services, such as Prodigy and Dow-Jones News/Retrieval, that also give current stock quotations.

Stock Quotations

Prices for NYSE, AMEX, and Nasdaq stocks are all quoted the same way: in eighths of a dollar, shown as fractions. (A change to decimal pricing, which is used in other global markets, is currently under consideration.) Exhibit 22-6 shows a portion of the March 1, 1994, stock quotations for NYSE-listed stocks, as they appeared in *The Wall Street Journal* on March 2, 1994. These quotations show not only the most recent price but also the highest and lowest price paid for the stock during the previous fifty-two weeks, the annual dividend, the dividend yield, the price/earnings ratio, the day's trading volume, high and low prices for the day, and the change from the previous day's closing price. The **price/earnings (P/E) ratio** is calculated by dividing the current market price by earnings per share. A company's P/E ratio should be compared to those of other companies in the same industry.

price/earnings (P/E) ratio Relationship between the current market price of a stock and its earnings per share; calculated by dividing the price by earnings per share.

To understand how to read stock quotations, follow the listing for the common stock of Chrysler Corporation in Exhibit 22-6, highlighted in blue. The stock traded at a high of 63 1/2 ($63.50) and a low of 37 ($37.00) over the previous fifty-two weeks. It paid annual dividends of $0.80, a 1.4 percent dividend yield. (Note that these columns are blank for Chyron, a biotechnology firm, which doesn't pay a dividend.) On March 1, Chrysler's P/E ratio was 8, and 1,638,000 shares (16380 × 100) were traded. On that date the stock traded at a high of 57 1/4 ($57.25), a low of

Means this is preferred stock issue

Means stock reached new high for year on day quoted.

High and low prices for previous 52 weeks

Abbreviated company name

Symbol for the company

Annual dividends per share for past 12 months

Dividend yield (dividend as percentage of price per share)

Price/earnings ratio

$$\left(\frac{\text{market price}}{\text{earnings per share}}\right)$$

Volume of shares traded on given day, in hundreds

High and low prices for day's trading

Closing (final) price for day

Net change in price from previous day

| | 52 Weeks | | | | | Yld | | Vol | | | | Net |
	Hi	Lo	Stock	Sym	Div	%	PE	100s	Hi	Lo	Close	Chg
	27 1/4	17 1/8	Chesapke Cp	CSK	.72	2.9	56	418	27 7/8	24 1/2	24 3/4	+ 1/4
	17 1/2	13 1/2	ChesapkUtil	CPK	88f	6.1	13	12	14 1/2	14 1/4	14 1/2	...
	98 3/4	75 1/4	Chevron	CHV	3.70f	4.3	22	6297	87	84 5/8	85 1/8	−1 1/2
	15 1/2	9	Chic	JNS		...	14	39	12 7/8	12 3/4	12 7/8	− 1/8
	28 1/8	19	ChicageNoWst	CNW		...	29	225	27 1/2	26 1/2	26 5/8	− 7/8
	56 1/2	29 1/8	ChileFd	CH	1.45e	3.1	...	692	48 7/8	46 1/4	46 1/2	−1 3/4
	133 3/4	61 1/2	ChileTelefonos	CTC	2.19e	1.9	...	1729	118	112 7/8	113 1/2	−3 3/4
	28 3/4	15 5/8	ChinaFund	CHN	.91e	4.4	...	822	21 1/8	20 1/4	20 1/2	−1
n	29	12 1/4	ChinaTire	TIR	.02p	.1	...	733	19 7/8	18 3/4	19 1/8	− 7/8
	17 7/8	10	ChiquitaBrd	CQB	.20	1.2	dd	4036	17 1/2	16 7/8	17 1/4	− 3/8
n▲	56 1/4	51 1/4	ChiquitaBrd pfA			...	...	295	56 1/2	54 1/2	55 1/4	−1
▲	18	11 5/8	ChiquitaBrd pf		.41e	2.3	...	407	18 1/8	17 1/2	17 3/4	− 1/4
	10 1/4	6 3/4	ChockFull	CHF	.23t	3.2	dd	259	7 1/4	7	7 1/4	+ 1/4
	43 3/4	30 5/8	ChrisCrft	CCN	.98t	2.6	7	176	37 1/2	37 1/8	37 3/8	+ 1/4
	31 1/8	22 5/8	Christiana	CST		...	37	1	26	26	26	...
	63 1/2	37	Chrysler	C	.80t	1.4	8	16380	57 1/4	55 7/8	56 3/8	− 5/8
	96 3/8	73	Chubb	CB	1.72	2.3	19	1719	73 3/4	73	73 1/8	− 1/8
	32 7/8	22 7/8	Church&Dwt	CHD	.44	1.9	16	745	23 3/4	23 1/8	23 3/8	+ 1/4
	1	7/16	Chyron	CHY		...	...	61	3/4	5/8	11/16	− 1/16
	43 3/4	33 5/8	Citicorp Inc	CER	2.46	7.2	13	290	34 1/2	33 5/8	34 1/8	+ 1/4
	24 3/8	15 1/2	CincBell	CSN	.80	5.0	dd	786	16 3/8	15 3/4	15 7/8	− 5/8
	29 5/8	24 1/8	CincGE	CIN	1.72	7.1	dd	1126	24 5/8	24 1/4	24 3/8	− 1/8
	62	53 1/4	CincGE pfA		4.00	7.3	...	z130	54 1/2	54 1/2	54 1/2	− 1/2
	70 3/4	61	CincGE pfB		4.75	7.4	...	z120	64	64	64	− 1/4
	103	96	CincGE pfD		7.44	7.4	...	z30	101	101	101	+ 1/2
	29 5/8	19 1/4	CincMilacron	CMZ	.36	1.5	dd	778	24 1/8	23 5/8	24 1/8	+ 1/4
	3 3/4	1 1/8	CineplxOde	CPX		...	dd	1312	3	2 7/8	2 7/8	...
s	33 7/8	16 1/2	CircuitCity	CC	.08	.4	14	377	19 1/8	18 5/8	18 5/8	− 3/8
s	49 3/4	27 1/2	Circus	CIR		...	27	3851	37 1/2	36	36 3/8	− 7/8
	44 1/8	25 3/4	Citicorp	CCI		...	11	11473	41 3/8	40 3/8	40 3/8	−1 1/8
	92 1/2	81 1/4	Citicorp pf		6.00	6.5	...	24	92 3/8	91 3/4	92 1/8	...
	100 3/4	92 1/4	Citicorp pfA		7.00	7.0	...	2	99 3/4	99 1/4	99 3/4	+ 1/4
	27 5/8	25 1/2	Citicorp pfC		2.28	8.8	...	33	26	25 7/8	25 7/8	...
	28 3/4	26	Citicorp pfD		2.27	8.4	...	155	27 1/4	26 7/8	27	...
n	26 3/4	24 3/8	Citicorp pfE		2.00	7.9	...	222	25 1/2	25 1/8	25 1/4	+ 7/8

▨ **Exhibit 22-6**
Listed Stock Quotes

55 7/8 ($55.875), and closed at 56 3/8 ($56.375). The closing (final) price was 5/8 of a point, or 62.5 cents, below the previous day's closing price.

Preferred stocks are listed with common stocks. The letters *pf* or *pr* after the company's name identify a preferred stock. Look at the "Chiquita Brd pfA" listing highlighted in purple in Exhibit 22-6. Companies may have a number of preferred stock issues, each identified by a letter. The highlighted listing is series A for Chiquita Brands. Preferred stock quotes appear only when the preferred stock has been traded on the given day. Note the arrow pointing up in the left margin. It shows that the stock set a new high for the year on March 1.

Bond Quotations

Bond quotations are also included in *The Wall Street Journal* and other financial publications. Exhibit 22-7 shows quotations for NYSE bonds trading on March 1, 1994. The labels indicate how to interpret the quotations. The numbers after the issuer's name are the coupon (interest) rate and maturity. For the highlighted Bell South issue, "6 1/4 03" means that this bond has an annual interest rate of 6.25 percent and that it matures in the year 2003. Many companies have more than one issue of bonds outstanding. Notice that Bell South has five different bond series listed.

Bond prices are expressed as a percentage of the par value (principal). A closing price above 100 means the bond is selling at more than its purchase price (at a *premium*). A par value below 100 is less than the purchase price (the bond is selling at a *discount*). The price of this Bell South bond on March 1 is 98 1/4, or $982.50; it is trading at a discount.

Treasury and other government bonds are also listed in the securities quotations pages. Their listings are similar to corporate bond listings.

Mutual Fund Quotations

net asset value (NAV) The price at which each share of a mutual fund can be bought or sold.

Price quotations for mutual funds differ from stock price quotations, as shown in Exhibit 22-8. Mutual fund share prices are quoted in dollars and cents and trade at their NAV, or **net asset value**. NAV is the price at which each share of the mutual fund can be bought or sold. Note that the Fidelity Capital & Income (CpInc) Fund has no "load" (NL), or sales charge. The Fidelity Advisor Growth Opportunities (GrOpp) Fund, on the other hand, has a load. That's why the NAV and the offer price are different. *The Wall Street Journal* also lists performance data provided by Lipper Analytical Services. On Monday, the fund charges and expense ratios are shown, while on Tuesday through Friday the quotations include return statistics for different time periods, ranging from four weeks to five years, and rank compared to other funds with the same investment objectives.

MARKET AVERAGES AND INDEXES

market averages Numbers used to measure the general behavior of the market, by using the arithmetic average price behavior of a group of securities at a given point in time.

market indexes Numbers used to measure the price behavior of a group of securities relative to a base value and give a general measure of the performance of the market.

"How's the market doing today?" The question is commonly asked by people interested in the securities market. An easy way to monitor general market conditions is to follow market averages and indexes, which provide a convenient way to gauge the general mood of the market by summarizing the price behavior of a group of securities. **Market averages** use the arithmetic average price of the securities at a given point in time to track market movements. **Market indexes** measure the current price behavior of a group of securities relative to a base value set at an earlier point in time. The level of an average or index at any given time is less important than its behavior—its movement up and down—over time.

Exhibit 22-7
Bond Quotations

Source: *Wall Street Journal*, 2 March 1994, p. C16. Reprinted by permission of *The Wall Street Journal*, © 1994 Dow Jones & Company, Inc. All Rights Reserved Worldwide.

Means this is convertible issue

Means this is a zero-coupon issue

Net change in price since previous day

Closing price for the day

Number of bonds traded

Abbreviated company name; annual interest rate and maturity date; current yield

| | | CORPORATION BONDS Volume, $45,740,00 | | |
| | | | | Net |
Bond	Cur Yld	Vol	Close	Chg
AForP 5s30	7.6	15	66	+ 1/2
AMR 9s16	8.6	77	104 1/2	− 1/8
AMR 8.10s98	7.7	25	105 3/4	− 1/4
Actava 9 7/8 97	9.8	30	100 5/8	− 1/4
Actava 9 1/2 98	9.5	56	99 7/8	...
AirbF 6 3/4 01	cv	22	113 1/2	−1
AlskAr 6 7/8 14	cv	76	86	− 3/4
AlskAr zr06	...	149	39 3/4	− 1/8
Albnylnt 5s02	cv	22	96	− 1/2
AlldC zr96	...	25	90 1/2	...
AlldC zr2000	...	72	64	− 7/8
AlldC zr95	...	15	92 7/8	...
AlldC zr97	...	85	81 3/8	−1
AlldC zr99	...	5	70 1/2	−1
AlldC zr01	...	10	61 1/8	− 3/8
AlldC zr05	...	20	45 1/2	+ 7/8
AlldC zr09	...	275	32 3/8	− 1/4
AlegCp 6 1/2 14	cv	50	102 1/2	...
Allwst 7 1/4 14	cv	25	91 1/2	...
AMAX 14 1/2 94	13.6	20	107	+1
AmBrnd 8 1/2 03	7.5	5	112 7/8	+2
AmBrnd 5 1/4 95	5.2	50	100 1/8	− 1/4
ACyan 8 3/8 06	8.2	1	101 3/4	+ 1/4
ATT 4 3/4 98	4.9	20	96	− 1/2
ATT 4 3/8 96	4.5	11	98 1/4	+ 1/8
ATT 4 3/8 99	4.7	100	92 7/8	+ 1/8
ATT 6s00	6.0	164	100 3/8	...
ATT 5 1/8 01	5.5	91	92 7/8	−1
ATT 8 5/8 31	7.8	56	110 1/2	− 1/2
ATT 7 1/8 02	6.9	192	103 3/4	− 3/4
ATT 8 1/8 22	7.7	311	106	− 3/8
ATT 8 1/8 24	7.6	114	106 3/8	− 5/8
ATT 4 1/2 96	4.5	40	99 3/8	− 1/8
Amoco 8 5/8 16	7.8	13	110	−2
AmocoCda 7 3/8 13	6.4	4	114 1/2	−1 1/2
Anhr 8 5/8 16	8.2	40	105 3/4	− 1/4
AnnTaylr 8 3/4 00	8.8	55	100	−1
Arml 9.2s00	9.2	20	100 3/8	− 1/4
Arml 8 1/2 01	8.9	15	96	−1 3/4
AshO 6 3/4 14	cv	2	101 3/4	...
Atchsn 4s95	4.1	3	98 5/8	− 1/8
AuburnHl 12 3/8 20f	...	5	152 1/2	−1 3/4
AutDt zr12	...	21	41 1/4	+ 1/4
Bally 10s06f	cv	63	97 1/4	− 1/2
BncFla 9s03	cv	1	120	−1 3/4
Barold 8s03	7.4	100	108	−3 1/4
BellsoT 7 7/8 03	7.7	123	103	− 1/2
Bellso 6 1/4 03	6.4	97	98 1/4	−1
BellsouT 7 1/2 33	7.4	10	101 1/4	+ 3/4
Bellso 5 7/8 09	6.4	74	91 5/8	− 1/2
Bellso 6 3/4 33	7.4	95	91 3/8	− 5/8
BstBuy 8 5/8 00	8.8	1070	98 5/8	−1

Dow Jones Industrial Average (DJIA) Market average consisting of an average of the stock prices of thirty corporations listed on the New York Stock Exchange.

The most widely used market average is the **Dow Jones Industrial Average (DJIA)**. It measures the stock prices of a group of thirty large, well-known NYSE corporations (listed in Exhibit 22-9). The companies in the DJIA are chosen for their total market value and broad public ownership. The DJIA is calculated by adding the closing price of each of the 30

Net change in NAV from previous quotation

Offer price (includes sales charge)

Net asset value

Investment objective

Indicates additional sales charges to buy fund

Fund name

Total return data from Lipper Analytical Services: year-to-date, periodic returns, performance rank

Indicates redemption fee to sell fund

Means there is no sales charge; offer price is same as NAV

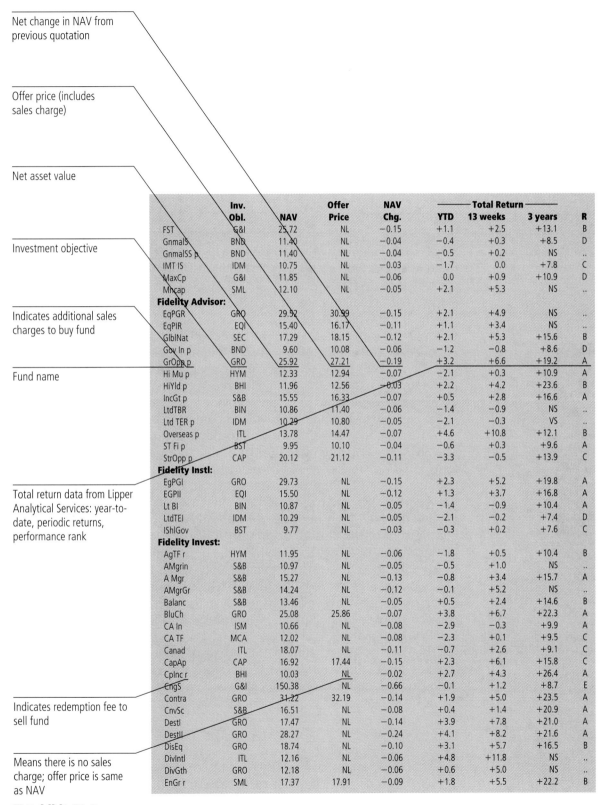

	Inv. Obl.	NAV	Offer Price	NAV Chg.	YTD	13 weeks	3 years	R
FST	G&I	25.72	NL	−0.15	+1.1	+2.5	+13.1	B
GnmalS	BND	11.40	NL	−0.04	−0.4	+0.3	+8.5	D
GnmalSS p	BND	11.40	NL	−0.04	−0.5	+0.2	NS	..
IMT IS	IDM	10.75	NL	−0.03	−1.7	0.0	+7.8	C
MaxCp	G&I	11.85	NL	−0.06	0.0	+0.9	+10.9	D
Mncap	SML	12.10	NL	−0.05	+2.1	+5.3	NS	..
Fidelity Advisor:								
EqPGR	GRO	29.52	30.99	−0.15	+2.1	+4.9	NS	..
EqPIR	EQI	15.40	16.17	−0.11	+1.1	+3.4	NS	..
GlblNat	SEC	17.29	18.15	−0.12	+2.1	+5.3	+15.6	B
Gov In p	BND	9.60	10.08	−0.06	−1.2	−0.8	+8.6	D
GrOpp p	GRO	25.92	27.21	−0.19	+3.2	+6.6	+19.2	A
Hi Mu p	HYM	12.33	12.94	−0.07	−2.1	+0.3	+10.9	A
HiYld p	BHI	11.96	12.56	−0.03	+2.2	+4.2	+23.6	B
IncGt p	S&B	15.55	16.33	−0.07	+0.5	+2.8	+16.6	A
LtdTBR	BIN	10.86	11.40	−0.06	−1.4	−0.9	NS	..
Ltd TER p	IDM	10.29	10.80	−0.05	−2.1	−0.3	VS	..
Overseas p	ITL	13.78	14.47	−0.07	+4.6	+10.8	+12.1	B
ST Fi p	BST	9.95	10.10	−0.04	−0.6	+0.3	+9.6	A
StrOpp p	CAP	20.12	21.12	−0.11	−3.3	−0.5	+13.9	C
Fidelity Instl:								
EgPGI	GRO	29.73	NL	−0.15	+2.3	+5.2	+19.8	A
EGPII	EQI	15.50	NL	−0.12	+1.3	+3.7	+16.8	A
Lt BI	BIN	10.87	NL	−0.05	−1.4	−0.9	+10.4	A
LtdTEI	IDM	10.29	NL	−0.05	−2.1	−0.2	+7.4	D
IShlGov	BST	9.77	NL	−0.03	−0.3	+0.2	+7.6	C
Fidelity Invest:								
AgTF r	HYM	11.95	NL	−0.06	−1.8	+0.5	+10.4	B
AMgrin	S&B	10.97	NL	−0.05	−0.5	+1.0	NS	..
A Mgr	S&B	15.27	NL	−0.13	−0.8	+3.4	+15.7	A
AMgrGr	S&B	14.24	NL	−0.12	−0.1	+5.2	NS	..
Balanc	S&B	13.46	NL	−0.05	+0.5	+2.4	+14.6	B
BluCh	GRO	25.08	25.86	−0.07	+3.8	+6.7	+22.3	A
CA In	ISM	10.66	NL	−0.08	−2.9	−0.3	+9.9	A
CA TF	MCA	12.02	NL	−0.08	−2.3	+0.1	+9.5	C
Canad	ITL	18.07	NL	−0.11	−0.7	+2.6	+9.1	C
CapAp	CAP	16.92	17.44	−0.15	+2.3	+6.1	+15.8	C
CpInc r	BHI	10.03	NL	−0.02	+2.7	+4.3	+26.4	A
CngS	G&I	150.38	NL	−0.66	−0.1	+1.2	+8.7	E
Contra	GRO	31.22	32.19	−0.14	+1.9	+5.0	+23.5	A
CnvSc	S&B	16.51	NL	−0.08	+0.4	+1.4	+20.9	A
DestI	GRO	17.47	NL	−0.14	+3.9	+7.8	+21.0	A
DestII	GRO	28.27	NL	−0.24	+4.1	+8.2	+21.6	A
DisEq	GRO	18.74	NL	−0.10	+3.1	+5.7	+16.5	B
DivIntl	ITL	12.16	NL	−0.06	+4.8	+11.8	NS	..
DivGth	GRO	12.18	NL	−0.06	+0.6	+5.0	NS	..
EnGr r	SML	17.37	17.91	−0.09	+1.8	+5.5	+22.2	B

■ **Exhibit 22-8**
Mutual Fund Quotations

Source: *Wall Street Journal*, 2 March 1994, p. C24. Reprinted by permission of *The Wall Street Journal*, © 1994 Dow Jones & Company, Inc. All Rights Reserved Worldwide.

Alcoa	Eastman Kodak	J. P. Morgan & Co.
Allied Signal	Exxon	Philip Morris
American Express	General Electric	Procter & Gamble
AT&T	General Motors	Sears Roebuck
Bethlehem Steel	Goodyear	Texaco
Boeing	IBM	Union Carbide
Caterpillar	International Paper	United Technologies
Chevron	McDonald's	Westinghouse
Coca-Cola	Merck	Woolworth
Disney	Minnesota Mining and Manufacturing	
DuPont	(3M)	

▧ **Exhibit 22-9**
The 30 Stocks in the Dow Jones Industrial Average

Standard & Poor's 500 stock index Broad market index that includes 500 stocks listed on the New York Stock Exchange, the American Stock Exchange, and the over-the-counter market.

stocks and dividing by the DJIA divisor, a number that changes over time to adjust for events such as stock splits. As of March 1994, the DJIA divisor was 0.44418455.

The DJIA changes daily. If the DJIA closes at 1000 one day and at 1020 the next, the typical stock in the index would have moved up by 2 percent (20 ÷ 1000 = 2%). The DJIA exceeded 3900 for the first time in January 1994. Three other Dow Jones averages are a twenty-stock transportation average, a fifteen-stock utility average, and a composite average based on the sixty-five stocks in all three averages. Dow Jones introduced its World Index in January 1993 to provide a way to measure international stock performance. It tracks 2,200 companies, in 120 industry groups.

An important market index is **Standard & Poor's 500 stock index**. The S&P 500 is broader than the DJIA. It includes 400 industrial stocks, 20 transportation stocks, 40 public utility stocks, and 40 financial stocks. In addition to NYSE-listed companies, the S&P 500 also includes a small number of AMEX and Nasdaq stocks. Many market analysts prefer the S&P 500 index to the DJIA because of its broad base. It is calculated by dividing the sum of the closing market price of each stock by the sum of the market values of those stocks in the base period and multiplying the result by 10. Like the DJIA, it is meaningful only when compared to stock values at other time periods. In June 1991 S&P launched the MidCap 400 Index due to growing investor interest in stocks of medium size companies. Its composition is about two-thirds NYSE companies and one-third NASDAQ companies.

The NYSE, AMEX, and NASDAQ also have their own composite indexes. So do the London and Tokyo stock exchanges. Each is useful for analyzing the performance of its market.

Concept Check

- What are four popular sources of investment information? What information do they provide?
- What role do market averages and indexes play in the investment process? How do they differ? Distinguish between the Dow Jones Industrial Average and Standard & Poor's 500 stock index.

CURRENT ISSUES IN THE SECURITIES MARKETS

8   The securities markets are very complex. Most of the time they operate efficiently, handling half a billion or more transactions a day without problems. But the stock market crash of 1987 and the discovery of ethical abuses have uncovered some problems in the securities markets. In addition, some interesting trends will affect investors, investment firms, and the markets.

THE CRASH OF 1987 AND ITS AFTERMATH

As noted earlier, the general direction of the securities markets can be upward (bull market) or downward (bear market). The change from one type of market to the other is usually slow. But on "Black Monday"—October 19, 1987—the Dow Jones Industrial Average plunged 508 points (23 percent), the largest single-day decline in the market's history. Even the strongest companies' share prices dropped sharply. The volume of shares traded on the NYSE that day, 604 million, was the largest ever. The activity severely overloaded the exchange's computers. Some investors panicked and sold their stocks at a loss. Some small investors were scared out of the market for a while.

The causes for the October 1987 crash are still not clear. Some believe the federal government's inability to control the large budget and trade deficits undermined investor confidence. Others point to investor fears of inflation and rising interest rates. In the period right after the crash, program trading was identified as a major cause. **Program trading** uses computers to monitor securities prices and trading volumes and to automatically buy or sell stocks when certain conditions exist. Program trading involves huge numbers of shares at a time. It can result in rapid movements in securities prices. Research since the crash has shown that program trading accounted for only about 15 percent of the trading on October 19, not enough to cause such a rapid and large decline. All of these factors undoubtedly contributed to the crash, but no one may ever know what caused them all to occur on a single day.

To avoid a repeat of "Black Monday," the securities markets took several corrective actions. One was to create **circuit breakers**. Under certain conditions, they stop trading for a short cooling-off period to limit the amount of one day's drop in the market. For instance, the NYSE circuit breakers stop trading for an hour if the DJIA drops 250 points and two hours if it falls another 150 points. The capacity of the NYSE computer system was also upgraded to handle 1 billion shares per day, several times more than the normal volume. There is better communication between regulators and the exchanges, and small trades get priority in a crisis.[9] New rules for program trading were instituted, although this technique is no longer used much because it is not as profitable as it once was.[10] But these measures have little impact when investor "follow-the-leader" psychology triggers massive securities sales.

program trading Use of computers to monitor security prices and trading volumes and to automatically buy or sell stocks when certain conditions exist.

circuit breakers Temporary halts in securities trading for a cooling-off period when certain conditions exist on the New York Stock Exchange.

Investors have learned a valuable lesson from the 1987 crash: don't panic. The stock market recovered within a few months. Small investors are again actively trading stocks and seem better prepared to ride out the day-to-day ups and downs of the market.[11]

ETHICAL ISSUES

As discussed in Chapter 5, all businesses must be aware of the ethical considerations of their actions. In the late 1980s and early 1990s, several cases of unethical practices in the securities industry made news. Three major infractions involved insider trading, illegal bond trading, and fraud.

insider trading Use of information that is not available to the public to make profits on securities transactions.

Insider trading is the use of information that is not available to the general public to make profits on securities transactions. Insider trading is banned by the Securities and Exchange Act of 1934. Because of lax enforcement, however, several big insider trading scandals arose during the late 1980s. The best known of these involved Ivan Boesky, who made $80 million using information supplied by insiders. He was tried, sent to prison, and fined $100 million. As a result of this and other insider trading cases, a law was passed in 1988 that greatly increases the penalties for insider trading and gives the SEC more power to investigate and prosecute claims of illegal actions. The meaning of insider was expanded beyond a company's directors, employees, and their relatives to include anyone who gets private information about a company.

Not all trading by insiders is illegal, however. Top executives and other managers often own stock in their corporations. They must notify the SEC of their intent to buy and sell shares. The largest transactions are disclosed in *The Wall Street Journal*. For example, in January 1994, the president of Scientific-Atlanta Inc. bought 10,000 shares valued at $282,000, and a director of Columbia Healthcare sold 145,000 shares market valued at $5.5 million.[12] The SEC thus makes sure that directors and employees do not use information unavailable to the general public as the basis for their transactions.

In May 1991 the securities community was rocked by another scandal, this time involving bond trading. Salomon Brothers, a major Wall Street investment firm and primary dealer in government securities, used fake bond bids to buy over 90 percent of all two-year Treasury notes sold at one auction. The law limits sales by any one entity to 35 percent. Because Salomon Brothers controlled the market for these securities, other dealers had to pay higher prices for the bonds. The government investigated and found Salomon guilty. Several top executives, including Chief Executive Officer John Gutfreund, were found to have been aware of these illegal practices, dismissed, and fined. Many investors brought civil suits against the company. Reforms in bond trading practices have now been instituted to protect investors.

In 1993 and 1994, the SEC investigated Prudential Securities and other major brokerage firms about their limited partnerships sales during the 1980s. At issue was whether brokers were guilty of fraud because they misrepresented these high-risk investments, using high-pressure sales tactics to sell them to clients looking for safety and retirement income. The

SEC and all fifty states accused Prudential of widespread fraud. Prudential denied the charges that such fraud occurred throughout the company. It also claimed that many investors, who had to pass certain income qualifications to purchase these partnerships, were in fact sophisticated investors who could be expected to understand the risks of the partnerships. Prudential, which had already paid $270 million to some investors, chose to settle the case (without admitting guilt) by establishing a $330 million fund for investor claims.[13]

As a result of these and other problems within the securities industry, the investment community itself is developing and enforcing new ethical standards aimed at further reducing the potential for abuses in the financial marketplace.

WHAT LIES AHEAD FOR THE SECURITIES MARKETS?

Several other trends are changing the way securities markets operate. Of special importance are two interrelated trends: globalization of the securities markets and the move away from Wall Street.

Globalization

U.S. firms are part of a worldwide business community. The securities markets are no different. Improved communications and the elimination of many legal barriers are helping the securities markets go global. The number of securities listed on exchanges in more than one country is growing.

Foreign securities are now traded in the United States. Likewise, foreign investors can easily buy U.S. securities. Many investors are using foreign securities to diversify their portfolios.

As of mid-1993, U.S. investors' total overseas equity holdings were $210 billion. Among the most popular international investments are companies in the United Kingdom, Canada, Japan, and Hong Kong.[14] Emerging markets in Latin America (such as Brazil, Chile, and Mexico) and the Far East (China, Thailand, Singapore, and Malaysia) are also attracting large numbers of investors. Since investors can make international transactions with relative ease, they can look worldwide for the best investment returns. Soon they will be able to trade securities around the clock, on almost any exchange in the world. Also, many international mutual funds are available. U.S. investors, especially large institutions, routinely look at major foreign financial markets.

The Move Away from Wall Street

Wall Street—brokerage firms, investment bankers, and stock exchanges—has historically been the core of the securities industry. But globalization and automation are changing its role. Advances in computers and telecommunications technology have revolutionized the securities markets. They have allowed the organized stock exchanges and Nasdaq to execute trades more efficiently. In addition, much analysis of securities can now be done by computer.

Some individual and institutional traders now make direct transactions, without using brokers, securities exchanges, or Nasdaq, in what is called the **fourth market**. The fourth market is a direct outgrowth of advanced computer technology. Individual investors can use their own inexpensive, powerful microcomputers to get information that was once available only through securities firms. They can use computer databases and software to analyze securities themselves. Money managers and institutions like pension funds and mutual funds, with large amounts of money to invest, want to avoid large fees and low returns. Thus they are developing the ability to do in-house research and trading. They are also concerned about whether the stock exchanges can handle the large securities transactions volume they generate.[15] As a result, many are using electronic order-matching systems or trading directly with each other to find the best prices for their clients. Instinet and Posit, the two largest alternative electronic exchanges, currently handle about 90 million shares a day and are growing rapidly.[16] The savings found in using the fourth market can be considerable. Philadelphia money manager Theodore Aronson manages $659 million for individual and institutional clients. By doing two-thirds of his transactions off the exchanges, he saves them about $2.5 millon each year in fees.[17] Clearly, Wall Street, U.S.A.—long the Main Street of the investment world—is giving way to Any Street, Anywhere in the World.

Concept Check

- Discuss the importance of the Crash of 1987 and describe how program trading and circuit breakers relate to it.
- What is insider trading? Why have stricter laws and ethical standards been developed to regulate the securities industry?
- How are globalization and the move away from Wall Street changing the securities industry?

■ SUMMARY

1. Compare common stock, preferred stock, bonds, mutual funds, futures contracts, and options.

Common and preferred stocks represent ownership—equity—in a corporation. Common stockholders have voting rights, but their claim on profits and assets is residual, or junior to the claims of those holding other securities. Preferred stockholders receive a stated dividend. It must be paid before any dividends are distributed to common stockholders.

Bonds are a form of debt. Bondholders are creditors of the issuing organization, and their claims on profits and assets rank ahead of those of preferred and common stockholders. The corporation or government entity that issues the bonds must pay interest and repay the principal at maturity. Bonds may be secured or unsecured.

Common stocks are more risky than preferred stocks and bonds. They offer the potential for increased value due to growth in the stock price and income through dividend payments. But neither dividends nor price increases are guaranteed. Preferred stocks are usually bought for their dividend income rather than price appreciation. Bonds provide a steady source of income and the potential for price appreciation.

Mutual funds are investment companies that pool the funds of many investors to buy a diversified portfolio of securities. Each fund has its own investment goals. Investors choose mutual funds because they offer a convenient way to diversify and are professionally managed. Futures contracts are agreements to buy or sell commodities or financial instruments at a specified price on a certain date. They are very risky investments, because the price of the commodity or financial instrument may change drastically.

Options are contracts that give the holder the right to buy or sell a given number of shares of common stock at a set price by a certain date. They, too, are high-risk investments.

2. Describe the U.S. securities markets.
Securities markets allow stocks, bonds, and other securities to be bought and sold quickly and at a fair price. New issues are sold in the primary market. After that, securities are traded in the secondary market. Organized stock exchanges, like the New York Stock Exchange and the American Stock Exchange, are places where securities are resold. The over-the-counter market is a telecommunications network linking dealers throughout the United States. The most actively traded securities are listed on the Nasdaq system, so dealers and brokers can perform trades quickly and efficiently. Futures contracts are traded at commodities exchanges.

3. Explain the key securities market laws and regulatory agencies.
The Securities Act of 1933 protects investors by requiring disclosure of important information regarding new securities issues. The Securities Act of 1934 and its 1964 amendment created the Securities and Exchange Commission and granted it broad powers to regulate the organized securities exchanges and the over-the-counter market. The Investment Company Act of 1940 regulates investment companies such as mutual funds and places them under SEC control. The Investment Advisers Act was passed in the same year. The Securities Investor Protection Corporation is a private organization that protects investment clients from financial failure of a brokerage firm.

4. Understand investors and their goals.
The two main types of investors are individuals, who invest their own money, and institutional investors, professionals who are paid to manage other people's money. Investors do best when they set goals that consider personal factors and the amount of risk they are willing to accept. Three of the most common investment goals are income, growth, and safety.

5. Outline the steps involved in opening a brokerage account and making securities transactions.
Investors must first choose a brokerage firm and a stockbroker in that firm. Then they open a cash account or a margin account. In a cash account, all securities transactions are paid in full. Margin accounts allow

investors to put up 50 percent of the price of the securities and borrow the rest from the broker. The investor gives an order to buy or sell securities to the broker, who sends it to the stock exchange to be carried out or, in the case of an over-the-counter stock, finds the dealer with the best price.

6. Identify the main sources of investment information.

The most popular sources of investment information are economic and financial publications, like *The Wall Street Journal, Barron's, Business Week, Fortune, Smart Money,* and *Money.* Other sources are subscription services and investment newsletters, stockholders' reports, brokerage firm research reports, and security price quotations.

7. Understand how to interpret stock, bond, and mutual fund quotations.

Stock quotations show the highest and lowest prices paid for the stock during the previous fifty-two weeks, the annual dividend, the dividend yield, the price/earnings ratio, the day's trading volume, closing price, high and low prices for the day, and the change from the previous day's closing price. Bond quotations show the interest rate, maturity date, current yield, trading volume, closing price, and change from the prior day. Mutual fund quotations provide the fund's objectives, net asset value, offer price, change from the previous day, return data, and rank.

8. Discuss current issues facing the securities markets.

As a result of the stock market crash on October 19, 1987, the securities markets took such corrective actions as installing "circuit breakers" to halt trading if the Dow Jones Industrial Average drops rapidly. Unethical practices such as insider trading, illegal bond trading, and fraud led to tighter regulation of financial markets. Trends that are changing the way securities markets operate are globalization of the securities markets and the use of computers to make securities trades without using the services of Wall Street.

■ DISCUSSION QUESTIONS

1. You have just won $100,000 in your state lottery. In light of your personal situation (age, finances, family situation, and so on), discuss your investment goals and develop a plan for investing the money. Be specific about the types of investments you would choose, and justify your choices.

2. Nearly every investment vehicle has some degree of risk, and investors expect to be rewarded for the risk they take. Given your own personal situation, describe your "risk profile" (how much risk you are willing to take). What types of investments would match your risk profile? How does your risk profile compare with that of your parents? With those of your classmates?

3. Compare direct ownership of securities with mutual fund ownership. What are the advantages and disadvantages of each? For whom are mutual funds a good investment, and why?

4. The stock of Lowell Enterprises is selling at $60 per share. Exactly one year ago, it was selling for $50 per share. During the year, it paid cash dividends of $2.28 per share. Calculate the following:

  a. Current dividend yield
  b. Percentage increase in price during the year
  c. Total return (expressed as a percentage of the initial purchase price) that would have been earned on a share of Lowell Enterprises stock purchased at the beginning of the year and sold at the end of the year.

5. While having dinner at a Manhattan restaurant, you overhear two investment bankers at the next table. They are discussing the takeover of Bellamco Industries by Gildmart Corp., a deal that has not yet been announced. You have been thinking of buying Bellamco stock for a while, so the next day you buy 500 shares for $30 each. Two weeks later, Gildmart announces its acquisition of Bellamco at a price of $45 per share. Have you fairly earned a profit, or are you guilty of insider trading? What's wrong with insider trading?

■ CASE

The New Stockbroker

After graduating from college, you accept an offer from a stock brokerage firm in your home town. After a lengthy training period, you start advising investors. At 9 a.m. on your first day on the job, a couple comes in. Both work, and their combined income is high by local standards. They wish to invest $50,000. Their goal is to have enough money to send their six-month-old daughter to college when she is eighteen. At 11 a.m. your next appointment arrives. He is a recent retiree who has just received $50,000 in pension funds. He collects Social Security benefits each month. Aside from that, he has only his pension, which he wants to invest.

Questions
1. What would the investment goals of these customers probably be?
2. How risk-tolerant would the couple be? How about the retiree?
3. Make general investment recommendations to these customers. Specify the types of securities you would recommend, and defend your choices.
4. Discuss some of the ethical constraints you should consider when suggesting investments to your clients.

Your Career in Finance

If you have an interest in the dollars and cents of running a business, like to follow the daily ups and downs of the securities markets, or have a knack for numbers, the world of finance may be for you. Because businesses and individuals need many different financial services, you can choose from a wide variety of positions.

There are two basic career paths in finance. The first is *managerial finance,* which involves managing the finance function for manufacturing and service businesses that make or sell consumer and commercial products or provide nonfinancial services. The second is a career in the *financial services industry,* which creates and sells financial products and services. Banking, insurance, and securities are all financial service industries.

Until recently, the financial services area was the fastest growing area of finance. But the many changes in these industries—for example, mergers and financial difficulties—have slowed the growth of employment opportunities. Although new job creation is not expected to be so great as in the mid-to-late 1980s, business graduates can still find many interesting and challenging positions.

Dream Career: Financial Planner

Today's financial world is more complex than ever. Americans constantly face new investment opportunities, changes in tax laws, and revised employee benefit plans. The variety of savings plans, securities, mutual funds, insurance policies, real estate investments, and other options confuses and frustrates many people. They are concerned with preserving or increasing their financial assets, protecting their families, and planning for their retirement. In addition, many people do not have the time to do the research needed to make wise savings and investment decisions.

Enter the financial planner. He or she asks clients specific questions about their financial needs. The planner then advises them about budgeting, securities, insurance, real estate, taxes, and retirement and estate planning and prepares a comprehensive financial plan to meet their goals. The financial planner is paid a straight fee or a fee plus commission on the dollar amount handled.

Although financial planning is a rather new field, it has grown fast. More and more people seek professional advice on managing their personal financial assets.

Financial planners should be good at dealing with people, communicating, and problem solving. The two main certification programs for financial planners are the Certified Financial Planner (CFP) or the Chartered Financial Counselor (CFC) credential. Each requires approximately two years of

Exhibit 22-7
Bond Quotations

Source: *Wall Street Journal*, 2 March 1994, p. C16. Reprinted by permission of *The Wall Street Journal*, © 1994 Dow Jones & Company, Inc. All Rights Reserved Worldwide.

Means this is convertible issue

Means this is a zero-coupon issue

Net change in price since previous day

Closing price for the day

Number of bonds traded

Abbreviated company name; annual interest rate and maturity date; current yield

CORPORATION BONDS
Volume, $45,740,00

Bond	Cur Yld	Vol	Close	Net Chg
AForP 5s30	7.6	15	66	+ 1/2
AMR 9s16	8.6	77	104 1/2	− 1/8
AMR 8.10s98	7.7	25	105 3/4	− 1/2
Actava 9 7/8 97	9.8	30	100 5/8	− 1/4
Actava 9 1/2 98	9.5	56	99 7/8	...
AirbF 6 3/4 01	cv	22	113 1/2	−1
AlskAr 6 7/8 14	cv	76	86	− 3/4
AlskAr zr06	...	149	39 3/4	− 1/8
Albnylnt 5s02	cv	22	96	− 1/2
AlldC zr96	...	25	90 1/2	...
AlldC zr2000	...	72	64	− 7/8
AlldC zr95	...	15	92 7/8	...
AlldC zr97	...	85	81 3/8	−1
AlldC zr99	...	5	70 1/2	−1
AlldC zr01	...	10	61 1/8	− 3/8
AlldC zr05	...	20	45 1/2	+ 7/8
AlldC zr09	...	275	32 3/8	− 1/4
AlegCp 6 1/2 14	cv	50	102 1/2	...
Allwst 7 1/4 14	cv	25	91 1/2	...
AMAX 14 1/2 94	13.6	20	107	+1
AmBrnd 8 1/2 03	7.5	5	112 7/8	+2
AmBrnd 5 1/4 95	5.2	50	100 1/8	− 1/4
ACyan 8 3/8 06	8.2	1	101 3/4	+ 1/4
ATT 4 3/4 98	4.9	20	96	− 1/2
ATT 4 3/8 96	4.5	11	98 1/4	+ 1/8
ATT 4 3/8 99	4.7	100	92 7/8	+ 1/8
ATT 6s00	6.0	164	100 3/8	...
ATT 5 1/8 01	5.5	91	92 7/8	−1
ATT 8 5/8 31	7.8	56	110 1/2	− 1/2
ATT 7 1/8 02	6.9	192	103 3/4	− 3/4
ATT 8 1/8 22	7.7	311	106	− 3/8
ATT 8 1/8 24	7.6	114	106 3/8	− 5/8
ATT 4 1/2 96	4.5	40	99 3/8	− 1/8
Amoco 8 5/8 16	7.8	13	110	−2
AmocoCda 7 3/8 13	6.4	4	114 1/2	−1 1/2
Anhr 8 5/8 16	8.2	40	105 3/4	− 1/4
AnnTaylr 8 3/4 00	8.8	55	100	−1
Arml 9.2s00	9.2	20	100 3/8	− 1/8
Arml 8 1/2 01	8.9	15	96	−1 3/4
AshO 6 3/4 14	cv	2	101 3/4	...
Atchsn 4s95	4.1	3	98 5/8	− 1/8
AuburnHl 12 3/8 20f	...	5	152 1/2	−1 3/4
AutDt zr12	...	21	41 1/4	+ 1/4
Bally 10s06f	cv	63	92 1/2	− 1/2
BncFla 9s03	cv	1	120	...
Barold 8s03	7.4	100	108	−3 1/4
BellsoT 7 7/8 03	7.7	123	103	− 1/2
Bellso 6 1/4 03	6.4	97	98 1/4	−1
BellsouT 7 1/2 33	7.4	10	101 1/4	+ 3/4
Bellso 5 7/8 09	6.4	74	91 5/8	− 1/2
Bellso 6 3/4 33	7.4	95	91 3/8	− 5/8
BstBuy 8 5/8 00	8.8	1070	98 5/8	−1

The most widely used market average is the **Dow Jones Industrial Average (DJIA)**. It measures the stock prices of a group of thirty large, well-known NYSE corporations (listed in Exhibit 22-9). The companies in the DJIA are chosen for their total market value and broad public ownership. The DJIA is calculated by adding the closing price of each of the 30

appear only when the preferred stock has been traded on the given day. Note the arrow pointing up in the left margin. It shows that the stock set a new high for the year on March 1.

Bond Quotations

Bond quotations are also included in *The Wall Street Journal* and other financial publications. Exhibit 22-7 shows quotations for NYSE bonds trading on March 1, 1994. The labels indicate how to interpret the quotations. The numbers after the issuer's name are the coupon (interest) rate and maturity. For the highlighted Bell South issue, "6 1/4 03" means that this bond has an annual interest rate of 6.25 percent and that it matures in the year 2003. Many companies have more than one issue of bonds outstanding. Notice that Bell South has five different bond series listed.

Bond prices are expressed as a percentage of the par value (principal). A closing price above 100 means the bond is selling at more than its purchase price (at a *premium*). A par value below 100 is less than the purchase price (the bond is selling at a *discount*). The price of this Bell South bond on March 1 is 98 1/4, or $982.50; it is trading at a discount.

Treasury and other government bonds are also listed in the securities quotations pages. Their listings are similar to corporate bond listings.

Mutual Fund Quotations

net asset value (NAV) The price at which each share of a mutual fund can be bought or sold.

Price quotations for mutual funds differ from stock price quotations, as shown in Exhibit 22-8. Mutual fund share prices are quoted in dollars and cents and trade at their NAV, or **net asset value**. NAV is the price at which each share of the mutual fund can be bought or sold. Note that the Fidelity Capital & Income (CpInc) Fund has no "load" (NL), or sales charge. The Fidelity Advisor Growth Opportunities (GrOpp) Fund, on the other hand, has a load. That's why the NAV and the offer price are different. *The Wall Street Journal* also lists performance data provided by Lipper Analytical Services. On Monday, the fund charges and expense ratios are shown, while on Tuesday through Friday the quotations include return statistics for different time periods, ranging from four weeks to five years, and rank compared to other funds with the same investment objectives.

MARKET AVERAGES AND INDEXES

market averages Numbers used to measure the general behavior of the market, by using the arithmetic average price behavior of a group of securities at a given point in time.

market indexes Numbers used to measure the price behavior of a group of securities relative to a base value and give a general measure of the performance of the market.

"How's the market doing today?" The question is commonly asked by people interested in the securities market. An easy way to monitor general market conditions is to follow market averages and indexes, which provide a convenient way to gauge the general mood of the market by summarizing the price behavior of a group of securities. **Market averages** use the arithmetic average price of the securities at a given point in time to track market movements. **Market indexes** measure the current price behavior of a group of securities relative to a base value set at an earlier point in time. The level of an average or index at any given time is less important than its behavior—its movement up and down—over time.

■ Most large brokerages offer training programs that prepare stockbrokers for the licensing examination.

study and several tests. The accounting and banking fields also have certification programs.

- *Places of employment:* Large securities or insurance companies such as Merrill Lynch or Prudential in medium- to large-size cities throughout the U.S.; financial planners can also work independently in any area, although a population base of 50,000 or more is desirable.

- *Skills required:* Four-year degree is generally required, although it is possible to enroll in the CFP program without a bachelor's degree. Three years' professional experience in personal financial planning or a related field such as banking or accounting is required to enroll in the CFP program. To establish an independent practice, a

CPA (certified public accountant), CFP, or CFC credential is helpful.

- *Employment outlook through 2005:* Excellent.

- *Salaries:* $18,000–$25,000 for an entry-level position with a large firm; planners with experience and a good reputation can earn $100,000+.

Where the Opportunities Are

Bank Officer/Manager

About a quarter of all employees in banking are managers or officers. They have positions in retail branch management; consumer, business, or real estate lending; international banking; operations; trust services; public relations and marketing; and human resources. They oversee all service operations provided by banks, from individual checking accounts to import-export financing.

Consolidation in the banking industry and increased competition among banks has made customer service a top priority. Banks are looking for employees with good people skills who can maintain the highest quality standards. As banks adapt their services to meet customers' needs, the types of positions available will change to reflect the additional services.

- *Places of employment:* Throughout the U.S., with major opportunities in financial centers such as New York, Chicago, San Francisco, and Los Angeles.
- *Skills required:* Four-year degree or MBA. Many banks have management training programs that last 12 to 18 months, with promotion to the first officer level in about two to three years.
- *Employment outlook through 2005:* Average.
- *Salaries:* $18,000–$25,000 for trainees; $22,000–$35,000 with an MBA; $35,000+ for vice presidents. Salaries vary with the size of the bank (large banks typically pay more) and with the area of specialization.

Credit Manager

Over the years, buying on credit has become a common way of doing business. Consumers use credit to pay for houses, cars, appliances, and travel, as well as for everyday purchases. Most business purchases are also made on credit.

Credit managers set the firm's credit policies, decide whether to accept or reject credit applicants, and oversee the collection of accounts receivable. In extending credit, the credit manager or credit analyst analyzes detailed financial reports submitted by the applicant and reviews credit agency reports to determine the applicant's history in repaying debts. Credit managers usually start as credit analysts and advance as they gain experience.

- *Places of employment:* Throughout the country.
- *Skills required:* Generally a four-year degree in accounting or finance, but sometimes a two-year degree is acceptable.
- *Employment outlook through 2005:* Good.
- *Salaries:* $21,000–$31,000 for credit analysts; $24,000–$41,000 for assistant credit managers; $29,000–$62,000 for credit managers.

Corporate Financial Manager

There are many positions of financial responsibility in corporations of all types—manufacturing, trade, service, and financial institutions. The highest positions are finance manager, controller, vice president of finance, and treasurer. Assistant managers and financial analysts work with finance managers.

Financial managers are concerned with raising and spending money for the firm's operations. They prepare financial plans to determine what funds will be required for payroll, raw material purchases, other operating expenses, loan payments, and so on. Financial managers work closely with the accounting department.

Most people starting out in managerial finance begin as financial analysts in the planning and budgeting area. Larger firms tend to have financial analysts who specialize in one area—forecasting, short- or long-term borrowing, or capital budgeting, for example. Smaller firms may assign the analyst several areas of responsibility.

Financial managers should have math aptitude, analytical ability, communications skills, computer skills, and the ability to work independently.

- *Places of employment:* Throughout the U.S.
- *Skills required:* Four-year degree in business, with accounting or finance major preferred; many employers require an MBA for advancement.
- *Employment outlook through 2005:* Excellent.
- *Salaries:* $22,500–$30,000 for entry-level financial analysts; $25,000–$45,000 for MBAs; $50,000+ for higher-level positions.

Stockbroker or Securities Sales Representative

Stockbrokers and securities sales representatives handle

orders for clients who wish to buy and sell securities. They also advise customers on financial matters, supplying the latest stock and bond quotations and analyst reports. Stockbrokers are usually hired by brokerage firms, investment banks, mutual funds, and insurance companies. Job opportunities for brokers are also emerging in other financial institutions such as banks.

In addition to knowledge of financial analysis and investments, successful stockbrokers and securities sales representatives have good sales and interpersonal skills, self-confidence, and a high energy level. Most large brokerage firms offer a training program at the entry level that prepares the stockbroker to take a licensing examination.

- *Places of employment:* Opportunities are available in all medium- to large-size cities.
- *Skills required:* Generally a four-year degree, but a two-year degree may be acceptable at some smaller firms.
- *Employment outlook through 2005:* Average.
- *Salaries:* $15,000–$20,000 plus commissions for trainees; $50,000–$100,000+ for experienced brokers.

Securities Analyst

Securities analysts are experts who study stocks and bonds and make recommendations on what to buy or sell. They usually specialize in certain industries (such as energy, utilities, automotive, telecommunications, or high technology) and follow selected firms in those industries. They prepare reports on these industries and securities that take into account the competitive, economic, and political environments. They are employed by and act as advisers to securities brokerage firms, investment bankers, mutual funds, insurance companies, and other financial institutions. The Chartered Financial Analyst (CFA) designation is important to success in this field. It requires passing a series of tests.

- *Places of employment:* Principally New York, although securities analysts work for institutions throughout the U.S.
- *Skills required:* Four-year degree; an MBA is often required.
- *Employment outlook through 2005:* Average.
- *Salaries:* $30,000–$40,000 for junior analysts with an MBA; experienced analysts can earn $100,000+.

Part 9

Further Dimensions and Opportunities

Overview

Businesses do not operate in a vacuum. Their decisions are very much influenced by their environment. Some of their activities are actually regulated by government, while others are monitored by the businesses themselves in order to avoid legal or tax consequences. Federal, state, and local governments exercise direct controls over business for many reasons. Certain regulations are used to encourage and protect competition, others protect consumer rights. Such governmental controls are controversial. Some people think regulation suppresses business initiative and growth. In recent years the U.S. government has promoted a policy of deregulation. This has resulted in drastic changes in formerly regulated industries like airlines.

Our legal system affects the lives and activities of everyone in the United States. The law that protects the rights and property of individuals and businesses is one of the cornerstones of our society. Laws, as rules of conduct, are created and enforced by the government—local, state, and federal. In the United States, the judiciary is responsible for settling disputes by applying and interpreting points of law. Business law is the body of law that governs commercial activities and forms the basis for business decisions. This includes contract law, property law, agency law, tort law, product liability law, and bankruptcy law. Many business decisions are strongly influenced by legal concerns.

Taxes are assessed by all levels of government on both businesses and individuals. Business pay taxes on their profits as well as payroll taxes for their employees. Again, there is great controversy about the effect of taxes on the decisions businesses make concerning investment. Some experts feel that greater investment stimulates economic growth and are opposed to any taxes that discourage investment.

Business decision making is also influenced by risk. Managers who wish to avoid risks could produce only goods with a proven track record, but that strategy would stifle growth. A policy of risk reduction or loss prevention is one way to protect against financial loss. This means that a company adopts stringent safety measures to reduce accidents. These measures can include protective clothing and training for workers as well safety equipment within structures.

Some risks just cannot be reduced to acceptable levels, so the risk is transferred through the purchase of insurance. Insurance is provided by both the government and private insurance companies. Government programs include unemployment insurance, workers' compensation, and social security. Private insurance can be purchased to cover financial losses resulting from damage or loss of property, liability claims, illness or injury, disability, and death.

Legal constraints, government regulation and taxation, and risk are all factors that affect the creation and operation of a successful business. The next two chapters will examine these issues.

The Legal and Tax Environment

Learning Goals

After studying this chapter, you should be able to:

1 Describe the sources of law, the U.S. court system, business law and the Uniform Commercial Code, and nonjudicial methods of settling disputes.

2 Describe the elements of legally enforceable contracts, and explain how breaches of contract are settled.

3 Understand the key concepts of property law.

4 Discuss other key types of business law: agency law, tort law, product-liability law, and bankruptcy law.

5 Understand the government's role in regulating businesses, and discuss the impact of deregulation.

6 Explain the taxation of business income, and list four other types of taxes affecting business.

 Career Profile

Sarah Bowers has had a quick climb. In just two years she's risen from a temporary job as an executive secretary at The Andrew Jergens Company to her present position as legal and regulatory coordinator for the firm. Jergens, a subsidiary of the KAO Corporation of Tokyo, Japan, manufactures and markets a complete line of personal care and skin care products.

Sarah is responsible for a wide variety of matters at the company. She acts as a monitor for the marketing department, assuring that the claims the company makes in its advertising can be substantiated; she checks trademark documents as they relate to Jergens' products; and she confirms that Jergens' products sold in Mexico and Canada comply with NAFTA regulations and meet various quality standards.

Sarah also works with the outside legal counsel who ensure that Jergens stays up-to-date on current legislation. This is important, because regulations relative to consumer products are constantly evolving. Jergens regularly enrolls Sarah in seminars that deal with new legislation in order to keep her informed. They also provide in-house training on court issues. When combined with the firm's strict quality control measures, this kind of instruction helps Jergens avoid product liability claims.

Extensive legal and regulatory research is part of Sarah's day-to-day responsibilities. Although her major in college was recreational administration, the advertising, marketing, and other introductory business courses she took prepared her well for the job she's in now. Every day at Jergens she draws upon the research and evaluation skills she acquired while writing papers for school. Currently, she is working toward her MBA at night in order to broaden her knowledge of marketing.

Overview

This chapter describes the legal environment of business and explains the government's role in regulating and taxing businesses. The chapter opens with a discussion of the sources of law and its importance to business, the court system, and nonjudicial ways to settle disputes—through arbitration or mediation. Several areas of law that relate to business—contract law, property law, agency law, tort law, product-liability law, and bankruptcy law—are described. Next, the chapter examines government regulation of business. Finally, the taxation of business is explained.

LAWS: THE RULES OF SOCIETY

 Our legal system affects everyone who lives and does business in the United States. The smooth functioning of society depends on the law, which protects the rights of people and businesses. The purpose of law is to keep the system stable while allowing orderly change. The law defines which actions are allowed or banned and regulates some practices. It helps settle disputes. The legal system both shapes and is shaped by political, economic, and social systems. As Judge Learned Hand wrote in *The Spirit of Liberty,* "Without [the law] we cannot live; only with it can we insure the future which by right is ours."

laws Rules of conduct that are created and enforced by a controlling authority, usually the government.

In any society, **laws** are the rules of conduct created and enforced by a controlling authority, usually the government. They develop over time in response to the changing needs of people, property, and business. The legal system of the United States is thus the result of a long and continuing process. In each generation new social problems occur, and new laws are created to solve them. For instance, in the late 1800s corporations in certain industries, such as steel and oil, merged and became dominant. The Sherman Antitrust Act was passed in 1890 to control these powerful firms. Eighty years later, in 1970, Congress passed the National Environmental Policy Act. This law dealt with pollution problems, which no one had thought about in 1890. Today new areas of law are developing in the computer and telecommunications fields with regard to privacy issues.

Our laws arise from three main sources: judicial decisions (called *common law*), written legislation (called *statutory law*), and administrative rulings (called *administrative law*). As this chapter explains, businesses are subject to many laws and regulations. When major disputes arise, an individual or business can settle the case through the court system using the litigation process—bringing a lawsuit against another party—or through private methods such as arbitration and mediation. Understanding the legal environment in which businesses operate is therefore an important part of a business education.

THE MAIN SOURCES OF LAW

common law Body of unwritten law that has been developed out of court decisions rather than enacted by legislatures.

Common law is the body of unwritten law that has evolved out of judicial (court) decisions rather than votes by legislatures. It is also called case law. It developed in England and came to America with the colonists. All states except Louisiana, which follows the Napoleonic Code inherited from French settlers, follow the English system. Common law is based on community customs that were recognized and enforced by the courts. Even today, cases settled by the courts become *precedents* for settling similar cases in the future. The court system is responsible for interpreting common law in the United States. Many areas of business law—such as contracts, agency, and property (discussed later in the chapter)—are governed by common law.

statutory law Written law enacted by legislatures.

Statutory law is written law enacted by legislatures at all levels, from city and state governments to the federal government. Examples of statutory law are the federal and state constitutions, bills passed by Congress, and *ordinances*, which are laws enacted by local governments. Statutory law is the chief source of new laws in the United States. Among the business activities governed by statutory law are securities regulation, incorporation, sales, bankruptcy, and antitrust.

administrative law Rules, regulations, and orders passed by boards, commissions, and agencies of federal, state, and local governments.

Related to statutory law is **administrative law**, or the rules, regulations, and orders passed by boards, commissions, and agencies of federal, state, and local governments. The scope and influence of administrative law have expanded as the number of these government bodies has grown. Federal agencies issue more rulings and settle more disputes than the courts and legislatures combined. Some federal agencies that issue rules are the Civil Aeronautics Board, the Internal Revenue Service, the Securities and Exchange Commission, the Federal Trade Commission, and the National Labor Relations Board. When state public utilities commissions regulate electric, gas, water, and telephone companies, they are creating administrative law. Businesses are affected by many administrative rulings. For instance, food processors, drug manufacturers, and cosmetics companies must comply with regulations of the Food and Drug Administration.

■ Boards, commissions, and agencies of the government are responsible for passing administrative laws. These rules and regulations often affect business. Cosmetics companies, for instance, must comply with many regulations set by the Food and Drug Administration.

BUSINESS LAW

business law Body of law that refers to commercial dealings.

Business law is the body of law that governs commercial dealings. These laws provide a protective environment within which businesses can operate. They serve as guidelines for business decisions. Every businessperson should be familiar with the laws governing his or her field. Some laws, such as the Internal Revenue Code, apply to all businesses. Other types of business laws may apply to a specific industry, such as Federal Communications Commission laws that regulate radio and TV stations.

Uniform Commercial Code (UCC) Model statute that sets forth rules applying to commercial transactions between businesses and between individuals and businesses.

In 1952 the United States grouped many business laws into a model that could be used by all the states. The **Uniform Commercial Code (UCC)** sets forth the rules that apply to commercial transactions between businesses and between individuals and businesses. It has been adopted by forty-nine states; Louisiana uses only part of it. By standardizing laws, the UCC simplifies the process of doing business across state lines. It covers the sale of goods, bank deposits and collections, letters of credit, documents of title, and investment securities. Many articles of the UCC are covered later in the chapter.

THE COURT SYSTEM

The United States has a highly developed court system. This branch of government, the **judiciary**, is responsible for settling disputes by applying and interpreting points of law. Although court decisions are the basis for common law, the courts also answer questions left uncovered by statutes and administrative rulings. They have the power to assure that these laws don't violate federal or state constitutions.

judiciary Court system, which is responsible for settling disputes by applying and interpreting points of law.

The court system includes both federal and state courts. As shown in Exhibit 23-1, the organization of these two court systems is similar. Each has three levels: trial (lower) courts, appellate (intermediate) courts, and the Supreme Court. The courts are grouped on the basis of the types of cases over which they have jurisdiction.

Trial Courts

trial courts Courts of general jurisdiction; found in both the state and federal judiciaries.

Most court cases start in the **trial courts**, also called courts of general jurisdiction. The main federal trial courts are the U.S. district courts. There is at least one federal district court in each state. These courts hear cases involving serious federal crimes, immigration, postal regulations, disputes between citizens of different states, patents, copyrights, and bankruptcy. There are also specialized federal courts that handle tax matters, international trade, and claims against the United States.

The state equivalent of the U.S. district court is usually called the circuit court, although some states call it a superior, district, or common pleas court. At the local level, municipal, city, and justice of the peace courts settle minor criminal cases and civil (noncriminal) cases involving small amounts of money (small claims courts). A small claims court may be under the jurisdiction of the state, municipal, city, or county court system.

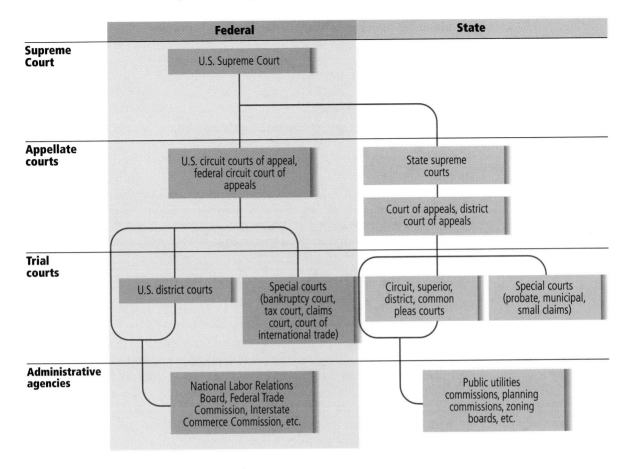

Federal		**State**
Supreme Court	U.S. Supreme Court	
Appellate courts	U.S. circuit courts of appeal, federal circuit court of appeals	State supreme courts Court of appeals, district court of appeals
Trial courts	U.S. district courts Special courts (bankruptcy court, tax court, claims court, court of international trade)	Circuit, superior, district, common pleas courts Special courts (probate, municipal, small claims)
Administrative agencies	National Labor Relations Board, Federal Trade Commission, Interstate Commerce Commission, etc.	Public utilities commissions, planning commissions, zoning boards, etc.

■ **Exhibit 23-1**
U.S. Court System

appellate courts (courts of appeal)
Courts to which a losing party in a trial court may appeal the decision; found in both the federal and state judiciaries.

Appellate Courts

The losing party in a case may appeal the trial court's decision to the next level in the judicial system, the **appellate courts (courts of appeal)**. There are twelve U.S. circuit courts of appeal. Cases that begin in a federal district court are appealed to the court of appeal for that district. These courts may also review orders from administrative agencies. Likewise, the states have appellate courts and supreme courts for cases tried in state district or superior courts.

No cases start in appellate courts. Their purpose is to review decisions of the lower courts and affirm, reverse, or modify the rulings.

The Supreme Court

The U.S. Supreme Court is the highest court in the nation. It is the only court called for in the U.S. Constitution. Any cases involving ambassadors, public ministers, or consuls or involving a state are heard directly by the Supreme Court. Its main function is to review decisions by the U.S. circuit courts of appeal. Parties not satisfied with a decision of a state supreme court can appeal to the U.S. Supreme Court. But the Supreme Court accepts only those cases that it believes will have the greatest effect on the country, only about 200 of the thousands of appeals it gets each year.

Many issues that affect businesses are brought before the Supreme Court. During the Court's 1993–1994 term, it heard cases on such issues as intellectual property rights, sexual harassment in the workplace, and employee privacy rights.

Administrative Agencies

Administrative agencies have limited judicial powers to regulate their special areas. These agencies exist at the federal, state, and local levels. For example, in early 1994 Florida's insurance department brought charges of fraudulent sales tactics against Metropolitan Life Insurance Company agents, accusing them of misleading customers into buying life insurance by calling it retirement accounts.[1] Disputes are settled at hearings or inquiries, which are similar to trials. Decisions of administrative agencies can be appealed to trial or appellate courts.

NONJUDICIAL METHODS OF SETTLING DISPUTES

Settling lawsuits by going to court is an expensive and time-consuming process. Even if the case is settled prior to the actual trial—as are about 57 percent, according to a recent survey by Price Waterhouse of 200 major corporations[2]—the legal expenses involved in preparing for trial are sizable. Therefore, many companies now use private arbitration and mediation firms as alternatives to litigation. Private firms offer these services, which are a high growth area within the legal profession.

arbitration Method of settling disputes whereby the parties agree to present their case to an impartial third party and are required to accept the arbitrator's decision.

mediation Method of settling disputes whereby the parties present their case to a neutral mediator but are not bound by the mediator's decision.

With **arbitration**, the parties agree to present their case to an impartial third party and are required to accept the arbitrator's decision. **Mediation** is similar, but the parties are not bound by the mediator's decision. The mediator suggests alternative solutions and helps the parties negotiate a settlement. Mediation is a more flexible approach than arbitration, allowing for compromise. If the parties cannot reach a settlement, they can then go to court, an option not available in most arbitration cases.

In addition to saving time and money, corporations like the confidentiality of testimony and settlement terms in these proceedings. Arbitration and mediation also allow businesses and medical professionals to avoid jury trials, which can result in large settlements in certain types of lawsuits, such as personal injury, discrimination, medical malpractice, and product liability. Some corporations—Travelers Insurance, ITT, Hughes, and Rockwell International, for example—require nonunion employees to agree to use arbitration for any discrimination claims.[3] Arbitration is used extensively in the securities industry to settle disputes between investors and brokers. The medical profession is also increasing its use of arbitration, to avoid lengthy and expensive malpractice suits.

In 1992, over 40,000 civil (noncriminal) cases were settled by the four major firms specializing in nonjudicial dispute resolution. A Center for Public Resources study of 406 firms revealed that they saved over $150 million in legal costs from 1990 to 1992. For example, Pacific Gas & Electric (PG&E) has reduced the amounts it has paid in settlements about 25 percent from 1988 to 1993 due in large part to its increased use of litigation alternatives.[4]

Concept Check

- What is law? Distinguish among the three basic sources of law.
- Define business law and the Uniform Commercial Code.
- Describe the court system in the United States.
- Explain how arbitration and mediation are used to settle legal disputes.

CONTRACT LAW

Linda Price, a twenty-two-year-old college student, is looking at a new car with a sticker price of $12,000. After some negotiating, she and the salesperson agree on a price of $11,000, and the salesperson writes up a contract, which they both sign. Has Linda legally bought the car for $11,000? The answer is yes, because the transaction meets all the requirements for a valid contract.

A **contract** is an agreement that sets forth the relationship between parties regarding the performance of a specified action. The contract creates a legal obligation and is enforceable in a court of law. Contracts are an important part of business law. Contract law is also incorporated into other fields of business law, such as property and agency law (discussed later in this chapter). Some of the business transactions involving contracts are buying materials and property, selling goods, leasing equipment, and hiring consultants. The letter of agreement shown in Exhibit 23-2 is an example of a contract.

contract Legal agreement, enforceable by law, that sets forth the relationship between parties regarding the performance of a specific action.

■ **Exhibit 23-2**
Sample Contract

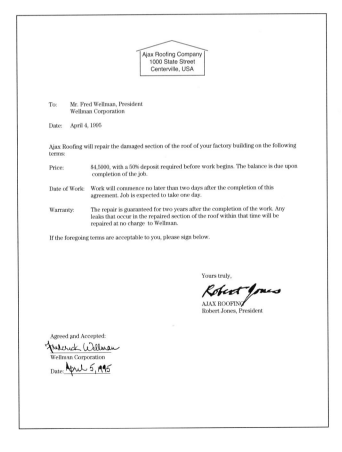

■ A contract creates a legal obligation and is enforceable in a court of law. Contracts can be express (written or spoken) or implied. You enter into an implied contract when you order a meal in a restaurant, because it is assumed that you will pay the price shown on the menu for your food.

express contract Contract whose terms are indicated by either written or spoken words.

implied contract Contract whose terms are indicated by the acts and conduct of the parties.

A contract can be an **express contract**, which specifies the terms of the agreement in either written or spoken words, or an **implied contract**, which depends on the acts and conduct of the parties to show agreement. An example of an express contract is the written sales contract for Linda Price's new car. An implied contract would exist if you ordered and received a sandwich at Jason's Grill. You and the restaurant would then have an implied contract that you will pay the price shown on the restaurant's menu in exchange for an edible sandwich.

CONTRACT REQUIREMENTS

Businesses deal with contracts all the time. Thus it's important to know the requirements of a valid contract. To be legally enforceable, a contract must cover all of the following:

- *Mutual assent:* Voluntary agreement by both parties to the terms of the contract. Each party to the contract must have entered into it freely, without duress. Using physical or economic harm to force the signing of the contract—threatening injury or refusing to place another large order, for instance—invalidates a contract. Likewise, fraud—misrepresenting the facts of a transaction—makes a contract unenforceable. Telling a prospective used-car buyer that the brakes are new when in fact they have not been replaced makes the contract of sale invalid.
- *Capacity:* Legal ability of a party to enter into contracts. The law says minors (children under eighteen), mental incompetents, drug and alcohol addicts, and convicts cannot enter into contracts.

- *Consideration:* Exchange of some legal value or benefit between the parties. Consideration can be in the form of money, goods, or a legal right given up. Say that an electronics manufacturer agrees to rent an industrial building for a year at a monthly rent of $1,500. Its consideration is the rent payment of $1,500, and the building owner's consideration is permission to occupy the space. But if you offer to type a term paper for a friend for free and your offer is accepted, there is no contract. Your friend has not given up anything, so you are not legally bound to honor the deal.
- *Legal purpose:* Absence of illegality. The purpose of the contract must be legal in order to be valid. It cannot require performance of an illegal act. A contract to smuggle drugs into a state for a specified amount of money would not be legally enforceable.
- *Legal form:* Oral or written form, as required. Many contracts can be oral. For instance, an oral contract exists when Bridge Corp. orders office supplies by phone from Ace Stationery Store and Ace delivers the requested goods. Written contracts include leases, sales contracts, and property deeds. Some types of contracts must be in writing to be legally binding. In most states, written contracts are required for the sale of goods costing more than $500, for the sale of land, for contract performance that cannot be made within a year, and for guarantees to pay the debts of someone else.

As you can see, Linda Price's car purchase meets all the requirements for a valid contract. Both parties have freely agreed to the terms of the contract. Linda is not a minor and presumably does not fit any of the other categories of incapacity. Both parties are giving consideration, Linda by paying the money and the salesperson by turning over the car to her. The purchase of the car is a legal activity. And the written contract is the correct form, because the cost of the car is over $500.

BREACH OF CONTRACT

breach of contract Failure of one party to a contract to fulfill its terms.

A **breach of contract** occurs when one party to a contract fails (without legal excuse) to fulfill the terms of the agreement. It gives the other party the right to seek a remedy in the courts. There are three legal remedies for breach of contract:

damages Money awarded to a party harmed by a breach of contract.

- *Payment of **damages:*** Money awarded to the party who was harmed by the breach of contract, to cover losses incurred because the contract wasn't fulfilled. Suppose that Ajax Roofing contracts with Fred Wellman to fix the large hole in the roof of his factory within a certain period (see sample contract, Exhibit 23-2). But the roofing crew doesn't show up as promised. Then a thunderstorm four days after the contract is signed causes $45,000 in damage to Wellman's machinery. Wellman can sue for damages to cover the costs of the water damage because Ajax breached the contract.

specific performance
Court-ordered remedy to a
breach of contract, requiring
the party breaching the contract to perform the duties
specified in it.

restitution Remedy to
breach of contract in which
the contract is canceled and
the situation is restored to its
precontract status.

- ***Specific performance*** of the contract: A court order requiring the breaching party to perform the duties under the terms of the contract. Specific performance is the most common method of settling a breach of contract. Wellman might ask the court to direct Ajax to fix the roof at the price and conditions in the contract.
- ***Restitution:*** Canceling the contract and returning to the situation that existed before the contract. If one party fails to perform under the contract, neither party has any further obligation to the other. Because Ajax failed to fix Wellman's roof under the terms of the contract, Wellman does not owe Ajax any money. Ajax must return the 50 percent deposit it got when Wellman signed the contract.

SALES CONTRACTS

sales contracts Contracts
for the transfer of goods
from a seller to a buyer for a
specified price.

The most common contract in American business is the sales contract. **Sales contracts**—contracts for the transfer of goods from a seller to a buyer for a specified price—are used millions of times each day in the ordinary course of business. These contracts are governed by common law, statutory law (most notably the Uniform Commercial Code), and English merchant law (a system of rules and customs that evolved from the activities of early traders).

The UCC and Sales Contracts

Article 2 of the UCC includes the main legal points governing sales contracts. It defines *goods* as tangible property, not services or intangible property like stocks and bonds. (Real estate, although tangible, is treated separately.) It defines *sales* as transactions in which title to goods is transferred. According to the UCC, a valid sales contract must include both the transfer of title and consideration (the price). The sales law set forth in the UCC applies to sales for either cash or credit. Businesses that sell goods must consider the consequences of both sales law and contract law when they draw up sales agreements with their customers.

Article 2 also says when a sales contract must be in writing. The rules for written contracts are complex. The most important one, however, is that sales for more than $500 require a written contract. In many cases, it is best to use written contracts for other sales as well to prevent disputes about contract terms.

Warranties

Article 2 of the UCC also covers *warranties*, or representations in sales contracts about the character, quality, performance, or title of the goods. The two types of warranties covered in Article 2 are express and implied warranties.

As discussed in Chapter 15, *express warranties* are specific statements of fact or promises about the product by the seller. This form of warranty is considered part of the sales transaction that influences the buyer. Express warranties appear in the form of statements that can be interpreted as fact. The statement "This machine will process 1,000 gallons of

Exhibit 23-3

Sample Warranty

Source: Courtesy Thompson Consumer Electronics, Inc.

Limited Warranty

What your warranty covers:
• Any defect in material or workmanship.

For how long after your purchase:
• 90 days for labor charges.
• One year for parts.
• Two years for picture tube.
The warranty period for rental units begins with the first rental.

What we will do:
• Pay any Authorized RCA Television Servicenter the labor charges to repair your television.
• Pay any Authorized RCA Television Servicenter for the new or, at our option, rebuilt replacement parts and picture tube required to repair your television.

How you get service:
• Request in home service from any Authorized RCA Television Servicenter. To identify your nearest Authorized RCA Television Servicenter, ask your Dealer, look in the Yellow Pages, or call 1-800-336-1900.
• Show the service technician your evidence of purchase date.

What your warranty does not cover:
• Customer instruction. (Your Owner's Manual clearly describes how to install, adjust, and operate your television. Any additional information should be obtained from your Dealer.)
• Installation and related adjustments.
• Signal reception problems not caused by your television.
• Damage from misuse or neglect.
• Remote control batteries.
• A television that has been modified or incorporated into other products or is used for institutional or other commercial purposes.
• A television purchased or serviced outside the USA.

How state law relates to this warranty:
• This warranty gives you specific legal rights, and you also may have other rights that vary from state to state.

If you purchased your television in Canada:
• The Canadian Warranty applies in place of this Warranty.

Si un livret d'instructions en français n'est pas inclus avec votre appareil, vous pouvez en obtenir un (INDIQUER LE NUMÉRO DE MODÈLE, VOTRE NOM, ET VOTRE ADRESSE) en vous adressant à:

Thomson Électronique Grand Public du Canada
Service des données techniques
6540 Tomken Road
Mississauga, Ontario, Canada
L5T 2E9

RCA
For your nearest RCA dealer or Authorized RCA Servicenter call toll free in U.S.A.
1 800 336 1900

RCA Thomson Consumer Electronics
600 N Sherman Dr, PO Box 1976
Indianapolis, IN 46206-1976

1991 Thomson Consumer Electronics, Inc.
Trademark(s) Registered
Marca(s) Registrada(s)
Part Number 1Q57 176-01A

paint per hour" is an express warranty, as is the printed warranty that comes with a computer or a telephone answering machine. Exhibit 23-3 is a sample of an express warranty.

Implied warranties are neither written nor oral. These guarantees are imposed on sales transactions by statute or court decision. They promise that the product will perform up to expected standards. For instance, a man bought a used car from a dealer, and the next day the transmission fell out as he was driving on the highway. The dealer fixed the car, but a week later the brakes failed. The man sued the car dealer. The courts ruled in favor of the car owner, because any car without a working transmission or brakes is not fit for the ordinary purpose of driving.[5] Similarly, if a customer asks to buy a copier to handle 5,000 copies per month, she relies on the salesperson to sell her a copier that meets those needs. The salesperson implicitly warrants that the copier purchased is appropriate for that volume.

Implied warranties can be excluded or changed by the seller, but only in clear terms, in writing, and before the sale. Suppose Drainwell Pump Company makes a pump that should be used only for oil and other heavy liquids. A customer who doesn't know about the design of the pump might assume that it can also be used for lighter liquids like gasoline and water. If Drainwell doesn't want to warrant the pump for use with light liquids, it must state in writing, before the sale, that the pump is not intended for use with light liquids.

Concept Check

- What is a contract? Describe the requirements for a valid contract.
- What are the three remedies for breach of contract?
- Define a sales contract. When must one be in writing? Distinguish between express and implied warranties in sales contracts.

PROPERTY LAW

One of the basic rights of the free-enterprise system is the right to own and use property. Property is used by businesses to produce and sell goods and services in order to make a profit. The rights and duties of owning, using, and selling property are covered by **property law**.

property law Law covering the ownership, use, and sale of property.

TYPES OF PROPERTY

property Rights and interests in anything that can be owned.

real property Land and everything permanently attached to it, such as buildings; real estate.

personal property Movable property, such as inventory, furnishings, and machinery.

tangible personal property Personal property that has physical substance.

intangible personal property Personal property that has no physical substance.

Property refers to the rights and interests in any object that can be owned. The two main types of property are real property and personal property. **Real property** (also called real estate) is land and everything permanently attached to it, such as buildings. It may be bought or leased. The lease of the property does not convey ownership rights to renters, but it does give renters the right to use the property as if it were their own.

Personal property is property that is movable. Inventory, furnishings, automobiles, and machinery are examples of personal property. It may be tangible or intangible. **Tangible personal property** has physical substance. Some examples are furniture, computers, and delivery trucks. **Intangible personal property** is something that has no physical substance but can be owned. Examples are stocks and bonds, accounts receivable, and *intellectual property*—books, songs, ideas, and other intellectual, creative products. Patents, copyrights, and trademarks, which are forms of intellectual property, are covered later in this section.

TRANSFERRING AND ACQUIRING PROPERTY

Most transfers of property take place in the normal course of business. The sale of goods is a common transfer of ownership by a business. Other transfers of property are less common. For instance, a firm may decide to relocate its headquarters and want to sell its building.

The transfer of real property is more complex than the transfer of personal property. First, the sales contract must be in writing. Second, whether the transaction involves a sale or a gift, the transfer of real property must be made by *deed*, a signed document that gives the new owner the title to the property. The deed is usually recorded in the office of the county official where the property is located.

Property can also be transferred through a *will*, the formal document that directs the transfer of a person's property at the time of death. It gen-

■ The musical *Tommy* is considered to be the intellectual property of its creators. They have been granted a copyright by the government, which gives them the exclusive right to use, produce, or sell their creation. Books, songs, and other creative products are also protected in this manner.

erally covers all property, both real and personal. Small businesses can be transferred by will to the owner's heirs.

As mentioned earlier, transfers of personal property usually result from ordinary business dealings. The bill of sale is proof of the transfer of personal property. Personal property can also be transferred by will, by gift, or by creation. *Creation* refers to getting personal property rights by creating something that can be patented (a new process or invention) or copyrighted (this textbook, for example). Trademarks can also be included in this category.

PATENTS, COPYRIGHTS, AND TRADEMARKS

The U.S. Constitution protects authors, inventors, and creators of other intellectual property by giving them the rights to their creative works. Patents, copyrights, and registration of trademarks and servicemarks are legal protection for key business assets.

patent Grant of the exclusive right to manufacture, use, and sell an invention for seventeen years.

A **patent** gives an inventor the exclusive right to manufacture, use, and sell an invention for seventeen years. The U.S. Patent Office, a government agency, grants patents for ideas that meet its requirements of being new, unique, and useful. The physical process, machine, or formula is what is patented. Patent rights—pharmaceutical companies' rights to produce drugs they discover, for example—are considered intangible personal property.

Patent protection can be quite valuable—or costly, depending on which side you're on. SciMed Life Systems, Inc., for example, lost suits brought by units of Eli Lilly and Pfizer for infringing on their patents for coronary catheters. In March 1994 the court ordered SciMed to stop making a catheter that accounted for 10 percent of its sales and to pay Pfizer damages of up to $66 million. SciMed had lost a similar case in 1991 and was ordered to pay the Eli Lilly unit $48 million.[6] Other cases involve even larger sums; in 1993 Litton Industries, Inc., won $1.2 billion from Honeywell Inc.

A **copyright** is also granted by the government. It is an exclusive right, shown by the symbol ©, given to a writer, artist, composer, or playwright to use, produce, and sell his or her creation. Works protected by copyright include printed materials (books, magazine articles, lectures), works of art, photographs, and movies. Under current copyright law, the copyright is issued for the life of the creator plus fifty years after the creator's death.

Patents and copyrights, considered intellectual property, are the subject of many lawsuits today. Electronics companies and individual inventors have filed over 100 patent and copyright infringement suits against Japanese firms. In 1992, Honeywell was awarded $300 million from Minolta Camera Co. and ten other Japanese companies for their unauthorized use of patented autofocus technology. In 1993 Eastman Kodak sued Sony for patent infringement for VCR and camcorder recording heads, and IBM sued Kyocera for selling personal computers with proprietary IBM operating system software.[7]

A **trademark** is a design, name, or other distinctive mark that a manufacturer uses to identify its goods in the marketplace. Apple Computer's multicolored apple logo (symbol) is an example of a trademark. A **servicemark** is a symbol, name, or design that identifies a *service* rather than a tangible object. The Travelers Insurance Company umbrella logo is an example of a servicemark.

Most companies identify their trademark with the ® symbol in company ads. This symbol shows that the trademark is registered with the Register of Copyrights, Copyright Office, Library of Congress. They use the trademark followed by a generic description: Fritos corn chips, Xerox copiers, Scotch brand cellophane tape, Kleenex tissues.

Trademarks are valuable because they create uniqueness in the minds of customers. Companies don't want a trademark to become so well known that it is used to describe all similar types of products. For instance, *Coke* is often used to refer to any cola soft drink, not just those produced by the Coca-Cola Company. Companies spend millions of dollars each year to keep their trademarks from becoming *generic words*, terms used to identify a product class rather than the specific product. Coca-Cola employs many investigators and files seventy to eighty lawsuits each year to prevent its trademarks from becoming generic words.

Once a trademark becomes generic (which a court decides), it is public property and can be used by any person or company. Names that were once trademarked but are now generic include *aspirin, thermos, linoleum,* and *toll house cookies*.

---

copyright Grant of the exclusive right to use, produce, and sell an artistic creation, such as a piece of art, music, or literature.

trademark Legally exclusive design, name, or other distinctive mark that a manufacturer uses to identify its products in the marketplace.

servicemark Legally exclusive symbol, name, or design that identifies a service in the marketplace.

Concept Check

- Define the two types of property. What are the two categories of personal property?
- How do patents, copyrights, and trademarks protect businesses?

OTHER TYPES OF BUSINESS LAW

 Contract and property law are the main types of law that firms encounter. But several other areas of law also influence business activities. These include agency law, tort law, product-liability law, and bankruptcy law.

AGENCY LAW

Businesses often employ someone to act on their behalf, as their *agent*. **Agency** is the legal relationship in which one person or business (the principal) authorizes another person or business (the agent) to act as a representative. The agency relationship is formalized in a contract, which must meet the standards described earlier. Businesses often use agency relationships in real estate, insurance, advertising, and travel transactions. For instance, a firm may enter into a contract with a realtor that gives the realtor the exclusive right to sell the firm's property. In this case, the firm is the principal and the realtor is the agent. Or a firm might use an employment agency to hire its personnel or use manufacturers' representatives to sell the company's product. Whatever the specific task for which the agent is hired, the principal is responsible for the actions of the agent.

agency Legal relationship in which one person (the principal) authorizes another person (the agent) to act as a representative.

TORT LAW

tort Private act that harms people or their property.

A **tort** is a civil, or private, act that harms other people or their property. The harm may involve physical injury, emotional distress, invasion of privacy, or *defamation* (injuring a person's character by publication of false statements). The injured party may sue the wrongdoer to recover damages for the harm or loss. A tort is not the result of a breach of contract, which would be settled under contract law. Torts are part of common law. Examples of tort cases are medical malpractice, *slander* (an untrue oral statement that damages a person's reputation), *libel* (an untrue written statement that damages a person's reputation), product liability (discussed in the next section), and fraud.

A tort is generally not a crime, although some acts can be both torts and crimes. (Assault and battery, for instance, is a criminal act that would be prosecuted by the state and also a tort because of the injury to the person.) Torts are private wrongs and are settled in civil courts. *Crimes* are violations of public law punishable by the state or county in the criminal courts. The purpose of criminal law is to punish the person who committed the crime. The purpose of tort law is to provide remedies to the injured party.

For a tort to exist and damages to be recovered, the harm must be done through either negligence or deliberate intent. *Negligence* occurs when reasonable care is not taken for the safety of others. For instance, a woman attending a New York Mets baseball game was struck on the head by a foul ball that came through a hole in the screen behind home plate.

The court ruled that a sports team charging admission has an obligation to provide structures free from defects and seating that protects spectators from danger. The Mets were found negligent.[8] Negligence does not apply when an injury is caused by an unavoidable accident, an event that was not intended and could not have been prevented even if the person used reasonable care. This area of tort law is quite controversial, because the definition of negligence leaves much room for interpretation.

The other basis for bringing a tort case is *deliberate intent*, an act designed to harm another person (physically or mentally) or his or her property. Slander, defamation, fraud, battery, and assault are torts involving deliberate intent. For example, a business that falsifies its financial statements to get a bank loan has committed the tort of fraud.

One area of tort law—*business torts*—involves wrongful interference with someone's business rights that damages a business's reputation or does financial harm. This area tries to prevent unfair competition. Business torts include interference with contractual relations, damage to a business's reputation, and unauthorized use of a person's name or picture. One of the largest cases based on interference with contractual relations was brought by Pennzoil against Texaco Oil Company. Texaco was accused of interfering with a 1984 merger agreement between Pennzoil and Getty Oil. The jury awarded Pennzoil $10.53 billion—an amount so large that Texaco filed bankruptcy to get even. The suit was settled for $3 billion in 1987.

Defamation arises when one party makes false statements about another's business or profession. Say that business at O'Shea's Irish Pub has plummeted over the past month. A customer shows Katie O'Shea, the owner, a letter written by Tom Grady, a competitor. This letter states that O'Shea's has been downgraded by the health department. The accusations are untrue. In fact, O'Shea's has just received excellent ratings from the health inspector. If O'Shea can prove that Grady's statements are both false and intended to hurt her business, she can sue for libel. She can also seek damages for any loss of business that she can prove.

PRODUCT-LIABILITY LAW

product liability Liability of manufacturers and sellers for defects in the products they make and sell.

Product liability refers to manufacturers' and sellers' responsibility for defects in the products they make and sell. It has become a specialized area of law combining aspects of contracts, warranties, torts, and statutory law (at both the state and federal levels). A product-liability suit may be based on negligence or strict liability (both of which are torts) or misrepresentation or breach of warranty (part of contract law).

strict liability Liability of a manufacturer or seller for any personal injuries or property damage caused by defective products or packaging, even if care has been used to prevent such defects.

An important concept in product-liability law is **strict liability**. A manufacturer or seller is liable for any personal injury or property damage caused by defective products or packaging—even if all possible care has been used to prevent such defects. The definition of *defective* is quite broad. It includes manufacturing and design defects and inadequate instructions on product use or warnings of danger.

Product liability suits are very costly. Over 100,000 product-liability cases were filed against hundreds of companies that made or used asbestos, a substance once used widely in insulation, brake linings, textiles, and other products that causes lung disease and cancer. Eighteen companies were forced into bankruptcy as a result of asbestos-related lawsuits, and the total cost of asbestos cases to defendants and their insurers exceeds $10 billion (most of which was paid not to victims but to lawyers and experts). Another series of cases relates to the safety of silicone breast implants, which was questioned after cases of leakage were reported. As of early 1994, over 7,000 lawsuits had been filed against manufacturers, including Dow Corning, Bristol Myers-Squibb, Baxter Healthcare, and 3M, and this number was increasing by about 200 each month. The amount victims will receive is expected to reach $4 billion, the largest single product liability settlement to date in the United States.[9]

Many product liability suits result from the publicity following large settlements, which encourages others to jump on the litigation bandwagon. For example, General Motors was sued by thirty-eight groups of truck owners after it was ordered to pay $105 million in the case of a teen who died when a GM truck gas tank exploded in a crash. GM chose to settle rather than get involved in the many trials.[10]

As a result of the increase in both the number of product-liability cases and the size of the awards, the cost of product-liability insurance has also increased. Businesses are concerned about the increase in multimillion-dollar jury awards. They claim these settlements keep companies from developing and marketing new products and are a threat to America's ability to compete. Thus businesses have successfully lobbied for laws in many states that limit the dollar amount of awards and require better proof of product defects. In addition, since 1989 fewer juries are awarding large settlements in injury lawsuits. From 1987 to 1992, the percentage of product liability suits won by alleged injury victims dropped from 54 percent to 43 percent.[11]

Product liability also applies to technology, and cases on computer performance are becoming more common, as the Technology Trends box on the next page indicates.

BANKRUPTCY LAW

bankruptcy Legal procedure by which individuals or businesses that cannot meet their financial obligations are relieved of their debts.

Congress has given financially distressed firms and individuals a way to make a fresh start. **Bankruptcy** is the legal procedure by which individuals or businesses that cannot meet their financial obligations are relieved of their debts. A bankruptcy court distributes any assets to the creditors.

Bankruptcy can be either voluntary or involuntary. In a *voluntary bankruptcy*, the debtor files a petition with the court, stating that debts exceed assets. The petition asks the court to declare the debtor bankrupt. In an *involuntary bankruptcy*, the creditors file the bankruptcy petition.

The Bankruptcy Reform Act of 1978, amended in 1984 and 1986, provides for the quick and efficient resolution of bankruptcy cases. Under this act, the two types of bankruptcy proceedings available to businesses

Computer Chaos

Like any other product, computers can malfunction. When they do, it's often disastrous—and costly—for business. As a result, a new type of product liability law is developing as companies file lawsuits against computer and software vendors for damages caused by computer products.

The dependency between hardware and software firms and their customers often leads to troublesome situations. The user has to rely on the seller's expertise, and the vendor has to base its recommendations on what the user says it needs. Attorneys representing software manufacturers claim that often buyers don't communicate clearly about what they need or are unrealistic in their expectations.

Consider the case of Kane Carpet Co., once the fourth largest carpet distributor in the United States. Kane sued a now-defunct division of McDonnell Douglas Corp. for selling it a $308,000 inventory control software package that gave inaccurate information about what products were in stock, making it impossible to fill orders promptly and accurately. This problem destroyed Kane's credibility with its retailers, who took their business elsewhere, and caused such chaos that the company went out of business a year and a half later. The defendant claimed that Kane was already in financial difficulty and the software did not cause the problem. As of early 1994, the case had not yet been settled.

In another case, General Motors' data processing subsidiary, EDS Corp., contracted with the Florida Department of Health and Rehabilitative Services to design and install the country's largest social services computer system. EDS sued the agency for withholding a $46 million payment. The agency countersued for breach of contract, claiming that the system cost twice the original price—yet couldn't handle the necessary transaction volume. EDS asserts that it complied with the terms of its contract and that the agency badly underestimated the number of residents requiring state aid in 1993. The resulting errors and delays led to $17.5 million in federal penalties. The state contends that EDS was so eager to win the large contract that it oversold its capabilities.

Cases like these emphasize the importance of detailed contracts that clearly set forth exactly what the vendor will provide and the cost of the services and equipment. Vendors now try to include warranty disclaimers that prevent the buyer from suing for economic losses.[12]

are *Chapter 7* (liquidation) and *Chapter 11* (reorganization). Most bankruptcies, an estimated 70 percent, use Chapter 7. After the sale of any assets, the cash proceeds are given first to secured creditors and then to unsecured creditors.

A firm that opts to reorganize under Chapter 11 works with its creditors to develop a plan for paying part of its debts and writing off the rest. The reorganization plan must be approved by the bankruptcy court. This often takes considerable time. For example, Lone Star Industries Inc. filed Chapter 11 in 1990. Its plan of reorganization was finally approved in February 1994. Under the plan, unsecured creditors will receive 85 to 100 percent of the amounts owed, preferred stockholders will recover 45 to 60 percent of their investment, and common stockholders' ownership will be cut to about 5 percent.[13]

Chapter 11 can be used for either voluntary or involuntary bankruptcy. If a workable reorganization plan cannot be developed, the firm's assets are liquidated under Chapter 7. In some cases, the threat of liquidation helps the parties come to terms.

- In what types of circumstances does agency law apply?
- What is a tort? Describe the two elements that form the basis for tort liability.
- Discuss the importance of product-liability law to businesses. What is strict liability?
- Briefly describe the main chapters of bankruptcy law.

GOVERNMENT REGULATION OF BUSINESS

5 Numerous government laws and agencies regulate business activities. Major federal agencies include the Environmental Protection Agency (discussed in Chapter 10), the Equal Opportunity Employment Commission (Chapter 12), the National Labor Relations Board (Chapter 13), the Federal Deposit Insurance Corporation (Chapter 20), the Securities and Exchange Commission (Chapter 22), and the Federal Trade Commission (discussed below). There are many others.

Federal, state, and local governments exercise control over businesses for many reasons. Among them are the desire to protect small firms from unfair competition, to protect consumer rights, and to prevent such unfair practices as price-fixing.

The cost to business of complying with government regulation can be quite high. For example, in 1989 Textron, with revenues over $8 billion, announced its intent to acquire Avdel, a $250 million rivet manufacturer. The FTC, concerned that the resulting company could possibly reduce competition in its industry segment, issued an injunction that kept Textron from acquiring control of Avdel until the investigation was completed. Through October 1993, Textron had spent $5 million in legal fees and $70 million in interest related to financing the acquisition.[14]

States also regulate businesses. For example, in 1993 an Arkansas court ruled against giant retailer Wal-Mart for violating its Unfair Trade Practices Act. The court determined that Wal-Mart followed a predatory pricing strategy that adversely affected the ability of three independent pharmacies to compete.[15]

Government controls are controversial. Some people maintain that government is smothering business with red tape and that there should be less government regulation. They feel that the government should limit its role and allow the market forces of supply and demand to determine what products are offered and by whom. Others feel that regulation has not gone far enough, that firms are often unethical and must be kept in line through strict government control.

REGULATION OF COMPETITION

antitrust regulation
Laws that keep companies from entering into agreements to control trade through a monopoly.

Many regulations seek to keep the marketplace free from influences that would restrict competition. They include **antitrust regulation**, laws that keep companies from entering into agreements to control trade through a monopoly. The first act regulating competition was the Sherman Antitrust Act, passed in 1890 to prevent large companies from dominating an industry so that smaller firms would find it hard to compete. This broad act banned monopolies and contracts, mergers, or conspiracies in restraint of trade. In 1914 the Clayton Act added to the more general provisions of the Sherman Antitrust Act. It outlawed the following:

price discrimination Illegal practice of offering a customer discounts that are not offered to all other purchasers buying on similar terms.

- *Price discrimination:* Offering a customer discounts that are not offered to all other purchasers buying on similar terms.
- *Exclusive dealing:* Refusing to let the buyer purchase a competitor's products for resale.
- *Tying contracts:* Requiring buyers to purchase merchandise they may not want in order to get the products they do want.
- *The purchase of stock in competing corporations* in such quantity that it would reduce competition.

exclusive dealing Illegal practice of refusing to allow a buyer to purchase a competitor's products for resale.

tying contracts Illegal contracts that require buyers to purchase merchandise they may not want in order to get the products they do want.

The 1950 *Celler-Kefauver Act* amended the Clayton Act. It bans the purchase of one firm by another if the resulting merger decreases competition within the industry. As a result, all corporate acquisitions are subject to regulatory approval before they can be finalized.

Most antitrust actions are taken by the U.S. Department of Justice, based on federal law. Violations of the antitrust acts are punishable by fines, imprisonment, or civil damage payments that can be as high as three times the actual damage amount. These outcomes give defendants an incentive to resolve cases. In a recent antitrust suit, the Justice Department accused six major airlines—American, Delta, Continental, Northwest, Trans World, and Alaska—of using a jointly-owned computer reservation system to negotiate future fares with each other, a practice that the Justice Department claimed raised ticket prices considerably. The price-fixing case was settled in March 1994 when the airlines, who did not admit or deny guilt, agreed not to announce future fares.[16]

The *Federal Trade Commission Act*, also passed in 1914, bans unfair trade practices. This act created the Federal Trade Commission (FTC), an independent five-member board with the power to define and monitor unfair trade practices, such as those prohibited by the Sherman and Clayton acts. The FTC investigates complaints and can issue rulings called *cease-and-desist orders* to force companies to stop unfair business practices. Its powers have grown over the years.

Today the FTC is one of the most important agencies regulating the competitive practices of business. In a recent FTC case YKK, Inc., the largest U.S. zipper manufacturer, was charged with trying to fix prices with its chief rival, Talon, Inc. The case was settled when YKK agreed to stop its practice of offering free installation equipment to customers, which is considered a form of price discounting. YKK had asked Talon to do the same. The case was notable because it represented an expansion of FTC enforcement to investigations of "invitations to collude" to set prices, rather than actual price fixing.[17]

REGULATION OF MARKETING ACTIVITIES AND CONSUMER RIGHTS

A number of federal laws directly affect the promotion and pricing of products. The *Wheeler-Lea Act* of 1938 amended the Federal Trade Commission Act and gave the FTC authority to regulate advertising. As discussed in Chapter 17, the FTC monitors companies' advertisements for false or misleading claims.

The most important law in the area of pricing is the *Robinson-Patman Act*, a federal law passed in 1936 that tightened the Clayton Act's prohibitions against price discrimination. An exception is made for circumstances like discounts for quantity purchases, as long as the discounts do not lessen competition. But a manufacturer cannot sell at a lower price to one company just because that company buys all its merchandise from the manufacturer. Also, if one firm is offered quantity discounts, all firms buying that quantity of goods must get the discounts. The FTC and the antitrust division of the Justice Department monitor pricing.

Many other laws affect the marketing practices of businesses and protect consumers' rights. There are also credit laws that focus on disclosure and fairness. Exhibit 23-4 summarizes some of the legislation in these areas.

■ **Exhibit 23-4**
Key Marketing and Consumer Protection Legislation

Pure Food and Drug Act (1906)	Created the Food and Drug Administration (FDA); protects consumers against the interstate sale of unsafe and adulterated foods and drugs
Food, Drug, and Cosmetic Act (1938)	Expanded the power of the FDA to cover cosmetics and therapeutic devices and to establish standards for food products
Flammable Fabrics Act (1953)	Prohibits sale or manufacture of clothing made of dangerously flammable fabric
Child Protection Act (1966)	Prohibits sale of harmful toys and gives FDA the right to remove dangerous products from the marketplace
Cigarette Labeling Act (1965)	Requires cigarette manufacturers to put labels warning consumers about health hazards on cigarette packages
Fair Packaging and Labeling Act (1966)	Regulates labeling and packaging of consumer products
Consumer Credit Protection Act (Truth-in-Lending Act) (1968)	Requires lenders to fully disclose to borrowers the loan terms and the costs of borrowing (interest rate, application fees, etc.)
Fair Credit Reporting Act (1971)	Requires consumers denied credit on the basis of reports from credit agencies to be given access to their reports and allowed to correct inaccurate information
Consumer Product Safety Act (1972)	Created the Consumer Product Safety Commission, an independent federal agency, to establish and enforce consumer product safety standards
Equal Credit Opportunity Act (1975)	Prohibits denial of credit on the basis of gender, marital status, race, religion, age, or national origin
Magnuson-Moss Warranty Act (1975)	Requires that warranties be written in clear language and that terms be fully disclosed

HOW BUSINESS INFLUENCES GOVERNMENT

lobbies Organizations that try to convince legislators to support the interests of their group.

Because of the big influence the government can have on business operations and profitability, businesses make their opinions on proposed laws known to federal, state, and local legislators. **Lobbies**, organizations that try to convince legislators to support the group's interests, actively campaign against laws they believe to be harmful.

Lobbies can be industry groups, trade associations, or independent consultants hired by corporations. Pro-business lobbies include the U.S. Chamber of Commerce, the Business Roundtable (a group of 200 large-company CEOs), the National Association of Wholesalers and Distributors, the American Medical Association, and many others. Some lobbies, such as the Sierra Club and other environmental groups, can be considered anti-business. Others—such as the American Association of Retired Persons (AARP)—promote the needs of special constituencies. Diverse groups sometimes form coalitions to lobby on specific issues, in order to get more attention from lawmakers than any one industry group could. For example, the Clinton administration health care plan was supported by such groups as organized labor, large insurance companies, and senior citizens' organizations, while small businesses, drug companies, hospitals, trial lawyers, and insurance agents were among those who opposed it.[18]

Does business lobbying benefit the nation? There is no clear answer. Some believe that businesses must educate legislators on business issues. They want lawmakers to have all the facts—not just those of anti-business interests—before they vote on issues that affect the nation's economy. Others argue that lobbying wastes money that could be put to other, productive uses.

DEREGULATION OF INDUSTRIES

deregulation Removal of rules and regulations involving business competition.

Over the past decade, the U.S. government has actively promoted **deregulation**, the removal of rules and regulations involving business competition. Deregulation has drastically changed some once-regulated industries (especially the transportation, telecommunications, and financial services industries) and created many new competitors. The result has been entries into and exits from some industries. Deregulation in the financial services industry, discussed in Chapter 20, eliminated many of the differences between banks and other financial institutions and increased competition.

Deregulation has also had a big impact in various transportation industries. In the airline industry, the number of airlines soared after passage of the Airline Deregulation Act in 1978, which removed restrictions on routes and ticket prices. Many large airlines left the less profitable routes. Their places were taken by new, smaller airlines. Price competition increased. But the increased competition, higher fuel costs, economic conditions, and price wars made it hard for many airlines, both new and established, to survive. Similarly, trucking and railroads were deregulated in 1980.

Although thousands of small trucking firms started operating, more than 300 large ones went bankrupt. The price wars resulting from the increase in firms has forced older companies to slash costs.

An area that is currently subject to regulation—but may be ripe for deregulation—is the telecommunications industry. For example, phone companies are prohibited from selling cable televisions programs within their own service area, and cable television companies can't sell phone switching or local phone services. In response to the changes in this industry due to the information superhighway and mergers and joint ventures between phone and cable firms, Congress is reviewing current legislation to determine whether eliminating some of this regulation will increase or decrease competition.[19] In the case of cable television, the Federal Communications Commission deregulated the industry in the mid-1980s but, as rates climbed, decided in 1992 to re-regulate it.

Consumers often benefit from deregulation. Increased competition often means lower prices. Businesses also benefit because they have more freedom to operate and can avoid the costs associated with government regulations. But more competition can also make it hard for small or weak firms to survive.

Concept Check
- How does the government regulate competition and marketing activities?
- Define lobbying, and explain how businesses use it.
- What is deregulation, and how does it affect businesses and consumers?

TAXATION OF BUSINESS

Taxes are sometimes seen as the price we pay to live in this country. Taxes are assessed by all levels of government on both business and individuals, and they are used to pay for the services provided by government. The federal government is the largest collector of taxes, accounting for 54 percent of all tax dollars. States are next, followed closely by local government taxes. Since 1985, local taxes have risen at a faster rate—an average of 8.1 percent per year—than state and federal taxes (6.3 percent and 6.1 percent. respectively).[20] The average American family pays about 37 percent of its income for taxes, 28 percent to the federal government and 9 percent to state and local governments.

Just about anything can be taxed. Medieval kings taxed salt, for example. Today the most common taxes are those on personal and business income. Exhibit 23-5 shows the sources of tax revenues. Individual income taxes are the biggest source of tax revenues for the federal government. Sales taxes are state and local governments' biggest revenue source.

The government uses changes in the tax code to promote its goals. For instance, if some of the interest earned on savings accounts is not taxed,

■ **Exhibit 23-5**
Sources of Tax Revenue

Source: Federal data from *Federal Reserve Bulletin* (Washington, D.C., Board of Governors of the Federal Reserve System), January 1994, p. A29. State data from U.S. Department of the Census, *Statistical Abstract of the United States: 1993*, 113th ed. (Washington, D.C.: Government Printing Office, 1993), p. 297.

Federal tax revenues

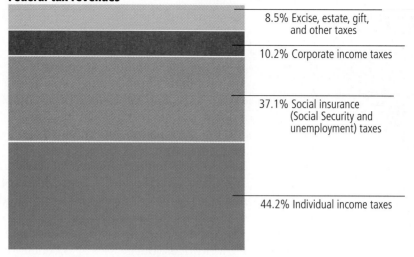

8.5% Excise, estate, gift, and other taxes

10.2% Corporate income taxes

37.1% Social insurance (Social Security and unemployment) taxes

44.2% Individual income taxes

State and local tax revenues

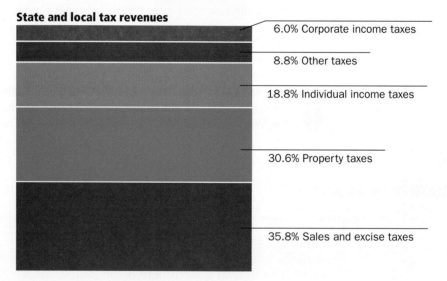

6.0% Corporate income taxes

8.8% Other taxes

18.8% Individual income taxes

30.6% Property taxes

35.8% Sales and excise taxes

people are encouraged to save more. Similarly, tax incentives for business can increase capital investment.

INCOME TAXES

income taxes Taxes based on the income received by businesses and individuals.

Income taxes are based on the income received by businesses and individuals. The income taxes paid to the federal government are set by Congress, regulated by the Internal Revenue Code, and collected by the Internal Revenue Service. These taxes are *progressive*, meaning that rates increase as income increases. Most of the states and some large cities also

Tax Tradeoffs

Do a state's tax policies affect its economic climate? First-term New Jersey governor Christine Todd Whitman thinks so. Her campaign platform included proposals to reduce state income taxes by 30 percent over a three-year period, reversing a ten-year increase in state and local taxes. Other states, including Georgia, Arizona, and Massachusetts, are also considering income tax cuts.

New evidence supports Whitman's contention that lower tax rates lead to stronger economic growth. A recent study by *Business Week* found a significant difference between low- and high-tax states in the rate of private sector job creation since 1985. The ten states with the lowest tax burden (the percentage of personal income represented by state and local taxes) averaged 22 percent job growth, compared to only 13 percent for the ten states with the highest tax burden.

In fact, there is room for many states to reduce taxes. The state and local tax burden is at a twenty-year high, due to increases during the recession to balance state budgets. As the national economy improves, rising personal and corporate incomes create a larger pool of taxable income for the states. Lower taxes also send a positive message about the state's attitude toward the business community. States with high taxes find themselves at a disadvantage when it comes to attracting new businesses.

Yet reducing taxes is not without its pitfalls. Obviously, lower taxes mean less revenue to spend on public programs. For example, New Jersey's three-year tax cut package would cost about $1.5 billion, sharply increasing the state's budget deficit. Such large revenue reductions typically require major cuts in education, social services, transportation, and similar services—services that are necessary to attract and retain businesses. Supporters of lower state taxes believe the stimulus to economic growth, especially in the entrepreneurial sector, will eventually generate enough additional tax revenue to make up the difference. Only time will tell whether the tradeoff—increased economic activity versus possible loss of public services—makes economic sense.[21]

collect income taxes from individuals and businesses. The state and local governments set their own rules and tax rates. Many states are looking at the relationship between tax rates and economic performance, as discussed in the Trends in Business Today box.

A dual system of tax rates exists for businesses. As discussed in Chapter 6, sole proprietorships and partnerships are not taxed as businesses, because the tax laws do not distinguish between the business entities and their owners. The income of these firms is taxed as the income of the people who own them. Under the tax law passed in 1993, tax rates on individual income range from 15 to 39.6 percent. In contrast, corporations pay income taxes as businesses. The owner and the corporation are separate taxable entities. The federal income tax rates for corporations range from 15 percent for firms with a taxable income of less than $50,000 to 35 percent for firms with a taxable income over $10 million. Not-for-profit corporations are exempt from federal taxes.

The gross income of a business may consist of both ordinary income and capital gains. *Ordinary income* is income earned from the sale of a firm's goods or services. It is taxable at the full individual or corporate tax rate. A **capital gain** is the profit made when an asset such as equipment, real estate, or securities is sold for more than its original purchase price. In the past, long-term capital gains—profits on assets held for more than six months—were taxed at lower rates than ordinary income. But the Tax Reform Act of 1986 stopped the special treatment of capital gains. Now they are taxed at the same rates as ordinary income. Some experts believe that lower tax rates on capital gains encourage investment and stimulate economic growth. In general, those who support business favor a reduction in the capital gains tax. Those who take the side of workers against big business tend to want capital gains taxed at the full amount. This issue is a political football that gets tossed about almost every fall when Congress is passing the budget for the coming year.

capital gain Profit made when an asset is sold for more than its original purchase price.

OTHER TYPES OF TAXES

Besides income taxes, individuals and businesses pay a number of other taxes. The four main types are property taxes, payroll taxes, sales taxes, and excise taxes.

property taxes Taxes imposed by state and local governments on real and personal property.

Property taxes are assessed on real and personal property, based on their value. They raise quite a bit of revenue for state and local governments, as shown in Exhibit 23-5. Most states tax land and buildings. Property taxes may be based on fair market value (what a buyer would pay), a percentage of fair market value, or replacement value (what it would cost today to rebuild or buy something like the original). The value on which the taxes are based is the *assessed value*.

payroll taxes Employer's share of Social Security taxes and federal and state unemployment taxes.

Any business that has employees and meets a payroll must pay **payroll taxes**, the employer's share of Social Security taxes and federal and state unemployment taxes. These taxes must be paid on wages, salaries, and commissions. State unemployment taxes are based on the number of employees in a firm who have become eligible for unemployment benefits. A firm that has never had an employee become eligible for unemployment will pay a low rate of state unemployment taxes. The firm's experience with employment benefits does not affect federal unemployment tax rates.

sales taxes Taxes imposed by states, counties, and cities on goods when they are sold; calculated as a percentage of the sales price.

Sales taxes are levied on goods when they are sold and are a percentage of the sales price. These taxes are imposed by states, counties, and cities. They vary in amount and in what is considered taxable. For instance, some states have no sales tax. Others tax some categories (such as appliances) but not others (such as clothes). Still others tax all retail products except food, magazines, and prescription drugs. Sales taxes increase the cost of goods to the consumer. Businesses bear the burden of collecting sales taxes and sending them to the government.

■ Excise taxes placed on various items—cigarettes, airline tickets, guns—can be used to raise revenue when the government doesn't want to change the income-tax rate. Often these taxes help pay for services connected to the item taxed. Excise taxes on gasoline, for example, are used to construct and maintain the country's highway system.

excise taxes Taxes placed on specific items (such as gasoline and alcoholic beverages) by federal, state, or local governments.

Excise taxes are placed on specific items, such as gasoline, alcoholic beverages, cigarettes, airline tickets, cars, and guns. They can be assessed by federal, state, and local governments. In many cases, these taxes help pay for services related to the item taxed. For instance, gasoline excise taxes are often used to build and repair highways. Other excise taxes— like those on alcoholic beverages, cigarettes, and guns—are used to control practices that may cause harm. Excise taxes can be used to raise revenues when the government doesn't want to make big changes in income tax rates. For example, in 1990 the federal government increased excise taxes on gasoline and other petroleum products, alcoholic beverages, and cigarettes.

Concept Check

- What is income tax? Explain the dual system of income taxation for businesses.
- Briefly describe property, payroll, sales, and excise taxes.

■ SUMMARY

1. Describe the sources of law, the U.S. court system, business law and the Uniform Commercial Code, and nonjudicial methods of settling disputes.

Laws are the rules governing a society's conduct that are created and enforced by a controlling authority. The three main sources of law are common law, or unwritten law based on court decisions; statutory law, or

Key Terms

administrative law 743

agency 755

antitrust regulation 760

appellate courts 745

continued

written legislation passed by governments; and administrative law, or written regulations passed by administrative agencies of federal, state, and local governments. The U.S. court system includes both federal and state courts, each organized into three levels. The courts settle disputes by applying and interpreting laws. Most cases start in trial courts. Decisions can be appealed to appellate courts. The U.S. Supreme Court is the nation's highest court and the court of final appeal. In addition to the courts, administrative agencies have judicial powers within their specialized areas.

Business law refers to all laws that regulate commercial transactions. All businesses must consider the legal implications of their activities. The Uniform Commercial Code provides a model for laws governing certain business activities. Because it has been accepted by most states, the UCC simplifies interstate transactions.

Arbitration and mediation are two ways to resolve legal disputes using private firms. The decision of an arbitrator is binding, while that of a mediator is not.

2. Describe the elements of legally enforceable contracts, and explain how breaches of contract are settled.

A contract is an agreement between two or more parties that meets five requirements: mutual assent, capacity, consideration, legal purpose, and legal form. If one party breaches the contract terms, the remedies are damages (paying for the losses that arose because the contract wasn't fulfilled), specific performance (fulfilling the terms of the agreement), or restitution (canceling the contract and restoring any money paid).

3. Understand the key concepts of property law.

Real property is land and everything permanently attached to it. Personal property is movable property. Personal property can be tangible (having physical substance) or intangible (having no physical substance, like securities and ideas). Property law governs the rights and duties of owning, using, and selling property. Transfers of real property require a deed conveying title to the new owner. The law also protects intellectual property—personal property that is created—through patents, copyrights, and trademarks.

4. Discuss other key types of business law: agency law, tort law, product-liability law, and bankruptcy law.

Agency law governs the relationship that arises when one person or firm hires another to act as a representative. The agency agreement is formalized in a contract. Tort law settles disputes involving civil acts that harm people or their property. Torts include physical injury, mental anguish, and defamation. Tort cases are based on either negligence or deliberate intent. Product-liability law governs the responsibility of manufacturers and sellers for product defects—even if all possible care has been used to prevent such defects. Bankruptcy law gives businesses or individuals who cannot meet their financial obligations a way to be relieved of their debts.

Bankruptcies can be either voluntary or involuntary. The two main options for filing for bankruptcy are Chapter 7 (liquidation of assets) and Chapter 11 (reorganization).

5. Understand the government's role in regulating businesses, and discuss the impact of deregulation.

The government regulates business to protect firms from unfair competition and such practices as price-fixing and deceptive advertising. Laws to protect consumer rights are another important area of government control. Recently, the government has removed many restrictive regulations. The industries most affected by deregulation include financial services, transportation, and telecommunications. Deregulation often results in increased competition and lower prices for consumers.

6. Explain the taxation of business income, and list four other types of taxes affecting business.

Businesses pay income taxes on profits. The income of sole proprietorships and partnerships is taxed as income to the people who own them. Corporations are taxed as businesses. There are different tax regulations and rates for individuals and corporations. Four other types of taxes affecting business are property taxes, payroll taxes, sales taxes, and excise taxes.

■ DISCUSSION QUESTIONS

1. Fred Jones had a used car for sale. Susan Williams offered him $7,500 for the car. He asked for $9,500, and she countered with $8,500. Jones said fine, and they shook hands on the deal. The next day Mark Evans came to look at the car and offered $9,000 for it. Because Jones had no written contract with Williams, he accepted the higher offer. When Williams came to pay for the car, Jones told her he sold it for a higher price. Did Susan Williams have a valid contract that met the five essential criteria? If not, what should she have done to make the deal? If so, what steps can she take to remedy the breach of contract?

2. A construction company was demolishing a building. The crew was very experienced and took all the usual precautions when using the ball and crane to knock down the walls. Nevertheless, some bricks flew loose and damaged the building next door. That building's owners sued the construction company for negligence. Can they collect damages?

3. You own a manufacturing company with serious cash flow problems. Your creditors are demanding payment immediately. You are confident that, with some additional time, you could work out your problems. How could you use the bankruptcy laws to get out of this mess?

4. Imagine that you are in Congress and will be voting on bills to further deregulate various industries. What factors would you consider in deciding whether deregulation is beneficial or not? Do you think that, in general, the government should have a larger role in regulating business, or can businesses be trusted to regulate themselves?

5. Which size of business benefits most from the current corporate income tax rates? Why? How can legislators use tax laws to influence business activity?

6. Do you think not-for-profit organizations should be exempt from all taxation? Should activities that compete directly with for-profit companies, such as health clubs run by YMCAs, be taxed differently?

■ CASE

Deregulation Dilemma

The October 1993 announcement of a $21.4 billion merger between Bell Atlantic, a "Baby Bell" regional phone company, and Telecommunications Inc. (TCI), the nation's largest cable television firm, raised questions about government regulation of telecommunications and media firms. The merger, however, fell through in February 1994. Two rounds of cable rate cuts legislated by Congress were expected to reduce TCI's annual cash flow by at least $225 million. The change in expected cash flow made TCI a less attractive merger candidate.

The cable television industry had been de-regulated in 1986. The industry is set up so that a single cable operator wins the right to serve a specified geographical area. Some legislators felt that this lack of competition requires regulation in order to protect consumers and to bring rising cable television rates under control. One piece of evidence cited in support of this view was a General Accounting Office study which showed that basic service rates had jumped 61 percent from 1986 to 1991. Accordingly, Congress passed the Cable Act of 1992 to re-regulate cable rates.

Opponents of cable regulation say the new regulations place unfair restrictions on cable companies. These limits come at an especially critical time, when companies are ready to spend billions of dollars for new technologies that bring subscribers more channels and services. They predict that overregulation will eventually result in fewer choices and higher prices.

In fact, soon after the Act became effective, about 30 percent of cable subscribers saw their rates *increase*. The reasons for the rate increases are unclear. The Federal Communications Commission (FCC), Congress, and cable operators all blamed each other.

The Cable Act is just one example of telecommunications regulation. With the potential for more joint ventures and mergers between telephone, media, and cable firms, Congress must determine what types of regulation are appropriate and which existing barriers to remove. Those who favor greater regulation believe that combining technologies will create huge companies and reduce competition. Others believe that competition within a free market system will do a better job of preventing abuses. The outcome of these decisions will be crucial for the future of the telecommunications industry and the information superhighway.[22]

Questions

1. Discuss the pros and cons of imposing government regulations on telecommunications companies. What are the issues that Congress must weigh?
2. How might we ensure fair prices to consumers without regulation?
3. How can government encourage innovation in a regulated industry?

Risk and Insurance

Career Profile

Anita Cannon-Hopkins is a financial consultant in the risk management department of Chemed Corporation. She obtained the position after making an important connection in a college course called Executive Forum. As part of the course, she and her classmates interviewed the CEOs of several companies. Before conducting each interview, the students thoroughly analyzed the firms, reviewing their annual and other financial reports. Chemed was one of the companies Anita researched. Shortly after interviewing the firm's CEO, she sent him a thank you note and inquired about career opportunities. Not too long after that, she was hired at Chemed.

Chemed Corporation is a diversified public corporation with businesses in medical- and dental-supply manufacturing and distribution; plumbing, drain cleaning, and appliance and air-conditioning repair and maintenance through the sale of service contracts; and sanitary maintenance products and services.

Anita administers various lines of insurance for Chemed's subsidiaries. Her primary responsibility is to pass the company's insurance costs on to the subsidiaries in an equitable manner. She also works with the company's insurance broker to make sure that Chemed's potential risk is covered. Anita gathers the information she needs through the chief financial officers and comptrollers of Chemed's subsidiaries. The risks she is confronted with are generally in primary casualty lines: workers' compensation, automobile liability, and general liability. Part of the crucial information she needs to do her job includes how many vehicles of what type require coverage and how many employees are at risk for various work-related injuries.

Anita's degree in operations management gave her a solid background for this position. The skills she perfected in college help her to forecast costs while assessing the different insurance plans available to Chemed's subsidiaries. Courses in writing and communication have also been useful, because making complex financial data understandable in order to pass it on to others is crucial to Anita's role at Chemed.

Overview

It is impossible to avoid all risks, but individuals and businesses can minimize risks or buy protection—called insurance—against them. Although some risks are uninsurable, many others are insurable. This chapter discusses insurable risks and the types of insurance available to cover them. It begins with the definition of risk and explains the concept of risk management. Basic insurance concepts and a description of the insurance industry are presented next. Then the chapter describes the three main types of insurance—property and liability, health, and life—and the types of coverage offered by each.

RISK MANAGEMENT

risk management Analyzing a firm's operations, evaluating the potential risks, and forming strategies to minimize losses.

Every day, businesses and individuals are exposed to many different kinds of risk. Investors who buy stocks or speculate in commodities may earn a profit, but they also take the risk of losing all or part of their money. Illness is another type of risk, involving financial loss from not only the cost of medical care but also the loss of income. Businesses, too, are exposed to many types of risk. Market risks, such as lower demand for a product or worsening economic conditions, can hurt a firm. Other risks involve customers, who could be injured on a company's premises or by a company's product. Like homes and cars owned by individuals, business property can be damaged or lost through fire, floods, and theft. Businesses must also protect themselves against losses from theft by dishonest employees. The loss of a key employee is another risk, especially for small firms.

Every business is faced with risks like these. **Risk management** means analyzing the firm's operations, evaluating the potential risks, and figuring out how to minimize losses. In today's complex business environment, the concern for public and employee welfare and the potential for lawsuits have both increased. Risk management thus plays a vital role in the overall management of a business.

WHAT IS RISK?

risk In insurance, the chance of financial loss due to a peril.

speculative risk Chance of either loss or gain.

Individuals and firms need to protect themselves against the economic effects of certain types of risk. In an insurance sense, **risk** (sometimes called *pure risk*) is the chance of financial loss due to a peril. Insurable risks include fire, theft, auto accident, injury or illness, a lawsuit, or death. **Speculative risk** is the chance of either loss or gain. Someone who buys stock in the hope of later selling it at a profit is taking a speculative risk. This type of risk cannot be insured against.

MANAGING RISK

risk avoidance Staying away from situations that can lead to loss.

Risk is part of life. Nevertheless, people have several ways to deal with it. One is **risk avoidance**, or staying away from situations that can lead to loss. For instance, a person can avoid the risk of a serious injury by choosing not to go skydiving. Kinder-Care, a nationwide day-care chain, could avoid risk by not transporting children to and from school or taking them

■ One practical way for a company to manage risk is to adopt a policy of risk reduction. This means coming up with safety measures that will cut down on accidents on the job. For a construction company, this might mean that workers would be required to wear hard hats, safety glasses, and other protective gear.

risk assumption Bearing a risk without insurance; self-insurance.

self-insurance Assuming risk against certain types of losses rather than buying insurance.

on field trips. Manufacturers who wish to avoid risks could produce only goods that have a proven track record. But these risk-avoidance strategies could stifle business growth. Thus risk avoidance is not good for all risks.

A more practical way to handle many types of risks is **risk assumption**. The willingness to bear a risk without insurance is also called **self-insurance**. Many large firms with warehouses or stores spread out over the United States—Sears or K mart, for instance—may choose not to insure them. They assume that, even if disaster strikes one location, the others won't be harmed. The losses will probably be less than the insurance premiums for all the locations. Many companies self-insure because it is cheaper to assume some risks than to insure against them. Many can no longer afford the same level of insurance they had in the past. Some choose to pay small claims themselves and insure only for catastrophic losses. Others "go naked," paying for all claims from company funds. This is clearly the most risky strategy. A big claim could cripple the firm or lead to bankruptcy.

risk reduction Reducing or eliminating the potential for financial loss.

A policy of **risk reduction**, or loss prevention, is another way to protect against financial loss. Companies adopt safety measures to reduce accidents. Construction workers are required to wear hard hats and safety glasses. Airlines keep their aircraft in good condition and require thorough training programs for pilots and flight attendants. Hotels install smoke alarms, sprinkler systems, and firewalls to protect guests and minimize fire damage.

risk transference Paying someone else to bear some or all of the risk of financial loss.

Finally, many risks can't be avoided, assumed, or reduced to acceptable levels. **Risk transference** is paying someone else to bear some or all of the risk of financial loss. One good prospect for risk transference, for example, is a surgeon, who faces the risk of a malpractice suit every time he or she performs an operation. A business that risks loss of or damage to goods being shipped to a customer is another good prospect. The way to transfer risk is to get **insurance**. Individuals and organizations can pay a fee (a *premium*) and get the promise of compensation for certain financial losses. The companies that take on the risks are called *insurance companies*. Insurance companies are professional risk bearers.

insurance In return for a fee (premium), guaranteed compensation for financial losses that arise from specified conditions.

Concept Check

- What is risk? Distinguish between pure risk and speculative risk.
- Describe four ways to manage risk.

INSURANCE CONCEPTS

insurance policies Written agreements that specify the risks the insurer will bear for the insured, the benefits, and the premiums.

Insurance policies are the written agreements that specify what is being covered by insurance. A policy defines the risks that the insurance company will bear for the insured party, the benefits of the policy (the maximum amount that it will pay in the event of a loss), and the premium (the cost to the insured for coverage). Any demand for payment for losses covered by the policy is a *claim*.

underwriting Reviewing insurance policy applications and choosing those that meet the company's risk criteria.

Before issuing a policy, an insurance company reviews the applications of those who want a policy and selects those that meet its standards. This **underwriting** process also determines the level of coverage and the premiums. Each company sets its own underwriting standards based on its experience. For instance, a life insurance company may decide not to accept an applicant who has had a heart attack within five years (or to charge a 50 to 75 percent higher premium). A property insurer may refuse to issue a policy on homes near brush-filled canyons, which present above-average fire hazards.

insurable interest Chance of suffering a loss if a particular peril occurs.

To get insurance, the applicant must have an **insurable interest**—the chance of suffering a loss if a particular peril occurs. In most cases, a person cannot insure the life of a friend, because the friend's death would not be considered a financial loss. But business partners can get life insurance on each other's lives because the death of one of them would have a financial impact on their firm.

2 INSURABLE RISKS

Insurance companies are professional risk takers, but they won't provide coverage against all types of risk. Some risks are insurable, some are not. For instance, changes in political or economic conditions are not insurable. An **insurable risk** is one that an insurance company will cover. For a risk to be insurable, it must meet these criteria:

insurable risk Risk that an insurance company will cover.

- *The loss must not be under the control of the insured:* The loss must be accidental—that is, unexpected and occurring by chance. Insurance companies do not cover losses purposely caused by the insured party. No insurance company will pay for the loss of a clothing store that the insured set on fire. Nor will most companies pay life insurance benefits for a suicide.
- *There must be many similar exposures to that peril:* Insurance companies study the rates of deaths, auto accidents, fires, floods, and many other perils. They know about how many of these perils will occur each year. Of course, they don't know which people or properties will suffer losses. But the **law of large numbers** lets them predict the likelihood that the peril will occur and then calculate premiums. Suppose that an insurance company has 150 policies in Morton, Iowa. The company knows from past experience that these policyholders are likely to have twelve car accidents a year and that the average payment for a claim in Morton has been $1,000. The total claims for one year's car accidents in Morton would be $12,000 (12 accidents $\times$ $1,000). Thus the company would charge each policyholder a premium of at least $80 ($12,000 $\div$ 150). Profits and administrative expenses would make the premium somewhat higher.

law of large numbers Statistical principle that a predictable number of perils will occur in a large group.

- *Losses must be financially measurable:* The dollar amount of potential losses must be known so the insurance company can figure the premiums. Life insurance is for a fixed amount specified at the time the policy is bought. Otherwise, the company and the *beneficiary* (the one who gets the funds) would have to agree on the value of the deceased's life at the time of death. Premiums have to be calculated before then, however.
- *The peril must not be likely to affect all the insured parties at the same time:* Insurance companies must spread out their risks by insuring many people and businesses in many locations. This strategy helps minimize the chance that a single calamity will wipe out the insurance company.
- *The potential loss must be significant:* Insurance companies cannot afford to insure trivial things for small amounts. Many policies have **a deductible**, an amount that the insured must pay before insurance benefits begin.

deductible Specified amount that the insured must pay before insurance benefits begin.

- *The company must have the right to set standards for insurance coverage:* Insurance companies can refuse to cover people with health problems like AIDS, cancer, or heart trouble; a poor driving record; or a dangerous job or hobby. They can also charge higher premiums because of the higher risks they are covering.

PREMIUM COSTS

Insurance policies must be economical—relatively low in cost compared to the benefits—so that people will want to buy them. Yet the premiums must also cover the risks that the insurance company faces. Insurance companies collect statistics on many perils. Then specially trained mathematicians called *actuaries* use the law of large numbers to develop actuarial tables. These tables show how likely each peril is. Actuarial tables are the basis for calculating premiums. For example, a mortality table showing average life expectancy and the expected number of deaths per 1,000 people at given ages is used to set life insurance premiums.

Almost every homeowner buys insurance to cover the perils of fire, theft, vandalism, and other home-related risks. With such a large pool of policyholders, homeowners' policies are usually inexpensive. Annual premiums are about 0.5 percent (or less) of the value of the home. This low cost encourages people to buy policies and thereby helps spread the insurance companies' risk over many homes throughout the country.

When setting premiums, insurers also look at the risk characteristics of certain groups, to assess the probability of loss for those groups. For instance, smokers tend to die younger than nonsmokers do and thus pay higher life insurance premiums. Female drivers under the age of twenty-five have a lower rate of accidents than male drivers of the same age, so their car insurance premiums are lower. In some cases, this has caused considerable controversy. For example, life and health insurers want to screen for AIDS, a disease that is very costly to treat and is likely to kill a new policyholder before he or she has paid enough premiums into a policy. Whether AIDS should be treated differently from other chronic diseases is the subject of ongoing debate.

Concept Check

- What are the key elements of an insurance policy? Why do insurance companies underwrite policies?
- Discuss the concept of insurable risks and the law of large numbers. Name the six criteria for insurable risks.
- How do insurance companies determine premium rates?

THE INSURANCE INDUSTRY

3 Insurers can be either public or private. Public insurance coverage is offered by specialized government agencies. The federal government is in fact the largest single insurer in the United States. Private insurance coverage is provided by privately organized (nongovernment) companies.

PUBLIC INSURANCE

About $425 billion a year is collected by government insurers. Government-sponsored insurance falls into two general categories: social insurance programs and other programs. Social insurance provides protection for problems beyond the scope of private insurers. These programs include unemployment insurance, workers' compensation, and Social Security. Other government programs provide insurance for risks that may not be adequately covered by private insurance. These programs include flood insurance, crop insurance, mortgage insurance, pension insurance, and property and liability coverage for high-crime areas. Deposit insurance, discussed in Chapter 20, is another form of public insurance.

Unemployment Insurance

unemployment insurance State insurance program that pays laid-off workers weekly benefits while they seek new jobs.

Every state has an **unemployment insurance** program that pays laid-off workers weekly benefits while they seek new jobs. Persons who terminate their employment voluntarily or are fired for cause are not eligible for unemployment insurance. These programs also provide job counseling and placement services. The benefits usually start a week after a person has lost a job and continue for twenty-six to thirty-nine weeks, depending on the state. The size of the weekly benefit depends on the workers' previous income and varies from state to state. Unemployment insurance is funded by payroll taxes levied on employers.

Workers' Compensation

workers' compensation Insurance, required of employers, that covers job-related injuries and diseases.

All employers have to fund **workers' compensation** insurance. It covers the expenses of job-related injuries and diseases, including medical costs, rehabilitation, and job retraining if necessary. It also provides disability income benefits (salary and wage payments) for workers who can't perform their jobs. Every state has laws requiring employers to buy this insurance or to be self-insured (have enough resources to pay workers' compensation claims). Workers' compensation insurance is available from private insurers or, in some states, from a state-sponsored fund. A company's premium is based on the amount of its payroll and the types of risks present in the workplace. For instance, a construction company would pay a higher premium for workers' compensation insurance than would a jewelry store.

Recently the cost of workers' compensation insurance premiums has risen. During the 1980s, the total amount paid in premiums almost doubled, while the total amount paid for claims tripled. From 1988 to 1992, the average cost per workers' compensation claim jumped from about $17,000 to almost $26,000. The increase was largely due to rising medical costs. The number of claims rose as well. Many large companies have turned to self-insurance in order to lower costs. Small businesses, however, typically cannot afford to self-insure and have been especially hard hit by the increase in premiums. Some states provide workers' compensation pools for companies who can't get coverage elsewhere. Another strategy that helps small companies contain workers' compensation premium costs is to form self-insurance funds for groups of companies. The fund members pool their resources and hire an administrator who contracts for the necessary services. These funds require that members are trained in and follow loss reduction procedures, including monitoring workplace safety and dealing effectively with injured workers.[1]

Social Security

The federal government handles **Social Security** insurance. It provides retirement, disability, death, and health insurance benefits. Officially called Old-Age, Survivors, Disability, and Health Insurance (OASDHI), Social Security is funded by equal contributions from workers and employers. These benefits go mostly to people over sixty-five, although they are available to younger people who are disabled. More than 90 percent of all U.S. workers and their families are eligible to qualify for Social Security benefits.

A health insurance program for those over sixty-five was added to Social Security in 1965. It is administered through **Medicare**. Medicare has two parts, hospital insurance and medical insurance (for doctors' and other medical services). The hospital insurance is financed through the Social Security tax. The medical insurance is financed through government contributions and monthly premiums paid by those who wish to have this coverage. Because Medicare pays only part of the insured's medical expenses, many people buy *supplemental insurance* from private insurance companies.

PRIVATE INSURANCE COMPANIES

Private insurance companies sell property and liability insurance, health insurance, and life insurance. Private insurers collect about $500 billion in premiums each year. Their total assets are $2.2 trillion. Life and health insurance companies dominate the industry, accounting for about 70 percent of total assets. Exhibit 24-1 lists the nation's largest insurance companies. Regulation of private insurance companies is under the control of the states and thus varies from state to state.

There are two basic ownership structures for private insurance companies: stockholder and mutual. Just like other publicly owned corporations, **stock insurance companies** are profit-oriented companies

■ **Exhibit 24-1**
Ten Largest U.S. Insurance Companies

Source: "The Service 500," *Fortune*, 31 May 1993, pp. 214, 218.

Company	Assets (in millions)
Prudential of America	$154,779.4
Metropolitan Life	118,178.3
Aetna Life & Casualty	89,928.2
American International Group	79,835.2
CIGNA	69,827.0
Teachers Insurance and Annuity	61,776.7
Travelers Corp.	53,602.0
New York Life	46,925.0
Equitable Life Insurance	46,624.0
Connecticut General Life	44,075.5

owned by stockholders. The stockholders do not have to be policyholders, and the policyholders do not have to be stockholders. Their profits come from insurance premiums in excess of claim payments and operating expenses and from investments in securities and real estate. Aetna Life & Casualty is the largest stockholder-owned insurance company in the United States, with assets of about $90 billion. Other major stock insurance companies are Allstate Insurance, CIGNA Corporation, Continental Insurance, and Fireman's Fund Insurance. Of about 5,000 insurance companies in the United States, most are stock insurance companies.

mutual insurance companies Not-for-profit insurance companies owned collectively by their policyholders.

The rest are **mutual insurance companies**, which are owned by their policyholders. They are not-for-profit organizations and chartered by each state. Any excess income is used to reduce premiums, retained to finance future operations, or returned to the policyholder-owners as dividends. The policyholders elect the board of directors, who manage the company. Most of the large life insurance companies in the United States are mutuals, including John Hancock, Metropolitan Life, New York Life, and Prudential Life. State Farm, the largest auto insurer, is also a mutual insurance company.

4   PROBLEMS FACING THE INSURANCE INDUSTRY

For many years the insurance industry was stable, conservative, and predictable. Insurance companies offered a limited number of policy types, collected the premiums, and invested them in long-term securities that earned a respectable return. But in the late 1980s, the two main sectors of the industry—life and health companies and property and liability companies—came under financial pressure, but for different reasons.

All insurance companies invest the money they receive in premiums, and the low interest rate environment of the early- to mid-1990s sharply reduced their investment income. With sales of traditional life insurance policies flat, life insurers began offering more complex and varied policies with higher returns to policyholders. These policies were good for consumers but less profitable for insurers, who compete with other types of financial institutions for savers' dollars. They also exposed the companies to interest rate risk. To boost profitability, many companies took more risks in underwriting and in investments, turning to real estate and junk bonds that promised high returns. As was the case with savings and loan associations, the collapse of the junk-bond market in 1990 and the drop in real estate values left many life insurers in weakened financial condition.

Although property and liability companies had stronger investments than life insurers, the price of their policies and the huge growth in liability lawsuits strained their resources. To gain market share, many property and liability companies set their rates too low. As a result, profits declined. Record numbers of catastrophe claims due to hurricanes in 1992, fires and floods in 1993, and winter storms and the Los Angeles earthquake in 1994 further strained these companies' reserves for future claims, which are not predictable and may not be known for many years. For example, Hurricane Andrew in 1992 alone accounted for $16.5 billion of the year's $23

■ The 1993 floods in the Midwest added to the insurance industry's recent woes. Billions of dollars in catastrophic claims were filed by individuals and businesses hurt by this disaster. This put a strain on many insurance companies' cash reserves, which they will need to pay out future claims.

billion in catastrophe claims, and damage from the 1994 earthquake was estimated at over $7 billion for just the first quarter of the year.[2]

Liability claims arising from pollution damage are also a problem for property and casualty insurers. Under the 1980 Superfund Act that regulates environmental cleanup, insurance companies could be hit with massive claim payouts. Courts have interpreted the clause in commercial liability insurance policies that requires insurers to cover "sudden and accidental events" to extend to environmental cleanup, even if the problem is caused by slow leakage over many years. Insurers claim that their policies were intended to cover only specific accidents, such as the crash of a truck carrying toxic wastes. The potential costs of environmental claims are unpredictable and huge. Through mid-1993, about 75 percent of the $15 billion spent under Superfund went to legal and related costs, and only about 200 of the 1,300 identified sites had been cleaned up. The major insurers are working with Congress and federal regulators to revise this onerous pollution clean-up program, and they have proposed that businesses, insurance companies, and the government sponsor a special fund for future settlements.[3]

However, the insurance industry managed to avoid the crisis that hit the banking industry and is stronger now than it was in 1990. Only a small number of companies failed, and most companies have reduced their junk bond and problem real estate holdings. In late 1992 the National Association of Insurance Commissioners, a group of state regulators that sets standards for the industry, established new minimum capital (equity) requirements based on the riskiness of a company's investments and operations. The greater a company's holdings of higher-risk assets such as common stock, junk bonds, real estate, and mortgages, the higher its required capital. Insurers are therefore investing more cautiously, resulting in lower returns that not only curtail profit growth but also reduce yields to policyholders. The future result may be higher premiums.[4]

Insurance companies are trying to solve their individual problems through a variety of strategies. For example, Equitable Life, one of the largest mutual companies, changed to a stock company and sold equity to the public to raise additional capital. Many companies are pulling out of unprofitable markets such as homeowners' and automobile insurance for individuals, either totally or in some markets. Others are using total quality management concepts to improve their operating efficiency, as the nearby Quality Management Trends box discusses.

Concept Check

- What does public insurance cover and why? Discuss the three main forms of public insurance.
- Distinguish between stock and mutual insurance companies.
- Discuss the problems facing the insurance industry.

TRENDS

Quality Management

New Policies for Quality

Faced with lower profits, insurance companies are looking for ways to reduce costs and improve efficiency. Total quality management, with its focus on satisfying customer needs, has been a logical route to achieving these goals.

Sun Life of Canada redesigned its business practices to emphasize quality at its U.S. headquarters in Wellesley, Massachusetts. Because serving customers was identified as the only business process, Sun's changes focused on better ways to provide its affluent policyholders with high-quality, quick, efficient service. It reorganized employees into eight-person teams trained to handle all policyholder questions. Because customers don't have to be transferred from specialist to specialist, problems can be resolved in less time. This pleased customers and increased representatives' productivity.

Business process redesign was coupled with efficient use of technology to reduce costs and improve service to both insurance agents and policyholders at The New England, a Boston-based life insurer. A new system gave agents access to home-office client information databases from their PCs. With better information, they could give personal, timely service to customers. Agents can also use a special desktop publishing system to prepare high-quality, customized sales presentation with graphics and color. Policyholders were pleased with the establishment of a customer service center they can call toll-free. Specially-trained representatives respond immediately to requests for account information and other policyholder requests. Agents now spend less time on paperwork and more time on building customer relationships.[5]

PROPERTY AND LIABILITY INSURANCE

5 Americans pay over $230 billion a year for property and liability insurance. Over 3,500 companies offer property and liability policies. This type of insurance is important for businesses, which wish to protect against losses of property and lawsuits arising from harm to other people.

property insurance
Insurance that covers financial losses from damage to or destruction of the insured's assets.

liability insurance Insurance that covers financial losses from injuries to others and damage to or destruction of others' property when the insured is the cause.

Property and liability insurance is a broad category. **Property insurance** covers financial losses from damage to or destruction of the insured's assets as a result of specified perils. Fire insurance is an example. It would pay the insured up to the policy amount for losses resulting from a fire. **Liability insurance** covers financial losses from injuries to others and damage to or destruction of others' property when the insured is considered to be the cause. It also covers the insured's legal defense fees up to the maximum amount stated in the policy. Automobile liability insurance is an example. It would pay for a fence damaged when an insured person lost control of his or her car, for instance. Commercial and product liability insurance also fall into this category. Commercial liability insurance covers a variety of damage claims, including harm to the environment from pollution. In the case of product liability, if a defective furnace exploded and damaged a home, the manufacturer might be liable for the damages. If the manufacturer were insured, the insurance company would cover the losses or pay to dispute the claim in court.

Businesses buy many types of property and liability insurance. These protect against loss of property due to fire, theft, accidents, or employee dishonesty and financial losses arising from liability cases. Individuals buy property and liability insurance on their homes and cars.

HOME AND BUILDING INSURANCE

home and building insurance Insurance that protects property owners from both property and liability losses caused by a variety of perils.

Home and building insurance protects property owners from financial losses caused by a variety of perils. Homeowners, landlords, and owners of all types of business property buy this type of insurance for protection against both property damage and liability losses.

Originally, home and building insurance covered only fires. Coverage has now been extended to windstorms, lightning, hurricanes, vandalism, riots and other civil disturbances, frozen water pipes, and falling airplanes. Coverage for earthquakes and floods is also available. Losses caused by wars and nuclear power plant accidents still are not covered. (However, special insurance pools created by property and liability insurers do provide some coverage for losses from nuclear accidents.)

The losses discussed thus far are basically property losses. Building owners also buy liability insurance for protection against financial losses arising from their liability for the injury of others. For instance, if a person broke an arm by falling on the ice in front of an apartment building, the landlord's property insurance policy would cover any claim. This type of liability insurance is usually included in homeowners' policies as well as landlords' and businesses' property insurance policies.

coinsurance Insurance that requires the property owner to buy an amount of insurance coverage equal to a specified percentage of the value of the property.

Property insurance policies usually include a coinsurance clause. **Coinsurance** requires the property owner to buy insurance coverage equal to a certain percentage of the value of the property. Often policyholders insure buildings for less than their full value as a way to cut premium costs. They do so because fire or other disasters may damage only part of the property. But the insurance policy covers the entire building. Insurers limit the payout if the property is underinsured. They use coinsurance clauses as an incentive for businesses to maintain full insurance on their buildings. For instance, some fire insurance policies have an 80 percent coinsurance clause. If the owner of a building valued at $400,000 buys a policy with coverage equal to at least $320,000 (80% × $400,000), he or she will collect the full amount of any partial loss. If the owner buys a policy for less coverage, the insurance company will pay for only part of the partial loss.

BUSINESS INTERRUPTION INSURANCE

business interruption insurance Optional insurance coverage that protects business owners from losses occurring when the business must be closed temporarily after property damage.

Another type of protection important to businesses is **business interruption insurance**. This optional coverage is often offered with fire insurance. It protects business owners from losses occurring when the business must be closed temporarily after property damage. A great deal of business income can be lost while a business is closed to repair the damage. Business interruption insurance may cover such costs as rental of temporary facilities, wage and salary payments to employees, payments for leased equipment, fixed payments (for instance, rent and loans), and profits that would have been earned during the period. *Contingent business interruption insurance* covers losses to the insured in the event of property damage to a major supplier or customer.

AUTOMOBILE INSURANCE

All fifty states have financial responsibility laws that require drivers to show proof of the ability to pay the costs (up to a limit) of any accidents for which they are responsible. Most drivers buy automobile insurance to get that proof of responsibility.

automobile insurance Insurance that covers financial losses from car-related perils.

Automobile insurance covers financial losses from a number of automobile-related perils, including accidents, theft, fire, and liability lawsuits. The two main types of automobile insurance are liability insurance and physical damage insurance. *Automobile liability insurance* protects the insured from financial losses caused by automobile-related injuries to others or damage to their property. The maximum payment limits are set by each policy. A $50,000/$100,000 policy, for instance, will pay up to $50,000 for each person injured in an accident but a total of $100,000 per accident, no matter how many people are involved.

Automobile physical damage insurance covers damage to or loss of the policyholder's vehicle from collision, theft, fire, or other perils. The two types of damage coverage are *comprehensive*, which covers losses due to fire, floods, theft, and vandalism, and *collision*, which covers damage caused by colliding with another vehicle or object.

Automobile insurance rates generally depend on the driver's age, marital status, gender, area of residence, and driving record. Young male drivers who live in cities and who have had more than one traffic ticket are charged the highest rates. This group historically has been involved in the most accidents.

About half the states have passed laws requiring **no-fault automobile insurance**. It covers the insured's financial losses resulting from automobile accidents, regardless of who was responsible. These laws also limit the right of accident victims to sue for damages. Suits can be filed only if injuries are severe. Supporters of no-fault insurance claim that it reduces premiums. But some states have repealed their no-fault laws because rates increased.

no-fault automobile insurance Insurance that covers the insured's financial losses resulting from automobile accidents regardless of who was responsible for the accident.

MARINE INSURANCE

marine insurance Insurance that protects goods in transit as well as movable personal property.

The term **marine insurance** is somewhat misleading, because it protects not only shipments by water but also shipments over land and even objects that are not being shipped. *Ocean marine insurance* covers shipowners if their ship or its cargo is lost or damaged. *Inland marine insurance* covers loss or damage to goods being transported by rail, truck, airplane, or inland barge, as well as goods in storage awaiting transportation. It also covers movable personal property, like jewelry, under special policies called "floaters" that are attached to homeowners' policies.

THEFT INSURANCE, FIDELITY AND SURETY BONDS, AND TITLE INSURANCE

theft insurance Insurance that protects businesses against losses from an act of stealing.

Businesses also want to protect their property against financial losses due to crime. **Theft insurance** is the broadest coverage and protects businesses against losses from an act of stealing. Businesses can also buy more limited types of theft insurance. *Burglary insurance* covers losses of and damage to property resulting from forcible entry into the insured's property. *Robbery insurance* covers losses due to unlawful taking of the insured's property by either force or threat of force. Burglaries usually are committed after business hours, robberies during business hours.

What if a dishonest employee steals from his or her employer? This situation is covered by a *fidelity bond*, an agreement that insures a company against theft committed by an employee who handles company money. If a restaurant manager is bonded for $50,000 and steals $60,000, for example, the restaurant will recover all but $10,000 of the loss from the insurance company. Banks, loan companies, and retail businesses that employ cashiers typically buy fidelity bonds.

A *surety bond*, also called a *performance bond*, is an agreement to reimburse a firm for nonperformance of acts specified in a contract. This form of insurance is most common in the construction industry. Contractors buy surety bonds to cover themselves in case the project they are working on is not completed by the specified date or does not meet specified standards. In practice, the insurance company often pays another contractor to finish the job or to redo shoddy work when the bonded contractor fails to perform. The property owner for whom the contractor is working may also get an additional financial settlement.

Title insurance protects the buyer of real estate against losses caused by a defect in the title—that is, a claim against the property that prevents the transfer of ownership from seller to purchaser. It eliminates the need to search legal records to be sure that the seller was actually the owner of (had clear title to) the property. Title insurance is generally purchased when a person buys a home.

OTHER TYPES OF LIABILITY INSURANCE

Businesses and businesspeople often protect themselves with three special types of liability insurance: umbrella personal liability insurance, professional liability insurance, and product-liability insurance.

Personal liability claims are a large portion of all liability claims. Many property insurance policies limit the amount paid for personal injury claims, and this amount may not be enough. **Umbrella personal liability insurance** increases the amount of liability coverage, to $1 million or more, above the amount paid by the homeowner's policy.

umbrella personal liability insurance Insurance that increases the amount of liability coverage above the amount paid by a homeowner's policy.

Many malpractice lawsuits are filed each year against professionals in fields like medicine, law, architecture, and dentistry. Corporate officers and directors have also been the target of malpractice lawsuits. **Professional liability insurance** covers financial losses resulting from alleged malpractice. It pays for legal fees and court-awarded damages up to specific limits. *Directors and officers insurance* is a type of professional liability insurance designed to protect top corporate management.

professional liability insurance Insurance that covers financial losses resulting from alleged malpractice in the performance of the insured's professional services.

Premiums for professional liability insurance have skyrocketed lately. The number of suits against corporate officers and directors has increased in recent years, and it has become harder for companies to buy insurance policies at reasonable rates to protect executives and directors. In New York City and other large urban areas, malpractice insurance rates for obstetricians are so high that a number of doctors have decided to stop delivering babies.

product-liability insurance Insurance that covers financial losses incurred by producers or sellers of goods or services due to injury or damage resulting from the use of the covered product.

Product-liability insurance covers the financial losses of producers or sellers when someone claims injury or damage resulting from use of the covered product. (The legal basis for product liability was discussed in Chapter 23.) Cases involve many types of claims. For example, a woman was awarded $3.25 million from Bic Corp. because one of its lighters exploded in her pocket, burning her badly.[6] As mentioned in Chapter 23, suits relating to asbestos and silicone breast implants cost companies many billions of dollars. Product-liability insurance covered a large portion of the monetary awards in these cases.

The cost of product-liability insurance has soared in recent years because of increased claims and large awards. As a result, many companies can no longer afford product-liability coverage. Some are choosing to fight the cases in court rather than settle out of court. Bic was the target of numerous lawsuits, which continued to be filed years after the product-liability case was closed in 1986. After Bic adopted a "don't settle" policy, the number of cases dropped 57 percent.[7] Some large corporations have formed a Product Liability Advisory Council, which takes on about twenty-five cases a year. It has won two-thirds of those cases for the manufacturers. And, the Product Liability Coordinating Committee, a lobbying coalition of insurance, manufacturing, and pharmaceutical companies, is working for the reform of current product liability laws.[8]

- Distinguish between property and liability insurance coverage. Why should businesses have both?
- Briefly describe the coverage provided by the main types of property and liability insurance.

HEALTH INSURANCE

6 Like other insurable perils, loss of health can bring financial ruin. The cost of health care has risen much faster than the cost of living in general, doubling between 1982 and 1992. The total cost of health care in the United States in 1992 was about $820 billion.[9] For many, medical expenses may come at the worst possible time. During a serious illness, earnings may be lost because of disability. **Health insurance** covers some of the losses resulting from illness or injury. About 85 percent of all Americans are covered by some form of health insurance.

health insurance Insurance that covers financial losses resulting from illness or injury.

TYPES OF HEALTH INSURANCE

To help meet the high and rising costs of health care, six basic types of health insurance policies are written:

- *Regular medical expense insurance:* Pays all or a portion of the doctor fees for nonsurgical care, laboratory tests, x-rays, and prescription drugs. Routine examinations are typically not covered. This type of insurance is usually included with other types of health insurance and not issued as a separate policy. In addition to the premium, the insured person has to pay for services up to the amount of the *deductible*, which typically ranges from $100 to $1,000. The insurance then pays 80 to 100 percent of covered medical costs. Many people choose higher deductibles in order to pay lower premiums.
- *Hospitalization insurance:* Covers room fees, the cost of nursing care, operating room charges, and other hospital service charges. Most policies do not pay the whole hospital bill. Some have a deductible, and many limit coverage to 80 percent of the total bill. Most limit room fees to the semiprivate rate or put a dollar limit on the daily room rate.
- *Surgical insurance:* Covers surgical fees charged by the surgeon, anesthesiologist, and other physicians. (Hospitalization for surgery is covered by hospitalization insurance.) To reduce costs, many insur-

■ Because the cost of medical care in the U.S. has risen so much faster than the general cost of living, health insurance has become a necessity for most people. The government has now stepped in, proposing several different programs designed to ensure that every American has access to basic health care.

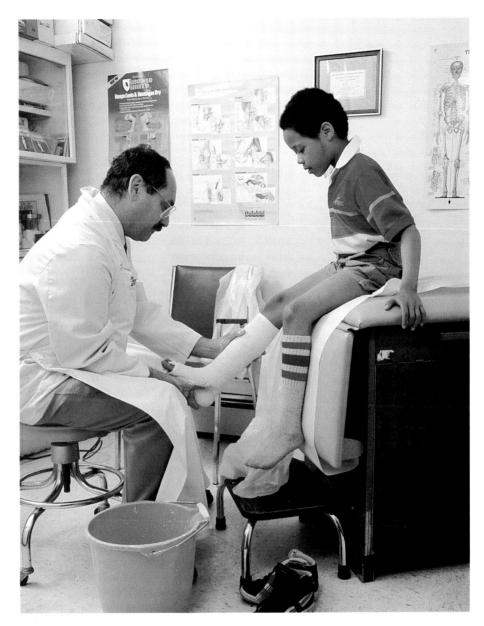

ance companies require second opinions to confirm the need for elective (nonemergency) surgery. If patients do not get a second opinion, the insurance company may refuse payment. Another way to reduce costs is to perform some types of surgery on an outpatient basis, thereby avoiding the high cost of a hospital stay. Some insurance companies will pay only a small amount or nothing if what they consider outpatient surgery is done on an inpatient basis. Others cover a higher percentage of the costs if the operation is done on an outpatient basis.

- *Major medical insurance:* Introduced in 1951 to cover financial losses that exceed the limits on hospitalization and surgical insurance. It covers all hospital costs, doctor fees, and other medical expenses up to a specific limit, such as $1 million. More than 160 million Americans have major medical policies. They are available at low cost because most people don't have to use them. These policies are written either as an addition to basic medical, surgical, and hospitalization insurance or as part of a total coverage plan.

- *Dental insurance:* Pays for a percentage of dental expenses, usually 50 to 80 percent, after payment of a deductible. This coverage is one of the most popular and fastest-growing types of insurance. Most dental plans are offered as an employee benefit.

disability insurance
Insurance that provides monthly payments to people unable to work as a result of illness or accident.

- ***Disability insurance:*** Provides monthly payments to those who are unable to work as a result of illness or accident. This type of insurance is usually offered by employers but is also available to the self-employed. It typically has a waiting period before income payments begin. All states also have disability income insurance as part of their workers' compensation program.

SOURCES OF HEALTH INSURANCE COVERAGE

Health insurance is provided by public and private insurance companies. Public health insurance programs include Social Security, workers' compensation, and Medicaid. Medicaid is a welfare program that pays the medical bills of the poor. It is funded by federal and state governments. Private insurance coverage is provided by commercial insurance companies, by Blue Cross/Blue Shield, and by managed care programs.

Private Insurance and Blue Cross/Blue Shield

Private insurance companies offer many different types of plans. Companies like Aetna Life and Casualty, Prudential, and Equitable Life provide policies covering all or some of the types of insurance just described.

Blue Cross/Blue Shield
Group of not-for-profit health insurance plans that contract with subscribers and with member hospitals and doctors.

Blue Cross/Blue Shield is a group of not-for-profit health insurance plans that contract with both subscribers and member hospitals and doctors. No disability coverage is offered by Blue Cross/Blue Shield. The premiums are often lower than premiums for other health insurance plans. Blue Cross/Blue Shield differs from other health insurers by being not-for-profit and by negotiating prices in advance with member hospitals and physicians. Because of the contracts with hospitals, subscribers must use member hospitals for nonemergency care to receive full benefits. About 40 percent of the population is covered by one of over seventy-three separate Blue Cross/Blue Shield organizations, which operate within a particular geographic region. In most regions they work together, with Blue Cross providing hospitalization and Blue Shield paying surgical and medical costs.

group insurance Private insurance coverage available to employees of a firm or government or to members of a trade association or similar organization.

These policies can be bought by individuals or through **group insurance** available to the employees of a firm or the government or to members of a trade association or similar organization. Employers typically pay some of the health insurance premiums, and employees pay the rest. Group policies usually cost less than individual policies.

Managed Care Programs

The cost of providing health insurance for employees has become a big burden for businesses. In just one year, from 1991 to 1992, the total average cost of health benefits per employee rose 10 percent—over three times the inflation rate—to $3,968 per year.[10] To control costs, firms are paying less of the premiums, requiring authorization before nonemergency hospitalization, and turning to **managed care programs**, which monitor treatment and limit the choice of doctors. Unlike traditional health insurance plans, in which the insured person can choose any physician, managed care programs generally pay only for services provided by doctors who are part of the plan. The two most popular forms of managed care programs are health maintenance organizations and preferred provider organizations. Membership in these plans has grown rapidly, increasing from 28 percent of all health insurance plans in 1988 to 51 percent in 1992.[11]

Health maintenance organizations (HMOs) are prepaid medical expense plans that offer almost unlimited use of specified health care facilities and services for a very low per-visit fee, around $2 to $10. HMOs get a monthly fee for each subscriber, rather than being paid on a per-service basis. These organizations employ their own doctors, who work at a central facility. Some HMOs even have their own hospitals. They favor preventive medicine and try to control health care costs by keeping their subscribers healthy. Their doctors are paid salaries and are encouraged to keep expenses down.

HMOs are one of the fastest-growing types of health care coverage today because of their emphasis on cost control and the wide range of benefits they provide. As of late 1993, about 45 million people were enrolled in HMOs, compared to only 10.2 million in 1982.[12] A federal law passed in 1973 requires companies with twenty-five or more employees to offer HMOs as an option if they are available in the area. Well-known HMOs include Kaiser-Permanente, CIGNA, and New York's Health Insurance Plan.

A **preferred provider organization (PPO)** is a cross between an HMO and a traditional insurance plan. PPOs offer complete health care services to subscribers within a network of physicians and hospitals. PPOs are most often a part of employee benefit plans. The sponsor of a PPO—an insurer, an HMO, an employer, a Blue Cross/Blue Shield group—negotiates for a variety of doctor and hospital services at a discount of 10 to 20 percent. Subscribers can choose from this group of approved providers. The cost savings are passed on in the form of lower premiums. The ability to choose from a large group of health care providers makes these plans more popular than HMOs.

It appears that those companies that are turning to managed care networks to control their health insurance costs are getting the results they were looking for. HMO costs rose 8.8 percent in 1992, compared to 14.2 percent for traditional plans. Premiums, too, are rising at a slower pace: 8.1 percent in 1993 versus 10.6 percent in 1992.[13]

managed care programs Health insurance programs that monitor medical treatment and limit the choice of doctors.

health maintenance organizations (HMOs) Prepaid medical expense plans that offer subscribers complete and almost unlimited use of specified health care facilities and services for very low per-visit fees.

preferred provider organization (PPO) Form of health care coverage that offers complete health care services to its subscribers within a network of physicians and hospitals.

ISSUES IN HEALTH INSURANCE

The high costs of health care and health insurance have become a big problem for many individuals, businesses, and the federal government. Spending on health care now accounts for 14 percent of the U.S. gross domestic product and is projected to reach 19 percent by 2000. The government's share of these costs is rising especially quickly. By 1995, federal health programs will represent the government's largest expenditure category, exceeding even defense and Social Security.[14] Reasons for the cost increases include longer life spans and new, more costly life-saving technology, surgical procedures, and drug therapies. Another reason for increasing costs is claims fraud. The Technology Trends box explains how health insurers use technology to find phony claims.

TRENDS

Technology

Software Sleuths

Health insurers are cracking down on claims fraud, which costs them $50 billion each year and can lower profit margins by 2 to 10 percent. Because insurers may have less freedom to raise premiums to cover the cost of fraud with the coming of health care reform, they are looking for new ways to fight this problem.

Many companies now rely on computer software that uncovers fake claims by quickly analyzing millions of claims for suspicious trends and patterns in billing and treatment. For example, a program might compare patient and doctor Zip codes and flag any that represent unusually long distances. The number of claims physicians file for various types of procedures can be tracked and compared to their peers, thereby identifying possible irregularities. Software used by Travelers' Insurance monitors thirty factors that could signal fraud, including office visits on holidays and claims from one doctor for treating several family members on the same day, which could indicate overcharging. Aetna's sophisticated program finds an average of 500 potential cases of fraud in the seven million claims it examines each month. In 1992 alone, the program helped the company recover $5.7 billion in fraudulent payments.

Companies with these fraud-detection programs recognize their growing attraction to other insurers. Travelers is marketing its software to other firms. AdminaStar Solutions, an Indianapolis firm with software that detects Medicare fraud for the federal government, adapted its product for private insurance companies. IBM also has a service to analyze health care provider billing and medical practices. For example, its system identified a southern California chiropractor whose average charge of $5,264 far exceeded the area's $1,184 average and who took twice as many x-rays.

Experts say that these systems could also help fight automobile insurance fraud, another major problem. A large number of claims filed for accident and stolen cars are in fact fraudulent. In Massachusetts, for example, an estimated 40 percent of all auto insurance claims are fraudulent. Software may soon cut that number and help relieve pressure to raise premiums for car insurance as it has for health insurance.[15]

Today an estimated 30 million Americans have no health insurance. Another 20 million are underinsured. Those being squeezed most are middle-income families, self-employed persons, and small businesses. They lack the market clout of larger groups and have a harder time buying affordable coverage. Fewer companies are willing to insure small groups, and those that do may charge very high premiums.

One solution is special small-business health insurance programs that combine companies into purchasing cooperatives. California's Health Insurance Plan is the first statewide program of this type. Employers who voluntarily join the cooperatives find that as part of a larger group they have more bargaining power with insurers. Insurers are competing to serve these cooperatives, allowing them to reduce premiums for their members at a time when most small firms are seeing their rates increase.[16]

national health insurance Federally sponsored health insurance plan for citizens.

Another possible answer to this dilemma is **national health insurance**, a federally sponsored, wide-ranging health insurance plan. Countries like Canada and Great Britain have national health care programs, sometimes called socialized medicine. In October 1993 the Clinton administration submitted to Congress a health care bill that featured health insurance coverage for all Americans, regardless of whether they are employed or have existing health problems. The plan emphasized managed care programs and preventive care. It also included quality and cost controls. Employers would be required to pay a certain percentage of insurance costs for all employees, including part-time workers. This requirement could put a strain on small businesses. Although universal coverage and simplified billing and claim filing procedures have broad support, the form the insurance program would take—and the methods of paying for it—generated considerable disagreement from the business community. Many feared that greater government involvement in what should be a market-driven solution would result in a costly and inefficient system. Within six months, it was obvious that many of the plan's original proposals were not acceptable. As of July 1994, debate on the plan and counterproposals to it continued. Its final form was uncertain.

Concept Check
- What are the three main sources of health insurance?
- What are the pros and cons of national health insurance?

LIFE INSURANCE

life insurance Insurance that provides a specific amount of money to the insured person's beneficiary or estate upon his or her death.

Life insurance provides a specific amount of money on the death of the insured person. The money goes to the beneficiary or estate that the insured has chosen. People buy life insurance to meet two needs: protection (income for the insured's family) and savings for the future. The amount of life insurance a person can buy is limited only by what he or she is willing to pay.

About two-thirds of all Americans have some life insurance to protect their family against the financial losses caused by the premature death of the breadwinner. Life insurance coverage in force in the U.S. totals about $10 trillion. Life insurance is included in most employee benefit plans and is also bought by individuals. To get an individual life insurance policy, the applicant usually has to qualify on medical terms. Group plans do not normally require medical examinations. About 2,000 companies sell life insurance, although about 40 percent of it is sold by the eight largest companies.

TYPES OF LIFE INSURANCE

The types of life insurance policies available to individuals include term, whole, universal, and variable life insurance. Businesses buy term, credit, and key-person life insurance. Types of life insurance differ, as shown in Exhibit 24-2, in the level of protection versus savings and cost. Exhibit 24-3 shows differences among premiums.

cash value Amount of money from a life insurance policy that is paid to the policyholder if the policy is canceled or that can be borrowed by the policyholder at low interest rates; surrender value.

Types of life insurance also differ in their cash value. **Cash value** (or surrender value) is the amount that is paid to the policyholder if the policy is canceled or that can be borrowed by the policyholder at low interest rates. For some types of insurance, part of the premium is invested. The interest earned on this investment accumulates, with the investment portion, as cash value. Thus some life insurance policies have, in effect, a savings feature.

The main types of life insurance and their features are:

term life insurance Life insurance that covers the insured's life for a fixed amount and a specific period.

- **Term life insurance:** As the name implies, it covers the insured's life for a fixed amount and a specific period, typically five to twenty years. It has no cash value. When the term ends, protection stops, unless the policy is renewed or a new policy is bought. The annual premiums for term insurance go up with age. Thus it provides inexpensive coverage for young people but may not be cost-effective for older people. The goal of term insurance is to provide a lot of coverage for a limited period, often when a family's children are young. Most group insurance plans are term policies.

■ Exhibit 24-2
Protection versus Savings in Different Types of Life Insurance

Source: Mark R. Greene and James S. Trieschmann, *Risk and Insurance* (Cincinnati: South-Western, 1988), p. 241.

Low premium
No savings
High protection

Term insurance

Medium-size
premium, savings, and
protection

Whole life insurance

High premium
Large savings
Low protection

Universal life insurance

■ Exhibit 24-3

Life Insurance Premiums
(for Adult Males)

Source: (Based on 1993 information from
109 companies; not all companies offer
products in each category.) Life Insurance
Marketing and Research Association, Inc.,
*Monthly Survey of Life Insurance Sales in
the United States* (Hartford, Conn: Life
Insurance Marketing and Research
Association, Inc., 1994), p. 2.

Type of Policy	Average Size Policy	Premium per Policy
Term life	$181,224	$ 487
Whole life	42,140	750
Universal life	98,946	1,138
Variable life	156,816	1,924
Variable universal life	129,185	1,826

whole life insurance
Life insurance that covers the
insured's life for his or her
whole life and that accumulates savings; straight life insurance.

**universal life insur-
ance** Combination of term
life insurance and a tax-deferred savings plan in which
premiums are invested and
earn, in effect, interest.

variable life insurance
Combination of life insurance
and a savings plan in which
the policyholder can designate how much of the pre-
mium should be allocated for
insurance and how much
should be invested.

- ***Whole life insurance:*** Also called straight life insurance, this type covers the insured's entire life. In addition to death protection, it has a cash value that increases over the life of the policy. Whole life is much more expensive than term insurance, and the interest rate used to determine its cash value is small—usually 4 to 6 percent. But the premiums can be handled in many different ways. Often they are paid in installments and remain level over the life of a policy. A variation called *limited payment life insurance* requires a higher premium for a certain period, such as twenty years or up to age sixty-five. After that, no more premiums have to be paid.

- ***Universal life insurance:*** One of the fastest-growing forms of life insurance during the 1980s, universal life insurance is a combination of term life insurance and a tax-deferred savings plan. It was developed to help insurance companies compete with other financial service institutions for investment funds. The premiums go into a fund similar to a mutual fund. This fund is credited with the policyholder's share of any investment earnings, after a deduction for expenses. The cash value is then invested in short-term and medium-term securities rather than in the long-term securities commonly used in the insurance industry. Thus the cash value accumulates interest at current market rates. The death benefit is equal to the amount paid by term insurance plus any cash value that has accumulated at the time of the insured's death. Universal life policy premiums are very flexible. They are based on the amount of insurance coverage desired and the amount the insured wishes to save. However, when interest rates began to fall, lower investment returns required policyholders to pay higher premiums to maintain the desired coverage levels.

- ***Variable life insurance:*** Like whole and universal life, this type combines life insurance with a savings feature. But unlike universal life insurance, it lets the policyholder decide how much of the premium should go to insurance and how much should be invested in the cash account. He or she also has a choice of how to invest these funds. Most companies offering variable life policies have a wide range of investment options. Thus variable life insurance offers the highest level of investment returns. But unlike whole or universal life policies, it does not guarantee a minimum return. Many variable life policies specify a minimum death benefit. But both the amount of insurance coverage provided and the cash value vary with the profits and losses being earned on the investment account. A popular newer type of life insurance, *variable universal life insurance,* combines features of variable and universal life. Policyholders can vary the premium amount during the term of the policy, giving them even greater flexibility.

credit life insurance
Insurance that guarantees repayment of the amount due on a loan if the borrower dies.

- ***Credit life insurance:*** This type guarantees repayment of the amount due on a loan if the borrower dies (or, in some policies, becomes disabled). It is bought by lenders, but the premium usually becomes part of the borrower's loan cost. The value of the insurance declines as the loan is repaid, since it is intended to cover only the unpaid balance of the loan.

key-person life insurance Term life insurance on the key employees of a firm, with the firm named as beneficiary.

- ***Key-person life insurance:*** Businesses often insure the lives of key employees, such as top executives, salespeople, inventors, and researchers. The death of a key person could seriously limit the income or value of a firm. To protect themselves, businesses buy term insurance policies that name the company as beneficiary. In the case of a partnership, which is dissolved when a partner dies, key-person insurance is often bought for each partner. The amount of the policy lets the surviving partner buy the partnership interest from the estate of the deceased. Thus the business can keep operating.

 Concept Check

- What are the two main reasons for buying life insurance? Which types of policies meet each need?
- Briefly compare the main types of life insurance policies.

■ SUMMARY

1. Define risk, and explain why individuals and businesses buy insurance.

Risk is the chance for financial loss due to a peril. Both individuals and businesses need to protect themselves against several types of risks. Many of these—death, poor health, property damage—can be covered by insurance, which pays the insured up to a specified amount in the event of loss from a particular peril. Buying insurance transfers the risk of loss from the insured to the insurance company.

2. Discuss the four ways of managing risk, and tell what makes a risk insurable.

Risk can be managed by avoiding situations known to be risky, by assuming the responsibility for losses due to certain types of risk (called self-insurance), by reducing it through taking safety measures, and by transferring it to an insurance company. The six criteria for insurable risks are the loss must be accidental (not under the control of the insured), there must be a large number of similar exposures to a particular peril, the loss must be financially measurable, the chances of the peril striking all the insured parties at once must be very small, the amount of loss must be significant, and the insurance company must be able to set the criteria under which it will issue coverage.

3. Distinguish between public and private insurance companies.

Public insurance is provided by government agencies. It falls into two general categories: social insurance and insurance for risks that cannot properly be covered by private insurance. Social insurance programs include unemployment insurance, workers' compensation, and Social Security. Other programs offer flood, crop, and crime insurance.

Private insurance companies can have one of two forms of ownership. Stock companies are profit-oriented firms whose shares are owned by stockholders. The owners of mutual insurance companies are the policyholders. They benefit from any excess profits, which are paid as dividends or used to reduce their premiums. Private insurers offer property, liability, health, and life insurance.

4. Understand the problems facing insurance companies.

Many insurance companies have felt financial pressure recently. To compete for funds with other financial institutions, life insurance companies began offering policies that earned higher returns on invested premiums. As interest rates rose, insurance companies' profits declined. Life insurers invested in real estate and junk bonds to earn higher returns, but suffered losses when those asset values fell. Property and liability insurers lost profits by setting premiums too low to cover the sharp increase in liability claims.

5. Explain the difference between property and liability insurance, and describe the main types of coverage.

Property insurance covers losses arising from damage to property owned by the insured person or business. Liability insurance covers losses due to injuries to others or their property determined to be caused by the insured. The main types of property and liability insurance are home and building, business interruption, automobile, marine, theft, fidelity and surety bonds, personal liability, professional liability, and product liability.

6. Understand what health insurance covers and where it can be obtained.

Health insurance protects against losses due to illness or injury. Coverage for medical expenses is divided into regular medical, hospitalization, surgical, and major medical insurance. These are often combined into one policy. Many companies also offer their employees dental insurance. Disability insurance provides monthly payments to cover loss of income during an extended illness. Health insurance can be bought by individuals or by employers, who typically pay for part of employees' premium cost. Sources of health insurance include private insurers, Blue Cross/Blue Shield, and managed care programs such as health maintenance and preferred provider organizations.

7. Define life insurance, and identify the forms it may take.

Life insurance pays the amount of the policy to a beneficiary when the insured person dies. In addition to the death benefit, some types of life insurance include a savings feature. The main types of life insurance are term life (protection only), whole life (protection and savings), universal life (protection and savings), variable life (protection and savings), credit life (protection, bought by lenders, with premiums typically part of the borrower's loan cost), and key-person insurance (protection, bought by businesses).

■ DISCUSSION QUESTIONS

1. Name some risks you take every day. What steps can you take to avoid or reduce these risks? Against which can you obtain insurance?

2. Classify each of the following as an insurable or uninsurable risk. Justify your answers.

  a. Loss of income due to a strike by union workers
  b. Permanent disability caused by a work-related injury
  c. Collapse of a building due to improper architectural design
  d. Loss of income resulting from a decrease in demand for a product due to war
  e. Injury caused by a defective product

3. You are the owner of a fast-food franchise that employs twenty-five people. Discuss the types of risks you could encounter, both insurable and uninsurable. What risk-management techniques would you use? Describe the types of insurance you would need and the protection each offers. In what cases might you self-insure?

4. Drug manufacturers have been found liable for side effects they could not have known about when a drug was invented. Cigarette companies have been sued by relatives of people who died from lung cancer, despite labels on cigarette packages warning consumers of the dangers of tobacco. To what extent do you think these businesses should be responsible for the products they make and the injuries that could result?

5. A big issue for businesses today is controlling the cost of group health insurance. Suggested remedies include limiting the amount people can sue for in-hospital and physician malpractice cases, increasing deductibles, requiring second opinions for surgery and preapproved nonemergency hospitalization, and using managed care options, such as HMOs and PPOs. Discuss how each of these can reduce costs. Which do you think are the best options? Are they fair?

6. You have decided to buy life insurance. Compare the advantages and disadvantages of term, whole life, universal life, and variable life insurance. Explain which one best meets your needs, taking into account your personal situation.

■ CASE

A Metropolitan Mess

In August 1993 insurance regulators in Florida began investigating Metropolitan Life Insurance Company for charges of deceptive sales practices, which that state considers fraud. Agents in the company's Tampa office misled nurses into buying life insurance by calling it a tax-deferred retirement plan. Some buyers of these policies had no need for life insurance but did require retirement benefits. The success of the Tampa office—in one year its manager made almost $950,000—attracted other Met Life offices, which copied its methods. The manager, who was subsequently dismissed by the company, denied any wrongdoing and claimed that his selling strategies were widespread at the insurer.

Met Life, also under investigation in at least thirteen other states, fired seven executives and has offered refunds to 60,000 policyholders, at a potential cost of $40 million. In Georgia it paid a $250,000 fine to the Georgia insurance department. Met Life President Ted Athanassiades admits that the company should have cracked down on the improper sales tactics when they surfaced in 1991.

In another case, a Texas jury ordered New York Life to pay $21 million to a widow who lost $65,000. (The case was later settled for a lesser, undisclosed amount.) She and other policyholders were defrauded by its agent, who admitted lying to and forging signatures of customers to sell more expensive policies.

This case marked a change in attitude toward insurance agent fraud, which appears to be a widespread practice in the life insurance industry. Agents, who often call themselves "financial advisers," can sell more life insurance by packaging it as a "private pension plan." They show customers examples of expected policy performance that may contain misleading information or use overly optimistic interest rate assumptions that inflate potential investment returns.

The companies claim that most abuses are caused by a few individual "rogue" agents driven by greed. However, the companies themselves are increasingly coming under fire for failure to properly monitor and control their agents. Federal and state regulators are currently considering new laws to control insurance sales and to make companies accountable for their agents.[17]

Questions

1. Should insurance companies be liable for the actions of their agents? What steps can they take to monitor and control their agents' selling strategies?
2. How can buyers of insurance policies protect themselves against fraudulent or misleading sales tactics?

Your Career in Law or Insurance

The legal and insurance fields offer business students many career opportunities. The rapid pace of change in the law and the many new government regulations have created a need for attorneys and paralegals. In the insurance industry, companies are offering a wider variety of financial products. Many think of insurance agents as financial planners, advising on a broad range of products. The insurance industry offers many types of jobs, including insurance agent, underwriter, claims representative, and actuary. Other companies often need risk managers to coordinate their insurance programs.

Dream Career: Risk Manager

As the business environment has become more complex, risk management has become more important for many firms. Risk management is much more than deciding which insurance policies to buy and for how much. Risk managers must know all about their companies' operations and risks. Then they determine the best risk management techniques (avoidance, reduction of hazards, self-insurance, commercial insurance). They develop and administer plans for controlling risk. Most companies assign only property and liability risks to risk managers, whereas others also include group life and health insurance in the risk-management department.

A key responsibility of risk managers is managing the commercial insurance program—choosing policies and coverages, handling claim settlements, controlling costs, and reviewing and updating the policies. Having a risk manager who can take an objective view of the company's requirements is an advantage in dealing with insurance agents and brokers.

- *Places of employment:* Throughout the U.S., especially in large firms.
- *Skills required:* Four-year degree.
- *Employment outlook through 2005:* Above average.
- *Salaries:* $25,000–$30,000 for entry level; $60,000–$70,000 for experienced managers.

Where The Opportunities Are

Attorney

Attorneys are professionals who interpret the law for their individual and business clients. They help companies comply with the many federal, state, and local laws that regulate their operations and represent them in lawsuits. They also prepare and review contracts and other legal documents, such as leases and deeds. Lawyers often specialize in one area of law, such as tax, securities, international, environmental, or insurance law. They may work for a law firm or have a private practice, working with a number of clients, or they may be employed by a corporation to do its legal work.

Attorneys must pass a state's bar examination to practice in that state. Good analytical ability and communications skills, both written and oral, are important for potential lawyers.

- *Places of employment:* Throughout the U.S.
- *Skills required:* Four-year undergraduate degree plus three-year law degree.
- *Employment outlook through 2005:* Above average.
- *Salaries:* $30,000–$50,000 for beginning corporate attorneys; law firms in big cities pay much more. Experienced lawyers and specialists can earn $75,000–$150,000+.

Paralegal

Paralegals assist attorneys in many areas of legal work. They help with research and analysis of information for a trial and with preparation of legal documents such as contracts, mortgages, and loan agreements. Most paralegals work for law firms, although some corporations—especially in the financial services industry—also hire paralegals. The government also employs paralegals, many of whom work for administrative agencies. In large firms, paralegals may specialize in one area of the law, such as real estate, taxation, estate plan-

ning, family law, or corporate law. Paralegals in smaller firms typically handle a variety of responsibilities. Paralegals should have good research, analytical, and communications skills.

Becoming a paralegal requires special training, either through a formal educational program or on-the-job training. The American Bar Association accredits paralegal training programs, which are offered by over 600 colleges, universities, law schools, community colleges, and specialized paralegal schools. Some programs require a four-year degree, although many accept applicants with a high school diploma or an associate's degree. Most formal programs take two years. Students with a four-year degree can often complete the training in less time. The National Association of Legal Assistants awards the certified legal assistant (CLA) designation to paralegals who meet education and experience requirements and pass a two-day examination.

- *Places of employment:* Throughout the U.S.
- *Skills required:* Specialized training program, either through a formal course offered by an educational institution or on-the-job training. Some programs require a two-year or four-year degree for admission.
- *Employment outlook through 2005:* Above average.

- *Salaries:* $20,000–$23,000 to start; experienced paralegals earn $25,000–$30,000+.

Insurance Agent and Broker

Insurance agents and brokers evaluate customers' insurance needs for protection against various perils—property damage, illness, injury, and death, to name a few—and design programs to meet those needs. They interview insurance applicants, help with claims and settlements, and collect premiums. An agent usually works for a single insurance company. A broker is independent, representing several companies. Some agents specialize in either life or property insurance, while others may offer many types of policies.

Most major insurance companies offer training programs and require continuing education to keep up-to-date with new product lines. Certification programs lead to the certified life underwriter (CLU) and chartered property casualty underwriter (CPCU) designations. These designations are recognized marks of achievement for insurance professionals.

- *Places of employment:* Throughout the U.S. Positions are more numerous in states with insurance company home offices, such as New York, Connecticut, Massachusetts, and Illinois.
- *Skills required:* Two-year degree, although some

companies prefer a four-year degree.

- *Employment outlook through 2005:* Average.
- *Salaries:* $15,000–$23,000 for trainees; $30,000–$75,000+ for experienced agents.

Underwriter

Insurance companies assume billions of dollars in risks each year. Underwriters decide which applicants represent an acceptable level of risk for the company to assume. They specialize in one of three areas: life, health, or property insurance. To make their decisions, underwriters analyze insurance applications, medical information, and actuarial studies (reports that describe the probability of certain types of loss). They also outline the terms of contracts, including the amount of premiums.

Underwriters are important to an insurance company's overall profitability. If they appraise risks too conservatively, their company may lose business to competitors. If they are too liberal and accept high-risk business, the company may have to pay more in claims.

- *Places of employment:* Best opportunities are in major insurance company centers—New York, Boston, Hartford, San Francisco, Chicago, Dallas, and Philadelphia.
- *Skills required:* Generally a four-year degree, although a two-year

degree is sometimes acceptable.

- *Employment outlook through 2005:* Average.
- *Salaries:* $24,000–$38,000; $40,000+ for managers.

Actuary

Why are car insurance premiums higher for younger drivers? How much more should a person with diabetes pay for life insurance? What should a fire insurance policy for a particular class of office building cost? Actuaries provide the answers to these and similar questions. They collect and analyze statistics to calculate the probability that certain risks will occur—death, illness, property loss or damage, and other perils. They determine the expected loss from a specific peril, and this information forms the basis for setting premiums. About half of all actuaries work for insurance companies. The rest work as independent consultants, for the government, or for corporations. Most specialize in either life and health insurance, property and casualty insurance, or pension planning.

Actuaries need good math skills and courses in statistics. Professional certification programs offered by the Society of Actuaries (life and health), the Casualty Actuarial Society (property and liability), and the American Society of Pension Actuaries (pension planning) require passing a series of examinations over a five-to ten-year period.

- *Places of employment:* Best opportunities are in major insurance company centers—New York, Boston, Hartford, San Francisco, Chicago, Dallas, and Philadelphia.
- *Skills required:* Four-year degree with major in actuarial science, mathematics, or statistics preferred.
- *Employment outlook through 2005:* Excellent.
- *Salaries:* $24,000–$28,000 for trainees who have not passed any actuarial exams; $30,000 for those passing one or two exams while in college; $43,000 with associate status (five to seven exams passed, depending on specialty); $62,000 for fellows (all exams passed); as high as $100,000+ for top actuarial executives.

Claims Representative

Fair and fast settlement of all claims helps insurance companies to meet their commitments to policyholders and protect their own financial position. The people who investigate claims, negotiate settlements with policyholders, and authorize payments are known as claims representatives. They include claims adjusters and claims examiners.

When property and liability insurance companies receive a claim, the claims adjuster determines whether the policy covers it and the amount of the loss. Adjusters

A potential lawyer should have good analytical ability communication skills, both oral and written.

use reports, physical evidence, and the testimony of witnesses in investigating a claim. When their company is liable, they negotiate with the claimant to settle the case. Adjusters must make sure that settlements reflect the claimant's actual loss.

In life and health insurance companies, the counterpart of the claims adjuster is the claims examiner, who investigates questionable claims or those exceeding a specified amount. Examiners may check claim applications for completeness and accuracy, interview medical specialists, and calculate benefit payments.

- *Places of employment:* Claims adjuster positions are found throughout the U.S.; claims examiner positions are located in most large cities.
- *Skills required:* Two-year degree, but many companies now prefer a four-year degree.
- *Employment outlook through 2005:* Average.
- *Salaries:* $22,000–$42,000, depending on type of insurance; $43,000+ for claims supervisors and managers.

Epilogue

Your Career

 Getting Started...

James Roberson, a musician, founded Rebuild/Rejoice—a Los Angeles gospel choir that unites Korean and black youths—following the riots triggered by the Rodney King trial. In 1993, he also started a record label, Just Do It! Records, which so far has one gospel choir recording to its credit.

Raised in Dallas, Mr. Roberson took part in the Head Start program and learned to sing and play piano with his gospel church choir. He attended the University of Texas at Austin on a scholarship, then landed a job at Capitol Records ("Only after bothering them for three months," he says).

Unhappy with an office job, he sang backup for two years for blues singer Maxine Otis. Then, while getting his MBA at the University of California at Los Angeles last year, Mr. Roberson received a $3,000 grant from the city's art fund to start his choir. "My friends look at me like I'm some freak of nature ... but they're just afraid of doing their own thing," he says. "This is what I have to do."[1]

SELF-ASSESSMENT

In a few years, many of you will go through what James Roberson has just experienced. That is, you will find your first job after graduation and start your career in business either working for someone else or starting your own company. Preparing for a career can be stressful if your approach is haphazard. The simple, step-by-step process that follows will make finding your dream job a bit easier.

WHO AM I?

Exhibit 1 shows the process that can lead to finding the right job. The first step is to ask "Who am I?" This step is the start of *self-assessment*, examining your likes and dislikes and basic values. Some specific questions might be these: Do I want to help society? Do I want to help make the world a better place? Do I want to help other people directly? Is it important for me to be seen as part of a big corporation? Do I prefer working indoors or outdoors? Do I like to meet new people, or do I want to work alone? Your answers can offer good insights.

WHAT CAN I DO?

After deciding what your values are, you can take the second step in career planning. Ask "What can I do?" This question is the start of *skill assessment*, evaluating your key abilities and characteristics for dealing successfully with problems, tasks, and interactions with other people. Many skills—for instance, the ability to speak clearly and strongly—are valuable in many occupations.

Be sure to consider the work experience you already have: part-time jobs while going to school, summer jobs, volunteer jobs, internships (short-term jobs for students, related to their major field of study). These jobs teach you skills and make you more attractive to potential employers. It's never too early or too late to take a part-time job in your chosen field. For instance, someone with an interest in accounting would do well to try a part-time job with a CPA firm.

In addition to examining job-related skills, you should also look at leisure activities. Some possible questions: Am I good at golf? Do I enjoy

Exhibit 1
Preparing for a Career

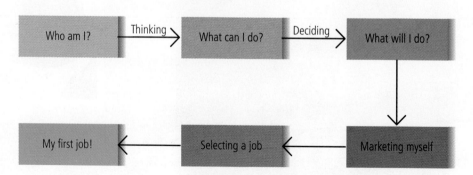

sailing? Tennis? Racquetball? In some businesses, transactions are made during leisure hours. Being able to play a skillful, or at least adequate, game of golf or tennis may be an asset in some fields.

WHAT WILL I DO?

The third step in career planning is to ask "What will I do?" You need to consider not only a general type of work but also your lifestyle and leisure goals. If you're a person who likes to be outdoors most of the time, you might be very unhappy in a career that requires eight hours a day in an office. Someone who likes living in small towns may have a problem working for a big corporation with headquarters in Los Angeles or New York City or Chicago.

You might start answering the question "What will I do?" by studying the *Career Employment Opportunities Directory—Business Administration*. The directory lists several hundred up-to-date sources of employment with businesses, government agencies, and professional organizations.

Another important resource is the *Occupational Outlook Handbook*, published every two years by the U.S. Department of Labor. The introduction in the current *Handbook* projects job opportunities by industry through the year 2000. The *Handbook* is divided into nineteen occupational clusters describing 200 jobs (with a section on military occupations). Among the clusters are education, sales and marketing, transportation, health, and social services. Each job description tells about the nature of the work, working conditions, required training, other qualifications, chances for advancement, employment outlook, earnings, related occupations, and sources of more information. The *Handbook* also describes work in more than thirty-five industries, grouped according to major divisions in the economy.

Yet another good source of career information is the career appendix at the end of each part of this book. These sections contain short job descriptions in the style used by the *Occupational Outlook Handbook*. They also tell what parts of the country are most likely to have openings in certain fields, the skills required, the employment outlook through 2000, and salary information. Each career appendix features a "dream career," a career worth striving for.

MARKETING YOURSELF

As graduation nears, students start thinking about getting in touch with prospective employers. Colleges and universities help by setting up a placement office (also called an office of career planning or an office of student services). A placement office tests and counsels students, lists part-time and summer jobs, and coordinates visits by company recruiters. It is also likely to suggest ways to use employment letters, resumes, and job interviews to advantage.

EMPLOYMENT LETTERS

Employers tell business professors that communication skills are of prime importance in making hiring decisions. To show off your skills when writing letters in your job search, follow these guidelines:

- Design your letters to be work-centered and employer-centered, not self-centered. As marketing tools, they should address the needs of employers and evoke a desire to learn more about you.
- Never give responsibility for your job search to anyone else. Do all the writing yourself, and follow up with employers on your own.
- Always address your letters to a specific person, with his or her correct title and business address. Call the human-resource department of the company to check if you're not sure of these details.
- Use high-quality stationery and envelopes.
- Keep each letter to one page. Take out extra words, and avoid rehashing material from your resume.
- Produce error-free, clean copy. Ask a friend to proofread your letter to be doubly sure that you haven't missed any errors.
- Tailor your letters for each case. Generic, mass-produced letters are unprofessional.
- Show appreciation to the employer for considering your application, for granting you an interview, and so on.
- Always keep your reader in mind. Make your letters easy to read and attractive.
- Be timely and prompt. Show that you know how to do business for yourself and, by implication, for others.
- Be honest. Always be able to back up your claims with evidence and specific examples from your experience.[2]

Overall, you are trying to communicate that you are a responsible person with a positive attitude who knows how to operate in a professional environment.

Several types of letters are important in the job-search process. One is the *networking letter* (see Exhibit 2). It is designed to get you information interviews—not job interviews—where you can meet people who can give you specific information about your intended career. Your reasons for wanting to meet with this person must be genuine and sincere. Information interviewing, or "networking," is a good way to do research on the job market, to refine your career goals, and to uncover information about the prospects in an industry or a region. Information interviewing is not a magical shortcut to employment. It requires solid preparation and much effort. But the networking letter is the first step in marketing yourself.

Once you have uncovered some job prospects, you may send an application letter and a resume. (Exhibit 3 shows a sample application letter.) The letter should open with a paragraph that will arouse interest and tell the reason for the letter (the enclosed resume). It should also show some knowledge of the company and explain the reasons for your interest in it.

132 Arapahoe Drive
Dallas, TX 75206
April 5, 1995

Ms. Kathryn A. Bonde, Manager
Barney, Smith and Jones, P.C.
Certified Public Accountants
1201 Highway 157, Suite 300
Dallas, TX 75214

Dear Ms. Bonde:

Dr. Schumacker, professor of accounting at the University of Texas, suggested that I contact you. He thought you would be in an excellent position, as an alumna, to help me with a career decision.

As a fourth-year accounting student, I am exploring which career path to pursue. Public accounting, management accounting, and IRS work all sound interesting to me at this point, but I want to go into my campus interviews next semester with a clear sense of direction. I would like to get your advice on the long-term career implications of each path as well as a better handle on the day-to-day activities of a CPA.

I will call you next week to see if we can arrange a brief meeting at your convenience. Your advice as an alumna and a successful accountant will mean a great deal to me.

Sincerely,

Michael C Wright

Michael C. Wright

The second paragraph should describe what in your background makes you a good candidate. It should also state what you want in a job. Finally, it should pinpoint the parts of the resume that will be of special interest to this employer.

The last paragraph should say something about a follow-up. It may request an application form and an appointment for an interview. It may say that you will wait to hear from the firm. Better yet, it may say that you will call or come by to talk with the person.

■ **Exhibit 3**
Sample Application Letter

P.O. Box 23411
Arlington, TX 76019
May 28, 1995

Mr. Robert J. Walker
Labor Relations Manager
Dynamics Corporation
Chicago, Illinois 60605

Dear Mr. Walker:

Dr. Randall Powell, professor of business administration at the University of Texas at Arlington, recently suggested that I write you concerning your opening and my interest in a labor relations assistant position. I have a B.A. degree in management and courses in labor economics, collective bargaining, labor law, and personnel. I am confident that I could make a positive contribution to your company. The part played by Dynamics Corporation in the development of the Tycho III rocket booster and the series of articles on your company in The Wall Street Journal and Fortune have been of great interest to me.

During the last two summers, I worked as a general laborer on a production line, once in a unionized shop and once in an unorganized plant. My ability to appreciate several points of view on labor problems should prove to be a major asset in my future career performance. Before I left my last summer job, my supervisor recommended that I be hired as a first-line foreman after graduation. Although I am enthusiastic about the foreman's position, I think my energies and resourcefulness might be better suited to handling union-management problems as a third party in the grievance procedure. This has been a goal throughout my four-year college career.

I would very much like to talk with you to show why I am a strong candidate for the position. Any Friday or Monday should be ideal for an interview appointment. I will call you in three days to see if your schedule might be open, or you can call me at (817) 555-2090. I look forward to meeting with you.

Sincerely,

Rebecca A Gray

Rebecca A. Gray

RESUMES

The goal of the application letter is to get the prospective employer to look at your resume, which summarizes your education, career to date, achievements, job-related activities, and goals. To both interest and inform prospective employers, the resume should be well organized, visually appealing, and brief (usually no more than one page for a recent graduate).

Your aim in sending a resume is to get not a job, but an interview. The employer wants to know who you are, what you want to do, and what you can do. Thus the resume should include positive information about your skills and accomplishments—in school, work, and your personal life.

There is no single format for a resume. Yet each one should begin with your name, address, and telephone number. This information should be followed by a clear statement of your objectives in terms of the job title or job responsibilities you are seeking or functional areas of the firm you wish to work in. A list of references or a statement that references will be supplied on request should be the last information in the resume. If you are interested in more than one field or have several different objectives, you will need to develop a resume for each one.

■ **Exhibit 4**
Sample Resume

Cheryl K. Westover
6512 West Second Street
Arlington, TX 76021
(555) 277-6745

Objective:
A position that would let me use skills in conducting public relations, copywriting, preparing news releases, organizing, and coordinating and promoting events.

Education:
Graduate of the University of Texas at Arlington with a bachelor of arts degree in journalism and a minor in business; GPA in journalism 3.7, overall GPA 3.5

Experience

Public Relations:
As a public relations director for Junior Achievement of Tarrant County, I have increased publicity for the organization in area newspapers, in-house publications of local businesses, high school newspapers, radio, and television by making good media contacts.

Copywriting, News Releases, and Photography:
I have published articles in the newspapers of the colleges I attended and have also written Junior Achievement press releases for area newspapers. I have had training in photography and own a 35mm camera.

Organizing:
My duties as membership chairman for a newcomers' club included organizing and directing a committee that contacted about 100 new residents each month. I maintained all records of contacts with prospective members and 250 active members. I have been active in Girl Scouts, church, school, women's clubs, and a hospital auxiliary.

Coordinating and Promoting Events:
I coordinated the efforts of Junior Achievement members and the Clean City Commission to mount a clean-up campaign in downtown Arlington. This was done in preparation for the 20th World Gymnastics championships. Three television stations covered the event, as did a Fort Worth newspaper.

Personal Information:
I enjoy designing and sewing my own clothes, playing tennis, and swimming. My health is excellent.

References:
Submitted on request.

The sample resume in Exhibit 4 emphasizes the applicant's job experience. Although some of the jobs were probably unpaid, they provided important experience. They show the person's qualifications for the job she's applying for.

JOB INTERVIEWS

Once the resume has achieved its goal—getting you an interview—you need to focus on making a good presentation in person. Look at the interview as a chance to describe your knowledge and skills and interpret them in terms of the employer's specific needs. To make this kind of presentation, you need to do some homework. You need to find out about the firm's history, product lines, and the like. The library is a good source for this information; the reference librarian can point you to appropriate books. You might also seach databases of business periodicals and newspapers for stories about the company in the past year or so.

Also, if you know about the different types of interviews, you can respond better to the interviewer's questions (or lack of them). The two main types are directive and nondirective. A *directive interview* is used to get specific information about the applicant's knowledge, skills, academic work, and job experience. A *nondirective interview* avoids direct questioning and prompts the applicant to discuss interests, ideas, values, priorities, and personal traits. (The interviewer may even stay completely silent at the start of the interview, forcing the applicant to begin the conversation.) A single session may include both types of interviews, but usually the focus is on one.

An interview tends to have three parts: ice-breaking (about five minutes), in which the interviewer tries to put the applicant at ease; questioning (directly or indirectly) by the interviewer; and questioning by the applicant. Almost every recruiter you meet will be trying to rate you in five to ten areas. The questions will be designed to assess your skills and personality.

For the interview you should dress conservatively. Plan to arrive about ten to fifteen minutes ahead of time. Try to relax. Smile and make eye contact with (but do not stare at) the interviewer. Body language is an important communicator. The placement of your hands and feet and your overall posture say a good deal about you.

Many firms start with a *screening interview,* a rather short interview (about thirty minutes) to decide whether to invite you back for a second interview. Only about 20 percent of job applicants are invited back. The second interview is a half day or a day of meetings set up by the human-resource department with managers in different departments. After the meetings, someone from the human-resource department will discuss other application materials with you and tell you when a letter of acceptance or rejection is likely to be sent. (The wait may be weeks or even months.) Many applicants send follow-up letters in the meantime to show they are still interested in the firm.

CHOOSING A JOB

Hard work and a little luck may pay off with multiple job offers. Your happy dilemma is deciding which one is best for you. Start by considering the FACTS:

- *Fit:* Do the job and the employer fit your skills, interests, and lifestyle?
- *Advancement and growth:* Will you have the chance to develop your talents and move up within the organization?
- *Compensation:* Is the employer offering a competitive salary and benefits package?
- *Training:* Will the employer provide you with the tools needed to be successful on the job?
- *Site:* Is the job location a good match for your lifestyle and your pocketbook?[3]

The toughest part of assessing a job's *fit* is to see it clearly. "Make sure you remove your rose-colored glasses," says Jean Eisel, director of career services at Arizona State University. "Students sometimes get wooed by the 'honeymoon' experience. They get excited by the company that picks them up in a limo and puts them up in a nice hotel," she says. "Later, they find that the company expects them to start at 7:30 a.m. each day and put in sixty-hour workweeks."[4] No matter how impressive the company, she adds, you have to be able to work there day in and day out.

Make sure you get an idea of what the future holds for you at each company. Some organizations, especially larger ones, have clearly defined paths for *advancement.* At many smaller organizations, the path is less obvious. As the company grows, people may be either promoted quickly or left to flounder. Be sure you have an idea of what it takes to move up before accepting any offers. Find out what each company's top performers are like and how you compare.

Compensation is always a big part of any job decision. A classic mistake made by many graduates is to say that a $29,000 salary is better than a $26,000 salary. It might not be, depending on the local cost of living. Costs of living vary widely, as shown in Exhibit 5. Some of the less expensive places to live are Colorado Springs, Amarillo, Texas, and Tulsa, Oklahoma. A job transfer at the same salary from one of these three cities to New York City or San Diego would greatly reduce your standard of living.

Don't forget to consider benefits as part of the compensation package. These might include health care coverage, dental coverage, life insurance, disability coverage, stock options, pension plans, transportation allowances, vacation time, sick leave, and tuition reimbursement, to name a few. Analyze what benefits you need, and then be sure your prospective employer can meet those basic needs.

Another factor to consider is *training.* Some companies handle training informally, "on the job," with the help of experienced staff members.

Average City, U.S.A.	100.0

Alabama
Birmingham	100.9
Huntsville	98.5

Alaska
Anchorage	129.2

Arizona
Phoenix	102.3
Tucson	106.6

Arkansas
Fayetteville	91.1
Little Rock	90.0

California
Bakersfield	110.5
Los Angeles/Long Beach	126.7
Palm Springs	114.8
Riverside City	112.3
San Diego	129.1

Colorado
Boulder	117.5
Colorado Springs	99.6
Denver	105.9

Connecticut
Hartford	129.1

Delaware
Wilmington	113.2

District of Columbia
Washington, D.C.	135.1

Florida
Jacksonville	96.4
Miami	111.8
Orlando	99.0
Tampa	98.9
West Palm Beach	110.0

Georgia
Atlanta	98.4

Idaho
Boise	104.2

Illinois
Bloomington/Normal	103.1
Champaign/Urbana	100.8
Peoria	104.1
Rockford	108.1
Schaumberg	119.9

Indiana
Indianapolis	97.3
South Bend	94.0

Iowa
Des Moines	104.2

Kansas
Lawrence	94.3

Kentucky
Lexington	100.3
Louisville	91.5

Louisiana
Baton Rouge	101.3
New Orleans	94.4

Comparing salary offers

$$\frac{\text{(City \#1)}}{\text{(City \#2)}} \quad \frac{\text{Index \#} \times \text{Salary}}{\text{Index \#}} = \$ \underline{}$$

Sample Equation:

- How much does a person in Atlanta need to earn annually to have the buying power of someone making $25,000 a year in San Diego?

$$\frac{\text{Atlanta}}{\text{San Diego}} \quad \frac{98.4 \times \$25,000}{129.1} = \$19,055$$

- How much does a person in San Diego need to earn annually to have the buying power of someone making $25,000 a year in Atlanta?

$$\frac{\text{San Diego}}{\text{Atlanta}} \quad \frac{129.1 \times \$25,000}{98.4} = \$32,800$$

Maryland
Baltimore	105.9

Massachusetts
Boston	142.1

Michigan
Benton Harbor/ St. Joseph	106.4
Detroit	116.6
Lansing	103.9

Minnesota
Minneapolis	102.5
St. Paul	100.2

Missouri
Kansas City	98.9
St. Louis	96.7

Montana
Billings	103.4

Nebraska
Lincoln	89.7
Omaha	92.4

Nevada
Las Vegas	109.9
Reno/Sparks	109.0

New Hampshire
Manchester	111.4

New Mexico
Albuquerque	103.9
Santa Fe	110.8

New York
Albany	113.0
Buffalo	114.8
New York City	208.7
Syracuse	103.1

North Carolina
Charlotte	101.6
Raleigh/Durham	98.3
Winston-Salem	95.8

North Dakota
Fargo	97.1

Ohio
Cincinnati	105.1
Cleveland	109.1
Columbus	110.9

Oklahoma
Oklahoma City	93.3
Tulsa	90.2

Oregon
Portland	108.8
Salem	98.9

Pennsylvania
Allentown/Bethlehem	105.8
Harrisburg	104.9
Philadelphia	127.5
Pittsburgh	111.2

South Carolina
Charleston	99.8
Columbia	95.2

South Dakota
Sioux Falls	96.6

Tennessee
Knoxville	92.2
Memphis	98.3
Nashville	90.8

Texas
Amarillo	89.4
Dallas	104.4
El Paso	103.0
Fort Worth	93.2
Houston	96.7
Lubbock	92.9
San Antonio	94.0

Utah
Provo/Orem	93.8
Salt Lake City	98.0

Vermont
Montpelier/Barre	109.2

Virginia
Prince Willliam	114.8
Richmond/Petersburg	107.5
Roanoke	94.6

Washington
Seattle	116.2
Spokane	104.3

West Virginia
Charleston	99.6

Wisconsin
Green Bay	97.7
La Crosse	99.9
Madison	113.8
Milwaukee	105.1

Wyoming
Cheyenne	96.7

■ **Exhibit 5**

Cost of Living in Selected
U.S. Cities

Source: "Cost-of-Living Comparisons,"
Managing Your Career (Spring/Summer
1994), p. 31.

Others offer formal programs. New employees complete a set of in-house courses, sometimes over six months or a year. Still other firms offer a combination of both.

Next to salary, where you work is often the biggest concern. Of course, as noted above, *site* determines the buying power of your earnings. Also remember that after work you'll want to do things you enjoy. Give careful thought to such factors as climate, transportation, traffic, and cultural and sporting events.

STARTING A NEW JOB

No time is more crucial, and possibly nerve-racking, than the first few months at a new job. During this breaking-in period, the employer decides whether the new employee is valuable enough to keep and, if so, in what capacity. Sometimes the employee's whole future with the company rides on the efforts of the first few weeks or months.

Most firms offer some sort of formal orientation. But generally speaking, they expect employees to learn the following quickly—and often on their own: the firm's goals; the firm's organization, including the new person's place in the chain of authority and responsibility; and basic personnel policies, such as coffee breaks, overtime, and parking.

Here are a few tips on making your first job rewarding and productive:

- *Listen and learn*: When you first walk into your new job, let your eyes and ears take everything in. Do people refer to one another by first names, or is the company more formal? How do people dress? Do the people you work with drop into one another's open offices for informal chats about business matters? Or have you entered a "memo mill," where anything of substance is put in writing and talks with other employees are scheduled through secretaries? Size up where the power lies. Who seems to most often assume a leadership role? Who is the person others turn to for advice? Why has that person achieved that position? What traits have made this person a "political leader"? Don't be misled by what others say, but also don't dismiss their evaluations. Make your own judgments based on what you see and hear. Then put it all together: your observations and others' comments.
- *Do unto others*: Be nice. Nice people are usually the last to be fired and among the first to be promoted. Don't be pleasant only with those who can help you in the company. Be nice to everyone. You never know who can help you or give you information that will turn out to be useful. Genuinely nice people make routine job assignments, and especially pressure-filled ones, more pleasant. And people who are dealt with pleasantly usually respond in kind.
- *Follow procedures*: If every new employee tried to change tried-and-true methods to suit his or her whims, the firm would quickly be in chaos. Individual needs must take a back seat to established procedures. Devote yourself to getting things done within the system.

Every boss understands that a new employee needs time to adjust. But the more quickly you start accomplishing things, the more quickly the boss will realize that you were the right person to hire.[5]

- *Dress for success*: Clothing in *Vogue* and *GQ* look great at movie premieres and boat launches. At the office, conservative attire never fails. A blue or gray suit, white or blue shirt or blouse, and black or blue shoes (low heels) send a professional message. If you want to make a fashion statement, wear a red tie or scarf. The exceptions are small, easy-going companies that respect individuality and creative or fashion-conscious companies where looking good is important. But even if your boss allows denim and T-shirts, you'll make a better impression on customers and co-workers if you dress nicely.[6]

- *Review your performance*: Think of an official performance review as a chance to get the pat on the back you so richly deserve. It's also a great time to realign your duties and career goals. If your first-year anniversary passes without a formal meeting with your boss, ask for one. Your boss probably just forgot, even though many companies require such a meeting. Prepare for the review by listing the goals you hope to accomplish and assessing your progress since the last review. Then speak openly about what you can expect to achieve in the coming year.[7]

So there you have it—some solid tips to help you launch a successful career. Good luck in the exciting world of business!

REFERENCES

Prologue

1. Joseph Shapiro, "Just Fix It," *U.S. News & World Report,* 22 February 1993, p. 52.
2. U.S. Department of Commerce, Bureau of the Census, *Statistical Abstract of the United States, 1992,* 112th ed. (Washington, D.C.: Government Printing Office, 1992), p. 381.
3. Fred R. Bleakely, "Number of Affluent Households to Jump and Spending to Rise, Study Indicates," *Wall Street Journal,* 13 October 1993, p. A2.
4. Amy Saltzman, "Family Friendliness," *U.S. News & World Report,* 22 February 1993, p. 60.
5. Based on population data from U.S. Department of Commerce, Bureau of the Census, *Statistical Abstract of the United States, 1992,* 112th ed. (Washington, D.C.: Government Printing Office, 1992), p. 14.
6. Kenneth Labich, "The New Unemployed," *Fortune,* 8 March 1993, p. 43.
7. Farrell Kramer, "Two Big Toy Makers to Be Playmates," *The San Diego Union-Tribune,* 20 August 1993, p. C1.
8. "Farmers Are Back in the Green," *Business Week,* 11 June 1990, pp. 18–19.
9. Alice La Plante, "TeleConfrontation-ing," *Forbes ASAP,* 13 September 1993, pp. 111–126.
10. Walter Kiechel III, "How We Will Work in the Year 2000," *Fortune,* 17 May 1993, p. 46.
11. Neal Templin, "A Decisive Response to Crisis Brought Ford Enhanced Productivity," *Wall Street Journal,* 15 December 1992, p. A1.

Chapter 1

1. Gail DeGeorge et al., "Wayne's World: Busting Beyond Video," *Business Week,* 1 November 1993, pp. 122–124.
2. Paul Ingrassia and Douglas Lavin, "Neon May Be a Bright Light for Chrysler," *Wall Street Journal,* 23 April 1993, p. B7.
3. Alan Deutschman, "Bill Gates' Next Challenge," *Fortune,* 28 December 1993, p. 31.
4. Victoria Pope, "Tracking Down Business," *U.S. News & World Report,* 30 August 1993, pp. 60–61.
5. Neela Banerjee, "Russia Is Short of Many Things, but Not Opportunities," *Wall Street Journal,* 9 September 1993, p. B2.

6. "A Portrait of America," *Business Week: Reinventing America 1992* (Special Issue), p. 54.
7. Howard Gleckman et al., "The Technology Payoff," *Business Week,* 14 June 1993, p. 57.
8. Myron Magnet, "Why Job Growth Is Stalled," *Fortune,* 9 March 1993, p. 51.
9. Adapted from Kenneth Labich, "The Best Cities for Knowledge Workers," *Fortune,* 15 November 1993, pp. 50–56; and Kevin Kelly et al., "Hot Spots," *Business Week,* 19 October 1992, pp. 80–83.
10. Stefan Fatsis, "New Wave of Mergers Bears No Resemblance to 1980s Barbarians," *San Diego Daily Transcript,* October 18, 1993, p. 1.
11. The Quaker Oats Company, *1992 Annual Report,* p. 4.
12. "Twenty-Twenty Hindsight," Small Business Supplement, *Wall Street Journal,* 15 October 1993, p. R4.
13. Jennifer Cody, "Family Matters," Small Business Supplement, *Wall Street Journal,* 15 October 1993, p. R20.
14. Walter Kiechel III, "How We Will Work in the Year 2000," *Fortune,* 17 May 1993, pp. 39–52; and Shawn Tully, "The Modular Corporation," *Fortune,* 8 February 1993, p. 106.
15. Based on "Privatizing Schools," *The San Diego Union-Tribune,* 7 November 1993, p. B6; and "Making the Minneapolis Schools Private," *Newsweek,* 15 November 1993, p. 67.

Chapter 2

1. David Hage, "An Uphill Struggle," *U.S. News & World Report,* 8 November 1993, p. 64.
2. Alfred L. Malabre, Jr., "The Outlook: Expansion May Prove Long-Distance Runner," *Wall Street Journal,* 8 November 1993, p. A1.
3. Lucinda Harper, "Producer Prices Dropped by 0.2% during October," *Wall Street Journal,* 10 November 1993, p. A2.
4. Timothy Aeppel, "U.S. Aluminum Makers Find World Market a Scary Place," *Wall Street Journal,* 8 November 1993, p. B4.
5. G. Paschal Zachary and Bob Ortega, "Workplace Revolution Boosts Productivity at Cost of Job Security," *Wall Street Journal,* 10 March 1993, p. A1; Elizabeth Lesly et al., "The Nimble Giants." *Business Week,* 28 March 1994, p. 66.
6. Tom Martin and Deborah Greenwood, "The World Economy

in Charts," *Fortune,* 26 July 1993, pp. 87–88.

7. David Wessel, "Federal Deficit Shrank in Fiscal 1993 to below Predictions of Two Agencies," *Wall Street Journal,* 29 October 1993, p. A2.

8. Suneel Ratan, "How to Really Cut the Budget Deficit," *Fortune,* 4 October 1993, p. 101.

9. David Wessel, "White House Sees '96 Deficit of $180 Billion," *Wall Street Journal,* 2 September 1993, p. A2.

10. Ratan, p. 104.

11. Michael Mandel et al., "How to Get America Growing Again," *Business Week/Reinventing America 1992* (Special Issue), p. 23.

12. Christopher Farrell and Michael Mandel, "What's Wrong?" *Business Week,* 2 August 1993, p. 56.

13. Gene Koretz, "Why America's Craving for Imports Is Likely to Grow," *Business Week,* 2 August 1993, p. 14.

14. Al Ehrbar, " 'Re-Engineering' Gives Forms New Efficiency, Workers the Pink Slip," *Wall Street Journal,* 16 March 1993, p. A12.

15. This section based on Myron Magnet, "Good News for the Service Economy," *Fortune,* 3 May 1993, pp. 47–52.

16. This section based on Warren Cohen, "Exporting Know-How," *U.S. News & World Report,* 30 August/6 September 1993, pp. 53, 56; and Ralph T. King, Jr., "U.S. Service Exports Are Growing Rapidly, but Almost Unnoticed, *Wall Street Journal,* 21 April 1993, pp. A1, A6.

17. Marc Levinson, "The Great Trade Deficit Hoax of '93," *Newsweek,* 15 November 1993, pp. 48, 50.

18. Richman, p. 54.

19. Linda Grant, "Profiting in Peacetime," *U.S. News & World Report,* 1 November 1993, pp. 60–62.

20. Brian O'Reilly, "Your New Global Work Force," *Fortune,* 14 December 1992, pp. 62–64.

21. Ralph T. King Jr., "Job Retraining Linked Closely to Employers Works in Cincinnati," *Wall Street Journal,* 19 March 1993, pp. A1, A7.

Part 1 Career Appendix

1. Personal contact with Joe Alfrey, 12 April 1994.

2. Paul Lim, "Some New Grads Turn Entrepreneur, Not Employee," *Wall Street Journal,* 25 June 1992, p. B2.

Chapter 3

1. Martha Farnsworth Riche, "We're All Minorities Now," *American Demographics,* October 1991, pp. 26–33.

2. "The Immigrants," *Business Week,* 13 July 1992, pp. 114–122; and "Immigrant Tide Surges in '80s," *USA Today,* 29 May 1992, p. 1A.

3. "Immigrants," pp. 114–122; "Immigrant Tide," p. 1A; and "Is Immigration Hurting the U.S.?" *Fortune,* 9 August 1993, pp. 76–79.

4. "Immigrants," p. 117.

5. Riche, p. 28.

6. James Allen and Eugene Turner, "Where Diversity Reigns," *American Demographics,* August 1990, pp. 34–38.

7. William O'Hare, "Reaching for the Dream," *American Demographics,* January 1992, pp. 32–36.

8. Ibid., pp. 32–36.

9. Ibid., pp. 32–36.

10. Riche, p. 28.

11. William O'Hare, Kelvin Pollard, Taynia Mann, and Mary Kent, "African Americans in the 1990s," *Population Bulletin,* July 1991, pp. 2–22.

12. "Booming, Suburban, and Black," *American Demographics,* September 1992, pp. 30–36.

13. Judith Waldrop, "Shades of Black," *American Demographics,* September 1990, pp. 30–34.

14. "Blacks' Family Incomes Grew During 1980s, Census Says," *Fort Worth Star Telegram,* 25 July 1992, p. A3.

15. William O'Hare, "In the Black," *American Demographics,* November 1989, pp. 24–25, 27–29.

16. "The Changing Marketplace," *Cincinnati Enquirer,* 28 September, 1992, p. E6.

17. William Dunn, "The Move Toward Ethnic Marketing," *Nation's Business,* July 1992, p. 400.

18. Carolyn Phillips, "Data Gap," *Wall Street Journal,* 19 February, 1993, p. R18.

19. Adapted from "Six Myths about Black Consumers," *Adweek's Marketing Week,* 6 May 1991, pp. 16–19.

20. "Former Pizza Hut Official Takes Big Franchise Slice," *Wall Street Journal,* 24 March 1992, p. B1.

21. "After Demographic Shift, Atlanta Mall Restyles Itself as Black Shopping Center," *Wall Street Journal,* 26 February 1992, pp. B1, B5.

22. Fred Bleakley, "Medical Maverick," *Wall Street Journal,* 19 February 1993, pp. R17, R20.

23. "The Largest Minority," *American Demographics,* February 1993, p. 59.

24. "The Mexican Way," *American Demographics,* May 1992, p. 4.

25. "Mexican Way," p. 4.

26. "One Million Hispanic Club," *American Demographics,* February 1991, p. 59.

27. "Habla Español?" *Target Marketing,* October 1991, pp. 10–14.

28. "The United States of Miami," *Adweek's Marketing Week,* 15 July, 1991, pp. 19–22.

29. "Hispanics' Tale of Two Cities," *US News and World Report,* 25 May 1992, pp. 40–41.

30. "United States of Miami," p. 20.

31. "To Reach Minorities, Try Busting Myths," *American Demographics,* April 1992, pp. 14–15.

32. "How to Speak to Hispanics," *American Demographics,* February 1990, pp. 40–41.

33. Thelma Snuggs, "Minority Markets: Define the Consumer of the 21st Century," *Credit,* January/February 1992, pp. 8–10.

34. Stuart Livingston, "Marketing to the Hispanic Community," *Journal of Business Strategy,* March/April 1992, pp. 54–57.

35. Elizabeth Roberts, "Different Strokes," *Adweek's Marketing Week,* 9 July 1990, p. 41.

36. "Targeting Hispanics: NutraSweet Educates while Coke Titillates," *Marketing News,* 11 November 1991, pp. 1, 2.

37. Greg Muirhead, "Mexican-American Influx Offers Chance for Growth," *Progressive Grocer,* April 1992, p. 4.

38. "Asian Americans," *CQ Researcher,* 13 December 1991, pp. 947–964.

39. "Asian Americans Increase Rapidly," *The Futurist,* September–October 1991, pp. 51–53.

40. This discussion adapted from William O'Hare, "A New Look at Asian Americans," *American Demographics,* October 1990, pp. 26–31. Reprinted with permission (c) American Demographics, October 1990. For subscription information, please call (800) 828–1131.

41. O'Hare, "New Look," pp. 26–31.

42. "People Patterns," *Wall Street Journal,* 28 September 1992, p. B1.

43. "Asian Americans," p. 953.

44. "Why Asians Can Prosper Where Blacks Fail," *Wall Street Journal,* 28 May 1992, p. A10.

45. "The California Asian Market," *American Demographics,* October 1990, pp. 34–37.
46. Jerry Goodbody, "Taking the Pulse of Asian Americans," *Adweek's Marketing Week,* 12 August 1991, p. 32.
47. Goodbody, p. 32.
48. "Suddenly, Asian-Americans Are a Marketer's Dream," *Business Week,* 17 June 1991, pp. 54–55.
49. Goodbody, p. 32.
50. "Suddenly," p. 55.
51. "Marketers Say Budgets Hinder Targeting of Asian Americans," *Marketing News,* 30 March 1992,p. 2.
52. Nejdet Delener and James Neelankavil, "Informational Sources and Media Uses: A Comparison Between Asian and Hispanic Subcultures," *Journal of Advertising Research,* June/July 1990, pp. 45–52.
53. "Suddenly," p. 54.
54. "American Dreams," *Wall Street Journal,* 16 June 1992, pp. A1, A5.
55. "American Indians in the 1990s," *American Demographics,* December 1991, pp. 26–34.
56. Wayne Cascio, *Managing Human Resources: Productivity, Quality of Work Life, Profits,* 3rd ed. (New York: McGraw-Hill, 1992), p. 58.
57. Towers Perrin & Hudson Institute, *Workforce 2000: Competing in a Seller's Market: Is Corporate America Prepared?* (Valhalla, NY: Towers Perrin, 1990).
58. "Promoting Cultural Differences at Fannie Mae," *Washington Post,* 24 August 1992, p. WB8.
59. Alvin Hill and James Scott, "Ten Strategies for Managers in a Multicultural Workforce," *HR Focus,* August 1992, pp. 6–8. Reprinted by permission of publisher, from *HR Focus,* August 1992 ©1992. American Management Association, New York. All rights reserved.
60. Alice Cuneo, "Diverse By Design," *Business Week/Reinventing America 1992,* 23 October 1992, p. 72.
61. "Diverse," p. 72.
62. This case is developed from Barbara Walker and William Hanson, "Valuing Differences at Digital Equipment Corporation," in Susan E. Jackson and Associates, eds., *Diversity in the Workplace: Human Resources Initiatives* (New York: The Guilford Press), pp. 119–137.

Chapter 4

1. "Fact Sheet," *Business America,* 13 September 1993, p. 18.
2. "U.S. Exporters Keep On Rolling," *Fortune,* 14 June 1993, p. 131.
3. "Will Tough Talk Mean Trade Wars?" *Fortune,* 8 March 1993, p. 94.
4. "Why Detroit Doesn't Need the Protection It Wants," *Business Week,* 8 February 1993, p. 32.
5. "Steel Rulings Dump on America," *Wall Street Journal,* 23 June 1993, p. A14.
6. Ibid.
7. "U.S. Duties on Korean Semiconductors Raise Double-Edged Sword to Dumping," *Wall Street Journal,* 19 February 1993, p. A9.
8. "GATT's Payoff," *Fortune,* 7 February 1994, p. 28.
9. "Clinton's Trade Route," *Business Week,* 26 July 1993, p. 25.
10. "Getting Tough," *Wall Street Journal,* 8 June 1993, pp. A1, A8.
11. "How Clinton Is Shaking Up Trade," *Fortune,* 31 May 1993, pp. 103–108.
12. "Road to Unification," *Sky,* June 1993, pp. 31–42.
13. "North American Marketers Await Trade Pact," *Marketing News,* 10 May 1993, pp. 1, 10.
14. "Salinas Wary of Treaty Review," *Fort Worth Star Telegram,* 21 March 1993, pp. J1, J12.
15. "How NAFTA Will Help America," *Fortune,* 19 April 1993, pp. 95–102.
16. Ibid.; Bradley Schiller, *The Macro Economy Today,* 5th ed. (New York: McGraw-Hill, 1991), pp. 490–506; "The Global Economy: Who Gets Hurt?" *Business Week,* 10 August 1992, pp. 48–53; "Big Move to Free Markets in Latin America," pp. 50–55; Herbert Baum, "Borderless North America," *Marketing Management,* Winter 1992, pp. 46–48; "Jolt to NAFTA," *Wall Street Journal,* 1 July 1993, pp. A1, A8; and Gary Becker, "NAFTA: The Pollution Issue Is Just a Smokescreen," *Business Week,* 9 August 1993, p. 16.
17. "Little Companies, Big Exports," *Business Week,* 13 April 1993, pp. 70–73.
18. "Making Global Alliances Work," *Fortune,* 17 December 1990, pp. 121–122.
19. Joel Bleeke and David Ernst, "The Way to Win in Cross-Border Alliances," *Harvard Business Review,* November–December 1991, p. 130.
20. "FedEx: Europe Nearly Killed the Messenger," *Business Week,* 25 May 1992, p. 124.
21. "Pizza in Japan Is Adapted to Local Tastes," *Wall Street Journal,* 4 June 1993, p. B1.
22. "Campbell: Now It's M-m-Global," *Business Week,* 15 March 1993, pp. 52–54.
23. Emily Thornton, "Japan's Struggle to Be Creative," *Fortune,* 19 April 1992, pp. 129–134.
24. "The Stateless Corporation," *Business Week,* 14 May 1990, pp. 98–105.
25. Neil King, Jr., "K mart's Czech Invasion Lurches Along," *Wall Street Journal,* 8 June 1993, p. A11.

Chapter 5

1. Stanley Modic, "Movers and Shakers of Corporate Social Responsibility," *Business and Society Review,* Spring 1990, p. 63.
2. "The Payoff from a Good Reputation," *Fortune,* 10 February 1992, pp. 73–76.
3. "Methods of Marketing Infant Formula Land Abbott in Hot Water," *Wall Street Journal,* 25 May 1993, pp. A1, A6.
4. "Joe Camel's Bad Press Could be Boosting the Brand," *Wall Street Journal,* 14 May 1993, pp. B1, B5.
5. "Novello Throws Down the Gauntlet," *Adweek's Marketing Week,* 16 March 1992, pp. 4–5.
6. "A Kinder, Gentler Generation of Executives," *Business Week,* 23 April 1990, p. 86.
7. "It's No Fad: Environmentalism Is Now a Fact of Corporate Life," *Marketing News,* 15 October 1990, p. 7.
8. Carl Frankel, "Blueprint For Green Marketing," *American Demographics,* April 1993, pp. 34–37.
9. "Disposing of the Green Myth," *Adweek's Marketing Week,* 13 April 1992, pp. 20–21.
10. Ibid.
11. Thomas A. Stewart, "Using Market Forces to Save Nature," *Fortune,* 14 January 1991, pp. 42–44.
12. Kevin Kerr, "Thinking Green is No Longer Just a Hippie Dream," *Adweek's Marketing Week,* 9 July 1990, p. 18.
13. Faye Rice, "Who Scores Best On the Environment," *Fortune,* 26 July 1993, pp. 114–116.
14. Ibid.
15. Ibid.
16. General Motors Public Interest Report, 1993.
17. Ibid.

18. "Companies That Serve You Best," *Services Marketing Today,* July/August 1993, p. 4.

19. Cyndee Miller, "U.S. Firms Lag In Meeting Global Quality Standards," *Marketing News,* 15 February 1993, pp. 1, 6.

20. Quotes taken from Charles E. Watson, "Managing with Integrity: Social Responsibilities of Business as Seen by America's CEO's," *Business Horizons,* July–August 1991, pp. 99–109.

21. "Three Decades After the Equal Pay Act, Women's Wages Remain Far From Parity," *Wall Street Journal,* 9 June 1993, pp. B1, B3.

22. "Executive Women Make Major Gains in Pay and Status," *Wall Street Journal,* 30 June 1993, p. A3.

23. Anne Fisher, "Sexual Harassment—What To Do About It," *Fortune,* 23 August 1993, pp. 84–88.

24. Ibid.

25. "Disability Docket," *Wall Street Journal,* 27 July 1993, p. A1.

26. "Disabilities Act Helps—But Not Much," *Wall Street Journal,* 19 July 1993, pp. B1, B8.

27. "Executive Pay," *Business Week,* 26 April 1993, pp. 56–57.

28. "Executives Win, Workers Lose," *Industry Week,* 17 July 1989, p. 19.

29. Laurie Petersen, "The Town That Maxwell House Left," *Adweek's Marketing Week,* 6 August 1990, pp. 19–22.

30. "Inspired From Above, ServiceMaster Dignifies Those Below," *Wall Street Journal,* 8 May 1990, p. A21.

31. "More Big Businesses Set Up Ethics Offices," *Wall Street Journal,* 10 May 1993, p. B1.

32. Kenneth Labich, "The New Crises in Business Ethics," *Fortune,* 20 April 1992, pp. 167–176.

33. Ibid.

34. Joseph Pereira, "Social Responsibility and Need for Low Cost Clash at Stride Rite," *Wall Street Journal,* 28 May 1993, pp. A1, A4.

Part 2 Career Appendix

1. This section taken from John James Arthur, "International Careers: Not All Is Glamour," *CPC Annual (1989–90),* 33rd ed., pp. 61–64.

2. "Working in Europe after Graduation," *Managing Your Career,* Spring 1991, pp. 18, 20.

3. Will Cantrell and Francine Modderno, "Landing An International Internship," *Managing Your Career,* Fall 1993, p. 17.

4. Ibid.

5. The NAFTA material is taken from Jeff Wood and Beth Pratt, "Head South, Young Graduate," *Managing Your Career,* Fall 1992, pp. 15–17.

6. Ibid.

Chapter 6

1. Lee Berton and Joann S. Lublin, "Seeking Shelter: Partnership Structure Is Called in Question as Liability Risk Rises," *Wall Street Journal,* 10 June 1992, p. A1.

2. John R. Dorfman, "Master Limited Partnerships Regain Fans Thanks to Special Treatment of Payouts," *Wall Street Journal,* 19 August 1993, pp. C1–C2.

3. Timothy L. O'Brien, "Franchises Spearhead Renewed Popularity of Co-Ops," *Wall Street Journal,* 29 November 1993, p. B2.

4. Brenton R. Schlender, "How Toshiba Makes Alliances Work," *Fortune,* 4 October 1993, pp. 116–120.

5. This section based on: "LLCs Authorized: Beneficial Alternative to Partnership or Corporation," *Gray, Cary, Ames, & Frye Quarterly,* Summer 1993, pp. 1, 5, 7; and John R. Emshwiller, "New Kind of Company Attracts Many—Some Legal, Some Not," *Wall Street Journal,* 8 November 1993, pp. B1, B2.

6. Randall Smith, "Higher Stock Prices Are Feeding a Revival of Merger Activity," *Wall Street Journal,* 14 October 1993, p. A6.

7. Michael Waldholz and George Anders, "Merck to Purchase Medco in $6 Billion Transaction," *Wall Street Journal,* 29 July 1993, p. A3.

8. Annetta Miller et al., "What Do You Do with $1 Billion?" *Newsweek,* 30 August 1993, p. 47.

9. Richard Gibson, "Dean Foods Will Buy Birds Eye Brand from Philip Morris Unit for $140 Million," *Wall Street Journal,* 2 November 1993, p. A6.

10. Smith, p. A6.

11. Suzanne Woolley, "Deal, Anyone?" *The 1993 Business Week 1000* (Special Issue), p. 36.

12. Personal interview with William Sinkula, Executive Vice President, The Kroger Co., 21 May 1993.

13. Manjeet Kripalani, "Utility Merger Mania," *Forbes,* 6 December 1993, p. 54.

14. Smith, p. A6.

15. William J. Cook, "Plugging in for Profit," *U.S. News & World Report,* 25 October 1993, pp. 46–47.

16. Linda Grant, "Corporate Connections," *U.S. News & World Report,* 2 August 1993, p. 47.

Chapter 7

1. Barbara Marsh, "Sleepless in Chicago," *Wall Street Journal Reports: Small Business,* 15 October 1993, p. R18.

2. Alan Deutschmann, "The Next Big Info Tech Battle," *Fortune,* 29 November 1993, pp. 40, 46.

3. Charles McCoy, "Entrepreneur Smells Aroma of Success in Coffee Bars," *Wall Street Journal,* 8 January 1993, p. B2; Ken Ohlson, "Bean Scene," *Entrepreneur,* December 1993, p. 90.

4. Don L. Boroughs, "Racing Against the Wind," *U.S. News & World Report,* 5 October 1992, p. 86.

5. Ibid., p. 108.

6. Paul Lim, "Some New Grads Turn Entrepreneur, Not Employee," *Wall Street Journal,* 25 June 1992, p. B2.

7. John A. Byrne, "Introduction," *Business Week/Enterprise 1993* (Special Issue), pp. 14, 16.

8. Becky Johnson, "These Temps Don't Type, But They're Handy in the Lab," *Business Week,* 24 May 1993, p. 68.

9. Ibid., p. 12.

10. Ronald Rosenberg, "Re-Emerging Business," *The Boston Globe,* 30 June 1993, pp. 44–45.

11. Charles Burck, "The Real World of the Entrepreneur," *Fortune,* 5 April 1993, p. 70.

12. Burck, pp. 62–63.

13. Frank Green, "Publisher Has Finger on Pulse of Medical Specialties," *The San Diego Union-Tribune,* 25 May 1993, p. C-14.

14. Mary Martin, "Rebirth in Chair City," *The Boston Sunday Globe,* 27 June 1993, pp. 54–55.

15. "Twenty-Twenty Hindsight," *Wall Street Journal Reports: Small Business,* 15 October 1993, p. R4.

16. Brent Bowers, "Regulation Play," *Wall Street Journal Reports: Small Business,* 15 October 1993, p. R16.

17. Marsh, p. R18.

18. Annetta Miller et al., "Now: The Brick Wall," *Newsweek,* 24 August 1992, pp. 54–56; Barbara Marsh, "Gender Gap," *Wall Street Journal Reports: Small Business,* 16 October 1992, p. R20.

19. Eugene Carlson, "Turned Down," *Wall Street Journal Reports: Black Entrepreneurship,* 19 February 1993, p. R1.

20. Eugene Carlson, "SBA Introduces Its 'Microloan' Program," *Wall Street Journal,* 3 June 1992, p. B2.
21. Dave Kansas, "Don't Believe It," *Wall Street Journal Reports: Small Business,* 15 October 1993, p. R8.
22. Guen Sublette, "15 Hottest Businesses for 1994," *Entrepreneur,* December 1993, pp. 74, 80.
23. Michael Kinsman, "Starbucks' Benefits, Pay a Premium Blend," *The San Diego Union-Tribune,* 11 June 1993, p. C-1.
24. Lisa J. Moore, "Selling Abroad," *U.S. News & World Report,* 2 March 1992, p. 66.
25. Terrian Barnes-Bryant, "A Two-Way Street," *MBE,* September/October 1993, pp. 62, 64.
26. Jeffrey A. Tannenbaum, "Chain Reaction," *Wall Street Journal Reports: Small Business,* 15 October 1993, p. R6.
27. Caroline Clarke, "Giant Steps for Black Franchisees," *Black Enterprise,* September 1993, pp. 45–48.
28. Jeffrey A. Tanenbaum, "Financial Claim Requirement Considered by Regulators," (Focus on Franchising Column), *Wall Street Journal,* 10 September 1993, p. B2.
29. Valerie Reitman, "India Anticipates the Arrival of the Beefless Big Mac," *Wall Street Journal,* 20 October 1993, pp. B1, B9; Eleena de Lisser, "In Australia, U.S. Fast Food Firms Slow Down," *Wall Street Journal,* 20 October 1993, pp. B1, B9; Diane Lindquist, "Fast Fit," *The San Diego Union-Tribune,* 24 October 1993, pp. J1, J2.
30. Jeffrey A. Tannenbaum, "Nutri/System Franchisees Live Franchiser's Nightmare," *Wall Street Journal,* 3 May 1993, p. B2.
31. Jeffrey A. Tannenbaum, "Once Red-Hot PIP Faces Legal Assault by Franchisees," *Wall Street Journal,* 8 April 1993, p. B2.
32. Adrienne S. Harris, "Hot Franchises You Can Run from Your Home," *Black Enterprise,* September 1993, pp. 62–64.

Part 3 Career Appendix

1. Abby Christopher, "Jeremy Jaech: Technician," *Inc.,* August 1993, p. 76.
2. Alan Farnham, "He Did It His Way," *Fortune,* 2 May 1994, p. 132.
3. Rod Riggs, "Specialty Publisher Crafts Needlework Books Galore," *San Diego Union Tribune,* 9 March 1993, p. C16.

Chapter 8

1. James Near, "Wendy's Successful 'Mop Bucket Attitude'," *Wall Street Journal,* 27 April 1992, p. B1.
2. Eckhard Pfeiffer, "My Turning Point: The Compaq Turnaround," *Audacity,* Spring 1993, p. 2.
3. "Steve Job's Vision, So On Target at Apple, Now Is Falling Short," *Wall Street Journal,* 25 May 1993.
4. "25 Executives to Watch," *Business Week 1000* (1993), p. 75.
5. "Sprawling Bureaucracy Eats Up Most Profits of Girl Scout Cookies," *Wall Street Journal,* 13 May 1993, pp. A1, A4.
6. John Welch, "Managing," *Fortune,* 25 March 1990, p. 30.
7. John Wilke, "Corporate Misfits Who Run Cabletron Play a Rough Game," *Wall Street Journal,* 9 April 1993, pp. A1, A10.
8. Ibid.
9. Ibid.
10. Paul Hofheinz, "Europe's Tough New Managers," *Fortune,* 6 September 1993, pp. 111–116.
11. John Sedgwick, "Time Is On My Mind," *Business Month,* August 1990, pp. 74–75; "8 Minutes Worth of Work," *U.S. News & World Report,* 22 May 1989, p. 81.
12. Brian Dumaine, "The New Non-Manager Managers," *Fortune,* 22 February 1993, p. 84.

Chapter 9

1. Thomas Stewart, "Reengineering: The Hot New Managing Tool," *Fortune,* 23 August 1993, pp. 41–48.
2. Brian Dumaine, "The New Turnaround Champs," *Fortune,* 16 July 1990, pp. 36–39.
3. James Quinn and Peggy Paquette, "Technology in Services: Creating Organizational Revolutions," *Sloan Management Review,* Winter 1990, pp. 67–78; and "The Technology Payoff," *Business Week,* 14 June 1993, pp. 57–68.
4. Andrew DuBrin and Duane Ireland, *Management and Organization,* 2nd ed. (Cincinnati: South-Western Publishing, 1993), p. 183.
5. John Ketteringham and P. Ranganath Nayak, *Breakthroughs* (New York: Rawbon and Associates, 1986).
6. "The Virtual Corporation," *Business Week,* 8 February 1993, p. 100.
7. "The Virtual Corporation," pp. 99–102; and "Here's a Virtual Model for America's Industrial Giants," *Newsweek,* 23 August 1993, p. 40.

8. Scott McCartney, "Lab Partners," *Wall Street Journal,* 15 July 1993, pp. A1, A4.

Chapter 10

1. James B. Treece, "Improving the Soul of an Old Machine," *Business Week,* 25 October 1993, pp. 134–136.
2. Michael Selz, "Small Manufacturers Display the Nimbleness the Times Require," *Wall Street Journal,* 29 December 1993, p. A1.
3. Erle Norton, "Small, Flexible Plants May Play Crucial Role in US Manufacturing," *Wall Street Journal,* 13 January 1993, pp. A1, A6.
4. Peter Coy et al., "In the Labs, the Fight to Spend Less, Get More," *Business Week,* 28 June 1993, p. 102.
5. Timothy Noah, "Clear Benefits of Clean Air Act Come at a Cost," *Wall Street Journal,* 15 November 1993, p. B1, B5.
6. James M. Burcke, "Preaching the Gospel of Conservation," *Business Insurance,* 26 April 1993, pp. 123–124.
7. David Hage and Linda Grant, "How to Make America Work," *U.S. News & World Report,* 6 December 1993, pp. 49–50.
8. Amal Kumar Naj, "Some Manufacturers Drop Efforts to Adopt Japanese Techniques," *Wall Street Journal,* 7 May 1993, pp. A1, A6.
9. Otis Port, "The Responsive Factory," *Business Week/Enterprise 1993,* p. 49.
10. Andrew Kupfer, "A Robot Inspector for Airplanes," *Fortune,* 3 May 1993, p. 93.
11. Shawn Tully, "The Modular Corporation," *Fortune,* 8 February 1993, p. 112.
12. Annette Kostyzak Shimada, "Digging Up, Digging Into Fast MRP II," *Manufacturing Systems,* October 1993, pp. 62–66.
13. Howard Gleckman et al., "The Technology Payoff," *Business Week,* 14 June 1993, pp. 60–61.
14. "Business Bulletin," *Wall Street Journal,* 4 November 1993, p. A1.
15. Stephen Baker, "A Surgeon Whose Hands Never Shake," *Business Week,* 4 October 1993, p. 111.
16. Kathleen Deveny, "Man Walked on the Moon but Man Can't Make Enough Devil's Food Cookie Cakes," *Wall Street Journal,* 29 September 1993, pp. B1, B12; Maria Mooshil, "Snapple Grapples with Rigors of Success," *Wall Street Journal,* 20 August 1993, p. A5D.

17. Jim Impoco, "How Utah Created a Mountain of Jobs," *U.S. News & World Report,* 22 February 1993, p. 43–44.
18. David Woodruff and John Templeman, "Why Mercedes Is Alabama-Bound," *Business Week,* 11 October 1993, pp. 138–139.
19. Gregory E. David, "Supplier Management: Xerox," *Financial World,* 28 September 1993, p. 62.
20. Nanette Byrnes, "Inventory Management: Campbell Soup," *Financial World,* 28 September 1993, p. 52.
21. Richard E. White, "An Empirical Assessment of JIT in U.S. Manufacturers," *Production & Inventory Management Journal,* Second Quarter 1993, p. 38.
22. Jeremy Main, "Manufacturing the Right Way," *Fortune,* 21 May 1990, p. 56.
23. Rahul Jacob, "TQM: More than a Dying Fad?" *Fortune,* 18 October 1993, pp. 66–68, 72.
24. Ronald Fink, "Group Therapy: That's Benchmarking," *Financial World,* 28 September 1993, pp. 42–47.
25. Ron Winslow, "Health Care Providers Try Industrial Tactics to Reduce Their Costs," *Wall Street Journal,* 3 November 1993, pp. A1, A12.
26. Ronald Henkoff, "The Hot New Seal of Quality," *Fortune,* 28 June 1993, pp. 116–117.
27. Barbara Marsh, "Allen Edmonds Shoe Tries 'Just-in-Time' Production," *Wall Street Journal,* 4 March 1993, p. B2.

Chapter 11

1. Andrall E. Pearson, "Six Basics for General Managers," *Harvard Business Review,* July–August 1990, pp. 94–101.
2. Joseph Gies, "Automating the Worker," *American Heritage of Invention and Technology,* Winter 1991, pp. 56–63.
3. "Fear and Stress in the Office Take Toll," *Wall Street Journal,* 6 November 1990, p. B1.
4. "Farewell, Fast Track," *Business Week,* 10 December 1990, p. 200.
5. "Is Your Boss Spying on You?" *Business Week,* 15 January 1990, pp. 74–75; and Gabriella Stern, "P&G Keeps Tabs on Workers, Others, New Book Asserts," *Wall Street Journal,* 7 September 1993, pp. A3, A6.

6. Adapted from Andrew DuBrin and Duane Ireland, *Management and Organization,* 2nd ed. (Cincinnati: South-Western Publishing, 1993), pp. 576–578.
7. Robert Johnson, "Tenneco Hired a CEO From Outside, and He Is Refocusing the Firm," *Wall Street Journal,* 29 March 1993, pp. A1, A14.
8. "The Fight of His Life," *Business Week,* 20 September 1993, pp. 55–64.
9. Carol Hymowitz, "Which Corporate Culture Fits You?" *Wall Street Journal,* 17 July 1989, p. B1.
10. Adapted from David Holt, *Management Principles and Practices,* 2nd ed. (Englewood Cliffs, N.J.: Prentice-Hall, 1990), pp. 433–434.
11. "The Search for the Organization of Tomorrow," *Fortune,* 18 May 1992, pp. 92–98.
12. Alan Farnham, "Mary Kay's Lessons in Leadership," *Fortune,* 20 September 1993, pp. 68–77.
13. James A. Wilson and Nancy S. Elman, "Organizational Benefits of Mentoring," *The Executive,* November 1990, pp. 88–94.
14. Pascal Zachary, "Agony and Ecstasy of 200 Code Writers Beget Windows NT," *Wall Street Journal,* 26 May 1993, pp. A1, A6.

Chapter 12

1. "Disability Docket," *Wall Street Journal,* 27 July 1993, p. A1.
2. "Sure Unpaid Leave Sounds Simple, But . . . ," *Business Week,* 9 August 1993, pp. 32–34.
3. Susan Chira, "Family Leave Is Law," *New York Times,* 15 August 1993, p. E3.
4. Warren Brown, "How to Write an Affirmative Action Plan," *American Demographics,* March 1993, pp. 56–59.
5. "Managers Navigate Uncharted Waters Trying to Resolve Work-Family Conflicts," *Wall Street Journal,* 7 December 1992, pp. B1, B7.
6. Chuck Hawkins, "We Had to Recognize That People Have Lives," *Business Week,* 28 June 28 1993, p. 88; and Jaclyn Fierman, "Are Companies Less Family Friendly?" *Fortune,* 21 March 1994, pp. 64–67.
7. "What the Boss Knows About You," *Fortune,* 9 August 1993, pp. 88–93.
8. "More Employers Check Credit Histories of Job Seekers to Judge

Their Character," *Wall Street Journal,* 30 May 1990, p. B1.
9. Tony Lee, "Making an Impression," *Managing Your Career* (New York: *Wall Street Journal,* Spring 1989), pp. 30–31.
10. Ibid.
11. Ronald Henkoff, "Companies That Train Best," *Fortune,* 22 March 1993, pp. 62–75.
12. Ibid.
13. Ibid.
14. "Companies Discover That Some Firings Backfire Into Costly Defamation Suits," *Wall Street Journal,* 8 May 1993, pp. B1, B14.
15. "Employee Benefits for a Changing Work Force," *Business Week,* 5 November 1990, p. 37.
16. This case is taken from Joan Rigdon, "Using New Kinds of Corporate Alchemy, Some Firms Turn Lesser Lights Into Stars," *Wall Street Journal,* 3 May 1993, pp. B1, B6.

Chapter 13

1. Telephone conversation with the Bureau of National Affairs on November 5, 1993.
2. "What US Worry? Big Unions' Leaders Overlook Bad News, Opt for Status Quo," *Wall Street Journal,* 5 October 1993, pp. B1, B6.
3. Ibid.
4. Dana Milbank, "Unions' Woes Suggest How the Labor Force in U.S. Is Shifting," *Wall Street Journal,* 5 May 1992, pp. A1, A4.
5. "Racketeering Suit Is Settled by Teamsters," *Wall Street Journal,* 14 March 1989, pp. A1, A6.
6. "Auto Pact Leaves GM Hard Choice: Go Along or Confront the Union," *Wall Street Journal,* 17 September 1993, p. A1.
7. Kevin Salwen, "To Small Firms, Idea of Cooperating With Labor is Foreign," *Wall Street Journal,* 27 July 1993, pp. A1, A8.
8. Ibid.
9. Ibid.
10. Ibid.
11. Diane Crispell, "Workers in 2000," *American Demographics,* March 1990, pp. 36–40.
12. "Labor Deals That Offer a Break From Us vs. Them," *Business Week,* 2 August 1993, p. 30.
13. Jennifer McEnroe, "Split-Shift Parenting," *American Demographics,* February 1991, pp. 50–52.
14. "A Decisive Response to Crises Brought Ford Enhanced

Productivity," *Wall Street Journal,* 15 December 1992, pp. A1, A13.

15. "The Strange Bedfellows Backing Workplace Reform," *Business Week,* 30 April 1990, p. 57.

16. Derived from an actual arbitration hearing. All names and places have been changed to protect identities.

Chapter 14

1. Cheryl Hall, "Hospital Uses a Little Magic on Service," *Dallas Morning News,* 18 July 1993, pp. 1H, 5H, 7H.

2. "How to Deal with Tough Customers," *Fortune,* 3 December 1990, pp. 38–48.

3. "Shades of Green," *Wall Street Journal,* 2 August 1991, pp. A1, A8.

4. "Will Consumers Ever Buy Again?" *Brand Week,* 27 July 1992, p. 36.

5. "Trading Fat Paychecks for Free Time," *Wall Street Journal,* 5 August 1991, p. B1; also see "Women Change Places," *American Demographics,* November 1992, pp. 46–51.

6. "Work Force 2005," *American Demographics,* May 1992, p. 59.

7. Ruth Hamel, "Raging against Aging," *American Demographics,* March 1992, pp. 42–45; see also "New Study on Today's Maturity Market," *Service Marketing Newsletter,* Summer 1990, p. 3.

8. Michael Major, "Promoting to the Mature Market," *Promo,* November 1990, p. 7.

9. "American Maturity," *American Demographics,* March 1993, pp. 31–43.

10. "Home Alone–with $660 Billion," *Business Week,* 29 July 1991, pp. 76–77.

11. Ibid.

12. "Americans on the Move," *American Demographics,* June 1990, pp. 46–48.

13. "The Incredible Shrinking Middle Class," *American Demographics,* May 1992, pp. 34–39.

14. "The World's Best Brand," *Fortune,* 31 May 1993, pp. 44–54.

15. "Camp Hyatt," *American Demographics,* January 1993, pp. 50–51.

16. "Those Little Kids Have Big Pockets," *Wall Street Journal,* 26 August 1992, p. B1.

17. "New Ways to Reach Children," *American Demographics,* August 1993, pp. 50–54.

18. "Marketing to Young Adults," *American Demographics,* April 1993, pp. 50–53.

19. "How Spending Changes during Middle Age," *Wall Street Journal,* 14 January 1992, p. B1.

20. Laura Zinn, "This Bud's for You. No, Not You—Her," *Business Week,* 4 November 1991, p. 86.

21. "The New Recipe at Campbell Soup," *AdWeek's Marketing Week,* 11 June 1990, p. 4.

22. "Frito's Micro Move," *AdWeek's Marketing Week,* 12 February 1990, p. 44.

23. Adapted from William Wilson and Xiaoyan Zhao, "Perestroika and Research: Ivan's Opinion Counts," *CASRO Journal,* 1991, pp. 27–31.

24. Lisa Marie Petersen, "Previews of Coming Attractions," *Brandweek,* 15 March 1993, pp. 22–23.

Chapter 15

1. "What's in a Brand?" *American Demographics,* May 1993, p. 32.

2. "ABC's of Brand Names," *Wall Street Journal,* May 1994.

3. "Flops," *Business Week,* 16 August 1993, pp. 76–82.

4. Lawrence Ingrassia, "A Recovering Gillette Hopes for Vindication in a High-Tech Razor," *Wall Street Journal,* 29 September 1990, pp. A1, A4.

5. Richard Gibson, "Pinning Down Costs of Product Introductions," *Wall Street Journal,* 26 October 1993, p. B1.

6. "China Coast Restaurants May Mushroom," *Wall Street Journal,* 19 April 1993, pp. B1, B5.

7. Partially adapted from "Value Pricing Is Hot as Shrewd Consumers Seek Low-Cost Quality," *Wall Street Journal,* 12 March 1991, pp. A1, A5; "Value Marketing: Quality, Service, and Fair Pricing are the Keys to Selling in the '90s," *Business Week,* 11 November 1991, pp. 132–140; and "GM, Pitching Value, Scores Cavalier Upset," *Wall Street Journal,* 11 May 1993, pp. B1, B2.

8. Alix Freedman, "Peddling Dreams: A Marketing Giant Uses Its Sales Prowess to Profit on Poverty," *Wall Street Journal,* 22 September 1993, pp. A1, A14.

9. John Wilke, "Beech's Sleekly Styled Starship Fails to Take Off with Corporate Customers," *Wall Street Journal,* 29 September 1993, pp. B1, B5.

Chapter 16

1. Patricia Sellers, "Pepsi Keeps On Going After No. 1," *Fortune,* 11

March 1993, pp. 62–70.

2. Bill Saporito, "Is Wal-Mart Unstoppable?" *Fortune,* 6 May 1991, pp. 50–59.

3. "Warehouse Club War Leaves Few Standing, and They Are Bruised," *Wall Street Journal,* 18 November 1993, pp. A1, A6; and "Sizing Up Profits," *Brandweek,* 4 May 1993, p. 32.

4. Lorne Manly, "Selling in the Stores of the Future," *Adweek,* 20 January 1992, pp. 12–13; and Richard S. Teitelbaum, "Companies to Watch: Catalina Marketing," *Fortune,* 18 May 1992, p. 89.

5. This section adapted from Laurie Petersen, "21st Century Supermarket Shopping," *Adweek's Marketing Week,* 9 March 1992, p. 9; and Howard Schlossberg, "Tomorrow's Retailing Technologies on Display Today at Smart Store," *Marketing News,* 20 January 1992, p. 2.

6. Michael McCarthy, "James Bond Hits the Supermarket: Stores Snoop on Shoppers' Habits to Boost Sales," *Wall Street Journal,* 25 August 1993, pp. B1, B8; and Francine Schwadel, "K mart Testing Radar to Track Shopper Traffic," *Wall Street Journal,* 24 September 1991, pp. B1, B5.

7. "Retailing Will Never Be the Same," *Business Week,* 26 July 1993, pp. 54–60; and Patrick M. Reilly, "Home Shoppers to Be Given Yet Another Service," *Wall Street Journal,* 14 January 1994, p. B1.

8. Matt Moffett, "U.S. Firms Yell Olé to Future in Mexico," *Wall Street Journal,* 8 March 1993, pp. B1, B5; and Matt Moffett, "Chic Star of Mexican Retailing: Sears Roebuck," *Wall Street Journal,* 8 March 1993, pp. B1, B5.

9. Roger Cohen, "Pizza and Persistence Win in Hungary," *New York Times,* 5 May 1992, pp. D1, D9.

10. "U.S. Discount Retailers Are Targeting Europe and Its Fat Margins," *Wall Street Journal,* 20 September 1993, pp. A1, A4.

11. Gabriella Stern, "P&G Mulls Plan to Cut Costs of Distribution," *Wall Street Journal,* 8 November 1993.

Chapter 17

1. "Flops," *Business Week,* 16 August 1993, pp. 76–82.

2. "Too Many Think the Bunny Is Duracell's, Not Eveready's," *Wall Street Journal,* 31 July 1990, p. B1.

3. "Pond's Intros: $40 Million," *Brandweek,* 8 November 1993, p. 3.

4. "Boxed In at Jack-in-the-Box," *Business Week,* 15 February 1993, p. 40.

5. "Blockbuster Goes Interactive," *Marketing News,* 6 December 1993, p. 1.

6. "Roster For Super Bowl Fills," *Wall Street Journal,* 13 December 1993, p. B6.

7. Eben Shapiro, "FTC Staff Recommends Ban of Joe Camel Campaign," *Wall Street Journal,* 11 August 1993, pp. B1, B5; Eben Shapiro, "Cigarette Makers Outfit Smokers in Icons, Eluding Warning and Enraging Activists," *Wall Street Journal,* 27 September 1993, pp. B1, B4; and "Joe Camel Can't Light Up Children in Q Ratings," *Advertising Age,* 1 March 1993, p. 8.

8. Pat Sloan, "Costly Controversies," *Advertising Age,* 22 March 1993, p. 52.

9. "Coupons: Are They Too Popular?" *Advertising Age,* 15 February 15, 1993, p. 32.

10. Oliver Teves, "Filipinos Take To Streets Over Botched Pepsi Promotion," *Dallas Morning News,* 29 July 1993, p. 15D; Bob Drogin, "You Got the Right One … Opps," *Fort Worth Star Telegram,* 27 July 1993, pp. 1–2; and Michael McCarthy, "PepsiCo Is Facing Mounting Lawsuits From Botched Promotion In Philippines," *Wall Street Journal,* 28 July 1993, p. B6.

11. "Expositions In Today's Marketing Mix," pamphlet published by the Trade Show Bureau, Denver, Colorado, 1993.

12. "Corridor Talk," *Adweek's Marketing Week,* 6 August 1990, p. 62.

13. Laura Bird, "Critics Shoot At New Colt 45 Campaign," *Wall Street Journal,* 17 February 1993, pp. B1, B8.

Chapter 18

1. William M. Bulkeley, "Computers Start to Lift U.S. Productivity," *Wall Street Journal,* 1 March 1993, p. B10.

2. Alice LaPlante, "Teleconfrontation-ing," *Forbes ASAP,* 13 September 1993, p. 112.

3. Sharen Kindel, "World without End," *Financial World,* 9 November 1993, p. 48.

4. Peter Nulty, "When to Murder Your Mainframe," *Fortune,* 1 November 1993, p. 114.

5. Jennifer DeJong, "The Right Connection," *Inc./Technology Guide,* Winter 1994, pp. 48–50.

6. Ibid., pp. 48, 52–54.

7. John W. Verity, "Getting Work to Go with the Flow," *Business Week,* 21 June 1993, p. 156.

8. Martha E. Mangelsdorf, "Higher Math," *Inc.,* December 1993, pp. 111, 114.

9. Ronald Fink, "Data Processing: PepsiCo," *Financial World,* 29 September 1992.

10. Mary Lu Carnevale, "World-Wide Web," *Wall Street Journal: Technology Report,* 15 November 1993, p. R7.

11. David H. Freedman, "Culture of Urgency," *Forbes ASAP,* 13 September 1993, pp. 27–28.

12. Adapted from Vic Sussman, "Policing the Digital World," *U.S. News & World Report,* 6 December 1993, pp. 68–70; Joan Connell, "Cyberethics," *San Diego Union-Tribune,* 10 December 1993, p. E1.

13. Patrick Marshall, "Stay in Touch," *Inc. 1994 Guide to Office Technology,* Winter 1994, p. 60.

14. Alison L. Sprout, "Saving Time around the Clock," *Fortune,* 13 December 1993, p. 157.

15. Sandra D. Atchison, "The Care and Feeding of 'Lone Eagles,' " *Business Week,* 15 November, 1993, p. 58; Phil Patton, " 'Virtual Office' Is the Latest in Work Styles," *The San Diego Union Tribune,* 1 November 1993.

16. David H. Freedman, "An Unusual Way to Run a Ski Business," *Forbes ASAP,* 7 December 1992, pp. 27–32.

17. Sharen Kindel, "Keep the Ball Rolling," *Financial World,* 4 August 1992, p. 60.

18. Sharen Kindel, "The Door into Your Company," *Financial World,* 21 July 1992.

Chapter 19

1. Adapted from "Daimler Plays Ball," *The Economist,* 27 March 1993, p. 76; "Daimler Bends," *The Economist,* 3 April 1993, p. 76; William Glasgall, "Daimler-Benz Opens Up," *Business Week,* 12 April 1993, p. 82; Stephen Kindel, "Daimler-Benz: Drang nach Westen für Kapital," *Financial World,* 27 April 1993, pp. 18–20; "Daimler listing opens the door," *Euromoney,* May 1993, p. 10.

2. Lee Berton, "Paramount Deal to Cut Buyer's Future Profits," *The Wall Street Journal,* 28 December 1993, p. A2; Eric S. Hardy, "Good Riddance to Goodwill," *Forbes,* 22 November 1993, p. 202.

3. Timothy K. Smith and Erle Norton, "One Baseball Statistic that Remains a Mystery: The Bottom Line," *Wall Street Journal,* 2 April 1993, pp. A1, A6.

4. Jill Andresky Fraser, "Straight Talk," *Inc.,* March 1990, p. 97.

Part 7 Career Appendix

1. Sources for information systems jobs: "Hot Tracks in 20 Professions," *U.S. News & World Report,* 26 October 1992, p. 104; and "The 25 Hottest Careers," *Working Woman,* July 1993, p. 42. Source for salary information: *1994 Salary Guide,* Robert Half International Inc., pp. 4–9, 11–15.

Chapter 20

1. Kenneth H. Bacon, "Banks' Declining Role in Economy Worries Fed, May Hurt Firms," *Wall Street Journal,* 9 July 1993, p. A1.

2. Adapted from Myron Magnet, "Good News for the Service Economy," *Fortune,* 3 May 1993, p. 50; Howard Gleckman et al., "The Technology Payoff," *Business Week,* 14 June 1993, p. 60.

3. Donald T. Savage, "Interstate Banking: A Status Report," *Federal Reserve Bulletin,* December 1993, p. 1086.

4. Roger Fillion, "Bank Plan Would Aid Poor Areas," *San Diego Union-Tribune,* 9 December 1993, p. C1.

5. Kenneth H. Bacon and John R. Wilkes, "Fed Gives Bias Laws New Clout as It Blocks a Bank Acquisition," *Wall Street Journal,* 17 November 1993, p. A1; Kenneth H. Bacon, "Shawmut Settles Charges of Bias in Its Lending Practices," *Wall Street Journal,* 14 December 1993, p. A2.

6. Albert R. Karr, "Administration Raises Request for S&L Bailout," *Wall Street Journal,* 17 March 1993, p. A2.

7. Therese Eiben and John Wyatt, "How the Industries Stack Up," *Fortune,* 12 July 1993, p. 84; Kelley Holland, "It's a Bank-Eat-Bank World," *Business Week,* 11 January 1993, p. 101.

8. Ralph T. King Jr. and Steven Lipin, "Corporate Banking, Given Up for Dead, Is Reinventing Itself," *Wall Street Journal,* 31 January 1994, p. A6.

9. William Glasgall and Bill Javetski, " 'Shipwrecks and Disasters,' " *Business Week,* 5 July 1993, pp. 94–95.

10. Richard C. Morais, "Citi über Alles," *Forbes,* 17 January 1994, p. 50.
11. Bernard Baumohl, "Are Banks Obsolete?" *Time,* 28 June 1993, pp. 49–50; Holland, "It's a Bank-Eat-Bank World," p. 101.
12. King, pp. A1, A6.
13. Adapted from Jeanne Saddler, "Bank Regulators to Expand Access to 'Character' Loans," *Wall Street Journal,* 19 July 1994, p. B2; Suzanne Alexander Ryan, "Bank of Boston Ties Fortunes to Loans for Small Firms," *Wall Street Journal,* 3 February 1994, p. B4.
14. Steven Lipin and Marj Charlier, "As National Banking Nears, Mergers Sweep Across State Borders," *Wall Street Journal,* 22 July 1992, p. A1.
15. Savage, pp. 1075, 1089.
16. Kenneth H. Bacon, "U.S. Comptroller Favors Letting Banks Sell Insurance, Other Financial Services," *Wall Street Journal,* 14 September 1993, p. C18.

Chapter 21

1. Interview with Sherrlyn Dunn, Vice President, Finance, Hunter Industries, San Marcos, California, 18 January 1994.
2. Michael Selz, "Small Firms Hit Foreign Obstacles in Billing Overseas," *Wall Street Journal,* 8 December 1992, p. B2; and Jill Andresky Fraser, "By the Minute Monitoring," *Inc.,* June 1993, p. 45.
3. Interview with Christopher H. Savage, Controller, Technical Operations, The Gillette Company, Boston, Massachusetts, 20 December 1994.
4. "How to Pick a Factor," *Inc.,* February 1994, p. 89.
5. Fred R. Bleakley, "Large Firms Will Continue to Cut Debt, Limit Capital Spending, Survey Shows," *Wall Street Journal,* 22 April 1993, p. A2.
6. Udayan Gupta, "Enterprise: Funds Flourish for Community Development Groups," *Wall Street Journal,* 8 March 1993, p. B2.
7. Richard A. Melcher et al., "Does Scott Beck Have Another Winning Recipe?" *Business Week,* 13 December 1993, p. 100.
8. Adapted from: Udayan Gupta, "Foundations Becoming Fount of Venture Funding," *Wall Street Journal,* 10 March 1992, p. B1; Guen Sublette, "Hidden Wealth," *Entrepreneur,* August 1993, pp. 94–101.
9. Joan C. Szabo, "Nothing Ventured, Nothing Gained," *Nation's Business,* June 1993, p. 28.
10. "Coast-to-Coast Angels," *Inc.,* September 1993, p. 36; and "On-Line Pitches to Investors," *Inc.,* January 1994, p. 101.
11. Michael Schuman, " 'Bill Gates Doesn't Need My Help,' " *Forbes,* 11 April 1994, p. 122.

Chapter 22

1. Earl C. Gottschalk, Jr., "Many 'Nice Guy' Funds Fail to Make Nice Profits," *Wall Street Journal,* 7 July 1993, p. C1; "A Fund That Does Well by Doing Good," *Fortune,* 13 December 1993, p. 40.
2. Statistics on the organized exchanges and Nasdaq provided through personal contact with the research departments of the NYSE, AMEX, and Nasdaq.
3. Adapted from Elisabeth Rubinfien, "Enterprising Comrades," *Wall Street Journal,* 24 September 1993, pp. R8–R9.
4. New York Stock Exchange, Research & Planning Division, *1993 Fact Book* (New York: New York Stock Exchange), April 1994; and Susan E. Kuhn, "The Perilous New Stock Market," *Fortune,* 27 December 1993, pp. 48–49.
5. New York Stock Exchange, Research & Planning Division, *1993 Fact Book* (New York: New York Stock Exchange), April 1994.
6. *Standard & Poors Stock Market Encyclopedia* (New York: Standard & Poors Corp.), Winter 1993, pp. 11–12.
7. Ibid., pp. 5–6.
8. Adapted from Sharen Kindel, "The Telephone Game," *Financial World,* 13 October 1992, pp. 74–75; Sharen Kindel, "The Alchemists at Bear Stearns," *Financial World,* 7 December 1993, pp. 74–76.
9. Kevin G. Salwen, "Safeguards Aim to Avert Another Crash," *Wall Street Journal,* 16 October 1992, pp. C1, C18.
10. George Anders, "Trading Moves Blamed in Crash of 1987 Tamed," *Wall Street Journal,* 16 October 1992, p. C18.
11. Douglas R. Sease, "Black Monday Taught Investors to Lose Fear," *Wall Street Journal,* 16 October 1992, p. C1.
12. "Insider Trading Spotlight," *Wall Street Journal,* 2 March 194, p. C27.
13. Michael Siconolfi, "Memos Reveal Prudential Sales Tactics," *Wall Street Journal,* 15 July 1993, p. C1; Michael Siconolfi, "Prudential Plans to Reject Some Claims," *Wall Street Journal,* 17 December 1993, p. C1; Michael Siconolfi, "Merrill's Partnership Sales in '80s Studied by Regulators," *Wall Street Journal,* 27 January 1994, p. C1.
14. Michael R. Sesit, "Americans Snap Up Securities Overseas at Record Pace," *Wall Street Journal,* 19 October 1993, p. C1.
15. Paul Gibson, "Floored," *Financial World,* 15 February 1994, p. 46.
16. Ibid., p. 47.
17. Ibid., p. 48.

Part 8 Career Appendix

1. Source of salary information: *1994 Salary Guide,* Robert Half International Inc., pp. 7–10.

Chapter 23

1. Greg Steinmetz, "Metropolitan Life Agents' Sales Practices Called Deceptive," *Wall Street Journal,* 10 March 1994, p. A4.
2. "Early Endings," *Wall Street Journal,* 11 February 1994, p. B7.
3. Steven A. Holmes, "Arbitration Becomes '90s Corporate Policy," *San Diego Union-Tribune,* 18 March 1994, p. A1.
4. Ellen Joan Pollock, "Mediation Firms Alter the Legal Landscape," *Wall Street Journal,* 22 March 1993, p. B4.
5. Len Young Smith et al., *Smith and Roberson's Business Law,* 7th ed. (St. Paul, Minn.: West, 1988), p. 6.
6. James P. Miller, "SciMed Ordered to Pay $66 Million to Pfizer Unit for Patent Infringement," *Wall Street Journal,* 8 March 1994, p. B5.
7. Neil Gross, "Patent Showdown Pending," *Business Week,* 24 May 1993, pp. 96–97.
8. Smith et al., pp. 161–162.
9. "Settlement Is Disputed in Breast Implants Suit," *San Diego Union-Tribune,* 18 March 1994, p. A20.
10. Linda Himelstein, "Monkey See, Monkey Sue," *Business Week,* 7 February 1994, p. 112.
11. Edward Felsenthal, "Juries Display Less Sympathy in Injury Claims," *Wall Street Journal,* 21 March 1994, pp. B1, B6.
12. Milo Geyelin, "Faulty Software Means Business for Litigators," *Wall Street Journal,* 21 January 1994, pp. B1, B6.
13. "Bankruptcy Judge Confirms Firm's Reorganization Plan," *Wall Street Journal,* 18 February 1994, p. B4

14. "Federal Trade Commission," *Financial World,* 26 October 1993, p. 42.

15. Bob Ortega, "Wal-Mart Loses a Case on Pricing," *Wall Street Journal,* 13 October 1993, p. A3.

16. Martin Tolchin, "Airlines Settle U.S. Price-Fixing Suit," *San Diego Union-Tribune,* 18 March 1994, p. C1.

17. Joe Davidson, "Two Companies Settle Charges of Trying to Fix Prices after Unusual FTC Action," *Wall Street Journal,* 26 March 1993, p. A4.

18. Ann Reilly Dowd, "Congress' Fight over Your Future," *Fortune,* 18 October 1993, p. 60.

19. Daniel Pearl, "Spurred by Bell-TCI Deal, Congress Moves Toward Ending Cable TV-Phone Barrier . . . ," *Wall Street Journal,* 21 October 1993, p. A18.

20. Lenore Schiff, "Taxes Grow More Local," *Fortune,* 4 October 1993, p. 24.

21. Michael J. Mandel and Geoffrey Smith, "The Rush to Roll Back Taxes," *Business Week,* 7 February 1994, pp. 114–115.

22. "Regulation 101," *San Diego Union-Tribune,* 1 October 1993, p. B6; Diane Dustin, "Cable TV Rates Up for 30% across U.S.," *San Diego Union-Tribune,* 20 October 1993, p. C1; Mark Lewyn, "Media Mergers: Why Washington Should Butt Out," *Business Week,* 1 November 1993, p. 37; Mark Lendler et al., "Collapse on the Info Highway," *Business Week,* 7 March 1994, pp. 42–43.

Chapter 24

1. Greg Steinmetz, "Small Firms Find a Strategy for Workers' Compensation," *Wall Street Journal,* 16 November 1993, p. B2.

2. Leslie Scism, "Insurers' Losses on Catastrophes Reach $7 Billion," *Wall Street Journal,* 29 March 1994, p. A2.

3. Chris Roush, "The Hurricane Called Superfund," *Business Week,* 2 August 1993, pp. 74–75.

4. Virginia Finegold and Michael K. Ozanian, "Less Risk, Less . . . ," *Financial World,* 28 September 1993, pp. 32–34; Suzanne Wooley, "Will Insurers Buy This Policy?" *Business Week,* 28 March 1994, p. 112.

5. Linda Grant, "New Jewel in the Crown," *U.S. News & World Report,* 28 February 1994, p. 56; Jerry Bowles, "Quality 93: Meeting Customer Needs through Technology at The New England" (Special Advertising Supplement), *Fortune,* 20 September 1993, pp. 136–138; Howard Gleckman et al., "The Technology Payoff," *Business Week,* 14 June 1993, p. 60.

6. Linda Himelstein, "Monkey See, Money Sue," *Business Week,* 7 February 1994, p. 112.

7. Ibid., p. 114.

8. Milo Geyelin, "Product Liability Groups Take Up Arms," *Wall Street Journal,* 29 January 1993, p. B1.

9. Hilary Stout, "Clinton's Health Plan Must Face Huge Costs of a Person's Last Days," *Wall Street Journal,* 22 April 1993, p. A1.

10. Ron Winslow, "Corporate Health Cost Rise Is Called Lowest in Five Years; Role of HMOs Cited," *Wall Street Journal,* 2 March 1993, p. B2.

11. Linda Grant, "Avoiding the Wreckage," *U.S. News & World Report,* 21 June 1993, p. 52.

12. "Enrollment in HMOs Spurted Almost 10% in 1993, Report Says," *Wall Street Journal,* 10 December 1993, p. A2.

13. Winslow, p. B2; "Enrollment in HMOs," p. A2.

14. Susan Dentzer, "Grim Fairy Tales about Health Costs," *U.S. News & World Report,* 10 May 1993, p. 61.

15. Chris Roush, "Call It Bogus 1-2-3," *Business Week,* 13 December 1994, p. 97; Peter Kerr, "Car-dumping Piling Up Across Nation," *Dayton Daily News,* 15 February 1992, p. D12.

16. Leslie Scism, "Small-Business Program in California Cuts Health Premiums by Average 6.3%," *Wall Street Journal,* 24 March 1994, p. B2.

17. Greg Steinmetz, "Life Insurers Now Find They Are Held Liable for Abuses by Agents," *Wall Street Journal,* 21 January 1994, pp. A1, A6; Steinmetz, "Met Life Got Caught, Others Sent Same Letter," *Wall Street Journal,* 6 January 1994, pp. B1, B3; Jane Bryant Quinn, "Yes, They're Out to Get You," *Newsweek,* 24 January 1994, p. 51.

Epilogue

1. Christina Duff, "Working Against the Odds," *Wall Street Journal,* 28 July 1993, p. A6.

2. William Banis, "The Art of Writing Job-Search Letters," *CPC Annual (1989– 90),* 33rd ed., p. 43.

3. Patricia Carr, "Eeny, Meany, Miney, Mo," *Managing Your Career,* Spring 1990, pp. 36–37.

4. Ibid.

5. "Listen and learn," "Do unto others," and "Follow procedures" excerpted from Robert Half, "After the Job Is Yours," *Managing Your Career,* Spring 1990, pp. 23–24.

6. Excerpted from Tony Lee, "An A-to-Z Guide to the Working World," *Managing Your Career,* Spring 1991, pp. 21, 24–26.

7. Ibid.

GLOSSARY

A

absolute advantage Ability to produce and sell a product that no other country can produce or that no other country can produce at such a low cost.

accountability Obligation to report back to one's supervisor the results of responsibilities undertaken.

accounting Process of collecting, recording, classifying, summarizing, reporting, and analyzing financial activities.

accounting equation Mathematical statement of the relationship among the three main accounting elements: Assets = Liabilities + Owners' equity.

accounts Categories of items that appear in the financial statements.

accounts payable Short-term trade credit extended to the buyer by the seller of products.

accounts receivable Sales made by the firm for which payment has not yet been received.

acculturation The process of adapting to the local culture.

acid-test (quick) ratio Ratio of current assets less inventory to total current liabilities; measures the firm's ability to pay current debts without selling inventory.

acquisition Purchase of a firm by a corporation or investor group.

activity ratios Ratios that measure how quickly a firm's resources are converted into cash or sales.

administrative distribution system Vertical marketing system in which a strong organization takes an informal leadership role in setting the policies of the distribution channel.

administrative law Rules, regulations, and orders passed by boards, commissions, and agencies of federal, state, and local governments.

advertising Any paid form of nonpersonal presentation by an identified sponsor, which may be transmitted by any of a number of different media.

advertising agencies Companies that help create ads and place them in the media.

advertising media Channels through which advertising is carried to prospective customers; include newspapers, magazines, radio, TV, outdoor advertising, direct mail.

advocacy advertising Advertising that takes a stand on certain social or economic issues.

affirmative action Laws that require firms to make special efforts to recruit, hire, and promote women and members of minority groups.

affirmative action programs Programs set up by employers to expand job opportunities for women and minorities.

agency Legal relationship in which one person (the principal) authorizes another person (the agent) to act as a representative.

agency shop Place of employment where the employee does not have to join the union but must pay the union a fee.

agents Sales representatives of manufacturers and wholesalers.

altered workweeks Major departures from the standard eight-hour-a-day, five-days-a week work schedule.

American Federation of Labor (AFL) Labor union, founded in 1881, that organized workers within skilled trades and encouraged unions to function much like businesses.

Americans with Disabilities Act Federal law that prohibits discrimination against disabled persons.

annual report Yearly document that provides a variety of information about a firm's financial condition, performance, and operations.

antitrust regulation Laws that keep companies from entering into agreements to control trade through a monopoly.

appellate courts (courts of appeal) Courts to which a losing party in a trial court may appeal the decision; found in both the federal and state judiciaries.

application software Program that makes a computer do the work that computer users require.

arbitration Method of settling disputes whereby the parties agree to present their case to an impartial third party and are required to accept the arbitrator's decision.

arbitration Settlement of labor-management disputes by having a third party make a binding decision.

articles of incorporation Legal description of a corporation filed with the state in which it is incorporated.

assembly lines Conveyor systems that move products to each work station in the production process.

assessment center Evaluation of managerial talent through an intensive period of exercises and tests.

assets Things of value owned by a firm.

auditing Branch of accounting that reviews the records used to prepare a firm's financial statements.

authority The right, granted by the organization to a manager and acknowledged by the employees, to request action.

autocratic leadership style Decision style in which managers make all the decisions and order employees to implement the solutions.

automated teller machine (ATM) Electronic banking machine that allows customers to make deposits, withdrawals, and other transactions around the clock, seven days a week.

automation Replacement of workers with machines; use of machines to do work with minimum human intervention.

automobile insurance Insurance that covers financial losses from car-related perils.

auxiliary storage system Hardware that provides long-term storage for programs and data; usually consists of some combination of floppy disk drives and hard disk drives.

B

backward integration Acquisition by a wholesaler or retailer of control over production of the products it sells.

balance of payments Difference between a country's total payments to other countries and its total receipts from other countries.

balance of trade Difference between the value of a country's exports and the value of its imports over some period.

balance sheet Financial statement that summarizes a firm's financial position at a specific point in time, providing detail on the items that make up the accounting equation.

bank charter License from either the federal government or a state government that lets a bank do business.

bank examiners Employees of the FDIC who review the financial records and management practices of member banks at least once a year to assure compliance with FDIC rules.

bank holding company Corporation that owns two or more different banks, usually allowed to cross state lines to do business.

bankruptcy Legal procedure by which individuals or businesses that cannot meet their financial obligations are relieved of their debts.

bargaining unit Group of employees eligible to vote in a union election and represented by a particular union.

barriers to entry Factors that prevent new firms from competing equally with the existing firm in a monopoly.

batch processing Updating a database by collecting the data over some period and then processing them all at the same time.

bear markets Securities markets characterized by falling prices.

benchmarking Measuring the products, services, and procedures of one's own company against the best companies to identify areas for improvement.

benefit segmentation Division of a market based on what a product will do rather than on consumer characteristics.

bill of material List of components required to make a product.

binary numbers Numbers (0 and 1) used to represent all data in a computer's central processing unit.

bit Binary digit; amount of memory required to store a single binary 0 or 1.

blacklists Lists of workers involved with unions, circulated among employers to keep those workers from being hired.

Blue Cross/Blue Shield Group of not-for-profit health insurance plans that contract with subscribers and with member hospitals and doctors.

board of directors Governing authority of a corporation, elected by the stockholders.

bond ratings Letter grades assigned to bond issues to rate their investment quality.

bonds Long-term debt obligations for corporations and governments.

bookkeeping Systematic recording of a firm's financial transactions.

brainstorming Process for generating new ideas by having a group think of as many ideas as possible, with criticism and evaluation held until later.

brand Product identifier in the form of words, names, symbols, or designs.

brand loyalty Preference for a particular brand.

breach of contract Failure of one party to a contract to fulfill its terms.

breakeven point Point at which costs are covered and additional sales result in profit.

breaking bulk Breaking down large shipments of goods into smaller, more usable quantities.

brokerage firms Financial organizations that buy and sell securities and provide related advice.

brokers Middlemen who bring together buyers and sellers.

budgets Formal written forecasts of revenues and expenses.

bull markets Securities markets characterized by rising prices.

bundling Pricing strategy of grouping two or more products together and pricing them as one.

business Economic process that involves assembling and using productive resources to create goods and services that can satisfy society's needs and wants.

business cycles Changes upward and downward in business activity.

business ethics Standards for judging the rightness or wrongness of conduct in business practices, institutions, and actions.

business interruption insurance Optional insurance coverage that protects business owners from losses occurring when the business must be closed temporarily after property damage.

business law Body of law that refers to commercial dealings.

bylaws Legal and managerial guidelines of a corporation.

byte Eight bits; amount of memory required to store the code representing one alphabetic character.

C

CAD/CAM systems Computer systems that integrate the entire design, testing, and manufacturing process.

cafeteria benefits plan Benefits plan in which employees choose their own benefits, up to a certain cost per employee.

canned presentations Memorized sales presentations.

capital Tools, machinery, equipment, and buildings used to produce goods and services and get them to the consumer.

capital budgeting Process of evaluating and choosing the long-term expenditures that offer the best returns and meet the goal of maximizing the firm's value.

capital budgets Forecasts for planned fixed-asset outlays over several years.

capital expenditures Investments in long-lived assets, such as land, buildings, and equipment.

capital gain Profit made when an asset is sold for more than its original purchase price.

capitalism Economic system based on competition in the marketplace and private ownership of the factors of production.

capital products Industrial products that are usually large and expensive and have a long life span.

capital structure Mix of long-term debt and equity.

cash budgets Forecasts of a firm's cash receipts and cash expenses.

cash flows Flows of cash into and out of a firm.

cash management Making sure that enough cash is available to pay bills as they come due.

cash rebates Price reductions made after consumers buy the product.

cash value Amount of money from a life insurance policy that is paid to the policyholder if the policy is canceled or that can be borrowed by the policyholder at low interest rates; surrender value.

CD-ROM (compact disk, read-only memory) Data storage device holding up to 680 megabytes on a single 4 3/4(plastic disk which is read with a laser beam.

centralization Practice of assigning only a limited amount of authority to lower-level managers.

central processing unit (CPU) Part of a computer system that computes.

certificates of deposit (CDs) Time deposits that pay a specified interest rate in exchange for leaving a given amount on deposit for a specified period.

certified management accountant (CMA) Professional accountant certified by the National Association of Accountants.

certified public accountant (CPA) Professional accountant certified by the American Institute of Certified Public Accountants.

chain of command Series of superior-subordinate relationships within a hierarchy.

circuit breakers Temporary halts in securities trading for a cooling-off period when certain conditions exist on the New York Stock Exchange.

circular flow Flow of inputs from households to businesses in return for money in the form of rent, wages, interest, and profits and flow of outputs from businesses to households in return for money in the form of spending.

closed shop Place of employment where only union members can be hired; made illegal by the Taft-Hartley Act.

closely owned firm Firm whose common stock is owned by a small group of investors.

coinsurance Insurance that requires the property owner to buy an amount of insurance coverage equal to a specified percentage of the value of the property.

collective bargaining Process of negotiating labor agreements that provide for compensation and working conditions mutually acceptable to the union and to management.

commercial banks Profit-oriented financial institutions that accept customer deposits, make loans to consumers and businesses, invest in securities, and provide other financial services.

commercial paper Short-term, unsecured IOU sold by large, financially strong corporations.

committee organization Organization structure in which authority and responsibility are held by a group of workers rather than a single manager.

commodities exchanges Places where futures contracts are traded.

common law Body of unwritten law that has been developed out of court decisions rather than enacted by legislatures.

common-size income statement Income statement that expresses each item as a percentage of some given base, such as sales.

common stock A security that represents an ownership interest in a corporation.

communism Economic system in which the factors of production are owned collectively and the people receive economic benefits according to their needs and contribute according to their abilities.

comparable worth Concept that employees should be paid the same for jobs that are similar in worth to the employer.

comparative advertising Product advertising in which the company's product is compared with competing, named products.

compressed workweek Workweek of either the normal number of hours squeezed into fewer than five days or fewer hours and fewer days per week.

computer-aided design (CAD) Use of computers to design and test new products and modify existing ones.

computer-aided manufacturing (CAM) Use of computers to develop and control production processes.

computer-integrated manufacturing (CIM) Manufacturing system that uses computer systems to automate the entire manufacturing process.

computers Machines that accurately process data at very high speeds without direct human intervention.

computer virus Computer program that copies itself into other software and thereby spreads to other computer systems, corrupting them.

conceptual skills Ability to view an organization as a whole, to understand how its parts fit together, and to see how it relates to other organizations.

conciliation Process in which a specialist helps management and the union focus on the issues in dispute and acts as a go-between.

concurrent engineering Using cross-functional teams to design both the product and its manufacturing process at the same time.

conglomerate merger Combining of firms in unrelated industries to reduce risk by diversifying operations.

conglomerate union Union, such as the Teamsters Union, that represents a wide variety of workers and industries.

Congress of Industrial Organizations (CIO) Labor union that broke away from the AFL in 1935 and organized workers along industry lines.

consumer behavior Actions people take in buying and using products.

consumerism Organized effort by citizens, businesses, and government to protect consumers.

consumer orientation Idea that planning should identify a product's likely consumers and supply goods or services designed to meet their needs and wants.

consumer price index (CPI) Index of the prices of a "market basket" of goods and services bought by typical urban consumers.

consumer products Goods and services purchased and used by the end user.

containerization Packing and sealing goods in large, standard-size containers that are transported without being unpacked until they reach their final destination.

contests Skilled competitions among consumers for various prizes.

contingency plans Plans that identify courses of action to be taken if events disrupt the completion of a strategic or tactical plan.

continuous improvement (kaizen) Idea, originated in Japan, that teams of workers look for small, inexpensive changes to improve production processes.

continuous process Production process that uses long production runs without shutting down equipment.

contract Legal agreement, enforceable by law, that sets forth the relationship between parties regarding the performance of a specific action.

contractionary policy Monetary policy used to restrict the money supply and slow economic growth.

contract manufacturing Private-label manufacturing in which a foreign company produces goods to which the domestic firm attaches its brand name.

contractual distribution system Vertical marketing system consisting of a network of independent firms that coordinate their distribution activities by contractual agreement.

controlling Managerial activity of ensuring that the organization's goals are being met, by monitoring progress toward them and correcting deviations from the plan if necessary.

convenience products Relatively inexpensive products that require little shopping effort.

convertible bonds Bonds that may be exchanged for a specified number of shares of common stock.

cooperative Organization formed by individuals or businesses with similar interests to reduce costs and gain economic power through collective ownership.

copyright Grant of the exclusive right to use, produce, and sell an artistic creation, such as a piece of art, music, or literature.

corporate campaign Attempt to disrupt the business dealings of a firm with which a labor dispute is in progress.

corporate culture Set of attitudes, values, and standards of accepted behavior that distinguishes one organization from another.

corporate distribution system Vertical marketing system in which one firm owns the whole channel of distribution.

corporate restructuring Expanding or contracting a firm's operations or changing its ownership structure.

corporation Legal business entity with a life separate from its owners, which limits the owners' liability.

corrective advertising Advertising run to correct false impressions left by previous ads.

cost of capital The minimum rate of return the firm must earn on its investments to maintain its market value and attract investors.

cost of goods sold Total expense incurred in purchasing or producing a firm's goods or services.

cost-of-living adjustment (COLA) Automatic wage increase as the cost of living rises.

cost-push inflation Increase in prices caused by increases in production costs.

countertrade Trading arrangement in which part or all of the payment for goods or services is in the form of other goods or services.

coupons Price reductions designed to stimulate immediate sales.

CPM (cost per thousand) Rate at which advertising costs are quoted, figured per thousand members of an audience.

craft union Union that represents workers in a single craft or occupation.

credit life insurance Insurance that guarantees repayment of the amount due on a loan if the borrower dies.

credit unions Not-for-profit, member-owned financial cooperatives.

crisis management Scramble for answers to business problems within a short time frame.

critical path Longest path through the activities identified in the production process.

critical path method (CPM) Scheduling technique that breaks a project into a sequence of activities and estimates the total time needed to complete the project.

currency Cash held in the form of coins and paper money.

current assets Assets that can or will be converted to cash within the next twelve months.

current liabilities Debts due within one year of the date of the balance sheet on which they're listed.

current ratio Ratio of total current assets to total current liabilities; measures the firm's ability to pay current debts.

customs unions Associations with reduced tariff and nontariff barriers for member nations and with common policies for trade outside the union.

cyclical unemployment Unemployment caused by a downturn in the business cycle.

D

damages Money awarded to a party harmed by a breach of contract.

data Numerous facts that are part of an information system.

database software Software that organizes information so it can easily be sorted.

data processing system Part of an MIS system that updates the records in a database and processes large amounts of data into the information required by managers.

dealer brands Brands that carry the wholesaler's or retailer's name; private brands.

debentures Unsecured bonds.

debit cards Plastic cards used to transfer funds from a customer's bank account directly to a merchant's account in payment for goods and services.

debt Borrowed funds that must be repaid with interest over a stated period.

debt ratios Ratios that measure the degree and effect of the firm's use of debt to finance its operations.

debt-to-equity ratio Ratio of total liabilities to owners' equity; measures the relationship between the amount of debt financing and the amount of equity financing.

decentralization Practice of assigning considerable authority and decision-making freedom to lower-level managers.

decertification election Election that allows workers to end their representation by a union.

decision support system System that provides several kinds of decision-making information and allows its users to ask "what if" questions.

deductible Specified amount that the insured must pay before insurance benefits begin.

dehiring Method of termination in which the employer makes the job so unpleasant that the employee quits.

delegation Distribution of job duties and authority to subordinates.

demand Quantity of a good or service that people are willing to buy at various prices.

demand curve Graph of the relationship between quantity demanded and price.

demand deposits Money kept in bank checking accounts that can be withdrawn by depositors on demand.

demand-pull inflation Increase in prices that occurs when the demand for goods and services is greater than the supply.

demographic segmentation Division of a market by such variables as age, education, gender, income, and household size.

demography Study of vital statistics, such as ages, births, deaths, and locations of people.

departmentalization Grouping jobs under the authority of one manager for the purposes of planning, coordination, and control.

depreciation Process that allocates the original cost of a fixed asset to the years in which it is expected to generate revenues.

deregulation Removal of rules and regulations involving business competition.

design for disassembly (DFD) Making products with simple parts and materials so they are easy and cheap to take apart and recycle.

desktop publishing Using microcomputers to design and produce published materials, including both text and graphics.

detailing Physical stocking of merchandise by delivery personnel rather than store personnel.

devaluation Reduction of a currency's value relative to another.

differential advantage Set of unique features of a com- pany and its products that the target market perceives as important and better than the competition.

direct foreign investment Active ownership of a foreign company or foreign manufacturing or marketing facilities.

directing Managerial activity of guiding others to achieve specific objectives.

direct marketing (direct-response marketing) Variety of approaches, such as catalogs, direct mail, and telephone sales, used to promote a product and get an immediate response from the buyer.

disability insurance Insurance that provides monthly payments to people unable to work as a result of illness or accident.

discount rate Interest rate the Federal Reserve charges member banks to borrow from it.

discrimination Unfair and unequal treatment of certain classes of people.

distribution centers Warehouses that specialize in changing shipment sizes but do not store goods.

distribution channel Series of marketing organizations through which goods and services pass on their way from producers to end users.

distribution strategy Decisions about how to deliver a good or service to the consumer or industrial user.

diversification Combining securities that have different patterns and amounts of return.

divestiture Selling selected operating units for either strategic or financial reasons.

dividends The part of profits of a corporation that is distributed to stockholders.

dividend yield Measure used to assess the dividends paid on common stock; calculated by dividing the current annual dividend by the market price of the stock.

division of labor Process of dividing work and assigning tasks to workers.

double-entry bookkeeping System of bookkeeping in which every transaction changes two accounts or records.

Dow Jones Industrial Average (DJIA) Market average consisting of an average of the stock prices of thirty corporations listed on the New York Stock Exchange.

dumping Charging a lower price for a product (perhaps below cost) in foreign markets than at home.

E

earnings per share (EPS) Ratio of net profit to the number of shares of common stock outstanding; measures the number of dollars earned per outstanding share of common stock.

economic growth Increase in a nation's output of goods and services.

economics Study of how people use scarce or limited resources to produce and distribute goods and services.

economies of scale Tendency for the cost per unit to decrease when large quantities of the item are produced.

electronic funds transfer systems (EFTS) Networks of telephone lines and computers that help make financial transactions.

electronic mail (E-mail) Computer networks through which written messages are recorded and transmitted.

embargo Complete ban on importing a product into a country or exporting it to a foreign country.

employee associations Labor organizations whose members work in federal, state, county, and municipal government agencies.

employee-centered managers Managers who are more concerned about their subordinates than about the details of their group's tasks.

employee orientation program Training program designed to acquaint new employees with the company.

employee services "Extra" services offered by companies to improve employee morale and working conditions.

employment agencies Private firms that help match job applicants with job openings.

entrepreneur A person who takes the risk of starting and managing a business in order to make a profit; a risk taker who seeks profit by combining natural resources, labor, and capital to produce goods or services.

Equal Employment Opportunity Commission Federal agency that investigates and resolves charges of employment discrimination.

equilibrium Point at which quantity demanded equals quantity supplied.

equity Funds raised through the sale of ownership interests in a business.

equity theory Management theory that explains motivation as related to workers' perceptions of how fairly they are treated compared with coworkers.

esteem needs Needs for the respect of others and for a sense of accomplishment and achievement; fourth level in Maslow's hierarchy.

exchange Process in which two parties give something of value to each other to satisfy their needs.

exchange rate Value of one currency in terms of another.

excise taxes Taxes placed on specific items (such as gasoline and alcoholic beverages) by federal, state, or local governments.

exclusive dealing Illegal practice of refusing to allow a buyer to purchase a competitor's products for resale.

exclusive distribution Market coverage consisting of one or two dealers per area.

executive search firms Private firms that work mainly with employers to recruit people for middle- and top-management jobs.

expansionary policy Monetary policy used to increase the money supply and stimulate economic growth.

expectancy theory Management theory that motivation and job performance depend on how employers view their workers.

expense items Industrial products that are smaller and less expensive than capital products and typically have a life span of less than a year.

expenses Costs incurred by a business in the course of generating revenues.

expert system Computer system that gives managers advice like that they would get from a human consultant.

exports Goods and services sold to other countries.

express contract Contract whose terms are indicated by either written or spoken words.

express warranty Written guarantee of the quality of a good or service.

external financing Money raised from sources outside the firm.

F

factoring Outright sale of a firm's accounts receivable to a financial institution that will assume the risks and expenses of collecting the money owed.

factors of production Four basic inputs used by business: natural resources, labor, capital, and entrepreneurship.

Fair Labor Standards Act Federal law that sets the minimum wage.

Family and Medical Leave Act Federal law that requires employers to grant unpaid leave to certain employees for family and medical reasons.

federal budget deficit Shortfall when total expenditures for government programs exceed the revenues received from taxes.

Federal Deposit Insurance Corporation (FDIC) Corporation established in 1933 to insure the deposits of commercial banks.

federal funds Excess funds in a bank's Federal Reserve account that may be loaned for a short term to other banks.

federal funds rate Interest rate charged on the loan of federal funds.

Federal Reserve System (the Fed) Central banking system in the United States which prints money and controls the amount in circulation.

Federal Savings and Loan Insurance Corporation (FSLIC) Corporation that insured the deposits of savings and loan associations from 1934 to 1988, when it went bankrupt.

Federal Trade Commission Federal agency that oversees advertising of products sold across state lines.

finance companies Financial institutions that make short-term loans for which the borrower puts up tangible assets as security.

financial accounting Branch of accounting that prepares financial reports used by managers and outside parties.

Financial Accounting Standards Board (FASB) Seven-member board that establishes standards for accounting procedures.

financial intermediation Process in which financial institutions help the suppliers and demanders of funds make transactions.

financial management Determining the most effective ways to acquire and use funds to achieve the firm's goals.

financial risk Chance that the firm will be unable to make scheduled interest and principal payments on its debt.

first-in, first-out (FIFO) Inventory valuation method that assigns the cost of the earliest bought or produced goods to the items sold.

fiscal policy Government program of taxation and spending, which can be used to stimulate the economy.

fiscal year The 12-month period used by a firm for accounting purposes.

fixed assets Assets used by a firm for longer than a year.

fixed-cost contribution Selling price per unit (revenue) minus the variable costs per unit.

fixed costs Costs that do not vary with different levels of output.

fixed-position layout Facility layout in which the product stays in one place and workers and machinery move to it as needed.

flanker brand Product that uses a new brand name but is introduced into a product category in which the organization already has products.

flat organization structure Organization structure with a wide span of control, few managerial levels, and a short chain of command.

flexible manufacturing system (FMS) Manufacturing system that integrates computers, robots, machine tools, and materials- and parts-handling machinery.

flextime Work schedule in which employees work during a core period of the day and schedule the rest of their work hours as they please.

float Advantage gained from the time it takes a check to clear and the amount be withdrawn from the check writer's account.

focus groups Groups of people from target markets who are brought together to discuss products and other marketing ideas.

form utility Transforming a good or service into a more desirable or usable form.

forward integration Acquisition by a manufacturer of a middleman closer to the target market.

four p's The four elements of the marketing mix: product, price, promotion, and place.

fourth market Services that allow individual and institutional investors to buy and sell securities without using brokers, securities exchanges, or the National Association of Securities Dealers Automated Quotation (Nasdaq) system.

franchise agreement Contract authorizing the franchisee to use the franchisor's business name and its trademark and logo in exchange for specified payments.

franchise extension Product introduced in a new category using an existing brand name.

franchisee Individual or company that sells the franchised good or service in a certain area.

franchising Business arrangement between a company that supplies a good or service and the individual or company that sells the good or service in a specified area.

franchisor Company that supplies the franchised product.

free-rein (laissez-faire) leadership style Decision style in which managers turn over all authority and control to employees.

free trade The policy of permitting people of a country to buy and sell where they please, without government restriction.

free-trade zones Areas formed by trade associations in which there are few, if any, duties or rules to restrict trade among the partners.

frictional unemployment Short-term, voluntary unemployment, unrelated to the business cycle.

friendly merger Combining of firms in which the target company supports the proposal of the acquiring company.

fringe benefits Employee benefits beyond wages or salaries, including insurance, pensions, and paid sick leave.

full employment Having jobs for all who are willing and able to work.

full warranty Warranty that meets certain minimum federal standards, including repair or replacement of defective products.

functional authority Combination of line and staff authority in which specialists are given the authority to supervise some specialized area of activity.

futures contracts Agreements to buy or sell and deliver specific quantities of commodities or financial futures at an agreed price at a future date.

G

Gantt charts Scheduling technique that uses bar graphs plotted on a time line to show the relationship between scheduled and actual production.

General Agreement on Tariffs and Trade (GATT) Multinational agreement passed in 1947 to reduce tariffs and other barriers to international trade.

general and administrative expenses Business expenses that are neither cost of goods sold nor selling expenses.

general partners Those partners in a limited partnership who have unlimited liability.

general partnership Partnership in which all partners share in the management and profits.

generally accepted accounting principles (GAAP) Standardized rules of accounting for preparation of financial statements, established by the Financial Accounting Standards Board.

generic products Products that carry no brand name, come in plain containers, and sell for much less than brand-name products.

geographic segmentation Division of a market based on region of the country, city or county size, market density, or climate.

give-backs Worker benefits removed from union contracts.

glass ceiling A barrier of subtle discrimination that impedes upward movement.

goal orientation Idea that a firm should be consumer oriented only to the extent that being so also achieves corporate goals.

golden parachute strategy Promise of expensive compensation packages to managers if they lose their jobs in a takeover, intended to make a firm less attractive as a takeover target.

goods Tangible items manufactured by businesses.

grievance Formal complaint by an employee or a union that management has violated some part of the labor contract.

gross domestic product (GDP) Monetary value of all final goods and services produced within a nation annually.

gross profit (gross margin) Amount a firm earns after paying to produce or buy goods but before deducting operating expenses; the difference between net sales and the cost of goods.

gross sales Total dollar amount of a company's sales.

group cohesiveness Degree to which the members of a group want to remain in it and the tendency of group members to resist outside influences.

group insurance Private insurance coverage available to employees of a firm or government or to members of a trade association or similar organization.

Group of Seven (G7) The seven economic superpowers, who meet regularly to set broad economic policies.

H

hardware Machine component of a computerized information system.

Hawthorne effect Improved work performance resulting from an improved attitude.

health insurance Insurance that covers financial losses resulting from illness or injury.

health maintenance organizations (HMOs) Prepaid medical expense plans that offer subscribers complete and almost unlimited use of specified health care facilities and services for very low per-visit fees.

hierarchy of needs Sequence of five human needs, as proposed by Maslow—physiological, safety, social, esteem, and self-actualization needs.

high-yield, or junk, bonds High-risk, high-return bonds.

holding company Firm that holds the stock of various operating companies and may provide financial and administrative support but not be involved with day-to-day operations.

home and building insurance Insurance that protects property owners from both property and liability losses caused by a variety of perils.

horizontal merger Combining of firms in which companies in the same industry merge to improve operations.

hostile takeover Combining of firms in which the target company does not welcome the proposal of the acquiring company and tries to block the transaction.

human relations How people interact with one another and how managers interact with employees to make the organization and the employees more effective.

human-relations skills Skills used in working with people to accomplish the organization's goals.

human-resource management Process of hiring, developing, motivating, and evaluating people to achieve organizational goals.

human-resource planning Creating a strategy for meeting a firm's future human-resource needs.

I

implied contract Contract whose terms are indicated by the acts and conduct of the parties.

implied warranty Unwritten guarantee that a good or service is fit for the purpose for which it was sold.

import quota Limit on the quantity of certain goods that can be imported.

imports Goods and services bought from other countries.

income statement Summary of revenues and expenses, showing profit or loss.

income taxes Taxes based on the income received by businesses and individuals.

industrial distributors Independent wholesalers that buy related product lines from many manufacturers and sell them to industrial users.

industrial products Products bought for use in producing other goods and services, for operating a business, or for reselling to other organizations.

Industrial Revolution Massive shift from home-based industries to the factory system, which began in England in the mid-1700s and in the United States in the mid-1800s.

industrial union Union that represents workers in a single industry, regardless of their occupation or skill level.

inflation General upward movement of prices.

informal leaders Leaders who emerge from a group because they understand member concerns and can communicate these concerns to others.

informal organization Relationships within an organization that are based on friendship or circumstances, that result in informal channels of communication, and that do not show up on an organization chart.

information Data that have been processed into a meaningful and useful form.

information systems Methods and equipment that provide information about all aspects of a firm's operations.

injunction Court order banning certain activities.

innovative maturity Use of creative marketing strategies to prolong the life of a product.

insider trading Use of information that is not available to the public to make profits on securities transactions.

institutional advertising Advertising that creates a favorable picture of a company and its ideals, services, and roles in the community.

institutional investors Investment professionals who are paid to manage other people's money.

insurable interest Chance of suffering a loss if a particular peril occurs.

insurable risk Risk that an insurance company will cover.

insurance In return for a fee (premium), guaranteed compensation for financial losses that arise from specified conditions.

insurance policies Written agreements that specify the risks the insurer will bear for the insured, the benefits, and the premiums.

intangible assets Long-term assets, such as trademarks and patents, that have no physical existence.

intangible personal property Personal property that has no physical substance.

intensive distribution Market coverage in which a manufacturer's products are sold virtually everywhere.

interest Fixed amount of money that the issuer of a bond must pay bondholders; coupon rate.

intermittent process Production process that uses short production runs for batches of different products.

internal financing Profits reinvested in a business; retained earnings.

International Monetary Fund (IMF) International bank that gives short-term financing to countries with balance-of-trade problems.

international union Union with membership outside the United States.

intrapreneurs Creative, risk-taking individuals allowed to work as entrepreneurs within an organization.

inventory management Process of determining the right amount of inventory and of ordering, receiving, storing, and keeping track of it.

inventory turnover ratio Ratio of cost of goods sold to average inventory; measures the speed with which inventory is turned into sales.

investment Securities bought for their predictable levels of return and market values over the long term.

investment banker Organization that specializes in selling new security issues.

J

job analysis Study of the tasks required to do a job well.

job-centered managers Managers who direct their efforts toward what is necessary for completing a task.

job description List of the tasks and responsibilities of a job.

job enlargement Expansion of the number of tasks involved in a job so workers have more job satisfaction.

job enrichment Redesign of jobs to provide workers with greater authority, responsibility, and challenge and a chance for more personal achievement.

job evaluation Systematic comparison of jobs to determine reasonable pay rates.

job-maintenance factors According to Herzberg, aspects of the work environment, such as working conditions and salary, that are required to keep workers in a job.

job rotation Reassignment of workers to several different jobs over time.

job satisfiers According to Herzberg, job factors, such as recognition and responsibility, that motivate workers to work harder.

job specification List of the qualifications a person must have to fill a job.

joint venture Business owned by two or more firms or investors (or governments). Often formed to undertake a specific project.

journal Listing of financial transactions in chronological order.

judiciary Court system, which is responsible for settling disputes by applying and interpreting points of law.

just-in-time (JIT) system Inventory system that schedules materials to arrive just as they are needed.

K

key-person life insurance Term life insurance on the key employees of a firm, with the firm named as beneficiary.

Knights of Labor First major national labor organization, founded in 1869.

knowledge workers Highly trained employees who manage, use, or operate new technologies.

L

labor Economic contributions of people working with their minds and muscles.

labor union Organization that represents workers in labor disputes over wages, hours, and working conditions.

Landrum-Griffin Act Federal legislation passed in 1959 that dealt mostly with the internal affairs of labor unions, such as the rights of union members and rules for electing officers.

laptop (notebook) computers Portable computers smaller than desktop computers.

last-in, first-out (LIFO) Inventory valuation method that assigns the cost of the most recently bought or produced goods to the items sold.

law of large numbers Statistical principle that a predictable number of perils will occur in a large group.

laws Rules of conduct that are created and enforced by a controlling authority, usually the government.

layoff Temporary separation of an employee from a job, arranged by the employer.

leader pricing Pricing strategy of pricing products below the normal markup or even below cost to attract customers.

leadership Ability to influence and direct others to attain specific organizational goals.

leadership style Relatively consistent behavior pattern that characterizes a leader.

ledger Accounting record that contains all of a company's separate accounts.

leverage Use of debt to finance an investment and increase the company's rate of return.

leveraged buyouts (LBOs) Mergers financed by large amounts of borrowed money.

liabilities Debts; what a firm owes to its creditors.

liability insurance Insurance that covers financial losses from injuries to others and damage to or destruction of others' property when the insured is the cause.

licensing Agreement in which a firm (licensee) buys or rents the right to use the patent, trademark, production process, brand name, product, or company name of another firm (licensor).

life insurance Insurance that provides a specific amount of money to the insured person's beneficiary or estate upon his or her death.

limited liability company (LLC) Business entity that provides liability protection to its owners but is taxed like a partnership.

limited partners Those partners in a limited partnership whose liability is limited to the amount of their investment and who do not participate in day-to-day management of the firm.

limited partnership Partnership that has two types of partners—general and limited.

line-and-staff organization Organizational design that combines the direct flow of authority of a line organization with staff groups who support the line departments.

line authority Right to make decisions and issue orders about line functions.

line extension Product using an existing brand name in an existing category but produced in a new flavor, size, or model.

line of credit Agreement stating the maximum amount of unsecured short-term borrowing a firm may do during a given period if the bank has money to lend when the firm wants it.

line organization Organizational design with direct, clear lines of authority and communication flowing from the top managers downward.

liquidity Speed with which an asset can be converted to cash.

liquidity ratios Ratios that measure the firm's ability to pay its short-term debts as they come due.

lobbies Organizations that try to convince legislators to support the interests of their group.

local area network (LAN) Computer network connecting a group of computers within one work site, allowing them to exchange data and share hardware and software.

local union Branch of a national union, organized in a specific area or plant.

lockout Refusal by management to let workers enter a plant or building to work.

long-term forecasts Projections of the firm's financial activities over two to ten years; strategic plans.

long-term liabilities Debts that come due more than one year after the date of the balance sheet on which they're listed.

loss leader Product priced below cost.

M

M1 The basic money supply: currency held by the public, demand deposits, and traveler's checks.

M2 An expanded measure of money supply, including M1 plus most time deposits (those smaller than $100,000).

M3 The broadest measure of money supply, consisting of M2 plus large time deposits (certificates of deposit over $100,000).

machine language Binary codes (0 and 1) used to store data in a computer's main memory.

macroeconomics Study of the economy as a whole.

mainframe computers Computers typically housed in several large cabinets, which usually require specially built rooms.

make-or-buy decision Question of whether a firm should make the parts needed in manufacturing its products or buy them from outside sources.

managed care programs Health insurance programs that monitor medical treatment and limit the choice of doctors.

management Process of coordinating a firm's human and other resources to accomplish its goals.

management by objectives (MBO) Program in which employees help set goals for their own performance and at specified intervals check their performance against the goals.

management information system (MIS) Computer system that collects and stores key data and produces information needed by managers for analysis, control, and decision making.

management reporting system System that uses collected data to produce decision-making information in the form of reports.

managerial accounting Branch of accounting that provides information used by a firm's managers to evaluate and make operating decisions.

managerial hierarchy Levels of management within the organization: top, middle, supervisory.

managers Employees of a firm who are responsible for coordinating resources.

manufacturer brands Brands owned by national or regional manufacturers and widely distributed; also called national brands.

manufacturers Firms that convert raw materials and component parts to finished products.

manufacturers' representatives (manufacturers' agents) People who represent noncompeting manufacturers and function independently rather than as salaried employees of the manufacturers.

manufacturers' sales branches Wholesalers owned and completely controlled by a manufacturer.

manufacturing resource planning (MRPII) Computerized system that integrates data from many departments and generates management reports.

margin requirements Minimum percentage of the value of securities that must be paid in cash by an investor, as determined by the Federal Reserve.

marine insurance Insurance that protects goods in transit as well as movable personal property.

marketable securities Short-term investments that can easily be converted into cash, such as Treasury bills, certificates of deposit, and commercial paper.

market averages Numbers used to measure the general behavior of the market, by using the arithmetic average price behavior of a group of securities at a given point in time.

market coverage Numbers of dealers used to distribute a product in a particular area.

market indexes Numbers used to measure the price behavior of a group of securities relative to a base value and give a general measure of the performance of the market.

marketing Process of planning and executing the conception, pricing, promotion, and distribution of ideas, goods, and services to create exchanges that satisfy individual and organizational objectives.

marketing concept Idea that a firm first identifies consumer needs and then produces goods or services that satisfy them.

marketing mix Blend of product offering, pricing, promotional methods, and distribution system that will reach a specific group of consumers.

marketing research Collecting, recording, and analyzing data important in marketing goods and services and communicating the resulting information to management.

market segmentation Process of separating, identifying, and evaluating the layers of a market in order to design a marketing mix.

markup pricing Addition of a certain percentage to a product's cost to arrive at a new price.

mass production Ability to produce many goods at once.

master limited partnership (MLP) Partnership that is taxed like a partnership, operates like a corporation, and has units publicly traded on a stock exchange.

materials requirement planning (MRP) Computerized information system for controlling inventory by comparing forecasts of production needs to inventory on hand.

matrix organization Permanent organization structure that brings people from different departments to work on special projects.

mechanization Use of machines for work previously done by people.

mediation Method of settling disputes whereby the parties present their case to a neutral mediator but are not bound by the mediator's decision. Often used to help bring about concession and compromise during labor disputes (between unions and management).

Medicare Social Security health insurance program for those over sixty-five.

mentoring Teaching a newer, younger employee about the firm.

merchant wholesalers Independent wholesalers that buy products from manufacturers on their own account and then resell them to other businesses.

merger Combination of two or more firms to form one new company, which often has a new corporate identity.

microcomputers Computers small enough to fit on an office desk; also called personal computers (PCs) and desktop computers.

microeconomics Study of particular markets.

middle managers Managers who are concerned with implementing the plans and policies of top managers and who oversee lower-level managers.

minicomputers Computers about the size of a file cabinet, too large to fit on a desktop but small enough to fit in a typical office.

mission General purpose or reason for an organization's existence.

mixed economies Economies that use more than one economic system, typically capitalism and socialism.

modem Hardware that connects a computer to a phone line so users in different locations can transfer data.

monetary policy Government programs for controlling the amount of money in circulation in a nation's economy.

money Anything, regardless of form, that is acceptable as payment for goods and services.

money market deposit accounts Savings accounts that allow limited check writing, earn interest at market rates, and are subject to minimum balance requirements.

monopolistic competition Form of capitalism in which a large number of firms offer products that are close but not identical substitutes and entry is relatively easy.

morale Mental attitude toward work and people.

mortgage bonds Bonds secured by a specific property of the issuing corporation.

mortgage loan Long-term loan secured by real estate as collateral.

motivation Stimulation and direction of behavior through encouragement, incentives, and reinforcement.

multiculturalism The recognition and acceptance of a variety of cultures that are roughly equally represented in a particular region.

multinational corporations Corporations that move resources, goods, services, and skills across national boundaries without regard to the country in which they are headquartered.

municipal bonds Bonds are issued by states, cities, counties, and other state and local government agencies.

mutual-aid pact Pooling of resources within an industry to help cover the costs of a member company whose workers go on strike.

mutual fund Financial service organization that pools the proceeds from selling its shares and invests them in a varied collection of securities.

mutual insurance companies Not-for-profit insurance companies owned collectively by their policyholders.

N

National Advertising Division (NAD) Division of the Council of Better Business Bureaus that handles advertising complaints from consumers and advertisers.

National Advertising Review Board (NARB) Group to which deadlocked or unsatisfactory cases from the NAD can be appealed.

National Association of Securities Dealers Automated Quotation (Nasdaq) system Telecommunications system that links OTC dealers with one another and with securities brokers.

national bank Bank chartered by the U.S. Treasury Department.

National Credit Union Administration (NCUA) Corporation established in 1934 to insure credit union deposits.

national debt Cumulative total of past budget deficits, minus any surpluses.

national health insurance Federally sponsored health insurance plan for citizens.

nationalism Sense of national consciousness that puts the interests of one's country ahead of international considerations.

National Labor Relations Board (NLRB) Federal agency that investigates charges of unfair labor practices and supervises union certification elections.

national union Group of many unions in a particular industry, skilled trade, or geographic area.

natural resources Commodities that are useful inputs in their natural state.

needs theory of motivation Theory that people act to satisfy their unmet needs.

negotiated order of withdrawal (NOW) account Interest-bearing checking account that can be held by individuals, but not businesses, and that is subject to service fees and minimum balance requirements.

net asset value (NAV) The price at which each share of a mutual fund can be bought or sold.

net loss Amount by which expenses exceed revenues.

net profit Amount by which revenues exceed expenses; net income.

net profit margin Ratio of net profit to net sales; measures the percentage of each sales dollar remaining after all expenses have been deducted.

net sales Dollar amount left after deducting sales discounts and returns and allowances from gross sales.

networking Using informal contacts inside and outside an organization.

net working capital Difference between total current assets and total current liabilities; measures the firm's overall liquidity.

networks Terminals, computers, and other equipment that use communications channels to share data.

new product Product that has a new brand name but is introduced into a product category new to the organization.

no-fault automobile insurance Insurance that covers the insured's financial losses resulting from automobile accidents regardless of who was responsible for the accident.

nominal GDP Measure of GDP that uses current market prices.

norms Standards of behavior or performance.

Norris-LaGuardia Act Federal legislation passed in 1932 that ended the use of injunctions by employers and declared yellow-dog contracts unenforceable.

North American Free Trade Agreement (NAFTA) Treaty that eliminates trade barriers among the United States, Canada, and Mexico.

notepad computers The smallest, handheld computers.

O

objectives Measurable targets to be achieved within a certain time frame.

Occupational Safety and Health Act Federal law that requires employers to provide a workplace free of health and safety hazards.

odd-even pricing Setting a price below the next whole number to influence consumers' perceptions of a product.

odd lots Blocks of fewer than 100 shares of stock.

office automation system Tools—such as word processing, E-mail, or fax—used by a company for better communication.

Office of Federal Contract Compliance Programs Federal agency that polices firms with U.S. government contracts to make sure job applicants and employees get fair treatment.

officers High-level employees of a corporation, who are responsible for implementing corporate goals and policies.

off-the-job training Employment training that takes place away from the job site.

oligopoly Form of capitalism in which a few firms produce most of the output and large capital requirements limit the number of firms.

on-line processing Updating a database by processing each transaction when the data about it become available.

on-the-job training Employment training that takes place at the job site and tends to be directly related to the job.

open market operations Purchase and sale of U.S. government bonds by the Federal Reserve.

open shop Place of employment where workers do not have to join the union nor pay a fee.

operating budgets Forecasts of profits, which combine sales forecasts with estimates of production costs and operating expenses.

operating expenses Expenses of operating a business that are not directly related to the production or purchase of its products.

operating system Collection of system software instructions.

operations management Managing the conversion process that turns inputs into goods and services.

options Contracts that entitle their holders to buy or sell specified quantities of financial instruments at a set price during a specified time.

order cycle time Time between placing an order and receiving the order in good condition.

organizational behavior Human behavior in an organized setting.

organization chart Depiction of the relationships among tasks and those given authority to do those tasks in a formal organization.

organized stock exchanges Places where securities are bought and sold.

organizing Managerial activity of arranging a firm's human and material resources to carry out its plans.

over-the-counter (OTC) market Telecommunications network that links securities dealers throughout the United States for the purpose of buying and selling securities.

owners' equity Total amount of the owners' investment in the firm, less any liabilities; net worth.

P

parent company Firm that controls most or all of another corporation's stock.

participative leadership style Decision style in which managers share decision making with group members through a democratic process, consensus, or consultation.

partnership Association of two or more persons as co-owners of a business.

partnership agreement Written statement of the terms and conditions of a partnership.

patent Grant of the exclusive right to manufacture, use, and sell an invention for seventeen years.

payroll taxes Employer's share of Social Security taxes and federal and state unemployment taxes.

penetration pricing Pricing strategy of selling a new product at a low price in the hope of achieving large sales volume.

pension funds Pools of money set aside to pay retirement benefits to corporate or government employees or to union members.

Pension Reform Act Federal law that protects the retirement income of employees and retirees.

pensions Retirement income paid to former workers.

perfect (pure) competition Form of capitalism in which a large number of small firms sell similar products, buyers and sellers have good information about the market, and entry or exit is easy.

performance appraisals Comparisons of actual and expected performance, used to make decisions about compensation, promotion, and other job changes.

perpetual inventory Continuously updated list of inventory levels, orders, sales, and receipts for all major items of a firm's inventory.

personal property Movable property, such as inventory, furnishings, and machinery.

personal selling Face-to-face sales presentation to a prospective customer.

physical distribution All business activities concerned with transporting raw materials, component parts, and finished inventory so they arrive at a designated place when needed and in usable condition.

physiological needs Most basic human needs for food, shelter, and clothing; first level of needs in Maslow's hierarchy.

picketing Union weapon in which union members form a line in front of an employer's site and try to persuade others to stop doing business with the firm.

piecework payment Method of payment in which employees are paid by the amount they produce.

place utility Having a good or service where consumers would like to buy or use it.

planning Managerial activity of deciding what needs to be done, how, when, and by whom.

point-of-purchase (POP) displays Promotional devices designed to stimulate immediate sales.

poison pill strategy Defense against hostile takeover in which the target firm acts to make itself less desirable for acquisition.

political skills Ability of a manager to get enough power to reach his or her goals.

possession utility Making it possible for consumers to complete a transaction and gain the right to use the product.

power The ability to influence others to take action.

preferential tariff Tariff that offers advantages to one nation (or several) over other nations.

preferred provider organization (PPO) Form of health care coverage that offers complete health care services to its subscribers within a network of physicians and hospitals.

preferred stock Form of equity capital that gives preferential treatment to holders over owners of common stock and pays fixed dividends.

premiums Gifts or prizes to consumers who buy a product, which add value to the purchase.

prestige pricing Raising the price of a product so consumers will perceive it as being of higher quality, status, or value.

price Perceived value that is exchanged for something else.

price discrimination Illegal practice of offering a customer discounts that are not offered to all other purchasers buying on similar terms.

price/earnings (P/E) ratio Relationship between the current market price of a stock and its earnings per share; calculated by dividing the price by earnings per share.

price skimming Pricing strategy of charging a high introductory price for a new product.

pricing strategy Decisions about how to price a good or service, determined by demand and by cost.

primary boycott Effort to keep people from buying the products of a firm with which the union has a dispute.

primary data Research data collected directly from the original source for the current project.

primary market Market in which new securities are sold to the public.

prime rate of interest Base rate charged by banks for short-term commercial loans to their most credit-worthy business borrowers.

principal Borrowed amount of money, on which the issuer of a bond pays interest; par value.

principle of comparative advantage Idea that all countries will benefit from producing and trading what each can produce best.

private accountants Accountants employed within business organizations.

privately owned firm Firm whose common stock is not available to the general public.

proactive managers Managers who anticipate problems, threats, and opportunities and take advance action.

process layout Facility layout that groups together all workers who perform similar tasks and moves products from one work station to another.

producer price index (PPI) Index that measures the prices paid by producers and wholesalers for commodities.

product Any want-satisfying good or service, along with its perceived tangible and intangible attributes and benefits.

product advertising Advertising of a specific good or service.

product (assembly-line) layout Facility layout in which work stations or departments are arranged in a line, through which products pass in sequence.

production Creation of goods and services by converting inputs to outputs.

production control Coordination of materials, equipment, and human resources to achieve production efficiency.

production orientation Idea that the firm should produce what it does best and then aggressively try to sell the product, based primarily on price.

productivity Output of goods and services per unit of labor.

product liability Liability of manufacturers and sellers for defects in the products they make and sell.

product-liability insurance Insurance that covers financial losses incurred by producers or sellers of goods or services due to injury or damage resulting from the use of the covered product.

product life cycle Series of stages in a product's sales and profits over a period of time, consisting of introduction, growth, maturity, and decline (and death).

product strategy Decisions about specific elements of a product or service, such as brand names, packaging, warranty, and service.

professional liability insurance Insurance that covers financial losses resulting from alleged malpractice in the performance of the insured's professional services.

profit Reward to businesses for providing what consumers are willing to buy.

profitability ratios Ratios that measure the profitability of the firm.

profit maximization Production of units of output for as long as the revenue from selling them is greater than the cost of producing them.

programs Instructions, prepared in advance, that allow computers to work continuously.

program trading Use of computers to monitor security prices and trading volumes and to automatically buy or sell stocks when certain conditions exist.

project management Temporary organization structure that brings together people from various parts of a company to work on a special project.

promotion Marketing activity that stimulates demand for a firm's goods or services; upward move in an organization to a position with more authority, responsibility, and pay.

promotional mix Combination of advertising, personal selling, sales promotion, and public relations used to promote a product.

promotional strategy Plan for informing, persuading, or reminding the target market about a good or service to stimulate action.

promotion strategy Decisions about how to advertise and sell a good or service.

property Rights and interests in anything that can be owned.

property insurance Insurance that covers financial losses from damage to or destruction of the insured's assets.

property law Law covering the ownership, use, and sale of property.

property taxes Taxes imposed by state and local governments on real and personal property.

prospecting Looking for sales prospects.

protected classes Specific groups of people with legal protection against employment discrimination under various federal laws.

protectionism The policy of protecting home industries from outside competition through the setting of trade barriers.

protective tariff Tax levied on imports to make them less attractive to buyers than domestic goods.

psychographic segmentation Division of a market based on personality or lifestyle.

psychological contract Unwritten expectations of an employee or an employer.

public accountants Independent accountants who provide accounting services to organizations and individuals for a fee.

publicity Information about a company or product that appears in the news media and is not directly paid for by the company.

public relations Any communication or activity intended chiefly to win goodwill or prestige for a company or person.

publicly owned firm Firm whose common stock is owned by a broad group of unrelated investors.

pull strategy Manufacturer's attempt to stimulate consumer demand to get wider distribution of a product.

purchasing power Value of what money can buy.

pure monopoly Form of capitalism in which a single firm accounts for all of an industry's sales.

push strategy Manufacturer's use of aggressive personal selling and advertising to convince a wholesaler or retailer to carry its merchandise.

Q

qualifying questions Questions used by salespeople to find genuine sales prospects.

quality circles Technique that brings together small groups of employees to discuss, analyze, and recommend solutions to quality problems in their area.

quality control Creating quality standards and measuring finished goods or services against those standards.

quality-of-work-life programs Processes and techniques designed to enhance job performance and commitment to the organization.

quasi-public corporation Business operated and often subsidized by a unit of local, state, or federal government.

R

rank-and-file Union members who are not elected officials.

ratio analysis Calculation and interpretation of financial ratios to assess a firm's financial performance and condition.

reactive managers Managers who do not respond to problems until the damage has been done.

real GDP Measure of GDP that adjusts for price changes.

real property Land and everything permanently attached to it, such as buildings; real estate.

recession Period of decline in GDP that lasts six months or longer.

recruitment Attempt to find and attract qualified applicants in the external labor market.

reengineering The redesign of business processes to improve operations.

reminder advertising Advertising used to keep the product name in the public's mind.

repetitive process Production process that uses pre-assembled modules.

reserve requirement Percentage of deposits that member banks of the Federal Reserve must hold in reserve.

resignation Voluntary departure of an employer from a job.

responsibility Obligation to perform delegated duties and to handle one's assigned authority.

responsible consumption Efficient use of resources by consumers and businesses with a view to the future.

restitution Remedy to breach of contract in which the contract is canceled and the situation is restored to its precontract status.

retailers Firms that sell goods to consumers and to industrial users for their own consumption.

retained earnings Total profits of a firm since its beginning minus all dividends paid to stockholders.

retirement Permanent separation of an employee from the company, usually at the end of his or her career.

return The opportunity for profit.

return on equity (ROE) Ratio of net profit to total owners' equity; measures the rate of return that owners receive on their investment.

revenues Dollar amount of sales plus any other income received from other sources.

revolving credit agreement Guaranteed line of credit.

rights offerings Direct sales of new issues of common stock by the issuing corporation to its existing stockholders.

right-to-work laws State laws that allow employees to work at a unionized company without having to join the union.

risk The potential for loss, or the chance that an investment will not achieve the expected level of return.

risk assumption Bearing a risk without insurance; self-insurance.

risk avoidance Staying away from situations that can lead to loss.

risk management Analyzing a firm's operations, evaluating the potential risks, and forming strategies to minimize losses.

risk reduction Reducing or eliminating the potential for financial loss.

risk-return trade-off Idea that the higher the risk of an investment is, the greater the return that is required.

risk transference Paying someone else to bear some or all of the risk of financial loss.

robots Computer-controlled machines programmed to perform tasks independent of human control.

round lots Blocks of 100 shares of stock.

S

S corporation Business entity that provides limited liability to its stockholders but whose profits and losses are taxed as the personal income of the stockholders.

safety needs Needs for security, protection from physical harm, and avoidance of the unexpected; second level in Maslow's hierarchy.

salary Payment to managerial and professional employees, set through job evaluation and not tied to any specific number of work hours.

sales contracts Contracts for the transfer of goods from a seller to a buyer for a specified price.

sales leads Inquiries about a firm's products generated by the firm's advertising and promotion.

sales promotions Marketing events or sales efforts—other than advertising, personal selling, and public relations—that stimulate consumer buying.

sales prospects Companies and people most likely to buy a salesperson's offerings.

sales taxes Taxes imposed by states, counties, and cities on goods when they are sold; calculated as a percentage of the sales price.

samples Free gifts of a product that are distributed to consumers to gain public acceptance of the product.

savings and loan associations (S&Ls) Type of thrift institution chartered by either the federal government or a state government.

Savings Association Insurance Fund (SAIF) Corporation established after the demise of the FSLIC to insure thrift institutions.

savings banks State-chartered thrift institutions that tend to make fewer residential real estate loans and more stock and bond investments than S&Ls do.

screening Checking new ideas against the firm's new-product goals and long-range strategies.

seasonal unemployment Periodic unemployment caused by seasonal variations in certain industries.

secondary boycott Boycott of companies doing business with a firm that is the subject of a primary boycott.

secondary data Research data collected for a project other than the current one.

secondary market Market in which already-issued securities are bought and sold.

secured bonds Corporate bonds that pledge specific assets as collateral.

secured loans Loans that require the borrower to pledge specific assets as collateral, or security.

securities Certificates issued by corporations or governments that represent either equity or debt investments.

selective credit controls Power of the Federal Reserve to regulate credit terms on certain types of loans made by banks and other institutions.

selective distribution Market coverage consisting of a limited number of dealers (but more than one or two) per area.

self-actualization needs Needs for fulfillment, for living up to one's potential, and for using one's capabilities to the highest degree; fifth and highest level in Maslow's hierarchy.

self-insurance Assuming risk against certain types of losses rather than buying insurance.

selling expenses Expenses directly related to marketing and distributing the company's products.

seniority Length of an employee's continuous service with a firm.

separation Employee's leave-taking, due to resignation, layoff, termination, or retirement.

servicemark Legally exclusive symbol, name, or design that identifies a service in the marketplace.

services Intangible items provided by organizations for their customers.

shopping products Products that are bought after a brand-to-brand and store-to-store comparison.

shop stewards Elected union officials who represent union members to management when workers have complaints.

short-term forecasts Projections of revenues, costs of goods, and operating expenses over a one-year period; operating plans.

sick-out Union weapon in which members claim they are not working because of illness.

single-payment note One-time loan repaid in a lump sum at the loan's maturity date; a form of short-term financing.

single-source research Marketing research that monitors the promotion that panel members are exposed to and what they buy.

small business Business that is owned by an individual or small group of investors, independently managed, locally based, and of little influence in its industry; its size may vary, from fewer than 500 to fewer than 100 employees.

Small Business Administration (SBA) Main government agency that helps small businesses through a broad range of activities.

social audit Systematic assessment of company activities that have social impact.

socialism Economic system in which the basic industries are owned by the government or by the private sector under strong government control.

socialization Process by which a new group member learns the basic goals of the group and the preferred means of achieving these goals.

social marketing Application of marketing theories and techniques to social issues and causes.

social needs Needs for belonging (acceptance by others) and for giving and receiving friendship and love; third level in Maslow's hierarchy.

social responsibility Concern of businesses for the welfare of society as a whole.

Social Security Federal insurance program that provides retirement, disability, death, and health insurance benefits, funded by equal contributions from workers and employers.

software Program of instructions that make computers perform.

sole proprietorships Businesses established, owned, operated, and often financed by a single individual.

span of control The number of employees reporting directly to a manager.

specialization Division of the production process into the smallest possible activities so that each worker performs only one task.

specialization of labor Dividing the firm's primary task into subunits that can be repeated easily and efficiently.

specialty products Products for which consumers search long and hard and for which they refuse to accept substitutes.

specific performance Court-ordered remedy to a breach of contract, requiring the party breaching the contract to perform the duties specified in it.

speculation Securities bought for high returns within a short time.

speculative risk Chance of either loss or gain.

spreadsheet software Software that automatically calculates rows and columns of numbers.

staff authority Right to advise and assist line managers and staff people.

staff personnel People in an organization who provide advice and specialized support services to line personnel.

Standard & Poor's 500 stock index Broad market index that includes 500 stocks listed on the New York Stock Exchange, the American Stock Exchange, and the over-the-counter market.

standardization Use of interchangeable parts.

standard of living Per-person level of material well-being of a country; measured by its output of goods and services divided by its total population.

state bank Bank chartered by the state in which it is based.

statement of cash flows Financial statement that summarizes the amounts of money flowing into and out of a firm.

statistical quality control (SQC) System that uses statistical techniques to test for quality.

statutory law Written law enacted by legislatures.

stockbroker Person licensed to buy and sell securities on behalf of clients.

stock dividends Payments to existing stockholders of a dividend in the form of stock rather than cash.

stockholders Owners of a corporation, who hold shares of stock that provide certain rights; sometimes called shareholders.

stock insurance companies Profit-oriented insurance companies owned by stockholders.

stock-purchase options Employee rights to buy a set number of shares of the firm's stock at a fixed price by a certain time.

strategic planning Creation of long-range, comprehensive objectives and development of long-term courses of action and allocation of resources to achieve those objectives.

strict liability Liability of a manufacturer or seller for any personal injuries or property damage caused by defective products or packaging, even if care has been used to prevent such defects.

strike Temporary work stoppage.

strikebreakers Nonunion employees hired to replace striking union workers; also called scabs.

structural unemployment Involuntary unemployment caused by the mismatch between available jobs and the skills of available workers.

subsidiary Corporation whose stock is largely or totally controlled by another firm.

supercomputers Specialized computers, of varying size, that very quickly compute complex scientific problems.

supervisors Lowest level of managers, responsible for managing operating employees.

supply Quantity of a good or service that businesses will make available at various prices.

supply curve Graph of the relationship between quantity supplied and price.

sweepstakes Consumer competitions whose winners are picked on the basis of chance.

sympathy strike Strike mounted by workers not directly involved in a collective bargaining dispute to support strikers who are directly involved.

system software Program that supports application software with instructions needed by all applications.

T

tactical planning Short-range, detailed planning based on strategic planning decisions.

Taft-Hartley Act Federal legislation passed in 1947 that prohibited unions from engaging in unfair practices.

tall organization structure Organization structure with a narrow span of control, many managerial levels, and a long chain of command.

tangible personal property Personal property that has physical substance.

target market Specific group of consumers toward which a firm directs its marketing efforts.

target return on investment Pricing objective in which the price is set to give the company the desired profitability in terms of return on its money.

tariff Tax levied by a nation on imported goods.

tax accounting Branch of accounting that develops tax strategies, prepares tax returns, and assesses the tax consequences of business deals.

technical skills Specialized knowledge and ability that a person brings to a job.

tender offer Direct offer to buy some or all of a target company's stock at a price above the market price.

termination Permanent separation of an employee from a job, arranged by the employer.

term life insurance Life insurance that covers the insured's life for a fixed amount and a specific period.

term loan Business loan with a maturity of more than one year.

theft insurance Insurance that protects businesses against losses from an act of stealing.

Theory X Management theory that assumes people do not like to work and that managers must closely control workers' behavior.

Theory Y Management theory that assumes people like to work and that they will do so when managers encourage learning and self-development.

Theory Z Management theory that combines U.S. and Japanese management styles.

thrift institutions Financial institutions (savings banks and savings and loan associations) that offer savings accounts and interest-bearing checking accounts.

time deposits Money kept on deposit at banks that earns interest but cannot be withdrawn on demand.

time utility Having a good or service available when consumers want it.

top managers Relatively small group of managers at the head of an organization.

tort Private act that harms people or their property.

total cost Sum of total variable costs plus total fixed costs.

total profit Total revenue minus total cost.

total quality management (TQM) The application of quality principles to all aspects of a company's operations to achieve greater efficiency and profitability.

total revenue Selling price per unit times the number of units sold.

trade credit Credit extended to the buyer by the seller of products; a form of short-term financing entered as an account payable.

trade deficit An excess of imports over exports.

trademark Legally exclusive design, name, or other distinctive mark that a manufacturer uses to identify its products in the marketplace.

trademark Legally exclusive design, name, or other identifying mark associated with a company's brand.

trade shows Meetings that give manufacturers and wholesalers the chance to display their products to a large audience of potential buyers at a relatively low cost.

trade surplus An excess of exports over imports.

transfer Sideways move in an organization to a position with about the same salary and at about the same level.

trial balance Summary of ledger totals for each account, used to confirm the accuracy of the accounting figures.

trial courts Courts of general jurisdiction; found in both the state and federal judiciaries.

tying contracts Illegal contracts that require buyers to purchase merchandise they may not want in order to get the products they do want.

U

umbrella personal liability insurance Insurance that increases the amount of liability coverage above the amount paid by a homeowner's policy.

unbundling Pricing strategy of reducing the bundle of services that accompany a basic product.

underwriting Reviewing insurance policy applications and choosing those that meet the company's risk criteria; the process, undertaken by investment bankers, of buying securities from corporations and reselling them to the public.

unemployment insurance State insurance program that pays laid-off workers weekly benefits while they seek new jobs.

unemployment rate Percentage of the total labor force that is not working but actively looking for work.

unfair labor practices Measures designed to keep workers from joining a union; banned by the Wagner Act.

Uniform Commercial Code (UCC) Model statute that sets forth rules applying to commercial transactions between businesses and between individuals and businesses.

union certification election Election, by secret ballot, that determines whether workers want to be represented by a union.

union shop Place of employment where nonunion people can be hired but must join the union within a specified period.

United Europe Trade agreement of the European Community that standardizes trade rules and taxes.

unity of command Principle that everyone in an organization reports to and gets instructions from only one boss.

universal life insurance Combination of term life insurance and a tax-deferred savings plan in which premiums are invested and earn, in effect, interest.

unsecured loans Loans obtained without the borrower's pledge of specific assets as security.

utility Ability of a good or service to satisfy consumer desires.

V

value marketing Offering the target market a product or service of high quality at a fair price and with good customer service.

variable costs Costs that change with different levels of output.

variable life insurance Combination of life insurance and a savings plan in which the policyholder can designate how much of the premium should be allocated for insurance and how much should be invested.

venture capital Financing obtained, typically by a small, growing firm, from investors that provide money in exchange for stock and a voice in management of the company.

vertical marketing system Planned, organized, formalized distribution channel.

vertical merger Combining of firms in which a company acquires a firm in the same industry that is involved in an earlier or later stage of the production or sales process.

vestibule training Off-the-job training in which trainees learn on the actual equipment they will use or on models of it.

virtual corporation Network of independent companies linked to share skills, costs, and market access.

volume segmentation Division of a market based on the amount of product bought.

voting rights Right of common stockholders to cast one vote for each share of stock owned.

W

wages Payments to lower-level employees based on the number of hours worked.

Wagner Act Federal legislation passed in 1935 that allowed the formation of unions and provided for certification elections.

warranty Guarantee of the quality of a good or service.

wellness programs Company-sponsored programs that help employees in personal areas of their lives.

white knight strategy Defense against hostile takeover in which the target firm finds a more suitable acquirer.

whole life insurance Life insurance that covers the insured's life for his or her whole life and that accumulates savings; straight life insurance.

wholesalers Firms that sell finished goods to retailers, manufacturers, and institutions.

wide area network (WAN) Computer network connecting computers at different work sites, allowing them to exchange data and share hardware and software.

wildcat strike Strike by local members of a national union while the labor contract is in effect, in violation of the contract.

word processing Using microcomputers to write, edit, and format documents.

workers' compensation Insurance, required of employers, that covers job-related injuries and diseases.

work groups Groups created to accomplish a specific task.

World Bank International bank that offers developing nations low-interest-rate loans to help build infrastructure and relieve debt.

Y

yellow-dog contracts Agreements by employees that, as a condition of being hired, they would not join a labor union; declared unenforceable by the Norris-LaGuardia Act.

COMPANY INDEX

SUBJECT INDEX

PHOTO ACKNOWLEDGMENTS

For permission to reproduce the photographs on the pages indicated, acknowledgment is made to the following:

215   © 1992 Alan Levenson
219   © Michael Tamborrino/Leo de Wys, Inc.
225   Courtesy of McDonald's
228   *(left and right)* KFC Corporation
238   © Ilene Ehrlich

Part 4   © Todd Joyce
242   © Todd Joyce
246   © Andy Sacks/Tony Stone Images
248   Photo by John Swart, 1991/ALLSPORT USA
252   © 1990 Ron Chapple/FPG International
256   © Joe McNally. All Rights Reserved.
259   *(left)* © 1990 Lou Jones/The Image Bank;
       (right) © Peter Sibbald/Sygma
263   © John Abbott
272   © Todd Joyce
275   © Doug Milner
284   Reuters/Bettmann
290   © James Schnepf
293   Photo Courtesy of 3M
300   © Todd Joyce
302   Photo Courtesy of ALCOA
307   © 1993 Steve Winter/Black Star
308   © Randy Olson
312   © John Warden/Tony Stone Images
318   Courtesy of International Business Machines
       Corporation
321   The Cincinnati Museum of Natural History
325   The Ritz-Carlton is a federally registered trademark
       of The Ritz-Carlton Hotel Company
337   © 1988 Gabe Palmer/Photo Network

Part 5   © Todd Joyce
340   © Todd Joyce
343   © Bruce Ayres/Tony Stone Images
344   Courtesy of A.T. & T. Archives
350   © Charles Gupton/Tony Stone Images
353   © Farnsworth/The Image Works
355   © 1994 Jim Henson Productions
360   © Rob Kinmonth
368   © Todd Joyce
370   © Greg Pease/Tony Stone Images
374   © Michael Newman/PhotoEdit
381   © Amy C. Etra/PhotoEdit
388   © 1991 Walter Bibikow/The Image Bank
395   © Myrleen Ferguson Cate/PhotoEdit
400   Johnson & Johnson
406   © Todd Joyce
410   UPI/Bettmann Newsphotos
422   © Charles Gupton/Tony Stone Images
425   © 1989 Randy Taylor/Gamma Liaison
436   Photo Network

Part 6   © Todd Joyce
440   © Todd Joyce
443   Dominos Pizza Inc.
450   © Bob Daemmrich/Uniphoto Picture Agency
455   Outdoor Advertising Association of America
458   © John Coletti/Stock, Boston Inc.
468   © Todd Joyce
470   © 1993 Philip Bailey/The Stock Market
481   © Peter Yates/SABA
493   © 1992 Peter Beck/The Stock Market

502   © Todd Joyce
508   © Andy Sacks/Tony Stone Images
510   Jaguar 1994 (Model)
518   © Elliott Kaufman
530   © Todd Joyce
533   © Seth Resnick/Stock, Boston, Inc.
537   BMW of North America Inc.
545   Photography by Alan Brown/Photonics
549   LEGO Systems, Inc.
562   © 1991 Michael Krasowitz/FPG International

Part 7   © Todd Joyce
566   © Todd Joyce
570   PI Systems Corporation
575   Courtesy of International Business Machines
       Corporation
580   © 1994 David Fields
586   Photography by Alan Brown/Photonics
594   © Todd Joyce
596   © Michael Newman/PhotoEdit
614   © Larry Lefever/Grant Heilman
615   Photography by Alan Brown/Photonics

Part 8   © Todd Joyce
632   © Todd Joyce
634   © Steve Vidler/Leo de Wys, Inc.
640   © 1986 Chris Jones/The Stock Market
646   Courtesy of PNC Bank
657   Springer/Bettmann Film Archive
668   © Todd Joyce
671   Photography by Alan Brown/Photonics
678   Courtesy of Intel Corporation
680   © David Young-Wolfe/PhotoEdit
685   *The Wall Street Journal*
698   © Todd Joyce Studio
700   © Ralph Mercer/Tony Stone Images
710   © Jon Riley/Tony Stone Images
716   © Bob Daemmrich/Stock, Boston, Inc.
718   The New York Stock Exchange
735   © 1992 Michael Melford/The Image Bank

Part 9   © Todd Joyce
740   © Todd Joyce
743   Uniphoto Picture Agency
753   Marcus/Bryan-Brown
772   © Todd Joyce
775   © Wendt Worldwide
782   © Eastcott/Momatiuk/Woodfin Camp & Associates,
       Inc.
789   © Michael Heron/The Stock Market
803   © 1991 Jim Pickerell/Stock, Boston, Inc.